1001 RESTAURANTS
YOU MUST EXPERIENCE BEFORE YOU DIE

1001 RESTAURANTS
YOU MUST EXPERIENCE BEFORE YOU DIE

GENERAL EDITOR JENNY LINFORD

FOREWORD BY JAY RAYNER

⬅ Le Meurice, Paris

CASSELL
ILLUSTRATED

A Quintessence Book

First published in Great Britain in 2014 by Cassell Illustrated
A division of Octopus Group Limited
Enedavour House, 189 Shaftesbury Avenue
London, WC2H 8JY
www.octopusbooks.co.uk

An Hachette UK Company
www.hachette.co.uk

ISBN: 978-1-84403-764-3
QSS.KRES

A CIP catalogue record for this book is available from the British Library.

This book was designed and produced by
Quintessence Editions Ltd.
6 Blundell Street
London N7 9BH
www.1001beforeyoudie.com

Project Editor	Katharina Hahn
Editors	Emma Clegg, Katharina Hahn, Carol King, Frank Ritter, Henry Russell, Dorothy Stannard
Designers	Sarah Holland, Damian Jaques
Editorial Director	Jane Laing
Publisher	Mark Fletcher

Colour reproduction by KHL Chroma Graphics Pte Ltd., Singapore
Printed in China by Midas Printing International Ltd.

Contents

Foreword | Jay Rayner

Those of us with an overly developed interest in our lunch can measure out our lives in great restaurant meals. For me it's the pastrami sandwich, the size of my own head, that I ate at the gloriously scuffed Katz's deli in New York, the meat cut for me by men with forearms like fire logs. It's the miraculous spun omelette of artichoke and the chicken breasts cooked over open coals in a puddle of frothing butter at Sostanza, an old white-tiled trattoria which has been on the same site in Florence since 1869. It is the parade of tiny gastronomic miracles at L'Astrance, the remarkably unglossy Michelin three star in Paris— oh, that langoustine bouillon—which restored my faith in cooking of high ambition.

Each of these meals, and so many more besides, managed the same trick: they didn't just feed my unreasonable appetites, they gave me a very specific sense of place, a memory that was so much more than just sight and sound. It was about taste and texture and culture. It was about the people I was eating among. Instead of just allowing me to spectate on another tourist spot it put me right at the heart of the action. Each of these meals reaffirmed my life-long love of restaurants.

This book contains the potential for 1001 experiences just like that. From Egypt to South Africa, from Los Angeles to Philadelphia, by way of Phoenix, Arizona, and Oxford, Mississippi, from Kyoto to Singapore, its pages are filled with glorious eating possibilities. Not that everybody will love every single one. It's not called 1001 restaurants "you MUST eat at before you die" or "1001 restaurants you'd be an idiot to miss." Restaurants are at their very best when they are simply trying to be themselves, rather than all things to all people. Try to please as many customers as possible and you head inexorably towards a lowest common denominator of wipe-down laminated menus or all-you-can-eat buffets where lumps of animals that died in vain fester beneath heat lamps.

What this book is not is a succession of gastro-palaces, where you pay as much for the thick tablecloths and the tinkle of the heavy-leaded glassware as you do for the food on the plate. There is some of that. Thomas Keller's French Laundry in California is here, as it should be; Keller is one of the greatest chefs in America, his food a master class in poise and good taste. So is El Celler de Can Roca, north of Barcelona, considered by many to the best high-end restaurant in the world. But if they are included it is because they do so much more than offer a tedious "me too" kind of luxury. Throw enough cash at the situation and you can be pelted with truffles and lobster for as long as you like. A great restaurant meal takes more than just tiresomely indulgent shopping. More importantly, the list also includes places like Cal Pep, the grand daddy of Barcelonan tapas restaurants where all is clatter and bash. And yes, there may be a nod to Heston Blumenthal's snail porridge at the modernist temple that is the Fat Duck in the quintessentially English village of Bray in Berkshire. But the simpler pleasures of his pub, the Hind's Head, with its big-fisted steak and kidney pudding gets equal billing. There's even a listing for the Company Shed, a shack on the Essex coast serving the best seafood, which is so spartan you have to bring not just your own wine but also your own bread.

For this is the thing. People with appetite know that great food does not always come on thick tablecloths. Indeed, they know that most of the time, humble and un-showy—no tablecloths at all—wins out. The challenge is finding the good stuff. That for me is one of the joys of restaurants: that sense of anticipation, when you sit down at an empty table with only a few words on a sheet of paper to guide you. Could this be the meal that stops the world?

Of course, it's easy for me to talk up the pleasures of taking a chance on lunch; a lot of the time I'm doing it with someone else's money. It's always good to have advice from those who have been there before, which is where this book comes in. It can help you shorten the odds and, between great meals, give you a bit of reading material to make you dream about the next one. So should you try to eat in every single restaurant listed here? Probably not. But you could have a lot of fun trying.

Introduction | Jenny Linford

Restaurants hold a particular place in our affections. We visit them to celebrate special occasions in our lives, from birthdays to anniversaries, to woo loved ones, to indulge in people-watching and conspicuous consumption, and for consolation and comfort. The recollection of an convivial meal at a good restaurant will linger on in the mind for years after the actual event. As such, restaurants arouse strong feelings. Everyone, after all, has at least one favorite restaurant, which he or she would recommend warmly. Equally, though, the responses restaurants arouse are deeply subjective, with one person's favorite another's abomination. Putting together this book, therefore, is stepping into an area of contention, offering much scope for stimulating debate.

When it came to selecting the 1001 restaurants you must experience before you die, our contributors around the world—a well-dined collection of restaurant reviewers, food writers, travel writers, journalists, inveterate eater-outers, and bloggers—were asked to suggest "iconic" restaurants they knew, ranging from humble but much-loved gems to luxurious havens of fine dining, with their on-the-ground knowledge and input forming the base of the selections. The result is a wonderfully wide-ranging selection of restaurants. Part of this diversity comes about from the globe-trotting nature of the book. The breadth of the definition of "iconic" has also allowed for a genuine and fascinating spread in terms of types of restaurants.

Naturally, this book contains entries for some of the world's most luxurious and grandest restaurants, such as Le Meurice in Paris, Eleven Madison Park in New York, La Pergola in Rome, or Louis XV in Monaco. Here, too, are diners' places of gastronomic desire, restaurants from around the world that feature on people's dream lists: the wonderful El Celler de Can Roca in Girona, Spain, the French Laundry in California's Napa Valley, New York City's haute-cuisine, game-changer Eleven Madison Park, L'Enclume in Cartmel, a small village in England, the trend-setting Momofuku Ko in New York, and so on.

Restaurants showcase the culinary talents of great chefs, and we have become familiar with the concept of the "celebrity chef"—someone who arouses such interest in his or her cooking that he or she has a following, with diners tracking him or her

Key to Symbols	Approximate cost per person for a 2-course meal (without wine)
$	20 USD or less
$$	20–55 USD
$$$	55–80 USD
$$$$	80–150 USD
$$$$$	over 150 USD

wherever he or she works. Within the pages of this book, therefore, we have included restaurants because they offer diners the chance to enjoy the vision of a notable chef. There are chefs such as Kunio Tokuoka of Kitcho in Kyoto, Japan, eminent for his *kaiseki*, and Paul Bocuse in Lyon, France, offering personal yet classic expressions of his country's great cuisine. Equally, we feature chefs who are exploring new frontiers in the restaurant world, such as René Redzepi at Noma in Copenhagen, Denmark, with his deep-rooted emphasis on foraging and seasonality; Heston Blumenthal, who at the Fat Duck in Bray, England, has done so much to promote molecular gastronomy; the witty creativity of Massimo Bottura of Osteria Francescana, Modena, Italy; Andre Chang who champions his thought-provoking "Octaphilosophy" at Andre in Singapore; Andoni Luis Aduriz of Mugaritz in San Sebastian, Spain, noted for his inventive playfulness; and Alex Atala at D.O.M. in São Paulo, Brazil, celebrating the rich, exciting treasure trove of indigenous ingredients from the Amazon region.

The great and the good of the restaurant world are well-represented in this book. Here, too, are historic institutions, from venerable Japanese restaurants that can trace their history back centuries to Parisian establishments to Ottoman restaurants in Turkey to Rules, London's oldest restaurant. Our definition of the term "iconic," however, also allows the spotlight to be shined on more down-to-earth establishments, those restaurants that do not offer haute cuisine and fine dining, yet which are, nevertheless, much-loved, loyally patronized establishments, serving excellent food without any pretensions. Many of these are insider gems, enjoyed by those in the know, offering authentic, engaging, and enjoyable dining experiences. Within these pages, you will find restaurants of this type championed all over the world. Read about Nick's Café, an ever-bustling all-American diner in Los Angeles; the glories of memorably tasty, perfectly cooked, crispy, garlic-smothered *gai tod*, or deep-fried chicken, in Bangkok's Soi Polo Chicken; Lisbon's beloved local institution Cervejaria Ramiro, with its noted *prego* (steak sandwich); traditional community restaurant La Nueva Palomino in Arequipa, Peru; and Kwan Kee, Hong Kong, specializing in clay pot rice.

Where appropriate, we have broadened the term "restaurant" to include the most basic eatery. For example, street food stalls in Southeast Asia, an authentic expression of that magnificent and fascinating cuisine, are represented. Food absolutely does not have to be grand or complex in order to give pleasure. Descriptions of dishes such as *bhel puri* in Mumbai or a Turkish kebab from a restaurant tracing its history back to the nineteenth century, founded by the man who invented the döner kebab, or a rich-textured, barbecued eel in Japan bring home vividly the satisfaction of good food cooked well.

One of the pleasures of putting together an international collection of restaurants on this scale is that it offers an opportunity to celebrate the sense of place. Food, after all, plays a huge and important part in expressing national identities. One only has to think of cuisines such as Japanese, French, Indian, or Spanish to get a sense of the diversity offered by restaurants. National cuisines are an expression of terroir, rooted in local geography, climate, and agriculture. Strikingly, a recurrent theme throughout many of the entries is the importance placed by restaurants on sourcing local and seasonal ingredients, from the freshest produce to the finest fish, seafood, meat, and poultry. This approach is found in restaurants ranging from a small, rural eatery in Puglia, Italy, to a three Michelin-starred French restaurant. Eating out while away offers travelers a chance, so to speak, to taste the country they are visiting. It is not surprising that often one's most vivid memories of a vacation abroad are centered on meals that one enjoyed there, whether it's of a flavorful bowl of pasta carbonara, eaten with relish in a Roman trattoria after a day seeing the splendid sights of that historic city, a signature pastrami on rye at Katz's legendary deli in New York, soaking in the city's atmosphere, or a mellow breakfast of scrambled eggs at Bills in Sydney.

In the pages of this book, you will find classic eating establishments that epitomize their national cuisine: cozy Parisian bistros, historic Viennese cafés, a British fish-and-chip shop, cheerfully carnivorous Argentinian steakhouses, Italian trattorias, Chinese noodle bars, lively Spanish tapas bars, and a Korean barbecued beef restaurant. Many of the restaurants chosen for this book are specialists known for one particular dish, whether ceviche in Peru, sushi in Japan, barbecued meats in America, pho in Vietnam, grilled Bratwurst in Germany, hummus in Israel, or smørrebrød (open sandwiches) in Denmark. There is a depth to the entries, with local and regional dishes highlighted. In the Italian section, for example, you will discover where to eat the best ragù in Bologna, pizza in Naples, and radicchio in Treviso. The richness of America's regional cuisine is well-represented in entries featuring shrimp and grits in Charleston, po 'boys in New Orleans, oysters in San Francisco, lobster in Boston, and pizza in Chicago. In an increasingly homogenous world, the diversity of eating places and the food they serve is a welcome reminder of the sense of excitement and exploration that food and travel offer.

Restaurants, of course, are not just about food—the dining out experience is made up of far more than simply the quality of what is on the plate. As good restaurateurs know, an excellent atmosphere and ambience are also key to creating contented diners. A sense of hospitality is a hallmark of the best restaurants. The importance of service is a constant theme, again expressed in many ways throughout this book. There is the friendly, democratic hospitality displayed to all customers taken into the fold at E. Pellicci's, the vintage café in London's East End, the warm personal welcome offered by Mariana and her husband Peter Esterhuizen at their home-based restaurant Marianas in Stanford, South Africa, as well as by Caterina Lanteri at her restaurant San Giorgio in Cervo, Italy, and the formal, smooth-as-silk service offered by haute-cuisine restaurants. Interestingly, there is a move in many high-end restaurants toward a more relaxed informality in service, as witnessed by Jason Atherton's popular London restaurant Pollen Street Social.

Memorable locations, too, are often part of a restaurant's appeal. Glancing through this book you will find restaurants in an extraordinary range of settings: a restaurant in South Africa's Kruger National Park, where diners looking out over the bushveld can spot elephants, lions, and cheetahs; a Beijing establishment dedicated to a Chinese opera singer housed in the former home of a Qing Dynasty courtesan; a Parisian restaurant located on the second floor of that most iconic of French landmarks, the Eiffel Tower; field-to-fork dining surrounded by vegetable fields on an organic vegetable farm in Devon; elegant dining inside a beautiful palazzo by the Grand Canal in Venice, Italy; an idyllic park setting for a much-loved restaurant in Calgary, Canada; and memorable feasting on magnificent food in the splendor of a historic fort in Jaipur, India. Panoramas, too, play their part, from New Zealand's The Sugar Club, perched high above Auckland's harbor, to Icebergs, Sydney, Australia, looking out over the crashing breakers of the Pacific Ocean.

What is also apparent from editing this book is the vitality of the eating out scene all around the world. Read the entries for cosmopolitan cities such as New York and London, and you will be struck by the energy of the restaurant scene. In both these great cities, there are wonderful classic restaurants, enjoyed for their sense of tradition, but equally, flourishing alongside these establishments, there are more youthful places, offering innovative approaches to eating out, shaking up preconceptions.

The boundaries within the restaurant world are changing in so many ways. Unlikely urban sites, from Victorian granaries to warehouses, are having new life breathed into them as they are transformed into restaurants. Cuisines are being played with all around the world, from Joe Beef in Montreal, Canada, delighting diners with its witty carnivorous menu, to Albert Adrià's Tickets, reinventing tapas in Barcelona, Spain. Food, it seems, lends itself to creativity, and the restaurants in this book bear witness to that. This book is filled with restaurants of which memories are made. Enjoy the exploration.

Index of Restaurants by Country

The sheer variety of places for eating out in North and South America is truly impressive. From breakfast in a vintage L.A. diner to feasting in an Argentinian steak house, and from tasting innovative food in the hippest of New York eateries to discovering the culinary riches of the Amazon Basin—there's much to enjoy.

The Americas

Commander's Palace, New Orleans, United States.

Sobo | Sophisticated bohemian cuisine in a relaxed setting

Location Tofino   **Signature dish** Crispy blue-corn tortilla taco with spicy wild fish and seasonal fruit salsa |

"I want people to eat my food and feel good enough to jump in that kayak and enjoy an adventure."

Lisa Ahier, chef and co-owner of Sobo

Hailing from New Brunswick in eastern Canada, Artie Ahier met his Texas-born wife Lisa in 1993 when they were both working on a yacht in Florida. Brought together by their shared interests in travel, nature, wildlife, and great food, the Ahiers moved to Tofino on the west coast of Vancouver Island, renowned for its pristine rain forest and ocean surf. There, in 2003, they opened their business in a well-equipped purple catering truck. News of the fresh, healthy, and flavorful food served in an eclectic environment soon reached visitors and media, and they were named one of the top ten new restaurants in Canada that year.

Sobo, short for "sophisticate bohemian," finally moved to a permanent and upscale location among Tofino's fishing and eco-tourism community in 2007. The Ahiers bring together their unique blend of maritime mettle and passion for the Canadian Southwest in a restaurant that uses seasonal and sustainable ingredients from various local purveyors.

The new location is a complete contrast to the stifling, space-restricted truck in which the business started. The spacious, contemporary, post-and-beam interior is sided by full-length windows overlooking Tofino's quaint buildings and the surrounding old-growth forests. This is not a formal restaurant but rather an upscale diner, with a chalkboard menu that constantly changes to reflect the local fishermen's catch and the seasonal produce from the farms.

Sobo's comforting chowder consists of a creamy, dill-infused broth brimming with smoked fish, which itself changes depending on the local catch. A hearty kale salad lashed with quinoa and local hazelnuts comes dressed tellingly with a tart lemon dressing and grilled halloumi. Oysters that are harvested from the pristine cold waters mere yards away are served freshly shucked with a Champagne Mignonette sauce or lightly broiled with salmon bacon and a delicate miso mayonnaise. **NF**

⬆ Sobo's tacos unusually combine fish and fruit.

The Pointe | Glorious locally caught seafood with Pacific views

Location Tofino **Signature dish** Shellfish and potato *nage* (stock) | $$$

The Pointe Restaurant at Tofino's Wikaninnish Inn takes full advantage of one of the most naturally majestic spots on Vancouver Island. The restaurant is a large, airy space that overlooks the town's fabled Chesterman Beach. Beyond the sand, the breathtaking view of the Pacific Ocean seems to go on forever, providing diners with a continually changing backdrop from summer to the storm season.

Tofino is a laidback tourist town, a former hippie haven known for its arts and crafts shops and friendly, informal attitude. The challenge for The Pointe was how to keep everything that was great about such a relaxed atmosphere while encouraging the pampered elegance expected of fine-dining establishments. It has succeeded. Thanks to a relationship with the Tofino-Ucluelet Culinary Guild, the menu blends a sophisticated approach with farm-fresh, organic ingredients produced on the island.

Everyone knows that a walk on the beach is one of the best ways to work up an appetite. The Pointe's eclectic menu offers any number of satisfying solutions to hunger in the realm of locally caught seafood, everything from freshly shucked oysters—harvested from farms that are so close you can drop by for a visit—to such indigenous delights as albacore tuna crudo and Clayoquat Sound shrimp pasta. And, just in case you are in a romantic mood, a tempting fried salmon collar for two is available.

There is also a Champagne brunch every Sunday that delights in playing with convention—try the buttermilk pancakes featuring Italian plums, toasted almonds, and mascarpone Chantilly, or the "Breakfast Poutine," which includes crisp pork belly.

In keeping with The Pointe's philosophy of preparing all edibles in-house, fresh bread is made each morning by the hotel's pastry team. The extensive wine list favors British Columbia vintages, ensuring a thoroughly local experience. **BJM**

"Much of the fresh seafood is fished from the very waters overlooked by The Pointe . . ."

tofinoadventuremap.com

[↑] The Pointe: fine dining with panoramic ocean views.

Sooke Harbour House |
An inspiring taste of Vancouver Island

Location Sooke **Signature dish** Eclectic tasting menus | ❸❸❸

This intimate restaurant and inn, founded in 1979, less than an hour away from Victoria on Vancouver Island, is located in a picturesque fishing town surrounded by forest. Owners Sinclair and Frédérique Philip are renowned for their spectacular garden, from which they harvest edible flowers, herbs, and vegetables for their striking dishes, which also draw inspiration from the foods of the indigenous peoples of the region.

The dining room, overlooking the entrance to Sooke harbor, is country rustic and comfortable, with beam ceilings of natural wood, a fireplace made of large beach stones, and candelabra highlighting the crisp linens, delicate crystal, and the brilliant offerings from the innovative and imaginative kitchen.

"This enchanting retreat is a plain, whitewashed clapboard farmhouse dating back to 1929."

ila-chateau.com

The inn is committed to using only foods from the southwestern tip of Vancouver Island, a policy that has proved challenging at times, yet has also brought rewards. Ingredients include foraged wild greens and pine mushrooms from the rain forest, uncommon seafood from by-catch nets, and golden salmonberries and huckleberries from forest trails.

Although the restaurant has a deep and extensive international cellar, it is the province's wines that excel. They are paired with such standout dishes as shellfish steamed with a juice of Riesling and heirloom carrot, served with honey cider-pickled purple cabbage, and hyssop-marinated and alderwood-grilled local veal, with a Granny Smith apple and caraway sauce. **NF**

Ulla | Lively, contemporary
Canadian cuisine popular with hipsters

Location Victoria **Signature dish** Scallop boudin blanc with Shimiji mushrooms | ❸❸❸

Ulla restaurant is located in a historic building in the heart of the oldest Chinatown in Canada, that of Victoria on Vancouver Island. Here, chef Brad Holmes and partner Sahara Tamarin have transformed hyper-local island cuisine into edgy, contemporary fare. Holmes delights in well-structured, technically perfect dishes that celebrate his exemplary organic and seasonal ingredients and "ethically raised proteins."

Opened in 2010, Ulla changed the way diners thought about their cuisine, as well as changing the identity of its neighborhood. Holmes and Tamarin created a distinctly modern, urban room for the mainly young hipsters and culinary aficionados of the city. In terms of decor and atmosphere, this is West Coast mixed in with a bit of New York's Soho, with hand-hewn fir tables, shelves of cookbooks, and modern street art accented by whimsical overhanging globe lighting and bentwood seating.

Holmes uses modern techniques to bring out classic flavors. Start with bites of crispy polenta cubes, lightly seasoned with sea salt and truffle mayonnaise, or their version of edamame (fresh chickpeas), picked green and fried in their delicate skins. A vibrant pea soup is kissed with smoked crème fraiche in place of bacon. A herb-encrusted halibut is livened up with an unexpected crispy brandade, a wonderful upmarket take on fish and fries.

Dishes change on the basis of availability and seasonality, but two dishes that put in regular appearances are the tender local octopus, with green chickpeas, black chickpea hummus, a Romesco sauce, and olive powder, and the sublime scallop boudin blanc, with Shimiji mushrooms, squash puree, pickled squash cubes, pumpkin seeds, and potato puree. **NF**

▣ Ulla's signature dish of scallop boudin blanc.

Le Crocodile | Elegant yet affordable French cuisine

Location Vancouver **Signature dish** Garlic-sautéed frog's legs | ❸❺

Vancouver's Le Crocodile wears its classical heritage like a badge of honor. And rightly so. For more than thirty years, the intimate space has offered locals the ultimate in French cuisine at a surprisingly modest price. Less than $40 (£25) will secure an entree—not much for the kind of food that can send critics into rapture. The Zagat restaurant survey suggested that chef and owner Michel Jacob deserved a knighthood for the perfection of his cuisine and superb service.

Ignoring the current trend, Jacob continues to hold Le Crocodile's staff to the highest standards. The setting is white linen, the silverware dazzling. The waiters are impeccable in waistcoats and cravats bearing the discreet logo of a miniature crocodile. The

> *"I don't use tongs…. Tongs can squeeze the meat and it's not an elegant tool. It's not very classy."*
>
> Michel Jacob, chef and owner of Le Crocodile

restaurant's doggie bag looks like it came straight from a shopping expedition to Hermès. At Le Crocodile, men still dine out in upscale blazers. The luxurious menu, featuring such classics as Alsatian onion pie, garlic-sautéed frog's legs, and oven-roasted bone marrow, is steeped in the kind of tradition that compels the patron to rise to the occasion.

The restaurant is celebrated for its deep list of French wines, but it is the exquisite detail of each dish, as pleasing to the eye as it is to the palate, which you will go away remembering. While the culinary touch is undeniably rich, it is light enough to allow you room to finish off the evening with a signature touch—a tiny, crocodile-shaped chocolate. **BJM**

Vij's | Creative, contemporary Indian food well worth the wait

Location Vancouver **Signature dish** Vij's lamb popsicles | ❸❺

How can you tell that Vij's is the most popular Indian restaurant in Vancouver? Even in the rain, the lines typically stretch down the block. Proprietor Vikram Vij refuses to take reservations. His guests have included everyone from novelist Julian Barnes to former Canadian Prime Minister Pierre Trudeau, but Vij believes strongly in his own brand of culinary democracy. He has turned away everyone from rock stars to famous talk-show hosts, and even his family is expected to stand in line.

Actually, many locals consider waiting in line to be part of the ritual. It is not uncommon to see hipsters in woolen hats and horn-rimmmed glasses striking up a conversation with young parents pushing a baby carriage. To the uninitiated, the idea of waiting in line in a typical Vancouver downpour may be inconceivable, but, here's the thing: once you get in, the food and attentive service are beyond worth it.

Any further delay you might encounter is softened by a glass of wine and an array of lovely snacks as you wait for your table in the lively dining area. The service is Western, with a welcome touch of old-school Indian hospitality provided by Vij himself. One of his favorite phrases is, "At your service," and he delivers with a conviction that helped Vij's to earn a *New York Times* review placing it "easily among the finest Indian restaurants in the world."

The food is best described as traditional Indian but with a contemporary spin that can border on whimsical. It is difficult to select a favorite in the stunning selection of appetizers, but the samosas—filled with lamb and beef and sautéed with fennel, cloves, and sumac—are unforgettable. Highlights from the inventive list of entrees include the Rajasthani spicy-style goat and the braised beef short ribs with roasted okra, walnuts, and jellybeans. **BJM**

Blue Water Cafe | Eastern seafood cuisine meets its

Western equivalent in a stylish former warehouse

Location Vancouver **Signature dish** Seafood tower |
$$$

Housed in a historic brick-and-beam former warehouse in the vibrant Yaletown warehouse district of Vancouver, Blue Water Cafe, helmed by award-winning executive chef and culinary genius Frank Pabst, is committed to exclusively sourcing wild, sustainable seafood. The dining room offers views of the open kitchen and Japanese-styled Raw Bar.

Pabst has a reputation for serving the freshest and most viable wild coastal species of local seafood to be had in Vancouver. Blue Water Cafe has one of the best selections of raw oysters and sustainable caviar in the city, and is also known for its celebration of little-known sea species, as well as its unforgettable "seafood towers," or tiered stands overflowing with briny abundance and freshness.

This is a sophisticated operation, run with an impressive eye for detail. The restaurant's deep and diverse wine collection provides perfect pairings with such brilliant starters as Dungeness crab and white asparagus panna cotta, garnished with celery, peanuts, sultanas, and a green apple foam, or local Gulf Island swimming scallops, with the added Provençal touches of a tomato and caper relish and lemon butter with thyme. To follow might be a buttery sablefish lightly touched with a miso sake glaze, with edamame quinoa and shiitake mushrooms and a splash of bonito dashi laced with yuzu—celestial Asian bliss. But it is not all fish here: the kitchen also produces Kobe-style short ribs, braised in a sauce of chili, coffee, and anchovy and served with celeriac puree and fresh horseradish gremolata.

To complete the Blue Water Cafe culinary experience, it is mandatory to sample one of pastry chef Jean-Pierre Sanchez's appealing and whimsical dessert creations, which range from the rich and indulgent to the light and elegant. **NF**

"We offer 'unsung heroes'… such as mackerel, sardines, jellyfish, octopus, and sea urchin."

Frank Pabst, chef at Blue Water Cafe

⬆ A seafood tower—wonderfully fresh seafood on ice.

Bishop's | A much-loved institution noted for its warm welcome

Location Vancouver **Signature dish** Dungeness crab and celery salad | ❸❸❸

A culinary landmark on Vancouver's dining scene since 1984, Bishop's combines an understated elegance with an ongoing passion for indigenous West Coast cuisine. Generations of devoted patrons have walked past the familiar swirl of the restaurant's sign to be greeted warmly by owner John Bishop. A believer in old-school service, he is just as likely to help a patron with a coat as he is to suggest a particular dish. For many locals, Bishop's is the place to celebrate a special occasion while basking in the warmth of the welcome from their eponymous host.

The ambience is stylish and discreet, with immaculate tablecloths and white walls punctuated by vibrant splashes of local art. Service is attentive yet unhurried, and the lighting is charmingly subdued. This is a place where people can talk to each other and listen without having to strain. Bishop's is also delightfully unstuffy despite its iconic status: one of the knowledgeable veteran servers wears a collection of skull rings on most of his fingers. Apart from specials, you can count on the menu being both focused and comfortably streamlined.

The selections are composed of a few enduring favorites, such as the notably fresh beet salad with goats' cheese, dill, and Banyuls vinaigrette. Ron Shaw, chef de cuisine at Bishop's, believes in using only the best local ingredients—such as Pitt Meadows heirloom tomatoes—and allowing their flavor to shine through.

There are a couple of popular meat dishes on the menu, including an elk striploin, served in style with mushroom croquettes. But it is this restaurant's stellar treatment of fish—ranging from halibut and wild salmon to a memorably good Dungeness crab and celery salad—that keeps the locals happy and returning year after year. **BJM**

⬆ Bishop's restaurant is a Vancouver institution.

Go Fish | Great fish and fries from a cherished seafood shack

Location Vancouver **Signature dish** Fish and fries | $

Opened in 2004 by Vancouver chef Gord Martin, this appealingly eclectic seafood hut consists of a recycled shipping container overlooking the wonderful public market on the waterfront of Vancouver's Granville Island. It is here that Martin combines sustainable seafood with creative flavors in his imaginative recipes.

The outdoor seafood emporium is the result of a cooperative relationship with the nearby Fisherman's Wharf at False Creek. Both chef and fishermen had the laudable goal of offering excellent, seafood-based cuisine while raising awareness of the importance of eating local, seasonal, and sustainable seafood.

Eating here is a plain and simple affair when it comes to the surroundings, with diners taking their places on an open-air deck area in front of the hut. On bright and sunny days, eating al fresco like this is a pleasure; should the weather be colder, though, come prepared and wrap up warm. The weather never seems to be a deterrent, however, and Go Fish always has a line of people patiently waiting to enjoy once again the quality of the cooking: carefully sourced, prime, spanking-fresh fish and seafood, handled simply and intelligently. Pride of place goes to the exemplary fish and fries, consisting of local cod, wild salmon, and halibut, coated in a golden, crisp batter made with beer from the local Granville Island brewery.

Other temptations include Martin's signature sandwiches, ranging from a "Po' Boy"—grilled succulent local oysters, shredded lettuce, chipotle crema, sweet onion, and house-made tartare sauce—to char-grilled West Coast albacore tuna brushed with sweet chili ponzu glaze, spiced tomato salsa, and wasabi mayonnaise. Or Martin's delicious take on the fish taco with his grilled salmon tacones, garnished with salsa, chipotle crema, and house slaw, and rolled in a flour tortilla cone. **NF**

⬆ Fish and fries at Go Fish is a real treat.

Tojo's | Sensational sushi from a noted master of Japanese cuisine

Location Vancouver **Signature dish** Tojo's tuna | ❸❸❸

Vancouver restaurateur Hidekazu Tojo—known to his many patrons simply as "Tojo"—has been celebrated around the world for his masterful way with Japanese cuisine. Trained in Osaka, he has played host to an admiring Anthony Bourdain and taught Martha Stewart how to make sushi on her TV show.

There are now many Japanese restaurants in Vancouver but Tojo's, founded in 1988, remains the standard against which all others are measured. In a nod to Tojo's legendary skill in preparing tailor-made dishes before your eyes, the *Washington Post* called his cuisine "grander and more enticing than a geisha's dance." For many locals, a visit to Tojo's is a welcome chance to see a culinary master at the height of his

---

"The Japanese have a long history with sushi. [They made] many mistakes but they learned."

Hidekazu Tojo, chef and owner of Tojo's

---

powers. The dining area may be roomy, modern, and inviting, but part of the magic is watching Tojo up close as he works at the sushi bar, his knife skills being only one part of the amazing sushi-making ritual.

Here you can select from a menu set at the highest level of Japanese cuisine: a choice of artfully prepared versions of classic Japanese dishes. But what sets the menu apart at Tojo's is the contemporary West Coast spin on several of the dishes. The wild Pacific salmon is as close as you are going to get to an edible version of this city's culinary roots. Other standouts include the Canadian sablefish, complete with Tojo's "secret marinade," and halibut cheek sautéed in a creamy garlic teriyaki sauce. **BJM**

The Pear Tree | Fine dining with a personal touch

Location Burnaby **Signature dish** Local prawn "cappuccino" | ❸❸❸

Canadian-born chef Scott Jaeger established The Pear Tree, a comfortable suburban hideaway just minutes away from the hectic and competitive Vancouver downtown environment, in 1998. Serving high-end cuisine with classic West Coast contemporary elegance, The Pear Tree has gone on to win numerous awards, with Jaeger being chosen to represent Canada in the Bocuse d'Or world cooking contest in Lyon.

Careful sourcing of prime ingredients is integral to Jaeger's seasonally-changing menu. He works with local food producers, obtaining meat and poultry, fresh vegetables, fish and seafood, and fruit and herbs from them. Trained in classic French technique, Jaeger uses his fine ingredients to redefine classics in a simple and elegant way, with culinary twists originating in the city's multi-ethnic heritages. Thus, a local prawn "cappuccino" is a reinvention similar to a Japanese *chawanmushi*, with tender, sweet prawns enveloped by delicate dashi custard and fragrant prawn bisque foam. Plump, succulent Vancouver Island scallops are skillfully seared and caramelized with orange to top a richly flavorful double-smoked bacon risotto.

Serious comfort food, especially in the fall and winter, is also on offer here, in dishes such as braised beef short rib, cooked for thirty-six hours and partnered with potato rosti, a mushroom puree, and Pemberton salsify. Jaeger's desserts hail from classic French territory and include well-executed examples of dishes such as lemon tart or crème brûlée.

Jaeger's charming and welcoming wife Stephanie looks after the well-tuned front-of-house staff, who glide effortlessly through the comfortable spacious room, which is decorated in tones of light mustard and browns, accented by colorful local artwork. **NF**

⬰ Twice-cooked pork belly with a spot-shrimp cassoulet.

Araxi | Superlative dining amid the snowy slopes of a popular ski resort

Location Whistler   **Signature dish** Truffle fries | ❸❸❸

Araxi is a prominent fixture in the main square of Whistler, a world-renowned ski resort in British Columbia. It offers fine dining for anyone who wants to get close to pristine snow without sacrificing a welcome touch of elegance. Proprietor Jack Evrensel named the place in honor of Araxi, his wife, and everything about the place suggests a labor of love.

Araxi is a lively bar for kicking back after a day on the slopes, but here you can forget the pub grub that is often passed off as après ski fare—this is no place for slackers or shedders. The refined cuisine on offer is easily good enough to prevail without the assistance or distraction of the spectacular scenery. If you can manage to resist the addictive truffle fries, there is a wide variety of wonderful small plates to share. Araxi's innovative Raw Bar presents several varieties of oysters, as well as inviting takes on everything from spot shrimp harvested from the Pacific Ocean to a daily selection of the freshest sashimi.

Executive chef James Walt has put together a menu that relies heavily on local produce, whether it is the fresh vegetables from North Arm Farm or the organic beef from nearby Pemberton. Walt—formerly the executive chef at the Canadian embassy in Rome—has presented his cuisine at the James Beard House in New York. At Araxi, he puts the accent on fresh, indigenous ingredients that leave as little distance between harvest and table as possible.

Highlights from a wide-ranging choice of entrees include an organic white shrimp risotto with asparagus and chives; a superb roasted saddle of rabbit; and a beef tenderloin steak that might be the best you have ever tasted. The justly celebrated wine list—supervised by award-winning sommelier Samantha Rahn—offers a range of elegant wines that accompany the food perfectly. **BJM**

⬆ At Araxi you can savor fresh fish in snowy surroundings.

Bearfoot Bistro | A taste of the good life away from the cold

Location Whistler   **Signature dish** Vancouver Island black cod with Champagne cream | ❺❺❺❺

In the ski resort of Whistler, two-hours' drive north of Vancouver, Bearfoot Bistro is home to effervescent and bon-vivant owner André Saint-Jacques and his gifted executive chef, Melissa Craig. Saint-Jacques has been an important addition to Whistler since 1995. Dedicated to celebrating all the good things in life, he is as passionate about pleasure as he is about new experiences, stunning cuisine, attentive service, and the virtues of a spectacular wine list.

Meanwhile, Craig's culinary philosophy combines simplicity and sophistication with an element of surprise. Having established herself as one of the top names in Canadian cuisine, she is a commanding presence in her large kitchen, and is devoted to sourcing out the best seasonal ingredients from both home and abroad. With organic farm producers in the neighboring Pemberton Valley mainly supplying the restaurant, you can expect some brilliant and colorful dishes from Craig's creative kitchen brigade.

The restaurant, with its inviting chalet-style dining room, is showcased by the expansive open kitchen. Downstairs, in the impressive 20,000-bottle cellar, there is a private dining room where guests can experience the thrill of sabering a bottle of Champagne, or don parkas to keep warm in the country's only permanent ice room as they sample an exhilarating flight of sub-zero vodkas.

Craig has an à la carte menu, but it is her tasting menus that really shine. Start with local steelhead salmon, lightly smoked with textures of cauliflower grébiche and watercress, or wild scallop paired with a kataifi-wrapped shrimp with coconut, kohlrabi, kaffir lime, and cilantro. Pork tenderloin comes with a braised cheek croquette, rutabaga, apple mustard, and local beets. Finish with the tableside-prepared, signature nitro ice cream with Tahitian vanilla. **NF**

⊤ Bearfoot Bistro serves exquisite, inventive dishes.

Langdon Hall | Gorgeous produce in a glorious stately home

Location Cambridge   **Signature dish** Bison striploin with juniper jus | ⊖⊖⊖

"I love that something as simple as a perfectly ripe … fragrant, juicy tomato can get me excited."

Jason Bangerter, chef at Langdon Hall

⬆ Chef Jason Bangerter joined Langdon Hall in 2013 after running two restaurants in downtown Toronto.

➡ A wealth of edibles are raised on the Hall's estate.

History, beauty, and calm—Langdon Hall in Cambridge, Ontario, is an all-around restorative destination, whether for lunch, an evening meal, or a weekend break. Dating back to 1898, when it was designed as a country retreat, the stately building was purchased in 1989 by Mary and Bill Bennett, who restored and renovated it as a charming hotel. This beautiful property is frequently listed as among the loveliest places to stay in Canada, with seasoned travelers placing Langdon Hall on their list of North American favorites.

Eating here is a treat, too. Food "with a sense of place" is on offer at Langdon Hall, with Chef Jason Bangerter able to source many of the fine seasonal products he uses to such good effect—vegetables, fruits, herbs, and edible flowers—from the Hall's own magnificent kitchen gardens. Even the maple syrup is tapped from trees in the grounds. Thus, intelligent and meticulous sourcing, using a network of local foragers and food producers, is the backbone of the menu here, combined with classic, well-executed, haute cuisine techniques.

As might be expected, given the institution's pedigree, the dining room is a serenely elegant place in which to dine, with al fresco dining being an option should the weather permit. Smooth-running, attentive service adds to a sense of well-being.

Fine, flavorful meat, poultry, fish, and seafood are combined to good effect with ingredients such as heritage beets and foraged mushrooms. The beautifully presented dishes include bison striploin with juniper jus, and Digby scallops with Jerusalem artichoke fondue, toasted hazelnut, and black kale.

Desserts are cut from similarly harmonious cloth, and tend to be made from complementary elements: plum and hazelnuts, chocolate and peanuts. Such elegant comfort food provides the perfect way to round off a meal in such a setting. **BJM**

Joso's | Seafood dishes and a gallery of risqué artwork

Location Toronto   **Signature dish** Risotto cooked in cuttlefish ink | ❺❺❺❺

> *"Shirley surprised me by revealing that she was the muse present in some of Joso's artwork…"*

Mirella Radman, scribd.com

Joso's was founded by Joso Spralja in the 1960s; his son Leo and Leo's wife Shirley have turned this popular, family-run, high-end seafood restaurant into a Toronto culinary landmark, not only because of its exquisite dishes from the Dalmatian and Aegean coasts, but also because of its eclectic interior.

A family-run restaurant Joso's may be, but it is not necessarily a family restaurant unless you are prepared to introduce your children to a riot of nudity. Even Don Juan might find the decor in this two-story space somewhat over the top. The place is full of "adult" watercolors and oils, authentic Dalí and Picasso dirties from the 1970s, randy collages, and black-and-white photos of statuesque blondes in fishnet stockings—not to mention anatomically impossible bronzes, and buxom statues in ceramic and stone. Here, *Pirates of the Caribbean* meets the *Playboy* mansion in a maelstrom of sensual kitsch.

If you are perfectly content amid the nakedness, the way is clear to enjoy some of the best Mediterranean seafood in Toronto. Once seated, you are immediately presented with a platter of the freshest fish, along with a poetic explanation of the day's international fish selection. Sharing plates is a good way to enjoy what this superb restaurant has to offer, from grilled octopus and charred butterflied prawns to lightly fried calamari. Be sure to sample the memorably good dishes made with briny cuttlefish ink, such as the *spaghettini alla Siciliana*, a garlicky pasta nest enrobed in dark, sepia-toned sauce, and the signature black risotto, a perfectly cooked bowl of silver-black pearls of risotto rice.

The service is warm and hospitable, contributing considerably to the sense of well-being when eating here. Joso's certainly stands out as a feast for all the senses, from the visual to the gustatory. That the formula is highly successful is witnessed by the hordes of loyal customers that keep coming back. **NF**

⬆ Joso's serves fresh, simply grilled fish.

Scaramouche | Elegant dining in a restaurant of two stylish parts

Location Toronto   **Signature dish** Truffled gnocchi Parisienne | ❸❸❸❸

For more than thirty years, Scaramouche has been an institution of refinement and polished, attentive service, with a luxurious menu to match, showcasing chef and co-owner Keith Froggett's superb technique without a hint of showiness. Such is the place's standing among the local community that it is invariably buzzing with a crowd of contented diners. Froggett's experience and commitment to high standards shine consistently in the food on offer.

Scaramouche has become a restaurant with a dual personality in that the large dining room was altered and split into two separate environments: the ever elegant Scaramouche and its more casual counterpart, the Pasta Bar and Grill. The grand, vaulted dining room remains a place for romance, engagements, power business dinners, and the old establishment, while the sibling informal space makes for a terrific weeknight dinner destination. Whichever space diners are in, however, there are truly spectacular, glimmering views of the city of Toronto forming a memorable backdrop to the impeccable service and stellar cuisine executed with panache.

Diners in the Pasta Bar and Grill can enjoy superb dishes, such as homemade cavatelli, tossed with organic shrimp, bacon heady with smokiness, tomatoes, and zucchini and a rich peppercorn fettuccine enrobed with a splendid sauce of braised beef tenderloin, oyster mushrooms, and Madeira.

Those in the Scaramouche dining room may enjoy a squab with a succulent bacon-wrapped breast stuffed with foie gras and wild mushrooms, and a confit leg adorned with spring peas, leeks, and toasted faro. The desserts available to those in both rooms are spectacular, thoughtful, and creative—witness the Valrhona chocolate mousse with Earl Grey ice cream and lemon curd. But it is the legendary signature coconut cream pie that reigns supreme and is absolutely worth anyone's indulgence. **NF**

"To be treated like royalty against the setting sun on the city skyline is to know pleasure."

postcity.com

⬆ Presentation is key at Scaramouche.

Bosk | A hotel restaurant that is way out of the ordinary

Location Toronto   **Signature dish** Nova Scotia lobster gnocchi with lobster emulsion | ❸❸❸

"I cook because it fulfills something inside of me... making somebody happy."

Damon Campbell, chef at Bosk

⬆ The wine wall defines the layout of the room.

Restaurants associated with hotels tend not to be glorified unless they are in the company of such luminaries as Pierre Gagnaire or Alaine Ducasse. But among the exceptions is Bosk, the beautiful signature restaurant of the Shangri-La, Toronto. Executive chef Damon Campbell and chef de cuisine Jeff Kang both came from the kitchen of Vancouver's renowned Diva at The Met, and here they have used their experience of high-class dining to excellent effect.

With its elegant, wood-hued decor and soft, subtle lighting, Bosk (meaning a small wooded area) is a quiet, serene oasis in the heart of Toronto's busy financial district. It is in this dining room, with its well-spaced, contemporary tables draped in crisp linen that many Canadian power brokers sort out their deals alongside the city's socialite charity ladies. The room's design centerpiece is the stunning wine wall, which holds most of sommelier Mark Moffatt's list.

The seasonally changing menu reflects Campbell and Kang's West Coast focus on using high-quality ingredients, many of them sourced locally and regionally (such as "Ontario's gathered leaves") and served in elegant and accomplished dishes. For example, Campbell's stunning butter-poached lobster atop delicate gnocchi pillows is splashed with a foamed aromatic lobster sauce; the local duck breast, perfectly seared to an intense shade of port, is paired with roast peaches, earthy onions, and parsnips.

For a lunchtime treat, you could head to Bosk and enjoy the succulent porchetta sandwich, wonderfully spiced and stacked with havarti, mustard pesto, and pickled shallots. Dinner sees a more formal approach, with the opportunity to order à la carte, or savor a carefully constructed tasting menu offering dishes from caviar doughnut to roasted squab breast served with salsify, hazelnut, brussel leaves, and cherry puree. Courteous service adds to the smooth-as-silk dining experience: a hotel restaurant to recommend. **NF**

Lee | Asian-inspired cuisine in a nightclub ambience

Location Toronto　**Signature dish** Green chicken curry with crispy multigrain rice cakes and spicy tomato jam | 💲💲

International celebrity chef Susur Lee is known for his skill in blending textures and flavors in tantalizing dishes. Since 1987, when he opened Lotus, his first restaurant, he has showcased his renowned style of cuisine at his various restaurants in Singapore, New York, and Washington, D.C., as well as appearing on the popular TV series *Top Chef Masters*.

After a decade of consulting for one of Asia's top restaurant groups, the chef returned to Toronto in 2000 to open an elegant gastrodome, Susur. Four years later, he opened Lee. While distinctly chic in appearance, Lee is a more informal affair, in keeping with fine-dining trends. Lee has a relatively youthful and hipster clientele; the decor has a nightclub edge and the surroundings are dimly lit. The cuisine is Asian-inspired and characterized by the small plates, which are designed to be shared by diners. Lee Lounge, a bar area next door, effectively extends the restaurant by offering a chic urban watering hole, complete with rose velvet banquettes, in which diners can wait and enjoy a pre-meal, an eclectic, Asian-inspired cocktail, and a little people watching.

Susur Lee's cosmopolitan cooking and stylish presentation are totally in keeping with the sophisticated surroundings. Crab cakes are enlivened by a spiced tamarind glaze and smoked chili mayonnaise, while East Coast diver scallops are spice encrusted and served with a Chinese sweet bean pesto and crispy bacon. Vegetarians are amply provided for with well-constructed dishes such as a Mexican goat cheese tart, heirloom tomato and beet salad, and quinoa vegetable chow fan and Singaporean-style slaw. Lee finds constant inspiration in Southeast Asia's rich and varied cuisine, manifested in dishes such as his Assam Thai satay and his award-winning dish of green curry chicken with a crispy multigrain rice cake and spiced tomato jam—a memorably good combination. **NF**

"It makes me feel really good to see people of different cultures connecting through my food."

Susur Lee, chef and owner of Lee

⬆ Thai satay is one of many delicacies on offer.

River Café | Offering food as lovely as the parkland setting

Location Calgary **Signature dish** Olsen's High Country bison striploin | $$$

Located in Prince's Island Park, Calgary, River Café has been called "magical" for good reason. To start with, it has an idyllic location that offers what locals consider to be the best view in town, looking out over the magnificent Bow River. Having discovered this wonderful site, founder and proprietor Sal Howell set out to create a restaurant where it was possible to enjoy dining in a natural setting throughout the seasons. She has transformed what was initially a small, open-air café that only operated during the summer months into a year-round restaurant, while preserving the relaxed, airy feel of the original space. The lodgelike decor is appealingly rustic in style and includes a stone fireplace, an open kitchen, and a drinks cabinet made from the prow of a boat. One of the café's most popular features is its spacious terrace, on which a meal can be enjoyed in the company of an impressive array of largely indigenous plants.

The adventurous cuisine on offer here complements the café's spectacular surroundings, drawing inspiration and ingredients from the surrounding landscape. An eclectic, seasonally changing menu relies on an ever-expanding network of farmers and producers. The restaurant's culinary mission is to "explore, innovate, and evolve."

Alberta may be famous for its beef, but odds are that the café's Bite Ranch beef striploin, complemented by chanterelle fricassee and anchovy-roasted cauliflower, can rival any steak in the city. The game, in dishes such as the Olsen's High Country bison striploin and the wild boar tenderloin, also showcases the kitchen's skills to good effect. The inventive vegetable selection is similarly impressive. The careful sourcing of fine local ingredients, creatively cooked by a kitchen that is confident in what it does, makes eating here a pleasure. With its outstanding wine list, the River Café is sure to become any culinary explorer's favorite discovery. **BJM**

"We learn from our peers, and then there is the never-ending flow of fresh young enthusiasm..."

Sal Howell, owner of River Café

↑ The profusion of flowering plants surrounding River Café helps to create an atmosphere of tranquility.

→ An image used to promote River Café's "Roots and Shoots 2013" event, which celebrated the local *terroir*.

Au Pied de Cochon | Robust, French-influenced cuisine for carnivores

Location Montreal **Signature dish** Stuffed *pied de cochon* (pig's foot) with foie gras | **$**

Powerful and gutsy; earthy and gloriously calorific; and even meaty, big, and bouncy (to borrow from The Who): these are just several of the descriptions that could be flung at Au Pied de Cochon and its celebrity chef, Martin Picard. It should be said at the outset that vegetarians and vegans would have a difficult time at Au Pied de Cochon. The menu is packed with such fulsome dishes as deep-fried foie gras; pig's trotters de-boned, breaded, and then dipped into the deep fryer; and a smooth and creamy guinea fowl liver mousse. And those are just for starters. People take their places in the brasserielike surroundings—big mirrors, long bar, adjoining stools, and a regimented line of tables—to enjoy the varied carnivorous fare.

As for the mains, it is a case of when the going gets tough, the tough get going. How about the "melting pot," a rich and molten stew of pork belly, sausage, and black pudding, atop a hill of wantonly buttered mashed potatoes? Or perhaps it is time for one of the restaurant's favorites, the "duck in a can," whose name tells it as it is—duck breast and foie gras packed into a can and cooked, with the meat rare and juicy and the foie gras providing a smooth contrast. Other options include spicy bison tartare and foie gras *poutine*, which could be interpreted as an upmarket version of cheese melted over fries (although it is not recommended that Picard should be told that!). Desserts are equally uncompromising: witness the helpings of maple syrup-influenced sugar pie.

Despite all these calories, Au Pied de Cochon is one of Montreal's gastronomic standouts, a place for people with big appetites who like to eat with gusto. Certainly this is not a place for faint-hearted pickers and nibblers—there is a lip-smacking, rib-sticking, napkin-staining enthusiasm about the place, and Montreal is all the better for it. **ATJ**

⬆ The interior has a French brasserie vibe.

Joe Beef | Playful riffs on classic French cuisine, with an emphasis on meat

Location Montreal   **Signature dish** Foie gras "Double Down" | ❸❸

Walk in through Joe Beef's door and you know that you are somewhere a bit special: tables rammed close together; the walls a riot of quirky, found objects, posters, and curious art; menus scrawled over blackboard walls; a bison's head in the bathroom.

But make no mistake: the ramshackle rooms are the setting for some very serious cooking. Sure, some of it might come across as jokey, with its plays on "dude food." The famous foie gras "Double Down," modeled on a little number from KFC but with the chicken breasts replaced by fat lobes of liver, is possibly one of the richest things you will ever eat. This is a place where you can get "beer cheese" and cornflake eel nuggets; Joe Beef has even been known to serve oysters on vintage radios.

But this tongue-in-cheek approach belies the love that owners Frédéric Morin and David McMillan have for classic French technique. They describe their food as Bocusian-Lyonnaise, and it is fitting that

bilingual Montreal should be home to this happy marriage of France and North America. So you might find complex and vinous *lièvre à la royale* (royal hare); *pieds et paquets* (stewed sheep's feet and offal); or *turbot au vermouth*. There might be a challenging, burgundy-colored horse meat tartare. Joe Beef cures and smokes its own charcuterie, and grows its own produce in a garden on the site of a former crack den.

Morin and McMillan are as buzzed about wine as they are about their kitchen, craft beer, and eccentric cocktails. McMillan is rumored to "drink magnums of Chablis nightly" and has a finely honed appreciation of France's finest (it is a neat symmetry that they staked their claim in Montreal's previously sketchy Little Burgundy). Joe Beef is highly individual and some maintain that they don't "get it." Make up your own mind, and start by ordering the sausage martini. **MOL**

⬆ Joe Beef offers great food and a mellow atmosphere.

Schwartz's | Venerable delicatessen that pulls in the crowds

Location Montreal   **Signature dish** Smoked beef sandwich served on rye | $

"The value of Schwartz's lies in the fact that it is unchanged; it's one of the last of its kind."

David Sax, theglobeandmail.com

⊤ Schwartz's is a beloved Montreal institution.

This place is popular; you will probably have to line up to get in. The interior might seem nothing much to write home about—this is "only" a delicatessen, after all—but then you see that the walls are covered by framed photographs of celebrities who have visited, as well as various plaques and the occasional painting of the place. The ambience is undeniably cozy, and more than likely you will end up sharing a table with loyal locals or an excited bunch of tourists.

People wait patiently in line at Schwartz's simply because it has the best smoked meat sandwich in town, made with juicy, well-seasoned slices of kosher-style beef brisket that has been cured for ten days and then smoked. The meat comes sandwiched between two slices of fresh rye bread, with a dollop of sweet yellow mustard slapped on top. Accompaniments include fries, sweet and sour pickles, and a plate of homemade slaw. To drink? Forget about fine wine or craft beer: a can of black cherry soda is the preferred option, and, believe it or not, it works.

Behind the counter, at which you will find regulars perching on stools, men dressed in white catering gear move about, constantly cutting away at great slabs of smoked meat. The meaty aroma rises into the air, warm and spicy, arousing the taste buds. How would you like the meat? It can be served lean, medium, medium fat, or fat. Aficionados swear by the medium-fat offering, although there are some who say that the flavor is all in the fat.

Ribs, steak, and chicken are also on the menu, but it is the smoked beef that folk come for, and they have been coming for a long time. Reuben Schwartz first opened on Saint Laurent Boulevard in 1928, naming his establishment the Montreal Hebrew Delicatessen. Since then it has had several owners, but the delicatessen remains a pivotal, must-visit place. Foodie fashions may come and go, but Schwartz's is a still point in an ever-turning world. **ATJ**

Toqué! | Elegant and sophisticated dining, delivered in style

Location Montreal **Signature dish** Duck magret | ❸❸❸❸

One eats well in Montreal, whether snacking on the cheese-and-fries glory that is *poutine*, or stretching the wallet and expectations toward the higher end of the market, which is where Toqué! (the name means "crazy") enters the gastronomic fray. Established in 1993 by husband-and-wife team Normand Laprise and Christine Lamarche, it is a standout destination in the vibrant heart of Montreal's International District.

Toqué! is a brightly lit and elegantly designed space with crisp white tablecloths and burgundy red tones on the walls and carpet, the decor reminiscent of 1970s chic. Diners here expect the daily-changing menu to celebrate local and seasonally grown produce in dishes designed to look and taste good. A journey through the à la carte menu might start with a visit to the the countryside of Quebec province, where the fois gras is considered to be among the best in the world. Those with an inclination to pork might chance upon the smoked suckling pig cheek. There might be a soup, perhaps a rich and cream-textured one made with Jerusalem artichokes, or a lobster salad, fresh and salty-sweet with a tangy accompaniment.

For mains, there might be a succulent venison loin with Bordelaise sauce, or a plump and tender duck magret. The dessert menu might suggest quince mousse or a poached pear filled with vanilla goat cheese. The cellar is commodious here, and the sommelier will be on hand to suggest wine pairings for each of the courses you choose.

Toqué! also fields a daily tasting menu designed to showcase the gastronomic skills of what many regard as Montreal's top eating place. Meanwhile, Toqué! continues to build its reputation in other ways. There is a cookbook entitled *Toqué! Les artisans d'une gastronomie québécoise* (2012), and for those who prefer to eat in relatively casual surroundings, there is the sister restaurant Brasserie T!, which opened in 2010. Truly, one eats well in Montreal. **ATJ**

"I remember my first taste … Toqué! was like a guerrilla fighter battling the forces of tyranny."

Alan Richman, U.S. journalist and food writer

⬆ Comfortable tables for two in the Toqué! dining room.

L'Express | Parisian bistro cooking in the heart of French Canada

Location Montreal   **Signature dish** Steak and fries | $ $

> *"I can't tell you how happy I am to read through a menu like this. They do everything just right."*

Anthony Bourdain, chef and author

⬆ L'Express has a Parisian bistro atmosphere.

The glitter of lights reflected in the mirrors that line the walls; the black-and-white checkerboard tiling on the floor, across which glide the waiting staff in black waistcoats and white aprons and shirts; the rise and fall of voices as friends and families gather to enjoy belt-straining portions of vigorous dishes such as bone marrow, steak and fries, pork rillettes, duck confit, calf liver, and veal kidney in mustard sauce (not all at once, of course)—this is L'Express. And on every table a jar of tangy, sweet-and-sour cornichons, highly addictive and a perfect companion for the basket of bread brought to your table when you sit down.

All of these details and the accompanying ambience suggest that this could be a traditional Parisian bistro, perhaps in a lively arrondissement and overlooked by a landmark such as the Basilique du Sacré Coeur. A further sense of being in Paris comes from the fact that French is spoken all around. But this is an ocean away from Paris: we are in Canada, in the province of Quebec, downtown in a bustling part of central Montreal.

L'Express first opened its doors in this location in 1980. In the years that have since gone by, it has become—for want of a better word—a Montreal institution, a place dedicated to good eating with the emphasis on French cuisine. Here you will find bistro food, hearty and happily served—creamy, smooth chicken liver paté to start with, followed by a moist slab of steak in the company of crisp and yet fluffy fries. The waiter will be pleased to offer his or her thoughts on the accompanying wine (or beer, if you so wish). To finish with, how about *Ile flottante avec caramel*, a twist on the standard dish in which a crunchy caramel-coated hillock of molten meringue appears in a moat of vanilla-flavored crème sauce. Or there are other Canadian bistro staples: maple syrup pie, orange crème caramel, or lemon tart. One last thought: be sure to go with an appetite. **ATJ**

Chez Boulay | French bistro style meets Nordic cuisine

Location Quebec   **Signature dish** Confit bison cheeks | ❸❸❸

Chez Boulay subtitles itself as a "bistro boréal," and there is a mixture of two traditions here: the French bistro tradition, with its robust dishes and casual approach to dining, and the boreal (subarctic) tradition, which has a Nordic inspiration. The concept yields plenty of fresh and seasonal vegetables and berries alongside sustainable game—such as elk, duck, and bison—plus a goodly helping of fish. Interesting ingredients like wild ginger, Labrador tea spice, and burdock root find their way into the kitchen, and the boreal influence is also discernible in the modern decor: white tones on the walls, and a clean and unfussy layout. Chez Boulay's intriguing idea of a French–Nordic fusion quickly earned it the status of one of Quebec City's hottest dining spots.

Chez Boulay was created by chefs Jean-Luc Boulay and Arnaud Marchand. Both already had fine reputations when the restaurant opened in 2012, although Boulay has had several decades in the business compared to Marchand's mere ten years. They met in 2010 on the Canadian TV show *Les Chefs!*, where Marchand was a contestant and Boulay remains a judge. Discovering a mutual interest in Nordic cuisine, they decided to work together.

Try the signature gourmet platters: the meat version includes dried saucisson, pork rillettes, and dried goose breast, while the seafood one pulsates with smoked salmon cubes, haddock rillettes, mussels, and shrimp. On the main dinner menu, there might be marinated Arctic char carpaccio with elderberry vinegar or a bison tartare to start with, followed by confit goose and duck legs in a scalloped parsnip parmentier, or confit bison cheeks with a trilogy of celery (as a puree, confit, and grated). Conclude the adventure with iced nougat and wild berries, or a maple eclair. Chez Boulay is Nordic invention meets Quebecois French open-mindedness, and the result is multigastronomic. **ATJ**

"The pear tart persuaded us that it is not hell to live in the northern latitudes. Sometimes it is heaven!"

Stephanie Wood-Houde, lapresse.ca

⬆ The harmonious woods of Chez Boulay's dining room.

3660 on the Rise | Haute cuisine in colorful Hawaiian style

Location Honolulu   **Signature dish** *Ahi katsu* | 💲💲

Adding a touch of class to Hawaii's dining out scene, this acclaimed restaurant, with Executive Chef Russell Siu at its helm, has built up a notable reputation, and is best known for presenting fresh island ingredients with touches of Asian, European, and local flavorings.

Siu combines a wide-ranging palate of good-quality ingredients to colorful and inventive effect. Starters include ahi katsu and duo of foie gras. The former is high-quality yellowfin or bigeye tuna wrapped in nori (edible seaweed) and spinach, flash-fried, sliced, and placed over wasabi-ginger butter sauce. The latter is prepared in two ways—one piece pan-seared and served with mandarin orange marmalade, the other served with a *lilikoi* (passion fruit) gelée, a tart–sweet accompaniment that contrasts well with the richness of the foie gras.

Appropriately for an island-based cuisine, seafood is a particular highlight, with dishes such as the light and elegant Chinese steamed fillet of snapper recommended. The snapper is lightly seared before steaming, thus adding additional depth of flavor, and the sauce is subtly flavored with black beans.

Among other fish dishes are steamed shrimp and scallop *lau lau*, an inventive and upscale version of a Hawaiian favorite; tempura catfish with ponzu sauce; and pan-seared sesame crusted ahi, which comes with scallion and ginger, sizzling hot oil drizzle, shiitake mushroom broth, and is finished with a miso-grilled musubi.

Desserts are always a treat here. The Mile High Waialae Pie is one of the restaurant's signature indulgences, consisting of two layers of vanilla and coffee ice cream with macadamia brittle, gooey caramel, and luscious chocolate sauces. Service is attentive and friendly, helpful on all levels. This is a place in which to have a treat with a special meal. **MG**

⊤ The seafood at 3660 on the Rise is a speciality.

Chef Mavro | An accomplished taste of Provençe meets Pacific cuisine

Location Honolulu   **Signature dish** Indochine-style poached lobster | 🟢🟢🟢🟢

Despite its unglamorous location and discreet setting, Chef Mavro offers distinctly high-end, fine dining. George Mavrothalassitis, the eponymous French chef-owner, is a man with strong ideas about the right way to cook, so diners should be prepared to surrender themselves to his culinary vision.

The bill of fare, which changes substantially from season to season, is a synthesis of his native styles and Hawaii's prime ingredients. Heirloom tomatoes and live shrimp arrive at the back door daily, delivered by the farmers and fishermen who have harvested them.

Diners may choose from an assortment of menus, such as "From Land and Sea" or "Provençe and the Islands," with each dish paired with an appropriate wine. A "sustainable caviar" tasting accompanied, *naturellement*, with Champagne, makes a luxurious start to the meal. From the main courses, highlights include the elegantly plated Indochine-style poached Keahole lobster (Keahole is the westernmost point on

the Big Island of Hawaii). This dish is flavored with kaffir lime, lemongrass, tamarind, green papaya, and chervil. Another excellent choice would be the Wagyu beef medallions, with a Pinot noir essence, drizzled with a braised short rib chimichurri parsnip puree, and sided by pickled baby beet salad. Desserts continue the Franco-Polynesian theme, combining ingredients such as chocolate, mango, and guava with playful exuberance. Everything on offer at Chef Mavro is highly accomplished and characterized by imaginative combinations of flavors and a wide-ranging palate of ingredients.

Adding to the appeal of the experience is the smoothly professional service, admirably well-versed in the intricacies of the changing menu. Very much a special occasions restaurant, Chef Mavro offers some of Hawaii's finest food and should be savored. **MG**

⬆ Chef Mavro has a relaxed yet elegant ambience.

Alan Wong's | Island cooking by the godfather of Hawaiian cuisine

Location Honolulu　　**Signature dish** Da Bag　|　❸❸❸

For a taste of contemporary Hawaiian food, this smart restaurant, despite its unlikely, rather impersonal location in an office building, is the place to go. Chef Alan Wong—a founder member of "Hawaii Regional Cuisine," an influential movement by local chefs to re-invigorate the state's restaurant cuisine—is a key ambassador for this style of cooking. His approach draws on Hawaii's diverse ethnic roots as the inspiration for new dishes featuring local flavors and locally grown produce. Carefully cultivated, close relationships with local farmers and food producers pay dividends in the glorious, high-quality, fresh ingredients that are the foundation of his cooking.

Here one can sample Wong's trademark cooking, notably influenced by Asia, yet created with sophisticated French savoir faire. Starters to look out for include the tomato salad with li hing (preserved plum) vinaigrette. The cheekily named "Da Bag" employs the French *en papillote* cooking technique to create a flavorful combination of clams, smoky kalua pork, and shiitake mushrooms steamed together in a package. In a nice piece of restaurant theater, the waiter punctures the parcel tableside, releasing a rush of kalua-scented vapor to appetizing effect.

When it comes to the mains, an elegant option is ginger-crusted onaga (long-tail red snapper). Look out, too, for President Barack Obama's favorite dish here—twice-cooked short rib, a glorious combination of flavors and textures. Desserts such as lilikoi brulée continue the French-Asian theme, combining classic cooking techniques with ingredients such as tapioca and the tropical fruit for which Hawaii is famous.

Given how busy it can be here, service is efficient and knowledgeable. If booking for a special occasion, let the restaurant know in advance to receive a menu signed by the staff as a keepsake. **MG**

⬆ Alan Wong's led a revival of Hawaiian regional cuisine.

Town Restaurant | Local island food in a mellow holiday atmosphere

Location Honolulu **Signature dish** Hand-cut pasta, cured ono roe, summer squash, and string beans | ❸❸

Locally sourced ingredients are of ultra-importance here, organic whenever possible, and served with Hawaiian-style graciousness and friendliness (aka "Aloha"). The menu at this contemporary, casual American neighborhood bistro changes daily, allowing the chefs to make the most of the finest farm-grown and market-purchased ingredients.

You'll recognize inspiration from classic recipes of the Mediterranean. Town's cuisine is best described as Contemporary American with an Italian sensibility, where the ingredients are allowed to shine and nothing is wasted. Town offers hand-cut pasta and gnocchi, slow-braised meats and freshly-caught local seafood, complemented by a modest wine list that showcases small artisan producers and creative, hand-crafted cocktails. Underneath the relaxed appearance, the kitchen shows considerable intelligence and taste in its ever-changing menu, creating flavorful food which is enjoyable to eat.

In addition to the signature dish, menu highlights include baby arugula with beets, orange, fennel, mint, chickpeas, and ricotta salata; black mussels with fennel pastina and tomato in a Cinzano broth; and gnocchi with guanciale or a dish of sautéed, locally-grown hamakua mushrooms. Desserts are creamy and dreamy, with indulgences such as salted chocolate pretzel tart and milk and honey buttermilk panna cotta, both great ways to end almost any meal.

Just minutes from Waikiki, the Town has a bar and a dog-friendly patio for al fresco dining, where the seating is reserved for walk-in guests. The restaurant has become a favorite for upscale casual or impromptu dining as well as for special occasions, and has captured a loyal following. Portions are generous and prices are noticeably reasonable, adding to the relaxed atmosphere. **MG**

⬆ The breakfast burrito is a hearty option to start the day.

Salt Bar & Kitchen | Contemporary tapas given the Hawaii touch

Location Honolulu **Signature dish** Charcuterie board, chef's selection | 🅢🅢

"If you're celebrating anything at all, including being alive, this is probably the place to do it."

John Heckathorn, *Honolulu Magazine*

This popular bar and eatery brings the tapas bar concept to Hawaii in distinctive and contemporary style. Urban chic surroundings showcase local ingredients, with pride of place going to the on-trend charcuterie, made from locally sourced, corn-fed Shinsato Farm pork cured in-house. Another treat for carnivores is head cheese, which, in spite of its name, is chicken liver pâté and rich pork rillettes.

The ground floor of the establishment is essentially one long bar with a few counter seats. Upstairs, in what was formerly a loft space, are a few tables. The atmosphere on both floors is intimate and lively, with a constant buzz of people eating, drinking, and talking.

The menu is as pared down as the stripped-back surroundings. It offers a small selection of dishes, from nibbles such as oxtail empanadas, served with a nicely contrasting tomato and golden raisin chutney, to "big plates" that are full meals in themselves. The bar's locavore policy dictates that Hawaiian produce predominates throughout: the fish of the day is caught in the adjacent Pacific Ocean; nearly all the meat is from nearby farms.

The ingredients are simple, but the treatment of them is memorably flavorsome and lingers in the memory. Particular favorites include flash-fried oysters with a zingy lemon jam, and chicken with Big Island squash and salsa verde.

The drinks list adopts a similarly selective approach, with a restricted but carefully chosen range of wine and beers to complement the food. Nothing here is haphazard. The cocktail menu offers creations such as the Mezcal-laden "Flight to Mexico" and the whiskey-based "Smoking Goat."

In addition to its food and drink, the Salt Bar and Kitchen has a fashionable, big-city vibe that has made it one of Honolulu's most popular hangouts for lunch and dinner. **MG**

⬆ Salt Bar & Kitchen serves a range of light meals in addition to the popular charcuterie.

Le Pigeon | French-influenced comfort food

Location Portland   **Signature dish** Beef bourguignon | 🟊🟊

Portland is justifiably proud of Le Pigeon—the second word pronounced in the American, not the French way—which, soon after opening in 2006, cemented the city's place on the international culinary map. Chef Gabriel Rucker intertwines American classics, French bistro cooking, and his own innovative take on food to create a menu that is captivating and inventive. Rucker's talent was recognized by *Food and Wine Magazine*, which named him a Best New Chef (and later an "all-star"), and by the James Beard Foundation, which awarded him the titles of Rising Star Chef of the Year and Best Chef Northwest.

Le Pigeon's decor is informal and charming. A brick wall faces the copper-accented open kitchen, and at the rear of the restaurant are high shelves stacked with wine bottles, cookbooks, and mason jars containing pickles. Vintage painted bronze chandeliers hang from the lofted ceiling, and the bread plates are mismatched retro floral china. Diners sit at three communal tables, or can claim one of the ten coveted spots at the chef's counter and watch Rucker and his sous chefs in action.

The menu changes frequently according to the season and Rucker's whim. An early proponent of nose-to-tail eating, Rucker is famously fond of both offal and meat, and diners should expect dishes featuring tongue, heart, liver, or belly, but there is always a fish of the day as well as something for vegetarians. A menu mainstay is the beef bourguignon—a homage to, rather than a replication of, the classic French dish—in which beef cheeks are braised overnight in wine until meltingly tender, and served atop a rich potato gratin. For dessert, adventurous diners should not miss the profiteroles filled with foie gras ice cream. Service is attentive and professional, and the French-dominated wine list impressive. All in all, it is easy to understand why this appealing restaurant is a Portland favorite. **SW**

"It's more important to do what you do really well than to do a lot of different things kind of well."

Gabriel Rucker, chef at Le Pigeon

⬆ The signature beef bourguignon is topped with Gruyère cheese.

Ned Ludd | Seasonal, savory, and always wood-fired

Location Portland　**Signature dish** Whole roasted trout　| 💲💲

"Named for the founder of the Luddites ... this craft kitchen prepares low-tech food."

fodors.com

⤴ The cozy interior is perfect for a meal with friends.

Ned Ludd: American Craft Kitchen is run by Jason Helms, a chef in the vanguard of Oregon's burgeoning culinary scene. All his food is cooked to order in a wood-fired oven—the kitchen has no other source of heat. The resulting dishes are warm, complex, and built on a flavorful foundation of the best regional produce they can find.

The menu takes hyper-seasonal to new heights—dishes change weekly, if not more often, offering a right-in-the-moment dining experience. Leafy green salads that might elsewhere be unremarkable are here lifted to previously unimagined levels of tastiness. While seasonal additions and changes are rapid-fire, it's a safe bet that anything with pork in it will be spectacular year-round. Fish dishes—the whole trout is spectacular, however it's prepared— and meat pies are, along with virtually everything else available here, a treat for the senses, with the textural diversity that can be achieved only by a wood fire.

Portlanders have an enthusiasm for brunch that is widely held to be unmatched in the Western Hemisphere. Ned Ludd steps up to the plate here with a vegetable hash with eggs, smoked trout, and toast that is consummately satisfying. The menu is heavily weighted toward the savory, with frequent appearances of warm marinated olives, several varieties of smoked fish, and charred greens.

Ned Ludd takes a clever and very "Portland" (in other words, exceedingly hip) approach to dining, but the restaurant's unfaltering commitment to quality—from produce-sourcing to preparation—makes the experience substantial and enduringly memorable. The robust flavors of every wood-fired dish are complemented by a warm and intimate setting. Ned Ludd is perfect for small group dinners and long conversations over the finest seasonal, regionally sourced, and beautifully prepared dishes the verdant Pacific Northwest has to offer. **CR**

Nostrana | A true taste of Italy in Oregon

Location Portland **Signature dish** Gnocchi | [$][$]

Nostrana is widely acknowledged as one of the best Italian restaurants in the United States. It has achieved this distinction through the work of Cathy Whims, a chef with a discerning palate, a restrained hand, and an instinctive awareness that the fewer the ingredients in a dish, the greater the challenge in its preparation. This traditionally Italian insight particularly informs her acclaimed fresh pasta. Her scratch cooking is elevated to an even higher level by the wealth of sensational raw materials that abound in surrounding Oregon.

The restaurant's name is carefully chosen. *Nostrana* in Italian means "from our locality," and suggests a sense of place and of heritage. Almost all of the ingredients are locally sourced, but the cooking is done as it would be in Italy.

Whims has been a regular visitor to Italy for decades, immersing herself in that nation's unmatched food culture, gleaning secrets from chefs and home cooks, and including them in her own cooking. For example, in Rome, it is traditional to serve gnocchi on Thursdays, and that practice has been adopted at Nostrana. Whims' version is made with semolina in a classic recipe that is now hard to find, even in the Eternal City, and served with mozzarella, tomato, porcini mushrooms, rosemary, and cream—a heavenly combination.

Local trout, lamb, beef, and pork are all cooked with Italian methods. Polenta is combined with chestnut flour, as is done in Liguria and Tuscany. Lentils come from Umbria. Many desserts are fruit-based, as Italians would have them. There is an outstanding wine list combining Italian and Oregonian bottles. Wines by the glass might include a delicious white Ribolla Gialla, a silken red Rosso della Valtellina, and marvelous dessert wines such as Picolit. It is extremely unusual to find any of these drinks outside Italy. **FP**

"The Neapolitan-style pizza is outstanding, as are the antipasti and bruschetta."

Insiders' Guide: Portland, Oregon

↑ Bruschetta is a popular antipasto choice.

Pine State Biscuits |

Delicious Portland comfort food

Location Portland   **Signature dish** The Reggie sandwich | **$**

Pine State Biscuits serves warm biscuit sandwiches and generous plates of Southern comfort food, dished up with no regard for calorie count.

Created by North Carolina transplants Walt Alexander, Kevin Atchley, and Brian Snyder, Pine State Biscuits got its start at the Portland State University Farmers' Market, where people would line up for hours to buy its wares, all of which are made from locally sourced, sustainably farmed ingredients.

The vibe at Pine State Biscuits' current premises on 11th and SE Division is decidedly informal. Order from the cashier, grab your silverware and a cup of coffee, and take a seat at the long counter, where you can watch the cooks on the line. There are also diner-

---

"The Reggie Deluxe is … the Big Kahuna, the Mac Daddy, the Ozymandias of sandwiches."

Portland Food and Drink

---

style tables under retro-style lamps with custom-printed shades, and picnic tables in the outdoor area, which is heated in winter.

All the food is superb—the grits and cornmeal blueberry pancakes are memorably delicious—but the signature dish is the Reggie. Sandwiched between two flaky, fluffy biscuits are fried chicken, bacon, melted cheese, and rich sausage gravy. Serious contenders can opt for the Reggie Deluxe: a Reggie with an egg. Pine State Biscuits does cater to vegetarians—the Regina, a biscuit sandwich with an over-easy egg, braised Collard greens, and Texas Pete Hot Sauce—but meat—particularly the moist, crispy fried chicken—is the main attraction. **SW**

Olympic Provisions |

A meat-centric, Portland-style menu

Location Portland   **Signature dish** In-house cured salami—try them all | **$$**

Housed in a classically restored industrial building near the east bank of the Willamette River, Olympic Provisions is Portland's first true salumeria. It offers a range of rich dishes that are rooted in the long traditions of rustic Spanish and Mediterranean cuisine, and elevated further by the seasonal bounty of the Pacific Northwest.

Guests can drop in for an unbelievably good sandwich or linger over a traditional European-style seated dinner. The premises' sleek design, warmed by candlelight and natural wood tones, pairs well with the food on offer. The space combines a deli counter, a seating area, an open kitchen, and a small retail space—it's well laid out but minimally decorated, leaving all the more time to focus on the food.

Oregon-raised chef Alex Yoder takes an ingredient-driven approach to the award-winning menu. With an in-house delicatessen at his disposal, it's no surprise that many dishes highlight mouth-watering savory meats, with salted, pickled, cured, and smoked ingredients making their way into most dishes. The Chef's Choice Charcuterie Plate is a great value and serves as a tasty introduction to a wide range of products.

The entrée selections are few, but each item is carefully crafted and flavorful. While some vegetarian options are available, the menu is aimed principally at meat-eaters, highlighting not only the house-made charcuteries but also mussels, chicken, prime rib, and several other delicious, regionally sourced, and seasonal offerings.

Before you leave, make sure to pick up a salami or chorizo to take home—or try the *saucisson au chocolat*, a French-style dark chocolate ganache made with nuts, candied ginger, and red wine, which is sure to satisfy any sweet tooth. **CR**

Paley's Place | Characterful restaurant using high-quality local, organic, and seasonal ingredients

Location Portland   **Signature dish** Line-caught Columbia River wild salmon (seasonal) | 💲💲

This 50-seat restaurant offers creative and consistently delicious dishes in some of the most relaxed, even downright cozy, surroundings you'll ever encounter. Chef and owner Vitaly Paley was born in Kiev, Ukraine, immigrated to the United States in the 1970s, and learned his craft in New York and France. He eventually chose Portland, Oregon, as his base because of all the high-quality ingredients available in the surrounding area.

He and his wife Kimberly opened their restaurant in 1995. In almost two decades of operation, Paley's Place has earned numerous accolades, and in 2005 Paley himself won the prestigious James Beard Award for Best Chef Northwest. Reservations are a must in this intimate space, especially for seats on the veranda, a real treat in the warmer months of the year.

Paley's Place has exerted an undeniable influence on the emergence of the now widely recognized Pacific Northwest style of cuisine. The menu revolves around meats and produce sourced from organic, local, and sustainably run operations. A carefully curated cheese list never disappoints, and the house-made fruit and nut bar—which Paley created after failing to find a condiment worthy of his world-class selection of cheeses—is outstanding and is now available commercially.

It's difficult to pick a favorite from a menu this good, and offerings change seasonally, but Paley and executive chef Patrick McKee work wonders with salmon in a wide range of styles.

The natural bounty of the verdant Pacific Northwest, paired with consistently excellent service, make a visit to Paley's Place a warm, welcoming, and memorable experience. For those who can't make it there themselves, Vitaly and Kimberly have published *The Paley's Place Cookbook*. **CR**

"A restaurant is like an art piece ... walking into Paley's Place can be like walking into a Matisse."

Portland Food and Drink

⊞ Paley's Place salmon—painstakingly prepared and simply presented, like all Vitaly's work.

Pok Pok | A gloriously authentic taste of Thai street food in Oregon

Location Portland **Signature dish** "Ike's Vietnamese fish sauce chicken wings" | **$**

"This is a wonderful restaurant ... I've rarely had a dish here that was flawed in execution."

Portland Food and Drink

⬆ A tasty dish of boar rubbed with garlic, coriander root, and black pepper, and glazed with soy.

Chef Andy Ricker's obsession with the food he ate in northern Thailand has spawned what may be the most exciting Thai restaurant in the United States.

The legend of Pok Pok is nearly as good as the food. After a year-long love affair with Thailand, Ricker started cooking and selling Thai-style barbecue literally from his own backyard in 2005. He later expanded the restaurant into his sunken basement, lining the walls with laminated plywood and setting up a bar against the far wall. In 2011, he won a James Beard award, and in 2012, he opened outposts in New York's Lower East Side and Brooklyn.

The original Pok Pok—still located in Ricker's sprawling house in southeast Portland—feels like a restaurant one might find in Thailand. Diners can sit on the partially enclosed outdoor patio under a corrugated tin roof, or inside Ricker's low-ceilinged, dimly lit former basement. Ricker encourages patrons to eat from the restaurant's metal plates with their hands, or a fork and a spoon, as in Thailand.

Pok Pok's food is entirely different from what is served in almost every other Thai restaurant in the United States. The flavors are bold and exotic, with few concessions to finicky Western palates. Smoke from the charcoal grill plays a major role in the preparation of most dishes, green papaya salad gets a kick from pungent fermented black crabs and blistering-hot chili, and the drinking water is flavored with pandan, which lends a subtle taste of vanilla and toasted hay. Ike's Vietnamese fish sauce chicken wings—Pok Pok's caramel-sticky, tangy, addictive signature dish—may set the standard by which other wings are measured.

With its low prices, this audacious and unpretentious restaurant is, in the view of many seasoned diners, one of the most pleasurable dining experiences in North America. It has made Ricker a star and should not be missed. **SW**

Willows Inn | An unforgettable dining destination

Location Lummi Island **Signature dish** Cold smoked reef-net-caught salmon | ❺❺❺❺

Lummi Island in Washington's Puget Sound abounds with the extraordinary natural bounty of the Pacific Northwest. The water surrounding the island teems with salmon, mussels, oysters, and clams; among the rocks on the shoreline grow edible seaweeds and grasses. In summer, the hillsides are lush with native berries; in the woods and fields are wild mushrooms and herbs, cherries, apples, plums, quince, horseradish, and sunflowers. The Willows Inn, a small hundred-year-old restaurant, three and a half miles (5.6 km) from the Lummi ferry dock, sits on the gentle curve of a bay, gazing west across the water.

Blaine Wetzel, the head chef, sources almost all of the elements he uses to create his exquisite tasting menus from Lummi itself, working with local farmers and fishermen and traipsing daily across the island to forage for ingredients. A protégé of Rene Redzepi, whose Copenhagen restaurant, Noma, has repeatedly been named the best restaurant in the world, Wetzel saw a rare opportunity in a Craigslist ad for a chef at the old inn. The owner recognized Wetzel as a visionary, and gave him free creative rein. Wetzel eventually acquired the inn with a partner.

Wetzel's food is prepared with a Scandinavian precision and careful minimalism; each dish captures the essence of its ingredients, amplifying and exalting them. It is like tasting food for the first time. If diners wish, they can have a seasonal "juice pairing" with their meal; the juices are unusual and ambrosial.

Windows in the warm, understated dining room overlook the bay; at the opposite end is the kitchen. Through open doors, Wetzel and his team of chefs can be seen working at a gleaming stainless steel island, plating the dishes. They deliver the plates together with the friendly servers, who themselves do a marvelous job. A meal here is, above all, fun. The Willows Inn is a once-in-a-lifetime experience—a real marvel. **SW**

"The food at the Willows Inn is very good—and when it's not very good, it's exquisite."

Bethany Jean Clement, *The Stranger*

⬆ Stinging Nettles: a dish of salmonberry blossoms on a stew of nettles, woodruff leaves, and goat cheese.

Meadowood | Fine contemporary dining in California wine country

Location St. Helena **Signature dish** Yogurt black sesame shiso | ❺❺❺❺❺

"*[Kostow] commands the kitchen, creating dishes you won't find on any other menu.*"

Michael Bauer, *The San Francisco Chronicle*

⬆ Polished wood at the entrance to one of the world's most polished restaurants.

➡ Shellfish presented with wild flowers in appropriately conch-shaped receptacles.

Meadowood is a sprawling 250-acre (100-ha) resort in the California wine country. The dining room of its restaurant overlooks a golf course. Chef Christopher Kostow trained at Jardins des Sens in Montpellier, France, then worked as sous chef under Daniel Humm at Campton Place, San Francisco, before becoming head chef at Chez TJ in Mountain View, California, prior to his move to Meadowood in 2008.

The style of food at Meadowood is contemporary rather than classical French, and many of the vegetables served are grown in the hotel grounds. In 2011, the restaurant was awarded the ultimate three Michelin stars.

A typical meal there might begin with clam fritters with lettuce and lemon, the molluscs tender, and the citrus element very precisely judged. Razor clams are smoked and grilled over grapewood, garnished with Ossetra caviar, and served with whipped avocado, compressed grape, and shaved green almonds. The quality of Meadowood's ingredients is further demonstrated in a dish of seared scallop from Maine with asparagus and a pair of crayfish, served with poached chicken quenelles, sauce mousseline, and tarragon.

The kitchen is not constrained by traditional Gallic flavor combinations, and is happy to reach out further afield where appropriate. Among the most notable departures is duck rubbed with chermoula (a North African spice blend) and served with raw rhubarb, mustard, and celery leaf. The fowl benefits from the spicy kick of the mustard, while the rhubarb provides acidity to balance the richness of the meat.

Meadowood staff are relaxed but proficient, and there are more than 50 pages of wines available to complement your meal. The restaurant's elaborate but technically strong cooking makes excellent use of local produce, and offers a spectacular culinary tour that matches the restaurant's leafy natural setting. **AH**

Acquerello | Traditional Italian dining in the heart of San Francisco

Location San Francisco **Signature dish** Ridged pasta with black truffle, foie gras, and Marsala | ❺❺❺❺

Acquerello is a white-tablecloth, fine-dining institution in a city better known for casual comfort food. Located inside a former chapel with a vaulted wood-beamed ceiling adorned with copper and wrought iron, the restaurant provides classic trappings such as upholstered stools for ladies' purses and tableside cheese service from a glass-enclosed cart. The clientele is perhaps a little more conservative than the average San Franciscan, but most diners are there for special occasions—engagements, birthdays, and anniversaries that they want to celebrate in style.

The menu selections run the gamut of Italian cuisine from classic to contemporary. Among the most original creations are the rugosa squash budino with cranberry, brown butter, and hazelnut, and the smoked potato gnocchi with crispy sweetbreads, Maitake mushrooms, and pancetta cream.

Acquerello is the brainchild of co-owners Suzette Gresham-Tognetti and Giancarlo Paterlini. The former is known as a chef's chef, while the latter is widely acknowledged as the Bay Area's foremost expert on Italian wine, so it is he who has developed the restaurant's 1,900-bottle wine list. He will never steer you wrong.

When, in 2012, the State of California passed into law a ban on the sale of foie gras, because its creation involved the forced feeding of ducks, it looked like the end for Acquerello's celebrated black truffle signature dish. However, Chef de Cuisine Mark Pensa soon discovered that if he soaked duck livers in milk overnight, then blended them with Marsala, cream, and butter, he could mimic perfectly the rich flavor of the foie that formed the base of this most luxurious of pasta sauces. **MD**

◄ This dish satisfies California legal requirements.

R&G Lounge | Boisterous Cantonese family-style dining

Location San Francisco **Signature dish** Salt and pepper Dungeness crab | ❺❺

The popularity of R&G Lounge in San Francisco's Chinatown can be explained in just five words: salt and pepper Dungeness crab. With three floors of dining rooms filled with upward of 250 seats, there are few who visit this Cantonese-style restaurant without ordering the signature dish.

You first notice the tanks of live crabs when you walk through the front door. Once an order is placed, a whole crab is plucked from the tank, cracked, dipped in a salt and pepper batter with a secret recipe, and then deep-fried. There is no room for modesty or politeness once the plate of hot and crispy crab hits the table. This is the epitome of eat-with-your-hands, finger-licking deliciousness.

> *"A favorite stop for Chinese businessmen on expense accounts … always authentic."*
> *Fodor's Travel*

But this is just one of more than 150 items on the menu. Experienced diners avoid the more common Chinese dishes like mu shu pork and Mongolian beef, but opt instead for fresh seafood delicacies like glazed black cod, steamed clams with eggs, prawns with honey walnuts, abalone with mustard greens, and scallop fried rice.

The décor is basic and the service can seem brusque and frenetic, as there are always lines of eager diners out the front door. A single table might see four or five different waiters during the course of the meal, but few customers seem to notice. This is a restaurant for large groups, picking at mouthwatering dishes spinning around on the lazy Susan. **MD**

Greens Restaurant | Iconic vegetarian restaurant in San Francisco

Location San Francisco **Signature dish** Warm spinach salad | 🟢🟢

When Greens opened in 1979, it was the San Francisco Zen Center's first foray into the world of fine dining. The all-vegetarian restaurant was a groundbreaking move that demonstrated to the increasingly health- and environment-conscious residents of the Bay Area that their preferred diet did not have to be mean and minimalist. Since then, the restaurant's endlessly inventive dishes and the best-selling cookbooks by executive chef Annie Somerville have consistently demonstrated that a meatless menu can even surpass its carnivorous cousins.

Somerville, who took over the kitchen in 1985 from founding chef Deborah Madison, works closely with organic gardeners at Marin County's Green Gulch Farms, which are also part of the Zen Center network, to source freshly picked chard, leeks, winter squash, flowering herbs, and other ingredients. She also buys from other local growers and cheese makers. Greens' much-lauded wine cellar draws heavily from small, high-quality producers on the west coast of the United States and in Europe that use sustainable vineyard cultivation techniques.

Housed in a cavernous former machine shop that was formerly part of an army base, the restaurant is as striking as the seasonal menu. Built by Paul Discoe, a master craftsman and a Buddhist priest, it incorporates twelve varieties of wood and was constructed in the Japanese-joinery style, entirely without nails. The structure overlooks the San Francisco Marina, in sight of the Golden Gate Bridge and the Marin Headlands. From the plate to the Pacific coastline, the visual experience at Greens is stunning.

Greens Restaurant offers a spectacular experience from start to finish, with dishes rooted in the finest produce the Bay Area has to offer, together with an award-winning wine list and staggering views. **CR**

⬆ Even meat eaters love Greens vegetarian restaurant.

Bar Tartine | Farm-to-table casual dining at one of the world's best bakeries

Location San Francisco **Signature dish** *Lángos* (Hungarian-style deep-fried potato bread) | 💲💲

Chad Robertson and Elisabeth Prueitt are the co-owners of Tartine Bakery, which many consider to be the best bakery in the United States. Together, they opened Bar Tartine, a casual restaurant in the Mission District of San Francisco focused on farm-to-table dining with European influences. After a few initial chef changes, Robertson and Prueitt asked Nick Balla to take the helm. The owners were installing a 15,000-lb (6,800-kg) oven at the restaurant to be able to bake Central European-style whole-grain bread, and thought that Balla, with his Hungarian background and culinary experience, would be a perfect match.

They were right. Under Balla, Bar Tartine is now serving some of the most delicious food in a city filled with culinary superstars. Drawing inspiration from Robertson's wonderful baked goods, Balla uses bread to great effect in dishes like beef tartare on koji toast with bottarga, and creamed sardines on sprouted rye. The kitchen's output also features in the restaurant's decor. The wooden walls of the rustic dining room are lined with jars of house-pickled fruits and vegetables destined for the plate.

At lunchtime, Bar Tartine offers up exquisitely composed sandwiches. Favorites include a kale and yogurt smørrebrød with sunflower tahini or smoked sturgeon, quark, and fried onion on "everything" bread. For dinner, Balla has developed dishes that draw on Eastern European traditions while staying true to the bounty of the Northern California larder. To that end, instead of the potatoes and carrots that would traditionally appear in comforting goulash, Bar Tartine's version comes with breakfast radishes and baby purple turnips, and is garnished with a bone marrow crouton. Balla even grows heirloom red peppers on land he leases from a local winery, then dries, smokes, and grinds them into paprika. **MD**

⬆ Even the pickles at Bar Tartine are made with care.

Atelier Crenn | The poetry of food, expressed with distinctive creative flair

Location San Francisco **Signature dish** "A Walk in the Forest" | ❸❸❸❸

French-born chef Dominique Crenn cuts a stylish dash on San Francisco's highly competitive dining-out scene. She is the first female chef in the United States to have been awarded two Michelin stars. Her culinary capabilities are on display at her "workshop" restaurant in the residential area of Cow Hollow, just down from Pacific Heights.

Also in evidence is her literary talent: the written description of each seasonally changing tasting menu takes the form of a poem, composed by the chef, in which each line enigmatically and lyrically describes a different course.

Crenn puts as much thought into the design of each dish as she does to its ingredients. An example of this is her soup of charred onion poured around a comte dumpling, with cider jelly, black truffle from Périgord, and powdered Iberian ham with a little brioche on the side. This rich take on the classic French onion soup has an impressive depth of flavor,

the hint of ham and truffle combining with cheese to elevate the dish from its humble origins into something luxuriously enjoyable.

Another example of Crenn's originality is a cylinder of eggplant brushed with molasses, honey, and spices, and cooked over hot coals. It is served with crisp of dehydrated tomato, potato crisps, and a little sheep cheese—an unusual and successful take on the American barbecue, in which the smoky eggplant flavor combines well with the other elements. First among equals is her signature dish, "A Walk in the Forest," which may be modified according to seasonal availability, but comprises local mushrooms with pine-dusted meringue.

Dominique Crenn has a modern cooking style founded on a classical technique, so she knows which culinary rules can be bent successfully. **AH**

⬆ A sophisticated oyster leaf dish at Atelier Crenn.

Slanted Door | Eatin' by the dock of the bay

Location San Francisco **Signature dish** Shaking beef | 💲💲

Charles Phan had a small Vietnamese restaurant whose door probably became slanted when in-the-know foodies in San Francisco kept banging on it trying to get in. Then, opportunity knocked. Nearby, the abandoned Ferry Building was being restored to serve two purposes. One was its traditional function as a mooring for ferries from and to Sonoma, Napa, and other nearby jurisdictions.

The other was as the site of a market held every Saturday. Farmers from Napa and Sonoma brought in organic fruit, vegetables, rice, nuts, milk, cheese, and meat that was quickly sold to the city's food lovers. The Ferry Building became known as one of the best places in the United States to purchase fresh produce.

The proximity of this vast array of potential ingredients inspired Phan and other chefs to open restaurants in other parts of the Ferry Building that had been designated as retail outlets. Phan's door no longer slants, but people still clamor to get in.

Access to the freshest seafood and the bounty of the surrounding valleys encouraged Phan to raise the quality of his cooking several notches. Shrimp and crab spring rolls are not to be missed. Shaking beef (cubes of beef with watercress, red onion, and lime) are favorites of first-time visitors and regulars alike. Gossamer cellophane noodles with Dungeness crab, green onion, and sesame are pleasure on a plate.

Another favorite is wood oven-roasted Manila clams with Thai basil, crispy pork belly, and fresh chilies. The same oven is used to roast boneless short ribs of beef with curry, carrots, butternut squash, and turnips. Such dishes reveal the French influence on Vietnamese cuisine. The fish cooked whole in a banana leaf and flavored with cilantro, lime, green garlic, and green onion is as beautiful to the eye as to the palate. **FP**

⬆ The restaurant offers truly innovative Vietnamese food.

Benu | World-class, modern fine dining with strong Asian influences in a beautiful setting

Location San Francisco   **Signature dish** Shark's fin soup with Dungeness crab, Jinhua ham, and black truffle custard |

> *"Lee uses the modern techniques in all the right ways—they surprise but never distract …"*

Michael Bauer, *SF Gate*

⬆ Benu's pork belly kimchi with edible casing.

Benu has garnered more accolades in its first few years of existence than most other restaurants will receive in their entire histories. Chef and owner Corey Lee worked in Michelin three-star kitchens in England, France, and the United States until 2010, when he opened his own place in San Francisco. It is now widely regarded as the best Asian-inspired restaurant in North America.

Although Benu is housed in a beautiful historic building, the starkly modern dining room is notable only for its lack of color. The intent behind the design, or lack thereof, is to force diners to devote their full attention to the contents of the plates in front of them. Offering only a single seventeen-course tasting menu per night, Benu's glass-enclosed kitchen produces a succession of dishes that are artful homages to seasonality, evolution, and Asian heritage.

One of Benu's best dishes, served early in the meal, consists of layers of braised pork belly, crème fraîche, a chilled oyster and kimchi foam inside an edible jewel box made from dehydrated kimchi broth. Intended for consumption in a single bite, the dish is a mash-up of hot and cold, crispy and creamy, and salty and tangy flavors. It is a dumpling with a difference that gives diners an early adumbration of the treats in store. These may include lobster coral xiao long bao, an upscale version of the traditional soup dumpling, and abalone blanquette, a twist on the classically French veal stew.

Each course is enhanced by the beverage pairings, which are carefully chosen by wine director Yoon Ha. Ha, who, like Lee, is of Korean descent, deftly uses beer, sake, sherry, and port in addition to the expected wine to achieve the difficult feat of making the food taste even better than it would if eaten unaccompanied by alcohol. **MD**

Boulevard | San Francisco landmark with a global following

Location San Francisco **Signature dish** Grilled local Wild King salmon (seasonal) | ❸❸❺

Since the Boulevard Restaurant opened in 1993, it has become the darling of foodies and food critics alike. In the capable hands of Nancy Oakes, the owner and one of the United States' most recognized and celebrated chefs, it has climbed the ranks of culinary acclaim, garnering numerous prestigious nominations and awards each year.

The menu is a creative delight from start to finish, pairing American regional flavors with a French-influenced style. The overall effect is hearty and flavorful, with a visually compelling, almost sculptural presentation for every dish. All the food is world-class, but Oakes' seafood dishes are not to be missed. While tables are in demand—make a reservation if you can—and the space is often buzzing with activity, the service is consistently warm, friendly, and impeccable.

The building itself is steeped in history, as the only local structure to survive the infamous 1906 San Francisco earthquake and the subsequent fires that destroyed much of the city. As the story goes, the building was slated for destruction by firefighters hoping to halt nearby flames from spreading, but a quick-thinking saloon keeper convinced them to spare it—offering a generous trade of wine and whiskey in return for the favor. Vaulted brick ceilings, floral banquettes, and warm natural wood tones set the stage for Oakes' carefully curated menu and 500-bottle-strong wine list, with something for every pairing and every palate.

Always popular with locals, Boulevard soon became widely famous and attracted visitors from all over the world, especially after 2012, when it received the coveted James Beard Award for Outstanding Restaurant. Almost immediately, it shot to the top of the "must-try" list for the culinarily inclined on any visit to the city by the bay. **CR**

Frances | Neighborhood joint with pedigree and down-to-earth food

Location San Francisco **Signature dish** Smoked bacon beignets with maple chive crème fraiche | ❸❸❺

Melissa Perello became executive chef of Charles Nob Hill at the age of 25. She then took the same role at the Fifth Floor, where she remained until New Year's Eve 2006, when she hung up her toque. At that moment, she had no idea whether she would ever cook again professionally. Cook again she did, but only after taking over a tiny neighborhood restaurant space in San Francisco's Castro district and turning it into Frances, the best neighborhood bistro on the West Coast.

The cozy dining room is adorned with simple black-and-white photography hanging on white walls above long, dark wooden banquettes. The service is unpretentious, with waiters willing to gab it up or leave you be, depending on your mood. With just 16

> *"It's all good. No, it's all pretty wonderful. And it's always different, just like dinner at home."*
>
> John Mariani, *Esquire*

items on the menu, most of them priced well below the high of $28 (£17), Frances has been packed with diners ever since it first opened.

Favorite dishes include smoked bacon beignets with maple chive crème fraîche, a perfectly seared bavette steak with lemony risotto, grilled Nardello peppers, chanterelles, and fennel pesto, and a rich and creamy chicken liver mousse with grilled country bread. In a graceful nod to the deliciously affordable *vins de table* of French country dining, Frances' wine director Paul Einbund blends his own house red and white wines with Marco Cappelli from California's Miraflores Winery. The blends change according to the season, and diners pay only for what they drink. **MD**

Mission Beach Café |
Locally and seasonally sourced menu

Location San Francisco **Signature dish** Rabbit pot pie | ❸❸❸

Every day at the Mission Beach Café has two distinct halves. In the morning and at lunchtime, there are lines for brunch. Wild mushroom Benedict with caramelized onions and truffle mornay sauce is a bright and breezy dish that brightens up the mistiest of San Franciscan days, a creamy yet pleasingly earthy ensemble that comes with a side of fried potatoes. Alternatively, daytime diners might go for salty-sweet huevos with salsa rojo, tomatillo pico de gallo, and pulled pork. Those who still have room after either of these dishes might finish with a slice of Brooklyn blackout cake, which is just one of several awesome baked joys developed by Alan Carter, the café's renowned pastry chef.

"… a welcoming destination for modern urbanites looking for a distinctive neighborhood eatery."

Menu Freak

Come the evening, the mood changes. The light is softer and candles flicker in the shadows, while the menu also takes a different tack with a more classical approach (all dressed up with a typically Californian concern for fresh and seasonal ingredients, and a sense of fusion). Rabbit pot pie is undoubtedly a favorite: pliable, buttery pastry, juicy chunks of meat, and curls of rich rabbit reduction. Also commendable is the homemade pappardelle in a creamy sauce of asparagus, morels, and oven-toasted tomatoes.

Whether it's morning or night, the food that comes out of the café's kitchen is locally and seasonally sourced, as pretty as a picture, and bursting with flavor. You can't ask for more than that. **ATJ**

Seven Hills | Breakout Italian
from small neighborhood bistro

Location San Francisco **Signature dish** Ravioli uovo | ❸❸

San Francisco has been home to four generations of the Alioto family. Leaders in both politics and the restaurant industry, the Aliotos started out running a fish stall on the Wharf in 1925. It would have made sense, therefore, for Alexander Alioto to slide right into a management position at the family's eponymous seafood restaurant. Yet, after studying at the California Culinary Academy, with stages at the French Laundry, at various restaurants in Italy, and working for Ron Siegel at the Ritz-Carlton, he branched out on his own to open this 40-seat neighborhood Italian bistro.

Seven Hills is unadorned, with a simple glass chandelier and bare wooden tables. A large, ever-changing flower arrangement at the end of the four-seat bar is the only design flourish. Customers are a balanced mix of older diners from the surrounding Russian Hill neighborhood, and younger folks from further afield. The kitchen balances these disparate crowds by offering both traditional and updated dishes on the à la carte menu, which is divided into appetizers, salads, pastas, and entrées.

Classic Italian-American plates such as osso buco and spaghetti with sausage and tomato sauce are perfectly executed. So, too, are original creations such as seared polenta with poached egg and lamb, jalapeño and garlic cream, and raviolo uovo (an egg yolk and brown butter-filled pasta).

In 2010, when Seven Hills was awarded the title of best Italian restaurant in San Francisco, Alexander Alioto said that he would resist any subsequent temptation to raise prices or add expensive bottles to the simple wine list, because in his view the place would always be just a simple local bistro.

Be sure to sample the signature dessert: house-made ricotta with fresh orange segments drizzled with honey, candied pistachios, and filo chips. **MD**

Gary Danko | Classic yet Californian cooking in a top spot that is booked up for months ahead

Location San Francisco   **Signature dish** Glazed oysters with Ossetra caviar, salsify, and lettuce cream | ❸❸❸

Gary Danko's eponymous restaurant near Fisherman's Wharf has had a loyal following since it opened in 1999. The chef's résumé includes graduating from the Culinary Institute of America in Hyde Park, New York, and working at Chateau Souverain in Sonoma County and as chef of the Dining Room at the Ritz-Carlton, San Francisco. He now produces a range of dishes that are inspired by French, Mediterranean, and regional American cooking and which change to reflect local seasonal availability.

The beautifully presented seared ahi tuna with avocado, nori, enoki mushrooms, and lemon soy dressing exemplifies Danko's elegant and accomplished way with ingredients. The fish rests in a very fine citrus sauce, which has just the right level of acidity to balance the dish. Fruits and spices are used to add that extra touch of zest to classic ingredients, as in his cardamom-poached pears paired with lemon pepper duck breast, or his salmon crusted with horseradish and served with tangy dilled cucumbers and mustard sauce. Precise cooking, whether of Maine lobster, scallops, duck, beef, or venison, is a noticeable feature, as are the high-quality ingredients, from impressive seafood to luxuries such as Ossetra caviar, which accompanies oysters in his signature dish. Desserts, too, are classy affairs, with the much-loved soufflés well worth sampling.

The setting—a wood-paneled room—is smart without being elaborate or overly formal. The noticeably excellent service—warm and attentive and happy to guide diners through the menu before they make their choice—makes dining here more than just a gastronomic pleasure. Gary Danko has won numerous accolades, including a James Beard Award, and has established his restaurant as one of San Francisco's top food destinations. **AH**

> *"The wine list ... and the rooms are as memorable as the food and impeccable service."*
>
> Fodor's Travel

⬆ The tempting array of cheeses at Gary Danko is a wonderful way to round off a meal.

Coi | An intimate dining experience focused on the here and now

Location San Francisco **Signature dish** "Earth/Sea" | ❺❺❺❺❺

To step into the dining room at Coi is to enter the mind of one of the most creative chefs in the world. Daniel Patterson has earned five James Beard nominations, two Michelin stars, and a worldwide reputation as a pioneer of California cuisine. His gastronomy is informed by a strong belief in "flavors of place," and this philosophy determines that his creations are from locally sourced ingredients.

Coi (pronounced "kwah") is an old French word that loosely translates as "tranquil." This is an apt description of the monochromatically brown dining room lined with natural materials such as rice paper and grass-cloth wallpaper. The decor is deliberately understated in order to create an ambience in which diners can concentrate on the food. The lack of windows further contributes to the feeling of serenity that provides a striking contrast with the bustling intersection of Broadway and Montgomery Street on which the restaurant stands.

With only 28 seats in the room, there is a distinct level of intimacy with the staff—Coi has one employee for every two diners.

One 11-course vegetable-centric menu is offered each night. To start, diners are presented with a dish called "Pink Grapefruit." But the name is deceptively simple. On one side of the plate sits a small bowl filled with fresh grapefruit and tarragon topped with grapefruit sorbet and grapefruit mousse infused with black pepper and ginger. On the other side, is a drop of oil made from the same grapefruit, tarragon, ginger, and black pepper. Diners are invited to dab this on their wrists before eating.

The signature dish, entitled "Earth/Sea," is tofu made from soy milk coagulated with deep seawater to produce a soft savory curd. It is served with cherry tomatoes, olive oil, and seaweed. **MD**

⬆ Coi's decor is pure understated chic.

Zuni | Rustic, understated French and Italian food in simple surroundings

Location San Francisco   **Signature dish** Chicken roasted in a brick oven with warm bread salad | ❸❸❸

Opened in 1979, Zuni adopted the style for which it became renowned under chef Judy Rodgers, who between 1987 and her death in 2013 turned the restaurant toward rustic French- and Italian-based cooking, with dashes of Mexican, North African, and Middle Eastern influences.

Rodgers began cooking while an exchange student in France, where she lived with the family of Jean Troisgros, chef-patron of Les Frères Troisgros. He taught her the vital importance of understanding ingredients and the crucial differences between one example of a common foodstuff and another.

Rodgers started out as a chef at Chez Panisse in Berkeley, California, a restaurant that was highly influential in the development of what became known as "California Cuisine." Later, she worked in France and Italy, as well as New York, before moving to Zuni. Since her death, Zuni has been run by her business partner, Gilbert Pilgram.

The Zuni is the antithesis of flashy. The decor is nothing more than serviceably utilitarian and the cooking simple, almost rustic. But it is that simplicity that makes Zuni so wonderful. Few dishes contain more than four or five principal ingredients; there are no fancy processes or inventiveness for its own sake. The menu changes daily, but some dishes—notably house-cured anchovies with celery, Parmesan cheese, and olives—are ever present.

The restaurant names many of its suppliers on the menu as a tribute to the excellence of Californian produce. But if the produce is American, the cooking is European at heart. So is the excellent wine list, which gives more space to France and Italy than to the United States. The most all-American feature is the oyster and shellfish menu, which showcases outstanding produce from native waters. **RE**

⬆ Zuni's rustic signature dish of roast chicken and salad.

Hog Island Oyster Bar | Order half a dozen
oysters or more looking out over the bay

Location San Francisco **Signature dish** Sweetwater (Pacific) oysters |

"On a sunny day, is there anything better than sipping wine and eating oysters? Only if it's here …"

fodors.com

⬆ Watch the oysters being opened at the bar before tucking in.

It's all about the oysters. Although the Hog Island Bar offers clams, crab, seafood stew, and chowder, among other tempting menu items, the main reason for going there is to bask in the joy of bivalves, whether they be Sweetwater, Atlantics, or Kumamoto. For anyone who wants to assess the difference between oysters (some are sweeter than others), this is one of the best places in the world to study.

Conventionally, diners order six to start, but it's not unknown for them to order another six (and then even another half dozen), such is the allure of the tangy, creamy, briny, fresh-tasting oysters that Hog Island cultivates on its own farm in the village of Marshall, 40 miles (64 km) north of the city.

The whole operation was opened in 1983 by marine biologist John Finger and ocean farmer Terry Sawyer. It currently sells a total of more than three million oysters a year, mostly here but also at another outlet in Napa. Hog Island Oyster Bar's main produce is served either as nature intended, in the raw, or in a variety of baked dishes, including Bagna Cauda, which features butter, garlic, capers, and anchovy, and Casino, with paprika, bacon shallots, and thyme added to the mix. The oyster is Hog Island's world.

The ambience complements the food. The premises in the renovated Ferry Building Marketplace are modern, light, and airy, with tall ceilings. Both outside and inside the magnificent panorama of San Francisco Bay is clearly visible. Those who grab a stool at the bar also get a ringside view of the theater of oyster-opening as shucking goes on at speed while beers and wines are poured. In 2012, Hog Island collaborated with local brewery 21st Amendment to produce a sumptuous oyster stout. Such has been the success of this venture that the company doubled the size of its bar—bivalve heaven just got a bit bigger. **ATJ**

Millennium |

Upscale San Francisco vegetarian

Location San Francisco   **Signature dish** Creole smoked tempeh | 🟊🟊

Welcome to the Hotel California, a classy-looking joint in downtown San Francisco. Built before World War I, it is an ideal spot for a good night's rest, but it is also a destination for those who like to eat well. This is because the Millennium restaurant has its home here. Step into the stylish lobby and make your way toward an airy and elegant dining space, where the finest vegetarian and vegan dishes are served. Forget any outdated stereotypes of veggie cuisine, being an overload of pulse beans and raw carrots, the dishes that head chef Eric Tucker creates here are inventive and seasonal—meat might be absent but gastronomic know-how is the order of the day.

Given Tucker's preference for seasonal sourcing from local producers, the menu changes frequently. Starters might include parsnip and butternut squash fritters accompanied by parsnip-cumin hummus, or wild rice and black sesame nigiri in a sweet mirin glaze. For mains, you could try potato tikki cake with mustard green and black-eyed pea sabzi or potato and chard roulade with smoked leek and celery root cream, seared Brussels sprouts, and baby turnips.

Millennium's thoughtful and carefully considered approach doesn't end with the food: it reputedly has one of the best organic wine selections in the whole country as well as a carefully selected list of craft beers from local artisanal breweries for those who prefer the grain to the grape with their meals. While diners enjoy the ambience—think white tablecloths, red faux-leather blanquettes, a zinc bar, and decor that includes hanging recycled objects—the young and friendly staff zip about, taking orders, zooming about with plates, and adding to what makes Millennium such a complete gastronomic experience. **ATJ**

Mission Chinese Food |

No-holds-barred Chinese-American

Location San Francisco   **Signature dish** Kung pao pastrami | 🟊

This place started as a pop-up restaurant inside a dingy pre-existing Chinese take-out spot called Lung Shan. It is now the trendiest Chinese food restaurant in North America.

The menu, created by Korean-American chef Danny Bowien, is laden with spice, fat, salt, and heat—fiery heat. The dishes sound familiar, but they are distinctly original, a melting pot of wok-tossed flavors. Consider the kung pao pastrami, which is Sichuan by way of the Lower East Side, with caramelized chunks of cured pastrami sautéed with peanuts, chilies, celery, and potato. Western influences also appear in two fried rice preparations: salt cod with mackerel confit, and chicken with schmaltz and chicken livers.

> "Mr Bowien does to Chinese food what Led Zeppelin did to the blues."
>
> Pete Wells, *The New York Times*

Do not think that the cheap menu prices mean that Bowien is skimping on quality ingredients or technique. To make the General Tso's veal dish, for example, a rack of veal ribs is spit-roasted until meltingly tender. The ribs are then dry-fried until crispy before being smothered in a sauce made from chilies, leeks, and green onions. The ma po tofu, a classic peasant dish, is made rich with a mouth-numbing sauce studded with fresh ground Kurobuta pork shoulder.

Mission Chinese Food is the restaurant of the moment in the United States. It is multiethnic, communal, affordable, and original. It is American and Chinese in equal measure. **MD**

Swan Oyster Depot | Old-school San Francisco oyster bar

Location San Francisco   **Signature dish** Oysters on the half shell | 💲💲

"This century-old institution serves the freshest seafood imaginable … [it is] as informal as the docks."

Zagat

⬆ Oysters are served on the half shell with lemon.

From the outside, Swan Oyster Depot doesn't look like much. It's just a narrow storefront, no more than 15 feet (4.5 m) wide, in a busy commercial district. There are only eighteen stools pushed up against a long marble counter covered with bowls of oyster crackers, lemon wedges, and pots of prepared horseradish. At the front of the shop is an open-air seafood display case; at the back, a small kitchen where live Dungeness crabs are steamed and clam chowder is prepared. In between, there are a few taps for beer, an oyster shucking station, and a few shelves with plates, bowls, glassware, and condiments such as capers, hot sauce, horseradish, ketchup, wasabi, and soy sauce.

Despite its rather unprepossessing outward appearance, Swan Oyster Depot is a San Francisco seafood institution, plain and simple. The star of the limited menu is, of course, oysters—usually a selection of Miyagi, Blue Point, Kumamoto, and Olympia varieties—on the half shell. Other items include crab Louie salad, shrimp cocktail, smoked salmon, and an innovative Boston clam chowder made without flour.

Swan was originally opened in 1912 by four Danish brothers who used to make fresh seafood deliveries by horse-drawn cart. The bar is now run by two generations of the Sancimino family. The horse has gone, of course, but the company's truck can still be seen on the streets delivering cracked Dungeness crab, sand dabs, and other local delicacies to a host of San Francisco businesses.

In a nod to the truly outstanding vineyards of California, Swan offers a small but wonderful selection of wines, but most of the customers—a broad selection of locals and tourists—opt for a pint of the hometown beer, Anchor Steam, which is the perfect accompaniment to old-school fare of this kind. **MD**

State Bird Provisions | California cuisine meets the dim sum cart

Location San Francisco **Signature dish** Deep-fried quail | 🌑🌑

When State Bird Provisions released sixty consecutive days' worth of reservations all at one time and made them available online through the reservations site Rezbook, each and every one of the tables was booked within ninety minutes. They would probably have gone even faster than that, but the rush to reserve a table crashed Rezbook's servers. Such is life for the chefs and co-owners Stuart Brioza and Nicole Krasinski.

Part of the reason for the demand was a month-long closure of the restaurant for expansion and a complete redesign by Wylie Price, who added a raw bar and a new art deco front door complete with salvaged chrome handle. He also installed two alcove booths for larger parties.

This cosmetic work was good, but the fact remains that it is not the look of State Bird Provisions that attracts its hip and fashionable clientele, but the food—inspired bites on small plates served from roving dim sum carts. Highlights include delicious guinea hen dumplings with aromatic broth, rabbit and fontina croquettes, spicy kimchi yuba with smoked egg bottarga, charred octopus in tomato-chickpea salsa, and pork belly plum salad. This isn't fusion cooking, this is true California cuisine inspired by the melting pot that is the most ethnically diverse of the United States, with influences from China, Mexico, Japan, France, Italy, Spain, Korea, and the Middle East.

While the dim sum-style offerings change daily based on the seasons and product availability, diners may also order items ("Commandables") from a printed menu. No one should miss out on the house specialty, "CA state bird with provisions," a buttermilk-marinated quail crusted in pumpkin seeds and breadcrumbs, then deep fried and served with a sweet and sour onion jam, shaved Parmesan cheese, and cracked black pepper. **MD**

"Just about everything is a must-order item … You end up putting yourself in the chefs' hands."

Michael Bauer, *SF Gate*

⬆ Few people know that California's state bird is the quail.

SPQR | Sophisticated, soulful modern Italian dining in a casual atmosphere

Location San Francisco   **Signature dish** Smoked fettuccine with smoked bacon, sea urchin, and quail egg | 🟢🟢

"… a chic, friendly spot … with a dedicated neighborhood following of all ages."

Fodor's Travel

⬆ SPQR brings a stylish slice of Italy to the heart of San Francisco's Fillmore District.

The name comes from the initials of the Latin for "the Senate and the people of Rome," but SPQR's owner, restauranteur, and sommelier Shelley Lindgren is inspired and influenced not just by the Eternal City but by the whole of Italy. Her restaurant—opened by chef Nate Appleman and currently helmed by Matt Accarrino—is lauded for its broad-ranging and fresh take on Italian food and wine in all their forms.

The decor of the narrow premises matches that of most Italian osterias, with two columns of banquette-lined tables and a small, crook-shaped white marble bar in the back. The space can be noisy, and the diners are often boisterous, but these features only add to the informal charm.

While there are several creative antipasti dishes—note the guinea hen terrine with vin santo gelatina and the liver mousse and brioche *agrodolce* (a traditional sweet and sour sauce)—the house speciality is the pasta, which is all homemade. The fettuccine in the signature dish is made with flour that is smoked before being mixed and rolled. The result is a smoothly luxurious take on the classic carbonara in which the richness of the sauce is derived not from the quail's egg, the bacon, or the cream, but from the pureed sea urchin.

Enjoyment of the food at SPQR can be enhanced by sampling the accompanying wines, most of which have a strong Italian bias. The staple contents of the restaurant's cellar are bolstered every year with new discoveries made by Lindgren on her biannual visits to Italy's smaller, lesser-known producers.

SPQR's wine list is categorized by the ancient Roman road that is closest to each item's place of provenance. Many of the vintages are offered in three-ounce tastings, glasses, half carafes, and full bottles, allowing diners to mix and match according to their own preferences. However, they would be well advised just to let Lindgren pick their pairings. **MD**

Quince | Italian- and French-inspired tasting menus with Californian produce

Location San Francisco   **Signature dish** Trofie pasta with lobster and cockscomb | ❺❺❺❺❺

Rarely do fine dining restaurants improve with age, but Quince is an outstanding exception to this general rule.

Established in 2003, Quince occupies a historically landmarked brick and timber building dating from 1907 in San Francisco's Jackson Square neighborhood. The interior, which was redesigned by architect Olle Lundberg, is considered by many to be one of the city's most elegant enclosed spaces. The restaurant's kitchen can be observed through large glass windows from the public sidewalk fronting the building, giving diners a view of the preparation of the food that is soon to come their way.

While a few à la carte items are available at the bar, it is the tasting menus on offer in the main dining room that have won Quince, and its chef and co-owner Michael Tusk, praise, accolades, and Michelin stars. Diners are given three options: a nine-course "Garden Menu," comprised mainly of vegetable-based dishes highlighting the season's best produce from the Quince rooftop garden; a more classic nine-course "Quince menu," and a five-course menu that draws from both of the larger offerings. The genius of each is the way that each option brings the influences of France and Italy to bear on the seasonal bounty of Northern California.

Favorites on recent menus have included shelling bean cassoulet with wild nettle, olive, and chanterelle mushroom; Carpenteria abalone with matsutake mushroom, heart of palm, and hosui pear; and Saint-Canut Farms suckling pig with red cabbage, sweet potato, and Fuji apple.

It is the pasta dishes, however, that steal the show at Quince. Tusk made his name by mixing flour, eggs, and water into something that is greater than the sum of its parts. Above all, be sure not to miss the Trofie pasta with lobster and cockscomb (chicken livers), a regular on the menu. **MD**

"Don't pass up the cheese course—it's one of the city's finer selections."

Fodor's Travel

⤒ The dishes at Quince are tasty, artfully arranged compositions.

Tadich Grill | Classic Gold Rush-era seafooder serving power lunchers

Location San Francisco **Signature dish** Cioppino | $$

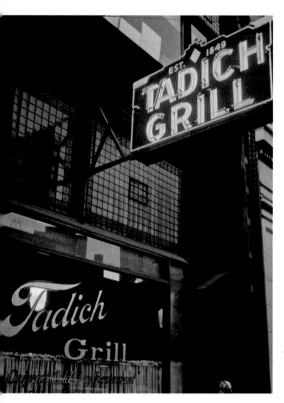

> "There's nothing trendy … but that doesn't keep 600 to 800 people from showing up daily."

Amanda Berne, *SF Gate*

⬆ Tadich Grill is already in its eighth location.

Legend has it that cioppino, San Francisco's iconic seafood stew, got its name when Italian-accented cooks working down on Fisherman's Wharf called upon the local fishermen to "chip in" a portion of their day's catch to fill the communal soup pot. Food historians, however, point to "*ciuppin*," a Ligurian word meaning "to chop" or "chopped," and suggest that it could signify a stew of mixed seafood, garlic, and tomatoes. Whatever the true etymology, most people agree that the cioppino at Tadich Grill is as good as it gets. The kitchen wouldn't produce more than 20,000 portions a year if it wasn't.

Tadich Grill, now in its eighth location, was founded in 1849 and is the third longest continuously operating restaurant in the United States. The current space has a long wooden bar running the length of the room and walls that are lined with dark wood paneling and oversized mirrors. Original Art Deco brass and milk-glass light fixtures hang from the ceiling. Tables are set with starched white tablecloths and a single bowl of lemon wedges. Waiters are dressed in pressed black pants, crisp white blazers, and strong neckties.

First-time visitors go for the history, but they return for the quality seafood. The attraction of everything on offer, whether it's stewed, broiled, sautéed, or baked, is, as the owners say: "If it's not fresh, it's not on the menu."

In addition to the cioppino, specialties include pan-fried sand dabs, charcoal broiled Petrale sole, and Dungeness crab à la Monza. Crab Louie salads and oysters Rockefeller are also very popular. Tadich Grill looks a lot like it did more than 100 years ago, and that's a good thing. In a city known for redefining cuisine and culinary technique, this restaurant stands as a beacon to a bygone era, and thus it has become a favored haunt for both the power lunch crowd and more casual evening diners. **MD**

Ton Kiang | Dim sum and then some

Location San Francisco **Signature dish** Clay pot casseroles | $

In a city with a population at least one-third Asian and an almost endless supply of choice ingredients, the potential for finding superb Chinese food is great. Ton Kiang always fulfills that promise, but for many years it was better known to native San Franciscans than to visitors because of its location in a residential neighborhood away from the familiar tourist trail. Today, however, increasing numbers are beating a path to its door.

The success of Ton Kiang can be attributed to its origins. The Hakka people of far northern China developed a cooking style using clay pots but, after several migrations to other parts of the country in the past thousand years, they incorporated other regional Chinese specialties and methods into their own cuisine. Many settled near Ton Kiang (East River) in Guangdong province in coastal southern China not far from Hong Kong. This meant the addition of seafood to the land-based flavors of the north.

The Ton Kiang menu reflects this diverse heritage. It includes *gao choy got* (shrimp and chive dumplings); *yeung qu dze* (shrimp-stuffed baby eggplants); and West Lake minced beef with crab meat soup.

Other favorites include steamed bacon with dried mustard greens, and whole Peking duck with steamed buns, deftly sliced at the table and served with hoisin sauce and, if desired, cucumber and green onion. Also popular are squash and duck; oxtail with carrot and celery; and sizzling onion chicken.

The traditional clay pot casseroles somehow concentrate flavors. The most bracing of these creations contains Pacific oysters, ginger, and scallions.

Although Ton Kiang is somewhat off the beaten track, the low-rent location helps keep prices down, especially for parties of six or more—and it can be argued that there are few finer aids to digestion at the conclusion of a gourmet extravaganza than a modest bill. **FP**

"*Ton Kiang is probably the number-one place in the city to have dim sum.*"

frommers.com

⊡ Be sure to sample the shrimp and chive dumplings.

Mustards Grill | Honest, sophisticated American fare

Location Napa Valley **Signature dish** Daily lamb, locally raised, done many different ways | ❸❸❸

Mustards Grill has been satisfying the appetites of hungry wine tasters since 1983. It serves a diverse clientele—locals, career winemakers, and chefs from up and down the Valley who eat here on their nights off—and assuredly walks the delicate line between fine dining and food for the people.

Owner and executive chef Cindy Pawlcyn is a trailblazer of farm-to-table cuisine, working tirelessly to prepare dishes informed by seasonal and regional availability, and, in the process, strengthening the relationship between diners and the natural bounty of the garden.

Long before "in-house gardens" became a staple of high-end dining establishments, Pawlcyn

> ## "Hyperflavored ... comfort classics with exotic spins come in heaping portions."
>
> frommers.com

cultivated her own plot, which expanded from small beginnings and now occupies 2 acres (0.8 ha) that produce an astounding amount of produce—in just one visual sweep, you can see the brightly-hued tops of beets and carrots, purple potatoes, melons, cabbages, and more, which make up no less than one-fifth of the fresh produce that is used every year in the bustling restaurant.

There's no better way to dine than to enjoy a dish made with produce harvested hours—or only minutes—before it arrives on the plate. It's these fresh ingredients and authentic flavors that have cemented Mustards' reputation as one of the Napa Valley's most consistent and desirable dining experiences. **CR**

La Tocque | Inspirational food and wine pairings in the Napa Valley

Location Napa Valley **Signature dish** Lamb loin with cumin-scented carrot puree and chickpea fries | ❸❸❸❸

We're in the middle of wine country here. The Napa Valley vineyards prosper and attract thousands of grape-loving tourists every year. Many of these oenophiles pass through Napa itself, and it's to La Toque—one of eight Michelin restaurants in the city—that those with a passion for matching food and wine will go to have their palates polished, preened, and amply rewarded.

La Toque opened toward the end of the 1990s and soon gained a formidable reputation for the superb cooking of head chef Ken Frank, who fused the modern Californian trend for fresh and seasonal ingredients with a contemporary European approach.

In 2008, the restaurant moved from its original premises in Rutherford to the Westin Verasa Napa Hotel, but the move had no effect on the cuisine, which still sources most of its ingredients from local farmers and suppliers.

The new La Toque's dining area has a design scheme that features subtle daubs of earth tones on the wall and plenty of light. The menus of the day offer several selections (there is also a Chef's Table Menu). Diners can opt for three- or four-course meals, all of which have exemplary pairings with wine. How about Angus beef tenderloin carpaccio with smoky aioli and grilled King Trumpet mushrooms paired with a Napa Valley Tempranillo Rose? Or maybe seared sea scallop with celery root, bacon, and wholegrain mustard—the wine choice here is a 2010 Chardonnay from Hyde Vineyard.

The range of choice is daunting, but those in the know often opt for the lamb loin with cumin scented carrot puree and chickpea fries—once named one of America's ten best dishes by *USA Today*—accompanied by a glass of 2006 Fincas de Ganuza Reserva from Rioja. **ATJ**

Etoile at Domaine Chandon | The original Napa
Valley fine-dining experience

Location Napa Valley   **Signature dish** Duck with fennel and chanterelles | 🅢🅢🅢

Today the Napa Valley enjoys a global reputation for fine cuisine, and has more landmark restaurants, award-winning chefs, and world-class wines than even the most fervent foodie could tackle in a single visit. But it was not always thus, and the restaurant that started the development of the region was Etoile, the culinary complement to Domaine Chandon, California's first sparkling wine house, which first opened in 1977.

Domaine Chandon is located in stunning surroundings and, perhaps even more appealingly, the restaurant is only a few steps away from the wine-tasting area. Etoile's reputation was originally established by iconic Wine Country chef Philippe Jeanty and later developed by Perry Hoffman.

Hoffman has garnered numerous accolades for his work, and is the youngest U.S. chef to receive a Michelin star. Drawing heavily from the gardens located just outside the kitchen, his hyper-seasonal approach to California cuisine pairs beautifully with the finest wines that Domaine Chandon and their neighbors have to offer. Hoffman is noted for his starters, particularly terrine of duck and artichokes with oxtail aspic and sweet white corn, a playful combination of a variety of textures. His signature dish, however, is a main course of duck with fennel, chanterelles, carrot, orange, and smoked honey.

The ingeniously curated dinner tasting menu developed by Etoile at Domaine Chandon provides some of the finest pairings of regional wines and innovative takes on classic dishes to be found anywhere in the Wine Country. The incomparable natural setting, the award-winning menu, and the extensive wine list offer a Napa Valley experience like no other, and demonstrate that, if there is one thing more exciting than heritage, it is the road ahead. **CR**

"… built for romance, with delicate orchids on each table and views of the wooded grounds."

Fodor's Travel

⬆ Domaine Chandon is situated in idyllic surroundings.

Tra Vigne | Where Tuscany meets the Napa Valley

Location Napa Valley **Signature dish** Sage-infused pappardelle with rabbit | ❺❺❺

First opened in 1989, Tra Vigne—from the Italian meaning literally "between vineyards"—lies nestled in the heart of the Napa Valley, overlooking a picturesque courtyard and neighbored by vine-covered, brick-laid buildings. The restaurant has delicately knit together two distinct but complementary regional cuisines with a seasonal and ingredient-driven slant to every dish.

The menu balances the lightness and vegetable-centric new Napa style with hearty, rich, and flavorful classic Tuscan fare, and offers a fresh take on traditional dishes from other parts of Europe that leaves visitors deeply satisfied, but still light on their feet, even after three or four courses. Although the restaurant stands near the Pacific coast of the United States, the setting is as Italian as Siena—truly the best of both worlds.

Chef Anthony "Nash" Cognetti has turned Tra Vigne into one of the most popular Wine Country eateries, a perennial attraction for locals and visitors alike. Born into a family of purveyors of fresh produce, Cognetti was taught from an early age that the main essentials of any great kitchen are the chef's awareness of the changes in the seasons and a willingness to adapt the menu accordingly.

He learned these lessons well. His appreciation of the visceral and tactile pleasures of food has earned sage-infused pappardelle with rabbit pride of place on the menu. Also highly recommended is the freshly pulled mozzarella. The pizzas and other wood-fire dishes never fail to impress.

The Tra Vigne experience is completed by the friendly and knowledgeable staff, who are always happy to recommend a wine pairing from an award-winning list that profiles the best of Tuscany and the Napa Valley. Brunch and lunch options on Sundays offer diners the opportunity to sample Cognetti's latest creations. **CR**

"It's a restaurant where you can find a menu that is both familiar and satisfying."

Michael Bauer, *Inside Scoop SF*

⬆ A lovely plate of rabbit pappardelle with Savoy cabbage and Parmesan cheese.

Redd | California roots with a European influence

Location Yountville **Signature dish** Carnaroli risotto with Maine lobster, lemon confit, and white truffle oil | $$$

Redd is the first solo venture by acclaimed chef Richard Reddington, who honed his culinary skills in the leading kitchens of Northern California, one of the world's most renowned fine dining regions. Since 2005, he has offered a menu of his own that is diverse in origin, finely honed throughout, and has a decidedly seasonal bent.

At the north end of Yountville's renowned "restaurant row," Redd stands out, even among such distinguished neighbors. Awarded a Michelin star between 2008 and 2013, the restaurant has been a favorite of locals, tourists, and critics alike. The food is, of course, exemplary, and the service is consistently warm and attentive. Meanwhile the space—from the sleek and polished exterior to the modern and decidedly chic indoor seating area, and an outdoor courtyard with a gurgling fountain—contibutes significantly to making Redd one of the finest holistic dining experiences the West Coast of the United States has to offer.

In true California style, Reddington has cultivated close relationships with farmers, artisans, and food producers in the surrounding area, and draws from culinary sensibilities honed in Europe and the Mediterranean to build a flavor-rich and varied menu. Selections veer less toward the conceptual, and more toward a contemporary take on comfort food, with fresh yet hearty dishes and a consistent depth of flavor. If you can't decide what to get—and with a menu built entirely of "must tries," the decision is never easy—the five-course tasting menu is a wonderful introduction to a range of food that is diverse in both flavor profile and ethnic style. The wine pairings highlight the considerable talents of the in-house wine director and the two sommeliers. Finally, the Sunday brunch is the perfect way to fuel up for a long day of wine tasting—and from here, you won't have far to travel. **CR**

"Redd presents polished comfort food in a simple, modern setting. Its wine . . . is some of the best . . ."

Wine Spectator

↑ The sashimi of hamachi yellowtail, sticky rice, edamame, and lime ginger sauce is a highlight.

The French Laundry | The definition of American fine dining

Location Yountville **Signature dish** "Oysters and pearls" | ❺❺❺❺❺

"… a culinary institution. Some of North America's finest chefs trained here."

theworlds50best.com

⬆ The sophisticated interior is set off against the original stone and timber structure.

➡ A beautifully presented dish featuring sashimi of kanpachi with salmon roe and radish.

There is scarcely enough space to list all of this restaurant's accolades: from Michelin stars and James Beard Awards for excellence in cuisine to "Best Restaurant" designations, The French Laundry and its chef, Thomas Keller, have earned them all. The humble stone and timber two-story structure that houses the eatery was originally built in 1900, serving as a residence, a French steam laundry, a bar, and even a brothel before becoming a restaurant. Inspired by the fine-dining destinations of the French countryside, Keller selected this 1,600-sq ft (150-sq m) space, with room for just 16 tables, because the ambience struck the right balance between "fine" and "comfortable."

Keller has said that he strives to be perfect in his cooking but mostly to make people happy. To best describe his cuisine the term "finesse" comes to mind—and the word is in fact defined on a sign hanging on the wall in the kitchen as "refinement and delicacy of performance, execution, or artisanship."

If you opt for the nine-course chef's tasting menu (a similar nine-course vegetarian menu is also available), the first course will invariably be Keller's signature dish of "oysters and pearls," a *sabayon* of pearl tapioca with Island Creek oysters and white sturgeon caviar. The next eight courses are determined by the changing seasons, but they are always playful in their composition.

Dishes including mac and cheese with butter-poached lobster and mascarpone-enriched orzo pasta or "tongue in cheek" of braised beef cheeks and veal tongue with baby leeks and horseradish cream elevate lighthearted comfort food to fine-dining status. No two ingredients are ever repeated in the course of a single evening, and each dish is just small enough to leave diners wanting another bite—until the next dish appears and it happens all over again. **MD**

Canlis | Breathtaking views and elegant dining in a historic restaurant

Location Seattle   **Signature dish** Peter Canlis prawns | ❺❺❺❺

Justifiably hailed as one of the most beautiful restaurants in the United States, Canlis has been the grande dame of Seattle's culinary scene since 1950. Built by preeminent Northwest architect Roland Terry, the restaurant is a stunning example of mid-century modern architecture. Through angled floor-to-ceiling windows, Canlis commands spectacular views of the Cascade mountain range.

The child of a Greek father and a Lebanese mother, Peter Canlis, the restaurant's founder, brought a Mediterranean brightness and elegance to his menu of modernized American classics. His signature Canlis salad is like a lighter Caesar, enlivened with herbs, crispy bacon, and a lemony dressing. The most requested item on the menu is Peter Canlis shrimps which are seared in a hot pan that is deglazed with vermouth, lime juice, and a touch of fresh chili, and then finished with a rich shrimp butter made with the shrimp shells.

Canlis's children, Mark and Brian, took over the business in 2005, and in 2008 they hired Eleven Madison Park's executive sous-chef, Jason Franey, as Canlis's fifth executive chef. Franey's modernist tasting menu has enabled Canlis to remain a contender in Seattle's formidable dining scene, while the à la carte menu continues to feature restrained, elegant preparations showcasing Northwest ingredients. In the cozy bar, casual diners can find dishes that are lighter on the wallet, stylish cocktails, and an impressive selection of Scotch malt whiskys.

Despite white tablecloths and a puzzling dress code—"We ask that gentlemen wear a suit or sport coat if possible. Many of our window tables require one"—Canlis is welcoming, thanks to the accommodating staff, a no-name coat check policy, and graceful tableside service. **SW**

⬆ Canlis is one of Seattle's must-visit restaurants.

Green Leaf | Thrillingly authentic Vietnamese food

Location Seattle   **Signature dish** *Bún dac biet* (combination vermicelli noodle salad) | **$**

Located behind an unprepossessing storefront, Green Leaf's tiny restaurant in Seattle's International District is just a step up from a hole in the wall, but it has delighted diners with its superb, fresh, and supremely authentic Vietnamese food since 2006. The interior is crowded but congenial, with bamboo-printed wallpaper, and friendly servers happy to offer advice. The extensive menu offers Vietnamese street food and regional specialities with a fine regard for authenticity.

A standout is *bánh xèo*, a fried rice flour and coconut crêpe scented with turmeric, folded like an omelet around pork, tiny shrimp, and bean sprouts, and eaten wrapped in lettuce with herbs and tangy *nuoc cham* dipping sauce. The pho is excellent, as are the bright green papaya, green mango, and lotus root salads, and many diners come just for the restaurant's signature dish, *bún dac biet*, a vermicelli noodle salad topped with shrimp skewered on sugar cane, grilled pork, pickled vegetables, and fried Asian shallots.

The restaurant also offers delicious and hard-to-find dishes from inland regions of Vietnam and the Mekong Delta, such as *bún bò hue*—a spicy beef noodle soup, which is served in the traditional style with beef shank, pig knuckle, and cubes of congealed pig blood—and *bún mam*, a thick and pungent fermented anchovy soup.

Another branch of Green Leaf in Seattle's Belltown neighborhood offers an expanded menu, including seafood—there is a spectacular whole Dungeness crab cooked with ginger and scallions—and Vietnamese desserts.

The original Green Leaf is packed with diners. As well as first-timers, there are repeat customers, food tourists drawn by the restaurant's considerable buzz, a significant number of Vietnamese, and—most telling—chefs from other restaurants. **SW**

⬆ Enjoy the gloriously tasty signature vermicelli salad.

Poppy | Innovative dining in top Capitol Hill neighborhood restaurant

Location Seattle   **Signature dish** Lavender duck leg with pomegranate red cabbage | ❸❸

At Poppy, chef-owner Jerry Traunfeld presents food quite unlike that of any other restaurant in Seattle. The menu revolves around thalis—multi-dish meals which are traditional in parts of India and Nepal. (A thali is the round plate on which the food is served.) Small portions of many dishes are presented on a single plate with nigella-poppy seed naan baked in the restaurant's tandoor.

One signature dish is a duck leg seasoned with lavender and lemon zest, served atop pomegranate-and-fennel-braised cabbage. Another is the addictive eggplant fries on the bar menu, which are lightly battered and drizzled with sea salt and honey. Traunfeld, a trained pastry chef, brings his inventive use of spice to the dessert thali, a beautiful, decadent assortment of sweet treats.

The restaurant's central concept was inspired when Traunfeld, a James Beard Best Chef Northwest, traveled in India. There he was struck by the balance that thalis achieve between flavors and textures. The food at Poppy reproduces this finely judged equilibrium. Collocations are influenced by produce that is in season, but not dictated by it: of far greater importance is the layering of spices and herbs. In the spring and summer, all of Poppy's herbs come from the restaurant's lush gardens in the back, where on sunny days patrons can dine outside.

The restaurant is at once cozy and spacious, elegant and inviting. High ceilings and tall plate-glass windows set off cool blond modernist wood furniture and deep red-orange walls. The kitchen is prominent, a sleek cube that juts into the restaurant itself, with a long high window that offers a partial view of the activity within.

Poppy uses rustic methods to produce metropolitan food. Providence Cicero summed up its appeal when she wrote in *The Seattle Times* that "it takes humble to haute levels." **SW**

"… somehow each small-portioned delight seems better than the last."

Fodor's Travel

⬆ Desserts are a sumptuous affair at Poppy.

Bar Sajor | Locavore cooking at its best, in an exquisite space

Location Seattle **Signature dish** Wood-fired rotisserie chicken with seasonal accompaniments | $$

Few chefs have done more to shape the way that food in Seattle restaurants is eaten, prepared, and—most importantly—sourced than Matthew Dillon. A *Food and Wine Magazine* Best New Chef, and winner of the James Beard Foundation award for Best Chef Northwest, Dillon is a former professional forager and dedicated locavore whose menus reflect the shifting seasons and the bounty of the temperate, pine-forested Pacific Northwest. At Bar Sajor, Dillon's third restaurant, in Seattle's historic Pioneer Square neighborhood, he draws influences from Northern Africa, Spain, and Portugal to create plates from seasonal ingredients that are considered, unexpected, and memorable.

The restaurant itself is an elegant, airy, high-ceilinged space with tables of polished hemlock and a zinc-topped bar opposite the large open kitchen. On the walls hang rococo *objets trouvés*, framed mirrors, and installations created by local artist Tamara Codor. The whole is dominated by a large wood-fired oven, rotisserie, and grill (there is no stove or range), where nearly all of the food—much of it from Dillon's own farm on Vashon Island—is prepared or finished.

Certain components appear in different iterations depending on the season and what is fresh. Thus rotisserie-roasted chicken, a signature dish, may be complemented by grilled persimmons and a nut-vinegar dressing one week, and by beets and caramelized butter the next. The delicious house-made smoked whole-milk yogurt may be the centerpiece of a starter, with rye crisps and pickled vegetables, or it may accompany braised and roasted bycatch octopus. Local herbs and wild berries are infused into vinegars and tinctures for the restaurant's cocktails. The wood-fired oven is also used to bake superb, rustic loaves of sourdough bread.

Dillon is at the height of his powers, and cooking the food he loves, and it shows. **SW**

"… embodies a paradigm shift in the larger dining scene, and one that's been a long time coming."

Allison Austin Scheff, *Seattle Magazine*

⊓ A beautifully presented dish with beetroot and leaves.

Shiro's | A Seattle treasure
serving superb traditional sushi

Location Seattle **Signature dish** Kasuzuke broiled black cod | ❸❺

When Shiro Kashiba immigrated from Japan in 1966, sushi was almost unknown in the United States. In the following year, he opened Seattle's first full-service sushi bar. In 1994, after opening other restaurants and achieving a reputation as one of the world's great sushi chefs, he opened the eponymous Shiro's in the Belltown neighborhood.

Born in Kyoto, Shiro trained as a sushi chef in Tokyo under the tutelage of Jiro Ono, owner of the three-Michelin-star Sukiyabashi Jiro. On arrival In the Pacific Northwest, Shiro was struck by the incredible abundance in its waters. He now sources most of his seafood locally, still going to the market daily to select the freshest fish.

> "Shiro's is Seattle's most iconic sushi restaurant. Chef Shiro Kashiba is a legend."
>
> FearlessCritic.com

The restaurant's decor is simple, with wood paneling and Japanese calligraphy on the back wall. At the room's center is the sushi bar; patrons begin lining up more than an hour before the restaurant opens to secure one of its eleven seats. (Customers who don't wish to line up can reserve seats at tables.)

The sushi is proudly traditional. Shiro discourages the use of soy sauce for dunking; it overpowers the fresh taste of the fish. He seasons the rice and paints the fish with nikiri—a house-made mixture of soy sauce, dashi, mirin, and sake—which perfectly enhances the flavor. The best way to eat is to order omakase—literally translated as "it's up to you"—in which the chef chooses everything for you. **SW**

The Walrus and the Carpenter | Oysters a-go-go

Location Seattle **Signature dish** Oysters fried in a cilantro aioli | ❸❺

Lines form early at this tiny, no-reservations eatery in Seattle's hip Ballard neighborhood, but it's worth the wait. Situated in a converted warehouse, the restaurant is flooded in the afternoon with light from the west-facing floor-to-ceiling windows. The walls are whimsically decorated with pen-and-ink drawings, including one of the eponymous Walrus, a salty fisherman with a taste for oysters. Diners sit on a high, sleek, gray banquette, or at the beautiful curved bar surrounding the open kitchen.

The Walrus and the Carpenter is first and foremost an oyster bar, but it is award-winning chef-owner Renée Erickson's French-influenced, seasonal, small plates, meant for sharing, that keep customers thronging back for more. The food is fresh and unfussy, and portions are generous. Signature dishes include spiced, cornmeal-crusted fried oysters, served piping hot with a cilantro aioli, and a delicate filet of smoked trout, garnished with home-pickled onion and a salad of lentils, crème fraîche, and walnuts.

Erickson displays an expert hand with seafood, and the menu principally emphasizes local clams, mussels, oysters, and fish, but meat-eaters can always find a classic steak tartare, and vegetable lovers should not miss the deep fried Brussels sprouts or the several excellent salads. For afters, there are local cheeses and simple desserts crafted for adult palates—roasted Medjool dates in clarified butter, flecked with salt, and rustic cakes and tarts made with seasonal ingredients and plenty of booze. To accompany this bounty, the restaurant features an excellent wine list, craft cocktails, and local beers.

The atmosphere is friendly, informal, and convivial, the service attentive. The Walrus and the Carpenter feels immediately like a favorite regular haunt, a place to which one hopes to return. **SW**

Matt's in the Market | Casual fine dining in the heart of Seattle's Pike Place Market

Location Seattle   **Signature dish** Cornmeal-crusted fried catfish sandwich | 💲💲

Even on a cloudy day, the view from Matt's in the Market is exceptional. The restaurant is situated on the top floor of the Corner Market Building in the heart of one of the oldest continuously operating public farmers' markets in the United States. Through large arched windows, diners look out over Elliott Bay and the Olympic Mountain Range, and the great clock that stands above the market's main entrance.

Owner Dan Bugge sources most of his ingredients from local producers, many within Pike Place Market itself, to create a delightful, fresh, seasonal menu. Lunch is informal and affordable. There are delicious sandwiches—don't miss the one with fried catfish, which has been on the menu since the restaurant opened in 1996—hearty soups, including an excellent gumbo, and composed plates for those seeking something more refined. By day, light from the corner windows fills the space, the old wooden rafters glow with reflected warmth, and the restaurant takes on the vibrancy and energy of its surroundings.

In the evenings, Matt's in the Market transforms into something altogether more romantic. Tucked away atop the shuttered market, the restaurant feels intimate, hidden. Diners perch around the beautiful wooden bar, or at tables near the lovely arched windows. There are small, seasonal plates—several of these can comprise a meal for two—and elegant, inventive entrées. Local seafood is prominently featured, as is the market's wonderful produce, all prepared with the deft and stylish touch distinctive of the Pacific Northwest, for which Matt's in the Market has become known.

The award-winning wine list is extraordinarily good, and the service always warm and professional. Matt's in the Market in many ways exemplifies the best of Seattle. **SW**

"Your first dinner at Matt's is like a first date you hope will never end."

Fodor's Travel

⬆ Top-class dining in a top-floor location.

Chez Panisse | Farm-to-table California-Mediterranean
cuisine at a legendary restaurant

Location Berkeley   **Signature dish** Baked goat cheese with garden lettuce |

$ $ $

"… lives up to its reputation and delivers a dining experience well worth the price."

Fodor's Travel

⬆ France transported to the Pacific coast on Chez Panisse's serving table.

Alice Waters' iconic restaurant opened in 1971 in the bohemian-chic university city of Berkeley, California, and became a legendary part of U.S. culinary history. Located in a two-story Craftsman-style house, the restaurant is welcoming: arriving is like walking into a dinner party in a French home—precisely the feeling that Waters has always tried to create.

Waters is a champion of the locavore movement, the influence of which is evident in every dish here. Since its inception, Chez Panisse has served only locally grown, impeccably fresh, organic food.

Upstairs, the informal café features a seasonal menu, fashioned by chefs Beth Wells and Nathan Alderson. Dishes vary daily, and are prepared in an open kitchen along one side of the dining room. They often include handmade pastas, pizzettas fired in the wood-burning oven, roasted poultry, fresh seafood soups and stews, and a deceptively simple yet excellent mixed green salad with baked goat cheese. Desserts celebrate fresh fruit in myriad ways. Try to get a table in the newly refurbished front porch in the shadow of the giant bunya bunya tree.

Downstairs, the restaurant serves a three- to four-course fixed dinner menu which changes daily. Chefs Jérôme Waag and Cal Peternell craft beautiful meals inspired by the local farmers' market. Guests—cosseted in the elegant wood-paneled dining room—savor dishes such as salmon carpaccio with anise hyssop, roasted duck with wild huckleberries, and red wine-poached pear tartlet.

The restaurant is named after Honoré Panisse, a character in Marcel Pagnol's 1930s movie trilogy *Marius, Fanny,* and *César.* Pagnol celebrated convivial dining in his films, and Chez Panisse is the epitome of that ethic, serving simple, fresh, California-style food to a knowledgeable, eclectic clientele. **PB**

Baumé | Deconstructed French cuisine meets molecular pan-Asia

Location Palo Alto   **Signature dish** Ratatouille with slow-poached egg | 🍷🍷🍷🍷🍷

Small is beautiful at Baumé: its dining area is minimalist in design, and there is room for only 22 diners. The restaurant has an almost nonchalant appearance, with large tinted windows and its name quietly settled above the main door. Inside, the orange and brown decor and ethereal background music exude tranquility. All in all, the look and atmosphere of the place make it hard to believe that it is home to some of the most accomplished and innovative food in the Bay Area, and that its chef, Bruno Chemel, is the possessor of two Michelin stars.

Chemel's dishes defy pigeonholing but may be summarized as a deconstruction of the classic cuisine of his native France, with added pan-Asian influences and a dash of molecular gastronomy (foam puts in an appearance here and there). Dining at Baumé is an adventure into a conceptual cuisine that reflects Chemel's interest in macrobiotic cooking (he studied it in Japan). Every dish is chosen and prepared for its flavor but also for its kindness to diners' digestion.

On arrival, diners are presented not with a conventional bill of fare but with a list of the ingredients that are being used that night in the 12-course tasting menu (there is a seasonal aspect to their availability) and a separate wine pairings menu. Dishes might include an assemblage of Asian pear, red pepper, and prosciutto that looks like an art installation; gazpacho served up like a cocktail, or ratatouille with egg slow-poached for half an hour at 62°F (16°C). Desserts are avant-garde, with intense evocations of seasonal fruit, as well as occasional billows of dry ice and crunchy textured ice creams.

None of this comes cheaply or quickly—Baumé is one of the world's most expensive restaurants, and dinner there cannot realistically be completed in less than three hours. **ATJ**

Chez TJ | Fine contemporary French cuisine in California

Location Mountain View   **Signature dish** Lobster consommé (seasonal) | 🍷🍷🍷

In 1982, working on a shoestring budget, George Aviet and Thomas J. McCombie opened Chez TJ in Mountain View, just south of San Francisco. It was an immediate success, and for food lovers throughout the Bay Area and beyond, it soon became not so much a restaurant as a way of gastronomic life.

As Chez TJ served its first happy visitors, the world of fine dining was undergoing a rapid revitalization. Quality of service was becoming an essential part of the five-star dining experience. Restaurants needed to do more than produce good food; they had also to be friendly and welcoming rather than aloof and exclusive. Chez TJ was among the first places to satisfy both criteria, and set the standard for the future.

"… Chez TJ is thoroughly modern, incorporating culinary innovation into its take on French cuisine."

Michelin Guide

Since McCombie's death in 1994, the staff has preserved his legacy, and ensured that diners leave Chez TJ with the feeling that they have been well fed and treated with courtesy and consideration.

Chez TJ's kitchen is currently commanded by Jarad Gallagher, a second-generation chef who learned as a child to hunt and forage for ingredients. An intimate understanding of seasonality and natural abundance informs his carefully crafted menu, highlighting the finest fresh products. Dishes offer a novel take on classic plates, informed by French flavor profiles and preparation methods. The lobster consommé is unmissable and so are the slow-baked tai snapper and anything with truffles. **CR**

Manresa | Sophisticated, contemporary dining, pulled off with panache

Location Los Gatos **Signature dish** Octopus *a la plancha* | ❸❸❸❸

"Kinch has a reputation as a genius. That's what his best friend, Wynton Marsalis, says, anyway."

GQ Magazine

⬆ Manresa's dishes are almost too pretty to eat.

➡ A culinary creation featuring delicate vegetables.

Manresa occupies premises on a quiet street in the prosperous community of Los Gatos, not far from San Jose, California. It takes its name from that of a beach near Santa Cruz where the restaurant's chef and owner, David Kinch, likes to surf. Kinch worked in Spain and with Marc Meneau at Espérance in Yonne, France, as well as at the Quilted Giraffe in Vero Beach, Florida, and at Hermes in San Francisco before opening his own Spanish restaurant prior to Manresa. His cooking style is modern but grounded in solid classical technique, with some influences from his regular trips to Japan.

There are no shortcuts at Manresa. Bread is made from scratch in the kitchen and this extra effort pays off in, for example, a fine levain loaf that has terrific texture and a superb crust. The technical skill shows in the little details, such as a nibble of superb Gorgonzola sable biscuits, which are bursting with cheese flavor and have excellent texture.

Octopus *a la plancha* is presented on a bed of wild rice with chrysanthemum pesto and a chicken broth gelée. This dish is so fresh that it lacks even a hint of the chewiness often associated with octopus. A "vegetable garden" dish is prettily presented with assorted leaves and flowers, plus a little pesto and lemon puree; every constituent comes from Manresa's own gardens.

The elaborate flavor combinations that characterize Manresa cuisine are displayed to maximum advantage in the suckling porcelet with green garlic panisse (a fried chickpea flour cake from the south of France), and in the unripe strawberries, with cream polenta and a meat jus perfumed with rhubarb puree. Manresa provides an impressive dining experience, with top ingredients and an assured technique. It is contemporary, but avoids the common pitfall of overreaching in the search for modernity. **AH**

Sierra Mar | Elegant coastal dining surrounded by untamed wilderness

Location Big Sur **Signature dish** Red abalone with dried tomato, basil, and brown butter | ❺❺❺❺

Henry Miller wrote of Big Sur that it is "the California that men dreamed of years ago . . . the face of the Earth as the Creator intended it to look." And there is little to gainsay him in the vista that confronts anyone seated in the Sierra Mar, a unique restaurant in the Post Ranch Inn, which stands high above the redwood-studded wilderness on this rugged and remote stretch of the Central California coast.

The decor is deliberately understated so as not to distract attention from the spectacular landscape just beyond the floor-to-ceiling windows. The only competition with the view is the menu, which for dinner provides two options. One is a traditional four-course prix fixe, which changes daily and offers choice and flexibility. With luck, one may be there on the nights that feature grilled ribeye steak with Gruyère potato gratin, Bordelaise sauce, and Choron Sabayon, or sesame-crusted rare ahi tuna with shallot soy sauce, wasabi butter, and crispy wonton salad.

The other possibility is the nine-course Taste of Big Sur tasting menu that highlights local ingredients from the surrounding coastal waters and mountains. Selections might include a carpaccio of fallow venison with gin sorbet, or morel mushrooms with ramp custard and asparagus soup.

What is quickly becoming a signature starter, "Roe, Roe, Roe" is a trio of rare and indigenous caviars—paddlefish and smoked cod roe on a baton of cucumber; herring roe with finger lime on a sliver of avocado; and smoked trout roe on mango—served side by side on a single plate.

Guests dining in the later part of the year should go for the local chanterelles that have been newly foraged from the Los Padres Wilderness, then pan-roasted and cooked into a warm mushroom broth to create a duo that highlights a seemingly simple risotto and seems to capture the very essence of Big Sur and Sierra Mar. **MD**

"This restaurant is so gorgeous and is in such an amazing location that it feels like a temple."

foodhoe.com

⬆ "Roe, Roe, Roe" is once, twice, three times a masterpiece.

➡ Sierra Mar is so well laid out that there are fine views even from the tables furthest from the windows.

La Super Rica Taqueria |
Julia Child's favorite taqueria

Location Santa Barbara **Signature dish** The Super Rica Especial | $

La Super Rica may not be the absolute best Mexican eatery in the United States, but, thanks to an endorsement of quality by cookery icon Julia Child, its place is cemented in California culinary history.

The small, turquoise-painted wood frame shack sits on Milpas street in a residential neighborhood on the east side of Santa Barbara. Diners walk up, order through a small window, help themselves to offerings from the salsa bar, and then wait until their number is called. The chalkboard menu hasn't changed much since the place first opened in 1980, founded by Isidoro Gonzales, a native of Jalisco, Mexico. Lines still form out the door every day, however, and if it ain't broke, Gonzales will tell you, don't fix it.

"… one of the most authentic Mexican home-cooking restaurants around."

Joanie Hudson, *The Santa Barbara Independent*

The undoubted star of the small operation is the woman working right behind the cash register, who rolls and presses thick, fresh tortillas from a pile of wet masa. The tortillas are griddled to order and served with almost every dish (always ask for extra).

The house specialty is the Super Rica Especial—a deconstructed chile relleno containing strips of al pastor pork mixed with roasted pasilla chiles and melted cheese, and then piled on the tortillas. Just don't miss the daily specials taped to the window right above where you place your order. That is where a few of the more unusual and traditional dishes, like pozole, banana leaf-wrapped tamales, and sopes, make their appearance. **MD**

Spago | Reinventing California
fine dining with inspired dishes

Location Beverly Hills **Signature dish** House smoked salmon pizza with crème fraîche and caviar | $$$

Spago is the flagship of Wolfgang Puck's empire , and probably always will be, at least for as long as the celebrity chef maintains a willingness to reinvent his best-known creation. The restaurant originally opened in 1982 on Sunset Strip in West Hollywood. In 1997, it moved to Canon Drive in Beverly Hills, where it maintained its popularity. But Puck, never a man to rest on his laurels, ignored the axiom "if it ain't broke, don't fix it," and closed down in 2012 so that the restaurant could be overhauled from top to bottom.

The latest Spago has been thoroughly re-imagined, with fresh decor and all-new market-driven menus featuring the best ingredients that California farmers, ranchers, and fisheries have to offer.

The new dining room, from designer-to-the-stars Waldo Fernandez, complements the new menu with a clean and simple aesthetic, incorporating natural elements to create an organic feel. In redesigning the bill of fare, Puck moved away from the fixed tasting menus at most other white tablecloth establishments and opted instead for an old-school Italian-style structure that enables diners to select appetizers, pastas, and entrées. Diners can cross continents in a single meal, juxtaposing dishes such as tempura soft shell crab with green curry vinaigrette, corn salad, and Thai basil, and grilled rack of lamb with harissa aioli, falafel "macaroons," and cucumber mint raita.

Puck's whimsical style still shines through in the new dishes. What looks like just another version of the achingly trendy roasted bone marrow is instead a clean marrow bone stuffed with a cold veal tartare and covered in a cap of smoked mascarpone cheese. But, don't worry, not everything has changed. The signature house smoked salmon pizza with crème fraîche and caviar is still available. But you now have to order it at the bar. **MD**

CUT | The Beverly Hills restaurant that pioneered modern, West Coast steakhouse cool

Location Beverly Hills   **Signature dish** True Japanese Wagyu ribeye steak |

$$$$

There are few restaurants in Los Angeles where people go to see and be seen and also walk away having had a good meal. Thanks to Austrian-born celebrity chef and restaurateur Wolfgang Puck and executive chef Lee Hefter, CUT, inside the famous Beverly Wilshire Hotel, is at the top of the list of places where you can do both.

This is not any old steakhouse; there are no mahogany walls or leather sofas anywhere in sight. Instead, the interior, designed by American architect Richard Meier, is starkly modern, from the swiveling black mesh-covered Eames chairs to the rotating collections of modern art hanging on the walls. (A recent CUT collection featured a nine-piece installation by John Baldessari.) Behind the scenes, Puck and Hefter curate a wide-range of steaks that are brought out front and displayed to the guests to help them choose exactly what they want. The selection includes grass-fed California Angus, 35-day dry-aged Nebraska corn fed beef, American Wagyu from Idaho, and authentic Wagyu from Miyazaki Prefecture, Japan.

Among other standouts on the menu are octopus carpaccio with pickled Romanesco and chorizo oil, bone marrow flan with parsley salad, and rotisserie poussin with roasted porcini mushrooms. CUT diners are almost sure to order hand-crafted cocktails from the restaurant's Sidebar, or wine from sommelier Dana Farner's 400-bottle selection that majors on reds.

CUT is quintessential Puck, and all Hollywood— just about the only place you'll have a better chance of seeing some movie stars is inside Warner Brothers Studios. But there's more to it than celebrity-spotting: the restaurant was awarded three stars by the food critics of *The Los Angeles Times* and won *Esquire*'s 2006 Restaurant of the Year award. **MD**

> *"Celebrity sightings are highly likely ... and the staff treat you like a million bucks."*
>
> Zagat

⤒ Tables at CUT meld into the lobby of the Beverly Hills Wilshire hotel.

Alibi Room | Roy Choi brings his taco truck magic to a fixed location

Location Culver City **Signature dish** Short rib taco | $

In the fall of 2008, chef Roy Choi burst onto the Los Angeles dining scene with his Kogi BBQ that was to become famous. It was not an ordinary restaurant with chairs and tables, or even walls and a door. No, Choi was cooking some of the city's best food in a roving taco truck, and offering fervent fans Korean barbecue tacos out on the highway.

Kogi's Korean tacos and quesadillas became icons of Los Angeles street food. The company's success paved the way for a gourmet food truck revolution that swept the United States.

For those who are not inclined to chase a truck around town, or those who just like a roof over their heads when eating dinner, Choi partnered with Los Angeles restaurateur Dave Reiss to bring the Kogi menu to Reiss's Alibi Room, a small but welcoming neighborhood watering hole with a triangle-shaped bar on the western edge of Culver City. The tiny kitchen not only makes classic Kogi taco truck fare, but

also offers select choices from some of Choi's other restaurants around town. The main focus of attention, naturally, is on the Kogi tacos.

The original Kogi short rib taco is made with two griddled homemade corn tortillas, caramelized Korean barbecued short ribs, fresh salsa, and a Napa cabbage slaw tossed in a chili-soy vinaigrette. Another popular choice is the spicy kimchi quesadilla, which Choi calls "the grandmother of them all." It consists of a fresh flour tortilla filled with jack and cheddar cheeses and added caramelized, buttered kimchi; the assemblage is griddled until it is melting and crispy. Before serving, it is cut into quarters and topped with a salsa roja and crushed sesame seeds. Such mash-ups of Mexican and Korean culinary traditions are classic Choi. Love it or loathe it, there may not be any better bar food around. **MD**

⬆ Top tacos but without a truck at the Alibi Room.

Bäco Mercat | A casual neighborhood restaurant with inventive food

Location Los Angeles **Signature dish** "Bäco" (flatbread sandwich) | $$

Bäco Mercat is a neighborhood restaurant that reflects its downtown Los Angeles locale: a comfortable mix of rustic charm and industrial chic that is casual and low key. Its small interior feels airy during the day, thanks to the tall ceilings and large windows, but transforms into a lovely, romantic hangout at night, lit mainly by Edison-style lights overhead. Its vintage tables are covered with simple brown paper stamped with the restaurant's logo and have matching chairs.

The room is lively, especially at dinner, and the food and drinks are inventive and fun. The seasonal menu, much like its neighborhood, is eclectic, with culinary influences from Mediterranean, Asian, Latin American, and Moroccan cuisines. Special attention is also paid to fresh local produce.

The lunch menu focuses on chef Josef Centeno's own creation, the so-called "bäco," a flatbread sandwich that is folded in half, resembling a hybrid of taco, gyro, and pizza. "The Original"—loaded with chunks of crispy pork belly, tender beef carnitas, and *salbitxada* (a Catalonian sauce made with tomatoes and almonds)—is reason enough to visit. The bäco dough is topped with smoked jalapeño and lamb or spiced beef, yam, and feta cheese, to make *coca*, the Spanish version of pizza. At dinner, the menu expands to include fish and meat entrées and a selection of vegetable plates featuring okra and Brussels sprouts.

The creativity and attention to detail extend to the bar as well. In addition to its signature cocktails, Bäco Mercat handpicks a selection of spirits, beer, and wine from around the world and even bottles its own line of soda pops.

The wildly flavorful dishes and inspired drinks selection have made Bäco Mercat both a hot spot and an oasis in downtown Los Angeles. **DT**

⬆ The popular signature Bäco flatbread sandwich.

Nick's Café |

A quintessential American diner

Location Los Angeles   **Signature dish** Ham and eggs | **$**

No trip to Nick's Café is complete without an order of its justly famous ham and eggs. This dish is so popular that, on the weekends, the line to sit at the horse-shoe counter runs out the door. It is served with hash brown or cottage fried potatoes on large breakfast plates, ready to be washed down with bottomless cups of coffee.

Situated on North Spring Street, just north of downtown Los Angeles, Nick's has been serving breakfasts and lunches since 1948. A mixture of railway workers, policemen, firemen, and hipsters rub shoulders at the counter, jostling for the jars of home-made salsa, which, like the ham, is also available to take away.

"… asked about 'noir' restaurants, the first place that came to mind was Nick's Cafe."

Jonathan Gold, *LA Weekly*

Other breakfast dishes include pancake stacks, huevos rancheros, omelettes, waffles, and skillet fries. The lunch menu features hot pastrami sandwiches, hot dogs, melts, a renowned one-pound burger, and a range of homemade soups and salads.

Nick's broad appeal is reflected in its clientele, which is a true cross-section of Angelenos. Its first-rate short-order cooking has an authenticity and an integrity that elevate it far above the average diner experience, and serve as a reminder of the qualities and character that have been lost as chain restaurants and diners have proliferated. Although self-praise is normally no praise, Nick's slogan is an apt summation: "Real Food, Real People, Real Diner." **KPH & FH**

Sqirl Café |

Tiny farm-to-table café

Location Los Angeles   **Signature dish** Kokuho Rose brown rice bowl | **$**

Much more than the sum of its humble parts, Sqirl Café serves the food of the moment, with complex flavors born of simple ingredients.

Before the building in which it stands became one of Los Angeles' best (and smallest) eateries, it was the commercial kitchen for Sqirl LA, which was widely acclaimed as the finest producer of confitures in the United States. The chef and owner of both businesses, Jessica Koslow, had previously made her name by sourcing fruit from organic farmers within a 350-mile (560-km) radius of her original kitchen on the Silver Lake/East Hollywood border and turning it into an extensive range of delectable jellies, jams, and preserves. Over time, Koslow expanded her business into new premises.

Sqirl's main room houses a coffee bar and pastry case with a communal table surrounded by 10 stools. Outside there is a small patio filled with bright orange folding tables and chairs.

The food is delicious yet healthy, familiar yet novel. There is toasted brioche with Sqirl jam and freshly milled almond hazelnut butter; seared young broccoli with cheddar and bread crumbs; or a prosciutto sandwich with romesco, homemade ricotta, and fresh greens on a flattened, crispy baguette. The signature dish is a bowl of perfectly cooked Kokuho Rose heirloom brown rice, each kernel of which is slicked with a bright and citrusy sorrel pesto, then gilded with house-preserved Meyer lemon, paper-thin slides of market radish, French sheep's milk feta, and topped with a poached egg. This description might read like a parody of faddish Los Angeles dining, but the reality of both the food and the ambience is the antithesis of pretension. Sqirl defies description—it can be appreciated only by experiencing it in person. **MD**

Philippe the Original | Home and reputed birthplace of the French dipped sandwich

Location Los Angeles **Signature dish** French-dipped sandwich | $

With its sawdust covered floor, refectory dining room and deli-style counter service, Philippe's is perhaps the most democratic restaurant in Los Angeles. Patrons from all walks of life come for the same thing, the famous French-dipped sandwich, which, it is claimed, was invented here in 1918.

According to legend, the then owner, Philippe Mathieu, accidentally dropped a sliced French roll into the roasting pan and soaked up the roasting juices while serving a policeman. The cop took the sandwich regardless, and then returned the following day with his friends, asking for more of the same.

In addition to the iconic sandwiches, which come filled with a choice of pork, beef, turkey, lamb, or ham, patrons can choose from an extensive menu, which includes soups, salads, chilies, stews, and a range of desserts—freshly baked fruit pies, tapioca, and classic American cakes. And, opening at 6 a.m., Philippe's also serves breakfast—French toast, pancake stacks, and fragrant, freshly baked cinnamon rolls.

The thing about Philippe's, however, is that while it may be historic, first opening in 1908 and serving from its current location since 1951, it wears its history as comfortably as a favorite sweater. (As staff like to say, only the prices have changed.)

The food comes fast, but it is not fast food. A Philippe's sandwich demands your time and attention (and a slather of the famous homemade mustard). For while Philippe's offers the most casual of casual dining, every item on its menu—from the dipping jus to the pickles and coleslaws, to a wine list carefully curated by third-generation owner Richard Binder—is prepared with the utmost care. Philippe's survives unchanged by virtue of the fact that it sticks to what it does, and does it very well. To visit once is to become a regular for life. **KPH & FH**

"Philippe's also is worth visiting just for its people-watching opportunities."

roadfood.com

⊤ Philippe the Original is on North Alameda Street near Los Angeles Union railroad station.

Rivera | Modern Latin cuisine served in downtown Los Angeles

Location Los Angeles **Signature dish** Homemade Mayan *tortillas florales* with Indian butter | $$$

"A knockout every time . . . this pan-Latin from genius chef Sedlar presents beautiful dishes."

Zagat

↑ Rivera is a popular dining destination for Latin food.

It's easy to think of Rivera as the definitive expression of chef John Sedlar's passion for Latin food, its culture and heritage. Sedlar originally came to prominence in the early 1980s with his first restaurant, Sainte Estephe, which combined the New Mexican and Spanish food he had grown up with in his hometown, Santa Fe, with his classical French training. As his fame increased, so too did his interest in and commitment to Hispanic and Meso-American culinary traditions.

The purpose of Rivera is to celebrate the spirit of these cuisines in all their forms around the world. The restaurant's menu is constantly evolving, and currently gives customers a choice of three menus, one Mexican-based, another inspired by South American methodology, and a traditional Old World Iberian offering. The signature dish from the first menu is *tortillas florales* with Indian butter. Other stand-out items include *bacalao negro fresco* (seared black cod), Venezuelan *arepas* (flatbread made of ground maize dough), *caracoles* (snails), and *vieiras Arabesque* (sea scallops with eggplant).

With its darkened Osvaldo Maiozzi-designed dining room, Rivera is a luxurious place. And with its attention to detail across every aspect of the restaurant, it has earned its place at the forefront of Los Angeles' gastronomic renaissance. Passion is a word that's thrown around all too freely in the food biz, but Sedlar is one of the few to whom it can be genuinely ascribed. He has founded the Museum Tamal on Grand Avenue, a collection of food-related artifacts of the Latin world. Meanwhile, his restaurant is constantly evolving, picking up new trends in the cultures from which it draws its inspiration and adopting rediscovered ancient practices. Thus Rivera is a paradox: a restaurant that has apparently achieved perfection, yet is constantly improving. **KPH & FH**

Taylor's Steak House
Old-school steakhouse in Koreatown

Location Los Angeles **Signature dish** Culotte (cap, top sirloin, or butcher's cut) steak | ❺❺

It's hardly surprising, given it was founded in 1953—moving to its current Koreatown location in 1970—that Taylor's exudes a deliciously old-school ambience. With its dark wood walls and Naugahyde booths, it feels from the first a perfect place for an icy Martini and a steak grilled just so. And in this Taylor's doesn't disappoint—it is, quite simply, one of LA's finest steakhouses.

While the menu features weekly specials and offers a range of appetizers, seafoods, and sides—including the chunky, juicy Taylor's crab cakes served with hollandaise and the justly famous Molly Dinner Salad (iceberg lettuce, tomatoes, onions, and blue cheese)—it is really all about the steak. And what makes Taylor's stand out above the competition is its attention to detail. If ever you've been exacting about how your steak should be cooked, this is the place to deliver your own slice of beefy Nirvana, done to your precisely specified T.

Taylor's prides itself especially on the culotte steak—sometimes also known as the cap steak, top sirloin, or the butcher's cut. With only two steaks a steer, it's a cut with which to treat yourself—ideally with the aforementioned Martini or a suitable red from the largely California-based wine list.

Los Angeles boasts a number of historic restaurants. But unlike several of them, Taylor's—an old favorite of Frank Sinatra, among other celebrities—does not trade on past glories. It survives and flourishes by continuing to be true to what it does, and doing it consistently well. It's aided in this by first-rate floor staff, many of whom have been on the team for years. As a famous restaurateur remarked: "This is the hospitality business. It's not hard. All you have to do is make people happy." And that's just what Taylor's does. **KPH & FH**

Park's BBQ | Classic Korean
barbecue done to perfection

Location Los Angeles **Signature dish** Gal-bi short rib beefsteak | ❺

Although Korea has one of the world's greatest cuisines, its fame has been slow to spread around the world. However, it has established a firm foothold in Los Angeles' Koreatown neighborhood, where Park's on Vermont Avenue is widely acknowledged as the producer of the best Korean barbecue outside Seoul.

The restaurant's speciality is fresh (sometimes marinated) meat (typically beef) cooked quickly over high heat on small charcoal and gas-fired grills built into the dining tables. While other Korean barbecue joints may serve lesser grades of beef, Park's promotes USDA Prime and American Wagyu. It's about quality over quantity here, and diners can taste the difference. The two most popular cuts for grilling at Park's are the

> "… the reason Park's is still the standard-bearer for Korean barbecue in this town is the meat."
>
> Besha Rodell, *LA Weekly*

gal-bi, a thinly sliced, but still bone-on short rib, and bulgogi, thinly cut slices of ribeye that are marinated in soy sauce, sesame oil, black pepper, ginger, sugar, and other seasonings. In keeping with Korean tradition, every meal comes with a complementary set of banchan (small bowls of cold side dishes), the two most common of which are kimchi and jap chae (glass noodles).

While Park's BBQ is located in an otherwise nondescript strip mall along a busy commercial corridor, this is not some hole-in-the-wall place waiting to be discovered. The framed celebrity headshots lining the walls are proof enough that Park's has made it in this movie-obsessed town. **MD**

Langer's Delicatessen |

Sublime hot pastrami sandwiches

Location Los Angeles **Signature dish** The #19 Sandwich | ❺❺

It is easier to assert that something is the best in the world than to substantiate the claim. Where food is concerned, excellence must always be a matter of opinion, but significantly there seems to be universal agreement that the best hot pastrami sandwiches on the planet are those served at Langer's Delicatessen in the Westlake neighborhood of Los Angeles.

It was the writer Nora Ephron who first drew the attention to Langer's in a 2002 article in *The New Yorker*. Readers figured that someone familiar with the celebrated delis of the Big Apple, such as Katz's and the Mill Basin, would know what she was talking about, and they soon discovered that she was right. While pastrami sandwiches top the bill of fare, they

---

"It is a matter of conventional wisdom: Langer's serves the best pastrami sandwich in America."

L. A. Weekly

---

aren't the only things to eat at Langer's: there are other deli classics, such as chopped liver, cheese blintzes, knishes, and matzo ball soup. But it's the pastrami that keeps the diners coming back. There are more than two dozen ways to order it; the most popular is the #19 on twice-baked Russian rye bread with coleslaw, Swiss cheese, and Russian-style dressing. Order with a house-made vanilla coke and a side of crinkle-cut fries.

Langer's decor is classic 1970s delicatessen, with brown vinyl banquettes and padded booths running the entire length of the 135-seat room. There is one seat at the counter, overlooking proceedings, that is reserved in perpetuity for Al Langer, the restaurant's founder, who died in 2007. **MD**

Lotería Grill |

Authentic regional Mexican favorites

Location Los Angeles **Signature dish** Probadita (a sampler of the restaurant's signature tacos) | ❺❺

The large, open dining room of Lotería Grill is a stark contrast to its beginnings as a tiny taquería with counter seating at the Farmers Market on Third Street. The spacious sit-down restaurant continues to celebrate the culinary traditions of Mexico, serving the authentic, made-from-scratch regional favorites that popularized the original stall. One notable change is the addition of a full bar, where diners can order margaritas while enjoying chef Jimmy Shaw's loving homage to the food he ate while growing up in Mexico City.

The interior, with high ceilings and an open kitchen, is elegant and the decor is festive. One wall is painted in a vibrant red but otherwise unadorned; the other walls are decorated with playful, oversized replicas of the cards used in *lotería*, the Mexican game of chance for which the restaurant is named.

Head outside to the patio, which looks out on Hollywood Boulevard, for some prime people-watching, or, for a bird's-eye view of the open kitchen, grab a seat at the long counter and watch chefs make fresh corn tortillas and other house specialties like sea bass with smoky and spicy Chile Morita sauce, or braised beef tongue in tomatillo sauce.

Shaw's tacos are legendary, made with fresh ingredients and bursting with bold flavors. Order the Probadita to sample twelve of the restaurant's signature tacos served on fresh, handmade mini corn tortillas. The griddle-toasted *chicharrón de queso* with jack cheeses is downright addictive. The bar, situated along the back wall, displays an impressive range of premium tequilas and mezcals. Choose one to sip, or try the popular spicy jalapeño margarita. For a truly authentic Mexican libation, opt for the Michelada classica, a mixture of fresh-squeezed lime juice, Worcestershire sauce, and Tapatio hot sauce. **DT**

Apple Pan | Signature burgers and pies since 1947 in a charming old-school restaurant

Location Los Angeles **Signature dish** Hickory burger with Tillamook cheddar cheese | $

Apple Pan, a family owned restaurant in West Los Angeles, opened in 1947 serving a simple menu of burgers, sandwiches, and pies in a quaint green-and-white ranch-style cottage. Diners sat atop red leather stools around a U-shaped counter that surrounded the red-bricked grill area. Burgers, served by men wearing white aprons and paper hats, were wrapped in paper and plunked down on the counter so that they stood on end.

Little has changed since then. The restaurant is still in its original location, and the menu is still largely the same as it ever was, though both the surrounding buildings and the prices of each item are notably higher than they were nearly seventy years ago.

The vintage charm remains, with the red stools, the old-fashioned cash registers, and the walls covered with paneling and plaid wallpaper. Generations of families have come here not only for wonderful food, but also for a trip down memory lane. It is not uncommon to overhear parents telling their children stories of how they, or even grandma and grandpa before them, sat at the very same counter and ate the very same burger.

Nothing at Apple Pan is fancy or super-sized, but everything there is made with quality ingredients. The two signature dishes—the Steak Burger with sweet relish and the (even better) Hickory Burger with Tillamook cheddar cheese and a tangy barbecue sauce—are consistently ranked among the top burgers in LA. Order fries and they will come out first, hot and crispy. The menu may be simple, but the fabulous burgers, pies, and nostalgic charm of the place keep Angelenos coming back for more. Reservations and credit cards are still not accepted, so bring cash. Lines can be long, but once inside, service is fast, courteous, and efficient. **DT**

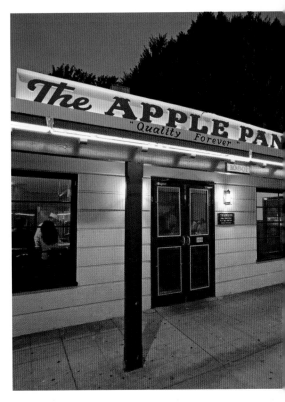

"… a classic American burger shack and hugely popular LA landmark."

frommers.com

⊡ Apple Pan offers an unmissable vintage experience.

Animal | Meat-centric small plates for the Hollywood hip crowd

Location Los Angeles **Signature dish** Poutine with oxtail gravy and cheddar | **$**

Jon Shook and Vinny Dotolo are the "Two Food Dudes" behind the popular Los Angeles restaurant Animal, which opened in 2008. Long-time friends who met while enrolled in the culinary program at the Art Institute of Fort Lauderdale, Florida, Shook and Dotolo first made their name in Los Angeles running a freewheeling catering business that was beloved by young Hollywood. Years before buffalo pig tails, braised beef tongue, and crispy pig ears were found on restaurant tables from coast to coast, Animal made these oddities a centerpiece of its cooking.

The small dining room at Animal is perhaps the sparsest in Los Angeles. Simple wood tables and chairs fill a rectangular space lit with exposed 120-watt

> *"Animal, the first restaurant to raise Boy Food to the level of a genuine cuisine."*
>
> Jonathan Gold, *LA Weekly*

light bulbs. There is nothing hanging on the walls and no sign on the building's exterior. In a town built on outward appearance, Animal has none.

The kitchen never loses sight of the primary focus of offering creative and comforting uses of lesser-utilized animal proteins popular with aficionados of the "nose-to-tail" school of cooking. The signature dish, poutine, is French fries covered with fresh cheese curds and topped with brown gravy. Other highlights include "buffalo-style" pig tails with celery and ranch dressing; veal brains with vadouvan (a spice mixture), apricot puree, and carrot; and marrow bone with chimichurri and caramelized onions. This is late-night munchie food for the cultured classes. **MD**

Lucques | Cal–Med cuisine in the former home of a silent film star

Location Los Angeles **Signature dish** Braised short ribs and horseradish cream | **$$$**

Suzanne Goin's and Caroline Styne's charming, chic, California-Mediterranean restaurant opened in 1998. Located in West Hollywood in a restored carriage house that once belonged to silent movie star Harold Lloyd, Lucques has a comfortable, rustic feel. The brick-lined walls, open-beamed ceilings, welcoming fireplace, and ivy-covered patio all contribute to making diners feel at home.

The seasonal menus are always inviting and intriguing. Goin is fond of braises with short ribs and oxtail, slow roasts, grilled meats, and fresh fish. Her soups are filled with healthy and tasty legumes—flageolet beans are a favorite. Her salads are bright and often combine fruit with ricotta, burrata, or fresh mozzarella.

Goin likes to layer flavors in her food, an effect she achieves through the use of spices from around the Mediterranean. You'll find a touch of Provençe in a rouille added to a soup or a tapenade atop a crostini; more classical French cooking in the fresh vegetable gratins, the confits, and the sauces; and a taste of Italy in her gnocchi, scaloppine, ossobuco, and bucatini. Spices of North Africa enliven many of the grilled dishes and enhance local delicacies such as Santa Barbara spot prawns. Desserts often showcase fruit at their peak in tarts, crumbles, gratins, and sorbets. The menu is well supported by an extensive wine list, adroitly overseen by Caroline Styne.

Lucques attracts an international clientele and the food-savvy LA crowd. The Sunday supper prix-fixe menu is a crowd favorite and excellent value. It's often the busiest night of the week, as regulars like to get their favorite table and settle in for a cozy meal. Be sure to book ahead. **PB**

→ Lucques offers a delightful dining experience.

Providence | An elegant seafooder thriving in an era of casual comfort food

Location Los Angeles **Signature dish** Salt-roasted live Santa Barbara spot prawn | $$$$

Providence is the fish-centric fine dining brainchild of two Michelin-star and James Beard Award-winning chef Michael Cimarusti. The restaurant is, in his words, "inspired by the natural abundance of coastal living," with a kitchen devoted to sourcing the world's best and most sustainable seafood (no bluefin tuna here). And while Cimarusti's technique is classically French, his ethos is decidedly Japanese, allowing pure ingredients to reveal what he calls "their own divine flavors, texture, and beauty."

The dining room is sleek and modern in muted brown. The fabric-lined walls are dotted with porcelain "barnacles" and the only burst of color comes in a pop of bright orange on the dining chairs and the coral-shaped candleholders on each table. The space is relatively quiet despite its smallness, and the service is professional but personable. There is no dress code, which alleviates the stuffiness that can sometimes be inhibiting in restaurants of this caliber.

Menu options range from a choose-your-own three-course prix fixe—with highlights being the clam "chowda" and the Japanese fresh water eel with grilled shiitake mushrooms, farm egg, and puffed rice—to a 16-course chef's tasting menu that changes regularly and is designed around the day's freshest catch. This is where Cimarusti truly shines, and it is the most likely place for diners to find his most famous dishes, notably the salt-roasted live Santa Barbara spot prawn with rosemary and lemon.

In what has become a Providence signature, each meal begins with a greyhound cocktail (grapefruit juice and vodka or gin) served in solidified hemispherical form on a small tasting spoon. This is an amuse-bouche with a difference and the serious underlying purpose of preparing diners for the whimsy and finesse of the main courses and accompanying wines and spirits that are still in store for them. **MD**

"If you're going with the tasting menu, don't read it beforehand. That way, it all comes as a surprise."

S. Irene Virbila, *Los Angeles Times*

↑ From the tasting menu: Japanese amberjack with tomatoes, fennel, and pickled matsutakes.

Musso & Frank Grill | Classic American food in vintage Hollywood setting

Location Los Angeles **Signature dish** Filet mignon from the grill | ❺❺❺

Founded in 1919 by Frank Toulet and Joseph Musso, this venerable establishment claims to be Hollywood's oldest restaurant. With its faded decor and dark wood interior, it is easy to imagine looking up from one's meal to see Douglas Fairbanks, Humphrey Bogart, or William Faulkner dining at the next booth. Currently owned and run by the great-grandchildren of John Musso, who bought the restaurant from its original owners in 1927, Musso & Frank's is an island of certainty in a city of restless and constant change.

Executive chef J.P. Amateau, only the third person to hold the position in the restaurant's history, is the custodian of a long tradition of American cooking. Grilled lamb kidneys—said to have been a favorite of Charlie Chaplin—appear alongside wood-grilled steaks, wedges of iceberg lettuce with blue cheese dressing, calves' liver, grenadine of beef, and Italian pastas. Daily specials, like Thursday's famous chicken pot pie, draw regulars like bees to honey. Do everything possible not to miss the mornings-only, gone-when-they're-gone flannel cakes—light, sweet, crêpe-like pancakes served fresh off the griddle.

The restaurant is divided into two rooms. In the dim lighting of the older room, it is easy to imagine the ghosts of writers past sitting in the mahogany booths, while the newer room, with its pheasant-patterned wallpaper, also houses the bar, which is home to what many say is the best martini in North America. Patrons may also sit by the wood-fired grill, where the masterful grill man Indolfo cooks steaks, fish, and other delicacies to perfection.

This is a restaurant with heart as well as history. Its service is impeccable. Its red-liveried wait staff and bartenders—some of whom have worked here for over fifty years—offer an old-school professionalism that is rare to find. If you go there once, you'll be sure to want a second visit. **KPH & FH**

"For the full M&F effect, sit at the counter or request table No. 1 in the west room."

frommers.com

⬆ A Hollywood institution, Musso & Frank has served stars from Greta Garbo to George Clooney.

Bestia | Popular, buzzing Los Angeles hot spot serving bold and adventurous Italian cuisine

Location Los Angeles   **Signature dish** Salumi, the chef's selection of house-cured meats, pickles, mostarda, and grilled bread | 💲💲

"… a serious restaurant turning out excellent, ingredient-driven Italian fare at a moderate price."

Time Out

⬆ The cavernous converted warehouse offers an industrial-chic setting for the rustic Italian food.

➡ Bestia's irresistible selection of house-cured salumi.

Bestia would be hard to find, located in an alley on the edge of downtown Los Angeles, were it not for the telltale line of cars at the valet stand outside it. Once inside this buzzing hot spot, you'll find a lively crowd sampling rustic Italian cuisine produced by the husband and wife team of executive chef Ori Menashe and pastry chef Genevieve Gergis.

Menashe's made-from-scratch food is extremely well executed, from the signature house-cured meats to the handmade pastas and pizzas. The pillowy agnolotti pasta—made with cacao and filled with braised oxtail and spaghetti rustichella, and cooked perfectly al dente—is rich and flavorful. Aside from the traditional ingredients of Italian cooking, the menu features numerous unexpected items, including chicken gizzards, beef and chicken hearts, sea urchin, and bottarga.

Not to be outdone, Gergis serves up a selection of enticing desserts, most notably the bittersweet chocolate budino with salted caramel and a drizzle of olive oil.

The open dining room can be described as glamorous meets industrial chic, with the aesthetics that one might expect from a restaurant housed, as this is, in a converted warehouse—brick walls, concrete floors, and exposed ducts. Slaughterhouse-inspired meat hook chandeliers add a playful touch. Outdoor seating is available on the balcony along the front and in the patio situated in the adjacent courtyard. Both locations are much quieter than the dining room.

Reservations are essential, so call a week or two in advance to secure your table. Get there early and make your way to the jam-packed custom-designed copper top bar and enjoy a handcrafted cocktail while you wait to be seated. **DT**

The Hungry Cat | First-rate raw bar and inventive seafood

Location Los Angeles **Signature dish** Maine lobster roll with a buttered, toasted roll | ❸❸

The Hungry Cat has sites in Santa Monica Canyon and Santa Barbara, but the branch tucked away off Hollywood's Vine Street is the original. Renowned for outstanding seafood, the cuisine reflects chef-proprietor David Lentz's Maryland roots, which he has fused to good effect with top California produce.

Keeping its decor minimal and low key, the better to draw attention to the quality of the food, The Hungry Cat offers an opulent raw bar—with crab, lobster, and a selection of fresh oysters from the United States, Canada, Mexico, and New Zealand—alongside caviars and a primarily seafood menu that changes week by week. The only constants are the lobster roll and the Pug Burger, a juicy beef patty served with blue cheese, bacon, and avocado.

Lentz's focus on seasonal quality ingredients ensures that this is a place deserving of repeated visits. Among the many recommendable entrées, look out particularly for the kabocha squash soup with chorizo-stuffed squid; Nantucket scallops with brown butter; mussels with braised fennel; and whole sea urchins, ethically sourced off the Santa Barbara coast.

While the cooking is consistently first rate, The Hungry Cat boasts an exceptional bar and one of the city's best curated wine lists, which is available by the glass or the carafe. Compiled by sommelier Tim Staehling, the list changes almost as often as the menu—the restaurant does not maintain a standing cellar—and offers undervalued gems such as Baden Gutedels and Edna Valley Viogniers. The cocktails deserve special mention, too: seasonal specials sit comfortably alongside classics, with the Pimlico (whiskey, lime, orange, and mint) being a favorite.

With its faultless service and friendly, intimate vibe, The Hungry Cat is a tranquil refuge from the bustle of Tinseltown. **KPH & FH**

⬆ Hollywood's The Hungry Cat is hidden in a courtyard.

Pizzeria Mozza | Creative Italian pizza in relaxed surroundings

Location Los Angeles **Signature dish** Pizza with squash blossoms, tomato, and burrata | $$

Pizzeria Mozza is a collaboration between famed chef Mario Batali and restaurateur Joe Bastianich, who together opened Babbo and Del Posto in New York City, and Nancy Silverton of La Brea Bakery fame. This casual pizza joint opened in 2006 to rave reviews for its creative Italian menu featuring wood-fired artisanal pizzas and pastas. It still draws the crowds.

Book ahead as reservations go quickly. The main dining room is small and gets loud enough to make conversation a challenge. The adjacent room, lined with wine bottles, is much quieter. The best seats in the house, however, are at the counter facing the wood-burning oven. Here guests can watch cooks skillfully poke and prod the dough into shape, artfully arrange fresh toppings, then slide the pizzas one by one into the oven.

The restaurant's Neapolitan-style pizzas are superb, with puffy crusts that are crisp and charred on the outside, while chewy and airy on the inside, and topped with market-fresh ingredients. Traditionalists will enjoy the classic Margherita pizza with mozzarella, tomato, and basil. For something out of the ordinary, try the pizzette topped with Ipswich clams and garlic, or the sweet Gorgonzola, fingerling potatoes, and radicchio pizza. The squash blossoms pizza with tomato and creamy burrata is another imaginative combination, forever popular with diners.

While pizza is the obvious draw, the antipasti, such as the roasted marrow bone and chicken liver bruschetta with *guanciale*, are also praiseworthy. Specials change daily, and include the Italian classics eggplant Parmigiana, pollo al forno with spicy peppers and broccolini, and lasagne al forno. For dessert, there is the superb and much-lauded butterscotch budino with sea salt and rosemary pine-nut cookies. **DT**

↑ Neapolitan-style pizza with a puffy crust at Mozza.

Picca | Modern cantina serving robust Peruvian food with touches of Japanese flair

Location Los Angeles   **Signature dish** *Chicharrón de pollo* (nuggets of marinated chicken fried and topped with salsa criolla) | ❺❺❺

"Some dishes feel like they should come with cartoon dialogue: Smash! Bang! Boom!"

S. Irene Virbila, *The Los Angeles Times*

⬆ A tasty Peruvian shrimp dish.

Chef Ricardo Zarate's journey from his native Lima, Peru, to California is a tale of perseverance, professionalism, and sheer cooking talent that would be incredible if it were not true. Picca is Zarate's second restaurant in Los Angeles. His first, Mo-Chica in Downtown's Mercado de Paloma, provided refined Peruvian comfort food. Inspired by the success of this enterprise, he acquired new premises on West Pico Boulevard and there set about creating a small-plate diner (*una picca* means "a nibble") that focuses mainly on *causa* (Peruvian sushi) and *anticuchos* (grilled skewered meats).

With its diverse and seasonally changing menu, Picca offers a fresh and exciting dining experience, showcasing Zarate's passion for Nikkei (Japanese-influenced Peruvian cooking).

Stand-out dishes include *anticuchos corazón* (grilled beef heart skewers with a walnut and rocoto pesto), *ceviche mixto* (seafood ceviche) with leche de tigre sauce, diver scallops *anticuchos* with aji amarillo aioli and wasabi peas, and *seco de cordero* (a lamb breast stew with canario beans and a coriander and Peruvian beer sauce).

Knowledgeable and efficient staff help guests navigate the well-structured menu, while signature (and often Pisco-based) cocktails created by Julian Cox ensure a lively pre-dinner bar scene.

Zarate is a chef imbued not only with Peru's extraordinarily diverse culinary heritage but also with European food culture as a result of 12 years' experience working in London restaurants, including the eponymous Gordon Ramsay and Pengelly's. In 2007, *Food & Wine Magazine* named Zarate one of its top ten emergent chefs. Picca's friendly atmosphere reflects his character, and his work displays mastery of even the most minute details of his art. **KPH & FH**

Night + Market |

Affordable, innovative Thai street food

Location Los Angeles   **Signature dish** *Nam kao tod* | ❸❸

Founded by chef Kris Yenbamroong, Night + Market is a "neighborhood café" on the western end of Sunset Strip that sells Thai street food—*aharn klam lao*, which roughly translates as "food to facilitate drinking." It is based inside Talesai, a more formal Thai restaurant with white tablecloths and an upscale menu belonging to Yenbamroong's parents.

The small dining room is austere, with cement floors, wooden picnic tables, and a few pieces of art hanging on the walls. The entire scene, from the decor through to the menu, is a homage to the famous night bazaars of Chang Mai and Bangkok. Because the restaurant is often filled with a younger, food-obsessed crowd, it get can fairly loud on the weekends, but that just adds to the atmosphere.

Night + Market is a restaurant for people who love spice and funk and heat in their food. Yenbamroong's most popular dish is nam kao tod, a crispy rice salad loaded with house-made sour pork sausage, chili, raw ginger, and peanuts. Also worthy of serious consideration is kor moo yang, which appears on the menu as "pork toro." This is a grilled, fatty pork collar served with a simple chili dipping sauce. Another commendable option is kao kluk gapi, a rice dish heavily seasoned with shrimp paste, candied pork, egg, green mango, bird's-eye chili, and cilantro.

Although these dishes are all designed to encourage the consumption of beer and whiskey, Night + Market also has some excellent wine offerings. The curated, affordable list features a number of lesser known, smaller bottlings, such as Frantz Saumon's Montlouis "Mineral+" Chenin blanc and L'Arpent Rouge from Clos Roche made from 100 percent Pineau d'Aunis, both from the Loire. After all, why facilitate drinking without offering something delicious to drink? **MD**

Chichen Itza |

Classic Yucatán in a food court

Location Los Angeles   **Signature dish** *Cochinita pibil* | ❸

Chichen Itza is situated in the back of the multicultural Mercado La Paloma in South Los Angeles. This open marketplace sits between a branch of the California Department of Motor Vehicles and a self-storage warehouse, so it isn't the first place you might look for what could be the single best pork dish in the western United States. But there it is, *cochinita pibil*—an achiote-marinated pork shoulder, seasoned with Seville oranges, garlic, black pepper, and allspice, wrapped in banana leaves and roasted until spoon tender. Served up in a pool of the orange-tinted pan drippings, with pickled red onions, steamed rice, black beans, corn tortillas, and habanero salsa, it is the perfect expression of the cuisine of Mexico's Yucatán Peninsula.

> ## *"I've had almost everything on the menu at Chichen Itza and I love every dish there."*
>
> Howard Meyers, *Consuming LA*

Chichen Itza chef and owner Gilberto Cetina practiced as a civil engineer near Cancún before moving to the United States and opening this eatery, which takes its name from that of an ancient Mayan city. A fast-casual food stand, Chichen Itza is open for breakfast, lunch, and dinner seven days a week. Diners order at the counter and then wait for their food in the market's colorful communal dining area.

Apart from pibil, other popular dishes are *panuchos*, an appetizer of crisp-fried corn tortillas, filled with black bean puree then topped with lettuce, turkey, pickled red onions, and avocado and tikin-xic, a white fish fillet marinated with lime juice and achiote, roasted and served on rice with a citrus jicama salad. **MD**

Addison del Mar | Splendid food in luxurious surroundings

Location San Diego **Signature dish** Kobe beef short rib | ❺❺❺❺

"... one of San Diego's most refined dining rooms, and the county's only AAA 5 Diamond restaurant."

frommers.com

⬆ Addison del Mar is set in a Mediterranean-style villa.

Dining at the Addison is an experience that engages all the senses. It starts as soon as you arrive at the opulent Grand Del Mar resort, which is where the restaurant makes its home. From the outside, the style is early twentieth-century Mediterranean Revival, with its arched windows and doorways and the warm glow of red brickwork; the architect Addison Mizner was a famous champion of this style and it is after him that the hotel's restaurant is named. Inside, there are plenty of marble fittings, period furniture, flowers, and a graceful, stately sense of calmness—once ensconced, there is a sense of leaving the hurly-burly of the outside world behind.

In charge of the kitchen is William Bradley, one of Relais & Châteaux's 160 Grand Chefs worldwide, who matches his passion for seasonal produce with a modern French style of cooking. He provides a choice of four tasting menus of three, four, seven, and ten courses. The component dishes change regularly, but among the occasional items that have been singled out for particular praise are the sensual sturgeon confit with caviar, and the signature dish, luscious Kobe beef short ribs, in which the meat is almost molten and comes off the bone with only the lightest of touches.

Other highlights have included a menu comprising three color–coordinated courses: Kumamoto oysters and horseradish, followed by caramelized cod with crispy kale, and concluding with a rich and soothing mascarpone mousse with candied pears and nougat. This is food as art, but it is also food for eating, and it is all served with a welcome and perhaps unexpected lack of pretension. With such a fabulous gastronomic experience, it's no surprise that Addison's wine cellar is also highly thought of—there are reputedly 37,000 bottles from which to choose. This is a restaurant that undoubtedly lives up to its high-end reputation. **ATJ**

Marine Room | Sweet surrender to the mystical power of three

Location San Diego **Signature dish** George's Bank diver scallops | ⬢⬢⬢

The superstitious say that misfortunes come in threes; but so, sometimes, do marvelous experiences. Take, for example, the Marine Room. If you're lucky enough to take your place for dinner at the right time, you will see the sun set behind the headland at the end of the La Jolla Shores bay. If dusk coincides with a rising tide, you will also be able to watch the ocean swelling and seething just below the windows. And then you will be presented with the third benison: a meal of artfully arranged French-influenced dishes. To start with perhaps another great threesome, the Ocean Trilogy Tasting, featuring juicy, salty-sweet slices of aromatic lobster, hamachi sashimi, and tuna tartare. Other starters could include steamed Pacific oysters, blue crab cake, five-mushroom casserole, or Oregon Kobe beef cheeks.

As for mains, the menu is an equally imaginative fusion of classical French and Californian, including Maine lobster tail served alongside aged Gouda polenta and absinthe butter, George's Bank diver scallops with pain d'espices and bourbon vanilla essence, and Cervena elk loin accompanied by wattleseed, bonito, and rhubarb preserve. Also recommended are tangerine-glazed organic tofu and rack of lamb with mission fig compote.

The Marine Room opened in 1941 and soon established itself as a regular destination for locals and visitors who flock to the spectacular seafront location to watch the regular showtime of crashing waves. Despite the restaurant's vulnerable position, the sea has only got the better of it twice: once in 1942, when excited waves smashed a window, and again in 1982, when an exceptionally high tide led to flooding. But such occasional mishaps have done nothing to dampen the ardor of diners for the Marine Room, with its light and airy interior, white tablecloths, and an unsurpassed backdrop of surf rolling in to the La Jolla Shores. **ATJ**

"… built for romance: you might even witness a marriage proposal or a wedding on the beach."

Fodor's Travel

⬆ Marine Room is renowned for its wonderful seafood.

Picasso | Fine Mediterranean food
amid Picasso originals and Vegas glitz

Location Las Vegas **Signature dish** Warm quail
salad with artichokes | ❸❸❸❸

Twist by Pierre Gagnaire |
Glamour dining in true Vegas style

Location Las Vegas **Signature dish** "Grand Dessert
Pierre Gagnaire" | ❸❸❸❸❸

Understatement is not a Las Vegas strongpoint, and this extraordinary restaurant has all the over-the-top qualities that make The Strip such an alluring venue. Part of the giant Bellagio casino hotel resort, it is themed around Spanish artist Pablo Picasso and features millions of dollars' worth of his paintings and ceramics on the walls. Set against the modern hotel complex, the restaurant achieves a semi-rustic style with exposed wooden beams, terracotta tiles, and lavish flower displays. The venue even served as a location for the movie *Ocean's Eleven*.

At the terrace tables, diners can enjoy a view of Bellagio's man-made lake, illuminated fountain show, and the replica Eiffel Tower. The food is no imitation,

---

> ## *"Serrano's cooking is a work of art that can proudly stand next to the masterpieces."*
>
> frommers.com

---

though. Michelin-starred Spanish chef Julian Serrano serves finely crafted dishes that are heavily influenced by French and Spanish cuisine. Dishes are artistically presented, served on white plates featuring dabs of color around the rim, resembling an artist's palette. Petit fours arrive on a silver tree, and butter pats are embossed with Picasso's signature.

The attention to detail throughout is impressive. Serrano's signature whole quail is served with roast artichoke, mashed avocado, pine nuts, four types of lettuce, grated carrot for color, and a sauce made from the roasting juices and flavored with vinegar. Some diners have been so impressed with this dish that they have ordered it for all four courses of their dinners. **SH**

High up on to the 23rd floor of the Mandarin Oriental hotel in the center of Las Vegas is Michelin-starred chef Pierre Gagnaire's first and only restaurant in the United States. It oozes pure Vegas glamour with its beautiful low-lit entrance and breathtaking views of the Strip. Every detail exudes stylish opulence, from the elegant porcelain and sleek tables to the translucent light globes.

Pierre Gagnaire's cooking has always defied definition. His cooking is light, modern French, and he has been described by some as "the philosopher poet of the restaurant world." Gagnaire draws on his love of jazz, philosophy, and art to express different nuances of a chosen ingredient. Every dish is made up of several smaller, complementary dishes that challenge diners to experience each ingredient afresh. "Degustation of tomato," for example, might include a raspberry and apricot sorbet to bring out the fruity notes of a delicate stuffed and baked tomato, which in turn plays with the textures, temperature, and flavor of a sliced fresh tomato with balsamic vinegar ice cream and summer shellfish.

The menus at Twist are fluid so that both Gagnaire and his chef de cuisine, Ryuki Kawasaki, can play with the best seasonal ingredients. The "Grand Dessert Pierre Gagnaire," however, is always on the menu, albeit with an ever-changing selection of components, such as Mojito granita with rhubarb fondue and caramelized pears.

Dining out in Las Vegas is as much about creating memories as it is about enjoying good food. Twist only opens at night, which adds to its sophisticated air. The calm, casino-free environment and beauty of the space make for an unforgettable experience. **SK**

▣ The stylish interior is matched by stunning views.

Pizzeria Bianco | A slice of pizza heaven in the Arizona desert

Location Phoenix   **Signature dish** Rosa Pizza |
❸❸

Chef Chris Bianco started his business in 1988 in the corner of a local grocery store in Phoenix, Arizona. His restaurant now occupies a lovely brick structure downtown and has become a Nirvana for pizza lovers the world over. *The New York Times* calls these some of the best pizzas in America, and Bianco himself was recently voted one of six international chefs who have changed the face of pizza through the years.

His pizzas—thin, crisp, and cooked in custom-built, wood-fired ovens—are as close to dough perfection as you can get. The signature Rosa Pizza with Parmigiano Reggiano, fresh rosemary, red onions, and Arizona pistachios displays a unique understanding of merging local sensibility with

---

"To call [Chris Bianco] a pizzaiolo is like saying Mark Twain had good penmanship."

Ed Levine

---

traditional methods. The result is a fatty, salty, crispy delight. The mozzarella is made on-site daily and many of the herbs are grown right there, too. The antipasto platter includes wood-fired vegetables, soppressata, and cheese with a side of bread made from in-house-milled Arizona heritage wheat. Bianco is renowned for his farm-to-plate philosophy and for his relationships with local producers, which allow him to offer the best ingredients.

Next door to the pizzeria, there is a bar where patrons can have a drink while they wait (and the wait may be long!). Bianco has opened two more establishments in other parts of Phoenix, but this is the one and only original. **KPH & FH**

Tarbell's | Everything you would want in a restaurant

Location Phoenix   **Signature dish** "Mr. Fish of the Moment" | ❸❸

Tarbell's has seriously good food with little pretense of being a great restaurant, and yet it is. Although it is based in Arizona, the Southwest is only one strand of the fabric of flavors woven by chef–owner Mark Tarbell, who was born in New England and had a classic culinary education in France. He now applies French techniques to American ingredients with impressive results.

But this restaurant is about more than the food. Tarbell himself believes in providing hospitality in the broadest sense, and his operation is widely praised for the welcome it provides to all its guests, and for the care and courtesy they receive throughout each meal.

Ingredients are selected with care and organic products are always at the top of the list. In a part of the United States that is best known for its large meat-laden plates, Tarbell's stands apart in its emphasis on fresh fish, superb vegetables, and excellent pizzas baked in a wood-fired oven. Two outstanding ways of starting a meal are the red pepper soup or the steamed mussels with white wine, shallots, and thyme.

Of course, there are also excellent meat offerings, especially of beef and poultry. Yet even carnivores may be tempted to give meat a pass when "The Earth's Best" is on offer. Each vegetable on this plate is prepared to bring out the best in its flavor and texture. For many regulars, "Mr. Fish of the Moment" from the Atlantic or Pacific oceans is the ideal choice, thanks to the freshness and supreme preparation of the fish.

Oenophiles favor Tarbell's for its superb cellar. The wine list is the first thing they consult, with foods then chosen based on the wine that has been ordered. Bottles are from most of the top regions of the world, but there are many small surprises, carefully chosen, that would be difficult to find in even the best restaurants in New York or London. **FP**

Full of Life Flatbread | Hidden farm-to-table gem offering organic flatbread in Los Alamos

Location Los Alamos **Signature dish** "The Beast" chocolate brownie | $$

A hand-painted wooden sign outside this restaurant bears the legend, "Eat good food," and that is exactly what you will do in this small, rustic-looking building in Los Alamos, an old stagecoach town one hour's drive north of Santa Barbara, California. There is a nostalgic quality about Flatbread, with its welcoming, whitewashed porch and long, zinc-lined bar. The dining room bustles with local winemakers, ranchers, farmers, and fresh food aficionados.

Clark Staub, a self-taught baker, opened his flatbread business in 2003. Three days a week, his cooks produce by hand organic flatbreads that are sold in gourmet markets up and down the West Coast. Then, Thursday through Sunday evenings, the large wood-lined production room is transformed into a restaurant with tables set up in full view of the mammoth 20-ton, 11-foot- (3.4-m) wide, wood-burning oven, in which all the restaurant's delicacies are cooked—not only the flatbreads, but also succulent combinations such as chanterelles and sugar snap peas with goat cheese and caramelized onions, rustic soups, hearty stews, spiny lobster, roasted vegetables, and other fresh produce from nearby fields. Sundays are particularly special, as Flatbread serves an ever-changing, seasonal dinner menu in addition to flatbreads and salads. Staub and head chef Spencer Johnston source all their ingredients from local farmers, ranchers, fishermen, and foragers.

This hidden gem in the heart of the Central Coast wine country also features more than 90 local wines, plus locally crafted beers. Diners should save room for dessert: Full of Life Flatbread is renowned for its delectable tarts, homemade ice creams, and "The Beast," a double chocolate brownie topped with marshmallow, slowly roasted in the oven, and served with vanilla ice cream. **PB**

"On weekend nights [it] can pull in hundreds of people from all over to get a taste of the organic fare."

LA Times

↑ The wood-burning oven is the center of the restaurant.

Frasca | Explore the delights of Friuli-Venezia Giulia in Colorado

Location Boulder   **Signature dish** Gnocchi with *cotechino*; *cjalsons* | 🅢🅢

"Sublime in every way, this Boulder must lives up to the hype ... Well worth the wait."

Zagat

⬆ A dish of *cjalsons*, a speciality of Friuli-Venezia Giulia.

In Friuli-Venezia Giulia (FVG), the northeasternmost region of Italy, adjacent to the borders with Austria and Slovenia, *frasca* is a branch. Traditionally, when wine is being sold, a branch is placed over the doorway of the winery, indicating that people can enter to buy wine and enjoy good food with it.

This restaurant is a monument to the food and wine of FVG in a most unlikely place: Boulder, Colorado. While it has expanded its menu to include some dishes from a few other parts of Italy, at its core it represents the remarkable combination of spices with ingredients from land and sea, paired with some of the world's great wines—it is this synthesis that makes FVG so special. While most Italian cookery is flavored with herbs, FVG has always used spices and just a judicious quantity of herbs.

Chef Lachlan Patterson and sommelier Bobby Stuckey understand exactly what makes FVG so unusual, and import those of its products that are inimitable—wine, polenta, montasio cheese, prosciutto di San Daniele—and combine them with local fish, vegetables, and meat (beef, pheasant, and especially lamb). Among the dishes that are unobtainable anywhere else outside FVG are *cjalsons* (a filled pasta akin to ravioli but containing ricotta, sultanas, cinnamon, nutmeg, rice, and chocolate); gnocchi with *cotechino* (a crumbly sausage made fragrant with rosemary and fennel); and *frico* (an addictive crisp made of montasio cheese).

The exemplary wine list features historic FVG varietals such as the whites Friulano (formerly Tocai), Ribolla Gialla, and Malvasia Istriana and the reds Refosco and Schioppettino. Having these wines available to pair with the food is a rare experience when one is far from the land in which the grapes (and other ingredients) have been produced. **FP**

Cochineal | Contemporary
cuisine in the heart of the desert

Location Marfa **Signature dish** *Chilaquiles* with roasted chicken | 🌑🌑

Schilo's Delicatessen |
A taste of Germany in Texas

Location San Antonio **Signature dish** Potato pancakes | 🌑

In the barren high deserts of West Texas, the tiny enclave of Marfa may be the last place one would expect to find a restaurant operated by a pair of Michelin-starred chefs. But there it is, tucked away in an adobe bungalow a block from the town's only traffic light.

Tom Rapp and Toshifumi Sakihara opened Cochineal in 2008 as a successor to their award-winning café États-Unis, a New York City mainstay known for its broad and exuberant take on rustic American cuisine. In Marfa, they continue their celebrated work inside a small open kitchen that provides quick access to both the dining area and the on-site vegetable garden.

Guests can choose between the shaded outdoor courtyard and the cozy minimalist dining room, a nod to Marfa's twentieth-century patron saint Donald Judd, a cryptic New York sculptor who relocated to this petite Texas town in the early 1970s. Menus change daily and focus on local raw ingredients. The chefs thrive on the challenge, crafting dishes rooted in North American culinary traditions while frequently referencing Mexico, which is just an hour's drive south. One evening might bring farm-raised barramundi, while another might feature chicken *chilaquiles*—a central Mexican casserole with fried tortilla chips, tomatillo sauce, and cream.

Be sure to peruse Cochineal's quirky wine list of some 250 bottles, which cover nearly every corner of the grape-growing world, to give even the most experienced connoisseurs plenty to discuss. And before you make your way back into the desert, perhaps to catch Marfa's mysterious "ghost lights" on Route 67, do treat yourself to Sakihara's renowned baked-to-order date pudding with rum caramel sauce—irresistible. **TR**

Perched above San Antonio's busy River Walk, Schilo's Delicatessen stands as a culinary monument to the city's rich German heritage. For nearly a century, the family-owned restaurant has served some the most beloved Reuben sandwiches and potato pancakes in the Lone Star State. The place was originally a saloon, until Prohibition forced Fritz Schilo to try his hand at cooking the German dishes of his youth. The menu is more or less the same today, offering classic deli fare as well as schnitzel and bratwurst platters.

The restaurant's interior—be sure to note the intricate tile-work on the floor—appears to have changed little since the Schilo clan first took over the downtown location. The open dining area, noted for

---

"This venerable downtown institution has been serving up … German soul food since 1917."

fodors.com

---

its decorative tin ceiling, maintains a steady flow of activity during breakfast, lunch, and dinner. At the rear of the space, an aging wood-paneled bar stocks Spaten and Warsteiner beers alongside Texas brews.

The deli counter that runs the length of the restaurant is tightly crammed with everything a sandwich will ever need, as well as surprising additions, such as pimento cheese and beef tongue. For breads, pick from sourdough, wheat, and Jewish rye. Lettuce, tomato, and sauerkraut are available on request. Schilo's shines after 5 p.m. with a special menu of German dinners, including paprika chicken. Be sure to stop by on Friday or Saturday evening to hear the live oompah band. **TR**

Qui | A synthesis of sumptuous Texan produce with delicate Asian gastronomical techniques

Location Austin **Signature dish** "Rabbit 7 Ways" | [$][$]

Chef Paul Qui runs his new flagship restaurant in Austin, Texas, collaboratively. He takes advice and happily delegates responsibility: he is possibly the world's most unassuming celebrity chef.

The premises have been designed with the city's slogan, "Keep Austin Weird," very much in mind—witness the 1970s'-style patio where walk-in guests can enjoy a craft cocktail, and the specially commissioned sculpture-turned-bike rack encircling a tree in the front yard. You can't help but have fun when dining at Qui, and neither can the obliging and personable staff.

One of the most popular dishes, destined for a permanent spot on the dinner menu, is the "Salmon Butter," oil-poached king salmon to be spread on crackers and topped with chopped egg, salmon roe, crème fraîche, pickled red onion, and Murray River pink salt. The kitchen's signature dish is "Rabbit 7 Ways"—a rich confit of the leg, a ballotine, two types of fermented sausage, fried rabbit belly, and a rabbit farce, all served with a bowl of leafy greens and herbs for wrapping and eating bossam-style after a dip in spicy carrot nuoc mam. The seventh and stand-alone preparation, a rabbit consommé, finishes out the dish.

One of the unique design elements in the restaurant is a slatted wall panel filled with handwritten tags hanging on hooks. Each of the tags bears the name of a single ingredient, and chefs are encouraged to play around with possible flavor pairings in their down time. This idea board can be the only explanation for what has become Qui's most popular dessert—a sundae sandwich that combines aged cheddar cheese ice cream with peanut praline, crispy waffles, and a drizzle of goat's milk caramel into one truly delicious combination. It may be unusual, but it is certainly wonderful. **MD**

"Paul Qui has introduced the vernacular of Asian street food to everyday menus."

Christopher Hughes, *The Boston Globe*

↑ Be sure to try Qui's signature dish, Rabbit 7 Ways.

Black's Barbecue |

Classic Texas barbecue restaurant

Location Lockhart **Signature dish** Barbecued homemade beef-and-pork sausage | **$**

The small town of Lockhart calls itself "The Barbecue Capital of Texas." In a state that takes meat grilled on wood fires very seriously, that's saying something.

The four acclaimed BBQ restaurants in Lockhart are estimated to serve a quarter of a million meals a year. That's in a town with a population of around 12,000 people. Lockhart's best-known and longest-established restaurant of this type is Black's, which occupies a big wooden building on Main Street and has been owned and run by the same family since 1932. The interior decor includes a display of Texas auto license plates, photographs of local high school football teams, and real longhorn cattle horns.

The food fits this down-home atmosphere perfectly: big portions of barbecued cuts of meat and homemade sausages. Customers line up with their plates to select from a wide range of side dishes, then order and pay for the meat at a counter. Everything is humble: plastic cutlery, polystyrene cups, paper plates, red checkered plastic table cloths, and free rolls of paper towels.

Owner Edgar Black still cooks the way his father did when the restaurant opened. He uses oak wood to fuel the brick barbecues, which cook meat that is seasoned only with salt and pepper. His wife Norma makes the thick red, sweet barbecue sauce, which is also sold in branded bottles and by mail order. In 1988, Edgar was named Lockhart's "Most Worthy Citizen."

Specialities here are beef brisket, pork ribs, and chicken, all infused with the oaky smoke from long sessions on the grill. Black's own beef-and-pork sausages are nationally renowned. Indeed, such is their reputation that in the 1960s, President Lyndon B. Johnson, a proud Texan, had Black's sausages specially flown to the White House for official barbecues. **SH**

Lonesome Dove |

A witty and creative taste of Texas

Location Fort Worth **Signature dish** Rabbit-rattlesnake sausage | **$$**

Lonesome Dove western bistro in the historic Fort Worth Stockyards embodies the very essence of twenty-first-century Texas—it is bold, brassy, and experimental, with an almost obsessive interest in the past. Anyone looking for a brief respite from the neighborhood's over-the-top cowboy culture will delight in this award-winning restaurant's casual and contemporary approach to the Western style, evidenced in both its atmosphere and its food.

Opened in 2000 by noted chef Tim Love, Lonesome Dove is a traditional upscale steakhouse that offers a variety of hand-cut chops and a classic à la carte menu of starchy sides. The Japanese Wagyu ribeyes, for one or two people, have become a much-

> *"If you can get to the Stockyards, you shouldn't miss dining [here] … sophisticated and exotic food."*
>
> fodors.com

discussed experience among Lone Star foodies. Just a simple New York strip or beef tenderloin, however, is more than enough to highlight the kitchen's skills.

Love relishes in taking guests on a wild ride through less familiar terrain, offering surprises such as rabbit-rattlesnake sausages, Rocky Mountain elk loin, and kangaroo carpaccio. While some of the menu detours may appear somewhat gimmicky at first, let your palate be the judge and enjoy the journey with a wine list brimming with California's best. Lonesome Dove truly shines when it takes on American comfort food: among the many quirky appetizers sit lobster-stuffed hushpuppies—a North Atlantic twist on a deep-fried staple from the southern United States. **TR**

Underbelly | A fascinating taste of New American Creole food

Location Houston   **Signature dish** Korean braised goat and dumplings | 💲💲

Underbelly will forever be known in Houston as the restaurant brave enough to fuse together the Texan city's varied and often disparate food cultures into a single culinary experience.

Proudly wearing its reputation as the "most diverse metropolis in the United States," Houston has a culinary landscape in which foodies can enjoy a bowl of Vietnamese pho, a plate of Nigerian fufu, and a stack of Salvadoran pupusas in adjacent blocks.

Chef Chris Shepherd launched Underbelly with the purpose of telling what he calls "the story of Houston food." The tale stretches from contemporary myriad global flavors back to the city's days as a shipping hub that linked Texas to other ports on the Gulf of Mexico. The result is an ever-changing menu of thoughtful combinations of regional flavors that Shepherd dubs "New American Creole." A typical night at Underbelly offers dishes ranging from Gulf shrimp and locally sourced grits to the restaurant's signature Korean braised goat and dumplings. Guests can order by plate or take advantage of Underbelly's family-style selections—full table servings that highlight the freshest items from local farms, ranches, and fishing boats.

Devoted carnivores will delight in farm-raised poultry and unique cuts of meat, all expertly butchered and smoked in-house. Crispy pork schnitzel and zampone ham—which reference Houston's historic German and Italian communities—make their way from the kitchen alongside pulled chicken in fish sauce and orders of spicy pork sausage with Szechuan sour cabbage.

Those looking for an adventurous seafood platter will need to try Underbelly's crispy bycatch, fried pieces of strange and unintentionally caught fish purchased from docks on the Gulf of Mexico. **TR**

⬆ Crispy whole triggerfish served at Underbelly.

Oxheart | Creative vegetable-focused cooking highlighting the Texas larder

Location Houston **Signature dish** Brassica leaves, pickled stems, goat whey, chrysanthemum, and herb oils | $$$

Chef Justin Yu first found his love for serving vegetables in a refined setting while working for Jeremy Fox at Ubuntu, the much-heralded vegetarian restaurant in Napa, California. He developed his passion for regional cooking while staging in Copenhagen, Denmark, the birthplace of hyper-Nordic cuisine. Luckily for diners in Houston, Texas, Yu brought both predispositions back to his hometown and there created Oxheart, the Warehouse District restaurant he runs with his wife, pastry chef Karen Man.

The Oxheart that gives the place its name is not the bovine innard but the heirloom variety of carrot. Thus from the outset, Yu is teaching diners that this is not going to be a normal Houston dining experience.

Guests at Oxheart choose from three menus: a four-course omnivorous menu focused on seasonal ingredients; a four-course vegetarian "garden" menu, and a seven-course chef's tasting menu that draws from both of the shorter meals.

The signature dish is raw brassica leaves and pickled stems, goat whey, chrysanthemum, and herb oils. This may sound like the curatorial comments on an exhibition label in an art gallery, but there is nothing pretentious about Oxheart. This beautifully presented dish tastes like a Texas childhood memory—raw florets of broccoli dipped in mother's best homemade ranch dressing. It is served with instructions to toss the ingredients together before eating.

Other noteworthy offerings include slowly roasted and pickled okra with smoked black garlic, crème fraîche, and "African blue" basil and mesquite-smoked catfish with cane syrup, collard green, oshitashi, mustards, and pickles. Dishes such as these, rather than the traditional vast steaks, are the stuff of life in the new Houston. **MD**

↑ Oxheart offers a no-fuss, inventive dining experience.

Bogart's Smokehouse |

Down-to-earth barbecue establishment

Location St. Louis **Signature dish** Rack of barbecued pork ribs with apricot glaze | $

Thanks to its huge portions of freshly barbecued meat, Bogart's has become an institution in St. Louis, Missouri. It stands on a downtown street corner near the famous Gateway Arch, Busch Stadium, and historic Soulard Farmers Market.

The exterior looks like an old shop front with a few tables along the pavement at the side; inside the big wood and glass doors, there are modest metal-topped tables equipped with plastic sauce bottles and towel dispensers. It's a small room, and such is Bogart's reputation that it often gets very cramped and busy. Diners have to sit wherever they can find a seat. The lines of people outside are usually given free samples while they wait.

"Try Bogart's breathtakingly good ribs, unsurpassed pulled pork, and stellar beef brisket."

Joe Bonwick, *St Louis Post-Dispatch*

The menu is displayed on blackboards, ordered and paid for at the counter, and served on metal trays or in plastic baskets, with side dishes in little separate bowls. The cutlery is black plastic.

It's all about simple barbecued meat here—as Bogart's says, "Our spin on America's favorite food." Customers order vast slabs of perfectly cooked pork ribs, rolls stuffed with turkey, beef, or pork, and even plates combining portions of different meats.

Side dishes include barbecued pork skins and deviled egg potato salad. Extra flavorings include apple sauce, hot "voodoo" sauce, and North Carolina-style vinegar sauce. Potato chips are supplied by the Billy Goat company; everything else is homemade. **SH**

Willie Mae's Scotch House |

Fried chicken in a New Orleans legend

Location New Orleans **Signature dish** Willie Mae's fried chicken | $

Willie Mae's Scotch House has become a Mecca for those seeking what the owners claim—and many magazine food critics acknowledge—to be the "World's Best Fried Chicken."

Willie Mae Seaton opened her legendary establishment in 1956 as a small bar. The following year, she moved the rapidly expanding enterprise to its current location in New Orleans' Fifth Ward, where she had space to offer hairstyling services in addition to the standard bar offerings. When the barbershop and beauty salon portion of the business closed in 1972, Willie Mae's Scotch House made its now legendary expansion into cooking.

For both better and worse, the long-standing foodie favorite saw major changes in 2005. In May of that year, the restaurant received the James Beard Foundation's American Icon award for the Southern Region. The local government of New Orleans, meanwhile, honored Seaton for her social and culinary contributions to the city. Then in August came devastation as Hurricane Katrina descended upon Louisiana. When the storm abated, Seaton returned to her restaurant to find it in near ruins.

Thanks to a committed team of volunteers and assistance from culinary preservation group Southern Foodways Alliance—which raised $200,000 (£120,000) for the rebuilding efforts—Willie Mae's triumphantly reopened its doors in April of 2007. Shortly afterward, Seaton turned over the reins of the business to her granddaughter, Kerry Seaton, under whose able direction the kitchen continues to serve up classic plates along with new additions, ranging from butter beans and breaded veal to smothered pork chops. The place is slightly out of the way and would be hard to find were it not for the long lines that form outside it whenever it is open (lunchtime only). **TR**

Antoine's | Opulent fine dining in one of America's oldest restaurants

Location New Orleans **Signature dish** Oysters Rockefeller | ❸❸❸

Antoine's has been an icon of New Orleans' grand dining tradition since it first opened its doors in 1840. This French Quarter institution has made some of the most enduring contributions to American culinary history, with dishes like artichoke eggs Sardou and twice-fried *pommes de terre soufflées*, both of which remain on the menu today.

But no plate is more associated with this restaurant than oysters Rockefeller, which was invented in Antoine's kitchen in 1899. Legend holds that Jules Alciatore, the son of founder Antoine Alciatore, devised the dish in the midst of a sudden snail shortage, using oysters in lieu of escargots. The younger Alciatore split open the shellfish, smothered them in bread crumbs and chopped greens, and then set them to bake. And thus was created a masterful platter so rich that it was named after the era's wealthiest man, oil tycoon John D. Rockefeller.

With 14 opulent dining rooms and seating for 800, the restaurant still smacks of bygone times, summoning visions of the Mardi Gras "krewes" that convened in their appointed spaces for decadent late-night bashes. The stand-out Rex Room—named for perhaps the most prominent of the city's old-line parade fraternities—features encased memorabilia from celebrations past set alongside hundreds of photographs of prominent restaurant guests. Competing krewes Proteus and the Twelfth Night Revelers also maintain eponymous dining rooms.

Unlike other long-standing city favorites such as Commander's Palace, Antoine's weathered Hurricane Katrina in 2005 relatively unscathed, reopening to an adoring crowd of 100 New Year's revelers on the eve of 2006. Since then, its fine service and presentation of classics dishes—from *escargots à la Bourguignonne* to baked Alaska—have continued uninterrupted. **TR**

"We have a sentimental soft spot for one of the first fine-dining restaurants in the New World."

frommers.com

⤒ The exterior of Antoine's on Rue St Louis.

Commander's Palace | Luxurious dining in atmospheric New Orleans

Location New Orleans   **Signature dish** Sugarcane-lacquered quail | 💲💲

For more than a century, Commander's Palace has stood in all its turquoise-and-white painted glory on a leafy residential street in the Garden District. It is a New Orleans institution and remains one of the top restaurants in the United States.

The menu of award-winning chef Tory McPhail mixes Louisiana Creole staples, such as turtle soup, gumbo, and shrimp remoulade, with innovative, seasonally inspired dishes. Almost every ingredient is sourced from producers nearby, while herbs travel a short way to the kitchen from a rooftop garden.

The restaurant's story begins in 1880 with Emile Commander, an area entrepreneur who opened a saloon to serve the neighborhood's well-heeled families. Two decades later, Commander's operation evolved into a renowned destination that drew gourmands from all corners of the globe. There followed two changes of management: one in the 1920s, during which its discreet dining rooms drew an eclectic mix of patrons ranging from riverboat captains to churchgoers, the other in the 1940s, the decade when many of the restaurant's most famous dishes were first created. Since 1974, Commander's Palace has been owned by the Brennans, a respected family of Louisiana restaurateurs, who have helped to launch the careers of acclaimed American chefs Paul Prudhomme and Emeril Lagasse. In 2005, Hurricane Katrina devastated the building. After a costly yearlong renovation, the beloved icon reopened as a symbol of the city's regeneration.

Known to locals simply as "Commander's," the restaurant enjoys a reputation for its popular weekend Jazz Brunches, during which guests enjoy live music from a roving band over Louisiana blue crab frittata and the house special, pecan and sugarcane-lacquered quail. **TR**

⬆ A handsome, much-loved New Orleans landmark.

Sylvain | A stylish, contemporary take on the American tavern

Location New Orleans   **Signature dish** Gulf shrimp *pirlou* and a bourbon crust | 💲💲

Though a relative newcomer to the New Orleans culinary scene, Sylvain has made a name for its refined approach to American tavern fare and its contributions to the city's thriving cocktail scene.

Nestled among the historic restaurants and tourist bars of the French Quarter, Sylvain sets itself apart as a one of the city's few upscale gastropubs. Placing its thoughtful comfort food on equal footing with a historically minded drinks menu, the small café has won the hearts of local foodies who are willing to cut through throngs of out-of-towners for a hangar steak with pickled watermelon and a Bourbon crusta.

Set in a two-hundred-year-old carriage house, Sylvain prides itself on recalling the neighborhood's noble and, later, bohemian past—from the days when Spanish colonial bureaucrats roamed nearby Jackson Square to the nights when author William Faulkner frequented its bars. Ever mindful of this evolving history, the restaurant offers classic regional dishes such as shrimp pirlou (a Louisiana rice pilaf) as well as modern-day twists like "Chick-Syl-vain," a nod to the popular American chicken-sandwich chain.

A revolving drinks menu—which may be a little difficult to read in the candle-lit interior—taps into the city's century-and-a-half of inventive cocktail culture. Bartenders behind the copper-top bar are ready to mix anything and everything, from a "Sazerac" (the "official cocktail" of New Orleans) to newer creations like a cinnamon-infused "Dead Man's Wallet." History buffs can ask for "Aunt Rose's Gingered Boom Boom," a jenever and ginger liqueur cocktail named for the notorious brothel magnate who once owned the building (and some say still haunts it.) No meal will feel complete without a "Sylvain Float," which incorporates root beer from Louisiana's beloved Abita Brewery, caramel ice cream, and ginger crisps. **TR**

⬆ Gulf shrimp and Louisiana popcorn rice at Sylvain.

Dooky Chase's | Miss Leah's Kitchen: great food that has inspired progressive thought and civil rights

Location New Orleans **Signature dish** Shrimp Clemenceau | $

"This was the place people like Ray Charles ... would come to after local shows."

frommers.com

⬆ Okra stew, a Southern classic.

Any restaurant may become famous for a variety of reasons. It might have a charismatic owner, wonderful decor, an epic wine list, or a storied past. Sometimes it is the chef but, when she or he moves on, admirers tend to follow. And then there are places like Dooky Chase's, which produces good food and has a special aura, but above all has Leah Chase.

Born in 1923, Leah married Edgar "Dooky" Chase, a jazz musician, in 1945, four years after this restaurant opened. Throughout her time in the restaurant, she has encouraged the work of African-American artists whose paintings adorn the walls. In the 1960s, thanks to Leah, Dooky Chase's became one of the few places in racially segregated New Orleans where civil rights activists of all colors could meet and plan without disruption. Leah nourished everyone who crossed her threshold with magnificent Creole cooking and remarkable versions of staple Southern classics such as fried chicken.

Today Dooky Chase's serves a lunch buffet from Tuesday through Friday, plus a special Friday evening meal that Leah often supervises. The buffet offers a rotating assortment of dishes, according to availability. These usually include fried chicken; red beans, rice, and sausage; gumbo z'herbes (a stew of turnips, mustard greens, and spinach); whitefish cakes; shrimp and lima beans; steamed okra; and shrimp Clemenceau (small shrimp, diced potatoes, peas, mushrooms, butter, and wine).

Desserts include peach cobbler, bread pudding, praline pudding, strawberry shortcake, and a simple but wonderful gingerbread.

Chase's motto is, "There are no secret recipes." That may be so, but the love and devotion that are added to the food here are unique ingredients that one can find only in Miss Leah's kitchen. **FP**

City Grocery | Defining the
way folks eat in the American South

Location Oxford **Signature dish** Shrimp and grits | ❸❺

William Faulkner, the most famous resident of Oxford, Mississippi, once noted that the aim of every artist is to arrest motion, which is life, and to hold it fixed. "The only immortality possible," he wrote, "is to leave something behind … that is immortal." John Currence, the chef and owner of City Grocery, will tell you in his colorful yet humble words that he has no such aspirations. But ask around this "postage stamp of native soil" and you will discover that Currence has dedicated himself to building what award-winning food writer and Oxford resident John T. Edge calls a "knitting back together of the tethers of community by way of food."

Whatever it is about Currence that attracts customers to Oxford from far and wide—it could be his collection of successful restaurants, the popular farmers' market that he helped to build, or the staple, subsistence ingredients that he works to elevate—he is undoubtedly a standard-bearer of Southern food and City Grocery is his flagship. Occupying an eighteenth-century livery stable on the main square, this is the place for food and drink.

Currence's classic dishes such as shrimp and grits and skillet-fried chicken pay homage to tradition, while his original dishes, like Bourbon-braised oxtail stew with smoked mushroom risotto cake, push Southern cuisine forward. Never one to rest on his laurels, Currence shuns trends in search of new levels of deliciousness that can come from vegetables and the wide variety of Southern seafood. He challenges himself to do better, and his diners to recognize that a dish of smoked beets with charred pecans and buttermilk-goat cheese crema can be as delicious as his ever popular corn and bacon fritters with comeback sauce. Even if this is all that Currence "leaves behind," we are certainly the better for it. **MD**

L'Etoile | Friend of the
farmer, beloved of the diner

Location Madison **Signature dish** Pork in many guises | ❺

Since 1976, L'Etoile has set trends in Madison and nationally. Its founding chef, Odessa Piper, is a farm-to-table pioneer who was one of the first Americans to encourage local farmers to produce cleaner, tastier food. As she developed her repertoire of dishes, she cultivated and taught young farmers and, especially, cheese makers in southern Wisconsin how their produce could best be used in cooking.

Piper also trained Tory Miller, her talented chef de cuisine. He has been in charge since 2005, and the food is now better than ever, partly because of his skills and partly because the quality of local agriculture is now as good as one can find anywhere in the United States.

"… crisp, stylish, and accessible … Just enjoy yourself and relish the regional goodness."

pursuitist.com

The pork from Willow Creek farm is transformed into prosciutto, salami, and lardons for salad. Pig's belly is breaded and deep-fried to become a tasty starter. Pork shoulder is the foundation of a rich sauce for perciatelli pasta. The pan-roasted pork chop with Yukon Gold mashed potatoes, bratwurst choucroute, and Riesling-mustard jus is gorgeous.

Outstanding beef is used for steaks and in a combination dish of braised short ribs and foie gras terrine. Locally sourced rainbow trout is a regular feature in preparations that change with the seasons. Vegetarians need not steer clear of L'Etoile. There is, in fact, a dazzling variety of dishes throughout the menu made with heirloom vegetables. **FP**

Dotty's Dumpling Dowry | A haven for handmade hamburgers

Location Madison **Signature dish** "Melting Pot" (hamburger with cheese, smoked bacon, and garlic sauce) | **⑤**

The people of Madison, Wisconsin, have a reputation for strength and friendliness—and for hearty appetites that match their temperaments. Dotty's Dumpling Dowry is their temple.

The state, known as "America's Dairyland," has cows that provide milk for all kinds of cheeses as well as excellent beef. It has also brewed some of the nation's best beers for more than 150 years. All these products are well represented on the menu at Dotty's, which, while it would probably not pass muster with cardiologists, represents a gold standard for what millions of Americans think of as their national dishes.

Although no true food lover would claim that any hamburger is the best—there are no reliable criteria for such a value judgment—the one on the menu at Dotty's bears favorable comparison with most.

Founded in 1969, Dotty's was among the first American burger joints to source its beef from individual farms rather than use mass-produced anonymous meat. Its best-selling burger is the "Melting Pot," topped with cheddar, Swiss, and provolone cheeses, local smoked bacon, and English garlic sauce. Alternatively, diners can create their own burgers with a variety of condiments, toppings, and sauces. These include "Heart Throb" (cream cheese, jalapeño, cilantro, garlic); "English Garlic" (mayonnaise, garlic, parsley); "Boomerang" (mustard, mayonnaise, black pepper, anchovies); "BBQ"; and "Ranch."

As an alternative to a burger, try Dotty's grilled bratwurst from Milwaukee or, for Friday night diners, the fish fry, which is made with walleye pike. Cheese curds (nuggets of white cheddar cheese, breaded and deep-fried) are an addictive classic. There is no better accompaniment than any of the restaurant's 20 beers from Wisconsin microbreweries, all of which are served ice cold in frosted glasses. **FP**

⬆ Dotty's boasts beautiful stained glass windows.

Au Cheval | A nouveau diner updates the classics

Location Chicago   **Signature dish** Cheeseburger | 💲💲

Diner-style burgers seem unlikely dishes to completely captivate the Chicago dining scene, but that is what happened when prolific restaurateur Brendan Sodikoff, who has a half dozen outlets in the city (and has more on the way), opened Au Cheval.

His aim was to put an upscale spin on diner classics, and while this restaurant, with its big booths, dark woods, dim lighting, and brick walls, looks nothing like a traditional eatery of that type, the old-school influences are evident on the menu.

There is the griddled cheeseburger, available as a single (two patties) or a double (three patties). The meat is topped with slices of cheese, pickles, and Dijonnaise. It is as simple as can be, but it demonstrates that restaurants do not need to add lots of crazy toppings to get it right.

Other highlights include the bologna sandwich, with fried house-made sausage stacked high in a soft bun—an elegant update on the lunchbox staple. A whole section on the menu is devoted to items "with eggs," and fried eggs can be added to everything, including the perfectly crisp fries smeared with rich Mornay sauce and the potato hash tossed with duck heart gravy. All the dishes on the menu pair perfectly with pints of beer, and the beer list is extensive, with a wide range of styles and many Midwest brands.

Around dinnertime, there is usually a long wait for a table, but customers can pass the intervening period elsewhere while awaiting a call from the hosts. And it is possible to wait over a beer at Haymarket Pub & Brewery, located kitty-corner to Au Cheval. Inside Au Cheval, booths line the walls and tables are clustered in the back, but the best seats in the house are at the bar, where the chefs put on a spectacular show—turning out dozens of perfect burgers an hour is hard, but they make it look easy. **AC**

⬆ Perfect burgers are the house speciality at Au Cheval.

Coalfire | Thin-crust pizza in a city known for its deep-dish fare

Location Chicago **Signature dish** 'Nduja pizza | $$

There are two kinds of pizza in Chicago—deep-dish and everything else. Visitors to the city always go for deep-dish, which was invented in the city, but native Chicagoans tend to prefer the others.

Among Chicago's growing number of thin-crust options, Coalfire is a standout. Ever since the coal-oven pizzeria opened in 2007, it has been turning out thin, blistered pizza on a perfectly chewy crust with a slightly crispy edge. Coalfire is equally suited to cozy date nights and large family dinners. The space is dimly lit, with large pieces of artwork on the dark walls; empty cans of peeled tomatoes on the tables serve as pizza stands.

The restaurant is a homage to the Neapolitan-style pizzerias for which New York and New Haven are known, but at Coalfire the pizzas are pulled out of the 800°F (430°C) oven with toppings that are distinctly Chicagoan. The sausages and cured meats, such as mortadella and prosciutto, which adorn most of the 14-inch (35-cm) pies are sourced from Publican Quality Meats, The Butcher & Larder, and other local purveyors. The 'Nduja pie has thin slices of spicy Calabrian salami that lends rich, savory flavors to the fresh mozzarella, tomato sauce, and chopped basil.

For vegetarians, the white pizza is a garlicky, herb-laden pie covered in three types of cheese and whole basil leaves, while the pesto pizza is topped with fresh pesto, mozzarella, ricotta, and kalamata olives. There is a build-your-own option, with mozzarella, goat, Gorgonzola, or ricotta cheese, a choice of vegetables, herbs, and meats, as well as eggs and anchovies.

The menu does not extend much beyond pizza—there are a handful of simple salads and cupcakes brought in from Chicago Cupcake for dessert—but that is no matter because the pizzas are the reason to go to Coalfire. **AC**

↑ White clam pizza at Chicago's Coalfire.

L20 | Luxurious seafood in sophisticated surroundings

Location Chicago **Signature dish** Ahi tuna tartare with avocado and caviar | ❺❺❺❺

This acclaimed Chicago restaurant oozes fine-dining elegance. Its stylish interior is a suitably contemporary setting for chef Matthew Kirkley's accomplished cooking. The restaurant's name stands for "Lake to Ocean," and seafood is a house specialty. Such is Kirkley's dedication to offering the freshest of fish in this land-locked city that he has installed two 100-gallon (378-liter), custom-made saltwater tanks.

Japanese influences abound, and Kirkley is known for his playful dishes, which are showcased in the tasting menu. The four-course prix-fixe menu offers a choice of two dishes in each course, with a meat option available for the mains. Begin with a lobster roll made with brioche, tender lobster salad, truffle aioli, and a little Romaine lettuce—a "sandwich" from which gourmet dreams are made. Follow this with Dover sole with cardoons (globe artichokes), mussels, and apple, and then, perhaps, ribeye with butternut squash gratin, onion, and marine cider.

Dishes here can be complex, as in the ahi tuna tartare, flavored with soy sauce and olive oil, then wrapped in shaved avocado, with Osetra caviar, edible flowers, and basil emulsion. Another characteristic dish is spiny lobster on a bavarois of matsutake mushrooms and mandarin, topped with a layer of mango gelee. The seasonally available lobster is sourced from Santa Barbara.

The harmonious flavor combinations are a tribute to the chefs' imagination and confidence, which carry through to truly mouth-watering desserts. These include lime parfait, cara cara orange, avocado, and tarragon, or a divine confection of apricots, génépi liqueur, marshmallow, and black lime. The silky smooth service matches the fabulous and artfully presented food, making eating at L20 both enjoyable and memorable. **AH**

⭱ Beautiful presentation is a characteristic of L20's cuisine.

Hot Doug's | Gourmet
sausages in a league of their own

Location Chicago **Signature dish** Foie gras and duck sausage with truffle aioli, foie gras mousse | **$**

Waiting in line for Hot Doug's is a rite of passage in Chicago—the restaurant opens at 10.30 A.M., and, on weekends, the hour-plus line starts before ten. The wait isn't nearly as long on weekdays. No matter the day or time, owner Doug Sohn will be taking orders behind a counter case filled with hot-dog trinkets and paraphernalia, including a hot-dog telephone. The affable, bespectacled Sohn is always ready to engage in conversation, helping to make the wait worthwhile.

There are two menus: the classics, named after celebrities or Chicago personalities, which are always available, and the daily specials featuring specialty sausages. There's a very solid Polish (named "The Elvis") and a great rendition of a Chicago dog dragged

---

> ## "The place is lively, bustling, and fun—the epicenter of the fine sausage movement."
>
> Chicago Tribune

---

through the garden—it's topped with mustard, relish, tomato, a pickle, celery salt, and peppers. Sohn substitutes caramelized onions for the standard raw ones. The dozen or so daily specials might include the hot sauce chicken sausage with smoked blue cheese and honey, or the kale and walnut pork sausage with sweet curry mustard and smoked Gouda. A decadent classic is the foie gras and sauterne duck sausage with truffle aioli, foie gras mousse, and fleur de sel. Other encased meats include alligator, veal, shrimp, rattlesnake, and elk. The thin, freshly cut fries, available with or without cheese sauce, garner almost as much praise as the meat, and on Fridays and Saturdays, the potatoes are cooked in rendered duck fat. **AC**

Alinea | Impressive cutting-edge
cuisine from a world-class talent

Location Chicago **Signature dish** Hot potato, cold potato, black truffle, butter | **$$$$$**

Alinea means new beginning, and this is what chef/owner Grant Achatz was looking for when he opened Alinea in 2005. Formerly a chef at the now defunct Trio and before that at The French Laundry, Achatz is a modern chef who embraces culinary innovations.

The restaurant occupies a town house in the north of Chicago. There is no regular menu. Instead, diners are taken on a culinary journey through a long and changing tasting menu of intricate dishes balancing flavors and textures to sensational effect. This might begin with steelhead trout roe with a sauce of cured grapefruit and spices, and Dijon mustard, with swede, slices of radish, and black licorice, delicately decorated with nasturtium flowers. The acidity from the grapefruit balances the richness of the roe, the radish provides an earthy note, the spices are carefully controlled.

Enormous time and effort goes into the cooking. Yuba (soy milk skin), for example, is fried into sticks and then wrapped in shrimp, pickled onion, *togarashi* (Japanese chili) powder, orange taffy (candy), and white and black sesame seeds. This is then fashioned into the shape of a quill pen that rests in an "ink well" of miso mayonnaise. But there is much more to this dish than exquisite presentation: the spices are carefully judged, the miso mayonnaise complements the shrimp, the yuba gives a firm, contrasting texture, and the chili lifts the dish with a perfectly judged zing.

The culinary trickery at Alinea is achieved with real flair, and the flavors are never forgotten among the wizardry; dishes have many elements, but they are logical and always there to add a useful texture or flavor. Alinea is considered one of the finest modern restaurants in the world at present. **AH**

➔ Artful presentation at Alinea.

The Purple Pig | Mediterranean small plates on the Magnificent Mile

Location Chicago **Signature dish** Pig's ear with crispy kale, pickled cherry peppers, and a fried egg | ❸❸❸

The tagline for the Purple Pig is "cheese, swine, and wine" and that sums up this bustling restaurant in the heart of Chicago perfectly. Wine is the drink of choice, and the list is well considered and accessible. In line with the European vibe, the wines span the Mediterranean, with choices from Greece, Croatia, and Serbia, as well as from more traditional wine-producing countries such as France, Spain, and Italy.

Order a glass at the bar, because there's almost certainly going to be a wait—the restaurant hasn't slowed in popularity since it opened in 2010. This is in part due to the all-star lineup of Chicago chefs behind the place. Mia Francesca's chef Scott Harris, Spiaggia's Tony Mantuano, and Jimmy Bannos and Jimmy Bannos Jr. of Heaven on Seven have pooled their talents to create a tantalizing lineup of Mediterranean small plates designed for sharing.

As the name of the restaurant suggests, the emphasis is on pork. The signature dish is the pig's ear—crunchy strips of pig's ear tossed with crispy kale and pickled cherry peppers, topped by a fried egg, which adds a creamy element. Much of the menu is like a tour through the rest of the animal—there's morcilla with apples and beans, a comforting dish of milk-braised pork shoulder with mashed potatoes, pork sweetbreads with apricots, and pork neck bone. But there are nonpork options as well, such as tangy whipped feta with cucumber salad or octopus with green beans. The long list includes a small number of dolci, such as Grandma D's chocolate cake.

The room has a warm glow, and most seating is at communal tables. Eating at the Purple Pig is much like being at a large family dinner, where everyone jostles for the last bite of turkey leg confit. **AC**

◄ Pork sweetbreads with apricots and fennel.

Lula Café | Farm dining in a neighborhood setting

Location Chicago **Signature dish** Vegetarian tasting menu | ❸❸❸

Charred eggplants roasted in embers, savory corn flan, butter-roasted radishes—at Lula Café, vegetables are treated as reverently as meats. One of the leaders in the farm-to-table movement in Chicago, Lula's make the most of local suppliers, such as Intelligentsia Coffee, Three Sisters Garden, Gunthorp Farms, and Bennison's Bakery.

Chefs Jason Hammel and Amalea Tshilds opened the restaurant in a tiny storefront in Logan Square as a labor of love in 1999. They began with a simple menu of soups, salads, and brunch items made on a four-burner stove with thrift cookware. Slowly, they grew their following, expanded their menus, and added to the restaurant's space.

"There are few restaurants as creative or wide-reaching in what they seek to achieve."

Chicago Sun Times

There are two menus—a café menu with staples, such as roast chicken and a turkey sandwich with avocado and bacon, and a changing specials menu. You can combine dishes from both. Select baked French feta sitting in a tangy jalapeño-basil oil from the café menu and smear it over grilled bread while diving into a plate of roasted eggplant puree with lamb pancetta. The menu also features a six-course vegetarian tasting menu that celebrates seasonality.

In the evening, sitting down to a meal in the dark, cozy dining room feels like a special, celebratory night out. But the restaurant also operates as a casual café, where it's possible to drop in for a gourmet breakfast or a delicious light lunch. **AC**

Fat Rice | A captivating Chinese-Portuguese fusion restaurant

Location Chicago   **Signature dish** *Arroz gordo* (rice layered with meat and seafood) | ❸❸❸

When Abraham Conlon and Adrienne Lo opened their Macanese restaurant, Chicagoans did not know what to expect. While the two had been cooking in the city with their pop-up dinner series X-Marx for a few years, the menus had been diverse. Macanese cuisine—a fusion of Chinese and Portuguese cooking that developed with Portuguese traders bringing spices back from Macau, a colony of Portugal in the sixteenth century—was something new.

For diners, a Macanese restaurant means a menu of small and large plates that are perfect for sharing. Expect bowls of fiery pickles, including sour chili cabbage and mixed Sichuan pickle, fat noodles, seriously addictive rice noodles that are chewy and coated with XO sauce, a Chinese chili fish sauce that is simultaneously salty, savory, and sweet, and char-grilled piri piri chicken in a pepper and tomato sauce, served with potatoes and peanuts. The restaurant's namesake dish is *arroz gordo* ("fat rice"), a big, layered rice dish packed with sausage, chicken, pork, clams, shrimp, and other meats and seafood. It comes with pickles, eggs, and sauces, designed for sharing.

A word about sharing—make sure you like your dining companions, because you'll likely be at Fat Rice for quite a while. There are no reservations, so you will probably have to wait for a table until you can snag a bar seat or a table in the rustic and colorful dining space, which is decorated with tchotchkes and vintage kitchenware.

Fat Rice operates an unmarked waiting space nearby, where guests can get a drink (try the Kalimotxo, a sangrialike drink made with Rioja, Coke, and lemon), and a bowl of coconut curry cashews or smoked paprika almonds and other small bites. The nibbles, which are from Mama's Nuts, a side project of Lo's, makes the wait go a little faster. **AC**

⬆ Euro-Asian comfort food from Chicago's Fat Rice.

Bang Bang Pie Shop | Comfort cooking at the cutest spot in Chicago

Location Chicago　**Signature dish** Sausage pie　| **$**

Nostalgic desserts such as cupcakes have been on the rise in Chicago since the turn of the century, but this sunny little shop in Logan Square has brought back pie, in a big, delicious way.

The pie menu at Bang Bang Pie Shop changes to reflect the seasons, but there is always a fruit, cream, and chocolate variety available, by the slice or whole. Within these certainties, the flavors change daily. A typical choice might be coconut cream pie, apple pie, or a chocolate salted caramel.

The pies are made with leaf lard—the highest quality lard that is key to the meltingly light pie crusts—or graham cracker crust, which is used for cream pies. There is also a daily savory option, such as *burek*, a flaky Turkish pie filled with spinach and feta, or perhaps a traditional chicken pot pie.

Bang Bang does a brisk trade in sweet and savory biscuits and, as good as the pies are, for many customers, it is baker and co-owner Megan Miller's

biscuits, made with house-churned butter, which are the scene-stealers. Lightly crisp on the outside, soft and pillowy inside, the biscuits are served still warm from the oven with a choice of savory and sweet toppings. Favorite savory versions are sausage and gravy, smoked ham, and candied bacon from Indianapolis' Smoking Goose Meatery. For a sweet treat, take a biscuit to the jam and butter bar for a dollop of plum jam and sorghum butter. Bang Bang roasts its own coffee blend, available hot as well as iced on tap, and homemade pickles are sold by the jar.

Vintage decor decorates the walls, and there are wooden tables and bright red chairs. In summer, there are picnic tables in the backyard. Whether stopping off for coffee and a slice of pie after an evening out or having a biscuit brunch, eating at Bang Bang Pie Shop always feels like a treat. **AC**

⬆ Enjoy a multitude of pies at Bang Bang Pie Shop.

Blackbird | Seasonal dining at a Chicago icon

Location Chicago **Signature dish** Corned beef tongue | 🟢🟢🟢🟢🟢

"When food is the criterion, Paul Kahan's restaurant belongs at the top of anyone's list."

Chicago Tribune

⬆ The cool, clean lines of Blackbird.

Chef Paul Kahan has his name on many restaurants—wine-focused Avec; The Publican, a beer, pork, and oyster hall; the wildly popular taco joint Big Star; and Publican Quality Meats, a butcher shop/café—but it is the high-end Blackbird that is the truest expression of his culinary vision.

The restaurant is part of the One Off Hospitality Group, a partnership between Kahan, restaurateur Donnie Madia, and wine steward Eduard Seitan. Its clean architecture and decor—a long white room with a wall of tables on one side and more tables grouped by the open kitchen—form a simple, modern backdrop for the sophisticated cuisine. Behind the bar, mixologist Kyle Davidson helms a changing cocktail program, setting the taste buds tingling with concoctions such as a whiskey sour topped with a layer of smoked meringue or an absinthe frappé.

Chef de cuisine David Posey oversees a seasonal menu of beautifully constructed plates that are at once elegant and playful. Options may include corned beef tongue served with yeasted mustard and brioche in a deconstructed sandwich; wood-grilled sturgeon with chicken wing; crispy suckling pig with celeriac risotto, granny smith apple, hazelnut and black truffle; or roasted monkfish with poached shrimp, endive, buttermilk, and capers.

Dana Cree handles the dessert menu. There are nods to childhood, with banana pudding and bubblegum ice cream among more sophisticated choices. Melding dessert and cheese courses to stunning effect, Cree's pretzel-raspberry-cow's milk cheese makes a fine finish to the meal.

A ten-course tasting menu pulls dishes from the main menu, while the surprisingly good lunch deal offering three courses at a very reasonable price almost makes it hard to justify an elaborate dinner. But not quite. **AC**

Longman & Eagle | Midwest cuisine in a homey inn

Location Chicago **Signature dish** Wild boar sloppy joe | ❸❸❸

With a menu of pâtés, roasted chicken, and whiskey cocktails, Longman & Eagle epitomizes Midwestern cuisine. Dishes are made with local ingredients and utilize all parts of the animal, and it doesn't cost a fortune to dine there. The restaurant forms part of an inn, which has six small rooms with tape decks (mixed tapes supplied), Apple TVs, and contemporary art on the walls. The cool vibe extends into the dining room, where brick walls, a wooden ceiling, and a long wooden bar give the space a rustic-chic feel.

While the menu incorporates hearty-sounding dishes such as wild boar sloppy joes, venison pâté, and *confit tête de cochon* (confit of pig's head), chef Jared Wentworth makes them taste, and look, elegant through spot-on execution and details such as crispy sage and pickled jalapeño topping the sloppy joe.

If you can't make dinner, come for brunch. Fried chicken and waffles is taken to a new level with a sweet potato-pork belly hash, while the whole hog crepinette—a little package of meat wrapped in caul fat—sits in a pool of maple jus.

Longman & Eagle's window proclaims "Eat, Drink, Whiskey," and the passion for whiskey is evident. More than 140 different types are available, and it is used in a long list of cocktails .

Because getting a table at Longman & Eagle is notoriously difficult, Wentworth has opened up its back area, dubbed OSB, or Off-Site Bar, a sixteen-seat, thirty-person space with a patio, where customers can wait for a table or stop off for a quick snack. There's a very simple menu that includes oysters, fried smelt, rillettes, and cheese plates. On weekends the sous chefs take over the space, creating a pop-up sausage shop on Saturday, with a menu that changes weekly, and a pop-up donut shop on Sunday. An inn, a bar, a restaurant, a doughnut shop—visiting Longman & Eagle aims to offer something for everyone. What's not to like? **AC**

"*Wentworth's menu of elevated American bar classics has been a smash hit.*"

The Independent

⬆ The ultimate sloppy joe at Longman & Eagle.

Topolobampo | Sophisticated Mexican food from
Chicago's most celebrated chef

Location Chicago **Signature dish** Roasted Atlantic stripe sea bass in yellow mole with Chesapeake Bay oysters, braised fennel, and crispy mushrooms | ❺❺❺❺❺

"Topolobampo's food is a world apart from the clichéd taco and burrito fare you find elsewhere."

Chicago Tribune

Rick Bayless, host of the TV series *Mexico–One Plate at a Time* and author of eight cookbooks, is arguably Chicago's best-known chef. He is also one of the most accessible, with a range of restaurants, from sandwich shops to mid-range eateries dotted around the city. Topolobampo, his highest end restaurant, lies behind a discreet doorway in Frontera Grill, another Mexican restaurant owned by him.

While the cuisine at each of Bayless' restaurants is authentic, Topolobampo shows there is much more to Mexican food than street food. Ingredients are seasonal and the menu states their provenance.

The menu opens with a raw bar—pristine oysters, served with limes and a smoky *mignonette* (sauce made with shallots, cracked pepper, and vinegar), and several styles of ceviche. First courses range from silky cauliflower soup to *sopa Azteca*, a bowl of chili broth filled with chicken, avocado, and cheese. Lamb and fish come with complex *mole* sauces, while desserts finish on a playful note. Try the ice cream with "tres leches" cake or papaya-lime sorbet with pineapple, kiwi, pomegranate seeds, and prickly pear broth.

The dishes are gorgeously plated, and sauces are poured tableside. While many high-end restaurants focus on building their wines, Topolobampo has created an excellent drinks list. The cocktail menu focuses on mezcal and tequila, with different kinds of margaritas—shaken and poured at the table—as well as sangrias and Palomas. Rounding out the list are Mexican beers and a beer that Bayless brewed with Goose Island Brewery specifically to pair with his food.

The room is as elegant as the food, with white tablecloths and large colorful paintings on the walls, and a sense of quiet reverence pervades. Dine at Topolobampo to understand what Mexican food is really about. **AC**

⬆ Warm colors create a convivial dining space.

Birrieria Reyes de Ocotlan
Succulent goat in a no-frills setting

Location Chicago   **Signature dish** *Birria* with a side order of freshly made tortillas | $

The cartoon goat head on the sign of the Birrieria Reyes de Ocotlan provides a clue to what's on the menu here—goat stew, goat tacos, and goat meat by the pound to wrap up in warm tortillas. The restaurant is as casual as can be—there's a take-out counter, a couple of televisions silently playing football games, and a dozen tables crammed into the back. A goat head peers down between framed photographs on the white tiled walls.

Located in Pilsen, a neighborhood with a large Mexican population that is filled with tiny *taquerias* (taco shops), Reyes de Ocotlan sets itself apart by specializing in *birria*, a traditional Mexican street food consisting of large chunks of roasted meat—in this case goat, bone-in—in a rich red broth made with spicy dried peppers and topped with a handful of raw onions and chopped cilantro. A bowl of dried chilies and a bottle of smoky hot sauce are set on each table, and slices of lime, onions tossed with habanero peppers, and more cilantro are served on the side, so diners can adjust the heat to their liking. To cut the spice a little bit and mop up the juices order a side of freshly made tortillas. A roll of paper towels is set on each table, and they're necessary if you really dig into the stew.

The rest of the short menu mainly comprises tacos. Different cuts of goat meat—tongue, liver, and head—are wrapped in a double layer of soft tortilla shells with freshly chopped cilantro and onion. Generous helpings of meat makes them quite substantial, and just a couple of tacos can make a satisfying meal. You can quench your thirst with a glass of freshly made horchata or pineapple juice. Dining at Birrieria Reyes de Ocotlan makes for a quick, casual, and filling meal, but it's a memorable one, and very affordable. **AC**

Manny's Cafeteria & Delicatessen
A gem of a deli

Location Chicago   **Signature dish** Corned beef sandwich | $

A meal at Manny's Cafeteria & Delicatessen is one of the quintessential Chicago dining experiences. It's where politicians hold meetings, and U.S. presidents stage appearances on trips through town. It's open from 6 A.M. to 8 P.M. and bustling at all hours.

The approach is casual. Grab a tray, slide it along the counter, stopping to load soups and entrees, or make a beeline for the man in a white apron and hat filling sandwiches with a tower of just-sliced, paper-thin corned beef, leaving room for Jell-O and pie.

Manny's was opened in 1942 by a Russian-born restaurateur, and is now run by the fourth generation of the same family. You could be forgiven for thinking that nothing has changed very much over the years.

> *"You go for comfort food … everything comes in oversized portions so bring an appetite."*
>
> *Chicago Tribune*

There are photos and news clippings on the walls and layer cakes for dessert. Entrees are old school classics such as roast beef, liver and onions, or spaghetti and meatballs. The corned beef sandwich is the best in the city. What feels like an insurmountable quantity of meat is placed between two slices of soft rye bread. Cheese is optional and mustard can be added from the bottles on the tables. Breakfast is popular. Beyond traditional eggs, pancakes, and omelets, there's fried matzo brei with onions or sausage, cheese blintzes, and bagels and lox.

Staff clear the tables and the cashier is located on the way out the door—it's one of the simplest dining experiences in the city, and one of the best **AC**

Big Bob Gibson Bar-B-Que | Award-winning hickory-smoked
barbecue and sauces in Alabama

Location Decatur (Alabama)   **Signature dish** Hickory-smoked barbecued pork |

"A peppery, mayo-based sauce transforms smoked whole chicken into something ethereal."

Chicago Tribune

Big Bob Gibson is an institution in Decatur.

"Big" is indeed a good word to describe this homespun northern Alabama institution. The plates of hickory-smoked barbecue are served in generous proportions with substantial sides and with drinks refilled gratis. The restaurant, which was opened in 1925 by 6-and-a-half-foot (2-meter), 300-pound (136-kg) Bob Gibson, is an expansive spread of a place with plenty of large and cushy booths and dining tables for parties of all sizes (in number and individual girth). Even the Big Bob Gibson parking lot is huge. However, you'll still find a line out the door and maybe a short wait for a parking spot, especially if you're heading over on a Sunday afternoon after church.

People come from miles around for "world championship" meats and sauces. From the "best original white sauce" in the state to the "best ribs in America," a long list of accolades and awards stretches through the decades and across the menu. Choose from half a rack of ribs; sandwiches, potatoes, or salads piled with pulled pork, beef brisket, chicken, or turkey and topped by mustard, habanero red, or a white sauce made with a cider vinegar and horseradish base; or a bowl of spicy stew. If you have room, finish with a slice of lemon, chocolate, or coconut pie.

The restaurant's cookbook, *Big Bob Gibson's BBQ Book* by Chris Lilly (husband of Big Bob's great granddaughter Amy, with whom Chris co-runs the Gibson empire), was recognized as the 2009 Book of the Year by the National Barbecue Association. *The Wall Street Journal*, Martha Stewart, the *Today Show*, and many more in the media have all taken notice. Nevertheless, Big Bob's eponymous eatery keeps its folksy charm. If the original Sixth Avenue location is slammed when you go, there's a second restaurant on nearby Danville Road. A third Big Bob Gibson Bar-B-Q outlet is in Monroe, North Carolina. **CO**

The Catbird Seat |

Sitting pretty in the Music City

Location Nashville **Signature dish** "Hot Chicken" |
❺❺❺❺

If there was ever a seat we wanted to land on in Nashville, it's The Catbird Seat. Who wouldn't want to be sitting pretty in one of the best restaurants in the American South? More and more these days, restaurant designers are bringing diners in direct contact with the chefs who prepare their meals. The Catbird Seat is leading this trend with thirty-two seats set around a U-shaped kitchen counter where Chef Erik Anderson and his team produce their dishes.

The restaurant offers just one seven-course tasting menu each night. Steering clear of the current tendency to focus only on local ingredients, Anderson's kitchen embraces the creativity that comes with having the world as its larder. The kitchen is, in the chef's words, always striving to offer guests something that looks familiar but tastes different, or tastes familiar but looks different. This concept shines through in the signature amuse bouche, "Hot Chicken." The resulting bite, served at the start of each meal, is a crispy crackling of chicken skin, brushed with sorghum and covered with chili flakes and paprika, then topped with "Wonder Bread" puree and dill salt. It's a tip of the hat to Nashville's most famous food and the introduction to the whimsy that is yet to come.

Other popular dishes include abalone with redeye gravy, pigeon with roasted porcini, and hay-infused yogurt and sturgeon with clams and blood sausage. Despite the use of abalone and other ingredients rarely seen in the South, Anderson and his crew never lose sight of their southern roots. A favorite dessert, served at the end of most meals, pairs spherified bourbon with wedges of vanilla cake, cherry crisps, and charred oak ice cream. When you're in the South, why just serve the bourbon when you can also give diners the true flavor of the oak barrel in which it was aged? **MD**

Prince's Hot Chicken |

The heat is on in Nashville

Location Nashville **Signature dish** Spicy fried chicken | ❺

There are few restaurants in the world where the question of what you are going to eat has only one answer. At Prince's Hot Chicken, set inside a small strip mall on the east side of Nashville, Tennessee, that answer is chicken. Hot chicken to be exact. But do you order it mild, medium, hot, or extra-hot? How you answer that question could dictate how the rest of your day goes.

Nashville's hot chicken isn't for the faint of heart. Most places around town marinate their chicken in a thick, wet cayenne paste before dredging the pieces in flour and frying them in hot oil. Prince's, which is the standard-bearer, brines its chicken, then flours it, fries it to order, and slathers it with a secret layer of super

"There are many pretenders to the hot chicken throne in Nashville but this great original is still king."

Condé Nast Traveler

hot spices. The resulting chicken, which is served simply with cheap white bread and dill pickle slices, has the color of rusted, molten lava. The heat registers somewhere near molten lava, too.

Back in the 1930s, the story goes, founder Thornton Prince was caught cheating on his "lady friend" with another woman. In revenge for his betrayal, the girlfriend cooked up a batch of his favorite Sunday fried chicken and laced it with a strong dose of cayenne pepper. The only problem was that Thornton loved every spicy bite and asked for more. Thankfully, that recipe has been passed down through generations to the current owner, André Prince Jeffries, Thornton's grandniece. **MD**

5 & 10 | A Canadian-born celebrity chef at work in an historic mansion

Location Athens (Georgia) **Signature dish** "Snackies," Frogmore Stew | $$

Hugh Acheson is the rare chef who manages everything from multiple restaurant ownership to TV appearances and writing cookbooks without losing his good-guy personality or the youthful vigor that is part of his brand. Even more extraordinary, he is a Canadian who cooks like a Southerner.

Everything Acheson does is worth the trip, but nothing is quite as representative of his style as the restaurant he started in a somewhat funky location in Five Points and relocated to the historic Hawthorne House built by renowned architect Fred Orr in the early 1900s on what is now the University of Georgia Fraternity Row. There are enough fireplaces, mantels, and porches to suit romantic notions of the South,

---

"… it remains Acheson's finest achievement and is, more than ever, a true destination."

atlantamagazine.com

---

but everything has been handled with a light touch. There is a fun bar and a small café, too.

Dinner might begin with the famous "snackies" (pimento cheese crostini with candied bacon, Anson Mills caramel popcorn seasoned with cayenne, and boiled peanut hummus with Georgia olive oil among them), move on to fresh corn soup garnished with Tybee Island shrimp and spruce tips, and then to the sorghum-glazed pork ribs with turnip, radish, and spiced pecans, although there are many other evolved regional specialties to choose. For dessert, apple pie comes with cranberry-caramel swirl ice cream and the pecan streusel and sweet potato bread pudding is rich with dates, molasses, and real vanilla. **CL**

Busy Bee Café | Southern comfort food in downtown Atlanta

Location Atlanta **Signature dish** Fried chicken, smothered pork chop, collard greens | $

Local politicians, national celebrities, and humble folk come to worship at this altar of Southern cooking in Atlanta, as they have since Lucy Jackson founded Busy Bee in 1947. They have their favorite table, their favorite waitress, and their favorite dish that they always order. Some people simply swear by the glossy cornbread muffins that are included with the meal; others are fanatic about the soft yeast rolls with honey spread. Everybody drinks iced tea, lemonade, or a mixture of both.

The house specialty is fried chicken. Marinated for twelve hours and lightly breaded before being cooked in peanut oil to a sumptuous shade of gold, it is the epitome of soul cuisine, especially when served with fresh collard greens and rich macaroni and cheese. All the classics are here, from pork chops (fried or smothered) to stewed oxtails, fried fish (whiting, tilapia, or catfish), candied yams, fried green tomatoes, cornbread dressing, and the kind of sweet tea you could drink by the bucket.

The place is always busy with people who linger over the last morsels on their vegetable plate as if they couldn't bear to see the last of their buttered okra, creamed corn, carrot soufflé, or string beans disappear. Lovers of old-fashioned banana pudding, red velvet cake with cream cheese icing, and sugar-sweet peach cobbler are in for a treat, and the nostalgia-inducing decor casts a spell on all who come fresh from a visit to the King Center or other memorials to the civil rights era.

Be prepared to eat early (dinner is served until 7 p.m.) and try to beat the crowds by avoiding prime times such as Sunday after church or any day when there is an event at nearby Spelman or Morehouse College. If you can't get a table, and the line's too long, there's take out, too. **CL**

Bacchanalia | Modern American in a former meatpacking factory taking farm-to-table dining to a new level

Location Atlanta   **Signature dish** Gulf crab fritters with Thai pepper, avocado, and coconut | ❸❸❸

Co-chefs Anne Quatrano and Clifford Harrison took a huge creative risk when they moved their fine-dining restaurant from Buckhead to the Westside in 2000. Then the area was best known for its meatpacking and warehousing facilities along a still active railroad track. But restaurant-goers embraced the romance and mystery of a massive utilitarian complex reborn as a place of timeless glamor, and Bacchanalia soon became hot.

Customers enter the belly of the building through the restaurant's own market—filled with tempting produce from Quatrano and Harrison's Summerland farm in Cartersville—and emerge into a gorgeously lit space with a long bar overlooking a glassed-in kitchen. Smart banquettes and dramatic drapes soften the industrial look. Knowledgeable staff crisscross the dining space.

Taking advantage of their own farm produce, Quatrano and Harrison change their five-course menu to reflect the sudden availability of glorious seasonal produce. On any given day, you might find lightly cured hamachi with kohlrabi and benne seeds; confit foie gras terrine with Georgia pear; Gulf crab fritters with Thai pepper, avocado and coconut; and squab with chestnut and sour cherries—all reflecting a sensibility in which the local and the global are part of the same sophisticated conversation.

The house-made charcuterie and the cheese cart are the best in the city, and the dessert course includes a sensational Valrhona chocolate cake with mint ice cream. Stunning wine pairings bring much joy to those who come to celebrate one of life's milestones or to reward themselves with a solo dinner at the bar (the only place where you can order à la carte). Bacchanalia feels fresh, effortless, and deeply rooted in the culture of Atlanta. **CL**

"This near flawless Westside New American keeps it fresh year after year."

Zagat

⤒ Bacchanalia offers a sophisticated dining experience.

Cakes & Ale | Big-time sophistication in a small town
setting intent on celebrating the good things in life

Location Decatur (Georgia) **Signature dish** Arancini, potato gnocchi, North Carolina trout |

"The food here rarely overreaches and is driven by what's growing in the local fields."

The New York Times

⬆ Cakes & Ale restaurant and bakery —a gastronomic corner of suburban Atlanta.

This attractively pared-down restaurant may be in the heart of a vibrant community close to downtown Atlanta, but it would be equally at ease in the Bay Area or the Napa Valley near San Francisco, where its owner, Billy Allin, came of age as a chef.

Of all the chefs in Atlanta, Allin is the one who most walks his own path without looking at what everybody else is doing. The name of this subtle contemporary American restaurant alludes to a passage in William Shakespeare's *Twelfth Night* and reflects Allin's belief that the best things in life are achievable by simple means.

The value of working with fresh local ingredients, including vegetables grown in his own large garden, is never far from his mind. Whether you are nibbling *arancini* rice balls with citrus and fennel pollen, slurping perfect cold-water oysters, or sharing a splendid burrata with preserved squash, walnut oil vinaigrette, and dandelion greens, you won't become a victim of sensory overload. You can approach a wonderful striped bass with cauliflower and cauliflower puree or a pork loin with cranberry beans, carrots, and turnip greens with your appreciative faculties still intact.

Always look for the many specials, which sometimes include marvelous potato gnocchi with duck ragú or billi bi mussels with sunchokes (Jerusalem artichokes) and mustard greens, to tap into the best of the season. Everything here is in keeping with Allin's reputation as a master of well-considered sensory experiences, from the wine, including by the glass and carafe, and the inventive cocktails, served in vintage glasses, to the purified water. The bread comes from the restaurant's own bakery next door. No detail has been overlooked in Allin's quest to make his guests feel pampered. **CL**

Zingerman's Roadhouse |

Regional American classics

Location Ann Arbor   **Signature dish** Pimento bacon
macaroni | ❸❺

Founded by the dynamic duo Ari Weinzweig and
Paul Saginaw, Zingerman's first made its name with its
deli, set up in Ann Arbor in 1982, to champion good
ingredients, from olive oil and cured meats to
farmhouse cheeses and freshly baked breads. Such
was the success of this vision that Zingerman's is now
a small food empire, with Zingerman's Roadhouse
offering customers a chance to sit down and dine on
dishes created according to the same ethos.

The concept is simple: Zingerman's serves
regional American classics—think corned beef hash,
"grits and bits" waffles, pickled green tomatoes. Prices
are likely to be higher here than they are in the diners
down the road, but the experience is totally different.
Chef Alex Young takes these American comfort foods
to new heights. "Really good American food" declares
the neon sign outside, and that's what is on offer here.

The careful sourcing of ingredients is key to
success. Grits come from South Carolina, the pork
from family farms in Iowa, crabs from Maryland, and
chickens from Amish farmers. A few miles west of the
Roadhouse is Zingerman's very own Cornman's Farm,
supplying the kitchen with fresh produce and meat,
including heritage tomatoes and pasture-reared beef.
This farm-to-fork approach to catering has gained
Chef Alex Young a national reputation as a champion
of American food.

Appealingly, the down-to-earth menu is matched
by relaxed, family-friendly surroundings. Diners return
for flavorful dishes such as the pit-smoked spare
ribs or the buttermilk fried chicken, followed by a
brownie sundae or rice pudding with maple syrup,
washed down with iced tea, root beer, or American
wines. Meals are enjoyed in simple, unpretentious
surroundings filled with the buzz of contented people
in conversation. **SH**

The Greenhouse Tavern

Creative farm-to-table locavorism

Location Cleveland   **Signature dish** Foie gras
steamed clams | ❸❺

Jonathan Sawyer, the chef and owner of Ohio's first
certified green restaurant, is passionate about
creating recipes that use ingredients produced within
miles, not days, of his kitchen door. As part of this
ethos, he endeavors to produce in-house almost any
ingredient that cannot be procured from the
surrounding region, including craft vinegar.

Cooking in the Midwest, Sawyer fetishizes nose-
to-tail meat-centric foods. Roasted pig's head with
barbecue sauce and a Flintstone-sized beef short rib
with brown butter popovers are just two of the
menu's heartier dishes. The signature foie gras
steamed clams with red onion brulee, house-made
late harvest viognier vinegar, and grilled bread is

> *"The … Greenhouse Tavern
> specializes in gutsy, vivacious
> American cooking."*
>
> fodors.com

another. But Sawyer is equally adept at cooking vegan
dishes, with offerings such as garden beets with
smoked apple, crispy red grain, and fermented black
bean and "cassoulet" with tofu, hominy, and white
beans also on the menu.

Sawyer's eco-consciousness extends to the front
of house as well. Almost everything is reclaimed. Old
church benches, bar tables, chandeliers, and a 1970s
Rock-Ola 444 Jukebox that spins 45s are just a few of
the many vintage items. The young, lively customers
who pack The Greenhouse Tavern on a nightly basis
believe in the food and this environmental message.
They know they are riding the leading wave of a new
Rust Belt food revolution. **MD**

Zuma | Top Japanese restaurant renowned for its celebrity clientele—but it's not all style over substance

Location Miami **Signature dish** Lobster roasted with shizo-ponzu butter | ❸❸❸

Zuma, an import from London (and Hong Kong, Dubai, Istanbul, and Bangkok), is a sizzling Japanese restaurant with spectacular design whose food can best be described as emphatic—its flavors go beyond merely bold. It opened in 2010 and remains one of downtown Miami's hot properties, drawing a great looking crowd of locals and tourists eagerly spending big bucks just to partake of the scene.

Zuma calls itself an *izakaya*, which in Japan is an informal place serving small plates (like tapas) whose function is to keep you upright while you drink sake and beer in excess. But Zuma is no ordinary *izakaya*, although you'll find myriad small plates: squid with green chili and lime; shrimp and black cod dumplings; sea bass sashimi with yuzu, salmon roe, and truffle oil; sweet-smoky pork belly skewers with yuzu mustard miso; and sweet corn with shiso butter. They are great for sharing, as is the shrimp tempura with freshwater eel, though you might want to keep this for yourself.

The restaurant has lofty ceilings and soft colors that allow its vast open kitchen to shine. The kitchen has three zones—a sushi bar, an energetic "robata" wood grill, and a large main kitchen full of gleaming equipment—while a bar and lounge overlooking the Miami River is a great place for creative cocktails. There's an immense menu of pristine sashimi and sushi, and the large assortments for the table are showstoppers. Main courses, such as sesame coated beef tenderloin with spicy soy sauce, miso-marinated black cod, and lobster roasted with shizo-ponzu butter, are beautifully plated.

Zuma was created by restaurant maestro Rainer Becker, who spent years studying the complexities of Japanese cooking and then modernized the experience into something that sounds exotic but tastes reassuringly familiar. **RG & MW**

"Waiters know the menu, from the hand-grated wasabi to the last rock chive sprout. "

miami.com

⬆ Zuma is one of Miami's hottest dining destinations.

Joe's Stone Crab |

Family favorite known for stone crab

Location Miami **Signature dish** Chilled stone crab claw with mustard sauce | $ $ $ $ $

Joe's restaurant is a simple establishment in an unremarkable low-rise building in Miami Beach. The dish that has made it famous is simple, too—boiled crab claws served with chunks of lemon and a pot of mustard mayonnaise.

Joe's Stone Crab restaurant in Miami Beach has been an acclaimed local institution since it opened in 1913. Initially, Joe Weiss's humble lunch counter in what was then an undeveloped part of Florida served local fish. As the Beach became more popular, Joe began experimenting with local crabs, which were plentiful and previously overlooked. The sweet-tasted stone crab claws were a big success with customers, and the restaurant built up a name for itself. Customers included Edgar Hoover, the Duke and Duchess of Windsor, and Al Capone.

The fifth generation of the Weiss family still work here, but the vital ingredient has become much scarcer. Today, crabbers take only one claw from the animal, then return it to the sea so that its claw can regrow. Some claws are as big as a human hand. They are boiled, chilled, and smashed by a mallet in three special places so that the shell can be easily peeled away. Popular side dishes include sweet potato fries with cinnamon sugar, creamed garlic spinach, and Brussels sprouts with pepper, bacon, and brown sugar butter sauce The menu has grown as the restaurant has moved upmarket. Joe's also operates a successful takeout service and mail-order shop for prepared meals that arrive complete with a mallet.

Diners sit in a large white-walled dining room, decorated with old photographs celebrating the restaurant's long family heritage. The enormous menu offers a wide range of dishes, but unsurprisingly most customers opt for crab claws, before rounding off with a slice of classic Key lime pie. **SH**

Bowen's Island Restaurant |

Delicious oysters galore

Location Charleston **Signature dish** Steamed oysters with Tabasco sauce | $

While standing in line at Bowen's—and there is always a line at Bowen's snaking down the zigzagging wooden ramp—customers tend to fantasize aloud about what they are going to order. Between swigs of canned beer, there's talk of fried shrimp and crab cakes, slathered with cocktail sauce and chased by "hush puppies" (cornbread balls). Someone will cite the fried fish.

But the real reason to brave the dark dirt road that leads to the screened-in porch that functions as a dining room has nothing to do with a fryer. During oyster season, Bowen's offers an all-you-can-eat special: customers who select it are handed a knife and white dish towel, then shown the way downstairs

> *"The rave-worthy, all-you-can-eat oysters are so fresh they might be accompanied by a little mud."*
>
> *Zagat*

to a dark, Dickensian chamber dominated by a gas-fueled griddle on which weathered cooks steam local oysters gathered in giant burlap sacks.

Seated at wooden tables, damp with oyster liquor and spilled Tabasco sauce, customers tuck into a bivalve feast. Carolina oysters are clustered, so each salty bunch is as knobby as a knotted silver chain. There's a hole carved into the center of each table for spent shells, and the cooks are forever circulating with another round, carried from the fire in a shovel. Establishments selling fried shrimp and hush puppies are rampant along the South Carolina coast, but only at Bowen's can eaters measure their seafood feasts in shovelfuls. **HR**

Husk | A trailblazer of the Southern revival

Location Charleston   **Signature dish** Cheeseburger | ❸❸❸

When Cook It Raw, an annual gathering of the world's leading avant-garde chefs, came to Charleston, its chefs prepared a dinner featuring ingredients meticulously foraged from low-country swamps and techniques that amounted to the culinary version of ice skating's quadruple axel. But after the meal, they all ate Husk cheeseburgers.

Husk, chef Sean Brock's first solo project, is a restaurant for folks who know restaurants. Located in a two-story Queen Anne house dating from 1893, in the heart of historic Charleston, the restaurant has bare wooden tables and dried okra pod centerpieces—touches that sometimes throw eaters who yoke culinary excellence to grandeur. But the dining room and the brick-walled bar, which set out to revive forgotten Charleston cocktails and became the city's best place to drink, are not prone to putting on airs. Instead, the focus is on the integrity of the ingredients and smart, playful cooking.

When Brock created Husk, he decreed anything grown or produced beyond the South would never enter his kitchen. This meant there was not any olive oil in the pantry. Brock and chef de cuisine Travis Grimes have relaxed the opening standards (and the South's artisan scene has grown, allowing the restaurant to buy olive oil from Texas), but Southern credentials rule: a meal might begin with fried pig's ears and benne seeds tucked into lettuce leaves or pimento cheese with pickled ramps (wild leeks).

Pickling is a recurring theme at Husk, along with other means of preserving, such as fermenting and smoking. Even eaters who just come for the burger get their pickle dose: bread-and-butter pickles top the deservedly legendary burger, starring patties ground from chuck steak and Benton's bacon and seated on a buttermilk benne seed bun. **HR**

⬆ Husk offers ingredient-driven Southern cuisine.

McCrady's | Impeccable modern cooking in a centuries-old tavern

Location Charleston   **Signature dish** Charleston ice cream | ❸❸❸❸

It is an American cliché to say of an establishment that "George Washington slept here." Fortunately, McCrady's does not peddle clichés. In the case of this historic tavern, the first president did not doze here, but ate well and drank Madeira.

Built in 1788 by an ex-convict, McCrady's later served as a coffeehouse and warehouse. It was vacant when its current owners took over the property in 2006. They installed Sean Brock as chef, allowing him to explore new trends in modern gastronomy, and for a time dinner at McCrady's meant foam. But Brock, who wears a radish tattoo, eventually scaled back his whiz-bang cooking and began to focus on just-harvested ingredients in more natural states.

Successive chefs de cuisine upheld Brock's vision, serving unadulterated steaks, pork chops, and local seafood. Few Southern kitchens are better at using the plate as a canvas. In late fall, the tasting menu presents different textures and colors, featuring huckleberry, pickled and served with aged squab and sunchokes, and elegant curlicues of local shrimp caught up in a butternut squash and benne composition. According to Brock, "Charleston ice cream"—ostensibly nothing more than rice—is everyone's favorite course, which he puts down to diners forging an appreciation of the region's founding crop, helped by the surrounding dishes and setting. At McCrady's, good looks and thoughtfulness are highly compatible.

It is impossible to get too thoughtful at a restaurant that has been serving hard drink since Washington's day. The inventive cocktail list includes a giddy mix of gin, homemade Mountain Dew vinegar, and St. Germain boba (tapioca). In honor of Edward McCrady's work as an importer of fortified wine, there is a choice of Madeiras. **HR**

⊞ McCrady's is listed as a national historic landmark.

Hominy Grill | A modest restaurant drawing international attention to Charleston with its pan-Southern cooking

Location Charleston **Signature dish** Shrimp and grits | $$

"Night after night … Stehling sends out handmade versions of myriad regional delicacies."

The New York Times

⬆ Shrimps and grits at Hominy Grill.

The defining grain of the low country is rice, but eaters at the esteemed Hominy Grill can be forgiven for thinking they are in corn country. Chef Robert Stehling in 1996 chose a maize-based name for his new restaurant, which eventually became an institution on the strength of its extraordinary shrimp and grits.

Meriting an exclamation point on the menu, the shrimp and grits are gussied up with mushrooms, scallions, bacon, and cheese. But it's the quality of the ingredients that distinguish the dish that has come to symbolize Charleston in American minds: Stehling, the first Charleston chef to win a Best Chef Southeast award from the James Beard Foundation, was a stickler for all that was fresh, local and seasonal long before it was trendy to know your farmer.

Stehling's cooking is traditional: at splashy culinary events where his colleagues serve up dishes sauced with reductions and finished with microgreens, Stehling has been known to bring a buttermilk pie. The pan-Southern menu at Hominy Grill includes jalapeño hush puppies with sorghum butter; grilled pimento cheese sandwiches; and catfish creole and fried chicken sandwiched between halves of a towering biscuit.

Hominy Grill pays careful attention to its squash casserole, stewed okra, and lima beans. A selection of vegetables paired with cornbread isn't especially fancy, but neither is the cheery, converted barber shop that houses the restaurant.

Hominy Grill draws its biggest crowds at brunch, when people patiently wait upward of an hour to sample tender homemade banana bread, tidy green tomato sandwiches, and the famous shrimp and grits. Fortunately, the restaurant mixes a mean bloody Mary, which is served from a take-out window on the holding patio. **HR**

Bertha's Kitchen | A bastion of classic low-country soul food

Location Charleston **Signature dish** Thick and spicy okra soup | $

Located well north of the Charleston depicted in glossy brochures, Bertha's Kitchen isn't designed for tourists. There are a few utilitarian tables, set with pepper vinegar and little else, but the vast majority of the cafeteria's customers are hungry wage earners who need to scurry back to work.

Yet culinary travelers who find their way to the boxy turquoise building will be rewarded with a low-country education unavailable to those who only sup on gentrified Southern dishes such as fried chicken and Coca Cola cake. At Bertha's, the region's cross-cultural history and unique geography are displayed on the steam table holding just-made red rice, lima beans, and peerless okra soup.

Akin to gumbo, okra soup is a thick mess of tomatoes, spices, and sliced okra, which shed their seeds and thicken the broth. Bertha's version of the classic dish is rich and deep, made to the specifications Albertha Grant established when she opened her restaurant in 1979. Although Grant passed away in 2007, her daughters still use her aluminum pots and pans.

Bertha's lists its specials on a handwritten board that stands near the front of the inevitable line, but the choices don't change much. There's a lush mac-and-cheese, soft as custard, smoky lima beans, simmered until their shells surrender, and hearty collard greens. Bertha's serves blocks of sweet cornbread, but the preferred starch is white rice.

There is lots of competition when it comes to great fried chicken in Charleston, but Bertha's owns the fried pork chop crown. The peppery chop, wearing a clean coat of seasoned fry, doesn't deserve to be rushed out the door: it's worth taking a seat to savor the output of one of the city's last great soul food joints. **HR**

FIG | A magnet for food and wine lovers near and far

Location Charleston **Signature dish** Tomato tarte tatin | $$$$

At FIG, food lovers are almost guaranteed to bump into fellow gourmands they have met elsewhere. At the top of most Charlestonians' list of favorite restaurants, it is a kind of culinary clubhouse.

Perhaps that's because the atmosphere is so amiable. FIG—the letters stand for "food is good," a motto as simple and honest as the restaurant's cooking—isn't overly casual, but the wooden chairs and earth-toned walls give the room a neighborhood bistro feel. Nobody here minds too much if guests share a loud laugh or strike up a conversation with guests at another table.

The food sets a high standard for ingredient-driven cuisine. Unlike chef Mike Lata's seafood restaurant, The Ordinary, FIG isn't specifically themed: French influences and local produce unify the menu. Among the emblematic dishes is a stunning tomato tarte tatin, which reminds eaters that tomatoes are rightly classified as fruit: the sweet, flaky-crusted pie, finished with fromage blanc and an olive tapenade, is made with tomatoes grown on nearby John's Island.

> *"Chef Mike Lata has the knack of making the region's seasonal bounty shine."*
>
> *Washington Flyer*

Other stalwarts on the menu are a hearty fish stew bobbing with shrimp, squid, and mussels, and a sticky sorghum cake: for a new spin on the British classic sticky toffee pudding, Lata glazes date cake with Kentucky sorghum syrup. FIG also offers one of the region's most intriguing wine lists, making it the perfect place to split a bottle with a friend. **HR**

Inn at Little Washington | A long-established
temple of gastronomy that never rests on its laurels

Location Washington (Virginia)   **Signature dish** "Gastronaut's Menu" | ❻❻❻❻

"Extraordinary cooking served by a fleet of cosseting waiters makes the inn an enchanting place."

Washington Post

⬆ Attention to detail is part of the inn's philosophy.

The Inn at Little Washington has collected so many stars and diamonds over the years that even the heavens might be a tad envious. There is virtually no exultation that hasn't been used to describe it. Indeed, adjectives such as sublime, intimate, rich, romantic, and even life-altering fail to capture all the magic that is consistently delivered to every guest at every table on every night.

Chef Patrick O'Connell has expertly orchestrated every aspect of his extraordinary inn, bringing the finest produce of the land to the most sumptuous setting in order to conjure culinary wizardry for his pampered guests.

O'Connell aims to excite all the senses. The Inn itself is an astonishing stage set by London designer Joyce Evans. In the inner sanctum—the kitchen—two kitchen tables, each seating six and flanked by a baronial fireplace, have a view of the chefs at work. The so-called Kitchen Table can be booked for a premium, though to do so might be to miss out on the theater of the main dining rooms.

For dinner, choose the three-course menu, or opt for the "Gastronaut's Menu"—ten chef-selected courses with wine pairings. You might find American osetra caviar with peekytoe crab and cucumber rillette; grilled breast of pigeon marinated in blueberry vinegar on a zucchini crêpe; curry-dusted veal sweetbreads with roasted local plums; and Virginia country ham and pappardelle pasta. Vegetarians are well served by the ten-course "Vegetarian Odyssey." If you can still manage dessert, weigh up the choices: perhaps grandmother's warm apple tart with buttermilk ice cream or a tingling pineapple lemongrass sorbet with pink peppercorn granita. The Inn at Little Washington presents unashamed luxury with exquisite taste. **CF**

Trummers on Main |
Southern charm with city influences

Location Clifton **Signature dish** Bacon-wrapped rabbit saddle with dumplings | **$$**

Main Street in Clifton, Virginia is four short blocks of Americana. The town grew up during the Civil War, when Union soldiers were posted to Devereux Station to hold off a Confederate invasion, and period architecture prevails.

Trummers on Main, which occupies the old Clifton Hotel, is no exception with its marvelous facade, including a spacious second floor balcony and charming front porches, intact. The interior, however, breaks the rules of quaint by being sleek and sophisticated. The reception doubles as the bar, in which old school Southern comfort mixes with New York City chic. The second floor dining area is spacious and airy with floor-to-vaulted-ceiling windows that enhance Trummers' seasonal philosophy with views over the garden. The third floor is an experimental space for pop-ups, such as an Austrian *Heuriger* (wine tavern) or a burger and milkshake bar. The restaurant's owners, Stefan and Victoria Trummer, like to surprise their customers.

The Trummers are omnipresent—in the warm greeting offered by Victoria at the door, in the sensual cocktails concocted by Stefan, and in the conversation that invariably gets going at one of the two communal tables in the dining space.

Chef Austin Fausett has created a four-part menu—seasonal, vegetarian, low country, and contemporary—and there is also a grand tasting menu with wine pairings. Offerings such as local rabbit ragout, bourbon-glazed sweetbreads, and pumpkin sherbet are just a few of the options on the menu one day in fall. The dishes are always influenced by season, local history, and Southern trends. Fausett packs a surprise with every dish and presentation, making a return visit for next season's menu a must. Or you could come for brunch on Sunday. **CF**

Quarterdeck |
A crab shack institution

Location Arlington **Signature dish** Maryland blue crabs | **$**

Anchored as it is between high-rise apartments at the back door of Fort Myer Army base, Quarterdeck is a bit of an anomaly. It's certainly far from the Chesapeake Bay. Nonetheless, it swells with all the culinary delights its name implies: from May through September, Maryland blue crabs, crusty with Old Bay seasoning, spill from plastic lunch trays as wait staff scurry across the floor to remove buckets of discarded shells and deliver fresh paper towels and cold pitchers of beer.

For over thirty years, ownership of the restaurant has passed, not through the family, but through a succession of family friends, bartenders, or managers, with Patrick Murrough, a former manager of Quarterdeck, now at the helm.

"Veteran servers know their customers and their product very well. All crabs are cooked to order."

northernvirginiamag.com

The Quarterdeck offers other fare to stay the hunger during the hour or so it takes for crabs to be delivered to the table, or for those too shy to dismantle a crab for eating. There are countless appetizers with and without signature crab meat—nicely steamed shrimp, scallops, jerk and fried catfish, as well as pizza and burgers. But until the end of crab season, it is rare to see a table without a pitcher of beer and crabs piled high on white butcher paper.

Dine on the patio in warmer months. There is no salt air or bay breeze, but the crack of the crab claw under the whack of a mallet among the conversation and laughter is evidence that the Quarterdeck is where the neighborhood crab shack has come of age. **CF**

Gadsby's Tavern | Where history is served

Location Alexandria **Signature dish** Roasted half duck with scalloped potatoes |

> "A true Revolutionary experience awaits at this historical Alexandria tavern. "

Zagat

⬆ You will be following in presidential footsteps here.

George Washington ate here, as did Thomas Jefferson, James Madison, James Monroe, Andrew Jackson, and other presidents and political notables. Maintained in period decor, and run by knowledgeable staff in colonial attire, Gadsby's Tavern is a history lesson open for brunch, lunch, and dinner. Established in 1785, the tavern, and then the tavern/hotel (now museum), was noted for the fine dining, rum punch, and the best accommodations in the area.

The adventure starts outside, at the corner of Cameron and Royal, where a brick-lined ice well once stored up to sixty-two tons of ice cut from the nearby Potomac River. Ice enabled Gadsby's to serve cold beverages and was sold to patrons.

The tavern was also known for its events—a tradition that continues 200 years later. Thanksgiving, Christmas, and the Birthnight Ball, marking Washington's birthday, are among the most popular public events at Gadsby's. However, it is almost impossible to visit the tavern when a social, musical, or theatrical event isn't being held or is in the last few days of planning.

Informal gatherings take place in the tap room and outdoor paddock while the dining rooms are representative of formal eighteenth-century dining. The menu is simple, with enough variety to suit all ages and tastes. First courses include Surrey Co. peanut soup with ginger and garlic and spinach in truffled honey and cider vinaigrette. George Washington's favorite features among the mains—roasted half duck with scalloped potatoes, corn pudding, *rotkraut* (red cabbage), and a cherry orange glacé. There are old-fashioned children's favorites, too, such as macaroni and cheese. George Washington might have been describing Gadsby's Tavern when he wrote, "My manner of living is plain and I do not mean to be put out of it. A glass of wine and a bit of mutton are always ready." **CF**

Old Ebbitt Grill | Everything a dining tavern should be—and more

Location Washington **Signature dish** Trout Parmesan | 💲💲

Established in 1856 as a boarding house, Old Ebbitt Grill is Washington, D.C.'s oldest saloon. It has moved locations several times, and in 1970 was saved from extinction when the saloon's contents were bought at auction by Stuart Davidson and John Laytham, owners of Clydes of Georgetown.

The new owners eventually moved the restaurant into its current Beaux-Arts building, a fitting home for its grand collection of antique beer steins, animal heads, said to have been bagged by Teddy Roosevelt, glass panels, paintings, and more. Period replicas such as the grand mahogany bar and the Victorian bentwood chairs complete the ambience.

An extensive menu of food and drink gives Old Ebbitt the feel of a neighborhood bar and grill where the neighborhood is the nation, if not the world. In the early evening a mix of office workers, politicos, tourists, executives, and D.C. citizenry come streaming through the revolving door eager to secure a mahogany and velvet booth. When packed, as is often the case, the 10-foot- (3-m-) high ceilings help absorb the noise levels, reducing it to a buzz of friendly chatter and laughter.

The food does not disappoint. It is simple yet imaginative, with old favorites and seasonal specials, all generously sized. Popular choices are the fried calamari appetizers, jumbo lump crab cakes, seafood jambalaya, and trout flash-fried in a Parmesan crust and served with a light hollandaise sauce. Pies, crumble, brownies and cheesecakes make up a familiar lineup of desserts.

The oyster bar carries its own unique experience, with a good choice of raw oysters that you can mix or match. These can be served at a table but not with the same fun and effect as at the oyster bar. The Old Ebbitt Grill, which also opens for breakfast and lunch, may sound like a tourist haunt, but it is a time-honored favorite of locals as well. **CF**

"The chilled bivalves—neatly shucked and typically offered in six or so varieties—are superb."

Washington Post

⊡ The Old Ebbitt Grill is everyone's favorite saloon.

The Tabard Inn | A long-established favorite worthy of a pilgrimage

Location Washington **Signature dish** Jumbo lump crab cake | ❸❸❸

Taking its name from the hostelry in Geoffrey Chaucer's medieval masterpiece, *The Canterbury Tales,* the ninety-one-year-old Tabard Inn in Washington has featured in more than a few modern novels, including John Grisham's *Pelican Brief.* Exposed beams, worn leather, and crisp white tablecloths falling to a checkered floor exude confidence, and like its namesake, the Tabard has a great sense of bonhomie.

Apart from being a quaint hotel, the Tabard is a highly respected restaurant. Whether in the stately Room 51, reserved for small private parties of up to fourteen people, in the main dining room, at the bar, or on the brick-walled patio, the inn is equally suited for a first date or anniversary, a power lunch, a family gathering, or a rare treat alone. An efficient bustle and muted conversations create a cozy intimacy

Executive Chef Paul Pelt all but grew up in the Tabard kitchen. He started as a line chef, left for a brief period, returned, and then took the lead. His approach is eclectic. The lunch and dinner menus feature hearty and traditional choices such as cassoulet or duck, but also highlight Italian, Asian, and Caribbean influences, with some Southern dishes. One might find jumbo lump crab cake with fried green tomatoes and black-eyed peas alongside soy sake braised short ribs, and there is always superb charcuterie and cheese. Pastry chef Huw Griffiths puts his own stamp on the menu, so leave room for desserts such as his multilayered dacquoise, or apple date cake.

The Tabard is frequently cited as the "best" or the "only" place for weekend brunch in Washington, D.C. The brunch menu includes fluffy homemade doughnuts and bagels with cured salmon, perfectly poached eggs with fried oysters, or flat iron steak. The Tabard Inn lives up to its namesake as a most appropriate first stop for any modern food pilgrim. **CF**

⬆ The Tabard Inn is a coveted and cozy brunch spot.

The Tombs | Georgetown's ageless college bar

Location Washington **Signature dish** Hoya salad | $$

Nearly every college town in the United States has a favorite college bar, most of which embody the particular spirit of the college and boast past patrons who went on to become famous—or infamous. The Tombs is no exception. Founded in 1962 by Georgetown alumnus Richard McCooey, the Tombs is part of a trio of restaurants—the others are 1789 and F. Scott's—occupying an 1800s federal-style townhouse, owned and operated by the Clyde's Restaurant Group. The Tombs, in the basement below 1789, is a comfortable favorite frequented by the Georgetown Hoyas (the sports teams that represent the university), faculty, locals, and tourists. It served as the inspiration for the bar in which the brat pack hang out in the classic coming-of-age movie *St. Elmo's Fire*.

Hoya memorabilia adorn the original brick walls, particularly from the crew teams who practice their sport along the Potomac. Game day for any Hoya event will be marked by large crowds with students and alumni sharing pitchers of beer, appetizers, or pizza while cheering their beloved team exuberantly. Do not be surprised to find a Jesuit priest or two among the crowd—founded by Jesuits, the university has a strong Jesuit tradition.

Clyde's favorites pack the menu, and so Tombs offers more than standard college bar fare. For dinner, choices might include Maine lobster, Delmonico cottage pie, and jumbo lump crab cakes. It also has an award-winning wine menu and desserts from pastry chef Ryan Westover. But there are plenty of bar food classics such as the Bulldog burger with beer-braised onions on a pretzel roll, and the Hoya salad—a cornucopia of ingredients served on a warm pizza crust. Sometimes, there are special events and pitchers of beer, to draw the college crowd and sustain the Tombs as Georgetown's college bar. **CF**

[↑] Sports memorabilia adorn the walls of Tombs bar.

The Monocle Restaurant |
Dining with the politicos

Location Washington   **Signature dish** Steak with wine sauce | ❸❸❸

Perhaps the best equalizer in a town known for political rivalry is a well-prepared steak. Located just shy of the back door to the Senate and a short walk from Union Station, The Monocle is a family concern that specializes in a few dishes done superbly well—mainly steak and seafood.

During the five decades since it opened, The Monocle has possibly seen more political figures breaking bread together, or at least in convivial cross table conversation, than any other restaurant in the capital. Signed photographs of ex-presidents, senators, members of Congress, and media folk line the burgundy colored walls; many of them doubtless heeded the words of wisdom stenciled along the

---

"The menu doesn't change with the seasons—heck, it doesn't even change with administrations. "

Washingtonian Magazine

---

cornices and beams, including "An empty stomach is not a good political advisor."

The staff, including long-time Maitre d' Nick Selimos, welcome newcomers and regulars with equal warmth, paving the way for a wonderful dining experience. The steaks are perfectly cooked, and come with a choice of three sauces. Lamb chops, pork rib, and calves' liver flesh out the meat options. The seafood is slightly more elaborate in presentation, with roasted Chesapeake Bay oysters in chardonnay curry sauce sometimes featuring alongside the salmon fillet and crab cakes. The Monocle's longevity is testimony to the Valanos family, the staff, and the good food served there. **CF**

Cityzen | Culinary magic
from a virtuoso chef

Location Washington   **Signature dish** Parker House rolls | ❸❸❸❸

This strikingly decorated, spacious restaurant on the ground floor the Mandarin Oriental Hotel is where Washington's movers and shakers like to lunch. Chef Eric Ziebold worked with the acclaimed chef Thomas Keller at the French Laundry in California and at Per Se in New York before opening Cityzen in 2002. It didn't take long for Ziebold's Washington debut to became a destination restaurant.

Ziebold's stylish contemporary cooking draws inspiration from Japanese, French, and Italian cuisine. In addition to the four-course menu, which changes frequently, there are two six-course tasting menus, one of which is vegetarian. They all feature seasonal produce and ingredients carefully sourced from around the U.S. Expect perfectly ripe tomatoes from Northern Neck on the western shore of Chesapeake Bay in nearby Virginia, Elysian Fields Farm lamb, and Broken Arrow Ranch quail, to name but a few. Each plate is pulled off with skill and flair.

Ziebold doesn't shy away from flavors with impact, or imaginative combinations. Roast squab is served with watermelon pickle, and venison might come with juniper pancakes and clementine tapenade. Desserts, too, display inventiveness and skill. How about "crispy winter squash beggar's purse" (quince velouté and autumn succotash) or an ethereal soufflé flavored with Meyer lemons or caramelized apple, depending on the season? Little touches such as the dainty Parker House rolls, elegantly presented in a box, add to the enjoyment of dining here.

The restaurant is proud of its extensive wine list, and has an eye-catching wall of wines. Sommelier Andy Myers is a knowledgeable and unintimidating guide who will pick the perfect pairing. The attentive and polished service is very much part of this sophisticated restaurant's appeal. **AH**

Woodberry Kitchen | A culinary ode to the natural bounty of the Chesapeake region

Location Baltimore **Signature dish** Liberty Delight Tavern steak with roasted carrots, cider beets, mustard greens, and creamed celery root | 🅢🅢🅢

One of the country's most ambitious—and most successful—farm-to-table restaurants occupies an old foundry in the unlikely setting of northwest Baltimore. Spike Gjerde's Woodberry Kitchen, which opened in 2007, practices sustainability to a degree that most chefs can only dream about. Virtually all of the restaurant's food comes from the Chesapeake region. To extend the local seasons, Gjerde maintains a heroic canning and preserving operation, banking sauerkraut, tomatoes, pickles, chutneys, and preserves for future use.

Nor does meat have much of a commute: every week, the restaurant purchases and butchers one steer and three hogs from nearby farms. The Chesapeake Bay supplies all the seafood.

All of this bounty is enhanced by a kitchen that is resolutely American and firmly tied to the region. "It's not as celebrated as other regional cuisines," says Gjerde, "but Chesapeake cooking happens to be one of the first great definable cuisines in this country. It's a 'creole' of Native American ingredients, African and Afro-Caribbean cooks, and European techniques."

Dining at Gjerde's restaurant is pure pleasure. The space is soaring and comfortable, part factory, part *Architectural Digest*. A wood-burning oven dominates the open kitchen. Servers are friendly, knowledgeable, and bursting to tell you where the rockfish (local parlance for striped bass) was caught.

The menu changes constantly, but you'll always find oysters, house-made charcuterie, wood-oven flatbreads, chicken and biscuits, deviled eggs, crab cakes, and what Gjerde calls the "tavern steak." "Because we butcher one steer every week," he explains, "the cut changes from day to day—one day a little bavette, the next a little skirt steak. It's always done in a cast-iron pan and it's always good." **EM**

"The farm-to-table concept on a grand, glamorous, and intense scale."

The Baltimore Sun

⬆ Spike Gjerde plates up at Woodberry Kitchen.

Fork | Contemporary dining that appeals to the mind as well as the taste buds

Location Philadelphia   **Signature dish** Peking-style Muscovy duck for two | ❸❸❸❸

*"[It is] current and fresh …
yet sophisticated in a
grown-up way."*

Philadelphia Inquirer

⬆ Whole roasted duck with Szechuan pepper-honey glaze—designed as a feast for two.

The Philadelphia culinary landscape is ever-changing, and Fork owner Ellen Yin has been riding the trends since 1997. Her latest triumph was to bring Chef Eli Kulp from New York City and commission a sophisticated makeover of the dining room.

Kulp has been warmly received by the national and local food critics. His menu divides into "bites," "raw bar," "to start," "handmade pasta," and "mains." He tantalizes all the senses with stellar ingredients, whimsical plating, and an intellectual take on the classics. His vitello tonnato consists of veal carpaccio, raw tuna, and tonnato sauce. The menu changes but it is always playful. Crisp radishes with butter are served on a bed of "dirt" made from ground black sesame and bitter chocolate. The grass-fed hangar steak is served with a "baked potato"—oven-roasted in the soil in which it was grown with herbs and spices, for deep, earthy flavor.

Chef Kulp says of his philosophy, "I treat each component of the dish as the 'star,' giving equal attention to vegetables, starches, and proteins to create a thoughtful, harmonious meal." Kulp features a nightly whole animal self-contained feast for two, a favorite being the whole roasted Muscovy duck with Szechuan pepper-honey glaze, served with a bitter greens salad. And he does mean whole—the liver is used in the sauce; the heart is grilled; and there is duck prosciutto available as well as confit and meatballs.

Kulp also includes a nightly selection of hand-made pasta, offering bold, unusual flavors such as burnt grain pappardelle with wild boar ragù, a dish inspired by southern Italy.

Strikingly decorated with signature oversize light shades and a giant mural evoking woodland birches in the soft sunset hues, this smart and attractive restaurant is a great place to enjoy inventive and delicious food. **LR**

Franklin Fountain | Vintage fun with sodas, sundaes, and banana splits

Location Philadelphia   **Signature dish** Banana split | ⑤

Walk through the door of this ice cream parlor and it feels as if you've stepped back in time, shedding at least a century, while putting on a pound in weight. Lovingly (and obsessively) reproduced by two brothers, Eric and Ryan Berley, this glorious, "vintage" ice cream parlor is a must-stop for kids and adult alike in the historic district of Old City, home of the Liberty Bell and Independence Hall.

Appropriately attired in uniforms and pill hats, the soda "jerks" serve up twenty-five flavors of soda by the glass and make banana splits following recipes created in 1904. Ice cream is packed in the original carton patented in 1894 by F.W. Wilcox and sundaes and splits are scooped into replicas of Victorian pressed glass. No plastics here.

Sitting at the oak tables and wire parlor chairs, you'll find there is much to amuse the eyes as well as the tongue. The store is filled with period pieces and replicas, including a belt-driven ceiling fan on the 1910 press-tinned ceiling with cherub faces and griffins.

The Fountain began churning ice cream in 2003 with milk and cream from family-owned dairy farms in the nearby agrarian counties of Berks and Lancaster. The results are sensational. Try the Southern Sympathizer—rum raisin and pistachio ice cream with pecans and pistachios smothered in hot caramel and studded with praline brittle.

Philadelphia has a storied relationship with ice cream that dates back to Thomas Jefferson, who liked to tinker with ice cream recipes. Historic nuggets accompany the ice cream, such as, "William Dreyer and Joseph Edy concocted the first batch of Rocky Road ice cream in 1929 following the great stock market crash to give consumers something to smile about during the impending Depression." The winter months see the menu turn toward hot drinks, cakes, and fruit pies wrapped in pastry so flaky that it shatters like glass when met with a fork. **LR**

"The wait can be excruciating but the reward is a truly artistic experience with a cherry on top."

Zagat

⬆ Franklin Fountain captures the flavors and experience of ice cream parlors of times gone by.

Reading Terminal Market

Rich pickings for the region's food lovers

Location Philadelphia **Signature dish** Amish specialties; DiNic's roast pork sandwich | $

Reading Terminal Market spreads over the ground floor and basement of a former train shed. Under one roof, you can indulge in snapper soup and fried clams at Pearl's Oyster Bar, hand-dipped ice cream from Bassets, America's oldest ice cream company, or sample a host of different ethnic cuisines.

You might query what came first here—the local chicken or the local egg. Did the market shape Philadelphian palates or the other way around? Fair Food, a leader in the locavore movement, started as a folding table selling items from a few farmers; it grew into an anchor stall selling produce, cheese, and meats.

The Amish merchants from nearby Lancaster are a signature feature of the market. They sell cake, pies,

> "The market was built to provide the people of the city with the bounty of the country."

Philadelphia Magazine

and produce in the section called Pennsylvania Dutch (religious observance keeps the stands closed on Sundays). Breakfast at The Dutch Eating Place will keep you going well into the afternoon, when you might have room for apple dumplings served with a pitcher of cream. For a lighter snack, do as New York chef Eric Ripert does when in town and visit Miller's Twist for a hand-rolled soft pretzel brushed with butter.

While there is a sit-down restaurant, your best bet is to wander the stalls, assemble a sampling, and grab a table in the community court. Order a roast pork sandwich from DiNic's and a Spataro's cheesesteak to taste side-by-side and decide for yourself which is the defining sandwich of the city. **LR**

Pumpkin

Intimate BYOB serving classic cuisine with exciting twists

Location Philadelphia **Signature dish** Seared scallops | $ $ $ $

For over a decade, Chef Ian Moroney and Hillary Bohr have quietly been putting their stamp on the city's culinary scene. Here at Pumpkin, their own venture, they have helped spark a vibrant nightlife in a once dreary neighborhood.

The two exemplify a Philadelphia tradition of the husband-and-wife BYOB—a small restaurant without a liquor license, so that investment start-up is minimal. Patrons enjoy bringing their own wine to pair with the menu, which is ever-changing according to what's just-picked, just-caught—or in the case of cheese or beef—perfectly aged.

The twenty-six seat dining room has matured along with chef Moroney's dishes, and both make understated use of local resources. A renovation made the tiled room quieter and hid the servers' station, while the local reclaimed wood paneling and sleek marble tables echo Moroney's use of impeccable local ingredients.

Moroney is passionately devoted to his kitchen, and you won't find him chasing after the celebrity moniker. He is an "old school" chef who taught himself classic cuisine, but the menu is far from stuffy. The ingredients for borscht turn into a chilled beet soup accented with a pickled cucumber, crème fraiche, and a translucent wisp of raw candy stripe beet. A sea bream filet rests on a bed of polenta surrounded in a pool of refined *acqua pazza* (lightly herbed broth) dotted with baby squash. A delicate salmon crudo adorned with a squid ink aioli and nasturtium shows off the artful, if sometimes slightly precious, presentation, but no ingredient is there unless it adds to the balance of texture, color, or flavor.

The Sunday five-course tasting menu is a favorite of regulars, and offers newcomers an excellent value introduction to this much-loved establishment. **LR**

Barbuzzo | Mediterranean-inspired fare that draws a late-night crowd to a cool corner of Philadelphia

Location Philadelphia **Signature dish** Uovo pizza | ❸❸❸

Chef Marcie Turney and her partner Valerie Safran have transformed a seedy city block into one of the happening destinations in Philadelphia's Center City. Starting with a small boutique in 2002, they now oversee an array of restaurants and shops, including the excellent Barbuzzo.

Reservations are a must in the convivial 75-seat dining room, although you can sometimes snare a spot at the chef's counter or bar, with a view into the wood-burning oven. All of the decor is handpicked and features reclaimed wood table tops, flooring salvaged from a harbor dock, and Italian marble counter tops.

Nominated for the prestigious James Beard Best Chef Mid-Atlantic in 2013, Turney has garnered national attention. She is devoted to regional flavors and fresh ingredients, and adapts dishes to suit the season. Uovo pizza, for example, will always sport a fresh egg, but summer vegetables make it lighter fare while winter ingredients such as Brussels sprout leaves and guanciale—cured pig cheeks—create something altogether heartier.

Leading the snacks and spreads section of the menu is the sheeps' milk ricotta on grilled country bread. Also here is pan-seared gnocchi with butternut squash. This is the first of the couple's restaurants to have a liquor license, and a very-well-thought-out, value-driven wine list showcases a range of quality Mediterranean offerings.

Be sure to save some room for dessert. Barbuzzo's Budino, a luscious salted caramel pudding with chocolate cookie bits, will have you craving for just one more bite. And, when making a reservation to do just that, plan some time before or after the meal to stroll the block and do a little shopping in its great boutiques. **LR**

"It captures the spirit, at once casual and sophisticated, that defines today's … dining scene."

Philadelphia Inquirer

⤒ Turney adapts her pizzas to reflect the seasons, here with a truffle and egg pizza.

Standard Tap | The simple pleasures of good food and fine draft beer

Location Philadelphia   **Signature dish** Fried smelts | ❸❸❸

It's all about the beer at Standard Tap, but the food could take an Oscar for best supporting role. Take the fried smelts. Made to order, they are first dunked in buttermilk, hand-breaded in crumbs, fried, and served with a remoulade. Paired with a locally crafted English-style pub ale, the richness of the dish is offset by balanced malt and hops.

William Reed and Paul Kimport opened their establishment in 1999, renovating an 1810 building that had been a tavern since 1850. Their eye for detail includes a bar they crafted out of Pennsylvania cherry wood. Their tavern soon drew attention. Beer lovers came here for the lines of draft beer that travel no farther than 100 miles (160 km); food lovers come for the simple but well-executed menu; locals come to catch up and throw some darts.

In best tavern style, Standard Tap has twenty lines serving up local draft beer from a 1956 beer engine, and there are always two cask-conditioned ales. Since these are all craft beers, they are served slightly warmer than most American beers, at about 42°F (6°C). Standard Tap is also one of the few bars in the city to have a Cask Marque Certificate—an international award for taverns serving the best cask ale. A full bar and wine is also available.

The kitchen eschews pretension, but does not stint on attention to detail. It includes duck confit, billed as "duck salad," and chicken pie—local chicken and carrots encased in flaky pastry that elevates a TV dinner standby to a sublime experience. There is a good mix of fish and shellfish, too. In spring, customers look for Pennsylvania trout on the menu.

The Tap can be credited for helping to revitalize the Northern Liberties neighborhood of Philadelphia, which draws a young, hip crowd. However, it remains a neighborhood tavern. **LR**

⭡ Try the wonderful duck salad with a glass of beer.

Vedge | A vegan restaurant for carnivores

Location Philadelphia   **Signature dish** Portobello carpaccio | 🌑🌑🌑🌑

Located in the classic European Deux Cheminées restaurant in an area that was once an outpost for Philadelphia's social elite, Vedge covers a lot of ground—literally and figuratively. While the space still retains Old World leaded glass and fireplace elegance, it has been stripped down to the essentials, with a marble bar and sleek white walls. Here Main Line dowagers in fur coats can rub elbows with tattooed vegan activists in perfect diplomacy, united by a love of what is on the plate.

Fans have watched chef Rich Landau and his wife and pastry chef Kate Jacoby evolve from their first restaurant featuring dishes heavy on the tofu and seitan to a current emphasis on vegetables. Landau composes a menu of small plates highlighted by "the dirt list"—created with farm vegetables barely out of the ground. Radishes are elevated to cult status in a sampler featuring a range of varieties and preparation, from raw to pickled and cooked.

Carnivores appreciate the Portobello carpaccio made from whisper-thin slices of mushroom fanned over a board and garnished with marble potatoes, caper *bagna càuda* (a warm Italian oil dip), and truffle mustard. The shaved, grilled, and smoked Brussels sprouts with mustard sauce have turned many a sprout-hater around. Jacoby's vegan desserts made without dairy likewise confound butter lovers.

While it may seem counterintuitive that vegetables would inspire a stellar wine list, Jacoby has discovered that wines coming from small producers with the same natural philosophy as the restaurant's cooking style work well. The couple resist the place being categorized as a vegan restaurant; it just happens to be vegetable focused. Says Jacoby, "It's about creating a restaurant for everyone with a focus on the food, not diet or lifestyle." **LR**

⤒ Portobello carpaccio—layers of flavor.

Sweet Lucy's Steakhouse | Southern barbecue in Philadelphia

Location Philadelphia **Signature dish** Pulled pork sandwich | $$

A Maryland native who lived in North Carolina and discovered the joys of pulled pork moves to Colorado and meets a girl from Philadelphia. The obvious ending is that they start a smokehouse in Philadelphia and live happily ever after. And this is pretty much how Jim and Brooke Higgins started Sweet Lucy's Smokehouse, a sit down and takeout restaurant in the outlying suburb known as the Great Northeast.

While the original barbecue was influenced by Jim's passion for authentic North Carolina barbecue, the couple travel to find new barbecue styles to add to their menu. Memphis baby back ribs crusted with a dry rub have become favorites along with a caramelized Texas brisket, and barbecue chicken.

"We are talking near perfection … fall-off-the-bone tenderness and sweet and smoky flavor."

CBS Philadelphia

"Consistency," says Jim Higgins, "is the trickiest part of the smoking. Every hunk of meat is different." To that end, meat is batch-cooked throughout the day over a hickory wood pit so that each piece is served at its peak, with the pink hew of properly smoked meat. Their cornbread is baked fresh every hour.

In a nod to the Philly palate, Sweet Lucy's also offers its version of the classic roast pork sandwich with broccoli rabe. Pulled pork is loaded on Italian bread and garnished with collard greens in a blending of Northern and Southern traditions. Can't decide what to order? Every Monday evening there's an all-you-can-eat buffet complete with an array of sides and assorted meats. **LR**

Vetri | Stellar Italian cuisine in an intimate setting

Location Philadelphia **Signature dish** Spinach gnocchi with brown butter | $$$$$

As the high prices indicate, what's on offer here isn't your nana's menu. Rather its genesis lies in chef-owner Marc Vetri's lengthy apprenticeship with top chefs in Bergamo, Italy. After perfecting his own technique with pasta, he returned to Philadelphia to open a small restaurant featuring Italian cuisine.

Vetri's spinach gnocchi with brown butter is a staple on the menu, a soft pillow so light that one is tempted to wonder why it doesn't float away. But it is Vetri's passionate commitment to fresh, seasonal ingredients and the possibilities they offer that have led him to develop his creative edge. You might find him experimenting with duck stuffed with chorizo or a charming flight of fancy in *caombasa* (dainty pasta shaped like doves) with quail and stone fruit.

Sommelier Jeff Benjamin, who has been at the restaurant since its inception and Marc Vetri's business partner since 2000, has firm views on what constitutes good service. Honored by the James Beard Foundation for the restaurant's front-of-house experience, he says he prefers to take the pretension out of high-end dining. He likes to add some fun to dining at Vetri while still maintaining an expectation of impeccable service.

This brick row home has been host to some of Philadelphia's finest restaurants for over four decades with Vetri occupying the space since 1998. Tuscan yellow walls and beamed ceilings are evocative of Italy while the commissioned Murano chandeliers provide understated elegance. With only 27 seats available, a reservation is a tough get, and the prix-fixe tasting menu is the sole option, but the first bite is confirmation enough that Vetri is, indeed, what many have called the finest Italian restaurant in the U.S. **LR**

➡ Spinach gnocchi with brown butter is a favorite.

Zahav | A sophisticated melting-pot cuisine inspired by the street vendors of Jerusalem

Location Philadelphia   **Signature dish** Deep-fried cauliflower served with herbed *labanah* (yogurt) | ❸❸❸

"No chef in the city is creating food as thrillingly personal and well executed."

Philadelphia Inquirer

⬆ Addictively good hummus served at Zahav.

The simple, understated decor of Jerusalem limestone and bustling market mural belies the sophisticated cuisine of this 2011 James Beard Best Chef Mid-Atlantic winner. Under chef patron Michael Solomonov's genius, cauliflower is elevated into a slightly sweet textural wonder: fried bits of crisp vegetable contrast with the smooth richness of *labanah* (strained yogurt) vibrantly colored and seasoned by pureeing with dill, parsley, chives, and mint.

Born in Israel and then raised in Pittsburgh, Pennsylvania, Solomonov returns to Israel for inspiration from the street food vendors. Zahav's ever-changing menu includes small plates of vegetables and meat rubbed in aromatic spices and grilled over coals. An adventurous diner can opt for the grilled duck hearts or crispy lamb's tongue, perhaps accompanied by roasted zucchini with feta; hazelnut and zucchini babaghanoush; or heirloom tomato salad with house-made ricotta.

Zahav is a feast for the eyes as well as the taste buds. Arranged like colorful gems in elaborate wrought-iron presenters, daily *salatim* (salads) are riffs on traditional pickles and salads, turning seasonal local produce into confounding explosions of flavor.

Once you have had Zahav's hummus you can never go back to the mass-market version. Several authentic versions, including a warm Turkish hummus with a pool of butter, pair with addictive *leffa*—bread baked to order in the wood-fired clay oven.

Although Solomonov and his business partner own other restaurants, he can still be found most nights in Zahav's open kitchen. For a glimpse of the master at work, opt for the ten-course tasting menu on Friday and Saturday nights, where four guests sit at a marble counter overlooking the kitchen and watch a feast prepared before their eyes. **LR**

Tacconelli's Pizzeria |

No frills, no fuss, and total satisfaction

Location Philadelphia **Signature dish** Tomato pie |
$

You say pizza; at Tacconelli's they say tomato pie. No doubt there have been feuds over the distinction, but according to John Tacconelli, a real tomato pie is a thin crust painted with tomato sauce, dusted with the tiniest bit of cheese, and topped with more sauce. He ought to know: Tacconelli is the fourth generation to bake pies in the brick oven here. His great-great-grandfather built the oven to bake bread upon coming to the U.S. in 1918.

The bread eventually gave way to the acclaimed tomato pie, with the recipe passing down through the family. The oven is heated throughout the day and then turned off when it reaches the required temperature so that residual heat cooks the pies. This limits the number of pies Tacconelli can make while still maintaining the quality, giving rise to the custom—considered fun by some and an annoyance by others—of ordering ahead to "reserve your dough," and then deciding what you will have on top of it once you arrive.

The menu includes white pie, which has no sauce and is simply adorned with cheese and lots of garlic. A popular favorite is the Margherita, with sauce, basil, and fresh mozzarella. It's possible to personalize your pie with toppings that include spinach, whole tomatoes, sweet peppers, onions, mushrooms, sausage, pepperoni, and prosciutto. That said, order more than three choices per pie and you'll be chastised for ruining the pie.

Tucked away in a small row house in the working class neighborhood of Port Richmond, Tacconnelli's is unremarkable in appearance. Patrons bring their own wine and beer to the intimate, homespun dining room. Pies can be ordered to take out, but eating them here, freshly cooked, is the best way to ensure the perfection of the crust. **LR**

Tierra Colombiana |

Authentic Latin flavors and salsa up top

Location Philadelphia **Signature dish** Bandeja tipica |
$$

Off the beaten path, Tierra Colombiana has long been Philadelphia's go-to for traditional Latin cuisine. Although the menu focuses on Colombian dishes, the kitchen prides itself on delivering a diversity of Latin and Caribbean flavors.

Be sure to come here with several people because you'll want to sneak a sample from everyone's plate, and it's a party kind of place. The *bandeja tipica,* a hearty plate of steak, pork, Colombian sausage, ground beef, and red beans, served with a cornmeal patty, egg, avocado, plantains, and rice, is the showstopper. But, at the other end of the scale, there's a cracking Cuban sandwich—crisp bread oozing with ham and cheese, accented with pickle.

"The tamales are the real prize. Unfold the banana-leaf wrapper and behold a meal in itself."

Philadelphia Inquirer

If the heavy meat menu is not to your taste, there is an extensive list of seafood, including several red snapper dishes. There is also a version of North American "surf and turf"—*churrasco colombiano con cola de langosta* (sirloin steak and lobster tail).

For variety, order a selection of appetizers as a complete meal. Good choices would be *tamal Colombiano,* a white tamale filled with pork; the arepa (cornmeal cake) stuffed with Colombian sausage; and the *ensalada verde en salsa mango,* a salad of spinach, watercress, and cucumber tossed in a mango dressing. The upstairs night club features salsa dancing on the weekends—a fine way to work off your meal and justify having one of the highly touted desserts. **LR**

ABC Kitchen | Ethical gets elegant at this farm-to-table high flier

Location New York **Signature dish** Roasted carrot and avocado salad with seeds, sour cream, and citrus | ❺❺❺

"The food is great. The room is pretty … The crowd runs high-wattage with net worth to match."

The New York Times

⬆ A tasty salad of roasted beets at ABC Kitchen.

Located in the spectacular ABC home store near the city's best farmer's market, ABC Kitchen became a game-changer the moment its first roasted carrot and avocado salad was served. Never before had New York's growing locavore movement been expressed in such elegant surroundings, or by one of the world's superstar chefs (Jean-Georges Vongerichten), with a curatorial commitment to quality.

With handmade porcelain dinnerware from a local artist, wood tables fashioned from fallen trees and recycled materials, bio-dynamic and organic wines, and a thriving rooftop garden, the restaurant subscribes to an ethos rooted in a "safe relationship with the environment and our table." These sensibilities come from store owner and visionary Paulette Cole and chief operating officer Amy Chender–both practicing Buddhists and devoted foodies. The hyper-seasonal menu is orchestrated by executive chef Dan Kluger.

The restaurant's eco-manifesto won't intrude on your dining experience, and most people flock here simply because the food is great. Young and old covet the intimate high-top tables near the bar, or dine leisurely in a softly lit dining room amid reclaimed artifacts. The menu offers five or six dishes per course, plus half a dozen pizzas. You will want to munch on impeccable crab toast with lemon aioli, share a wood-fired whole-wheat pizza with locally foraged mushrooms and poached egg, indulge in pretzel-dusted calamari, or dive into a bowl of roasted beets with house-made yogurt. Alternatively, elevate your taste buds with raw scallops, grapes and lemon verbena, or go for broke with fabulous wood-oven roasted Maine lobster anointed with lemon-chili vinaigrette. Be sure to read the back of the menu for a lesson in sustainability: the food is free of pesticides, synthetic fertilizers, antibiotics and hormones, and is GMO-free and humanely sourced. **RG & MW**

Asiate | An American-Asian hybrid with breathtaking views

Location New York **Signature dish** Butter-poached lobster | ❺❺❺

This restaurant on the thirty-fifth floor of the Mandarin Oriental hotel, with sensational views of Central Park and the glittering New York skyline, could easily get by on being a splendid room with a view and a mediocre menu. In fact, Burma-born executive chef Toni Robertson, American chef de cuisine Angie Berry, and wine director Annie Turso have turned it into a very good restaurant. They are a rare all-female triumvirate in a fine-dining setting.

The original identity of the kitchen was fashionable pan-Asian, but it has evolved to become elegant American with a pronounced Asian accent. While many of the building blocks of the dishes, such as fish, seafood, and perfect vegetables, are locally sourced, the flavorings are often redolent of Tokyo, Seoul, Hong Kong, or Bangkok, reflecting Robertson's Asian roots. Long Island duck with *pain perdu* (French toast) and pickled cherries is proudly local, while Atlantic halibut with soba mai (buckwheat noodles), surf clams, and citrus sabayon spans time zones. Lobster is poached in butter and might be paired with white polenta or parsnip puree and a lip-smacking kaffir lime emulsion.

The food is so beguiling that you might forget to look up from your plate at the million-dollar view. If you do, you will also see the famous wall of wine, a sparkling display of more than 1,300 bottles from Asiate's superb list.

Being a hotel restaurant, Asiate is open for breakfast, brunch, lunch, and dinner, with menus that evolve with the hour of the day and the season of the year. While the cooking is geared to the discerning cosmopolite, visitors from Asia can find dishes that are gentle reminders of home. Not surprisingly, prices can be as sky-high as the view, but New Yorkers in the know like to dress up and come here for the three-course prix-fixe lunch, which offers incredible value for money. **FP**

"Professional, attentive service helps foster an atmosphere of dreamlike luxury."

fodors.com

⬆ Asiate's impressive wall of wine.

Asian Jewels Seafood | A temple to the art of dim sum

Location New York　**Signature dish** Shrimp dumplings | ❸❸

Arguing about restaurants is one of New York's favorite sports, and one of the most hotly contested issues is where to go for dim sum. Between the city's three Chinatowns—in Manhattan, Queens, and Brooklyn—there are scores of excellent choices, each with passionate advocates. Asian Jewels is at or near the top of most lists, and justifiably so.

It is a huge restaurant, resplendent in red and gold furnishings and crystal chandeliers. The perpetual crowds ensure a wide selection of fresh dim sum, with more than eighty items to choose from. Diners do not see a menu, because all the food is placed in bamboo baskets, then stacked onto carts and wheeled through the dining room, in the traditional dim sum way. See something you like? Wave it over. Most dishes contain three or four delicious morsels.

It is impossible to go wrong with any of the shrimp offerings: *har gow* are the pleated, translucent dumplings through which one can just make out the

tender pink of a whole shrimp. The fried shrimp balls are served, improbably, with a garnish of Pringles potato chips. Even better (and no Pringles) are the steamed shrimp balls. Or try the same mixture pressed into curves of tender green pepper. Shrimp are rolled up in wide rice noodles and splashed with sweet soy sauce—treatment also lavished on pork. In fact, pork finds its way into rich dumplings, snowy steamed buns, and parcels of sticky rice cooked inside lotus leaves. Vegetable lovers will find plenty of bright, plant-based dishes, though many will have been augmented with bits of sausage or dried shrimp.

Asian Jewels serves dim sum from 9 A.M. to 4 P.M. weekdays, and 8 A.M. to 4 P.M. weekends. The dinner menu is similarly vast and specializes in seafood. Weekends are always busy, so arrive before 11 A.M. to avoid having to wait in line. **EM**

⤒　Dim sum arrives in traditional bamboo baskets.

Betony | This New American strives for perfection

Location New York   **Signature dish** Roasted chicken with chanterelles and black radish   💲💲💲

A two-story affair in the remains of a failed Russian restaurant, Betony is run by expats from Eleven Madison Park, an establishment with three Michelin stars. Their pedigrees show—from manager Eamon Rockey's attentive servers, to Bryce Shuman's dishes, whose simple descriptions belie complex flavors, pinpoint execution, and deep thinking.

Numerous dishes at Betony rise to levels of greatness. Marinated trout roe, rice, and cucumber emerges as a miniature still life astride a homemade puffed rice cracker; it is beautiful enough to wear. Chilled curls of voluptuous hot-smoked foie gras are adorned with seasonal accompaniments, such as mizuna, mustard greens, and kabocha squash glazed in kecap manis—an Indonesian soy sauce.

Roast chicken has become a competitive showstopper at upscale restaurants. Betony skips the razzmatazz and offers a perfectly shaped breast from a perfectly raised chicken. Brined and cooked, it rests upon *umami*-laden pureed chanterelles. Leg meat, mushrooms, dandelions, farro (like pearl barley), and a quail egg comprise a perfect side dish. The bird may change during colder months to duck or poussin.

Thatches of fresh dill might cover a butter-poached lobster; if so, a server will pour lobster sauce through the dill, transmitting flavor and bouquet to the meat below.

Betony's standout dish is its nothing-like-your-mother's short rib. Cooked *sous vide* (marinated in airtight plastic bags in water) with garlic and herbs for forty-eight hours until rare, the rib is then crisped over coals and carved like fine steak. Charred romaine and a fried sweetbread complete this amazing dish. It is possible to splurge on an expansive wine list but there is more in the affordable range than is typical for this caliber of restaurant. **RG & MW**

⬆ Marinated trout roe in a puffed rice cracker.

Chelsea Market | Artisan food experiences near the High Line

Location New York **Signature dish** Smorgasbord of seafood, breads, cured meats, and salads | 💲

Chelsea Market, which opened in an old Nabisco factory in 1997, is a venue for professional cooks and for bakers, fishmongers, butchers, and other wholesale suppliers to New York's food retailers. Inevitably, these tenants expanded to feed tourist hordes and office workers, and the result is a 425-foot-long (130-m) smorgasbord of food choices. Forty plus restaurants and vendors of interesting edibles flank a block-long, meandering indoor corridor. The Food Network's headquarters is upstairs.

Spend lots or a little: a few dollars will get you superb *adobada* (pork marinated in a chili sauce), sliced from a spit into a hand-pressed tortilla at Los Taco No. 1; a more expensive meal may include clambake for two with lobster, corn, and sausage at Cull & Pistol, which is attached to Lobster Place, a mind-boggling seafood shop-café where Asian visitors dismember cooked lobsters early in the morning. Bowery Kitchen, specializing in cookware,

also makes sandwiches at Bowery Eats: try its warm, juicy Four Ps: roast pork, prosciutto, provolone cheese, and roasted bell peppers on a baguette or focaccia.

Dickson's Farmstand deals in local meats and birds. Try its inventive sandwiches or buy slices of homemade ham or charcuterie and shop for go-withs throughout the market. Purchase a *piadina* (Italian flatbread) at Buon Italia—tops for all things Italian—or buy one of the sandwiches. Many vendors cook and bake here, so stock up on Sarabeth's famed preserves and bundt cakes, and sample Amy's singular semolina-fennel-raisin bread.

Among the restaurants, The Green Table's organic menu ranges from a mac-and-cheese to wild striped bass in pistou broth. Try clam toast at Cull & Pistol, made of grilled bread, aioli, littlenecks, and tasso ham. Friedman's lunch serves American classics. **RG & MW**

⬆ A convivial place for food shopping and dining.

Balthazar | A corner of Paris in downtown New York

Location New York **Signature dish** Steak frites | $$

You can find built-from-a-kit brasseries anywhere, and they feel phonier than Disney. But Balthazar, designed by Keith McNally, is as obsessively authentic as a line-for-line copy of the *Mona Lisa* done by Leonardo Da Vinci himself, right down to the crinkled paint. On the day it opened, Balthazar looked like it had been there for fifty years. Beyond trendy, it is a city-wide destination for meals at all hours, including a stellar brunch.

You will find well-heeled artists down from their lofts, Internet wizards down from their lofts, and decorators ransacking Soho to furnish their lofts—and people like you, all fitting in perfectly. Balthazar is democratic, so feel free to strike up a conversation with people at the next table.

The classic brasserie fare is of a very high order, with every dish well considered. There are lively salads and grand shellfish platters. Steak tartare, seared organic salmon, roasted chicken, chicken paillard with frisee, and even the hamburger—all are winners. Likewise, the wine list is cleverly tailored without a clunker in the lot.

McNally originally named the place "Balzar," but owners of the famous Balzar brasserie in Paris objected, hence the new name—which, if you're literate enough, will remind you of Lawrence Durrell's *Alexandria Quartet,* or of a supersize wine bottle holding 3 gallons (12 liters). Balthazar is always crowded, even between meals, so be sure to reserve well ahead or you'll have to wait for a table on a bench just outside the door. You might try waiting at the bar, but it, too, will be crammed with happy people.

Do not ignore the bread basket. McNally supplies restaurants all over New York with his bread, which is sold from the adjacent take-out shop. The pastries and sandwiches merit attention. **RG & MW**

⬆ Balthazar is a French-style brasserie with panache.

Bouley | The show goes on at this extraordinary restaurant in Tribeca

Location New York   **Signature dish** Chicken *en cocotte* on alfalfa and clover hay | 💲💲💲💲

Ease open the door and enter another world—an anteroom lined with perhaps a thousand fragrant apples. You've stepped from bustling Tribeca into sublime Bouley, whose vaulted dining room, rich carpets, and luxurious furniture welcome you to France. No other restaurant in New York feels like this.

David Bouley is highly idiosyncratic, and you must surrender yourself to his gastro-esthetic: high-concept, deeply complex, Asian-influenced dishes, assembled from unusual combinations of ingredients, follow one upon the other in astounding colors.

Inflated blini "biscuits" enclose smoked salmon, caviar, and white truffle honey, one extra milligram of which might unbalance the dish. A kuzu crisp with

---

"David Bouley's Tribeca" trailblazer is the epitome of refined, grown-up dining."

Zagat

---

melted Aligote and fingerling potatoes wears a hat of white truffle. Sea urchin roe and Osetra caviar float in a cloud of apple foam and yuzu (an Asian citrus fruit). Wild mushrooms and tuna belly are enrobed in coconut foam. Intense, thickened black truffle dashi coats porcini flan full of crabmeat.

And so it goes on: meltingly tender sardines on vegetable *escabeche* and raspberry vinegar, black cod with avocado miso and smoked milk, chicken steamed on alfalfa and clover hay in a sealed casserole. You may order à la carte, but a six-course dinner tasting menu is the way to go. A set price five-course lunch offers excellent value. Service is friendly and superb. **RG & MW**

Dizzy's Club Coca-Cola | Great food, great view, and all that jazz

Location New York   **Signature dish** Miss Mamie's fried chicken | 💲💲

Picture a stereotypical New York jazz venue: a cramped basement room, dimly lit, reeking of last night's beer, worn furniture, and cheap wine extortionately priced. That's not Dizzy's Club Coca-Cola. Named after legendary trumpeter Dizzy Gillespie, this place is sleekly designed and occupies a lofty space within the Frederick P. Rose Hall/Jazz at the Lincoln Center complex. On the fifth floor of Time-Warner Center, it boasts windows overlooking Central Park, reasonable elbow room, excellent acoustics, and good sight lines. The food may not be groundbreaking, but the music often is. Jazz great Wynton Marsalis considers this place home and often appears with his musicians.

The menu leans toward Southern favorites prepared by New York's largest caterer, Great Performances, in consultation with Spoonbread, an African-American caterer. You might start a jazzy evening with hot wings, blackened shrimp kale Caesar, fried green tomatoes with mozzarella and red pepper remoulade, or a triptych of authentically sassy gumbos. Mains also have a strong Southern accent: ultra-crispy fried chicken and collards; baby back ribs with baked macaroni and cheese; and blackened salmon with crawfish étouffée. The fried chicken alone is worth the trip, but do leave room for a helping of warm beignets.

The club has a good roster of draught beer and exuberant cocktails. There's bourbon infused with black cherries, Manhattan-style; a thirst-quenching "Dark & Stormy," made with dark rum and homemade ginger beer; and their signature "Dizzy Gillespie," prepared with mint-infused rum, fresh lime, and cane sugar—all priced unusually lower than at the city's upscale cocktail emporia. With jazz performances every night, you can come often and stay late. **RG & MW**

Daniel | Luxurious French cuisine from a modern master in a grand neoclassical setting

Location New York **Signature dish** Oven-baked black sea bass with syrah sauce | $$$$

Multi-Michelin-starred Daniel, the creation of Daniel Bouloud, has been wowing New Yorkers for twenty years. The restaurant—once the premises of the legendary Le Cirque, where Bouloud was executive chef for a while—is unashamedly grand, the menu is highly ambitious, and the service is superb.

Daniel is modern rather than classic French, and its menu brims with ingredients that would never cross the threshold of, say, La Grenouille. The cooking is globalized and highly complex. The go-withs alone make an enticing menu. Consider these accessories for black sea bass with syrah sauce: oregano-zucchini millefeuille, tempura cipollini, onion marmalade, and green-peppercorn-potato duchesse. With the duck breast come bing-cherry chutney with galangal, glazed daikon, poippini mushrooms, pistachios, and port jus. The food is as dressy as its customers.

Presentation at Daniel is always stunning. A tasting of heirloom tomatoes, for example, comes in three permutations, as does raw hamachi; a veal trio contains roasted tenderloin, braised cheeks, and sweetbreads, each with its own accompaniments; angus short ribs and wagyu tenderloin comprise a duo of beef (actually a trio if you count the smoked tongue accompaniment).

Desserts divide into fruit, chocolate, ice cream, and sorbet, or you can idle your way through a selection of superb American and imported cheeses. There are three-course, six-course, and seven-course menus offered at ascending price levels. In addition, an excellent three-course vegetarian menu is available. A less formal but very comfortable bar serves impeccable wines and various cocktails along with savory dishes and late-night desserts served à la carte. **RG & MW**

"*Daniel's cheese cart is one of the finest four-wheeled vehicles in New York.*"

The New York Times

⬆ Daniel's is a great choice for a celebratory night out.

RedFarm | Inventive Chinese food in New York's West Village

Location New York **Signature dish** "Pac-Man dumplings" | $$

Joe Ng is a savant of dim sum. He was discovered by prolific restaurateur Eddie Schoenfeld, an unlikely maven of Chinese food, at a cavernous restaurant in Brooklyn. Chinese crowds flocked there each weekend for Joe's amazingly creative dumplings.

The pair became partners at this compact West Village destination, and the dumplings, if anything, are even better. Joe's restless mind constantly spins new riffs on main courses using (mostly) Asian ingredients in nontraditional ways, so you'll want to order these, too.

Schoenfeld (aka Eddie Glasses) rarely drinks, but somehow he has assembled a repertoire of Asian-esque cocktails that are not to be missed. Have your waiter fetch some anthropomorphic dumplings (the "Pac-Man dumplings" resemble characters from the popular video game) while you peruse a short menu that is long on temptations. You'll want the spicy crispy beef, Kowloon filet mignon tarts, and a stunning dish of shrimp-stuffed chicken that is crisped with a layer of puffy rice. Equally enticing dishes are found on their ever-changing specials sheet.

The restaurant packs the maximum number of people into a minimum of space, so creature comforts are in short supply. This is offset by food designed for sharing, even though you may not want to relinquish any of the Creekstone Farms prime ribsteak that has been set in front of you. A long communal table runs down the center of the restaurant.

RedFarm does not accept reservations, but you can put your name on the list, and they'll call your mobile when a table is free. Explore one of the neighborhood bars while you wait or, better yet, pop downstairs where the owners have opened Decoy, which specializes in Peking duck. There may be room for a cocktail there—or even a table. **RG & MW**

↑ **Dumplings reference the Pac-Man arcade game.**

Junior's | Original New York cheesecake and other culinary classics

Location New York **Signature dish** New York cheesecake | $

Junior's, with its iconic cheesecake, opened in 1950, directly across from the Brooklyn Paramount Theater where Chuck Berry and Fats Domino made the world shake. The theater has gone, but Junior's and its earthshaking cheesecake live on.

Cheesecake is the quintessential New York dessert, perhaps as famed and synonymous with the city as the Yankees. What is called "New York Cheesecake" at a suburban mall simply is not. Generations of New Yorkers and visitors have made the pilgrimage to the Brooklyn branch to sample the dense, ultra-smooth cheesecake that rivaled the one served at Lindy's, a historically famous Times Square contender. The Junior's in Times Square is in close proximity to the Broadway theaters, and there are additional outlets in Grand Central Station and in a Connecticut casino.

Although you find mammoth hamburgers and sandwiches on the menu (good ones, too), the list of speciality main courses is interesting in that it is a catalog of what middle-class New Yorkers ate fifty years ago. After a complimentary basket of rolls, coleslaw, and pickles you will find such throwbacks as Hungarian goulash, brisket of beef with mushroom gravy, gussied up fried chicken, and broiled Roumanian tenderloin (better known as skirt steak).

But, if it is just the apotheosis of sumptuous, velvety cheesecake you're craving, there is an ample choice. The cheesecakes come in a variety of flavors and toppings (including a sugar-free one), but it is best to go with the plain version—why try to improve on perfection?—and savor it slowly. If you're with friends or family, you might order strawberry shortcake just for contrast. Should you become addicted (many people do), Junior's cheesecakes are also available via mail order. **RG & MW**

⊡ Junior's cheesecake is a staple for New Yorkers.

Eataly | Eat, drink, and shop in an acre of Italian food

Location New York   **Signature dish** Slow-roasted beef rib | ❸❸

Eataly is part grocery emporium, part restaurant, and totally Italian—from a vast collection of cheeses, olive oils, and condiments, to coffees and teas. With lofty ceilings, white tiled walls, and astounding food displays, you can hardly rest your eyes.

A chain of enormous food circuses in Italy, Eataly landed resoundingly in New York in 2010. The acre-plus food hall on Broadway and 23rd Street generated so much traffic that rents nearby skyrocketed.

Eataly's restaurants are organized by food groups. Near a retail display of fish is "Il Pesce." Order whole roasted fish, a good fritto misto, and seafood salads. Adjoining the meat department, "Rosticceria" serves daily sandwiches—maybe porchetta, or brisket with

> *"The cavernous Eataly is … a temple of all things Italian. Make a beeline for [the] sandwiches."*
>
> fodors.com

salsa verde, or Black Angus prime rib. Nearby is "Manzo," which has an ambitious meat-oriented menu: sweetbreads with lobster and corn, pork belly with peaches and caramelized onions, beef rib with polenta and barbaresco vinaigrette.

"Le Verdure," in the center of a photogenic greengrocer's, creates culinary magic with vegetables. Workers, up-to-here in flour, fashion wood-oven pizzas, signaling the entrance to "La Pizza and La Pasta." Pastas made in-house, or up-market imports, are cooked properly al dente. Expect a line. With a gelateria, a panini stand, and a rooftop beer garden, it is possible to lose your mind and empty your wallet. But what fun! **RG & MW**

Gotham Bar & Grill | A modern American stunner

Location New York   **Signature dish** Seafood salad with avocado and lemon vinaigrette | ❸❸❸

Gotham's great chef, Alfred Portale, virtually invented skyscraper plating nearly three decades ago, a style copied—for better or worse—by restaurants across America. But the foundations of his New American creations have always been deep, complex flavors and a technique that borders on wizardry. He has since abandoned his "edifice complex" in favor of simpler presentations, but his mastery carries on.

Gotham has garnered five consecutive three-star *New York Times* reviews and endless accolades from the food world. The vaguely postmodern room, regularly refreshed by co-owner Jerry Kretchmer, places Gotham among the best-designed and most interesting restaurants in the country. The lighting, filtered through parachute fabric, is bright by day and verges on romantic in the evening while maintaining a sparkle on the splendid food.

Despite its lofty cuisine, Gotham's staff is casually dressed. But don't be fooled: they know everything about every dish and can guide you through a comprehensive wine list, all the while making you feel like their best friend.

Don't miss Portale's legendary and complex seafood salad—ruby red shrimp risotto with tomato confit—or his squab with foie gras, gnocchi, and fennel-orange compote when the bird is in season.

Overlooking the dining spaces, Gotham's bar gets seriously busy during cocktail hour with its well-tailored selections of wine by the glass. You also can eat at the bar, which may be advisable for two reasons: reservations are generally hard to come by, and the food is expensive, so here's a chance to try a dish or two without plunging into an entire dinner. That said, the three-course Greenmarket Lunch (three choices for each course) is one of New York's great bargains. **RG & MW**

Brushstroke | A feast for the mind as well as the senses at this Japanese *kaiseki* restaurant in Tribeca

Location New York **Signature dish** *Chawan-mushi* topped with crab and black truffle dashi | ❺❺❺❺

Chef David Bouley has vicariously opened (and closed) a cluster of restaurants in an enclave at the edge of Tribeca. His highly successful Brushstroke specializes in Japanese *kaiseki*—a creative progression of intricate dishes, hot and cold, that contrast and complement taste, texture, color, and seasonality.

The restaurant is a collaboration between Bouley and Isao Yamada of the Tsuji Culinary Institute in Osaka, and staffed by students. The room has a pleasant social buzz, while numerous kitchen acolytes silently transform the mystical idea of each dish into its three-dimensional complexity. You see this clearly in a bowl of crab *chawan-mushi*, the flawless egg custard topped with a thickened, crabby, *umami*-rich black truffle dashi—heavy over light, spicy overlaying creamy. If large enough, it would, by itself, suffice as a supremely satisfying dinner.

Lobster tail in fragrant sea urchin sauce demands attention, for its accompanying lobster dumpling's chewiness is the antithesis of the delicacy you would otherwise expect. Yet it succeeds brilliantly. A sansho-pepper ponzu sauce tingles your tongue and rounds out the dish.

King salmon with salmon caviar in a rice-thickened broth and guinea hen in a broth with tofu skin and nicely textured rice are penultimate dishes. Desserts, including soy sauce and mirin ice creams, seem superfluous after these.

Brushstroke offers two eight-course menus (one is vegetarian) and a ten-course dinner. With the exception of sashimi, most dishes are cooked. The sommelier will seduce you with terrific wine and sake suggestions, but begin with a haunting tarragon-shiso-gin-lime cocktail. Searching for a sushi-only experience? Try Ichimura, a boîte secreted in a corner of Brushstroke with its own master. **RG & MW**

"The dishes, gorgeously plated on handmade Japanese stoneware, flow like parts of a symphony."

Time Out

⊡ Delectable morsels—pork cheek in a cider reduction with green apple puree.

Roberta's and Blanca | Sister restaurants in Brooklyn
offering contrasting yet equally worthwhile experiences

Location New York **Signature dish** Grilled Mangalitsa collar (at Roberta's); Aged beef drizzled with *vino cotto* (at Blanca) | 🟢🟢

"Roberta's is one of New York's most deeply satisfying Italian-American restaurants."

bloomberg.com

⬆ The distinctive exterior of Roberta's.

While not Brooklyn's first grunge restaurant, Roberta's is the stylistic archetype: ugly cinderblock building; iffy neighborhood, desolate streets now turning hot; semi-trailers clogging lumpy roads; concrete floor and exposed infrastructure; multilevel vegetable garden; uncomfortable picnic tables; lousy lighting; tattooed waitstaff; no reservations; and long waits. It's the ultimate locavore hipster joint—but with great food that makes getting here akin to a treasure hunt.

Roberta's is famed for its pizzas. They change often and, if you must, try "Speckenwolf" (smoked prosciutto, oregano, mushrooms, onions, and mozzarella) or "Amatriciana" (tomato, pecorino, guanciale, onion, chili). Instead, though, eschew the pizza and start with an impeccable salad (romaine, candied walnuts, pecorino, mint; or broccoli, kale, kohlrabi, anchovy), then move to the "Kitchen" dishes: boudin noir, pumpkin, buttermilk, pumpkin butter; striped bass, chestnuts, romanesco sauce; squid ink garganelli, eggplant, tomato, shiso. All have fresh, zinging flavors that mentally shift you into sync with the decor. Suddenly you ask, "Why can't all restaurants look like this?"

The wine list brims with obscurities and, in the spirit of adventure, ask your waiter about "orange wines." Attached to Roberta's is a sleek, separate restaurant called Blanca, open Wednesday through Saturday. Perched on a cushy stool at a twelve-seat counter, customers are served twenty or so tasting courses from a vast open kitchen. The food tends to be minimalist but with sharp flavors. The chef, Carlo Mirarchi, explores interesting combinations of textures, and adores well-aged meat and poultry, so there's a certain funk to many of his dishes that will reward sophisticated palates. Reservations are difficult because the restaurant books out for a month in a single day. **RG & MW**

Katz's Delicatessen |
A legendary New York deli

Location New York **Signature dish** Pastrami on rye with mustard | ❺❺

New York's Lower East Side used to be crammed with Jewish delicatessen, but out-migration and gentrification have pretty much eliminated them. If you don't know what true delis were like, journey to Houston Street for some living history.

Katz's has been in the Dell family for more than 125 years, serving pretty much the same smoked and cured meats. It is currently run by young Jake Dell, who left medical school to keep this icon alive. These days, its customers comprise an expanding crowd of tourists, hipsters, aging Jews from another era, and New Yorkers who understand what the real thing is.

On entering, each person is given a ticket. Don't lose yours or it will set you back a fair bit of cash. Ignore the hot dogs, knishes, or even corned beef, and head straight for the sharp-knived chap who carves the pastrami. In front of you is a tip cup. Ignore that, too, and instead observe how great pastrami is trimmed and sliced by hand—never by machine—something your average suburban "deli" can't do.

Pastrami is sometimes made from the same cut as corned beef, but strictly speaking it should come from the navel end of the brisket. It is brined, coated with a mind-boggling complexity of spices, smoked, and then steamed into succulence. You could assume that Meg Ryan's ecstatic reaction in *When Harry Met Sally*, which was filmed here, was induced by pastrami.

You need nothing on this impeccable sandwich except perhaps a dab of mustard and Katz's legendary sour pickles and tomatoes. If you are the type of person who can't resist deli combination sandwiches, take a flyer and top your pastrami with a scoop of chopped liver. Eat it slowly and savor history. The carver will have punched your ticket. Pay the cashier as you leave. **RG & MW**

Del Posto | A grand Italian
restaurant worthy of its reputation

Location New York **Signature dish** 100-layer lasagna *alla piastra* | ❺❺❺❺

In 2008, when grunge dominated restaurant designs, Del Posto opened with expanses of mahogany and marble, a central staircase, swashbuckling balconies, and a grand piano. But its the food that makes Del Posto, owned by restaurateurs Joe and Lidia Bastianich and Mario Batali, *The New York Times*'s only four-star Italian restaurant, with a Michelin star to boot.

Parties of up to four may dine à la carte, but other groupings must choose between tasting menus. Guests choose their antipasti, main courses, and desserts, and the table votes on two pastas, which are served to everyone. Before that, there's an avalanche of bites such as polenta and salt cod, crisped buffalo mozzarella, or chickpea fritters with tomato powder.

"A place to sit in luxury and drink Barolo, while eating food that bewilders and thrills."

The New York Times

Chef Mark Lander's pastas are unerringly excellent. Spaghetti with Jonah crab and jalapeños sounds un-Italian, but order it, along with orecchiette and lamb neck ragu with nubbins of orange carrots, toasted rye crumbs, and a spritz of tangerine oil. Their 100-layered lasagna is mightily famous.

The show continues with seasonal main courses like lobster with artichoke, almond, and basil, or Apician spiced duck with broiled endive, hazelnuts, and sour cherries. Desserts and petits fours from Brooks Headley are exquisitely thought provoking. Many dinner items appear on their prix-fixe lunch menu, which is a less expensive way to enjoy the experience. **RG & MW**

Serendipity 3 | Party central on the Upper East Side

Location New York   **Signature dish** Frrrozen hot chocolate | $$

"Serendipity 3 is one of the few places kids like that doesn't have a ride."

New York Magazine

⬆ Serendipity 3's trademark Frrrozen hot chocolate.

According to the dictionary, "serendipity," a made-up word, means "accidentally stumbling upon the pleasantly unexpected," and "camp" (as defined by Susan Sontag) means to "dethrone the serious" in an outrageous manner. This New York restaurant, going strong on East 60th Street since 1954, is both serendipitous and camp.

Serendipity 3 may have launched the notion of furnishing a restaurant with Victorian cast-offs, with lots and lots of frivolous stuff piled on top of other stuff. The menus are the size of a football field—with playful names such as "Frrrozen Hot Chocolate," "Apricot Smush," "Chicken Flambé," and "Foot-Long Hot Dogs" making sure customers get the point. Customers tend to comprise celebrities and Upper East Siders with their children, who contribute to the atmosphere of a perpetual birthday party, regardless of age.

The menu contains many old-time favorites—french toasted cream cheese sandwich with strawberries and apricot preserves; hamburger with caviar, sour cream, and cucumbers—along with middle-American staples such as nachos and chicken wings. But people come here for the desserts, specifically the famous frozen hot chocolate, the recipe for which, legend has it, was withheld from Jackie Kennedy (although it is in Serendipity's cookbook and for sale as a take-home kit). It is a spectacular, shakelike concoction designed for sharing with your tablemates. This is also true of the extravagant ice cream assemblages, including a massive banana split. The lemon icebox pie is also worth trying.

Unfortunately, you cannot make dessert-only reservations, and lines can be quite long, so you need to be patient. But, as a memento, you can buy the famous Hebrew eye-chart dish towel on the way out. **RG & MW**

Eleven Madison Park | Witty irony and gastronomic adventures

Location New York   **Signature dish** Glazed Normandy duck | ❺❺❺❺

Three Michelin stars and four from *The New York Times* are reasons enough to go to Eleven Madison Park. But proprietor Will Guidara and chef Daniel Humm believe four-hour tasting dinners can weary both mind and palate, so they have applied hijinks to their inventive 15-course meals.

Smoked sturgeon arrives under a bell jar swirling with smoke, accompanied by caviar and bagel crumbs, referencing New York's iconic brunch. An acolyte cook then appears at your table with ultra-orange carrots, and puts them through a meat grinder; tossed with smoked bluefish, mustard oil, pickled quail egg, grated horseradish, and sea salt, you have faux steak tartare. Venison is a study in black: a covered black pan concealing a charred, hollowed baguette that, top removed, reveals a venison fillet—theatrics that bring to mind David Copperfield pulling rabbits from hats. The restaurant pokes fun at locavorism, which it actually takes extremely seriously, as most ingredients come from farms in the region. A cheese course called "Greensward" is a basket packed with pretzel bread, mustard, grapes, and a bottle of craft beer—presumably a picnic in the park.

The waiters' patter and trickster presentations (they talk of "the dialogue of the dining experience") takes getting used to, but consider the oyster: bulgur wheat, sorrel, and frozen grape mignonette sound like impossible soul mates to the single bivalve in a bowl of ice, but the briny, crunchy, sweet-sour, and icy contrasts are electrifying. The lobster poached in lemon butter is voluptuous, the richness perfectly balanced by Brussels sprouts (pickled, shaved, pureed, and caramelized), while the duck, dry-aged for ten to fourteen days and glazed with lavender honey and Szechuan peppercorns, is truly memorable. Eleven Madison Park is at the top of the restaurant heap and reflective of New York's considerable dining prowess. **RG & MW**

> *"Inspired, coherent, and downright delicious … and, yes, the most fun."*
>
> *Time Out*

⬆ The restaurant's stunning art deco dining room.

Jean-Georges | World-class cuisine in ultra-chic surroundings

Location New York   **Signature dish** Caramelized scallops with cauliflower | 🄢🄢🄢🄢🄢

"Prepare to be open-mouthed … Nothing you encounter will fail to awe."

New York Magazine

⬆ The white, light, and effortlessly elegant dining room.

➡ Classic Jean-Georges—egg caviar.

Jean-Georges, the eponymous restaurant of world-class chef Jean-Georges Vongerichten, is the essence of sophistication and gastronomic marksmanship. The cuisine is uniquely his, melding French, Alsatian, and Asian influences. For decades, this superstar chef has been a pilot light of creativity, resulting in signature restaurants around the globe. Yet this exquisite jewel, located in Trump Tower on Central Park West, shines brightest.

Dinners in the ultra-chic dining room are expensive, but they are edible dream works. A genius at vibrantly combining ingredients that in lesser hands might jangle taste buds, Jean-Georges evokes confident suspense in diners. Caramelized scallops with cauliflower and caper-raisin emulsion, for example, has been widely copied but never surpassed. Any rendition of squab is worth having, and if garlic soup with frog legs is available, do not hesitate. Other intensely interesting dishes include sea urchin, jalapeño, and yuzu; shrimp with baby artichokes, lemon fennel emulsion, and paprika oil; sea trout and oyster tartare; and licorice-braised sweetbreads with ginger.

Service is a performance art at Jean-Georges. There are many bottled riches here, but the sommelier will guide you at any price level. Men must wear jackets, preserving the gestalt of the restaurant's well-heeled clientele. Yet, unlike in many other status places in New York City, dining at Jean-Georges is neither a stuffy nor a quasi-religious experience. It is wonderfully comfortable, and you may sit up straight or "lean in" to the magical vibes.

The front room, called Nougatine, is a more casual bar-café serving breakfast, lunch, and dinner. Its noonday meal and Sunday brunch are among New York's rare bargains and, weather permitting, its menu is served on the lovely terrace overlooking Central Park. **RG & MW**

The Breslin | Hip hotel
gastropub with scrumptious food

Location New York   **Signature dish** Lamb burger
with feta, cumin mayo, and thrice-cooked fries | **$$**

Yes, it will be crowded. No, they take no reservations. And, yes, you will wait in the well-beaten bar or the adjoining lobby of the Ace Hotel, where packs of twenty-somethings stare into every known electronic device. Yes, you want to eat here. The Breslin is April Bloomfield's encore to the Spotted Pig, the famed West Village gastropub. Here she has uplifted the concept of fatty, salty, notoriously not-so-healthy British pub food by making the stuff taste amazingly scrumptious.

There is fish on the menu, but most mains are aggressively macho. The lamb burger, coarse and slightly gamey, is topped with feta cheese and cumin mayonnaise, and comes with thrice-cooked fries. A

"You may need to pace yourself—and save half that pig's foot for lunch ..."

Time Out

---

signature dish of pig's foot for two is, in truth, the skin of the foot packed with porky things and deep fried.

Venturesome groups book the Chef's Table for an entire well-burnished suckling pig that is neatly dismembered for customers to pick out every last morsel of meat by hand. It comes with Caesar salad and anchovy croutons, Brussels sprouts with apple chutney, baby carrots, duck fat-fried potatoes, and two desserts for the survivors.

The place is dimly lit, assorted junk store memorabilia and animal taxidermy covers the walls, and there is a party mood. The wine list is good, but it is best to focus on the curated selection of draft beers. **RG & MW**

Ilili Restaurant | Modernist
Lebanese food by an acclaimed chef

Location New York   **Signature dish** Brussels sprouts
with grapes, fig jam, walnuts, and mint yogurt | **$$$**

Here is Lebanese food created with the same finesse and style as any three-Michelin-star French restaurant, and served in elegant surroundings on New York's Fifth Avenue. Chef and co-owner Philippe Massoud escaped the ravages of war-torn Beirut to study in New York and then traveled to cook in Paris, Marbella, and back again to Lebanon. Massoud grew up in his family's swank seaside hotel, the Coral Beach, where he first hung out in, and then fell in love with, the kitchen. His food exemplifies all of this.

Lebanese classics such as chicken taouk (a type of shawarma) are reimagined, the breast skewered and served with sumac garlic whip and fines herbs salad. Hummus gets turned into a royal main course with lobster, *honshimeji*, and oyster mushrooms. Massoud's favorite, steak tartare, is presented as three-dimensional architecture; it virtually melts in the mouth.

Massoud's mezze are among the best in the city: *Mouhamara* (eggplant with sundried peppers and pomegranate molasses), *chankleesh* (feta cheese with onions, tomato, and za'atar spices); *fattoush* (a pitta bread salad); and beef shawarma are first rate. But riffs on the classics really inspire: *kebab kerez* (lamb and beef meatballs with cherry sauce, kataifi pastry, and scallions); grilled octopus with lamb belly "pastrami," fennel, grapefruit and ramp vinaigrette; succulent lamb chops with *za'atar salsa verde* and roasted tomatoes. You'll want the mixed grill-for-two for yourself, with one of the restaurant's extraordinary wines from Lebanon's Bekaa Valley. You won't find this array of Lebanese vintages on any list in the city. Desserts prove to be as riveting as the rest of Massoud's evocative menu. The Ilili candy bar—chocolate ganache, fig caramel, pistachio, and dulce de leche—is a must. **RG & MW**

Gramercy Tavern | A standard-bearer of
New American dining and elegance

Location New York   **Signature dish** Smoked trout with cipollini puree
and pickled onions | ❺❺❺❺

When Danny Meyer opened Gramercy Tavern in 1994,
he introduced a style of restaurant that would be
copied countless times. If familiar today, the Tavern's
decor—brimming with folksy antiques—and its
hyper-seasonal menu were once revolutionary. Still
performed with genuine enthusiasm almost twenty
years later, Meyer's paradigm still seduces. The
Tavern's sustained success—and its Michelin star—
can be attributed to chef Michael Anthony and the
nearby Union Square Farmer's Market.

Menus change frequently, but the best dishes pair
straightforward classics with unexpected accessories.
Sweet cipollini puree beds unadorned house-smoked
trout, while bulgur and pistachios sneak into a
textbook beef tartare. A "down home" dish of pasture-
raised chicken and sausage, flourished with smoked
onion, exceeds the sum of its very chicken parts.

For the most creative path, opt for the vegetable
tasting menu, containing delights such as "Barely
Touched Vegetables" with olive, pine nut, lemon
ricotta, and sungold tomatoes. Ordered à la carte,
these earthy delights can make a lighter meal for
omnivores and vegetarians alike.

Do not overlook the tavern's front room, a more
casual space that beckons both locals and tourists.
Passers-by stop in for a glass of Champagne, linger for
a few small plates, or even opt for the tavern tasting
menu with beer pairings. Wherever you dine, save
room for artisanal cheese or a dessert. Individual apple
pie with vanilla ice cream is a specialty.

Service is ultra-professional but friendly in the
Meyer tradition, and thoughtful touches, such as tiny
take-home *bomboniere* ("favors") make Gramercy
Tavern a perennial favorite for celebrating any of life's
milestones. Its American pastoralism still soothes,
even if its traits can now be found citywide. **LM**

*"This chic tavern gives
classic American cuisine
a contemporary twist."*

Gayot

⬆ The vegetable tasting menu includes creative
   dishes such as this salad.

Momofuku Noodle Bar | Life-changing ramen for those who wait

Location New York **Signature dish** Momofuku ramen | 🟢🟢

On a stretch of First Avenue in Manhattan's East Village, Momofuku Noodle Bar announces itself with a line snaking down the block. Only those who order, in advance and online, whole-fried chicken dinners secure reserved tables. And so, hip locals and food-focused tourists wait patiently to taste the origins of David Chang's Korean-inflected culinary empire.

The Momofuku brand spreads as far as Toronto and Sydney. It includes the two-Michelin-starred *omakase*-style (leave the selection to the chef) restaurant Momofuku Ko; a magazine for the food-obsessed literati, *Lucky Peach* (which is what "momofuku" means); Momofuku Ssäm Bar; and Momofuku Milk Bar.

Founded in 2004, Chang's Momofuku noodle bar peddles simple-sounding dishes in unapologetically cramped quarters. A long bar, a few communal tables, and ubiquitous pale wood set a convivial scene. Although the menu fluctuates, a few pivotal dishes

are fixed. Chang has perfected the components that make Momofuku ramen worthy of its accolades: tender pork shoulder, fat slices of belly, custom-made alkaline noodles in an intense broth, and a perfect, slow-poached egg elevate this collegiate staple. Equally deserving of praise are the steamed pork buns, balanced with cucumber and lashings of sweet hoisin, which have inspired impersonations all over New York. The chicken dinners, intended for four to eight people, include two whole birds fried Korean style and Southern style, accompanied by *moo shu* pancakes, bibb lettuce, four sauces, and vegetables.

Momofuku's seats may be uncomfortable, its service brusquely efficient, and its soundtrack high decibel, but with his tiny shop, Chang introduced New York to a new kind of casual eating, one that is both humble and high end. **LM**

⬆ Effortlessly hip dining from David Chang.

Momofuko Ko | Rock-star chef David Chang's culinary triumph

Location New York　**Signature dish** Shaved foie gras with lychee | ❺❺❺❺

You can only make reservations online, and they go quickly. You cannot book a party of three. You cannot find the place. It seats twelve at a cramped counter. There are no menus and no substitutions. And no photos allowed. You should definitely go.

Ko's has one of New York's most exciting tasting menus—eighteen courses at lunch, where a meal stretches to four hours, fewer at dinner. You rarely see owner David Chang because he is tending his wider empire or investigating all things *umami* in a nearby laboratory, but you'll interact with several chefs, as they prepare and explain your cavalcade of dishes. Far Eastern ingredients abound in the kitchen, but none of the food tastes "Asian"—Chang calls it American, but nothing like you would imagine.

Be ready to relish a parade of the following dishes: Beets, crisp black trumpet mushrooms, raw horseradish, and grains of paradise; snapper, rye seeds and pickled radish; charred mackerel,

teeny rice balls, pickled shallots, and grated yuzu rind. Then might come raw oyster with smoked jalapeño foam; lobster with lobster sauce and yogurt with white chocolate; and shiitake tortelloni with buckwheat and brown butter-shiitake tea that will lift you off your seat.

And it does not stop there: sepia on the plancha with fennel, black olive seaweed paste, and nori powder; *chawan mushi* (a savory egg custard) overlaid with smoked dashi, raw shallots, and caviar; and leg of lamb slow-roasted with onion, chili, mint, basil, and mushroom powder, served with gentle cucumber kimchee. For dessert, try the Concord grape sorbet and white chocolate ganache. Each dish had a singular complexity that changes with each wonderful bite and each contains long flavors. Menus change frequently. **RG & MW**

⬆ Steamed pork is just one of many delicacies on offer.

Oceana | A classy celebration of fish and seafood near Rockefeller Center

Location New York **Signature dish** Taro-wrapped dorade | $$

"Always a gratifying spot for indulging in spectacular seafood . . ."

Michelin Guide

↑ Chef Pollinger at work in Oceana.

Oceana is a sprawling, modern seafood restaurant owned by the Livanos family, with Ben Pollinger, one of New York's youngest Michelin-starred chefs, at the helm. It has maintained its high-wire level of fish cookery and fine dining since its inception (in another location) in 1992. Huge windows and white drapery add warmth to the bright, sleek space and help you imagine ocean breezes wafting by.

Ben Pollinger brings formidable training under storied chefs Alain Ducasse and Gray Kunz. If you are lucky enough to snag the glass-roomed chef's table adjoining the kitchen, let Pollinger orchestrate a multi-course meal that might become a once-in-a-lifetime experience.

Oceana literally roams the world's oceans for its globally inflected menu. Devotees enjoy cumin-dusted Alaskan king salmon, crispy taro-wrapped dorade with coconut milk curry, and General Tso's lobster over black sticky rice. Tableside preparations for two include whole roasted branzino stuffed with mushrooms, spinach, olives, and lemon, and meltingly tender filet mignon. To begin the feast, order one of Oceana's towering shellfish extravaganzas and watch heads turn.

Up front, there's a capacious room with a raw bar and a drinking bar. A menu of small plates, highly popular at lunch and pre-theater, allows you to graze contentedly. Ditto the selection of oysters—usually a dozen varieties from distinctive shores. The bar itself specializes in gins—thirty at last count, which may be some sort of admirable record.

Architectural desserts provide sweet ballast, including pastry chef Jason Chan's irresistible, knockout Dulcey & Dark Chocolate Brownie Soufflé with malt ice cream and chocolate pearls. As a souvenir, you can purchase a copy of Chef Pollinger's cookbook, *School of Fish*. A meal at Oceana, after all, is an education. **RG & MW**

Red Rooster Harlem | Fab brunch in Harlem's emerging dining district

Location New York · **Signature dish** "Fried yardbird" | ❸❺

Marcus Samuelson's Red Rooster restaurant, near the southern border of Harlem, is a thriving social bridge between New York's diverse populations, with an affable ethnic mix in the clientele.

Previously head chef at the Scandinavian restaurant Aquavit, Samuelson designs menus that are also vivid bridges across cultures. You'll find ingredients from his native Ethiopia as well as from Sweden, where he grew up. There are dishes that reflect Harlem's gastronomy, with accents from the African continent and favorites from America's South.

The restaurant seems smaller than its notoriety suggests. There's a bright, lively watering hole up front, its back bar sheltering a comfy dining room behind. Ginny's, a speakeasy downstairs, features live music at night and a Sunday morning gospel buffet brunch at 10.30 A.M. and 12.30 P.M. There's gospel music upstairs, too, but no reservations. Yes, the A Train stops nearby. "Dress sharp," says the restaurant.

Favorite appetizers include fried chicken and waffles with chicken liver butter and fried green tomatoes with bacon and buttermilk dressing. An old-fashioned main course of chop suey isn't exactly a Chinatown rendition, but Helga's meatballs with lingonberries and braised cabbage will remind you of Scandinavia. Chili-lacquered pork chop, jerk chicken, fish and grits, and a rendition of fried chicken termed "Fried Yardbird" all represent the area's crosscurrents of flavors. If you're really hungry, try the Rooster noodles, a big bowl of ramen made with teff noodles, head-on shrimp, crab, and pork belly—teff being an indigenous high-protein grain of Ethiopia.

There are wines on tap and cocktails by the pitcher, including a negroni made with fig- and pear-infused bourbon, Campari, and sweet vermouth. Red Rooster's success has encouraged more new restaurants to open, so its area has the bustling vibe of an emerging dining district. **RG & MW**

"[A] jumping Harlem joint ... the scene's lively and the people-watching superb."

Zagat

⬆ "Fried yardbird"—Red Rooster's take on fried chicken.

Il Buco Alimentari e Vineria | A taste of Rome in the East Village

Location New York **Signature dish** Short ribs | $$

There is a lovely place like this near Campo de' Fiori in Rome—grocery-café up front, dining room below—but at Il Buco Alimentari e Vineria you save the airfare. Entry is through a food shop filled with spectacular breads, cured meats, and prepared foods, all homemade, and a scattering of small tables. Your nose will be lured by a wood-burning oven to a rustic dining space below. Both rooms will be crowded and noisy. The food will be as marvelous as your best memories of trattoria dining in Italy.

At dinner, there are starters like grilled quail with unexpected accompaniments, such as charred cherries and Sicilian pistachios; homemade ricotta with additions like Persian cucumber and white anchovies; and boards of the restaurant's own salumi.

Recommended mains include slow-roasted short ribs on a wooden plank with olives, celery, walnuts, and fresh horseradish, or the porchetta with raw peaches, charred onions, and pickled scapes.

With their excellent breadbasket, these two courses are filling, but do not skip the pasta. Look for pasta with *bottarga* (dried tuna roe); or with almonds, anchovies, capers, and tomatoes; or with house-cured salt cod, Meyer lemon, and fennel.

For morning people, there is *torta pasqualina* (a deep-fried pie with kale, eggs, and Parmesan); or porchetta and eggs with arugula, salsa verde and clothbound cheddar. Lunchtime enticements might include salt cod carpaccio with Meyer lemon, chili, and paper-thin flatbread; short rib sandwich with Gorgonzola and sweet-and-sour onions; or roast poussin with shishito peppers and pancetta. The proprietress, Donna Lennard, also owns Il Buco restaurant around the corner, but this one, known as the "alimentari" (delicatessen), is where to dine. A brief, intelligent wine list is full of lovely surprises. **RG & MW**

↑ A seriously appetizing taste of Italy at this deli/eatery.

Le Bernardin | Exquisite seafood in an upscale setting

Location New York **Signature dish** Yellowfin tuna with foie gras | ❺❺❺❺

In 1986, a stunning brother-and-sister import from Paris, Le Bernardin, turned American notions of how to cook seafood upside down. Their menu was built around a parade of raw and barely warmed fish, with gentle heat applied to its cooked dishes. Fabled chef Gilbert Le Coze died in 1994, but his sister Maguy carried on with renowned seafood chef Eric Ripert. Originally French to the core, Ripert's food has expanded geographically, incorporating accents from Southeast Asia to the Andes. His cooking is not duplicated anywhere in New York.

Le Bernardin is both formal and upscale in a city where almost all new restaurants tilt toward casual. In fact, a recent redesign is even more upscale than before. You will need a fat wallet to dine here, and men need to wear jackets.

Menus change often but are always filled with provocative delights. From the "Almost Raw" category, do not miss the thinly pounded tuna with foie gras. Or, if you do not mind paying a supplement, order shaved geoduck clam and caviar with a wasabi-citrus mousseline. Under "Barely Touched," there is octopus charred on a plancha with green olive and black garlic emulsion. And under "Lightly Cooked," the wild striped bass with Bhutanese red rice, green papaya salad, and a ginger-red wine sauce shows off Ripert's global curiosity—as does red snapper with charred green tomatoes and Baja shrimp sauce.

For a more casual experience, try the restaurant's elegant lounge, where an à la carte menu of delicious small plates offers wonderful choices—including a celebrated smoked salmon croque monsieur with golden Osetra caviar. Le Bernardin has three Michelin stars and has been awarded four stars by *The New York Times* five times—it could not be ranked any higher. **RG & MW**

⬆ Le Bernardin is one of the world's premier restaurants.

La Grenouille |

An elegant bastion of French cuisine

Location New York **Signature dish** *Quenelles de brochet* with caviar | ❺❺❺❺

Anthropological preservationists ought to sequester the DNA of this last-of-its-kind restaurant, for its formal "Le" and "La" competitors have all gone extinct. This is reason enough to visit La Grenouille, a bastion of classic, elegant French food on East 52nd Street for more than fifty years.

The excellent food resides in a time warp of floral bouquets and couture-clad clientele. This is the food Escoffier cooked: sweetbreads, frog legs, kidneys flamed in cognac, Dover sole filleted tableside, oxtails in red wine, legendary soufflés to order, and the Lyonnais classic *quenelles de brochet*—pike in a shellfish sauce topped with caviar. The restaurant has ignored every culinary trend, and has ignored the cult

---

"The dish is executed perfectly … a masterpiece devoid of irony or deconstructionist camp."

The New York Times

---

of celebrity chefdom. The person in charge is the owner, Charles Masson, who will be on the floor along with a brigade of captains, waiters, and attendees.

La Grenouille is celebrated for its extraordinary flowers and lighting, and each table has a peach-hued lamp to flatter the clientele's complexions, and to reflect their genuine and significant jewels. Men must wear jackets and smartphones logically are banished. There's a social hierarchy here, so regular guests are more equal than others when it comes to seating. At a more informal upstairs bar, there's an à la carte menu where some hors d'oeuvres and Champagne comprise an excellent order and no jackets are needed. **RG & MW**

Keens Steakhouse |

Old New York at its best

Location New York **Signature dish** Mutton chops | ❺❺❺

The part of Manhattan called "the West 30s" near Herald Square includes the Empire State Building, the flagship Macy's department store, and what is known as "the Garment District," where most of New York's fashion houses are found. Although this zone has an older feeling than most of midtown, it is almost entirely of the twentieth century apart from Keens, a robust survivor from 1885, when this area was the heart of the theater district.

When smoking was still part of the dining experience in New York, Keens was famous as a place where regular clients could have their own clay pipes stored between visits. Specially trained boys would deliver the pipe to the customer and then retrieve it as the bill was being paid. Today, the visitor can see more than 88,000 pipes that remain from former times.

Keens has several wood-paneled rooms and is comfortably spacious in a city full of restaurants that stack diners cheek by jowl. For the most part, the menu at Keens Steakhouse (which, until recently, was called Keens Chophouse) recalls a time of Falstaffian indulgence in meat, ale, and whiskey, favored by a clientele that included presidents, athletes, singers, actors, furriers, bankers, and even cowboys who found their way to town. Executive chef Bill Rodgers does not rest on the kitchen's past laurels, but faithfully upholds the care in the selection and preparation of ingredients before they are cooked.

Various cuts of top-quality beef, plus lamb chops, lobster, oysters, salmon, and Dover sole are fixtures on the menu, and all are expertly cooked. Desserts include key lime pie, crème brûlée, and dark chocolate mousse. But people travel great distances to Keens specifically to order the mutton chops. They might seem like a culinary anachronism to some, but they are, in fact, sensational. **FP**

Great N.Y. Noodle Town | Authentic Hong Kong-style noodles and roast meats in one of Chinatown's finest

Location New York   **Signature dish** Roast pork wonton noodle soup | $

Approach Great N.Y. Noodle Town from Bayard Street and you'll be beckoned by one of Chinatown's most tempting restaurant window displays: suspended from steel hooks is a flock of bronzed roast ducks and chickens, fat strips of *char siu* (barbecued pork) and burnished ribs, and glittering sides of whole pig.

Manning this meaty station is a cleaver-wielding fellow who expertly hacks up the wares and transfers them to waiting bowls and plates to be combined with noodles in myriad delicious ways. The noodle soups, with rich broth and thin egg noodles, are one of the city's best bargain lunches. You won't have to choose between the noodles and the ruffly, whole-shrimp-filled wontons—prices are so reasonable, you can have both. No soup for you? Fat noodles, thin noodles, wheat noodles, and rice noodles come steamed, stir-fried, or deep-fried, with all manner of meat, fish, and vegetables. And meat can be had on a bed of white rice.

Noodle Town has an extensive seafood menu as well. The salt-baked shrimp, squid, whole fish, and scallops are all delicious, although they are not baked but lightly battered, deep fried, and then dusted generously with salt. Among the vegetable choices, sautéed pea shoots (the vines and leaves of the pea plant) and *choy sum* (Chinese flowering cabbage) are highly recommended.

There's no lingering at this bustling establishment, modest in the extreme. You may have to wait for a table during peak noodle-slurping times, or you may wind up sharing a table with a Chinese family. (In which case, pay close attention: this is an opportunity to see items that are not on the printed English menu.) And if you find yourself with a yen for noodles on Thanksgiving or Christmas, or in the early hours, it's open every day of the year, until 4 A.M. **EM**

"*Noodletown lives up to its billing ... with expertly prepared Cantonese cooking.*"

New York Magazine

⊤ Roast pork wonton noodle soup—the perfect pick-me-up after a night on the town.

The Four Seasons Restaurant | A bastion of power

dining in a majestic landmark setting

Location New York **Signature dish** Crisp farmhouse duck for two | ❸❸❸

"… the town's power menagerie gather along the banquettes like sea lions on a rock."

New York Magazine

⤴ The bar with its rippling brass "curtain."

This quintessential New York restaurant is as grand and modern as it was when it opened in 1959. Its soaring interiors, designed by Philip Johnson and William Pahlman, are landmarked, as is the Seagram Building in which it is housed. Diners sit in the very same Brno chairs used by titans of industry, by literati, glitterati, and diplomati; the same tableware is in the Museum of Modern Art.

There are two restaurants, the Grill Room and the Pool Room. You should lunch in the former, where the food is simultaneously straightforward and sparkling, and dine in the latter, where meals tend to be showier. There's no bad seat in either.

The Four Seasons was launched by the influential restaurateur Joe Baum, and is now run by Alex von Bidder and Julian Niccolini. At the outset, menus, tablecloths, plantings, and uniforms changed each season (hence the name), which proved financially illogical. Locavorism was invented here before anyone knew the word: a mycologist foraged for mushrooms, cherry tomatoes, and baby avocados, and snow peas were introduced along with other then exotic ingredients and preparations.

Sophisticated seasonality still informs menus full of classics: perfect snapper, shatteringly crisp duck for two, bison filet with foie gras, impeccable Dover sole, all with perfectly balanced accompaniments. Starters such as crispy oysters in a yellow pepper sauce, spectacular burrata, and hamachi sashimi with watermelon are not to be missed.

The scale may be monumental, but generous table spacing provides intimacy. At night, dancing lights reflect from the pool and off the rippling brass curtains to produce an effect not duplicated anywhere—especially when the room is decorated for Christmas. **RG & MW**

Ippudo | Authentic Japanese ramen in a fun environment

Location New York **Signature dish** Akamaru modern ramen | $

In the last decade, the lowly foam cup of instant noodles has risen to an art form as ramen restaurants opened in droves in New York. You can start a serious argument regarding which one is "best." No such place exists, of course, but Ippudo is certainly among the top four or five ramen places in the city and probably the most fun.

Ramen vary from region to region in Japan; Ippudo's come from the southern island of Fukuoka, where people line up in the dark of night at little stands and carts for bowls of soup and noodles, which they slurp sitting on bridge chairs, rocks, or tree stumps. As in Fukuoka, Ippudo, an offshoot of a major Japanese chain, uses copious quantities of long-simmered pork bones to build their deep, rich, dense broth (called *tonkotsu*)—slightly nutty and flecked with a bit of fat—along with some unctuous pork and shreds of cabbage.

The place is rather large, energetically decorated, and buzzing with vitality. Chefs shout "welcome" from the open kitchen. The signature dish, Akamaru Modern, is their basic broth enlivened with scallions, soy, pork belly, fragrant garlic oil, and some miso paste for a blast of *umami*. The skinny noodles will be perfectly al dente and have the proper elastic snap to them. You can top this superlative bowl of soup-and-noodles with more braised pork belly or with a salted-boiled egg or a soft-poached egg.

Ippudo has other good things to eat. The pork buns are exemplary, as is the yellowtail sashimi (dinner only). There are two Ippudos in town, but the original one in the East Village is considered the better of the two. It takes no reservations, and a youngish crowd happily lines up for up to forty minutes at peak times. Parties of two may be seated at a communal table, and slurping with neighbors is no bad thing. **RG & MW**

Orso | A celebrity haven specializing in Sardinian cooking

Location New York **Signature dish** Grilled tuna with braised fennel | $$

Like Joe Allen, its sister restaurant next door, Orso has a clientele of show business people and those who love them. Orso has fewer tables and feels more exclusive, making it a haven for star actors and media people who enjoy the casual but tasty Italian cooking.

While there are dishes from many parts of Italy, the kitchen is especially adept at the lusty but refined cooking of Sardinia. Pizzas might be made of *carta da musica*—thin, crispy sheets of bread that Sardinians liken to music paper. It might be topped with fennel and *bottarga* (cured fish roe) dried eggs of tuna or mullet, another Sardinian specialty. *Malloreddus,* small chewy gnocchi, comes with a sauce of three types of wild mushroom and pecorino cheese.

"Fun late at night when the theater people come… after they have removed the make-up."

The New York Times

Main courses lean toward beef, veal, chicken, duck, and pork. Especially delicious is quail stuffed with sausage, broccoli rabe, pine nuts, corn, and farro, finished with a marsala sauce. Just as tasty, and much lighter, is the *tonno*—a wedge of grilled yellowfin tuna with braised fennel, couscous, tomato, and lemon.

Despite all the meat, vegetarians can do remarkably well at Orso, whether it is salad or pizza with vegetable and cheese toppings, or main courses made of a series of *contorni*, the side dishes made of everything green as well as with potatoes. Unmissable are the cannellini, sauteed white beans from Tuscany combined with rosemary and olive oil, made more savory when you add freshly ground black pepper. **FP**

Nobu | Archetype of a fusion empire that covers the world

Location New York **Signature dish** Black cod with miso | $$$

"... course after course of thrilling creations announcing pure and clean flavors."

Gayot

[↑] A glamorous, sophisticated dining experience.

[→] Black cod—sweet-salty and served with miso.

Toiling in an obscure strip mall in Los Angeles, Nobu Matsuhisa revolutionized how raw fish is served in the United States. He was brought to the dormant corner of Hudson and Franklin Streets in Tribeca in 1994 by actor Robert De Niro, whose film empire was housed around the corner, and Drew Nieporent, the famed restaurateur. The rest is fusion history: ceviche meets sashimi meets crudo.

In truth, Nobu imported well-established Peruvian techniques for serving raw fish that he learned while working in Lima. Visit that city's *cebicherias*, and you'll find astounding varieties of raw fish and crustaceans served with electrifying sauces tangy with citrus, pungent with peppers, and fragrant with cilantro and other herbs—all of which Nobu filtered through the lens of a talented Japanese chef.

This first Nobu restaurant was designed by David Rockwell, and with its intimate scale, abstract tree forms, and superb lighting, it has an uncanny, almost "extra" spatial dimension. Subsequent Nobus have ballooned to circus dimensions, including the branch on West 57th Street.

Baffled by the strange-sounding dishes? Then ask for help because you definitely want things you don't normally eat. If there's a *tiradito* on the cold part of the menu, go for it—these are colorful and saucy Peruvian takes on raw fish. Also try the "new style sashimi," which is drizzled with hot olive oil before serving. Have the restaurant's go-to cooked dish—black cod (sablefish) with miso, a sweet-salty-unctuous recipe. Sea urchin tempura, "pasta" made of julienned squid, and *umami* sea bass are also all worth the trip. With theatrical design, vibrant sound, and multi-ethnic seafood, Nobu venues are the antithesis of the holy experiences offered by the best sushi bars where there's only fish to focus on. You're certain to have more fun here. **RG & MW**

Joe Allen | Join the Broadway Babies in a New York classic

Location New York **Signature dish** La Scala salad | $

On West 46th Street, known locally as Restaurant Row, you can flip back the pages of the calendar in your mind and picture yourself in the 1950s, with guys and dolls stopping for a Manhattan cocktail here and New York strip steak there. Or the 1980s, with a chorus line of hoofers and warblers waiting for that big break in a show on Broadway, two blocks away. To experience all of this today, go to Joe Allen, where supporting players rub shoulders with stars.

Since 1965, Joe Allen has been a New York classic. Food tastes like Mom makes. She might serve black bean soup, or shrimp cocktail to start, then bring meat loaf with mashed potatoes, calves' liver and onions, or smoked salmon and scrambled eggs.

"This timeless Theater District joint is still a magnet for show-biz types … après-theater stargazing."

Zagat

You will also find escargots, cassoulet, and steak tartare, throwbacks to a time when Restaurant Row was home to several bistros offering French home cooking. La Scala salad is an anachronism from when Italian-style food was exotic. This large bowl of diced salami, provolone cheese, iceberg lettuce, chickpeas, and red pepper is a favorite. Dessert might be a berry cobbler, banana cream pie, or watermelon ices.

Look at the long brick wall covered with framed posters of stars in Broadway shows. This is the "Bomb Wall," so called because the shows were flops. This visual admonition reminds theater people that very little is guaranteed in show business, which is why the comfort food at Joe Allen feels so good. **FP**

WD 50 | Art meets science on the Lower East Side

Location New York **Signature dish** Foie gras with anchovies and cocoa nibs | $$$$

Chef Wylie Dufresne, noted wizard of centrifuges, dehydrators, carbonators, and vacuum apparatus, is credited with bringing "molecular gastronomy" to New York. Housed in a former Lower East Side bodega with rec-room plywood decor, WD50 is a throwaway, but you are here for something else—to have your palate provoked, your eyes fooled, and your expectations baffled.

A thousand words describing Dufresne's avant garde cooking would leave you no further informed than what has just been said. Each unruly dish is about two bites, precisely enough for your mind and tastebuds to wrap themselves around the seemingly contradictory ingredients.

No one in town does this better. Consider a teeny starter of saffron-coconut ice cream studded with poppy seeds and topped with caviar. Redolent of saffron, the ice cream defies you to quibble about it living harmoniously with caviar, which indeed it does. A single sea scallop, having undergone microsurgery, is accompanied by a neat square of carrot raviolo filled with incredibly intense carrot ooze. Beneath, a granola wafts fragrances of a bazaar in Marrakech. A dish of foie gras-anchovy-tarragon-cocoa nibs is an amazing amalgam of disparates that unite in a surf-and-turf.

There are two menus here—a thirteen-course dinner of the crew's most recent innovations and a seven-course dinner of WD50's older favorites. The restaurant generally fills with thirty-somethings having fun dissecting the mysterious flavors. You can assemble your own mini-feast at the bar by ordering any two courses for a fixed price (additions extra). The mixologists will concoct complex cocktails that match what you're eating. You might find Pink Moon—gin, rosé vermouth, lemon, and violet oils—the most intriguing nontraditional Martini ever. **RG & MW**

Tanoreen | Color and flavor combine in this refined take on Middle Eastern home cooking in Brooklyn

Location New York **Signature dish** Eggplant Napoleon | $$

A city of immigrants, New York is home to a number of Middle Eastern enclaves, all of which are well-served by good restaurants. Tanoreen is something else entirely. Chef-owner Rawia Bishara was raised in the Galilee, where her mother blended traditional Palestinian dishes with Mediterranean cuisine. That was Bishara's inspiration. In 1998, she opened a ten-seat eatery in Bay Ridge, a neighborhood that started out Norwegian, became Italian (it provided the backdrop—and illuminated dance floor—for *Saturday Night Fever*), and now has a large Arab-speaking population.

As Bay Ridge's Middle Eastern roots expanded, so did Tanoreen, evolving into a gracious restaurant with excellent service and a proper wine list that includes quite a few Lebanese bottles.

You could easily make a meal of the excellent appetizers: hummus, tabouleh, *fattoush* (a salad containing torn pitta bread), *mujadara* (a blend of rice, lentils, and frizzled onions), *muhammara* (a chunky spread of red peppers and walnuts). Particularly memorable creations are roasted cauliflower drizzled with lemon tahini and pomegranate molasses and fried Brussels sprouts with pomegranate-tahini yogurt and breadcrumbs. The eggplant Napoleon is a genius dish in which crisp, fried disks of eggplant are layered with smoky babaghanoush.

The most popular entree at Tanoreen is probably the lamb fetti, a delicious amalgam of shredded meat, toasted pita, rice cooked with broken vermicelli, yogurt-tahini sauce, and slivered almonds. If you don't see it among the daily specials, the chicken fetti is a satisfying alternative.

For dessert, it is worth the fifteen-minute wait for the baked-to-order *knafeh,* a little bunker of shredded filo concealing molten sweet cheese and topped with orange-blossom syrup and pistachios. **EM**

"Pickles come first . . . Palates jump to attention. They are greeted by plates and plates of appetizers."

The New York Times

↑ Caramelized cauliflower drizzled with lemon tahini and sweet pomegranate molasses.

Don Antonio by Starita | Fried pizza—a Neapolitan epiphany

Location New York   **Signature dish** Fried pizza topped with tomato sauce and smoked mozzarella | ❷❺

In *L'oro di Napoli* (*The Gold of Naples*), a Vittorio De Sica movie from the 1950s, a young Sophia Loren sensually flattens discs of pizza dough for her cuckold of a husband to drop into a vat of scalding oil. They promptly inflate and are sold without embellishment, to be eaten as a snack.

The set for the movie was a real-life restaurant, the Pizzeria Starita a Materdei in Naples, which has been baking (or frying) extraordinary pizza since 1910. But in the early 2000s, Antonio Starita—the shop's third-generation *pizzaiolo* (pizzamaker)—hit upon an ingenious third step. After frying the dough and decorating it, he pops the pie into an oven to warm the toppings and melt the cheeses.

A version of this fabled place lives on New York's West 50th Street, opened by Starita and his disciple Roberto Caporuscio. There, authentic Neapolitan pizzas parade from a wood-burning oven and out of a deep-fat fryer.

Don Antonio by Starita's specialty fried pizza, topped with an intense tomato sauce and imported smoked mozzarella (provola), is known as "Montanara Starita." The secret to the crust's lightness is palm oil, which can withstand the rigors of high temperature. It adds a delicate crispness that makes the dough billowy. There are other dishes to swoon over: *angioletti,* thumb-sized puffs of fried dough tossed with marinated cherry tomatoes, garlic, oregano, and arugula, homemade burrata, and gorgeous salads. There are more than fifty varieties of pizza available, including Pizza Sorrentina made with lemon slices, smoked buffalo mozzarella, and fresh basil. For dessert, try the pizza with ricotta, honey, and almonds.

Don Antonio by Starita takes no reservations, and crowds form early, often waiting on the sidewalk for one of its seventy seats. **RG & MW**

⭱ Authentic Neapolitan pizza in Midtown Manhattan.

Per Se | Exquisitely orchestrated multi-course dining

Location New York   **Signature dish** "Oysters and pearls" | ❺❺❺❺❺

A top New York restaurant in a glassy, glossy shopping mall? When superstar Thomas Keller transposed The French Laundry, possibly the best restaurant in the United States, from California's Napa Valley to the Time-Warner Center in New York, the city's food elite were ecstatic. The settings could not be more different, but the gastronomic spirit of both restaurants is identical. Pass through the enigmatic blue door at Per Se, and its luxurious ambience, glittering view of Central Park, flawless service, and extraordinary food merge into a singular experience. Meals in this jewel box designed by Adam Tihany can exceed four hours. There are two very pricey tasting menus (one vegetarian), and wine pushes the check even higher.

The "tongue-in-cheek" quotations on the menu indicate that things are not always what they seem. After a seductive foreplay of canapés, meals begin with Keller's signature "oysters and pearls"—a creamy, salty, groan-inducing "sabayon" of pearl tapioca with oysters and white sturgeon caviar. Dramatic processions of French/American morsels might include his much-imitated butter-poached lobster with hand-cut rigatoni and tomato raisins, or butter-poached scallop with *garniture à la blanquette de Saint-Jacques*. If you're lucky, "Calotte De Boeuf" will be served. This is a succulent cap surrounding the ribeye that butchers cleverly reserve for themselves; it will come with "interesting" accompaniments. A shoot-the-moon dish, foie gras terrine with black winter truffle glaze and demi-sec mission figs, is worth the supplement. Expect a tidal wave of desserts and *mignardises* (aka petits-fours) and an invitation to view the spare-no-expense kitchen.

Reservations are hard to get, but it is possible to sample some of these items individually along with cocktails in an elegant front room. **RG & MW**

⬆ Keller's urban interpretation of The French Laundry.

Union Square Cafe | Where food and the customer come first

Location New York   **Signature dish** Yellowfin tuna burger | 💲💲

The Union Square Cafe is the favorite restaurant of many New Yorkers, whether they have eaten there recently or not. Opened in 1985 in a neighborhood that it helped renew, it was revolutionary at its birth and is venerable now.

Created by restaurateur Danny Meyer as a New York trattoria with ingredients sourced from the nearby Union Square Greenmarket (itself once radical, now an institution), the Union Square Cafe's menu has the DNA of chef Michael Romano, who understood how to make humble ingredients sing.

Romano made pasta central to the menu, and it is some of the best in town, better than in many Italian restaurants: the ricotta gnocchi melt in the mouth,

---

"Greenmarket fresh New American food served by engaging staffers …"

Zagat

---

tagliarini, which come with truffles in season, are elegantly silken, tortelli are folded parcels of butternut squash or cheese. Main courses at USC call on carefully sourced products from land and sea, and are paired with tangy, crunchy vegetables bought that morning at the market. The iconic yellowfin tuna burger, with its ginger-mustard glaze, is a culinary trope from Tokyo to London but was born here.

The wine list is a marvel that ranges from food-friendly reds and whites by the glass to bargain bottles to classic big year Bordeaux dating back to 1945 and selling for nearly $10,000. Oenophiles, whether fat cats or lean cats, will find a bottle to make them purr. **FP**

Jungsik | Haute Korean in Zenlike surroundings

Location New York   **Signature dish** Crispy red snapper | 💲💲💲

If your notion of Korean food is lots of salty, garlicky, fermented things followed by explosively spicy casseroles and grilled meats, here's a radical change. Jungsik's Korean food is refined in a Frenchified manner and presented elegantly in a minimalist restaurant that once housed the legendary Chanterelle. It has two Michelin stars and an ambitious wine list. Its owner is an alumnus of Bouley and Aquavit, and Jungsik is an offshoot of a similarly ambitious nouvelle restaurant in Seoul.

After being criticized for heavy-handed pricing, there's now a tasting menu and an à la carte menu whose savory dishes are available in two sizes. It still is expensive, but you can order in proportion to your credit card limit.

This haute stuff is highly cerebral and more subtle than the Korean barbecue palaces uptown. Prosaic tomatoes and mozzarella morphs into *bibim*—a salad of greens, tomatoes, and an arresting arugula sorbet. Braised and grilled octopus is nicely piquant, and comes with ssamjang, a complex, spicy paste that is folded into a taming aioli. Sea urchin with crispy fried quinoa, seaweed rice, and a kick of kimchee is an exercise in texture, flavor, and aroma. Halibut, often bland, is enlivened here with seaweed powder and well-spiced anchovy broth.

With seared scales standing upright, snapper fillet looks like it's having a bad hair day, but you'll discover a shocking crispness after which the scales will shatter in your mouth; it comes in a brilliant green jalapeño-cilantro sauce. Don't miss Galbi, short ribs with little fried rice cakes and a smidgen of kimchee. Pork belly fanatics should try Hae Jang, Jungsik's version in a spicy, deeply flavored broth. Cocktails are creative and expensive, and desserts are limited but lovely. **RG & MW**

The River Café | New York's most romantic
restaurant with food and wine to match

Location New York **Signature dish** Yellowfin tuna with foie gras | ❺❺❺❺

In 1977, Michael (Buzzy) O'Keefe, one of New York's most fastidious restaurateurs, restored a dilapidated dock on a wasteland corner of Brooklyn, and created a world-class restaurant—The River Café. From the moment this stunningly simple barge opened its doors, it gained international attention as one of the world's most romantic restaurants. Nested under the Brooklyn Bridge, it overlooks the Manhattan skyline in all its glory. Here, one sits at beautiful tables with crisp white linens and table lamps that softly illuminate your companion and trickle light upon the water.

The River Café became a launching pad for what became known as "new American cuisine." This culinary movement was grounded on the teachings of great European chefs, but with an emphasis on the quality and provenance of its ingredients. Some of the country's best chefs created their identities here, including Larry Forgione, David Burke, and Charlie Palmer. But it was O'Keefe, playing impresario and conductor, who orchestrated the most professional service, maintained the café's glorious visage, and instituted one of the country's most outstanding wine programs directed for the last 35 by Joey DeLissio.

It all came to a screeching halt in 2012 when Hurricane Sandy inflicted grievous damage. But fourteen months later, the Café reopened its doors with the same hypnotic view and the highly regarded food of executive chef Brad Steelman. His modernist dishes include sea scallops with citrus, soy, Asian pear and coriander ice, and yellowfin tuna stuffed with foie gras and served with black truffle vinaigrette. Fish and seafood feature prominently, but rack of lamb, duck, and dry-aged strip steaks are also impressive, as is the chocolate marquise Brooklyn Bridge, served with a "black-and-white" ice cream soda to finish. This is a place to celebrate the good things in life. **RG & MW**

"Dining on the comfortably lounge-lit floating barge … is like living in a Woody Allen movie."

New York Magazine

⬆ The River Café is tucked under the Brooklyn Bridge.

Grand Central Oyster Bar | A seafood institution in a railroad station

Location New York **Signature dish** Oyster pan roast | $$

You step into history here—an architectural gem encased in an architectural gem. The Grand Central Oyster Bar lies on the lower level of the majestic Grand Central Terminal, a beaux-arts masterpiece that celebrated its 100th birthday in 2013. Like that station, the equally aged Oyster Bar's structure is a principal reason for visiting. A Spanish craftsman named "Guastavino" devised its ancient vaulted ceilings, but what holds their individual tiles in gravity-defying position is nearly miraculous. Beneath it, some 440 seats make the oyster bar New York's biggest seafood restaurant.

Equally miraculous are the ancient bowl-shaped cookers on view when you sit at the oyster bar's shellfish counter. Lined in steel and powered by steam, they turn out "pan roasts"—heady amalgams of shellfish (clams, shrimp, lobster, scallop, oyster, or a combination), cream, clam juice, and a dash of chili sauce that are made one at a time and served on toast.

The daily menu is like an encyclopedia of fresh fish. The daily specials tend to be gussied up more than necessary, so choose a fish and have it cooked as simply as possible. Wild striped bass is recommended, as is black cod, which rarely appears on menus.

Sampling the twenty-five different oysters on the menu (their provenance is posted above the shellfish counter), all priced by the piece, makes for a fun way to spend the afternoon.

The wine list features approximately 300 reds and whites from around the world, with many available by the glass. Or try a Bloody Mary oyster shooter.

As seafood goes, this is Le Bernardin's opposite—a feeding barn with little subtlety. Main courses are reasonably priced, and you get to enjoy the scene. The room has more energy at lunchtimes than in the evenings. **RG & MW**

↑ The beautiful vintage setting is part of the charm.

Peter Luger | The granddaddy of the New York steakhouse

Location New York **Signature dish** Porterhouse steak for two | 🅢🅢🅢

For more than 125 years, bloodthirsty carnivores have trekked to Brooklyn for Peter Luger's seductive steaks. Some can't seem to get enough of its beer hall atmosphere and gruff demeanor, while others swear by the meat's prime-quality pedigree and perfect aging. But the truth is, you go because it is the much-lauded granddaddy of all New York steakhouses, and for the sheer pleasure of saying that you've been.

The 1887 building is in a quiet backwater of trendy Williamsburg, and next to the off-ramp of the Williamsburg Bridge. The menu is so limited that you'll be thought a hick if you request one. Most people order steak for two or more, a great slab of porterhouse that is much copied across New York. This hallowed dish arrives already carved, ostensibly to show off its rosy interior and for easier sharing, but, in truth, shameless slathers of butter are melted into the meat's interstices, imparting an uncanny richness that perhaps was once supplied by superior marbling.

If you're not into sharing, the steak-for-one will serve you well, while the grilled fish (usually salmon) holds its own. Sides such as fried potatoes and creamed spinach are hedonistic and *de rigueur*. Virtually everyone orders the tomato onion salad, in season and out. The lunchtime hamburger is a real winner, made in part from the steaks' trimmings. Adding excess to excess, desserts all come *mit schlag*—meaning with billows of whipped cream.

The restaurant was bought at auction for a song in 1950 by Jewish businessman Sol Forman. His business was just across the street, and he wanted to entertain his clients. Today, it is owned by his three impressive daughters, and a granddaughter, who buys the meat. Be warned, the steakhouse is expensive, and you must pay cash or hope they'll accept a check; they don't take credit cards. **RG & MW**

⯅ The Driggs Dining Room in Brooklyn's Peter Luger.

P.J. Clarke's | Once a haunt of Frank Sinatra and Jackie Kennedy, this midtown old-timer is still going strong

Location New York   **Signature dish** Cheeseburger | $

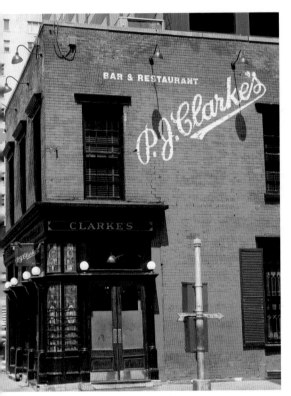

"The classic New York experience… with a Boddingtons and a bacon cheeseburger."

New York Magazine

P.J. Clarke's distinctive red brick premises.

"It's quarter-to-three (in the morning) and there's people in the place." If these words remind you of a classic song made famous by Frank Sinatra, P.J. Clarke's is the saloon where Johnny Mercer wrote it in 1941 and Ol' Blue Eyes held forth in the wee small hours of the morning.

For a joint that has been in business since 1884 in a red brick building erected in 1868, its mere existence is a miracle in midtown Manhattan, a part of town where nothing else is left of the New York of once upon a time. You will see the old broken cash register here and a wall of fading pictures of singers, showgirls, and boxers. Waiters wear the same long white aprons of a century ago.

A visit to the original P.J. Clarke's (accept no arriviste copy of recent vintage) is not a walk down memory lane, but a connection to a renewing tradition for a certain kind of New Yorker. Its patrons have a quiet swagger, born of their connection to the ghosts in the room: Mr. Sinatra at table 20 at 2 A.M., Louis Armstrong practicing his trumpet in the back at dawn; Mrs. Kennedy and her children having cheeseburgers at 2 P.M. In fact, that cheeseburger is the talismanic link to previous generations of customers, who feasted on the hand-formed patty, cooked in butter (or so it seems), overlaid with American cheese, and upon request also topped with smothered (sautéed) onions.

There is more good food available beyond the burgers. Daily specials that speak different culinary languages come and go: classic New England clam chowder, steaks, chops, seafood platters, and excellent spinach are all prime choices. Beer and ale on tap spark convivial banter in the front room and quiet reflection in the back. Here's looking at you, kid. **FP**

Shopsins | Top breakfast
in this diner in Lower Manhattan

Location New York **Signature dish** Mac-and-cheese pancakes with stuffing | **$**

Welcome to Shopsins, the ultimate quirky restaurant, serving great breakfasts and epic sandwiches. It randomly insults customers and from time to time summarily evicts them. Buried in the south corner of the Essex Street Market building on the Lower East Side, Shopsins has about fourteen seats and takes no reservations. They'll seat no more than four of you, and should your party exceed that number, you'll be invited to leave. Leave cell phones and cameras in your pockets and your food allergies at home. Don't ask questions. The menu features what feels like 1,000 items (there are fifty-one soups, twelve Tex-Mex breakfasts, and fifty specialty sandwiches, not to mention the cakes). With a kitchen the size of a walk-in closet, getting food served is a challenge, as is deciding what to order—which is what you do while waiting for a table.

The food is belly-busting and carb-laden. Most people go for signature mac-and-cheese pancakes, often stuffed with eggs and bacon, but you might try the unruly Quack pancakes with pecans, figs, and mango-pineapple bbq duck. If you would rather have sweets, there's the Original Slutty Cake (pumpkin, peanut butter, pistachios, cinnamon), or the Don Ho (macadamia, banana, piña colada cream cheese). You want these with their own hot sauce and maple syrup? Don't ask, just do it.

Sandwiches seem composed of ingredients that shouldn't belong together, but get along well here. There's Jihadboy (beef, pomegranate, tapenade, feta, pistachios, and tahini dressing) and Fat Darrell (chicken fingers, waffle fries, chorizo, tomato gravy, garlic jalapeño cheese bread).

Incidentally, if you see a disheveled fellow mumbling while slumped in a chair, that's Kenny Shopsin, the owner. **RG & MW**

TAO Downtown | Stage set
with pan-Asian food on the side

Location New York **Signature dish** Miso-glazed Chilean sea bass satays | **$$$**

Tao Las Vegas is the country's largest-grossing restaurant, but the latest, Tao Downtown New York, may be the most spectacular. For this you can thank David Rockwell, the most theatrical of designers. A massive reclining Buddha glares at your Martini in the lounge, while a Chinese Quan Yin statue with more arms than an octopus appears to move its limbs in a magical feat of illumination.

Seating 350, the place feels as vast as an army mess hall, but every surface is intriguingly Asian-esque and over-scaled, the lighting terrific, and the crowd boisterous. A massive central staircase accommodates several dining terraces from which lucky people watch the parade while slurping cocktails.

> *"This is not so much a restaurant as a nonstop party … the idea is to order many dishes and share."*
>
> The New York Times

Playing to tourists, the food is equally Asian-esque and mostly good, albeit mildly seasoned and inauthentically sweet. Main courses are expensive, and even stitching together a menu of small plates, dim sum, and cocktails may bruise your wallet. Glazed tuna and wild mushroom roll is a winner, as are "Cantonese" cauliflower, pork potstickers with black-and-white sesame seeds, vegetable gyoza, a hillock of braised five-spice short ribs, and a satay of miso-glazed Chilean sea bass, all decently portioned. Salmon and black bass main courses are excellent, and sushi from the high-wattage raw bar is fun. Order trendy Taiwanese shaved ice with fresh fruit and mochi to share for dessert. **RG & MW**

Russ & Daughters Café | Smoked fish and bagels on the Lower East Side

Location New York | **Signature dish** Smoked-salmon platters | 💲💲

After 100 years of selling first-rate smoked fish and other appetizing store classics to generations of New Yorkers to eat at home, the venerated Russ & Daughters has opened a café around the corner from its Lower East Side mini-emporium. Families are gathering around the restaurant's tables for platters of herring (pickled, mustard-dill, schmaltz, Holland, curry) and superlative smoked salmon (Scottish, Norwegian, Nova Scotia, Gaspe Nova, double-smoked Danish), and all the go-withs—bagels, bialys, cream-cheese spreads, homemade chopped liver, and chopped whitefish salad.

The sixty-five seat Russ & Daughter's Café feels a bit like an upscale luncheonette, but its menu extends into the realm of luxury, and diners can feast on various kinds of caviar (Osetra, Siberian, American, hackleback, salmon, wasabi-flavored) to dab onto *latkes* (potato pancakes) and blini, or to fold into various egg dishes. Should you demand aquavit for your herring (and you should), vodka for your smoked salmon, Champagne for your caviar, or gin for your gravlax, there is a well-tailored selection at the bar, and never mind that it looks like an old-fashioned soda fountain. The experience is so special that the Smithsonian Institution honored Russ & Daughters as part of New York's cultural heritage.

Niki Russ Federman and Josh Russ Tupper, the fourth generation of the family's proprietors, shuttle between the shop on Houston Street and the restaurant on Orchard Street—the restaurant occupying part of the long-gone Allen Street synagogue, smack in the middle of what once was a poverty-ridden Jewish ghetto. In the twenty-first century, the Lower East Side is full of bespoke cocktails, and hip boutiques interspersed among aging shops filled with bargain clothing. **RG & MW**

⬆ Russ & Daughters is a much-loved New York institution.

The Modern | Fine dining located at New York's Museum of Modern Art

Location New York   **Signature dish** Slow-poached farm egg in a jar | 💲💲

Situated immediately next to New York's Museum of Modern Art and sharing a view of its sculpture garden, The Modern has given new definition to the art of eating. Ever faithful to its name, it allows diners to choose their own style of eating, be it Impressionist, Cubist, or Expressionistic.

The room is divided by a wall of milky glass cubes. On one side, facing the garden, is the restaurant. On the other side is the bar. The restaurant has formal table settings and soft illumination. It also has high prices and exquisite dining on menus that are either à la carte or prix fixe. The bar has clean comfortable lines and the possibility to self-invent at tables and low banquets. Both have superb service.

The menu in the bar unfolds to form three cards, called "One," "Two," and "Three." They propose a choice of savory dishes of different sizes and character. A diner can select from any and all, as many or as few as appeals—call it "constructionist eating."

Chef Gabriel Kreuther brings flavors of his native Alsace and combines them with local foods to create an immensely appealing menu that ranges from modern takes on fatty traditional dishes to new works of art. The "Modern Liverwurst" could easily be called "Pork Velvet." Other choices include cauliflower soup with roasted hazelnuts, mascarpone, and white balsamic vinegar; monkfish with mushrooms and applewood-smoked bacon; beef cheek *sauerbraten*, which is essentially a German pot roast.

Similar enticements appear in the restaurant's tasting menus. Most diners on either side of the glass wall find their way to the iconic slow-poached farm egg in a jar with lobster, mushroom, and sea urchin froth. When eaten with a spoon, slowly, deliberately, and contemplatively, it reveals a level of artistry for which there are few words but many emotions. **FP**

⬆ Slow-poached egg in a jar is a signature dish.

Stella 34 | Grand trattoria inside New York's most popular department store

Location New York   **Signature dish** Porchetta from the wood-burning oven | 💲💲

Carved from hidden storage space, Macy's has built, at enormous expense, a 260-seat trattoria on its sixth floor looking onto the Empire State Building. With marble tiled floors and acres of white marble, the place projects a brilliant, modern shine. It has a take-out shop, a gelateria, a wine cellar, and an open kitchen with three wood-burning ovens.

It is run by Patina Restaurant Group, which also operates the acclaimed Lincoln uptown, and numerous restaurants in cultural institutions. It is busy, and not necessarily with shoppers; people go to Stella 34 specifically to eat, which is why it has a private elevator accessible via 35th Street.

Although its menu breaks no new ground, there are lots of good things to eat. There is pizza in profusion. They tend to be soft and puffy as in Naples, and good choices are the "Cavolfiore" (cauliflower with black pepper, and lemon) and "Barese" (tomatoes, sausage, broccoli rabe, and taleggio). But this is no mere pizza joint. A small plate of baby octopus with gigante beans and soppressata vinaigrette makes a great starter, as does the Caesar salad made with assertive escarole instead of romaine and marinated white anchovy and risotto balls with sausage and mozzarella.

The pasta can be made with gluten-free rice flour and among the interesting dishes is *strozzapreti con seppie* (elongated cavatelli with cuttlefish ink, hot pepper sauce, and breadcrumbs.) The porchetta suckling pig from one of the wood ovens with bitter green salad, gorgonzola, candied almonds, and bacon-sherry vinaigrette is satisfying, as is the rotisserie chicken. Wines by the glass are well chosen and, by New York standards, reasonably priced. The restaurant is open only until 9:30 P.M., so do not plan on going for a late dinner. **RG & MW**

⬆ Clean lines characterize the interior at Stella 34.

The Standard Grill | Hipster hotel dining in the Meatpacking district

Location New York **Signature dish** "Million Dollar" roast chicken for two | ❸❸

If you are walking New York's bustling new High Line (and you should), here's a great place to begin or end your journey. The Standard Hotel straddles this must-see promenade, with a great scene and a fantastic assemblage of places to eat and drink.

The Standard Grill, its main restaurant, will be packed whenever you want to go, so make reservations and hope your table is ready. Young New Yorkers party at this sprawling restaurant, often with six or more sexy things crammed into a banquette for four. Food from an open kitchen is good, waiters are helpful, and the rolling din exceeds anything an audiologist would approve.

First-timers gape at the penny-paved floor and wonder at its value. If your party is large, splurge on a punch bowl of cognac, peach puree, and cider. Start with grilled apricots with coppa and marcona almonds, or foie gras with balsamic cherries. Then consider swordfish with green olive and preserved lemon salsa, ribsteak for two, or pork chop with warm bacon-potato salad. Their popular "Million Dollar" chicken for two is finished with lemon-cayenne crème fraîche and croutons cooked in the chicken juices.

You can spin an entire evening at the hotel, for just outside is a rollicking beer garden, the noise of which puts Yankee Stadium to shame; it is standing room only after work and populated by even younger folk. In winter, the hotel's piazza becomes a small ice rink, which switches to an informal pizzeria in summer.

Topping the Standard, a sophisticated terrace bar offers fantastic Manhattan views, particularly around sunset. The drinks are excellent, the nibbles rather expensive, and there is live jazz later in the evening. Two essential reasons for going there are an Oscar-worthy video that accompanies the elevator ride and giggle-inducing bathrooms. **RG & MW**

⬆ The "Million Dollar" roast chicken in a black iron skillet.

The Spotted Pig | West Village gastropub with celebrity clout

Location New York **Signature dish** Chargrilled burger with Roquefort cheese and shoestring fries | 💲💲

One of Manhattan's best burgers is neither from a decades-old diner, nor from a venerable steakhouse. Beautifully charred and topped with oozing Roquefort cheese, it comes alongside shoestring fries studded with crispy slivers of garlic and fried rosemary leaves. You find it in a Michelin-starred gastropub in the heart of the West Village.

Gastropubs were launched in the early 1990s by venturesome English chefs who rejected their country's stereotypically stodgy fare—fish and chips and steak-and-kidney pie. By focusing on seasonal high-quality ingredients (with accents from Italy and France), they turned dreary pubs into exciting new places to eat. The Spotted Pig is among New York's best versions. Opened by music manager Ken Friedman and British chef April Bloomfield, with early backers including chef-restaurateur Mario Batali and Jay-Z, it has been buzzing since 2004. Bloomfield serves unapologetically rustic food.

In addition to the burger, try chicken liver toast as a seductive starter, or deviled eggs as a fun treat to share. Bloomfield's sheep's milk ricotta gnudi—inspired by her time at London's River Café—are light-as-air and widely praised. Nose-to-tail devotees should have the crispy pig's ear salad.

While Bloomfield has moved to more successes at The Breslin and John Dory Oyster Bar, the cozy Pig encapsulates her roots. Potted plants, piggy figurines, and banquettes covered in threadbare velvet all contribute to a whimsical aesthetic.

The handsome bar is raucous with beer aficionados plowing through an excellent list, and the kitchen keeps them fueled until 2 A.M. But it is the delightful food served atop the tiny tables that has New Yorkers and savvy tourists coming back for more. The Spotted Pig is especially popular for brunch. **LM**

⬆ The Spotted Pig is a gastropub with Italian undertones.

Minetta Tavern | New life breathed into an aged saloon

Location New York **Signature dish** "Black Label Burger" | $$

The Minetta Tavern was a Greenwich Village hot spot from 1937 through the 1980s but then began to falter. That is, until it was resurrected by impresario-restaurateur Keith McNally, known primarily for making new places look ravishingly old. At the Minetta Tavern, he buffed and polished what was authentically old and installed a French bistro/steakhouse menu that has kept the new incarnation packed since 2009. Its black-and-white checkered floor and caricature-filled walls attract a young clientele who understand how to dress up while dressing down.

The Tavern is justly famous for its "Black Label Burger," a flavorsome grind of aged skirt steak, rib steak, brisket, and who-knows-what-else, served with caramelized onions and pommes frites. The restaurant also is noted for its pedigree steaks, including a New York strip on the bone and a dry-aged côte de boeuf for two served with roasted marrow bones and gem lettuce salad. You can dine well without the steaks. Starters of oysters and truffled pork sausage, oxtail and foie gras terrine, and brandade of salt cod, potatoes, and truffles are worthy choices and properly French. Trout fillet meunière with crabmeat and brioche croutons, crisp pig's trotter with lentils and herb salad, and a variation on pasta carbonara are all standouts. If here for lunch or weekend brunch, do not miss the rendition of a French dip, multiple layers of rare sliced steak with horseradish in a garlic-rubbed baguette.

Your chances of snagging a table at this upscale neo-saloon are better at brunch than at other times. And, while you could order the usual two-eggs-any-style, why bother when there is black pudding clafoutis, or ham baked in hay with eggs and grits? A perfect excuse to pop a cork. **RG & MW**

⬆ The Tavern was a favorite of Ernest Hemingway's.

Marea | Luxurious fish and pasta and views of Central Park

Location New York **Signature dish** Fusilli with braised octopus and bone marrow | ❺❺❺❺

"'Memorable' is putting it mildly at this Columbus Circle stunner ... exquisite seafood and pasta."

Zagat

⬆ Dishes showcase the best of Italian regional cooking.

Launched in 2009, anchored by a glowing Egyptian onyx bar, and decorated with silver-dipped seashells, Marea (the name means "tide") sailed through a collapsing global economy. Recession? Not here, in this grown-up dining room overlooking Central Park.

This extraordinary Italian restaurant specializes in fish. In most seafood emporia, you are advised to choose simple preparations. But, because you will be spending a wad of money, you should opt for grandstanding, complex dishes, because renowned chef-owner Michael White is known for memorable, larger-than-life flavors. The profusion of menu choices makes ordering a challenge—snacks for sharing, eighteen different raw fish presentations, a section each for caviar and for truffles, seductive antipasti, regional oysters, a dozen divine pastas, and six fish preparations all precede the daily whole fish choices.

To begin, split an order of *ricci*—sea urchin crostini draped in warm lardo with a few grains of sea salt; its earthiness first rattles and then soothes all of your senses. Share a plate or two of raw fish: wahoo, wild mushrooms, and lobster roe, or go for bigeye tuna with oyster crema and crisp sunchokes for texture. Then order a dish of grilled octopus with smoked potatoes, pickled red onion, chilies, and tonnato sauce.

Do not miss the lusty house-made pastas, for they make suitable main courses. Standouts are fusilli with braised octopus enriched with bone marrow; *strozzapreti* with lump crab, sea urchin, and basil; and *francobolli*, which are ravioli of smoked ricotta and chestnuts with dried cherries.

Should you have room, try any fabulous fish dish or order the steak—a fifty-day-aged sirloin served with bone marrow *panzanella* that ranks among the best meat dishes in town. Dessert? Affogato with vanilla gelato, a shot of hot espresso, and a shot of Amaro. **RG & MW**

Totonno's | Classic pizza in Coney Island

Location New York **Signature dish** Pizza Margherita | $

There's probably more pizza in New York than anywhere else in America. You can get it round, square, or oval; by the inch, by the pound, by the pie, or by the piece; thick or thin; Roman, Neapolitan, Sicilian, or multi-national; and cooked on wood, gas, or coal. From this profusion, Totonno's distinguishes itself with history, stellar pies, and an offbeat location in Coney Island at the far end of Brooklyn.

The pizzas are classic New York pies—which requires some explanation. The pizza's puffy rim (properly called "bones") is resiliently chewy but not crispy, with charred bubbles verifying that live yeast has worked its magic; the bones will remain pliable long after leaving the oven. The base of the pizza, in this case fired in the thousand-degree heat of a coal oven, will be thin and crisp but not crackerlike. Slabs of fresh mozzarella and a topping of crushed San Marzano tomatoes will be applied with discretion and will cling to the dough rather than slither into your lap.

Founded in 1924 by pizzaiolo Antonio "Totonno" Pero, the restaurant was wrecked by fire in 2009 and then again by Hurricane Sandy in 2012. It looks as undecorated as always—random antique doodads, aged newspaper clippings, and pressed-tin walls and ceilings. With no reservations and no standing room, co-owner Cookie Ciminieri will politely suggest you line up outside.

A short menu hangs over the open kitchen, but old-timers order a Margherita and a white pizza of lusciously simple mozzarella and garlic. A small bottle of cheap Chianti matches the pizza perfectly. Bear in mind the limited opening hours when you visit.

There's plenty to do around Coney Island after your pizza. Partake of the legendary amusements, visit a Cyclone's baseball game, or stay out late and fall into a glitzy Russian nightclub in nearby Brighton Beach for another experience you should have before you die. **RG & MW**

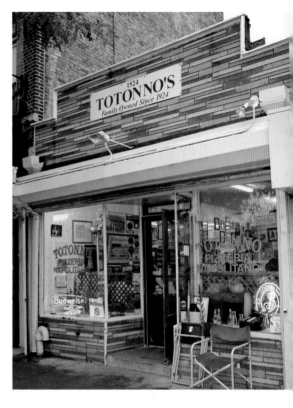

"The original Totonno's, one of the early giants of New York City's coal-oven pizza, is legendary."

The New York Times

⤒ Totonno's has hardly changed in more than 90 years.

Sushi Nakazawa |

Superb Greenwich Village sushi

Location New York   **Signature dish** Scallop with *yuzukosho* | ❸❸❸

Daisuke Nakazawa toiled for 11 years under the harsh gaze of sushi master Jiro Ono in Tokyo before becoming proprietor of Sushi Nakazawa in Greenwich Village. While in Japan, Nakazawa landed a bit part in a cult movie called *Jiro Dreams of Sushi*. Bald and monk-like, Nakazawa tears up when, after 200 fruitless tries, stone-faced Jiro approves his signature *tamago*—a fiendishly difficult layered and rolled "egg sushi."

Nakazawa was lured to New York by Alessandro Borgognone, who owns an Italian restaurant in the Bronx. Borgognone tracked down Nakazawa after seeing the movie, and installed him here in 2013.

It is a classic omakase restaurant. You get about twenty courses from an ever-changing array of raw

---

"The meal is like a wave, its gentle lulls rendering the crests all the more thrilling."

Time Out

---

material and you eat what you're given—which is glorious. You might encounter a fish that has been smoked over hay; scallops dabbed with *uzukosho*, an amalgam of yuzu peel and hot chilies; triggerfish topped with its liver; geoduck blow torched to the proper temperature; or barracuda from Tokyo.

Nakazawa has fun interacting with customers. He might toss live shrimp to jump around on your plate before sacrificing them. He might present a tray of sea urchins in their shells and let you pick your favorite before transforming it into something transcendent. There's an ambitious wine list, but you'd be wise to select the sake tasting that matches various styles of sake with the sushi. **RG & MW**

Louis' Lunch |

A venerated one-dish wonder

Location New Haven (Connecticut)   **Signature dish** Original hamburger sandwich | ❸

One fateful day in 1900, so the legend of this restaurant recalls, a businessman needing something to eat in a hurry dashed into Louis' Lunch wagon. Owner Louis Lassen grabbed a portion of minced steak trimmings, formed it into a patty, grilled it, and squashed the resulting chunk between two slices of bread. This is believed to be the first hamburger, a meat staple that has since become America's national dish. But Lassen's makeshift meat patty was no overnight sensation.

It took Lassen another seventeen years to graduate from his mobile catering wagon to a proper restaurant. The business has since moved again, but the fourth generation of Lassens still run Louis' Lunch.

The birthplace of the hamburger sandwich now serves only one dish. The esteemed Louis burger is made from a blend of minced steak, then clamped in wire frames and grilled upright on both sides at the same time, using antique gas stoves.

The "original burger" arrives between two square slices of toasted bread, instead of inside the usual bread bun. Here the burger is served with what the restaurant claims is the only acceptable garnish: cheese (in the form of spread), onion, tomato, and/or mustard, but never with modern interlopers such as ketchup or mayonnaise. Portions of French fries or salad are allowed.

Louis' Lunch is a small operation, seating a maximum of thirty. It's only open at lunchtimes and the decor is self-consciously worn and simple with bare brick walls, wooden tables and chairs, some of which are covered in carved graffiti, and an old unpainted wooden bar with cast-iron bar stools. The burgers however, are noticeably more expensive than in your average American diner—that must be the price of heritage. **SH**

Blue Hill at Stone Barns | The epitome of locavorism at the world's most luxe farm

Location Westchester **Signature dish** "Vegetables on a Fence" | ❸❸❸❸

Old Mr. Rockefeller had a farm. In fact, the Rockefellers owned the last working farm in Westchester County and rather than developing McMansions, they have preserved it for posterity. By spending money as only Rockefellers could, they turned 80 acres (32 hectares) into Stone Barns Center for Food and Agriculture, a nonprofit that trains farmers and children in the ethos of seasonal, anti-industrial, sustainable food. At the center of it is Blue Hill at Stone Barns, a restaurant in an immense dairy barn built in the 1930s.

Dining here, 35 miles (56 kilometers) from midtown, is only half the fun. Arrive early, wander the bucolic premises, and gaze upon Berkshire hogs, Finn-Dorset sheep, and a flock of contented chickens. Beneath the automated roof of a vast greenhouse, a dirt floor is planted with the country's most cosseted vegetables, awaiting their peak-time harvesting.

Headed by Dan Barber, the restaurant is the epitome of locavorism. You will not get a menu. Instead, there's a list of what's currently available. Tell your waiter what you would rather not eat, then choose between the "Farmer's Feast" or the "Grazing, Pecking, Rooting" options and wait for a cavalcade of dishes. First to appear might be "Vegetables on a Fence"—an unadorned array of just-harvested produce that sidesteps odd flavor combinations and molecular trickery. Instead, you must focus on the inherent attributes of what nature provides and how Barber combines them with subtlety and integrity.

Vegetables may be the stars, but house-made charcuterie explores how to use every bit of the farm's animals. Barber does endlessly interesting things with eggs, and gently cooked meat courses can be a rosy revelation. Desserts are artful expressions of seasonality and seduction. Jackets and ties for men preferred. **RG & MW**

"This place has presence, commanding beauty, and fantastic cuisine."

Gayot

⊞ Imaginative creations are artfully plated.

Nick & Toni's | The hottest table in the Hamptons

Location East Hampton **Signature dish** Wood-roasted local fish | $$$

"This sophisticated Italian-Med offers tasty meals to the über-trendy … in an upscale setting."

Zagat

[↑] Wood-roasted fish is the speciality at Nick & Toni's, served here with lentils and radish.

[→] The colorful mosaic above the wood-burning oven was created by local artist Eric Fischl.

On Saturday nights in summer, Hollywood stars and Wall Street titans converge on Nick & Toni's in East Hampton. As soon as it opened its doors in 1988, this place became a magnet for celebrities who "summer in the Hamptons," or maintain homes there. Paul McCartney, Martha Stewart, Steven Spielberg, Sarah Jessica Parker, Alec Baldwin, Billy Joel, and Richard Gere are all regulars. The restaurant could probably get by on star power alone, even if it wasn't one of the best restaurants on Long Island.

The narrow front room features a bar and the restaurant's famous wood-burning oven; the larger dining room is adjacent to a lovely covered patio where additional tables are placed in fine weather. Service is extremely professional (a rarity in the Hamptons), and even the hoi polloi are always treated with courtesy.

Long Island's East End is not only an upper-class enclave, but also a rich agricultural and wine-producing region. Nick & Toni's chef-partner Joseph Realmuto makes prodigious use of the local produce, wine, and seafood, and also maintains a fair-sized organic garden (he hosts a weekly farmers' market in the parking lot). His ever-changing menu is made up of equal parts rustic Italian and New American. Pastas and risottos are always recommended, as is anything issuing from the fantastic wood-burning oven, especially the wood-roasted fish. Vegetables are taken seriously here—vegetarians will not feel deprived in the least.

On summer weekends, especially in August, reservations are hard to come by, but the dozen outdoor tables are available on the night, so guests who show up without calling ahead can take advantage of these, if others don't beat them to it. They can enjoy a drink on the benches or wide steps outside the front door before their meal: it's a great opportunity for celebrity spotting. **EM**

Polly's Pancake Parlor | Iconic pancake house on a New Hampshire farm

Location Sugar Hill **Signature dish** "Pancake Sampler" | $

"This is a true New Hampshire breakfast spot . . . one step above the rest."

New Hampshire Magazine

↑ Polly's nestles in the countryside celebrated by the poet Robert Frost.

Only a few miles from the home of poet Robert Frost (now a museum worth a visit) is the home of poetry in pancakes—a few simple ingredients elevated to perfection set against the background that inspired Robert Frost's remarkable writing.

In 1938, when Wilfred "Sugar Bill" Dexter and his wife Polly turned their rustic barn into a quaint tea room, they were taking a road less traveled. But Polly's exceptional pancakes took top billing in no time. Little has changed for hungry travelers, who have been making the pancake pilgrimage for more than seventy-five years. Diners enjoy an idyllic view, overlooking the open fields of Hildex Farm, framed by the majestic White Mountains.

Polly's is now run by Kathie Alrich Cote, the fourth generation of the family. While there are omelets, eggs Benedict, and other breakfast offerings, it's really all about the pancakes: 3 inches (8 cm) in diameter, they are puffy, flavorful, and available in five varieties—plain, oatmeal buttermilk, buckwheat, whole wheat, and cornmeal, the last three organically grown and stone-ground. Add-ins include walnuts, blueberries, coconut, and chocolate chips. With twenty-five variations to ponder, it may take some willpower to settle for an order of six of the same.

The "Pancake Sampler" lets you mix-and-match any three batters and toppings. Your waitress actually makes them herself —in batches of three, so that a second serving arrives hot off the griddle just as you are finishing your first. For an additional two bucks you can get them gluten-free. Maple leaf-shaped pewter trays are filled with Polly's famous maple products to top your pancakes: pure maple butter, maple sugar, and maple syrup.

The restaurant does not take reservations on holidays or weekends, but last year more than 54,000 patrons decided to come anyway. It closes during winter so call ahead. **RG & MW**

Union Oyster House | America's oldest restaurant, where JFK dined

Location Boston **Signature dish** Half a dozen oysters on the half shell | ❺❺

The Union Oyster House was established on Union Street near Boston's waterfront in 1826. This makes it America's oldest restaurant in continuous use. The history of this old brick building goes even deeper. It is designated as a National Historical Landmark because it was a rebel headquarters before the War of Independence and the temporary home of a future king of France—Louis Philippe I.

America's oyster craze of the early nineteenth century led to oyster parlors opening in every town. This building changed use accordingly, and has been a Boston seafood institution ever since. It claims to have employed America's first waitress and to be the first place to supply toothpicks.

Politicians have long been among its patrons. In the early nineteenth century, Senator Daniel Webster was partial to the oysters here. In more recent times, as befits a New England establishment, it was popular with the Kennedy family. President John F. Kennedy had his own private booth, which is now marked with a plaque and flag.

Today, the venue trades actively on its venerable history and is a popular spot for tourists visiting Boston. The tables, chairs, beams, pillars, and paneling are all dark wood and gilt-framed oil paintings hang on the walls. A dimly lit historic ambience prevails.

Otherwise, the menu offers a wide range of New England classics, offering hearty portions of dishes such as clam chowder and Boston baked beans. Seafood is a particular specialty here, as befits its Boston location and history. Lobster, sourced from the restaurant's own pools, is offered in various incarnations: boiled, broiled, or transformed into grander creations such as lobster ravioli or lobster Newburg. There is even a "Ye Olde Seafood Platter." True to the restaurant's name, oysters continue to be popular here, served up in assorted guises, from freshly shucked and in their half shells to stewed. **SH**

"This culinary museum is a must-go for out-of-towners seeking legit chowder and oysters."

Zagat

⬆ Two plates of what the Union does best— half a dozen oysters on the half shell.

Neptune Oyster | Arguably the best seafood in Boston in a bustling little bar in the North End

Location Boston **Signature dish** Raw oyster selection |

*"This tiny spot delivers…
an eye-poppingly bold,
lip-smackingly rich repertoire."*

Gayot

⬆ Shellfish is the star of the show here.

The inventively conceived and presented dishes could have come from a glamorous uptown gourmet restaurant. Neptune Oyster, however, is a cramped bar with a few tables in an unloved part of town. It seats a maximum of forty-two. There's no booking, no waiting area, and no desserts. You can't even get a cup of coffee.

Somehow rising from its humble location, chef Michael Serpa's food bar has built a reputation as the best place in Boston for seafood. It is always busy, noisy, and packed. Some eat on stools at the bar, others squeeze around tables with strangers.

Guests can eat something simple but perfectly prepared such as battered fish and chips, or opt for a gastro treat like seared scallops from George's Bank off Cape Cod. The scallops are served on a bed of pear butter, duck confit, blue cheese, and baby Brussels sprouts. Or what about a white shrimp gazpacho with a rose harissa chili sauce, Greek yogurt, and green onion? More unusual ingredients such as cod cheeks or sea urchins sometimes surface.

Customers get a small sheet describing the characteristics of the different oysters available that day. The team of expert shuckers are renowned for their speed and grit-free efficiency. Many opt for a raw pick-and-mix selection of oyster varieties to compare flavors. Oysters crop up in other dishes, too: there can't be many places that serve a cheeseburger with fried oyster on the side.

Lobster roll, perhaps with a glass or two of Riesling from the long wine list, is a lunchtime favorite. Grilled brioche buns are stuffed with a mountain of lobster and served either Maine-style (cold, tossed in mayonnaise) or Connecticut-style (drizzled in hot butter). New Englanders also appreciate Neptune's version of their regional favorite: clam chowder. **SH**

No. 9 Park | Fine dining
in a smart Boston townhouse

Location Boston **Signature dish** Prune-stuffed gnocchi with foie gras beurre blanc and almonds | ❸❸❸

Discreetly housed in a smart townhouse in Boston's historic Beacon Hill, looking over Boston Common, this elegant restaurant offers a sophisticated dining appearance. The smart yet understated decor, with its dark wooden floors and antique chandeliers, sets the tone for eating here.

The restaurant's founder, the celebrated chef and restaurateur Barbara Lynch, looked to France and Italy for inspiration, producing a predominantly classical cuisine that makes the most of local ingredients. Having trained with chef Mario Bonello at Boston's St. Botolph Club, she worked at some of Boston's top restaurants and traveled to Italy where she learned about the country's cuisine before returning to Boston to become executive chef at Galleria Italiana. Lynch opened her own restaurant, No. 9 Park, in 1998 and gained a notable reputation and loyal following for her accomplished cuisine.

Sea bass from Oregon, for example, is paired with black olives and fennel flowers, with American caviar adding a touch of luxury. Roasted squab is combined with grilled corn, pork sausage, and cucumber. The quality of the ingredients shines through, as evident in the inherent sweetness of the diver-caught scallops.

The chef's tasting menu, which changes weekly, showcases technically accomplished dishes such as house-made bigoli pasta with celeriac, smoked salt cod, and Calabrian chili and grilled quail with chickpea farinata, rosemary, and anchovies. Desserts include chic takes on old favorites, from panna cotta, sorbets, and parfaits to excellent patisserie creations.

The setting for No. 9 Park is one of the prettiest in the city, and the understated classical cooking here matches the stylish surroundings. An impressive wine list and knowledgeable, well-trained staff add to the experience. **AH**

L'Espalier | Accomplished
modern New England-French cuisine

Location Boston **Signature dish** Scallops with red cabbage, apple raita, and cauliflower puree | ❸❸❸

Espalier sits at the pinnacle of the Boston dining scene. Its string of awards is testament to this. It also owns Apple Street Farm, an organic farm in nearby Essex, Massachusetts, and heirloom vegetables are delivered directly to the restaurant from the farm.

The cooking is quite classical in nature, with luxury ingredients to the fore. This is seen in tender Maine lobster, served with seafood chowder and topped with a few slices of prosciutto. A slab of foie gras terrine has a smooth texture and plenty of deep foie gras flavor, offered with a jelly of Sauternes and Mission figs, which provide some balancing acidity to the dish. Care is taken in the selection of ingredients, shown in a dish of plump, sweet diver-caught

> *"This is a place that takes a hot cuppa seriously—it employs a tea sommelier."*
>
> The Boston Globe

scallops, paired with tender red cabbage, an apple raita, and saffron cauliflower puree. The cabbage nicely balances the sweetness of the shellfish.

The kitchen is not rooted in the past, however. Asian influences are seen in a main course of marlin with miso broth, pak choi, and tender udon noodles. A meal at L'Espalier might conclude with a rich chocolate *millefeuille* made with Valrhona chocolate and served with praline ice cream. Over the years, the cooking at Espalier has maintained a consistently high standard, using high quality ingredients and demonstrating solid kitchen technique. Service is quite formal but still friendly, the dishes well paced. **AH**

Yankee Lobster | A down-to-earth haven for lovers of good seafood

Location Boston **Signature dish** Lobster mac and cheese | ❸❸

Boston's waterfront is packed with glossy seafood restaurants and bars. Hidden among the tourist chains and upscale eateries is this authentic fishermen's outlet, set up relatively recently by the Zanti family, who have been fishing out of Boston since the 1920s.

The restaurant is a simple room tacked on the side of Zanti's fish market. Shellfish are kept fresh in big seawater tanks at the rear, the menu is chalked on a board behind the counter, and the tables are adorned with napkin dispensers and bottles of sauce. Food comes on paper plates or in plastic baskets. Real ale comes in the bottle; wine in plastic glasses.

There are a few basic tables and metal chairs inside the cramped room, in a yard, and outside under

---

> *"Order something simple like clam chowder or a lobster roll, and you will not be disappointed."*
>
> *Lonely Planet*

---

an awning. Nevertheless seafood fans seek out Yankee Lobster for what many say is the widest selection of fresh and tasty seafood in the city.

There's no pretentiousness here; everything is served simply and effectively. A meal might involve a bowl of thick creamy chowder and a basket of fried scallops or sweet-fleshed lobster meat smeared with melted butter and served in a roll. Everything comes with coleslaw and beer batter fries. Other Yankee Lobster specialties include grilled tuna, fried shrimp, and crab cake sandwich. The signature macaroni and lobster dish uses diced lobster meat and a cheddar and Parmesan sauce with white wine, garlic, tomato, and onion, topped with breadcrumbs and baked. **SH**

Shaw's Fish & Lobster Wharf | Fresh lobster by the sea

Location New Harbor **Signature dish** Lobster roll | ❸

Fancy dining? Hell no. Shaw's is in Maine, down on New Harbor's fishing wharf, overlooking the small working harbor where the fishermen land their catch. From the outside, Shaw's looks like a couple of shacks joined together, with a big red plastic lobster over the entrance; inside, it's cafeteria clean. Orders for food are taken at the counter.

Shaw's might not have five-star looks, but the food it serves is star quality, especially when it comes to lobster. Lobsters are king in this joint, especially when the meat is shredded and mixed with a little bit of mayo and lemon juice and then laid to rest in a soft bun. The result is juicy and pliant in texture and touched with a gorgeous sea-fresh taste; aficionados reckon that Shaw's dishes up the best lobster roll on the Maine coastline.

You can also, of course, have lobster on its own, with single, twin, and triple lobster dinners available. They are served simply with drawn butter, salad, and a bread roll and butter. For something more warming, go for a bowl of lobster stew. Other than lobster, the menu includes crispy fried clams and silky chowder, seafood casserole, as well as salads (including lobster), a shrimp basket, steaks, burgers, many sandwiches, and desserts such as cheesecake and key lime pie. Daily specials are written on a board.

When the weather is fine, you can sit out on the deck to eat while taking in the view of the working harbor. You will not be alone in appreciating the surroundings. In the late 1990s, Hollywood descended on New Harbor to film scenes for the movie *Message in a Bottle*; that particular film had a sad ending but those that come to Shaw's feel nothing but contentment when biting into their fresh lobster. **ATJ**

➔ The fresh lobster roll is a must.

Biko | The best of two worlds in a tasty combination

Location Mexico City **Signature dish** Carrillera (pig's cheek) | ❸❸❸

The three chefs behind Biko—Mikel Alonso and Bruno Oteiza from the Basque country of Spain and Gerard Bellver from Catalonia—have been living and working in Mexico since the early 1990s and now feel properly settled in the country, with its rich world of flavors and traditions. They call their blend of cuisines "gatxupa," which literally means "fusion," and describe it as "evolution," but it is in effect much more radical than that. Bringing a playful enthusiasm to their creative cooking, they offer surprise and delight in equal measure: their dishes make use of the very best seasonal ingredients and are prepared with an in-depth knowledge of modern methods, applied with surgical precision and a free-spirited enthusiasm.

Diners can choose either a menu with a clear Basque influence or opt for the tasting menu, which offers beautiful surprises with every course; these may include jurel (a type of mackerel); foie gras with malted apple or pears soaked in sherry; delicate shrimp dishes; carrillera callejera (pig's cheek—a homage to tacos al pastor, a popular pork dish); quail with a popcorn crust; or veal with amaranth cream.

For dessert, the playfulness comes into its own: among the many creations to be savored are amazing chocolate spheres that burst in the mouth. Every course can be accompanied by a special wine from a list that has a distinct Basque element, but is truly eclectic and widely regarded as the most comprehensive in Mexico City.

The space is minimalist, with lots of wood, touches of metal, and warm, subtle lighting, creating an sophisticated environment in which to enjoy the meal. Such is the restaurant's following that there is also a private members' club—Casa Biko—tucked away within the restaurant where special meals, tastings, and private cookery classes are offered. **RR**

⬆ A pretty appetizer of scallop salad at Biko.

Fonda Don Chon | Pre-Hispanic dishes in a working-class dive

Location Mexico City   **Signature dish** Cactus worm tacos with avocado sauce | **$**

On an impoverished-looking street, Fonda Don Chon might seem a little downtrodden at first glance. But this humble restaurant is only a 15-minute walk from Zócalo, the cultural, geographic, and touristic heart of Mexico City, and has hosted some of the country's leading politicians as well as travelers with adventurous palates from all over the world.

Located near Mercado de la Merced, one of the world's largest food markets, Fonda Don Chon opened in the 1950s offering a basic menu of fresh ingredients sourced from the market and catering to the tastes and budgets of the Merced vendors. Strongly influenced first by the xipitecas counter-cultural movement of the 1960s, then by the wave of nationalistic pride in the 1970s, the Don Chon kitchen has always sought inspiration from the indigenous Nahuatl Indian heritage and developed a pre-Hispanic selection of attention-grabbing dishes. Having established a reputation for rootsy cooking, Fonda Don Chon became popular with Mexican electoral candidates keen to show that they could kick it with el pueblo. Their visits to Fonda Don Chon provided photo opportunities for the local press to show them sinking their teeth into ethnic cuisine that might be challenging for Western tastes.

Fonda Don Chon serves some conventional dishes, but is best known for Creole-Indian items such as *gusanos de maguey* (cactus worm tacos with avocado sauce). These are naturally an acquired taste, but can be commended for their crispy crunch. Also worth trying are *albóndigas de armadillo* (armadillo meatballs in mango sauce), *venado con huitlacoche* (venison with corn smut), and *escamoles de hormiga* (red ant roe), the "caviar of Mexico." Lunch during the week is the best time to go, with a morning browse through the market setting the tone for your meal. **CO**

⬆ The signature dish is not for the faint-hearted.

Pujol | Reviving tradition through culinary innovation

Location Mexico City **Signature dish** *Mole madre* | ❸❸❸

> *"A meal at Pujol is a culinary tour of Mexican cooking with Chef Olvera as your guide."*

A Life Worth Eating

⬆ The entrance to Olvera's innovative restaurant in an upmarket area of Mexico City.

➡ A creative take on a taco at Pujol.

At Pujol, top Mexican chef Enrique Olvera offers a reinterpretation of the popular traditional recipes of his country. To achieve this, he spent a long time researching and analyzing the typical ingredients of land and sea. Then, when he began to use them himself, he remained constant to the precept "waste not, want not": he is famous for always making the most of everything.

Step by step, Olvera combined innovative methods with ancient traditions, and thus created unique dishes that are unobtainable elsewhere. The resulting cuisine has earned Pujol a place in the world's top restaurant rankings.

There are short and long tasting menus, and for a full experience, it is best to go for the latter, which includes eleven courses, among them a hollowed-out pumpkin filled with grilled baby corn. Corn is the "taste of Mexico," the key ingredient in the country's cuisine, and it appears on Pujol's menu in many variations. The other prominent ingredient is the popular *mole* (a type of Mexican chili sauce served with a multitude of dishes). Olvera's version, the *mole madre*, consists of a permanently maintained base to which new *mole* keeps being added; it is then served with a tortilla alone—all that is needed is this dark, thick, aromatic sauce that is made following a tradition going back several thousand years. Other specialities include cubed ceviche (fish) with hoja santa herbs; toast with *escamoles* (ant larvae); green noodles with chili sauce and dried shrimp, and, for dessert, simple but exquisite fermented banana.

Beverages accompany the dishes perfectly and include not only carefully selected wine but also limited-edition beers. The space is minimalist, the dishes arrive in perfect time, and the service is faultless. Any visit will be an experience that stays in the diners' minds and will always be associated with their time in Mexico City. **RR**

Azul Condesa | Mexican regional dishes cooked with verve and imagination

Location Mexico City   **Signature dish** Roast duck stuffed fritters in *mole negro* |

"What is transcendent here is the mole negro. *It is so much more than a sauce. It is a heritage."*

Trevor Felch, trevsbistro.com

⬆ Azul Condesa serves imaginative cuisine in a no-frills environment.

When you eat at Azul Condesa, you dine in light, airy and modern surroundings: when the weather's fair (which it often is in Mexico City), take a table outdoors, where the sun shines and the bright green foliage provides a vivid contrast to the pale and cool neutral tones within.

But the real joy of dining here is the imaginative regional specializations of head chef Ricardo Muñoz Zurita, a cooking star with several books to his name, including the definitive dictionary of Mexican cuisine. Azul Condesa is his third restaurant, after Azul y Oro and Azul Histórico, and by general consent his greatest achievement to date.

The menus created by Zurita pay homage to Mexican cuisines that even Mexicans had forgotten or lost sight of, especially those of the southwestern state of Oaxaca, well known for its several varieties of *mole* sauce (as well as for its mescal). The state of Tabasco, famous for its fiery sauces, is also well represented: try as starter the *chaya tamalito*, a maize dumpling cooked Tabasco-style and topped with tomato sauce and cheese. Other options, especially for the adventurous, could be a spicy guacamole with grasshoppers or sea snails served with olive oil. For mains, you might want to try the roast duck stuffed fritters in an Oaxacan *mole negro* (black mole) sauce or maybe venison in a yellow mole.

Azul Condesa is very much a place where robust regional cuisine meets the modern imagination of Zurita. The chef is not just content with his regular menu either: every month sees a special festival celebrating certain ingredients such as chilies, mushrooms, or seafood. Even drinking here has a sense of occasion: how about a chicken breast mescal in a gourd, the vessel in which it is traditionally served? When you dine at Azul Condesa, you certainly eat and drink in style. **ATJ**

San Angel Inn |

Classic Mexican in a colonial hacienda

Location Mexico City **Signature dish** *Huitlacoche* | 💲💲💲

Leaving the bustle of avenues Revolución and Insurgentes behind, the first thing people walking up Altavista come across is the studio of Mexico's famous artist and muralist, Diego Rivera. Architecturally, the building looks as though it's part of the Bauhaus, with its industrial aesthetic, jagged roofs and shocking mauve walls.

Nestling up against this factorylike apparition is the San Angel Inn, a restaurant on the site of a seventeenth-century colonial Carmelite monastery, where Mexico Revolution leaders Pancho Villa and Emiliano Zapata signed a pact in 1910. It is now one of the country's most beautiful haciendas, with lush gardens and an elegant portico leading into a secluded patio courtyard off which radiate segments of elegant spaces—dining rooms, a bar, even a ballroom. Musicians play in a gracious area that's coolly tiled and crammed full of tinkling fountains and flowering agapanthus plants. Perfect Margaritas are served in silver carafes and ice buckets

Meanwhile, in the vast dining rooms, with their polished wood and starched white linen, hordes of waiters bring diners enormous trays of dishes that could include seafood ceviche Acapulco-style; Rockefeller shrimp and schnitzel; calf's brains with black butter, or the signature dish, *huitlacoche* (corn pancakes), which may be served with a variety of accompaniments.

The menu makes no attempt to compete with either the sharply regional street food that seems to fill almost every district of the city, or the cutting-edge deconstructed *mole* sauces currently produced by Mexico's leading chefs. The San Angel Inn offers only Mexican–international cuisine of the old order. It's nothing like trendy, but it makes perfect sense on its own terms, and few people who have ever dined here would want it any other way. **SFP**

MeroToro |

Baja California comes to Mexico City

Location Mexico City **Signature dish** Slow-roasted ribs | 💲💲

MeroToro? Literally translated, it means fish (mero) and bull (toro), but here in Mexico City's fashionable district of Condesa, Gabriela Cámara and Pablo Bueno's much-acclaimed restaurant is more than a mansion of surf and turf (even though its menu owes a lot to the cuisine of the coastal area of Baja California, as seen through an international prism). Yes, fish and steaks are grilled and beef ribs are roasted, while starters include a selection of seafood dishes; but, taken as a whole, head chef Jair Téllez's menu is a happy marriage between robust cuisine and the ethereal and endless quest for flavor.

Take, for example, his soup of white beans, sea urchin, and chorizo oil: this manages to be both silky and earthy. Alternatively, try the slow-cooked Iberian

> *"Chef Jair Téllez deftly shows off his skills with both seafood and meat dishes."*
>
> fodors.com

pork, served with braised lentils and a poached egg, with its sensuous mouth feel and bracing bite provided by the legumes. For mains, some swear by a juicy and sweet fillet of roast grouper resting on a bittersweet and creamy puree of cauliflower and chard; others prefer the salty-sweet Mexican risotto with shrimp (a reflection of Cámara's Italian roots).

This is Cámara and Bueno's second restaurant in Mexico City (the first was Contramar), and their reputation for offering great dining has drawn in a fashionable and food-literate crowd from the start. The place looks good as well: the outside is smart and contemporary while the interior offers a modern, modish, artistically distressed ambience. **ATJ**

Scotchies | Jamaican jerk chicken just as it should be

Location Montego Bay **Signature dish** Jerk chicken or jerk fish | **$**

Old barrels and chunky wooden benches under a makeshift thatched canopy, loud music, people drinking Red Stripe beer from the bottle, some locals playing dominoes—welcome to Scotchies, where dishes arrive wrapped in tin foil, with a plastic knife and fork. This may seem like the most basic Jamaican "jerk pit," but the food at Scotchies has been acclaimed as some of the finest of its kind in the world.

There are three sites: the original in Montego Bay, and two newer outposts in Kingston and Ocho Rios. In all three, the traditional cooking procedure is diligently followed: the meat is marinated overnight in a tenderizing mix of lemon and saltwater, then seasoned with a spicy "jerk" sauce that includes lemon, herbs, and hot bell peppers.

The whole split chickens are placed directly on a traditional Jamaican open-air barbecue of smoking sweetwood and pimento wood chips. Huge slabs of pork are treated the same. There is no grill and the meat is placed directly on the wood. Both are covered with sheets of corrugated iron while cooking, helping to capture the flavor of the wood in the meat. Some experts claim that it is in fact impossible to capture this exact flavor anywhere else without the same Caribbean wood.

The menu is limited to these two meats, sold by the quarter, half, and whole pound, or as a whole, half, or quarter bird. The only other "main course" available is chicken or pork sausage, or jerk fish, cooked with okra, onions, and tomatoes. Everything else on the one-page menu is a side dish: roast sweet potato, yam, or breadfruit, sweet corn, plantains, rice and peas, or rice and kidney beans, and "festival," which is a distinctive local cornbread fritter. **SH**

← Traditional jerk chicken served at Scotchies.

Gloria's Rendezvous | Sip fish tea and soak up the atmosphere

Region Kingston **Signature dish** Curried lobster | **$**

In Jamaican culture, "fine dining" means something very different from elsewhere: dining out is a lengthy social occasion to embrace conversation, leading to late-night entertainment. For this, many Jamaicans select one of Gloria's two seafood restaurants in Port Royal, considered one of the island's best places to eat. But visiting tourists may be surprised by the simplicity of the restaurant.

Forget fine table linen and white-glove service, at Gloria's Rendezvous you will sit on plastic chairs under a tent, on a road near the airport. Food is cooked in a ramshackle kitchen. Gloria's nearby beachside Top Spot at least has the luxury of interior dining space. Service is somewhat sparse, too: sometimes it is friendly and prompt, but more often it can be slow. The wait for food can stretch to an hour, and waitresses never write down orders, preferring to memorize them in a haphazard fashion. Locals, however, do not seem to mind, taking the chance to relax, chat, and drink some Red Stripe beer.

Everyone agrees on one thing, however: the food is worth waiting for. Fish is caught by Port Royal fishermen and served steamed, fried, or grilled. The menu features curried or grilled lobster, parrotfish, snapper, conch soup, and garlic or honey-jerked shrimp. Side dishes include local favorites such as rice and peas, grilled onions, okra, tomatoes, festival sweetbread, sweet potato pudding, and bammy flatbread. One of the more distinctive offerings is Gloria's fish tea that arrives in a cup to sip before the main course.

Weekends at Gloria's are famed as part of Port Royal's lively night scene, with music and dancing. On these busy nights, you can spot the locals in the know: they avoid long waits for their food by ordering over the phone before they arrive. **SH**

Marmalade | A sophisticated take on Puerto Rican cuisine

Location San Juan **Signature dish** White bean soup with truffle oil | $

"The restaurant is a labor of love … and it is evident in the flavors and attention to detail."

frommers.com

⬆ A sleek restaurant offering upmarket dining.

Well-traveled American owner and chef Peter Schintler set up his first restaurant on the island of Puerto Rico after working under six famous master chefs including Raymond Blanc, Gordon Ramsay, and Peter Timmins, and in kitchens as diverse as Le Cirque in Manhattan and Blu Restaurant in Singapore. Marmalade aims to honor the finest Puerto Rican fresh produce and recipes, but in a lighter, more sustainable way, avoiding the island's culinary tradition of deep-frying everything in sight.

Schintler's restaurant and wine bar is located on Calle Fortaleza, the main street in the picturesque heart of Old San Juan, the Spanish colonial part of the capital. Food is modern "Californian-French," using local farm produce and applying international inspiration from Schintler's master chef tutors.

The experience he gained at Italy's famous truffle restaurant, La Contea in Piedmont, reveals itself in the signature dish, a triumphant evolution of the humble Puerto Rican staple of white bean soup. Reviewers have described the creamy creation, which is flavored with black truffle oil, applewood-smoked bacon dust, garlic, thyme, onion, and celery, as a "life-changing experience." And Schintler's treatment of red snapper surely owes a little to his time in Singapore, where he was awarded the "Rising Star Chef of the Year." The fish is poached in a Thai curry and coconut broth, and served with jasmine rice and a spiced shrimp sesame dumpling.

The restaurant is modern and the ambience relaxed, with chic decor in an orange-and-white color scheme, and heavily cushioned benches. Schintler may serve the main courses himself and makes regular trips from the kitchen to chat with the diners. Guests can also linger in the stylish lounge to enjoy one of the innovative cocktails, such as the "Global Warming," which includes a triple pepper ice cube that heats up as you drink it. **SH**

Rainforest Hideaway | A romantic rainforest dining experience

Location Marigot Bay **Signature dish** Grilled swordfish with saltfish *brandade* | 💲💲

To get to Rainforest Hideaway, diners need to drive over a hill where a magnificent view opens up of the clear emerald green water of Marigot Bay, with yachts bobbing between palm trees, mangroves, and bleached wooden piers, all laid out like the ultimate "appetizer." By the time they have parked and taken the complimentary water taxi across to the al fresco restaurant on the far shore, most diners know they are in for something special.

Rainforest Hideaway spreads across a series of piers and boardwalks and right up into the rainforest. By night, the setting is especially awe-inspiring, with fairy lights shining in the trees, candles and hurricane lamps on the tables, and underwater lights revealing shoals of fish cavorting around the pier. This is clearly an extremely romantic venue. Does the food live up to the setting? It certainly does. In fact, the mix of exotic Caribbean flavors and classical French techniques is surprisingly sophisticated for such a remote spot that can only be reached by boat.

The kitchen is even able to show off a little with dishes like chili and lemongrass infused shrimps with herb and garlic risotto and ginger sauce, or pan-fried mahi-mahi with roasted spiced pumpkin, *tostones* (fried plantain slices), Creole *beurre blanc* and *callaloo* (a tropical vegetable) reduction.

The Swedish chef follows a policy of using mostly Caribbean produce in the starters, desserts, sauces, and side dishes, combined with mostly imported meat and fish, which is necessary to maintain a constant quality of supply that is normally unavailable on such a small island. Many fruits and herbs are grown in the restaurant garden. St. Lucian cocoa beans are rated highly in the world of chocolate production, so the island plantations supply the chocolate for desserts, such as white chocolate crème brûlée and dark chocolate cake. But more adventurous diners may opt for the "fried cheese ravioli" dessert. **SH**

> *"Exotic Caribbean tastes … are paired with French techniques at this upscale hideaway."*
>
> fodors.com

⬆ The view of Marigot Bay is spectacular.

The Cove | A true taste of Bajan cuisine in the chef's home

Location Cattlewash **Signature dish** Fish of the day in orange and ginger glaze | $$

How about visiting an award-winning Caribbean cookery writer for lunch at home? That option is readily available on Barbados. Cook, author, and local personality, Laurel-Ann Morley cooks lunches at The Cove restaurant overlooking the rugged east coast at Cattlewash. It is part of her charming home, a simple light-blue painted wooden building hidden among vegetation, but it is not easy to find: only a small sign points up the hill.

Diners are welcomed like old friends and served by Laurel-Ann's husband and daughters. The surroundings are modest: you can sit inside the whitewashed dining room with its bare wooden floor or on the terrace under a wooden veranda. Lunch is served from a limited menu written out on a blackboard, although Laurel-Ann often introduces the dishes herself and explains their history. On Sundays, The Cove serves a Bajan buffet lunch that attracts locals from all over the island and booking is essential.

The food is based on fresh, expertly prepared Bajan ingredients. You will find famous local specialities like stuffed crab backs, fried fillets of flying fish, and pepperpot stew. Shrimp can be lightly battered with a pepper jelly dip or served with coconut in a curry. Side dishes include sweet potato, Caribbean souse, and sweet-and-sour pickled beetroot.

There are less well-known Bajan dishes on offer, such as ground provision soup (made with yam, *eddoe*, and cassava) and *calaloo* soup (made from a Caribbean leaf vegetable). The fish of the day comes from Oistins fish market and may include the less familiar Caribbean *channa* or mahi-mahi, often served with Laurel-Ann's signature orange and ginger glaze. The concise dessert menu features the reliable crowd-pleasers of rum and raisin bread pudding, chocolate fudge pie, and lime cream tart. **SH**

[↑] The Cove is hidden away above the coastal highway.

Champers | Delicious food in fantasy tropical island surroundings

Location Christ Church   **Signature dish** Parmesan-crusted barracuda | ❺❺❺

Sitting down on an open terrace, perched right above the beach with palm trees swaying in the wind as waves crash on the sand below: for many visitors, Champers is like a Caribbean fantasy come true. But there is more to this traditional Bajan home than the spectacular views across Accra Beach: locals consider Champers the best place to eat on the whole south coast of the island.

There is plenty of seafood on offer, of course, from the signature barracuda to the typical Caribbean dishes of coconut shrimp with chili sauce or Cajun blackened mahi-mahi with rice. Flying fish, tuna, and scallops usually appear somewhere on the menu, too. Beyond the local specialities, Champers offers fish pie, Scottish smoked salmon, and crab crepes. More standard fare includes spiced pork chops with garlic mash and caramelized apple sauce and herb-crusted rack of lamb with new potato mash and broccoli florets.

The chef demonstrates a more international flair with dishes such as medley of seafood pasta with lobster, shrimp, clams, and mussels tossed in a Champagne and pesto cream, fillet of beef with garlic mash, cognac, and mustard cream, or camembert baked in puff pastry with spiced apples.

Expect hints of an American dining experience throughout, from "greeters" in the car park to massive portions. Lunch is dominated by local business people, whereas dinner is a more relaxed and romantic affair. The restaurant offers a lively downstairs eating area, with the more formal area on the level above. It is essential to book in advance to get one of the best tables overlooking the beach at any time of the day. If you can tear yourself away from the stunning ocean view, the restaurant owner is very proud of her gallery of local art. **SH**

⬆ Cheesecake with strawberry coulis at Champers.

Oistins Fish Fry | Fresh fish cooked on the spot, entertainment included

Location Oistins   **Signature dish** Barbecued swordfish | 💲

With its paper plates, plastic knives and forks, and not a printed menu in sight, it is clear this venue is not about haute cuisine. Yet Oistins Fish Fry is definitely one of the most memorable food experiences for anyone coming to explore Barbados.

Originally, Oistins was a quiet fishing village at the southern end of the island, known only for its big modern fish market. Tourists would stroll between the fishing boats, watching fishermen weaving nets and catches being unloaded. Gradually, a few stalls appeared alongside the market, barbecuing and selling some of the day's fish. The idea caught on with both tourists and locals, and has grown into a major island institution. The fish fry is now the second biggest tourist attraction on Barbados.

The recipe is still simple: around 30 vendors have set up stalls with names such as Uncle George's, Granny's, or Pat's Place. A big plate of fried or grilled fish is simply garnished with extras including salad, sweet potato, coleslaw, cucumber julienne, macaroni pie, and even chips. The fish on offer is likely to include marlin, swordfish, tuna, snapper, lobster, shrimp, mahi-mahi, and flying fish. Diners browse competing stalls to find what they want, then find a place to sit on shared benches and picnic tables. There is no wine list—the drink of choice is usually a bottle of local Banks beer or local rum.

The fish fry now operates day and night all through the week. If Saturday is busy, Friday can be absolutely frenetic. Expect long lines. Hotels run shuttle bus trips, locals may appear in bizarre fancy dress, craft and souvenir stands are open for business, and local bands, choirs, and DJs appear on makeshift stages. A few elderly locals sit at tables playing dominoes, but most people end up dancing at some point—an unmissable experience. **SH**

⬆ **Choose from different types of grilled fish at Oistins.**

Brown Sugar | Authentic Bajan classics in lively surroundings

Location Bridgetown **Signature dish** *Cou-cou* and flying fish | ❸❸

This is just the place for lovers of classic dishes such as macaroni pie, pepperpot (spiced meat) stew, and flying fish. And, if you think that may be a rather select few, you have not been to Barbados. These dishes are among the most popular specialities, and Brown Sugar is usually busy with local businesspeople.

The restaurant has been based in an old Bajan house just outside the capital for more than 45 years. It is not far from the beach, but there is no sea view as such. Instead, the fan-cooled interior and pretty patios are decked with flowers, ferns, and trickling water features. The homely atmosphere includes regular live music from Bridgetown musicians.

Lunch is usually very busy, with locals and visitors alike flocking to the restaurant, thanks to an extensive planter's buffet lunch of around 30 authentic Bajan and Creole specialities. Pride of place in this all-you-can-eat array goes to the national dish of *cou-cou*, a smooth, firm paste of cornmeal and okra, served with seasoned flying fish "roll-ups" that are poached in a court-bouillon. This distinctive Caribbean dish dates back to the times when inexpensive local ingredients were used to feed slaves.

Other local delicacies included in the buffet are pumpkin bread dumplings, peas and rice, fried plantains, *souse* (slow-cooked pork in a lime and vinegar broth), fish cakes, and the ever-popular pepperpot stew and macaroni pie.

Evenings are quieter affairs at Brown Sugar, offering candlelit dinners with an à la carte menu of yet more local specialities such as split pea soup with biscuits, coconut shrimp, lentil pea chili, and plantain-crusted mahi-mahi. Typical Bajan desserts round off the main courses: try the delicious pawpaw pie, or bread and butter pudding with rum sauce, one of Brown Sugar's most requested dishes. **SH**

⬆ Brown Sugar is set on the outskirts of Bridgetown.

Richard's Bake & Shark | The ultimate fried shark sandwich

Location Maracas Bay **Signature dish** Fried shark sandwich | ⑨

"Is this the world's best fish sandwich? For any fish-lover … Richard's is required eating."

Arthur Bovino, Daily Mail

⬆ The Bake & Shark sandwich is worth the wait.

To some, it is a simple fried fish sandwich to eat on the beach, like a Trinidadian version of fish and chips. To others, it is a distinctive delicacy that deserves its place alongside the culinary marvels of the world. But most people agree that the best place to sample bake and shark is at a spectacular palm-tree-lined white sand beach in Trinidad.

Richard's Bake & Shark is one of several stalls along the back of Maracas Bay beach and among many on the island—but it is one of the oldest and certainly the most famous of the lot. Richard's is now run by his son Gary, but the recipe and the reputation remain unchanged. The famous sandwich is made from simple ingredients: the "bake" (homemade bread) is made by dropping a dollop of raised dough (consisting of flour, water, baking powder, lard, yeast, and salt) into a pan of hot fat. The sizzling mass is then shaped into a crispy, oily bun (similar to Indian fried bread), which is filled with shark steak (usually black tip shark) that has been coated in flour and deep-fried.

Customers can help themselves from a vast array of sauces and accompaniments, layering as much as they like to create their own sandwich. The quality of these is said to be the secret of Richard's success: they range from garlic sauce, tamarind, chili sauce, mango chutney, and "chadon beni" (Mexican coriander) to sides of Trinidad-style "coleslaw" of seasoned and dressed grated cabbage and cucumber, cheese, various salads, or slices of pineapple. The whole glorious combination is usually washed down with an ice-cold beer.

The sandwiches can be consumed on one of the tables set up next to the stand or—even better—taken down to the beach. Before that, however, customers must beat the considerable lines: on weekends, they can be particularly long, as people come from all over the island to eat here. **SH**

Veni Mangé | Creative Caribbean cooking in colorful surroundings

Location Port of Spain **Signature dish** Stewed oxtail with dumplings | $ $

Veni Mangé stands on Ariapita Avenue, the lively restaurant strip in the center of Trinidad's capital, Port of Spain. It is an old clay-colored colonial house surrounded by exotic tropical plants. Inside, there is a relaxed Caribbean ambience: every chair seems to be painted a different color, the walls are crowded with local art, and, high above the diners' heads, ceiling fans keep the humid air moving.

Sadly, the restaurant's long-standing chef Allyson Hennessy passed away in 2011. Allyson was a major TV celebrity in Trinidad, famous for both reading the news and hosting chat shows. A Cordon Bleu-trained chef, she also had her own television cooking series. Together with her sister Roses Hezekiah, she launched the restaurant in 1980, calling it Veni Mangé, which is French patois for "come and eat." Roses, a Caribbean music producer, still runs the restaurant today.

The kitchen serves up a daily changing menu based around Caribbean specialities, so expect *callaloo* soup, crab backs, Creole lamb, and homemade desserts such as coconut bake and rum fruit trifle. Fresh fish includes red snapper, mahi-mahi, grouper, king fish, and shrimp. These are normally grilled and served with a tamarind, coconut, mango, or garlic sauce.

By Trinidad standards, this is an upmarket restaurant and prices are much higher than in small cafes that offer similar dishes, but, at Veni Mangé, everything is carefully prepared and well presented on homely decorated crockery. More creative offerings include saltfish accras (fritters) with Mexican coriander sauce, stewed beef in Guinness with dumplings, chicken with pineapple rum sauce, pork in ginger sauce, and black-eyed peas and nut croquettes with mango sauce. The fish broth with cassava, dumplings, and green figs is a must-try. Typical side dishes are Caribbean staples of macaroni pie, plantains, chickpeas, and beans and rice. **SH**

"The best lunches in town are served in this traditional West Indian house."

fodors.com

⬆ The food is prepared with care and served with pride.

Lo Nuestro | Classic Ecuadorian seafood in cozy surroundings

Location Guayaquil **Signature dish** Ceviche | $$

In the bustling port of Guayaquil, Ecuador's biggest city, culinary traditions are influenced by the seafood from the river and Pacific Ocean beyond. Hence, seafood is the focus at Lo Nuestro, one of the highest-rated restaurants in the city and very much an institution that pulls in locals and tourists alike. It is located in the trendy Urdesa district, along with many of the city's leading eateries.

The outside of the small whitewashed former residential villa is decorated with flags and giant potted palms, and pedestrians are beguiled by a big board displaying the daily specials. On the inside, the cozily cluttered decor is mainly pink and white, with wooden shutters and period furniture adding character, and walls covered with old prints and photographs. Prices are perhaps higher than at an average Ecuadorian restaurant, but there is a genuine, homely feel to the place.

Most diners order some ceviche to start, then ask for the catch of the day for their main course. Businessmen fill the restaurant at lunchtime, sometimes settling for a classic Latin American lunch that lasts several hours. The food is lovingly prepared and presented, sticking mainly to tried-and-tested local classics and ingredients.

The signature house ceviche is a medley of octopus, fish, shrimp, and calamari marinated in lime juice and served in an open clam shell topped with sweet red onion. Spiced crab claws come with a garlic dipping sauce and the sea bass is served with a crab sauce. Another winning dish is breaded *corvine con verde* (a local sea fish similar to snapper, breaded and served with vegetables, and topped with avocado). Other traditional favorites include homemade empanadas, *seco de chivo* (goat stew), and shrimp prepared in many ways. Bustling and convivial, this is a pleasant place to enjoy a taste of Ecuador. **SH**

La Choza | Ecuadorian food in a bright, cheerful family restaurant

Location Quito **Signature dish** Cheese soup | $$

The Pallares family has been serving high-quality traditional Ecuadorian food for more than forty years. Owner Diana Pallares says that the recipes have been passed down from her grandmother, although the classics are now mixed with plenty of modern influences. This large restaurant stands on one of the prime boulevards of Quito, across the street from the World Trade Center, and so is shrewdly geared up to cater to large groups of visiting businessmen. It has, however, also become something of a national institution for its championing of local cuisine.

Food is served at simple square wooden tables with white cloths and bright, traditional woven place mats and orange and green napkins. Dishes are carefully presented versions of favorites from the diverse regions of Ecuador, washed down with corn beer or fruit punch. Staple ingredients such as plantain, yucca, rice, and maize appear in many forms. Typical hearty dishes include fried plantain-flour turnover stuffed with cheese, marinated shrimp with garlic and onion, green pepper served with rice, fried yucca, and salad, and fried pigs' trotters with peas and peanut and onion sauce.

> *"The mood, music, and menu are strictly Ecuadorian ... Pastry stuffed with lobster is a speciality."*
>
> fodors.com

The spacious interior retains a rustic Andean feel, despite the colorful modern decor and shiny tiled floor. Old wooden doors, wooden ceiling beams, and local ceramic art displayed on the walls add to the atmosphere. There is also a big fireplace and a stage for folk music and dance performances. **SH**

Andrés Carne de Res | Where food and music come together to create an unforgettable experience

Location Chía   **Signature dish** *Picada rumbera* (grilled meat) | **❸❸❸**

The name Andrés refers to Andrés Jaramillo Flores, who founded this popular restaurant (in praise of which the Nobel Prize-winning author Gabriel García Márquez even created a rhyming slogan) more than 30 years ago. It is located about half an hour's drive from Bogotá, and specializes in Colombian food, and grilled meat in particular, accompanied by rumba music. The building is of gigantic proportions, and the decor somewhere between playful and kitsch, clearly designed to turn a meal into a memorable experience. The wooden tables are adorned with all manner of decorative objects (all for sale), and names and mottos on red heart-shaped illuminated signs. Once seated, you may find yourself sharing your food with "Frida Kahlo," "Diego Rivera," or "Marilyn Monroe"—or you may be crowned king or queen by the end of the evening. Anything can happen here.

While the atmosphere is lively, the food is truly delicious. The menu is all of 60 pages long, and fairly complicated, so it is best to ask for recommendations. The many tasty dishes include empanadas, *patacones* (fried green plantain), *pastel de yuca* (cassava casserole), mixed fried platter, *arepas de chócolo con queso* (corn cakes with cheese), consommé, and *picada with chicharrón* (pork crackling). For mains, you should order the *parrillada* (barbecued meat), or the *ajiaco con pollo* (potato stew with chicken). The excellent exotic fruit juices and typical desserts such as *merengón de guanábana* (merengue with guanabana fruit) in chocolate sauce are also worth trying.

The waiting staff (mostly made up of students) is efficient and pays attention to detail. There is all kinds of music played throughout the evening, and before you know it everyone is dancing along to a rumba. There is no need to worry about how much you can drink—the motto is to enjoy yourself, and there are chauffeurs at hand to drive you back home. **RR**

"This legendary steakhouse blows everyone away, even repeat visitors, for its fun atmosphere."

Lonely Planet

⊼ The colorful decor is part of the attraction.

Café Casa Veroes | A true taste of Venezuela in historic surroundings

Location Caracas **Signature dish** *Pabellón criollo* |

"Who can resist a few fritters filled with Carupanera black pudding and covered in llanero *cheese?"*

Edgardo Morales, chef and founder of Café Casa Veroes

⤒ The café is a tranquil refuge from the hectic streets.

With its characteristic flaky pastry and melt-in-the-mouth texture, *pastel de polvorosa* (chicken pot pie) is one the most refined and characteristic dishes of Venezuelan gastronomy. For a chance to sample this dish, much loved by Venezuelans, at its authentic best, take a tip from the locals and make your way to Café Casa Veroes at the heart of Caracas' historic center. The café is located on the grounds of a magnificent colonial mansion turned museum, the Casa de Estudio de la Storia de Venezuela. It is a small, friendly café, with only twelve tables, offering *pastel de polvorosa* and other traditional Venezuelan dishes to appreciative locals and curious visitors alike.

Another favorite on the café's regular menu is *pabellón criollo*, Venezuela's national dish, which consists of rice served with shredded beef and black beans, with fried plantains on the side. When prepared with love and understanding, as it is here, this simple, hearty dish is immensely satisfying.

Chef Edgardo Morales, who founded Café Casa Veroes, takes pride in his dedicated exploration of Venezuela's culinary traditions, witnessed by another outstanding dish in his repertoire, the gloriously flavorful *asado negro*: beef slow-cooked until tender with spices and unrefined sugar.

There are no alcoholic drinks on offer here, but instead a rich variety of tastes from the tropics in the shape of refreshing fruit juices and smoothies, made from Venezuelan fruits such as red mulberries, guava, pineapple, and naranjilla. Another option is the refreshing *el cachicamero*, brown sugarcane juice flavored with pineapple and ginger.

The café itself is modest and unpretentious, but what is on offer in this secluded place is a rare chance to discover the national dishes of Venezuela, cooked with love and eaten with relish. The fact that the café also serves extremely good coffee should help to persuade any waverers to give it a try. **RA**

Cega | A lesson in high-end Venezuelan food at a gastronomic institution

Location Caracas **Signature dish** *Talcarí de chivo* | ❸❸❸

Located on a peaceful street in downtown Caracas, housed in a 1930s art deco house designed by the pioneer Venezuelan architect Gustavo Wallis, is the Centro de Estudios Gastronómicos, or CEGA, Venezuela's first center of gastronomic studies. It was founded more than twenty-five years ago by José Rafael Lovera, who was also the founder of the Venezuelan Academy of Gastronomy.

At the study center, the Cega restaurant opens its doors just three days a week so that thirty privileged lunchtime diners can enjoy dishes prepared by student chefs training in top-class Venezuelan cooking. Customers are welcome to bring along their own wine to complement the meal. The students have every motivation to produce food of a very high culinary standard because they are evaluated for their performance at the dining room.

Flying the flag for Venezuelan cuisine, the menu here offers the curious a chance to sample the country's traditional dishes, ranging from folk fare to recipes from the colonial era. Equally, as befits a culinary institute aspiring to the highest standards, the food is carefully presented in a contemporary manner. Dishes such as *corbullón Caribeño*, a complex spicy soup, or a Venezuelan goat curry are re-interpreted and enhanced using haute-cuisine techniques. And customers can sample some of the dessert recipes of the Mantuanos—as the aristocratic descendants of the colonial Spanish conquerors are known—notably the Maria Luisa cake, a delicate biscuit filled with guava syrup and cream that was first seen in the mid-eighteenth century.

Despite its serious educational role, the restaurant is an engaging place in which to learn about high-end Venezuelan cuisine. Be warned, though, that electronic payment methods have not yet arrived at Cega, so be sure to bring cash—just as the Spanish conquistadores did centuries ago. **RA**

"Cooking, like many other human activities, is a wonderful combination of hands and brain."

José Rafael Lovera, founder of Cega

⬆ Cega prides itself on its take on Venezuelan dishes.

La Estancia | A venue popular with carnivore celebrities

Location Caracas   **Signature dish** *Parilla La Estancia* | 🌑🌑🌑

Housed in style in an ex-colonial home, complete with a courtyard filled with leafy palm trees, La Estancia offers hospitality to business executives and large family groups alike. Established in 1957 in the middle of the financial district of Caracas, the restaurant is regarded as Venezuela's exemplary steak-house and has long had a devoted following for its trademark grilled meats. The quality of the carefully sourced meat, and the extensive range of meat cuts on offer (including classic Argentinian ones), have made this place a carnivore's delight, enhanced by notably generous portions and courteous, polished, and experienced service. Such is the restaurant's reputation that many celebrities have dined here over the decades, including movie stars Catherine Deneuve and Yves Montand, who reportedly shared a delicious *parrilla* (dish of barbecued meat).

Although the menu offers well-rendered versions of classic dishes such as tournedos Rossini, snapper bonne femme, and steak stroganoff, it is the lovingly grilled, flavorful beef that is the star of the show. Classic accompaniments include *arepas* (cornmeal cakes), *tamales*, soft white cheese, yucca bread, and *congri*, a special Cuban rice with beans. To round off the meal, for diners who have any room left, desserts range from the simple and refreshing—fresh melon, peaches, and pineapple—to the indulgent, such as pancakes with *dulce de leche* or caramel flan.

Diners may sit in the large main hall, with its photos of celebrity diners, or opt for smaller rooms that have an Argentinian theme. Wherever you sit, there is a convivial buzz of friends and families enjoying themselves. La Estancia is a local institution for celebrating special occasions, from birthdays to wedding anniversaries. Don't spoil it by being in a hurry—this is a place for lingering. **RA**

⊡ A wide choice of wines is available at La Estancia.

Palms | Innovative cuisine from Venezuela's leading female chef

Location Caracas   **Signature dish** *Pollo laqueado en papelón* | ❺❺❺❺❺

Stepping into Palms is to enter the experimental personal laboratory of chef Helen Ibarra. Noted for her innovative creativity and ability to push culinary boundaries to delicious effect, Ibarra received her culinary education at the hands of such notable master chefs as Joël Robuchon and Gérard Vié. Within Venezuela, she is widely known, not least for being the first woman in the country to manage the kitchen of a five-star hotel. In 2012, she won the Gourmand World Cook Book Award in the female chef category with her book, *Cocina Extra-Ordinaria*.

"In professional cooking, a chef has to offer [the diner] different paths," she says. In her personal take on Venezuelan gastronomy, she likes to offer a menu of dishes inspired by literary references, and so feed the imagination and spirit as well as the palate; one such dish is her *Pollo laqueado en papelón* (laquered chicken with sugarcane and lemon). Julio Cortazar is one writer who has inspired her menus.

Among the starters to look out for are Ibarra's trademark take on *tequenos*, a popular snack made from dough and cheese, and here flavored with goat cheese. Ibarra mixes up French haute-cuisine culinary techniques and dishes with Venezuela's indigenous ingredients and rich history—a French-style duck confit may arrive paired with Creole-inspired bananas and plantain, French fries, and flakes of corn.

The dining room remains rooted in the 1990s, but the presentation of the food is of a distinctly twenty-first century character, and not without humor: *Fosforera*, a typical seafood soup, is presented with a "fisherman's net" of puff pastry, surrounded by cassava "sand;" as a whole, the dish resembles a Caribbean island floating in the sea. Ibarra's food is not designed simply to assuage the appetite; these are dishes to be savored, enjoyed, and discussed. **RA**

⭱ Dishes at Palms are designed to appeal to the eye.

Remanso do Bosque | A taste of the Amazon
with an innovative, contemporary twist

Location Belém **Signature dish** Grilled *filhote* (river fish) garnished with buttery cassava and *manteiguinha* beans salad | 💲💲

"A slice of the jungle in the heart of the city, [the restaurant] majors in Brazilian cuisine with a local slant."

theworlds50best.com

⬆ Dishes are made with Amazonian ingredients.

Amazonian cuisine is attracting huge curiosity worldwide because of its potential to provide diners with exciting, brand-new ingredients and flavors. Many of these novel foodstuffs can be tasted in Remanso do Bosque in Belém, the capital of Pará, located at the mouth of the Amazon River. The restaurant offers a thrilling opportunity to sample the region's incredible range of unique fruits, root vegetables, and fish from both the river and the sea.

The Castanho family opened their first restaurant, the thriving Remanso do Peixe (literally, "fish backwater") in a plain building on a tiny residential street, specializing in fish stews. Their latest venture, Remanso do Bosque ("forest backwater") is bigger, bolder, and better equipped, complete with a large kitchen, wood-burning oven, and charcoal grill. The menu is also more extensive, including even more specialties from the north of the country and featuring poultry and pork, as well as fish.

Chef brothers Thiago and Felipe Castanho, the sons of the founder, create typical regional dishes but also more innovative ones. Amazonian fish dishes are still the stars of the menu: try *filhote* (a massive river fish) or juicy *pescada amarela* (a type of hake) from the sea. They may be roasted in the oven, cooked on the grill, or simmered in one of the restaurant's famous pot stews. There are also meat delicacies, such as free-range chicken with rice cooked with *jambu* (a vegetable that has a light numbing effect) and pork belly roasted with brown sugar sauce, potatoes, cabbage, and *pirão de leite* (a milk puree). Local key ingredient cassava appears in many forms, for instance in *tucupi* sauce (extracted from wild manioc). Indigenous forest fruits such as *cupuaçu* and *bacuri* are also put to good use, soaked with cachaça in a cocktail, or simply as a refreshing fruit dessert. **JM**

Yemanjá | An authentic taste of traditional Bahian cuisine by the beach

Location Salvador   **Signature dish** *Moqueca* (seafood stew) | **$$**

The Brazilian state of Bahia has a very particular culture that is characterized by strong African influences, brought to Brazil during the era of slavery. These influences are apparent in music and dance, but also in the distinctive flavors of the cooking, and Yemanjá is the perfect place to discover all about this wonderful *cozinha bahiana*.

Yemanjá was first established in the 1960s, at a different address; since 1974, however, this popular restaurant has been in its current location, directly overlooking Salvador's beautiful Armação beach and serving as a perfect showcase for Bahian food. Dishes are characterized by the use of many typically African ingredients, such as dendê (African palm) oil, which lends a distinctive orange-red color. Typical dishes include *vatapá*, a paste made with nuts and dried shrimp, and *acarajé* dumplings made with black eyed peas deep-fried in palm oil—a popular snack that is often sold at street food stalls by women dressed in traditional white dresses.

Yemanjá offers all this and more. As befits its beachside location, fish and seafood are the speciality. In fact, the name of the restaurant, Yemanjá, in the local religion refers to the goddess of the seas, and so the focus of the menu is on her marine bounty, transformed into delicious dishes that express the region's rich history and traditions.

In the huge and lively dining room, customers can enjoy several versions of the local *moqueca* (a fish or seafood stew made with tomatoes, onions, coconut milk, and palm oil). Here you can sample it with all kinds of seafood: fish, shrimp, crab, octopus, oysters, soft shell crab, and lobster. Another must-try dish is *bobó de camarão*, a shrimp stew prepared with cooked, smooth-textured tapioca (cassava starch) cream. **JM**

Xapuri | Authentic, hearty food served in a rustic setting

Location Belo Horizonte   **Signature dish** *Vaca atolada* beef | **$**

Among Brazil's many regional cuisines, the one from the state of Minas Gerais in the east of the country (known as *cozinha mineira*), is one of the most influential. The region traces its history to mining activity in the eighteenth century and its people, the mineiros, are proud of the strong culinary tradition.

Probably the most authentic place to sample this delicious, earthy cuisine is Xapuri in the state capital of Belo Horizonte. Located in the area near the Pampulha architecture complex created by famous Brazilian architect Oscar Niemeyer, the restaurant is housed in a rustic-style building that resembles an old farmhouse with simple wooden tables underneath a thatched roof. It was set up in 1987, next to the owner's house,

> *"Heaping platters of traditional fare … this is the place for a mineiro dining experience."*
>
> frommers.com

and since then the cooking has remained unchanged, including popular snacks such as fried sausages and cassava dumplings.

Pork is a key local ingredient, and it forms the base for several dishes here: pork sirloin, marinated and roasted, is served with rice, kale, potatoes, and *tutu* (a bean stew with manioc flour); another hearty offering is fried pork ribs with rice, *feijão tropeiro* (beans mixed with manioc flour and bacon), kale, and boiled cassava. The most interesting dishes include *vaca atolada* (literally, "cow stuck in mud"), consisting of beef cooked with cassava, which forms a creamy gravy, and *galinha ao molho pardo* (chicken with brown gravy), made with the blood of the bird. **JM**

Roberta Sudbrack | Simple ingredients transformed into creative dishes

Location Rio de Janeiro   **Signature dish** Raw tuna wrapped in crystallized breadfruit | ❸❸❸❸

Born in the southern state of Rio Grande do Sul, Roberta Sudbrack came to fame as the chef de cuisine of the presidential palace in Brasilia during Fernando Henrique Cardoso's tenure, gaining a reputation among high society for her exquisite cooking. It was in 2001, when Sudbrack settled in Rio de Janeiro, and established her own, eponymous restaurant, that her original and innovative cooking became accessible to a wider audience.

The restaurant—now acknowledged as one of Rio's very best—is located in a modern yet intimate venue. On the second floor you can see the kitchen and the chef at work through a glass panel. Although Sudbrack's cuisine is characterized by many different techniques, she is resistant to using the cutting-edge kitchen equipment that is popular in modern restaurants. Instead, she prefers to produce dishes by updating old techniques with a minimalist twist and great economy of ingredients, resulting in a great

harmony of flavors. Sudbrack thoroughly researches all the Brazilian ingredients she uses, even the most humble ones. For the latter, she is always trying to find new and exciting uses. Her dishes usually feature banana, okra, brown sugar, or cornmeal, all cooked with imagination. The restaurant's set menu changes daily, reflecting the changing seasons.

Among the most exciting dishes created by Sudbrack are the raw tuna wrapped in crystallized breadfruit with cumaru (tonka bean) and mushroom consommé; fresh heart of palm with shrimp and free-range chicken egg; aged rice risotto with asparagus and tucupi (jus of cassava); grilled beefsteak with sauce Béarnaise and banana flour; and Brazilian chocolate with crystal chayote (christophene fruit). This is clever, contemporary Brazilian food, cooked with love and presented with flair. **JM**

⬆ A selection of delectable desserts at Roberta Sudbrack.

Mocotó | The place to go for rural Brazilian fare in the city

Location São Paulo   **Signature dish** *Mocofava* | $

Forty years ago, José Oliveira, a migrant from the poor north-eastern region of Brazil came to the wealthy city of São Paulo, where he opened a small shop selling typical ingredients of his region. In addition to these regional foodstuffs, he also sold a speciality called *caldo de mocotó* (calf's foot jelly soup). The demand for this dish became so great that soon the shop turned into a small bar, and then expanded to a larger property.

Today, Mocotó is recognized as the best restaurant in São Paulo for sampling the rural cuisine of north-eastern Brazil, in particular the state of Pernambuco. The authentic regional cuisine is now prepared by the founder's son, Rodrigo Oliveira, who studied gastronomy and gained experience working at various top restaurants. Oliveira uses sophisticated culinary techniques to perfect the simple cuisine from the land of his ancestors—the results are regional dishes created with flawless execution. Mocotó's most emblematic dish is *mocofava*, a *mocotó*

broth enhanced with fava beans, sausage, and bacon, a true masterpiece of comfort food. Other typical dishes are tapioca cubes, *escondidinho* (dried meat covered with mashed cassava); *baião de dois* (rice, beans, sausage, bacon, dried meat, and cheese curd), baked pork knuckle, and brown sugar ice cream.

Although it is located far from the more fashionable neighborhoods of São Paulo, Mocotó has become famous for the quality of its food as much as the notably low prices. Still a simple place, it also attracts loyal followers from among the richest people in the city, who travel across São Paulo, prepared to wait in line patiently for up to two hours to get a table, sharing the space with the more down-to-earth locals who continue to frequent their favorite neighborhood spot, just as they have been doing for decades. **JM**

⊡ A chance to sample food from Pernambuco in São Paulo.

Fasano | A sophisticated taste of "La dolce vita"

Location São Paulo   **Signature dish** Stuffed quail | ❺❺❺❺

Following the immigration wave of the late nineteenth century, São Paulo took on a strong Italian influence, which was also reflected in its cuisine. Down-to-earth restaurants offered cheap food such as pizza and hearty pasta and became very popular. At the other end of the spectrum, Fasano, the most elegant restaurant in Brazil and located in the most aristocratic neighborhood of São Paulo, is also Italian.

The restaurant is named after the family who over a century ago began serving food in the prestigious areas of the city. Today, Rogerio Fasano leads the operation, which encompasses several hotels and restaurants across Brazil and abroad.

The most iconic location, however, remains Fasano in São Paulo, now housed in the stylish hotel of the same name, which was opened by the family in 2003. The refined setting with its classic yet contemporary atmosphere is enjoyed by the Brazilian elite, and Fasano is eponymous with the best that the metropolis has to offer. The cuisine is based on traditional Italian fare, with ingredients of the highest quality, many imported directly from the source (such as truffles from Piedmont or tiny castraura artichoke buds from Venice). Italian classics such as breaded veal cutlet or *risotto alla parmigiana* (risotto with butter and Parmesan) are always immaculately executed here, but there is also room on the menu for other chef creations such as cream of asparagus with poached egg and shrimp, linguine with anchovies and bottarga, and quail stuffed with Tuscan bacon and basil with cauliflower gratin.

The mostly European wines are well chosen and among the best served in the country. Service in the salon (which boasts a skylight that can be opened if the weather allows) is courteous and efficient. Dining here is a thoroughly civilized experience. **JM**

⬆ The elegant dining space at Fasano.

Fogo de Chão | A carnivore's delight, showcasing Brazil's famous beef

Location São Paulo   **Signature dish** Slow-roasted beef ribs | 💲💲

Brazil is recognized the world over for the quality of its beef, which is still produced from free-range and grass-fed cattle, resulting in noticeably tasty meat. Anywhere you go in this vast country, you will find good *churrascarias* (steakhouses) to serve this prime beef, a tradition that was born in the southern state of Rio Grande do Sul, with its *gaúcho* (cowboy) style of rearing cattle on the wide plains.

While many of the best steakhouses serve meat à la carte, the more typical and popular way of serving *churrasco* is the "rodizio" concept, where a perpetual "rotation" of waiters walks among the tables offering diners the chance to sample all kinds of freshly grilled meat, cooked on skewers that are placed over charcoal embers.

Fogo de Chão originated in Rio Grande do Sul, and with nearly thirty branches in Brazil and the United States, it is one of the best examples of the *churrascaria* tradition. Very comfortable, with

good meat and great wines, the restaurant has a battalion of waiters offering successive cuts and promoting this gastronomic orgy, where you pay a fixed price for all you can eat. A caipirinha, made with Brazilian sugarcane spirit cachaça, lime, and sugar, is the perfect drink to kick off the meal.

Quality steaks, grilled to the right point, are served in various cuts. You can taste pork ribs and sausages, beef cuts such as rib-eye, sirloin, skirt steak, or rump steak, and huge, impressively tender slow-roasted beef ribs—not to the forget the *picanha* (cap of rump), a typical Brazilian cut.

To accompany all this tasty meat, go for traditional side dishes such as *pão de queijo* (warm cheese bread), farofa (fried and seasoned manioc flour), fried polenta, rice, and black beans. There is also a huge, splendid salad buffet. **JM**

⬆ A Brazilian *churrasco* is an essential experience.

D.O.M. | Thrillingly original and adventurous Brazilian cuisine

Location São Paulo **Signature dish** Oysters breaded with tapioca pearls | $$$$$

Alex Atala, one of the most famous Brazilian chefs, does not cook traditional Brazilian dishes in his celebrated restaurant, D.O.M. What he does offer is a distinctively Brazilian cuisine, in a modern form and attuned to contemporary trends. At the heart of his cooking is his passion for the Amazon, a region he knows much about and whose distinctive ingredients he uses to great effect.

Opened in 1999 in Jardins, the most upscale neighborhood of the city, the elegant D.O.M., with its refined setting, modern menu, and cosmopolitan audience, could be in any major city in the world—except for one thing: its Brazilian roots depend on a number of ingredients that would be very difficult to source outside of Brazil.

The tasting menu gathers foodstuffs that even Brazilians from outside the Amazon region will be unfamiliar with, as well as ingredients from other parts of the country, used to create incredible taste effects. Creations include *pupunha* (palm heart) "fettuccine" (the vegetable is sliced into strips like pasta ribbons) prepared with *manteiga de garrafa* (liquid butter from northeastern Brazil) and popcorn flour, oysters breaded with tapioca pearls (a by-product of cassava), cured beef with Brazil nut milk and *priprioca* (an Amazonian root essence), and *filhote* fish with *tucupi* (a liquid extracted from wild manioc) and tapioca. Not to forget the famous pineapple with Amazon ants—the ants add an amazing, surprising flavor that is similar to lemongrass.

To round off the meal, you might choose wasabi sorbet (a nod to the important Japanese influence on Brazil's culinary heritage) with *jaboticaba* (a fruit known as "Brazilian grape," which grows on tree trunks). To visit D.O.M. is to discover something about the essence of Brazil, as seen through the modern and sophisticated artistic lens of a true culinary original. **JM**

"I feel a kind of responsibility to show the amazing diversity of our produce."

Alex Atala, chef and owner of D.O.M.

[↑] The elegant, sleek interior of D.O.M.

Maní | Contemporary Brazilian haute cuisine in a very relaxed atmosphere

Location São Paulo **Signature dish** "Perfect egg" with *pupunha* (peach palm) foam | ❸❸❸

Alongside D.O.M., there is another São Paulo restaurant that truly represents the emergence of a modern Brazilian cuisine that gained the world's attention: Maní, headed by chefs Helena Rizzo and Daniel Redondo, who themselves typify the bridge between Brazilian tradition and the forefront of modern, international cuisine. Helena is from Brazil, and after starting her career as a cook in São Paulo, she worked in Italy and Spain (where she met Daniel) before returning to Brazil. Daniel is Catalan and received all his professional training in one of the best restaurants in the world, El Celler de Can Roca in Girona.

Maní is a restaurant that, unlike other places of the same level, has a very informal and unpretentious atmosphere: it is probably one of the most relaxed haute cuisine restaurants in the world. The cuisine reflects this warm atmosphere: it is light, colorful, and creative. The menu has à la carte dishes, but can be better appreciated if ordered in the sequence of small dishes offered in the tasting menu.

One of the specialities of Maní's cuisine is using quintessential Brazilian ingredients in new guises, sometimes with the help of cutting-edge techniques, or by simply "upgrading" culinary traditions. Among the dishes that are particularly well known are the "perfect egg" (cooked at length at a low temperature, resulting in a creamy consistency) with *pupunha* (peach palm) foam; lamb shank with gratin of *pupunha* and Brazilian-nut *farofa* (fried flour); and beef prime rib with cassava and banana consommé. Also be sure to look out for a fun version of the classic *feijoada* (a traditional bean and pork meat stew and typical Brazilian dish)—at Maní, it is made with bean spheres, pig foot carpaccio, and crunchy kale. Desserts such as eggnog ice cream with coconut foam (presented in an egg shape) are similarly creative and entertaining. **JM**

"… the cooking is both delightful and clever, and the restaurant is just as enchanting."

Financial Times

⊡ The airy sitting room extends into a lovely garden.

ámaZ | Amazon-influenced cuisine in the Peruvian capital

Location Lima **Signature dish** Amazon snails served with chorizo-flavored oil | ❸❸

Peruvian cuisine is not just about guinea pigs and Lima beans. It could be, if you want it to be, but gastronomically curious visitors to Peru's capital Lima would be better advised to get down to ámaZ, one of the hottest eating-out joints located in the fashionable gourmet district of Miraflores. There is a culinary boom—you might even say a food revolution—happening in Peru, and ámaZ is one of the names that peole shout about the most. Needless to say, the place fills up fast so booking is necessary.

Within the cool confines of a dining area that boasts what could be called a tropical ambience (with rattan fixtures, cool colors, and a sense that you could be on the patio of a Amazonian cabin waiting for the heat of the day to die down), head chef Pedro Miguel Schiaffino uses ingredients from the Amazon and turns the area's traditional cuisine on its head. This means new twists added to staples such as fried mashed green bananas, dried pork, and the Peruvian

version of ceviche, *tiradito*—for this, Schiaffino uses cashew nut oil, banana vinegar, and river shrimp broth. Sweet potato, more common for soaking up the juices, is replaced with banana.

Then there are the large snails scooped from the Amazon River, served in their shells and spotted with chorizo-infused oil. Lovely shrimp and scallops are cooked in banana leaves, while shreds of raw palm heart make for a refreshing salad. Desserts also make use of unusual fruits from the Amazon such as *cocona* (its taste has been described by some as "tomato in the company of a lemon"). The mood at ámaZ is relaxed and casual, as diners embark on their journeys of culinary discovery. Dishes are vibrant-looking, artistically arranged on the plate and, most importantly, they explode with flavor on the palate. **ATJ**

⬆ Be sure to try the Amazon snails at ámaZ.

Astrid & Gastón | A truly memorable culinary and cultural experience

Location Lima   **Signature dish** Ceviche "del amor"; "Chinese" guinea pig | ❸❸❸❸

Astrid & Gastón is the critically acclaimed flagship of talented chef Gastón Acurio, whose restaurant chain now spans the globe. Together with his wife, Astrid Gutsche, who orignally came from Germany, Acurio and his team take Peruvian cooking to perfection. Dining à la carte, customers can choose from dishes prepared with the best Peruvian produce.

However, the restaurant also has innovative themed tasting menus: one of them is named "The Journey" and tells, in culinary terms, the story of people who left Liguria, Italy, on a voyage to El Callao, Lima, to make a new life for themselves in Peru in the nineteenth century. The story is told in five acts over several courses. The first, "The Departure," refers to the emigrant standing at the port of Chiavari, Genoa, with a trunk filled with precious flavors to accompany him on his life-changing trip: bread with cheese and jam, or salt-dried fish. This is followed by "The Voyage," with *papa a la genovesa* (potato with a pine nut and basil

cream similar to pesto). Act three, "Integration," includes a fish stew known as *cioppino* in Italy and *chupín* in South America; this is followed by "Success," an incredible dish of pork with chincho (a herb similar to huacatay but with a milder flavor), eggplant, and apple. The final act, "The Return," celebrates the emigrant's triumphant return to the motherland and is marked by desserts such as frozen panettone. Every bite is an experience to savor.

"The Journey" is designed to be a pleasure for all five senses. The multi-talented team headed by chef Diego Muñoz works with great precision, and all the details of the tasting experience, including the music, are chosen with great care. It is difficult to capture the atmosphere of this place in words—you must go and visit it to appreciate its deserved status as one of the best restaurants in the world. **RR**

⬆ Enjoy sublime Peruvian cuisine in an elegant setting.

Central | For a true experience of *terroir*

Location Lima   **Signature dish** *Toma de mar* | ❸❸❸❸

"Central Restaurante ... doesn't even bother putting its name on the cedar door."

Tom Sietsema, washingtonpost.com

⊼ The relaxed, unpretentious decor at the Central.

Central has gathered many plaudits from around the world and is regarded as an outstanding Latin American restaurant. This is a tribute to the skills of chef Virgilio Martínez, who is dedicated to continuous exploration of South American ingredients in his meticulous yet simple cooking. His latest tasting menu, called "Mater Uno," demonstrates his skill in working with different *terroir* produce. Diners may never have tasted dishes such as these before. With his culinary creations, Martínez goes in search of the identity of the land and its unique products.

The tasting menu consists of thirteen courses, corresponding to locations at various levels of altitude; it even includes a unique type of bread made with coca leaves. "La Diversidad," at 30 feet (10 m) above sea level, consists of *toma de mar*, a dish made with raw scallops, kañihua (a crunchy seed), tumbo (banana passionfruit), and oysters with borage— a new, delicious version of Central's famous ceviche house special. At 4,000 feet (1,200 m), you get shrimp with sacha inchi (an indigenous, nutlike plant), herbs, and chia (a mintlike herb); at 15,000 feet (4,500 m), an inventive creamy dish made with frozen potato, paico (a herb), and mullaca (a root from the Andes). At 2,600 feet (800 m), the "Selva Roja" comprises paiche, airampo (a cactus fruit), and chonta (a type of fish); and at 12,500 feet (3,800 m), lamb with kiwicha (amaranth) and chamomile. The "Amazonia Pura," at 1,600 feet (500 m), offers Bahuaja nut and maca (a root). The dessert, at 8,200 feet (2,500 m), is made from cocoa, coca, and chirimoya fruit.

The menu is thoughtfully and skillfully devised to produce compatible, harmonious flavors, and the suggested drinks are carefully selected to match and enhance the food. The decor of the restaurant is minimalistic, and the best table is probably the one right by the kitchen, where you can see the kitchen staff in action making all those dishes. **RR**

Chez Wong | A taste of pure ceviche perfection

Location Lima   **Signature dish** Sole ceviche | 💲💲

Chez Wong is one of the underground (private) restaurants that enjoy true cult status in Peru. It is located in the La Victoria, Lima home of chef Javier Wong, who calls it his workshop. With only a handful of tables, it is necessary to book in advance; even if there happens to be an empty table, it will not be made available without a reservation. Chez Wong is about food and food alone, and there is nothing to distract from the essentials here, neither on the plate nor in the decor. Everyone knows that once they get past the door something very special awaits, namely some of the very best ceviche in the world, a verdict supported by locals and foreign visitors alike.

Wong only works at lunchtime, because in Peru the tradition is to serve ceviche for lunch, and he takes this rule very seriously. He says that the dining room should always be located next to the bedroom, because, after lunch, it is time for the siesta.

Part of the charm of dining here is the immediacy of the experience. The dishes are prepared within minutes from whole fish, using basic kitchen tools, in front of the guests. There is no menu as such: you can order from three starters and two mains; there is no more choice than that. The dishes are usually based on *lenguado* (sole), and sometimes octopus, which is so fresh that it is almost still alive—Wong's admirable motto is: "It needs to have been alive last night, or it's no good." The fish pieces are mixed with red onion, lemon juice, salt, and pepper; nothing else is allowed to affect their flavors.

Apart from ceviche, there is also a *tiradito* (sliced raw fish) starter, brushed with sesame oil. If you want a hot dish, you can have sole again, this time sautéed. There is no wine list, and there are no desserts, either, but that does not bother the many admirers who come all the way to La Victoria suburb to try these delicacies. If you are lucky, the master chef will even show you how to make the dishes. **RR**

"Every day you are in the kitchen, you discover something new."

Javier Wong, chef at Chez Wong

⬆ Javier Wong demonstrates his fish preparation skills.

La Mar Cebichería | Memorably fresh seafood in a Lima institution

Location Lima   **Signature dish** Ceviche tasting selection | ❸❸❸

The establishment of La Mar was a watershed moment for Lima: with this cevicheria, chef and international restaurateur Gastón Acurio firmly established his vision of making this type of restaurant a true destination for locals. La Mar is nothing short of a "temple" of Peruvian seafood. The setting is spectacular, and the immediate surroundings are perfect for tasting the freshest seafood, prepared as soon as it arrives and made using only a few other ingredients so that its essence is not lost.

The dishes are announced on a giant board and struck off when supplies run out—basically, you eat the dish of the day, and, if there is none left, you must return another time. Every morning, the catch of the day is delivered, and you could almost say that it comes with its own identity document: everyone knows who caught each fish and at exactly what time.

Over the year, the choice of ceviche is endless. You should try the classics, such as the one made from small *pejerrey* (sand smelt fish). Or go for the ceviche tasting selection (*degustación de cebiches*). If in season, this may include sea urchins that are so fresh that they taste sweet; black clams; *tiradito* (raw sliced fish) *chalaco* (with peppers) or in *leche de tigre* sauce; or glazed tuna *tiradito*. Afterward, you can continue with *causa olivar* (a Peruvian dish made with potato and olives) with grilled octopus, or *chupe de camarones* (shrimp stew), followed by the catch of the day.

Do not be put off by the ugliness of the fish; the best ones, such as *pejesapo* or *diablo*, may not look nice, but prepared in different ways, they are delicious (and the chef does not use any endangered marine species). There is an excellent selection of drinks to go with your meal. For dessert, choose from *picarones* (a type of donut); outstanding *buñuelos* (sweet fritters) made with pumpkin dough and covered in honey; or crème brûlée made with *chicha morada* (a sweet beverage derived from the native purple corn). **RR**

> *"… to immerse yourself in the genuine cebicheria experience there is nowhere better."*

theworlds50best.com

⊼ A stylish restaurant noted for its superb ceviche.

Maido | A fusion of Peruvian and Japanese flavors

Location Lima   **Signature dish** *Tiradito* of *pejerrey*; "nigiris de la tierra" | ❸❸❸

To truly understand Nikkei cooking—the fusion of Peruvian and Japanese cuisine—you must try this place. It is an encounter of two cultures and two histories that in coming together create beautiful new flavors. At Maido, you can explore the concept of Nikkei and what the restaurant calls a "third reality." The restaurant's founder is Mitsuharu Tsumura, or "Micha" as his friends call him, and he describes the venture as Japanese tradition with a Peruvian heart. The cuisine also shows additional Chinese influences, which make the mix of flavors and textures even more complex and unusual.

Maido means "welcome" in Japanese, a greeting that the staff will shout to you as you enter. You can try many types of excellent food here, but it is the fish and seafood, prepared with refined methods, which truly stand out. To immerse yourself in the cuisine, you can go à la carte, or you can choose one of the tasting menus that change according to the availability of ingredients. The *Tercera Realidad* (third reality) menu might be compared to a piece of music, with not a single note out of tune. There are fifteen different courses, starting with classic grilled octopus, followed by *hassun* (snails in *sillau* sauce); Nikkei ceviche; a delicious sandwich with *pejesapo* (a type of catfish); *cuy* (guinea pig) coated in peppercorn fruit with *rocoto* (Peruvian red bell peppers); *tiradito* (thinly sliced raw fish, similar to ceviche) of *pejerrey* (sand smelt) in *leche de tigre* sauce with cocona fruit; *nigiris de la tierra* (sushi from the land); duck with crispy bacon; and Wagyu beef *a lo pobre* (served with egg and fries). Dishes such as these demonstrate the restaurant's remarkable expertise in combining textures, aromas, and flavors.

In addition to the main dining area, there is a private dining room with tatami mats for those seeking a special experience, and a bar serves very good Pisco-based cocktails and herbal infusions. **RR**

"We have different flavors and different products ... but we also have avant-garde creativity."

Mitsuharu Tsumura, chef and Maido founder

⬆ Seafood served in a sea urchin shell.

La Nueva Palomino | Explore traditional Andean cuisine

Location Arequipa **Signature dish** *Chupe de camarones* | ❷❷

"*This sprawling* picantería *with [its] pleasant patios is a great place to come on the weekend.*"

fodors.com

⬆ Try authentic Andean food at La Nueva Palomino.

Using only the best and freshest local ingredients, La Nueva Palomino has been serving first-class regional Peruvian food since around 1899. Now under chef-proprietor Monica Huerta, it is spearheading the revival of Andean cuisine. It is a *picantería*—a family-run, traditional community restaurant typical of the Andes, and particularly the city of Arequipa, the heartland of Peruvian food. *Picanterías* are customarily run by Andean women serving local people all day long. Having started with one room in the colorful district of Yanahuara, La Nueva Palomino now spreads across three properties in a residential area just minutes from the pretty main square.

The decor is rustic with uneven walls, wooden ceilings made from eucalyptus logs, and cement flooring; the smell of the kitchen log fire scents the whole restaurant—do try to get a seat nearby so you can take a peek. This is a chance to try authentic *cocina andina* at its best. The *chupe de camarones* (shrimp chowder), with large Arequipa river shrimp, broad beans, fresco cheese, and huacatay, is memorably good. Chef Monica has also delved back in history to rediscover long-lost recipes such as the *quinoa chupe* chowder. *Rocoto relleno* (stuffed Rocoto bell pepper) and *ocopa* (boiled potatoes and egg in a sauce made with huacatay black mint, amarillo chili, and roasted peanut) delight customers at lunch time. Do try one of the *guisos* (stews), *zarzas* (pickled salads), or any dish from the wood-fired oven.

When it comes to food preparation, the restaurant lovingly follows tradition. There are no food blenders; all the mixing and blending is done by hand, using a large boulder and flat, stonelike pestle and mortar. Most of the dishes, including suckling pig, are cooked using wood-fired ovens and hobs. Generous helpings of dishes packed with flavor and a bustling atmosphere have made this restaurant a favorite of many. **MM**

El Garzón | A magical, idyllic escape with fire-cooked food

Location Garzón   **Signature dish** Braised *ojo de bife* (rib-eye steak) with chimichurri sauce | ❸❸❸

A picture-perfect town, Garzón seems to have leaped off the page of a magical realism novel. In fact, it is located in the Sierra de Carapé, in the interior of Uruguay, with rolling fields and green hills, cattle, and birds, plus the odd fox making an appearance at night. The rare commodity of absolute silence fills the landscape all around the spot where Argentine chef Francis Mallmann decided to set up this stylish small hotel and restaurant, in an abandoned former general goods store. Simplicity, good taste, and a setting that extends into the beautiful, well-maintained garden create a great outdoors dining experience.

The distinguishing characteristic of the restaurant, apart from the peaceful location, is the fire-based cooking. Mallmann prepares delicious dishes with a focus on the best local produce, simple execution, and clean flavors. Some foods, such as the homemade bread, empanadas, and pizzas, are cooked in a clay oven. Others come out of the "infiernillo" oven, a cast-iron arrangement that roasts food between two wood fires, one below it and one above, while preserving the flavors of the ingredients to perfection. Infiernillo meat dishes include *bife aplastado de cordero* (lamb steaks) with crushed potatoes and gremolata; *ojo de bife* (rib-eye steak) with chimichurri sauce; pork with soy sauce; and lamb with Criolla sauce. There are also tasty salads as accompaniments, and a selection of freshly prepared desserts.

At night, the atmosphere changes as dinner is served by candlelight, the experience becoming even more intimate and romantic. The carefully chosen menu of elegant dishes—such as tasty soups, spinach and mushroom cannelloni, grilled salmon, and oven-baked pork with brioche salad—is changed regularly. To finish it all off, see whether the classic Némesis chocolate cake is available, or yummy pancakes with caramelized *dulce de leche* sauce. This is a tranquil place to step out of hectic modern life for a while. **RR**

"I wanted to cook with Argentine ingredients and wood fires [as] gauchos and Indians cook…"

Francis Mallmann, chef and founder of El Garzón

⬆ El Garzón—a peaceful place to enjoy fine food.

Boragó | Flavorsome local produce worked into innovative dishes

Location Santiago de Chile **Signature dish** *Curanto* with Patagonian rainwater | ❸❸❸

"*[In Chile] we don't even know what we have up in the mountains. In the forest. Down in the sea.*"

Rodolfo Guzmán, chef and founder of Boragó

⬆ A basket of twigs with potato bread and a stock made using rainwater, for serving with *curanto*.

The stripped-down surroundings and serene, Zenlike atmosphere at Boragó belie the ambition of chef Rodolfo Guzmán and the efforts he has made. The concept of a creative chef is somewhat unusual in this place of traditional cooking, but the undaunted Guzmán is a true culinary explorer. Three times a week, he and his team set out to explore the neighboring countryside, returning with basketfuls of produce that he works into the best of regional cooking. He also makes longer trips, finding culinary treasures around the Chilean coast, mountains, and lakes and creating dishes with them. Guzmán feels equally at ease using modern methods and the traditional ones that he discovers in the villages.

The menu, which varies daily according to what Guzmán has found, consists of fourteen courses, served on rustic ceramic plates or large flat stones. You might get to taste *caldo de raíces de ulte* (a dish made from roots)—the flavor of the Pacific on a spoon—or citrus fruits with chlorophyll mayonnaise, or squid with parsley bread. The traditional *curanto*—a typical Chilean dish originally cooked by putting various ingredients in a well or hole in the ground and covering them with hot stones—is accompanied by a stock made using Patagonian rainwater. Next you can try conger eel, lima beans, and clam stew, and wood-smoked beefsteak. For dessert, try *rica rica de Atacama* (a meringue dessert made with *merkén*, a smoked chili pepper, and the Chilean *rica rica* herb); Patagonian fruits; or *espino coulant*, a dessert made with 60 percent Valrhona chocolate—a half-frozen ball that explodes in the mouth. This is so delicious that you may decide to skip the next step, a menthol sorbet that, while clearing the palate, also cancels the memory of the chocolate. Wines and juices made from unfamiliar fruits accompany each dish. This is a space to truly get to know the undiscovered, "virgin" Chile. **RR**

Tegui | A culinary haven hidden behind graffiti

Location Buenos Aires   **Signature dish** Grilled quail stuffed with ground corn | ❸❸❸

Tegui is the main restaurant of celebrated Argentinian chef Germán Martitegui, who spent some years abroad before returning to Buenos Aires and opening this showcase of his culinary skills. Reaching Tegui—undoubtedly one of Argentina's best restaurants—in the Palermo district of the city, you may be surprised to find an anonymous door set in a wall covered with colorful graffiti. To get in, you need to ring a bell and wait for someone to grant you entry.

The main space boasts very high black-and-white walls and a shiny black ceiling; illumination comes from lanterns and spotlights. The tables are simple but cozy, and the space opens up to a patio with large banana plants and marble tables. There is a bar and a lounge area with sofas, and providing a background to the dining area is an impressive wine collection behind glass. Every table has a view of the kitchen and the chef working together with his team of young cooks. Diners often start with a cocktail, because there are many unusual creations in addition to the classics.

The excellent wine list includes something to accompany every dish on the menu. You can choose one, two, or three dishes, or you can opt for the tasting menu with either Champagne or wine. The menu changes roughly every two weeks. You can sense the master's touch in all of the dishes, in both the visual presentation and the combination of flavors and aromas, especially in the unexpected use of popular ingredients to create unique combinations. Do try the warm oysters; the gnocchi made of ricotta, chestnut, and sweetbreads; the typical Argentinian *bife de lomo* steak with *quebracho* oil, chimichurri sauce, foil-baked potatoes, farofa (manioc paste), and egg; or the delicious roasted quail filled with ground corn, dried apricot puree, and Malbec sauce. Ask for dessert recommendations, which may include an incredible citrus and ginger tart with passion fruit sorbet and kumquat sauce. A cult restaurant, hidden from view. **RR**

"We [chefs] are Latin Americans who are not looking to Europe or the United States anymore."

Germán Martitegui, chef and founder of Tegui

⤒ The subtly lit wine collection reminds diners that Tegui takes its wines as seriously as its food.

Cabana Las Lilas | Memorable steak in a lively Argentinian steakhouse

Location Buenos Aires   **Signature dish** T-bone steak | ❸❸❸

You don't have to dress up like a gaucho to enjoy the enormously big and juicy slabs of beef that they put on your plate at Cabana Las Lilas. Be sure to come hungry, though, in order to concentrate properly on enjoying the hefty portions of steak alongside various accompaniments. How about a bowl of *papas soufflé*, a bit like puffed-up potato chips, or maybe some slices of home-baked bread with a variety of starters including cured ham and pickled vegetables; or maybe you will want to dip the wonderful bread into some chimichurri, the famous Argentinean hot sauce that practically dances on the tongue.

This is a lively place, popular with locals and tourists alike, situated in the former port area of Puerto Madero, which has been overhauled and transformed, and is now one of the fashionable districts of Buenos Aires, complete with glittering high-rise buildings designed by the likes of Norman Foster and Philippe Starck. The restaurant has a modern feel with its light, caramel wooden floor, soft neutral colors throughout, and an open kitchen where the chefs wielding sharp knives add to a sense of occasion. There is also a balcony overlooking the old port for some alfresco dining. This may be a steakhouse—but it is not just any old steakhouse.

When the steaks arrive (all meat is sourced from the restaurant's own ranch), they are juicy and tender, soft enough to cut with a fork, and cooked to perfection with just the right pinch of seasoning: this is truly a carnivore's paradise. Having gorged on meat—the T-bone steak dwarfs its plate, being a mammoth slab of meat—you might want to further indulge in a dessert (if you can); the crepes filled with sweet *dulce de leche* are especially tempting. And afterwards? It seems that a good walk is in order. **ATJ**

⊕ Cabana Las Lilas is very much a carnivore's delight.

Florería Atlántico | Flowers, cocktails, and all manner of grilled delicacies

Location Buenos Aires   **Signature dish** *Pechito de cerdo* (spare ribs with vegetables) | 💲💲

Arroyo is one of the prettiest streets in all of Buenos Aires. If you go there for a walk during the day, you will find this lovely florist-cum-wine store nestled among the art galleries, with lots of light and blooms everywhere. At 7.00 P.M., a door at the back of the store is opened and you can go down a flight of stairs to get to the cocktail bar, one of the best in Buenos Aires. The space is the brainchild of Julián Díaz, founder of the popular 878 bar/restaurant, and "Tato" Giovannoni: both are true heavyweights of the Argentinian cocktail scene. The bar also offers food, which is prepared on a grill dating from 1940.

The atmosphere harks back to bars of the nineteenth century when European immigrants would arrive just off the boat and go for a drink. The ceiling is unfinished and the walls dark, with a range of drawings of mythological sea creatures from ancient maps. The cutlery is marked with intricate designs, and a collection of glasses and bottles contributes to the ambience, together with the lively music. The cocktail list is arranged nationally to include the main European countries from which immigrants came—Spain, Italy, France, Britain, and Poland.

To accompany those cocktails, opt for tapas—for instance, grilled octopus with glazed potatoes and olive tapenade, or organic eggs from the countryside with *chistorra* (Basque cured sausage), tomatoes from La Plata, baby vegetables, and white truffle salt. Fish lovers can enjoy plates based on the catch of the day, and those who prefer meat can choose from grilled entrails or pork with pumpkin, baby carrot, sweetcorn, and dates. Desserts are also prepared on the grill: try the banana with goats' cheese and *dulce de leche*. Florería Atlántico is much more than a bar with an historic theme; this is a "gastro bar," with the very best cocktails and wines, and delicious food. **RR**

⬆ Discover this delightful "secret" bar and restaurant.

La Brigada | Arguably the best meat in the world

Location Buenos Aires   **Signature dish** *Corte especial* (special in-house cut steak) | ❸❸❸

Argentina is a country where the best *parrilleros* (specialists in barbecued meat) are revered as culinary gurus. To truly distinguish yourself as a *parrillero* in a place where cattle are still considered the sacred animals of the Pampas is no mean feat, but Hugo Echevarrieta has done it and owns one of the best *parrillas* in Buenos Aires. The decor consists of football paraphernalia, photographs of famous visitors, and plants, but people come here for the meat.

The waiters will know straight away that you are going to order the meat, and will arrange to cook it to your taste, although the owner always recommends medium rare. The meat arrives only with salt and no other additions; you can add chimichurri sauce if you wish, but you should first try the meat without anything else to appreciate the taste and to understand what makes Argentinian meat so special. Each cut arrives on a new, hot plate and with special cutlery; fries, the most popular accompaniment, are

served on the side, as are the salads. This is an opportunity to get to know Argentinian cuisine. Start the introduction to the local flavors with *empanadas* or *bocadillos de acelga fritos* (fried chard), followed by barbecued sweetbreads, *chinchulines* (intestine) of kid and lamb, *morcilla* (black pudding), and kidneys.

For the meat proper, you can get *entraña* (skirt steak), *ojo de bife* (rib-eye steak), or *vacío del fino* (flank steak). There are also two especially good cut options: the *corte especial* and the *redondito*; these do not feature on the menu but everyone knows about them, and the meat is so tender that you could cut it with a spoon. The desserts are Buenos Aires classics: *budín de pan* (bread pudding), *arroz con leche* (milk rice), and *queso y dulce* (cheese with sweet jelly). Echevarrieta also has some of the country's best wines for a perfect accompaniment to the meal. **RR**

⬆ A convivial space to enjoy superb barbecued meat.

La Cabrera | Excellent meat and original *cazuelitas*

Location Buenos Aires   **Signature dish** *Ojo de bife* (rib-eye steak) | ❺❺❺

This is not a steakhouse or *parrilla* in the traditional sense. Hungry gauchos do not come here after a day riding the Pampas, but you will find some of the best Argentinian meat, excellent wines, and the selection of *cazuelitas* (special side dishes) that lend the place its unique identity. Gastón Riveira is the chef who found his true expression in this type of cooking, at the same time managing to innovate the *parrilla*, which for the majority of Argentinians is a sacred concept.

This is a restaurant where it is best to go in a group and order many different dishes to share. The best appetizers are smoked cheese with *jamón* (ham), *morcilla* (black pudding), *chorizo criollo* (like Spanish sausage but without paprika), and *mollejas* (sweetbreads) served medium rare. For mains, *lomo madurado con hueso* (aged fillet steak on the bone), *colita de cuadril* (top of the rump), *entraña* (skirt steak), *ojo de bife* (rib eye), *bondiola de cerdo* (pork shoulder), *bife de chorizo* (rump steak), and *asado corte americana*

(a variation on rump steak) are on offer. There are also other cuts of dry-aged or Kobe beef available.

The cold *cazuelitas* are passed around on an enormous tray for people to help themselves as often as they like. Examples include tapenade, salads, garlic cloves in red wine, apple puree, tartar sauce, and pickled eggplant. Desserts include homemade ice cream—do try the *dulce de leche*. The wine cellar features some of the best Argentinian Malbecs, which are an ideal accompaniment for this type of food.

La Cabrera is very popular and although there is now a sister restaurant both get very busy, and it is advisable to make a reservation. The decor includes memorabilia and diagrams of cattle that illustrate the Argentinian meat cuts. Plates are displayed along the walls, signed by guests from all over the world— ample evidence of the restaurant's success. **RR**

⭱ The dark and cozy interior of La Cabrera.

Europe

From the traditional and historical to the truly innovative, when it comes to dining out, Europe has it all: the conviviality of Italian trattorias and Spanish tapas bars; the civilized formality of sumptuous French establishments; and the imaginative, sophisticated cuisine of exciting new restaurants in Denmark and Germany. Europe boasts a rich, memorable tapestry of culinary delights to explore.

← Le Jules Verne (Eiffel Tower), Paris, France.

Humarhúsid Restaurant | The star is lobster ... or is it langoustine?

Location Reykyavik   **Signature dish** Herb-crusted tenderloins of lamb and Icelandic lobster | ❺❺❺

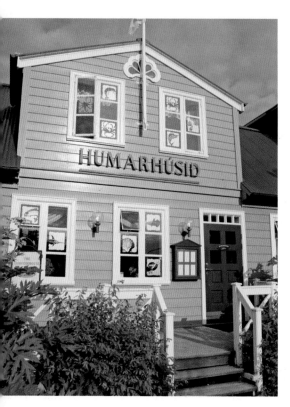

"One of the city's swankiest eateries ... top-notch cooking, slick service, and a good atmosphere."

Matt Warren, *The Independent*

⬆ A rural setting in the heart of town.

For more than twenty years, the Humarhúsid Restaurant—"The Lobster House"—has been serving fine shellfish cuisine in the center of Iceland's capital. Its traditional gray-painted wooden-framed building dates back to 1838, making it one of the oldest in the city. The interior retains a historic elegance, too. Amid the formal white linen and polished glassware, you'll find a cozy mix of rooms featuring quirky chandeliers, gilt-framed mirrors, oil paintings, wall tapestries, odd chairs, and plush cushions.

But there's nothing ancient about head chef Gudmundur Gunnarsson's fine creations. Among his more complex dishes is "Seafood Fantasy," which includes an eclectic mix of ingredients such as salmon, mussels, and Icelandic lobster with Jerusalem artichokes and five-spice lobster broth. Another highlight is deep-fried risotto and tomato cheese salad with chili ice cream and salted crackers. The innovative desserts include Icelandic cheeses with deep-fried seaweed, birch syrup, and thyme purée.

There are various fish, meat, and vegetarian dishes on the lunch and dinner menus, but the lobster is the star. A note of linguistic caution, however: Icelandic lobster is actually the smaller North Atlantic version, usually called langoustine.

This plentiful local ingredient appears in many wonderful forms here, including cream of lobster soup with garlic roasted lobster tails and in langoustine risotto, along with goats' cheese, rocket, pistachios, and Champagne foam. Icelandic lobsters may also arrive at the table with a wide range of side ingredients, including lamb, pork, oxtail, creamy barley, smoked duck, clams, horse, and even Iceland's most controversial delicacy, whale.

Other local specialities are less controversial: there are plenty of root vegetables, spotted catfish, baby Icelandic potatoes, blueberries and crowberries, and, of course, cod. **SH**

Solsiden | Serving up some of the world's finest seafood

Location Oslo **Signature dish** Seafood platter for the whole table | ❺❺❺❺

Few restaurants capture the striking beauty of Scandinavia's smallest capital better than Solsiden. The restaurant is open only between mid-May and September each year. However, during that short summer season, it embodies the collective Norwegian lust for sunshine, fine wines, and unrivaled seafood after a long and dark winter. Indeed, legend has it that Solsiden serves more Chablis than any other restaurant in the world.

Housed in an old port warehouse, with small tables stacked closely together to accommodate the overwhelming demand on warm days, the restaurant has sliding doors that may be opened to reveal the bustling Oslo harbor and the fjord just a few feet from from the diners' places. As a magnet for hipsters and financiers alike, Solsiden is ideal for people-watching. Regular diners return here year after year.

All the cuisine follows the simplest of recipes. It is exclusively seafood—no meat is on offer—and everything is cooked with almost no artifice, on the basis that the raw ingredients are of such high quality that they require only minimal adornment. The menu features an extensive à la carte menu as well as a set menu that changes daily, but it is generally agreed that the absolute must-try is the extravagant seafood platter, which features oysters, langoustines, hand-dived scallops, and lobsters—everything that makes cold-water marine fish such a treat. Served for two or more diners, the platter is presented on a bed of seaweed with freshly baked bread and aioli.

Solsiden is a large restaurant, yet it is nearly always filled to capacity and usually has only a few outside seats available for walk-in customers with no reservations. But anyone prepared to commit to an advance booking will be handsomely rewarded with top-quality unpretentious food in the appropriately low-key surroundings of a plainly decorated Norwegian quayside building. **ABN**

"… especially appealing on sunny midsummer evenings when sunlight streams onto the pier."

frommers.com

⬆ An eye for detail is a hallmark of Solsiden's service.

Maaemo | Humble ingredients lovingly prepared and beautifully presented

Location Oslo **Signature dish** Textures of oyster with dill and horseradish | [$][$][$][$][$]

"We said we wouldn't talk about Noma. They can do what they do and we'll do what we do."

Esben Holmboe Bang, head chef

Although it is uncertain who originated the now much-lauded Neo-Nordic cuisine—Noma in Copenhagen is most commonly credited as the trend-starter—there are few restaurants in the world that practice it as purely and uncompromisingly as Maaemo, a name that means "Mother Earth" in Old Finnish. Head chef Esben Holmboe Bang's team starts work every day foraging for herbs in local parks and nearby forests. All ingredients are ecological and sourced within a 60-mile (100-km) radius of the premises in the recently rejuvenated East End of Oslo.

With floor-to-celing glass walls on three sides, Maaemo offers panoramic views of the city skyline yet retains a sense of intimacy. This is not only a result of the delicate yet simple Nordic interior design elements, but is also a product of the staff's enthusiastic and welcoming demeanor. Above the dining room, in a glass-enclosed cube, highly visible chefs at work contribute to the spectacle.

Ingredients are treated with refinement and care. The kitchen is never afraid to let simple items shine. You may occasionally encounter local delicacies such as oysters and langoustines, but Maaemo's cuisine is defined by the new flavor profiles with which it promotes less well-known local produce. Highlights include frozen discs of tart and creamy cheese with orange-colored bleak roe, and a dessert consisting of silky-smooth butter ice cream served with sweet crumble and clarified butter poured tableside.

Maaemo is a glorious restaurant where dining is more than a meal—it is an experience. Frequently courses are created to evoke an emotion rather than simply to satisfy hunger. However, it's Neo-Nordic at its very core and assiduously local, always showcasing humble ingredients with meticulous technique and an almost obsessive attention to detail. Although an evening at Maaemo requires both time and planning, it's well worth the effort. **ABN**

↑ Esben Holmboe Bang champions Neo-Nordic cuisine.

→ An exquisite dish of fresh flowers and mushrooms.

Ice Hotel | Lapland ingredients in the Arctic snow

Location Jukkasjärvi   **Signature dish** Six-course tasting menu served on ice dishes | 🅢🅢🅢🅢🅢

"I use elk cheese from Swedish elk. I pick the rowanberries just outside the window!"

Richard Näslin, chef at the Ice Hotel

⬆ The distinctive flavors of Lapland ingredients are at the heart of the dishes, which are served on ice.

➡ The Ice Hotel's front doors, with antler handles.

The meal might start with a cold trio of fish roe and cream served on an ice dish. Following that are three different cuts of reindeer with local mushrooms, some lightly smoked elk, and breast of ptarmigan with lingonberry sauce. A dish of herb-marinated cheese might then be served, and finally a delicate lemon mousse with chocolate cake.

What would be a fine meal served in a normal restaurant becomes an extraordinary one when it is eaten in a remote spot, 125 miles (200 km) inside the Arctic Circle. This is Sweden's Ice Hotel, the first, the biggest, and the most acclaimed winter resort rebuilt on an annual basis from ice and snow. After more than twenty-three years of rebuilding, everyone knows by now that the hotel melts back into the river every spring. So don't look for this place in the summer—the hotel simply will not exist.

In the winter, though, you will find guests wandering around the rooms of carved ice in snowsuits. The bar serves its colorful cocktails in ice "glasses," and drinkers are warned not to let their lips linger on these for fear of getting stuck to them.

When it comes to the restaurant, however, there is a slight conceit involved; it is housed in a traditional wooden building. In winter, it is surrounded by snow-decked pines and flickering lanterns, but customers do not have to sit on, or eat at, furniture made from ice blocks, as they do in the hotel bar. And this part of the operation is open all-year-round.

The restaurant is quite formal, with crisp white linen, white crockery, and silver cutlery. Customers choose between a four-course or a six-course menu, both highlighting ingredients from Lapland such as moose, reindeer, Arctic char, and wild berries. The surprisingly good modern Scandinavian cuisine has garnered a shelf of awards. And anyone feeling less than excited by the unchallenging building can opt to eat his or her meal at a remote "wilderness camp." **SH**

Fäviken | Local produce rooted in tradition with an eye for innovation

Location Järpen   **Signature dish** Bone marrow with raw beef heart and grated turnips | ⦿⦿⦿⦿⦿

More than anything, Fäviken is defined by its harmonious coexistence with its harsh surroundings. In this inhospitable environment, produce is harvested at its prime and later dried, pickled, and cured as cupboards are filled before punishing winters. As stores are depleted, spring and the harvest returns once again. This cyclical unity with nature is as old as the Vikings themselves.

Possibly the most isolated serious restaurant in the world, Fäviken is housed within the grounds of a hunting chalet at the end of a dirt road, east of the small skiing hamlet of Åre, Sweden. It offers all the modern comforts while maintaining a uniquely rustic refinement. The six bedrooms are luxurious yet quaint. The dining room, with hams and herrings being dried from the ceiling, feels appropriately like a Valhalla.

The cooking is firmly rooted in Nordic traditions yet offers mind-blowing innovation, provoking with forgotten ingredients and techniques. Presentation is often simple with few, but pronounced, flavors. Depending on the season, you might be treated to local game in various states of preservation or succulent seafood from the nearby Norwegian coastline. Highlights include live scallop cooked in the shell over embers and salted herring aged for three years served with curd on rusks, not forgetting delectable trout roe served with pig's blood custard.

Fäviken Magasinet is an all-immersive dining experience unlike any other, its location adding to the sense of pilgrimage. Read a book in front of the fire or enjoy a soothing sauna before dinner. Awake the next morning to fresh mountain air and an equally eye-opening breakfast. Constantly at the mercy of the wilderness surrounding him, Chef Nilsson has created an adaptive approach to gourmet dining that's likely to provide a palate for a changing world. **ABN**

⊡ Simple rustic surroundings showcase the Nordic food.

Niklas Ekstedt | Uniquely creative, wood-fired delicacies

Location Stockholm   **Signature dish** Mussels and scallops on seaweed with oyster and hazelnut pesto | ❸❸❸

The open fire offers endless possibilities according to revolutionary chef Niklas Ekstedt, who collaborated with Rene Redzepi (of Noma fame) in his previous Michelin-starred restaurant in Stockholm. Here, he sets out to show dramatically how the most primitive of long-lost culinary techniques, cooking only with wood, can produce outstanding, elegant, and creative cuisine with distinct flavors. Ekstedt re-defines what makes great contemporary cooking.

Food is prepared either in the magnificent fire pit, a wood-fired oven, or on the wood-burning stove; there is absolutely no electricity or gas. Guests have spectacular views of the process, yet are protected from the smoke by a glass wall—it is a truly mesmerizing experience. What makes it especially intriguing, and even radical, is the fact that it is precisely the opposite of the complex "molecular cuisine" with its squiggles, foam, and tiny dishes. Expect Nordic elements such as lingonberries,

wild herbs, pine, and wild mushrooms transformed as ancient traditions meet modern Swedish cuisine. More recently, Ekstedt has also introduced a "stone age microwave"—a large, glass-fronted box with charcoal embers at the bottom that is connected to a chimney and can be controlled precisely—and a wood-fired, wind-up mechanical rotisserie. The interior is as decidedly rustic and stylish as the cooking.

Memorable dishes include a raw starter of sea cucumber, oyster, avocado, and parsley; chimney-smoked lobster tail served with lobster sashimi and oyster and hazelnut pesto; reindeer baked on glowing timbers; and beef on pear wood with chimney-smoked tomatoes and duck liver. Desserts also focus on fire: sourdough waffles are served with the local speciality of cloudberries and sourdough pancakes with flambéed fruit and salted caramel ice cream. **SP**

⬆ Squid cooked over fire, a characteristic treatment here.

Rosendals Trädgårdscafe | Homemade food in a beautiful garden

Location Stockholm   **Signature dish** Cinnamon buns | **$$**

"One can soak in a little history … by ambling along to the candy-colored Rosendal Palace."

yourlivingcity.com

⬆ Freshly made bread from the café's bakery is used for delicious sandwiches.

A hidden gem that Stockholmers love and tourists may easily miss, this rustic café is set in the rambling Rosendal's Garden on the leafy island of Djurgården, which is connected to the city center by a bridge. Set among apple orchards, a vineyard, and a rose garden packed with more than a hundred varieties of rare old roses, the café is the perfect place to end a walk on the island. It is incredibly popular on weekends, so try to go on a weekday to avoid the lines.

The food is served in the garden's big glasshouses, and you can eat in there, too. In the days of fall and winter, they are wonderfully cozy with candles everywhere. But if there is even a glimpse of sun, most people take their food to the nearby orchard and bask on the grass, or seek out a seat under a shady apple tree.

Only open during the day, the café serves home-cooked food with an emphasis on fresh ingredients. The menu changes every day, and as well as good soups and generously filled sandwiches, there are hearty salads and interesting meat and fish dishes. In summer, you might find Arctic char with couscous and sour cream, or a crisp salad with chunks of smoked mackerel; when the days turn colder, it might be slow-cooked lamb shanks with tender vegetables, or a creamy chicken casserole.

The cakes and pastries are legendary, and Stockholmers are happy to walk all the way here from the city center for a cup of coffee and a big, buttery cinnamon bun, or a slice of *kladdkaka* ("sticky cake"), a gooey chocolate cake that melts in the mouth.

All the food is organic, and much of it is very local—the chunky bread in your sandwich is from the café's own bakery, and there is a good chance that the vegetables in your salad were grown right there in the garden. There is also a shop selling bread and produce from the garden, so you can take a little bit of the Rosendal experience home with you. **FQ**

Fjäderholmarnas Krog | A taste of Sweden away from the city

Location Stockholm   **Signature dish** Toast Skagen | ⓢⓢ

Sitting on the wooden terrace, looking out to sea, you might easily imagine you were many miles from the nearest city, yet this island restaurant is just a twenty-five minute boat trip from the heart of downtown Stockholm. It is the perfect place to sample a little slice of what Stockholmers call *skärgårdslivet*, or life out in the archipelago of tiny islands that surround the Swedish capital. City folk flock here to spend long summer days sailing, swimming, and getting back to nature. On sunny days, the terrace is most in demand, but it is light and airy inside the restaurant, too, with big windows that make the most of the views.

The food here is designed to showcase the best Swedish seasonal produce. The fish, especially, is prepared in inventive ways—perhaps plaice pan-fried with cockles, or pepper- and cumin-cured salmon served with chanterelle mushrooms. Traditional Swedish dishes have their place, too; toast Skagen features plump shrimps with creamy dill mayonnaise, and there is a classic starter of three types of pickled herring served with new potatoes, mature cheese, and homemade crispbread. If you do not particularly like fish, there are excellent meat dishes, too.

Desserts range from petits fours—looking almost too beautiful to eat—to very simple, very Swedish berries with ice cream. And if you happen to emerge just in time to miss the next boat back to Stockholm (they depart once an hour), you can follow your meal with a stroll around the tiny island, or do as the Stockholmers do and snatch a few minutes of sunbathing on a cliff overlooking the ocean.

Fjäderholmarnas Krog is primarily a summer haunt, but if you are in Stockholm during December, it is worth hopping on the boat to sample the restaurant's traditional *Julbord*, or Christmas table. This buffet of classic festive dishes, including herrings, meatballs, and slow-cooked spiced ham, is a real taste of how the Swedish celebrate Christmas. **FQ**

"Fjäderholmarnas Krog … lies nestled among tool sheds and newly tarred boats."

mynewsdesk.com

⬆ The waterfront terrace of Fjäderholmarnas Krog is a fine introduction to life in the Stockholm archipelago.

Daniel Berlin Krog | Inspirational Nordic food in pastoral surroundings

Location Skane-Tranas   **Signature dish** Lightly baked cod with apple, beetroot, and kelp | 🅢🅢🅢

"[Dishes] dramatically simplistic in their construction and yet full of surprises and clever twists."

theworlds50best.com

⊡ Cooking in an open fire is just one of the innovative techniques that distinguish Daniel Berlin's cuisine.

In recent years, there has been much posturing and pontificating in the press about what is called the "new Nordic cuisine." To the onlooker, the movement can look like a lot of men with beards camping out in the woods and waxing primeval about how to slaughter chickens; the Spartan restaurants that they open and patronize are the kind that might have live prawns, moss, and bark on the menu.

Daniel Berlin is an altogether less hysterical practitioner of the art. His eponymous restaurant could be said to be in the middle of nowhere—a tiny hamlet in Österlen, the southeastern part of the Swedish province of Scania. The scene is still and pastoral, a verdant landscape dotted with red wooden barns that could be a snapshot from centuries ago. Yet his low-slung, whitewashed cottage, its serene little dining room boasting only five or so tables, is the scene of world-class cooking.

Witness the translucent, pure white sliver of local fish served with sea vegetables; the lamb with jus poured over it through bunches of freshly plucked herbs; the elderberry ice-pop served halfway through as a palate cleanser, enjoyed on a short stroll around the gardens where Berlin grows much of what appears on the plates. Each mouthful is clean, fresh, but complex; each plate is a thing of beauty.

Berlin is a major talent. His cooking is revelatory, intuitive, and very seasonal. I recall humble celeriac, baked in coals for six hours until it is transformed into a thing of smoky luxury, being "decapitated" tableside and distributed by Berlin himself before being bathed in an intense cheese cream—all done with modesty and grace. It is a family affair, and the affable man recommending the organic wines is Berlin's father. At the end of an extraordinary dinner, the chef even drove us back to our country inn—not as a special favor, but something frequently done. It is hard to imagine any of Berlin's peers managing that. **MOL**

Bastard | Vividly memorable foods served nose to tail

Location Malmö   **Signature dish** Bastard *planka* (charcuterie platter) | **$$**

The flavors at Bastard are not big, they are massive, a slap across the chops that will leave you beaming with surprised pleasure. Smokily charred slivers of beef heart, perhaps, punched up with garlic, capers, radicchio, and a sharp stab of vinegar. A tin of excellent anchovies is peeled open and served just so, with lashings of creamy, lactic Swedish butter, lemon quarters, and grilled homemade sourdough bread. Garnet-colored local venison comes raw in a vivid tartare. Even a bland-sounding chicken dish is topped with leaves of its skin, crisped with the most addictive of seasonings. Menus change daily, depending on what is fresh, but always feature the Bastard *planka*, a groaning board of rillettes, salami, cured hams, snowy lardo, pâtés, and headcheeses, served with piles of sourdough bread and butter scattered with sea salt.

Malmö is a forward-thinking city, renowned for its championing of green resources and its dynamic modern buildings. But Bastard is located in the medieval heart of the city, like a brash, confident upstart blowing raspberries at its stuffier neighbors. Owned by chef Andreas Dahlberg, it is the sort of place you might expect to find in the United States, in Brooklyn or Portland perhaps, so it delivers something of a frisson to find it in Sweden's third city.

The high-ceilinged room, with its rough-luxe mix of subway tiles and ornate wallpaper, vintage educational posters, and chandeliers, is always packed to the rafters with an appreciative, frequently raucous crowd (Bastard is also a choice destination for cocktails, and for its wine list, mostly of biodynamic and natural labels). There is a surprisingly pretty outdoor space wrought from a side alley, all fairy lights and rickety furniture; the staff are friendly and knowledgeable (not to mention drop-dead gorgeous). Why is the place called Bastard? No idea. But the name guarantees that you will remember it, just as you will Dahlberg's food. Come here hungry. **MOL**

"Dahlberg [works] miracles with bits of animal that are not, in essence, that appetizing."

wallpaper.com

⬆ A paradise for charcuterie connoisseurs, the Bastard *planka* includes some of Sweden's best cold meats.

Lasipalatsi | Where style and substance come together

Location Helsinki **Signature dish** *Vorschmack* (minced lamb with herring and onions) |

"…popular year round with lunching city suits; the terrace throngs during after-work drinks."

Lonely Planet

⬆ Lasipalatsi—a splendid, striking setting to sample Finnish food.

This restaurant is named after the building in which it is housed, the marvellous Lasipalatsi (which means "glass palace" in Finnish), opened in 1936. A central meeting point near the city's grand railway terminal, it also contains the state broadcasting studios, historic cinemas, cafés, and many appealing shops, including a wonderful organic food store.

The restaurant opened in 1998 in a room with sleek lines and high ceilings that make it at once classical and contemporary. The dining area is lit atmospherically, taking full advantage of the long hours of sunshine during the summer months and enhanced with the warm glow of candles and soft lighting when the days are short.

Chef Petri Simonen's cooking makes the most of the splendid bounty of Finland's forests, lakes, and seas to produce a range of food in which style and substance coexist harmoniously. If either of the main caviar dishes—*muikun mätiä* (with sour cream, chives, red onion, and black pepper) or vendace (a sardine-like freshwater whitefish, served with sour cream and a rusklike bread)—is on offer, do not miss it.

The main menu has superb offerings of meat and fish as well as desserts made from wonderful Finnish berries. Throughout the year, special menus highlight the best of each season, including asparagus, fresh fish, and reindeer.

Vorschmack, which can be ordered as an appetizer or a main course, tastes much better than the ingredients may suggest. Each Finn makes the dish with different meats, which might include lamb, beef, moose, or reindeer. At Lasipalatsi, it is minced lamb, simmered with onions, pickled herring, and salted anchovy, served with baked potato, sour cream, pickled cucumbers, and beets. Miraculously, it awakens the taste buds with sensations of fattiness, sweetness, saltiness, and cleansing notes of sourness all at the same moment. **FP**

Savoy | Fine dining by design

Location Helsinki　**Signature dish** Pan-cooked herring fillets | 💲💲

The choice of Helsinki as World Design Capital in 2012 was no more than the Finnish capital deserved: it had been leading fashion in this area for the greater part of the twentieth century. Witness Savoy, probably the most renowned restaurant in Finland, which opened in 1937 and in which almost everything—exterior, interior, fixtures, tables, chairs, glasses, and cutlery—was created or inspired by the nation's greatest architect, Alvar Aalto.

The most iconic item is the undulating Savoy vase, now generally known as the Aalto vase, which was created specifically for this restaurant. Just as discreetly beautiful are the golden bell pendant lamps that hang above most of the tables.

The terrace, fully open in summer and enclosed for the rest of the year, commands fine views of Helsinki's esplanade, the onion-dome buildings that date from the time of the Russian occupation, and the nearby harbor.

The proximity of the Baltic influences the menu, which majors in seafood. Herring, in its many guises, is the star. Perhaps the finest of its numerous manifestations here is as a fillet, lightly breaded in rye flour and then pan-cooked in butter. There is also a nonpareil plate of pickled herring that pairs beautifully with a glass of the local aquavit. Herring is a flavor note in *vorschmack*, the curiously addictive combination of minced meat (often, but not invariably, lamb), anchovies, and onions.

In addition to traditional Finnish fare, more unusual dishes are available to beguile eye and palate. Seared scallops served with blue mussel tortellini and fennel sauce is a wonderful composite of flavors, textures, and sensations. In the colder months, grouse and pike appear on the menu, along with reindeer fillets prepared in a variety of styles as entrées or as a delicious terrine served with Waldorf salad. **FP**

"The restaurant's decor exemplifies Finnish modernism ... Alvar Aalto designed every detail."

frommers.com

⤒ Herring is served in many different forms at the Savoy in Helsinki.

Noma | Haven of culinary surprise and delight

Location Copenhagen **Signature dish** Tartare of musk ox and wood sorrel | $$$$$

"Today, nature is our biggest inspiration. I see our restaurant having [a] pact with nature."

René Redzepi, chef and co-owner of Noma

↑ René Redzepi's use of foraged ingredients such as lichens has influenced chefs around the world.

→ Imaginative, intricate, and profoundly seasonal dishes are a Noma hallmark.

You are stepping across the cobbled streets of Christianshavn in Copenhagen. The wind whips up the sea and sends the clouds scudding across the sky. Ahead, in a weatherbeaten old warehouse, is Noma, a restaurant regularly ranked as the best in the world.

As dusk falls, soft light glows from the restaurant windows. Upstairs, shadowy forms move in the test kitchen, developing new ways to cook Nordic ingredients—roasting rhubarb root and yeast to create an *umami*-rich, fresh-tasting broth for shrimp; slow-cooking potatoes to create a pureed plumstone (almond) flavored pudding with plums.

Inside, the old beams arch above a simple, spacious dining room and an open-plan, high-tech kitchen. Waiters and chefs bring the succession of breathtakingly beautiful small dishes that make up the twenty-serving set menu. Every dish offers a surprise—the delicate crunch of fried reindeer moss, dusted with cep powder and dipped in roast juniper wood crème fraiche; or the exciting tingle of frozen salted wood ants, sandwiched with blueberry paste between nasturtium leaves. The ants act like sherbet on the accompanying blueberry ice.

Chef René Redzepi's culinary aim is to transport the diner to a time and place, were they to close their eyes and just eat. Thus, the taste of lobster consommé covered in peppery nasturtium petals evokes the end of summer, just as the flavor of his burned leek, with its grilled inner leaves brushed with cod's roe, conjures up November fires and sea spray.

Every dish is created from regional, seasonal ingredients, many of them wild, such as birch sap in spring or rose hips in autumn. Some of the foods, such as butter or beer, are the sublime-tasting produce of small, highly specialized artisans. In his reinterpretation of traditional Nordic techniques, such as pickling, drying, and salting, Redzepi is creating nothing less than a new style of cooking. **SK**

Kodbyens Fiskebar | Contemporary, stylish fish
dishes in Copenhagen's meatpacking district

Location Copenhagen   **Signature dish** Scallops with squash, artichokes, and cep mushrooms | 🟢🟢🟢🟢🟢

"As the night wears on, the restaurant morphs into a happening late-night party spot."

redvisitor.com

⬆ Beautiful Scandinavian fare at Fiskebar.

Kodbyens Fiskebar, which only opens at night, is a restaurant where you go to have fun. It occupies a low industrial building, next to a meat processing plant in Copenhagen's meatpacking district. Above the main door, large gray letters spell out "Kod og Flaeskehal" (meat and flesh). Set at the end of a windswept car park and surrounded by other industrial-looking units, it looks bleak, but don't be deceived. The area has become a magnet for restaurants, galleries, and clubs. And Kodbyens Fiskebar has become the place to hang out in Copenhagen—even the Crown Prince of Denmark is rumored to have been seen there.

Anders Selmer, a former Noma restaurant manager and sommelier, opened Kodbyens Fiskebar in 2009; the name translates as "meat town's fish bar." It offers delicious Nordic-influenced fish dishes and a wine list built around Selmer's favorite vineyards.

Inside, it is designer-scruffy. A central bar dominates the room, with tables, chairs, and battered black leather sofas lining the partially tiled white walls. A beautiful, cylindrical jellyfish tank and clever lighting and music create a cool vibe at night. In summer, trestle tables extend the restaurant outside.

The menu is short and good. There are small "raw" dishes—perfect for those hanging out at the bar—such as razor clams with fennel and hazelnuts, different types of oysters, and smoked trout roe with beach mustard and fine shavings of pickled purple carrot. The cooked dishes are perfectly balanced. Fish and fries, for example, is made with succulent smoked cod, while a fall dish of scallops tastes extra sweet with squash, artichokes, and cep mushrooms. Be sure to leave room for a pudding, such as the smoked buttermilk panna cotta with fresh blueberries and woodruff granite, or the pear crumble with cherry beetroot gel and almonds—they are gorgeous. **SK**

Tivolihallen | Classic smørrebrød in the heart of the Danish capital

Location Copenhagen **Signature dish** A wide selection of smørrebrød | 💲💲

Smørrebrød—open sandwiches—are an institution in Denmark, with many Danes taking homemade versions of them to work in their lunch boxes. Visitors looking to sample this iconic Danish speciality should head for Copenhagen's family-run Tivolihallen, in the historic heart of Copenhagen. Take a few steps down from street level and you enter a clublike space, evoking a bygone era: here are Danish antiques and design classics with tables set simply with white linen tablecloths. In a building dating back to the eighteenth century, the Mother Earth figure of owner Helle Vogt greets her regular clientele and tourists alike with warmth and charm, inviting them to enjoy her homemade Danish delicacies.

One of the joys of smørrebrød is the sheer range of toppings available. At Tivolihallen, there is a long list of options, with diners simply ticking off the ones they want to try. All the much-loved classics are here, freshly assembled and elegantly presented in all their colorful variety, and served the traditional way on either buttered rye bread or white bread. Seafood lovers are well served, from the seven different versions of herring to the smoked eel with scrambled egg or the pan-fried plaice. Meat toppings include rare roast beef, liver paté, a creamy chicken salad, and steak tartare with all the trimmings. A few more substantial main dishes, such as meatballs or roast pork with red cabbage, are offered at lunchtime, too.

Pondering the menu and choosing what to eat is part of the fun of dining here. Bear in mind that the restaurant does not offer smørrebrød in the evening; for dinner there is a short, homely menu of what is aptly described as "granny food with a twist," again championing classic Danish cuisine. When visiting Denmark, trying smørrebrød and discovering the appeal of this simple snack is a must. **KRM**

Geranium | Visually stunning and technically flawless food

Location Copenhagen **Signature dish** Jellied ham with tomato foam and tomato water | 💲💲💲💲💲

In 2010, Geranium, the restaurant of Bocuse d'Or-winning chef Rasmus Kofoed, moved slightly outside Copenhagen's center to the eighth floor of an office block connected to Parken, FC Copenhagen's football stadium. The entrance is shared with the building's resident offices, making for an unusual start to a meal. However, the space between tables is ample in a way that seems reminiscent of a bygone era. There is also a pleasing sense of a great, airy expanse, with floor-to-ceiling windows on two sides of the room and quite spectacular views of the trees of a nearby park.

The cuisine is expert, local, and seasonal, as is expected of a modern Nordic restaurant, but the menu is distinctly lighter and more elegant than that

---

"It's the process where we attempt to make everything as perfect as possible that excites me the most."

Rasmus Kofoed, chef and co-owner of Geranium

---

of rivals. Plates are adorned by seasonal flowers and petals (Geranium, of course, shares its name with a family of edible flowers). Tremendous skill is evident in the visually stunning presentations and impressive array of culinary techniques, yet the glorious ingredients are always given room to shine. Typical dishes are the melt-in-the-mouth local langoustine with juniper and red herbs and the jellied ham with tomato water that is poured tableside.

Geranium is an intriguing mix of the modern avant-garde and the charm and elegance of more venerable restaurants. Its dining experience can be more fulfilling than that of some cutting-edge peers, and it sure offers a nice change of pace. **ABN**

Ballymaloe House | Archetypal warm Irish hospitality
in the home of Ireland's first family of food

Location Shanagarry, Cork **Signature dish** Baked plaice with melted butter and summer herbs; carragreen moss pudding with crushed blueberries | ❸❸❸

"If someone came to my door with fresh fish, I took it. I would never send them away…"

Myrtle Allen, founder of Ballymaloe

⬆ Ballymaloe restaurant first opened to guests in 1964.

There is an incomparable warmth to the welcome at the dining room of the first family of Irish food, where sprightly matriarch Myrtle Allen, high goddess of Irish slow food and artisanal producers, still dines regularly. It is her home, after all, and her great passion for baking is evident in the exceptional Irish soda bread offered at the beginning of the meal with beautiful farmhouse-churned butter. And—joy of joys—there is genuine encouragement to try a little of everything you like from a bountiful dessert trolley.

The feel of dining in a much-cherished family dining room, surrounded by fantastic Irish art and polished wood furniture in keeping with the Georgian surroundings, is increased by there being a set menu. There is generally a soup (maybe vibrant spinach and rosemary), or an unusual salad, warm with lamb's kidney and caramelized shallots. Invariably there is fish, landed locally at Ballycotton: poached gray mullet, with definitive Hollandaise sauce and champ (here, potato mashed with peas and parsley); or plaice goujons with superlative, tangy tartare sauce. There may be a roast or game (in season, roast woodcock served with their innards, and sweet geranium jelly).

Always bear in mind both the mesmerizing array of desserts—temptations such as blood orange tart, profiteroles, raspberry jelly with fresh mint cream, and carragreen moss (a local seaweed) pudding—and the carefully selected cheeseboard, with fare from small artisanal producers that is unlikely to be available beyond the local farmer's market.

On Friday evenings, there is an hors d'oevres buffet specializing in shellfish from Kenmore Bay: lobster, prawns, and mussels, plus homemade pâtés and salads. Foodies and local families come to savor what is tantamount to an Irish gastro-pilgrimage, a truly memorable and thoroughly unstuffy event. **SP**

Farmgate Café |

An authentic taste of traditional Ireland

Location Cork **Signature dish** Corned beef and
parsley sauce with steamed jacket potatoes | $

The historic English Market in Cork is one of the oldest
covered markets in the world and has provided the
citizens of Cork with fine Irish produce since 1788.
Farmgate Café, one story up and overlooking the
market, was opened in 1994 by Kay Harte with the
premise of serving simple, traditional Irish food.
Essential to her ethos was that the food served should
link directly to produce from the market traders, so
that diners could see exactly where the ingredients
were coming from. Harte is an ambassador of Irish
food and was a founding member of the illustrious
Good Food Ireland organization.

The café offers both self-service and a more
formal dining room; both are perfect for lingering
over lunch to the sounds of the bustle below. The
blackboard changes daily and boasts a short, seasonal
menu that includes classic Irish dishes made with
homegrown and cured meats from the market
butchers, many of whom rear their own livestock.

Look forward to corned beef or mutton;
shepherd's pie; liver and bacon; tripe; or drisheen, a
spicy, pig's blood sausage. Irish potatoes feature
prominently and come in many guises: mashed, roast,
as champ (mashed with scallions), and colcannon
(mashed with cabbage). But the café is not for
carnivores alone. There is a daily catch of Irish fish and
seafood on offer, soups and chowders are
homemade, and sandwiches are hand-cut to order
using artisan or freshly baked soda bread. The cakes
and desserts are made in-house, and cheeses are Irish.

The approach at Farmgate Café has drawn an
endless stream of diners through the years. So
impressive is the fare that some even dine there six
days a week. They come for the good food, high-
quality fresh produce, the buzz of the market, and the
warmth of Harte's Irish hospitality. **EL**

Cafe Paradiso |

Truly creative vegetarian cuisine

Location Cork **Signature dish** Braised turnip galette
with mushrooms and pecans in red wine gravy | $$

Tucked away near a busy road in the city of Cork, this is
one of Britain and Ireland's most acclaimed vegetarian
restaurants. Run by patron-chef Denis Cotter, Cafe
Paradiso is, unusually, attractive to vegetarians and
carnivores alike. After eight years in banking, Cotter
left to pursue an alternative career, starting out at the
renowned vegetarian restaurant Cranks in London.
He returned to Cork an accomplished vegetarian chef
and, after a stint at the Quay Co-Op, he opened
Cafe Paradiso in 1993.

Cotter's intention was to focus on simplicity, in a
relaxed setting, while serving food of a fine-dining
standard. Crucially, he also wanted to disprove the
perceived restrictions of vegetarian cuisine. Twenty

> *"[A] stylish little restaurant … with an extensive choice of interesting, original vegetarian dishes."*
>
> Michelin Guide

years later, Cafe Paradiso has become a destination for
both dedicated regulars and visitors—so much so
that he opened a guesthouse above the restaurant
to accommodate them.

The food is refined and detailed, and intensely
flavorful, making use of local ingredients supplied by
the Gort-Na-Nain farm just south of Cork. Influences
from Cotter's time in New Zealand are evident in
dishes such as lime-grilled haloumi with spiced carrot
puree, dukkah, lentils, pickled orange, and sultana,
but you are as likely to find Italian-influenced cuisine
made with Irish ingredients, for example, in a dish
of parsnip ravioli with ginger butter, sprout tops,
and stout reduction. **NS**

Scarista House | A triumph of culinary arts on a remote Scottish island

Location Isle of Harris **Signature dish** Stornoway-landed turbot with langoustine butter sauce | $$

The food is widely acclaimed, with ultra-fresh seafood a speciality. The restaurant has culinary plaudits, and was judged one of the top ten places to eat by the sea by the *Times* newspaper. So why is Scarista not a more familiar name to restaurant followers? It is surely because this whitewashed old mansion is one of the United Kingdom's most remote restaurants. As if reaching Scotland's Outer Hebridian islands were not enough, visitors then face a long journey over the mountains of the Isle of Harris to reach Scarista Bay.

The trek is eventually rewarded by a sensational setting: the pretty little hotel stands alone at the center of a 3-mile (5-km) crescent of white shell beach, with a turquoise sea backed by misty mountains.

In this distant spot, long-standing owners Patricia and Tim Martin face a logistical battle to maintain culinary standards. Dinner therefore is a four-course set menu. Deviations are allowed for vegetarians, and with notice special diets are catered to. Vegetables, salads, and herbs are grown in the hotel garden and in other gardens on the island. Bread, cakes, jam, marmalade, ice cream, and yogurt are made in the kitchen. Perhaps the easiest part is stocking the cellar, which includes around eighty wide-ranging wines, costing for all budgets.

Years have been spent scouring neighboring islands and mainland lochs for ingredients. Happily, they are of the highest quality. Local Uist peat-smoked scallops and salmon, Scottish farmhouse cheeses, and Stornoway black pudding often appear on the menu.

The Martins' struggles against the odds are so successful that diners are not necessarily guests of the hotel. Customers travel huge distances to eat in the cozy dining rooms here, lured by dishes like quail with Armagnac mousse, or Sound of Harris lobster, eaten by candlelight in front of an open peat fire. **SH**

↑ **Scarista House—a hospitable haven on the Isle of Harris.**

The Three Chimneys | Fine Scottish cooking in an awe-inspiring place

Location Isle of Skye   **Signature dish** Hot marmalade pudding with Drambuie custard | ❸❸❸

Twelve hours from London, or six hours from Glasgow, is a long drive for a meal, but many have made the trek to enjoy the magnificent natural setting, food, and hospitality of the Three Chimneys restaurant on the Isle of Skye. Thankfully for travelers, there is also a guest house if they wish to stay.

With no restaurant experience at all, Eddie and Shirley Spears opened the Three Chimneys in 1984. Determined to provide outstanding Scottish food and hospitality, they overcame all the challenges, not least the remote location. Plaudits came quickly, including being listed in the Personal Top Five of Frank Bruni (restaurant critic of *The New York Times*) and twice in *Restaurant's* Top Fifty restaurants in the world.

The vernacular architecture of the whitewashed stone croft sits beautifully in the raw, unbridled beauty of its surroundings. The inside has rough-hewn walls, sisal flooring, and traditional coziness. The menus, sustained by local produce, pivot on seasonality and are steeped in the rich heritage of Scottish cooking. There is classic fare, with net-fresh local langoustines, oysters, scallops, crabs, and all things piscine; carnivores can delight in venison haunch, lamb, mallard, haggis with neeps (turnips); cheeses are Scottish.

But the food is not as straightforward as it seems. The Scottish fare, on closer inspection, reveals itself to be an eclectic mix of origin and style, classic and modern cooking. The risotto of razor clams (from Arisaig on the mainland) with a syboe (green onion) and mussel pakora is India, Italy, and Scotland all coming together on one plate.

Eddie and Shirley are now all but retired, but remain owners and directors of the Three Chimneys. Thankfully, their culinary ethos and high standards still reign supreme under chef director Michael Smith. **EL**

⬆ Characterful Scottish cuisine in a stone croft.

Andrew Fairlie at Gleneagles | Ultra-sophisticated hotel dining

Location Auchterarder   **Signature dish** Smoked lobster with lime butter | ❺❺❺❺❺

"Andrew blends the best in French and Scottish cooking … with outstanding ingredients."

Gleneagles website

⬆ Smoked lobster with lime butter is Fairlie's star dish.

Does Andrew Fairlie have it all? The setting of his restaurant is truly magnificent, on the grounds of the iconic Edwardian Gleneagles hotel with the heather-covered Scottish Highlands in the distance. He remains the only chef with two Michelin stars in Scotland and is highly respected among his discerning peers. His glamorous restaurant exudes confidence, with cooking that effortlessly combines classic techniques with influences from Fairlie's trips to Japan. Eating here is always a thoroughly enjoyable treat: beautifully cooked fine Scottish produce matched with extraordinarily friendly and cosseting, polished service.

The dining room is decorated in appetizing hues of chocolate, chestnut, and strawberry, with floor-to-ceiling silk drapes, intimate booths, and highly covetable paintings by contemporary Scottish artist Archie Forrest that add to a real sense of occasion.

Here diners can experience the pinnacle of contemporary gastronomy, and it is definitely advised to go all out with the tasting menu, preferably with matching wines. The tasting menu is actually better value than dining à la carte and gives diners the opportunity to try all the dishes that Fairlie considers his best for each season—including his signature dish of Orkney lobster smoked over whiskey barrel chips and baked with lime butter.

Luxurious ingredients prepared with an original and playful twist feature in dishes such as roasted hand-dived scallops with sea bass, a divine oyster parfait, and a pleasingly contrasting crunchy squid cracker, or the incredibly decadent foie gras "donut" in a piquant-sweet rhubarb sauce. Game comes directly from the Gleneagles Estate, and lamb is sourced from Fairlie's brother. The desserts are exquisite creations based around one single, flavorful ingredient, such as Scottish strawberries, and are always presented beautifully. **SP**

Martin Wishart | A committed chef showcasing fine Scottish produce

Location Edinburgh **Signature dish** Ceviche of halibut with mango and passion fruit | 💲💲💲

Martin Wishart's eponymous restaurant is set in a terrace in Leith, the old docks area of Edinburgh, a distinctly colorful area at one time but now much smartened up. Wishart trained in the kitchens of Le Gavroche and with Marco Pierre White before opening his own place in 1999. The restaurant gradually built a strong local reputation for its skillful cooking, being awarded a Michelin star in 2001 that it has retained ever since. The first-floor dining room is simple and unpretentious, with widely spaced tables set with crisp white linen. It is an unshowy setting for excellent cooking.

The menu is short and highly seasonal, making good use of the high-quality produce that abounds naturally in Scotland, such as Kilbrannan langoustines, roe deer venison, Shetland monkfish, and Scottish strawberries. An example of how Wishart uses this produce to good effect may be experienced with the flavorful, organic Shetland salmon, which has been smoked in the kitchen; konbu (kelp) vinegar and soused cucumber and malt powder give balance to the richness of the smoked fish.

A further example of using local produce in season is grouse cooked with a sauce flavored with Armagnac, served with cabbage, salsify, baby onions, and lardons. The grouse is pan-fried initially, to get a crisp skin, then cooked in the oven, before being finished for a couple of minutes in a pan. The bird, hung for less time than is common, does not have the over-gamey flavor that can easily occur with this ingredient. A meal might conclude in style with pink-grapefruit jelly served with honeycomb tuiles and passion-fruit cream, with melon sorbet and mandarin and passion-fruit foam.

Wishart is not a chef who seeks media attention, and he is mostly found in his kitchen rather than promoting his latest book deal. He produces a very high standard of food, marrying old-fashioned culinary technique to top-quality produce. **AH**

"There's no real magic to it. I keep things as simple as I can in my own mind and I keep them realistic."

Martin Wishart, chef and owner

⬆ Starfruit adorns a typically delicate Wishart dessert.

The Kitchin | Definitive seafood so fresh it is almost shocking

Location Edinburgh   **Signature dish** "Sea," pig's head, and langoustine | 💲💲

"From nature to plate" is the mantra of Michelin-starred chef Tom Kitchin, as fiercely committed to *terroir* as his mentor, Alain Ducasse, with whom he trained at Le Louis XV on the French Riviera. So proud is Kitchin of the freshness of his produce that diners are presented with a map of Scotland highlighting the exact sourcing of their ingredients, from Orkney scallops to Arisaig razor clams, known locally as "spoots." The cooking, influenced by classic French techniques, is bold yet elegant and accomplished. Langoustines are robustly presented in a signature dish in homage to chef Pierre Koffmann, with whom Kitchin also trained. A perfectly seasoned, boned, and rolled pig's head is served with a huge roasted langoustine tail and a paper-thin crispy pig's ear.

The ultimate starter is "Sea." In summer, this is a salad of heritage tomatoes and minutely diced vegetables with a "rock pool" of vibrant shellfish topped with an oyster and a "tide" of tomato consommé; in winter, it is sea vegetables, including sea aster and samphire. The fish main dishes are stunning, luxurious, and harmonious in texture—any fresher and they would leap off the plate. Diners book up to a year ahead to be among the first to taste the new-season game that Kitchin cooks so masterfully. Young grouse is properly cooked medium rare, accompanied by wild blueberries, girolles, the lightest bread sauce, and game chips. Desserts may be a classic lemon or pistachio soufflé, or gossamer-thin *millefeuille* with fragrant Blairgowrie strawberries.

The interior on Leith's quayside evokes the Scottish landscape, with heather and sea-blue hues. The animated buzz of chatter in the dining room and the knowledgeable, friendly staff (a good mix of Scottish and French, like the cuisine) add to the non-reverential informality. **SP**

⬆ The restaurant was formerly a whisky warehouse.

Magpie Cafe | Fish and chips, a resident ghost, and impressive views

Location Whitby **Signature dish** Fish and chips | $

The landmark, three-story, black-and-white building housing the Magpie Cafe in Whitby, a seaside town in North Yorkshire, dates back to the eighteenth century. All year round, and in all weathers, there is a long line of expectant diners waiting outside for a table.

Despite its age, the building has only housed a café (and, reputedly, a resident ghost) since 1939. The current owners, the Barker family, took over in 1954. The third generation of Barkers, spouses and children, still take care of all aspects of the business today.

Standing in line for a table at the Magpie is torture when you are hungry, with the appetizing scent of cooking fish and chips wafting past. However, the wait is never long. Inside, service is efficient, with numerous staff nipping deftly between tables tucked into every nook and cranny. There are additional tables up the steep, curving staircase on the top floor. A table by the window up here affords the best views of the town, the sea, the beach, and the famous ruins of Whitby Abbey, which are reputed to have been an inspiration for Bram Stoker's novel *Dracula*.

Fish and chips is the best-selling dish at the Magpie. Up to a thousand portions a day are cooked and served, either in the café or as a takeaway in the high summer. But alongside the fish and chips is an extensive menu with a variety of local fish and seafood dishes; freshly caught local lobster is always popular. Steaks, pasta, and vegetarian choices are available for those not wanting fish, and a tempting array of traditional British puddings is also on offer.

Given the volume of fish and chips sold at the Magpie, several boats in the harbor work exclusively to supply the café, practically catching fish to order for them. Is it any wonder, then, that the Magpie's fish and chips are supremely fresh and considered to be among the best in England? **EL**

⬆ Classic British vacation fare at its very best.

The Drunken Duck Inn | Modern food in a centuries-old coaching inn

Location Ambleside **Signature dish** Drunken duck to share | $$

"The kind of place anybody would like to find at the end of a day's walking . . ."

Jay Rayner, *Observer*

[↑] The welcoming inn is situated above Ambleside.

[→] Cherry-glazed duck is a dish to share and savor.

This well-weathered inn is perched high above the village and commands dramatic views over the surrounding Lakeland fells. Attracting a mix of seasoned walkers, food lovers, tourists, and locals, it is as much a popular watering hole as a destination famed for its outstanding modern British cuisine.

The interior is furnished simply yet elegantly with dark wood furniture, unclothed tables, and historical prints and artifacts. Tastefully appointed onsite accommodation adds to the charm of the rural idyll.

Lunch menus are informal affairs and include quality sandwiches served with fat fries, best enjoyed with one of the home-brewed beers—perhaps the Red Bull Terrier or Brathay Gold. Resolutely British, Sunday roasts are especially popular with families, the slow-roasted, locally sourced meat arriving on a chunky wooden board surrounded by all the trimmings, served from copper pans.

The dial is turned up for dinner, although the atmosphere remains relaxed, with the service friendly and on the ball. Chef Jonny Watson and his team put on a fine spread, featuring a roll call of local produce: perhaps Herdwick lamb from a nearby farm, Morecombe Bay shrimp, and Cartmel Valley smoked salmon. The much-acclaimed cherry-glazed duck for two to share is a perennial favorite—crisp skin on the breast yields to juicy, pink-cooked meat below, plated with delectable, slow-cooked, confited legs. This, along with the accompanying meaty gravy, tangy red cabbage, and crisp roast potatoes, sums up the style—unpretentious yet perfectly executed.

Highlights from the afternoon tea menu include freshly baked scones, full-flavored preserves, and the acclaimed sliced and buttered Borrowdale tea bread, studded with tea-steeped dried fruit. This spot is one of Cumbria's best-loved inns. It is no surprise that the rooms and restaurant tables are booked months in advance. **RGu**

L'Enclume | An idyllic, rural setting for thrilling
contemporary dining

Location Cartmel **Signature dish** Cartmel Valley venison with charcoal oil and fennel | ❺❺❺❺

L'Enclume is the ultimate gastronomic retreat, deep in the wilds of Cumbria in the medieval village of Cartmel. Chef Simon Rogan believes in reflecting the landscape on the plate. He uses local produce, grown and foraged, only at its point of seasonal perfection. This is contemporary naturalist cooking at its thrilling, trailblazing best. Precise technique and attention to the smallest detail is at the heart of his cuisine.

L'Enclume means "anvil" in French, and the 800-year-old building was originally a smithy. It is now an elegant restaurant with whitewashed walls and bare tables of beautiful local wood, with beguilingly tactile tableware designed by local craftspeople. Incredibly, all of the vegetables, herbs, fruit, and flowers in the dishes and, increasingly, the meat, too, come from Rogan's own 14 acres (6 ha) of farmland.

A meal at L'Enclume is a progression from snacks to larger dishes. Snacks might feature exquisite white pebbles with oyster cream, apple, and oyster leaf that tastes vividly of the sea. Main dishes include a playful cod "yolk" with watercress, runner beans, and grilled scallop, tangy with salt and vinegar, with cauliflower, raw scallop, and wood sorrel. Throughout, the vegetables and herbs—often mere micro-shoots with intense flavors—are central to the plate.

Herbs and foraged produce feature even in the unusual desserts, which pay homage to the season and the landscape, and are pleasingly light, layered, and barely sweet at all. Desserts may include plum with malt and brown sugar; anise hyssop, raspberry, and milk skin; meadow sweet, blueberry, buckler leaf sorrel, and walnut; and sea buckthorn, sweet cheese, and woodruff. Dining here feels very special; it is a poetic and joyful experience that put Cartmel firmly on the gastronomic map, even before Rogan took over the restaurant at Claridge's in London. **SP**

> *"Rogan's food is modernist ... and shows a commitment to the good stuff."*
>
> Jay Rayner, *Observer*

⬆ Contemporary naturalist cooking from Simon Rogan.

The Star Inn | A glorious taste of Yorkshire in a picturesque, ancient inn

Location Harome **Signature dish** Black pudding with foie gras, watercress, apple, and vanilla chutney | ❸❸❸

Andrew Pern, chef-owner of the highly acclaimed Star Inn in Harome, is a leading light in Britain's food scene. He and his former wife bought the extraordinarily pretty but near-derelict fourteenth-century thatched inn in 1996. Their painstaking restoration retained the low beams and walls and preserved the innate character of the place. Pern humbly claims that his tenure is only one chapter in the building's long history—but what an illustrious chapter it is.

When The Star Inn opened, British pubs were only just realizing the notion of serving good food—before then, although it had often been a part of the offering, it was rarely considered great. For Pern, it was not enough just to serve high-quality food; he placed great emphasis on regional and seasonal ingredients from North Yorkshire. This is now the accepted norm, but back then his approach and attitude were groundbreaking. Soon accolades, plaudits, and the first Michelin star ever awarded to a pub came his way. Pern expanded the business to include an award-winning boutique hotel, too.

Pern's signature dish of grilled black pudding with pan-fried foie gras epitomizes his cooking. The humble blood pudding is partnered with that most noble of ingredients, foie gras. The grassroots dish is served with local watercress and apples, a homemade chutney, and a scrumpy (rough cider) reduction. The cider is locally produced, sourced from the monks at nearby Ampleforth Abbey.

The well-earned success of The Star Inn has garnered it a loyal following, not least locally, with the people of Yorkshire who are justifiably proud of their county, the food it produces, and The Star. Eating at The Star is to become immersed in all that is wonderful about seasonal Yorkshire food in the hands of a master. **EL**

The Burlington, Devonshire Arms | Sublime setting and food

Location Bolton Abbey **Signature dish** Marinated scallop, avocado, radish, and pig's head croquette | ❸❸

The Burlington is the fine-dining restaurant of the Devonshire Arms Country House Hotel & Spa, part of the 30,000-acre (12,000-ha) Bolton Abbey estate of the Duke and Duchess of Devonshire. It has a Michelin star, four AA rosettes, and a 2,500-bin wine list. The meat, fish, and vegetables all come from the estate.

Head chef Adam Smith, former executive sous chef at the Ritz Hotel in London, is now making his mark here. His inspirational modern British food is classic, exemplified by his signature dish of marinated scallop, avocado, radish, and a pig's head croquette. The seasonally changing menu features marriages of flavors and textures that are executed with razor-sharp precision. Apples and lovage from the estate's

> *"[Adam Smith] is without doubt the very best chef that has been in my kitchens ... "*
>
> John Williams, executive chef, The Ritz

garden may share a plate with a Whitby crab, or a silky puree of homegrown cauliflower with an oyster.

There is a measure of formality (gents must wear a jacket) in the elegant, softly lit dining rooms. Drawings of classical architecture from the renowned Devonshire Collection at Chatsworth adorn the pale-colored walls, and the antique tables are dressed with designer silverware and crystal glasses. The adjacent airy conservatory has fine views of the gardens and the stunning Yorkshire Dales. This is a more relaxing space, but the dress code still applies. The service is excellent: The warm, attentive staff softens an establishment that might otherwise tend toward the reserved. Everyone knows what he or she is doing. **EL**

The Box Tree | Innovative food in a famous Yorkshire gem

Location Ilkley **Signature dish** Roasted scallops, celeriac puree, truffle, smoked eel, and Granny Smith apple | ⓈⓈⓈⓈ

> *"It is so important to retain the star; you never feel quite comfortable until you see it in writing."*
>
> Simon Guellar, head chef at the Box Tree

⬆ The Box Tree has a fine pedigree of notable chefs.

The Box Tree, Ilkley, occupies one of the oldest buildings in the town. Dating from 1712, it was home to various businesses until Malcolm Reid and partner Colin Long turned it into a fine-dining restaurant in 1962. It quickly became the North's most successful restaurant, gaining two Michelin stars almost immediately. Legendary British chefs Michael Truelove and Edward Denny made their mark on the menus, and the Box Tree was also pivotal in the early career of world-renowned chef Marco Pierre White.

Since then, the restaurant has ridden highs and endured lows (it lost its stars), but it has risen once again since passing into the careful hands of chef Simon Guellar and his wife, Rena, in 2004. A Michelin star has been earned, and awards and plaudits for the gastronomic gem have rolled in relentlessly since.

The plush decoration may be seemingly unchanged since the era of Reid and Long, but there has been a careful and considered cleanup. The cautious makeover has created a greater sense of space without making the low-ceilinged rooms feel any less cozy, warm, or inviting.

Simon Guellar's signature dish exemplifies his approach to cooking. Roasted scallops with celeriac puree add up to a classic and perfect marriage of flavors; truffle adds depth and elegance; smoked eel and Granny Smith apple are the twist, one that in the wrong hands would be a disaster.

Where Guellar has led, many chefs have followed. His seemingly simple food belies a more complex reality; it is accomplished, innovative, and exciting. French classic techniques underpin much of the cooking but without demanding undue attention.

The sublime cooking, coupled with an enviable wine cellar and the consummate front-of-house service—the product of Rena Guellar's expert eye and well-trained staff—seems set to ensure that the Box Tree will delight for years to come. **EL**

The Pipe and Glass Inn | A taste of Yorkshire in an historic hostelry

Location South Dalton   **Signature dish** Ginger burnt cream with rhubarb and sugar cakes | 💲💲

Until relatively recently, food critics considered East Yorkshire to be a culinary desert. All that changed with the arrival of James and Kate Mackenzie at The Pipe and Glass Inn, South Dalton, in 2006. Both had excellent reputations as protégés of the renowned Star Inn at Harome in North Yorkshire. Similarities between the two inns can be found in their buildings and pretty village locations, but that is as far as it goes.

It took but a short time for the talented pair (James in the kitchen and Kate front of the house) to put the inn and its area on the map. Among the plaudits arriving in quantity was the Michelin star, an elusive award that they had long coveted.

Despite its culinary fame, The Pipe and Glass remains firstly an inn. The floors are wooden and scrubbed, the furniture chunky and comfortable. The mirrors, lamps, and tasteful bric-a-brac are unobtrusive and soften any edges. Three separate dining areas are arranged to flow seamlessly into one, culminating in a glass conservatory with a table able to accommodate twenty-eight diners.

Eating at the inn is a relaxed and informal experience, but that does not mean that it is laid-back or casual. This is a professional team, and their friendly approach fronts a skillful operation. The menu is carefully crafted to tease and tempt the palette. Mackenzie is passionate about the freshness of his ingredients and where they are sourced. He cleverly balances flavors, textures, and tastes, often in unpredictable combinations: wild rabbit with cockles, halibut with oxtail, or haggis dressed up as a fritter.

Mackenzie's attention to provenance is seconded by his interest in his food's history. This is epitomized by his signature dish of ginger burned cream with Yorkshire rhubarb and East Yorkshire sugar cakes. The rhubarb is local, but the cakes were inspired by a 200-year-old recipe that the chef discovered in the archives of the nearby Beverley Town Council. **EL**

"We know what sells … that's why we have a proper prawn cocktail on the menu—because people love it."

James Mackenzie, chef and owner of The Pipe and Glass

⊼ Carefully crafted food is on offer here.

Whitelock's | Traditional British pub food in atmospheric surroundings

Location Leeds   **Signature dish** Pie made of beef and ale | ❸❺

The inn now known as Whitelock's Alehouse opened in 1715 as the Turk's Head. The Whitelock family took over the license in the late nineteenth century, the name was changed, and John Lupton Whitelock installed the now-famous ornate interior. A Victorian confection of highly polished brass, marble, etched glass, and leather, it remains almost unchanged today.

Unlike the decor, the food has periodically undergone change, and not always for the better. Any attempt to deviate from the established Britishness of the menu has resulted in failure; but, thankfully, these anomalies have been rare. Owner Ed Mason has long kept the menus rooted in traditional pub food, with a good smattering of local provenance to ensure good

---

"The Leeds equivalent of Fleet Street's Old Cheshire Cheese … It is the very heart of Leeds."

Sir John Betjeman, poet and broadcaster

---

quality. Service comes in the pub manner of ordering at the bar. Portions are hearty, and while wines are limited, ales (many of them local) are in abundance.

Robust sandwiches, fish and chips, ham hock, and black pudding with Scotch egg are just some of the regular dishes at lunch. They reappear at dinner time, where they share the menu with lighter, more contemporary dishes: salads, vegetarian options, and even a risotto. Sunday lunch includes the national dish of a roast meat, Yorkshire pudding, and gravy.

The longevity of Whitelock's is extraordinary, and the consistency of approach a joy. This is a place for anyone who appreciates food and drink well and truly rooted in its provider's heritage. **EL**

Hambleton Hall | Classic dining in a splendid Victorian country house

Location Hambleton   **Signature dish** Chanterelles with confit bacon, dandelion leaves, and quail eggs | ❸❺

Overlooking the Rutland Water reservoir (the largest artificial lake in Europe) is Hambleton Hall, a nineteenth-century hunting lodge now converted into a luxury hotel. It has a lovely terrace with landscaped gardens and a beautiful view over the water. The dining room is a gracious affair, with its high ceilings, thick carpet, and views over the garden.

Aaron Patterson is in charge of the kitchen, having started here in 1984 and taken over as head chef in 1992. The restaurant has retained its Michelin star since 1983. A meal might begin with a nibble of delicate tomato tart with Mozzarella and rich Mozzarella choux pastry. A starter might be a large, plump, sweet, sautéed scallop with onion puree, Puy lentils, lemongrass foam, and onion bhaji. The scallop has inherent sweetness, perfectly timed, with the onion bhaji a clever and original pairing, the foam adding a nice hint of spice to the dish.

Desserts continue the high standard. A passion-fruit soufflé with a lovely, light texture comes with a delicate passion-fruit ice cream accompaniment. The caramelized apple tart comprises very finely sliced apples on a good, rich pastry, sitting in a pool of caramel sauce, the top of which is browned with a blow-torch rather than caramelized during the cooking. The center of the tart has a scoop of perfect vanilla ice cream surrounded by blackberries, which add some welcome tartness to the dish.

There is an excellent wine list that features carefully chosen producers, with some kindly priced wines at the high end of the list. Hambleton Hall is a lovely place for a relaxing break, combining an elegant country setting with high-class cooking and very welcoming service. **AH**

▢ The picturesque garden setting of Hambleton Hall.

Sat Bains | Boldly creative flavor combinations
created by a culinary star

Location Nottingham **Signature dish** Ham, egg, and peas | ❸❸❸❸

Marvelously creative chef-proprietor Sat Bains has single-handedly put Nottingham on the culinary map with his eponymous restaurant. The converted Victorian barn may be virtually under an overpass, but it has great style, warmth, and polish. And Bains makes a virtue of his unexpected, unprepossessing location, even offering a dish that is named after the restaurant's zip code and made with foraged herbs from the nearby meadows and river banks.

Dining at Sat Bains is an occasion to suspend preconceptions and embrace outlandish ingredient and texture combinations, such as scallops with strawberries, cream, wood sorrel, and *sauce vierge*; with Bains' alchemy, they invariably work. Even the menu is divided, unconventionally, into salt, sweet, sour, bitter, and *umami*. Bains' signature bread is wonderfully moreish: a mix of malt and treacle sponge, served with hand-churned Lincolnshire butter.

Bains' ham-and-egg dish won the U.K. TV cooking competition *Great British Menu* with a perfect 10/10, and tasting it is *de rigeur*. This is no freeway roadside fare. Served with a runny duck egg and Jabugo ham, the peas arrive in three forms: braised in ham stock, made into minted sorbet, and as shoots. More provocative still is roe deer with roasted cauliflower, pear, blue cheese, and dark chocolate.

Plenty of dishes cross the boundary from savory to sweet, and the kitchen has a definite penchant for experimenting with chocolate—be sure to try the aerated chocolate in a kind of walnut whip with meringue and maple granite. Service, led by Sat's wife Amanda, is highly personable, sweet, and extremely well-informed. For an even greater insight into the originality and technical prowess of the kitchen, book the chef's table and watch as inventive dishes are prepared right in front of your eyes. **SP**

> *"It's not the genius of the chef you are observing. It takes craftsmanship to make it delicious."*

Sat Bains, chef and owner of Sat Bains

⬆ A dish of organic salmon in oyster sauce.

Morston Hall |
Bucolic country gardens and fresh crab

Location Holt **Signature dish** Saddle of lamb with hay-infused jus; passion-fruit soufflé with ice cream | ❸❸❸❸

From the sophisticated, pale gray conservatory of this Georgian flintstone restaurant/hotel is an arcadian vista of lupins, lavender, roses, and a lily pond. Morston Hall is run by Galton Blackiston, Norfolk's towering culinary hero, who was extolling the virtues of eating locally and seasonally long before it became fashionable. The menu is a showcase of Britain's rich heritage of ingredients: seafood from the nearby north Norfolk coast, samphire, or flavorful asparagus. Blackthorn serves a set-price, one-sitting dinner that is even better than a tasting menu because it changes at every service to reflect what is freshest. The portions are generous rather than dainty.

Here, the cooking is exquisitely nuanced, subtly incorporating the latest culinary techniques—sea trout as a confit cooked in olive oil with chervil, compressed watermelon with chervil—with the absolute precision and perfection that comes with classical training. A number of the staff, including head chef Richard Bembridge, have spent time with the legendary Roux brothers at both Le Gavroche and Waterside Inn, and their experience shines through.

There is exceptional attention to detail in the luxurious canapés, including lobster with tomato and wobbly micro Parmesan custards dressed with flowers. Savory sorbets are a regular feature, such as the zingy fresh pea paired with a marvelously savory bacon mousse. Desserts are artfully multifaceted, strictly seasonal, and thoroughly enjoyable—for example, the pistachio sponge crumbles with pistachio, cherry ice cream, and poached cherries, and a slice of vanilla pannacotta is a real treat.

The staff is young, knowledgeable, and charming. This is definitely a place for celebrations, so expect romantic tables for two balancing the Marigold Hotel graciously gray brigade. **SP**

Midsummer House |
Extraordinary quality and creativity

Location Cambridge **Signature dish** Roast quail, shallot puree, grapes, celery, and sourdough | ❸❸❸

Overlooking the lush green of Midsummer Common, in the heart of beautiful and historic Cambridge, this serene restaurant is one of the finest places to eat in England. Chef-patron Daniel Clifford has been at the helm for fifteen years, inspiring his peers, critics, and diners with exceptionally elegant, inventive cooking.

For the full experience, order one of the tasting menus and enjoy the ride; it will be a succession of delicately balanced dishes to bring the senses alive. The lightness of touch belies the effort and skill required to produce dishes at this level. Clifford works with what is in season, and his modern food is strongly rooted in classical techniques, using cleverly combined ingredients. In one dish, scallops, potatoes,

> *"An extremely well-run and likable restaurant presided over by an inventive, gifted chef … "*
>
> Matthew Norman, *Guardian*

and truffle are lined up inside a tender whole leek, with burned onion powder sprinkled on top. The intense and delicate ingredients are perfectly balanced. There are often many elements to a dish, but rather than being complicated, they provide surprises—as in the apple crumble, baked yogurt, and vanilla dessert, which hides a spoon of caramel at its base.

The Victorian villa that houses the restaurant is simple, peaceful, and comfortable. Many diners are there for special events, and all will have booked well in advance. There is an atmosphere of anticipation, yet the whole is given a sense of ease by staff who are relaxed and knowledgeable. The reputation of this exciting chef is justly earned. **CB**

Le Champignon Sauvage | An exquisite exercise in the craft of cooking

Location Cheltenham **Signature dish** Scallops with cauliflower puree, cumin veloute, and *ras el hanout* caramel | $$$

David Everitt-Matthias and his wife, Helen, opened Le Champignon Sauvage in a quiet Cheltenham terrace in 1987. The restaurant slowly built up an enviable reputation for simple but precise cooking, gaining a Michelin star in 1995 and a second in 2000, accolades that it has since retained.

The kitchen shows considerable attention to detail, starting with the bread, made from scratch in the kitchen for each service. Many top restaurants bring in their bread, yet this humble element of the meal, which remains on the table until the desserts arrive, often gives an indication of how much care a restaurant takes. The rolls, whether granary with a good crust or a soft brioche with bacon, are excellent.

The dishes here are based on the classics but show sophisticated touches. One example is roasted native lobster with confit of duck hearts, complemented by pumpkin and nougat velouté. This unusual combination of flavors works very well; the tender lobster contrasts with the richness of the duck heart confit, and the pumpkin adds a hint of sweetness. Another example is the Goosenargh duck, which is cooked beautifully pink and served with chicory caramelized in maple syrup, the duck resting on a bed of walnut mash. It is accompanied by a deep reduction of cooking juices, the slight bitterness of the chicory being an effective partner to the duck.

The high level of skill continues with dessert, so often the Achilles' heel of fine U.K. restaurants. A cylinder of passion-fruit cream with mango, served with a slice of caramelized mango, has a lovely taste. It is served with a smooth coconut sorbet, along with little cubes of fresh mango—a refreshing and successful combination. Champignon Sauvage is refreshingly unpretentious, content to produce carefully crafted food in a relaxed setting. **AH**

↑ Dishes are elegantly presented here.

The Hardwick | Gloriously flavorful food showcasing Welsh produce

Location Abergavenny   **Signature dish** Roast pork loin, slow-cooked pork belly | ❸❸❸

The Hardwick is located in a converted pub with accommodation, and it retains the cozy conviviality and beamed ceiling of its former incarnation, spruced up with rich textiles and leather. Chef-proprietor Stephen Terry was at Marcus Pierre White's legendary Harvey's in the 1980s, where so many Michelin-starred chefs earned their stripes. He also worked at Le Gavroche with Michel Roux, Jr., and at L'Arpège in Paris with Alain Passard, before taking the helm at Coast in Mayfair, a very fashionable place in the 1990s.

Terry's creativity and technical prowess remain as impressive as ever, and the sheer range of his menu is quite staggering, especially considering that it is insistently based on local produce.

Right from the first taste of the exceptional bread, supplied by Alex Gooch's bakery in nearby Hay-on-Wye, or the Black Mountains smoked salmon with laverbread and sesame rye, a meal at the Hardwick stands out as a treat. Throughout, flavors are punchy and distinctive, and the portions unusually generous. Some ingredient pairings are rarely seen on the same plate; cod with chanterelles, saddleback pork, and broad beans is a perfect example. The pork belly has outstanding crispy skin and is served without pretension with bubble and squeak. The ravenous will marvel at and relish the beef platter, with carpaccio of Herefordshire beef, seventy-two-hour cooked short ribs, an almost obscenely juicy burger, and oxtail suet pudding. There is a chocolate plate, too, offering mousse, brownie, and peanut and cherry parfait.

With the Brecon Beacon hills close by, all this indulgence may be compensated for by a brisk walk the next day. And the food is not all so robust; Terry has a light touch, too. One memorable dish is an elegant summer dessert with honey and amaretto enhancing the perfume of a perfect white peach. **SP**

⊡ Stephen Terry's cooking delivers flavors in style.

The Walnut Tree Inn | Good food to relish at a legendary Welsh venue

Location Abergavenny **Signature dish** Rack of lamb with sweetbreads and cromesqui | 🅢🅢

On the outskirts of Abergavenny, the Walnut Tree is one of the best-known restaurants in Wales. Chef and owner Franco Taruschio originally opened it in 1966, and diners were drawn from far and wide by the Italian food. The Walnut Tree went through some tough times following Taruschio's retirement in 2001, but its reputation is now fully restored, with the kitchen in the capable hands of Shaun Hill, whose culinary career includes, famously, his tiny, Michelin-starred restaurant, The Merchant House in Ludlow, where the kitchen contained him and him alone.

The à la carte menu, written in resolutely down-to-earth style, changes daily. It showcases an intelligently selected range of ingredients from seiwin (sea trout) and cockles to suckling pig and pigeon, with offal a particular favorite. The cooking style is simple, yet accurate; a slab of perfectly cooked halibut might be served with beurre blanc, new potatoes, green beans, and a little samphire, or a crab salad enlivened with just a touch of spice. Hill's assured culinary technique is demonstrated by precisely cooked roast quail, served with grapes to provide acidity and balance the richness of the fowl, with lettuce and a jus with plenty of flavor and little bits of bacon to add smoky richness. A more elaborate dish is rabbit pithier, consisting of excellent pastry and moist, carefully cooked rabbit meat, with julienned vegetables and a lovely rich sauce. The desserts also show Hill's precision and attention to detail. A lime curd and mango tart has a rich curd filling that shows just enough acidity from the lime, combined with very ripe Alphonso mango and good pastry.

The informal setting of the Walnut Tree (the website states that there is "no dress code or similar pomposity") is perfect for relaxing and admiring some understated yet serious cooking. **AH**

⬆ The Walnut Tree Inn serves delicious comfort food.

The Company Shed | Fine English seafood served fresh on the beach

Location West Mersea **Signature dish** Freshly shucked native oysters | $

Ever since the Romans came to prize the oysters from around Colchester, there has been a venerable tradition of farming them. Today, anyone in West Mersea who wants to enjoy oysters and other seafoods at remarkably reasonable prices heads to the Company Shed, founded by seventh-generation oysterman Richard Haward and run by his family. At first glance, this is just a simple wooden building on a pebbly beach, set among boatyards and seagulls.

The appetizing aroma of frying garlic that wafts from the Shed, and the line of people waiting for a table (no bookings are taken), suggest good things on offer. Inside, the setting is basic: a single room, with a wet-fish counter to one side, and a few tables covered by cheery, sea-themed oil cloths. Essentials such as malt vinegar, Tabasco, and paper towels for wiping hands are placed on every table. Invariably, the place is filled with diners of all ages, from couples to large family groups, companionably shelling prawns or langoustines or picking crabs. The etiquette is simple: bring your own bread and drink (fine white wines or soft drinks, the choice is yours), and help yourself to glasses from the shelf.

The hungry choose from a short menu of cold and hot seafood dishes, go and order at the counter, then wait for their dishes to arrive, brought by friendly, youthful waiting staff. Popular dishes include the generous seafood platter; sweet-fleshed tiger shrimp, freshly grilled with salt and herbs, served with garlic mayonnaise and rich giga oysters with cream and Parmesan. In season, the family's home-grown, flavorful native oysters are excellent. There is nothing fancy here, just fresh seafood served in a friendly, straightforward style. Having to check the tide table because the nearby causeway becomes impassable at high tide just adds to the sense of adventure. **JL**

↑ The Company Shed is supplied by local fishing boats.

Le Manoir aux Quat' Saisons | An exquisite sybaritic experience

Location Great Milton **Signature dish** Confit of salmon, apple, and lemon verbena | ❺❺❺❺❺

The mesmerizing vegetable gardens here, grand in scale, beauty, and diversity—growing everything from Japanese basil to amaranth—are at the heart of dining at Le Manoir. They epitomize chef Raymond Blanc's passion for discovering, showcasing, and preserving the best of vegetables, herbs, and fruits in his Oxfordshire Eden.

Sitting in the elegant conservatory and gazing out on the gardens is an idyllic experience, and one that sets the tone for dining here. On offer is pampering of the very highest order, yet the food is light, clean, and intelligently accentuated with herbs and spices, with unexpected touches that give finesse. It is luxurious but not overindulgent.

Canapés, enjoyed in the lounge among Matisse prints, are delightful tantalizers: miniature salt cod croquettes, Parmesan biscuits, Iberico ham, and melon. The menus are seasonal and reflect what is in its prime, whether it be a salad of just-picked salad leaves with scallops and langoustine, or baby beetroot terrine winningly partnered with horseradish sorbet. Blanc's long-lasting regard for Vietnam and Japan is apparent in the flavoring of many dishes, including a highly original dish of Cornish wild brill paired with courgette flowers stuffed with an ethereal fish and herb mousseline and wasabi emulsion. More classic choices include fillet of beef with truffles, Swiss chard, and girolles. The impressive cheese trolley plays on the Anglo-French dynamics of the kitchen, and the seasonal soufflé is unmissable for dessert. The extensive wine list runs to over 1,000 bottles and, unsurprisingly, is strong on French wines; the likes of Chassagne-Montrachet are offered by the glass with tasting menus.

Service is courteous, knowledgeable, and in tune with a dining room that is invariably full to capacity, with tables of families celebrating important milestones and couples on romantic trysts. **SP**

"If we meet at the table for good, simple ethical food, we can create a kinder society."

Raymond Blanc, chef patron of Le Manoir

⬆ Pan-fried sea bass, langoustines, and Asian greens.

➡ Path of anticipation: the grand entrance to Le Manoir aux Quat' Saisons, set amid beautiful gardens.

The Hand & Flowers | Rustic, modern cooking from the heart

Location Marlow   **Signature dish** Glazed omelette of smoked haddock and Parmesan | ⓈⓈ

The Hand & Flowers has the singular distinction of being the first pub awarded two Michelin stars. Chef-patron Tom Kerridge opened the informal and welcoming venue with his wife, Beth, in 2005; the first star came within a year of opening and the second followed in 2012.

Kerridge has built an exceptional reputation for his full-flavored, robust, modern cooking. Hailing from the West Country, he is fiercely proud of Britain's rich food heritage and uses many intriguing British ingredients. Herbs and flowers such as lovage, wild garlic, mustard leaf, and meadowsweet crop up, while ale, mead, hops, malt, and hay all appear to delicious effect across his menu. One clever dessert draws on the bitter notes of ale to balance out the rich sweetness of an intense chocolate cake.

The chef is renowned for his meat dishes. He makes inventive use of less familiar cuts, such as pig's head or sweetbreads, while more straightforward

dishes benefit from his attention to detail and genius for maximizing flavor. Kerridge's duck breast, served with peas and fries cooked in duck fat, won the highly prestigious *Great British Menu* TV competition to cook the main course at a banquet for Prince Charles.

Kerridge also champions British drinks by offering draft real ale. An elegant and fresh celery and dill gin, created with Ginstitute, shows what can be done when a pub classic is rethought by a great chef.

A weekday lunch menu chosen by the chef represents stunningly good value for food of this quality. Kerridge embodies a warmth and enthusiasm for food and has a ready desire to inspire others, too. The service and atmosphere at The Hand & Flowers are infused with his generous spirit. This gastronomic corner of England has four indulgent cottage suites, which offer the option of an overnight stay. **CB**

⊡ Michelin-standard dining in a gastropub setting.

The Royal Oak | Skillfully executed food in informal pub surroundings

Location Maidenhead   **Signature dish** Lasagna of wild rabbit with wood blewits and chervil | ❺❺

At first glance, the Royal Oak seems a surprising venue for top-class food. A rather stark-looking, roadside pub near Maidenhead, its exterior gives little indication of the culinary skills within. The decor inside is basic, too, with plenty of dark wood, a bar, and tables, with a few overlooking the garden. But what sets the Royal Oak apart is the team in the kitchen.

Head chef Dominic Chapman took over the Royal Oak in 2007, having worked as the first head chef of the Hinds Head, Heston Blumenthal's pub in Bray. Chapman has hospitality in his blood, coming from the family that owns the well-known Castle Hotel in Taunton. His skill quickly became evident at the Royal Oak, and in 2010 Michelin awarded the establishment a star; it was a rare accolade for a pub.

The cooking at the Royal Oak is characterized by high-grade ingredients, appealing classical British dishes, and impeccable culinary technique. Customers will find a Scotch egg here, this being a pub after all

but also more demanding fare. The rabbit and bacon pie is an excellent example of the cooking, with lovely golden-brown pastry covering a generous filling of rabbit meat and its juices, the flavor enhanced by the smokiness of the bacon. The emphasis on quality ingredients can be seen in a wild salmon fillet with peas, cooked accurately and with the sort of flavor that is entirely absent from the farmed salmon served by most British restaurants.

Desserts are particularly appealing here, one example being a cherry trifle with gorgeous sponge and summer fruits of very high quality. The essentially British dish is elevated to a high level by the quality of the produce and skillful technique. The Royal Oak is proof that top-quality food does not have to be especially elaborate or served in a stuffy, formal setting. It just needs to be very, very good. **AH**

⬆ The Royal Oak: a pub with hidden culinary assets.

Polpo | A hip London reinvention of a traditional Venetian *bàcaro*

Location London   **Signature dish** *Fritto misto* (fritter of meat, seafood, and vegetables) |

> *"I give thanks for these parades of small tastes, particularly here where the pricing is forgiving …"*
>
> Jay Rayner, *Observer*

⬆ Deftly cooked seafood is a forte of the menu here.

➡ Polpo offers the relaxed ambience of a *bàcaro*.

Tucked away in London's fashionable Soho district, Russell Norman's trailblazing first restaurant has set the bar high for the competition. Frequented by hip media types and food lovers alike, Polpo is the place to see and be seen.

A stylish interpretation of a traditional Venetian bar, or *bàcaro*, Polpo launched in 2009 in Beak Street premises once occupied by the Venetian painter Canaletto. The elegant and understated interior, designed with an astute eye by Norman himself, has exposed brick walls, reclaimed antique fittings, and simple wooden furnishings. The attention to detail is reflected in the menu, the wine list, and the service, which is young, cheerful, and efficient. Small, reasonably priced dishes, cooked to perfection, allow top-quality ingredients to shine through.

Traditional *cicchetti*, or Venetian bar snacks, head up the menu, such as an irresistible *crostino* with *baccalà mantecato*, a blend of codfish, olive oil, garlic, and parsley. Such foods evoke images of tiny restaurants overlooking canals, especially when accompanied by a glass of prosecco or a perfect Negroni. The Campari Bar in the basement offers the *cicchetti* menu plus a full range of wine and cocktails.

Meandering through the menu is like exploring Venice's back streets: you never quite know where you will end up. Spinach and Parmesan *pizzette* with soft egg lead to fennel salami and a fig and goat's cheese bruschetta, perhaps via octopus and potato salad or a plate of cured buffalo meats and mozzarella. *Fritto misto* and spicy pork and fennel meatballs, once tasted, cry out to be ordered again. The dilemma: is there room left for mackerel tartare with *pane carasau* ("music paper bread") before pudding?

The puddings (baked peach, orange, and almond cake) and smaller *dolci*—chocolate salami or ricotta crumble—strike just the right note, along with a *moscato* (muscat) or coffee, to end on. **SKi**

Dinner by Heston Blumenthal | Historic British cuisine, reinvented

Location London   **Signature dish** Salamugundy (chicken oysters, salsify, bone marrow, and horseradish cream) | ❺❺❺❺

Few would have thought that historic British dishes could be reinvigorated to become a much-emulated trend. But chefs Heston Blumenthal and Ashley Palmer-Watts (who worked with Blumenthal for many years at The Fat Duck) have the Midas touch, translating impressively scholarly research into magnificent creations on the plate. Their dishes are traditional, each with its date and source of inspiration cited on the menu, but reworked with a lighter touch, an injection of modern techniques, and a form of presentation that shows plenty of verve and wit.

Dinner's "meat fruit" (c. 1500) has acquired iconic status and is an absolute must. It is the most velvety of chicken liver parfaits, masterfully encapsulated in a mandarin jelly to resemble a perfect mandarin (the kind of joke that hugely amused banquet guests in the sixteenth century). The use of "ketchup" condiments to introduce a note of acidity to balance the intensity of dishes is both twenty-first-century

Blumenthal and authentic—witness the roast scallops with cucumber ketchup and borage (c. 1820). "Meat and flesh" (c. 1390) is a beautiful, deeply flavorsome starter of braised calves' tails in red wine and a heady saffron risotto. "Powdered duck" is glossy, glazed duck brined with period flavors, including clove and bay, and served with smoked fennel confit. "Beef royale" is profoundly satisfying: seventy-two-hour slow-cooked beef, piquant with anchovy and onion puree. "Tipsy cake" is a must for dessert: yeasty, fluffy, boozy, and served with caramelized pineapple.

There is a gargantuan clock mechanism in the glass-walled kitchen, visible to most of the dining room, and it is this that turns the vast stainless-steel spit on which the pineapples are theatrically turned and caramelized. For the culinary curious, this is a restaurant of dazzling artistry and theater. **SP**

⊤ At Dinner, sleek style meets cutting-edge cooking.

Rules | The best of British cuisine at London's oldest restaurant

Location London   **Signature dish** Wild roast duck with mustard sauce | ❸❸❸❸

Rules is not just a restaurant, it is an institution. Founded in 1798 and owned by just three families since then, it has cozily atmospheric dining rooms crammed full of ornamentation from its long and illustrious past. For many, the first impression is of a baronial hall or an eccentric private club.

Rules is so famous that people assume it must be coasting on its celebrity and making a living from gullible tourists in search of Ye Olde Englande. Happily, nothing could be further from the truth. Most people who have been eating here for a long time testify to its consistently high quality, both in its cooking and service. There is room for around ninety diners, and there are around ninety staff. Such a high staff–customer ratio shows full commitment to quality.

Rules is an unashamed and proud champion of great British produce and traditional British cooking. Anyone who wants rib of beef, steak and kidney pie, or old-fashioned steamed puddings should come here.

In season, Rules is also one of London's top restaurants for game, much of it coming (alongside glorious Belted Galloway beef) from its own Lartington Estate in Yorkshire. The dishes are not complicated, but it is hard to imagine them being done better. The cooking owes much to the cuisine of France, of course, but all grand British food owes a debt to that country.

Special mention needs to be made of the service. There is a remarkable quality here, especially among some of the longer-serving waiters, which is best described as respectful friendliness. But there is nothing but seriousness when it comes to the business of serving. If you order game, expect a solemn ritual as platters are passed and sauces and garnishes brought forth. And whatever you order, you will find a suitable bottle from the long, French-centered wine list. Rules is one of a kind. **RE**

⤴ A cherished British gastronomic institution.

Apsleys, A Heinz Beck Restaurant | A luxurious taste of Italy

Location London   **Signature dish** *Fagotelli carbonara* | 💲💲💲

"*Beck's reappraisal of Italian tradition still manages to turn heads ... Service is quietly assured.*"

Square Meal

⬆ Superb, elegant dishes include a delicate risotto.

Cocooned inside the stately Lanesborough Hotel at Hyde Park Corner, the Michelin-starred Apsleys, a Heinz Beck Restaurant, to cite its full title, is housed in a striking, glass-roofed, art deco dining room. The menu, created and overseen by renowned German chef Heinz Beck, holder of three Michelin stars at La Pergola in Rome, changes seasonally and is as elegant as the surroundings. This is Italian food passed through an haute-cuisine prism, to glittering effect.

Luxurious ingredients, such as lobster, foie gras, or Iberian suckling pig, are presented in dainty and intriguing forms. Beck's signature dish of *fagotelli carbonara*—a witty reworking of a Roman classic, enclosing pancetta-infused cream and egg within a parcel of fine-textured pasta—is a memorably delicious creation, not to be missed. Lunchtime diners might opt for two or three courses from the menu of the day. The full seven-course tasting menu, which changes with the seasons, offers a civilized and more leisurely meal, beginning perhaps with foie-gras terrine with smoked apple and amaretti, passing through Challans duck with Jerusalem artichoke and salsify, and rounding off in style with an Amadei Chuao chocolate dome. Chosen with discernment, the wine list offers an impressive range of fine wines—including a strong Italian selection—many of which can be enjoyed by the glass.

The setting here also adds to the allure. The dining room, with its immense glass roof, is a magnificent space that at the same time manages to feel intimate. During the day, light floods in from above, while at night, with the dark sky overhead, it has a romantic atmosphere. The efficient kitchen, headed by executive chef and Beck protégé Heros de Agostinis, is complemented by charming and attentive service that ensures that dishes arrive at well-paced intervals. All in all, a polished and elegant dining experience to match the surroundings. **JL**

St. John | London's pioneer of "nose-to-tail eating"

Location London **Signature dish** Roasted bone marrow and parsley salad | ❸❸❸

Few restaurants can claim to have changed the way food is viewed by a whole nation of diners, but St. John is one of them. Since its founding in 1994 by restaurateur Trevor Gulliver and self-trained chef Fergus Henderson, St. John has introduced tens of thousands to the idea that fine dining can be based on simplicity.

The credo of simplicity is apparent in the décor of this former smokehouse in London's trendy Smithfield district: white walls and a tall ceiling with no decoration, stripped wood floors, and industrial light fixtures. It is also apparent in the phrasing of the menu, which strips dishes down to the bare essentials: "Terrine," "Peas in the Pod," or "Summer Vegetables in a Bowl." There are no flowery adjectives or detailed descriptions, and the cooking itself—while demonstrating tremendous skill—presents top-quality ingredients in fairly simple preparations.

St. John is big and bustling, and nearly always crowded at lunch or dinner. You can sit at the bar and order snacks, great cocktails, and wine by the glass (the wine list is exclusively French and surprisingly reasonable). But eating in the main restaurant is what people come here for.

The cooking is famous for two reasons. One is its championing of British produce and British cooking, although some influences from continental Europe are also present. The other is what is termed "nose-to-tail eating"—using the parts of animals that many restaurants avoid: liver, kidney, and sweetbreads are some of the tamer kinds of offal served here. On some days, you might find chitterlings or spleen. The popular roasted bone marrow and parsley salad is never off the menu and is as good as any served in France. Meat dishes are straightforward and include wonderful pies, and there are always several fish and vegetarian dishes on the menu, which changes twice daily. **RE**

"St. John's cooking is sophisticated, concocting flavors that are delicate as well as rich."

Time Out

⬆ The roasted bone marrow is always on the menu.

Galvin at Windows |
Elegant dining and a glorious panorama

Location London   **Signature dish** Loch Duart salmon with Cornish crab, avocado cream, and fennel compote | ❺❺

As the name suggests, the view is very much part of the experience here. Housed at the top of the Hilton Hotel tower on Park Lane in London's Mayfair, this light, airy restaurant offers truly spectacular views over central London. The huge floor-to-ceiling windows allow diners to peer into the Queen's back garden, spy on the MI6 headquarters building, and glimpse Crystal Palace in the distance.

It is not merely the panoramic views, however, that bring diners here. The cooking is firmly in classical territory, with an appealing menu of carefully composed dishes, while service is commendably smooth. A meal might include a nicely balanced, refreshing dish of cured Loch Duart salmon topped

---

> *"[This] is a slick, smart restaurant. It's the sort any great world-class city like London ought to have."*
>
> Jay Rayner, *The London Magazine*

---

with Cornish crab, avocado cream, and fennel compote. Roasted monkfish comes garnished with orange-braised endive, cauliflower puree, pine nuts, shellfish reduction, and spiced oil and golden raisins, an interesting flavor combination to enliven the fish. Landes pigeon is combined with pastille, couscous, eggplant puree, and spiced harissa jus.

There is a subtle nod to contemporary food trends, as witnessed by the presence of hay-baked beetroot and the showcasing of natural wines on the wine list. Desserts, however, stay in classical territory, with a well-executed tarte tatin with properly caramelized apples and a luscious rum baba among the treats on offer. **AH**

The Ritz | Skillful cooking in opulent surroundings at a legendary hotel

Location London   **Signature dish** Lamb "Belle Epoque" | ❺❺❺

Many hotel restaurants drift along on autopilot, but The Ritz makes no such mistake with its impeccably high standard of cooking. The dining room is vast and opulent, with vaulted ceilings, marble pillars, huge mirrors, and thick carpets, and an extraordinarily beautiful private dining room is situated in William Kent House just next door, where the same menu is available. The formal service is extremely capable.

Chef John Williams has spent his career in top hotels, prior to the Ritz as head chef at Claridge's and working at The Berkeley, among others. He is a "chef's chef," shunning the limelight and focusing on the quality of the dishes emerging from his kitchen. The vast basement kitchens of the Ritz are tightly organized and draw on top-quality produce, such as live langoustines from Scotland, combined to great effect with broad beans and a subtle verbena sauce.

The considerable space and resources at The Ritz allow some culinary drama, as shown in a whole sea bass in pastry, carved at the table—a fishy version of Beef Wellington, with the pastry containing mushroom Duxelles, quail eggs, and lobster mousse, separated from the pastry by a layer of spinach. It is served with a *mireille* sauce (Béarnaise sauce with a reduction of lobster), showing the kitchen's considerable skill with time-consuming classical sauces.

A vast pastry-making section in the kitchens is wonderfully capable of creating elaborate dishes such as the Amedei chocolate ganache with chocolate sauce, tonka bean ice cream, and pear puree, a fantastically rich, flavorful dessert showing several textures of chocolate. The Ritz really has food to match its opulent surroundings: its restaurant glides along effortlessly like a Rolls-Royce. **AH**

➡ The irresistible Amedei chocolate ganache at The Ritz.

Hakkasan | A sophisticated taste of Chinese cuisine in a dazzling setting

Location London **Signature dish** Silver cod roasted with Champagne | **$$$**

> "[It] remains a benchmark against which all high-end Chinese restaurants should be judged."

Time Out

⬆ The dark, glamorous dining space at Hakkasan.

A contemporary, glamorous Cantonese restaurant with a luxurious edge. There's no other way to describe Hakkasan than as breathtakingly seductive on every level, from the first bite of luscious dim sum to the sleek, Christian Liaigre-designed lacquered wooden screens and the flattering low lighting. Hakkasan in Hanway Street was created by serial restaurateur Alan Yau and overturned all preconceived ideas of what a top-flight Chinese restaurant should be, providing a towering benchmark. Head chef Tong Chee Hwee, who arrived hot from Summer Pavilion, the famed restaurant in Singapore's Ritz-Carlton, is at the creative culinary helm, presiding over what has become a chic international mini empire. Hakkasan would make the perfect, glitzy James Bond hideout.

The delectable dim sum set the scene: XO scallop dumpling, asparagus lingzhi mushroom, *har gau* pork, shrimp *sui mai*, and Chinese chive and shrimp are all flavorsome and delicate in texture. Try the venison puffs, fried golden lobster roll, and salt-and-pepper squid. The menu is liberally littered with luxurious ingredients: even the stir-fry is made with sirloin beef and Merlot, while Peking Duck can be ordered with Beluga caviar and pancakes (and a second serving of XO sauce), green onion, and ginger. Order ahead for whole abalone with sea cucumber and asparagus. Black truffle roast duck imbued with five-spice is wondrously *umami*-rich, and jasmine tea-smoked pork ribs have an intriguing, delicate fragrance.

Clay-pot dishes are another highlight, whether luscious scallop and shrimp or ethereal homemade tofu. There are plenty of inventive vegetarian options: exotic mushroom stir-fry is accompanied by gai lan vegetables, lily bulb, and macadamia nuts. It is tempting to drink exotic cocktails throughout, but there is also a scintillating wine list to enjoy. Desserts are comparatively simple: go for the lemon pot with lemon curd or the softly hued macarons. **SP**

Le Gavroche | Wonderfully indulgent French cooking

Location London **Signature dish** Soufflé Suissesse | ❺❺❺❺

If you asked London's fifty top chefs to name their favorite restaurants in the capital, most of them would probably mention Le Gavroche. Founded in 1967 and in its present location since 1981, Le Gavroche has inspired a whole generation of restaurateurs and trained some of Britain's finest chefs.

The founders were brothers Michel and Albert Roux, who trained in their native France before moving to Britain. They always followed an unalterable principle: meticulous attention to detail in every area. The Roux brothers knew that they had to run the restaurant with military precision if they were to present customers with the kind of food, service, and comfort they expected. One famous example of their fanaticism is the fact that the whole restaurant is cleaned from top to bottom at the end of every day—and then again the next morning. Michel Roux left in the mid-1980s, and in 1991 the restaurant was taken over by Michel Roux, Jr., Albert's son.

The food began as traditional, classic rich French cuisine, becoming increasingly elaborate. Since Michel, Jr., took over, the food has gradually acquired a lighter approach and influences from Asian and North African cuisines have been incorporated, as evidenced in a dish of sautéed lobster served in a jus flavored with coconut and lemongrass. Despite these changes, the restaurant's most famous dish, Soufflé Suissesse, remains a fixture: it is a cheese soufflé that is cooked, and then cooked again with double cream.

Le Gavroche is a luxurious restaurant, with works by Miró and Picasso on the walls and expensive cutlery and tableware. Such detail does not come cheap, but the set lunch of three courses including wine is a remarkable bargain. The wine list is predictably rich in fabulous bottles, but also caters well to those on a lower budget. The ice creams and sorbets are so good they will make you cry, and the cheese trolley is the best in all of London. **RE**

"There's something reassuringly familiar ... diners come here to revel in fine food [and] comfort."

Square Meal

⊡ Attention to detail is evident in the table setting.

Chez Bruce | The definitive neighborhood restaurant

Location London   **Signature dish** Fillet of cod with olive oil mash | ❸❸❸

With its impeccable menu, stupendous cheese board, and interesting wine list, Chez Bruce is considered the gold standard of neighborhood restaurants. It is regularly judged the "chef's choice" for dining out. High praise indeed for owner Bruce Poole's gutsy take on modern Anglo-French cooking.

The look is more bistro than fine dining, but the crisp linen and fine glasses are indications that dining is taken very seriously here. There are lovely, serene views across the green of Wandsworth Common, an appealing place for working up an appetite or walking off a Sunday lunch. There are certain fixtures on the set menu that regulars won't let Poole change: the sweetbread starter, Paysanne (potato, bacon, and

---

"Doubtless some view our food as slightly old-fashioned … we take that as a compliment!"

Chez Bruce website

---

cheese) salad with gribiche (cold egg) sauce; deconstructed Niçoise salad with seared tuna; fillet of cod with olive oil mash; and côte de boeuf.

This is not a restaurant that aims to surprise, except in the consistent quality of the luxurious ingredients and the technical precision of its dishes. Expect glossy *risotto nero* with fennel, lemon, and star anise, roast turbot with crisp skin and silken chunks of fish, served with cocoa beans, bacon, and chestnuts, and deluxe comfort foods, including pork belly with choucroute. Simple and sublime desserts include hot chocolate with almond praline and vanilla bean ice cream and a mesmerizing choice of cheeses with homemade quince jelly. **SP**

Dabbous | Palate-challenging cuisine in hip surroundings

Location London   **Signature dish** Iberico pork with acorn caramel praline, turnip tops, and pickled apple | ❸❸❸

New-wave bistro Dabbous was a phenomenal hit from day one thanks to its thrilling, palate-challenging cooking that conjures up soil, hedgerow, pool, and tide. This is game-changing cooking that combines the best of trendy ingredients and techniques with new Nordic influences and chef Ollie Dabbous' classical roots. Dabbous trained with Raymond Blanc at Le Manoir aux Quat' Saisons and worked with Andoni Luis Aduriz at Mugaritz, Alain Passard at L'Arpège, and Rene Redzepi at Noma before running the kitchen at Agnar Sverrison's Textures in London.

Original and playful texture juxtapositions are key to what makes the food so thrilling. Dabbous' riff on lightly scrambled egg, mixed with earthy woodland mushrooms and smoked butter, presented nestling on a bed of hay, is ethereal. Even the most unassuming of ingredients—wild garlic—is transformed into a beautiful pine-infused consommé. There's clearly a huge fondness for accentuating *umami* flavors in the kitchen, especially in a complex dish of braised cuttlefish with white bean and radish. The cheese course is invariably excellent. Desserts offer clean, fragrant flavors with plenty of textural interest. A buckwheat waffle with smoked fudge sauce and sour cream provocatively combines toasty, sour, earthy, and subtly sweet. Chocolate ganache is partnered with sheep's milk ice cream and basil "moss."

Plenty of natural wines feature on an adventurous and fairly priced wine list and are invariably interesting. Dabbous' industrial chic interior is starkly different to many Michelin fine-dining rooms: unplastered walls, concrete floor, exposed copper piping, and bare wooden tables. Oskar's Bar downstairs serves quirky cocktails and classics—a limited menu offers a taste of Dabbous when getting a reservation for upstairs proves challenging. **SP**

Racine | The perfect Paris bistro set right in the heart of London

Location London   **Signature dish** Warm garlic and saffron mousse with mussels | ❸❸❸

Racine is the perfect Paris bistro. It turns out classic French bourgeois cuisine to a consistently high standard, the service is proud, polished, and professional, and the decor is quiet and understated. And the wine list is all French. There's just one thing slightly wrong with this picture: Racine is not in Paris but in Knightsbridge, London, just a few minutes' walk from Harrods department store and the Victoria and Albert Museum.

Racine owes its distinctive character to chef-patron Henry Harris. Harris worked for eight years under Simon Hopkinson, one of the seminal figures in modern British cooking, before opening Racine in 2002. Although widely regarded one of the best British chefs of his generation, he has not followed many of his contemporaries in pursuing a media career. Most of the time, he is to be found in the kitchen at Racine.

Racine is a place where carnivores will be very happy. Offal dishes such as calf brain and *tête de veau* (beef brain) are regular features, as are grilled rabbit with mustard sauce and smoked bacon (one of the most popular dishes) and côte de boeuf for two. But there are always a couple of fish dishes available, as well as a vegetarian main course.

Save space for one of the tempting desserts. They are always good, and Harris himself says of his crème caramel: "You may have had one as good, but I question whether there is one that is better. It's not often I stick my head above the parapet like that." In true "French fashion," Racine makes itself more accessible by offering a set lunch (and early dinner): two or three courses at less than you'd pay for a main course at some of London's pricier restaurants. That's just another thing that makes Racine one of the best restaurants in London. **RE**

"Few London restaurants deliver the bonhomie of a genuine Parisian bistro, with their panache."

Square Meal

⤒ Racine's star dish of warm garlic and saffron mousse with mussels.

Hibiscus | Remarkably inventive cooking that defies expectations

Location London   **Signature dish** Hazelnut and passion fruit *millefeuille* with butternut squash ice cream | ❸❸❸❸

Hibiscus began in Ludlow, Shropshire, a small town near the Welsh border known for its interest in good food, and attracted enthusiastic gastronomes from all over the country. Since the restaurant's move to London in 2007, the enthusiasm has continued to grow.

Chef Claude Bosi is acclaimed for breaking new ground in two principal ways: the unexpected appearance of fruit in savory dishes and the use of savory ingredients in sweet dishes. Therefore, you may find pairings such as lobster and apricot, crab and pickled melon sorbet, and mackerel with strawberry in appetizers or main courses. On the dessert menu, there might be a tart made with fresh peas or a basil ice cream. An amuse-bouche might consist of pineapple and hibiscus flower cola.

The other innovation is in the presentation of the menu, which changes with the seasons. Instead of a list of dishes, you get a list of ingredients with the most distinguished seasonal produce. First you decide how many courses you'd like—three, six, or eight—and then you tell the waiter about anything you don't like. The kitchen uses the chosen ingredients to make a meal that will be a surprise from beginning to end.

Some of the assembled flavors are startling—for example, in a dish of sea bass, eucalyptus, artichoke, pig's head, and Barigoule sauce. But they are not just for the chef's amusement: Bosi has a sure sense of what will work together and taste good. However unlikely some of the combinations may sound, they are certain to succeed.

The set lunch menu tends toward somewhat simpler cooking, especially in the desserts, but it still gives a good sense of Bosi's inventive approach. Wine comes mostly from France and is well chosen, but strongest in the upper price ranges. You can always order by the glass rather than the bottle, however. **RE**

⬆ Scallop with Morteau sausage, radish, and hazelnut crust.

Ottolenghi | Stylish, beautiful food that tastes as good as it looks

Location London   **Signature dish** Roasted eggplant with black garlic yogurt, fried chili, hazelnuts, and herbs | ⑨

When talented chefs Yotam Ottolenghi and Sami Tamimi opened their first, small deli-cum-café in a West London side street, it was a game changer for London's food scene. The pared-down, minimalist decor combined with strikingly displayed sweet and savory food that both looked beautiful and tasted wonderful, has been much imitated ever since. Opened in 2004, Ottolenghi Islington combines a take-away deli and restaurant, and retains its ability to pull in the locals with an alluring window display of cakes, pastries, and lovely swirled meringues.

Inside, the white-walled dining area is dominated by a long, white communal table with white seats. The stylish cool of the decor contrasts all the more with the vivid colors of the salads. At lunchtime, the formula is simple: no booking (so arrive early if you want to get a table). Once seated, choose from salads or a main course, such as seared beef fillet or quiche, also with salad. And what salads they have! Ingredients such as

eggplant, beetroot, and butternut squash are cleverly transformed into delightful dishes. Ottolenghi is widely known for his globetrotting-inspired use of ingredients such as pomegranate molasses, wasabi, barberries, sumac, and nori. As anyone who has browsed the Ottolenghi cookbooks will know, dishes are very carefully constructed indeed, with layered, intriguing combinations of texture and flavor. At dinner, there is a wider choice of dishes on offer.

The popular, relaxed weekend brunch is a great way to sample the food, with an enticing menu featuring *shakshuka* (a glorious combo of eggs baked with spiced tomatoes and peppers) or cinnamon French toast. Standards are high and the dishes deliver, while service is friendly and efficient. Leave room for the delectable cakes and pastries, such as the addictive chocolate and hazelnut brownie. **JL**

⬆ The vibrantly alluring salad display at Ottolenghi.

Grain Store | Sophisticated veg-centric dining for a metropolitan audience

Location London   **Signature dish** Sprouting beans and seeds, miso eggplant, citrus chicken skin, and potato wafer | 🄢🄢

One of the fascinating aspects of great cities is that they change continuously. The area behind King's Cross railway station typifies the ebb and flow of London life. Once a bustling Victorian goods yard in the nineteenth century, it had become a derelict and abandoned space by the late twentieth century, but has now had new life breathed into it by an imaginative redevelopment scheme. Chef Bruno Loubet's popular Grain Store is beautifully placed in the heart of it, very much part of the area's renaissance.

Housed in a high-ceilinged space that was once part of a granary, the building's industrial roots have been retained in the decor of bare brick walls, unvarnished wood, huge arched alcoves, and piping ducts overhead. An open-plan kitchen with chefs industriously at work spans one side of the space.

On offer is a gloriously wide-ranging, fashionably veg-centric menu, executed with verve and panache. Globe-trotting flavorings—date syrup, mustard oil,

dukkah—feature to transform and revitalize fresh produce from cauliflower to Jerusalem artichokes. Assorted textures and flavors make every inventive dish appealing: a rich, miso-flavored eggplant puree is contrasted with intense, fresh seeds and sprouts, fine potato wafers, and crisp, salty pieces of chicken skin.

In the summer months, the restaurant takes on a particularly appealing vibe, with light flooding in through the large windows and the chance to dine outside on the square. Weekend brunches, whatever the season, are particularly popular—think corn bread with tomato relish, crème fraîche, pickled cactus, and scrambled eggs, or rice milk porridge with succulent Agen prunes, date syrup, and toasted almonds. Diners range from families with children to young professionals sipping cocktails at the bar. This is jaunty, cosmopolitan food for a cosmopolitan city. **JL**

⬆ Beetroot with pink grapefruit, gherkins, and bottarga.

Pied à Terre | Dazzlingly inventive cooking in a small, sleek modern space

Location London   **Signature dish** Roasted breast and leg of quail, Douglas Fir puree, and hazelnut vinaigrette | ❸❸❸

Charlotte Street in London's historic Bloomsbury area has long been one of the city's busiest dining-out thoroughfares. Pied à Terre, founded in 1991, can almost be regarded as a grand old veteran of the street. But longevity hasn't bred complacency: the cooking at this tiny jewel of a restaurant (with just 42 covers in the main dining room) is as restlessly inventive as it was on day one. Bold creativity and artful presentation don't always go hand in hand with great flavor, but here they most certainly do.

Pied à Terre was created by David Moore, whose area of expertise is the front of house. He established a sleekly modern look from the start, which was maintained after the complete refurbishment following a catastrophic fire that closed down the restaurant for a year. A lovely big skylight bathes the room in light during the day.

Right from the start, the restaurant served food that combined the highest level of gastronomic artistry and daring with an intense focus on top quality in every single ingredient. This approach has remained consistent through the years.

Each chef has brought his own touch to the monthly changing menu, but the inventiveness and bold touch have been constant. You could almost feel a little dizzy just reading the names of the dishes: how about steak tartare with caramelized veal sweetbreads, barbecue mayonnaise, pickled salsify, and smoked eel? Or breast of chicken with sautéed scallops, red pepper, chorizo puree, and shellfish bisque? These say a lot about the approach to cooking, which juxtaposes flavors that may sound "wrong" together but create unexpected harmonies. As a result, a meal here will make you think about food in a new way. For budget-conscious diners, the set lunch is a real bargain. **RE**

⊤ **Dishes are artistically conceived and executed here.**

Pétrus | A luxurious, smooth-as-silk fine-dining experience in the heart of the West End

Location London   **Signature dish** Chocolate sphere with milk ice cream and honeycomb | ❺❺❺❺

"The real deal for high-end dining, this sophisticated … jewel is one for a special occasion."

Zagat

⬆ Presentation matches the ingredients at Pétrus.

Pétrus restaurant, named after the iconic Pomerol wine, was born out of a dispute between two of Britain's best-known chefs, Gordon Ramsay and Marcus Wareing. It was the name of the restaurant that the former owned and at which the latter cooked, but the pair had a much-publicized falling out. Wareing stayed put in the dining room of the Berkeley Hotel but Ramsay retained the rights to the Pétrus name. Not content with making Wareing change the name of his restaurant, in early 2010 Ramsay opened a new Pétrus just a minute's walk away.

Sometimes good things can come out of turbulent beginnings, and so it has proved here. Head chef Sean Burbidge honed his skills at Gordon Ramsay's flagship Royal Hospital Road restaurant, and now demonstrates his classical culinary training here. Witness, for example, the way that he is able to coax deep flavor out of such a simple dish as onion soup, topped with chives, adding a little onion at the base of the soup to improve texture.

Burbidge's dishes consistently show balance, as illustrated by an impressive crispy veal sweetbread with choucroute, served with carrots and a well-judged sherry vinegar sauce, the sourness of the sauce offsetting the richness of the sweetbread. An enjoyable dish with seemingly humble ingredients is pork fillet with Bayonne ham, black pudding, creamed cabbage, and Madeira sauce. The meat has wonderful flavor, the sauce is rich and deep, and the vegetable provides an earthy contrast.

The emphasis on rock-solid technique continues into the dessert stage of the meal, with the memorable chocolate sphere with milk ice cream and honeycomb a creative and delicious tour de force, adding a wonderful touch of drama to this stage of the meal. Pétrus, like its namesake wine, is all about a luxurious experience. **AH**

The Harwood Arms |
London boozer turned gastropub

Location London   **Signature dish** Scotch egg | 💲💲

The Harwood Arms was an unappealing local Fulham boozer until 2008, when it changed hands and the new owners transformed it from a drinking den into a gastropub. In the vanguard of this initiative was Stevie Williams, a talented young chef whose old boss at The Ledbury, Brett Graham, became one of the investors in this new project.

Co-owner Mike Robinson also runs The Pot Kiln, near Newbury, Berkshire, a country pub that is noted for its game. He is himself a keen hunter, and now supplies his London outlet with deer and rabbit. One of The Harwood Arms' stand-out main dishes is the shoulder of venison, slow cooked for five hours, stunningly tender, served with a rich venison jus and horseradish and paired with a delicate rack of venison smoked in hay.

Cooking of this level of skill did not go unremarked; and, in 2010, The Harwood Arms was awarded a Michelin star, a rarity for a pub. What is interesting is that the food is still very much hearty pub food: there are no fancy garnishes or linen tablecloths here. Indeed the best-known dish is a brilliant take on the old pub staple, the Scotch egg, in which the sausage meat filling is venison and the dish is cooked to order with a liquid egg center, a crisp bread crumb coating, and precise seasoning. This is a million miles from the Scotch egg that supermarkets serve, and started a trend toward up-market Scotch eggs in London pubs, although none of the rivals is a match for these originals.

The head chef changed in 2011, with Barry Fitzgerald taking over the reins, but he has maintained the same style. A meal might finish with Bramley apple doughnuts, the acidity of the apple cutting through the richness of the doughnut. More than anywhere else, The Harwood Arms has redefined the standard of pub food in London. **AH**

E. Pellicci | Legendary East End
café for a fry-up with a side of banter

Location London   **Signature dish** English breakfast | 💲

With its small frontage partially obscured by the Bethnal Green market stalls on the pavement, it is easy to walk past E. Pellicci. But it would be a pity to do so, because this is a famous institution, founded in 1900 by Priamo Pellicci and still run by his family.

Step inside and discover a gem from a bygone age, with fixtures and fittings, including beautiful golden-brown-toned marquetry commissioned in 1946—the premises have listed building status.

All customers—whether regulars or newcomers—are greeted with a friendly warmth by Nevio Junior, who keeps a shrewd and experienced eye on proceedings. Sit down at a spotlessly clean, formica-topped table—complete with the latest edition of *The Sun* daily newspaper, brown sauce, and ketchup—

> "... serves everything with a 'where everybody knows your name' smile. A truly special place."

House & Garden

choose from the classic caff options—ham, egg and chips, liver, and bacon—then soak up the atmosphere, of which Pellicci has a superabundance. Customers are a cross-section of society: builders in rough jackets, local families, old age pensioners, tourists, and artists. Over the decades, this tiny café has hosted all sorts, from local gangsters to soap stars.

All generations eat here, with children warmly welcomed, teased, and fussed over. Affectionate banter flies through the air. The food is freshly cooked to order and served in generous portions. Genuinely hospitable and gloriously democratic, this much-loved café is a place with heart and soul and should be treasured as such. **JL**

Moro | Modern British interpretation of Spanish and Moorish cuisine

Location London **Signature dish** Yogurt cake with pistachios and pomegranates | $ $ $

"... vibrantly fresh food that throws out surprising and pleasurable flavors at every turn."

Time Out

⬆ Moro offers al fresco, but the real action is inside.

Situated in the heart of bustling Exmouth Market in London's now-trendy Clerkenwell, Moro was opened in 1997 by husband and wife team Sam and Sam Clark after their inspirational three-month road trip through Spain and Morocco in a camper. Their decision to open a restaurant serving vividly flavorful cuisine in what was once a less-than-fashionable locale has paid dividends, with Moro having become a much-loved classic over the years, now with sibling Morito next door.

The understated, pared-down decor ensures that the focus is firmly on the food cooked in the open-plan kitchen at the back of the restaurant. The wood-fired oven and charcoal grills underpin Moro's cuisine: grilled quail and bream, roasted sea bass, and pork feature regularly. With bare walls, hard floors, and plain dark wood furniture, Moro can be noisy, but not too noisy: the buzz of conversation hovers at just the right level.

An extensive list of tapas is served all day at the bar to complement the outstanding selection of sherries and wines sourced from Spain and Portugal. Locals drop in for fino and jamón and to soak up the lively, informal atmosphere.

Dishes on the main menu offer traditional Moorish cuisine with a modern twist. Seasonal plates focus on the finest ingredients thoughtfully cooked, and service is knowledgeable and attentive with considered recommendations, particularly for pairing food and wine.

Flavors are memorable, from octopus summer salad with dill, paprika, and caperberries through Moroccan bread salad with argan oil and anchovies to desserts such as rosewater and cardamom ice cream. Clever use of spices elevates dishes such as charcoal grilled lamb accompanied by an eggplant and pomegranate *fattoush* and nut tarator. The signature dish is best enjoyed with a glass of moscatel. **SKi**

Wiltons | Sumptuous seafood in the most English place in Britain

Location London **Signature dish** Dover sole meunière | ❸❸❸❸

Wiltons is a blue-blooded bastion of British tradition. It has been operating in St. James's, the heart of London's gentleman's club land, since 1742. It was originally a seafood stall and was granted a royal warrant as purveyor of oysters to Queen Victoria. Now an opulent restaurant, it remains true to its own traditions, and it is almost de rigueur to start any meal there with Beau Brummell or Colchester Natives served with muslin-wrapped lemon and tabasco.

Other dishes showcase the best of British produce—potted shrimp, dressed crab, scallops with parsnip, raisins, and capers. Wiltons is the place to experience a proper sonorous beef consommé, served hot or cold. Caviar is a constant on the menu, served with buckwheat blini and sour cream. Fish lovers adore the deft serving of Dover sole meunière on the bone, the decadence of lobster Thermidor, and the poached wild turbot. Seasonal game—grouse, pheasant, and woodcock—is a speciality, too.

The restaurant prides itself on its silver service, *Downton Abbey*-style, with impeccably dressed staff deboning the sole at the table with consummate finesse. Dedicated trancheurs with highly polished carving trolleys serve the daily roasts, which run the gamut from salt-marsh lamb to salmon coulibac.

For pudding, the fruit crumble, the content of which varies according to the season, is highly recommended and is a particular favorite of French diners, who regard it as the height of chic. Alternatively or additionally, the savories are worth serious consideration. These include Scotch woodcock (scrambled eggs with anchovies on toast) and angels on horseback (bacon-wrapped prunes).

Anyone in search of the quintessence of Englishness, which is popularly regarded as elusive, need look no further than here. **SP**

Hedone | Inspiring food from a ground-breaking, self-taught chef

Location London **Signature dish** Turbot with potato skin emulsion and aged beef jus | ❸❸❸❸

Mikael Jonsson's Hedone attests that, if the food on the plate is based on the finest ingredients available, cooked with thought, intelligence, and perfect balance, it will attract diners from every corner of the globe.

Jonsson has received critical acclaim and is now mentioned alongside other great self-taught chefs such as Nico Ladenis, Raymond Blanc, and Heston Blumenthal. Mikael Jonsson's perfectionist obsession with creating good food in his restaurant is matched by accomplished culinary technique in the kitchen.

The homemade bread is on a par with that of the finest bakers in France and Hedone desserts show technical excellence and lightness of touch in the pastry section. The open kitchen allows Jonsson to

> *"Exciting. Everything we ate and drank lived up to that adjective. A series of excellent dishes ensued."*
>
> Nicholas Lander, *The Financial Times*

engage with patrons, creating a relaxed and convivial atmosphere. Service is assured and unfussy. Diners can opt for three courses or a series of tasting menus, including the carte blanche option, where the chef delivers his choice of dishes. Excellent well-kept cheeses can be chosen as an extra course with all menu options.

Highlights have included turbot with potato skin emulsion and aged beef jus, an intense gazpacho with dill sorbet, cuttlefish tagliatelle, roasted French squab pigeon with beetroot and cherries or with Jerusalem artichoke foam, a series of superb millefeuilles featuring seasonal berries, as well as a sensational chocolate bar. **DJ**

The Ivy | Theater restaurant par excellence with a star-studded history

Location London **Signature dish** Shepherd's pie with beef and lamb mince | ❸❸❸

In the late 1990s, The Ivy was as famous as the many celebrities who dined there. These days the A-list has mostly moved on—to sister restaurant Scott's in Mayfair, as well as to whatever the newest hot spot is on London's utterly transformed dining scene.

But, while you may no longer have a Hollywood actor sitting at the next table, The Ivy is back to doing what it does best: namely, being the preeminent theaterland restaurant in London's West End.

It's a place with an illustrious history: it opened in 1917 and was patronized by Noël Coward and Laurence Olivier. It fell out of fashion after World War II, but was revived in 1990 by Jeremy King and Christopher Corbin (who now own The Wolseley). Their coup was to design

---

> *"The modern British menu is full of scrumptious things, all delivered with know-how and style."*
>
> Tatler

---

a space that was brand new, but looked like it had played a part on the London stage since Sarah Bernhardt trod the boards. In no time, publishers, publicists, and anyone patient enough to reserve a table weeks in advance were eating in the same orbit as Nicole Kidman and Jack Nicholson. Those days are gone, but The Ivy has two trump cards that keep it current: staff who treat everyone like a celebrity and a culinary philosophy that focuses on the menu rather than the chefs.

Whoever is in the kitchen, the classic dishes are always here—duck and watermelon salad; steak tartare; shepherd's pie; iced berries with white-chocolate sauce. This continuity is key to The Ivy's longevity. **BMcC**

Tramshed | Contemporary British dining with modern British art

Location London **Signature dish** Indian rock chicken with stuffing and fries | ❸❸

There is a glorious audacity to British chef Mark Hix's Tramshed restaurant. To begin with, there is the building itself. Tucked away down a narrow side street in London's Hoxton district—once rough and ready, now seriously hip—it once housed the electricity generator for the tramway system.

The centerpiece of the cavernous space (high ceilings, metal girders) is a specially commissioned Damien Hirst artwork—a whole cow with a cockerel perched on its back inside a huge tank of formaldehyde on a tall plinth.

This installation reflects the main focal points of the menu—beef and chicken. While such a limited range could be dismissed as a gimmick and soon become tiresome, it is a tribute to Hix's vision that The Tramshed is perennially filled with diners and buzzing with conversation. The short, cleverly thought-out menu, with many of the dishes designed for sharing, is good. Starters include cock 'n' bull croquettes with chervil mustard and light Yorkshire pudding with whipped chicken livers, an intriguing combination that really works.

Careful sourcing shows in the quality of the meat and poultry here, so well-aged, Glenarm, marbled steaks, or rib on the bone are succulent and flavorful. The roasted Swainson House Farm chicken, for two to three people to share, arrives strikingly presented with its legs in the air to be carved at the table by one of the friendly waiting staff, accompanied by sage stuffing, irresistible fries, and gravy. The comfort food theme continues with desserts such as salted caramel fondue with marshmallows and doughnuts. Informal and affable, this is British dining out shaken up, energized, and thoroughly enjoyable. **JL**

↦ Damien Hirst's striking artwork dominates the space.

The Ledbury | Exceptional modern cooking, delivered with style

Location London **Signature dish** Grilled mackerel with pickled cucumber, Celtic mustard, and shiso | ❸❸❸

The Ledbury opened in 2005 in what, at the time, was the distinctly down-market Ladbroke Grove area of west London. Over the years, the area has gentrified, and, alongside it, The Ledbury has built up its reputation as one of the city's top restaurants.

The dining room is light and airy, with a few outside tables available when the weather is clement. The key to The Ledbury's success, however, has been Brett Graham, the gifted and affable Australian chef who has gained the restaurant an impressive two Michelin stars.

The menu is modern without being beholden to the latest culinary trends. A typical item is the single langoustine cooked in a red curry sauce with yogurt and a broccoli stem—natural partners that are restrained and delicate in flavor. Brett has a great awareness of and focus on ingredient quality, from heritage tomatoes to Galloway beef. He is particularly renowned for sourcing excellent game.

Exquisite culinary technique is displayed in dishes such as the pork jowl, which has been cooked for eight hours and is served with pork crackling, a lime reduction, scorched pear, and dandelion leaves. The pork is tender with deep flavor, the crackling is crisp, and the lime and pear give sufficient acidity to balance the richness of the pork.

Desserts can be more cutting-edge, and fine pastry technique is illustrated by brown sugar tart with poached Muscat grapes and stem ginger ice cream, a nice combination of flavors with the richness of the sugar balanced by the grapes and enlivened by the ginger. The Ledbury's cooking just gets better and better, and is now perhaps the toughest reservation to score in London. **AH**

◁ Excellent culinary technique is evident in the dishes.

Scott's | Glamorous British dining in a Mayfair institution

Location London **Signature dish** Dover sole meunière | ❸❸❸❸

Originally an oyster warehouse when it opened in Haymarket in 1851, Scott's has an illustrious history as a venerable seafood institution and is known as the place where writer Ian Fleming had his dry Martini shaken not stirred. Now a true Mayfair grande dame, it moved to its smart present location in 1968 and is arguably more glamorous than ever, with its Chartreuse green marble mosaic framing the ornate seafood bar designed by Martin Brudnozki. In the wood-paneled dining room, with gilded mirrors and British art adding to its chic, the menu is unexpectedly daring, catering to guests who incline toward more adventurous eating. Try sautéed monkfish cheeks with snails, bacon, and Bordelaise sauce, monkfish

> *"It's serving the right sort of food in the right sort of place, although, I think, rather expensively."*
>
> A. A. Gill, *The Sunday Times*

osso buco, or chocolate pots with rum madeleines. The classics are equally well done. As befits its origins, the kitchen excels when cooking fish, especially sole. Diners can enjoy the best of posh comfort food: haddock, colcannon, poached eggs, and grain mustard sauce, the very best fish and chips, game dishes, or a definitive rib eye and Béarnaise. Scott's is one of the few places still serving a splendid extravagant steak Bellini adorned with foie gras and truffles and, charmingly and unusually, savories— Welsh rarebit, herrings on toast—as an alternative or in addition to dessert. Desserts can be old favorites such as impeccable Bakewell tart or spectacular chocolate bombe and mandarin. **SP**

Bentley's | There's more to British seafood than fish and chips

Location London **Signature dish** Native oysters | 🅢🅢🅢🅢

It's often noted that, for the inhabitants of an island nation, the British are remarkably unfond of eating fish, unless it comes in batter and is deep-fried. Irish-born chef Richard Corrigan, however, is a champion of the produce of the British Isles, and since taking over Bentley's in 2005, he has dedicated the restaurant to proving that the fish and seafood from British waters are some of the best that the world has to offer. Most people believe that he has succeeded.

Bentley's has been plying its trade near the bright lights of Piccadilly Circus since 1916. It is a restaurant of two halves: a formal first-floor Grill, where the walls are covered in William Morris fabrics and the wooden floors glow with polish, and a ground-floor Oyster Bar, where the marble counter has been a feature since Bentley's first opened. (Outside is a covered and heated terrace; Corrigan might be able to make you rethink British ingredients, but there's nothing he can do about the weather.)

The Oyster Bar menu has a bistro feel; this is the place for the freshest seafood—dressed crab; grilled scallops; a dozen native oysters—along with simple plates such as sole goujons, smoked haddock, and Dover sole that are just the ticket before or after a West End show. Upstairs is fancier, with more luxe ingredients and cheffier treatments dictating the stiff prices: roast fillet of cod with razor-clam vinaigrette and a "Royal fish pie" that earns its regal moniker through the addition of lobster and tiger shrimp. There's also meat: Corrigan is just as enthusiastic about game as he is about fish and, in the fall, roast grouse with all the trimmings is as British a dish as you'll find.

Make time, too, for a snifter in Bentley's elegant cocktail bar—if you don't want to test the theory that oysters should be consumed with spirits, there are more than 20 cuvées of Champagne to try. **BMcC**

⬆ Bentley's is the Rolls-Royce of London fish restaurants.

Alain Ducasse, The Dorchester | Exceptional haute cuisine in Mayfair

Location London **Signature dish** Tournedos Rossini | ❸❸❸❸

Great hotels are expected to house great restaurants. To add luster to dining at The Dorchester, the hotel has gone for Alain Ducasse, the world-famous French chef with a glittering culinary career. He's a busy man, a globetrotter: as well as this three-Michelin-star restaurant at the beating heart of one of the world's most luxurious hotels, there are another twenty or so establishments around the world with which he is involved and which showcase and interpret his gastronomic ideals. Back in London, Executive Chef Jocelyn Herland is the man who brings Ducasse's culinary philosophy to life in a vibrant, creative way.

This means modern French cuisine, making use of high-quality seasonal produce, sourced from both the British Isles and France, dishes brushed onto the plate as an artist works on a canvas. The flavors of the dishes are matched with similarly creative aplomb: the langoustine ravioli in a ginger-lemongrass and smoked tea consommé combines seafood sweetness, spiciness, soft acidity, and a waft of smoke, while tournedos Rossini served with crunchy cos lettuce and Périgueux sauce has an earthy caramel-sweetness; the meat is moist and juicy and the lettuce adds a sparky texture. Fine ingredients, treated with respect and intelligence, are transformed into technically accomplished dishes.

The food is just part of the experience at this elegant hotel. The dining room is a calming influence, with its light colored wood fittings, ruffled white tablecloths, and the sort of exceptional service that comes with haute cuisine. An unusual centerpiece is the table lumière, an ovoid veil of cotton and fiber-optic strands that rises to the ceiling. Within this tentlike space, there is room for six exceptionally well-heeled diners to have their own dinner party in complete seclusion. **ATJ**

⬆ Special occasion dining inside the table lumière.

Gordon Ramsay | Famous London eatery offering refined haute cuisine

Location London **Signature dish** Ravioli of lobster, langoustine, and salmon in a bisque with caviar | $$$$

After developing a glowing reputation (and earning two Michelin stars) for his superb, classical French cooking at the restaurant Aubergine, in 1998 Gordon Ramsay and most of his team dramatically walked out. At the age of 31, Ramsay took over the Royal Hospital Road premises that used to house Pierre Koffmann's famous restaurant La Tante Claire. Within three years, he had earned the elusive third Michelin star, something just two restaurants in London were awarded in 2013.

Eventually, Ramsay decided to devote most of his time to his restaurant empire and television career, handing over the reins of the kitchen to his protégé, Clare Smyth. Smyth has maintained the elegant, classical style of cooking for which the restaurant became famous, yet has developed her own distinctive stylistic touches. While the setting is unassuming—an intimate, low-ceilinged room within a Chelsea terrace—diners are treated to a wonderful display of highly accomplished cuisine, delivered with understated yet attentive service. A luxurious starter is warm foie gras with sweetbreads, carrots, and almond foam and Cabernet Sauvignon vinegar. The foie gras is of the highest quality, with silky smooth texture and deep liver flavor. The sweetbreads have a gorgeous texture, with the vinegar giving the otherwise rich dish much-needed balance.

The degree of effort that goes into the cooking here can be seen in a pork dish in which the meat is prepared five separate ways: a sausage made from the the shoulder; roast loin with crushed new potato, bacon, and green onion; pork served with apple; pig cheeks wrapped in Savoy cabbage with Dijon mustard; and ham hock with pineapple, plus apple puree. This is a clever and perfectly balanced dish, the apple giving just the right level of acidity to offset the richness of the pork. Clare Smyth's cooking offers some of the most refined food in Britain. **AH**

"[Clare] has a level of composure that is intimidating, almost like a boxer entering the ring."

Gordon Ramsay, celebrity chef

[↑] The decor is deliberately low-key to avoid upstaging the cuisine.

[→] Five forms of pork in a single memorable dish.

La Trompette | A much-cherished neighborhood restaurant

Location London **Signature dish** Cornish cod with truffle butter, grilled leeks, cauliflower, and chanterelles | ❺❺❺

When La Trompette opened in 2001, few people believed that such an upmarket restaurant could succeed in any part of London other than the center. Chiswick—although prosperous enough, with a sprinkling of minor media celebrity residents—was seen as a district that could support only pizza chains and neighborhood restaurants. It was regarded as a bridge too far.

That was not a view shared by Nigel Platts-Martin, the Oxford-educated restaurateur and former lawyer who had branched out from The Square, a two-star Michelin restaurant in downtown Mayfair, to try his luck further out of town at Harveys (later Chez Bruce) on Wandsworth Common. The success of this venture—thanks to the work of the fledgling Marco Pierre White—encouraged Platts-Martin to see if he could achieve the same in another far-flung location.

From the start, La Trompette offered a simple menu of classical dishes, consistently turned out.

Although the restaurant has had several different chefs, including Ollie Coulard and Rob Weston, it has remained consistent and built a reputation for enjoyable food, friendly service, and a particularly good wine list priced at a modest mark-up level by London standards, with well-chosen growers and plenty of canny choices, including some real bargains at the upper end.

The menu offers dishes such as lightly seared slices of tuna served with anchovies, French beans, black olives, and crushed potato or a pleasantly sweet Orkney scallop with lightly curried parsnip puree. For dessert, you might be offered a refreshing dish of Alphonso mango with gingerbread, passion fruit, whipped ewe's milk yogurt, and lime. La Trompette has gained a Michelin star and attracted customers from all over the country. **AH**

⬆ Guineafowl served at La Trompette.

Launceston Place | An elegant food haven in the heart of London

Location London **Signature dish** Duck egg, peas, girolles, Pata Negra lardo, and duck fat toast | 💲💲

Prosperous Kensington has some surprisingly peaceful spots. One such is a little corner on Launceston Place, which, though only a short walk from bustling Kensington High Street, remains quiet and residential. The restaurant here occupies four separate nineteenth-century houses that have been connected to form an elongated dining room comprising several separate cozy areas.

Since it opened in 1986, the restaurant has hosted several talented chefs. The latest is Tim Allen, who joined in early 2012, after seven years at Whatley Manor in the Cotswolds. His talents were quickly recognized, with Launceston Place gaining a Michelin star just a year after he took over.

The cooking is precise, based on good-quality ingredients; the dishes have logical and appealing flavor combinations. One example is turbot served on the bone with asparagus, peas, broad beans, cep cream, and reduced Madeira. The delicate fish is complemented nicely by the vegetables; the cream adds an earthy note. This is a dish that brings out its luxury ingredients to the best advantage rather than trying to challenge the diner. In similar vein is the pork tenderloin served with crisp pig's head, cabbage pickled with a little cumin, truffled pork sauce, and a celeriac and truffle puree. The result is another sensible combination of well-balanced flavors, the hint of vinegar in the pickled cabbage bringing balance to the richness of the dish.

The relaxed atmosphere at Launceston Place fits well with the cooking, which is imaginative without succumbing to the temptation to distract the diner with culinary trickery. Put the bustling thoroughfare nearby out of your mind, relax, sit back in the comfortable chairs, and savor the restrained pleasures of fine dining in an oasis of tranquility. **AH**

⬆ Launceston Place exudes a sense of calm.

Locanda Locatelli | A seductive taste of Italy in the heart of London

Location London **Signature dish** Wild sea bass in salt and herb crust | $$

What could be more enticing? A restaurant that exudes glamor from every caramel-and-cappuccino leather banquette by designer David Collins, a devastingly handsome, leonine chef, Giorgio Locatelli, an A-list clientele of Hollywood stars, and yet a warm, convivial atmosphere that encourages family dining. It's always a great sign when the bread basket is swoon-worthy and the slender, house-made grissini are in a class of their own, not to mention the focaccia.

Start with unusual antipasti salads showcasing the best and most seasonal ingredients: cured pork neck with girolles; shrimp with fresh borlotti; puntarelle greens with anchovies and capers; or burrata with pumpkin and hazelnuts. Ox tongue with vividly verdant salsa verde is invariably on the menu, too. The soups—the lightest classic tortellini in crystal-clear brodo or chestnut, chickpea, and chili—are wonderful. The choice of pasta can seem somewhat overwhelming because they are all so tempting: cappellacci with pumpkin; aromatic clam linguine; veal ravioli with jus; truffle linguine. Risottos are dreamy, creamy, and decadent, and include some rare specialities from Locatelli's northern Italian upbringing in the village of Corgeno, including variations made with spectacularly rich Barolo wine, radicchio, and Castelmagno cheese.

Seasonal main dishes include spring lamb with morels, broad beans, and minted peas, chargrilled beef sirloin with Trevisano and polenta, and turbot with ceps. Desserts include tiramisu and an exceptional ricotta tart with cedron confit. Gelato are marvelous, too, whether limoncello, myrtle, truffle honey, or cassata. There's an unashamedly Italian bias to a wine list that combines the big hitters with some intriguing, worth-exploring boutique wines. There is a great choice of grappa, too. **SP**

↑ An elegant setting for accomplished cooking.

The River Café | The world's most lauded canteen for superlative Italian fare

Location London   **Signature dish** Wild sea bass with anchovy and rosemary sauce; chocolate nemesis | ❺❺❺❺❺

The River Café heralded the dawn of a new era in British restaurant design and cuisine. It was founded by Rose Gray and Ruth Rogers, whose architect husband Sir Richard Rogers originally designed the building as his company's staff canteen. The two women offered their favorite Italian cuisine and hired a succession of glittering chefs to prepare it—the list included Jamie Oliver, Theo Randall, and Stevie Parle.

The food soon gained a reputation, and so too did the space in which it was made and served. The vast open kitchen, shiny steel surfaces, bold blue floor, and industrial decor quickly became the model for a whole generation of new restaurants. And it has itself withstood the test of time—it still looks cool today.

Meanwhile, the menu was always vibrant, celebrating impeccably sourced, gloriously fresh ingredients. Burrata, offered here long before it became ubiquitous, is served, mesmerizingly, with wood-roast yellow peppers, yellow dattarini tomatoes, and golden oregano flowers. Pasta is a highlight, whether handmade ravioli with zucchini, buffalo ricotta, and zucchini flowers, tagliatelle with new season wet walnuts, or spaghetti with bottarga, tomato, and parsley.

A dish cooked in the immense wood-fried oven is a must. Rarely off the menu is wild sea bass with rosemary and anchovy sauce with borlotti beans and Sorrento tomatoes. Classic dishes may include slow-cooked veal shin with prosciutto, *risotto bianco*, and gremolata. There's always a discerningly selected choice of cheese, perhaps *pecorino di fossa*, buried in the ground to age. For dessert, the Amalfi lemon sorbet is memorable and the chocolate nemesis has few peers. The River Café is eyebrow-raisingly expensive, but demands to be experienced. **SP**

⬆ A hugely influential and much-loved restaurant.

Fifteen | Gutsy food in mellow surroundings the Jamie Oliver way

Location London **Signature dish** Homemade bread | ❸❸❸

"The vibe is upbeat, the decor bright and modern, and the food consistently great."

coolplaces.co.uk

⬆ A rhubarb eclair served at Fifteen.

At first glance, there is nothing particularly distinctive about Fifteen. Tucked away down a side street in now trendy Hoxton, it looks like any number of attractive restaurants that have sprung up there recently. In fact, though, it is a pioneering, philanthropic enterprise set up in 2002 by British TV chef Jamie Oliver. Fifteen is Oliver's laudable attempt to offer opportunities to young people from disadvantaged backgrounds to work in the restaurant world.

There is a cheerful and mellow vibe to this place. A comfy bar area in which to drink and enjoy tasty snacks, such as cured pig's cheek and walnuts, leads into a dining room that is dominated by a big wood-fired oven that plays an important part in the menu. Downstairs, with its dark wood floor, leather banquettes, and alcoves, has a cozy feel. Framed photographs of the foundation's alumni remind one of Fifteen's serious purpose, as does the open-plan kitchen, with its white-hatted apprentices busy at work.

The food is rustic in style and presentation. Good ingredients—including produce from Oliver's own garden—are transformed into dishes for a daily changing menu. This is simple, gutsy food that delivers on flavor: huge, juicy wood-baked mussels with charred spring onions offer smoky notes and a sweet, aromatic chili kick from a Thai-style sauce.

Oliver's love of Italian cuisine is evident in the textured bread—baked onsite and served with homemade butter and *crema di lardo*—and the hand-made pasta. Look out, too, for the excellent pizzas, with innovative toppings such as flavorful Irish Gubeen cheese and winter truffle or chard and smoked ricotta.

Service is friendly and the place buzzes with diners, including Jamie Oliver fans from abroad eager to visit this, his most personal restaurant. It's so smooth-running that you forget the educational aspect of it—which shows just how successful it is. **JL**

Marcus | Great food from a great chef, served with relaxed formality

Location London   **Signature dish** Seasonally changing menu | ❸❸❸

The considerable culinary talents of British chef Marcus Wareing are showcased in handsome style at this elegant restaurant, cocooned within the discreetly glamorous Berkeley Hotel in Knightsbridge. Previously known as "Marcus Wareing," 2014 saw the restaurant being refurbished and reopened as "Marcus." The move to first name terms is significant—it signals a move to a dining experience that is less formal than before, but definitely no less luxurious.

The sophisticated dining room, with its understated, subtle hues, notably comfortable and generously spacious leather banquettes, and striking pictures on the wall, is at once contemporary and classic. Just as the finest materials—marble, leather, and wood—have been chosen and carefully crafted for the restaurant, so impeccably sourced ingredients, from prime British meat such as Rhug Estate pork or Herdwick lamb, to seasonal produce, cooked with notable skill, are at the heart of the menu.

Wareing is noted for his formidable technique and perfectionist standards, creating clever, elegant, meticulously executed dishes, such as Galloway beef served with hispi (pointed) cabbage, baked potato foam, braised short rib, and marrow. The somewhat laconic names of dishes contrast with the complexity and finesse of their execution. Precision cooking is a hallmark of the kitchen, from a beautifully cooked piece of prime turbot, served with Dorset snails, potato gnocchi, and pickled shallot to the perfectly seared foie gras, served with mango puree.

The deft service, inspired by American restaurants such as Eleven Madison Park, is welcoming and accomplished. Wareing has restructured the menu to make it far more flexible, with lunchtime diners able to order à la carte. The full Marcus experience is also on offer, from the Taste menus to the splendid chef's table, from which you can watch Marcus and his brigade in action. **JL**

"I wanted to design something which was at the level of luxury fine dining but not stiff …"

Marcus Wareing

⬆ Galloway beef impresses in technique and flavor.

Sketch | Exuberant gourmet cuisine in an appropriately lavish setting

Location London **Signature dish** "Veal" tasting menu | ❸❸❸

On the ground floor of the Sketch building is a casual restaurant, bar, and pastry shop. Upstairs in the Lecture Room and Library is served some of the most elaborate food in London. Sketch is the creation of restaurateur Mourad Mazouz and Parisian chef Pierre Gagnaire, with day-to-day cooking run since 2012 by Romain Chapel. In 2013, the place was awarded two Michelin stars.

Gagnaire is noted for taking a particular ingredient and serving it in many variations. Laconic dish headings, such as "lamb," "beef," and "veal," with brief notes on what the dish contains, merely hint at the kitchen's creativity and sense of fun. Langoustine, for example, may appear in tartare form with crunchy

---

> "This place has a flair for quirky, good-humored design that's unexpected and delightful."

Martin Creed, *Daily Telegraph*

---

bok choy and spiced grapefruit syrup, as a mousseline with cardamom and strawberry cubes, as a jelly in a cup with edamame broad beans and peppered bisque, or grilled with dried bacon and pan-fried in beurre noisette with a powder of shells and a soubressade sausage.

Ingredients are of impeccable quality: the Challans duck, for example, is served with cumin and cinnamon sauce, red cabbage and blackcurrant marmalade, red onions, prune paste, roasted foie gras, and potatoes with coriander. Your meal might conclude with gianduja chocolate topped with caramel laced with balsamic vinegar, chocolate sorbet, and sharon fruit. **AH**

Tayyabs | Punjabi restaurant famed for its addictive lamb chops

Location London **Signature dish** Grilled lamb chops | ❸

With a neon sign over the door to attract diners who might otherwise miss it hidden away down a Whitechapel side street, Tayyabs is very much a local institution. Founded in 1972 as a small Punjabi café by Mohammed Tayyab, who had emigrated to Britain from Lahore, it is now run by his three sons.

The family's hard work over four decades has been rewarded by success and expansion; Tayyabs is now huge—spread out over three premises combined into one vast restaurant and over three floors, including a dimly lit basement area with a night club air to it. Such is its popularity that it now offers a take-away counter by the entrance. Not only is it vast, it is also perpetually busy, with a cosmopolitan throng eating the food with notable relish, while others line up patiently for tables to become free.

The aroma of cooking meat that greets you as you enter is a clue to the restaurant's appeal. Tayyabs has made a name for its great value spicy food. A steady stream of black-clad waiters bring iron platters of sizzling, freshly grilled meat to the tables. Be sure to sample the legendary lamb chops, which pack a piquant, spicy kick, are gloriously flavorful, and should be relished and nibbled to the bone. Other good things on offer include chicken tikka, fiery seekh kebab (minced lamb), and *karahi bhindi* (okra). Freshly baked breads, from traditional roti to light, puffy nan, are another simple pleasure here. Prices are so reasonable that it is all too easy to overorder, succumbing to the lure of dishes such as *nihari* (a lamb stew) or karahi jumbo shrimp. Despite the scale of its catering, Tayyabs is run with noticeable and commendable efficiency, surely another reason for its popularity. This is a restaurant that absolutely knows what it is doing and has a loyal clientele that loves everything about it. **JL**

Koffmann's, The Berkeley | Accomplished haute
cuisine from a revered British chef

Location London **Signature dish** Gascony-style pig's trotter stuffed with sweetbreads and morels | ❸❸❸

Londoners who love gastronomy adore Pierre Koffmann. Resident in London since 1970, Koffmann worked at Le Gavroche and then at the Waterside Inn. In 1977, he and his wife, Annie, opened La Tante Claire on the site now occupied by Gordon Ramsay. La Tante Claire won three Michelin stars before moving to the Berkeley Hotel in 1998. On the death of his wife in 2003, Koffmann—grief-stricken and exhausted—decided to retire. But the lure of the kitchen later proved irresistible, and, in 2010, he reopened at The Berkeley.

Koffmann grew up in Gascony in southwest France—a region known for fine ingredients (especially duck and pork) and rich, earthy cooking. The earthiness is certainly in evidence now in his much-imitated signature dish (created when he was at La Tante Claire) of pig's trotter stuffed with sweetbreads and morels, and in appetizers such as his Gascony-style black pudding croque monsieur with egg.

Such dishes attest that, if Koffmann's cooking could be summarized in a single word, that word would be "big." But he has always had a light touch, particularly with fish and shellfish, and that finesse has become even more noticeable in recent years. Cod might be steamed and served just with vegetables and a fennel consommé, for instance. Desserts are relatively simple, and very French. Most people go nuts for the pistachio soufflé, which is another long-standing signature dish.

The main menu changes monthly. Set lunch and pre- and post-theater menus provide low-cost food options, as usual. The wine is expensive, as you would expect in such an opulent setting, but there are lower-priced bottles to be found and a good selection by the glass and half-bottle carafe. **RE**

"All the dream French dishes are here, all … elevated to a level of rare refinement."

Ben McCormarck, *Daily Telegraph*

⬆ An impeccable pistachio soufflé at Koffmann's.

Quo Vadis | Seasonal comfort food in a vintage Soho restaurant

Location London   **Signature dish** Smoked eel and horseradish sandwich | 💲💲

With its Union Jacks flying jauntily outside, long frontage, and striped awning, Quo Vadis, right in the heart of London's Soho district, looks every inch what it is—a historic restaurant and a local landmark. Housed in buildings dating back to 1734 and during the nineteenth century home to Karl Marx, it has been a restaurant since 1926. This Soho institution has now had refreshing new life breathed into it under the ownership of the Hart brothers, with chef Jeremy Lee at the helm.

Inside, the dining room, with its vintage stained glass windows and beautiful, eye-catching flower arrangements, while undoubtedly elegant, also manages to feel comfortable—a difficult effect to achieve, and one that is central to this restaurant's entire approach. The appealingly illustrated menu is amended "daily and merrily," allowing Lee free rein to feature only the finest of discerningly sourced seasonal ingredients, such as salsify, blood oranges, sea trout, the freshest garden peas, and English asparagus. The laconic labeling of dishes—"grouse & co," "crab & mayonnaise," "salt duck, pickled prune"—signals Lee's unfussy approach, which is to allow the ingredients to shine through in truly tasty food that is easy to eat and enjoy. A notable comfort food angle is evident in hearty offerings, from the gloriously rich and addictive smoked eel and horseradish sandwich to the daily changing pie with buttery mash.

Dining here is a convivial experience, with the room almost invariably full of people and buzzing with conversation, and the tall, distinctive figure of chef Jeremy Lee frequently emerging from the kitchen to chat with diners. "What we want is folk coming to eat good food in a good room and leaving wreathed in smiles," says Lee simply. And in that, Quo Vadis succeeds admirably. **JL**

⭱ A rare sight: an empty table at Quo Vadis.

Pollen Street Social | Sophisticated modern British cuisine

Location London **Signature dish** Full English breakfast (part of the set lunch) | 💲💲

Jason Atherton is a chef with a devoted following. After his success at Gordon Ramsay's Maze, the opening of this restaurant, his first solo venture, was eagerly anticipated in the world of fine dining.

Atherton's witty and intelligent cooking reflects the stylish refinement of its Mayfair surroundings, while also being playfully creative and delivering satisfying depths of flavor. The seasonally changing menus genuinely chart the shift through the year, offering superb ingredients such as impeccably cooked red-legged partridge and exquisite English asparagus presented in dishes that are at once sophisticated and gloriously eatable. Flexibly, diners can choose to eat a series of courses or opt for a selection of small dishes, thus creating their own tasting menu. Soups here are always worth ordering, such as the intensely tasty chervil root soup, textured with duck rillette, nuts, and seeds, accompanied by a smoked ricotta tartine.

The set lunch, with its generous range of extras, offers excellent value and is a wonderful way to experience the great man's cooking. Atherton himself can often be glimpsed at the pass. The desserts are a particular highlight, and diners have the option of moving from the main restaurant to the separate dessert bar in order to witness their preparation. The sorbets are glorious, especially the citrus ones, but more complex creations, such as the toffee apples with liquorice ice cream, spiced cream stout reduction, almond, and ginger soil are also at once light and enticing.

The atmosphere is convivial—Pollen Street is social in more than just its name. One leaves the restaurant feeling thoroughly spoiled by the beautiful food and the charming service, purring with contentment and with a sense that life is good. **JL**

⬆ Oysters from Fowey, Cornwall, served "hot and cold."

The Wolseley | Impeccable comfort food in the classiest of surroundings

Location London   **Signature dish** Kedgeree | ❸❸

With its prestigious location and its air of historic grandeur, The Wolseley looks as if it has been on Piccadilly for hundreds of years. But, in fact, it was opened in 2003 by expert restaurateurs Chris Corbin and Jeremy King.

In effect, The Wolseley is a British take on the Parisian brasserie, offering a flexible, overlapping set of menus throughout the day, enabling diners to drop in at any time between early breakfast and late dinner. On offer here is upmarket comfort food, drawing inspiration from Britain, France, and Austria, and featuring classic dishes such as eggs Benedict, schnitzel, kedgeree, and *moules à la normande*. Desserts and sweet treats include such popular retro joys as Black Forest gateau, apple strudel, and banana split. Dishes arrive beautifully presented, with an appropriate level of pomp and ceremony.

The charm of this easy-to-enjoy food is accompanied by the appeal of the setting. What was a magnificent, high-domed 1920s Wolseley car showroom, complete with beautiful fittings and black-and-white marble floors, is now a glorious restaurant with huge pillars, impressive chandeliers, and a perpetual buzz of conversation. It is the perfect showcase for all the delightful drama of a bustling eating place: smartly-dressed staff in black-and-white uniforms taking orders, dishes being brought to table, customers arriving and departing—an ideal spot for people-watching.

Ever since it opened, this has been a place where people come for a treat, whether bringing an elderly aunt out for a proper tea or a celebratory post-theater meal. With its cleverly devised menus, gorgeous setting, and attentive service, The Wolseley, appropriately for its setting, purrs like an expensive, well-maintained motor car. **JL**

⬆ Beautiful interiors are part of The Wolseley's appeal.

The Square | One of the gastronomic capitals of the world

Location London　**Signature dish** Dorset crab lasagne with shellfish cappuccino and Champagne foam　| ❸❸❸❸

Classic French training informs The Square's menu, yet it's thrillingly contemporary, too, with astute nods to pickling, fermenting, and bringing vegetables more central to the plate. From the very first impeccable cone of foie gras offered as an amuse-bouche, this is serious and refined cooking to relish and savor. Each and every course surprises, delights, and astonishes with its precision and finely nuanced flavor.

Pigeon is offered as a tartare and ballotine with its textures matched by pickled vegetables, chestnuts, and truffle, providing richness and subtle crunch. Pastas are superb and equally creative: hand-cut chestnut *strozzapreti* with rabbit and the decadent fat of Lardo di Colonnata and Périgord truffle. Philip Howard, the chef and co-owner, indulges his customers with expensive ingredients, exactingly sourced: fillet of turbot with smoked celeriac milk puree and truffle and hazelnut pesto; roast Cornish sea bass with artichoke, salsify, and white truffle butter; and short rib of beef with

fermented ceps and bone marrow exemplify his approach. Desserts are as intricate and clever as the rest of the meal, yet refreshingly light: Brillat-Savarin cheesecake with passion fruit, lime, and coconut; banana soufflé with stout ice cream and gingerbread; glazed pear with *dulce de leche* ice cream, salted caramel mousse, and coffee.

Although the wine list is strongest in Champagne, Burgundy, and Bordeaux, it's adventurous, too, with extraordinary wines from unfamiliar *terroirs*, including an ambrosial dessert wine from Cyprus.

The sobriety of the dining room—with notably well-spaced tables—is enlivened by fabulous paintings and engaging, confidently knowledgeable staff. No wonder The Square remains a favorite, not only with gastronomes, but also with many of the world's most discerning chefs. **SP**

⬆ Beef with onions, kale, ceps, bone marrow, and parsley.

Hind's Head | Pub food with a characteristically inventive Blumenthal twist

Location Bray **Signature dish** Oxtail and kidney pudding | ❸❸❸

"… it's hard not to feel like a Tudor monarch and want to feast accordingly."

Kate Robinson, *Daily Telegraph*

⬆ A country pub with a major difference.

It may be a Tudor beamed inn in a little hamlet, but this is no ordinary pub. First off, it is in Bray, the village with the most Michelin stars in Britain, and, what's more, it is masterminded by quirky culinary eccentric Heston Blumenthal, who is as fascinated by historic dishes and the national culinary heritage as he is by applying scientific technique and a sense of playful theater to his dishes. It is best to request a downstairs table, as this offers more of the genuine pub atmosphere, with its dark paneling and enveloping leather banquettes.

Chef Kevin Love has an amazing pedigree, including cooking with the late Santa Santamaria at his legendary three-star Can Fabes in Barcelona and at Gordon Ramsay in Chelsea, London, so expect impeccably executed, profoundly flavored, and instinctively composed dishes that belie their simplicity and are often daring in their make-up. Starters of scallop tartare with white chocolate, soused mackerel with pickled lemon and horseradish, and snail hash are hardly standard pub fare. The proper suet oxtail pudding is epic and should be experienced. Lighter appetites are catered to with fine pescatarian ensembles, including plaice sautéed with potato puree, samphire, and shrimp. Devotees of Blumenthal's triple-cooked chips may like to order veal sirloin on bone and buttered cabbage as a distinctly different take on the old English standard.

Desserts, too, are a treat here. The famous Quaking Pudding is based on a medieval blancmange scented with rosewater and wobbles suggestively on the plate, while mulled wine and chocolate slush alludes nostalgically to children's treats made even more special by the addition of the sublimely rich caramel Millionaire's Shortbread to dip. Hind's Head serves up astoundingly good food and is an exhilarating step into the world of period culinary drama in inimitable, fun style. **SP**

The Waterside Inn | Gourmet dining at Roux's legendary establishment

Location Bray **Signature dish** Le Menu Exceptionnel | ❸❸❸❸

On a bank of the Thames in the pretty Berkshire village of Bray is the aptly named Waterside Inn, which in 1985 became the second restaurant in Britain to be awarded three Michelin stars, an accolade that it has retained ever since.

The setting is enchanting, with a little summerhouse just by the water, where you can have a glass of Champagne as you consider the menu. There is even a pier for guests who arrive by boat. The dining room overlooks the river, the waiting staff are formally dressed, and the dining room is luxuriously appointed, with perfectly ironed linen tablecloths.

When The Waterside Inn opened, its chef was Michel Roux, who was inspired to spread his wings by his success in central London at Le Gavroche. Although he has now handed the culinary reins over to his son Alain, the classical French cooking style remains unchanged. Expect top-quality ingredients and intricate, labor-intensive cooking in dishes such as Challons duck that is spit-roasted and carved at the table, served with prunes, Puy lentils, and a Grand Chartreuse jus. Another example of the fine technique in the kitchen can be seen in a tart of crab with langoustines, the shellfish having lovely inherent sweetness that is nicely balanced by a precisely seasoned herb emulsion.

The Roux dynasty of chefs is famed in particular for its pastry skills, so expect the dessert course to be the highlight. Enjoy a flawlessly light soufflé or a dish such as roasted wild cherries served with a Kirsch sorbet on a delicate biscuit tuile.

This establishment was one of the restaurants that first put Britain on the culinary map, and it remains a place of pilgrimage for the nation's gastronomes. On a summer's day, The Waterside Inn is the perfect setting for an indulgent, luxurious meal. More than a quarter of a century after opening, it continues to weave its magic. **AH**

"Food that … holds to traditional values of coherence, correlation, and euphony."

Matthew Fort, *Guardian*

⬆ Rabbit on celeriac fondant with glazed chestnuts.

The Fat Duck | Inventive cooking from a master of molecular gastronomy

Location Bray **Signature dish** "Sound of the Sea" | $$$$$

Heston Blumenthal is that rarest of creatures, a self-taught chef who won a Michelin star for his little restaurant in the sleepy Berkshire village of Bray, initially serving bistro food with the odd inventive twist. But he didn't stop there, growing in culinary ambition and gaining a second, then a third Michelin star for cooking that was undeniably original and creative to the brink of madness in the eyes of some. Certainly no one had ever contemplated putting a plate of snail porridge or bacon and egg ice cream on a menu before, yet somehow these odd-sounding combinations worked.

The dining room, in a listed building, is tiny, with a low ceiling and exposed wooden beams. It seats just 35 guests. A huge brigade of chefs toil over the sophisticated tasting menu that is now the only offering from the kitchen. A jelly of quail and cream of langoustine with pea puree and chicken liver parfait shows that Blumenthal is perfectly capable of making high-quality classical food if he puts his mind to it. This particular dish is an homage to French culinary legend Alain Chapel. More in character, though, is Blumenthal's imaginative *Alice In Wonderland*-inspired mock turtle soup, made of beef stock freeze-dried and wrapped in edible gold leaf, served with "tea" of beef stock, which melts the gold leaf and, when poured, completes a complex soup of ox tongue and vegetables.

Service from a well-drilled front-of-house team leads diners gently through all the theatricality. Blumenthal has brought a playful sense of invention to the world of restaurant cooking, his food original and exciting yet always impeccably precise, like a perfectly executed magic trick. The Fat Duck has put a very British form of modern cooking on the culinary map of the world. **AH**

↑ Jelly of quail and crayfish cream, with accompaniments.

The Harrow at Little Bedwyn | A delicious gem in the Cotswolds

Location Marlborough   **Signature dish** Poached lobster with cardamom, carrot, and white truffle | ❸❸❸

The Harrow at Little Bedwyn—a village near Marlborough, Wiltshire—was opened in 1998 by husband-and-wife team Roger and Sue Jones, who both had backgrounds in private catering. He headed the kitchen, she ran the front of house. The restaurant was awarded a Michelin star in 2007 and has retained it ever since.

There is a small garden terrace where you can have a drink as you browse the menu and wine list. The latter is quite extensive and includes some relative bargains tucked away within its upper reaches.

The dining room is cozy, and the service is unobtrusive and low-key. The cooking style is simple, with the emphasis on choosing good-quality British ingredients and letting them shine without polish. One example is a salad of cured Somerset eel with cured Kelmscott ham and a Waldorf salad—a nice combination of ingredients, without any culinary flourishes or ostentation.

Another example is seared foie gras, scallop, and black pudding. The single diver-caught scallop is lightly pan-fried to allow its natural sweetness to come through, the pairing with the black pudding bringing a pleasing combination of earthy and seafood tastes, with an extra dimension from a smear of reduced Pedro Ximénez sherry.

The Harrow at Little Bedwyn is pleasingly restrained in its approach. It avoids gastronomic pyrotechnics and is no follower of ingredient fashions. Here, food is to be enjoyed: the dishes are appealing and the ingredients carefully selected so that the elements complement each other rather than show off how avant-garde and clever the chef is. The pretty country setting and the unfailingly friendly welcome make this an appealing venue in which to enjoy a relaxing lunch or dinner. **AH**

⬆ A dish of lobster and white truffle.

The Sportsman | An off-the-beaten-track gastronomic destination

Location Faversham **Signature dish** Slip soles with seaweed butter | ❸❸❸

In 1999, chef-patron Stephen Harris took over this run-down pub on the marshes by an old coastal road near Faversham, Kent, and turned it into an informal restaurant offering truly outstanding, ingredients-driven cuisine at reasonable prices. Under his aegis, The Sportsman soon drew favorable comparisons with some of the icons of British gastronomy in remote locations, such as Joyce Molyneux's The Carved Angel in Dartmouth, Devon, and the Taruschios' The Walnut Tree Inn near Abergavenny, Wales.

As a chef, Harris is self-taught but clearly well educated. His work and style are influenced by a range of leading chefs, including Nico Ladenis, Marco Pierre White, and Gordon Ramsay.

"This is not a place to pass through; it is a place to savor, to have dinner in: a Kentish bulwark."

Ed Cumming, *Daily Telegraph*

One of the benefits of The Sportsman's location is that it has superb ingredients almost on its doorstep. Fish is sourced from boats that land a stone's throw away; most of the meat and vegetables are from local farms that work closely with the restaurant. Hams are cured in-house using home-prepared sea salt.

Menu highlights include slip soles with seaweed butter; turbot with asparagus and smoked turbot roe sauce; pork belly with apple sauce; and an extraordinarily fine lemon tart. The cheeses are always top-notch. The Sportsman is a tied house (all its alcohol comes from a single supplier), so the wine list is limited; but, on payment of a small corkage fee, customers may bring their own bottles. **DJ**

The Latymer at Pennyhill Park | Opulent country house hotel

Location Surrey **Signature dish** "Continental breakfast" | ❸❸❸

Graciously situated in 123 acres (50 ha) of gently rolling green hills, Pennyhill Park is a luxurious country house hotel and spa near Bagshot, Surrey. Among its claims to fame are its appearance in the 1964 James Bond film *Goldfinger*, with Odd Job's steel-rimmed hat decapitating one of its statues. Within the 1849 manor house is The Latymer, the hotel's main restaurant—an atmospheric, wood-paneled dining room complete with exposed beams and well-spaced tables, high-quality cutlery and glassware, and no distracting music. Showcased in these grand surroundings are the considerable culinary talents of chef Michael Wignall, who took over in 2007 and under whose leadership The Latymer gained its first Michelin star in 2009 and a second in 2013.

The cooking style is elaborate and involved, with high-quality ingredients a noticeable feature. An example is the tuna rolled out in a cannelloni shape, with lime and soy sauce, octopus, ginger marshmallow, and Osetra caviar. Flavors are combined with flair and achieve remarkable balance—as in the ballotine of grouse served with a little smoked duck, tiny pieces of beetroot, and a butternut squash sorbet. As befits food of this quality, service here is professional and excellent.

Desserts continue the sophisticated theme. The humble chocolate fondant is enlivened with a little popping candy inside, and served with a pineapple beignet, coconut sorbet, and sabayon. Modern technique is shown in a dish called "continental breakfast," which comprises pink grapefruit jelly, yogurt sorbet, pain perdu with cinnamon, a parfait of cornflakes, lemon curd pancake, and a little foam of pain au chocolat. Wignall is an outstanding British chef; the Latymer is an outstanding British location: perfect synergy. **AH**

Old Spot | The perfect English market town restaurant in England's second smallest city

Location Wells   **Signature dish** Pork belly and Morteau sausage, onion puree, choucroute, and juniper sauce | ❷❷

In a prime position with fine views from the back windows of the toweringly ornate west front of Wells Cathedral and the elegant Cathedral Close, this small, compact restaurant has been in existence since 2006, when it was started by Ian and Clare Bates. It's neither trendy nor flashy, but it is the sort of solid no-nonsense place that every neighborhood should possess and clutch to its heart. The interior is neat but not showy, and newspapers are spread out along the bar counter. But it's the food that singles the place out.

Chef Ian worked for Michel Guérard in France and for Simon Hopkinson at Bibendum in London, and now produces wonderfully understated yet skillful cooking. The menu changes weekly, making the most of seasonal produce and locally sourced ingredients, such as the offal of which Ian is particularly fond.

The format here is short, just four or five dishes per course, and the descriptions are plain and unfussy; Bates dips his toe into a bit of French, a bit of Italian, and a bit of plain old English, and mixes in barely the slightest hint of a twist. Fine pastry often crops up, sometimes in the form of tartlets with local cheese such as Harborne Blue or Caerphilly paired with leeks. Alternatively, it might appear as a *feuilleté* filled with deviled lamb's kidneys. Add in a hearty soup, an elegant salad, a roast meat, and a fine fish dish, and that's about as extensive as the Old Spot menu gets.

But small is beautiful. This really is the embodiment of a perfect country restaurant that manages to keep it simple but do it magnificently well. And with two courses at lunchtime very reasonably priced indeed, it's excellent value, too. Most restaurant reviewers find something to cavil about, even in the world's greatest restaurants, perhaps to reassure readers that they retain their critical faculties. But for the Old Spot, the praise is unanimous. **SFP**

"There's nothing ... unusual about the food served here— except that it's utterly brilliant."

Jay Rayner, *Observer*

⤒ Pork belly served with red cabbage.

The West House | Inventive food and stunning flavors

Location Biddenden **Signature dish** Grilled John Dory fillet, cauliflower, raisins, onion bhaji, curry oil | $$

> *"It's an unstuffy platform for Garrett's confident, fine-tuned modern cooking."*
>
> Square Meal

⊼ A dish of oak-smoked haddock.

Housed in a fifteenth-century timber-framed weaver's cottage in the picture-perfect village of Biddenden in Kent, this Michelin-starred restaurant serves British food with international élan, pulling in a clientele that includes enthusiastic locals, foodies, and visitors to nearby Sissinghurst Castle, Vita Sackville-West's former home.

Chef-patron Graham Garrett, who has cooked for rock stars and royalty, established the West House in 2002. His constant aim is to be as seasonal as possible and to source the best produce. Kent—prime farming land, adjacent to the sea and dubbed the "Garden of England"—gives him scope to do that in style. Among the things that most excite him are the first asparagus, the very short season for elderflowers, and local birds and deer during game season. He supports artisans in France and Spain when their products inspire, but he is even more thrilled by local ingredients, such as the fish that comes in from day boats along the nearby coastline.

Garrett adds complementary, but not always traditional, elements to his dishes to create an elegant dance of flavors. Delicate oak-smoked haddock from a celebrated local smokehouse is enlivened by a Dijon mayonnaise dressing, leafy, sweet green pea shoots, the savory crunch of lardons, and the iron-rich coastal tang of rock samphire pickled in-house.

Garrett's food shows his British heritage in details such as the pork dripping offered in addition to the butter that accompanies the warm homemade bread. Garrett's wife and son run the front of house with warmth and charm. This part of Kent is all rolling hills and hedgerows, oak beams, and red brick, and has been officially designated "an area of outstanding natural beauty." In this inspiring location, Garrett has harnessed his own prodigious energy to the creation of truly beautiful food that is well worth making a detour for. **CB**

Royal Oak | Gastropub where the locals provide ingredients

Location Bishopstone **Signature dish** Slow roast organic saddleback pork belly | **⑤**

The Royal Oak stands on a winding country lane in Bishopstone on the rolling Wiltshire Downs in southern England. Diners at this Michelin Bib Gourmand-rated village gastro pub might expect the chefs to buy their raw materials from exclusive markets or specialist suppliers. However, many of the Royal Oak's ingredients come from the backyards of the cottages surrounding it. The kitchen works on a system where green-fingered locals are given seeds, then trade their best garden produce over the bar in return for food and drink.

This genuine commitment to local sourcing is explained by the pub's ownership: the proprietor, Helen Browning, is also the owner of the adjacent farm, which she has turned into an award-winning organic showcase that provides beef, veal, lamb, and pork, plus milk, cream, and butter to the kitchen. Add in the pub's own allotment produce and the chickens that freely range around the garden, and around ninety percent of everything sold at the Royal Oak is local and organic.

Browning's produce dominates the menu, of course, including her 35-day-aged steaks, humanely reared veal, and homemade sausages, but trimmings might include Wiltshire hedgerow plunder like nasturtium salad or tarragon mayonnaise. The young and enthusiastic staff also finds time to make bread, cure bacon, and even bake beans.

The food is served on a mixed collection of old wooden tables in a casual pub atmosphere. That lack of pretension extends to many of the dishes: veal might be served as a burger, liver could come with potato and broad bean hash, and zucchini flowers might be deep-fried in batter.

Time your visit right, and you may stumble upon one of the quirky occasional events at the pub, including overnight stays in the pig huts and pig races around the village. **SH**

"What motivates me the most [about farming] is allowing our animals as good a life as possible."

Helen Browning, proprietor and farmer

⬆ The Royal Oak is a proper gastro pub.

Burgh Island Hotel | An art deco gem on a private island

Location Kingsbridge   **Signature dish** Poached lobster tail, lobster mousse, chickpea, and red pepper salad | $ $

"It's an adventure coming here. You have to accept being cut off twice a day."

Deborah Clark, co-owner of Burgh Island Hotel

⊞ A gloriously atmospheric dining experience.

This four-star art deco hotel on its own tiny island, just over 300 yards (300 m) off the south Devon coast near Kingsbridge, advertises itself as "80 years and three-and-a-half hours from London." Indeed, the prewar style is so pervasive that today many guests feel obliged to dress in period costume to dine.

Arriving at the 26-acre (10.5 ha) grassy island is part of the fun. At low tide, you are driven by Land Rover across the wet sands; at high tide, you clamber onto an ancient improvised tractor with seats raised 12 ft (3.6 m) above the waves on stilts.

But it's that Roaring Thirties aura that provides the main appeal. Burgh Island's heydays were when Edward VIII wooed Mrs. Simpson in the Palm Court, Noël Coward played piano in the ballroom, Agatha Christie wrote best-selling whodunits in the cliff-top gardens, and the Harry Roy Band played the Charleston on a floodlit floating platform in the middle of the seawater rock pool. This was the decade when Burgh Island was hailed as "the smartest hotel west of The Ritz."

That spirit lives on in the black-tie, jazz-and-cocktails atmosphere beneath the stained glass dome amid Bakelite fittings, polished chrome, and shiny parquet floors. Spot the pencil moustaches and white pearls, and keep something in reserve for the energetic post-dinner dancing.

The kitchen uses local produce. Lobsters, crabs, and scallops are caught in the waters around the island and kept in the hotel's own seawater lagoon. Salad leaves and herbs grow in the hotel's polytunnel above. In total, around 80 percent of ingredients are sourced within 20 miles (32 km).

Service has been described by one reviewer as "Jeevesian," but the food is up to date. The daily changing menu is an eclectic array of modern British and international innovation, ranging from asparagus soup with a poached egg to Parmesan custard. **SH**

Riverford Field Kitchen | Delicious field-to-plate dining

Location Buckfastleigh **Signature dish** Slow roast shoulder of lamb with smoked tomatoes and spiced eggplant | **$**

This restaurant occupies a simple, wooden outbuilding in the middle of muddy vegetable fields near Buckfastleigh, Devon. Diners sit on long benches at communal tables and share heaped serving dishes of hearty, seasonal food. Its unique selling point is simple but captivating—you eat what is grown in the fields around you.

This homely venue is at the center of Riverford Farm, headquarters of one of Britain's largest organic vegetable suppliers. Around 40,000 of the nation's homes take delivery of Riverford boxes of organic vegetables every week.

The enterprise is the brainchild of charismatic farmer Guy Watson, who launched it in the 1980s as a one-man smallholding. Since then, it has grown into a country-wide business and a thriving visitor attraction—during the holiday season, there are farm tours, cookery demonstrations, pick-and-cook days, children's planting events, nature walks, and trailer rides. It even sells its own cookbooks.

The restaurant is a family affair—one of Guy's brothers, Oliver, has a dairy farm next door and another brother, Ben, runs a local chain of butcher and farm deli shops. The real stars, however, are the organic vegetables, freshly picked each day from the fields around the restaurant.

The kitchen is run with verve, efficiency, and imagination. While you might expect carrots and beets served with their tops on, you may well be surprised by potatoes, garlic, and bay cooked in parchment, or by braised artichokes with polenta and romesco. Every meal comes with five different vegetable side dishes. And the quality of the main dishes, such as slow-cooked hand of pork stuffed with fennel and bacon, has left critics gasping. Among the admirers of Riverford's cooking is global celebrity chef Gordon Ramsay, who remarked after a visit: "I knew it would be good ... but not that good." **SH**

"... unbeatable, especially the veg. My only complaint is it's so delicious I eat too much!"

Harden's

⊼ Great food in communal surroundings.

Hix Oyster and Fish House | British seafood with Jurassic coast views

Location Lyme Regis **Signature dish** Fish house pie | ❸❸❸

"After months of reviewing London restaurants, I found it a vision of Paradise."

John Walsh, *The Independent*

⤒ Diners can enjoy stunning views of Lyme Regis harbor.

Having made his name at such famous London restaurants as Le Caprice and The Ivy, Dorset-born chef and restaurateur Mark Hix has returned to his roots in style. Visitors to the picturesque seaside town of Lyme Regis, famously featured in Jane Austen's novel *Persuasion*, can now make their way up through the town's park to his wonderfully situated restaurant. Simply styled, with stripped wooden floor and white wood furniture, it is a bright, light space with a friendly, relaxed vibe and an appealing beach shack air to it. Diners here look through glass walls out over Lyme Regis harbor, with its famous Cobb, and feast their eyes on stunning views of the Jurassic coastline stretching into the distance.

As befits its coastal position, the restaurant majors in spanking fresh fish and seafood, sourced from local fishermen. Hix championed the use of British produce long before its current fashionability, and the menu is studded with indigenous artisan food and drink. Moreover, Hix is a master of presenting his creations in an accessible, affable way. A meal here might start with freshly shucked assorted oysters—Devon Yealmes, Brownsea Islands, Portland Pearls—or a rich-tasting, classic French-style fish soup, served with Berkswell cheese, saffron mayonnaise, and croutons.

When it comes to main courses, Hix is famous for his stylish renditions of comfort food. A stand-out dish is the Fish House Pie, a luxuriously indulgent version of the old classic. Many dishes are even simpler creations that rely on the quality of their ingredients to shine. Among the top desserts are treacle tart and fruit pies. Also well worth sampling are the jellies, which often arrive in deliciously tipsy forms through the addition of Somerset Kingston Black (a cider brandy aperitif) or perry. Sitting here, especially on a fine summer's day, eating fish and seafood lovingly sourced from the very seascape at which one is looking, is a fine example of British spirit-of-place dining. **JL**

Gidleigh Park | Sophisticated fine dining in the picturesque West Country

Location Chagford **Signature dish** Dartmoor lamb with Boulangère potato; confit shoulder | ❺❺❺❺

Gidleigh Park was created as a labor of love by Paula and Kay Henderson, who found a beautiful but neglected sixteenth-century manor house at Chagford, on the edge of Dartmoor, and in 1977 transformed it into a boutique hotel with a restaurant. The head chef is the supremely talented Michael Caines, whose work gained the restaurant in 1994 two Michelin stars, which it has retained ever since.

You reach Gidleigh Park house down a narrow, winding country road, at the end of which the timber-framed Tudor building is set on a slope with a stream running in front of it. This is a rural idyll, and, on a summer's day, you can have a relaxing drink on the pretty terrace as you contemplate the menu and feel that life is sweet. The once vast wine list with its rare Californian wines at bargain prices has now been streamlined, but there are still some reasonably priced vintages to try before your meal as you contemplate the lovely view.

The cooking here is classical in style, using the best and freshest, carefully sourced local produce to fine effect. You might encounter a main course of sea bass with a zucchini flower stuffed with scallop mousse, gazpacho, and a garnish of lobster, fennel, and asparagus. One of the most acclaimed dishes is squab of pigeon with pea puree, wild garlic, and Madeira sauce. Another is the wild mushroom ravioli with poached quails' eggs and mushroom velouté. Dessert might be hazelnut and milk chocolate parfait and dark chocolate mousse on a chocolate sable biscuit with white chocolate ice cream. Presentation is always one of the strongest points.

Gidleigh Park is without doubt one of Britain's most iconic country house hotels, a place that combines lovely West Country scenery, fine cooking, and excellent wine. The high service standards here complete the overall package. It is a place in which to relax and be pampered. **AH**

"Michael Caines' cuisine is approachable, sensational and worth every penny. "

Fiona Duncan, *Daily Telegraph*

⬆ Michael Caines, head chef at Gidleigh Park.

Nathan Outlaw | Stylish modern seafood on the north Cornish coast

Location Rock   **Signature dish** Wild Cornish turbot with seaweed and oyster sauce | ❺❺❺❺

Nathan Outlaw the chef is famous for his love of cooking fish; Nathan Outlaw the restaurant is ideally positioned to capitalize on the labors of local fisherman. Their combined achievements were acknowledged in 2011 with the award of a prestigious second Michelin star.

The premises are in the St. Enodoc Hotel above the estuary of the Camel River in the picturesque village of Rock, Cornwall. The interior is intimate and the service hospitable and charming. Behind the scenes, Chris Simpson presides over a small and efficient team in the kitchen.

Fresh fish and seafood, bought from Cornish day boats, are the focus of the cooking. Indeed, all that is on offer is a seafood tasting menu of four fish courses followed by cheese and two desserts. The aim is to showcase the pleasures of truly fresh, locally caught fish and seafood in style, with diners taken through a carefully paced progression of courses. Well thought-out dishes such as cod, kohlrabi, and curry, or turbot with ham hock and spring piccalilli reflect Outlaw the chef's flair for combining ingredients to memorably tasty effect. Touches such as the "oyster mayonnaise" dressing, made with oyster juice, show his characteristic skill at maximizing flavor.

Seasonal produce, such as foraged wild garlic, St. Enodoc asparagus, or winter root vegetables, is used with flair and creativity, with the restaurant's own kitchen garden playing an important role in the menu. The cooking does not depend on gimmickry or elaborate garnishes, but allows diners to appreciate really top-quality, carefully prepared seafood. Perhaps the sole drawback to Nathan Outlaw's is that it is open only for dinner and only on certain days of the week. Demand for tables therefore greatly outstrips supply, and booking ahead is essential. **AH**

⊼ Fish goes from day boat to table in a matter of hours.

Seafood Restaurant | The Cornish restaurant championing seafood

Location Padstow **Signature dish** Padstow Lobster, grilled with fine herbs or steamed with mayonnaise | ❺❺❺❺

This is the bait used by TV chef Rick Stein to get the British hooked on fish and seafood. His success has been so great that the town in which he established himself, Padstow, Cornwall, is now often referred to in the popular press and broadcast media as "Padstein."

Stein's influence is now pervasive, but this is the restaurant where it all began—a double conservatory room, adorned with plenty of contemporary art and an elliptical seafood and sashimi bar in its center, and offering glorious views across the bay.

While carefully sourced, supremely fresh, local fish and seafood are the stars of the show, the dishes draw their inspiration far more widely—from traditional British and classical French to recipes inspired by Stein's TV travels to Goa, Thailand, and beyond.

Start with sweet-fleshed Helford shrimp, dipped in lemon and garlic aioli and eaten in their entirety, head to tail, Ponthilly oysters, and Sennen Cove squid with chili and mint. Follow them with a distinctly rich Newlyn fish pie, crammed with monkfish and scallops in a truffle-infused creamy sauce. More adventurous palates may crave refreshing crab, wakame, cucumber, and dashi salad with wasabi, Madras stone bass, tomato and tamarind curry, or Singapore chili crab for which napkins tucked into chins are advised—it is utterly delicious, piquant, and almost unbelievably messy!

Given the restaurant's reputation, it seems almost sacrilege not to eat fish here, but there are soups, terrines, and 30-day-aged rib eye on offer for confirmed carnivores. Desserts such as saffron and cardamom bread-and-butter pudding showcase Stein's eclectic creativity in mixing traditions from all over the world to stunning effect. Just don't expect to see Rick Stein working at the pass too often, as he divides his time between Cornwall and Australia. **SP**

⊡ The hotbed of Britain's seafood revolution.

The Seahorse | The freshest of seafood served with confident simplicity

Location Dartmouth　**Signature dish** Scallops seahorse-style | 💲💲

"The wild langoustines [at The Seahorse] are bigger than Mike Tyson's fists."

Jasper Gerard, *Daily Telegraph*

⬆ A restaurant where diners can relax and enjoy top-notch fish and seafood.

➡ Scallops—the house speciality.

Dartmouth, the buzzing but delightful town on the banks of the Dart River in Devon, is home to many versions of classic fish and chips, but the destination restaurant for those with a piscatorial appetite is The Seahorse. Having a prime position on the waterfront and serving excellent seafood, it's a popular place with both locals and visitors. The overwhelming impression you get on entering is that you'll be looked after. The welcome is warm, the interior is cozy, and diners are comfortable and relaxed. It's all very assured and far from try-hard. As is the food. Mitch Tonks and Mat Prowse, the owners and chefs, believe in keeping it simple, and when the fish is this fresh, it would indeed be foolish to do otherwise. So there's always a choice of something caught that day, simply grilled.

The chefs travel widely and often, and The Seahorse menu is regularly updated to incorporate their latest discoveries and enthusiasms. Thus there may be some anchoïade, the anchovy spread, on the table to go with the bread, or perhaps some burrata, the fresh Italian cheese, as part of a caprese salad.

Such incidentals come and go; the constant is seasonal ingredients at their best. Expect brill in spring, spider crab in May, native lobster during the summer, sardines from late summer to early fall, and the eagerly anticipated Dover sole and lemon sole to herald the start of winter.

Although the menu naturally has a strong fish focus, there is always a meat option, and the sweetbreads are highly regarded by those in the know. To finish, choose from discerningly chosen and perfectly served cheeses as well as a dessert menu with the likes of expertly crafted panna cotta or roasted fruit. In addition to a daily-changing aperitif and an interesting and competitively priced choice of wine by the glass or by the carafe, the wine list is carefully considered with an extensive range of well-chosen European labels. **CS**

Hell Bay | Discover seafood heaven at the mouth of Hell

Location Bryher **Signature dish** Hell Bay bouillabaisse with warm crusty bread | $$

Sailors named it Hell. This rocky bay on the most westerly inhabited Scilly Isle faces brazenly into the Atlantic fury. Waves crash in with a momentum undiminished since leaving North America. Locals say shipwrecks outnumber people here.

One might think that the construction of a luxury hotel in such a location, huddled among ancient rocks, facing west into storms, would be a recipe for financial ruin. Yet on an island half-a-mile (1 km) wide and only the height of a tree, it is a remarkably civilized outpost. The style is New England beach house: low-rise, with pastel paints, wooden verandas, ample use of driftwood, and bare wooden floors.

The restaurant may look into the mouth of Hell but is a heavenly place to be. It is decorated with Malabar fabrics, Lloyd Loom furniture, and a superior collection of modern British art, celebrating the island's bohemian painters' colony. There's a light and airy atmosphere and a casual, bistro style of service.

The food is better than you'd expect in Hell. With three AA rosettes, it's the highest rated in the Scillies, albeit in the remotest spot. Many diners are lured via water taxis from more populous islands.

The hotel maintains strong links with local produce. It runs food-foraging breaks and has a fresh shellfish shack on the beach; it keeps chickens and gets guests to collect their own breakfast eggs.

Seafood such as mackerel, monkfish, scallop, and crab are specialities, but so, too, in this ultra-mild, well-watered climate, are the island's meat and vegetables. Dishes ranges from the enticingly simple, like moules marinière and warm crusty bread, featuring mussels freshly harvested from Cornish rocks, to more complex creations such as braised shoulder and roasted loin of lamb served with butternut squash fondant, spiced lentils, and rosemary lamb jus. **SH**

↑ A serene vision of the mouth of Hell.

Star Castle Hotel | Where diners can watch the owner catch the mains

Location St. Mary's **Signature dish** St. Mary's lobster Thermidor | 💲💲

Many restaurateurs claim to be committed to low food miles and the use of local produce, but few of them carry it to the extremes of Robert Francis, owner of the four-star Star Castle Hotel. This small sixteenth-century fortress commands the approaches to St. Mary's, the largest of the Scilly Isles, 28 miles (45 km) off England's south-western tip.

Francis skippers the hotel's own fishing boat, the *Gallos*, sailing past the restaurant windows daily to catch lobsters and crabs around the island. These are served the same day.

More than that, he has planted his own 2-acre (0.8-ha) market garden a little way across the island. Here he sows more than 10,000 fruit and vegetable seeds annually to keep his kitchen stocked with ultra-fresh ingredients. And if that's not enough, the indomitable owner is an oenophile who has traveled the world to select the wines for the Star's acclaimed cellar. He has since studied to become a qualified winemaker. In 2007, Francis planted more than 7,000 vines in an 8-acre (3-ha) south-facing patch of the island and in 2014, the hotel's own first vintage was produced.

Apart from Francis' personal efforts, the Star's chef uses meat from a farm on St. Mary's and fish from the island's fishermen. Most of the kitchen's ingredients come from this tiny area of no more than a 5-mile (8-km) radius.

Guests can dine in the old exposed-stone-walled restaurant in front of an open fire or in the sunny conservatory with wicker chairs and an overhead grape vine. They are also invited to visit the owner's flourishing vegetable field and vineyard. The most intrepid of them are even allowed to join Francis on his fishing expeditions and personally select the ingredients of their evening dinner. **SH**

⬆ Robert Francis on board the *Gallos*.

De Lindenhof | A peaceful place to enjoy pure flavors

Location Giethoorn   **Signature dish** Pike perch with smoked eel and mint | ❺❺❺❺❺

De Lindenhof is a two-star Michelin restaurant set in exquisite English gardens just beyond the center of the picturesque village of Giethoorn (known as the "Venice of the North"—it has no roads, only canals, bridges, and bike paths). It would be hard to find a more restful spot to enjoy the bounty of the region.

Patron-chef Martin Kruithof is known both for his pure, clean, and inventive take on the classics and his cavalcade of amuse-bouches, such as wasabi macarons with eel. The restaurant's à la carte menu includes "cannibal toast" (steak tartare with Espelette pepper), oxtail-stuffed cannelloni with mushroom sauce—a classic Kruithof creation—and lemon and passion fruit soufflé. Also available is a four-course "Lindenhof menu"; an eight-course "Ziel en Zaligheid" (Soul and Sanctification) menu, with dishes such as langoustine with fennel and lime and guinea fowl with green curry and rice; and the full De Lindenhof experience in the form of the twelve-course "Martin's Choice" tasting menu. Oenophiles will be impressed by the wine list.

De Lindenhof, formerly a farmhouse, has a beamed ceiling, oak floor, and characterful windows overlooking a fragrant kitchen garden, where many of the herbs, edible flowers, and vegetables used in the kitchen are grown. The mood in this temple of gastronomy is quiet and formal, as are its diners. The service is warm and welcoming, yet unobtrusive and refreshingly pretention-free. In warmer months, a table may be booked on the lovely garden patio, which looks out over the restaurant's leafy garden and canal. Also on offer is a guided canal tour on the restaurant's sloop, which comes with a packed picnic. And visitors reluctant to leave this idyllic spot have the option of extending their visit with a stay in one of De Lindenhof's comfortable on-site suites. **KE**

⬆ Farmhouse features have been retained in the decor.

De Librije | Witty and creative modernist cuisine in a former monastery

Location Zwolle   **Signature dish** Foie gras, North Sea crab, and fermented red cabbage juice | ❸❸❸❸

De Librije (Dutch for "the library") is located in a sixteenth-century building that was originally a Dominican monastery in the heart of Zwolle. Head chef Jonnie Boer joined the restaurant in 1986. He and his wife Therese, who both grew up in the area, then bought the restaurant in the early nineties and turned it into a highly successful operation that has won many accolades, including three Michelin stars.

The dining room is characterized by a very tall ceiling with plenty of natural light coming in through the high windows and a large central chandelier that dominates the room. The menu is firmly in modernist territory, and the creative chef's creations are complemented by an impressive 800-label wine list.

Mayonnaise of basil topped with tartare of beef, cream of oyster, *pomme soufflé*, oyster, and oyster leaf is a dish that harks back to the early days of De Librije—and it is, intriguingly, "plated" at the table directly onto the hand of the diner. Monkfish is served with a jus made from rollmop herring and prepared with *baharat* (a Middle Eastern blend spice mix that includes paprika). This unusual dish combines the traditionally Dutch ingredient of herring with spices and the more luxurious monkfish. A little drama may be provided in the form of beef from a dairy cow that is cooked at the table, on a hot stone, and served with potato crisp, mushrooms, and bone marrow.

A meal might conclude with a deconstructed apple pie, with the individual elements offering up tasty surprises such as a "clove" that is actually made from chocolate and a "vanilla pod" that is in fact vanilla jelly. More than just culinary trickery, the flavors of the apple and the vanilla ice cream create an excellent combination. De Librije offers a journey of exploration into exotic flavor pairings and highly skilled modern cooking. **AH**

⬆ The venerable setting is part of the restaurant's appeal.

De Culinaire Werkplaats | Design-led Dutch dining

Location Amsterdam   **Signature dish** Black food | ❸❸❸❸

"Discover and experience in five dishes—transparency, stones, pearls, water, and essence…"

"Sign of the Times" menu, deculinairewerkplaats.nl

⬆ Founders Marjolein Wintjes and Eric Meursing explore the creative possibilities of vegetarian food.

➡ Imaginative and inventive food, strikingly presented.

This concept restaurant, truly at the cutting edge of food, design, and art, is unlike any other in the Netherlands. Design duo Marjolein Wintjes and Eric Meursing insist on calling their award-winning restaurant/design studio an "eat-initiative." If that makes De Culinaire Werkplaats ("the culinary workplace") sound awfully pretentious, it really is not. The down-to-earth mentality that the Dutch are famed for is at play here. Guests casually share a communal table in the open kitchen of the studio, and they help themselves to organic wine from a selection on the counter. There are no waiters, so diners have to carry their own plates. The democratic approach even extends to letting customers decide how much to pay for their food.

To experience a five-course "eat inspiration," take a tram to Staatsliedenbuurt, west of Amsterdam's center, where an airy atelier awaits, with industrial steel, light wood, artsy edible fabric swatches, and "inspirational" quotes aimed at making visitors think about "the future of food." The tasting menu consists of three savory and two sweet dishes, and always includes a "sneak preview," usually a flatbread with a topping or spread that reveals something about the menu's conceptual theme. The theme changes every six to eight weeks, and always features organic or fair-trade grains, fruits, and vegetables that are in season and sourced locally from small-scale farms. So far, no meat or fish have featured. Past themes have included "Just in Time," "Urban Landscapes," and the most famous theme, "Black," from which the proprietors have retained their signature usage of naturally black ingredients, such as black quinoa, blackberries, black sesames, black salt, and black pasta.

Each theme is revealed in the choice of ingredients, shapes, colors, and tastes, and also in how the food is consumed. Portions are medium sized to avoid waste, but customers may order seconds. **KE**

De Kas | Fresh farm-to-table food, literally grown next door

Location Amsterdam **Signature dish** Seasonal, daily changing menu | ❸❸❸

The clue is in the name, which simply means "the greenhouse." Set in leafy Frankendael Park, De Kas is a former municipal nursery that was given a stylish makeover by Dutch designer Piet Boon. Now an Amsterdam institution, the restaurant attracts a mix of suited executives, local foodies, and tourists who cannot help but admire the impressive 26-foot- (8-m-) high glass conservatory.

De Kas has delighted diners for over a decade with its farm-to-table approach. More than a dozen varieties of fragrant heirloom tomatoes grow on the vine by the entrance of the restaurant, making it immediately clear that the focus is on the very freshest of local ingredients. The three-course set menu is based on the day's harvest from the on-site nursery and herb garden, plus other local suppliers. The cooking style is inspired by rural Mediterranean cuisines, with particular emphasis on so-called "forgotten vegetables," such as beets, celeriac, and samphire, prepared in ways that retain their flavors.

Served on the patio facing the herb garden, with rose-ringed parakeets swooping overhead and storks nesting nearby, a meal might begin with warm, crusty bread, grassy olive oil, and fruity green olives. Then come asparagus with heirloom beets and crisp potato croquettes, or scallops with samphire.

A main course of spiced spring chicken features bright orange carrot oil, which adds an earthy note. The high culinary standards carry through to the desserts, such as panna cotta topped with blueberries and juicy strawberries that are startlingly alive with flavor. Rounding off the meal is coffee served with a tray of madeleines, sugar-coated fruit pastilles, and pastries. **KE**

◁ A glass house setting for lovingly sourced food.

Greetje | Updated traditional Dutch cuisine in a nostalgic dining room

Location Amsterdam **Signature dish** "Greetje's Grote Finale" | ❸❸

Dutch still-life paintings from centuries past create an impression of a nation devoted to delicious food. In recent decades, that impression was often belied by the reality of Dutch restaurant cooking, but that is changing. Local chefs have rediscovered homegrown ingredients and are returning to comforting classics.

There is nowhere better in the capital to enjoy a taste of authentic Dutch food, prepared with care and a modern touch, than Greetje, situated in an historic canal house and named for the mother of the proprietor. Locals and tourists looking for a taste of the old Holland rub shoulders in an interior designed to look like a traditional Dutch dining room, with blue Delft tiles, chandeliers, bouquets of fresh flowers,

---

"Greetje takes old-fashioned classics and makes them into something [to be] proud of …"

Vicky Hampton, *Guardian*

---

candles, and dark wood. Friendly servers explain dishes from a menu featuring indigenous ingredients such as Beemster lamb, Zaanse mustard, mackerel, samphire, Opperdoezer Ronder potatoes, garden herbs such as purslane, parsley, tarragon, and chervil, and spices such as cinnamon, mace, cloves, and nutmeg, a legacy of the country's historic trade with the East Indies.

Greetje serves hearty dishes such as a Beemster hare stew with pearl onions and red cabbage, and the "Grote Finale" (big finish), a selection of desserts for two, might include treats such as strawberries marinated in Dutch genever with tarragon; crème brûlée with natural licorice root extract and licorice ice cream; and red summer fruits with organic yogurt. **KE**

Ciel Bleu | Elegant fine dining with panoramic city views

Location Amsterdam   **Signature dish** Cornetto of scallop | ❺❺❺❺

"A chic restaurant … experience stylish service and delicious creative cuisine."

Michelin Guide

⬆ One of the chefs at work in the Ciel Bleu kitchen.

➡ Desserts are delicate, imaginative creations.

Ciel Bleu is situated on the 23rd floor of the Japanese-owned luxury hotel Okura, with panorama windows along one side of the dining room affording a fine view over Amsterdam. The space is luxurious, with generously spaced tables set with fine linen tablecloths and comfortable chairs. Head chef and manager Onno Kokmeijer trained at family-run restaurants before joining Ciel Bleu. It is due to him that the restaurant has gained and retained two Michelin stars. He offers an extensive menu that changes four times per year.

The cooking makes use of select ingredients and has some modern touches, but nothing that jars. In the unusual pairing of deep-fried soft-shell crab with avocado and beansprout salad, or the exquisite deep-fried foie gras and langoustine with spicy mango chutney, the unusual blends of flavors work well together.

The focus on first-class ingredients is also evident in dishes such as cornetto of scallop with truffle mascarpone: a single cooked scallop is served with green pea coulis, black truffle, and Parmesan mousse. The scallop and pea flavors harmonize, and the Parmesan is not too dominant.

Interesting flavors are also balanced skillfully in a dish of fried turbot on farm bread, topped with Iberian *pata negra* ham and served with Lardo di Colonnata, glazed black salsify, and a dressing of Amontillado sherry, the latter providing a clever contrast to the richness of the *pata negra*. Fried sweetbreads in Pedro Ximénez sherry on a mousse of celeriac showcase masterfully juxtaposed flavors and textures. At Ciel Bleu, the standard of the cooking definitely matches the spectacular view.

The waiters are very attentive and responsive, and the sommelier is extremely knowledgeable, happy to make a recommendation from the comprehensive wine list to match the chosen dishes. **AH**

Lute | Inventive culinary pyrotechnics in a former gunpowder factory

Location Amstelveen   **Signature dish** Tasting menu of five signature dishes | ❸❸❸❸

Celebrity chef Peter Lute is a jury member of the Dutch version of the hit TV series *MasterChef*. His eponymous restaurant is housed in the eighteenth-century stables of what was once a gunpowder factory on a bank of the Amstel river. The space was transformed into a stylish restaurant by architect Winy Maas of MVRDV and interior designer Eline Strijkers.

Lute maintains that the restaurant's industrial setting inspires an "authentic approach;" rather than being led by outside trends, it is dictated by what the chef personally sees, hears, and feels from day to day. Today, the former gunpowder factory produces fireworks that are served on a plate. Lute's philosophy of authenticity is rooted in his cooking. He believes in finding the best local products and then fine-tuning and refining these ingredients to intensify their flavors; the results are presented to guests in stunning and mouthwatering arrangements. Highlights might include a delicate truffle soup; a feather-light take on

shrimp tempura; airy lemon polenta; and a passion-fruit and chocolate dessert, beautifully presented on a slate platter and tasting as good as it looks. In summer, for a delightful al fresco dining experience, reserve a table on the restaurant's elegantly shaded terrace, which was designed using natural materials and luxurious Bisazza glass mosaics.

The thoughtfully designed restaurant, which has been operating since 2002, was the realization of a dream for the chef–owner, whose vision is to increase guests' enjoyment with an experience that engages all their senses—a restaurant visit with added value. That may sound a simple proposition, but it is a challenge to achieve it on a daily basis, according to Lute, whose intuitive approach extends to the service. Indeed, it is the restaurateur's wish that every guest feels as welcome as his friends and family. **KE**

⬆ **The stylish surroundings showcase Lute's food.**

Blauw | Traditional Indonesian cuisine in a classically modern establishment

Location Utrecht   **Signature dish** Indonesian rice table | **❺❺**

Indonesian food is the favorite adopted cuisine of the Netherlands (in much the same way that Indian cooking is in the United Kingdom). In fact, the connection with the former Dutch East Indies is so strong that it has long become a tradition for Dutch hosts to take guests to an Indonesian restaurant for a "taste of the Netherlands." Restaurant Blauw melds a taste of the past with contemporary decor, proving popular with a varied clientele from students to suited sophisticates.

It is a coming home of sorts for owner Stefan Vreugdenburg, who was born in the Netherlands and whose forebears lived in Java. The restaurant's name, which means "blue," might confuse those entering the chili-red restaurant, which also features a large portrait of Vreugdenburg's family back in colonial times. In fact, the name refers to the family's Indonesian bloodline, which often shows itself by way of a temporary blue-tinged birthmark.

Order the *rijsttafel* ("rice table"), a unique Dutch–Indonesian hybrid of a dozen or more dishes from across the Indonesian island group; its menu was created in colonial times to give visiting dignitaries a taste of what the "Spice Islands" had to offer. At Blauw, there are three "rice tables" to choose from—seafood, vegetarian, and mixed—along with other meat, seafood, and vegetable-based dishes. The series of chili-spiked dishes, which soon start arriving at the table in sleek, boat-shaped vessels, may include aromatic *babi ketjap* (a pork stew made with sweetened soy sauce); *satay kambing* (a meltingly tender goat satay); and *spekkoekijs* (ice cream with the flavors of the beloved Indonesian layered spiced cake). You may not recall every dish you sample, but you will certainly leave Blauw sated and with lingering memories of lime, lemongrass, and galangal. **KE**

⬆ Be sure to order the *rijsttafel* at Blauw.

In Den Rustwat | Fine food and a 400-year heritage of hospitality

Location Rotterdam   **Signature dish** Seasonally changing menu | 💲💲💲

"Passion is a prerequisite for any true gourmet experience. Everything has to be right, period!"

Marcel van Zomeren, chef and co-owner

⬆ Marcel van Zomeren is proud of his food.

Who would have believed that, a mere stone's throw from the bustling, skyscraper-dominated center of Rotterdam, a landmark restaurant is housed in a venerable establishment where guests have been made to feel at home for more than four centuries? In Den Rustwat, which also refers to itself as IDRW, is situated in one of the best-preserved historic buildings of Rotterdam, a former inn with a history that dates back to 1597. The thatch-roofed restaurant is surrounded by a lush garden, adjacent to an arboretum, which between them boast more than 4,000 varieties of trees, shrubs, and plants.

Inside, the restaurant has a nostalgic ambiance, with warm, subdued colors, a dark stone floor, and classic white-tableclothed tables with remarkably comfortable armchair seating. In Den Rustwat's calling card is its consistent, expert level of hospitality. The extremely amiable staff walk the line between professionalism and familiarity with ease, and clearly have a passion for their calling.

The cuisine at IDRW is modern, with a French education. "Love and time are my most expensive ingredients," says chef and co-owner Marcel van Zomeren. "Good products are the foundation of everything we do." Classic dishes are reinterpreted through a locavore lens focused on seasonal Dutch products, such as roasted Dutch Wagyu beef with naan bread and tossed herbs; whole lobster, which is first smoked by the table and then served with a salad of tomatoes, cauliflower, egg, and an Iberico ham sauce; tonka bean cannelloni; and delicious candied rhubarb and strawberries with yogurt-tarragon ice cream.

An unexpected oasis of calm in one of the Netherlands' largest cities, IDRW is sure to appeal to lovers of gastronomy and history, and is best suited to the leisurely pace of a romantic meal. Book a table on the gorgeous garden terrace in warmer months. **KE**

Inter Scaldes | Art on a plate

Location Kruiningen   **Signature dish** Scallop prepared in the shell with black truffle | ❺❺❺❺❺

It is a culinary cliché to describe beautiful food as "art on a plate," yet the genuine passion that patron chef Jannis Brevet has for art is reflected in many of the artfully constructed dishes he has created for the Michelin two-star restaurant Inter Scaldes. He even published a cookbook, entitled *Cuisine & Art*, in 2009. "Looking at art feeds the mind, loving art enriches life," says Brevet, who frequently contemplates his growing collection of abstract art in search of visual elements that he might choose to incorporate in his cooking. Indeed, amid the art adorning the walls of the renowned restaurant, his well-heeled clientele might easily find themselves sitting next to the artwork that inspired the look of the dish they are about to eat.

The setting is equally beautiful. Surrounded by an immaculate English garden, the restaurant's thatch-roofed former farmhouse sits on a sliver of pretty polder land in the Scheldt estuary; hence, its Latin name, which means "between the Scheldt Rivers." Inside, the decor is noticeably understated, with classic caramel and cream-colored furnishings and impeccable dinnerware.

The cooking style is a modern take on the French tradition with an occasional Asian touch. Carefully chosen local ingredients such as lamb, samphire, sea lavender, fruit, and cheese are sourced from the surrounding Beveland polder. The restaurant is in Zeeland province, and there is a particular emphasis on seafood—Zeeland is famous for its mussels, Oosterschelde lobster, oysters, and fish from the local waters. All are used to create memorable dishes at Inter Scaldes; try the Zeeland lobster in Sauternes.

Co-owner Claudia Brevet goes out of her way to ensure that guests leave with a smile. Her charm, combined with her husband's precise cooking and the perfect pairings of prize-winning sommelier Koen van der Plas, make an experience at Inter Scaldes one of pure perfection. **KE**

> *"I wouldn't say I copy paintings, but I am inspired … by their colors, shades, and structures."*

Jannis Brevet, chef and co-owner

⬆ Jannis Brevet in the Inter Scaldes kitchen.

De Karmeliet | Classic Belgian fine dining in a city of canals

Location Bruges   **Signature dish** Oysters and poached quail's egg with caviar | ❸❸❸❸

The historic city of Bruges is home to some of Belgium's top dining destinations. De Karmeliet moved to its current premises, a classical townhouse with marble floors and high ceilings, in 1992. Its owner and head chef is Geert Van Hecke, who worked under legendary chef Alain Chapel before opening his first restaurant in Belgium in 1983. Van Hecke won a Michelin star in 1985, another in 1989, and the ultimate accolade of three Michelin stars in 1996.

The style of cooking is generally classical French, though in recent years influences from Japan have shown themselves in some dishes. The food can be relatively simple, and is generally not overloaded with superfluous garnishes.

One delicious example is a starter of risotto with morels, not in itself a complex dish, but here featuring morels of the highest quality, the rice having absorbed just the right amount of the superb chicken stock in the cooking process. Seasonality is shown in a spring dish of white asparagus with fresh morels, arranged with a smooth, creamy sabayon of potato inside a container of asparagus; the chicken juice used is perfumed with nutmeg. The garnish consists of perfectly cooked shrimps, some basil oil, and squid ink juice.

This being Belgium, a lot of attention goes into the perfectly kept cheese trolley, with plenty of turnover to ensure that the cheeses are in optimal condition. For dessert you might choose a light chocolate soufflé, cooked evenly and with the rich, dark chocolate flavor coming through strongly.

De Karmeliet is a place where you can appreciate the traditions of classical cookery, and indeed you will be constantly reminded of history as you stroll through the pretty streets of Bruges after enjoying your meal. **AH**

⬆ The chocolate soufflé is a delicious treat.

Aux Armes de Bruxelles | Belgian classics in an authentic brasserie

Location Brussels   **Signature dish** Mussels marinières | ❸❸❸

Located in one of the most touristic streets of Brussels, near the UNESCO World Heritage site of Grand Place, this 1921 institution offers simple Belgian dishes generously presented in a brasserie atmosphere. The Veulemans family, who owned the venue until 2005, started the trend of serving mussels marinières at the table in individual iron pots. Steamed in a broth traditionally flavored with onions, celery, and wine, the mussels are served with thickly cut fries. Locals take an empty mussel shell to extract the next one.

The extensive menu offers a fine assortment of Belgian classics, such as the famous croquettes de crevettes, which is North Sea shrimps served simply in the typical way, with a piece of lemon and fried curly parsley. Other favorites include tomatoes with gray shrimps, cheese croquettes, beef stew with Brussels gueuze beer, steak tartare, and *waterzooi*, a stew of poultry, fish, or lobster.

The restaurant is split into three rooms. The first, the emblematic art deco main area, features private wooden booths with seats covered in green leather; the second, often called the "Flemish room," is much brighter due to surrounding windows with stained-glass insets; the third room is narrow and more intimate. Waiters, impeccably dressed in white jackets, chat with the regulars, some of whom come every Sunday. Original patrons may regret the departure of the founding family, but the new owners have succeeded in retaining the authentic atmosphere.

You can try one of the numerous Belgian beers on offer; alternatively, the wine list has a "coups de coeur" section suggesting three different wines. For dessert try the flambéed crêpes with Mandarine Napoléon liqueur, prepared at the table. A gourmet show that never disappoints. **MF**

⬆ *Waterzooi*, a Belgian speciality, made here with poultry.

Comme Chez Soi | The flagship of Belgian haute cuisine

Location Brussels   **Signature dish** Sole in a Riesling mousseline sauce with gray North Sea shrimps | ❸❸❸❸

Set in a townhouse in the heart of Brussels since 1936, this elegant, Michelin-starred restaurant remains the top place to discover fine Belgian cuisine. Laurence, the daughter of celebrated chef Pierre Wynants and wife of current chef Lionel Rigolet, is there to welcome you. The main restaurant is designed in the Art Nouveau style with mirrors, wood paneling, and green stained glass. Customers may also dine in a private salon, or at a table in the open-plan, stainless-steel kitchen. Watching the choreographed ballet of chefs preparing the finest of dishes is highly recommended.

Rigolet, the fourth-generation chef, continues the restaurant's tradition of using the finest seasonal and luxury ingredients, imaginatively prepared and creatively presented. The menu showcases a mix of Wynants's signature dishes, clearly marked, such as salad of North Sea lobster with black truffles and potatoes and Rigolet's new creations. One of the most exquisite dishes on the menu was jointly created by the two chefs: a potato mousseline with crab, shrimps, and Royal Belgian caviar with white oyster butter and chives. The five- and six-course tasting menus are new creations, bringing new flavors and spices: examples are breast of Landes pigeon with cubeb pepper and Guinness, chanterelles, and Romanesco flowers and roasted wild halibut, Gillardeau oysters, artichoke, and Taggiasche olives.

Before he handed over to Rigolet, Wynants was also the maître sommelier—and the wine list is mind-blowing. The wine cellar offers one of the biggest European collections of Bordeaux *grand cru* wines, including those from the Pétrus vineyard. Desserts continue the pampering: Rigolet's lime soufflé granita with mojito perfume is a real firework of flavors. **MF**

⬆ The restaurant's beautiful Art Nouveau interior.

L'Idiot du Village | Inventive food in a colorful, intimate venue

Location Brussels   **Signature dish** Escalope of warm foie gras with pepper and vanilla | ❸❸❸

One of Brussels' best-kept secrets, this atmospheric restaurant, hidden in a quiet street, is ideally located between the shops of the Sablon and the popular Marolles flea market. In his small kitchen, co-owner and chef Alain Gascoin prepares imaginative dishes from local ingredients, keeping an eye on customers through a small opening, while Olivier Le Bret, his business partner, takes care of the guests.

Gascoin wants to surprise his clients: "They should not feel bored when they eat," he says. But that never happens here. The restaurant's name sets the tone, and the chef's creativity and sense of humor are reflected in both the s-etting and the food. The main room, predominantly blue, casual, and warm, features a large crystal chandelier. Thick red curtains frame the windows, while on the wall a painting of a dog with a human body, by the Belgian artist Thierry Poncelet, looks like an ancestral portrait. Gascoin is French and loves to adapt traditional Belgian recipes

and ingredients by preparing them in exotic ways. This creates a seasonal menu showcasing a wonderful mix of flavors. Thankfully, the escalope of foie gras with pepper and vanilla is offered throughout the year. It is perfectly cooked, even slightly crispy on the outside, and deliciously smooth inside.

Other highlights include carpaccio of sea bass and scampi, with lime and coconut milk; roasted lobster with spices or the lobster ball with green cabbage; roasted pigeon with mango and a touch of chocolate; and turbot with mussels.

Dessert favorites at L'Idiot du Village include iced meringue with salty caramel; *stoemp*, traditionally a potato-based dish, here given a twist to create a delicious dessert of red fruits; and the classic, delightfully thin apple tart served with ice cream. This is a place with real soul. **MF**

⊓ The dining room is dark and cozy yet elegant.

Historischer Weinkeller |
Robust dishes in a Hanseatic setting

Location Lübeck   **Signature dish** Grilled plaice
from the Baltic Sea | ❸❸

Not one but two restaurants are found in the historic wine cellars lying beneath the Holy Spirit Hospital of Lübeck, which has a history going back to the medieval Hanseatic League (it was originally built in 1286). If you want potatoes, you must visit the Kartoffelkeller. Here, in a candlelit, brick-ceilinged vault of indeterminate age, they are made into pancakes and dumplings, as well as mashed and roasted in a variety of local and regional styles. There is a gratifying robustness about what accompanies them, too—how about mash with Lübeck sausages, sauerkraut, and fried onions, or maybe fried potatoes with a pork fillet, creamed mushrooms, vegetables, and hollandaise sauce? Lighter dishes (if there can be such a thing with the humble potato) include a gutsy potato salad with turkey, or yet more fried potatoes with freshly fried herrings. This is food for cold winters, and is not for those who watch their calories.

Fancy a change of scene? The other restaurant (called Der Butt, which translates as "the flounder") is, as the name suggests, more concerned with fish, which is not surprising given Lübeck's long links with the sea. Starters include a creamy fish soup and pickled herrings served with—naturally—a potato pancake and sour cream. Typical mains are grilled Baltic Sea plaice, North Sea sole, or, in a switch to a freshwater species, a fillet of perch served with rosemary-flavored potatoes. Meat dishes include venison, steak, and duck.

As well as covering two gastronomic bases, owners Joachim and Christa Berger know how to exploit the Historischer Weinkeller's unique atmosphere. Rooms may be hired for special celebratory dinners with the serving staff dressed up in medieval costume; at such events, diners can pretend they have returned to Hanseatic Lübeck. **ATJ**

Fischereihafen | Popular
family-owned harbor fish restaurant

Location Hamburg   **Signature dish** Lobster
Thermidor | ❸❸❸

In Hamburg harbor, and along the steel-gray Elbe River, boats and barges ply back and forth from the open sea. The riverside Fischereihafen restaurant has a terrace from which, on sunny days, diners can keep an eye on the passing ships. In cooler weather they go inside, up a flight of stairs, and view the harbor and river from a space of white-shirted waiters, dizzying cocktails, and a shoal of seafood and fish dishes. Plates are piled high with lobster claws ready to be cracked, and devotees swear blind that the lobster Thermidor here is the best in the West. Smoked eel with scrambled egg and fried bread on the side is a classic starter, while the turbot served with Pommery mustard sauce has always made plenty of friends. In

> *"Along the Grosse Elbstrasse there is now an animated quarter that attracts food lovers …"*
>
> travel.michelin.com

the adjoining oyster bar, you can sit on a stool, sip on a cocktail, and indulge in a plate of salty, briny bivalves.

Rüdiger Kowalke opened the doors in 1981, and, as the years passed, Fischereihafen became *the* place to eat fish in Hamburg; he handed over control to his son in 1987 but still pops in several days a week. Regulars don't say they are going to Fischereihafen, but to "Kowalke." The ambience is calm and soothing, with the numerous framed marine paintings joined by a scattering of photos of former customers, such as Mikhail Gorbachev, Helmut Kohl, Sean Connery, and Franz Beckenbauer. In some restaurants, such mementoes can seem garish, but here they blend in with the elegant and friendly mood. **ATJ**

Jacobs | Contemporary, elegant fine dining in a peaceful
setting overlooking the Elbe River

Location Hamburg **Signature dish** Venison with ginger mash, cabbage, and turnip, with a reduction of cooking juices and grated horseradish | ❸❸❸❸

Jacobs restaurant resides in an eighteenth-century merchant's house on the banks of the Elbe River. Its main dining room has a high ceiling, generously spaced tables, and windows overlooking the river. Jacobs, under the guidance of head chef Thomas Martin, was awarded its first Michelin star in 1998 and a second star in 2011. There is an unusually extensive wine list, with a particularly fine selection of German Rieslings to accompany your meal. The food here is firmly in classical territory, made with high-grade ingredients and involving some intensely flavored sauces that are time-consuming to make.

A meal might begin with a poached egg on a macaroni base, with chanterelle mushrooms, broccoli, ham, and celeriac sauce. For a fish course, you might try John Dory with a deeply flavored pressed tomato; a sauce of saffron and bay leaf; and tapenade, with lemon zest providing balancing acidity. Culinary theater may appear in the form of a whole turbot, carved at the tableside and served with beurre blanc, carrots, baby cep mushroom, and onion. Meat dishes get the same level of attention: venison comes served with ginger mash, cabbage, and turnip, along with a rich reduction of the cooking juices; some freshly grated horseradish provides bite.

You might finish with a dessert of exotic fruits, with pineapple, honey melon, and watermelon; or cocoa sorbet and mango; or a sorbet of mango and tamarind. But leave a little room, because after that a large trolley appears, loaded with a huge array of tempting petits fours and a selection of ice creams.

The kitchen at Jacobs showcases high-grade ingredients and demonstrates strong classical cooking skills, producing attractively presented dishes that consistently taste superb. The service more than matches the high standard of the food. **AH**

"A gourmet is as pleased to have a well-prepared sausage as an exclusive Breton turbot."

Thomas Martin, chef at Jacobs

⬆ Roast ox shoulder with lemon polenta.

Burgermeister |

Fresh burgers in an unusual location

Location Berlin   **Signature dish** Bacon cheeseburger
with sautéed onions | **$**

Berlin has seen a boom in burger joints in recent years, and Burgermeister can lay claim to being one of the first. It may also be the only fast-food stand in the city that is housed in a former public toilet. Co-owner Cebrail Karabelli, a veteran of the Berlin restaurant scene, thought the disused nineteenth-century structure would make an ideal site for his next gastronomic business venture. It took some effort to convince the city government to let him lease the landmarked building, but Burgermeister has thrived ever since it opened in 2005.

Originally, Karabelli offered "currywurst" (sausage with ketchup and curry powder) as well as burgers, but soon he was concentrating on what sold best: the burgers. Refining his product, he focused on improving quality while keeping prices affordable. Now Burgermeister has its own butcher's store, where the beef is ground fresh each day and formed into thin patties. The sesame-seed buns are baked exclusively for Burgermeister by a local Canadian-owned bakery. The result is a flavorful hamburger reminiscent of the well-known U.S. fast-food chains, but everything is taken a step further by using fresh, high-quality ingredients. The beef tastes like real beef, the bacon is crispy, and the homemade ketchup-mayonnaise sauce adds a distinctive, slightly sweet counterpoint.

The tasty burgers are just one key to Burgermeister's success; its unique location is another. Karabelli's witty transformation of the one-time sanitary facility has left its historical character intact, and the green filigreed structure is a rare surviving example of the Berlin public architecture of its time. Its position on a traffic island on a busy road, near a well-used subway stop and within walking distance of the Kreuzberg district, a popular neighborhood for partygoers, is another big draw. **TO**

Theodor Tucher |

German cuisine in the heart of Berlin

Location Berlin   **Signature dish** Sautéed scallops with
black pudding, marinated beetroot, and potato | **$$**

Theodor Tucher seems to pose more questions than answers. Is it a restaurant, with German-orientated dishes and a lively, unpretentious ambience that attracts both passing tourists and savvy locals? Is it a bar, where good German wines and the exemplary Bavarian beers of Weihenstephan can be studied in the golden gleam of a modernistic interior? Is it a library, with its tightly packed shelves of books keeping watch among the tables in a gallery above the main dining area? Or is it a statement of how far Germany has changed since 1989, as it squeezes into what was once a no-man's-land and is now the bustling thoroughfare between the cleaned-up Brandenburg Gate and Unter den Linden?

"The glam gold interior has huge windows, tall pillars, a private dining room, and even a library …"

Guardian

The varied menu includes plump and juicy currywurst, sourced from a city butcher; potato soup with sour cream in the style of old Berlin; salty-sweet, falling-off-the-bone pork knuckle with potato mash; meatballs in a creamy caper and beetroot sauce; chicken with Riesling cabbage; and sautéed scallops with black pudding. A vegetarian menu includes a tomato soufflé with goat cheese and a wheat risotto.

There is a definite fizz and freshness about Tucher, but let us return to the earlier questions, and consider the answers. Theodor Tucher is all of those things; but, first and foremost, it is a restaurant whose dishes celebrate both the muscular and delicate nature of German cuisine and the revival of Berlin life. **ATJ**

Gugelhof | An outpost of the hearty cuisine of Alsace-Lorraine in the German capital

Location Berlin **Signature dish** *Baeckeoffe*, a stew featuring pork, beef, and lamb, served with root vegetables matured in Alsace Riesling wine | 💲💲

From 1871 until 1945, the French province of Alsace-Lorraine yo-yoed between French and German ownership. Now, located in Prenzlauer Berg in the former East Berlin, this handsome, rustically endowed restaurant specializes in Alsace cuisine with the odd German touch. Served in a warm ambience of wood paneling, stucco pillars, and muted brown hues, dishes such as Alsatian onion soup, the famous pizza-like *tarte flambée*, and *choucroute* (sauerkraut) attract both local people and homesick travelers eager to remind themselves of the tastes of home.

This is a rumbustious, hearty cuisine that no Berliner would find unfamiliar. The young waiting staff whizz around the tables with plates piled high with juicy smoked sausages, succulent pork cutlets, and earthy black pudding; these are eagerly devoured and washed down by glasses of lustrous, aromatic Gewürztraminer. *Baeckeoffe* is also a speciality of the house, a meaty belter of a stew featuring cuts of pork, beef, and lamb served with helpings of root vegetables that have been matured in Riesling (produced in Alsace, of course); the pot is sealed with dough during cooking. For those who want a dish of international renown in the 1970s, Gugelhof's own fondue can be ordered. Featuring raclette, Emmental, and Gruyère cheeses, it is rich, unctuous, and silken in the way it greets the palate.

Booking is always recommended for this pleasing establishment, although it is doubtful that, back in 2000, one of Gugelhof's more illustrious diners needed to telephone in advance. On a visit to Berlin, the then U.S. President Bill Clinton asked German Chancellor Gerhard Schröder to suggest somewhere to eat in Prenzlauer Berg. Gugelhof was put forward, and Clinton thoroughly enjoyed himself, reportedly indulging in a helping of *choucroute*. **ATJ**

"Some guests come specially because of the goat roast … others because of the Baeckeoffe.*"*

garcon24.de

⊞ The dough-sealed pot of the speciality, *Baeckeoffe*.

Henne Alt-Berliner Wirtshaus | The best chicken in town

Location Berlin **Signature dish** Fried chicken and potato salad |

"Henne's decor appears barely touched since ... Marlene Dietrich first sang 'Falling In Love Again.'"

Melissa Frost, somamagazine.com

⬆ Paintings and curiosities from the early twentieth century line the interior of the restaurant.

➡ Henne's entrance loudly proclaims the restaurant's enthusiasm for the local Schultheiss Pilsener.

Chicken is the main attraction at the aptly named Henne (the word is German for "hen"), although here it will not be just any old bird. For a start, the chickens are organically raised. In the kitchen, they are marinated in buttermilk before being fried and served as halves alongside either potato or cabbage salad, all at a reasonable price. There are other items on the menu—currywurst or meatballs are available—but it is for the chicken that people flock here (there is no option for vegetarians unless you count the salad). On the plate the chicken is a deep golden color and has a crispy, crunchy skin, while the meat is juicy and bursts with flavor.

Diners should expect to wait some time for their bird to reach the table because each one is cooked freshly; some customers minimize their wait by booking ahead. For those customers who do not resort to this, there is plenty in the place to admire after they just turn up and grab a seat among the communal tables. For a start, Henne, being located in the hipster's area of Kreuzberg, was literally feet from the old Berlin Wall. But the restaurant also has a history going back to the years before World War I, and has managed to survive revolution, hyper inflation, two world wars, and the Cold War. Inside, Henne is a traditional Berlin pub with dark wood panels, on which all manner of framed photos and pictures hang, while the comings and goings of the white-shirted staff are illuminated by old lamps. There is also a garden for when the weather becomes benevolent. Meanwhile, beer is the order of the day as an accompaniment for the chicken, and many customers opt for the locally brewed Schultheiss Pilsener.

When President John F. Kennedy was in Berlin in 1962, he was invited to visit Henne but his advisers wrote back to say that he would be too busy. That letter (now framed) can be seen on the wall behind the bar. He had no idea what he missed. **ATJ**

Café Einstein | A civilized place for food and conversation

Location Berlin **Signature dish** Apple strudel | $$

Housed in an elegant nineteenth-century villa in Berlin's Schöneberg district, Café Einstein is an oasis of Viennese coffeehouse culture in the German capital. Grab yourself one of the newspapers hanging from a rack in the foyer, choose a spot in the main dining room or perhaps the cozy library room, and settle in for an experience that recalls a bygone era.

Café Einstein was opened in 1978 by an expatriate Austrian eager to recreate an important part of her country's culture: the "Kaffeehaus," a place where generations of Viennese went for coffee, food, and—crucially—conversation and intellectual debate; a place where artists, writers, and thinkers could meet with their peers and discuss their ideas and plans. The choice of location for Café Einstein was an excellent one; the villa was one of only a few on its street to survive Allied bombing raids, and it boasts a history that includes a stint as an illegal gambling casino.

The café has changed hands a few times since its start, but the current owners are continuing the path established by its founder. Traditional Viennese offerings such as Wiener Schnitzel, Tafelspitz, and apple strudel are combined with modern pan-European influences, and seasonal ingredients are used. That combination of the new and the old is echoed in Café Einstein's decor. The villa's original fittings, woodwork, and plaster detailing have been carefully maintained without the place being made to feel like a museum. The café's leafy garden area is a popular attraction in the warmer months.

An institution of the former West Berlin, Café Einstein continues to be patronized by an eclectic range of guests—academics to businessmen, senior citizens to teenagers, artists to politicians. Famous actors are known to go there for celebrations, perhaps drawn by the fact that movie director Quentin Tarantino used the upstairs Lebensstern bar as a set for his 2009 film *Inglourious Basterds.* **TO**

"The effect [is completed by] slightly snobbish waiters gliding across squeaking parquet floors."

fodors.com

[↑] Café Einstein is located in Berlin's Schöneberg district.

Fischers Fritz | Memorably good gourmet dining in the German capital

Location Berlin   **Signature dish** Supreme of Atlantic turbot, black chanterelles, and Béarnaise sauce | ❸❸❸

Fischers Fritz in Berlin's Regent Hotel has held two Michelin stars since 2008. In charge of the kitchens is Christian Lohse, who trained with some world-class chefs in France, including Guy Savoy and Marc Meneau. He was previously head chef of Zur Windmühle in Bad Oeynhausen, Rhine-Westphalia, and is noted for his mastery of seafood cookery.

The dining room is traditional, with wood paneling, a high ceiling, chandeliers, and comfortable classical chairs. A meal might begin with a slab of terrine of foie gras topped with a transparent crisp layer of smoked eel with pepper caramel and eggplant jam. You might continue with a bouillon of Atlantic langoustine with ravioli of lardo and langoustines with Japanese pepper, garnished with a little artichoke, enoki mushroom, and coriander.

At times, the kitchen ventures off the familiar path, as seen in a dish of baked egg on smooth basil mash, the egg soft inside its crisp outer shell, with tartare of prawn and red mullet and a saffron sauce. This is a bold and unusual set of flavors, but they work harmoniously together. One of the many excellent fish dishes is gilthead bream, served with carrots, mushrooms, carefully cooked leek, and a zucchini flower stuffed with tartare of the bream.

The high technical standard of the cooking is maintained at the dessert stage. This is shown in a refreshing dish of chilled citrus soup with ginger and lime, with a cucumber sponge that has a distinct taste of ginger. This is accompanied by a silk-smooth and intensely flavored white chocolate ice cream garnished with juniper. Fischers Fritz combines impeccably sourced ingredients with consistently high technical skills, creatively linking flavor combinations that work well together. The grand room and formal yet welcoming service combine to make this one of the top dining destinations in the German capital. **AH**

"Subtle and sophisticated … the chef cooks with the ardent lyricism of a culinary troubadour."

Frommer's Germany

⬆ A selection of fruity desserts at Fischers Fritz.

Borchardt | A Maxim's-style buzz in the heart of Berlin

Location Berlin   **Signature dish** Wiener Schnitzel | $$

"The catering pedigree of Roland Mary's Borchardt stretches back to the reign of Kaiser Wilhelm II …"

60by80.com

A visit to Borchardt is always an occasion—it is definitely a place to be noticed, somewhere to be on equal dining terms with celebrities ranging from politicians to pop stars. But people do not go to Borchardt just for a spell of stargazing while picking at the remains of a lukewarm meal. The food is seriously good here, while the decor—some suggest it has more than a hint of the atmosphere of *fin de siècle* Berlin—is grand and eye-catching without being stuffy. For a start, look at the marble columns standing like sentries beneath a ceiling that rises to the heavens. Tread the tiled floor with its Art Nouveau flourishes, and settle yourself in one of the oxblood red banquette seats. There is a hustle and bustle of waiting staff wheeling their way between tables, while diners lick their lips as they fall in love with a Wiener Schnitzel or a juicy fillet steak accompanied by sweet potato fries. Borchardt offers the diner a restaurant and theater in equal measure.

The original Borchardt was established in 1853, but nearly a hundred years later it was destroyed in the fighting at the end of World War II. In East Berlin, it was subsequently rebuilt and used as a training center for chefs, but in 1992, after much renovation, it opened next door to its original site on Französische Strasse with the aim of bringing a Maxim's-style sense of classic dining to Berlin.

The menu embraces both classical French cuisine and traditional German cooking. Typical dishes are poached lobster with bouillabaisse, oysters, steak tartare, calf's liver, and Wiener Schnitzel (which the regulars rate as the best in the city). Those with a penchant for grilled meats are also well served with a foot-stompingly successful selection of grilled steaks. Eating at Borchardt is not cheap, and it is always advisable to book, but those who enjoy a sense of occasion, a bout of people watching, and fine food will want to return time and time again. **ATJ**

⬆ Borchardt offers good food and people-watching.

Cookies Cream | Adventurous vegetarian cuisine for food lovers

Location Berlin **Signature dish** Parmesan dumplings with artichoke and barbecued tomato | 🟡🟡

The Cookies Cream experience is unique, and begins with the challenge of actually getting there. Located in Berlin's central Mitte district, in what was once the French Cultural Institute in the former East Berlin, the entrance is tucked away in an alley between the Westin Grand Hotel and the Komische Oper, requiring you to summon sufficient courage to venture down it. Once you have found the right door, you ring the bell to be allowed into what is the famed Cookies nightclub, then climb the stairs to the restaurant.

There, you are greeted by waiting staff dressed in casual black clothing, and a decor that contrasts candles, starched white tablecloths, and flower arrangements with the plainly visible elements of the room's ventilation and electrical systems. That high-tech architectural display of what is usually hidden is echoed by the wide, doorless entrance to the kitchen, which allows guests at many of the tables to observe their meals being prepared.

And what meals they turn out to be. With the curious journey already having raised visitors' expectations that they are in for something special, the food at Cookies Cream does not disappoint. Head chef Stefan Hentschel deliberately eschews standard vegetarian restaurant fare—pasta, rice, tofu—and instead focuses on seasonal vegetables, which he often prepares as if they were meat. The result is a short, modern, and sophisticated menu featuring surprising combinations of flavors and textures. The menu changes according to whatever is available and in season, and can feature intriguing details, such as a charcoal foam, or a soft-boiled quail egg tucked into a fluffy brioche. Most of the dishes can be prepared to accommodate vegans, although the owner, also named Cookie, says that a large proportion of the guests are not vegetarians at all, but adventurous diners wishing to try something new. At Cookies Cream, the thrills continue after you sit down. **TO**

"My grandparents had a garden, and I was fascinated to see veggies grow as a kid."

Stefan Hentschel, chef at Cookies Cream

⬆ Diners can watch their food being prepared.

Café Anna Blume | Encourage romance to blossom
over breakfast with flowers

Location Berlin   **Signature dish** "Anna Blume" breakfast for two or four people |

"Delicate odors waft through the café … petals and other flower parts turn up in the beverages."

slowtravelberlin.com

⬆ The generous "Anna Blume" breakfast option.

Berlin has no shortage of cozy cafés with yummy cakes, a relaxed atmosphere, and outdoor seating, but Café Anna Blume may be the only one in the city where you can get an artfully arranged flower bouquet along with your caffè latte. Co-owner Britta Biebach says that the inspiration for this unusual pairing came from her background as a landscape architect, as well as a desire to go into business with her husband, who owns an adjacent café and bakery. Anna Blume—*Blume* is German for "flower," and the name came from a poem by Dadaist Kurt Schwitters—opened in 2005, but its elegant Art Nouveau decor makes it feel as though it has been here for generations. The flower vases in wall niches, red leatherette banquettes, and a red velvet-draped corner area are just perfect for small groups and special celebrations. Outside, there is seating beneath a huge old chestnut tree. The café takes up part of a generously sized corner on a leafy street in the Prenzlauer Berg district.

The menu features cakes and other sweet delights, as well as savory dishes such as soups, salads, and entrées; the dinner menu changes every few weeks. The basis of the cooking is German but the dishes are given an international twist. The most popular meal of the day is breakfast, particularly the "Anna Blume," a continental-style option for two or four people featuring a selection of gourmet cheeses, cold meats, fresh fruit, homemade jam, bread, and scrambled eggs, all served on a tiered cake stand.

A glass door separates the café from the flower store, itself worth a visit, which is dominated by stunning seasonal flowers and a large metal chandelier decorated with roses. The florists sell natural-looking, custom-made arrangements until the store's closing time, after which the café staff are able to provide pre-made bouquets. **TO**

Ganymed | French-style
brasserie food by the Spree River

Location Berlin **Signature dish** Chateaubriand | ❸❸

Ganymed Brasserie is a restaurant for all seasons. During the summer, when the city's trees are green and fully in leaf, the riverside terrace of this stately brasserie soothes diners with a view of the slowly flowing, somnolent Spree River. Across the river, on the other side of the bank, stands the Reichstag, at once a historic survivor and a statement of the new Germany. During the colder months, with the winds blasting through Berlin's wide streets like ethereal boy racers, it is time to retire inside, where the crisp white tablecloths and Art Nouveau mosaics and details evoke a touch of Parisian glamor.

The theme inspired by the City of Light is continued by the menu, which trills with the melodies of classic French cuisine. Here, a luscious Chateaubriand with mustard sauce, green beans, and gratin Dauphinois; there, fillet steaks with a pleasing yin and yang of meatiness and sweetness and served with homemade Béarnaise sauce or shallots braised in red wine. Those diners wanting fish and seafood dishes are also likely to be leaving in a happy mood. The prawns are juicy, the lobster is frank and fulsome in its assault on the taste buds, and who knows what the kitchen does to make the sea bream so succulent.

It may seem as though Ganymed has been hosting French fine dining for an extremely long time, but, until the end of World War I, it was a place frequented by workers from the shipyards. It was not until 1931 that it was established under its current name as a swanky place to eat good food. Come the end of the World War II, however, it had been blown to bits, just like most of central Berlin's old stagers. Adrift in the east, and with the Berliner Ensemble as a neighbor, it became a hangout for the likes of Bertolt Brecht and Kurt Weill. Yet, with the reunification of Berlin and refurbishment, it is anchored once more at the center of the city's gastronomic galaxy. **ATJ**

Rogacki | A slice of Berlin
history with standing room only

Location Berlin **Signature dish** Smoked fish | ❸

If you are looking for an authentic, unpretentious Berlin dining experience, look no further than Rogacki, an institution in Berlin's Charlottenburg district since 1928. Part market hall, part dining hall with stand-up tables, Rogacki started by smoking and selling fish. While home-smoked fish remains the core of its business, the offerings have expanded to include a dizzying, overwhelming array of food.

A cafeteria-style counter area serves traditional German-style meals, such as pork knuckle, various sausages, and four different kinds of potato salad. Two smaller counters offer more international-style gourmet dishes, as well as raw oysters or a plate laden with items from the market stalls. More types of fresh, smoked, pickled, and otherwise prepared fish are

> *"Workers are busy filleting herring, slicing cucumbers, shaving cabbage, and carving meat ..."*
> The New York Times

available than you may ever have imagined existed. There are also preserved meats, fresh meats (including venison and wild boar), poultry, cheeses, homemade salads, and baked goods.

Everything can be purchased to take home, but it is much more fun to eat there, standing at one of the tables, elbow to elbow with a cross-section of Berlin society. Dietmar Rogacki, grandson of the founders, says the standing tables are a holdover from the 1960s, when the food hall still lacked toilets and German law required establishments with a certain number of seats to have sanitary facilities. Walking into Rogacki, with its 1980s-style decor and signs, feels like walking back into the history of West Berlin. **TO**

Konnopke's Imbiss | Enjoy a Berlin snack and watch the world go by

Location Berlin   **Signature dish** Currywurst | $

*"The stand has survived…
Hitler's Third Reich and the
East German dictatorship."*

spiegel.de

⬆ Currywurst and fries: Berlin's great social leveler.

No visit to Berlin would be complete without sampling "Currywurst"—skinless, fried pork sausage sliced into pieces, then covered with ketchup and curry powder. There are as many opinions on where to get the best Currywurst as there are claims regarding who invented it. But the sausage stand known as Konnopke's Imbiss has them all beat in terms of location and historical tradition.

This Berlin institution started in 1930 when company founder Max Konnopke began selling various types of sausages on the street from a mobile stand. After World War II, Konnopke's moved to the permanent site that it still occupies, a traffic island in a busy intersection, below a subway line in the Prenzlauer Berg district. In 1960, this became the first sausage stand in East Berlin to offer Currywurst—a West Berlin invention—and it was hugely successful. It became an attraction for every visitor to East Berlin, with long lines of hungry customers waiting patiently at almost every hour of the day.

Konnopke's survived the upheaval of the fall of the Berlin Wall and German reunification with what current co-owner Dagmar Konnopke (Max's granddaughter) describes as a mixture of "reliability, tenacity, and tradition." They may have expanded the menu to include things like potato salad and crispy, paprika-flavored fries, and offered their curry powder in five different degrees of spiciness, but the focus has remained on what Konnopke's calls its "staple food": the Currywurst.

Dagmar Konnopke says that many of her regular customers feel that the atmosphere of the location adds to their enjoyment of their Currywurst: subway trains rumbling overhead, cars and bicycles whizzing past, pigeons milling around. Hers is a thoroughly democratic customer base: everyone is equal before their humble ketchup-covered sausage, whether tourist, construction worker, or bank employee. **TO**

Lutter & Wegner | A classic restaurant in central Berlin

Location Berlin **Signature dish** Wiener Schnitzel | $\textbf{\$}$$\textbf{\$}$

A triumvirate of solid pillars march across the middle of the main dining space, their top halves sporting colorful and expressive paintings that are supposed to represent wine, women, and song. That said, the ambience of Lutter & Wegner is more relaxed than such an observation would suggest. This is a place where the murmur of conversation is respected and not smothered by canned music, and where the subject under discussion is more than likely to be the Austro-German regional dishes being served.

Here, potato soup, a creamy and silky dish, is a popular starter, while the mains include such favorites as *Sauerbraten* (a German pot roast of long-marinated beef, traditionally served with red cabbage or potato dumplings) and Wiener Schnitzel, accompanied by a potato salad. The latter dish is reckoned by those who know about such things to be the best in Berlin; the Schnitzel is a substantial presence on the plate, with the veal tender and as light as air, juicy, and pliable on the palate, with a breadcrumb coating that provides a pleasing crunch. There are other equally excellent dishes on the menu, but it is the Wiener Schnitzel that keeps the gastronomic juices flowing. In between mouthfuls, diners can glance through the large restaurant windows at the grand edifices and human theater of the adjoining Gendarmenmarkt.

Lutter & Wegner has been the name of a Berlin establishment since 1811, when Christopher Lutter and August F. Wegner opened a wine tavern. The venue's reputation as a place to wine and dine grew throughout the nineteenth century (its selection of wines remains peerless to this day), and one story has it that the name "Sekt" for sparkling wine was coined here. The original Lutter & Wegner building was destroyed in World War II, but a new embodiment opened at the current address in the mid-1990s. It remains an essential destination for both hungry tourists and knowing Berliners. **ATJ**

"It seemed that every German within earshot … had ordered the exact same thing: the Schnitzel."

Stuart Emmrich, *The New York Times*

⬆ Wiener Schnitzel with a side dish of potato salad.

Coselpalais | Coffee and cake in an elegant Baroque setting

Location Dresden   **Signature dish** Boiled beef with horseradish sauce and potato dumplings | ❸❸

Baroque and roll: do as Dresdeners do and drop into the Grand Café Coselpalais for a coffee and slice of cake during the afternoon. The coffee is rich and fragrant, while just looking at the display of tarts (such as blueberry, black cherry, and apple) and strudels can add inches to the waist. Cream? *Natürlich*.

If the weather is benign, grab a table outside and gaze in admiration at the adjoining Frauenkirche Lutheran church, which dominates this part of Dresden. Or, inside, there are four main eating areas, all elegantly Baroque with glittering chandeliers, oil paintings on the walls, displays of Dresden porcelain, and gilded furnishings.

Yet there is more to the Coselpalais than coffee and cake. The menu might be called modern Central European. There are Saxony specialities, such as Dresden meatloaf, or boiled beef with horseradish sauce and potato dumplings; but, in a deliberate echo of how this once-isolated part of Germany has opened itself to the world, the menu also features such fusions as tuna carpaccio and duck breast with mango and cilantro sauce.

Naturally, given the Coselpalais's position, tourists make their way across the courtyard to the hotel rooms, but this is also a popular place for Dresdeners. Further attractions here include the wine list, which unusually features a selection of Saxony wines, and a store from which homemade Dresdener *Stollen* (fruit cake) can be sent directly to anyone in the world who appreciates coffee and cake.

The eighteenth-century palace itself was largely destroyed during an Allied bombing raid toward the end of World War II. Like the adjoining Frauenkirche, it was rebuilt after Germany was reunified. This miracle of resurrection can be contemplated while sampling an impressive Torte for your sweet tooth. **ATJ**

⬆ **The sumptuous, airy dining room at Coselpalais.**

Alte Meister | A creative menu in an artistic ambience

Location Dresden   **Signature dish** Free-range chicken breast with Gorgonzola-flavored spinach | ❸❸

High ceilings, walls in muted pastel colors, arched alcoves, plenty of light—both natural and artificial—and staff gliding rather than rushing about. As people sit down to eat in the calm and elegant surroundings of Alte Meister, they might think they were in a museum or gallery space. In fact, situated within Dresden's famous Baroque Zwinger Palace (all totally rebuilt after World War II), the Alte Meister restaurant adjoins its namesake picture gallery, with its paintings by the likes of Dürer, Holbein, Rubens, and Rembrandt.

Some might argue that this close proximity to the great masters of painting has rubbed off on the kitchen here. Dishes that combine fresh local ingredients with cuisines from around the world are as prettily presented as any of the pictures hanging in the neighborhood. White plates pulsate with bright, vivid greens, salmon pinks, pastel yellows, and dark brooding browns. A starter might be a dreamy swirl of cream-of-carrot soup dotted with braised rabbit liver;

a main dish could be a grilled fillet of sea bass alongside vegetables infused with coconut curry, or a juicy, free-range chicken breast partnered with a creamy yet earthy sauté of Gorgonzola-flavored spinach. The bright colors continue to bedazzle in desserts such as the umber-flecked crème brûlée.

This kind of artistry happens during the evening, but the Alte Meister also opens for lunch. At this time, the menu is more laid back, but the roast veal liver with melted onions has the capacity to melt lunchtime hearts, and the Parmesan risotto with fried mushrooms and morels is certain to send the once-hungry out into the afternoon well satisfied. Looking around the Zwinger and considering Alte Meister's place within it, you would think that it had been here forever—in fact, the restaurant only opened in 2001 but has become one of Dresden's top eateries. **ATJ**

⬆ Alfresco dining around a statue of Carl Maria von Weber.

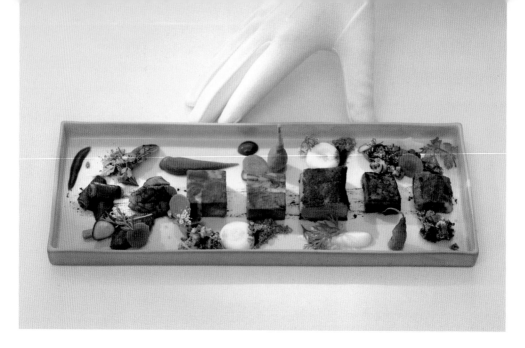

La Vie | Deconstructed dishes that look as good as they taste

Location Osnabrück **Signature dish** Saddle of venison with turnip, avocado, and grapefruit | ❸❸❸❸

It is an ideal name, la vie (the restaurant presents its name in lower case); after all, time passed in a restaurant of this caliber (it has three Michelin stars) may be regarded as time belonging to another, more glorious life, in a place far from mundane care. It is time spent with food that is dressed, designed, and delivered as though the kitchen staff had been trained at an academy of the fine arts.

The white plates bear bold strokes of color: pine-needle green, jet black, snow white, blood red, salmon pink, and sunset orange. In contrast, the decor comes from a calmer palette of muted cream and caramels, although in places the occasional modern canvas raises the volume. A picture starts to emerge of la vie. This is the home of dishes that have been deconstructed (also referred to as molecular gastronomy, a more fashionable term for the process).

Do try the saddle of venison with turnip, avocado, and grapefruit; or a bouillabaisse featuring calamari, gurnard, anchovies, saffron potatoes, and deep-fried noodles, all of which spent time in a bouillabaisse stock, and all of whose constituent parts are displayed on the plate like a minimalist artwork. Then there is a banana milkshake flavored with cilantro, kaffir lime, and caramelized chocolate. Equally serious are the wines that sleep the sleep of the just in the most ancient, 600-year-old part of the building.

The restaurant's building, right in the center of Osnabrück, was actually redesigned in a classical style 200 years ago. Head chef Thomas Bühner took over in 2006. It already had one Michelin star, and a second followed a year later. Bühner is passionate about the original, pure flavor of his ingredients, which accounts for the deconstructed nature of the dishes. The set menus include one at lunch and two in the evening, with the latter two offering a series of tasters. **ATJ**

⊤ **Lamb in different guises, artfully presented.**

Vendôme | Sophisticated dining based on impressive culinary technique

Location Bergisch Gladbach **Signature dish** Venison with pine-needle jelly and celery cream | ❸❸❸❸

Tucked away on one side of the stately hotel Schloss Bensberg near Bergisch Gladbach is Vendôme, a little restaurant with big ambition. Vendôme is the creation of chef Joachim Wissler, who moved here in 2001 after having earned two Michelin stars at Marcobrunn restaurant in Eltville in the Rheingau. In just five years, Wissler won Vendôme three Michelin stars.

The dining room at Schloss Bensberg is opulent, with the tables unusually large and generously spaced; the number of diners is restricted to fewer than thirty to ensure that the kitchen can provide superlative, precise attention to its customers. This is particularly important because the tasting menus are extremely elaborate, with as many as two dozen small but beautifully crafted dishes being served. Examples include Parmesan "coral," shaped like a coral reef, alongside goose-liver panna cotta, which has a silky texture and a deep liver flavor, and Parmesan candyfloss. This might be followed by a delicate

cuttlefish salad with candied peanuts, cucumber, roasted green onion, and miso cream. Although the cooking is rooted in modern French technique, there are nods to German cuisine in dishes such as the "Leipziger Allerlei," a hotchpotch of stone crayfish with crumbs of mustard-seed bread, morels, and a dazzlingly intense shellfish bouillon.

The technical skill of the kitchen is obvious in the "paper" of roast pork, a delicate, ultra-thin layer of meat that flakes apart when touched and yet melts in the mouth to leave a deep pork taste on the tongue. Vendôme produces some of the most elaborate food in the world, yet its complex dishes deliver a consistently superb dining experience. Gastronomic delights combined with flawless service and a classy wine list—Vendôme emerges as one of the top restaurants on the world dining scene. **AH**

⬆ Vendôme's signature dish of venison.

Villa Merton | Seasonal cuisine with an emphasis on foraging

Location Frankfurt **Signature dish** Venison with green elderberries | ❺❺❺❺

Villa Merton, the restaurant of Frankfurt's Union International Club in a building of the same name, typifies the growing gastronomic achievements of German chefs. Innovative chef Matthias Schmidt scours the neighboring hills, forests, and rivers for the ingredients that make up his handsome looking, multi-flavored dishes. There are foraged elements in the two tasting menus (one is called *Roh*, or "raw," and the other *Stoff, or* "stuff")—celery with an emulsion of currant bush; garlic mustard; salad juice; fir tips; beechnuts and buttermilk; apple with stinging nettle; oat flakes; blossom pollen; grapeseed oil; or green elderberries. Schmidt is equally zealous about seasonability and sustainability. The food is arranged creatively on the plate, and it might initially feel as though you are eating an artwork, but Schmidt's use of unusual items such as fir tips, dandelion buds, and lovage dismisses any suspicions of culinary pretension.

The restaurant is located in what is known as the diplomatic district of Frankfurt, and for many diners that means a cab ride from the city center. It occupies a mansion that was built by one Richard Merton in the 1920s; inside, tall French windows look out onto a green park and its venerable trees, while high ceilings, a warming, nostalgic, fall color scheme on the walls, crisp white tablecloths, and mirrors endow a trio of eating spaces with a comfortable sense of elegance and good taste. The food is complemented by a pulse-quickening selection of wines from the breadth of Europe, with offerings both from new vinous kids on the block and the more traditional winemakers. As befits such a restaurant, a table at Villa Merton does not come cheap, but, on the other hand, a dinner there is an experience that lingers long in the memory. **ATJ**

← Villa Merton, home of the eponymous restaurant.

Spezial-Keller | Robust dishes served with home-brewed beer

Location Bamberg **Signature dish** Smoked ham knuckle with sauerkraut | ❺❺

Cozy is the word for the Spezial-Keller: ash-colored wood paneling; ceramic mugs lining the walls; an old-fashioned, green-tiled oven squatting in the corner of one room; and, drifting through the air, sleepy, warm aromas of roast meat. Staff, carrying great plates of food and massive steins of home-brewed *Rauchbier* (smoked beer, a Bamberg speciality), dart between tables occupied by locals and well-informed tourists. Windows look out onto the red roofs and spires of the ancient city, and, come the summer, everyone takes to the beer garden.

The Loehr family has been in charge for several generations, but the cellar and associated brewery actually go back to the early 1500s. There is a certain

> *"Quite a hike out of town, but the superb* Rauchbier *served here is your reward, along with the views."*
>
> Lonely Planet

magic about a place like this where good food and drink have been dispensed for centuries.

The food is robust and brawny. A big favorite is the smoked ham knuckle: it has delicious crispy skin, beneath which the juicy, luscious meat falls off the bone with ease—regulars claim that this is the best in Bamberg. Heaps of sauerkraut, accompanied by firm yet pliable potato dumplings, keep the ham company. Other choices on the compact menu include roast duck, Viennese veal escalope, and homemade potato salad. Another tempting option is the traditional Bamberg brunch of *Weisswurst*—white sausages—for which a refreshing glass of home-brewed Weissbier is a necessary accompaniment. **ATJ**

Victor's | Exquisite dining inspired by Japanese and French cuisine

Location Perl-Nennig　**Signature dish** Shrimps with cucumber, yogurt, and lemon | ❸❸❸❸

A casino complex near Germany's border with Luxembourg is the unlikely home of Victor's Gourmet-Restaurant, one of Germany's top eateries. The restaurant, a short walk from the casino itself, is situated in the Schloss Berg, an attractive, historic building with a pretty courtyard. Head chef is Christian Bau, who gained a coveted third Michelin star for Victor's in 2006 and has maintained this level of cuisine ever since. So seriously does the chef take this achievement that he has had the three Michelin star symbols tattooed on his arm.

The dining room at Victor's is quiet and seats just a couple of dozen guests at large, generously spaced tables. Bau's cooking is rooted in French classical cuisine, but the influence of Japan also comes through in certain dishes. Ingredient quality is paramount, and only the very finest produce is used.

One old favorite is a little nibble of beef tartare with quail egg and Osetra caviar, a beautifully balanced creation. Another is Parmesan foam with duck liver; a remarkable depth of flavor is obtained from the liver, with the foam adding another dimension of relish to this sumptuous dish.

The Asian influence is evident in a toro tuna roll served with soy marshmallow and quinoa, and pickles, wasabi cream, and Japanese mayonnaise; the balance of Eastern spices is carefully orchestrated. The emphasis on top-quality ingredients may also be seen in the stunning Sisteron lamb from Provence, France, with the lamb belly and sweetbreads combined with mushrooms and a yam and black garlic crumble.

Victor's Gourmet-Restaurant presents some of the most exquisite foods to be found, not just in Germany, but in the whole of Europe. Whether or not you choose to saunter down to the casino for gambling, there is no risk involved in a meal at Victor's. **AH**

⊞　A delicate starter of scallop served at Victor's.

Amador | Edgy cooking on the edge of town

Location Mannheim   **Signature dish** Langoustine, radish, Lustenauer mustard, and leek | ❺❺❺❺❺

Don't allow yourself to be deterred if you seem to be approaching an industrial wasteland on the wrong side of town while trying to track down this most elusive of Michelin three-star restaurants. What has the appearance of a disused warehouse is, in fact, the exterior of one of Germany's foremost culinary powerhouses. Walk through the elegantly rusting metal doorway, and you will be introduced to a radically different state of affairs. Inside, you will find a gleaming, white, cathedral-like space, with each table placed on its own circular red rug. What seem to be groups of oversized air ducts jut out from the floor.

Restaurant Amador is the creation of chef Juan Amador, who was born in Germany to Spanish parents. One of his formative experiences was a visit to El Bulli, and it is easy to see parallels here with the cooking of Ferran Adrià. A plate of vinegar-flavored macaroons might be served with what initially appears to be a tube of toothpaste—it is, in fact, a tube of light cream cheese. It follows that the menus are given elliptical titles, such as "Snapshot" or "Retrospective," and the dishes are listed simply as a roll-call of their ingredients—John Dory/parsley/aioli/Iberico ham, for example. But the flavors are heavenly, bridging the gap between the robust and the delicate. The wine list, itself a talking point in its binding of ostrich leather, is drawn up by Master of Wine Michael Broadbent and unusually offers only wines from Germany and Spain.

It turns out that the restaurant's similarity to a modern art gallery space is not accidental. Two vast doors open to reveal an even larger space beyond the main dining room that is home to one of the largest private art collections in Germany, with vast canvasses and installations by Joseph Beuys and Anselm Kiefer. Amador is truly a feast for all the senses. **SFP**

⬆ The immaculate white interior features red highlights.

Leopold | Pfalz hospitality brought beautifully up to date

Location Deidesheim **Signature dish** Pfalz classics and new interpretations of old favorites | ❸❸❸

"This lovely vaulted restaurant is a long-standing favorite on Germany's southern wine route."

viamichelin.co.uk

⬆ Amuse-bouches from the Leopold kitchen.

Few evenings are better spent than on the courtyard terrace of Deidesheim's Restaurant Leopold. Sitting alongside the Jugendstil villa of the Weingut von Winning winery, Leopold strikes the perfect balance between modern German style and Pfalz joie de vivre.

Leopold is located just beyond the half-timbered heart of Deidesheim, one of Germany's most famous and picturesque wine villages. It was to Deidesheim that German ex-chancellor Helmut Kohl used to bring foreign dignitaries to charm them with *Pfälzer Saumagen*, the local speciality of stuffed pig's stomach. Dining around here can be hidebound or free-wheeling, but Leopold's modern, clean-cut style is refreshing, appealing, and successful.

Dining al fresco on the terrace cannot be beaten, but the restaurant's interior, in the tastefully renovated former stables of the estate, is equally comfortable, with vaulted ceilings lending a sense of space and lightness. Well-executed updates of traditional German favorites include *Tafelspitzsülze*, a set terrine of beef. Oxtail often features, and so does the obligatory Pfalz trinity of *Leberknödel*, *Bratwurst*, and *Saumagen*—liver dumplings, sausage, and pig's stomach. For the latter, marjoram-flavored pork and potato are simmered inside a pig's stomach, then sliced, fried, and served with sauerkraut and *Bratkartoffeln*, or crispy sautéed potatoes. Dry-aged steaks from Swabian bulls are a big draw, as is steak tartare. Modern inflections appear in Japanese-inspired fish dishes and Mediterranean-styled pasta and gnocchi interpretations.

Proximity to the winery means, of course, that the excellent local dry Rieslings feature heavily. Explore the superb selection of aged bottles from historic single sites like Ungeheuer or Pechstein, or try a pinot noir from the limestone soils of nearby Laumersheim. Von Winning's own multi-layered sauvignon blanc testifies that you are in one of Germany's best wineries. **AK**

Bratwurstherzle | Beechwood-grilled sausages in a Nuremberg institution

Location Nuremberg   **Signature dish** Original Bratwurst with sauerkraut and horseradish | ❸❸

As most people with more than a passing interest in food know, there is no such thing as an ordinary sausage in Germany. But while there are said to be hundreds of different sausage styles to be found around the country, at Bratwurstherzle, in the old center of Nuremberg, just one style is enough to bring in the crowds. This is the original Nuremberger Bratwurst, a juicy, subtly spicy, smaller-than-average sausage that is grilled over an open fire. The Bratwurst has Protected Geographical Indication status, which means that it has to be produced in and around Nuremberg to qualify for the name "Nuremberger."

In the slightly rustic, Gothic-lite confines of Bratwurstherzle—lots of wood, antlers, mullioned glass, and settlelike seating—the beechwood grill is kept going all day, and as a consequence the appetizing aroma of roast meat wafts about the rooms like a wraith. This might explain why, even though it sits in the middle of one of the more popular touristic parts of the city, it is a place where locals outnumber visitors—such is the pull of its luscious Bratwurst, made with premium local pork.

The sausages have always been placed on tin plates, usually in groups of six, eight, ten, or twelve, in the company of substantial and sustaining sour-sweet rounds of sauerkraut, creamy potato salad, and piled-up dollops of bracing horseradish sauce. In the colder months, the glow of the fire adds a sense of safety and security to the meal; come summer, customers carry their tin plates outside and combine their sausage scoffing with people watching.

The original Bratwurstherzle, built in the early sixteenth century, was destroyed during World War II bombing raids. As Germany rose from the ashes, so did Bratwurstherzle, reopening in its current location in 1954. It has been thriving ever since, a true beacon for those who love to snack on that far from ordinary sausage, the Nuremberger. **ATJ**

"The take-away variant is called … 'three in a roll'—a prime example of Franconian directness."

Jefferson Chase, news.de

⬆ Try a traditional Bratwurst straight from the grill.

Berg | Fresh ingredients and seasonal dishes

Location Stuttgart   **Signature dish** Venison with chestnut cream |

> *"We want to interest younger people in fine dining, in addition to our loyal guests."*

Philip Berg, owner of Restaurant Berg

⬆ An example of Berg's quirky food presentation.

Berg means "mountain" in German, and with a name like that prospective diners might expect to be eating in an Alpinelike ambience, complete with antlers on the wall and cowbells ringing in the background. Thankfully, that is not the case at this highly regarded Stuttgart restaurant, which is actually named after its owner, Philip Berg. Faux-Alpine knick-knacks are conspicuously absent from the simple, veering-toward-minimalist interior, where calm, tranquil white walls are offset by well-polished, chestnut-colored wood. This place of clean lines and understated modernity has its own quiet sense of style, and the outside terrace has an equally restful feel.

Up until 2011, Berg was known as the one-Michelin-starred Breitenbach, named for the then-owner and head chef, Benjamin Breitenbach. He moved on, but local foodies were soon reassured when his restaurant manager and sommelier Philip Berg took over the reins. The result has been a continuation of the line of happy diners traipsing in through the front door—even without the Michelin star, which Berg says he is not actively chasing.

If there is a philosophy here (and it seems that most haute-cuisine restaurants are obliged to have one in the modern era), it refers to the best use of fresh ingredients and their seasonal sourcing, as well as being creative and imaginative about the collaborations on the plate. So fried scallops stand sentinel over a scattering of pumpkin pieces; a rose-pink slice of venison lounges on a bed of chestnut cream; a compact chocolate tart is served hand in glove with a baked apple sorbet. The menu is small and changes regularly, and is all the better for it.

Given Philip Berg's earlier occupation as a sommelier, it is not surprising that the wine list is monstrously good. In conclusion, you can climb as many mountains as you like, but, when in Stuttgart, there is only one Berg worthy of your attention. **ATJ**

Wielandshöhe | Swabian cuisine with an international flavor

Location Stuttgart **Signature dish** Ox roulade with mustard sauce | ❺❺❺❺

Viewed from outside, there is really little about the Wielandshöhe to excite the imagination. It simply has the look of a modern hotel with its clean lines and fresh white paint, and it is almost anonymous in the way it sits on a steep street in the Degerloch area of Stuttgart (it is not easy to park, and customers are better taking a taxi). Once inside, however, an elegant ambience may be discerned: high windows let in light and provide stunning views of the city and surrounding countryside; starched white tablecloths and the glitter of well-polished cutlery add to the sense of occasion; and, most importantly, there is the susurration of appreciative diners as they eat. Meanwhile, Wielandshöhe's head chef and founder Vincent Klink is often seen moving among the tables to make sure that everyone is happy.

Klink turns out to be a bit of a gastronomic personality: a TV chef, a writer, and a great advocate of seasonal cooking, organic produce, and flavor—all of which are very important to his restaurant. For Klink, a meal has to taste good rather than look like something more at home in an art gallery or science laboratory. His menu, which changes monthly, is influenced both by regional Swabian cuisine and cuisines from further afield.

Starters might include a snow-pea and shrimp soup, a Hokkaido pumpkin soup with pumpkin-seed oil, or minestrone with basil and olives. Mains could feature trout caught in a river of the Black Forest, or game brought in by hunters from outside the city boundary (one example is venison, which is baked in herbs). Other meats are sourced locally, with roulade of ox served in mustard sauce being a favorite. However, Klink would never refuse fish caught in the Atlantic, or meats from outside the state; for him, it is all about quality and taste. Wielandshöhe is a place where robust cuisine and ethical sourcing come together to form a single, unified whole. **ATJ**

"Vincent Klink is the Emeril Lagasse of Swabia. Local gourmets love their TV chef…"

worldguide.eu

⬆ Swabian fare with a creative touch.

Röttele's | Elegant and innovative dining in a Renaissance château

Location Baden-Baden **Signature dish** Quail, artichoke salad, cep *empanada*, and elderberries | 🆂🆂🆂🆂

Röttele's Restaurant, set in the impressive Schloss Neuweier, is located on the edge of the Riesling vineyards of Neuweier village in Baden-Baden. Schloss Neuweier belongs to the eponymous neighboring winery that cultivates, among others, this historic single site, known as Mauerberg. The winery's tasting room is on the same courtyard as the restaurant, and you should not miss the opportunity of a tasting. The traditional-method sparkling Riesling is a perfect aperitif for chef Armin Röttele's international cuisine.

Röttele cooked in numerous fine-dining restaurants across Europe before settling back home in the Black Forest. He combines French, Mediterranean, and Asian influences to intriguing effect. You may find quail with an artichoke salad, cep *empanada*, and elderberries; curried tuna with lemon grass and baked king prawns; or a cocktail of lobster, octopus, and veal sweetbreads with wild mushrooms and parsnip. A perceived prevalence of lobster and foie gras may be attributed to the international jet set that frequents the spas and casinos of Baden-Baden.

Experimental compositions may have earned the internationally trained chef his Michelin star, but the simplicity of Röttele's whole baked market-fresh fish, carved at the table and served over two courses, first with an olive-and-potato puree and vegetables, then with chanterelle risotto and cream of langoustines, is an equal winner. The wide selection of European cheeses deserves a mention, as do the inventive desserts and the attentive but unobtrusive service.

The wine list naturally features Schloss Neuweier's own wines, but not exclusively: the choice is as international as the cuisine. Post-dinner, the bar in the vaulted cellar is the perfect place for a digestif. Here the cuisine may be modern but the period surroundings add to the ambience and deserve savoring. **AK**

Zum Alde Gott | A rural retreat majoring in local produce

Location Baden-Baden **Signature dish** Pheasant with kale puree | 🆂🆂

Sometimes it is not very difficult for a restaurant to get it right. At Zum Alde Gott, the food is served in a compact dining room with twelve tables (there is also a summer terrace); the ambience is upmarket, punctuated by the clink of glasses being refilled with the locally produced Riesling. The satisfaction of the diners is easy to see, and chef and owner Wilfried Serr, who has been here for more than three decades, certainly likes to make people happy.

From the outside, Zum Alde Gott has the look of an alpine chalet with its snow-unfriendly steep roof; this is wine country and vineyards lead off in all directions. It is cozy inside, with comfortable, cushioned chairs, subtle artistic touches on the walls,

> *"Wilfried Serr … mixes his palette of flavors with astounding skill and imagination."*
>
> Frommer's Germany

and sunflowers on the tables in the summer. The smiles on the faces of diners only broaden when Serr and his team produce their appetizing dishes.

This is rural Germany, just south of Baden-Baden, and we are in the village of Neuweier. The regional cuisine is not ignored, but France is not far away and the menu is open to other influences. Pheasant (local game is plentiful) with kale puree and chestnuts is a warming dish for the cold months; the trout caught in the rivers of the nearby Black Forest are plump and juicy; then there is the lobster lasagna, homemade foie gras, and rabbit stuffed with snails. As you would expect, given the proliferation of vineyards, the drinks list features many locally produced wines. **ATJ**

Bareiss | Impeccable food at the center of German haute cuisine in an idyllic Black Forest village

Location Baiersbronn **Signature dish** Wild duck glazed and served with chestnut sauce and mushroom dumpling, with confit of duck on a bed of diced vegetables | ❸❸❸❸

The little Black Forest village of Baiersbronn is an exquisite spot, with the pretty Murg River meandering through the scenery and forest pines and firs scenting the air. Baiersbronn is also home to the Hotel Bareiss, an attractive establishment that boasts a very fine restaurant. Chef Claus-Peter Lumpp, having initially trained at Bareiss, worked at restaurants around Europe before returning to take over its kitchen in 1992. Under his guidance, the reputation of the kitchen has grown in stature, culminating in a third Michelin star being awarded in 2007. The dining room is cozy and looks out over the nearby conifers.

The cooking style is French, but there are influences from elsewhere. This variety can be seen in a dish of tuna prepared in three ways: a cube of tuna with a red pepper jus; tartare of tuna with wasabi cream; and tuna loin marinated with spices. Modern touches are evident in a terrine of silky foie gras served with frozen "air" of liver and port wine jelly, sweet-corn mousse, and a goose-liver foam with toasted brioche; here, the balance of the richness of the foie gras with the sweet corn is very skillful.

The impeccable sourcing of ingredients is demonstrated in a dish of poached langoustines, served with a ratatouille of diced vegetables and resting in an octopus sauce, with a little potato disk under each langoustine; the crustaceans have a superb flavor. A main course might be wild duck glazed and served with a chestnut sauce and a mushroom dumpling, along with an intense confit of duck on a bed of diced vegetables.

Bareiss combines top-class cooking with one of the prettiest locations for a restaurant to be found anywhere. Service is impeccable, and even the wine markups are sympathetic. Without doubt, this is a special restaurant in a gorgeous location. **AH**

"As someone who had gone through the 'Bareiss mill,' it was a great challenge for me to take over."

Claus-Peter Lumpp, chef at Bareiss

⤴ The appealingly cozy dining room at Bareiss.

Schwarzwaldstube | Gastronomic adventures in the Black Forest

Location Baiersbronn-Tonbach **Signature dish** Pancetta-coated fillet of venison | ❺❺❺❺❺

"You fight all year [for a Michelin star] like a man possessed and never know for sure if it works."

Harald Wohlfahrt, chef at Schwarzwaldstube

⬆ Michelin three-star chef Harald Wohlfahrt puts the finishing touches to an experimental dish.

➡ Smoked char with char caviar and wild herbs.

Standards are high at Schwarzwaldstube, one of four restaurants on-site at the Black Forest hotel of Traube Tonbach, which was founded by the Finkbeiner family at the end of the eighteenth century (they remain at the helm). In the elegant and luxurious confines of Schwarzwaldstube's dining area, there is a similar sense of continuity (though spanning rather fewer years) because head chef Harald Wohlfahrt has managed to keep hold of three Michelin stars since 1992, a gastronomic feat that has led to his recognition as perhaps Germany's best chef.

The style of food may be described as classic French cuisine shaking hands with regional Black Forest produce, with the addition of a modern German cuisine that is adventurous but does not reject tradition; there are also hints of Asian fusion. This is confident cuisine: the tasting menu can include eclectic treats such as frogs' legs in tempura; fried duck liver with kumquat compote; gently smoked red mullet with imperial caviar crème fraîche; and puff pastry filled with guinea-fowl mousse.

Choices on the set menu might include succulent, well-aged beef glistening with a rose-colored sheen, or crispy pancetta coating a fillet of venison, served with a piquant star-anise sauce. But demonstrating how German cooking no longer conforms to the old cliché of meat and yet more meat, the restaurant also has a good selection of vegetarian dishes imaginative enough to tempt the most red-blooded of carnivores—how about fried forest-mushroom risotto with parsley sauce, or ravioli stuffed with artichoke puree and white truffles from Alba?

There is a superb wine list compiled by the hotel's award-winning sommelier, Stéphane Gass, who is passionate about discovering and promoting local winemakers. With all this food and wine to celebrate, is it any wonder that the Schwarzwaldstube has maintained its place among the stars? **ATJ**

Zum Franziskaner |
Robust Bavarian cuisine

Location Munich **Signature dish** Crispy grilled duck with red cabbage, apple, and potato dumplings | ❸❸

There is a lot to take in at the beer-hall restaurant Zum Franziskaner, close to Max-Joseph-Platz in the center of Munich. It engages all the senses—a glass of beer on the table, glinting in the light, snowy foam atop; warming roasting aromas drifting out of the kitchen; the appreciative murmurs of the diners mingling with the scrape of cutlery on broad-brimmed plates.

Even though wine is available, this is Munich and beer is the favored accompaniment to most of the dishes. Franziskaner's sprightly *Weissbier* (white beer, made using malted wheat rather than barley) enjoys center stage alongside plates heaped with chunky cuts of pork hock, halves of crispy roast chicken, generous helpings of juicy, salty sauerkraut, and the lustrous *Weisswürste* (white sausages filled with veal, onion, and parsley, typically served with sweet mustard and fresh pretzels). The *Weisswürste* are considered the best in town and are very popular for a mid-morning snack with a glass of *Weissbier*. Exceptionally hungry menu browsers might consider ordering the dish called *Schmankerlpfand'l*, which roughly translates as "the delicacy of the house," a helping of suckling pig, duck, pork hock, and rib steak sausages, accompanied by potato dumplings, red cabbage, sauerkraut, and brown sauce.

Zum Franziskaner has existed for a couple of centuries, and the decor of its rooms is a mixture of muted colors, dark wood paneling, framed photographs of yesteryear, and displays of plates and jugs, all contributing to the homely atmosphere that Bavarians seem to like so much. This is a place where both tourists and Munich citizens come to be refreshed and revived. The music of a traditional Bavarian band is regularly to be heard playing in the background, and sometimes diners get up to dance, perhaps hoping to work off their massive meal. **ATJ**

Boettner's |
Munich beacon of civilized gastronomy

Location Munich **Signature dish** Pike dumplings with spinach and lobster gratin | ❸❸❸

Boettner's opened in 1901 during the time of Kaiser Wilhelm and the so-called Belle Époque. A tumultuous century later, Boettner's remains a beacon of French-influenced Bavarian cuisine. Current chef and owner Frank Hartung is the fourth generation of his family to be in charge since Alfred Hugo Boettner opened the doors.

In the 1990s, Boettner's moved to its present home in a Renaissance-era building in the center of Munich. The decor has an old-fashioned, traditional feel, with pride of place given to the original solemn dark wood fittings. Tables are draped in starched white cloths, upon which folded napkins stand like sentries. The friendly waiting staff dismiss any

> *"Traditional dishes are prepared in classical style ... there is a great wine list and a lovely garden."*
>
> travel.yahoo.com

suspicion of fussiness, however, and such is the quality of the food that the clientele are all smiles.

What might they be enjoying? Perhaps the veal steak with truffle sauce, pike dumplings with spinach and lobster gratin, or that classic of French cuisine, lobster Thermidor. Freshness and seasonality are prized, and the fall menu is sprinkled with mushroom and porcini dishes. The dessert list features sweet and rich dishes like chocolate mousse or hazelnut nougat parfait. There is also the "action menu," five courses paired with five different wines for a reasonable price. Sample dishes include truffled duck breast, fried red mullet, a shellfish mousse with avocado cream, and poached plums with a poppy seed parfait. **ATJ**

Dallmayr | Classic modern cuisine in a Michelin-starred Munich institution

Location Munich **Signature dish** Saddle of fawn with red curry blood sausage and quince | ❺❺❺❺

Dallmayr is both an occasion and an institution. A delicatessen was established on its site in the early years of the eighteenth century. A century after that, in 1870, Alois Dallmayr was the new owner, and even though he sold it in 1895, it is his name that has remained. The original building was destroyed during World War II, but restored in 1950. The restaurant, situated on the first floor, is more recent.

On the ground floor, the Dallmayr delicatessen resembles great emporia like Fortnum & Mason in London or Gastronome No 1 at Moscow's GUM. All manner of caviars, cheeses, chocolates, meats, wines, and spirits call out to the browsing customers, notably at the indoor fountain with its live crayfish. Upstairs, the Michelin-starred Restaurant Dallmayr maintains similarly high standards, with creative chef Diethard Urbansky leading the kitchen brigade to great acclaim.

The restaurant's ambience is set by crisp white tablecloths, comfortable chairs, formal but friendly staff, hand-painted porcelain plates, and hand-blown wine glasses. The menu shares that attention to detail and sense of elegance. A flurry of amuse-bouches veer toward the molecular (wild salmon with brown-bread cream; horseradish and wheatgrass or deer liver with cocoa), while the main dishes are a combination of classic and modern: saddle of venison with red curry blood sausage and quince or beef, goose liver, tarragon, and pineapple.

This is French classicism with a modern makeover. The restaurant is also home to an astutely considered list of 600 wines, chosen by sommelier Julien Morlat, to accompany the dishes. Above the circulating delicatessen clientele, Dallmayr's diners come and go, wowed by the culinary designs of Urbansky and his dedicated team. **ATJ**

"Dallmayr is quite simply the best delicatessen in Munich! Urbansky's classic modern cuisine is artful …"

Michelin Guide

⊼ A pretty dessert of rhubarb and coconut ice cream.

Tantris | A German haute-cuisine landmark with dramatic decor and fine wines

Location Munich   **Signature dish** Turbot with aubergine puree and olive jus |

ⓈⓈⓈⓈ

> "Tantris serves Munich's finest cuisine … the cooking is subtle and original."

frommers.com

⊡ The dining room is furnished in red and black.

Restaurant Tantris in Munich has become a key part of German culinary heritage. It opened in 1971, and has employed some of Germany's most talented chefs, including Eckart Witzigmann and Heinz Winkler, who both went on to found Michelin three-star restaurants of their own. Since 1991, the kitchen had been in the capable hands of Hans Haas, who has earned two Michelin stars for the restaurant.

The modern dining room, by architect Justus Dahinden, is quite striking, with plenty of space and a bold use of red and black. The lengthy wine list includes some very fine German wines as well as a good range of French classics, all priced relatively modestly. The service is very professional, efficient, and eager to make your visit a memorable one.

The cooking style relies on top-quality ingredients and avoids over-complication. There is, for example, a starter consisting of a little filo pastry cornet of marinated salmon with a hint of dill; the effect is dazzlingly fresh, with the acidity of the marinade balancing the salmon beautifully. Tantris's attention to ingredients is also shown in a starter of scallops with mango and avocado; the scallops are lightly seared and retain their natural sweetness, the Thai mango is of the highest quality, and a citrus dressing acts as a foil to the sweetness of the scallops. The superb kitchen technique is illustrated by the delicate texture of the ravioli used in a dish of quail egg and peas, accompanied by baby morels. A meal might finish with a refreshing dish of biscuit tuiles stuffed with mango mousse and passion-fruit sorbet.

Tantris is without doubt the finest restaurant in Munich, as it has been for decades, acting as a culinary beacon that draws diners from far and wide. Few restaurants may be said to have maintained such a high standard for such a long period of time. **AH**

Schwarzer Adler |

Unmissable gastronomic institution

Location Kaiserstuhl **Signature dish** Tournedos Rossini | ❸❸❸❸

Records show that there has been a *Gaststube* (inn) here at the Schwarzer Adler for centuries. Run for generations by the visionary Keller family, who always kept the inn alongside their winery, this was one of the first Baden restaurants to garner a Michelin star, which it has held without interruption since 1969.

The cuisine is resolutely traditional French, but favors local ingredients. And what could seem like a throwback to another era works perfectly in practice: Tournedos Rossini made with local Kaiserstuhl veal and black Périgord truffles is as much a highlight as truffled chicken in a salt crust, or—as all the menus also give the French in acknowledgement of border-crossing gourmets from nearby Alsace and Switzerland—*Turbot de l'Atlantique poêlé à la Bordelaise*.

Local asparagus, fresh crayfish, and game are used when in season. But even more famous than the food is the exceptionally well-stocked cellar of mature Bordeaux and Burgundy wines. That they represent excellent value is due to the Schwarzer Adler being not only a working winery famous for its Grau- and Spätburgunder—pinot gris and pinot noir, respectively—but also one of Germany's foremost wine merchants, with longstanding ties to the best wineries in France and Italy. Rare vintages are a speciality, as are large-format bottles, all aged in the specially dug mountain cellar. The restaurant, the wine list, and the wonderful young sommelière, Melanie Wagner, have all won innumerable accolades.

The Schwarzer Adler is a must-visit institution, and just across the street is Winzerhaus Rebstock, a beautifully restored barn in which Schwarzer Adler staff execute almost-forgotten Baden specialities with no less care than is lavished on the Michelin-starred food of the main restaurant. Try *Eingemachtes Kalbfleisch* (veal ragout) or braised hare. **AK**

Zehner's Stube |

A Black Forest star

Location Pfaffenweiler **Signature dish** Atlantic turbot with lobster foam | ❸❸❸❸

The Zehner in question is chef Fritz Zehner, who set up his eponymous *Stube* (which roughly translates as "room") in the Black Forest village of Pfaffenweiler in 1988. He had already gained a Michelin star, which soon followed him to his new place, a fifteenth-century house with crow-stepped gables. The star has remained in place, and visitors to Zehner's Stube can see why. Black Forest food has been dogged by unfavorable preconceptions of stodginess (especially the sticky, creamy gâteau, good as it tastes), but the dishes at Zehner's Stube are in a different class, a fresh, brightly expressed cross-cultural sine wave of flavors.

The vaulted dining room has a calm and collected air with its cool marble floor, pale, almost flowery

---

"Zehner describes his cooking as 'ohne Schickimicki'— *without messing about."*

Condé Nast Traveller

---

curtains, and murmur of appreciative diners. Dinner might start with a dreamy, salty-sweet foie gras terrine, matched with fragrant and lightly acidic quince jelly; or maybe some Falstaffian-sized scallops resting on a bed of tart, tangy celery puree, with a brush of mild yet still exhilarating Thai curry sauce.

The mains are a further demonstration of the balance between tradition and the modern. Delicate Atlantic turbot is contrasted by lobster foam, while saddle of venison is offset by morels and savoy cabbage. Something to drink? The restaurant is a great champion of exemplary wines from the Baden region. Desserts include chocolate soufflé and yogurt ice or elderflower sabayon on apricots. **ATJ**

Romantik Hotel Spielweg | Baden cuisine at the highest level

Location Münstertal **Signature dish** Consommé of local red deer with juniper dumplings and cep ravioli | $$$

No other place encapsulates Black Forest hospitality like Spielweg: this old *Gaststube* (inn) still retains an original tiled oven and wood-paneled walls, with the handwritten menus offering seasonal Baden cuisine. The origins of this historic inn are humble, but the Fuchs family have succeeded in creating a dining experience at the highest level without sacrificing a jot of authenticity. That is a rare feat, and diners are attracted from far and wide.

Münstertal, a quiet valley still dominated by farming and forestry, provides an idyllic backdrop. Local specialties like Black Forest trout and fir-smoked ham are almost always on the menu, but chef and owner Karl-Josef Fuchs is best known for the game. An avid hunter and expert venison cook himself, he has authored a book on the subject. Thus, you can have a Wiener Schnitzel of wild boar, or refined variations on the venison theme, such as a consommé of the local red deer with juniper dumplings and cep ravioli.

The restaurant boasts its own cheese dairy where Fuchs makes and ages soft and hard cheeses from the milk of the local Hinterwälder cows. This old Black Forest breed also finds its way onto the meat menu, as carpaccio, veal terrine, or steak. Charcuterie is another speciality; do not miss the *Blutwurst* (savory black pudding), which is often served with veal sweetbreads as a starter. Nor should you leave without trying the Black Forest gâteau, with a liberal dash of cherry eau de vie. A well-chosen wine list, majoring on the best Baden wines, especially the local Spätburgunder, or pinot noir, completes the experience.

Hands-on cookery workshops in butchery, sausage making, venison barbecuing, and Christmas bakery, as well as themed weekends: nose-to-tail eating of pork is celebrated in spring, while fall weekends are dedicated to duck dishes. **AK**

[↑] Romantik Hotel Spielweg pays great attention to detail.

Residenz Heinz Winkler | Bavarian center of culinary delight

Location Aschau im Chiemgau   **Signature dish** Lobster carpaccio with lemon verveine | ❺❺❺❺

Few chefs ever gain the elusive third Michelin star, but, in 1981, Heinz Winkler achieved this in style. At the age of just thirty-two, he was the youngest chef ever to be awarded this accolade (although this has since been bettered by Massimiliano Alajmo of Le Calandre). Born in the Tyrol, Winkler had trained at Paul Bocuse and then worked at Restaurant Tantris in Munich under the legendary Eckart Witzigmann, himself the third-ever non-French chef to earn three Michelin stars. Despite his Italian roots, Winkler's cooking style is rooted firmly in classical French cuisine. Having gained three stars as head chef of Tantris, he left to open his own establishment in 1991.

Residenz Heinz Winkler is located in the Bavarian countryside between Salzburg and Munich. Its bright yellow walls contain an attractive courtyard garden, and it is possible to stay overnight here after enjoying some dazzling cooking. Chef Winkler's cooking is known for its light touch, as shown by little nibbles—

a stunning yellow-pepper mousse, marinated salmon laced with ginger, and diced vegetables infused with a hint of spice and encased in pastry. You might continue with scallops wrapped in lasagne, or a whole sea bass cooked in a salt shell and served with a cream and chive sauce.

Meat lovers will appreciate the whole duckling, cooked perfectly, filleted at the table, and served with a finely judged balsamic dressing that balances the richness of the duck beautifully. A meal might finish with "tears" of chocolate, fried fondant spheres served in a biscuit case with a coconut ice cream.

Residenz Heinz Winkler's combination of an attractive country setting, attentive service, and technically superb cooking has made it a culinary destination for epicures across Europe and beyond. A visit is an unforgettable experience. **ATJ**

⬆ Assorted nibbles are served before the main meal.

A L'Huîtrière | Long-standing Lille landmark of seafood cuisine

Location Lille **Signature dish** Roast turbot with Burgundy snails and apples | ❺❺❺❺

> *"This sophisticated restaurant is well known for its fabulous seafood and wine cellar."*

Lonely Planet

Take a walk through the old streets of Lille and you'll find A L'Huîtrière, the city's famous Michelin-starred seafood restaurant. Stop and look before going in. The frontage is art deco and the restaurant is a survivor of the two world wars that passed this way (it opened in 1907); also, the colorful strip of ceramic tiles depicting fishes in the water is apparently unchanged since it was installed in 1940. Time to eat. Inside, there's a timelessness and sense of elegance about the dining room, with smart French Imperial chairs, crisp white tablecloths, glittering crystal chandeliers, and caramel-blonde wooden paneling.

Those nervous that this kind of smartness may encourage a hushed preciousness will be comforted by the fact that, to reach the restaurant, you have to pass through the more boisterous front, where all manner of fish and seafood are on display and for sale, and there is also a lively bar. This yin-and-yang contrast between the two spaces certainly helps to ground any attempts at pretension.

A L'Huîtrière translates as "the oyster shop," and while these beautiful bivalves are much in evidence on the menu, the seafood dishes also sparkle on the palate. You can try a fresh-tasting Saint-Jacques tartare with sesame and beet, or a Saint-Jacques hamburger with foie gras and horseradish cream (the scallop tartare is also served with Périgord black truffle). Then there is bouillabaisse, meaty and sturdy, fried blue lobster with tarragon, and a robust roast turbot accompanied by Burgundy snails and apple.

All is fresh and fragrant, precisely cooked and delicately flavored, luscious dishes that have some regulars claiming A L'Huîtrière is the best seafood restaurant in the world. Amid this piscatorial paradise, meat eaters are not forgotten, with beef Rossini and noisettes of venison and roasted pigeon breast on the menu. However, for the true devotee of A L'Huîtrière, it's life on the ocean wave every time. **ATJ**

⬆ A distinctive landmark, A L'Huîtrière is not only a restaurant, but a specialist delicatessen.

La Grenouillère | Daringly modernist culinary fireworks

Location Montreuil sur Mer   **Signature dish** Lobster barely smoked over juniper branches | ❻❻❻❻

The building of La Grenouillère simply takes your breath away. Designed by renowned theater designer Patrick Bouchain, this astonishing extension to the modest, family-run, Picardy-timbered farmhouse next to the river seemingly brings the outside in, with walls resembling wavering tree branches. The dining room is dominated by an extraordinary central clockwork fireplace housing a single flame, and by masses of tiny LED lights hung from steel rafters.

In this striking setting, Alexandre Gauthier's cooking also pushes boundaries. The food has an edgy use of flavor, texture, and color, with much emphasis on mixing raw with molten sauces and liberal use of wild herbs—all accentuating the sense of bringing the landscape into the room. A succession of small, breathtakingly beautiful plates may include raw monkfish wrapped in shavings of asparagus, buttery John Dory with lightly smoked spinach and wild herbs adding a slightly bitter balance, and gossamer-thin parsley raviolo with a molten egg yolk. Harking back to simpler times, there are frogs' legs sauteed in butter and lemon, a token reminder of the cooking of Alex's father, Roland.

The produce is exceptional, exemplified in dishes such as Boulogne lamb served with potato puree, ash-dusted mushrooms, and spring truffles. There are surprises, too, one involving nettles and honey—but it would be a shame to reveal this. Desserts also thrill with their inventiveness—look out especially for the towering concoction of meringue resting on sea buckthorn mousse, accompanied by wild marjoram and tart sea buckthorn puree.

Eating here is an occasion that is full of delights, and unexpected flavors and pairings. Some may find the cooking challenging, yet it is always exhilarating and refreshing and captures the precise essence of its exemplary ingredients—very much the future of modernist French gastronomy. **SP**

> *"The dining room is as right-now as the cooking. It's all glass and wood and rusted metal…."*

John Lanchester, *Guardian*

⤒ A creation from Alexandre Gauthier for La Grenouillère: bread made with hemp flour.

Restaurant Gill | An atmospheric, gastronomic haven in historic Rouen

Location Rouen **Signature dish** Pigeon roasted *à la Rouennaise* | ❸❸❸

> *"The minimalist decor . . . is an appropriate backdrop for the sophisticated cuisine."*

frommers.com

⬆ Roast pigeon is the speciality of Restaurant Gill.

If Rouen, with its wonderful medieval houses in streets that are centuries old, is one of northern France's cultural gems, then Restaurant Gill is its culinary diamond. This acclaimed restaurant is a tiny gastronomic haven. What is more, it is just a short stroll from Rouen Cathedral, famously depicted by Impressionist painter Claude Monet, and the Place du Vieux Marché, where French martyr Joan of Arc was burned at the stake in 1431.

Gilles and Sylvie Tournadre created Restaurant Gill, in a building that they say resembles a safe, on the right bank of the River Seine, and they have been thrilling the Rouennais—Rouen's denizens—with their excellent menus for decades now. This is a small restaurant, with a honey and dark caramel-hued decor, sparkling glassware for fine wine, crisp white linens, soft lighting, and white orchids on the tables—all this gives it a supreme feel of intimacy.

Chef Gilles's cooking bears the hallmarks of a cook who is trained in the French classics, while also being thoroughly contemporary, innovative, and exciting. He loves technology almost as much as food, and his kitchen is cutting-edge. Gilles likes to keep things simple, allowing natural flavors and textures to shine. Typically, his menu will feature warm oysters with a subtle spicy dressing, or traditional hare terrine with foie gras medallions as an appetizer, these guaranteed to set the scene for the good food to follow.

The restaurant's speciality dish is pigeon roasted *à la Rouennaise* with seared foie gras. This might tempt as a main course, or perhaps instead try a fillet of John Dory cooked Meunière-style, with cabbage in a creamy smoked haddock sauce, or maybe a slow-cooked saddle of lamb with fricassée vegetables, chickpea mouse, and a medley of lemon and dates. Desserts are ingenious and delicious, and include one of Gilles's favorites, his traditional soufflé with Père Toutain Calvados and an apple mousse. **CFr**

Sa Qua Na | The Zen of seafood in Normandy

Location Honfleur   **Signature dish** Poached lobster with lime and coconut broth | $$$$

In the small, picturesque port of Honfleur, it is a pleasure to find a seafood restaurant with this level of creativity and flair. The unusual and wittily punning name is derived from *saveur* (flavor), *qualité* (quality), and *na* (short for nature), and sounds the same as *sakana*, which is Japanese for fish. The name is a clue to chef Alexandre Bourdas' culinary experience—he worked for the renowned Michel Bras, not only in France but also in Toya in northern Japan. While the decor in this intimate restaurant is serene and minimalistic, diners here enjoy accomplished cooking in the form of two tasting menus, characterized by surprising combinations of flavors and techniques.

Bourdas has drawn on his time in Japan to create an innovative menu, drawing on classic French cooking methods, while using a flavor palette with noticeable Eastern influences. Flavorings are used to enhance carefully sourced local ingredients, such as fish and seafood. Poached monkfish, for example, might be served surrounded by a pool of a delicately aromatic coconut broth, flavored with cilantro, lovage, and lemongrass. Excellent local, carefully roasted, free-range chicken is partnered with Tarbais beans, cabbage shoots, and kaffir lime leaves with a spicy jus. Dourade is enlivened by yuzu, and beef is made fragrant by green cardamom—the menu, changing daily, offers a series of cleverly executed, well-judged and sophisticated dishes that tantalize and intrigue. There is a notable purity of flavor to Boudas' cooking. An intelligently chosen wine list and the hospitable and warm service add to the charm.

The desserts don't disappoint, either. Bourdas' experience as a pastry chef ensures a high standard of technique while, again, his imagination shines through. Creations such as marshmallow, mandarin sorbet, cream, and matcha are delectable delights to savor. Undoubtedly, this Normandy restaurant is one of France's most exciting culinary destinations. **AH**

"Surprising combinations attest to Bourdas' far-flung influences … bien sûr, reserve well in advance."

fodors.com

⬆ Sublime seafood and minimal decor at Sa Qua Na.

La Rapière

Tiny historic Normandy eatery

Location Bayeux   **Signature dish** French beef fillet, *Périgueux* sauce with truffle | ❸❸❸

If you like your restaurants cozy and packed with history, then La Rapière won't disappoint—this tiny Bayeux venue has more than 500 years under its belt, having been around from before the time of King Louis XIII. Housed in one of the quaintest alleys, it is lined by soft, creamy stone houses.

Inside, you'll find warm caramel-hued walls, gorgeous stone feature walls, a fireplace, and carved oak timbers, bathed in candlelight after sunset. It's a fitting backdrop for the antique-style chairs and wooden tables attired with crisp white linen.

There are two small dining areas that reverberate with the reassuring hum of appreciative diners. Hosts Simon and Linda Boudet have created a venue where

---

"In a late-1400s mansion … this atmospheric restaurant specializes in Normandy staples."

Lonely Planet

---

the flavors and textures of meat, fish, and other local produce unite in harmony, with dishes presented with great flair. Linda's attentive team and her knowledge of wine add to the package—no surprise, then, that tables are booked well in advance.

Chef Simon Boudet's menu excels in French gastronomy. Start with a cocktail of half-cooked duck foie gras from southwest France partnered with homemade raison and nut bread and apple and red onion chutney, then proceed to roasted guinea fowl in wine or king scallops served in a cast-iron pot. Desserts to round things off might include a mousse of toffee, honey, and chocolate or a vanilla cheesecake served warm with a salted-butter toffee ice cream. **CFr**

Le Parc Brasserie

Haute Champagne-Ardennes cuisine

Location Reims   **Signature dish** Haddock with creamed chicken, truffles, and pear | ❸❸❸❸

Le Parc Brasserie is housed in a splendid nineteenth-century château that is set in acres of rich countryside in the Champagne-Ardennes region of France. A beautiful space of cream and caramel hues, tapestries, tables dressed in fine white linen, chandeliers, and vast flower displays, it lives up to its surroundings in elegant style.

Guests enjoy panoramic views of the château's grounds from the restaurant's almost floor-to-ceiling windows, each of them lavishly dressed. The extravagant setting befits the menu of fine food and wine, impeccably served by courteous waiters.

Chef Phillipe Mille, a Michelin-starred chef who grew up on a farm not far from Le Parc, and developed his overwhelming passion for fine and wholesome food at a very young age, offers exquisite menus championing classic French haute cuisine.

Along with Mille's à la carte menu, luxurious specialities can be found on the Tradition et Gourmandise collection of Ardennes delicacies as well as the white truffle menu. Mille describes his cuisine as "gourmandize"—meaning to eat and enjoy—with the emphasis on flavor and fine seasonal ingredients.

Dishes such as duck foie gras with local pears or Saint-Jacques scallops with sea urchins might be followed by a rack of pork with Ardennes ham, or Le Parc's signature dish of hot-cold haddock with creamed chicken, truffles, and a lightly poached pear. The dishes are paired with top-notch French wines and, naturally, local Champagne. Reims is famous for its network of caves and tunnels beneath the city dating back to Roman times, and it is here that thousands of bottles of Champagne are aged. The resulting vintages are much sought after the world over, and are a distinctive feature of the cellar offered to guests at Le Parc. **CFr**

Le Pavé d'Auge | A rural celebration of Normandy's robust flavors and gutsy gastronomy

Location Beuvron en Auge   **Signature dish** Veal shank simmered in local cider | ❸❸❸

Here in the heart of Normandy's verdant countryside, in the center of the beautiful and tranquil village of Beuvron en Auge, Le Pavé d'Auge is a calm and cordial celebration of local and seasonal produce that is orchestrated by chef Jérôme Bansard. Before settling down to eat, it is recommended that aspiring diners have a look around the village. It is remarkably well preserved, with its half-timbered houses and quiet streets, and this outside wander will act as a suitable appetite boost. From the outside, the restaurant's black-and-white half-timbered walls and steeply pitched roof make you half expect medieval peasants in clogs to come dancing through the door.

Sightseeing over, it's time to eat. In the roomy dining room, a traditional space with Imperial-style chairs, exposed beams, and alcoves, Normandy's robust cuisine is lionized with gusto and style, with Bansard adding his own touches, which have given the restaurant a Michelin star. You might want to start with a selection of oysters or perhaps pan-fried foie gras accompanied by figs; then there could be a slice of pig's trotter with homemade mustard and sautéed mushrooms, a sturdy and hearty dish. Mains? Veal shank simmered in local cider is a regular on the menu, as is roast duck fillet, fabulously flavored dishes that are at the heart of the region's cuisine.

To mix things up a little, there might be roasted monkfish with a tagine of vegetables, or beef and oysters in broth. For dessert, many who visit swear by the Grand Marnier soufflé, a creamy, tangy, light-as-air treat. And, if you have any remaining space, don't forget the cheese board, featuring a slice of le Pavé d'Auge, the smooth and buttery cheese the restaurant is named after. Afterward, a stroll through the silent streets of Beuvron en Auge provides a fitting conclusion to a magnificent experience. **ATJ**

"The Pavé d'Auge serves unabashed meat-heavy feasts in splendid surroundings."

Greg Ward, *Daily Telegraph*

⬆ The restaurant features the region's typical half-timbered exterior.

Les Avisés | Fine dining in the heart of the Selosse champagne estate

Location Avise **Signature dish** Chicken with a crushed walnut crust and Champagne | ❺❺❺❺

Looking for exquisite Champagnes and a gastronomic menu bursting with regional flavors? Then visit Les Avizés, a nineteenth-century château with a white classical façade, views over the Selosse estate vineyards, a labyrinth of underground cellars, and one of the Côte des Blanc's finest Champagne houses.

Owners Anselme and Corinne Selosse know their Champagne; Anselme's father, Jacques Selosse, created the domain that bears his name. The family's extensive vineyards yield almost 60,000 bottles of Champagne every year. Together with the expertise of chef Stéphane Rossillon and his wife Nathalie, the couple has created one of the most respected auberges in the region. A seriously stylish space with

---

"The aim is ... to find the delicate and precise balance between the presentation and the dish."

Anselme Selosse, owner of Les Avises

---

wooden floors and a contemporary decor that blends with the house's classical architecture, it is the perfect setting to enjoy gastronomy at its best.

Chef Stéphane Rossillon changes his menu daily, with dishes designed to complement the Champagne and embody the region. For an appetizer, taste a wedge of artfully presented local game terrine or a mushroom soup with quail, topped with a lightly poached egg. Then choose chicken in a crust of crushed walnuts, turbot in a light Meunière sauce of butter, flat leaf parsley and lemon, or filet mignon cooked pink with carrot and potato puree. Classic French cheeses and desserts like black cherry clafoutis or crème brûlée will finish things off beautifully. **CFr**

Alain Ducasse au Plaza Athénée | Luxurious fine dining

Location Paris **Signature dish** Langoustines with caviar | ❺❺❺❺❺

For those in quest of a truly grand Parisian dining experience, the Plaza Athénée delivers in style. This is the flagship restaurant of famed French chef Alain Ducasse, whose culinary skills have been widely acclaimed, and the restaurant has been awarded three Michelin stars. Such is his reputation that, as is now de rigeur among top chefs, his restaurant empire extends around the globe. Ducasse has made a name for his precise culinary execution and his emphasis on impeccably sourced ingredients.

Luxurious ingredients, as one would expect in a restaurant of this caliber, are very much on show, and skilfully handled. So, for example, diners might enjoy a a dish of langoustine flesh, served cold, shaped into cylinders, and topped with caviar. To the side, offering a contrast of temperatures and textures, is a glass of warm langoustine consommé, delicately flavored with ginger and lemongrass. The natural sweetness of the langoustines contrasts nicely with the salty caviar, complemented by the aromatic broth. The flawless produce invariably shines in the simplest of presentations, perhaps a pair of precisely seasoned scallops with black truffles, served both raw and cooked, the latter with a light, truffle-flavored jus accompanied by potatoes and leeks. This dish serves to highlight the sensational quality of the shellfish.

Impeccable cheeses are on offer, and desserts demonstrate classic culinary techniques, ensuring that meals are rounded off in style. The restaurant also boasts a cellar of 35,000 bottles of wine, with a knowledgeable sommelier on hand to offer guidance. The exemplary service, with unwaveringly helpful, knowledgeable, and professional staff, makes dining here a thoroughly pleasurable experience. **AH**

➡ Luxurious ingredients, presented with flair.

Au Boeuf Couronné | A carnivore's delight in the heart of Paris

Location Paris **Signature dish** Country-style chicken liver pâté | ❸❸❸

> "You'll find bon vivants from all over Paris in the buzzy dining room…"

fodors.com

⬆ The traditional interior of Au Boeuf Couronné makes for a classic French dining experience.

Au Boeuf Couronné, as its name suggests, is a culinary establishment where meat in all its forms—braised, roasted, or lovingly transformed into a flavorful pâté—is celebrated with considerable gusto. Its location in Villete, a district which was historically home to Paris's abattoirs and meat markets, is appropriate indeed.

Chef Christophe Joulie knows his meat, and the menu here features nearly a dozen different cuts of beef alone. His 10.5-ounce (300-gram) steak, expertly cooked and served with a shallot confit, is a popular choice among diners. Those craving even more generous portions of beef are well served by offerings such as *Chateaubriand des bidochards* at 24.5 ounces (700 grams) and rib roast at over 2 pounds (1 kilo), which can be shared. Dining here is definitely not for those counting calories or craving salad. The decor, like the menu, is traditional and unpretentious—with dark wooden chairs and white linen tablecloths—a simple setting in which to savor classic French cuisine.

As one would expect, much emphasis is placed on the quality of the meat, which is carefully sourced from reputable Parisian butchers, with the cuts of beef matured to maximize both flavor and tenderness.

Appetizers are distinctly hearty affairs. Country-style chicken liver pâté, made to a recipe handed down from Christophe Jolie's grandmother, is a constant, while bone marrow arrives served simply and to the point with Guérande sea salt and toast. Main dish choices include rump steak in a creamy béarnaise sauce, or Fort des Halles sirloin steak, or rib steak with flat leaf parsley and red wine and shallot sauce. Christophe's veal with a ravigote sauce, or duck breast portions with fondant carrots are confidently executed offerings, plus his popular freshly made beef burgers. Desserts consist of classic French treats such as crêpe Suzette flambéed in Grand Marnier or crème brûlée with bourbon cream. **CFr**

Au Petit Fer à Cheval | An iconic bistro created by a self-made man

Location Paris   **Signature dish** *Confit de canard* | ❸❸

Au Petit Fer à Cheval is the sort of bistro that you always hope to find in Paris, but rarely do. Set on a narrow street lined with cafés and boutiques, blink and you'll miss the well-worn, bottle-green frontage with its curlicues of gold lettering and a scant handful of chairs on the pavement outside under a slightly shabby canopy. The first of five venues opened in the area under the leadership of hyperactive self-made restaurateur Xavier Denamur, the bistro stands on the site of a former coffee and chocolate trader dating back to 1903, making it a perfect symbol of the area's successful gentrification.

Inside is the highly polished, horseshoe-shaped bar that gives the bistro its name, and that seems to be propping up a couple of regulars at any time of the day. When you pull up a chair in the tiny dining room at the back, with its battered wooden furniture, and visit the highly memorable—and not always pleasantly so—metal-plated toilet inspired by Jules Verne, you feel as if you're taking a seat in a real piece of France.

The menu plays it straight down the line of bistro classics, while firmly stating its commitment to organic produce and seasonal vegetables from a farm just outside Paris. There's Mariage Frères tea and hot chocolate in the mornings, with boiled eggs and fromage blanc, then throughout the day and night are sandwiches with hams, pâtés, and cheeses and a no-nonsense selection of well-executed steak, foie gras, and other jazz standards.

It is unlikely that anyone has ever left Au Petit Fer à Cheval unhappy after having been served a plate of their signature *confit de canard*—that salt-cured, slow-cooked, fat-fried Gascony dish that so many places get wrong. Here, it is the perfect way to punctuate a trip to the Marais, the medieval merchants' quarter that has become a hangout for Paris's "bobos"—bourgeois bohemians. **EH**

"… this is Paris like in films or dreams. It mirrors the city of today and the one from yesterday."

madaboutparis.com

⬆ Au Petit Fer à Cheval has a tiny entrance and a few hotly contested pavement tables.

Bistro Paul Bert | Simple bistrot perfection
and an unbeatable lunchtime menu

Location Paris **Signature dish** *Paris Brest* (choux pastry with noisette cream) | 💲💲

"This heart-warming bistro gets it right almost down to the last crumb."

Time Out

⬆ A classic bistro experience at Paul Bert.

Perhaps Paris' best-loved bistrot, Bistro Paul Bert retains much of its busy bonhomie thanks to the near constant jovial presence of bistrot owner Bernard Auboyneau. He is rarely far from his time-warp, zinc-topped bar or, in summer, one of the terrasse tables outside. He also oversees the seafood bar, l'Ecailler du Bistro, adjacent to the main restaurant, and the recently opened "6 Paul Bert" 219 yards (200 m) further along the street. This is a more canteenlike version of the bistro, with a small, beautifully stocked deli counter that is open on Mondays.

At the original address, all the style codes of the Parisian bistro are religiously respected, from the multi-colored patterned tiles to the mirrors, white tablecloths, and leather banquettes. While the decor charms your pants off (less so the service), the unbeatable lunch menu will answer all your prayers for proper French bistro food. Kidneys served whole and pink, steak tartare, tender milk-fed lamb roasted in a cast-iron Staub, straight-up steak and chips, or a towering Paris Brest are all on offer, and, at lunchtime, there are some competitive deals. Special mention goes to the huge, daunting *îles flottantes* and subtle homemade sorbets and ice creams.

Other dishes, the fish in particular, are treated with a lighter, more modern touch, like the pollock fillet, left raw, sliced thinly, and sensitively flavored with Asian herbs and spices. "Simple ingredients, treated well" should be such an easy promise to keep in a country with such natural produce; but, if many places manage to spoil the plainest tomato salad, cep omelette, or Grand Marnier souffle, Paul Bert is not one of them. In fact, simple perfection is what it does best. There is an impressively large wine list (although a more limited choice by the glass), with many rare and delightful bottles that do the plates proud. **TD**

Brasserie Benoit |

Small brasserie with classic French dining

Location Paris   **Signature dish** Scrambled eggs and Périgord truffles | 💰💰

In 2005, Alain Ducasse took over one of the jewels of Paris' small brasseries and ensured its survival—some would say supremacy—in the classic French dining stakes. Brasserie Benoit celebrated its centenary in 2012 and, until Ducasse's takeover, the restaurant had belonged to three generations of the Petit family. The beautiful interior—resplendent with engraved glass, gleaming bronze, copper features, and huge mirrors—has been wonderfully preserved, with a lovely wood-paneled salon upstairs for bigger parties.

But it is downstairs where you really want to be, reading *Le Canard Enchaîné* that's left at your disposal, soaking up a little slice of Parisian life, imagining (or spotting) some of Paris' literary and political figures who use Benoit as a regular eating and drinking venue. Many of the dishes are served at the table with Monsieur Petit's original utensils and tableware. Fish is taken off the bone, côtes de veau carved, and crêpes Suzettes flambéed in front of you. And, if it's the season and your budget stretches to it, know that the truffles shaved onto your omelette or set on a warm buttered sourdough tartine are fabulous at chez Benoit.

The bistro has a Michelin star, still the only authentic bistro in Paris to have one, and the cooking lives up to the accolade. At lunchtime, there's a well-priced prix fixe menu, but it's hard to resist those great French classics such as veal tongue Lucullus with braised romaine salad and mustard cream, sweetbreads sautéed with coxcomb and chicken kidneys, foie gras and truffled jus, huge and succulent Burgundy snails in herb and garlic butter, or a superlative pâté en croute à la carte. The wine list is, predictably, as impressive, even if the ancient cellars, where full barrels used to be stored, has been transformed into modernized kitchens for continued dining delight. Merci, Monsieur Ducasse. **TD**

Brasserie Lipp |

Political drama in St. Germain des Prés

Location Paris   **Signature dish** *Choucroute* and beer | 💰💰

Sitting on the Boulevard St. Germain, opposite Café de Flore and Café les Deux Magots, Lipp is a key player in the glittering history of St. Germain des Prés. Opened in the 1920s and decorated with elaborate mosaics, Rococo chandeliers, ceilings with African hunting scenes, and enormous tilted mirrors with optimal views of Paris's Who's Who, it remains at the center of political and literary life. François Mitterrand was a long and faithful customer, often lunching there with Mazarine, the daughter of his long-term mistress.

Dining at chez Lipp can be disconcerting. No other Parisian restaurant has such an openly subjective seating system, following rules known only to the brisk waiters and the maître d'. If you show up with a French government minister, you could predict a table in

---

"Everybody should go at least once to this archetypical brasserie in Saint Germain."

Zagat

"Paradise." If your guest is Mick Jagger, you might find yourself in the right-hand part, the "Aquarium." If you are pleasant and well-dressed but unknown to the staff, then "Purgatory" is likely, the windowless room at the back. If you are wearing shorts and an "I love Paris" T shirt, you will end up in the room known as "Hell."

The food remains steadily down to earth, with brasserie standards of Bismarck herrings with onions and juniper, foie gras stuffed pig's trotter roasted in bread crumbs, and steak tartare prepared à la minute. All this is unceremoniously plonked before you—this is a place to eat and converse, not "lunch" or "dine" with stuffy decorum. **TD**

Le Galopin | A relaxed and charming example of the "new" Paris bistro

Location Paris   **Signature dish** Grilled eel | ❸❸❸

Parisian chef Romain Tischenko has cut a path through the French culinary landscape, having worked variously in respected establishments in Normandy, Nice, and Megeve, finally ending up as second-in-command of Michelin-starred chef William Ledeuil's Ze Kitchen Galerie. What really propelled him into the public eye, though, was when he became champion of the French version of *MasterChef* in 2010—this made the reserved cook a household name, and allowed him to open his own tiny table.

Le Galopin is located in a pleasant villagelike square in an area between the trendy Canal Saint Martin and the multi-cultural Belleville. The small dining room of the bistro draws French foodies from afar, with its all-exposed brick and minimal decor, a countertop that is perfect for aperos, and an open kitchen where Tischenko creates a seven-dish market menu that is changed daily (including two amuse-bouches, an appetizer, fish, meat, and two desserts).

Brother Maxime operates the bistro service—he was a world traveler who dropped his anchor and then discovered a passion for natural, biodynamic wines at the legendary Le Chateaubriand restaurant in Paris' 11th arrondissement before partnering with his brother at Le Galopin. Dishes are always inventive, seasonal, and minimalist (with rarely more than three ingredients), and often feature unusual produce and riffs on classics such as salted cod poppers with yuzu or grilled eel with pleurotte mushrooms.

Downstairs, in the cellar, are two tables d'hôtes for private events. It is not unusual to see neighbors popping in for a glass of wine at the counter or Tischenko coming out of the kitchen to serve the dishes himself and talk shop. The easy, relaxed feel of this local table is very much part of the new Paris bistro vibe: it's all about delicious, casual food. **TD**

⊕ The chic dining room at Le Galopin.

Chez Jenny | Relaxed dining with a taste of Alsace at this Parisian brasserie

Location Paris **Signature dish** *Choucroute* "Chez Jenny" (sauerkraut) | ❸❸❸

Chez Jenny is by no means the oldest of Paris' brasseries, bustling Alsace-style restaurants where the menu prominently features shellfish and *choucroute*. Founded in 1931, it's a mere baby when compared to nineteenth-century gems Lipp and Bofinger. Nor is it as famous as some of its older counterparts. But, if you want the authentic brasserie experience, with the focus on food rather than glamor, head to Chez Jenny.

The decor is unique among Paris brasseries, with its paneled walls, marquetry, and distinctive frescoes and wooden sculptures that have been there since the beginning. Though very large, it is on two floors, so you don't feel you're in the middle of a huge crowd—and the comfortable banquettes make it seem as if you're in a room of your own.

As in any proper Alsatian brasserie, the menu gives pride of place to shellfish (gorgeous platters of oysters or mixed crustacea) and to huge plates of *choucroute* garnished with various combinations of

meat or fish. Chez Jenny also serves authentic Alsatian *flammeküeche*, a cross between a quiche and a pizza, topped with crème fraîche, fromage blanc, and onions.

It is not all Alsace on the menu, however. Chez Jenny takes enormous pride in its onion soup "Tradition," which is almost a meal in itself. And the steak tartare is as good as you will get in Paris, chopped by hand for a pleasingly coarse texture.

Chez Jenny is a Paris institution, and you are therefore likely to be surrounded by more Parisians than tourists. One large table might include three generations, right down to babies in high chairs, while another might have a group of old friends who give the impression that they have come regularly every week for several decades. That feeling of dining among the locals is all part of the attraction of this wonderful brasserie. **RE**

⬆ **Chez Jenny offers an authentic brasserie experience.**

Allard | Classic gastro dining in a stylish Parisian bistro

Location Paris **Signature dish** *Canard de Challans aux olives* (duck with olives) | ❺❺❺

With its relaxed, buzzy feel and delectable bistro cuisine, Allard is something of a legend in St. Germain des Près. It was founded in 1932 by Marthe Allard, a Burgundian peasant who adored cooking and brought her family recipes to the capital. Today, it is one of the latest Alain Ducasse eateries, offering visitors top gastronomy not far from Notre Dame.

The country-chic decor cuts quite a dash. Chocolate brown and cream with terracotta accents is the color theme, coupled with sepia photographs and hat hooks, bric-à-brac, and rustic-style lighting that throws a glow over this classic French bistro scene.

Chef Laëtitia Rouabah steps up to the plate with French classics, including Challans duck with olives

---

"The food is superb: try a dozen snails, some cuisses de grenouilles, or poulet de Bresse."

Lonely Planet

---

and lamb with flageolet beans and coq au vin, fixtures that see devoted regulars returning to Allard time and again. Laëtitia also offers fresh, contemporary brasserie-style food, with expert wine pairing by sommelier Jonathan Belhassein. Meunière-style sole with lemon, or grilled red salmon with a Béarnaise sauce, or a fillet of beef served with a light pepper sauce all feature. Topping and tailing these might be appetizer dishes of pâté en croute, marinated salmon, preserved duck foie gras with toasted country bread, or coddled eggs with wild mushrooms and garlic bread. For dessert, there's an accomplished crème brûlée, pan-seared seasonal fruit, or rum savarin with lightly whipped Chantilly cream. **CFr**

Benoit | Serious classical cooking in a legendary bistro

Location Paris **Signature dish** Snails in the shell with butter and herbs | ❺❺❺

Benoit would almost be a pastiche of itself if it wasn't so perfectly done—the gleam of the polished brass fittings, the curve of the wooden bar, the deep blush of the red banquettes, the flick of linen napkins being shaken out, the ceiling painted with scenes of blue skies and fluffy white clouds. Just a stone's throw from the Hôtel de Ville, Benoit has been open since 1912, and it takes its history seriously. In its most recent incarnation, it has joined the empire of Alain Ducasse. He installed chef Eric Azoug in the kitchen, charged with maintaining Benoit's reputation as one of the most distinguished vanguards of the Parisian bistro tradition, and proud owner of a Michelin star. If you hit the à la carte and the wine list with intent, you can rack up a significant bill, but the wallet-friendly institution of a more affordable set-lunch menu persists.

What all this means is not the weight of pomp and formality, but a serious and sophisticated dedication to dishes that might seem tired or clichéd elsewhere, and no holding back on the butter, cream, and booze. There will always be calf's head *en ravigote* on the menu, and fat escargots with their heart-stopping pools of garlicky butter to mop up with handfuls of bread. Slow-cooked beef cheek almost melts on your fork, and huge doorstops of pale, fluffy Savarin cake come with Chantilly cream spooned from a pot and a choice of two Armagnacs to slosh over it—and the bottle left on the table, just in case. You'll also see the roots of this kind of cooking—the instinct to feed lavishly from a communal pot— in many of the dishes. Things like *pâté en croute* or *cassoulet maison* are dished up tableside from their baking dishes, the whole experience striking a memorable balance between luxury and comfort. **EH**

⬌ Profiteroles Benoit served with hot chocolate sauce.

L'Escargot Montorgueil | A brasserie known for snails and frogs' legs

Location Paris **Signature dish** *Gueusaille de Kouikette* (potatoes stuffed with snails in cream and parsley sauce) | $$$

"'Le tout Paris' loves the perfectly seasoned grenadine of monkfish stuffed with plump juicy snails . . . "

bonjourparis.com

↑ The Empire style of L'Escargot d'Or's black wooden façade and gold typography sets the scene.

Opened in 1832, the restaurant was bought in 1919 by Claude Terrail, also the owner of the mythical La Tour d'Argent. The venue rapidly became a Parisian society institution, and the headquarters of various partying personalities of the time such as Sarah Bernhardt, Sacha Guitry, Marcel Proust, and Georges Feydeau. Back in those days, the restaurant was called L'Escargot d'Or, and since that time little has changed in terms of its superb Empire period decor. The black wooden façade; the black and white tiles; the wood paneling; the tall, engraved mirrors; the comfortable, red-velvet banquettes; the fancy candelabras; and the wooden ceilings are all carefully preserved. There is a succession of salons downstairs (the farthest one is the quietest and most cozy), and there is a beautiful wooden staircase leading to a larger room upstairs, and a broad terrasse on the pedestrian rue de Montorgueil for warmer days.

The food at L'Escargot Montorgueil is honest brasserie style, with dishes such as eggs mayonnaise, foie gras terrine, roast bone marrow, beef tartare, *sole Meunière*, crêpe Suzette, frogs' legs, and *canard à l'orange*. The clientele is a mixture of older Parisians nostalgic for the old days and international visitors—most of whom arrive from visiting the Pompidou Centre nearby—as they wander around the city. Most of all, here is where to come if you love snails, or if you would like a serious introduction to them.

Served in cute spirals, you can order from six to three dozen snails (good luck), flavored with three different sauces—classic flat leaf parsley and garlic (it is worth noting that the chef has a light hand with the garlic), a light curry or, brace yourself, Roquefort. Snails turn up in the *oeufs meurettes* (eggs cooked in red wine), and the most famous dish, potatoes stuffed with snails in a cream and parsley sauce, is called "gueusaille de Kouikette" in homage to Claude Terrail's sister, Kouikette Terrail. **TD**

Chez Casimir | A straight-talking, absurdly generous local gem

Location Paris **Signature dish** Pigeon cassoulet | $$

Most people rushing to and from the Gare du Nord in pursuit of star connections will neglect to explore the boulevards around the bustling station. This is a shame, because if you stray just a few minutes away from the unlovely rue de Dunkerque, the rue de Belzunce hosts three venues from one of Paris' best-known and loved restaurateurs. Thierry Breton is a top-drawer professional who has chosen down-to-earth local bistros over Michelin stars. The original, Chez Casimir, is wedged in a corner opposite the Eglise Saint Vincent de Paul, and doesn't look like anything special, although the pavement seats under the green-and-white-striped canopy are inviting. The best meal to stop by for is brunch, which has almost legendary status among those in the know.

Rather than the various spins on eggs and pancakes that are sweeping the numerous self-consciously trendy venues across the city (bruncher is a standard verb nowadays), a lazy late morning at Chez Casimir is an unmissable opportunity (provided you're very hungry) to sample a stunning range of produce from the buffet table. You can take your pick from cheeses and charcuterie, pâtés and crêpes, salads and quiches, breads and pickles and much more, while the unapologetically grumpy waiter delivers a whole series of hot dishes to the table. A coddled egg, perhaps, and an individual cast-iron pot of pigeon cassoulet, a bowl of mussels, and maybe a steaming mug of fish soup.

First-timers often fail to pace themselves—a mistake, because desserts (past the bar and around the corner) take up two enormous, groaning shelves, flanked with piles of fresh fruit and a gently bubbling pot of melted chocolate to go with all the flans and tarts and pies and mousses. You help yourself to water at the bar, and order and collect your wine and coffee there as well. There are no frills, just a serious dedication to filling your plate, and filling it well. **EH**

"Thierry Breton's bright, easygoing bistro is popular with polished Parisian professionals … "

fodors.com

⬆ The buffet table at Chez Casimir includes an array of excellent cheeses.

Guy Savoy | Superb haute cuisine from a master of French cuisine with an emphasis on flavor

Location Paris   **Signature dish** Artichoke and black truffle soup | ❺❺❺❺

For visitors to Paris in search of a quintessentially French, exceptional haute-cuisine experience, a visit to acclaimed chef Guy Savoy's eponymous restaurant is surely on their "to do" list. Having worked at the famous Maison Troisgros restaurant in Roanne, with Pierre Troisgros as an important mentor, Savoy set up his own restaurant in Paris, which has retained three Michelin stars since 2002. Savoy himself has mentored a number of leading chefs, including Britain's Gordon Ramsay. While Savoy now has a global restaurant empire, his beloved Paris restaurant, in which every detail of food, decor, and service has been carefully thought out, is the place in which to enjoy his cuisine.

Savoy is known for his classic culinary technique and ability to coax out flavors from the most humble ingredients. So a dainty serving of turnip and carrot emulsion with ginger, lemongrass, and lemon salt delivers an intense experience. Luxurious ingredients are also to the fore. His signature dish, artichoke and black truffle soup, arrives served with brioche with mushrooms and truffles, a gloriously rich, satisfying creation—creamy textured, with the earthy notes of artichoke and truffle complemented by *umami*-rich Parmesan shavings. The main courses on offer then demonstrate Savoy's ability to transform ingredients into taste creations that linger on in the memory.

Desserts, too, whether light, fruit-based creations or richer ones such as chocolate fondant, show the kitchen's impressive technique and Savoy's skill at creating food that is thoroughly enjoyable to eat. As one would expect in a French restaurant of this standing, the cheese board, a glorious array of French cheeses at their best, is truly impressive. The attentive, thoughtful, unstintingly professional service at Guy Savoy is part of the restaurant's appeal. This is French gastronomy in glorious form. **AH**

> *" In this haute-cuisine restaurant … plates are imaginative works of contemporary art."*
>
> Zagat

⬆ An exquisite langoustine and cauliflower creation by Guy Savoy.

Chez Georges |

A generous taste of bistrot cuisine

Location Paris **Signature dish** Salmon in sorrel sauce | ❷❷

A few years ago, Chez Georges's many fans trembled in fear at the bistrot's first change of owner since opening in 1964. Would it stay the same? Would it be spoiled for ever? No need to worry; all is well with this classic bistrot.

The jovial Maitre d', Angelo Belloni, still presides at Chez Georges in Paris' rue de Mail. Moreover, the high sepia walls of the two long and narrow rooms are just as they were, along with the bustling service of the athletic, uniformed waitresses and the Rabelaisian portions of the honest French bistrot cuisine that is served here. Of course, the place is constantly buzzing with a crowd of international visitors—eating at Chez Georges is a sort of Parisian rite of passage. In fact, this is so much the case that you will be hard pushed at times to hear any French from anyone but those taking your order.

But this really doesn't matter, because the service and food are as joyous and greedy as the ambiance in the noisy room. Everyone shares the common goal of eating the seriously good food and wine. Huge bowls of cornichons and crème fraîche circulate around the tables, accompanying the smoked salmon, preserved smoked herring, or *terrine de museau*. With a simple plate of egg mayonnaise or *oeufs en gelée*, you can order your wine in pewter pots, and no one will frown if you prefer a glass of beer with your leeks and vinaigrette. (Expensive) fish and meat dishes are mostly served as plain as plain can be, but the taste and freshness of the produce is consistently irreproachable.

The classic desserts of tarte au citron, tarte tatin, and chocolate mousse are, predictably, heavenly—if you can make it that far. Just make sure that, if do you decide to start a plate, you finish it, too, or the waitress might get angry with you. **TD**

Chez l'Ami Jean |

Memorable food from a master chef

Location Paris **Signature dish** *Riz au lait* (rice pudding) with caramel | ❸❸❸

On an unassuming side street in Paris's chic 7th arrondissement is Chez l'Ami Jean, a cramped little Basque-inspired restaurant. Together, locals and jet-setting foodies crowd the woodsy old-school dining room, shoulder to shoulder, for delicious, impeccably sourced produce cooked by one of the City of Light's reigning gastro-bistro master chefs, Stéphane Jégo.

L'Ami Jean is not to be taken lightly. Servings are by turns generous and over-the-top, precise and delicate, from the traditional *côte de boeuf* (veal shank) to more inventive dishes such as crab meat with cep mushrooms and *Vache qui Rit* emulsion. Chez l'Ami Jean allows participation in the chaotic ambiance that is Jégo's life for those serious about eating well and

> *"Reserve in advance and arrive hungry because the Basque dishes served are anything but light."*
>
> frommers.com

drinking too much. Even those waiting for tables at the bar counter are offered homemade charcuterie from niche producer Eric Ospital with their aperitifs.

Jégo doesn't mess around; he commands his staff with a frenetic energy, one eye on the stoves, the other on the dining room from his seat in the closet-sized open kitchen, from which he shouts and cooks. He rules with an iron hand, knows each producer by first name, and does exactly what he feels whether or not it follows culinary convention. Some may find it a mite confusing to navigate the extensive menu and choose between trad and cutting edge, but L'Ami Jean is a bistro after its owner's heart: it takes you in and embraces you, cajoles you, and satisfies you. **TD**

Hélène Darroze | Pleasurable food from a fêted chef

Location Paris **Signature dish** Roast chicken with Espelette pepper | $$$

"A simple pavé of herb-crusted sturgeon cuts like marshmallow and tastes as sweet as scallop . . ."

Terry Durack, *The Independent*

Hélène Darroze never planned to become a chef, but the great, revered chef Alain Ducasse decided otherwise. She was training in hotel management with Ducasse in Monaco, but after a short stage in his kitchen, which was meant only to give her experience in all sides of the business, Ducasse spotted her obvious culinary talent and urged her to cook.

Hélène took over the family auberge in Les Landes and then opened her restaurant Hélène Darroze in Paris in 2000. Success and Michelin stars followed—one in Paris, two at The Connaught in London—making Darroze one of France's most famous and fêted women chefs ever. Her restaurant on rue d'Assas (a stone's throw from the infamous Hôtel Lutetia, which was HQ to the Gestapo during World War II) is welcoming and warm, cozy even, with deep reds and purples decorating the two floors. Darroze cooks and creates from instinct, "from her heart", she likes to say, interpreting over and over the fine produce she grew up with in Les Landes.

Strongly influenced by this region, close to Bordeaux and the Basque country, and seemingly blessed by the food gods, Darroze's cooking highlights foie gras, ceps and truffles from Périgord, lamb from the Pyrénées, caviar from Aquitaine, Basque bell peppers, olive oil, chocolate, and, of course, *piment d'Espelette*, the gently smoky Basque-country chili pepper, which Hélène made trendy in France almost single-handedly. A master of roasting meat, Hélène's roast chicken dishes should not be missed, and along with her faithful pastry chef, Scotsman Kirk Whittle, the extreme sensual pleasure of her cooking continues right through dessert. Then comes the moment to try a vintage Armagnac from the cellars of Hélène's uncle, cousin, or brother, all three of whom are producers and *négociants* (wine merchants) in her home region—this will round off your meal here in rich, mellow style. **TD**

↑ Hélène Darroze's famous, eponymous restaurant is a welcoming and hospitable haven.

Café de Flore | A literary legend on a Left Bank boulevard

Location Paris **Signature dish** Le Flore croque monsieur | ❸❸❸

Camus, Sartre, De Beauvoir, Prévert, Hemingway, Capote, Dalí, Lacan, Deneuve, Bacall, Depp, Coppola, Gainsbourg—what do they have in common? Why they all patronized the Café de Flore, often using it as their office or second home. Reading this list of great names in art, literature, film, and philosophy is like leafing through some of the great movements that have shaped modern French society and culture. Surrealism was debated here, and existentialism, and *La Nouvelle Vague*. Anyone who was anyone would have stopped by in the café's heyday—even Chinese premier Chou En-lai was a regular in the 1920s. This is why the Flore's iconic green-and-white canopy, its unchanged mirrors, mahogany and white-aproned waiters, and red banquettes haunt the imaginations of so many visitors to Paris.

Founded in 1887 and named after a nearby sculpture of Flora, goddess of flowers and springtime, the Flore had an extraordinary run as one of the most celebrated intellectual coffeehouses in the city (along with its nearby rival, Les Deux Magots), and still attracts celebrities today. This makes it an essential pilgrimage for those sensitive to the place's traditions (it still hosts an annual literary prize), and the stellar roster of diners that it has welcomed over the years.

Inevitably, its modern incarnation is more in keeping with its setting in Saint Germain des Prés—now an extremely trendy neighborhood—and its popularity with tourists than it is with the penniless writers and artists of yesteryear. If Sartre and De Beauvoir had been able to keep up their habit of breakfast, lunch, and dinner at the Flore today, it is fairly certain that the bill would plunge them into the depths of existentialist despair. But the vast, classically Parisian café menu of drinks, Champagnes, cocktails, breakfasts (including eggs fourteen different ways), hot and cold buffets, cheeses, salads, ice creams, and desserts certainly has everything to please. **EH**

" … you'll find mocktails, great coffee, salads, croques monsieur, pasta, and veggie burgers."

Lonely Planet

⬆ Legendary greats Camus, Sartre, and Hemingway were among the regulars at this iconic café.

Restaurant Chartier | An historic, egalitarian institution
with an emphasis on reasonably priced food

Location Paris **Signature dish** Leeks vinaigrette |

" … *the only fin-de-siécle* bouillon *to remain true to its mission of serving cheap, sustaining food."*

fodors.com

⬆ The illuminated entrance at Restaurant Chartier.

Chartier is one of the last authentic Paris *bouillons* (traditional eateries) to have retained its original decor and purpose. It is a tall, beautifully preserved, noisy dining hall, clad in dark shiny wood, with high brass cradles for coats and bags sitting above the rows of tables. The building is historically listed, and still intact are the sideboards in the 319-seat dining room, with their wooden drawers, where regulars used to keep their fabric napkins. An upstairs mezzanine, bathed in daylight from the glass-paneled ceiling, is good for larger groups once they have braved the formidable lines, which often snake through the courtyard and spill onto the rue du Faubourg Montmartre outside.

There are no reservations taken at chez Chartier. Built to feed the Parisian workers of the quartier, visitors are still here to be fed, quickly and cheaply, in the Parisian tradition, certainly not spoiled or "hosted." In fact, there are occasions where you might feel you are barely being welcomed. But, since the restaurant's opening in 1896, Chartier still keeps its promise of a bowl of soup for a single euro.

The rest of Chartier's menu is cheap, following a good plain French style, with dishes such as *oeufs mayonnaise; les escargots;* leeks in vinaigrette; steak and chips; veal liver and boiled potatoes; chocolate mousse; and tarte tatin. It is true that Chartier can be a bit hit and miss as far as freshness is concerned, and you never quite know when a tin or a freezer packet may have helped speed your dish through its time in the kitchen and onto the table before you. Still, this egalitarian eating institution maintains a powerful draw. It is fast and filling—and a little thrilling, too, as the room fills and empties at breakneck speed, with orders and bills scribbled on paper tablecloths as elegantly attired, long-aproned waiters swirl around the floor with their trays held high. **TD**

L'Astrance | Innovative fine dining in appealingly laid-back surroundings

Location Paris **Signature dish** *Millefeuille* of mushrooms and foie gras | ❸❸❸❸

Chef Pascal Barbot caused a stir back in 2007, when at the age of thirty-five, and only seven years after opening, he picked up a third Michelin star in L'Astrance's laid-back surroundings. There is no stuffy, silver service here. Instead, there are twenty-five covers in an airy, modern space in an out-of-the-way street just off the edge of the Seine in Paris' 16th arrondissement. The restaurant's ultra-relaxed service then knocked a couple of decades off the usual age of star-collecting diners. Barbot trained under Alain Passard, and traveled and cooked extensively in the Far East, Australia, and the U.K. before settling in Paris.

These influences show in his cooking. His use of spices as salt and Asian fusion ingredients, and his dislike of the standard French-style sauces used at the beginning of the century, were revolutionary. They are still to be found in his cooking in light and subtle touches, but perhaps Barbot's trademark today lies more in his contrasts of raw and cooked, herbs, juices, and infusions. Lobster is served in an autumn vegetable broth, grilled calamari with mango, and papaya and pineapple with pepper foam.

L'Astrance's signature dish is a beautifully simple *millefeuille* of raw mushroom with marinated foie gras. L'Astrance is an alpine flower, and the desserts often carry floral and vegetal notes, just like the potato puree with fromage blanc, or the ginger ice cream and citrus tarte, delicately decorated with petals. The menu is set, an increasingly common practice these days, but still extremely rare for a three-star restaurant.

This gives Barbot free rein to interpret what is good and in season, and allows a certain pace to install itself during the meal. The process is helped along by a service that never feels rushed or tense, thanks also to the talent of Barbot's business partner, manager, and sommelier Christophe Rohat. **TD**

Le Baratin | A tiny bistrot with a cult reputation serving French classics

Location Paris **Signature dish** Monkfish roasted on the bone with Espelette pepper | ❸❸

On a cobbled sidestreet high on la rue de Belleville in north-east Paris, this bistrot has become the very definition of cult. Perhaps an unlikely spot for such a fashionable address, this shabby, characterful part of town is not yet gentrified, nestled among Chinese and Thai restaurants and supermarkets.

Maintaining its deep banquettes and high, curved bar, owners Raquel Carena and Philippe Pinoteau recently gave Le Baratin a facelift, renovating the tiny kitchen where there was only room for Raquel and a commis. So diners can once again enjoy the inventive cooking and the selection of organic and natural wines. Famously gruff (be warned), Philippe lights up instantly if you take an informed interest in his wines.

> *"Le Baratin attracts gourmands from all over Paris—so be sure to book …"*
>
> *Time Out*

Carena is self-taught, but the influence of Breton chef Olivier Roellinger, known for his use of spices, is clear. Her cooking centers on generous French classics and irreproachable fish and meat, prepared perfectly yet simply (often raw), with touches of Asian spices and condiments. There is a mackerel tartare with smoked Tosazu vinaigrette, and *mallard* with ginger and redcurrant jelly and lightly roasted monkfish tail, served with the most delicate of vinaigrettes and Basque chili pepper. For comfort, diners can choose the red wine and mushroom rabbit stew or daube of ox cheek and oxtail, and to finish the delectably simple desserts of bitter chocolate cream, cherry compote, or roast figs. **TD**

Kitchen Galerie Bis | Asian meets French with defining Parisian finesse

Location Paris **Signature dish** A daily changing starter of Asian/French fusion cuisine chosen by the chef | 💲💲

" … dishes are sophisticated, colorful, and elegant … fusing the flavors of France and Asia."

Time Out

⬆ The Asian/French bistro style of Kitchen Galerie Bis mixes East and West in a refined French package.

Kitchen Galerie Bis sits next to its Michelin-starred sister restaurant Ze Kitchen Galerie on rue des Grands Augustins. Located in the 6th arrondissement, an area renowned for its elegant boutiques and galleries, this is an ideal spot to enjoy lunch or dinner in the city.

Under the keen eye of William Ledeuil in the kitchen and Marin Simon at the front of the house, KGB joined the pre-existing Ze Kitchen Galerie in 2009, allowing the team to expand their successful concept of Asian/French bistro cooking, but with lower prices and a brisker service. Ledeuil is an art enthusiast, and KGB is filled with specially commissioned pictures that infuse color and atmosphere into this bright, modern space. Even the logo, by jazz musician and artist Daniel Humair, adds a laid-back but cultural style.

The food is equally intriguing—inspired by the flavors and techniques of Asian cuisine, the approach is a marriage of ingredients from East and West served in a refined French manner. Tamarind, lemongrass, ginger, mikan pepper, and orange-flower water can be found across the KGB menu, infusing both sweet and savory dishes with aromatic delicacy. Memorable examples include a main course of confit and grilled quail with pear and Sancho pepper, and a dessert of apple and tamarind cappuccino with walnut-wine emulsion and ginger ice cream.

In the evening, there is a tasting menu, at lunch a shorter prix fixe menu offering excellent value for two or three courses. It is inadvisable to miss the appetizer, beause the KGB "zors d'oeuvre" is the signature dish. A daily changing plate of assorted dishes, the offering contains four mini portions and a chance to taste a wider range of these fresh, precise dishes.

The knowledgeable, welcoming, and efficient staff are used to serving a happy crowd of elegant and colorful Parisians. Kitchen Galerie Bis is a relaxed and happy place to eat, with great value food that is both refined and interesting. **CB**

L'Atelier de Joël Robuchon | Flagship enterprise of a rock star chef

Location Paris   **Signature dish** Caramelized quail stuffed with foie gras and truffled mashed potato | $$$$

Joël Robuchon's reputation precedes him, perhaps more than any other chef in Paris. The sheer weight of the numbers attached to his career is startling—the man holds more Michelin stars than any other chef in the world in a dozen restaurants in as many cities, from Las Vegas to Tokyo. His atelier (workshop) is one of the concepts he has reproduced globally to enormous acclaim—but this branch in Saint Germain des Prés, an extremely well-heeled Left Bank area of Paris that has some thrilling nineteenth-century bohemian credentials, is the original. This is where Robuchon is best known for paving the way for a whole new era in high-end French cookery, leaving behind the overwrought attempts of nouvelle cuisine and putting ingredients center stage in a way that continues to inspire cooks today.

Robuchon took his first "retirement" in 1995, and you might be forgiven for feeling that the venue's hyper-masculine decor, all red and black and dark wood, hasn't moved on much since then. Forty scarlet leather high stools are placed around an open kitchen, with serried ranks of wine bottles arranged on the walls behind diners and glowing jars of preserves and pickles on shelves above the chefs. The best—if most expensive—way to do Joël Robuchon is as Joël Robuchon intended, which means letting the kitchen display its chops through the multi-course *dégustation* (tasting) menu. All the dishes here are small and intense, showcasing a single ingredient (the menu leads each description with *"l'aubergine"* (eggplant) or *"la langoustine"* or *"le pigeon,"* with an exact execution that can manage to make the ingredient taste more like itself than you ever thought possible. Robuchon embraces global influences—*la volaille* comes in a Japanese gyoza and Asian-spiced bouillon—but his heart remains firmly in France and in celebrating its culinary traditions, while also expressing them in some unexpected forms. **EH**

"…this red-and-black-lacquer space has a bento-box-meets-tapas aesthetic."

fodors.com

⬆ Joël Robuchon's Indian rosewood counter gives diners front row seats as their food is prepared.

L'Arpège | Alain Passard's genius flows "from potager to plate"

Location Paris   **Signature dish** *Tarte bouquet de roses* ("Rose" apple tart) | ❺❺❺❺

World-renowned chef Alain Passard trained under classical teachers Gaston Boyer and Alain Senderens, finally buying the rather unassuming restaurant L'Arpège from Senderens in 1986. It has since become a cornerstone of French gastronomy—a mixture of a 7th-arrondissement luxury canteen and discreet salon that welcomes an array of significant French figures, from politicians to businessmen.

The mischievous, energetic Passard, who is now an instrumental figure in training and inspiring young chefs all over the world, is in his kitchen every day, often popping out toward the end of service to chat with a friend who has dropped in for lunch. But, if the atmosphere can be light-hearted and cozy, it does not take away from the precision and artistry in the plates.

Passard steadily collected his Michelin stars until he was awarded the ultimate three stars in 1996. He has retained them ever since, even as he switched, controversially, the thrust of his dishes from meat and fish (his pigeon in a sugared almond crust was his first famous dish) to vegetables in 2001. In 2002, he started growing his own vegetables in a superb walled garden in the Sarthe.

More than a decade later, Passard now has three gardens, which supply the restaurant with a significant amount of produce, ensuring the Alain Passard signature phrase *du potager à l'assiette,* "from potager to plate." Let the chef himself take you through what his gardens are making him cook that day—this may mean a four-hour lunch, so be warned. Brace yourself also for the bill, but this is the inevitable price to pay for such an immaculate level of service and unparalleled quality of produce. Don't miss his chaud-froid egg (or L'Arpège egg, an interpretation of *oeuf à la coque*) with maple syrup, chicken in hay, and the exquisite rose-petal apple tart. **TD**

⬆ A delicate dish of scallops and truffles at L'Arpège.

Le Dôme | Exceptional fish at an archetypal Parisian institution

Location Paris **Signature dish** *Fruits de mer* | 😊😊

Le Dôme, on its prepossessing corner location on boulevard du Montparnasse, is one of the grand old cafés of Paris, with a distinctive 1930s art deco styling. Today, Le Dôme retains its reputation for great food, specializing in *fruits de mer* (seafood) and fish.

Locals and the ceaseless stream of international visitors alike find a comfortable retreat here, an escape from the movements of the frantic city outside. From early morning breakfast right through into the late hours of the night, it is possible to stop for anything, from a café and croissant on the terrace to one of La Dôme's many classic dishes. There is an extensive and excellent selection of *fruits de mer*, and if you don't have time to stop and take your time over a plate of oysters, then you can buy them to take home from the fabulous fish shop attached to the main restaurant.

When choosing lunch or dinner, the first stage is to assess what is the catch of the day. All the fish is sourced naturally from the French coast, unless it is marked otherwise. Alternatively, you can opt for one of the traditional regional fish dishes that are a speciality of the house. A good choice would be *mouclade*, the creamier cousin of *moules marinière*, which marries the sweet, plump shellfish with a saffron-infused sauce with just a hint of curry. The mussels used here are *moules de bouchots*, which are cultivated in clusters on wooden posts. These grow more slowly, and closer to the shore, producing mussels that are significantly richer and more complex in flavor than those raised on rope in deep water.

It is the attention to detail that makes this grande dame of Parisian dining a delightful place in which to spend time. With its warm interior of brass, wood, and glowing lamps, and the terrace overlooking the Parisian artery that is the boulevard du Montparnasse, this is a metropolitan café of distinction. **CB**

⬆ The sophisticated art deco interior of Le Dôme.

L'Ambroisie | Refined haute cuisine in surroundings to match

Location Paris **Signature dish** Roast langoustines with sesame wafer | ❸❸❸

The most formal of the elite Parisian three-Michelin-star group, this restaurant is tucked behind the arches of the splendid seventeenth-century Place des Vosges in the Marais that is home to many major figures in French politics and public life. You could be forgiven for thinking that not much has changed in at least a couple of centuries, but the restaurant was given a complete makeover about ten years ago (with the design based on a pseudo-Roman-banquet-hall look), and the interior is now clad in antique wood paneling, plasterwork, Aubusson tapestries, and chandeliers.

All this pomp is perfectly befitting of Ambroisie's haute cuisine, and this is one of the few remaining restaurants where this level of dining exists. The extreme luxury of the produce (think lobster, caviar, truffles, Champagne) and the refinement of their execution and presentation is extremely rare in France, and well nigh impossible to find outside the country. There are also three high-ceilinged adjoining salons, with a private room for larger parties and an invisibly delineated pecking order of tables.

Let's just say that if you are wearing a rucksack as opposed to Chanel, you might find yourself seated next to a very rowdy table of tourists. But whatever your attire, prepare to be thoroughly looked up and down as you arrive, and you will be addressed by your name. The slight haughtiness from the staff is all part of the experience, in fact a small price to pay for the extreme delight of the dishes you are about to savor. The most famous dishes are the langoustines in sesame puff pastry with a light curry sauce as an appetizer and a light chocolate tarte for dessert. Between those masterpieces, you might find it hard to choose between the sole with Alba truffle, the lobster with pumpkin and chestnuts with devil sauce, or the Lozère lamb with sweetbreads and gnocchi. **TD**

⬆ Sumptuous tapestries adorn the walls of the restaurant.

Le Chateaubriand | The temple of bistronomy

Location Paris   **Signature dish** Chocolate cake with olive oil and fleur de sel | ❻❻❻❻

Imagine a poster child for the new bistronomic cuisine that swept through Paris and changed forever the face of Gallic fine dining, and think of Inaki Aizpitarte. This cooler-than-thou, self-taught chef first discovered his passion while working as a dish washer in a Tel Aviv restaurant. He then rocked the restaurant scene in style when he opened Le Chateaubriand in 2006 in this forgotten pocket of the 11th arondissement.

The 1930s-style bistro, consistently ranked above a gaggle of Michelin-starred establishments in various best-of-lists, is one of the hardest tables to book in town. This is thanks to Aizpitarte's highly personal, unpretentious, and often unpredictable menu, which changes daily and marries pristine ingredients in original ways. Dishes such as red berry piperade or foie gras in miso soup show the Basque chef's eye for showcasing high-quality products while combining them in often unexpected ways, although always with his own inimitable technical flair.

Picky diners beware that this destination table is not for those who are faint of heart in their dining preferences. The menu is strictly no choice (although allergies are catered for) and pared down with the freshest seasonal produce, often featuring raw fish and meat. There are no tablecloths, service is of the bearded and tattooed hipster variety, and the natural wine-heavy list sometimes needs some navigating, but this is one hot spot that leaves no one indifferent.

Despite the iconoclastic nature of this dining establishment, Le Chateaubriand provides a veritable snapshot of the best of modern French cooking. Dining reservations are among the most difficult to obtain in town; but, after the first sitting, walk-ins are accepted from 9.30 P.M. While waiting, it is best to pass the time at the next-door Rem-Koolhaas designed natural wine bar, Le Dauphin. **TD**

⬆ Innovative, characterful dining is on offer here.

La Fontaine de Mars | Enjoy classic French dishes in a charming bistrot

Location Paris **Signature dish** Duck confit | 💲💲

> " 'It's like being in a movie about Paris,' murmur those charmed by the prototypic bistro look … "

zagat.com

⬆ La Fontaine de Mars offers a delightful Parisian dining experience.

When it comes to a taste of Paris, rue St. Dominique, in the otherwise mostly sedate 7th arrondissement, has everything going for it: picture-postcard views of the iconic Eiffel Tower at almost every turn, terrific restaurants and food shopping, and a Parisian site of note to visit at either end of the road, namely the Ecole Militaire and Les Invalides.

La Fontaine de Mars has the considerateness to stay open for seven days a week, including the summer month of August, which sees so many places close for vacation, and so it is an exemplary spot for a long, lazy lunch in the middle of an extended *balade*. Since its opening in 1908, this charming, friendly bistro has retained all of its appeal through various renovations and extensions as well as the much-publicized visit of the Obamas in 2009. Its decor is reassuringly pure French bistrot, with its wood-paneled walls, deep red-leather banquettes, and red-checked tablecloths on tables that spill out from all sides onto the pavements of the rue St. Dominique.

The *fontane* (fountain) in the bistrot's name sits to one side of the restaurant, and the tables on the terrasse under the stone arcades are one of the most pleasant places to linger on a hot summer's day, cooled by the tinkling of the fountain's water spray. The cuisine is Parisian bistrot with a gentle selection of local produce (and, indeed, some very good wines) from the southwest of France—duck confit, magret de canard, and foie gras pepper are all on the menu, and there is an excellent cassoulet from Toulouse.

More than anything, this is a perfect rendezvous to enjoy some impeccably created bistrot classics. These include *oeufs en meurette* (eggs cooked in red wine sauce), giant Burgundy snails in garlic butter, *boudin noir* (black sausage) from famous charcutier Christian Parra, *andouillettes*, *blanquette de veau* (veal blanquette), and one of the very best roast lamb dishes in Paris. **TD**

Le Comptoir du Relais | Luxurious comfort food in a bijou bistro

Location Paris **Signature dish** *Cochon au lait aux lentilles* (roast suckling pig with lentils) | ❸❸❸

Le Comptoir du Relais is a viable contender for the best bistro in Paris. This unique, iconoclastic venue also has a comforting aspect, where local gourmands and food critics rub elbows with tourists, and where everyone will find their gustatory pleasure.

Chef Yves Camdeborde virtually created France's gastro-bistro revolution with his far-flung La Régalade, which was among the first to offer top-flight products (similar to those in Michelin-starred establishments, minus the truffles and caviar) along with affordable, generous menus (although with a limited choice) for the general dining public. His training at the Hôtel de Crillon and the exceptional value prices have ensured this bistro has been fully booked up for a decade.

When he moved to the Left Bank and opened the Hôtel Le Relais Saint Germain, with its art deco dining room dubbed Le Comptoir, it was the equivalent of a culinary earthquake. The forty-seater bijou dining room is open daily for lunch (walk-ins only) and has a vast menu of seasonal, luxurious comfort food. A typical meal might start with homemade charcuterie from cult producer Eric Ospital, or crab *rémoulade,* and continue with scallops roasted in their shells with algae butter, or a juicy steak with Béarnaise.

In the evening, the restaurant is often booked months in advance for the tasting-menu-only dinner, where Camdeborde takes off his gloves and hits your taste buds with reinvented classics and sometimes edgy cooking: fried eggs with black truffles, sashimi quality raw scallops with Espelette pepper, milk-fed lamb from the Pyrénnées with fresh peas. Then there are mind-blowing desserts, as well as good renditions of crowd-pleasing favorites such as rice pudding with caramel sauce. If you show up *sans reservation,* bide your time at the wine bar next door, L'Avant Comptoir, a friendly standing-room-only joint, where they'll ply you with natural wine and tapas until a seat becomes available in Le Comptoir du Relais. **TD**

" … the single dinner sitting … features a five-course set menu of haute-cuisine food."

fodors.com

⬆ Seriously accomplished cooking, enjoyed in intimate surroundings at Le Comptoir du Relais.

La Rotonde | Historic Parisian venue serving classic dishes all day

Location Paris **Signature dish** Steak tartare | ❸❸

This grand Parisian brasserie, with its red awnings, art deco sign, and curving frontage takes its place among the celebrated places to eat on the boulevard du Montparnasse. Open all day, this is an ideal venue to rest in between forays into the heart of Paris.

La Rotonde sits directly opposite Le Dôme; while over the road fish is the star, here the steak tartare is legendary. It is not unusual to find steak tartare in Paris. However, it is the quality of the dish in this venue that sets it apart. The various elements are brought to the table, chopped, mixed, and prepared following your order on a serving table to one side. As well as offering wonderful dinner theater, it also ensures exceptional freshness, essential for a really good steak tartare.

"… the ancient Rotonde … has become a favored destination for partying Parisians."

Time Out

Other French classics are onion soup and *sole Meunière*, with a cheese course of Saint-Marcellin, finishing with ice creams and sorbets from celebrated maker Berthillon. You can also choose a *formule* (set menu), where you can put together an appetizer, main course, and dessert for less than the à la carte menu.

La Rotonde wears its history with pride, and has changed little since 1911. Over the past century, the red-velvet banquettes and fringed brass light fittings have borne witness to Parisian figures such as Chaïm Soutine, Amedeo Modigliani, Jean Cocteau, and the Ballets Russes, who have all passed into its red-painted interior, sat on wicker chairs on the terrace enjoying a café noisette, and watched the city go by. **CB**

Le Meurice | Elegant cuisine in stunningly sumptuous surroundings

Location Paris **Signature dish** Guinea fowl and foie gras pâté *en croute* | ❸❸❸❸

In 1835, Augustin Meurice installed a new luxury hotel under the vaulted pavement of rue de Rivoli, overlooking Les Tuileries. The location was close to the most prestigious shopping areas and attracted artists, writers, sovereigns, and aristocrats from all over the world. Le Meurice's restaurant is in the magnificent Salon Pompadour, inspired by the Salon de la Paix in the Château de Versailles. White and gold paneling, towering mirrors and oil paintings, marble pillars, and gold-embossed bronze decorations make this the most stunning, glittering dining room in Paris.

After a successful period under Michelin-starred chef Yannick Alléno, the restaurant was recently taken over by Alain Ducasse. He has removed some of the Philippe Starck elements that had previously been introduced, redirecting the focus toward sumptuous period beauty.

Head chef Christophe Saintagne brings with him an ultra-refined celebration of French *terroir*, creating a luxury version of the farm-to-table international cooking wave. The style is light, playful, and luxurious. Simple ingredients are used with meticulous care and cooked with extreme precision. Salt-steamed root vegetables arrive in cast-iron pots, with long silver forks with which to skewer them. Semi-raw scallops come with a lavish shaving of Alba truffle on a simple souffléd buckwheat crêpe; an optimal ripeness camembert is served with perfectly seasoned lettuce and Christophe Vasseur's Pain des Amis. The chocolate dessert uses Premier and Grand Crus from Alain Ducasse's Bastille chocolate atelier. The service is affable and efficient. Le Meurice is a deliciously romantic, modern Parisian experience and not to be missed—if your wallet can take the strain. **TD**

➜ Le Meurice embodies a delightful, romantic style.

Le Cinq | Luxe, high French cuisine in palatial surroundings

Location Paris **Signature dish** *Pithiviers* of grouse, partridge, hen pheasant, and foie gras | ❺❺❺❺❺

The sumptuous walk through the Four Seasons Hotel George V lobby and "galerie"—a long, tapestry-clad salon with sofas and armchairs—leads you to the impressive doors of Le Cinq's dining room. If you are a man and are not wearing a jacket and tie, you will be lent one by the restaurant before being allowed to take your seat, as Le Cinq is one of the last formal rooms where a dress code is strictly imposed. The restaurant's high ceilings, palm trees, oil paintings, marble-painted columns, crystal chandeliers, and arched, draped windows opening onto the hotel courtyard combine to transport you to a world of the most immaculate luxury.

Thankfully, chef Eric Briffard's two-Michelin-star cuisine does justice to the magnificent surroundings. Briffard holds the distinction *Meilleur Ouvrier de France* (MOF), meaning "best French craftsman," a unique and prestigious award in France. Briffard trained with Joël Robuchon and spent many years in Japan, so his highly classical haute-cuisine française is tinged with the Japanese precision and architecture that so many great French chefs have absorbed.

His *pithiviers* is a sort of ultimate game pie that requires days of preparation, made with foie gras, chestnut honey, and three different birds (grouse, partridge, and hen pheasant). This and his roast lamb, slow cooked for seventeen hours, are perhaps the most famous dishes on the menu. There is also the grandiose *chariot des mignardises*, a two-tiered trolley full of sweets, lollipops, sugared fruits, nuts, and petit fours served after dessert. But his masterful handling of the most simple fruit and vegetables—often chosen personally by Briffard at the nearby, très chic Marché d'Iéna in avenue du Président Wilson—also satisfy the smaller appetites of business lunchers who haven't planned a siesta after their meal. **TD**

⬆ **The glittering, palatial dining room of Le Cinq.**

Le Train Bleu | A Belle Epoque gem set in a bustling train station

Location Paris   **Signature dish** Beef tartare | ❸❸❸

The Exposition Universelle in 1889 brought to Paris some of its most ambitious and enduring Art Nouveau architectural projects, many of which form the most iconic parts of the metropolis today. There are the sweeping, majestic Grand Palais and Petit Palais galleries, the Pont Alexandre III, and the Gare de Lyon, one of Paris' six major train stations and today a humming modern transport hub. Set among the arrivals boards and ticket booths, Le Train Bleu is a delightful eccentricity.

Opening at the station in 1901, this venue is a gorgeous example of the spirit of the age, which was able to simultaneously celebrate the past as well as welcome a wealth of fresh, new ideas for the future. So in between the ostentatious gilt and velvet and the carvings in the grand, high-ceilinged room of Le Train Blue, you will also encounter forty-one oil paintings of trains, railways, and significant events from the turn of the twentieth century.

Coco Chanel, Brigitte Bardot, Jean Cocteau, and Salvador Dalí have all been regulars here. There is something utterly irresistible and romantic about the place, from the sweeping double staircase to the fat golden cherubs on every cornice.

You pass the seafood display on your way in—all crushed ice and beady eyes—but that's not all that's on offer. Global influences abound: a fillet of mullet with fennel and tomatoes crowned with a tempura zucchini flower; cod marinated in gazpacho; or Scottish salmon cooked with coconut and red curry. The meat dishes are less avant-garde—veal, chicken, steak, and lamb are cooked with solid classic flavors, while desserts are pure nostalgia—eclair, rum baba, *millefeuille*, meringue, and brioche trifle. After more than a century, Le Train Bleu still straddles the old and the new, and attracts the beau monde of Paris. **EH**

⬆ The glorious, ornate ceiling is a feast for the eyes.

Pierre Gagnaire | A temple of world gastronomy
showcasing a master chef's cuisine

Location Paris   **Signature dish** "Le Grand Dessert de Pierre Gagnaire" (eight desserts based on traditional patisserie) | ❸❸❸❸

"If you want to venture to the frontier of contemporary luxe cooking … dinner here is a must."

fodors.com

⬆ Delicate sea bream carpaccio at Pierre Gagnaire.

Just off of the densely packed (with tourists) avenue des Champs Elysées, hidden in the womb of the tiny Hotel Balzac, lies one of the temples of world gastronomy, run by the enigmatic Pierre Gagnaire. Despite the fact that Gagnaire runs or owns thirteen restaurants around the world, from Berlin to Tokyo, this cosseted, modern lair, encased in brown lacquer and decorated with doodles from the chef, is undoubtedly *la maison mère*, bringing well-heeled gastronauts from the four corners of the globe to try the chef's unique and challenging cuisine.

Gagnaire is a firm believer in fine French produce and old-school techniques, but his travels and his experimentations with French food scientist Hervé have undoubtedly propelled his cuisine into the future. So Gagnaire fearlessly sends out strange and imaginative dishes, some of pure genius, others flawed, but always interesting.

Appetizers might include seaweed jelly with razor clams and baby mackerel, or perhaps a refreshing pear flavored with dwarf Artemisia, Thai grapefruit, cheese, pineapple, and calamansi. Mains are more anchored in the traditional. Perhaps an impeccably cooked veal rump roasted with orange sliced at the tableside, served on a watercress puree, and accompanied by an unctuous burrata-cheese ice cream with celery root, Siam squash, and Cremona mustard.

Gagnaire personally inspects every plate and is the spitting image of a mad scientist with his long, white hair, ever gesticulating, tasting, and observing, in a constant state of motion, whether backstage or in the dining room. There is no doubt that a meal at chez Gagnaire is an exceptional experience, by turns exciting, surprising, satisfying, and even sometimes frustrating, but one which leaves its imprint on your culinary brain for some time. **TD**

Passage 53 | Simple ingredients are elevated in an unusual venue

Location Paris **Signature dish** *Velouté de potimarron* (creamy soup of winter squash with cheese) | ❸❸❸❸

There is something of the Far Eastern temple about Passage 53. The white-painted, doll's-house-like space, with its narrow spiral staircase is hushed and tranquil—there's a single stem of blossom in the window, and everything is laid out just so. Even the crockery is remarkable, eggshell thin, in pleasingly unexpected shapes and textures.

No surprise, then, to learn that the kitchen talent comes from Shinichi Sato, the first Japanese chef to earn two Michelin stars in France. He learned from the best, at l'Astrance in Paris and Mugaritz in Spain. This classical and modern juxtaposition is reflected in the location in Passage des Panoramas, an eighteenth-century, glass-covered arcade known for its stamp collectors' boutiques and vast range of restaurants. Of these, Passage 53 is the most distinguished and least ostentatious—the signage is discreet and the white blinds are permanently lowered.

The set menus range from simply indulgent to lavishly extravagant. You can stick to the set menu or choose from the tasting dishes, matched wines, or an extra such as that day's truffle delivery brought to the table squatting in a glass jar and wafted under your nose. Whichever you choose, you will receive a series of pitch-perfect dishes that run from classical to startlingly inventive, with charming extra titbits like freshly baked miniature madeleines, all butter and treacly crunch, or a stunning amuse-bouche of chilled pumpkin soup layered into a tiny oval cup with fromage blanc so that it looks like an egg. The separate courses all sing out clearly—oysters with fennel and green-apple mousse, or a delicately scented crème brûlée with an ambrosial scoop of honey sorbet, crowned with a twist of spun sugar. A meal that will linger in the memory, because it is about more than simple greed or technique. **EH**

Le Voltaire | An historic Parisian address, perfect for people watching

Location Paris **Signature dish** *Oeuf mayonnaise* | ❸❸❸

The superbly dreamy setting and historical heritage of this rather claustrophically cozy restaurant continues to charm Parisians and visitors. Nestled on the Quai Voltaire, at the Left Bank corner of Le Pont Royal, this offers a perfect midday stop between visits to the Louvre and the Musée d'Orsay.

As you step down through the tiny entrance of Le Voltaire, you can choose between quick-and-simple dishes or take your time in the more gastro section. Either way, the atmosphere is inimitable, with elder Parisian literati, loud tourists, and, during Paris Fashion Week, fashion editors, celebrities, and supermodels. Tables are cramped, the tableware satisfyingly old-fashioned and ornate, and the service pretty much par

---

"Clubby, expensive, and fun, this elegant hideaway … pulls in a chic French and American crowd."

Zagat

---

for the course in Paris, unless you are Anna Wintour, that is. Thankfully, the food and the history are good enough to make up for any froideur from the staff.

The greatest curiosity here is the bargain *oeuf mayonnaise*, a nod to more egalitarian dining times, which comes beautifully garnished with crudités on a flowery plate. The price of everything else, from coffee to a (very good) roast chicken and crisp chips, will well make up for any savings you've made by choosing the cheaper egg dish. But the classics are well executed, and you cannot go wrong with the salmon steak and Béarnaise sauce, mushooms in olive-oil vinaigrette with generous Parmesan shavings, or the tarte tatin and crème fraîche. **TD**

Mollard | Gloriously ornate decor and a slice of Parisian history

Location Paris **Signature dish** "Omelette Surprise" (Norwegian omelette) | 💲💲💲

The significance of this gorgeously ornate art deco brasserie is forever linked to the Gare St. Lazare across the street. Opened in 1895 as the St. Lazare quartier, then the most chic and modern in Paris, business was booming, and Parisians flocked to enjoy the impressive decor of this newly created restaurant.

Architect Jean Niermans commissioned mosaics of scenes from Deauville, St. Germain en Laye, and Ville d'Avray, all destinations reached from St. Lazare, and he also designed the banquettes and furniture. The glittering decor was judged old-fashioned after World War II, and was hidden away behind paint and panels. In 1965, it was once again revealed, almost completely intact, and restored to its former glory.

" … the desserts are deliciously retro, ranging from crêpes Suzette to omelette norvégienne… "

Time Out

Mollard is now a protected historical monument and the Gare St. Lazare has had a new facelift. The atmosphere and hazy, sepia light of the mirrors and mosaics give the brasserie a dreamy feel, above the noise of travelers and tourists. Huge trays of oysters and seafood, prepared at the ice-clad outdoor bar, are hoisted high by white-aproned waiters zigzagging their way around the tables. The food is less than gastronomic, so stick to the simple dishes (avoid the fish à la carte and the house wines by the glass), and the oysters and seafood. "Omelette Surprise," the signature dish, is a fun, swan-shaped Norwegian omelette, with ice cream encased in Italian meringue, flambéed, and brought alight to the table. **TD**

Restaurant Chaumette | A taste of French bourgeois cuisine

Location Paris **Signature dish** Pot au feu | 💲💲

Chaumette is one of the last outposts of mondaine restaurant life, arriving before the great *bon chic, bons gens* (bcbg) expanses of the 16th arrondissement hit the Périphérique. This is the lunchtime canteen for many radio and TV journalists from nearby La Maison de la Radio and TF1 studios, while, in the evening, it morphs into a neighborhood restaurant for the elegant (older) locals.

This authentic Lyonnais bouchon was founded in the 1930s by Madame Chaumette, friend of the great and the good from France's cinema industry. There are still framed letters of praise on the walls in the toilets written from an expanse of stars, including Brassens, Arletty, and Jean Marais, and the decor has hardly changed since its inception, even after Madame Chaumette's death in the 1980s. The comfortable banquettes, a winding iron staircase, wood panels, old photos, mirrors on the walls, a zinc-rimmed bar, and the traditional French bourgeois cuisine rich with *jus courts*, veal, and fish stocks, Chaumette will satisfy your appetite and your clichéd bistrot dreams.

The low awning over the long, wood-encased windows of the façade creates a cozy inside/out terrasse that spills right out over the pavement in summer, inviting you to stroll along the Seine to the nearby Eiffel Tower and Champ de Mars. There's a great value prix-fixe menu at lunchtime, and, in the evening, the menu stretches itself over typical bistro dishes with a twist such as pan-fried veal kidneys with small clams, roast chicken breast with chorizo coulis, and cabbage stuffed with crab meat. Or you can stick to true classics such as chicken liver terrine with confit onion puree, *pot au feu* (the house speciality made with three meats, five vegetables, and an egg-white clarified bouillon), steak with Béarnaise sauce, and vanilla *millefeuille*. **TD**

Prunier | Extravagant seafood and a long-established supplier of the very best caviar

Location Paris **Signature dish** Caviar | ❸❸❸

This exquisite art deco jewel of a restaurant—decked out in a gold-flecked, sea-blue façade—is steeped in history and protected by a French historic monument classification. It was built in 1925 by Alfred Prunier, more than fifty years after he had opened his first oyster house on rue d'Antin. Glittering its way through the end of the century—and especially during the Franco-Russian alliance of 1892—Prunier started to import caviar for his ever-growing Russian clientele.

After many ups and downs, fast forward to 2000, when La Maison Prunier was bought by Pierre Bergé, then president of Yves Saint Laurent Couture. Bergé, passionate about caviar (and the new owner of a sturgeon farm in the Dordogne), promptly entered Prunier into partnership with Caviar House, ensuring many happy and prosperous years ahead. The dark, very formal, verging-on-strict room—with its art deco trappings; high, twinkling walls; and stiff, brown-checked fabric banquettes—is still where the ultra-rich come for their caviar. Prunier sells its own and many other brands, these days preferring farmed sturgeon from the U.S. and Europe to an unreliably produced and unecological "wild" Russian supply.

The restaurant specializes in *"tout ce qui vient de la mer"* (everything from the sea), and enjoying the good-value, three-course lunchtime menu is an accessible treat for a more modest budget. You can sample fresh crab meat tartare, light small clam broth, perfect John Dory with steamed artichokes and cresson jus, and perhaps 1.75 ounces (50 grams) of Prunier's excellent caviar "Tradition." If oysters are your preference, you can choose them from the long, marble-festooned shellfish bar that greets you as you enter, mirroring its caviar counterpart across the room. The choice of wines and Champagnes is as you would expect it to be, extensive and expensive. **TD**

> *" This chic and expensive … seafood extravaganza boasts a gorgeous art deco dining room."*
>
> Zagat

⬆ The beautiful art deco façade of Prunier.

Le Jules Verne | Make this restaurant No. 1 on your Parisian dining-out list

Location Paris **Signature dish** *L'Ecrou* chocolate and praline dessert | ❺❺❺❺❺

> "The fish shimmers as if it were a giant pearl, its texture satisfyingly chewy …"

Jasper Gerard, *Daily Telegraph*

⬆ A sumptuous dish of lobster, celery, and black truffle with remoulade and Gala apple salad.

➡ Le Jules Verne comes with panoramic views from the second floor of the Eiffel Tower.

If ever there were a destination restaurant, then it is Le Jules Verne. Part of Alain Ducasse's extended empire, there's just no more memorable Parisian address, a breathtaking 137 yards (125 m) up, on the second floor of the Eiffel Tower. Visitors take the heated, padded elevator up through the south tower of the Eiffel Tower until they reach their tables, and this is certainly a great prelude, with truly mind-blowing views across the city. That it is possible to run a restaurant perched in such a place is on its own extraordinary, and that it should be a gastronomic experience is an added bonus. Le Jules Verne is also a culinary feat, because no flame is allowed in the kitchens at this altitude. So the elements of each dish are assembled in the kitchens below the southern tower and are then taken up to the second floor for final assembly.

Do not, therefore, make any requests for flame-grilled or flambéed ingredients—in fact even a green salad on the side—because diners must stick to the menu. The latter is studded with French classics, some served exactly as you would expect, whereas others are given a light makeover. The Challans duck, for example, is cooked in a cast-iron *cocotte* with turnips and apples; the beef *tournedos* are prepared with foie gras, souffléed potatoes, and *sauce périgueux;* the Breton lobster is accompanied by cocoa beans and a light bisque; and the salmon served with caviar and sorrel sauce. The signature dessert "L'Ecrou" (the bolt) is a geometrically shaped chocolate mousse and ganache creation with crispy *feuillantine* and praline.

Almost everyone here is celebrating something, giving the rooms a rather febrile feel, despite the fact that dress codes seem to be forgotten. The helpful service is well used to providing candles for birthday cakes and keeping a subtle eye out for marriage proposals. Try to score a table right by the window in order to savor this truly Parisian dining experience at its panoramic best. **TD**

Polidor | Pick a good bottle of wine, look around you, and step back in time

Location Paris   **Signature dish** *Blanquette de veau* (veal ragout) | ❸❸

One of the oldest Paris *bouillons*, the stunning interior of Polidor has hardly shifted since it opened in 1845. Its fate as an unmissable Parisian landmark was sealed when Woody Allen used it as a location in his madly successful *Midnight in Paris*, and it really does reek of history and romance.

It is not hard to imagine back in time Verlaine, Hugo, and Rimbaud drinking and debating at every red-checked table; Vian, Jarry, Queneau, and Ionesco holding meetings of the Collège de Pataphysique ("imaginary science college"); or groups of Mai 1968 students striding across the ancient patterned tiles to organize their social revolution. Set in the heart of the university quarter near l'Odéon, there is a lovely, laid-back, bohemian feel to Polidor, following the same style as those bars and bistrots frequented by Parisian students. Visitors are less numerous now, however.

Such is Polidor's historical and literary legacy that it has become a sort of museum or pilgrimage restaurant, with eighty percent now filled by visitors who sit together at the long communal tables in the center of the restaurant. This has pushed up the prices.

The menu of bistrot staples is almost unchanged from its heyday, with specials set on the same days since forever. Tuesdays and Fridays welcome *hachis parmentier* (shepherd's pie), Mondays see black sausage and mashed potato, then tripe arrives on Wednesdays, Auvergne sausage and lentils on Thursdays, and roast lamb and beans on the weekend. The three-course lunch menu is simple—celery remoulade, beef bourguignon, and fruit tarte—while the evening adds a little chic with smoked salmon, duck confit, and tarte tatin. You can sniff out a decent bottle of wine from the old-fashioned Polidor wine cellar next door, and then pretend you are a poet or a novelist for a heady hour or two. **TD**

⬆ Polidor provides the classic Paris *bouillon* experience.

Tour d'Argent | Historic dining in the heart of the French capital

Location Paris **Signature dish** *Canard au sang, pommes soufflés* (roast duck, soufflé fried potatoes) | ❺❺❺❺

Tour d'Argent is the oldest restaurant in the city, and perhaps the most important slice of the history of Parisian dining. Its history goes right back to 1580, when Monsieur Rourteau opened a tavern built with silvery stone from the Champagne region. Here, discoveries were made: Henry III learned to use a fork, Henry IV enjoyed *poule au pot*, and Richelieu found that a whole ox could be cooked in thirty different ways. Destroyed during the Revolution, the restaurant was reborn during the Second Empire thanks to the Maître d'Hôtel and subsequent owner, Frédéric Delair, who defined and established forever the recipe of the venue's famous roast duck, *canard au sang*, a linchpin of the menu and, indeed, the establishment.

Fast-forward to 1947, and young Claude Terrail inherits the maison, moved by his father André to the sixth floor of the building. Terrail installed the wraparound, floor-to-ceiling windows that gave the restaurant its breathtaking views over the Paris rooftops, the Seine, and Notre Dame. Terrail's sense of spectacle brought glamor and international prestige to the restaurant, adding artists, Hollywood stars, and heads of state to the already impressive "we were here" gallery (this is on show on the ground floor of the building and worth a look). Today, it is more for the history and the show that people visit Tour d'Argent.

The split-level room that sits bathed in Paris' buttery light is splendid and lively. The waistcoats and tails of the waiting staff and the two "duck theaters"—canopied stands where the *canards au sang* are prepared—give you the feeling that you are making a stage entrance. Your (numbered) duck is carved and served at your table on a silver and mahogany chariot, no less, and crêpes Suzettes are also spectacularly flambéed at the tableside. Both these dishes are essential fare for the full Tour d'Argent experience. **TD**

⬆ A dish of langoustines at Paris' oldest restaurant.

Ribouldingue | A modest
bistro specializing in offal

Location Paris **Signature dish** *Tête de veau* (beef brain) | ❸❸❸

Paris is full of restaurants renowned for glitz, glamor, noise, and bustle, but La Ribouldingue is special because it is so small and unassuming. The Left Bank location couldn't be better, just a short walk from the Seine and with a view of Notre Dame at the front door. (All the more reason to grab a table outside if the weather is good.) Inside, the restaurant is wood-paneled, with a decorative motif of a leaping man.

For offal lovers, this is heaven on Earth. Most days you can expect not just bistro classics of sweetbreads, tripe, and brains, but more unusual offal such as cow's udder and pig's snout or ear. Each is given expert and distinctive treatment—the brains might be fried or poached, for example, and can be served hot or cold.

" … usually full of people, including critics and chefs, who love simple, honest bistro fare."

Time Out

You don't have to love offal to come here. Fish dishes are also recommended for first and second courses, and the vegetable soup (served from a huge tureen) is reliably good. So are the desserts, which tend toward slightly decadent richness, and the cheese selection on a wooden board is a pair of perfectly chosen specimens with a lovely mixed salad. Wines can be found at reasonable prices (for Paris).

Two minor warnings: on some days, the offal offering is smaller than usual, so those seeking less-familiar examples might be disappointed; and you might sometimes have to wait a little for your food. But these are the tiniest of complaints. And the venue's diminutive size makes booking *de rigueur*. **RE**

Maxim's | Belle Epoque restaurant
immortalized by Woody Allen

Location Paris **Signature dish** *La selle d'agneau "Belle Otero"* (roast lamb) | ❸❸❸

If ever there were a restaurant where the food really does not matter, it is Maxim's. This restaurant has always been more of a temple of enjoyment. Nowadays open only in the evenings, it caters more to groups of tourists and corporate gatherings than the glittering *Tout Paris* of yesterday.

You can book small tables and eat à la carte, in which case stick to classics such as melon and serrano ham, sea bass carpaccio, red mullet and ratatouille, or pot-roast Bresse chicken with tarragon butter and potato puree for two. Alternatively, you can enjoy overpriced dishes with liberal scatterings of caviar, lobster, langoustines, and foie gras. This will create a spectacle and allow you to experience this worthy jewel of the Belle Epoque, most recently brought to life on screen by Woody Allen's *Midnight in Paris*.

Maxim's was redecorated for the Paris Exposition Universelle in 1900. Maxime Gaillard brought in artists from l'Ecole de Nancy and transformed the interior, most notably with the splendid glass ceiling, painted wall frescoes, cut-glass mirrors, and the bronze and copper decorations in grand Art Nouveau style. Upstairs, chambres d'amour (now private salons) were built for courtisans, the most famous of whom had dishes named after them on the menu! Proust, Guitry, and Cocteau were regulars before the restaurant was requisitioned, then becoming the favorite spot for German officers during the occupation. When Paris was liberated, the jet set returned en force. Onassis, Callas, and Marlene Dietrich among many others, contributed to its ascendency, until in the sixties and seventies, it became the most glamorous and most expensive restaurant in the world. Pierre Cardin then took over, spreading the brand around the globe. In 1979, it was registered, and henceforth has been protected as a national historical monument. **TD**

Restaurant Michel Rostang | Bourgeoise cuisine
by the latest star of the Rostang dynasty

Location Paris **Signature dish** *Pain de mie* black truffle sandwich | ❸❸❸❸

Michel Rostang grew up in Sassenage, near Grenoble, in his parents' hotel-restaurant. Four generations of Rostang chefs came before him and Michel first learned his skills with his own father, Jo, in the Alps, and later at famous Parisian maisons, Lucas Carton and Lasserre. In 1978, he opened his own restaurant on a quiet corner in the 17th arrondissement. His restaurant today is one of the last Parisian temples of bourgeoise cuisine, although it is interesting to know that Rostang was the first Michelin-starred chef to introduce *prix-fixe* menus—and even branch out into secondary bistrots, as so many chefs do today.

The restaurant is a formal yet warm space, with dark wood, a hushed atmosphere, and attentive, accomplished, old-style service—this often includes a greeting by Michel's wife as you arrive. Rostang's cooking revolves around contrasts between cooked and raw, sea and land, with a penchant toward the cuisine of Lyonnais, Savoie, and Provence.

A specialist of black-and-white cooking truffles, Michel's simple *pain de mie* black truffle sandwich has become a modern classic, even though it is packaged and sold in season at La Grande Epicerie de Paris as the ultimate luxury fast food. In the restaurant, as well as the truffles, you will also find some noble French classics—wild game, Breton lobster, Bresse chicken, Loire valley asparagus, and ceps from Périgord. Never mind hipster bistronomy, this is where you can come to enjoy woodcock, wild boar, or roasted roe deer, all of which have been prepared in the same way for decades. Apart from roasted meats and the cultish truffle sandwich, don't miss the pan-fried foie gras with mandarin segments, souffléed *quenelles de brochet* (pike dumplings) with cream of lobster sauce, and an exquisite warm salted caramel soufflé with pear sorbet. **TD**

" … exquisite, artfully presented classics, including an incredible truffle menu in season."

Zagat

⬆ Michel Rostang continues a long line of Rostang chefs.

Septime | Contemporary cuisine is the deal at this foodies' favorite bistro

Location Paris **Signature dish** Piedmont hazelnuts with mushrooms, blackberries, and *zabaglione* | ⓢⓢⓢ

Bijou it may be, but what Septime lacks in space, it more than makes up for in personality. Run by Bertrand Grébaut, rock music fan and celebrated chef, whose take on modern gastronomy has become legendary, Septime opened just a few years ago and is now one of the "must-go" bistros in Paris.

Septime lies on the Right Bank in the trendy Bastille district, just a ten-minute walk from the Ile de la Cité and its magnificent Notre Dame Cathedral. The decor comprises gnarled wooden tables topped with exquisite glassware and large white candles, shiny hanging nautical-style lanterns, lots of mirrors, and modern art. Rock music adds to the lively ambiance.

Septime's menu is an inviting selection of small plates that change daily according to the seasons and the whim of the chef. Diners can order just one or two plates, or indulge in a feast of many. The temptation is to go for the carte blanche menu, where five courses are brought to your table, each chosen by Bertrand

himself. Artfully presented plates are likely to include Dordogne pork slow-cooked for forty-eight hours, drenched in anchovy cream, and accompanied by zucchini and turnip slices, or perhaps veal coupled with trout eggs or a huge bowl of bouillon with tasty chunks of mushrooms, seafood, and oysters. There is also an extensive wine list offering complementary pairings to individual flavors.

One of Bertrand's favorite savory dishes is crushed Piedmont hazelnuts pan-fired with flavorsome mushrooms such as porcini or chanterelles to which wild blackberries, tarragon, or wild sorrel are added, and the dish is then topped with a whipped smoked egg *zabaglione*. The desserts are equally imaginative creations—savory pumpkin puree topped with sweet sherbet is a consistently popular diners' request and is well worth sampling. **CFr**

⬆ The understated rustic interior has an urban touch.

Verjus | From supper club to world-class restaurant, this still feels like home

Location Paris **Signature dish** Skillet-cooked duck, smoked celery root, orange, rye, red cabbage sauerkraut | ❸❸❸

Set over two floors of an exquisite old townhouse, just a few moments walk from the classical columns and manicured gardens of the Palais Royale, Verjus fits in easily with the neighborhood's more distinguished addresses. You find your way there via a discreet iron gate, up some well-worn stone steps, and through an understated gray-painted doorway. The wine bar downstairs is reached from the street below.

The American owners Braden Perkins and Laura Adrian used to run a supper club in Paris called Hidden Kitchen, and its success led them to found Verjus in 2012. It has now become one of Paris' new generation of young, hip restaurants, with its international chefs performing confident riffs on French dishes and inventing plenty of their own.

The dining room is chic but not stuffy; the wine bar has its own, lighter menus. The eight-course *dégustation* (tasting) menu offers a masterful, unpretentious tour de force—depending on the season, strips of banka trout might recall Scandinavia when paired with salty roe and smoked potatoes, or speak of something wilder, teamed with chanterelles, chilies, chives, and roasted corn. Familiar flavors on the page—lemon cake with blueberries, Greek yogurt sorbet, and lavender honey, for example—always surprise on the plate, without overdoing the drama.

Downstairs in the wine bar, at lunchtime, you can try sandwiches that are soaked in nostalgia for Perkins and Adrian—"Mr Chang's Buns (East Village, NY)," with braised pork belly, steamed Chinese buns, hoisin sauce, pickles, and scallions, or "Midnight Cuban (Seattle, WA)," with pork shoulder, garlic mayo, cilantro, and chilies. Be it a full-blown restaurant meal or a snack and a glass of something, Verjus is about feeding you extremely well, in an atmosphere that is faultlessly professional and always warm. **EH**

⤒ Discreet, chic surroundings showcase excellent cooking.

Taillevent |

Savor luxury in grand French tradition

Location Paris **Signature dish** Lobster boudin, fennel, and steamed lobster with a light bisque | ❺❺❺❺❺

One of Paris' most famous gastronomic restaurants, Taillevent was created in 1946 by André Vrinat, a key figure of Parisian and French gastronomy. It gained its first Michelin star in 1948 and held three from 1973 until 2007, the year before Vrinat passed away. Today, his daughter Valerie manages the Taillevent holding, including restaurants and wine bars in Paris and Tokyo. A succession of great chefs (Philippe Legendre, Michel del Burgo, and Alain Solivérès) have run the impressive kitchens, which also inspired the makers of the popular Pixar film *Ratatouille.*

Originally a *hôtel particulier*, entering Taillevent feels like arriving at a very grand great aunt's house for lunch, greeted by the friendliest butler in the world. The clientele, however, is *Vieux Paris* businessmen and politicians—and you can almost smell the power.

" … this grande dame basks in renewed freshness under brilliant chef Alain Solivérès."

fodors.com

The two restaurant salons were spruced up in 2004 with light, Louis XVI wood paneling and contemporary sculptures and paintings. The service is immaculate, and service à table with meat, fish, and some desserts prepared at the time follows a mesmerizing, formal style. Dishes such as crayfish and frogs' legs in pastry or *tourte* of jugged hare *à la Royale* are created in the grand French tradition, without the complicated techno-finicky elements so prevalent in starry international restaurants. Savor, too, the fabulous wine list from the extensive Taillevent cellars, which hold over 1800 references. **TD**

Breizh Café |

Breton crêpes meet Japanese fusion

Location Cancale **Signature dish** Buckwheat galette with Breton ham | ❺❺❺❺

Humble Breton pancakes are usually eaten in the street or as a budget dish in a tourist restaurant. In this western region of France, the local speciality is known as a galette when savory, with simple fillings like cheese or ham. Sweet pancakes, called crêpes, are usually stuffed with jelly or honey. On the grand old seafront promenade of Cancale, however, crêpes reach a gourmet level. Overlooking the oyster beds and harbor wall, Breizh Café is an intriguing mix of rustic Breton tradition and minimalist Japanese style.

Downstairs, it's all crêpes, served with an unusual precision in a minimalist Japanese style. Ingredients are organic versions of the traditional, with optional additions for the adventurous. These range from the interesting (pine nuts and blue cheese) to the more outrageous (fried eggs or Japanese *yuzu* citrus butter). Buckwheat galettes are chopped into neat sections and served on slates.

Upstairs, things are more formally Eastern. Diners remove their shoes, and they can eat at the bar facing the open Japanese kitchen or kneel at low tables with the option of chopsticks. Tall windows look out across the Bay of Mont St. Michel. The upstairs menu is a sophisticated fusion of Japanese and Breton. Lobsters caught from the waters outside the window are served in a velouté, in a tall mug with a wooden spoon, and Cancale oysters are lined up for eating on a long black slate plate. Duck breast portions come with noodles on a bed of Japanese vegetables, and the scallops are topped with a tiny yellow flower.

Upstairs, dishes can be paired with wine or sake; downstairs, there's an extensive menu of traditional pancake accompaniments, cider or Calvados. Founder Bertrand Larcher's eclectic formula has been a great success, earning a Michelin star in Cancale, with offshoots of Breizh opened in Paris and Japan. **SH**

Maison des Tanneurs | Classic Alsace *choucroute garnie*
at an ancient timbered mansion by the river

Location Strasbourg   **Signature dish** Duck liver *Belle Strasbourgeoise* | ❸❸❸

The magnificent, heavily timbered mansion at the side of the River Ill on Strasbourg's Grande Ile houses one of the city's finest restaurants. Built in 1572, during the reign of King Charles IX, the Maison des Tanneurs was a tannery that supplied the city with shoe leather. The stench in those days must have been unbearable, but today the only aromas emanating from the building are those of top-quality *choucroute garnie* (dressed sauerkraut).

Since opening in 1946, the Maison des Tanneurs has built a reputation among gourmands for a menu of traditional Strasbourg specialities. Resplendent with solid-oak panels and beams, red soft furnishings, and lead-light windows, the service in the dining hall is calm and assured, the setting creating a gracious atmosphere. Summer dining can also be enjoyed on the terrace, with a view of the boats going to and fro on the river below.

The various flavors and textures on the menu fuse seamlessly together. Choose an appetizer from rich terrine of duck with hazelnuts, *tarte a l'oignon*, or *escargots* delicately cooked in Riesling and garlic butter. To follow, there are veal kidneys in an Alsatian white-wine sauce, guinea fowl with green bell peppers, or the signature dish *Belle Strasbourgeoise*, duck liver braised slowly with local herbs. All these dishes demonstrate a firm emphasis on the present as well as some cleverly honed modern ideas.

Strasbourg's sauerkraut staple is never far away, served, for example, with the Alsatian pork dish *Baeckeoffe* and a dish with neat little twirls of dough and beef with Provençal herbs called *Fleischnackas*. Finally, maintain the Strasbourg tradition right to the end of the meal with the marbled cake *Kougelhopf* with homemade ice cream, or the traditional Alsatian apple and cream tart drizzled with fruit coulis. **CFr**

"We recommend crayfish tails in court bouillon and coq au Riesling (chicken, white wine, and noodles)."

frommers.com

⊡ Overlooking the river Ill, the splendid Maison des Tanneurs offers summertime dining on the terrace.

Au Crocodile | Inspired gastronomic creations at a Strasbourg legend with a long-standing pedigree

Location Strasbourg **Signature dish** Blue lobster cannelloni | ❸❸❸

"Artistically presented seasonal specialities have won Au Crocodile a Michelin star."

Lonely Planet

⬆ Au Crocodile is a gourmet destination.

Au Crocodile is something of a legend in Strasbourg, having had its gastronomic repertoire celebrated by the world's foremost food critics for almost a hundred years. So, when Michelin-starred chef Phillippe Bohrer took over this super-elegant restaurant in 2010, he certainly had a reputation to uphold; a task which he has managed to do in style—inspired gastronomic creations are not in short supply here.

The glorious seventeenth-century mansion that houses the restaurant is packed full of fascinating period details, such as golden oak paneling, stucco walls, ornate ceilings, and Old Masters. And, yes, there is indeed a stuffed crocodile that hangs in the foyer, which is said to have been brought back by a local general in the late 1700s after a stint with Napoleon Bonaparte's army in Egypt.

The restaurant offers a classic dining experience. Chef Phillippe Bohrer, who hails from Alsace and trained under some of the country's finest chefs, offers an assortment of amuse-bouches to pave the way for the elegant dishes to follow. These include foie gras presented with a crumbled nut coat and drizzled with a plum spiced wine sauce; an ingot of roasted duck breast portions in a poached fig sauce; blue lobster cannelloni; or a dish of succulent grilled turbot presented with a creamy chestnut sauce. These are just a handful of creations that might feature on the six-course Menu Gourmand and the ten-course Menu d'Agrément set menus.

A freshly baked streusel with chocolate ganache and sweet ice cream, a chocolate mousse with a praline crisp and *yuzu* juice, or red-berry coulis are among the range of desserts that might bring the Au Crocodile experience to a close. Along the way, the 65,000-bottle wine cellar will yield the most perfect liquid accompaniment. **CFr**

L'Auberge de l'Ill

A classic French family auberge

Location Illhaeusern **Signature dish** Salmon soufflé "Auberge de l'Ill" | ❺❺❺❺

From its origins as a simple family inn on the bridge serving *matelote*, a freshwater fish stew, the Auberge de l'Ill steadily established itself as a force to be reckoned with. Their first Michelin star came in 1952, the second in 1957, and, in 1967, it completed the hat trick, holding three Michelin stars ever since.

This is the quintessential French family auberge, owned and run by members of the Haeberlin clan: Marc is in the kitchen, sister Danielle and wife Isabelle receive guests at the door, while uncle Jean-Pierre still does his rounds of the dining room.

Europe's royalty and celebrities from all over the world have dined at L'Auberge de L'Ill—indeed, their photographs grace the walls outside the dining room. But, one of the joys of the Auberge is that it remains a family inn at heart, quite unspoiled by its considerable fame: in fact, your table neighbors are just as likely to be locals who have saved up for a special occasion as a group of international celebrities. The best option is lunch, when you can appreciate the views out onto the garden and the manicured lawns that sweep down to the river, fringed by weeping willows.

The cuisine at L'Auberge de L'Ill is classic French (souffléd salmon or lobster Prince Vladimir, created by Marc's father Paul Haeberlin), and is firmly rooted in Alsace (good examples being foie gras scooped straight from its decorated pottery terrine or rack of suckling pig with a pretzel crust). There is also plenty of room for culinary innovations, such as ginger-infused lobster with mango and apple salad or sole and fresh cannelloni filled with burrata on a bed of fava beans and tomato. The encyclopedic wine list is rich in Alsace's top growths, and there are enough Burgundies and Bordeaux to make the hearts of the most demanding wine connoisseurs beat with anticipation and excitement. **SS**

Aux Crieurs de Vin

Superb wine and gastro-bistro cuisine

Location Troyes **Signature dish** Homemade *andouillettes* | ❺❺❺

Aux Crieurs de Vin is a Troyes institution, a picturesque town of cobbled alleys, open squares, and half-timbered sixteenth-century houses. Larmandier-Bernier and Jacques Selosse are among the upscale Champagnes, Christian Binner and Domaine des Vignes du Maye are top wines from Alsace and Burgundy, and there are wines from Beaujolais, Rhone, and the Loire.

Owners Jean-Michel Wilmes and Franck Windel specialize in natural wine. Each vintage they store, sell in their shop, or serve in their gastro-bistro has been selected for its pure ingredients and organic growth. Their passion for all things natural extends to the food, whether it is a case of *andouillettes* (homemade coarse

> *"Choose a bottle of wine before pairing it with a good, simple dish …"*
>
> Michelin Guide

pork sausages, wine, and onions) or the range of main courses. Chef Françoise Wilmes shares Jean-Michel and her son Franck's vision, and creates blissful, unpretentious dishes using the purest of ingredients.

Platters of sliced smoked sausages with sautéed potato wedges, savory mushroom-filled crêpes, plates of delicate brie or camembert, or light foie gras with salad might appear as appetizers on the menu, which changes daily. Slow-braised *paleron de boeuf* served with a light sauce or zesty lemon confit of chicken or parmentier-style lamb might tempt as mains, with a meal culminating in desserts like homemade apple tart. Dishes are designed to complement and not detract from the amazing flavors of the wine. **CFr**

Les Bons Enfants | Confident flavors and upscale
gastronomy with contemporary flair

Location Saint-Julien-du-Sault | **Signature dish** Duck foie gras | ❸❸❸

"This informal restaurant cooks up wonderful regional dishes, all in a convivial atmosphere."

Lonely Planet

⬆ Some seriously good food is on offer here.

Once, the residents of nineteenth-century Saint-Julien-du-Sault in Burgundy, France would have come to this place to socialize over a drink. Now the residents, known locally as Saltusiens, come here to eat upscale gastronomic cuisine. That's because Les Bon Enfants occupies an imposing 200-year-old red brick property, formerly an inn, secreted amid the narrow streets of this pretty French village that was transformed a few years back by local food-lover Pierre-François Lobies. It is now a haven for gourmets.

Monsieur Lobies and chef Ryo Nagahama have created a place where diners feel cocooned. Soft, creamy walls are dotted with paintings; the subtle lighting around the linen-attired tables reflects in the glassware; there are antiques and edgy objects d'arts by local artisans; and doors that open out onto the village. It is also somewhere to enjoy good Burgundy cuisine with a contemporary, often Asian, twist.

Textbook duck foie gras is one of the classic appetizers that might kick off the experience of dining at this stylish eatery. Other alternatives are Saint-Jacques scallops with a cream of cauliflower and consommé jelly, or local *andouillettes*. You could then try mains of crispy pig's head delicately cooked in a wine sauce, salmon marinated and served with crispy seaweed, chicken infused with lemon and balsamic, or perfectly cooked steak with an onion and fennel fondue. All the dishes boast confident flavor combinations and are artfully plated.

Bringing things to a close might be a selection of French cheeses and desserts of melt-in-the-mouth chocolate fudge topped with strawberries and cream, homemade vanilla crème brûlée with pistachio nuts, or a freshly baked fruit pie with sherbet. Monsieur Lobies also offers a wide selection of Burgundy vintages to enhance the flavor of each course. **CFr**

Le Bistrot des Grands Crus |

Trendy bistro food and wine

Location Chablis **Signature dish** *Rognons de veau* (veal kidneys) | ❺❺❺

A bright and breezy sort of place, Le Bistrot des Grands Crus, owned by the hotel-restaurant Hostellerie des Clos a few minutes walk away, can be found in the heart of Chablis, in the northernmost wine district of Burgundy. Almost all the grapevines in Chablis are Chardonnay grapes, which are transformed into one of the world's most celebrated dry white wines.

Le Bistrot des Grands Crus' small but select wine list excels with aromatic Chablis vintages, including Grand Cru and Premier Cru selections aged in oak barrels. All bottles are available by the glass to enable diners to sample some of the region's finest. The bistro's respected chef, Michel Vignaud, has devised a menu that is designed to enhance local wines. Dishes are traditional to the region, plus there's a smattering of modern plates that work for the trendy set who often gather here for informal socializing.

Le Bistrot des Grands Crus' contemporary decor gives it a vibe. Heavy, cream-colored wooden ceiling beams and walls, golden wood floors, and table accessories in accents of red, green, and turquoise make for a fun feel, while, downstairs, the cellar, with its arched honey stone walkways and bottle-lined walls, provides a second dining area. In summer, a garden terrace tempts al fresco-style dining.

Chef Vignaud's menus are always written on blackboards. *Rognons de veau*, his signature dish of veal kidneys cooked perfectly and presented in a light wine sauce, is a fixture. Appetizers typically come in the form of eggs poached in Pinot Noir, or delicious Burgundy snails—*les escargots de Bourgogne*—served with garlic croutons, or rabbit terrain with hazelnuts. An innovative selection of main courses might feature local delicacy braised Chablis sausage, or a soufflé of cod with mussels, or trout cooked in wine. Chablis sherbet concludes a meal here perfectly. **CFr**

L'Herbe Rouge |

Rustic food and superb Touraine wines

Location Valaire **Signature dish** Red bell peppers stuffed with cod brandade | ❺

Tucked in a perfectly peaceful spot in a corner of the Touraine, close to the epic Chaumont, this is the restaurant you have been longing to come across. Chef patron Cécile Argondico has created a real find. The food is simple and easy on the wallet. The modesty of the place belies the quality of the food, cooked with a focused palate and attention to detail.

A tomato salad will be made of three varieties and fresh basil, sea salt, and good olive oil will be the perfect accompaniment. The local duck foie gras doesn't get better, and needs no undue adornments.

There are more complex dishes, but the ethos is simple. Presentation is straightforward, but clean and precise. Garnishes are absent, unless they contribute

---

"Good, honest country food and lovely natural wines from the surrounding regions of the Loire."

foodtourist.com

---

to the dish. A salad of quinoa and peas forms a neat circle, enhanced with a bright citrus dressing. A dessert of *La Faisselle*, an unctuous soft white cheese, is served drizzled with an ooze of bright saffron infused honey to complement its milky simplicity.

Argondico is married to Thierry Puzelat, a fine local vigneron. His well-regarded labels Clos du Tue-Boeuf and Puzelat-Bonhomme are served here, as are other bottles chosen with a love for the region's natural wines. The relaxed rooms and large shaded outdoor terrace are decorated with stylish reclaimed pieces. At L'Herbe Rouge, a mixture of locals and tourists count themselves lucky to be eating and drinking so well in the French countryside. **CB**

L'Espérance | Organic produce celebrated at a beautiful
Burgundy chateau with historic views

Location St. Père sous Vézelay   **Signature dish** *Cromesquis* with foie gras | ❺❺❺

"The vegetables are likely to convert die-hard carnivores to vegetarianism."

gayot.com

⬆ Visitors to L'Espérance can look out through the huge picture windows onto the glorious gardens.

L'Espérance is one of the region's noted restaurants. Its easy, elegant ambiance and organic, gastronomic cuisine by celebrated chef Marc Meneau has truly put it on the map. Meneau's speciality is taking ancient Burgundy recipes and giving them a contemporary twist with organic ingredients, presenting them as exquisite plates with fine local wines.

The restaurant is housed in a château with stone floors and a magnificent conservatory dining space. Round tables are dressed in fine linen and lavish flower displays. The real show-stopper here, though, is the views. Beyond the richly planted gardens that surround the house are historic buildings, including La Madeleine Vézelay, an eleventh-century abbey and a masterpiece of Burgundian Romanesque architecture.

The organic produce served at L'Espérance couldn't be fresher, picked daily from Potager Biâu Kitchen Garden, the restaurant's organic garden that Meneau, a keen gardener, has designed and nurtured. Lemons, apples, and strawberries grow next to carrots, leeks, and Jerusalem artichokes. The organic cuisine extends to meat, fish, seafood, and cheeses sourced from reputable suppliers.

Homemade croquettes—*cromesquis*—with foie gras is one of Meneau's favored appetizers, which typically he would follow with a mains selection of veal fillet baked in caramel, poached chicken with truffles, or the classic regional beef in red wine dish, *boeuf à la Bourguignonne*, each accompanied by a puree of vegetables from the garden. The next option on L'Espérance's menu is a cheese course that might comprise platters of brie, camembert, and the Burgundian soft cheese *Époisses de Bourgogne*, while desserts take the form of piquant peppered strawberries or sweet apple tarte Tatin. Diners always leave content. **CFr**

Casse-Cailloux |
An intimate setting for local produce

Location Tours **Signature dish** Jugged hare |
💲💲

Presided over by the husband and wife team of Patricia and Hervé Chardonneau, this small and well-loved restaurant is at the heart of the historic city of Tours. In a region famed for its food and wine, Casse-Cailloux makes the most out of all that is local. A stone's throw from the covered food market in Tours, itself a temple of fresh ingredients and wonderful places to wander, Casse-Cailloux is the perfect place to stop during a tour of the city.

An egalitarian and welcoming spot, the clientele is predominantly local. Those in the know, from those seeking a working lunch to local winemakers who appreciate its well-sourced Touraine wine, come here for Hervé's superb cooking.

The food showcases the best of the region, using seasonal ingredients at their peak. The fish cuisine is a great strength, and they make delicious use of varieties such as pollack, which are outside the usual menu staples. The tempting menu is based on traditional fare, but the precise cooking has a well-judged modern touch and dishes are presented without undue fuss. There is a great generosity of spirit and attention to detail where it counts.

For example, a dish of jugged hare is made in the traditional way, stuffed with foie gras and stewed with red wine. This dish is so popular that, during the season it is on the menu, despite the restaurant's small number of covers, it goes through 10.5 gallons (40 l) of wine a week in its preparation.

The room itself is simple, but comfortable and light. Bread is piled into linen-lined baskets and the chef is visible, happy at his work, through a large hatch into the kitchen. When you combine Patricia's warm welcome and Hervé's precise, full-flavored cooking in a place where it is easy to pass the time, you have the recipe for a perfect local restaurant. **CB**

Ferme de la Ruchotte |
Serious classics in a rustic farmhouse

Location Bligny sur Ouche **Signature dish** Braised veal in a creamy tarragon sauce | 💲💲💲

If the thought of dining on classic dishes in a rustic stone French farmhouse set in a forest just outside the historic Bligny sur Ouche in Burgundy fires your imagination, then a trip to La Ferme de la Ruchotte is sure to leave you with treasured memories. Chef Frédéric Menager, together with his wife Eva and their team, have created a restaurant where good food and wine rules. It's a stylish place, with heavy golden oak beams, stone walls, menus on blackboards, bare wooden tables, and antiques, while the odd piece of contemporary art adds a cutting-edge touch.

Here, the meat, dairy products, and produce that finds itself in the country kitchen of chef Menager is creatively presented on the plate for diners to enjoy,

---

"No restaurant can compete with the seasonality of dishes or the freshness of their produce."

tasteburgundy.com

---

and doesn't get much fresher. *Mouton Solognot* lamb, *porc Gascon* (pork), and poultry like Barbarie duck, *rouge des Ardennes* (turkey), and *poussins et démarrés* (chicken) come from the La Ruchotte farm, vegetables are grown and picked fresh daily, eggs are collected, and herbs picked.

The expansive menu takes in unfussy Burgundy classics like *boeuf à la Bourguignonne*, braised veal in a creamy tarragon sauce, *coq au vin*, and a haunch of venison with fondant potato. Bread is made fresh daily using organic flour, and local cheeses and homemade desserts add the finishing touches. La Ferme de la Ruchotte's wine list is expansive, too, with many vintages sourced from organic producers. **CFr**

Loiseau des Vignes | Rare vintages accompany classic Burgundy food

Location Beaune **Signature dish** *Escargots de Bourgogne* | ❸❸❸❸

"The menu includes such delights as oeufs meurette selon Loiseau … *"*

fodors.com

⤒ Chef Mourad creates elegantly plated creations, as in this salmon dish.

➡ The interior of Loiseau de Vignes with its oak beams, stone walls, and immaculately dressed tables.

After you have taken a stroll around the picturesque town of Beaune, a table awaits you in Michelin-starred Loiseau de Vignes. This eatery will bowl you over with its gastronomic menu and magnificent "library" of fine wines. The vintages, many of them rare ones such as those from Jean-François Coche-Dury or Domaine Raveneau, are displayed behind glass in illuminated wooden bookcases and dominate the restaurant's chic decor. Gnarled oak ceiling beams, stone walls, and tables dressed in crisp linen add to the immaculate interior styling, and the floor-to-ceiling windows look out over the gardens. The scene is accented by chairs, lavishly upholstered in terracotta. Loiseau des Vignes is a seriously elegant place.

Founded by celebrated restaurateur Dominique Loiseau, Loiseau des Vignes offers guests wine by the glass, allowing the sampling of different vintages, each served at the right temperature, or the enjoyment of wines with each course. Chef Mourad Haddouche excels in *gastronomie Bourguignonne*, designed to work in harmony with the fine wines.

Chef Mourad's Discovery menu might kick off with appetizers of foie gras served with spiced plums, *escargots de Bourgogne* (wild Burgundy snails) served with lashings of garlic, or *oeuf meurette selon Loiseau*, a dish of lightly poached eggs in a flavorsome sauce, followed by mains of Burgundian classics like *boeuf à la Bourguignonne* cooked with prime cuts of beef and braised in a full-bodied red wine, or the chicken and mushroom in wine dish *coq au vin*, accompanied by finely sliced vegetable chips and decorated with edible ribbons and flowers.

There are twenty or so choices of cheese, including the soft cheese *Époisses de Bourgogne*, and desserts that typically comprise platters of mini chocolate eclairs, almond cake, or zesty lemon tart. Coffee served with thumbnail-sized chocolate macaroons brings things to a very satisfying close. **CFr**

Ma Cuisine | Where Burgundy wines and classic dishes work in perfect harmony

Location Beaune   **Signature dish** *Boeuf à la Bourguignonne* | ❸❸❸

" ... *enjoys a reputation for well-prepared regional food and an impressively varied wine cellar.*"

frommers.com

⬆ *Boeuf à la Bourguignonne* is a traditional Burgundy stew and Ma Cuisine's signature dish.

This trendy gastro-brasserie, housed in a beautifully renovated stable that dates back to medieval times, is where locals, many of them wine producers, flock for some of the finest food and wine in Beaune. The attraction is not only chef Fabienne Escoffier's menu of country-house Burgundy dishes, albeit all cooked and served with an imaginative and modern twist, but also to enjoy a good bottle of wine.

Ma Cuisine is famous for its fabulously laden cellar, bursting to the seams with some 800 different wine vintages, most from the Burgundy region. Its wine list is a triumph, and, in France, that's no mean feat. Pierre Escoffier, Fabienne's partner, is a sommelier par excellence and adores the wines produced from the Pinot Noir and Chardonnay grapes in the valleys in and around Beaune. Among his favorites are Côte de Beaune vintages and Premier Cru from Puligny-Montrachet and Chassagne-Montratchet.

Pierre chooses his wines with precision so that they complement the dishes Fabienne Escoffier creates for the ever-changing Ma Cuisine menu. Burgundy classics like *boeuf à la Bourguignonne,* cooked with tender cuts of beef and braised in a full-bodied red wine, is Fabienne's signature dish and rarely fails to appear. Other mains might include *coq au vin* (chicken and mushrooms cooked slowly in wine), braised veal escalope, or roasted breast of duck, each plated with considerable artistic flair.

To top and tail the mains, you can start with *Escargots de Bourgogne* (wild Burgundy snails) with lashings of garlic. Other appetizers are black truffle with egg, compôte of rabbit with tarragon and *Époisses de Bourgogne*. Then, continuing the classic-with-a-twist theme, choose desserts of crème brûlée with chocolate, crème caramel with raspberries, or glazed French apple tart with cinnamon sherbet. **CFr**

La Promenade |

Regional food and wine to savor

Location Le Petit Pressigny **Signature dish** *Roast géline de Touraine* (roast chicken) | ❸❸❸

La Promenade, led by father and son chefs Jacky and Fabrice Dallais, has long been established as an exceptional destination for fine regional food and wine. In the depths of beautiful, unspoiled countryside in central France, it is the venue for all manner of special occasions, indulgent Sunday lunches, and travelers' pilgrimages.

With its Michelin star and reputation of many decades, there are certain expectations; these are unerringly met. Eating here is a treat. Canapés such as a lollipop of crisped potato with olive begin a meal that does not scrimp on the extras. An amuse-bouche such as a delicate cep bouillon with foie gras will "delight the mouth." This sense of occasion lasts until the final bite, with excellent petit fours or a mini madeleine creating memories to savor.

The cooking is French and suitably refined, but there is also an uncommon lightness of touch. The finest local ingredients are cooked to perfection, and Jacky Dallais proudly showcases the best of the region. Wild boar is cooked as a chop, simply but perfectly. The local *géline*, a particularly flavorsome and succulent black chicken, is roasted with lemon.

Touraine and Saumur-Champigny wines add to the strength of La Promenade, along with the tremendously helpful sommelier, Xavier Fortin, who has a peerless knowledge of these wines and a justifiably celebrated reputation. Those in the know travel to La Promenade for an unmatched selection of bottles, many of which would otherwise be hard to come by. If you decide to get a good bottle of wine here, your investment will prove its worth. In two spacious and unfussy rooms, the Dallais family and their brilliant sommelier do all they can to make this remarkable institution a restaurant that lingers long in the memory. **CB**

Maison Lameloise |

All the riches of Burgundy on a plate

Location Chagny **Signature dish** *Tarte soufflé* with calamansi fruit and orange | ❸❸❸

Equidistant between Beaune and Chalon sur Saône in Burgundy is the small, sleepy market town of Chagny. Sitting on the tiny main square is a fine hotel and restaurant that has been in the family since Pierre and Denise Lameloise took over the Hôtel du Commerce in 1921. Several generations later, the manager is Frédérick Lamy, a nephew of the family, and he shares the operation with chef Eric Pras. Pras himself has a fine track record, having worked at Maison Troisgros in Roanne and Le Relais Bernard Loiseau in Saulieu.

From the outside, the building is plain, with just a few clipped box balls as ornamentation, while, on the inside, this is very much a restaurant with rooms. The accommodation is lovely, but plays second fiddle to a

"Chosen as the world's favorite restaurant by reviewers posting ratings on TripAdvisor."

reuters.com

charming set of dining rooms that serve some superb French food. Mind you, the wines are just as good, but the neighboring villages do have names like Santenay, Chassagne Montrachet, and Puligny Montrachet.

Right from the start, it's the distinction of the ingredients that shines through—homemade breads, excellent duck foie gras, venison from nearby Sologne, or Poularde de Bresse with white truffles and a cardoon gratin. Cheese and desserts are as impressive. This is rarefied contemporary cooking that draws from a firmly rooted classical base. Eric Pras' aim is simple, to "continue the history of the establishment and uphold the current level of excellence." A fine intention, and one he appears to be achieving. **ATJ**

Maison Troisgros | Family restaurant with high culinary standards

Location Roanne   **Signature dish** Charolais beef fillet with Fleurie wine sauce | ❸❸❸❸

> "The food and wine come in a compelling format, the menu the same size as a large paperback."

jancisrobinson.com

⬆ The restaurant's dining area is a subtly sophisticated affair.

➡ Maison Troisgros dishes are plated with panache.

Family businesses all too often come and go, and especially in the restaurant trade, but the Troisgros family have been at the forefront of Roanne's gastronomic excellence since the 1930s, when the grandfather of current head chef Michel Troisgros set up a hotel-restaurant opposite the railway station in this small town in the Loire. A handy spot indeed, as La Maison Troisgros has become a place of pilgrimage over the last few decades, as Michelin stars and various other accolades have been heaped on it.

Classical French cuisine could be an easy way to describe the menu, perhaps with a touch of nouvelle cuisine—there's certainly an artful minimalism in the way the dishes are presented. Strips of pickled vegetables lie like candy stripes on the bone-white plates, while three plump ravioli seem to be forming a circle, as if engaged in an endless dance. This plated modernism also extends to the ambience of the restaurant—retro tulip chairs surround circular tables, while the color scheme is a soothing light caramel with off-white flooring. Despite the retro chic styling, La Maison Troisglos is not the sort of place that lives on past glories. Before he took over from his father, Michel Troisgros traveled the world and worked with various master chefs. Everything that he brought back was an eclectic vision of the dishes that he wanted to serve.

There are three menu options when you settle down at the table: there is the à la carte, which might include oysters in a *dashi* bouillon or sautéed frogs' legs with tamarind satay as an appetizer, followed by veal ear and sweetbreads with truffle, or a molten piece of Charolais beef fillet with Fleurie wine sauce. Then there is the menu of the month, using whatever is fresh and seasonal, while the market menu makes an appearance on certain days of the week. Whatever dishes you choose, the result will create art on the plate as well as heaven on the palate. **ATJ**

Flocons de Sel | Stunning food with Alpine views to match

Location Megève　**Signature dish** *Biscuit de brochet et de lotte du Léman* | ❸❸❸

"Emmanuel Renaut's three-star Flocons de Sel … brings new meaning to … haute cuisine."

fodors.com

⬆ Flocons de Sel serves dishes of creative subtlety, often garnished with seasonal herbs and flowers.

Flocons de Sel is very much a restaurant with a view. It is strikingly located on a hillside near the appealing town of Megève in the French Alps, and looks out over the mountains, with their snowy peaks. The appeal for diners who make their way here, (including, naturally, winter sports enthusiasts), however, is distinctly culinary. Emmanuel Renaut, the restaurant's owner and head chef, is the holder of the prestigious *Meilleur Ouvrier de France* (MOF), meaning "best French craftsman," accolade, and the restaurant here has been awarded three Michelin stars.

The setting is rustic chalet in style, as befits its Alpine surroundings. In fine weather, diners can begin their meal here by sitting and enjoying a drink on the terrace, grazing on dainty nibbles and soaking up the splendors of the scenery. The dining room is marked by clean simple lines—there is considerable wood in evidence, as well as white walls and big windows, allowing the natural light to flood in.

The cooking here is, on the whole, modern in style, as witnessed by dishes such as monkfish and pike "cookies" with an onion and mushroom emulsion and a rich seafood jus. Monsieur Renaut's classic training, however, comes through in other offerings such as an impeccable *pithivier* of precisely seasoned cep mushrooms, or a well-executed plate of sweetbreads with mushrooms. The local *terroir* is a source of inspiration, with Renaut working with a team of foragers as well as sourcing ingredients from local farmers and growers. Dishes here often feature seasonal herbs, flowers, and plants such as marigold, nasturtium, violets, and pine, elegantly used in refined ways. Desserts artfully combine ingredients to create dainty concoctions, which are appealingly plated.

The service is polished, with dishes from the tasting menu arriving at a steady pace. The setting is spectacular, and Flocons de Sel is certainly a restaurant at the pinnacle of the French culinary scene. **AH**

Paul Bocuse | Family restaurant with a robust style of nouvelle cuisine

Location Collonges au Mont D'or **Signature dish** Truffle soup | ❺❺❺❺❺

In the world of French haute cuisine, chef Paul Bocuse is a respected and venerated figure. Born into a family of chefs and having trained at Mère Brazier and La Pyramide, he returned in 1959 to the family restaurant just outside Lyon. Under his direction, it went from no stars in 1960 to three Michelin stars in 1965, an accolade that it has retained. Bocuse is credited as a leading figure in modernizing and lightening French cuisine; his name is often associated with "la nouvelle cuisine," although his robust style bears little relation to the fanciful excesses of that movement. The Bocuse d'Or cooking competition, which he established in 1987, is also one of the most prestigious culinary titles.

Eye-catchingly housed in an impressive, brightly decorated building with Paul Bocuse in huge letters across the top, this family restaurant is the place to visit for those wishing to experience his cuisine. The dining room, ornately decorated in fin-de-siècle style, is a grand showcase for Bocuse's cooking, with formal and impeccable service to match.

The cooking here is unashamedly traditional in style, with menus ranging from Menu Bourgeois to Grand Tradition Classique. A signature dish is the truffle soup VGE, created by Bocuse for France's President, Valerie Giscard D'Estaing, in 1975, a luxurious concoction flavored with black Périgueux truffle and foie gras, arriving with the bowl covered in a pastry case. Breaking the pastry releases the glorious aroma of truffles, a moment of culinary theater to savor. Luxurious ingredients, such as foie gras, meticulously cooked turbot, Bresse chicken, and lobster are all features of the menu.

Desserts, billed as "delicacies, temptations, fantasies, and chocolates," arrive with due pomp and ceremony on a convoy of trolleys with cherry clafoutis, delicate fruit tarts, and rich chocolate gateau. Eating here is an unashamedly luxurious and quintessentially French experience. **AH**

"Whether the namesake chef is on site or not, the standards ... continue to reach for the skies."

frommer.com

⤒ A mural outside the restaurant in Collonges au Mont d'Or depicting chef Paul Bocuse himself.

La Rotonde | Fine dining
in luxurious surroundings

Location Lyon **Signature dish** Soft-boiled smoked egg with truffle and mushroom mousse | ❸❸❸❸

Acclaimed French chef Philippe Gauvreau started work in his uncle's pastry shop. His career accelerated rapidly, and, after years working with Jacques Maximin at the Negresco in Nice, Gauvreau finally got the chance to run his own restaurant in Lyon in 1993.

His new gourmet venue was housed in the Vert Casino, amid exclusive park land on the outskirts of Lyon. In 2009, it moved into a spectacular semi-circular room in the luxury spa hotel next door; but, after three years, moved again to a refurbished art deco dining room back on the first floor of the casino. The new grand dining room has well-spaced tables, tall windows, and large gilded mirrors. The atmosphere is formal and diners are attired smartly.

"The Autour des Epices menu shows the potential of Gauvreau and his talent to play with flavors."

gayot.com

Gauvreau holds two Michelin stars and is known for occupying the middle ground between old-school French cuisine and the new wave of eclectic cooks. His food has a classical balance of ingredients but with adventurous personal touches. Gauvreau is renowned for creating unfamiliar taste combinations, like veal with cocoa, sardines marinated in aniseed, lobster and asparagus, scallops with Chardonnay vinegar, or monkfish with hazelnut sauce. The dishes are immaculately prepared and presented creatively; shellfish might arrive on a brick of ice, a perfect lemon soufflé can be accompanied by a delicate lemon sorbet, or rum baba served with baked pineapple. It all makes for an intriguing, if expensive, experience. **SH**

La Palagrie | Unpretentious
brasserie menu at a fantastic bistro

Location Lyon **Signature dish** Lake Geneva fera on hot stone with pumpkin puree | ❸❸❸

La Palagrie is a seriously chic bistro created within what was once one of Lyon's finest grocery stores. Renowned for its groundbreaking cuisine, it is regarded as being at the forefront of the Lyonnaise "bistronomy" scene. By day, the light from its high, arched windows highlights the simplicity of its contemporary soft cream decor, rustic wooden tables and flooring, wall art, and its open kitchen. By evening La Palagrie is bathed in dramatic lighting, with the promise of a cozy eatery within.

Confident, unpretentious brasserie dining is the deal here, and it's all built on fine seasonal French ingredients, often fish and always with a modern twist. Lunch and dinner menus change daily, and might feature black olive and haddock risotto as an appetizer, proceeding to dishes of spicy hot crusted haddock with green onions, pan-seared scallops with chervil or mackerel, and broccoli with wasabi, all of which hit the spot. Texture and flavors work in harmony here, complemented by super wines, and it's all down to the passion and skill of chef Guillaume Monjure and sommelier Chrystel Barnier.

Monjure, who has worked with some of the best in Paris and Morocco, likes to push the boundaries; so, when not out scouring for the freshest local produce, he is busy reinventing his culinary repertoire. His succulent blue lobster from Brittany, his signature fera from Lake Geneva served over a hot stone with a pumpkin puree, or his pan-fried blood sausage topped with orange trout eggs offer an insight into his spirited imagination and dedication to his art.

Enjoyable and memorable desserts like mini madeleines drenched in Grand Marnier, chocolate soufflé, or meringue topped with chestnut mousse, plus excellent homemade breads, demonstrate this as a bistro that's firing on all cylinders. **CFr**

Brasserie Georges | Historic brasserie serving local classics and home-brewed beer

Location Lyon   **Signature dish** Pork and pistachio sausage in white wine sauce with mashed potato | ❸❸

"It's enormous!" is usually the first impression of Brasserie Georges. That's because this is claimed to be one of the largest brasseries in the world; it seats more than 700 diners, and its record serving for one day is more than 2,500 meals. Yet this mega-restaurant is the oldest brasserie in the city. It was built in 1836 by an Alsace brewing company. Its construction was a major architectural adventure of the time: the ceiling of 837 square yards (700 sq. m) has no pillars and was supported by roof beams of four huge fir trees that were pulled from Provence by oxen.

The brasserie stands next to the railway station, and huge neon letters, a sign added just after World War II, spell out the name on the façade as if it were a 1950s dance hall, so it's easy to spot. Inside, there's one big room. It retains an art deco theme, with rows of red padded leatherette bench seats, hand-painted decorative ceilings, and lots of mirrors and floor-to-ceiling windows. The atmosphere is lively, if traditional, with waiters in white shirts, black bow ties, and waistcoats rushing around at speed.

Following tradition, Brasserie Georges still brews its own beer in tanks in full view of the customers, but it is also widely acclaimed for its food. The menu is indeed surprisingly sophisticated for such a large, affordable, and popular venue. You might start with homemade foie-gras or chicken liver cake with Madeira sauce, calf's head with caper and herb sauce might follow, or perhaps pike quenelles with mushroom sauce. There are plenty of local specialities, too, including local pork and pistachio sausages, calf's foot salad, and cream cheese with shallots and chives.

The brasserie has two other odd claims to fame: in 1986, it served the biggest sauerkraut in the world, and, in 1996, it dished up the largest baked Alaska. So this brasserie is huge in delivery as well as reputation. **SH**

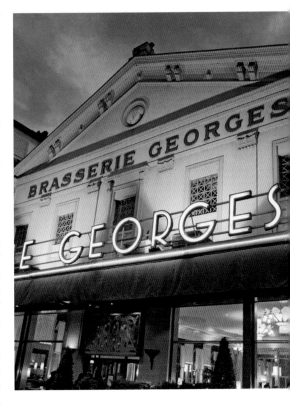

"Meals range from hearty veal stew or sauerkraut and sausage to more refined fare."

fodors.com

⬆ The brasserie's eye-catching façade cannot be missed.

Café Comptoir Abel | Traditional Lyonnaise bistro food in a *bouchon*

Location Lyon   **Signature dish** Lyonnaise *andouillettes* with "Bercy" sauce | ❺❺

It takes something special to become a culinary institution in the gourmet city of Lyon. Café Comptoir Abel is a favorite of locals because it retains the charm and style of a simple café of times gone by.

This is a *bouchon*, a type of traditional Lyonnaise bistro serving meaty local specialities, like sausages, duck pâté, and roast pork. There are twenty officially recognized *bouchons* in the city (plus at least as many that claim to be for the sake of tourists), but Café Comptoir Abel is the oldest and most authentic. Created by "Mere Abel" in 1928, it stands on a cobbled street corner just next to an arch and looks like the sort of bar that Maigret would have frequented.

The dimly lit interior of Café Comptoir Abel creates the impression of another rich slice of history. The bare wooden parquet floor and the old furniture are worn and dark. A creaky wooden spiral staircase leads to the first floor. Even the walls are made of dark wood paneling, decorated with blackboards, mirrors, and a selection of old metal advertisements. Chef Alain Vigneron's menu is traditional. He arrived when he was nineteen and has spent his whole career perfecting Lyonnaise classics, like *quenelle de brochet* (pike quenelle), the fish in a creamy mousse served with a browned crust, and sautéed veal liver or kidneys. Appetizers include a Lyonnaise salad with bacon and warm boiled egg added to the greenery, or artichokes with a slab of foie gras.

The presentation probably hasn't changed since Vigneron opened. Chicken and beef dishes come with morel mushrooms, *andouillettes* with a shallot and white wine sauce, and carpaccio with fried apples. A popular accompaniment is a rice pilaf flavored with a chicken broth, and many dishes arrive at the table sizzling in the skillet they were baked in. All in all, a deliciously retro experience. **SH**

⬆ The wood-clad interior of Café Comptoir Abel.

Restaurant Régis & Jacques Marcon | A hilltop gourmet haven

Location Saint-Bonnet-le-Froid **Signature dish** Mallard with carrots, polenta, and porcini mushrooms | $$$$$

On a hill above the village of Saint-Bonnet-le-Froid stands the three-star Restaurant Régis & Jacques Marcon, a hilltop haven of exemplary food, most of it sourced from the surrounding countryside. From outside the restaurant and adjoining hotel, the view is of a modern-looking, minimalist establishment of untreated timbers, glass, and steel. On clear days, the views of the hills in this part of the Auvergne are phenomenal, something that the light and airy dining room capitalizes on, with its large wall-to-ceiling windows. It is a stark modern space, with the views providing a softer contrast, while the ceiling is dotted with tiny sparkles of light.

The cooking is modern French and beautifully presented. Bone white plates are dotted with edible flowers and the odd exclamation mark of foam, with juicy, succulent pieces of lamb, duck, or beef. There are also plenty of creations involving all manner of fungi, which Régis has usually gone out and picked himself. So it is no surprise to discover that a tasting menu is a mirror of this love of all things mycological. For instance, you might be offered zucchini filled with girolles, char poached with mushrooms, and lamb with cep granita. Then there is dessert: mushroom chocolates might sound wrong but they are popular, as are the lentils caviar in Verveine liqueur.

This is not mushroom madness for the sake of it, but a bold and innovative take on flavors and textures, exploring how they work with each other. As well as the tasting menu, there is the Vellave menu consisting of an appetizer, mains, cheese (all rustic and local), and dessert—here such delights as crab cannelloni and duck served in two ways enthrall. And after the meal is over and you're back outside, satisfied, enjoy the starry night (fingers crossed) and the land cloaked in darkness. You will be back. **ATJ**

[↑] **A dish of mushroom fricassee, artfully presented.**

Maison Pic |
Fine dining from a notable talent

Location Valence **Signature dish** Brie de Meaux with Bourbon vanilla | ❺❺❺❺❺

Restaurant Maison Pic is a restaurant with a family pedigree. Founded in 1889 by chef Ann-Sophie Pic's great-grandmother, Sophie, her grandfather André Pic gained three Michelin stars in 1934 and her father Jacques Pic did the same in 1973. Until recently, Pic had slipped to two stars; but, in 2007, Anne-Sophie won the restaurant a precious third star, making her France's only female chef to do so. The family history resonates when dining here—diners pass a wall of family photographs—yet the setting is contemporary, serene, harmonious, and tastefully decorated.

Anne-Sophie's cooking is known for its elegance and subtlety. A characteristic offering is *La betterave plurielle*, yellow and candy-striped Chioggia beets,

---

"Anne-Sophie Pic has been called a fireball … bringing modern touches to classical dishes."

frommers.com

---

with the natural sweetness of the beets cut by an acidic touch of Blue Mountain coffee and tangy barberries. Seafood is a feature, such as langoustines with rhubarb and Tasmanian pepper. Formidable classic cooking mixes with imaginative creativity—think violet sea urchins in a fine sorrel jelly fluid egg with cubeb pepper. And don't miss the indulgent *Brie de meaux* with Bourbon vanilla.

Desserts are similarly refined, including offerings such as lager beer and caramel, a witty take on France's classic *Ile Flottante*, a beer-infused mousse with soft, rich caramel and crunchy hazelnut cookie. Anne-Sophie Pic is carrying on her family's culinary artistry with flair and panache. **AH**

L'Envers du Décor |
Fabulous wine and unpretentious dining

Location Saint-Émilion **Signature dish** *Canelé de Bordeaux* | ❺❺❺

Housed in a glorious, centuries-old building that sits among Romanesque churches, L'Envers du Décor is a haunt of trendy locals as well as visitors to the historic town of Saint-Émilion. This bar à vins and brasserie offers a vast choice of wines by the glass, so you can pop in after a bit of sightseeing, sit at the bar, and enjoy a glass of local red or white. If you are partaking of its Bordeaux-inspired menu, you can also select the best vintage for your course.

Run by François des Ligneris, the son of a count, this eatery has become something of a legend since it opened in 1987. Unpretentious brasserie dining is the deal here. Fresh local produce is transformed into imaginative dishes, with their roots deep in the heritage of Bordeaux, and accompanied by the finest local wines, mainly from the Merlot and Cabernet Franc grapes. Dine inside in the cozy restaurant amusingly decorated with wooden wine boxes or al fresco-style in its stone-walled courtyard, which becomes an especially intimate space during the long summer evenings.

Appetizers take the form of oysters, a speciality from Bordeaux's Arcachon Bay—these are delicious with a local dry white wine, along with platters of sliced meat, seafood plates, or creamy foie gras. Typically, these first courses proceed mains of *confit de cunard* (duck), Charolais beef, lamb in a Bordelaise sauce accompanied by sautéed potatoes, *mignon de porc* in a creamy morel sauce, or slow-braised rib of veal, with the local smoked sausages *andouillettes*.

Traditional recipes resurface in the choice of desserts. Homemade *canelé de Bordeaux*, a cake made from a creamy batter and baked in a fluted copper mold, is a signature offering at L'Envers du Décor, along with a mouthwatering fig tart or rich chocolate cake. Diners leave full and content. **CFr**

Le Chapon Fin | Michelin-starred modern
cuisine in a Belle Epoque landmark

Location Bordeaux **Signature dish** Pigeon off the bone with a medley
of white beans and mushrooms | ❸❸❸

Le Chapon Fin (the "fine cockerel") has a long and colorful history. The restaurant was founded in 1825 in one of the smartest areas of the city of Bordeaux. By the early twentieth century, it was a fashionable high society haunt for celebrities of the day, like Toulouse-Lautrec, Clemenceau, and Sarah Bernhardt. Such was Le Chapon Fin's prestige that British and Spanish monarchs were also customers.

Today, under young chef Nicolas Frion, it is a Michelin-starred restaurant, offering a menu inspired by the culinary heritage of southwestern France. The food is well-executed, contemporary fine cuisine, but still the most distinctive feature of the restaurant—and a major attraction of the venue—is the famous interior: customers dine in an Art Nouveau rocky grotto created in 1901. This extraordinary room is decorated with ornate latticework and plants. The ceiling rises 25 feet (7.5 m) to a full-length skylight flooding the linen-covered tables and upholstered high-back chairs with natural light. This Belle Epoque chamber has been declared a French National Monument. This is a popular magnet for Bordeaux visitors, and also serves as an inspiration for Frion to produce an innovative and artful menu.

The southwestern influence makes its presence felt on the menu in ingredients such as foie gras, offal —kidneys, sweetbreads, pigs' trotters—and game such as pigeon and hare. Frion presents these rich and luxurious foodstuffs with style, elegantly constructed dishes with intriguing flavor combinations.

As one would expect, the wine list is a particular pleasure. The renowned wine cellar is dominated, of course, by great Bordeaux vintages. The sommelier gives guided tours of the stone vaulted basements, recommended as an excellent way of whetting your thirst and preparing your palate for dining. **SH**

"This is where visiting presidents dine … classy food served with bow-tied panache."

Anthony Peregrine, *Daily Telegraph*

⬆ Nicolas Frion worked with Paul Bocuse, Gérard Boyer, and Thierry Marx before joining Le Chapon Fin.

La Tupina | Classic rustic cooking from southwest France in a city restaurant

Location Bordeaux   **Signature dish** Barbecued duck breast portions with chips cooked in duck fat | ❸❸❸

La Tupina feels like it has been transplanted from a tiny village into the heart of Bordeaux. Chef Jean-Pierre Xiradakis' restaurant brings old-school rustic cooking from southwest France into the city.

You'll find La Tupina in an ancient, narrow cobbled street very near the river. There are the standard fair-weather tables outside, but inside the furniture looks as if it has come straight from a farmhouse, with the walls cluttered with old photos and country artifacts. Customers take a seat by a big open fire where meat rotates on spits. This one is mainly for show, but there is another real open roti fire working in the kitchen, which, with its grand wooden farmhouse table, also looks as if it belongs in an old French country house.

La Tupina means "kettle" in Basque. Here it refers to the cauldron that hangs by the fire, slowly warming soup in a traditional peasant way. The smell of the steaming broth permeates the eatery's quaint little rooms. Xiradakis' personal mssion is to gather the best ingredients of the region—naturally this includes Bordeaux wines, as well as fish from Bordeaux's Gironde Estuary, corn-fattened ducks, and chickens that roam freely around local farms, the traditionally hunted hares, pigeons, pheasants, partridges, renowned Bigorre "black pigs," and vegetables from the region's country markets.

The cooking style is often rural, too, with meat grilled over a vine wood fire while the accompanying French fries are cooked in duck fat. Menus here are full of simple classics such as slow-roasted lamb in its own juices, spit-roasted beef, and *pot-au-feu* stew.

Despite its rustic style, prices are high at La Tupina, reflecting its revered reputation, although the lunchtime set-menu deals are reasonable. Nearby, there are other outposts of Xiradakis' food empire in the form of a café, grocery, wine-bar, and bistro. **SH**

⬆ The space is decorated with photos and knick-knacks.

Michel Bras | Refined cooking drawn from a primitive landscape

Location Laguiole   **Signature dish** *Gargouillou* (a blend of young vegetables, herbs, flowers, and seeds) | ❺❺❺❺❺

Father and son Michel and Sébastien Bras run their eponymously named hotel and restaurant in the heart of the southern Massif Central region of Aubrac. It is a desolate, wind-swept plateau with glacial lakes and its own breed of cattle. Situated right at its heart is Michel Bras, a building that looks as if it has just been beamed in from another planet: expansive walls of glass, shardlike shapes cantilevered out over the hillside, and other architectural forms that seem almost to blend into and merge with the wild meadow landscape. The garden is untamed and naturalistic, while inside all is quietly humming with a sense of well-being that's rare to find within the restaurant business (the staff are encouraged to participate in their own cycling club).

The building may appear to have been dropped in from somewhere quite alien, but the inspiration for the cooking truly reflects what is on the doorstep, with vegetables and herbs given just as much prominence as meat. Typical dishes, for example,

might be a cep tart with walnut oil, or kohlrabi with confit orange. And then, of course, there's the local beef, which is braised with seasonal vegetables and served with a truffle jus. It is eaten using a traditional Laguiole knife, which was used by local shepherds in the fourteenth century. Ingredients are first class and the deftness with which they are cooked is impressive.

Many commentators have referred to Michel Bras' "holistic" approach to cooking and to his love of the region where he was born. He has said that this deep sense of *terroir* was born out of the fact that the Aubrac region produces so little, and therefore one has to make the best of what is available.

When planning a trip to Michel Bras, bear in mind that the hotel has only a dozen bedrooms, and both these and the seats in the restaurant require booking well in advance. **SP**

⬆ Michel Bras is housed in a striking building.

La Bonne Etape

From Provençal organic garden to plate

Location Château-Arnoux-Saint-Auban
Signature dish Lamb in Provençal herb juice | ❸❸❸❸

An elegant seventeenth-century hotel, La Bonne Etape has little balconies, ivy-covered stone walls, and almond-green wooden shutters. With its honey-hued walls and antique furniture, it is the epitome of period elegance. Heavy golden oak ceiling beams dominate and windows are lavishly dressed. In the kitchen, chef Jany Glaize uses vegetables from the organic garden, honey from the beehives, and fruit from the trees outside—these ingredients are then transformed into dishes for the Michelin-starred restaurant.

Jany prepares authentic Provençal recipes handed down from his grandmother, Gabrielle, and desserts from his confectioner father, Pierre, with each dish given a modern, gastronomic twist. Jany also has 6,000

"This is a voyage for the senses and a natural stepping stone to reaching perfect happiness."

jpmoser.com

---

bottles of wine to complement the dishes, in what he describes as one of the best wine cellars in France.

La Bonne Etape's menu is ambitious, reflecting Jany's confidence and culinary expertise. Guests might start with guinea fowl in lavender oil supreme or pan-fried duck foie gras and rhubarb in truffle oil, followed by roasted pigeon with hazelnut mash or local lamb cooked in a traditional savory juice with Provençal herbs. Alternatively, fish lovers can enjoy mackerel marinated in lemon or local snails in garlic for starters, with sea bream tornadoes with mussels or monkfish poached in oregano oil to follow. The finale is cheese and a dessert selection that features a delectable lavender-scented honey ice cream. **CFr**

Le Bistro de Lagarde

Creative regional cuisine

Location Lagarde d'Apt **Signature dish** Roasted Ventoux pork | ❸❸

Where once nuclear missiles hid in silos high up on the Albion plateau in the middle of the Vaucluse is now host to a thoroughly more benevolent guest. Le Bistrot de Lagarde is located in a former bunker that has been transformed into a rustic-looking and simply decorated restaurant 1,203 yards (1,100 m) high above the land. Here, head chef Lloyd Tropeano is free to indulge in his passion for regionally influenced dishes featuring local produce from the surrounding farms, sun-warmed hillsides, and fertile plains that spread down to the Mediterranean.

This is a lonely and lovely spot, reached by a road that was originally built to transport the missiles. There's a refreshingly austere look about the interior, with its solid wooden furniture, tiled floor, and beams traversing the ceiling, but the food is colorful and sings with the rich flavors of this fertile part of southeastern France.

Ventoux pork is slowly roasted over an open fire and emerges soft, sweet, and juicy; seasonal vegetables are simmered in their own juices; gilt-headed bream is grilled and served with a scattering of herbs. Various interpretations of duck, venison, lamb, trout, brandade, langoustines, and steaks all take their turn in the menu's spotlight, which changes every couple or months or so depending on what Tropeano can source. Despite its isolation, Le Bistrot de Lagarde is a popular spot for lunch and dinner (the prices tend to bump up a bit during the latter slot).

Let us not forget dessert: chocolate crème brûlée makes an appearance, rich, dark and solicitous in the way it leaves the palate purring. A sense of playfulness emerges with a slice of "reversed" lemon tart topped with several balls of white meringue. Dishes such as these give a sense of the joy and creativity that is at work in this restaurant high up in the clouds. **ATJ**

La Bastide de Moustiers | Alain Ducasse's country
hideaway offering the freshest Provençal cuisine

Location Bordeaux   **Signature dish** Sautéed rabbit served with fennel mousse and edible flowers | ❸❸❸

The setting for La Bastide de Moustiers in the Alpes de Haute Provence region of France is idyllic: fields of scented lavender and groves of gnarled olive trees as far as the eye can see (with deer making an occasional appearance) and a quiet country lane. It was the scene that captured renowned chef Alain Ducasse when he first caught sight of the charming seventeenth-century stone bastide that became his home and then went on to house this upscale restaurant.

Everything about the restaurant makes it the kind of place you want to spend time in. There is the crisp white decor with accents of terracotta, fine antiques, walls adorned with contemporary art, a beautifully cultivated four-acre garden, and, of course, the creative, gastronomic cuisine. Attention to detail is everything. The day-to-day running of the place is in the hands of Jérémy Barbet, while the kitchen is the playground of chef Christophe Martin, who is passionate when it comes to sourcing local fresh produce. What Christophe can't find in La Bastide de Moustiers' own kitchen gardens, he sources at local farmers' markets. A speciality is his imaginative use of edible flowers.

Authentic Provençal cuisine is presented in the form of three lunch and dinner menus, with dishes prepared using olive oil from the estate's own groves. A delicious brandade made with cod, cream of garlic, and wild herbs, or a risotto made with fresh garden produce might lead the way as appetizers. These might be followed by a main of succulent rabbit sautéed and served with fennel mousse, or duck breast portions or pigeon roasted to perfection with figs and beets, each artfully presented on the plate. Diners can then round off their meal with an impeccable selection of local Provençal cheese or elegant desserts. **CFr**

> *"Vegetables, herbs, and flowers are plucked from the gardens to ornament delectable dishes."*
>
> *Mr. & Mrs. Smith*

⊡ The menu features seasonally changing ingredients, including freshly harvested produce from the garden.

Restaurant Prévôt | Upscale
eatery in France's "melon country"

Location Cavaillon **Signature dish** Melon with lobster bouillabaisse | ❸❸❸

There is no doubt that fresh melon is the favored produce at the Restaurant Prévôt. In fact, this stylish eatery in the center of Cavaillon is famous for its creative approach to using this super-healthy fruit. The interior uses soft lavender hues and tables are dressed in yellow linen. Paintings adorn the walls, fresh flowers are everywhere, and ceramic melons are quirkily displayed. Chef Jean-Jacques Prévôt, whose family founded the restaurant in a glorious stone-built, blue-shuttered melonnier in 1981, is passionate about food, especially melons.

In the summer, when the cantaloupe-style local melons are in season, you might find roasted melon drizzled with lobster bouillabaisse, or veal and melon

---

> *"The Restaurant Prévôt is a seriously good spot, serving excellent regional food."*
>
> Anthony Peregrine, *Daily Telegraph*

---

confit with the trimmings. Each side of the main course might be an appetizer of squid stuffed with chicken and pine nuts with a melon puree, and then a meringue dome with a melon foam with roasted almond ice cream, or melon balls in a melon basket.

When Cavaillon melon is out of season, Jean-Jacques creates dishes with springtime asparagus, autumnal mushrooms, and winter truffles, and there is an exhaustive à la carte menu. Daughter Sandra-Rose is as enthusiastic about the wine cellar, with wines from regions such as Burgundy and Provence joined by delicate square bottles of Le Melanis, a delicious light aperitif made from almonds, spices, and (yes, you've guessed it) melon. **CFr**

Mirazur | Culinary Eden
perched on the dazzling Riviera

Location Menton **Signature dish** Quinoa and cep risotto with parsley brioche | ❹❹❹❹

Incredibly, this extraordinary sun-drenched location was once a modest café on the French-Italian border. The Argentinian-born, classically French-trained chef Mauro Colagreco deftly spotted its astounding potential. He then transformed it into a gastronomic destination with one of the most wonderful organic kitchen gardens in the world, teetering on steep terraces on the cliffs of the Côte d'Azur. Here grow all manner of heritage vegetables, including a variety of tomatoes, fruits, herbs, and edible flowers. Colagreco's vegetable-centric cuisine pays homage to his culinary mentor, the brilliant Alain Passard of L'Arpège, with whom he worked for several years in Paris. Colagreco excels in light, clean, fresh flavors, delivered with sublime balance and texture, and his dishes often use the citrus fruits synonymous with Menton.

The triple-level restaurant has mesmerizing, panoramic views over the azure Mediterranean, so it is fitting that fish features prominently. So snacks may include fresh anchovies and langoustine "bon-bons." The menu is entirely based on produce at its vibrant peak in the garden. Zingy, grassy asparagus with citrus and apple and a vanilla honey yogurt sauce is both highly original and beautifully pure and refreshing. Langoustine tails are citrus roasted, served with an orange puree and, typically, a ragout of young peas and fava beans. Luxurious roast turbot arrives simply, with an exquisite onion butter sauce and cucumber.

The desserts are equally colorful and fragrant, especially musky saffron cream with almond foam, orange-flower brioche, and orange sabayon. The whole restaurant seems suffused with joy at its magical setting and its glorious produce, making it a very difficult place to leave. **SP**

➡ Mirazur's terrace has a view over the Mediterranean.

Hostellerie Jérôme | Fine seafood in an inn frequented by Napoleon

Location La Turbie   **Signature dish** Sea bass with zucchini flower compote | ❺❺❺❺

" …this twelfth-century presbytery is the perfect overnight stopover for dedicated foodies."

frommers.com

⤒ Fresh, local produce is the essential starting point for all dishes, including peach pie.

Hostellerie Jérôme can be found in the center of the medieval town of La Turbie, sitting surrounded by stone cottages, perched high above the coastline of the French Riviera. The views across the rooftops toward neighboring Monaco, with yachts catching the breeze in the azure sea below, are dazzling.

The Hostellerie Jérôme trails an impressive history, housed in a glorious stone building dating from the thirteenth century, it was once part of a presbytery, and home to the friars of Lérins Abbey. Indeed, it is said Napoleon Bonaparte once stayed here in 1796. Today, its guests may not be quite so famous, well not all of them anyway, but they are welcomed without exception by owners Bruno and Marion Cirino.

Step inside the inn's restaurant and it gets even better. Seriously elegant, the interior is dominated by a magnificent vaulted ceiling painted with frescos that are reminiscent of the work of Italian painters. Here, diners enjoy the classic haute cuisine of Provençe, all the time surrounded by paintings and antiques from the eighteenth and nineteenth centuries, and with a view onto the prettiest of terraces.

Chef Bruno has a passion for sourcing fresh local produce, and, when not in the kitchen, he is almost always to be found in the local market selecting fresh produce. Carefully selected, notably fresh fish and shellfish, such as excellent sea bass or lobster, is a particular highlight of Hostellerie Jérôme, ingredients then transformed by the kitchen into elegant dishes. Bruno's signature creation is sea bass with zucchini flower compote, but diners can also enjoy the flavor and textures he creates in dishes such as lobster with lemon and plums, shrimp with jasmine, and his roasted duck foie gras. He offers a prix-fixe menu, and, for those looking for a veritable feast, his La Grande tasting menu can involve a dozen or more small plates of dishes containing delights such as almond-crusted shrimp, truffles, and pigeon slices. **CFr**

La Colombe d'Or | A true one-off—art collection meets Provençal cooking

Location Saint-Paul-de-Vence **Signature dish** Hors d'oeuvre platter with basket of crudités and anchovies | ❸❸❸❸

Painting rather than singing for one's supper really was the order of the day at this charming, timbered rose stone inn. This was a mecca for many of the world's most celebrated artists, who came to live on the Riviera in the 1940s to draw the extraordinary light of the coast. The chef-proprietor Paul Roux (it is still owned by the same art-loving family) of La Colombe d'Or ("The Golden Dove") willingly accepted artworks in exchange for hospitality, and the dining room became a favorite retreat of Picasso, Matisse, and Chagall. Yves Montand and Simone Signoret also met and married here. It is utterly thrilling to dine among original Mirós and Braques, either in the disarmingly simple yet elegant wooden paneled dining room or on the vast garden terrace shaded by fig trees, flanked by a ceramic mural by Fernand Léger.

The menu sticks stoically to classic Provençal dishes. Start with soupe au pistou, foie gras, or the generous platter of hors d'oeuvres, popular at lunch and more than enough for two, and brought to the table with flourish. Expect at least fifteen white ceramic dishes with raw vegetable crudités with anchovies, grilled bell peppers, stuffed eggplant, caramelized onions, anchovies, chickpeas, charcuterie, and much more. Bringing beautiful ingredients to the fore rather than impressing with technique is the core of the à la carte menu, with grilled dourade or roast chicken with gratin dauphinois warm favorites. A rabbit fricassée with blood red sauce and tagliatelle is also a regular fixture. There is a touch of theater about the service, with dover sole expertly deboned and rack of lamb carved at the table. Soufflés are a speciality, as well as fruit tart and refreshing lemon sorbet.

Staff are considerate and seemingly never star-struck, as this is a favored haunt of many big movie stars and art-world names, with discretion famously assured. Henri Matisse once called La Colombe d'Or "a small paradise"—who could argue with that? **SP**

" … so perfect overall that you haven't really been to the Riviera until you've stayed or dined here."

fodors.com

⬆ The charming dining room at La Colombe d'Or is a lovely spot in which to enjoy the local cuisine.

Le Chantecler, Le Negresco | A palatial Provençal restaurant offering an opulent dining experience

Location Nice   **Signature dish** Herb-crusted sole and crayfish with zucchini and caramelized eggplant | ❸❸❸

"Ensure you're in a grand mood if you're going to splash out: every dish is an exquisite creation."

Lonely Planet

⬆ The Negresco hotel has been a highlight of Nice's promenade des Anglais for over a century.

Le Negresco stands, in jaw-droppingly beautiful and palatial style, in pole position for the best views of the French Riviera's Baie des Angles in Nice. This sets the scene perfectly for what can only be described as the gastronomic extravaganza to be found in the hotel's Le Chantecler restaurant.

The contemporary cuisine of chef Jean-Denis Rieubland is driven by the fine produce and traditions of Provence. Choose between the à la carte and tasting menus, and expect artfully presented plates of beauty. You might find appetizers of lightly cooked duck foie gras with truffle, Jura white wine jelly and homemade brioche with chestnuts, sea scallops with pink garlic and cream of squash, or crab and mango cannelloni with Sturia caviar and lime cream.

Herb-crusted sole and crayfish with local zucchini dusted with basil and caramelized eggplant is one of Chef Rieubland's dinner specialties. Meat lovers will relish the fillet of beef cooked with nori seaweed in a white port Bordelaise sauce, or venison roasted with bell peppers served with vegetables and candied tangerine, all with wine pairings suggested by the sommelier from Le Chantecler's 15,000-bottle cellar. The finale might be opera cake with raspberries or gingerbread soufflé flambéed with Cointreau.

Le Chantecler's decor is as much a feast for the eyes as the menu is for the palate. Opulent settings for fine dining rarely get better than this. The dining room has intricately carved woodwork dating from 1751; some panels are left natural, others are exquisitely painted and gold-leafed as they would have been in the eighteenth century. There are lavishly attired windows, plush carver chairs, crisp pink linens, and carpets to sink your feet into, plus bronze statues on the tables. Combined with the haute-cuisine cooking, this is a luxuriously extravagant experience. **CFr**

La Merenda | Legendary eatery offering authentic Niçoise cooking

Location Nice **Signature dish** Tarte de Menton | ❸❸❸

La Merenda in old Nice has a confident ambiance, and a menu so refined that it has been drawing in local gourmands for decades. The fact that the restaurant has no telephone and diners have to make their way to the rue Raoul Bosio in order to make their dinner reservation, or risk not getting a table, might put many off, but not those who are already acquainted with the gastronomic offerings of La Merenda.

Chef Dominique Le Stanc trained under some of France's finest chefs—including Michel Husser (Le Cerf), Marc Haeberlin (L'Auberge de L'Ill), Alain Chapel, and Alain Senderens—before acquiring La Merenda, which in Nicoise dialect means "delicious morsel." He has also achieved two Michelin stars along the way. Taking his inspiration from authentic regional Nicoise cuisine, Dominique changes the menu constantly and writes his specials of the day by hand on a blackboard in the corner only once he has selected fresh produce from the market.

Le Stanc's partner Danielle greets diners as they enter. There might be a tomato tart as an appetizer, perhaps followed by stuffed sardines, ratatouille, or fritters of zucchini flowers. Another day might see *la tarte de Menton*, the speciality dish of onion, herbs, and garlic tart with black olives from the groves of Nice.

The setting is rustic; stepping inside is a little like entering a traditional French bistro where time has stood still. Wooden tables barely a yard apart are dressed with red cloths and flowers, with little stools, oil lamp-style lighting giving an intimate glow, pictures on the walls, and an open kitchen where Le Stanc can be seen creating his dishes. These elements all combine to give an easygoing feel.

La Merenda is where locals eat. It is a place to linger, relish authentic Nicoise food, and engage in conversation with your neighboring diners. **CFr**

L'Amphitryon | A gastronomic gem in Toulouse's suburbia

Location Colomiers **Signature dish** Lamb with dates and lemon roasted in mint powder | ❸❸❸❸

Amid the Toulouse suburbs, L'Amphitryon hides itself away, but fails to escape those after gastronomic excellence; it does have two Michelin stars, after all. Airbus and the Cité de l'Espace Museum is nearby, but L'Amphitryon maintains a feeling of greenness and nature, tranquility and well-being, offering a pleasant escape from the day-to-day realities of modern living.

Inside, the dining room has a luminous ambience, helped by the glass walls and ceiling. It's a modern-looking place, a clean, fresh environment that doesn't distract from the food. Ah, yes, the food—under head chef Yannick Delpech, L'Amphitryon has won a reputation (and a brace of stars) for its dedication to fine, fresh produce to create sublime dishes. Changing

> *"Inside, it's understated, upmarket chic, inventive food and excellent service."*
>
> Amy Fetzer, *Guardian*

seasonally, the menu ensures that ingredients are at their flavorful best. You might come across lamb cooked with dates and lemon and dusted in mint powder, or how about cod cooked two ways with salted and cured fish roe?

Fresh sardine and morel cream is a favorite appetizer, and there's always a luxurious riff on foie gras, with truffles also taking a bow when in season. The dishes are served with impeccable design, laid out on snow-white plates as if art-school training was a prerequisite for working in the kitchen. The wines proffered as matches for the dishes are all local and often rather special. L'Amphitryon is special, too, and continues to go from strength to strength. **ATJ**

Michel Sarran | Creative cuisine from a talented chef

Location Toulouse **Signature dish** Poached sea bass with creamy polenta and lobster sauce |

> " ... Mediterranean formulas suited to the rhythms and reasons of modern living."

fodors.com

⬆ Michel Sarran describes itself as more of a house than a restaurant.

➡ Accomplished and sophisticated modern French cuisine, served with élan.

It's lunchtime, or it might be dinner. It doesn't really matter, because whatever the time of day you can be sure there will always be a happy hum of diners ooh-ing and aah-ing over their plates in the easygoing, elegant aura of the two dining rooms at Michel Sarran's eponymous restaurant. Located in a modest, homely looking nineteenth-century house a few minutes walk from the River Garonne, Michel Sarran has been based here since 1995; in that time, he's gained a reputation as one of the best chefs in France, along with a couple of Michelin stars.

The food at Michel Sarran is modern French cuisine served with true artistry, dishes that have the look of still lives with splashes of color; although, after the initial viewing, it is time to eat them. For appetizers, you might want to try the creamy, silky foie gras soup, pieces of the rich pâté floating like islands of desire in the warm liquid, or maybe you'll go for the lobster tartare with its accompaniment of chilled bisque and tangy orange zest.

What about mains? Well, the poached sea bass sits on a base of smooth polenta, soft and yielding to the touch of the fork, and light and sweet on the palate. There is also a trio of scallops roasted on "grains" of celery accompanied by mooli and scatterings of white truffle from Alba, creating a remarkable concord of sea-fresh sweetness and deep booming earthiness in the mouth. Other dishes include a casserole of *Noir de Bigorre* pork, calf ribs, and tender lamb from the Ayeron region, northeast of Toulouse.

There is an à la carte menu and two lunchtime menus, one entitled "Saveurs," the other "Surprise"— these consist of four courses: a main, cheese, and two desserts. It is, however, no surprise to discover that, at the same time as attracting committed gourmands, Michel Sarran is a place that politicians and film stars also like to frequent; after all, good food knows no social boundaries. **ATJ**

Le Relais des Moines | Gastronomic retreat in the heart of Provence

Location Les Arcs sur Argens **Signature dish** Chocolate spheres with citrus mousse and sorbet | ❸❸❸

It is hard to think of a more appealing way to acquaint yourself with the tastes of Provence than to head for Les Arcs sur Argens, the delightful partially walled medieval capital of Côtes de Provence, and seek out Le Relais des Moines. The stone country house standing in acres of rich park land and vineyards that is now home to the brasserie has been an enchanting retreat since the sixteenth century. Once it was the home of aristocracy; now it is a gastronomic haven.

Chef Sébastien Sanjou and his team have put Le Relais des Moines firmly on the Provençal gastronomy map. Here, guests enjoy such appetizers as shrimp in zucchini cannelloni or beef consommé, proceeding to fresh fish from Saint-Jean-de-Luz with asparagus cooked Provençal style, or breast of pigeon, artfully fanned on the plate. Between each course, as amuse-bouches, single-mouthful tasters are brought to the table, consisting of a local oyster, expertly poached, or a langoustine and smoked eel sampler.

The flavors and textures of these busy dishes fuse together harmoniously, with the refined gastronomic momentum continuing right through to the desserts. A speciality is chocolate spheres with citrus mousse filling, served warm with sorbet. The whole dining experience is heightened further by the sommelier and his pertinent advice on the best wine for each course. Around 2,000 bottles of 230 wines are kept at their optimum temperature in caves that are carved naturally into the rock beneath the country house.

The two dining rooms—complete with stone walls, archways, vast fireplaces, and a modern terrace with impressive views across the vineyards—can accommodate over a hundred diners, and yet the restaurant's feel is also one of intimacy. Locals, known as Arcois, have known about this retreat for years, and visitors are delighted to be in on the secret. **CFr**

⬆ A dish of scallops served at Le Relais des Moines.

Chez Fonfon | A chance to sample authentic bouillabaisse in its city of origin

Location Marseille **Signature dish** Marseille bouillabaisse | ❸❸❸

While this cozy fish restaurant, with its crisp linens and terracotta-hued decor, comes with some attention-grabbing nautical artifacts on the walls, the real showstopper here is the superb location. Chez Fonfon is right by the water at Vallon des Auffes, one of Marseille's tiny fishing coves. Boats laden with fishing nets are moored up right on the doorstep, and huge windows frame the picturesque scene. The catches on the menu at Chez Fonfon are brought ashore just hours before they are served, landed just yards away, so the freshness of the fish and shellfish here is a given.

Chez Fonfon is known especially for its authentic bouillabaisse, a fish dish that Chef Alexandre Pinna—who runs the family business, created in 1952—first started cooking as a child. Crammed full of octopus, monkfish, conger eel, and rascasse (scorpion fish), plus a handful of sea urchins, and simmered in wine, olive oil, garlic, tomato, and saffron, this classic, rich French fish stew originated right here in Marseille.

The fish-loving diners at Chez Fonfon can choose to enjoy amuse-bouches and sip a memorable vintage from the restaurant's upscale wine list. The latter, designed to complement the taste and textures of the fish dishes, also offers a peaceful moment of expectation while waiting for the hearty bouillabaisse to arrive. This is traditionally served as a broth with the fish removed and brought to the table as a side plate, with an accompaniment of toast.

There is no doubt that Pinna knows his fish and uses the ocean's abundant larder to excellent effect. Along with his signature bouillabaisse, his menu of fish dishes is what diners book here weeks in advance to experience. Risotto with asparagus, shrimp and Parmesan, oysters with a creamy mix of mushrooms, Champagne, and hazelnuts, or monkfish and mozzarella skewers with pasta are just some of the favorites. **CFr**

⬆ **Chez Fonfon is situated on the waterfront.**

L'Epuisette | Landmark restaurant on the water's edge that wows with imaginative fish dishes

Location Marseille   **Signature dish** *Bourride du Vallon* | ❸❸❸

"*Guillaume Sourrieu has … a big reputation (and a Michelin star) for sophisticated cooking.*"

fodors.com

⬆ L'Epuisette has a beautiful view of the fishing boats in the port of Vallon des Auffes.

The Mediterranean Sea is just a pebble's throw away, so it is only fitting that the fresh fish brought ashore in the harbor of Vallon des Auffes is showcased on L'Epuisette's tempting menu. You might be drawn to an appetizer of sliced yellowfin tuna with foie gras, or perhaps lightly-seared Breton scallops with a caviar and leek mousse. For mains, you might choose grilled lobster liberally sprinkled with spices and served with a creamy crab meat sauce and lemon potatoes, or, alternatively, sea bass cooked in walnut wine, served with a medley of mushrooms and spinach.

L'Epuisette is perched on a rock with the sea just a short distance below, where the colorful fishing boats pass by. For decades now, this restaurant has wowed the region's food-lovers with gastronomic dishes from the Mediterranean. Chef Guillaume Sourrieu, who took over the reins a few years back, has become something of a legend in Marseille. His motto is that all dishes served to diners should be sophisticated, artful, and modern, but above all else of the finest standard. Sourrieu explains, "I establish a harmony between these three essential elements: the core product, the filling, and sauce, giving priority to the freshness and quality of the products." His signature dish *bourride du Vallon* (poached yellow bass, monkfish, and mussels) ticks all these boxes.

The creativity continues right through to dessert, with the pastry chef offering concoctions such as chocolate pie topped with pepper ice, or crisp pastry puff filled with pear sitting neatly on a crème brûlée.

Sourrieu's deftly skillful hand in the kitchen is complemented by the input of Bruno Dukan, the award-winning sommelier, who knows his wine and takes his inspiration for appropriate vintages from the menus created by Sourrieu. These two are a winning team indeed. **CFr**

Vague d'Or | Traditional
Provençal cuisine with a Michelin twist

Location St. Tropez **Signature dish** Sisteron lamb |
❸❸❸❸❸

Surrounded by lawns and mature palm trees, and looking out over the brilliant turquoise sea of St. Tropez, the seriously upscale Résidence de la Pinède offers the full luxury package. Here, you can relax, mingle with celebs, and dine on Provençal cuisine so exquisite that it has earned chef Arnaud Donckele the culinary accolade of three Michelin stars for his work in the beautiful La Vague d'Or restaurant.

Chef Donckele champions Provençal cuisine. He takes authentic recipes that have been handed down through the generations and, with a wave of his magic wand, transforms them into modern, creative, and wholesome dishes of gastronomic elegance. Fresh fish brought ashore nearby, meat from local farmers, and produce grown in the countryside of Provence form the menu's foundation. There is no compromise in Donckele's kitchen when it comes to quality.

Baby lobster and sea mullet served as two courses typically feature on the fish menu. This can be served cold as slices in yuzu juice, and hot with caviar pearls and a shellfish broth-infused salicornia and verbena mixed salad. Donckele has assembled a similar partnership on the meat menu—for example, lamb from Sisteron prepared with local herbs, eggplant, and tomato as an appetizer, and drizzled with a savory pepper sauce as a main course. Each comes with a fine wine suggestion.

La Vague d'Or, with its calm, neutral decor and panoramic views of the bay, exudes an invitation to linger. Cocooned and relaxed, diners should be perfectly primed to enjoy one of the restaurant's desserts, created fresh and presented on the plate as nothing less than a work of art. Creations, such as hot soufflé of rhubarb and green apple drizzled with lime, or a tart topped with strawberry and lime mousse and grated lemon, are truly to be savored. **CFr**

Auberge du Vieux Puits |
Glorious food in a tranquil, remote village

Location Fontjoncouse **Signature dish** *Oeuf de poule pourri* (egg with truffle and mushroom puree) | ❸❸❸❸

Deep in Languedoc Roussillon, amid rugged, craggy mountains, the isolated village of Fontjoncouse is home to the Auberge du Vieux Puits, a restaurant and inn showcasing the culinary talents of Gilles Goujon, its chef-patron. Goujon and his wife, Marie-Christine, took over the restaurant in 1992. Since then, their hard work and dedication to producing wonderful food has seen many plaudits, including three Michelin stars.

As befits its remote and rural location, the dining room is rustic in style, with a stone floor and exposed wooden beams, in character a country location rather than a grand, formal temple of gastronomy.

Goujon is known for his way with high-quality, seasonal ingredients, and uses an extensive network

> *"If you love excellent food and wine, there can be no finer restaurant in the south of France."*
>
> golanguedoc.com

of local food producers. A deceptively simple dish such as tomatoes, using five different varieties, served with sweet onion and basil sorbet demonstrates the importance of the produce to the combination of flavors, from the perfectly ripe tomatoes to the onion and aromatic basil. Main courses are similarly assured, dishes in which the quality of the ingredients shines through, as does the expertise and technical skill.

Make sure to leave room for two final stages. Desserts include elegant creations such as chocolate sable with Tahiti vanilla cream and local raspberries. Finally, the splendid cheese trolley, offering a seasonally varied selection of local cheeses, is a tour de force. This is indeed food that is worth a special journey. **AH**

Le Louis XV | Truly luxurious dining, with food to surpass a lavish interior

Location Monte Carlo **Signature dish** Provençal vegetables with black truffle | $$$$$

It is impossible not to rub the eyes in disbelief at the peerless opulence of chef Alain Ducasse's flagship restaurant in the Hotel de Paris, overlooking the Ferrari-jammed Place de Casino in Monte Carlo. A riot of sumptuous marble, gold, mirrors, and chandeliers, it makes every diner feel like a million dollars.

When the restaurant opened back in 1987, Prince Rainier of Monaco challenged Ducasse to create the world's first Michelin three-star restaurant within four years. Ducasse achieved this daunting feat in less than three years, and his food remains flawlessly brilliant.

The cuisine, based around the terroir of the Riveria, is far more contemporary, or even simple, than the room might suggest. Examples include asparagus pasta with an intense morel sauce; beautifully cooked sea bass, zingy with Menton lemon, basil, and olives; and a pot of vegetables with a pastry topping that is broken at the table to reveal exquisitely sweet baby carrots, artichokes, turnips, and fava beans.

The devil is in the incredible details, from the hand-blown glass bowl of crudités, cut to maximize their flavors and dipped in a tapenade of Niçoise olives, to paper-thin bread imprinted like handmade paper. There is a vast cheese board and desserts are exceptional, from the rich chocolate croustillant to crisp, caramelized ravioli filled with passion fruit. White-gloved waiters use gold scissors to clip a verveine plant and make a digestif, served in a gold teapot and accompanied by tiny lemon tarts, canelés, madeleines, marshmallows, and macarons.

The wine list runs to more than 400 of the most impressive wines in the world, and the set menu includes so many extras that it could be called the most extraordinary gastronomic bargain on Earth. Many of Ducasse's Michelin three-starred peers cite this as their most memorable meal. **SP**

↑ Star chef Alain Ducasse at work in the kitchen.

Silvio Nickol | A mecca for food and wine lovers alike

Location Vienna **Signature dish** *Vogelfrei* (guinea fowl, beets, and walnuts) | ❺❺❺❺

The Silvio Nickol restaurant inside the magnificent Palais Coburg claims to have the largest cellar—and more wine—than any other restaurant in Europe. There are at least 60,000 bottles, including some of the rarest ones to be found anywhere: a Rüdesheimer Apostelwein from 1727 is thought to be the oldest drinkable bottle in the world. There are many French wines that it would be difficult to locate in France, and all the Château d'Yquem vintages produced from 1893 to 2001. There is also a significant number of bottles of the legendary 1945 Château Mouton-Rothschild.

Although many undoubtedly come here to drink wine that cannot be tasted elsewhere, it would be unfair to refer to this ultra-exclusive dining experience as a night in a wine restaurant. The cuisine of chef Silvio Nickol is up to the challenge of serving food that will make the wines taste even better. He proposes tasting menus, with or without wine pairings, of five, seven, or nine courses, and these come at a set price.

You may then drink a bottle ordered from the wine list, or opt for a different glass to pair with each course, chosen by the restaurant and billed separately.

Among the dishes that might appear are duck liver with macadamia, walnut, fragolino grapes, and marigold; monkfish with parsley, spinach, miso, and buckwheat; squab with Savoy cabbage, cranberries, beetroot, and juniper; cucumber with tapioca, coconut, coriander, and juniper; or scallop with rice, orange, cauliflower, and peanut. The *Vogelfrei* combines Guinea fowl, beets, and walnuts. Each creation invites you to pause and savor it.

Two special chef's tables offer a closed-circuit transmission of what is happening in the kitchen, which will fascinate food lovers, just as their oenophile friends are transported in reverie by the many glasses of extraordinary elixirs. **FP**

⬆ Silvio Nickol is housed inside an historic palace.

Café Central | Enjoy the atmosphere in a classic Viennese café

Location Vienna **Signature dish** Wiener Schnitzel |

"*Both Trotsky and Hitler sipped coffee under Café Central's magnificent arches.*"

bbc.co.uk

⬆ The glorious interior of Café Central is not to be missed.

Café Central has a mood and moment for every part of the day. In the morning, those with time to spare take a newspaper and order a typical Viennese coffee such as *Melange* and pass the time of day musing and watching the world go by. The Bohemian poet Peter Altenberg (1859–1919) did just that, and he is commemorated by a life-sized sculpture that some may notice sitting placidly among today's coffeehouse idlers. Other famous regulars included Trotsky, Freud, and Arthur Schnitzler.

Come lunchtime, both office workers and tourists stroll in and take their places among the gleaming marble columns that rise up to the vaulted ceiling; after having a look around, they consider lunch. This is very much a traditional Viennese café, with a history that goes back to the middle of the nineteenth century. Lunch might start with a bowl of nourishing sauerkraut soup with loin of pork, followed by salmon trout fillet in the company of balsamic lentils, spinach, and bacon sauce; others might plump for the cream of corn soup with smoked paprika oil, followed by ricotta ravioli and brown butter. Afterward, and weather permitting, there is a good chance that the afternoon will deserve a brisk walk around the beauty of central Vienna; but if the weather denies this, it is quite possible just to snooze in an armchair.

Come evening, the mood changes once more; the lights come on and the waiters begin to glide about with bottles of wine or beer to hand, and plates of food held out like benedictions. Now is the time to contemplate a ragout of venison with red cabbage, or pan-fried carp in thyme batter, or indeed the traditional Wiener Schnitzel. But remember that, because you are in Vienna, you must leave ample room for dessert: here, a serving of apple strudel or a chocolate torte is more than a mere pudding. Café Central: the ghosts come back for more here, and after you have enjoyed the experience, so will you. **ATJ**

Café Demel | Historic Viennese café offering sweet delights

Location Vienna   **Signature dish** *Apfelstrudel* and hot chocolate; "Annatorte" | 🄢🄢

Soft and pliant, sweet and sticky apple strudel; rich and unctuous chocolate cake; pastries that look like miniature works of art: you know you're in the heart of an historical establishment as soon as you enter Café Demel. Founded in 1786, the café was moved from Michaelermarkt to its current location among exclusive shops on the upscale Kohlmarkt in the 1850s. It is well known for its elaborate, creative window displays that feature sweet wares as well as elegant packaging. Through the years, during war, revolution, royal patronage, political upheaval, and recession, Café Demel and its white-clad waitresses, known as *Demelinerinnen*, have remained constant in an ever-changing world.

Inside, the café boasts a mixture of classical and art deco furnishings across three floors: glittering ornate chandeliers cast their light on decadent displays of pastries in pastel colors, waiting to be chosen underneath shiny glass cases. The mahogany bar is mirror-backed, the ceilings are high, there's the ever-present aroma of coffee and chocolate, and the murmuring of shoppers who pop in for cake or tourists who just want to gawk at the place. It is as if World War I, or II, never happened in here, although the glass panels on the first floor that allow customers to see the chocolatiers and bakers at work is a small concession to modernity. There is a small museum covering the café's history on the premises.

Most people come for the varied pastries and cakes—the rich chocolate *Annatorte* is named after Anna Demel—with coffee or a hot chocolate, but what about something more substantial? The menu also features hearty Austrian classics (not too heavy in their elegant execution here), including Wiener Schnitzel, veal goulash, roasted fillet of char, and ricotta ravioli. And while you eat or just sip a coffee, this venerable old place carries on as it has for centuries. **ATJ**

"An elegant, regal café within sight of the Hofburg … It wins marks for the sheer creativity of its sweets."

Lonely Planet

⊡ Coffee and cake at Demel is the ultimate treat.

Steirereck | A wonderful taste of Austria in a parkland setting

Location Vienna   **Signature dish** Char with beeswax, yellow carrot "pollen," and sour cream | **$ $ $**

"Alpine sorrel, tree spinach, and sea purslane [are used in the] highly botanical tasting menus."

gourmettraveller.com.au

⬆ Chef Heinz Reitbauer grows unusual plants for his dishes in a special terrace garden in the park.

➡ Steirereck is housed in Art Nouveau splendor.

Set in the beautiful Stadtpark in Vienna, Steirereck is often nominated as the best restaurant in Austria. Along with the more casual Meierei (milk bar), it offers gratifying, innovative food that can be a real bargain or very expensive, depending on when you go.

Each day, Meierei has one of the best breakfasts in town, served until noon. Freshly pressed juices practically sing with the flavor and fragrance of gorgeous native or tropical fruit. The soft-boiled egg with sour cream and foie gras is three spoonfuls of decadence. Then, at noon, the menu switches to lunch. An apple strudel issues from the oven at 1.00 PM. At 2.00 PM, a freshly baked *Topfenstrudel* (cheese curd strudel) appears, to be joined throughout the day and evening by Austrian classics such as Wiener Schnitzel and goulash, along with certain dishes from the ambitious Steirereck menu. Cheese lovers will savor the quality and quantity of the Austrian offerings as well as those from Italy and France.

At Steirereck itself, prices at lunch, and especially in the evening, can be as lofty as the cooking is audacious. The most famous dish is the *Saibling* (char) with beeswax, yellow carrot "pollen," and sour cream—few visitors will have encountered this heady combination of tastes and textures before. Just as remarkable is the barbecued sturgeon with kohlrabi, quinoa, and elderberry, this last being a fundamental and characteristic flavor of Austrian cuisine.

Chef Heinz Reitbauer has a farm in Styria, with its own small country inn. Many of the meats and vegetables at Steirereck come from there, most notably the succulent lamb; in contrast, the beef comes from a farm in the Austrian alps. Both the beef served with salsify, figs, and celery and the braised and roasted veal with fermented white asparagus and crunchy elderflower are unforgettable. As to be expected in Vienna, the desserts are stunning. The wine list is ample and service is first-rate. **FP**

Lindenhofkeller | French-Swiss cuisine in an understated cellar restaurant

Location Zurich **Signature dish** Slow-roast saddle of Swiss veal with herb butter | $$$

"Outstanding meals await at this upmarket venue . . . where the wine list has depth and breadth."

Zagat

Lindenhofkeller is a renowned traditional restaurant in Lindenhof hill, part of the historic center of Zurich and the original site of the town settlement overlooking the Limmat River. Located in the cellar of a fourteenth-century house on a steep side street, the restaurant has been in business since 1860. The city has expanded in all directions since then, but this small eatery still has a big reputation in Switzerland. Since 1996, manager, chef, and sommelier René Hofer has been in charge of the kitchen, providing the finest classic French-Swiss cuisine.

From the stepped pavement, a modest entrance leads into a small vaulted room with tables placed between arches and pillars. The decor is understated, but all the components of a fine-dining experience are in place: widely spaced tables, crisp white linen, and sparkling glassware. The only individual touch is a display of various wine labels attached to one wall. In fine weather, the dining space extends into an internal courtyard surrounded by apartments, sometimes with the homely touch of the neighbors' washing hung out to dry.

The restaurant's signature dish is the rack of Swiss veal, oven-cooked at a low temperature for many hours; it has to be ordered the day before. The long cooking time makes for wonderfully tender, pink meat on the inside and a distinctive crispy crust. It is served with liquid herb butter and a choice of side dishes, including saffron rice, egg noodles, or salad. The chef's mastery of meat and game dishes is evident throughout the menu: other tasty offerings may include grilled bison fillet, carpaccio of beef with truffles, or lamb salad with bacon dressing.

Hofer is also a true wine enthusiast, and his restaurant is known for its 600-strong selection of wines displayed in an impressive 27-page wine list that includes many little-known Swiss vintages—a chance to explore the finest wines of the country. **SH**

↑ The restaurant is located in the historic Lindenhof hill district of Zurich.

Hôtel Georges Wenger | Not an average railroad hotel

Location Jura **Signature dish** Venison prepared three ways with red cabbage and pepper sauce | ❸❸❸

Georges and Andrea Wenger's restaurant, situated in the Swiss village of Le Noirmont in the rugged Franches Montagnes district of the Jura, is a place of sincere charm and warmth that wears its two Michelin stars lightly. Originally, this was the station hotel: the local service, known affectionately as *le petit train rouge qui bouge* (the little red train that moves), still stops just outside the door of the restaurant, a distinct advantage in that it allows guests to relax, enjoy their meal and wines, and then take the train home.

However they come, the people who find their way up to these wild Jurassic heights do not come here to see or be seen. They come rather for a taste of Georges Wenger's honest, locally rooted, exquisitely prepared food, served with quiet, unshowy assurance by Andrea Wenger and her deft young team.

This is a chef who is a staunch champion of local products. At different moments throughout the year, asparagus, wild garlic, fresh morels, lake fish, lamb and veal, game, wild mushrooms, and a selection of local raw-milk cheeses, the majority raised on nearby farms or foraged from the fields and forests, are featured on his menus. Fish and shellfish come directly from the French coastline several times a week. The wine list, comprising more than seven hundred options, is strong on Swiss and French wines, particularly those of neighboring Burgundy.

Each year in November, when farms throughout the Jura region would traditionally kill a pig and put up provisions for winter, the Wengers offer their celebrated and always over-subscribed nine-course "Menu St. Martin." This is an all-pork extravaganza drawing on locally raised organic meat, prepared in the true Martinmas spirit and including head "cheese" (actually a terrine made from head meats), homemade sausage, black pudding, pork roast, and sauerkraut, all interpreted with a two-star touch and served with great good humor. **SS**

"Tomme au foin—*a mountain cheese left to ripen in hay—made its comeback on [Wenger's] menu.*"

vacation.hotwire.com

⬆ Chef Georges Wenger delights in using local produce for his dishes and desserts.

Hôtel de Ville | Impeccable
food in a legendary Swiss restaurant

Location Crissier **Signature dish** "Scarlet" tomato pulp and pip consommé with Imperial Osetra caviar | ❸❸❸❺

The Hôtel de Ville, in the little town of Crissier near Lausanne, is in itself a chapter of restaurant history, having over the years hosted legendary chefs Frédy Girardet, who set up the restaurant in 1971, and, from 1996, his protégé Philippe Rochat. From 2012, it has been in the capable hands of Benoît Violier, who has worked here for twenty years, having trained under Joël Robuchon. In each of its eras it has retained the ultimate three Michelin stars.

The restaurant has a policy of closing for a few weeks each year, when the staff take their vacations, so there are no "off nights," and the waiters are so superbly trained that one other (nameless) three-star Michelin restaurant sends its managers here to see

---

"Nothing can be definitively acquired; everything must be done all over again every day."

Benoît Violier, chef at Hôtel de Ville

---

what service perfection should look like. When it comes to classical French cooking, the Hôtel de Ville at Crissier is at the pinnacle. The cooking is firmly in classical territory, based on impeccable ingredients. and clearly illustrated by an amuse-bouche of Rose de Berne tomatoes and guacamole, served on silver spoons. A dish of ravioli filled with cep mushroom and hazelnut has a terrific flavor and delicate texture.

The impeccable quality of the ingredients is also seen in a large langoustine from Brittany, served with a wonderful lemon sauce flavored with ginger. For dessert opt for mixed red fruits atop a layer of vanilla ice cream and a ring of biscuit, with black currant jelly and silky strawberry puree. **AH**

Chesery | Glorious cuisine
served in a stylish mountain chalet

Location Gstaad **Signature dish** Hot chocolate cake with kumquats | ❸❸❸❺

Chesery's slogan promises "the fine art of simplicity," so some may find it surprising that truffle-stuffed brie and terrine of quail and foie gras with sweet and sour pumpkin are on the menu. Simplicity hunters beware: here in Gstaad, normal standards do not apply.

Actually, Robert Speth's long-standing Michelin-starred restaurant is fairly homely and even good value by the surreal norms of this jet-set mountain retreat. At the Bellevue across the road, a glass of cognac can cost as much as $1,600 (£1,000), so Chesery's wine, from around $80 (£50) a bottle, must seem embarrassingly cheap to some guests.

The restaurant is located in the Aga Khan's former luxury chalet, somewhere between Bernie Ecclestone's hillside villa and Roger Federer's favorite spa. In true Gstaad style, Chesery looks too big to be a restaurant, although the neatly maintained geranium flower boxes do soften its imposing frontage. Inside, it is all light wood, simple fabrics, and well spaced tables. Speth has run the kitchen since opening, back in 1984; his wife, Suzanne, manages the front of the house.

The dishes have evolved into a unique blend of classic haute cuisine and Speth's individual sparkle. Expect local game presented with flair: venison on Savoy cabbage with vinegar and plum sauce; and whole roast duck accompanied by Asian-style vegetables. Look out for Scottish grouse with sauerkraut, or Australian sirloin with mango and onion confit. Similarly, cod may come with miso, and octopus with sweet potato. Speth delivers food to the homes of local billionaires— but nonbillionaires may find this restaurant to be their best chance of sampling his inventive cooking. **SH**

▣ The Chesery is located in one of the many luxury chalets of Gstaad.

Restaurant Didier de Courten | High-end Swiss cuisine

Location Valais **Signature dish** Duck foie gras fondant with quince jelly, figs, and spiced apples | ❸❸❸

"Creating a dish is realizing a fantasy, pursuing intentions and desires... monotony is [my] ruin."

Didier de Courten, chef and owner

⬆ The Hôtel Terminus houses both Didier de Courten's brasserie and his elegant restaurant.

➡ Visual finesse has helped lead to two Michelin stars.

The Hôtel Terminus, a classic, primrose-yellow building in the town of Sierre in the wine-growing Swiss canton of Valais, was built in 1870, revamped in 2005, and now houses the two restaurants of star chef Didier de Courten, along with a wine bar.

At the front, and spilling joyously out onto the sidewalk whenever the town enjoys one of its frequent sunny days, is de Courten's brasserie, L'Atelier Gourmand, which is always packed with a largely local crowd. Eating at L'Atelier is a great way to experience the mastery of this celebrated chef without breaking the bank. In back is the Michelin two-star Restaurant Didier de Courten, which draws a discerning and well-heeled clientele from all over Switzerland and beyond.

In both the brasserie and the restaurant, the food is stamped with de Courten's style: French at heart but with slight accents from neighboring Italy. De Courten's cuisine is pared down, creatively modernized, and driven by a passionate and near-obsessive quest for perfection. Unlike many starred chefs, de Courten is not to be found welcoming guests at the door, or doing a lap of honor of the dining room after the meal. Where he likes to be is either working in his kitchen or high up in the Val d'Anniviers, where he has a weekend chalet.

The menu shadows the seasons and draws on the finest raw materials: typical dishes include scallops on black Venere rice with a shellfish–chorizo emulsion; lobster claws and rillettes with black olive jelly; filet of chamois (goat) and tiny sausages made from the shoulder, with an apricot confit; and veal with truffled parsnip puree. Desserts, often fruit-based or chocolate-infused, are artful combinations of flavors, colors, textures, and serving temperatures. Every dish is presented as if it were a contemporary still life.

The Valais is Switzerland's prime wine-growing region, and the wine list offers the chance to sample some of its finest and rarest bottles. **SS**

Trattoria Altavilla | A warm welcome and generous dishes

Location Bianzone   **Signature dish** *Sciatt* | ❺❺

On a Sunday afternoon in summer, you can almost hear a pin drop in the quiet hillside town of Bianzone—unless you happen to be near the terrace of Trattoria Altavilla with its buzz of happy diners clinking glasses, clattering cutlery and crockery, and with diners shouting out exclamations of delight at the food served at Anna Bertola's restaurant.

Although the trattoria has an understated and laid-back vibe, dishes are well researched and prepared with an enthusiasm and diligence that has secured the place a devoted following. You don't have to be a regular to feel at home. The dishes are among the finest local foods, confidently transformed into generous dishes.

The trattoria is known throughout the province for serving some of the best *pizzoccheri* (short buckwheat pasta similar to tagliatelle, served with cheese, potatoes, and cabbage), and for the tasty *sciatt* (balls of deep-fried cheese in buckwheat flour),

served here as the lightest of fritters with unctuous cheese, nestling on a bed of finely shredded chicory dressed with olive oil and wine vinegar. Bresaola and local, hand-picked mushrooms feature in various dishes as do top-quality meats of pork, beef, lamb, and sometimes venison. There is a good selection of cheeses, including Valtellina Casera and Bitto, a Lombard cheese speciality.

Homemade desserts include delicious ice cream flavored with Braulio, the local digestif. The wine list is extensive and varied, with a strong emphasis on local labels, which is no surprise; as the trattoria overlooks a valley of vineyards. Inside, in the cozy Valtellina Room, you can learn more about the local products at various wine tastings. For those who enjoy a cigar after their meal, there is also a dedicated cigar room. **CS**

⬆ *Sciatt* served with chicory from the garden.

Locanda dell' Isola Comacina | Simply great food in a lake setting

Location Ossuccio   **Signature dish** Fresh vegetable antipasti | ❸❸❸

Benvenuto Puricelli's unique restaurant stands on a tiny island amid the dramatic scenery of Italy's grandest lake, Como. Diners arrive on a small ferry and need to clamber up the stone steps to the Locanda. Tables are set on a lakeside terrace or in the high-ceilinged stone dining room, which is covered in paintings and photos of Puricelli with various celebrity guests including George Clooney, Brad Pitt, and Elton John. The five-course set menu is the only option available—and it has not changed since the restaurant opened in 1947.

If that is not unusual enough, around 900 years ago, the whole island was cursed by a local bishop, and the legend of the curse resurfaced when two early backers of the restaurant died suddenly. Since then, the ancient curse is being "defeated" by a fiery exorcism ritual that is enacted after every meal: at the sound of a bell, Puricelli dons a woollen bobble hat and tartan waistcoat, and retells the tale of the curse while setting fire to a pot of brandy. This is then served to the customers with coffee and sugar.

From all this, you might expect rather uncommon food; but, in fact, it is surprisingly wonderful simple Italian cuisine. Start with an array of fresh seasonal vegetable antipasti, served in small bowls decorated with painted flowers and accompanied by wood-smoked prosciutto and bresaola that has been dried in the restaurant cellar. Next, you might opt for wood-grilled trout followed by chicken fried in an iron pan and roasted in a wood oven, served unpretentiously with salad, lemon, salt, pepper, and olive oil.

A huge Parmesan then appears and each diner is given a chunk to round off the meal. For dessert, opt for fresh fruit with the finest ice cream and delicate homemade cream sauce made to an original island recipe. Local white wine is served throughout. **SH**

⬆ Guests can dine right by the water's edge.

Al Sorriso | Elegant Italian haute cuisine near Lago Maggiore

Location Soriso **Signature dish** Potatoes with egg, Parmesan, and white Alba truffles | ❸❸❸❸

"Fans of the Piedmont and the mountains will be in their element in this restaurant."

Michelin Guide

⏏ Desserts are beautifully presented.

At Al Sorriso, chef Luisa Valazza is in charge in the kitchen, and her husband Angelo runs the front of house with help from their daughter Paola. The family-run restaurant opened in 1981, in the quiet village of Soriso near Lago Maggiore, some 50 miles (80 km) from Milan. It gained a first Michelin star very soon after opening, followed by a second and third. Luisa is a self-taught chef who completed an art degree before deciding on cooking as a career.

The dining room is characterized by well-spaced tables and pink tablecloths, with a wine list of more than 600 labels. In addition to the à la carte menu, there are two set menu options on offer, one focusing on seafood, the other on meat.

The deceptively simple cooking relies on the superb produce that the area has to offer—for instance, in a simple dish of cannelloni with local tomato and basil, the intense flavor of the tomatoes is remarkable. Tartare of Piedmontese Fassone beef is served with a Parmesan tuile nest of salad leaves and *vitello tonnato* (veal and tuna) sauce, the delicate tuile and salad dressing balancing out the richness of the beef.

The technical skill of the chef is evident in a dish that appears to be pasta, but is actually made with scallops that are cut into pastalike strands before cooking. The scallops are sourced south of Venice, and have a lovely inherent sweetness. A classic dish, pumpkin risotto with gorgonzola, is masterfully enhanced with a dash of 25-year-old balsamic vinegar, and the stock used for cooking the rice is superb. Be sure not to miss the excellent cheese selection.

The ingredients used at this restaurant are excellent and the cooking technique is impeccable. There are no chef gimmicks here, but that is the restaurant's strength. Al Sorriso is a particularly lovely place to enjoy a meal, showcasing the flavors of Italy at their very best. **AH**

Piccolo Lago | Enticing cuisine in a charming lakeside setting

Location Lago di Mergozzo **Signature dish** Cheese flan | ❸❸❸❸

Lake Mergozzo is one of the prettiest of the Italian lakes, and Piccolo Lago is situated about halfway down the lakeside, facing an imposing hillside. The restaurant has been run by the same family since 1974, with Marco Sacco as head chef following in the footsteps of his father Bruno, and boasting two Michelin stars.

The dining room has several tables with breathtaking lake views and floor-to-ceiling windows that create a truly striking setting. There is also a pretty outside terrace overlooking the lake, where you can have a drink and browse the menu as you look over the gorgeous scenery.

The cooking style is quite modern, taking Italian classics and reinventing them with a twist. Cheese flan is made with a local cheese and served with celeriac and red berries (to provide a balancing acidity), and flavored with a touch of mustard. A deconstructed carbonara consists of freshly made pasta topped with smoked ham, and an eggshell to one side containing a sauce of egg yolk, Parmesan, and gin. The superb pasta and ham work well together, with a sauce that has just the right level of richness. Other dishes worth mentioning are sturgeon with kohlrabi and vanilla cream and "Milanese-style" quail with endive.

You may want to go for the wonderful selection of micro-desserts. Alternatively, there is a raspberry, white chocolate, and Bacardi cake or rum baba, the popular classic, presented in a lighter take that also includes slivers of mango, pink grapefruit, custard cream, and pineapple sorbet, with mint—a refreshing and delicate composition.

Piccolo Lago is a lovely dining experience, with a stunning location, innovative and very enjoyable food, and friendly service. It is no exaggeration to say that it has one of the prettiest settings of any restaurant in the world. **AH**

"Past and present are intertwined everywhere ... the chef's creations tell the story of the territory."

Piccolo Lago website

⬆ Reinvented classic recipes are Piccolo Lago's forte.

Villa Crespi | Classic fine dining with stunning lake vistas

Location Orta San Giulio **Signature dish** Pigeon and foie gras with cocoa beans and Banyuls sauce | ❸❸❸❸

"Staying at this Moorish caprice, topped with an aqua onion dome, is to give oneself over to opulence."

Lonely Planet

⬆ A perfect lakeside setting for a romantic meal.

Villa Crespi is just a few minutes' walk up the slope from the banks of beautiful Lake Orta. The Moorish building was built by a successful cotton trader in 1879, who spent a lot of time in Persia, and features some very elaborate arabesque stonework. Nowadays it houses a luxury hotel and restaurant, where head chef Antonino Cannavacciuolo reigns in the kitchen, while his wife Cinzia runs the front of house. Before working here, Cannavacciuolo trained with Marc Haeberlin at the famous Auberge de L'Ill in France and at the restaurant of the Grand Hotel Quisisana on Capri.

At the back of the building is an extensive garden with a view over the lake and a terrace where you can have a drink before dinner. As well as admiring the panorama, you will need some time to fully appreciate the huge wine list, which includes more than a thousand different selections, with 250 Champagnes and sparkling wines.

The cooking is classical Mediterranean, making good use of the excellent local ingredients. A meal might start with a skewer of langoustine and scallop with green onion and lemon, served with shredded celeriac and a centrifuged Granny Smith apple sauce. The shellfish is of impeccable quality, perfectly cooked, and the apple sauce provides a gentle balance to the dish.

An unusual but effective pairing is red mullet with turnip tops, mash, and smoked cheese. This is not an obvious flavor combination, but the cheese is carefully restrained, the turnip tops provide a good balance to the richness of the mash, and the fish is perfectly cooked and seasoned.

The picturesque lakeside setting is magical, the ingredients are of a high standard, and the cooking technique is hard to fault. Combined with top-class service, a meal at Villa Crespi is a true gourmet delight. **AH**

Al Cacciatore della Subida | Sophisticated cooking and top wines

Location Cormons　**Signature dish** Veal shank　| ❸❸❸

Situated only steps from the Slovenian border, Al Cacciatore della Subida elevates home cooking to high art. It is also a true temple to the food and wine of Friuli-Venezia Giulia. This small region in the northeastern corner of Italy takes its influences from Venice, Austria, and the nearby Slavic countries, and yet maintains a character all of its own.

More than in any other part of Italy, the innovative use of spices and herbs in the cooking makes for remarkably sophisticated, unusual flavors. Examples might include veal with cinnamon or venison with nutmeg as main courses, or a yeast cake filled with ricotta and tarragon.

Italy's best white wines and some excellent reds are produced in the region, many of them in the gorgeous Collio zone that surrounds the town of Cormons. Vintners are experts in local cuisine and will make wines that pair with the flavors: Cabernet Franc to go with nutmeg and Sauvignon blanc to be paired with saffron.

La Subida is run with great passion and dedication by Josko and Loredana Sirk and their family. Josko travels the region to source exquisite foods produced in small quantities. The prosciutto made by his friend Gigi d'Osvaldo, for example, is hard to find anywhere else. As Josko slices it into silken ribbons by hand, you realize that the reason it tastes so good has partly to do with how carefully it is cut.

The food is strictly local but stunningly refined. *Frico*, a sort of crisp made with local Montasio cheeses of different ages, is irresistible. When apricots or plums are in season, they are used to fill large but delicate *gnocchi di susine*, which are served with butter, cinnamon, and smoked ricotta cheese. The meltingly tender *stinco di vitello* (veal shank) is worth the trip alone, but there are countless other attractions from delicious starters to tasty desserts, all paired with amazing wines. **FP**

"This restaurant successfully combines old traditions with an innovative modern approach."

Michelin Guide

⬆ The dining room at La Subida is cozy and rustic.

Trattoria Visconti | Refined food in a family restaurant

Location Ambivere   **Signature dish** Nonna Ida's *casoncelli* | 💲💲

Trattoria Visconti is a quiet, civilized, and relaxed affair. In the summer, when eating out on the beautiful terrace in the idyllic garden, surrounded by fragrant trees and plants, it is hard not to feel that all is right with the world. When the weather is cooler, you can eat inside where tables are generously spaced.

This is a family restaurant in both senses: it is run by the Visconti family, and the professional yet friendly staff ensure that families with however many young children are made to feel welcome and comfortable. But then it is also possible to imagine romantic dinners here. Either way, diners benefit from a cosseted few hours in a refined yet welcoming setting. The menu is varied and creatively considered.

You may choose to start with an antipasto from a selection of homemade salumi or fresh anchovies, or opt for the wild boar terrine, followed by one of the primi, perhaps fresh tagliollni with spring vegetables or a classic Milanese risotto, pea soup with salt cod, risotto with quail, pumpkin gnocchi with sage, or perhaps tripe. The star dish is Nonna Ida's *casoncelli*, a filled pasta with butter and sage.

For the secondi, there may be asparagus with polenta on offer, beef cooked in olive oil with polenta, wild rabbit, or kidneys. Visconti also offers a vertical tasting of one-, three-, and five-year matured Bitto as an option for the cheese course. Desserts may include various tarts with homemade jam or a delicious pistachio *semifreddo*.

There is an interesting wine list to choose from, and Daniele Visconti will help with expert advice should it be needed. If you had not noticed them right away, when you leave, be sure to look out for the two quirky scarecrows near the front door. This may be fine dining, but the atmosphere is far from stuffy. **CS**

⬆ Enjoy the refined yet welcoming atmosphere.

Ristorante Baretto di San Vigilio | A lesson in simple style

Location Bergamo   **Signature dish** Beef with olive oil and polenta | ❸❸

Baretto di San Vigilio perches at the very top of the Città Alta (upper city) of Bergamo. It takes two funicular rides and a pair of sturdy shoes to get here, but, once you have arrived, you will feel truly rewarded: you can choose to sit under a flowery, umbrella-covered pergola, with a 360-degree view of beautiful Bergamo stretching before you, or you might opt for a table in the very elegant dining room.

Tables are covered in fine linen, colorful flower arrangements are dotted around wooden dressers, the wine list showcases the very best of Italian wines, and the waiters are trained to listen with great attention. If you would like to see how an excellent restaurant is run—this is the ideal.

The menu is short and simple, showcasing local and regional ingredients simply and authentically, in season, and with minimum fuss but maximum technical know-how. As you ponder what to order, listening to the birdsong outside and admiring the chic guests, the waiters bring out tasty amuse-bouches to go with a pre-dinner prosecco or Campari cocktail.

The chefs create some excellent risotti, pasta dishes, charcuterie, and warm salads as starters, and the beef and freshwater fish dishes are a tour de force. Do leave room for dessert, though: the fresh fruit salads, zabaione, chocolate cake, and Italian trifle are all worth sampling.

What is so wonderful about this little restaurant is the consistency of everything it offers: you can dine here for both lunch and dinner every day of the week, and the standard will always be high. The place is also frequented by many locals—always a very good sign, particularly as they choose Baretto for weddings, christenings, and other family occasions. You will still be talking about this restaurant long after you return home. **SdS**

⬆ The appealing dining room at Baretto di San Vigilio.

Da Vittorio | Creative high-end cuisine presented with flair

Location Brusaporto **Signature dish** *Paccheri* | ❸❸❸❸

"… an elegant villa surrounded by extensive grounds, offering a perfect oasis of wellness."

relaischateaux.com

⬆ Da Vittorio boasts an impressive wine cellar with nearly 3,000 labels.

➡ The terrace is ideal for al fresco dining.

Da Vittorio is set in a striking location not far from the historic town of Bergamo, on a hillside with a lovely garden terrace and a pool. It was established in 1966 by the parents of the current chef duo, Enrico and Roberto Cerea, who specialize in seafood. The quality of their cooking has been recognized with three Michelin stars.

The cooking makes great use of the terrific local ingredients: *paccheri* (pasta tubes) are cooked with wonderful local tomatoes and a little basil, and served with 36-month-aged Parmesan cheese and just a hint of chili for an extra kick.

A trio of sweet langoustines is prepared in a variety of styles: as tempura; cooked with couscous, lemon, and rosemary; and served with a little balsamic vinegar: In each case, the cooking of the shellfish is precise. Sea bass is cooked at the table in a cast-iron pot that has a layer of very hot stones at the bottom; water is then poured over the stones and the pot covered, the resulting steam cooking the sea bass. The wild bass is infused with herbs and served simply with a selection of diced vegetables.

Those who prefer meat may opt for a beef tartare from Piedmont beef with a caper crisp and a dash of Worcestershire sauce. Superb ingredients like these do not need complex treatment. The menu is regularly updated to reflect changes in the season and to explore new culinary themes. The vast wine list offers almost 3,000 separate wines to accompany the dishes, with 15,000 bottles kept in a temperature-and-humidity-controlled cellar.

Desserts are offered from a pretty stand in the garden: wild strawberry sponge makes use of the local seasonal fruit, or you may choose silky dark chocolate ice cream or a delicate apple tart. Da Vittorio makes the most of its lovely hillside setting, and the very high-caliber cooking showcases the excellent ingredients of the region. **AH**

Toni del Spin | The irresistible charm of timeless tradition

Location Treviso **Signature dish** Vicentina-style stockfish with polenta | **$$**

From the moment you cross the threshold at Toni del Spin, you know you are in for a treat. High-beamed ceilings, rusticated stone walls, chalked menu boards, and the mingled aromas of rich game roasts and freshly laundered table linen are all tell-tale signs of solid, dependable Veneto cuisine. And nowhere is the cuisine more dependable than at Toni del Spin. Here the traditions are as old as the 130-year-old walls, and Alfredo Sturlese, the restaurant's proprietor since 1986, has no intention of changing them.

Hearty pigeon broth, roast duck and goose, pan-stewed rabbit, thick bean soup, and wild mushroom risotto are just some of the local specialities prepared by the restaurant's long-standing chef, Guido Severin, in addition to the erstwhile owner's signature dish of Vicentina-style stockfish (prepared with onion and milk). In the old days, Toni's dish was so popular that it earned him and his restaurant the nickname "del spin" (the cod bone):

being too busy to bone the fish properly, he opted instead to keep customers happy by offering them a free glass of wine for every ten bones they found.

Nowadays, Guido is far too attentive to take such liberties, even if the menu has expanded considerably to pay homage to Treviso's claim to culinary fame, radicchio. When in season, these slender and succulent stems fill the restaurant's menu with a range of delicacies from risottos and lasagnas, to grilled side dishes, crispy salads, and veal stews.

To accompany all these gastronomical delights, there is an excellent, 300-label wine list, selected by Alfredo's professional sommelier son. Father and son are also renowned for their fierce competition when creating Treviso's other masterpiece—tiramisu. No matter who wins, this exquisitely creamy dessert is the perfect way to end a perfect meal. **DJS**

⊼ Treviso's Toni del Spin is a traditional trattoria.

Osteria della Villetta | Flavor and tradition in a charming osteria

Location Palazzolo sull'Oglio **Signature dish** *Tris* of beef patty, stuffed Savoy cabbage, and beef cheek | ❸❸❸

A few steps from the railway station in the small town of Palazzolo sull'Oglio, you will find the eye-catching pale green building that has housed Osteria della Villetta for over a century. Maurizio and Grazia, the current owners, are the fourth generation of the Rossi family, who have run this osteria (albeit in another location) for even longer. If you are looking for traditional food from Brescia, served by true experts, look no further.

This is a popular small restaurant with a strong local following. The food stays within its comfort zone but it receives rapturous praise. Ingredients come principally from personally known local producers, and everything is full of flavor, integrity, and tradition.

The day's specials are written and updated on a small blackboard, and may include vegetable minestrone with pesto; gnocchi with butter and sage; beef in oil with polenta; and in winter homemade *cotechino* (cooked sausage often served with lentils)

or *bollito misto* (mixed meats and vegetable in a broth). The signature dish is a *tris* (trio) of a beef patty, a roulade of pork-stuffed Savoy cabbage, and a boiled beef cheek with salsa verde. Harking back to the days when nothing was wasted and leftovers were used creatively, it remains a local favorite.

The wine list has an emphasis on Franciacorta, and numerous wines are served by the glass. To round off the meal in the summer, there are some good artisan cheeses and strawberry tarts or baked stuffed peaches on offer.

It is a truly charming and relaxed space with conversation-inspiring artwork on the walls, imposing cabinets full of bottles and glasses, evocative black and white photos of the family in past decades, and large worn wooden tables. You can see why diners return time and again. **CS**

⬆ Dining here is a pleasantly informal affair.

Ristorante Macelleria Motta | A destination for discerning carnivores

Location Bellinzago   **Signature dish** Tartare of Piedmont beef three ways | 💲💲

"Meat specialities in all their guises take pride of place in this excellent restaurant."

Michelin Guide

⬆ Various charcuterie and meat products are on display.

➡ The beef tartare is strikingly presented.

Vegetarians look away now, meat lovers gather round. If you know that in Italian "macelleria" means "butcher," you already have the right idea. This place is owned and run by Sergio Motta, who is indeed a butcher, and the first sight to meet diners on entering this restaurant is a dramatic floor-to-ceiling refrigerated display of huge slabs of meat: legs of beef, hams, and sides of various carcasses. The idea is clear: opening a restaurant followed on from running a butcher's shop.

Walking past the raw meat display, you enter the restaurant itself, with its sedate color palette and pristine white table linen. Here you can enjoy a menu that also includes some interesting vegetable side dishes—but that is not what you have come for. Choose from homemade salumi, beef prosciutto with artichokes in oil or with wild asparagus, depending on the season, risotto with saffron and marrow, beef liver sautéed with sage and plums, spleen with *pinzimonio* (mixed raw vegetables), grilled heart, tripe with poppy seeds and lemon rind, *ossobuco*, or a 10oz (300g) burger.

The restaurant specializes in beef and ox meat, specifically from the oxen that Sergio buys at auction in neighboring Piedmont. He slaughters them throughout the year, and is happy to explain any part of the process or his meat-buying criteria. If he is around, you may receive an informative lesson, complete with photos, of what to look for when buying animals for meat, how they are killed, and how to prepare them for consumption. If you are squeamish, you may wish to skip this part.

If you have room for dessert after all that meat, do try the house tiramisu, the almond *semifreddo* with saffron sauce, or the pannacotta. A carefully considered wine list—unsurprisingly predominantly red—proves that this is much more than an afterthought of a restaurant. **CS**

Due Colombe | An elegant setting for beautifully presented food and a taste of local grappa

Location Borgonato   **Signature dish** *Il manzo all'olio del Due Colombe con polenta* ("Due Colombe" beef in oil with polenta) | ❺❺❺❺

"Due Colombe is a Michelin-starred fine-dining haven housed in a fourteenth-century watermill."

Mr. & Mrs. Smith

⤒ A converted watermill houses this stylish restaurant and grappa tasting bar.

The small village of Borgonato is located in the region of Franciacorta in Lombardy, which is famous for producing some of Italy's best sparkling wines. There are two very good reasons to make the journey here: one is to visit the restaurant Due Colombe to taste the excellent food prepared by chef Stefano Cerveni. The other is to visit the grappa distillery of Borgo Antico San Vitale, where you can learn all about the distilling process and get a taste of Franciacorta grappa. The distillery and the restaurant are actually in the same lovingly and tastefully restored group of buildings (originally a watermill), so there is no need to make a detour.

The dining room is on the first floor of the main building, overlooking the grappa tasting bar. The tables are large and well spaced, and the food is cooked with consummate skill, packed with flavor, and beautifully presented. Choose from delicacies such as rabbit ravioli with butter, sage, and crispy Parmesan; creamy risotto with squid ink; ginger- and saffron-marinated scampi; homemade tagliatelle; or dried sardines from Lake Iseo with candied tomatoes and toast.

Star dishes such as the beef in oil with polenta—a recipe from Cerveni's grandmother, Elvira, dating from 1955—and the vibrantly colored purple potato and shrimp with Franciacorta sauce make reference to the wine-making area in which the restaurant is situated and to its culinary history. Be sure to order a glass of Franciacorta bubbly while you peruse the menu or opt for a local grappa to finish.

After your meal, you can wander over the immaculately kept lawn or around the elegant garden to fully appreciate the atmosphere of this quiet little haven. The ambience is stylish and civilized, and great attention to detail is evident everywhere. **CS**

Al Pont de Ferr | Spectacular cuisine in an unpretentious context

Location Milan **Signature dish** Candied red Tropea onion | 🍷🍷🍷

Al Pont de Ferr is a charming eatery located on the banks of Milan's pretty Naviglio Grande canal in the Navigli district. This strangely bucolic area, packed with rough and ready cafés and bistros, is the place to be when you wish to escape the city's fashion hype and let your hair down.

Al Pont de Ferr happily embraces the party spirit with a cozy atmosphere, sturdy furniture, and wine bottles lining the walls of this classic Italian tavern. Run for over twenty-six years by its sommelier patron, Maida Mercuri (known locally as "Our Lady of the Navigli"), this restaurant offers friendly service, an excellent wine list, and some show-stopping cuisine prepared by Uruguayan chef Matias Perdomo.

With his tousled hair and easy manner, Matias looks very relaxed, but he goes to great lengths with his cooking. Over the years, he has worked hard to lift the restaurant's reputation from "just risotto or cutlets" to what he describes as "crazy, exciting gastronomic journeys." The result is a much-coveted Michelin star and satisfied customers who can enjoy reasonably priced taster menus offering dishes that are as unusual as they are spectacular.

"My cuisine is fun, almost bothersome," Perdomo says—so do not be surprised if your Tropea onion turns out to be a caramel bubble, your amberjack and foie gras looks like a mini mosaic, or your "green pea dessert" is served in a trowel.

This is all part of the experience, created by the perfect duo: both experts in their own field and with a genuine love for what they do. Add to this, a complete lack of pretension and a childlike sense of pure fun, and you will soon see why Al Pont de Ferr has become one of Milan's most popular restaurants. After all, relaxed sophistication is a rare and sought-after quality. **DJS**

Ristorante Cracco | Miniature works of art to stun the senses

Location Milan **Signature dish** Saffron risotto | 🍷🍷🍷🍷🍷

In recent years, Carlo Cracco has become a household name in Italy. Numerous TV appearances have turned him into the archetypal master chef, but his international reputation still rests firmly on the superb cuisine served at his smart Milanese restaurant.

Carlo's success is based on an almost maniacal attention to fresh ingredients and detail, combined with sublimely artistic presentation. At Cracco, you are served miniature works of art. Ingredients are presented on the plate in orderly ranks of taste and texture or swirled into dizzying kaleidoscopes of shape and color, punctuated by artistic squirts and squiggles. The effect is stunning, and your taste buds will rejoice as the combinations are heavenly.

> *"Cracco scores big with this seductive Italian a few steps away from the Duomo."*
>
> Zagat

Oysters with figs and sage butter, Campari-marinated shrimp, and beetroot-soused scallops are among the mouthwatering innovations, but the apotheosis of the restaurant's cuisine are the rice dishes: a succulently creamy version of the classic Milanese saffron risotto is a revelation, as is Carlo's sea urchin and squid ink risotto, or rice with cocoa, lemon, and anchovy. The wine list, incidentally, is extremely impressive for a restaurant of this size.

This is alchemy of the highest order, tastefully matched by the restaurant's comfortable yet prestigious interiors that fuse the sober linearity of contemporary Italian minimalism with a warm hint of the Orient. **DJS**

Il Luogo di Aimo e Nadia | Italian food taken to stylish perfection

Location Milan **Signature dish** Spaghettoni of durum wheat with green onion and hot pepper sauce | ❸❸❸

"… one of the best dining experiences you'll ever have, from start to finish."

Zagat

⬆ Striking modern art adorns the walls at Il Luogo di Aimo e Nadia.

Il Luogo di Aimo e Nadia, located in one of the quieter areas of Milan, was established in 1962 by chef Aimo Moroni and his wife Nadia. The food is rooted in Italian tradition, and initially the cooking style was that of the couple's native Tuscany, but over time it developed to take in influences from other regions of Italy. The restaurant now holds two Michelin stars, and great care goes into the wine selection as much as the food (the excellent sommelier has even published two books on the wines of Italy). The sleek but cozy dining room is characterized by striking modern art adorning the walls.

A typical meal may begin with white bean soup from Tuscany with alpine char and dried mullet roe: a warming, comforting dish. Spaghettoni made with Cavalieri durum wheat is a remarkably simple yet delicious dish, served with a green onion and hot pepper sauce, olive oil, and basil from Liguria: the sauce provides just the right degree of bite to lift the flavor of the dish, and the seasoning is precise. This is a daringly simple dish to serve in a top restaurant, but it really works beautifully.

Stewed *totani* (squid) with Sicilian almond and artichokes is soft without a hint of chewiness, the flavors working together harmoniously. Diners may continue with oxtail stewed in Barolo wine, encased in a ring of delicate, silky *pomme purée*. The meat is slow-cooked and the silky mash a perfect accompaniment to the oxtail.

A truly inventive dessert worth trying is "Dolci Ortaggi," which consists of an eggplant hemisphere with chocolate, basil, and lemon balm sorbet. Another tasty option is the chestnut "kiss," with almond sorbet and a smoothly textured mousse. Service is superb, always friendly and attentive. This is what Italian food is all about—straightforward dishes elevated to a high level by great attention to detail in the kitchen. **AH**

Il Ristorante Trussardi alla Scala | Sophistication on all levels

Location Milan **Signature dish** Sea bream with gold, ginger, and saffron jelly | ❸❸❸❸

Just like its home, Milan, Il Ristorante Trussardi alla Scala is urbane, sophisticated, and fashionable. The elegant white decor, light wood floors, and design-conscious tableware and chairs are all immaculate, while the long wall of windows overlooks the world-famous Piazza della Scala, making a bold design statement.

The establishment is frequented by a cosmopolitan clientele and has an air of casual elegance. But, unlike many designer eateries, Trussardi alla Scala is no mere meeting point for fashion victims. This restaurant takes its cuisine very seriously, and its startlingly original, Michelin-starred menu is created by one of Italy's brightest young chefs.

Luigi Taglienti has worked with many of the great French and Italian chefs and won Italy's Young Chef of the Year award. The seasonal menu he creates here reflects the mood of contemporary chic that permeates the restaurant. Inventive but also respectful of tried-and-tested tradition, Luigi aims to simply "thrill my guests," and this he does by personally selecting only the freshest organic ingredients and masterfully balancing them in dishes that are remarkable for their flavor and imaginative creativity.

The result is a whole new taste horizon, with adventurous pasta combinations, such as squash and pickled cherry ravioli, or turnip and shrimp and veal sausage tortelli, and palate-rocking flavor explosions, such as veal snout braised with spumante, mackerel, and black truffle, saddle of venison with pear eau de vie, oyster water, and sauce poivrade, or Luigi's signature raw sea bream with gold, ginger, and saffron jelly.

Sophisticated taste in a sophisticated ambience for a sophisticated clientele: an evening at Trussardi alla Scala is a true experience of culinary excellence in a classy setting. **DJS**

"The location could not be more central or prestigious … excellent pre- or post-opera."

concierge.com

⬆ The star dish of sea bream is a decadent treat sprinkled with gold.

Il Desco | A must-try destination for risotto lovers

Location Verona   **Signature dish** Risotto with local celery, warm *guanciale*, and allspice |

"*Il Desco offers highly creative cuisine made with a variety of the best ingredients [of] the Veneto.*"

frommers.com

⬆ The elegant dining room at Il Desco.

Il Desco is a family-run restaurant in a 15th-centry building in the heart of Verona, drawing on local produce for its excellent regional dishes. Chef Elia Rizzo trained with the legendary Gualtiero Marchesi (the first Italian chef to be awarded three Michelin stars), and Il Desco has won two Michelin stars. Nowadays, Elia's son Matteo is in charge in the kitchen, while Elia's wife runs the front of house. The elegant dining room boasts an ornate, decorated wooden ceiling.

The cooking is innovative, making use of the best ingredients the Veneto has to offer. Start with freshly baked bread and a range of interesting amuse-bouches. One of the star dishes is linguine of lobster with lime and coriander, a great example of the chef's cooking style, with very tender lobster and the lime providing a pleasant acidic kick. Scampi is no cliché here: the Il Desco version features superb langoustines, deep-fried in a light batter and served with a green salad, the dish being elevated by the quality of the langoustines.

Meat dishes may include venison with pearl onions or stuffed pigeon, but the house speciality is clearly risotto: made not with arborio or carnaroli rice but Vialone Nano, a local japonica rice from Verona. The result is top-class risotto, with incredibly tender rice, prepared with wonderfully flavored chicken stock and enriched with seasonal vegatables.

Desserts are superlative. You might choose to finish your meal with delicate *millefeuille* of apple and ginger chutney, with a lovely thin pastry and just a hint of ginger enriching the apple flavor.

Service is friendly and capable, and the chef is very much present in the dining room while staff carefully attend to the needs of the customers. This restaurant provides a good example of the classic cooking of the region, featuring high-quality ingredients and first-rate technique. **AH**

12 Apostoli | Spread the gospel of exclusive dining

Location Verona   **Signature dish** *Risotto alla sbirraglia* (with chicken and celeriac) | ❻❻❻❻

Tucked away in a quiet street behind Verona's picturesque Piazza delle Erbe market, 12 Apostoli accepts its role as the city's signature eatery with grace and dignity. From the discreet grandeur of its stained-glass entrance to the barrel-vaulted, jewelry-box majesty of its interiors, this is a restaurant that exudes exclusive class and style.

Everything here is steeped in history, even the restaurant's name: the "twelve apostles" was the nickname given to a group of tradesmen who met here to do business in the mid-eighteenth century. At that time, the establishment was little more than a tavern, but when Antonio Gioco took over in 1925, he began a process that has culminated, three generations later, in an exemplary experience of fine dining.

The service is flawless, and the carefully compiled menu of time-honored local classics and modern creations includes dishes ranging from ricotta-filled ravioli, pasta and bean soup, and Amarone-braised duck to fish delicacies, such as tuna with zucchini flowers and monkfish with figs. The dessert trolley is a magnificent feast of irresistible delights.

A princely wine list accompanies the menu, and recently the restaurant's wine cellar has become a particular point of pride following the discovery of a series of ancient ruins within it, including remnants of a Roman temple and road, and of a medieval tower built from stone blocks taken from the collapsed outer wall of the city's famous amphitheatre.

A distinguished institution such as this one attracts a similarly distinguished clientele: various members of Europe's royal families and a long line of celebrities have graced the tables throughout the years, from Greta Garbo to Barbra Streisand. All affirm the merits of the restaurant's excellent cuisine, and so after 260 years, instead of twelve faithful customers this grand old institution now attracts many more. **DJS**

"Here the twelve tradesmen did business, over a dish of pasta and beans and a glass of Valpolicella."

12 Apostoli website

⬆ Historic surroundings add to the atmosphere.

Locanda Cipriani | An elegant haven on the island of Torcello

Location Torcello **Signature dish** John Dory fillet "alla Carlina" | ❺❺❺❺

"There is a lot to like about the high-class Locanda Cipriani… the specialities are done to perfection."

Time Out

The boat trip from Venice across the lagoon to the island of Torcello takes about 40 minutes. Centuries ago, this island used to be an important center of the region, with several thousand inhabitants, seven churches, and a cathedral. Today, it is notably peaceful—a lush green island with only a few inhabitants, visited on weekends by tourists who usually come to see the glorious Byzantine basilica. However, gourmets in the know will also find their way to the Locanda Cipriani inn and restaurant, where they can enjoy the tranquil surroundings and unique setting.

You can also book one of the exclusive, simple yet charming rooms at the Locanda to stay a little longer and follow in the footsteps of famous guests such as Ernest Hemingway who used to spend long periods of time here to write. The current restaurateur, Bonifacio Brass, is the grandson of Giuseppe Cipriani who founded the world-famous Harry's Bar and, just like his grandfather, he is a master when it comes to creating a welcoming yet discreet atmosphere.

This renowned and impressively consistent restaurant is elegant without being showy, as befits its peaceful, isolated setting. Despite its legendary reputation, it is both calm and welcoming—in short, the perfect dining destination. The tables are set on the veranda and in the well-tended garden looking out toward the church of Santa Fosca.

Flavors are combined beautifully in classic specialities, including delicate zucchini flowers filled with shrimp, creamy risotto "alla torcellana" (with vegetables from the estuary), John Dory fillet "alla Carlina" (with cherry tomatoes and capers), or sea bass fillet with artichokes. Be sure not to miss the superlative *meringata* (merengue cake) for dessert, the perfect finishing touch for this civilized dining experience. **MS**

⬆ Al fresco dining in an idyllic setting on Torcello.

Osteria alle Testiere | A diminutive gem of fine Venetian cooking

Location Venice   **Signature dish** Mollusk with ginger | ❸❸❸

This tiny Venetian restaurant located just around the corner from the Campo Santa Maria Formosa is going from strength to strength. There are just nine small wooden tables, set in elegant osteria fashion with black paper table mats and slim long-stem wine glasses, and the walls are adorned with the "testiere," from which the restaurant takes its name: old headboards that were removed from beds and are now used as decoration.

Friends and business partners Bruno and Luca make a perfect team, combining their respective passions. The latter runs the front of house while the former works his magic in the kitchen, where he is the master of herbs: there is a never-ending supply of fresh seasonal greens such as radishes or leek, as well as wild herbs including mint and coriander to add flavor to the small menu of fresh fish. Only fresh fish is used and the dishes can vary considerably from season to season.

Examples include scallops with orange and red onion; small gnocchi with *mazzancolle* shrimp and wild fennel; *caparòssoli* clams tossed with ginger; linguine with monkfish and cinnamon; John Dory fillet with juniper, pink pepper, mint, and fennel in orange and lemon juice; and a simple but delicious mixed grilled seafood platter of fish and shellfish for those who are not enthusiastic about sauces and juices. Everything is prepared with immaculate care, and with the very best ingredients. Luca will happily explain every nuance of the menu in perfect English and help you choose a wine, his great passion.

There is a different cheese on offer every week, providing the perfect excuse for ordering a lovely red wine to round off the meal. Those who prefer a sweet finish can opt for a lemon and meringue tart, *crema rosàda* (a traditional but almost forgotten Venetian recipe made with egg-based cream), or tiramisu. Now you just need to get a table! **MS**

"… experience this true gem with its exceptional, extremely fresh and inventive seafood dishes."

Zagat

⬆ Intimate dining at Osteria alle Testiere.

Ridotto |
Insider's secret to be savored

Location Venice **Signature dish** *Tubetti* in goby stock with aromatic herbs from the lagoon | ❸❸❸

The culinary talents of chef-patron Gianni Bonaccorsi are showcased in this intimate Venetian restaurant, named after the waiting room in a theater where the audience gathers in the interval. In contrast to Bonaccorsi's big and bustling pizzeria Aciugheta, this tiny venture is very much a personal project to allow him to explore his love of food: there are only 18 covers to ensure the best possible attention to detail in dishes that he has carefully put together.

Superb local ingredients are the base for Bonaccorsi's cooking. He pays homage to traditional dishes, but there is an appealingly creative lightness of touch in the way he plays with flavors and textures. The superb homemade pasta is a highlight, and includes *spaghetti neri* colored with squid ink, served with sea urchin roe and candied peppers, and intensly flavored *tubetti* (pasta tubes) cooked in fish stock.

One can find excellent meat here as well as the famous Venetian fish and seafood. Diners are given the choice of a "menu di mare" (seafood) or "mare e terra" (seafood and meat). Carnivorous options might include succulent suckling pig paired with green apple and raspberries, or roast rabbit with artichokes and chanterelle mushrooms. The fish is always fresh and cooked with precision in dishes such as fresh cod with *baccalà* (salt cod) and black smoked lentils.

Be sure to explore Bonaccorsi's well-stocked wine cellar with its painstakingly selected vintages to accompany the various dishes. The dolci also push the boundaries: try the strawberry soup with cardamom crumble and bay-infused ice cream or the house tiramisu, which is made without eggs, dairy products, or sugar. Innovative in concept and accomplished in execution, this is food with personality. **MS**

Boccadoro |
Tranquil food haven in a pretty spot

Location Venice **Signature dish** Black-and-white *gnocchetti* with goby fillets | ❸❸❸

One of the charms of exploring Venice is the sense that one might stumble upon a hidden gem anywhere—a beautiful church or, indeed, an excellent restaurant. Tucked away in a characteristic maze of narrow streets, on a lovely little square close to the exquisite Santa Maria dei Miracoli church, with its stunning mosaics, is Boccadoro, a pretty restaurant where you can sit underneath a sprawling vine. Although the interior is cozy, you may want to sit outside and soak up the atmosphere.

The food is as colorful and pretty as its surroundings. There is a short but carefully put-together menu, fresh ingredients are sourced on the day, with an emphasis on fish and seafood, as is

---

"Take a seat beneath the pleasant pergola on this quiet square for the freshest of seafood."

Lonely Planet

---

traditional in Venice. Antipasti are a glorious showcase of the sheer variety of seafood to be found in the lagoon: tiny baby octopus, delicate spider crab, shrimp, raw fish, and sautéed mussels and clams.

Among the primi, the homemade pasta stands out: try black tagliolini with scallops and artichokes or lasagnette with hand-chopped steak; but the quality of the pasta is so outstanding that even simple tagliatelle with fresh tomato is memorable. The secondi also follow the "fresh and seasonal" mantra, with the quality of the ingredients shining through in deceptively simple dishes such as John Dory fillet with potato and zucchini flowers, wild sea bream with honey, or sea bass marinated in pepper. **MS**

Da Fiore | A true Venetian treasure of beautifully prepared dishes executed to a high standard

Location Venice   **Signature dish** Tagliolini with *moscardini* in ink | 🆂🆂

Nothing distracts from the food at Da Fiore: there is no panorama or extensive view, just a spacious, elegant room with a calm atmosphere and subtle lighting. Da Fiore has always been a favorite of discerning locals, and has remained so even now that it is regarded a top-rated international restaurant by connoisseurs.

The secret of Da Fiore's success lies in the combination of passion for food, dedicated research (done by Mara Martin in the kitchen) and the friendly reception by Maurizio Martin who runs the front of house. The menu is regularly updated without losing any of its character, retaining old favorites that still manage to pleasantly surprise the regulars. When you take a look at your fellow diners, you can see how they concentrate on their food, rather than just eat it, as if to understand the secret of its preparation—but Mara, who is confident and truly passionate about her cooking, is not worried about anyone trying to guess her recipes.

Antipasti include scampi and marinated salmon, *canoce* (mantis shrimp), *garusoli* (sea snails), *moscardini* (small octopus), and *schie* shrimp with polenta. There is an unusually wide selection of primi: try one of the various seafood risottos—for example, risotto with scampi and porcini mushrooms.

The fish theme continues through the second course options, masterfully cooked dishes such as oven-baked turbot with potato crust, sea bass *al cartoccio* (cooked in a "parcel" of aluminum foil), and, depending on the season, fried *canestrei* clams, *moeche* (soft-shell crabs), or squid. All dishes are traditional but executed to a high standard that is hard to find elsewhere. Add to this the homemade desserts and tempting wine list, and the memory of your meal may become a pleasant blur. **MS**

"Da Fiore's modern take on Venetian cuisine certainly merits its international reputation."

fodors.com

⬆ A dish of scallops served at Da Fiore.

Al Covo | Superb seafood from the lagoon served with flair

Location Venice **Signature dish** Sea bass tartare with celery and fennel | ❸❸❸

Discreetly tucked away, this intimate restaurant is frequented by Venetian gourmets as well as by tourists in the know. You can get there by strolling along the Riva degli Schiavoni from San Marco toward the Giardini della Biennale, taking in the breathtaking views and turning left just before the Arsenal and into the small square of Campiello della Pescaria.

In good weather, you can dine outside on the terrace overlooking the square, but the elegant interior is also worth seeing: the two cozy rooms have exposed bricks and low ceilings with dimmed lights, and are decorated with paintings and fresh flowers. The setting is classic, but the cooking is creative.

If you cannot tell your squid from your octopus, you have come to the right place: you can learn all there is to know about the local specialities from restaurant owner Cesare Benelli, who is committed to championing produce from the Veneto. The kitchen is open, and you won't find a trace of canned food,

animal fat, or artificial ingredients of any kind. Only fresh fish is used in traditional dishes that also include nearly forgotten recipes. Everything is designed to showcase the quality of incredibly fresh ingredients.

Choose from sashimi-style raw fish, fresh vegetables, fish soup, gnocchi with goby fillets, *anguilla in umido* (stewed eel), and various fried and grilled fish. Cesare likes to be inventive, putting together local produce with ingredients that are more typical of the south, resulting in combinations such as fried zucchini flowers with buffalo ricotta from Cilento and mint.

Careful sourcing means that carnivores are also well catered to: some notable meat dishes on the menu include rigatoni with Sambucano lamb and peppers from Carmagnola and *scamone* beef steak. Be sure to sample the respectable wine list. **MS**

⬆ Al Covo is a cozy, hidden gem of a restaurant.

Corte Sconta | Fine Venetian fare in a vine-covered courtyard

Location Venice   **Signature dish** Sautéed clams with ginger | ❸❸❸

Living up to its name, which means "hidden courtyard" in Italian, this restaurant is indeed tucked away in between some houses, with a lovely courtyard dining area covered by a sprawling vine. First opened in 1980, it has since transformed from a humble family-run trattoria into a renowned eatery while still retaining "rebellious" touches such as napkins made of paper instead of fabric.

You can marvel at the ingredients that will soon grace your plate on a counter by the entrance: freshly cooked shellfish, shrimp, *schie* shrimp, *canoce* (mantis shrimp), spider crab, meatballs, and various desserts. Chef Eugenio Oro rules the kitchen; the menu is rich in typical lagoon dishes, but with a fresh, innovative twist, carefully prepared and combined with delicate flavors. The restaurant has not forgotten to include vegetarian and vegan options.

The antipasti tasting selection gives diners a chance to try the best traditional dishes: spider crab paté; gurbell marinated with aromatic herbs; tuna marinated in balsamic vinegar and juniper berries; sautéed local clams with ginger; steamed spider crab; and a steamed seafood platter of mantis shrimp, cuttlefish roe, octopus, and dried codfish mousse.

Pasta is made daily: try the gnocchetti with monkfish and fresh peas or tagliolini with mantis shrimp and artichoke. For the main course, opt for grilled fish, *fritto misto* (mixed fried seafood), or *bisàto sull'aria* (a small eel cooked in balsamic vinegar and laurel); mullet with lemon and cardamom; or flan of carrot, zucchini, and dill with black truffle. To round it all off, there is a selection of a dozen Italian cheeses, exquisite desserts, and the traditional zabaione with Venetian biscuits. Not to forget the excellent wine cellar—you will probably have to come back for another meal to fully appreciate the whole menu. **MS**

⬆ Diners can sit under the sprawling vine in the courtyard.

Vini da Gigio | An informal and unpretentious taste of Venetian cuisine

Location Venice **Signature dish** Risotto with seasonal ingredients | ❺❺❺

Run with generous hospitality by brother and sister Paolo and Laura Lazzari, this popular restaurant is perpetually busy, buzzing with contented diners enjoying the traditional Venetian cooking on offer. There are no outside tables, but the interior is cozy, with brick walls, wooden furnishings, and large windows affording a glimpse of the architectural splendor outside. Service is friendly and unhurried, allowing diners to linger over their food and enjoy long conversations.

As the restaurant's name implies, wines are a forte here. You could start by studying the noteworthy wine list with its local specialities, many of them from small producers, and then build your meal around your wine choice—or choose the dishes first and accompany them with recommended wines.

This is one of few restaurants in Venice that puts equal emphasis on fish and meat dishes, so it is a perfect choice for those who are looking to sample one of the impressive red wines, perhaps with *ossobuco*, *fegato alla veneziana* (Venetian-style liver), or lamb cutlet. Among the fish specialities, you will find a classic Venetian seafood antipasti platter (including *canestrelli* clams, cod croquettes, *canoce* mantis shrimp, and *schie* shrimp) and raw fish.

Last, but definitely not least, there are various types of risotto with seasonal ingredients on offer— for example, with scampi and porcini mushrooms, or pumpkin and asparagus tips—and always cooked "all'onda" (soft), as is the custom in Venetian cooking. For cheese lovers, there is a refined selection from small suppliers sourced by Paolo that includes raw milk cheese, mountain cheeses, or cheese with herbs, all of which can be sampled with a glass of wine or an artisan beer. Without being flashy, this restaurant offers genuinely excellent Venetian food. **MS**

⊡ Vini da Gigio is in the Cannaregio district of Venice.

Wildner | Venetian specialities served with an unforgettable view

Location Venice   **Signature dish** Grilled octopus with red onion salad, lentils, and steamed potatoes | ❸❸❸

The area around Venice's St. Mark's Square, thronged with tourists and souvenir stands, might not be the best place to linger. Those in the know, however, will head for an inconspicuous building closeby that offers a wonderful instant escape from the crowds: the light-filled veranda of the Wildner is a serene haven from the hustle and bustle. The tables look out over St. Mark's Basin and the island of San Giorgio Maggiore, and in the evening the candlelight creates an even more magical atmosphere.

Luca Fullin, the manager, took over the family enterprise after gaining extensive experience abroad, and has very much rooted the restaurant in its region, both in terms of ingredients and recipes. The menu showcases traditional Venetian dishes, so this is a chance to try local specialities such as excellent *baccalà mantecato* (creamed salt cod), scampi and *sarde in saor* (Venetian-style sweet-sour scampi and sardines), seafood risotto, or *fegato alla veneziana*

(Venetian-style fried liver with onions). Preference is given to organic produce and local foodstuffs, with Luca committed to championing slow food ingredients. Look out for fine produce, such as exquisite purple artichokes from the island of Sant' Erasmo (just a short distance away in the northern lagoon), the typical "Biancoperla" polenta, or "La Granda" beef (a type of beef from the Piedmont).

All the fish comes from the Adriatic, and is available grilled, fried, or oven-baked, and daily specials are put together with fresh, seasonal ingredients from the Rialto market. The extensive wine list includes organically and biodynamically produced wines. Finally, do not leave without trying one of the desserts created by Mamma Donatella—the only question is: should you go for tiramisu or *bavarese* (Bavarois cream)? **MS**

⬆ The impressive panorama with San Giorgio Maggiore.

Venissa | Stylish contemporary dining in the Venetian lagoon

Location Venice   **Signature dish** Mackerel confit | ❺❺❺❺❺

"A bucolic idyll … This delightful setting is reflected in the cuisine, which is simple and unfussy."

Michelin Guide

⬆ The estate comprises a vegetable and herb garden as well as a vineyard.

➡ Dishes are beautifully presented at Venissa.

The pleasantly green island of Mazzorbo is located in the northern lagoon of Venice and connected to the larger island of Burano with a bridge. Like many of the other small islands in the lagoon, it had its heyday in the Middle Ages and then fell into a slow decline as the main island of Venice gained more importance. Nowadays, however, in this pretty, sleepy spot, you can find the distinctly chic Venissa. A futuristic hotel and restaurant, it forms part of a vineyard estate, which in turn is part of a historic and cultural restoration project that was initiated by the prosecco producer Bisol of Treviso, who initiated the planting of a new, gloriously verdant vineyard on the island.

In the restaurant's understated yet elegant surroundings, diners can enjoy accomplished and contemporary cooking that showcases excellent Italian ingredients. Venissa's executive chef, Arianna Dalla Valeria, presents a refined take on Venetian cuisine, with a seasonal menu that changes daily and is based on the finest local ingredients. The waters of the lagoon offer rich pickings when it comes to fish and seafood (mullet, eel, and *moeche* crab, among others), and in a nod to local sourcing and the project's agricultural roots, many of the vegetables and herbs used in the kitchen are cultivated in the estate's own garden, while the nearby island of Sant'Erasmo, legendary for its artichokes, is another source of notably flavorful fresh produce.

The magic of Dalla Valeria's cooking lies in transforming these prime foodstuffs in unexpected ways, surprising diners with artfully arranged artichoke leaves that could at first be mistaken for rose petals, or vivid beetroot-colored rectangles that turn out to be squid. As you would expect, the wine list also offers a unique opportunity to sample the wines that are made from the grapes of the estate's vineyard, which complement the delicate dishes perfectly. **MS**

Quadri | Picture-postcard dining in St. Mark's Square

Location Venice **Signature dish** Cappuccino of baby shrimp and curried clams | ❺❺❺❺❺

"… one of the legendary restaurants in Italy: Quadri [is] a name steeped in history."

fodors.com

⊡ Chef Silvio Giavedoni is in charge in the kitchen.

Right in the middle of Venice's St Mark's Square—which was memorably described by Napoleon as Europe's most beautiful dining room—looking out to the Basilica with the arches of the Procuratie Vecchie to your left, you will find this historic establishment, gloriously decked out with sumptuous stucco and rooms full of mirrors and late eighteenth-century paintings of carnival scenes. You have to come here at least once when visiting Venice, if only to simply enjoy an excellent aperitif such as the Verdini, which is the Quadri's refreshing take on the more famous Bellini. Prepared with apple, celery, and prosecco, it is the perfect drink to start your evening .

St. Mark's Square is one of the lower-lying areas in Venice, and can be affected by *acqua alta*, but there is no need to worry: if this happens, the staff will make sure you reach the place safe and dry, and you get the added bonus of seeing the imposing buildings of the square reflected in the water—an unforgettable image.

Since 2008, the Alajmo brothers, known for adding color to their ventures, have been in charge of the establishment. They offer international gourmets a chance to taste their cuisine in a unique setting, made more special by the fact that this is the only restaurant among the cafes in the square.

For an informal meal downstairs, try the excellent club sandwich with *vitello tonnato* (veal with tuna). Alternatively, for a more leisurely experience, you can go up to the elegant restaurant for a proper meal. Enjoy one of the delicious tasting menus and soak up the atmosphere and view of the piazza as you sample innovative dishes such as cappuccino of baby shrimp and curried clams; rack of lamb with herbs, crispy vegetables, and ricotta with tomato basil pesto; fried langoustine rolls with basil bottarga, almond, and oregano sauce; or fried vegetables with carrot zabaione and balsamic vinegar. **MS**

Osteria L'Orto dei Mori | Sicily meets Venice in a tasty combination

Location Venice   **Signature dish** Sea bass fillet with herbs and basil sauce | 🟢🟢

A favorite with many locals for its affordability, this friendly restaurant is headed by a Sicilian chef, Lorenzo Cipolla, who has created his own special fusion of Sicilian-Venetian cuisine. Located in the Cannaregio district of Venice, the building is literally next door to the birthplace of Tintoretto, and just a few steps away from the beautiful Madonna dell'Orto church.

In the summer, the little square opening out onto the canal is at its most charming and picturesque, with the bridge and a small kiosk adding an appealing touch to this classic Venetian scene. As befits a neighborhood establishment, families are welcome: the kids can play in the square while the adults enjoy their dinner. The interior of the osteria is fitted with original lighting and subtle touches of color that create an appealing atmosphere.

What you get here is lovingly prepared, simple, authentic cooking based on excellent seasonal ingredients, but with a good pinch of originality. This may include dishes such as aubergine *parmigiana* timbale with buffalo mozzarella or gnocchetti with scallops, courgette, and leek. Lorenzo also happily serves up excellent versions of ever-popular Venetian classics such as *fegato alla veneziana* (Venetian-style liver) with polenta.

Other star dishes worth sampling are the excellent carpaccio of scampi, tagliolini pasta with *nero di seppia* (squid ink), and delicate sole on a bed of *riso Venere* (black rice). The dessert menu offers temptations such as *crespelle* (crepes) with custard cream and mixed berries, or ricotta mousse with pears cooked in red wine. The wine list boasts Venetian and Friulian specialities to pair with your food of choice, and there is also Champagne for toasting special family occasions, as well as whisky and rum for a post-prandial glass or two to linger on and enjoy the restaurant's convivial charms for a little longer. **MS**

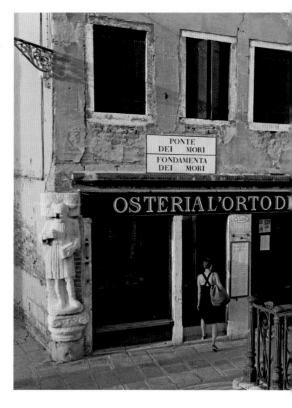

"A little off the tourist track, this warrants a visit for delicious classic plates and original pasta dishes."

Zagat

⊡ L'Orto dei Mori is tucked away in a quiet part of Venice.

Aman Canal Grande
Venice | Dine in a glorious palazzo

Location Venice   **Signature dish** Beef *tataki* with ponzu sauce | ❸❸❸❸

The Aman Resort hotel chain is world-renowned for its high standard of luxury and originality, and the Aman Canal Grande Venice certainly lives up to this. For the Venice venture, the Palazzo Papadopoli was chosen, a grand five-storey structure situated directly on the Canal Grande, with some parts still occupied by members of the Papadopoli family. There is an exclusive private garden opening out onto the canal (one of very few gardens directly on the canal) and another, more secluded one to the back of the building, near the "land entrance."

You will most likely arrive by boat, on the canal side, but if you are planning to get there by land, make sure to bring a good map to navigate your way. The building has been painstakingly restored to its former grandeur while creating the right ambience for its modern function. Beyond the 24 elegant rooms—one even boasts a fresco by Tiepolo—there are various relaxation zones for reading, eating, chatting, playing games, or taking an aperitif. In fact, there is no reception as such: things are more informal and fluid here, but very efficient nonetheless.

The restaurant takes up most of the *piano nobile*, looking out over the Canal Grande, with large high-ceilinged dining rooms decorated with beautiful frescoes and striking chandeliers. Low tables with comfortable chairs provide the perfect setting to enjoy the exquisite dishes and impeccable service. As one might expect, fresh fish and seafood is at the heart of the cooking, and chef Naoki Okumura draws culinary inspiration from Japan and Thailand as well as Venice's traditional maritime cuisine, so you will find *spaghetti alle vongole* alongside elegantly presented, delicate Japanese dishes, including sushi and sashimi, and Thai-inspired shrimp rice with tamarind. A stylish dining experience in the heart of La Serenissima. **MS**

Locanda Vecchia Pavia
"Al Mulino" | Truly stellar cuisine

Location Pavia   **Signature dish** Boned veil shank stewed in Bonarda sauce | ❸❸❸❸

"Al Mulino" is an epic country eatery. Idyllically set in a charming old millhouse, surrounded by manicured lawns and just a stone's throw from the beautiful Gothic Certosa di Pavia abbey, the restaurant is romantic, stylish, and a distinctive gourmet treat.

Oreste Corradi, the elegant maitre d', accompanies guests to a table in the airy dining room with red terracotta floors, antique wooden roof beams, and plump, green upholstered chairs. There is also a smaller VIP room, a larger room upstairs for special occasions, and a fabulous terrace.

Many of the guests are city slickers from nearby Milan in search of country air, and the "Al Mulino" menu soon has them dreaming with its canny

> *"I want to carry guests away on a dizzy voyage through the tastes and flavors of Italian tradition."*
>
> Oreste Corradi, manager of Locanda Vecchia Pavia

combination of Michelin-starred sophistication and natural wholesomeness. Oreste's wife, Anna Maria, produces spectacular dishes that range from lasagnette with artichokes or porcini mushrooms to succulent *agnolotti* pasta parcels, all accompanied by an impressive wine list of over 1,000 labels.

A triumph of culinary research is the "risotto alla certosina," a spectacular monks' recipe from the abbey that blends frog legs, crayfish, and mushrooms into a delicious risotto. Refined meat and fish courses follow, including roast pigeon and wine-stewed veal, and the feast ends with a succulent *zabaglione semifreddo*, or the perfectly named Torta Paradiso. A sublimely satisfying experience. **DJS**

Locanda delle Grazie | Mantuan favorites served
with gusto and old-fashioned hospitality

Location Curtatone **Signature dish** Pumpkin tortelli | ❺❺

If you like your countryside restaurants traditional and dependable, head to the small town of Curtatone on the outskirts of Mantova, where you will find the Locanda delle Grazie, run by Fernando and Daniela Alighieri with help from their daughter Anita. It is a firm favorite with local families, especially on weekends. Everyone is made to feel welcome (no problem at all to have dinner for one here), and although the staff are busy, they are efficient and always find the time to chat with guests at every table, whether to explain the menu to first-time visitors, or to enquire after family news or how the crops are coming along. It is old-fashioned, comfortable, and cozy.

There is nothing trendy or fickle about the place: the tablecloths are flowery, the bread baskets are lined with doilies, and, if you order freshly caught lake fish, it will be filleted at your table. For all the professionalism in evidence, there is also likely to be some spirited and playful chatter.

The menu is traditionally Mantuan, varying according to seasonal changes: salami from Mantova, pumpkin tortelli served with butter and sage, *risotto alla pilota* (with sausages), tagliatelle with duck ragout, maccheroncini pasta with wild boar or hare ragout, slow-cooked horse meat with polenta, pike in salsa verde, or wild boar or hare stew with polenta.

To round off the meal, try the *sbrisolana*, a crumbly shortbreadlike cake that is arguably the most typical of Mantuan desserts and is sometimes served with warm *zabaglione*. Alternatively, there is a delicious liquorice *semifreddo* with chocolate flakes. On your way out, you can buy some homemade delicacies to take home, such as grissini and *schiacciatine* (large flattened breadsticks), or the incredible *sbrisolana*. **CS**

"This restaurant is particularly popular for its Mantuan specialities such as pike."

Michelin Guide

⬆ Dining at this much-loved local restaurant is an informal affair.

Del Cambio | Gracious dining in a truly venerable Italian institution

Location Turin **Signature dish** *Finanziera alla Cavour* |

😊😊😊😊😊

"Crimson velvet, glittering chandeliers … and a timeless air greet you at this grande dame."

Lonely Planet

⬆ Del Cambio is located in the center of Turin.

Turin's exquisite Ristorante Del Cambio is the epitome of exclusive elegance. Located in the city's graceful and airy Piazza Carignano, it is the kind of institution that offers a truly unique dining experience.

Originally opened in 1757 as a café for the theater next door, Del Cambio is more than a hundred years older than the state of Italy itself. Over the centuries, its sumptuous interiors and dripping chandeliers have welcomed all the nation's big names, from Casanova to Verdi and Puccini, from the Agnelli (Fiat) family to Count Camillo Cavour, the politician who was instrumental in unifying Italy. He was such an aficionado that he had his own private table at the restaurant and even lent his name to the rich signature dish, the *finanziera alla Cavour*, which is made with chicken liver.

With such a glittering and eventful history, and two hundred and fifty years under her belt, this grand old lady began to look a little worn, so in 2013 an ambitious renovation project was launched. A true labor of love, the result enhances all Del Cambio's former pomp with the bright new lights of sophisticated contemporary comfort. A cocktail bar was also opened on the first floor, with a portrait of the ever-present Count Cavour.

The restaurant's menu has been entrusted to one of Italy's most exciting young chefs, Matteo Baronetto. Born into a family of Fiat factory workers, Matteo has the ideal combination of a youthful sense of adventure and local savvy. His aim, in his own words, is "to merge innovation and tradition in the name of simplicity," and that is exactly what the menu does.

Enjoy the sophistication of the dishes, drink in the exquisite interiors, and raise a glass of excellent Barbera to the spirit of Cavour to thank him for championing such an excellent institution. **DJS**

Dal Pescatore Santini |

Stunning food in an idyllic setting

Location Canneto sull'Oglio **Signature dish** Marinated
eel | ❸❸❸❸

Dal Pescatore is situated in an isolated spot in the countryside east of Milan in the Parco Oglio nature reserve, between Cremona and Mantua. Owner and restaurant manager Antonio Santini's grandparents opened a restaurant on this spot in 1925, and changed the name to Dal Pescatore in 1960. The kitchen is run by Nadia Santini, who has held three Michelin stars at the restaurant since the mid-1990s. She was trained by her husband's grandmother (who was running the restaurant in the 1970s), never having cooked professionally before then.

Eating here feels almost like visiting a friend's house—albeit one who can cook superbly. The building has an attractive terrace and a garden in the back, and, while you have a drink, you might encounter the family's Golden Retriever and cat.

In the dining room, generously spaced tables look out over the garden. The cooking style is deceptively simple, showcasing the very finest ingredients, which can be seen in a starter of eggplant and tomato with olive oil, basil, and thyme, featuring dazzling tomatoes and just enough lemon to balance the flavor—a very simple dish, perfectly done. The ever popular pumpkin (*zucca*) tortelli also delight with clear flavors that make you appreciate all the ingredients.

Cooking skill is also demonstrated with a classic risotto with peas, porcini mushrooms, and sweet herbs, the peas providing a beautiful sweetness and the rice cooked to perfection. Main courses may include cold lobster in Champagne jelly or marinated eel with pickled ginger and caviar Baerri Royal. To conclude the meal, you could opt for the delicious, light orange soufflé with passion fruit coulis. Dal Pescatore is a truly magical place, and the natural beauty of the setting is complemented by the stunning cooking. **AH**

Paolo & Barbara |

Classic regional cuisine served with style

Location Sanremo **Signature dish** *Sardenaira* |
❸❸❸❸

This Ligurian restaurant takes its name from the husband-and-wife team, Paolo and Barbara Masieri, who have been running what was once Paolo's father's restaurant in the town of Sanremo since 1988. They take great pride in sourcing fresh fish and shellfish, such as sea urchin and shrimp, from local fishermen, beef from a Piedmont breed of cattle, woodcock and wood pigeon from the Maritime Alps, and vegetables from their farm at Alta Val Nervia.

Naturally, the food changes with the seasons (be sure to try the sheep ricotta in spring and Montèbore, a type of Ligurian cheese, in the autumn), but guests can always expect tasty, light dishes that are complex in their composition, but also a nod to traditional

---

"The fish is so fresh that I serve it raw, following recipes that I personally develop …"

Paolo Masieri, owner of Paolo & Barbara

Ligurian cuisine. Among those are: *carpaccio di alalunga ai porcini* (tuna carpaccio with porcini mushrooms); baby shrimp from Sanremo in a cream of Jerusalem artichoke with a bitter orange confit, flower, and herb salad; squid stuffed with wild green herbs, Castelvittorio bean cream and pimpinella oil; poached egg with sea urchin, shrimp, and crispy leeks; and a delicate pear mousse with wild blackberry sauce and pistachio cream. The eternally popular *Sardenaira* pizza is made with stone-milled organic flour.

The owners are warm hosts, eager to explain the subtleties of olive oil and mushrooms. Their skill and enthusiasm, together with the elegant style of the restaurant, have won them a Michelin star. **CK**

Al Castello | The "king of tubers" in a truly princely setting

Location Grinzane Cavour **Signature dish** White truffle with an egg, Parmesan, and hazelnut mousse | ❺❺❺

It would be difficult to find a more spectacular location for a restaurant than Grinzane Cavour in Piedmont, the home of Al Castello. Located in a grand thirteenth-century castle close to Alba, the restaurant offers dramatic medieval interiors and breathtaking views over the surrounding hills and vineyards.

Both the castle and vineyards owe their preservation to the indefatigable Count Cavour who restored everything here during his time as mayor. The village now carries his name as does the massive stone fortress that houses a small collection of his possessions, a curious museum dedicated to truffles and local gastronomy, and the best stocked regional wine cellar in Piedmont. The castle also boasts an

---

"… well worth a visit for a fine meal, a taste of superb wine, [and] a glimpse of history."

realfoodtraveler.com

---

exclusive restaurant, where those truffles and local specialties can be relished in exquisite dishes prepared by the Michelin-starred chef Alessandro Boglione.

The fascinating tuber with its aromatic, pale beige flesh is a gourmet's dream—from late September to January, it can be savored with a veal tartare, grated over poached eggs, blended into a sage and butter pasta sauce, or enriching a light egg and Parmesan mousse. Veal cheek and black truffle complete a decadent meal leading up to a grand finale of Gianduia chocolate with dried orange. The food is gracefully served in a comfortable atmosphere, and the wine list boasts an excellent selection of local Nebbiolo, Barbera, Dolcetto, and Barolo vintages. **DJS**

Antica Corte Pallavicina | A royal taste of Italian charcuterie

Location Parma **Signature dish** Culatello | ❺❺❺❺

Crossing a drawbridge to reach the dining room of this restaurant gives new meaning to the phrase "making a grand entrance"—especially when guests are greeted by some rather satisfied-looking black iron pigs in the cobbled courtyard that hint at the dishes to come. This is a proper medieval castle, complete with turrets, dating from the fourteenth century and owned by the Spigaroli family.

The speciality, *culatello*, is the jewel in Emilia Romagna's crown of cured meats; more prized even than Parma ham, it comes from the rump of the black pigs that graze in the 500 acres of farmland surrounding the castle. It is artisanally produced and matured in the cellar, and there is a long list of illustrious regular customers. You can ask to see it in the cellar, and see if you can spot famous names such as star chefs Alain Ducasse and Massimo Bottura, and Britain's Prince Charles, a firm devotee.

The particular humidity of the river-bank setting imbues the *cullatello* with a distinctive, rich muskiness. The restaurant's star dish is the selection of different ages of *culatello*: 26-month Mora Romagnola breed, 30-month Cinta Senese, and 37-month black pig arranged enticingly on a raised platter and served with homemade seasonal vegetable pickles and ultra-thin, moreish *carta da musica*.

Other specialities include frogs' legs, snails with soft polenta, and guineafowl marinated in juniper and rosemary, wrapped in *culatello*, and baked in Po River clay, or a slow-cooked beef stew recipe dating back four generations and served with white polenta. The grand conservatory setting within the courtyard of the castle, with its majestic candelabras, has beguiling views of the river and the countryside beyond where the precious pigs roam freely. It is a fine place to dream of being lord or lady of the manor. **SP**

La Greppia | Try centuries-old Parmesan recipes
at the court of stately dining

Location Parma **Signature dish** *Tortelli di erbette* | **$$$**

Nowhere upholds the grand traditions of Parmesan cuisine with such refined dignity as La Greppia. This small, unassuming restaurant in the heart of the charming old town welcomes guests with a simple but graceful decor of white tablecloths, antique furniture, and wooden roof beams.

At first glance, it may seem more homely than majestic, but behind a window at the rear of the room, Chef Paolo Colà and owner Pier Paolo Chiariotti create exquisite dishes based on recipes that date back to the heyday of the Duchy of Parma and the heady pomp of the seventeenth-century court. The stern aristocrats certainly took their stomachs seriously, and the rich and exciting combinations of tastes and temperatures in these dishes are an absolute delight.

Tortelli al savor are succulent pasta parcels of chestnut, apple, and grape must while *cappuccino di baccalà* adds a witty twist to the ancient combination of stockfish and creamed potato by adding a touch of curry sauce and serving it in a cappuccino cup with a sprinkle of cocoa on top. Other dishes worth trying are pan-stewed goat, veal with caramelized balsamic vinegar, and classic local pasta specialties, such as *anolini parmigiani* or the restaurant's signature chard and ricotta-filled *tortelli di erbette*.

Naturally, this being Parma, the banquet would not be complete without platters of the finest Parma ham and exquisite 36-month–aged Parmesan cheese. And, last but by no means least, comes the impressive dessert tray, laden with endless temptations, such as pears poached in red wine with a Parmesan cheese mousse or delectable morsels of almond, amaretti, and bitter orange preserve, known as *bocca di dama*. La Greppia offers a real feast, and Guido Barilla, head of the world's leading pasta company, is often seen dining here—these are indeed delicacies fit for a king. **DJS**

"This terrific spot offers up some of the best Parmesan cooking … the dessert tray delivers some stunners."

frommers.com

⬆ Homemade pasta is laid out in the kitchen.

Ristorante Cocchi | A truly blissful, elegant culinary experience

Location Parma **Signature dish** *Bollito misto* | ❸❸

Ristorante Cocchi is located within Parma's Hotel Daniel. There may be more famous restaurants in town, but few provide the same culinary thrills that you can experience here. A meal at Cocchi proceeds almost like a Verdi opera, with each course as an "act." Take it slowly to savor the whole experience.

The "overture" would be salumi: a platter of prosciutto di Parma and other cured meats. "Act One" could be tortelli, delicious folded fresh pasta parcels that might contain chard, spiced pumpkin, meat, or cheese—if you want to try different variations, you can order a *bis* (two types) or *tris* (three). In the colder months, "Act Two" is provided by the cart offering *bollito misto*, an assortment of boiled meats with

---

"This restaurant is the pride of the town … rustic in style and pleasantly secluded."

Michelin Guide

---

condiments, triumphantly navigating the tables. You will be offered slices of meat from parts of the cow, pig, and chicken that you may never have pondered but will not be able to resist in this tasty form.

Accompanying sauces include *salsa verde* (herbs, capers, oil, and boiled egg), *pearà* (beef broth, bread crumbs, beef marrow, butter, and pepper), and *mostarda* (ripe fruit with mustard oil). Vegetables are steamed or baked, and always crowned with Parmigiano Reggiano, the "King of Cheeses." "Act Three," the desserts, varies with the seasons. You could try the crumbly, nutty *torta sbrisolona* or the delicate *zabaglione*, which is made to order and has the glorious golden color of the historic town buildings. **FP**

Ristorante Guido | Refined Piedmont cuisine in a royal setting

Location Serralunga d'Alba **Signature dish** *Agnolotti di Lidia al sugo d'arrosto* | ❸❸❸❸❸

Ristorante Guido was founded in 1960, in the small Italian town of Costigliole d'Asti in southern Piedmont, by Guido Alciati and his future wife, Lidia Vanzino. They aimed to create a modern restaurant, with dishes using fresh seasonal produce and making reference to traditional cooking. In a move that was innovative for the time, the couple served a fixed menu to clients by reservation only. They soon acquired a formidable reputation in Italy as masters of the culinary arts and cornerstones of Piedmont cuisine.

The couple's sons, Ugo and Piero, have continued their parents' vision, but in 2013 the restaurant was relocated to the sumptuous surroundings of the Villa Reale in the Piedmontese village of Serralunga d'Alba. The nineteenth-century building is the former hunting lodge of King Vittorio Emanuele II and his wife, Rosa "La Bela Rosin" Vercellana, and now forms part of the Fontanafredda nature reserve and vineyard. The restaurant is located on the first floor of the villa and the Alciati brothers have decorated it in a dramatic modern style that shows off to great advantage the high ceilings and period touches, including beautiful chandeliers and frescoes. Dishes are presented superbly—they are as good to look at as they are to taste.

Guests can sample dishes that make reference to tradition, such as the silky handmade *agnolotti di Lidia al sugo d'arrosto* (*agnolotti* pasta in beef broth, a type of ravioli typical of the region), or oven-roasted lamb with taggiasca olive oil, as well as a range of tasty desserts. The divine *fiordilatte mantecato al momento* is a plain but delicious cow's milk ice cream, made just before it is served; it is low in fat and uses no emulsions. This is innovative cuisine with firm roots in the traditions and flavors of the region. **CK**

Piazza Duomo | Witty modernist cuisine served in the heart of truffle country

Location Alba **Signature dish** Truffle menu | 💲💲💲💲

The picturesque town of Alba in Piedmont is world-famous for its peerless white truffles. You will find this three-Michelin star restaurant in the heart of the old town, in a maze of narrow streets near the cathedral of San Lorenzo. The entrance is discreet, rather in the style of an American Prohibition-era speakeasy—you need to ring the bell and state your name.

Chef-patron Enrico Crippa trained with Antoine Westermann at Le Buerehiesel in Strasbourg and Michel Bras at Laguiole. He has also worked with the legendary Ferran Adrià at El Bulli and Gualtiero Marchesi in Milan, so he has experience of some very high-profile kitchens. Crippa opened Marchesi's restaurant in Kobe and stayed in Japan for three years before returning to Italy and opening his own restaurant in 2005.

Piazza Duomo was awarded its first Michelin star in 2006, and two more in the following years. The cooking style is unashamedly modernist, with the latest in culinary gadgetry used to construct unusual textures in the elaborate dishes. This is particulary evident in a dish of shrimp with olive oil cream, olive cubes, cuttlefish sauce, fennel, and yogurt powder. An entire "truffle menu" pays homage to the fine tuber.

Another example of the playful nature of the cooking can be seen in a dish of braised veal cheeks with chestnuts or pasta with Fassone beef, Parmesan foam cream, and "tomato" sauce: in reality, the sauce is made with red bell peppers. The wonderful Piedmontese beef used shows that ingredient quality is always paramount. Classical dishes are very well executed, as can be seen in delicate gnocchi with slivers of zucchini. The extensive wine list offers many options to complement your meal; there are 125 different Champagnes alone. Conclude with a treat—milk dessert with caramel and milk merengue. **AH**

"For a chef, being here is magical. People are used to eating well … the local produce is spectacular."

Enrico Crippa, chef at Piazza Duomo

⬆ The elegant dining room at Piazza Duomo.

Osteria Francescana | A wonderfully innovative dining experience

Location Modena   **Signature dish** Foie gras "camouflaged" with hare, chestnut, and herbs | ❺❺❺❺❺

Osteria Francescana is the achievement of one ambitious man: Massimo Bottura. Ever since he opened this small, sophisticated restaurant in his home town of Modena in 1995, he has claimed just about every award in the gourmet universe. Three Michelin stars and "International Chef of the Year"—the accolades are impressive.

To some, Bottura is a genius, others have called him "bonkers," but whatever your view, there is no denying the wit and artistry of his approach. "I want to tell a visual story to help diners understand the products I use and the territory I come from," he says—and many of his dishes do just that. For example, the succulent "Journey to Modena" that tells the tale of an eel swimming up the Po River and picking up apples, grapes, and corn on the way.

"Five Ages of Parmigiano Reggiano cheese" is a similar gastronomic journey in time, created through a masterly presentation of five different-aged Parmesan cheeses that are wittily transformed to create varying tastes and textures. Despite such dazzling creativity, Bottura is quick to emphasize the quality of the produce and the importance of local tradition in his cooking. He values and works closely with *terroir*, preserving regional identity, but, at the same time, he reminds young chefs of the need to dream and evolve in their cuisine.

This motto of "feet on the ground, head in the clouds" is present everywhere at Osteria Francescana, from the actual dishes to the interior of the twelve-table dining room, where the stylishly austere, gray-and-white decor is offset by exciting contemporary artworks. Tradition and innovation, vision and experience—Bottura sees all art as a complex marriage of diverse ingredients, and his mesmerizing gourmet creations are no exception. **DJS**

⬆ Iced basil with buffalo mozzarella powder and flowers.

Ristorante Pappagallo | Tradition out of its comfort zone

Location Bologna   **Signature dish** *Parmigiana di melanzane scomposta* | ❸❸❸

Striking the right balance between tradition and innovation is a challenge that few restaurants meet as successfully as the Pappagallo in Bologna. Housed in a splendid fourteenth-century palazzo, just a stone's throw from the city's emblematic two towers, this establishment has a long reputation of fine dining, certified by the autographed smiling portraits of celebrities that line the walls.

Instead of overawing the young head chef, however, the Pappagallo's heritage seems only to inspire Pietro Cocchiarella. Founding his menu on the region's classic dishes, Pietro constantly breaks new ground by choosing the freshest ingredients and emphasizing their natural colors and tastes. A perfect example of this is his *parmigiana di melanzane scomposta*, a very tasty reworking of a local classic that presents the three main ingredients of Parmesan, tomato, and eggplant in separate layers with the usual cheese topping at the bottom.

This focus on natural flavor is apparent in all Pietro's dishes, such as the exquisite buttered gnocchi with fresh tomato and basil and his superb herb-breaded rack of lamb. Like most Bolognese institutions, the Pappagallo has a reputation for meat, but Pietro has pushed back frontiers here, too, by adding a seductive range of fish specialties. Many of these depend on the fresh catch of the day, which he selects himself from the busy stalls in the nearby medieval market, but some—such as the seared tuna steak with a touch of lavender honey—have become as much a part of this charming establishment as its vaulted ceilings and dripping chandeliers.

Elegant without being pompous, Pappagallo is a restaurant that makes you feel special. A fine selection of wines, the attentive service, and irresistible desserts complete the dining experience. **DJS**

⬆ A selection of dainty desserts at Pappagallo.

Ristorante Diana |

Bolognese cuisine beyond meat sauce

Location Bologna **Signature dish** *Spuma di Mortadella* | 💲💲💲

Located in the center of Bologna's main street in Via Indipendenza, Ristorante Diana occupies the heart of this city in more ways than one. Originally opened in 1909 as a café, the restaurant was taken over in 1973 by local salumi king Ivo Galletti and soon became the city's benchmark for haute cuisine.

Bologna may be famous all over the world for the ubiquitous dish of Spaghetti Bolognese, but local inhabitants remain unaware of their global notoriety, partly because none of them would ever dream of serving their prized meat sauce with shop-bought spaghetti rather than fresh tagliatelle, and partly because their real culinary pride and joy is a massive, 10-in (25-cm) diameter sausage—the mortadella.

Not surprisingly, Ristorante Diana is a shrine to this local wonder: starters include an exquisite mortadella mousse (*spuma di mortadella*), a gourmet's dream. With a clear focus on local specialities, the restaurant even provides guests with a separate menu for traditional Bolognese fare. This includes all the local favorites, such as tortellini in broth, lasagne verdi, and the famous *carrello dei bolliti*, a trolley offering a selection of boiled meats served with salsa verde (a parsley, caper, and anchovy sauce).

These delicacies are masterfully prepared by the restaurant's long-standing chef, Mauro Fabbri, who has received numerous accolades and titles over the years, including "President of the Golden Rolling Pin" and even "World Ambassador for Tagliatelle al Ragù."

Naturally, such grand cuisine demands an equally grand setting, and Ristorante Diana complies, with its elegant "Great Gatsby" atmosphere enhanced by high stucco ceilings, classic tableware, and, of course, impeccable service. In short, this is a genuine Bolognese treat. **DJS**

Trattoria Serghei |

A rare pearl of quiet perfection

Location Bologna **Signature dish** *Tagliatelle al ragù* | 💲💲

Friendly, intimate, and cozy, Bologna's Trattoria Serghei is a gem. This tiny restaurant seats a mere 28 guests in a space no bigger than a living room, but the tables are never cramped, and, when you take your seat, you feel that everything is just as it should be, from the cypress-wood paneling to the crisp, hand-printed table linen, and the graceful service provided by siblings Diana and Saverio Pasotti.

Like so many Italian eateries, Serghei is a family-run institution; a particularly deep tie seems to bind the Pasottis to their work. Their father, Sergio, fitted the restaurant out himself in 1967, initially opening it as a tavern, but two years later his wife, Ida, started working her rolling pin, and a new era of culinary

---

"This trattoria is a bastion of traditional Bolognese cuisine … Don't miss the tortelloni."

concierge.com

---

refinement began. No one makes pasta like Ida Pasotti, at least in Bologna. Every morning, she rolls out great golden pasta sheets, then cuts them into tagliatelle strips or squares for her exquisite tortelloni.

Over 80 now, she shows no signs of stopping and often mingles with the guests later in the evening, rather like Alfred Hitchcock appearing in one of his movies. Marcello Mastroianni always ate here when in Bologna, and the restaurant's unusual name harks back to a visit by the Bolshoi Ballet, who insisted on toasting "Serghei" (Sergio) after every course. And who can blame them? After some unforgettable pasta, stuffed zucchini, and a perfect *semifreddo* you may be tempted to raise a glass to Serghei yourself. **DJS**

Da Laura | Fresh seafood dishes served in a picturesque, isolated cove right by the sea

Location San Fruttuoso **Signature dish** *Fritto misto di pesce* | 🟡🟡

Talk about isolated—the tiny Ligurian village of San Fruttuoso is hidden away in a cozy cove on the Portofino peninsula. To get there, you need to either take a ferry from Portofino or walk, but it is well worth the extra effort, especially if lunch at Da Laura is your reward.

Situated right on the beach, with the ebb and flow of the waves along with the voices of contented diners the sole soundtrack, this unpretentious family-owned trattoria comprises a number of tables simply set out underneath the arches of the medieval abbey that is supposed to hold the remains of the saint after whom the village is named. There is also a compact outdoor terrace, plus a shack of sorts, where the bar is housed. Such is Da Laura's closeness to the sea it is not unheard-of for diners to take a dip in the sea in between courses.

Given the fantastic location, it comes as no surprise that fresh seafood and fish dishes make up the majority of Da Laura's menu (although regulars are also known to rave about the lasagne with homemade pesto sauce). For starters, you can choose from a ravishing selection of anchovies, calamari, and tuna, all juicy, fresh, and pliant, with just a hint of briny saltiness. Or you may go for a luscious helping of spaghetti daubed with a tangy seafood sauce that includes wonderful clams, mussels, and sea urchin.

For the main course, you should dive into plates of grilled squid or octopus, or possibly a helping of crisp fried fish and seafood (the famous *fritto misto di pesce*), the salty scent and taste of which provide a gastronomic "counterpoint" to the waves that lap onto the shore just some feet away. Even though it is only open for lunch, this is the kind of place you never want to leave. **ATJ**

"The unique location alone makes a visit worthwhile. You can even eat in your bathing suit…"

ilmangione.it

⬆ Lunch by the sea in the idyllic setting of San Fruttuoso.

La Terrazza, Hotel Splendido | Dine in the heart of the Riviera

Location Portofino **Signature dish** "Spaghetti alla Elizabeth Taylor" | ❺❺❺❺

> *"One of Italy's most glamorous retreats … La Terrazza is the ideal place to enjoy superb cooking."*
>
> CN Traveller

⊞ Beautiful views are on the menu at La Terrazza.

Getting a table at La Terrazza—this is the high life. One of two restaurants at the stylish five-star Hotel Splendido in Portofino (there is also a cocktail bar), La Terrazza is a place where film stars (both dead and alive) have come and gone for decades. Inside, the dining experience is more formal, with smart waiting staff gliding about as silent as ghosts, while a piano plays in the background.

However, when the weather is clement (this is the Italian Riviera after all, and the clemency of its climate is well-established), it pays to take a table outside on the terrace, where breathtaking views of Portofino bay stretch out glimmering below. Meanwhile luxury yachts and other, more down-to-earth boats drift in and out, adding to the sense of languor.

Acclaimed head chef Corrado Corti has a passion for the freshest seafood and fish; he is also unmoved by the developments in trend-influenced international cuisine. Classic Ligurian dishes such as seafood salad with olive oil and lemon sauce and ravioli filled with vegetables and herbs accompanied by walnut sauce demonstrate his belief in the multiple joys of regional cuisine.

Elsewhere, the menu could perhaps be described as "new wave traditional," with John Dory ravioli in red mullet sauce, the catch of the day in a mixed grill, and fillet of beef in Barolo wine sauce getting the appetite going. One of the rare nods to the hotel's history of visiting celebrities is a dish named "Spaghetti alla Elizabeth Taylor," which features three varieties of fresh tomatoes and was originally requested by the movie diva herself.

To round off your meal, there are some cheeses, sourced from artisanal farms, and desserts made fresh every day. This may be the high life, but there is a solid integrity and intelligence to the food and the ambience that makes La Terrazza much more than just a "place to be seen." **ATJ**

Nigo Pezigo | Enticing new dishes inspired by tradition

Location Fosdinovo **Signature dish** Tagliatelle with rabbit, pine nuts, olives, and fresh thyme | **$$**

The tiny restaurant of Nigo Pezigo pokes out from the medieval walls of Fosdinovo like a child peeping out from under his mother's apron. Dominated by the massive towers of the Malaspina castle on one side and the heart-stopping view of the Ligurian coastline on the other, the restaurant boasts a unique sea and mountain setting.

Nigo Pezigo is run by a charming young couple who are extremely enthusiastic about their work. Federico waits on the tables while his wife Alice works in the kitchen, creating a fascinating menu with love and flair, following a philosophy of cherishing local heritage that is also expressed in the name of the restaurant: "Nigo Pezigo" is a line from an old, local rhyming dialect that remains popular, although nowadays few can decipher its meaning. It is this attraction to an almost forgotten history that inspires Alice's cuisine.

Creating local dishes is a way of reviving traditions, but it also means committing to zero food miles. Nearly everything is sourced from nearby farms and local fishermen. The result is a stunning seasonal menu, with tasty dishes ranging from marinated anchovies and grilled monkfish to testaroli pasta with pesto, rabbit, pheasant, or hare sauce and an exquisite hazelnut and duck terrine served with a leaf and fruit salad.

Needless to say, Alice prepares everything herself, including the bread, pasta, and a range of irresistible desserts, such as the delicious strawberry and crème Chantilly *millefeuille*. The refinement of the menu is matched by the restaurant's interior: dark wood furniture and crisp table linen offset the natural stone of the vaulted ceiling to create a sober but tasteful atmosphere. Federico says he likes to think of Nigo Pezigo as a constantly evolving experience. Looking back to the past, for this couple, is the best way of inspiring and developing their own cuisine. **DJS**

"A beautiful location ... weather-permitting, the views stretch all the way to Corsica."

ilmangione.it

⬆ Filled pasta is made lovingly by hand.

Ristorante San Giorgio

Gorgeous food with a view

Location Cervo **Signature dish** Gnocchetti with seafood sauce | ❸❸❸

This may well be the Italian restaurant of your dreams. Perched near the top of a hill town that looks out over a deep-blue bay on the Italian Riviera, the menu combines perfect fish and seafood with excellent herbs and vegetables from inland. All dishes are prepared with olive oil from nearby Taggia and Badalucco, arguably Italy's best.

However, none of the fine ingredients alone could make for such a gourmet experience if they were not subject to the culinary wisdom of the lovely Caterina Lanteri, instantly recognizable by her large glasses and huge smile, who founded this restaurant in the 1960s. Caterina is assisted by her son, Alessandro, who runs the restaurant with a quiet passion underpinned by a

---

"A classy restaurant … with a cuisine that reinterprets Ligurian tradition with inspiration."

ilmangione.it

---

strong emphasis on first-class ingredients, sourced daily from the market in nearby Oneglia. Thimble-sized gnocchetti are accompanied by a vibrant seafood sauce, with a carefully considered amount of hot red pepper and Parmesan putting paid to the rule that fish and cheese should not be combined.

This being the Italian Riviera, there are some incomparable herbs—especially the basil, transformed into lovely pesto—that provide Caterina with a palette of flavor to pair superbly with the fish and vegetables. For dessert, try the exquisite mousse of fresh hazelnuts, prepared only when the best nuts are available. A meal here is such a gratifying experience that you might not even notice the gorgeous views. **FP**

Eco del Mare

An exclusive treat for all the senses

Location Lerici **Signature dish** Parchment-baked sea bass | ❸❸❸

The Eco del Mare provides one of Italy's most exclusive beach cuisine experiences. Located in a small, private cove on the jagged stretch of coastline known as the Gulf of Poets, this stylish "beach club" (as its owner, Francesca Mozer, defines it) is a unique combination of natural beauty and refined dining. Reached either by boat or in the convenient elevator that takes you down from road to beach level, the restaurant sprawls lazily along the seashore, leaving space in front for a scattering of loungers.

Undoubtedly the first thing that strikes you is the booming of the waves—the "eco del mare"—as the sea is so close and the sound naturally magnified by the curve of the cliffs. It was this that attracted Francesca's father in the early 1950s, when he bought the cove and set up a series of beach huts.

The stunning location was an immediate success, but in 2006 Francesca decided to raise the stakes. Closing the place for almost four years, she turned the huts into suites, enlarged the kitchen, employed a new chef, and lovingly created a distinctive ambience of ready-rusted canopies, stick-weave chairs, weathered wood tables, and beach-scavenged logs. Reopened in 2010, the establishment has fulfilled Francesca's dream of creating a restaurant that offers "culinary excellence and refinement as well as that most exclusive of qualities—freedom."

Fresh fish naturally dominates the menu and changes daily according to the catch of the day. The masterpiece is the local morone (sea bass), grilled or baked, but the mullet, fried anchovies, shrimp ragout, and seafood timbales are all equally exquisite. Unadulterated nature, total privacy, and gourmet cuisine—what more could you want? **DJS**

→ Beautifully presented seafood served by the sea.

Ristorante Majore | Celebrating pork in many variations

Location Chiaramonte Gulfi **Signature dish** *Gelatina Majore (di maiale)* | $

Chiaramonte Gulfi is a hill town on the top of Monte Arcibessi in southeast Sicily, known for its spectacular views across the island, which have earned it the nickname "The Balcony of Sicily." However, it also has another claim to fame thanks to the Ristorante Majore, which produces dishes made from pork that attract locals, tourists, and food lovers to the small town.

Ristorante Majore is located on one of the medieval streets just off the town square. The entrance leads straight into the kitchen, where cherry tomatoes simmer and pork chops sizzle in large brass pots, exuding a wondrous aroma. The smaller dining room is a delight in its homely intimacy with traditional decor and intricate *trompe l'oeil* frescoes. It first opened in 1896, at a time when every family kept a pig at home and knew the secrets of curing and salting its meat during the winter. Four generations later, the restaurant is still in the hands of the family.

> *"In a splendid setting of green pine groves ... Majore continues its unique tradition of cooking pork."*
>
> Ristorante Majore website

Dining here is a memorable experience; you can marvel at the numerous ways to eat pork (and wash it down with wine). The *ravioli al sugo di maiale* consists of pasta stuffed with ricotta in a pork sauce with basil and tomatoes; the *costata ripiena* is a pork chop stuffed with pork sausage and minced pork; the *capicollo* a piquant salami with black pepper. The most remarkable dish is *gelatina Majore*, the restaurant's superb take on pork gelatine, with pistachio. Truly unforgettable, and an incredible bargain. **CK**

Magnolia | Achingly cool and witty food creations

Location Cesenatico **Signature dish** Lobster and lemon verbena linguine | $$$

"Genius, when young, is divine," said Benjamin Disraeli and never has this been more true than at Alberto Faccani's restaurant, Magnolia. Alberto, one of the brightest young stars on Italy's culinary firmament, opened this stylish institution in his hometown of Cesenatico on the Adriatic coast when he was just 26. To say that this was bold is something of an understatement, as Italy is known for favoring gray-bearded experience over youthful zest. But Alberto is Alberto. Just two years later, he was awarded his first Michelin star, and, several years later, the restaurant is just as cool and excitingly innovative as when it opened.

"I want to offer my guests what I would like to be served myself," says Alberto. "I want them to enjoy the experience. I want them to have fun." And fun these dishes certainly are with their witty combinations of flavors and textures that shake the senses.

Freshly caught fish dominates the menu, and the best way to explore Alberto's talents are his taster menus. These five-, seven- or ten-course experiences bombard the palate with explosions of taste and color. Amberjack with raspberry and cucumber, monkfish with pesto and cherry tomatoes, calamari carbonara, scallops with leek and truffles, and tuna with red currant and green onions are just some of the options, as the menu changes monthly.

Alberto is truly dedicated to his guests. The dining experience is enhanced with tastefully designed contemporary interiors and stylish tableware. To cater to all budgets, he also organizes bistro evenings, and if you yearn to discover the magician's secrets, you can sign up for a cookery course and learn how it is done from the maestro himself. **DJS**

→ Aesthetic presentation is paramount at Magnolia.

Da Delfina | Traditional Tuscan cooking in a spectacular setting

Location Artimino **Signature dish** *Rigatina acciugata con fagioli di Sorana* | ❸❸❸

Situated in the small village of Artimino, a 45-minute drive from Florence, Da Delfina's out-of-the-way location only adds to its charm. Dining on the terrace with its panoramic views across the olive groves of the Tuscan hills feels like being inside a landscape painting. You also get an excellent view of the Medici Villa known as "La Ferdinanda"—a place that has played an important role in the history of this family-run restaurant.

Delfina Cioni (née Giusta), the founder, was born in 1909 in a farmhouse that formed part of the Medici Villa estate. After her father died, when she was still a child, she went into service at the villa, working for a family of Venetian nobles. There, Delfina learned to cook and, over the years, she added refinement to the rustic dishes she prepared, which were based on peasant food. She began to cook for hunters who visited the villa, and when it became a tourist attraction in the 1950s, she started to cook for tourists, too. Her cuisine proved such a success that in 1975, Delfina and her gamekeeper husband, Baldino, renovated a stone building nearby and opened it as the Ristorante Da Delfina. Nowadays, Delfina's son, Carlo, is in charge (Delfina herself worked until she was over a hundred years old), and he continues to create dishes based on traditional Tuscan dishes.

Guests can watch the cooking thanks to an open kitchen, with meat being grilled or spit-roasted over an open fire. The menu changes with the seasons, with some ingredients sourced from the restaurant's orchard and vegetable patch. Among the tasty dishes on offer are *terrina di coniglio* (rabbit terrine), duck macaroni, and *rigatina acciugata con fagioli di Sorana* (bacon and anchovies with creamy Sorana beans). For dessert, try the lovely *torta Mantovana* served with a hot sauce. **CK**

Trattoria Sostanza | A true Aladdin's cave of Tuscan delights

Location Florence **Signature dish** *Tortino di carciofi* (artichoke tart) | ❸❸

In a place as inundated with tourist menus as Florence, seekers of culinary gems need to look a bit harder for that special gourmet experience. Trattoria Sostanza is well off the beaten tourist track—like Aladdin's cave, the unassuming entrance belies the wonders within.

Opened in 1869, this is one of a few taverns in Florence to have preserved its typical, late nineteenth-century style. The space is small and narrow, with original white marble-topped tables and walls lined with white tiles and dubious artwork; also, to reach the bathroom, you have to cross the kitchen. The restaurant does not accept credit cards or serve coffee, but it does offer a wonderfully relaxed atmosphere and old-fashioned pride in its cuisine. As

> *"People have been lining up at the long communal tables since 1869 to enjoy huge amounts of food."*
>
> frommers.com

in most trattorias, the menu is handwritten and changes with seasonal produce, but certain specialties are fixtures, such as the delicious *tortino di carciofi*, melt-in-the-mouth butter-fried chicken, and the classic *bistecca alla fiorentina*. Two fingers high and weighing about a pound, the mammoth T-bone is chopped to order by chef Mario and tossed on the grill to be carefully turned so as not to lose a drop of the succulent juices.

The result is a meatfest like no other, but, if you are tempted to lick your fingers, beware! Decades ago, cook Guido Campolmi was observed doing the same and was immediately labeled *troia*, or "whore." Some locals still call the trattoria "i'troia" to this day. **DJS**

Enoteca Pinchiorri | All the best things come in pairs at this popular enoteca and restaurant

Location Florence   **Signature dish** "Mora Romagnola" suckling pig with zucchini and marinated onions | 𝕾𝕾𝕾𝕾𝕾

Enoteca Pinchiorri is arguably Florence's most illustrious gastronomic destination. Originally opened in 1972, the establishment owes its success to a simple but effective mantra that "two is better than one." To begin with, this enoteca is not just a wine cellar (although is has one of the best-stocked cellars in Europe), but also a highly acclaimed restaurant.

Similarly, it is run by a team of two masters, Giorgio Pinchiorri, the restaurant's much-respected founder, and Annie Féolde, his wife and the first female chef in Italy to receive three Michelin stars. There is also the combined force of two nationalities and their cultures at work: the enoteca is unquestionably Italian—Giorgio was born near Modena—but Annie was brought up in Nice and instinctively adds a breath of French culinary adventure. For thirty-five years, Annie and Giorgio have shared their passion for combining fine wine and gourmet cuisine, and the result is one of the most exclusive dining experiences in the world.

Everything at Enoteca Pinchiorri is special, from the majestic fifteenth-century interiors to the flawless service and expert sommeliers who discreetly guide guests through the cellar's stock of over 4,000 labels. Then, of course, there is the cuisine that teases the senses with its extraordinary à la carte dishes and twenty-course "Whispers of Spring" taster menu. This wondrous flight of gastronomic creativity is prepared by two chefs—Italo Bassi and Riccardo Monco—and includes exciting flavor combinations, from ricotta, sweetbread, and walnut ravioli to octopus with pumpkin and coffee, or crisp, candied pigeon thighs. As Annie Féolde herself says: "Taste is a multifaceted experience fed by all our senses." Without doubt, the experience of an evening in the grandeur of Enoteca Pinchiorri is far more than the sum of its parts. **DJS**

"One of Florence's temples of gourmet dining, this ... restaurant will [also] delight wine enthusiasts."

Michelin Guide

⬆ Culinary creativity at Enoteca Pinchiorri.

L'Erbhosteria | Enjoy an authentic and pretty taste of the wild

Location Badia Tedalda   **Signature dish** Nettle ravioli with creamed silene and calendula flowers | ❸❸

Like any rare and original experience, L'Erbhosteria can be rather elusive. Located high up in the Tuscan Apennines in a tiny, stone-built hamlet, this restaurant has limited opening hours, and you should always phone before setting out. But if you do make the pilgrimage, you will soon realize why inveterate forager Piero Valentini could not possibly have opened his fascinating eatery anywhere else.

Sitting down for one of Piero's meals is like finding a secret door to Nature's larder. The aromas that drift in from the kitchen are strong and earthy, and the appetizer salads stun the senses with their dazzling colors and tastes. Burnet, borage, and yarrow are just some of the wondrous ingredients used, and garnishes of dandelions, violets, primroses, and daisies are spectacularly pretty.

For pasta, try the delicious nettle ravioli in creamed silene leaves and calendula flowers or the wild mushroom tagliatelle dressed with Jerusalem artichoke tubers and marjoram. Plump pheasant breast comes with black truffles and juniper berries followed by tempura-fried elderflowers.

This is a cuisine that deliberately chooses simplicity and freshness over artifice. "The secret," says Piero, "is to let the ingredients speak for themselves." Nearly all of them are gathered only a few hours before they are served. Considering the altitude, this may seem unbelievable, but Piero is keen to stress the abundance of nature. "The menu is a continual surprise," he states, "and picking flowers in spring is very different to digging tubers in a snowdrift."

This is all part of a philosophy where everything is given just the time it needs, and a leisurely lunch becomes an opportunity to talk, savor some excellent wine, and enjoy an atmosphere of friendly well-being. L'Erbhosteria is a natural tonic for body and soul. **DJS**

⬆ Salads at L'Erbhosteria are almost too lovely to eat.

Cucinaà | Delicious contemporary Umbrian dining in an informal setting

Location Foligno   **Signature dish** Organic truffled egg with bruschetta powder and hazelnut pesto | ❸❸

Cucinaà's location, in the middle of a nondescript road, may not look too promising at first; but, the moment you enter the stylish, light-filled restaurant, it becomes clear that this is a serious place serving top-quality food in a pared-back, relaxed setting. The three culinary stars behind Cucinaà cover all the bases: chef Marco Gubbiotti (who has earned a Michelin star), pastry chef Andrea Santilli, and sommelier Ivan Pizzoni have moved away from an haute cuisine environment to create a place where the focus is simply on the food.

You can have a meal here, shop for some carefully chosen gastronomic specialities, including a fine selection of wines and olive oil, or order a selection of dishes to take away. Open continuously from early in the morning, Cucinaà is perfect for an excellent coffee and sinfully good pastries for breakfast, a quick snack, or a restorative drink with culinary inspiration later in the day.

Expertly cooked traditional main dishes and a changing array of salads and vegetables mean that lunchtimes are particularly busy. Workers flock here to enjoy perennial classics including aubergine, basil, and mozzarella parmigiana, pasta with chickpeas and salt cod, or crunchy lamb cutlets with thyme. Some opt for the Umbrian speciality of *pasta frascarelli* (made with semolina) with mushrooms or truffles.

Seasonality is key to the menu—if something is only available for a few days, then that's even more reason to get excited. Pride in the local ingredients and immediate gastronomic history is paramount, but these values have been put into an approachable and casual setting. Eating here is an excellent, modern way to experience some of the best food that Umbria has to offer. Be sure to finish your meal with a slice of the chocolate *crescionda* tart with amaretti and ricotta. **CS**

⊡ **Umbrian dishes are prepared with seasonal produce.**

Enoteca L'Alchimista | The magic of lovingly sourced food and wine

Location Montefalco   **Signature dish** "Pretend carbonara" strangozzi | ❸❸

Whether eating on the shaded terrace in the summer heat, observing the daily life of Montefalco on the Piazza del Comune, or seated in the cozy basement in winter, there is always a delicious choice of Umbrian specialities on offer at the family-run L'Alchimista. Owner and sommelier Cristina Magnini works closely with nearby winemakers so there is an interesting and varied selection of wines for sale in the Alchimista shop as well as an ever-changing offer of wines by the glass. Be sure to try some of the lovely wines made from local Grechetto and Sagrantino grapes.

There are also olive oil tastings at L'Alchimista. The "alchemist" of the restaurant's name is Patrizia Moretti, Cristina's mother, who does indeed magically transform local ingredients into inventive yet straightforward dishes that just beg to be eaten. Strangozzi, the long pasta traditionally found between Foligno and Spello, appears frequently on the menu, and is usually served simply with superb locally grown vegetables and seasoned with a fruity olive oil. The team at L'Alchimista work closely with small local suppliers, among them an artisan producer of *fiore molle della Valnerina*, a cow's milk cheese with saffron based on a recipe that is seven hundred years old. Patrizia uses it with pancetta and a small amount of zucchini to make her "pretend carbonara" (usually made with pecorino) strangozzi.

Stuffed zucchini flowers and summer salads are particularly delicious, and Patrizia's warming soups made from traditionally used legumes such as Roveja peas from Cascia or Trasimeno beans are perfect cold-season fare. In October, she uses black celery from Trevi, which is only available for a short time, in a parmigiana dish with meat and sausages. Diners are advised to leave room for Patrizia's exquisite fruit tarts, perfect with an espresso. **CS**

⊕ L'Alchimista is located on a corner of Piazza del Comune.

Vespasia | Savor Umbrian delicacies in elegant surroundings

Location Norcia **Signature dish** Wild Roveja pea soup with sheep ricotta gnocchi | ❸❸❸

Vespasia's comfortable interior, with its muted, calming color palette, provides a welcome respite from the crowds of visitors who regularly flock to Norcia. The hometown of St. Benedict (San Benedetto) attracts not only religious tourists but also gourmets in search of the culinary delights that this town is widely known for (the term *norcineria* has come to mean expert pork butchery throughout Italy).

The restaurant is part of the stylish Palazzo Seneca Hotel, courtesy of the Bianconi family, who have run hotels and restaurants in Norcia for seven generations, but is rapidly becoming a destination in its own right. This is hardly surprising given that the menu contains some of the finest local specialities, and the owners have forged strong relationships with the best suppliers. Fittingly, evocative black-and-white portraits of their regular suppliers are displayed for all to see. The delightful, secluded courtyard is ideal for an aperitivo and a relaxed perusal of the menu while you wait for your table. Drinks are served with an artfully presented choice of nibbles that includes a few slices of coppa, olives, and pecorino.

The previously abandoned but meticulously restored building provides a beautiful setting and a magnet for truffle seekers and gourmets looking to savor the porcine delicacies of Norcia. The monthly changing menu always features local pork and truffles (either winter or summer truffles), and may include Castelluccio lentils from nearby Piano Grande. Choose from fresh tagliolini with black Norcia truffles, a hazelnut and truffle mousse, spit-roasted lamb from the Sibillini Mountains with a Castelluccio lentil soufflé, local unpasteurized goat's and sheep's cheese, or a dessert made with beer produced by the town's Benedictine monks; plenty of inspiration for a shopping spree in the nearby gourmet food shops. **CS**

⬆ Vespasia serves Umbrian and Norcia specialities.

Tredici Gradi |

Food and cheese in perfect harmony

Location Viterbo **Signature dish** Cured meat and cheese board | $

Viterbo is a beautiful, historic town northeast of Rome, and visitors to the capital would be well advised to make the journey to see its medieval center—and to dine at this unpretentious, formidable trattoria.

Tredici gradi means "thirteen degrees"— what the proprietors consider the ideal percentage of alcohol in wine. While experts may swoon over more powerful wines with intense grape saturation and higher degrees of alcohol, most Italians view wine as an accompaniment to food that should not overpower it.

Many people come to enjoy one of the many excellent wines available by the glass with a *tagliere* (cutting board) of *salumi e formaggi*, carefully selected cured meat from throughout Italy and local cheeses made of cow's or sheep's milk. Sample the susianella from Viterbo and three types of prosciutto, from Carpegna, Parma, and San Daniele. It is best to limit the size of your *tagliere*, though, to save room for magnificent fieno pasta, tagliatelle, or fettuccine.

"This baronial-esque dining den, complete with velvet drapes, is a safe bet for authentic . . . grub."

Lonely Planet

For secondi, try the porchetta—mouthwateringly good suckling pig flavored with wild fennel, best with a glass of local white wine and a portion of greens gathered seasonally (and often from the wild) that lend a characteristic bite to meals that might otherwise be quite rich. For dessert, *crostata di visciole e mandorle* is a scrumptious tart made only when the dark local cherries are available and paired with almonds. Or you could go for more cheese. **FP**

L'Archeologia |

Fine dining in a historic location

Location Rome **Signature dish** "Antique hors d'oeuvres" | $$$

The Via Appia was one of the first roads ever built, connecting the ancient capital of the Roman Empire with the vital Mediterranean port of Brindisi. Today, the uneven cobbles and flagstones of the stretch of road closest to Rome are preserved as a historic park.

Right alongside the Via Appia Antica you will find L'Archeologia, a highly rated restaurant run by the Casavecchia family since it opened; nowadays, Marco Casavecchia is in charge. The eatery uses its enviable position to its advantage: ancient busts, monuments, and stone relics are dotted around the garden, and more classical reproductions abound inside among dark wooden beams, pillars, stone archways, and old fireplaces.

L'Archeologia may not actually date back to ancient times, but it is very old in "restaurant years." It opened in 1890 in a former staging post for changing horses, and today's customers can dine in the shade of a wisteria that is said to be three hundred years old.

Amid all this heritage, it is a pleasant surprise to find that the food is modern, fresh, and innovative. Look out for gnocchi with squid and tomato, beef carpaccio with layers of Parmesan, and diced grouper with fettuccine. Other dishes include cuttlefish soup with shellfish and *strangozzi alla pecorara* (a distinctive handmade pasta served with garlic, pepper, ham, and pecorino). The long, hollow *cavatelli* pasta is said to have been invented by Marco's grandmother.

Some dishes are proudly ancient in origin: a selection of "antique hors d'oeuvres," for example, is based on a classic dish for eighteenth-century merchants who stopped off at the coaching post and includes traditional delicacies of wild boar sausage, deer salami, and Umbrian salami. **SH**

[→] L'Archeologia is set on the atmospheric Via Appia.

Roscioli | An authentic taste of Rome in a historic deli

Location Rome **Signature dish** Spaghetti carbonara | $$

"More like a Caravaggio painting than a place of business . . . top-quality comestibles."

fodors.com

[↑] A multitude of tasty goods is laid out at the counter.

Roscioli is the kind of authentic local eatery that you dream of finding on your culinary travels, but hardly ever do. Originally a bakery and delicatessen with a 150-year history offering a wide range of charcuterie, cheese, and olive oil along with baked goods, it started out on a separate site. Its current format goes back to 2002, when Alessandro and Pierluigi Roscioli decided to add a restaurant to their shop, resulting in a narrow dining room with exposed brickwork, tightly packed tables, and tiled floor.

Jazz music is usually playing in the background, and countless wine bottles line the shelves. Although the menu seems to offer just a few wines, if you do ask for a list, two huge books will appear, revealing an extensive range of fine wines, many barely more than their retail price. The wine cellar itself is located downstairs, with a few tables set out among the collection of bottles.

Roscioli is also a bakery, so the bread does not disappoint: you can choose from a mix of rustic brown slices with a lovely crust and some superb buttery focaccia, offered with outstanding mozzarella. For the primo, you could try the spaghetti carbonara—a true delight with a lovely texture, made with high-quality bacon and fine Parmesan cheese.

Amatriciana pasta, another classic, is also excellent, with a rich tomato sauce that complements the guanciale and pecorino cheese; fettuccine with white truffles is a simple dish that lets the heady truffle fragrance speak for itself. You might also want to sample a slab of Mediterranean tuna, served with carefully cooked zucchini, carrots, and cauliflower.

To finish your meal, opt for the tiramisu with its deep coffee flavor: it is deliciously creamy but not too rich, with a sprinkling of chocolate on top. Service is relaxed and friendly: this is not fancy food, but the ingredients are terrific and there is a real honesty to the cooking. **AH**

Trattoria Perilli | Authentic Roman trattoria food with plenty of meat dishes

Location Rome   **Signature dish** Rigatoni alla carbonara | 🟢🟢

A 390 A.D. travel tip from St. Augustine may seem a rather obscure recommendation for a modern-day restaurant, but nowhere is his maxim of "when in Rome do as the Romans do" more pertinent than at Trattoria Perilli. After all, no self-respecting centurion would have dreamed of trying eclectic gourmet fare when he could be tucking a serviette under his chin and just burying his nose in a bowl of Perilli's deliciously saucy pasta.

Trattoria Perilli has been serving food in the Testaccio district of Rome since 1911, and nobody guards the local culinary traditions more closely. Until the late 1970s, this area was the center of Rome's extensive meat trade, and slaughterhouse workers were often paid in off-cuts—the so-called fifth quarter (*quinto quarto*)—so many of the specialties are not for the faint-hearted: *coratella* is an exquisite combination of sautéed lamb heart and artichokes, *pajata* sauce is made with veal intestines, *animelle* are fried sweetbreads, and *coda alla vaccinara* is a hearty oxtail stew.

But, if all this seems a little bit much, do not fear: Perilli also serves a spectacular roast lamb, zingy puntarelle (endive), and plump globe artichokes. Its signature pasta is the mouthwatering rigatoni alla carbonara, not made with bacon but with guanciale from Amatrice or cured pork jowl, a local delicacy that is also used in the restaurant's other chin-licking Roman classic, bucatini all' amatriciana.

These marvels as well as the excellent local "Castelli Romani" house wines are served by old-school waiters in black trousers and bow ties who seem as timeless as the Roman scenes depicted on the walls. Their professional ease and ready humor could come straight out of Federico Fellini's *La Dolce Vita*, and if they think you look hungry, they might even serve you your pasta in the large bowl that it was mixed in. **DJS**

"A typical Roman trattoria in the most typical Roman district … generous portions, great quality."

ilmangione.it

⬆ Trattoria Perilli is in Rome's Testaccio district.

La Pergola | Accomplished, sophisticated food with a panorama

Location Rome **Signature dish** Fagotelli "La Pergola" | ❺❺❺❺

La Pergola is part of the Hilton Cavalieri hotel, which is perched at the top of Monte Mario, overlooking the city. In the lavishly decorated dining room, all of Rome sprawls beneath you, with St. Peter's Basilica just one of many visible landmarks. Chef Heinz Beck originally trained at Heinz Winkler before moving to La Pergola, which subsequently gained three Michelin stars. Beck holds lectures on nutrition at a local university, and there is a definite lightness to his cooking style.

Dishes are served on vermeil plates and paintings, vases, and other assorted artworks are dotted around the space to create a unique, sophisticated atmosphere. Your meal might start with duck liver terrine with smoked apple, almonds, and amaretti with stunning flavors, the apple providing just enough acidity. Fagotelli "La Pergola" is a signature dish with remarkably light pasta. It combines fagotelli pasta with elements of the quintessential Roman carbonara: bacon and eggs are tucked inside the

pasta casing to create a successful modern take on a beloved classic. If you prefer fish, a warm emincé of sea bass with vegetables marinated in olive oil features perfectly cooked fish served with excellent vegetables to complete the dish.

Another example of the chef's skill is the black cod with marinated anchovy vinaigrette and sweet chili pepper: the pepper lifts the taste of the cod, but not too much—it works superbly. To complement the dishes, the immense wine cellar boasts as many as 3,000 wines and a total of 60,000 stored bottles.

To conclude the meal, you could go for a wonderfully refreshing dessert of ricotta cheese puff with diced pear. Pergola is a sumptuous experience, in a glorious setting, with a beautifully appointed dining room and superb service to complement the highly skilled cooking. **AH**

⊡ A pretty dish of fried zucchini flower at La Pergola.

Enoteca Ferrara | Great wine and inspired cooking in Trastevere

Location Rome   **Signature dish** Swordfish with cinnamon and pine nuts | ❸❸

On a cobbled piazza among the narrow lanes of Rome's fashionable Trastevere district, you will find a small ancient building. Inside, it opens up into a series of connected dining rooms like Doctor Who's Tardis. Among the maze of rooms on different levels is a bar, a delicatessen, a restaurant, a wine bar, and a trattoria—and, if that's not enough, you can sit in a wicker chair in the square outside.

Inside, the fifteenth-century building tables are laid out under a dark beamed wooden ceiling, between grand brick arches, and alongside white-washed walls. Chef Maria Paolillo is an authority on classic Italian recipes and her sister Lina is a sommelier—she compiled a wine list that goes back to World War II. Enoteca Ferrara was once judged Italy's finest wine shop. The enormous wine cellar is visible through metal grilles beneath the restaurant. At quiet times, diners can take a tour of this atmospheric basement, which is at the street level

of ancient Rome, and choose a bottle from two huge bound books—one for white, one for red—listing the history and characteristics of each of the available 1,600 wines.

Some people just come for the wine, and perhaps some antipasti to go with it, but the cooking is highly acclaimed and well worth trying. In the osteria, guests can sample versions of traditional Italian peasant food, known as *cucina povera*, which includes flavorsome bean soups, fresh pasta, and stews. The menu at the restaurant proper is more modern: dishes might include a delicate "pasta tower" with pork, mushrooms, and vegetables; swordfish fillets with cinnamon and pine nuts; or fried zucchini and squash flowers. Watch out for the speciality dessert, *zuppa inglese*—an irresistible cold trifle submerged in a sauce of hot chocolate. **SH**

⬆ The "pasta tower" can be paired with an exquisite wine.

Da Felice a Testaccio | Classic Roman cuisine in a chic restaurant

Location Rome **Signature dish** *Gricia* (cured pig's cheeks) ravioli | ❺❺❺❺

Da Felice was opened in 1936 on a street corner in the Testaccio district of Rome, far from the tourist crowds, by the notoriously grumpy Felice Trivelloni. Felice was renowned for putting fake "reserved" signs on tables in order to turn away anyone he didn't like. At the time, it was a basic workers' trattoria but it slowly gained a reputation for good home-style cooking. Thankfully, Felice's son Franco, who runs the restaurant these days, is more welcoming. Strangers are no longer turned away at the door—unless of course the restaurant is fully booked, which nowadays it often is.

The place has had a stylish makeover since then, too, but the focus is still on high-quality versions of Roman classics with a menu that changes daily. Chef Salvatore Tiscione produces special dishes for each day of the week: for example, Monday appears to be the day for fettuccine with artichokes and roast lamb's head; Friday is the time to try octopus with potatoes or fettuccelle with mussels and pecorino; Saturday is

the day for the restaurant's signature dish, *gricia* ravioli, delicious pasta parcels of cured pork cheek served with tomato, ricotta, and basil.

In addition to these, traditional staples such as pasta *cacio e pepe*, all'amatriciana, and carbonara are always on the menu. Meat lovers should try the oven-baked lamb with potatoes. Be sure to also leave room for the famous tiramasu, served in a pretty, tall glass.

Nowadays, the restaurant is a modern, urban eatery with a black-and-white tiled floor, burnished bar, and industrial-style metal pendant lights. The crockery is more traditional, depicting motifs of a hunting scene, the table linen is crisp white, and the chairs simple dark wood. Staff wear uniform black, and the atmosphere is bustling yet relaxed. The wine list is surprisingly extensive, so take your time to choose a wine to accompany your meal. **SH**

⬆ A taste of Rome at this long-established eatery.

Cecilia Metella | A popular local restaurant with a lively atmosphere

Location Rome   **Signature dish** *Scrigno alla Cecilia* | ❸❸❸

Named after the nearby Mausoleum of Caecilia Metella—the daughter of an ancient Roman consul who died young and had a splendid monument built in her memory—the Cecilia Metella restaurant and bar is located on the Via Appia near Rome's early Christian catacombs. Founded in 1966 by the Graziani family who still run the place, the restaurant is a no-nonsense venue with two large rooms that are popular with locals for family celebrations, including wedding receptions and banquets, with avuncular staff at hand.

The food is good value, but it is the surroundings that make Cecilia Metella a true destination in Italy's bustling capital. Visitors will find a haven of green in the large gardens, complete with a bubbling fountain, shady walkways, rambling vines, lawns, and large terracotta pots and flower tubs—this lovely spot is perfect for whiling away a few hours dining alfresco. Guests can choose from a wide range of dishes that include an antipasti buffet of grilled vegetables, salami, and bruschetta. The menu comprises Italian classic dishes including *melanzane alla parmigiana* (eggplant, tomato, and Parmesan) and tiramisu, as well as Roman specialties, such as *saltimbocca alla romana* (veal and sage cooked in Marsala and butter). Various grilled meat and fish dishes are also on offer.

Cecilia Metella's signature dish, *scrigno alla Cecilia*, is allegedly inspired by the tower of the mausoleum, and has become so famous that it has made it into several cookery books as a top pasta recipe. In Italian, a *scrigno* is a container that contains precious objects—for example, a jewelry box. Here, the "jewel" of *scrigno alla Cecilia* is served in terracotta bowls—a rich bake of green capellini pasta, cream, and mozzarella, layered with crepes and covered in tomato sauce and thinly sliced prosciutto. **CK**

⬆ A traditional dish of *saltimbocca alla romana.*

Al Ristoro degli Angeli | Classic Roman cooking

with plenty of modern twists

Location Rome **Signature dish** *Cacio e pepe* | ❷❷

> *"The vibe and decor are old-style French bistro, but the food is resolutely Italian."*

Time Out

⤒ A plate of *cacio e pepe* pasta, a Roman classic.

This former prewar grocery store on a street corner in the up-and-coming district of Garbatella has been reborn as an acclaimed combination of traditional trattoria and chic modern bistro. Garbatella used to be a workers' district that was built up in the 1920s. Recently, it has become more gentrified, and many restaurants and clubs have sprung up.

Right opposite the revamped Palladium theater, Al Ristoro degli Angeli was one of the first new ventures—and it is still renowned as one of the best. Despite its acclaim, it has a warm, friendly atmosphere, which is helped by the decor of period wooden furniture, pictures, and books about the history of the Garbatella district. The restaurant owners even organize a walking tour of the area every Sunday morning.

Chef Federico Sparaco's menu is a mix of modern ideas and Roman classic recipes, with a heavy emphasis on organic ingredients. So you will find dishes such as fried calamari with *passatina di ceci* (chickpea puree) or *straccetti di maiale* (sautéed strips of pork) flavored with thyme, lemon, and toasted almonds. There are some flourishes such as zucchini flowers stuffed with ricciola (amberjack) or fish stew with couscous, offset by homely dishes including *patate della garbatella* (traditional roast potatoes) or *semifreddo* for dessert.

The house speciality is a version of the classic Roman *cacio e pepe* pasta: the pasta is simply flavored with black pepper and pecorino cheese, and in Sparaco's hands ends up forming a crunchy crust on top. Combined with a small but interesting wine list, and some trendy design touches of quotations painted on the walls, it all makes for a popular dining experience, and the small restaurant is packed with locals most nights. **SH**

Il Tempio di Iside |

Top seafood in smart surroundings

Location Rome   **Signature dish** *Spaghetti al riccio* |
🩸🩸🩸

Il Tempio di Iside near the Colosseum is the place where Romans head to eat good fresh seafood. It is known in particular for its starters of raw fish and its oysters. Owner Francesco Tripodi is aware that his clients rely on being able to dine on seaside-quality fish, so he drives to two fish markets daily to ensure the finest catch. Il Tempio di Iside's decor is a mix of old and new, with neutral colors and modern furnishings that complement the stonewall interior, with its vaulted ceiling and series of stone arches. In warm weather, guests can dine alfresco.

The antipasti starters vary according to the catch of the day and may consist of raw, hot, or cold dishes, including *tartare di tonno* (tuna tartare), *carpaccio di gamberi* (shrimp carpaccio), and *orecchie di Venere* (abalone). Among the pasta dishes on offer are *spaghetti al riccio* (with sea urchins), *scialatielli con uova di Sanpietro e scampi* (long, flat-sided spaghetti with John Dory roe and shrimp), and *fusilli napoletani con pomodori ciliegini* (fusilli pasta Neapolitan-style with cherry tomatoes). Main courses change constantly. Desserts may include *cassata* (ricotta cake) and stuffed ricotta *cannoli*. The food is tasty and the portions are generous—you could easily make a meal from the antipasti alone

The atmosphere is lively and when large groups of Italians eat here, it verges on the boisterous. The restaurant is busy throughout the day, attracting a lunchtime crowd of businessmen. At any time, it is advisable to make a reservation to be sure to get a table. Given that Il Tempio di Iside is mainly frequented by locals rather than tourists, it might be worth brushing up on your restaurant Italian, especially the names of various fish and shellfish, to confidently navigate the menu and get the most out of the experience. **CK**

Renato e Luisa |

Discover culinary magic in this trattoria

Location Rome   **Signature dish** *Cacio e pepe; fiori di zucca* | 🩸🩸

It is not easy to find the entrance to Renato Astrologo's understated restaurant, Renato e Luisa. The unassuming doorway is located in a small lane off Largo Argentina near the Pantheon, in the heart of Rome. Inside, at first it may seem like any other Roman trattoria, with its dark wooden ceiling and wall paneling, high shelves of wine bottles, and hanging display of copper pans. The atmosphere is noisy and friendly rather than trendy.

Then the food starts arriving, and shatters all preconceptions. Renato's starters might include a small tower of potato, dyed black with squid ink, standing in a splash of bright green pesto and contrasting red cherry tomato slices, and topped by a

---

> *"A favorite among in-the-know Romans, this backstreet trattoria is always packed."*
>
> Lonely Planet

---

loop of octopus tentacle. Or perhaps a dish of breaded and fried tuna and sardine balls served on pureed celeriac and baby spinach. It quickly becomes apparent that this is no simple trattoria. In fact, many reviewers cite Renato's food as their favorite in the capital. That's some accolade for a tiny restaurant with seriously cheap house wine.

The small but daily changing menu is still firmly based in trattoria territory, offering exquisite versions of classics, but breaking new ground with many dishes. Salmon, for example, will be served with pasta and chicory and a slither of melted provolone cheese. Smoked tuna salad comes with melon and linguine carbonara is served with truffles. **SH**

Osteria La Carbonara | Classic family cooking in a Roman osteria

Location Rome **Signature dish** Spaghetti carbonara | ❸❸

"Generous portions of traditional homemade pastas … the experience here is never dull."

cntraveler.com

A plate of spaghetti carbonara in this lively old restaurant has become one of the ultimate visitor experiences in the Italian capital, and tourists are often found lining up outside long before it opens. But there is a lot more to La Carbonara than its namesake pasta dish. This typical osteria was founded in 1906, and its unashamedly old-fashioned kitchen still serves a range of Roman classics, such as *cacio e pepe* (cheese and pepper) pasta, homemade potato gnocchi, baccalà (cod), and pasta with pistachio and tomato.

It is a family restaurant, run in true Italian style with mother Teresa Rossi in charge of the kitchen and her husband, son, and daughter working alongside. Located in the picturesque Campo de' Fiori, from the outside, it first appears to be just another humble bar, although there is a large shaded area for eating outside. Once you enter, it quickly becomes obvious how popular the place is: the walls are covered in graffiti and cartoons praising the restaurant. The simple wooden tables are covered with paper tablecloths, and customers sit under entire hams dangling from the vaulted brick ceiling. Upstairs is almost a different world, with its smart dining room in minimalist decor, boasting views across the square below—but for the truly authentic atmosphere, stay with the throng downstairs.

It is certainly a bustling place to eat, and a great opportunity to try traditional dishes, expertly cooked with the best and freshest ingredients: the house *frittura*, a selection of battered vegetables including pumpkin, eggplant, and artichoke, or the deep-fried artichokes with stuffed zucchini flowers. If you do opt for the classic carbonara, which originated in Rome, it definitely won't disappoint: the pasta is cooked typically al dente and the creamy egg, cheese, and bacon sauce is generously topped with grated Parmesan. **SH**

⬆ The star dish—spaghetti carbonara.

Ristochicco | Where Vatican priests go for lunch

Location Rome **Signature dish** Rigatoni norcina | ❸❸

"Tourist restaurants disgrace and degrade the best cuisine in the world, damaging the image of our country," writes Alexander Vaccini, son of the Ristochicco owner, on his blog. And when you visit this family-run restaurant in a busy cobbled street near the Vatican, you see a sign outside that announces in no uncertain terms that they serve "no pizza, no lasagne, no sandwich, no house wine." The menu also educates any visitors who are brave enough to enter about proper Italian dining etiquette: Ristochicco will not serve cappuccino with pasta or make up separate bills.

This somewhat strict attitude is redeemed by the high quality of the food and service, which explains why Ristochicco is a local favorite—even priests from the Vatican come here for a plate of pasta—and, ironically, also with visitors in search of an authentic Italian restaurant among the countless tourist venues. This is Rome's most determinedly local restaurant. A few tables are placed under an awning and some hanging flower baskets for dining in the summer; inside, the simple dining room is traditional and cozy. Tables are small, set close together, and covered with characteristic red-and-white checked linen. The ceiling is high and beamed, the brick walls are lined with dark cupboards full of wine, and the floor is made up of bare red tiles.

Chef and owner Roberto Vaccini's reasonably priced menu offers classic Roman fare, including al dente spaghetti carbonara and *cacio e pepe*, mixed bruschetta, and the speciality of rigatoni norcina (pasta with a creamy mushroom sauce and walnuts). He is also interested in reinterpreting ancient Roman recipes (look out for the "tuna of Marco Aurelio"). In addition to the classics, other popular dishes on the menu include bucatini pasta with mussels and pecorino, gnocchi with sausage, and meatballs in a black truffle and porcini sauce. **SH**

"Our philosophy is to reproduce the dishes belonging to the papal and Roman tradition."

Ristochicco website

⬆ Ristochicco is the go-to place for authentic food.

Il Cormorano | The pick of the local catch

Location Castelsardo   **Signature dish** Spaghetti with lobster "alla castellanese" | ❺❺❺❺

"While you savor your meal, you may hear the locals speak in their ancient Catalan dialect."

Il Cormorano website

⬆ Spaghetti with lobster is a popular choice at Il Cormorano.

Considering the excellence of the cuisine on offer, Il Cormorano is a remarkably unobtrusive restaurant. Bearing in mind the breathtaking panorama of the local coastline, with its jagged black cliffs and crag-top castle, you may be slightly reluctant to head to the quiet backstreet where it is located. A brief glimpse at the dishes around you, however, will soon banish any doubts—Il Cormorano not only serves incomparable Sardinian cuisine; it does so with a rare level of style and panache.

Praised for good reason, the restaurant's chef, Diana Serra, is fanatical about the freshness of her fish, selecting it personally from the nearby harbor's morning catch and carefully adapting the menu to the seasons. Seafood crudités are sensational and the rustic local pasta shapes served with gurnard, squid and zucchini flowers, mussels, shrimp, or her signature lobster "alla castellanese" are all equally tempting. These delights are followed by exciting main courses, such as hand-fished red snapper with chestnuts and wild porcini, grilled squid with pumpkin and mushrooms, or a simple fried or grilled fish fillet from the day's catch.

The decor pays a coy tribute to its seafood menu, with a tasteful combination of lobster pot lampshades, brightly colored walls, and draped fishing nets. The atmosphere is discreet and relaxed, with stylish, contemporary tableware and comfortable seating; in the summer, you can also dine on the veranda. The restaurant's owner, Renato Pinna, is an entertaining and patient host and is only too happy to explain the Sardinian specialties and the impressive wine list, which boasts over 350 labels and includes many bottles from local, niche production wineries. And if you have not yet tasted *sebadas*, the intriguing Sardinian cheese-filled pastry dessert served with local honey, then this is the place to do so. **DJS**

Peppe Zullo | Simple food with the freshest ingredients in rural Puglia

Location Orsara di Puglia   **Signature dish** Borage Parmigiana; rigatoni norcina | ❸❸

It is impossible to eat at Peppe Zullo's and not be aware of the man himself. When Peppe gave his name to the restaurant, he did so firmly believing that every detail of every meal was his responsibility—and the restaurant is indeed an extension of his enthusiastic, larger-than-life personality. Peppe is never far from the stove or tending the small piece of land with its gardens that provides most of the ingredients he needs for his wonderful dishes. His cooking involves magical transformation, but is straightforward and unfussy at the same time. When you visit, you may even get to see him in action in the open kitchen.

This is undoubtedly the place to go for simple, uncomplicated food, and it makes sense: the freshness of the produce means the flavors are clean and vibrant. Alongside the vegetables, Peppe also leaves lots of space for wild plants to thrive in the gardens—for instance tiny but flavorsome wild peas. He also cultivates a huge array of herbs, many of which you're unlikely to have ever heard of, let alone seen elsewhere.

The growing of fruit and vegetables and rearing of livestock is done with an all-consuming enthusiasm, as is the cultivation of superb olive oil and wine. Depending on the time of year, you could be offered a choice of dishes such as wild asparagus with Peppe's own olive oil, pasta with beans and sivoni greens, cardoncelli mushrooms, caciocavallo cheese with pumpkin jam and honey, or local lamb with roasted potatoes.

There is not much served in the restaurant that does not come from Peppe's own production; but, when he needs larger quantities of produce, he sources it locally—very locally, in fact: every year he enlists the help of his neighbors to make passata from their tomatoes so that he has a sufficient supply for his restaurant for the whole year. **CS**

"Peppe takes all the raw materials from his gardens ... a meal becomes a journey of discovery."

Peppe Zullo website

⬆ The freshest of fresh ingredients feature on the menu, as seen in the signature borage dish.

Antichi Sapori | A culinary revelation in a rural Pugliese hamlet

Location Montegrosso **Signature dish** "Burnt wheat" orecchiette with fava beans, black olives, and ricotta | ❸❸

"An original trattoria decorated in rural style and serving regional specialities such as orecchiette."

Michelin Guide

⬆ Be sure to try the orecchiette here.

To get a table at Pietro Zito's Antichi Sapori, booking is absolutely essential. Given that it is located in a small hamlet and quite some distance from the nearest major town, that requirement gives an indication of the restaurant's culinary reputation. A casual space serving simple, seasonal, and traditional food, it is also good value for money. This is partly because a significant amount of the produce that is used in the kitchen travels only a few feet from Pietro's own gardens—many of the vegetables on your plate will have been plucked just hours before you get to eat them.

The food is shaped by the local culture and farming traditions; there is always some deep green extra virgin olive oil on the table as an essential condiment for pretty much everything. In a region where antipasti are taken very seriously, the selection of starter dishes is the stuff of culinary legend. Depending on the time of year, you might choose from fried zucchini with mint, ricotta with caramelized celery, or perhaps artisan-produced capocollo. Leave room for the pasta dishes, though, especially the Pugliese orecchiette ("little ears") pasta with vegetables or legumes, such as dried fava beans, which are also used for *puré di fave*, another regional favorite. Follow with a secondo, perhaps excellent veal, pork, and fennel sausages. There is a variety of desserts available and coffee is served with caramelized almonds.

Pietro and his restaurant are a galvanizing force behind various community food initiatives. Every August, for example, a big party is organized where everyone turns their tomato harvest into passata for the coming year. It is this loyal support of the neighborhood along with local artisan cheese and salumi makers that not only guarantees excellent food at Antichi Sapori, but a very warm and welcoming atmosphere. **CS**

Ristorante Bufi | A secluded and peaceful setting for expertly cooked food

Location Molfetta **Signature dish** *Ciambotto* (fish soup) | ❸❸❸

Ristorante Bufi in the center of the coastal town of Molfetta may have an unprepossessing exterior, but venture over the threshold and you will find some of the best cooking in town. Salvatore Bufi, who was born and bred here, particularly excels with dishes featuring local fish and vegetables, but there are many other joys on offer, the excellent bread basket with homemade grissini, for example. The very best ingredients are prepared in a simple style and served with an admirable lack of pretension.

The menu itself has no fancy wording, just a straightforward description of what comprises each dish: octopus salad with red onion, celery, and olives; green beans with salt cod and tomatoes; roasted eggplant parmigiana with pinenuts, pancetta, and pecorino; salad of roasted cuttlefish with zucchini and mint; and tagliolini with sea urchins. Salvatore's signature dish expresses his enthusiasm for local ingredients and ancient recipes: *ciambotto*, the traditional fish soup of Molfetta, is turned into an exquisite dish. Originally a humble meal prepared with small, inexpensive fish added to stock, olive oil, garlic, parsley, and tomatoes, it has evolved over time and now includes more pricey fish such as scampi and scorpion fish; it is also made more filling with the addition of broken spaghetti.

In the summer, a secluded and shaded courtyard makes for wonderful outside dining away from the bustle and traffic of the town. When it is too cold for sitting outside, the clean white interior with its vaulted ceiling offers a haven of peacefulness in which to escape the world for the duration of your meal. To finish, you may want to opt for a carefully chosen selection of cheeses, or sample the fine desserts—perhaps a few scoops of the delicious homemade ice cream, which comes in many tempting flavors: vanilla, mandarin, hazelnut and rum, or chocolate and cardamom. **CS**

> "Three factors are key to Bufi's success: very fresh fish, seasonal greens, and exceptional olive oil."

amioparere.com

⬆ The restaurant's signature dish of *ciambotto*.

Don Alfonso 1890 | A splendid taste of southern Italy

Location Sant'Agata sui Due Golfi **Signature dish** "Vesuvio di rigatoni" | ❸❸❸❸

"… a luxurious enclave in the heart of Sant'Agata. Dishes are made from excellent produce."

Michelin Guide

⬆ The elegant facade of Don Alfonso 1890.

➡ The "vesuvio di rigatoni" is a feast for the eyes.

Don Alfonso 1890 is located in the sleepy village of Sant'Agata sui Due Golfi, which is perched on a picturesque promontory between the Gulf of Naples and the Gulf of Salerno. The kitchen is headed by Alfonso Iaccarino, the founder's grandson (named after his grandfather), and his son Ernesto, with Alfonso's wife Livia running the front of house. This is a family business that was originally a simple family hotel; the restaurant in its current form started in 1982 and now holds two Michelin stars.

The emphasis is on local cuisine and produce. Many of the ingredients come directly from the family farm, "Le Peracciole," established in 1986 a few miles away on the coast near Positano and opposite Capri. The superb quality of the local ingredients is evident in a simple tomato focaccia, which is airily light, with just the right amount of salt, and generously topped with a stunning tomato sauce. These tomatoes are grown on the farm, and picked and brought to the restaurant every day to ensure perfect freshness. A meal might include delights such as lobster tempura—perfectly cooked lobster in a crisp tempura batter, served with a lemon, orange, and honey sauce on the side, the streaks of dark, sweet, and sour sauce providing the right balance of flavors. The "vesuvio di rigatoni" is a very popular choice and is as pretty to look at as it is flavorful to eat.

The wine cellar in the basement is worth seeing—and not just because of its vast 25,000 bottle collection: the cellar comprises a series of chambers that date back to the fifteenth century, with a stone staircase descending down a series of flights, with wine bottles at each level, and leading to an old well that these days is used for aging cheese.

Service is of a very high standard, with staff genuinely passionate about the food that is served. This restaurant is a delightful place to sample the very best of Italian produce and hospitality. **AH**

L'Antica Pizzeria da Michele | Simply great pizza in the heart of Naples

Location Naples **Signature dish** Pizza Margherita | 💲

In 1870, Salvatore Condurro opened a pizzeria in Naples and thus started a tradition of making some of Italy's most sought-after pizza. Thirty-six years later, his son Michele moved the family business to a different site and re-branded it as L'Antica Pizzeria da Michele. Since then, this tiny eatery in the heart of ancient Naples, with its marble tabletops, communal wooden seating, and thin yet ever-present cloud of yeast in the air, has been wowing both local and visiting foodies.

More than a century of continued success (and minimal innovation) suggests that they know how to do one thing, and do it well. In fact, two things: customers may choose between the Margherita (with tomato, basil, and mozzarella) and the Marinara (with tomato, oregano, and garlic), the only options available. For the full Napoli experience, go for the classic Margherita—ask for "doppia" (double) mozzarella—and marvel at the ever so slightly charred edges of the gummy crust that overlaps the rim of your twelve-inch plate, as the warm sauce mingles with the melted fresh cheese. This is the ultimate Margherita. Made with "Type 00" wheat flour and topped with a sauce made from San Marzano tomatoes grown on the slopes of Mount Vesuvius, cow's milk mozzarella from the nearby farms of Agerola, seed oil, water, yeast, and sea salt, it is a study in simplicity.

But, naturally, the perfect pizza depends on the skill of the pizza chefs, and what they do with those few essential ingredients: kneading the dough and leavening it, stoking the flames in the wood-fired oven to exactly the right temperature, positioning the pizza to maximize the baking time, and knowing precisely how long to keep them in the oven—the result is arguably the best pizza on the planet. **CO**

⬆ Pizza perfection at L'Antica Pizzeria da Michele.

Torre del Saracino | Innovative cuisine on the Amalfi coast

Location Vico Equense   **Signature dish** Rum baba | ❺❺❺❺

Torre del Saracino is situated on the coast in Vico Equense, a small town a few miles from Sorrento, with a splendid view over the Gulf of Naples. The restaurant is built in and around an ancient watchtower (the "torre"), and boasts an extensive wine cellar opposite the main dining room. It has become a key culinary destination on the Amalfi coast, with the technically skilled cooking making the most of the terrific local seafood. Established in 1992, the restaurant has earned two Michelin stars. Chef Gennaro Esposito's cuisine emphasizes the local seafood and has some modern touches.

You might want to start your meal with a nibble of locally caught amberjack, served on tomato cream and a light basil sauce—a simple but wonderfully flavorsome dish. Esposito's skill is also evident in rabbit ravioli with caramelized onions: the pasta parcels have a lovely texture and the onions provide a hint of balancing sweetness. Red mullet, another terrific

dish, is prettily presented: finely chopped up with spinach, bell peppers, and zucchini, then shaped into a neat block topped with mixed leaves.

Desserts are a strong suit of the restaurant. For a fruity finish, you might want to try the excellent mandarin sorbet with its delicate color and deep flavor. But the unmissable sweet speciality of the house is the pretty rum baba, served with wild strawberries and *crema pasticcera* (custard) rather than Chantilly cream. The baba is incredibly light and moist, with just the right amount of rum.

The petit fours, often served as an afterthought elsewhere, are also truly classy here: they might include a moist almond cake, flaky pastry rolls filled with cream, miniature mixed fruit tarts with superb red fruits and smooth *crema pasticcera*, or excellent hazelnut macaroons. **AH**

⬆ A tempting dessert of rum baba with wild strawberries.

Da Adolfo | A boat ride and simple food on the beach

Location Positano   **Signature dish** Grilled mozzarella on a lemon leaf | 💲💲

To get to Da Adolfo, you need to take a shuttle boat from Positano—look out for the red fish bearing its name on a mast at the beachside jetty. A gentle twenty-minute ride then carries you away from the tourist frenzy in town to a small cove with just two restaurants.

On a sunny day, it is best to get there with plenty of time to spare before lunch and enough time for another break before you return, because for a nominal fee you can hire a sun lounger and relax with a book, or go for a swim. What better way is there to work up an appetite? There are some showers and changing facilities if you want to spruce yourself up before your meal; but, in any case, the vibe is casual—just as it should be on the beach.

With its delightful terrace and tiny kitchen in full view up several rocky steps, Da Adolfo is a wonderful spot. The joy of eating fresh fish with the salty smell of the sea, and the sound of the crashing waves

and happy swimmers in the background, is hard to beat. And the food itself is fantastic.

Simplicity is key: uncomplicated fish and vegetable combinations for pasta and grilled fish with squeaky fresh salads feature on the day's menu, which is chalked on a blackboard: options may include marinated anchovies, grilled mozzarella on a lemon leaf, pasta with clams and pumpkin, or the simple yet perfect catch of the day, seasoned with olive oil and fragrant Amalfi lemons. In this beautiful setting, and with such wonderful ingredients, who would want anything more complex?

After lunch, it is time for a coffee and perhaps a limoncello, or even a brief snooze on the sand, before you take the shuttle back to Positano. Great food and a wonderfully relaxing time sandwiched in between two boat rides— just perfect. **CS**

⬆ Mozzarella on a lemon leaf is the house speciality.

Da Tuccino | Culinary wonders by the Adriatic

Location Polignano a Mare   **Signature dish** Carpaccio of scorpion fish with tuna prosciutto | ❸❸❸

Sitting on Da Tuccino's bright and airy terrace in the beautiful coastal town of Polignano a Mare, overlooking the Adriatic with nothing but a marina interrupting the expanse of blue in front of you while you enjoy a plate of fish, would be enough to keep most people happy. But Da Tuccino has a special delight up its sleeve: *pesce crudo* (raw fish). Foodies travel from far and wide to enjoy this speciality at this restaurant.

Forget what you know about sashimi or "raw fish for beginners," as the locals call it, and immerse yourself in a gastronomic tradition that in recent years has soared in popularity. Located on the outskirts of town and run by the charming and efficient Centrone family, this is a destination restaurant for those in the know. To get the most out of your dining experience, rather than choose from the menu, you should go up to the fresh fish display and join the animated discussion with staff over the latest catch,

or just watch the enthusiastic and knowledgeable regulars debate their preferences. The raw antipasti alone may be enough for an entire meal.

Should you feel nervous about consuming raw fish—many people do—then fear not, nobody will force you. Whatever is served raw will also be cooked, should you wish, and prepared with conviction and passion. In fact, even the most ardent crudo fans can reach saturation point and might send raw mussels, shrimps, or octopus to the kitchen, to be promptly returned in cooked form.

Among the excellent cooked dishes are orecchiette, often served with clams and zucchini flowers, long pasta with frutti di mare, or simply a fillet of whatever fish takes your fancy, grilled and served with a salad and some fresh, local olive oil. Be sure to also try a *sgroppino* cocktail. **CS**

⬆ Fish dishes are beautifully presented with flowers.

Cumpà Cosimo | The gold standard of Italian classics

Location Ravello **Signature dish** *Assaggio di primi* | 💲💲

High above the Amalfi Coast, in the beautiful town of Ravello, Netta Bottone has presided over her family's trattoria, Cumpà Cosimo, since the late 1960s. Netta (nobody calls her Signora Bottone) produces dishes of what might be called typical Italian fare—but her renditions are the gold standard.

In Netta's kitchen, straightforward cheese ravioli, spaghetti with tomato sauce, or pizza can inspire song: the food she prepares is delicious yet delicate. Netta usually mingles with the diners and makes suggestions; the uninitiated may think she is telling them what to order, but she knows what is best on any given day—and that is what she will recommend.

The secret is that Netta picks the best ingredients available, and she is lucky to live in a place that has some of the most sublime tomatoes, lemons, and vegetables at hand for most of the year. The sea provides a daily catch of wonderful fish and seafood and the excellent beef and magnificent mozzarella

comes from just inland. All the pasta dishes are so good that having just one means missing out on the others. But there is a solution: the *assaggio di primi*, a tasting selection of up to seven different pastas. Many are based on tomato, mozzarella, and ricotta, but each dish manages to exalt these ingredients in subtly different ways.

For mains, you might want to try the succulent steak with local tomatoes, greens, and potatoes from nearby Avellino that are considered the nation's best. The famed Amalfi lemons are the star of many desserts, including cakes, gelato, and the lovely house limoncello— perfect for rounding off your meal.

Red and white wines from Ravello combine well with Netta's food, and you can also sample excellent regional wines made from Aglianico, Coda di Volpe, Fiano, Greco, and Taurasi grapes. **FP**

⬆ Cumpà Cosimo is a Ravello institution.

Cibus | One of the best cheese boards in Italy

Location Ceglie Messapica   **Signature dish** Fettucce of Mennelle olives with fava beans and pecorino | ❸❸

It used to be a challenge for nonlocals to find Cibus, but since it has become a gastronomic institution, clear signs from Piazza Plebiscito in the center of Ceglie Messapica have been put up, indicating which narrow alleyways of the old town you need to take. And thank goodness for that. Lillino Sillibello's casual restaurant is a must for anybody who is interested in good Pugliese food, and it is a real mecca for cheese lovers. A table on the covered outside terrace is a treat in the summer, when you can benefit from the cool air; in the winter, you can sit close to the cheese store inside and take a closer look at the goods.

Lillino makes an impressive number of excellent and varied cheeses himself as well as sourcing some from the best artisan producers, and can talk you through any detail you'd like to know about them: how they were made, who made them, and what best to drink with them. But before you reach the cheese course, being in Puglia, you need to factor in some serious antipasti—and the Cibus antipasti platter is renowned. On it you may find a small grain salad with zucchini, carrots, bell peppers, and cacioricotta cheese shavings, a vegetable mix in a dressing made with Coratina olive oil, celery cream with capocollo from nearby Martina Franca, and—if you are very lucky and come at the right time of year—stracciatella cheese with grated Murgia truffles.

After that, move on to fava bean puree with seasonal vegetables, spaghettini with wild asparagus, or linguine with organic chard and cicerchia beans (an antique and recently rediscovered legume), and then perhaps on to rabbit with tomatoes and olives, roast pork with lampagioni bulbs, or a platter of mixed roast meat. Be sure to save room for one of the best cheese boards in Italy and the superb fig ice cream. **CS**

⬆ A taste of Puglia, tucked away in Ceglie Messapica.

Antica Focacceria San Francesco | Palermitano classics

Location Palermo **Signature dish** *Sarde a beccafico* | 💲💲

Adjoining a piazza opposite the thirteenth-century Church of San Francesco di Assisi, Antica Focacceria San Francesco is closely linked to its ecclesiastic neighbor. In 1834, the church gave one of its buildings to the *monsù* (the princes' chef), Antonino Alaimo, who opened a restaurant serving traditional Palermitano peasant food. It proved popular among the aristocracy and elite. Since then, distinguished names including Luigi Pirandello, Sophia Loren, and even Hillary Clinton have dined here. Perhaps the most notable customer was Giuseppe Garibaldi, who visited in 1860 en route to the mainland on his quest to form a united Italy. Alaimo's descendants, the Conticello family, renovated the restaurant in 1902, and it is now run by brothers Fabio and Vincenzo.

The building boasts a Liberty-style decor and is divided into two parts: upstairs you find the ritzy Sala Florio, downstairs is a self-service area with tiled walls and floors, iron chairs, wooden benches, and marble-topped tables. It is usually full of locals and in the summer guests can eat outside in the piazza.

There are numerous dishes on offer from pasta and salads to meat and fish. The menu boasts Palermitano specialties such as *pani cà meusa*, a sandwich made with sweet focaccia bread, boiled calf's spleen, and grated caciocavallo cheese, which may be an acquired taste for some. Other local fare includes potato croquettes, light panelle chickpea fritters, and a soft goat's cheese salad. The *sarde a beccafico* (sardines stuffed with bread crumbs, pine nuts, raisins, sugar, and lemon juice) is a triumph of complementary flavors and textures. Desserts include cannoli, cassata, and pistachio mousse.

Another reason to visit is to support the courageous Vincenzo, who made a stand against the mafia by refusing to pay protection money. **CK**

⬆ A venerable Palermo eatery with a local following.

Ristorante Il Saraceno | Dining on the rocks

Location Cefalù **Signature dish** Fresh grilled tuna | 💲💲

The picturesque fishing port of Cefalù on the northern coast of Sicily, underneath the glowering crags of the La Rocca mountain, has become a tourist destination in recent years, as much for its sandy beach as the beauty of the Norman cathedral in the main square. Despite the influx of visitors, it is still possible to eat well at local restaurants, and among the best is the Ristorante Il Saraceno. Although it appears modest from the outside, the restaurant's veranda and terrace offer spectacular views across the Tyrrhenian Sea.

The service is prompt and the staff are pleasant even when temperatures go above a sweltering 110°F (43°C) degrees at the height of summer. The menu is varied, offering pasta and pizza, as well as various meat and fish dishes. Classic Sicilian fare is the order of the day, including bruschetta, *caponata* (a dish of eggplant and olives), spaghetti with *vongole* (clams) or with *ricci di mare* (sea urchins), grilled swordfish,

and grilled sea bass. The grilled tuna, available only when in season, is particularly notable.

There are numerous restaurants scattered along the shore of Cefalù with views out over the sea, but what makes Il Saraceno truly special is its innovative layout. Dining at sea usually involves a boat ride, but for those who prefer keeping their feet on land, this restaurant offers the next best thing—the terrace has forty tables extending along a wooden gangway across the rocks and leading right out to the water.

As a romantic spot to sip an aperitivo, enjoy a leisurely meal, watch the sunset, or pass the time under the beautiful night sky while listening to the sound of the waves, this is hard to beat. Given the lovely, unusual ambience, booking a table in advance is advisable during the busy summer months right up until September. **CK**

⬆ Watch the sunset from your table on the gangway.

Casale Villa Rainò | Artisan cooking on a Sicilian farm

Location Gangi **Signature dish** *Stigliole* | 🟢🟢

"See cheese- and sausage-making, olive-pressing, and many more artisan traditions first hand ..."

Condé Nast Traveller

⬆ The building has been restored with loving care.

Situated in the valley of Mount Marone in the heart of Sicily, Casale Villa Rainò is surrounded by the wooded countryside and the mountains of the Parco Naturale Regionale delle Madonie, a few miles from the pretty medieval hilltop town of Gangi. This rural retreat is the result of a labor of love on behalf of its owners Aldo and Nina Conte. The couple restored a prestigious nineteenth-century farmhouse complete with large grounds that include an olive grove. The house was once home to the Li Destri, a noble family, and hosted famous guests including Benito Mussolini and a Russian tsar. Nowadays, it is open to ordinary folk as an agriturismo and restaurant, renovated carefully with period furniture. Guests can take part in cookery classes and observe centuries-old agricultural practices.

The restaurant, with its stone walls and ceramic-tile floor, has a homely, rustic feel. The food epitomizes Sicilian country cooking and a meal soon turns into a veritable feast: a normal offering includes several starters, two pasta dishes, and two meat dishes of grilled or roasted meats and sausages. What is on the menu changes seasonally, as all dishes are made from local produce, from *involtini di melanzane* (eggplant rolls) to *caponata* (eggplant stew) and creamy *risotto alla zucca* (risotto with pumpkin). Guests can sample ricotta cheese so fresh that it is still warm on the plate, or try regional delicacies such as crumbly *panelle* (fried chickpea fritters) and tender *stigliole* (grilled kebabs made from lamb's intestine), served with lemon and salt. All of this can be washed down with a few glasses of local wine.

To wind up the meal, there are usually several dessert courses to choose from; you might want to try the light *cannoli*, sample some sweet, pear-shaped caciocavallo cheese, or order one of the huge plates of wonderfully fresh fruit. Finish it off in true Italian style—with a tiny shot of dark espresso. This is rural Sicily at its best. **CK**

Trattoria La Grotta | Fresh seafood in a volcanic seaside grotto

Location Santa Maria La Scala **Signature dish** *Spaghetti al nero delle seppie* | ❺❺

Located in a grotto of black volcanic lava rock, Trattoria La Grotta is run by Carmelo Strano, known to locals as "Don Carmelo," and his son, Rosario. Carmelo is the third generation of his family to take charge of the restaurant in the tiny Sicilian fishing village of Santa Maria La Scala, north of Catania. To get there, it is a 15-minute stroll from Acireale on the "Riviera of the Cyclops." Walking down to the coast, through a nature reserve, is just enough to build up an appetite while you take in the spectacular views of the Ionian Sea.

Trattoria La Grotta is renowned for its excellent seafood and fish—the house specialities are *insalata di mare* (seafood salad with lemon and olive oil), mixed fried fish, fish soup, pasta with clams, grilled fish, and *spaghetti al nero delle seppie* (spaghetti with cuttlefish ink). Guests can choose dishes from the menu or take a look at the catch of the day, which may include lobster or shrimp, and is displayed in a freezer tray beside the open-plan kitchen, with its whitewashed grotto walls. (Fresh fish is charged by weight as is common throughout Italy.) The spaghetti with cuttlefish ink is superb, as is the grilled fish, and it is fun to eat in the dining room surrounded by the jagged black rock of the grotto walls. In the summer, of course, it is possible to eat outside. The restaurant is usually busy, frequented by Sicilians having a lazy lunch out or enjoying a celebratory meal with family and friends.

In fact, Trattoria La Grotta is mainly a place for the locals because Santa Maria La Scala is a fishing village rather than a tourist destination, and visitors may well see fishermen repairing their nets in a nearby grotto. This is a charming little restaurant in a very pretty location and it is well worth a visit for a real taste of Sicilian life as well as very good food. It is advisable to make a reservation; the space fills up fast with eager customers. **CK**

"The dining area is atmospherically set in a cave ... [and] the food is superb.

Lonely Planet

⤒ Santa Maria La Scala is a working fishing village.

Al Mazarì | Sicilian fish dishes and sweet delights at a family-run restaurant

Location Syracuse **Signature dish** *Spaghetti cu la sàissa e li milinciani fritti* | ❸❸

Al Mazarì is located in Ortigia, a small island within the Sicilian town of Syracuse, on a side street off the main square—it can be missed easily, which would be a pity. Opened in 2006, it is run by the Roccafiorita family who moved here from Mazara del Vallo in the faraway province of Trapani on the southwest coast of Sicily. The menu consists of classic local dishes plus Trapani specialities with Arabic influences, such as couscous.

The sensation on entering the lobby and adjoining small dining room is that you are in an elegant home complete with chandeliers, oil paintings, and various knickknacks. There is a relaxed ambience and jazz music plays softly, never intrusively, in the background. Ludovico, the head of the family, welcomes guests with his son, maître d' Enzo, while his wife, Silvana, works in the kitchen, aided by her other son, sommelier Peppe.

Starters may include vegetable dishes, which vary according to the seasons—perhaps grilled eggplant, bell peppers, or wild fennel. The fish starters may include marinated swordfish, breaded mussels, or juicy grilled shrimp. For main courses choose from excellent *sàiddi a beccaficu* (boned sardines in bread crumbs with grapes, pine nuts, and cherry tomatoes) and flavor-packed *spaghetti cu la sàissa e li milinciani fritti* (homemade spaghetti with sweet cherry tomatoes and fried eggplant). Desserts change daily and are to die for: go for the traditional cassata, a tangy lemon tart, or the surprisingly light tiramisu.

Enzo is on hand to suggest aperitivi, wines, and liqueurs. It is a good idea to take his advice, because he knows the right drinks to complement your choices, whether red Nero d'Avola or sweet Malvasia dessert wine. Round off the meal with a zing: espresso is served with some grappa on the rim of the cup. **CK**

Osteria da Mariano | Classic regional cooking in a lively atmosphere

Location Syracuse **Signature dish** *Pasta alle mandorle* | ❸❸

Osteria da Mariano is a real find. Snuggled in a side street in Syracuse's Ortigia, it is where the locals go for celebratory dinners and lazy lunches. The menu is based on local produce from the surrounding Monti Iblei area, known for its honey, olives, citrus fruit, cheese, and almonds, and changes with the seasons.

Two large, stonewalled rooms are decorated in a rustic fashion, creating an intimate feel; but, for most of the year, it is possible to eat outside in a narrow alley festooned with fairy lights, in a lively atmosphere thanks to the constantly chattering Sicilians and the locale's attentive owner, who often jokes with guests.

Starters include a mixed plate that may feature fresh ricotta, grilled vegetables, bruschetta, caciocavallo

---

"…waiters squeeze past tightly packed tables, dishing out earthy country food to boisterous diners."

Lonely Planet

---

from Ragusa, salami, *impanata* (broccoli pie), and *caponata*. The main courses range from seafood such as octopus, mussels, swordfish, squid, and shrimp to grilled meats, including lamb, veal, rabbit, and pork. Be sure to try the signature dish, *pasta alle mandorle* (pasta with almond sauce): the subtly sweet taste and nutty, creamy texture of the sauce combined with the corkscrew-shaped pasta makes for a memorable dish.

At the end of a meal, guests are likely to be presented with some chunks of *torrone*, a sweet, chewy nougat made with toasted almonds and honey, or *ghiugghiulena* nougat made from honey and sesame seeds, washed down with local liqueur in a plastic cup. **CK**

Terraliva | A charming taste of the Sicilian countryside in an agriturismo restaurant

Location Buccheri **Signature dish** Ravioli with zucchini flowers and sheep ricotta | 💲💲

Terraliva in the Sicilian countryside near the small hilltop town of Buccheri is both an agriturismo and a restaurant. A working farm, it was opened in its current form by Tino Cavarra and Giuseppina Frontino in 2008. Located in a tranquil spot among hills, vineyards, and olive groves, the eighteenth-century farmhouse was built from hand-cut tuff, limestone, and volcanic rock. The restaurant is open both to staying guests and the general public. The stone-arched space has a rustic charm, and the terrace is a pleasant spot for a relaxing meal.

There is no standard menu. Instead, Cavarra offers a daily changing choice of traditional Sicilian dishes selected according to the seasons and using fresh produce from the farm. Terraliva's wines, jellies, fruit, herbs, vegetables, and award-winning olive oil are all used to great effect. Tasty starters such as bruschetta with baby plum tomatoes, pecorino with olive oil, potato croquettes stuffed with mozzarella, zucchini rolls, and spicy olives are an enticing hint of what is to come. Exemplary ingredients are combined in wonderful dishes such as ravioli with zucchini flowers and sheep ricotta with olive oil, toasted bread crumbs, and almonds; breaded beef roulade, stuffed with crispy vegetables; and scamorza cheese accompanied by an orange salad with pine nuts, Pantelleria raisins, and red onion. Desserts include crumbly fresh ricotta in a drizzle of chocolate sauce or superior homemade strawberry ice cream.

Given that there is no set menu, a visit to Terraliva means guests are in for a surprise—but they are unlikely to be disappointed. The staff is friendly, the atmosphere is homely, and the food represents the best of Sicilian cuisine. On a balmy summer's evening, when dinner is accompanied by the chirping song of cicadas, Terraliva truly feels idyllic. **CK**

"The old farmhouse is surrounded by hilly country where you can feel a sense of peace ..."

Terraliva website

⬆ Wines from Terraliva's own vineyards accompany the delicious food.

Il Duomo | A gem of a restaurant in an enchanting Sicilian town

Location Ragusa **Signature dish** Pasta with sea urchins | ❸❸❸

Sicily is undeniably beautiful. But the baroque towns of southeast Sicily are something else altogether—they are ravishing. Ragusa is an exquisite example, all honeyed stone and exuberant ornamentation. Behind the *duomo* (cathedral), in one of the town's most enchanting squares, is this eatery of the same name, owned by chef and local hero Ciccio Sultano.

Many agree that Italian food is at its best when celebrating the glorious ingredients without too much primping and posturing. In his jewel box of a restaurant, Sultano walks the tightrope between letting Sicily's blisteringly good produce (pistachios, tomatoes, almonds, lemons, figs, ricotta and other cheeses, unimpeachable seafood, meat from Nebrodi, and tuna from Marzamemi) speak for itself while also creating complex dishes prepared with intricate technique. He mines the island's history for dishes that may have been long forgotten, often with Spanish or Moorish influences, bringing them back to

life in delicious creations. From the breads baked with heirloom wheat varieties through the limpid local extra virgin olive oil, which somehow manages to taste like concentrated Sicilian tomatoes, to the pasta dishes that unite the thwack of carb satisfaction with preternatural delicacy (if sea urchins are in season, be sure to try them), Sultano's cooking, issued from his postage-stamp sized kitchen, will leave you dazzled. And his take on the island's beloved *cannoli* is a crisp, creamy dream.

Il Duomo's small, interlinked parlors are decorated with antiques and dark "English-style" wallpaper, providing a seductive setting for some of Italy's most creative cooking. Michelin stars aside (and Il Duomo boasts two), Ciccio Sultano stays true to his roots and to his cooking style. Dishes can be paired with excellent wines. **MOL**

⬆ Pasta with tuna roe and lemon verbena.

Federico II | Classic Sicilian cuisine in a medieval setting

Location Ragusa **Signature dish** *Pasta alle sarde* | ❸❸

Federico II is tucked away in the heart of the baroque town of Ragusa, in a peaceful spot adjacent to the Giardino Ibleo, which is featured in the popular TV series *Inspector Montalbano*. During the summer, it is possible to eat on the vine-covered, stonewalled terrace that offers some welcome shade and a great view of the garden.

The restaurant with the regal name is set in a grand old palazzo, with white stone walls and tiled floors. It is named after Frederick II of Hohenstaufen, King of Sicily and Holy Roman Emperor, and the owners have decorated the interior with care to create a medieval ambience with suits of armour, weaponry, and tapestries on display. A small goldfish pond adds a charming, relaxing note.

Federico II is run by a charming husband-and-wife team. The service is warm, welcoming, and friendly. If you have to wait a little while for your order, it is good to know that this is because the food is being cooked with fresh, local produce, and that some bruschetta and various other nibbles will most likely be served while you wait. The menu changes according to the season and focuses on Sicilian and Ragusa classics, such as pappardelle with porcini mushrooms and *coniglio alla stimpirata* (rabbit braised with vegetables). A salad of juicy Sicilian blood-oranges, pungent olive oil, and olives is truly divine, as are the melt-in-the-mouth *cannoli*.

The restaurant's signature dish is the unmissable *pasta alle sarde* (pasta with sardines)—it is outstanding and leaves diners wanting to return to sample it again. The dish is prepared following the classic recipe, with bucatini pasta, sardines, saffron, pine nuts, wild fennel, sultanas, and toasted bread crumbs. Here, the dish is a revelation: a flavorful, sweet, and sour sensation for the taste buds. **CK**

⬆ Be sure to try the signature *pasta alle sarde*.

Ristorante Hosteria delle Grazie | Top-quality pasta and wine

Location Vittoria **Signature dish** *Trafilati al bronzo* pasta | 🟡🟡

It would be easy to miss the delights that Ristorante Hosteria delle Grazie, in the Sicilian town of Vittoria in the provice of Ragusa, has to offer because of its unassuming exterior. But, as with many places in Sicily, a humble entrance is no indication of what may lie inside a building. A simple doorway under an awning reveals a staircase that leads to the restaurant on the first floor. The elegant interior is an impressive example of the Art Nouveau style (known as Liberty in Italy), with its polychrome, floral-patterned tiled floors, frescoed ceilings, and intricate ceramic and glass lamp fittings.

The food is based around typical regional dishes, with a focus on seasonal produce and fresh fish from the nearby fish market at Scoglitti on the Mediterranean coast. But it is the pasta dishes that triumph here, made using the old *trafilati al bronzo* method, whereby the pasta is drawn through a bronze mold rather than one made of Teflon.

Consequently, the texture of the pasta is grainy, not smooth, and the sauce sticks better to the surface, enhancing the flavors.

Of the pasta dishes on the menu, the pennette with *ciliegini* (cherry tomatoes), pesto, and pistachio is a perfect combination of nutty crunch and sweet flavors. Other sauces to consider for your pasta are *nero di seppia* (cuttlefish ink) and fresh ricotta; *capuliato* (a conserve of thick-cut, sun-dried tomatoes and extra virgin olive oil), saffron, and basil; and swordfish, mint, *ciliegini*, and eggplant. Other dishes include pizza and couscous with fish sauce.

Vittoria is renowned for its wine, and the house red is an excellent, smooth Cerasuolo di Vittoria. The Ristorante Hosteria delle Grazie may be off the beaten track, but it is a glorious venue where you are guaranteed to eat well. **CK**

⬆ *Trafilati al bronzo* pasta is the speciality of the house.

La Moresca, Relais Torre Marabino | Refined dining in a tower

Location Ispica Ragusa **Signature dish** *Carpaccio di baccalà* | 💲💲

The historic Relais Torre Marabino is a glistening white stone structure in Sicily's Iblei countryside with views of the nearby sea. In the sixteenth century, it was a watch tower used to monitor the approach of the Barbary Corsairs (North African pirates) as well as the arrival of ships transporting grain. Later, it became a monastery, then a baron's home, and in 1988 it was turned into an organic farm. In 2007, the tower was restored and transformed into an agriturismo.

The restaurant La Moresca is part of the Relais Torre Marabino agriturismo and is open to everyone, although reservations are necessary. The decor is modern, with a nod to the rural setting in the form of various antique farm tools, wooden bread-making appliances, and ceramic plates. Guests can also dine outside, on a stone-flagged terrace in the garden.

The joy of eating at an agriturismo is that you get to eat meals that are made with its own seasonal produce. The dishes are prepared using the superb produce grown on the farm, from vegetables such as tomatoes, artichokes, carrots, and fennel to fresh fruit, including melons, oranges, and lemons. The farm also produces honey, jelly, and olive oil, as well as Nero d'Avola and Chardonnay wines, and an award-winning Muscat. In short, a cornucopia of Sicilian food.

Although the setting is rustic, the food is not: La Moresca offers innovative cuisine that is exquisitely presented. You could start a meal with oysters served with lemons from the garden and bruschetta of homemade bread with fennel, oregano, tomatoes, and scamorza dressed with extra virgin olive oil. Mains include *carpaccio di baccalà* (thinly sliced salt cod) on a bed of julienne salad, homemade pasta with artichokes and cured fish roe, and roast octopus steamed with cherry tomatoes and fennel. Round off the meal with carob panna cotta with almond sauce. **CK**

⬆ A dish of salt cod "cappuccino" at La Moresca.

Fattoria delle Torri |

Superb Sicilian diffusion cuisine

Location Modica   **Signature dish** *Fare u lebbru 'nciucculattatu* | ❸❸❸

Tucked away at the end of a small cul-de-sac, Fattoria delle Torri is a place frequented by the cognoscenti. The unassuming entrance via a small door and up a spiral staircase belies the delights of the food, and ambience, of a place that should satisfy any gourmet.

Located in a nineteenth-century palazzo, the restaurant boasts a spacious white interior with vaulted arches, looking out over a small lemon grove in a walled courtyard where guests can dine alfresco. The owner, Peppe Barone, opened the establishment in 1987. He is one of the trailblazing Sicilian chefs who revamped traditional cooking by adding a nouvelle cuisine twist to combine flavors and textures in innovative and mouthwatering ways. Such is his

---

"This is one of Modica's smartest restaurants … the seafood is particularly gorgeous."

Lonely Planet

---

reputation that he has featured in *The New York Times* and mentored many of the region's leading chefs. Barone is an attentive host, always on hand to suggest what to eat and which wine to select.

You many want to try a modern twist on a traditional dish, *fare u lebbru 'nciucculattatu* (rabbit cooked in a sauce made from Modica chocolate), light fava bean and ricotta tortelloni, tender black pork from the Nebrodi region, and, for dessert, melting warm chocolate cake or tangy almond mousse. There may be as many as six courses on the fish and meat tasting menus. The quality of the food here is comparable to that of the top restaurants in the capitals of the world. **CK**

Ristorante Torre d'Oriente |

Traditional Sicilian cuisine with a twist

Location Modica   **Signature dish** *Gambero in crosta di capelli d'angelo* | ❸❸

Modica's Ristorante Torre d'Oriente lies at the foot of the town's tiny castle, in one of its many steep, narrow alleys. The restaurant's location offers a stunning panorama across the bell towers and roofs of one of Sicily's baroque towns renowned for their curvaceous architecture. Depending on the weather, guests can eat indoors or al fresco on one of two terraces overlooking a lemon grove with superb views of what locals call Modica's *presepe*—a nativity scene. Gazing at the buildings, terraces, palm trees, prickly pear cacti, and gardens that tumble down the slopes, you can see how the analogy came about: it is like looking at a series of doll's houses with balconies sporting color-coordinated washing lines and flower pots, not unlike the small nativity structures found in churches around Christmas. Inside, the restaurant is decorated in a minimalist, modern style.

Opened in 2004 by brothers Giorgio and Meno Iabichino, it was later sold to chef Maurizio Urso, although the siblings still help in the kitchen. Urso continues to create traditional Sicilian cuisine with a contemporary twist, using seasonal local produce. His creations include *arancini* rice balls with a subtle pistachio base, melting gnocchi with swordfish, spaghetti with creamy ricotta and fava beans, seared tuna with a sesame-seed crust, and a rich chocolate fondant made from Modica's own speciality chocolate that contains no dairy. The sensational signature dish is *gambero in crosta di capelli d'angelo* (shrimp in an angel hair pasta crust). It is a dish that looks and tastes fabulous, consisting of fat shrimp on a bed of mashed potato that supports a treelike structure of delicate angel hair pasta strands cooked in local honey and a reduction of Nero d'Avola. **CK**

➭ Modica is one of Sicily's most picturesque towns.

Taverna La Cialoma | Traditional fish dishes in a charming, tiny piazza

Location Marzamemi   **Signature dish** Grilled tuna | ❺❺

Marzamemi, in southeastern Sicily, is populated by only a few hundred people, but in summer these numbers swell as visitors flock to this charming spot, with its small harbor full of colorful boats and picturesque Piazza Regina Margherita square, where Taverna La Cialoma is located. The restaurant has a view across the piazza—ideal for people-watching.

The name "La Cialoma" refers to a song that local fishermen used to sing while hauling tuna into their nets at a time when Marzamemi was one of the most important tuna fishing ports on the island. Although tuna fishing has declined in recent years, tuna (and other fish) is still key to Taverna La Cialoma's menu. Diners can choose from a handwritten menu that changes daily according to the seasons. The dishes are prepared by the granddaughter of the village's last *rais* (the captain of the tuna-fishing fleet). For starters, guests can sample dishes such as *melanzane in agrodolce*, creamy golden and tangy sweet and sour eggplant, or tiny white smelt fish that glide on the palate.

The grilled tuna is freshly caught and guaranteed to melt in the mouth; it is also served in a sauce of olives and tomatoes. All ingredients are sourced from local produce, including tiny, sweet cherry tomatoes grown only a few miles along the coast at Pachino—they are so prized, they have been awarded "Indicazione Geografica Protetta" (Protected Geographical Indication) status. The wines are also of local origin, with the red Nero d'Avola being a favorite for its light but plummy flavor.

During the summer months, it is advisable to book a table, because discerning locals often visit on weekends, knowing very well that they can have an excellent meal, in a gorgeous piazza, for a reasonable price. **CK**

⬆ La Cialoma: alfresco dining in a peaceful fishing village.

Restaurant de Mondion, Xara Palace | Dine with celebrities

Location Mdina   **Signature dish** Braised Maltese snails with asparagus, liquorice, and mustard essence | ❸❸❸❸

You enter the medieval citadel of Mdina by going over a narrow bridge across a moat and through the fortified gatehouse. Within the city walls, in the traffic-free alleyways between the looming convents and monasteries, is a small palace that was built right into the turreted ramparts in the Middle Ages, when the crusading Knights Hospitallers ruled this small Mediterranean island.

Now converted into a luxury hotel, Xara Palace includes Restaurant de Mondion, regularly judged Malta's best eatery. Guests sit high up on the rooftop and terraces atop the city walls, looking down on the island, with the lights of Valetta twinkling in the distance.

Chefs (and brothers) Kevin and Adrian Bonello serve modern Mediterranean food to Xara Palace's international guests and wealthy visitors from across the island. It is an exclusive venue, only open for dinner, and no children are allowed—which has helped De Mondion's reputation as a romantic dinner spot. It has become a favorite of jet-setting celebrities including Roger Moore, Sharon Stone, and Bruce Willis, and newspapers delighted in the fact that Brad Pitt dined here with Jennifer Aniston and Angelina Jolie—on separate occasions.

In keeping with the clientele, the menu is showy and expensive, but short. The skills of the kitchen are evident in roast lamb with roasted salsify, rocket, garlic, and lemon puree, venison scented with lime, and fresh local fish served with lemongrass velouté. Pan-fried foie gras is presented on a white port brulee and vegetables may arrive as pickled ribbons or domes. But the Bonello brothers ensure that humble local ingredients such as shellfish, rabbit, snails, and mushrooms also get included frequently. After dinner, the unspoiled maze of "The Silent City" is perfect for a romantic stroll. **SH**

⬆ Presentation is key at Restaurant de Mondion.

Arzak | Both family restaurant and the epicenter of Basque cuisine

Location San Sebastian   **Signature dish** Cromlech, manioc, and huitlacoche | ❺❺❺❺

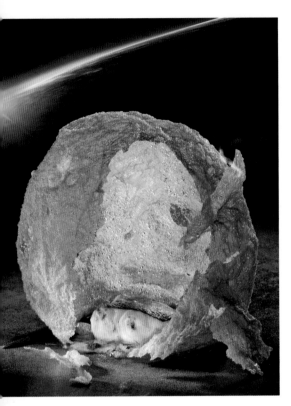

"Cooking, apart from being an art, has to be fun and it has to transmit pleasure ..."

Juan Mari Arzak, chef and owner of Arzak

⬆ "Stranded hake" is served in a lettuce-covered sphere.

➡ The truly impressive Arzak wine cellars store thousands of bottles of wine.

Arzak is dining tantamount to a wild adventure in color, texture, technique, sound, and flavor. Chef Juan Mari Arzak is internationally recognized as the culinary guru of Basque cuisine. Here, together with his charming and dazzlingly talented daughter Elena Arzak, voted best female chef in the world in 2012, they retain a truly hands-on role. The emphasis is firmly on teasing the best out of local Basque traditions and ingredients, yet Juan Mari delights in incorporating unusual herbs, spices, and condiments.

The restaurant is in an unfashionable suburb of San Sebastian, and its exterior is unexpectedly modest, essentially a converted family home dating back to when Juan Mari's great-grandparents first opened a taverna here. Inside, however, it is ultra-modern, dark and seductive, with polished concrete walls bearing the fossil-like imprints of cutlery.

Diners are piqued by colorful snacks served on modernist metal sculptures. A glass bottle of raspberry puree, corked and infused with melon and jamon, is an Alice-in-Wonderlandlike curiosity. Cromlech, manioc, and huitlacoche is an extremely clever, inventive, and delectable dish; the prehistoric stones of the Basque coast are represented by a crisp shell of manioc, a Brazilian root vegetable, stuffed with an indulgent combination of onion, green tea, and foie gras. Fish courses are sensational in taste and presentation, whether the white tuna with beautiful baked, dried garlic petals in different colors, or the monkfish with a spectacular "balloon" of reduced fish stock and parsley, which is burst at the table.

Desserts are equally playful: chocolate marbles served with amaranth and oregano; a huge ball of chocolate truffle containing carob; and the surprise of melon with wrinkled dried tomatoes, sumac, lime, and crunchy chia (a plant related to mint). The sommelier suggests wines to go with the tasting menu. It all adds up to a truly unconventional dining experience. **SP**

Ganbara | Definitive *pintxo* bar that always delivers on flavor

Location San Sebastian   **Signature dish** Deviled spider-crab tart | ❸❸

The crowds passing in and out are a good indicator that Ganbara is a cut above the myriad *pintxo* (bar snack) places offering a bewildering choice of temptations in San Sebastian's charming Old Town. Just try a few *gildas* (a typical Basque *pintxo* skewer of olive, salt-cured anchovy, and guindilla chili pepper)—a specialty of the house. Seeing chef Elena Arzak at the bar with a plate of cep and girolle mushrooms and runny egg—she and her father, celebrity chef Juan Mari Arzak, run a restaurant downstairs—is confirmation that Ganbara's father, mother, and son team are offering something special.

The *pintxos* are resolutely seasonal and made from impeccable, carefully sourced ingredients. Although the spread across the marble bar is alluring, including the gloriously savory mini croissants of Iberian ham ordered by almost every diner, the specials, such as the decidedly piquant deviled spider-crab tarts constantly delivered piping hot from the kitchen, are unmissable. Even more impressive are the fish delicacies that Basque connoisseurs seek out: neck of hake in mesmerizingly light egg batter (reportedly one of Juan Mari Arzak's favorites); *kokotxas*, or hake throats, gelatinous with a wisp of smoke from the grill, wobbly, juicy, and saline, served with a *pil-pil* garlic and parsley sauce; red shrimp simply sautéed, sweet, delicate, and rich; and belly of tuna marinated in lemon and olive oil. Drink with *txakoli*, a local wine from Getaria that is poured from a great height to display its gentle effervescence and acidity.

As befits the caliber of the cooking, the room is elegant in pale wood enlivened by original artwork. There are a few bar seats, but locals prefer to stand at the bar, discarding paper napkins as they eat. For a more sedate and sedentary experience, it is possible to savor the talented Arzaks' food downstairs. **SP**

⬆ Locals stand at the bar to eat at Ganbara.

Mugaritz | Highly innovative food that challenges the senses

Location Errerteria   **Signature dish** Roasted and perfumed veal | ❺❺❺❺

In this stunning restaurant in the Basque Country, complete with vast vegetable gardens, chef Andoni Aduriz likes to play with nature, time, and emotions. The tasting menu is one of serious, high-end gastronomy, yet delivered wittily throughout. Beautiful yet bizarre plate sculptures are laid on each table, and the waiting staff advise that the first nibbles—from crisp real fish bones with lemon and garlic to a rich toast of bone marrow with herbs and horseradish ash—must be eaten with the fingers to experience them most intensely.

What is so utterly memorable is how the essence of each ingredient is captured. Ice shreds with scarlet shrimp perfume perfectly convey the experience of sucking the juice from shrimp heads. There are many unexpected combinations of flavors and visual tricks: crab with macadamias and pink peppercorns; succulent hake loin with tiger nut and concentrated clam juice; and what appears to be a crème caramel

yet is, outrageously, savory duck juice with wobbly tofu. Other dishes are poetic expressions of seasonal Basque ingredients, presented with extreme panache, with many of the ingredients fresh from the gardens. Highlights may include red mullet in a butter of its own liver, almonds, and bread; and "the cow and the grass," a beautiful piece of beef draped with a verdant herb sauce. Wherever possible, diners are invited into the vast kitchen, where they can watch how their next course is prepared. Be prepared for a "game" mid-meal at the table; the winner receives an extravagant treat to accompany the next course.

Desserts are delicious, whether the frozen almond turrón or "vanilla fern" with crisp crystallized ferns masquerading as vanilla pods. The trump card is a dramatic presentation in towering wooden vessels of petits fours as the seven deadly sins. **SP**

⬆ Fried pieces of beef tendon served on thorny branches.

Martín Berasategui |
High-class culinary wizardry to savor

Location San Sebastian   **Signature dish** *Millefeuille* of eel, foie gras, green onion, and green apple | ❸❸❸❸

Michelin star-adorned chef Martín Berasategui's eponymous restaurant is discreetly housed in a modern building in a residential area. Born in San Sebastian, Berasategui trained in France, and worked with Michel Guérard in Bordeaux and Alain Ducasse in Monaco. A standard bearer of Spanish avant-garde cuisine, he applies technical brilliance without ever forgetting the importance of balancing the flavors in the dishes he makes with the finest local ingredients.

A meal might begin with one of the restaurant's signature dishes: a neat, rectangular slab of smoked eel, foie gras, green onion, and green apple, a pleasing combination of tastes and textures, with the apple providing just the right amount of acidity to

> *"[It is important to] know your tradition well, because traditions are like a house's foundations."*
>
> Martín Berasategui, chef and owner

counterbalance the richness of the foie gras. The considerable technical skills of the kitchen are illustrated by dishes such as the liquid-centered raviolo of onion and squid ink, served with a consommé of squid poured around the sphere and a single squid-ink chip on one side.

Further culinary wizardry is seen in a dish of sole served off the bone alongside smoked fish snout and little spheres of mild green chili. More traditional dishes impress, too, such as the flavorful pigeon with wild mushrooms and dainty, delicate-textured pasta parcels with truffle, the mushrooms being an earthy addition to the richness of the pigeon. An impressive taste of haute cuisine from a Spanish master. **AH**

Ibai | Superb seafood in a tucked-away gem of a restaurant

Location San Sebastian   **Signature dish** *Kokotxas al pil-pil* (hake throats in a fish-oil, garlic sauce) | ❸❸

There is something very appealing about discovering a "secret" gastronomic gem, and Ibai is certainly one of those. Tucked away in the basement of a modest tapas bar in central San Sebastian, Ibai takes the definition of "intimate" to an extreme—this restaurant has a mere eight tables. Adding to its intriguing reputation, it opens only for weekday lunches, there is no menu, no English is spoken, and it is notoriously difficult to get a reservation. Furthermore, there is no wine list; at one side of the modest dining room, with its stone-tiled floor and exposed beams, there is instead a row of bottles from which to choose.

Ibai is a family-run business that has been catering to those in the know since 1983, with chef Alicio Garro invariably using the highest possible quality of local ingredients. The reason for the restaurant's cult following first becomes clear when one samples the *pintxos* (snacks) served there. Take, for example, a simple yet stunning dish of lobster, served at room temperature with a lemon dressing. The flavor of the lobster is superb, the flesh beautifully tender, with the lemon providing just the right kick of acidity to counterbalance the sweetness of the crustacean. The seafood is quite simply a pleasure to eat; witness the terrific dish of fried squid, cooked to tender perfection. The restaurant is famed for its way with fish: for example, sole is cooked whole and served with a little butter, then filleted at the table. Again, the fish is of dazzling quality and precisely cooked.

The cooking is simple, but why would anyone want to distract from such superb ingredients? A chef's job should be to let the produce speak for itself. The quality of the ingredients at Ibai would shame many Michelin three-star restaurants. The setting and the cooking may be straightforward, but it is a delight to eat food of such quality. **AH**

Akelare | Enchanting food from one of Spain's most innovative chefs, with a sensational sea view

Location San Sebastian **Signature dish** Shrimp flambéed in a red-wine spirit and served with a French bean puree | ❺❺❺❺❺

The name of this restaurant means "coven" (as in witchcraft), and, as testified by its three Michelin stars, the cooking there certainly enchants. On show are the considerable culinary talents of chef Pedro Subijana, who was born in San Sebastian. Subijana initially planned to study medicine, but switched to a course in hospitality in Madrid. Medicine's loss was catering's gain. He worked for a time at a few simple restaurants in the Basque region and Madrid before becoming chef de cuisine at Akelare in 1975, an exciting time for New Basque Cuisine. He has since gone on to achieve an impressive reputation.

The cooking at Akelare offers an intriguing blend of traditional and modernist, using the finest local ingredients, including herbs and fresh produce from the restaurant's own vegetable garden. The care taken when sourcing ingredients is obvious in the variety of top-quality wild mushrooms used in a dish of "pasta" made with red bell peppers, which is served topped by the mushrooms and slivers of Parmesan cheese. Also impressive is the sheer quality of the foie gras used for a dish of sautéed foie gras with "salt and pepper," which are flakes of puffed rice and sugar. Subijana's classic approach may be seen in a dish of high-quality shrimp cooked at the table in an iron pot, flambéed in a red-wine spirit, and served with a French bean puree. And the modernist side of the kitchen may be seen in the shellfish "caught" in a net made from rice flour, or the apple tart wrapped in edible paper made from chocolate and apple.

Akelare's location, perched in the hills near to San Sebastian, is very much part of the wow factor. From the restaurant, there is a spectacular view of the sea, so try to reserve a table by a window when making a reservation. The combination of Subijana's cuisine and the enticing ocean prospect is irresistible. **AH**

"Never believe that you're on top and know everything, that no one can teach you anything."

Pedro Subijana, chef at Akelare

⬆ Akelare's remarkable "distilled lobster" dish is prepared at the table in a coffee vacuum siphon.

Bodegón Alejandro |
A contemporary take on the taverna

Location San Sebastian **Signature dish** Glazed veal cheek with potato and bacon terrine | 🪙🪙

Zuberoa | Luxury dining in
the heart of the Basque Country

Location Oiartzun **Signature dish** Roast scallop on onion cream with caramelized endive | 🪙🪙🪙🪙

Down some stairs in the heart of the Old Town of San Sebastian—a city with so much to offer lovers of good food—Bodegón Alejandro is the quintessential taverna, cozy and comforting in its welcome. However, it offers traditional dishes seasoned with a splash of innovation and sophisticated culinary technique. Behind the scenes, Michelin three-star chef Andoni Luis Aduriz of the restaurant Mugaritz has a supervisory role, and his presence is felt in the sophistication of the cooking.

Charming, smiling staff supply marinated anchovies with the fish-centric menu, an appealing taste of the piscine treats to come. Standout starters include a fish soup brimming with clams, shrimp, mussels, and garlic-rich hake; and an unusual combination of cherry tomato stuffed with squid, roasted in its juice on creamy rice with squid ink and Idziabal cheese sauce, the acidity and freshness of the tomato offsetting the rich sauce. Strikingly dramatic is the fresh squid stewed in its own ink, which lives up to its appearance with the requisite deep savoriness. The grilled hake on potatoes with virgin olive oil and citrus vinaigrette is an elegant, beautifully balanced dish. For dessert, do not miss the junket prepared at the table with fresh local milk and rennet. It arrives with a jar of Basque honey, a nutcracker, and bowl of fresh walnuts for DIY action. Equally irresistible is the caramelized French toast soaked in fresh cream and egg yolk, with lemon thyme ice cream.

The pale-yellow room, decorated with tiled pictures and furnished with chunky wooden furniture, invites long investigation of the reasonably priced wine list. Endearingly, along with the check are brought malted milk and cookies—a hospitable touch that sums up the spirit of the place. A really charming, unpretentious gem. **SP**

Few things feel more special than being ensconced within the walls of this 600-year-old stone country house in the remote heart of the Basque Country. The dining room is all dark wood, thick stone walls, and acres of rich linens. Those who choose to dine on the terrace find themselves amid ancient oak trees.

Chef Hilario Arbelaitz is a master of old-school Basque cooking. His passion is for cooking the traditional dishes of the region using top-quality ingredients: Cantabrian sardines on tomato tarts with smoked Idiazabal cheese salad, or roast crayfish on vichyssoise with vanilla ravioli. Arbelaitz coaxes magnificent flavors from everything he touches. The result is a decadent menu built on a series of rich-

> *"The atmosphere is unpretentious: just a few friends sitting down to dine simply—but very, very well."*
>
> fodors.com

seeming dishes that do not skimp on portion size. But it is cleverer than that, with Arbelaitz's artful use of fresh, seasonal ingredients balancing the luxury treats: examples are a creamy veloutte of sea urchins; roast scallops with truffled onion cream; Iberian pancetta with smoked pumpkin; poached eggs on cream of foie gras; roast sole with cockle vinaigrette; roast pigeon on fig bread; and a drunken cake topped with bitter-almond foam and coconut ice cream.

The wine list is equally extravagant—the cellar is stocked with some 3,000 different bottles—but people do not dine at Zuberoa for something light and bright. Feasting like this is not for every day, and that is what makes it so wonderfully naughty. **TS**

Elkano | Superb seafood cooked with loving care over a charcoal fire

Location Getaria **Signature dish** Turbot grilled on the bone and served with sea salt, olive oil, and cider vinegar | ❸❸❸

It is always a pleasure to eat at a good seafood restaurant, and in the appealing coastal town of Getaria, the traveler finds Elkano. With its stone-tiled floor and net drapes, the restaurant has a simple, old-fashioned appearance, but do not be deceived: it offers the chance to enjoy some fine piscine dining.

The love of seafood shared by most Spaniards is exemplified there by the care taken in sourcing the finest fish and seafood. Starters include marinated tuna, with a notably excellent flavor, and a rich, dark-colored fish soup, based on a carefully prepared and exemplary fishbone stock.

The highlights of the Elkano menu are the foods that are cooked on open-air charcoal grills. Best of all is the eye-catching grilled turbot; the whole fish is cooked with remarkable precision on the charcoal grill and served on the bone. This is as simple a dish as can be imagined, with no sauce or garnish as an accompaniment, but it is nevertheless stunning. The quality of the fish is obvious, as is the perfect timing of the cooking, the charcoal leaving just a hint of smokiness and the flesh firm and cooked through beautifully. Elkano justly prides itself on the quality of all its fish and seafood, from the hake and red mullet to the spiny lobster and goose barnacles. The fish available will change according to the season, so in the fall customers might be offered sole, while in the spring it might be the lightly steamed clams from Galicia that stand out on the menu.

Mirroring the care taken in the kitchen, the service is polite and capable. Another happy aspect of this restaurant is the fairly priced wine list; in particular, the top Spanish wines are remarkably reasonable. Elkano is the kind of restaurant that focuses on prime ingredients and careful cooking rather than making dishes appear pretty. It is a seafood lover's delight. **AH**

"The turbot is cooked on the oak charcoal ashes very slowly, without touching the fire ..."

Ceylan Milor, gastromondiale.com

⬆ Enjoy beautifully cooked fish in Elkano's comfortable dining room.

Etxebarri | Grilled food taken to heavenly heights

Location Vizkaya **Signature dish** Smoked baby eels | ❸❸❸❸❸

Hidden away in the hills of the Basque Country and handsomely housed in solid, rustic style, Asador Etxebarri has gained an international reputation for the food it produces using just one cooking technique, namely grilling. This is the magnificent obsession of self-taught chef and owner Victor Arguinzoniz. With the aid of two wood-fired ovens and a custom grill, he uses a variety of woods to impart specific and appropriate flavors to whatever ingredients are being cooked. Arguinzoniz takes a pure approach, carefully selecting the ingredients to be grilled in order to bring out their flavor.

The simplicity of the kitchen's culinary philosophy is mirrored by the peaceful, civilized upstairs dining room, with its dark wooden beams, wooden floor, and well-spaced tables spread with white linen tablecloths. Outside there are magnificent views of rugged mountains that offer a spectacular natural backdrop to some memorable cooking.

The daily-changing menu showcases seasonal ingredients selected because they are at their optimum. A meal might begin with *chorizo* (spicy sausage) on toast, then continue through delights such as a solitary, stunningly fresh, Palamós shrimp simply grilled and served whole, the flesh sweet and delicious; baby octopus; and a perfectly cooked piece of *umami*-rich beef fillet. The deceptive simplicity of the culinary approach, the quality of the ingredients, and the care taken in the cooking mean that diners can savor each ingredient as it appears. Desserts continue the grilled and smoked theme: try the apple tart with smoked ice cream.

Service is attentive throughout and the excellent wine list is an additional pleasure. As a restaurant, Etxebarri is one of a kind, where Arguinzoniz takes the grilling of food to a sophisticated level. **AH**

⊼ The views add to the dining experience.

Azurmendi | Sensational fine dining with home-grown produce at its core

Location Bilbao   **Signature dish** Egg cooked from within by a truffle consommé | ❸❸❸❸

Azurmendi is a sleek and stylish vision of a restaurant, located in a dramatic hilltop setting. Alongside the restaurant is a vegetable and herb garden with a computer-controlled greenhouse in which many of the vegetables used by the restaurant are grown.

Since it opened in 2005, Azurmendi has had a meteoric rise up the Michelin ladder. It was awarded a first star in 2008, a second in 2011, and a third in 2013. Azurmendi's chef, Eneko Atxa, was born in the Basque Country, and he has worked at top restaurants such as Etxebarri and Martín Berasategui.

The food showcases Atxa's considerable culinary technique via wittily conceived and technically accomplished dishes. To start, diners are served an amuse-bouche "picnic," presented in a dainty hamper. The skill of the kitchen is shown by dishes such as a truffled egg presented on a spoon, the egg yolk having been injected with a truffle consommé that cooks the egg from the inside outward.

As befits the idyllic rural surroundings, there is an emphasis on vegetables. One dish, called "the garden," takes parts of vegetables grown on the premises and sets them out as a little garden on a slate. Zucchini, cauliflower, carrots, broccoli, peas, and cherry tomatoes variously appear in a "soil" made from dehydrated beetroot, and tiny potatoes are buried within the soil. A meal might conclude with an "egg flan" dessert, which is a white chocolate egg served with caramelized nuts, or an intensely flavored coffee pudding with rum ice cream.

The service is impeccable, and the waiters friendly and knowledgeable. The wine list is impressive, and showcases fine Spanish wines to good effect. The food at Azurmendi is remarkably assured, the produce exceptional, and the cooking technique a delight. It is a world-class restaurant. **AH**

⬆ Ingredients are presented with panache at Azurmendi.

Casa Marcial | Michelin-starred, updated Asturian
mountain cuisine in a remote pueblo

Location Arriondas   **Signature dish** *Llámpares* (limpets with potato, chives, and cider sauce) | ❺❺❺❺

"… one of the great restaurants along the northern coast of Spain, an unexpected discovery …"

Frommer's

⬆ A simple setting for complex cuisine.

Narrow winding roads lead from Spain's north coast up into the Picos de Europa mountains to the Manzano family's restaurant, hidden deep in the forested foothills. The Casa Marcial restaurant in Asturias is part of an old farmhouse that was once a shop run by Nacho Manzano's grandparents. His parents started serving simple local food there, and then Nacho, helped by his sisters Olga and Sandra, turned it into an acclaimed shrine to Asturian cuisine that has won two Michelin stars.

Nacho has three Michelin stars to his name thanks to the acclaimed offshoot he runs in the regional museum in Gijón with another sister, Esther. He is also involved in running the Ibérica restaurant chain in London. Nevertheless, the remote mountain restaurant is closest to the heart of his cooking. It is there that he, then aged 13 years, devised his first recipe: cornstarch cakes fried in olive oil with stewed onion and Cabrales cheese. Years later, the dish is on the menu at Casa Marcial. Such dishes epitomize Nacho's approach: a dedication to traditional Asturian ingredients and techniques, mixed with modern expertise and innovation, to produce delicate, crispy versions of hearty mountain classics. For example, Nacho's take on the traditional *fabada*—a stew of haricot bean, *chorizo* (spicy sausage), blood sausage, cabbage, and ham—uses crisp bacon and raw vegetables in a vinaigrette to add texture and contrast.

Throughout his tasting menus, Nacho gives a new dimension to local classics such as *pitu de caleya* (free-range chicken), which is braised until it assumes a deep brown hue. Some of Nacho's creations go way beyond the local repertoire. His icy cucumber soup is poured around a sorbet of green bell pepper, and pigeon is served marinated in seaweed, kalamata olives, and sardines. **SH**

La Nueva Allandesa |
Robust food in the mountains

Location Pola de Allande   **Signature dish** *Repollo relleno* (cabbage stuffed with sausage) | 🟊🟊🟊

The prospect of a meal at a 1950s hotel in a small country town does not usually inspire much culinary excitement. However, this otherwise unremarkable hotel in a rural backwater has an acclaimed restaurant that has become known as a food-lovers' destination in its own right. La Nueva Allandesa has a reputation (as well as assorted culinary awards) for serving the best Asturian specialities made using authentic, high-quality local ingredients.

The hotel stands in a narrow street of the historic riverside town of Pola de Allande, a picturesque point on tourist itineraries of the Cantabrian mountains. The restaurant is on the ground floor, housed in a large, high-ceilinged room divided by pillars, with shiny floor tiles and high-backed wooden chairs. On one side, there is a view of the Río Nison, which runs right behind the hotel.

La Nueva Allandesa's restaurant serves a set Asturian tasting menu that demonstrates the region's robust mountain food, dominated by spicy sausages and cabbages.

The reasonably priced degustation menu starts with a chunk of local morcilla pork sausage pâté. Next comes pote Asturiano, a thick white bean, potato, and cabbage stew. That is followed by *fabada*, a warming haricot bean and *chorizo* (spicy sausage) casserole with added ham and tomatoes, flavored with garlic and paprika. The house specialty, *repollo relleno*, is a steamed ball of chopped spicy sausages, onion, garlic, and mushrooms wrapped in cabbage leaves. Then things take a sweet turn with a plate of *frisuellos* (thin pancakes). The meal ends with a slice of sweet and gooey hazelnut tart. Everything is accompanied by a young, local red wine. Finally, coffee and brandy are essential for digesting this hearty food. Take note and be sure to arrive hungry. **SH**

Verde Galicia Pulperia |
Down-to-earth Galician institution

Location Ordes   **Signature dish** *Pulpo a feira* (octopus stew) | 🟊🟊

Galicia, the most northwesterly region of Spain, is renowned for its seafood, including, in addition to standard fare, lesser-known delicacies such as *percebes* (gooseneck barnacles), *navajas* (razor shell clams), and *berberechos* (heart clams).

Above all, Galicia is famous for its *pulpo* (octopus), and many of its towns have *pulperías*—cafés serving octopus dishes in basic, informal surroundings.

The Verde Galicia Pulperia in Ordes is often cited as the best place in the region to experience this speciality. It is a typically humble restaurant-cum-bar. The entrance beneath a women's clothes shop leads into a dark basement full of wooden furniture and paper tablecloths.

> "… don't run away from octopus. This is a food that has legs. Embrace it."

Spanish Food World

The menu features other typical Galician dishes, including *chipirones* (baby squid), *raxo* (pork, potatoes, and bell peppers), and *pinchos morunos* (spiced pork cubes), but visitors often arrive to find everyone in the restaurant tucking into octopus in various forms. For hardcore octopus eaters, there are hefty chunks of tentacles, with the suckers intact and almost no adornment. For the squeamish, there is *pulpo y gambas* (octopus with shrimp) or barbecued octopus with seasoning.

Most locals, however, choose *pulpo a feira*, a traditional preparation in which the octopus is tenderized by pounding, then boiled and served simply with olive oil, paprika, and salt. **SH**

Tira do Cordel | Galician
seafood delicacies on the beach

Location Finisterre **Signature dish** *Percebes* (goose barnacles) | ❸❸❸

Goose barnacles from the Coast of Death? Said in English, this delicacy from verdant Galicia on Spain's craggy Atlantic edge sounds like something a person would eat only if he or she was starving and lost. However, when uttered in Spanish—*"percebes de la Costa da Morte"*—mouths start to water. Anyone who loves seafood will lust after *percebes*. Yielding flavors as evocative as they are delicious, a lightly boiled and sparingly seasoned mound of *percebes* is the gustatory equivalent of a seaside vacation. *Percebes* are the ultimate gourmand finger food: people who enjoy slurping oysters and cracking into lobster shells will find the traditional twist-and-pinch method of eating goose barnacles a sheer delight.

"… without any shadow of a doubt, one of the finest fish and seafood restaurants in all Spain."

Adrian McManus, *Spanish Food and Travel File*

Not so much a seasonal product as one that is dangerous to harvest (it is called the "Coast of Death" for a reason), *percebes* are a limited speciality. They need to be prepared quickly, too. Finding them fresh anywhere beyond Galician markets and eateries is rare; which is where Tira do Cordel comes into its own.

Tira do Cordel is a restaurant located about a mile (1.5 km) from Cape Finisterre. The family-run establishment brings the distinctive tastes of Galicia to the table with cordial and appreciative service. Its long grill sits prominently along an open kitchen for diners to admire the gorgeous catches of the day cooking upon it. Equally impressive is the list of local wines that pair perfectly with the items on the menu. **CO**

Compartir | Casual dining
with a taste of the New Wave

Location Cadaqués **Signature dish** House-marinated sardines in *horchata* (tigernut milk) | ❸❸❸

Compartir has the feel of a good old-fashioned Mediterranean tavern, but it has an unusual pedigree as the pet project of Mateu Casañas, Eduard Xatruch, and Oriol Castro, three chefs who came hot out of El Bulli near the town of Roses when that restaurant closed for the last time in 2012. Unsurprisingly, the food at Compartir is far from the usual taverna fodder.

Combining traditional dishes from the Empordà region of Catalonia—of which the rocky cliffs, idyllic coves, and fabulous seafood of the Costa Brava make up the coastal portion—with contemporary Catalan cooking inspired by the brave new world of El Bulli, this is arguably some of the most exciting, yet laid-back dining in the land. With its breezy, slate-floored terrace, linen cushions, and woven grass lanterns that recall the bars of Ibiza, it is more beach-chic than stiff dining room, and cleverly recalls the golden years of one of the Costa Brava's livelier towns. Cadaqués was a hot spot in the early twentieth century when Salvador Dalí, Federico García Lorca, Pablo Picasso, and Man Ray would hang out here, mixing their work with long *sobremesas* (postprandial relaxation the Spanish way.)

Modern diners will linger, too, the better to savor dishes such as sardines caught just off the coast, marinated in-house, and topped with little pearls of orange that pop like caviar; robustly flavored beetroot salad with strawberries, almonds, and roasted garlic, all plucked from the surrounding countryside; and tiny breaded rabbit chops, fried and served with a bowl of zingy apple aioli.

In contrast to the formality of El Bulli, the atmosphere at Compartir is relaxed. This restaurant is all about sharing flavors, techniques, experiences, and good times in an easily accessible package. **TS**

⊡ Compartir is a place to linger in charming Cadaqués.

Mas Pau | Tradition meets modern in a sixteenth-century farmhouse

Location Figueres **Signature dish** Pork trotter stuffed with crayfish | ❸❸❸❸

There is a good reason why Catalan cuisine is considered one of the best in Spain. The region has exceptional fish and seafood, abundant olive groves, vineyards, and fruit orchards, and, particularly in the Empordà district, excellent pasture for meat and dairy products. It is thus a natural place for chefs to choose as their place of work. Among the regional dishes for which it is celebrated is *mar i muntanya*—a combination of seafood and land produce, such as the crackling of pork trotter stuffed with crayfish that is the star of the menu at Mas Pau.

This restaurant was established in 1960 by the Reig family, dedicated gourmands, in part of their sixteenth-century stone farmhouse nestled in the

---

"Mas Pau is special in its combination of excellent food and enchanting setting."

Michael Jacobs, *The Daily Telegraph*

---

countryside near Girona. Later, they appointed Toni Gerez as maître d' and Xavier Sagristà as chef de cuisine, both of whom had formerly been at the famously radical El Bulli restaurant. As one would therefore expect, the cooking style at Mas Pau has lots of contemporary flourishes, although the flavors remain staunchly Empordàn.

Apart from the signature dish, main course highlights include salt-cod fritters with honey and a *romescada* of grilled fish enlivened by a luscious sauce of pounded hazelnuts, nyora peppers, and garlic. Do not miss the pre-dinner snack of sweet pork sausages infused with apple (a regional specialty often given to guests on their departure). **TS**

Rafa's | *A la plancha* seafood heaven on the Costa Brava

Location Roses **Signature dish** Grilled John Dory in olive oil | ❸❸

Rafa's may be close to the legendary El Bulli, with its challenging and wildly creative haute cuisine; but, while the latter became world famous, many prefer the seafood cooked *a la plancha* (grilled on a metal plate) at Rafa's in Roses.

Rather than scaling culinary heights, a meal at Rafa's is simply about the sheer pleasure of eating and drinking. The restaurant is so understated that it does not bother with much in the way of signage; but, once located in the back streets, diners will be amply rewarded with some of the finest fish they have ever eaten. When Ferran Adrià was head chef at El Bulli, he used to regularly eat at Rafa's. What better recommendation can there be?

The small dining room is bare, furnished with heavy wooden benches and little by way of decoration. There is a fleeting aroma of smokiness and a brusque but warm welcome from the single, matronly server. Do not go looking for a menu—there is not one as such, just the best of what is sparkiest and sweetest from the sea that morning: delicate little lilac *tellinas* (bivalve molluscs), fruity clams, cuttlefish, langoustines, and *carabineros* (shrimps). The fish—bass, bream, turbot, John Dory, sardines, and anchovies—have only a slick of grassy olive oil by way of adornment; it is all they need.

The smoky squid is dreamy: its tentacles just-charred and its interior as tender as a caress. Rafa's knows the exact second to remove the fish from the blistering heat, making even gurnard taste luxurious. The only accompaniments are crisp local white wines and rich, fruity reds. (Want a Garnacha with monkfish? Nobody will bat an eyelid.) Or perhaps there will be some bread or tomato salad. Order some Iberian ham. It may be simple, but Rafa's food really is a feast for all the senses. **MOL**

Els Casals | Farm-to-fork dining stylishly elevated to the highest level

Location Berguedà **Signature dish** Farm-reared chicken roasted *en cocotte* | ❸❸❸

Few places take farm-to-fork dining quite as seriously as Els Casals. When farmer-chef Oriol Rovira and his brothers and sisters had the opportunity to reimagine the family business (their mother Dolors Prat looks after a guesthouse), they wanted to do something that minimized the gap between food production and what appears on the plate. They set up a vast organic garden with an ample supply of livestock in order to demonstrate not only that sustainable, ethical farming was better for people and the environment, but also that it tastes wonderful.

They first hit the headlines as producers of exceptional organic charcuterie, which they began selling to discerning bars and restaurants in Barcelona. But it was too far from source, so they decided to convert their farmhouse, a handsome stone *masia* outside the little town of Sagàs just south of the French border, into a hotel and restaurant.

Curiously, Els Casals has remained under the radar outside Catalonia, despite holding a Michelin star since 2007. Some places are destined to remain known only to local insiders, but those willing to make the journey—and it is tucked away in a fairly remote part of the region—will be amply rewarded. From the minute one bumps up the property's country lane, where cows munch in the hedgerows, past fields of verdant crops and on, up to an old farmhouse framed by the mighty Pyrenees, it is obvious this is a restaurant that is connected to the land deeply.

Rovira's cooking is largely about showcasing the product he so lovingly rears and grows. It is the simple things that stand out: a rocket salad strewn with fresh, green almonds; jamón from his own pigs; a bowl of creamy white beans with homemade pork sausages; and cannelloni made with guinea hen meat. Els Casals is the essence of what farm-to-fork signifies. **TS**

"The main focus at Els Casals is to emphasize a powerful bond between cuisine and countryside."

The International Poor Chef School Project

⬆ *Cotnes* (pork rind), a Catalan speciality, at Els Casals.

El Celler de Can Roca | Wonderful world-class dining
at a restaurant created by three brothers

Location Girona   **Signature dish** Iberian suckling pig |

" … a masterpiece of culinary dexterity, and brilliant food and wine matching."

Nicholas Lander, *Financial Times*

⬆ A tempting apple dessert at El Celler de Can Roca.

This legendary restaurant is the creation of the three Roca brothers—head chef Joan, sommelier Josep, and patissier Jordi. Opened in 1986, its latest incarnation is in a purpose-built building to which they moved in 2007. There, they work with thirty chefs to produce the intelligent and creative cuisine that has won them international acclaim.

The sleek, contemporary dining room is in the shape of a triangle around a central tree-filled courtyard. The food is as stylish and well designed as the surroundings. Take, for example, a dish such as veal steak tartare. At El Celler de Can Roca, the meat is served as a rectangular slab on which are dots of mustard ice cream, mustard leaves, spicy tomato ketchup, caper compote, Sichuan pepper, a little lemon compote to provide acidity, praline cream, and oloroso sherry, with a garnish of small fried potatoes and smoked paprika. A pool of meat Béarnaise sauce completes a complex set of flavor combinations in perfect balance, the mixture of richness, acidity, and spice just right, the fried potatoes providing a crunchy texture contrast, the meat itself of superb quality. There is a witty verve and inventiveness to all the food here: the Roca brothers always remember that their customers must enjoy the dining experience.

El Celler de Can Roca is justly noted for the quality of its wine and food matching, with the vast wine cellar, in which some 60,000 bottles are stored, a formidable resource and one that Josep uses intelligently to good effect. In short, this Catalan restaurant is superb, with terrific ingredients, high levels of culinary skill, well-judged flavor combinations, and exquisite food presentation. Classy service and a dazzling wine list complete the dining experience here, which justly sees devoted followers of fine food flocking through its doors. **AH**

Restaurant Gaig | Elegant
dining room serving Catalan classics
Location Barcelona **Signature dish** Squab rice
with porcini mushrooms | ❸❸❸

Carles Gaig began his rise to stardom in the early 1970s, when he took over the Taberna d'en Gaig, which his family had owned and run since 1869. In 1993, he was awarded a Michelin star.

In 1989, he oversaw a complete renovation of the place, which he then renamed Restaurant Gaig. In 2004, he moved the enterprise to the Hotel Cram on Carrer Aribau in downtown Barcelona. There, the restaurant thrived until the global economic recession reduced his business and inspired a move to new premises approximately a mile (1.5 km) away on Carrer de Córsega.

Gaig then began to explore the possibilities of a cuisine that applied rustic techniques to traditional, locally sourced ingredients. He was motivated partly by personal interest and partly by his belief that diners were beginning to tire of the avant-garde molecular gastronomy adopted by places such as El Bulli, El Celler de Can Roca, and Sant Pau, and would welcome a return to old favorites.

He was soon proved right when the new Restaurant Gaig was filled to capacity every night with customers keen to sample newly revived old standards including *botifarra amb mongetes de ganxet* (sausage with white beans); *perdiu amb vinagreta calenta* (partridge with warm vinaigrette); and *tartar de llobarro i gamba* (sea bass and shrimp tartare). Other Gaig dishes are available nowhere else in Barcelona: for example, locally caught woodcock, roasted in the traditional manner with its head still attached (aficionados like to scoop out the brain) and pig trotters served with black turnips.

Gaig's sole concession to modernity is the decor, which is stylishly contemporary, with generously spaced tables laid with thick, snowy linen and plump comfy dining armchairs. **TS**

Bar Mut | Sensational food
in a tapas bar with star quality
Location Barcelona **Signature dish** *Carpaccio de huevos fritos* (potatoes topped with broken eggs) | ❸❸❸

Some places have star quality, and Barcelona's Bar Mut is one such place. True, the smoked glass, the antique wood shelves, and the marble tabletops give it a more glamorous air than more traditional tapas bars, and the fact that it is actor Robert de Niro's favorite bar in Barcelona adds a certain sparkle. The food is sensational, and the staff provide an object lesson in what hospitality should be. However, there is even more to it than that. In 2006, when owner Kim Díaz opened Bar Mut, he set out to create a retreat that offered an escape from the real world, even if only for a little while. He believes that his customers should feel special every second they are under his roof.

> *"... this elegant retro space [is] everything a great tapas bar or restaurant should be."*
>
> fodors.com

Díaz is the consummate host, flitting from group to group, suggesting daily specials or, if asked to do so, taking control of the order himself. Expect the finest ingredients treated with reverence and refreshingly free of fuss: a dish of tender clams bathed in sherry with the gentle heat of guindilla chili peppers and garlic just showing through; a slab of suckling pig running with juices; Bar Mut's signature *carpaccio de huevos fritos* (matchstick potatoes topped with broken eggs and truffle oil); or tender white beans covered with a shaving of *mojama* (cured tuna loin). Lucky diners are even invited upstairs to Mutis, a clandestine cocktail bar in a Belle Epoque apartment, acclaimed by the drinking cognoscenti. **TS**

Cal Pep | Exemplary tapas in a Barcelona institution

Location Barcelona   **Signature dish** *Botifarra* (pork sausage) with duck foie gras and white beans | **$$**

Cal Pep is tucked away in a quiet street in the Barri Gòtic area of Barcelona, near the seafront. It was set up in 1977 by Josep "Pep" Manubens and showcases Mediterranean food in tapas style. Originally, "tapas" was a term for slices of bread or meat served with sherry by bar owners who made a point of providing ham that was particularly salty in order to encourage more drinking. In contemporary times, tapas bars offer a wide variety of dishes, and Cal Pep is regarded as the best of its type in Barcelona.

Cal Pep has a back room with a dining table, but the lively atmosphere is best enjoyed at the counter. There is no menu, the emphasis being on fresh seafood delivered daily from the city market.

> *"It's getting a foot in the door here that's the problem—there can be lines around the square."*
>
> Lonely Planet

Waiters advise what dishes are available that day. Customers might be offered a simple dish of peas with shrimp, artichokes, and broad beans. The classic dish of chicken or ham croquettes is there, too, ideally accompanied either by one of Spain's excellent red wines or a glass of sherry. Slices of beef fillet are cooked simply and served with fried potatoes, and cod arrives with spinach and *alioli* (garlic mayonnaise). The signature dish is *botifarra* (pork sausage), with duck foie gras and white beans with port reduction.

Tapas bars can be found not only in Spain but all over the world. Cal Pep is one of the restaurants that has done the most to establish the global reputation of this style of cuisine. **AH**

Casa Leopoldo | Historic place recalling Barcelona's golden years

Location Barcelona   **Signature dish** Suquet of fish and bull-tail Casa Leopoldo-style | **$$$**

Leopoldo Gil opened his emblematic restaurant in 1929 in what was then the most bohemian, although at times fairly insalubrious, neighborhood in the city of Barcelona. His commitment to traditional home cooking was a risk—on the first day, he served only two customers—but one that paid off eventually. The place became the favored haunt of artists and writers, actors and singers performing at the Liceu opera house nearby, and bullfighters, many of whom are immortalized in portraits hanging on the walls of the blue-and-yellow tiled dining rooms.

Casa Leopoldo is run by Gil's granddaughter, Rosa, and while the crowd may not be quite so famous, the restaurant still draws a loyal clientele of Catalan and international gourmands.

Products sourced every day in the Boqueria food market reflect the changing seasons and the culinary history of Catalonia in dishes such as hare in chocolate sauce, *cap-i-pota* (stewed head and hoof of pork), and *arroz brut* ("dirty" rice studded with baby cuttlefish and artichokes that give it its distinctive grubby color).

The lunch menu is hale, hearty, and reasonably priced, with mammoth portions of classics such as *revueltos* (creamy scrambled eggs studded with wild mushrooms) and stewed beef cheeks. Although lively by day, Casa Leopoldo really comes into its own at night, when diners dive into shared platters of little fried fish, anchovies in vinegar, and *pa amb tomaquet* (toasted bread rubbed with tomato, garlic, and olive oil), followed by dishes such as deeply savory stewed bull's tail. The extensive wine is strongest on Riojas, Albariños, and Priorats, which are among Rosa Gil's own favorite pressings.

With its determinedly untrendy approach to restaurant dining, Casa Leopoldo belongs to a bygone era, but discerning diners still revere the past. **TS**

Kaiku | Top-notch creative seafood dishes in the regenerated fisherman's quarter of Barcelona

Location Barcelona   **Signature dish** Smoked rice paella with wild mushrooms and artichokes | ❸❸

Glass windows fringed by bottle-green shutters, white paper tablecloths fluttering in the breeze, uninterrupted sea views, there is something of the old-fashioned Spanish fantasy about Kaiku. Reassuringly nontrendy it is all a Mediterranean seaside restaurant should be, and more—sitting down to a meal at a table on the seaside terrace that overlooks the beach is a must.

Basque chef Hugo Pla's cooking is in a league of its own, taking sustainable fish, much of it sourced from La Barceloneta, and turning it into a distinctive style of modern seafood cuisine. The product may be local, but he embraces influences from all over the world with gusto, particularly the fresh, zippy brightness of Asian dishes.

He grills *zamburiñas* (tiny, pinky-nail sized scallops) and drizzles over a yuzu vinaigrette, steams mussels in lemon and ginger, fries sea anemones in tempura batter to dip in mango aioli, scatters slivers of raw sea bream with poppy seeds and sundried tomatoes, and combines locally smoked rice with monkfish and rock mussels, or artichokes and wild mushrooms to create fall on a plate. All can be complemented by wine selected from a reasonably priced list.

Given the largesse of Pla's creative sparkle and its impeccable results, it is something of a miracle he has managed to remain relatively unknown, but that is also a big part of the appeal. Kaiku attracts a faithful, local clientele—and Catalans are nothing if not fastidious when it comes to the perfection of the fish and seafood they eat—making it almost impossible to get in without a reservation.

In a city overrun with tourists, places like Kaiku are a gift, combining old-school values of friendly service and an informal atmosphere with twenty-first century panache and creativity. **TS**

"… seeking it out is worth your while; the seafood here is excellent and the value is ironclad."

Fodor's Travel

⬆ *Chanquetes* (deep-fried goby fish) topped with a brace of fried eggs.

7 Portes | A taste of Barcelona's Belle Epoque with phenomenal rice dishes

Location Barcelona **Signature dish** Paella Parellada | ❸❸❸

In Barcelona, as in Paris, London, or New York, there are certain restaurants that have achieved fame worldwide thanks in no small part to the people that have passed through them. It is almost easier to draw up a list of who has not eaten at 7 Portes than who has, with a guest book strewn with compliments penned by the singer Lou Reed, actress Bo Derek, and even the late Spanish king, Juan de Borbón. It remains one of the city's best-loved and most iconic restaurants.

Situated in a stately, arcaded block dating back to the mid-nineteenth century it was the fantasy of one Josep Xifré i Cases, a Catalan businessman who made it his home, his office, and—for good measure—added a luxury café with no less than seven doors through which to lure the public, inspired by those he had seen in Paris. It changed hands several times over the years, but it was always top of the list of VIPs passing through, especially once it fell into the hands of the great gourmand Paco Parellada, the city's

answer to Escoffier, in the early 1940s. High-profile guests followed, and in true twenty-first century style, visitors can flick through a digital guest book on the restaurant website, but nothing beats the paper one.

The black-and-white tile floor, the frilly, tangerine-colored lampshades, and liveried waiters seem to belong to another era, which is all part of the thrill of eating here. It offers a taste of the Belle Epoque, Barcelona's golden age, and it still offers an authentic flavor of Catalunya, though it is most celebrated for rice dishes. Paella Parellada, seen on so many menus in Barcelona, was invented at 7 Portes as a nobleman's version of the dish. All the bones and shells are removed to prepare paella Parellada before serving, leaving diners with a clean, elegant rice dish fitting of their position and, presumably, their outfits. This is still the best place in town to try it. **TS**

⬆ Barcelona's 7 Portes is a much-loved institution.

Barraca | A modern classic for fish and rice dishes

Location Barcelona **Signature dish** Fish and seafood paella | ❸❸❸

The Spanish *chiringuito* (beach bar) has undergone dramatic changes. Gone are the sandy sardine shacks and in their place is a more sophisticated seaside dining room serving top-notch rice and seafood dishes. Barraca is the result of a collaboration between the pioneering Woki Organic Market that owns the property, and the chef Xavier Pellicer, whose pedigree has seen him in the position of head chef at the one-starred ABaC and the two-starred Can Fabes. Pellicer is back in the city he loves best, overseeing the cuisine at Barraca with chef Rafa de Valicourt. Both are passionate about organic ingredients, sustainable fishing, and biodynamic and natural wines, resulting in one of the most interesting lists in Barcelona. Little wonder the restaurant has been swiftly embraced by food-loving locals as a modern classic.

The elegant, first-floor dining room has uninterrupted views of the Mediterranean, reflected pleasingly on a palette of natural wood and stone plateware, glittering aquamarine glasses, and windows that span the length of the room letting in fresh sea breezes. Lunchtime is a convivial feast that goes on for hours, starting with snacks to share such as feather-light *buñuelos de bacalao* (salt-cod fritters), cockles, mussels, clams flash fried with garlic and guindilla chili peppers to add zing, and briny Cantabrian anchovies laid across impossibly crisp *pan con tomate* (bread with tomato). Afterward, out come crowd-sized pans of rice, cooked to al dente, chewy perfection and studded with artichokes, sausage, and cuttlefish, inky *arròs negre* (seafood and rice cooked with squid ink) enriched with dollops of aioli, and a classic paella studded generously with local fish and seafood. After the wonder years of molecular gastronomy, there is a return to grassroots cooking in Barcelona, and Barraca does it with flair. **TS**

⬆ Classic paella by the sea at Barraca in Barcelona.

Ca L'Isidre | A neighborhood classic with a modern outlook

Location Barcelona **Signature dish** Monkfish *suquet* (fish stew) with potatoes and clams | ❸❸❸

Nothing captures the essence of Barcelona life more than gathering friends around the table of one of the city's iconic restaurants. Ca l'Isidre is one of the old guard: an intimate and elegant neighborhood classic with wood-paneled dining rooms, Persian rugs on the floor, and vases of fresh flowers. It has been built on old-fashioned family values and meticulously executed dishes that make guests feel right at home. Since opening in March 1970, ostensibly to feed the theatergoers on the nearby Parallel, the place has thrived and, although it has never been one for nouvelle cuisine, molecular fireworks, or towering presentations, it manages to seem more modern than ever with each passing year.

Long before the locavore movement became fashionable, Isidre Gironés and his wife Montserrat Salvó had evolved their dishes to reflect tastes for a lighter style of cooking that showcases regional products. Catalans, passionate about the provenance of regional products, come for the three-course lunch menu, gourmet travelers seek it out for a taste of the authentic, and critics never fault it.

A bowl of sweet tender peas grown just along the coast and cutely nicknamed "Maresme caviar" are topped with a sliver of truffle plucked from the volcanic earth of the Garrotxa; a bright, tomato gazpacho comes garnished with chunks of lobster and crunchy vegetable toasts; and grilled diver scallops pair beautifully with briny oyster leaves. These are contrasted by a confident approach to nose-to-tail in the form of lamb's brains with black butter and meltingly soft and unctuous pig's trotters stuffed with porcini.

Seriously crowd-pleasing stuff with deep, traditional roots, but the owners' sights are set firmly on the future. Long may it be so. **TS**

⬆ Ca L'Isidre exemplifies stylish, elegant dining.

El Quim de la Boquería | An uncommon restaurant in a market

Location Barcelona   **Signature dish** Eggs with baby squid | $$

In 1987, when Quim Márquez Durán leased a tiny stall in Barcelona's La Boquería, the oldest and largest food market in Spain, he only had space for two burners, a sink, a cash register, a small display case, and a narrow counter at which five diners could eat at once. Yet, from the beginning, he showed a rare gift for understanding the particular characteristics and challenges inherent in every ingredient he handled.

Placing Márquez in a superb food market was like offering a master painter an infinite palette of colors. For Márquez, though, the palate mattered more than the palette. Despite limited space and equipment, he managed to create astonishing dishes by combining flavors and textures that were unexpected. Strips of lamb pan-cooked quickly in dark beer so they were fork-tender and had a slightly malty taste. When tiny fresh clams were available, he would steam them using cava, the Catalan sparkling wine. They took on a lemony sweetness and the fragrance of verbena.

Word spread, and Barcelonans waited patiently for a stool to discover what inspiration Márquez had that day—inevitably based on encountering a new ingredient as he roamed the market. No restaurant in Spain has access to fresher food. In 2000, a larger stall with eighteen seats became available. Márquez expanded, managing to increase the dishes on offer while improving their variety and quality. He and four young men (including his two sons) rotate balletically as they perfectly cook and serve a range of magnificent fish, seafood, meat, and vegetables.

As Márquez's place is open only for breakfast and lunch, most diners eat at least one course of fried eggs topped with their choice of Spanish ham, caramelized foie gras, wild mushrooms, fried whitebait, or tender baby squid made glorious when slathered with golden egg yolks. **FP**

⬆ The fresh food here is definitely worth waiting for.

Koy Shunka | Artful *kaiseki* cuisine with a Mediterranean twist

Location Barcelona **Signature dish** Japanese noodles with *espardeñas* (sea cucumbers) | ❺❺❺❺

Chef Hideki Matsuhisa got his first Michelin star in 2013 placing Koy Shunka firmly at the top end of Japanese restaurants in Spain. Born in Tokyo into a family of restaurateurs, Matsuhisa moved to Barcelona in 1997 as co-owner of Shunka, the first serious sushi restaurant in the city and one that became a favorite among the city's top chefs, Ferran Adrià and the late Santi Santamaria among them. When Matsuhisa opened Koy Shunka in 2008, it was to parlay his talents into a fine-dining experience that could integrate the culinary influences of his adopted land. The resulting *kaiseki*—a carefully structured, multi-course cuisine celebrated for meticulous preparation and presentation—is an ingenious fusion that combines

---

"… order at least eight dishes to get an idea of all the wonderful things they do here with sushi."

Time Out

---

the delicacy of Japanese techniques with more robust Iberian flavors such as Pata Negra ham, succulent Palamós shrimp, and organic, farmed caviar from the Rio Frío in Andalucia.

Sleek, slate-gray dining rooms wrap around an island bar with the best views of chefs preparing each dish with intrinsic precision. Koy Shunka offers a choice of two tasting menus, which roll out in a series of choreographed dishes that balance taste, texture, and temperature with seasonal ingredients such as silky nyumen soup noodles with *espardeñas* (sea cucumbers), diaphanous slivers of boat-fresh sashimi, snowy white slabs of wild Mediterranean turbot, and butter-tender chunks of Wagyu beef. **TS**

Cañete | Bustling tapas bar with southern style hospitality

Location Barcelona **Signature dish** Sweetbreads, shrimp, and artichokes | ❺❺❺

This cozy, tiled tapas bar with its pocket-sized Andaluz patio took Barcelona by storm when it opened in 2010. Hailing from Andalucia, the bar oozes the joie de vivre of the south, and it was crammed from the get-go with folk looking for tapas with provenance that was a step up from the ubiquitous *patatas bravas* (cubes of potato in a spicy, tomato sauce), *pimientos de padrón* (small green peppers), and deep-fried squid rings.

It has become the haunt of aficionados, with chefs working full throttle from an open kitchen behind the bar to deliver pristine Catalan seafood such as shrimp from Barceloneta cooked in sea water and local squid with white beans from the Maresme, as well as Andaluz classics like fried anchovies, lacy shrimp fritters (*tortas*) from the seaside towns near Cadiz, and heartier meat dishes like bull tail in red wine. On special occasions, a whole roast *cochinillo* (suckling pig) with butter-tender flesh contrasted by the crunchiest skin delicately spiced with cloves and garlic graces the bar top. There is an intriguing European wine list, too, featuring several natural wines, and plenty by the glass, including a Billecart-Salmon Champagne, although it is a shame not to see any sherry given the provenance of the menu.

Still, eating in Spain transcends the physicality of merely putting things in one's mouth. It is about friendship, conversation, and on-the-table emotions, and Cañete bristles with them all, so much so that it has expanded operations, incorporating the original Cañete Barra, where people can go for a quick lunch or supper at the bar, or Cañete Mantel (meaning "tablecloth"), where friends and families gather round the table and settle in for several hours. In terms of price, it may not be as modest as the tapas bars of the south, but few places capture the spirit of Spanish conviviality with such aplomb. **TS**

Hofmann | Accomplished food and optimum service from a cookery-school restaurant

Location Barcelona   **Signature dish** Homemade bread | ❸❸❸

Mey Hofmann was born in Germany but moved to Barcelona as a professional caterer. She set up Hofmann in 1982 as a cross between cookery school and restaurant. The team in the kitchen is a mix of experienced chefs and a large number of trainees from the school. The dining room has a tiled floor, low ceiling, and wood-paneled dining room, with black upholstery.

The numerous hands in the kitchen allow for elaborate plating and presentation of dishes. It also means that the bread is all made from scratch and is excellent: a typical selection includes focaccia, ewe's milk cheese roll, delicate brioche with bacon, an olive bread, and a sesame roll.

Warm *tarte fine* (thin tart) of sardines, onions, and tomato has very light pastry and high-quality sardines possessing great flavor, a fine example of what can be done with humble but good ingredients, presented skillfully. This might be followed by morels stewed with foie gras, which features liver and mushrooms in a cream sauce with a few chives as garnish.

A main course might be high-quality pigeon served with spicy onion chutney and caramelized onion, served with a crispy leg of pigeon as a texture contrast. A meal might conclude with a pretty dessert of crispy chocolate stuffed with coconut, liquid toffee, and a praline hazelnut ice cream with a spun sugar bag and toasted hazelnuts.

The army of chefs available comes to the fore at the end of the meal with an elaborate selection of petit fours. This might include a superb passion-fruit jelly; a delicate biscuit, chocolate truffle with praline wafer; or lemon curd on a biscuit base with a chocolate garnish. The service at Hofmann is efficient and friendly. It is a delightful restaurant, offering classy food in an unusual and fun environment. **AH**

"Unbelievable menu and a staff that tries very hard because they're being graded!"

Orange Coast Magazine

⊡ The Michelin-starred Hofmann is renowned for its beautifully plated food, including cheesecake.

Cinc Sentits | Classic fine dining meets thoroughly modern Catalan cooking

Location Barcelona **Signature dish** Diver scallop on Jerusalem artichoke puree with onion and Iberian ham | ❸❸❸

Within Barcelona's fine-dining circuit, few chefs execute their tasting menu so generously as Jordi Artal at Cinc Sentits. The Catalan-Canadian chef is self-taught, passionate about his Catalan roots—he opened the restaurant together with his mother, Rosa, and sister, Amèlia, after relocating to Barcelona from San Francisco in 2004—and serves some of the most innovatively contemporary Catalan cooking based on locally and sustainably sourced products.

The dining room is sleek, elegant, and somewhat dark with spotlights focused on the tables to keep diners attention on the food, while shimmering gold, chain-link lanterns add a sense of luxury and glamour to what is otherwise a fairly minimal space. Tables are amply spaced and laid traditionally with thick white linens and Riedel glassware. There is no music. In many respects, it is classic Michelin dining but with an air of expectation that ensures a frisson of excitement and edginess.

Artal's signature snack is a layered shot of *flor de sal* (sea salt), Canadian maple syrup, and a foamy cava syllabub that makes for a genius appetite sharpener before the tasting menu continues in a series of prodigiously talented creations. His is a journey through the seasons, across land and sea, manifest in dishes elevated with haute techniques like smoked potato and silky egg custard topped with sustainable caviar from the Val d'Aran, trout smoked over Maresme pine with cucumber pickles and fresh goat cheese, and suckling pork cooked *sous vide* (under vacuum). Vegetables like Jerusalem artichokes, wild onions, Girona apples, and sweet tomatoes get equal billing alongside more obvious luxuries such as Galician diver scallops and foie gras, suckling lamb and Araíz pigeon, artisan cheeses and jewel-like fruits. Combined with an artful wine pairing, Cinc Sentits is an unforgettable experience, and, in terms of price-quality ratio, arguably the best deal in Barcelona. **TS**

"Simply sublime, this takes you on a roller-coaster ride to bliss, delighting at every turn ..."

Zagat

⬆ Cinc Sentits' tasting menu offers a delightful journey through land and sea.

➡ The decor is sleek and stylish.

Quimet & Quimet | Top tapas
in a tiny neighborhood bodega

Location Barcelona   **Signature dish** Shrimp *montadito* (bread rolls with cheese, shrimp, honey, and caviar) | 🟢🟢

Many years ago, two prestigious American food critics got into a fight over who had discovered Quimet & Quimet first. Whoever it was, word spread fast, and it is safe to say that it remains one of the most popular tapas bars in Barcelona. This would be less surprising were it not for the fact that owner Quim's specialty are *conservas* (seafood in a can)—a gourmet product that is much revered across Spain, but one that can leave unsuspecting foreigners cold. In Quim's hands however, the seemingly humble, no-cook tapas are elevated to the sublime, like a *montadito* piece of small bread topped with confit tomatoes, luscious canned tomatoes, and chopped capers. Add to this a handful of other stellar ingredients—gourmet artichoke

---

"This lively bodega is justly famed for its unique and exquisite montaditos … "

Guardian

---

hearts; balsamic onions; plump, boiled shrimp perhaps drizzled with truffled honey; or a coarse pork pâté with candied chestnuts—and this truly is some of the finest tapas in the land.

Quimet & Quimet opened in the 1960s, first as a small *bodega* where locals went to buy their wine. Over the years, a few snacks were offered to go with a tumbler of wine from the barrel, or a glass of *vermut* (local vermouth) on tap, which were so good, they began to take over. People flocked to the tiny bar lined from floor to ceiling with wine bottles, and wedged themselves around a couple of high tables for a lunchtime aperitif or pre-dinner snack, which quickly became the main act. **TS**

Pakta | New Wave *nikkei*
with a laid-back soul

Location Barcelona   **Signature dish** Squid nigiri (sushi) with huacatay salt and Iberian pork dumplings | 🟢🟢🟢🟢

Albert Adrià worked at his elder brother's highly influential restaurant El Bulli, and was instrumental in its meteoric rise to being voted the world's best three times. Described as "the most talented chef I know" by Danish chef Rene Redzepi of Noma, Adrià is finally getting his day in the sun and building a culinary empire of his own.

Pakta is based on *nikkei* cuisine dating back to the first wave of Japanese immigrants into Peru, who created their own fusion of the two culinary cultures. In Adrià's hands, it is an haute expression of the food, embracing the elegance and delicacy of Japanese dishes with the most robust flavors of South America. But he has taken a fresh approach to the fine-dining ambience.

The restaurant has the coziness and informality of a Japanese *izakaya* (pub) or an Andean bar, reminding patrons that eating out, even at this level, should be fun. Designed by Barcelona firm El Equipo Creativo, a mere thirty-two covers are shoehorned into a tiny dining room where the ceiling and walls are crisscrossed by colorful yarns, wooden tables are left bare, and the bar, where many of the dishes are prepared, is the beating heart of the place. Heading the kitchen with Adrià are Jorge Muñoz and Kyoko Ii from Peru and Japan, respectively, who had both been working at the Adrià brothers' tapas bar, Tickets. The trio generate a buzz that few other fine-dining establishments can. Dishes like squid sashimi with huacatay salt and lime, sea bass ceviche with a tangy kumquat *leche de tigre* (tiger's milk), and suckling-pork *gyoza* (dumplings) attack the senses on multiple levels. It is taste, texture, temperature, unusual ingredients, and unlikely combinations that conspire to seduce the senses, making this little restaurant one of the most exciting places to eat in Europe. **TS**

Sant Pau | Three-Michelin starred dining at a restaurant run by one of Spain's greatest chefs

Location Barcelona **Signature dish** Dentex with capers, olives, and vermouth | ❺❺❺❺❺

The world of fine dining is peculiar in having comparatively few female chefs, a situation that is happily changing, albeit rather slowly. Just outside of Barcelona, however, in the little seaside town of Sant Pol de Mar, Carme Ruscalleda has long been recognized as one of the best chefs in Spain. With a sister restaurant in Madrid, headed by her son Raül Balam, and another in Tokyo, it is still to the original that serious gourmands make their pilgrimage.

Situated in a classical nineteenth-century, Mediterranean villa on the seafront with a verdant garden off the main dining room, it is a welcome breath of fresh air after the city, but still close enough to go to for lunch. The light-filled space provides a pleasing backdrop to a tasting menu built out of a reverence for local ingredients, particularly the fruit and vegetables that grow in the market gardens of the Maresme coast, and a keen awareness of the seasons. Compared to many of Spain's top chefs, Ruscalleda's great skill is in her lightness of touch and coaxing deep flavors from seemingly simple ingredients. The Catalan restaurant mirrors the delicate techniques learned in Japan, while the Tokyo arm bursts with bright Mediterranean flavors. The two kitchens complement each other supremely well, a nod to the trend for Catalan-Japanese fusion that has become a part of the Barcelona restaurant scene, applied the other way around.

Dishes like Romesco dashi with kelp and wild chanterelle mushrooms, or a riff on the Catalan classic of slow-roast duck with pears, updated with the sour-salty addition of purslane and bright acidity of yuzu, sage and lemon marshmallows, and licorice and sherbet sticks show the restaurant at its very best. This is an icon of Catalan cuisine in the twenty-first century and all that it embraces. **TS**

"I like my dishes to be a bit playful, and to make the diners smile ..."

Carme Ruscalleda, chef and founder of Sant Pau

⬆ Witty and creative food from an acclaimed chef.

Tickets | Tapas from Spanish master chefs

Location Barcelona   **Signature dish** Spherico olives, lobster escabeche, and pork jowl steamed buns | ❸❸❸

When El Bulli—one of the world's most feted restaurants—shut its door forever at the end of the summer of 2012, it weighed heavy on those who had never managed to get a table. Fortunately, the Adrià brothers who ran it are never ones to sit on their laurels, as the opening of their tapas bar in Barcelona, Tickets, would prove.

Conceived as a homage to the nation's favorite pastime—to "tapear" (to bar hop, snacking and sipping en route)—it was designed as a series of small bars, each with its own specialty: fish and seafood at one, crisp croquettes and silky ham at another, and echoes of the lauded mothership in the form of gossamer thin slivers of tuna that look like ham, oysters dressed with passion fruit caipirinha, delicate little "mushrooms" sprouting from grassy granita, and golden quail's eggs topped with caviar. In addition to finger food and oysters, there are also desserts on offer, including cheescake with lemongrass sorbet.

Dining at Tickets is the ultimate trip into an edible fairground with candy-colored dining chairs, flash-bulb lights, and cotton-candy machines. Yet it is also a place where the service is as elegant as the presentation, where the key driver of the project, chef Albert Adrià, is often to be seen working the stoves, and where his elder brother, legendary El Bulli chef Ferran, is perched at the bar quaffing vintage cava with a couple of his chef friends.

Like all the best tapas bars, Tickets does not take itself too seriously. It is a place to stimulate the senses and the taste buds; but, above all, it is a place to have fun. Unsurprisingly, since the nanosecond it opened, it has been one of the most popular eateries in Barcleona, with everyone from local foodies to international gastronauts clamoring for the chance to sample some of the Adrià brothers' creations. **TS**

⬆ The colorful interior at Tickets has a fairground vibe.

Rías de Galicia | A showcase for the finest bounty from Spain's three seas

Location Barcelona **Signature dish** Spider-crab *canellones* and soupy rice with velvet crabs | ❸❸❸

Since opening in 1986, Rías de Galicia has become regarded as the best fish and seafood restaurant in Barcelona. The Iglesias family who own it are lifelong friends of the Adrìa brothers of El Bulli fame, and a collaboration between the two families has seen them add the Cañota tapas bar and the Espai Kru raw-food bar to their little enclave of restaurants in Poble Sec. However, the flagship is still Rias de Galica, which remains deeply rooted in sourcing and serving exceptional fish and seafood from the Iberian Peninsula.

An elegant dining room on an oyster and purple palette is flanked by polished partitions recalling the minimal elegance of Japanese Ryokan, although the large oil paintings depicting landscapes of three Spanish seas—the Cantabrian, the Atlantic, and the Mediterranean—leaves no doubt of the restaurant's provenance. This reverence for product is showcased within vast glass cabinets piled high with fish and seafood given a modern makeover: mysterious *percebes* (gooseneck barnacles) from the rocky shores of Galicia need nothing to make them more exciting, neither do hot pink Palamós shrimp cooked on a slab of salt. But tender *espardeñas* (sea cucumbers), popularized by Ferran Adrià and beloved by chefs all over Spain, do well with potatoes slow cooked in olive oil perfumed by cilantro, as do slippery, tiny *angulas* (baby eels) from the Basque country, with their traditional partners of garlic and chili.

Raw scallops are punched up by the wild, briny tang of sea urchins from the Costa Brava, plump anchovies from the Cantabrian come on shaved ice spiked with lemon, sweet *navajas* (razor clams) are enhanced by a smidgen of smoked salt, and wild *dorada* (gilthead bream) sashimi is given spark with the addition of a jalapeño chili-pepper dressing. **TS**

⭱ Rías de Galicia is known for the quality of its seafood.

Víctor Gutiérrez |

Creative Peruvian food in Salamanca

Location Salamanca **Signature dish** Scallop ceviche | 🆂🆂

Tucked away in the picturesque old streets of the medieval heart of Salamanca, this tiny restaurant, which seats twenty diners in its minimalist dining room, offers some striking food.

Peruvian chef Víctor Gutiérrez, whose talents are on show in this, his eponymous Michelin-starred restaurant, draws on Peru's richly diverse cuisine for inspiration, with influences ranging from Inca to Japanese to Mediterranean and Spanish. He enjoys experimenting with both striking flavor combinations and imaginative presentation. This is a Peruvian chef who can pair cod with sea-urchin ice cream and Oreo cookies with guacamole, but also serves a simple scallop lime ceviche as a course in its own right.

"Justifiably exclusive vibe with emphasis on innovative dishes with plenty of colorful drizzle."

Lonely Planet

Admittedly, the presentation is not simple: the scallop arrives on a plate covering a glass bowl containing a live, swimming goldfish.

Diners can choose from assorted set tasting menus, a format which gives Gutiérrez the chance to showcase his culinary creativity. Ingredients which a diner might encounter during a meal range from flavorful Iberian ham to delicate grouper sushi, from Asian-style *tocino* (bacon) rolls to tasty veal steak. The tasting menu could include: crab ravioli and suckling pig interspersed with a cold green tea and vanilla palette cleanser, fish in coconut, yellow chili sashimi, a baked potato, foie gras with port-and-mango ice cream, and petit fours hidden in a little metal box. **SH**

Bodega de la Ardosa |

Traditional tapas staples in Malasaña

Location Madrid **Signature dish** *Tortilla española* (Spanish omelet) | 🆂

The area of Malasaña is Madrid's ever-changing hipsterville, but past the secondhand boutiques, pseudo-Mexican quesadilla joints, and Franco-Japanese fusion eateries, one locale refuses to follow fads, the Bodega de la Ardosa.

The bar's pedigree is impeccable, and it is said to have been frequented by Spanish artist Francisco de Goya. The clientele has changed in the more than 200 hundred years La Ardosa has been open, but little else has. That is why Madrid's trendies go here—to drop their pretensions for an evening of Spanish staples.

La Ardosa's decoration is a treasure trove of trinkets charting its history. There are league tables of pub games no longer played, and a back wall lined with what must be every brand of beer ever drunk in the bar. An immutable love of beer is evident in the addition of Scottish craft beer BrewDog on tap, one of the few modern trappings in the bar.

Although plenty of restaurants have tried to reinvent the Spanish omelet, there is such a thing as a perfect *tortilla española*, and at La Ardosa Spain's perennial classic is consistently excellent. Just cooked on the outside and still gooey in the center, all other tortillas can be measured for quality and tradition against this one. La Ardosa's *salmorejo*—gazpacho's lesser known but heartier brother made with tomato, bread, a little garlic, and vinegar—is fantastic. And do not forget a selection of their freshly made *croquetas*: crispy croquettes filled with a creamy béchamel sauce and spiked with a choice of cabrales Asturian blue cheese, Iberian ham, shrimp, or *cecina* (cured beef.)

And, a little secret—if the bar area is too crowded, which it inevitably will be, it is fine to climb under the bar and enter the little den at the back, where a speakeasylike room awaits those with the gall to do such a thing. **DC**

El Arrozal | The best restaurant in Madrid to eat paella cooked to order

Location Madrid   **Signature dish** *Paella valenciana* (artichokes, green beans, red and green bell peppers, white beans, and chicken with bomba rice) | ❸❺

No dish is more identified with Spain than paella, and one of the best places to try it is El Arrozal, a charming paella restaurant in Madrid's La Latina district. The proprietor, Juan Antonio Pastor, serves the gamut of Spain's rice dishes. Traditionalists can opt for the classic meat *paella valenciana*, the original paella that was invented in the Albufera rice fields around Valencia. Seafood lovers can try the *paella de marisco*, and those who can never decide can choose that happy compromise, the *paella mixta* (mixed paella.) Vegetarians are not left out because the *paella de verduras* is especially for them, while coeliacs can eat with ease as the entire menu is gluten free.

But there is more to rice dishes in Spain than just paella, and El Arrozal serves them all. *Arroz a la banda*, an Alicante dish consisting of rice cooked in fish broth and served with shrimp, or the king of rice dishes, *arroz con bogavante* (rice with lobster), are also available. One of the advantages of El Arrozal is that it is possible to order all of these because it serves excellent individual paellas. Most good restaurants in Spain will not serve paella for less than two people, but at El Arrozal everyone can order his or her own paella, or share several. All paellas are cooked freshly to order—many restaurants do not do so—with freshly prepared ingredients every time. For the *paella valenciana*, artichokes, green beans, red and green bell peppers, white beans, and chicken are briefly stir-fried with bomba rice. The tomato and saffron broth is then added and the dish is left to cook. As is traditional, the paella is not stirred while it is cooked, allowing for a an essential crispy bottom to develop.

El Arrozal also runs paella classes in English, so students can take the secret of how to make perfect paella home with them. **DC**

> *"Take the set menu for a good value meal of paella, salad, and tapas."*
>
> gospain.about.com

⬆ In the summer months, diners can eat outside on the terrace at Madrid's El Arrozal restaurant.

Casa Ciriaco | Castilian
classics at a traditional taverna

Location Madrid **Signature dish** *Cochinillo* (suckling pig) | 💰💰

Casa Ciriaco is on the ground floor of an old block on the busy Calle Mayor in Madrid's city center, not far from the Royal Palace. The building is famous in Madrid for an assassination attempt on King Alfonso XIII as his wedding procession passed by in 1906. An anarchist threw a bomb at him from an upstairs window. The king—and the restaurant—escaped unscathed. Local chef Ciriaco Muñoz took over an existing bar and started serving food there in 1917. His descendants still run it as one of the most traditional restaurants in the Spanish capital.

The Muñoz family continues to serve the same range of old-time Castilian dishes. Expect hefty portions of classics like suckling pig, partridge and

---

"Nouvelle cuisine here means anything being served in 1900 …"

frommers.com

---

butter beans, hare with white beans, chicken in almond sauce, and a chickpea stew that—by obscure tradition—is only prepared on Tuesdays. There is a renowned cellar of classic Spanish wines, too.

The restaurant retains an old-fashioned layout. Guests enter under a red awning over the pavement, into a narrow area by the bar. It leads into the wider dining room beyond. The wooden floor, whitewashed walls, and dark wooden chairs keep it simple, although the walls are decorated with bullfighting souvenirs and photos of famous names that have eaten there, including Spanish royalty and writers. Contemporary clientele include businessmen having lunch or tourists looking for a taste of traditional Madrid. **SH**

Taberna de la Daniela Goya | Traditional stew year round

Location Madrid **Signature dish** *Cocido madrileño* (chickpea stew) | 💰💰

The original Taberna de la Daniela Goya is found in the wealthy and prestigious Salamanca district of Madrid, just off Calle Goya, one of the city's main shopping areas. From the outside, the old signage and dark wooden doors make Taberna de la Daniela Goya look like a traditional bar; from the inside, the bright downlighters, zinc bar, and modern tiled walls seem to belong to a breezy café. The truth is somewhere in between. It is a restaurant that is popular for light meals and snacks with passing locals.

Taberna de la Daniela Goya has become known for one specialty, announced in big letters above the door: the local dish "*cocido.*" Normally, the dish is served in winter as a traditional stew based around chickpeas with various chunks of meat added. However, at Taberna de la Daniela Goya, *cocido* becomes a full meal and is served all year round. Order it at Taberna de la Daniela Goya to receive a tureen of chicken vermicelli soup, a plate of chickpea and vegetables (this could include potato, carrot, tomato, and cabbage), and a bowl of meats, often including chicken, beef, ham, *chorizo* (spicy sausage), black pudding, and morcilla sausage. Some eat the trio separately, some like to have them at the same time and mix ingredients as if it was a stew. The children's menu even includes an infant version of *cocido*.

The formula has been a big hit in Madrid, and the "Daniela" name appears on three other restaurants in the capital. Yet there is more to the chain than chickpeas. For snacking, there is a range of more than seventy different tapas, canapés, and *raciones* (large portions of tapas). For full dining, there is a menu that includes gazpacho, noodle soup, tripe, Basque cod with *pil-pil* (garlic and chili) sauce, and a range of homemade desserts, such as *tarta de manzana* (apple pie) and *arroz con leche* (rice pudding). **SH**

El Club Allard | Witty, stylish molecular cuisine in one of Madrid's most prestigious gourmet temples

Location Madrid   **Signature dish** Eggs with bread and pancetta served over potato cream sauce | ❸❸❸❸

Overlooking Madrid's Plaza de España, El Club Allard is handsomely housed on the second floor of a grand historic building, the Modernist Casa Gallardo that dates to 1908. Its prestigious address hints at its roots as a private club, established in 1998. In 2003, however, El Club Allard opened its doors to the general public and, under its Basque head chef, Diego Guerrero, began garnering Michelin stars.

Diners ascend to the restaurant up a flight of stairs to be greeted by a discreetly luxurious, formal, high-ceilinged dining room, complete with chandeliers, thick carpet, and tables, spaced widely apart, set with crisply ironed white tablecloths.

Despite the traditional setting, the food is modernist, offered in the form of assorted tasting menus. Diners might begin a meal with Spanish truffle with foie gras and shredded venison, served over a base of tomatillo smoke that is released when served, the foie gras tasting properly of liver but neither too strong nor overly smoky: a carefully made and enjoyable dish.

Guerrero has a playful strand to his cooking, as witnessed in his little culinary joke in a dish called, "Babybel," which looks like the popular ellipsoid cheese encased in red wax. In reality, it has a coating of beetroot, but inside is high-quality, rich-tasting Camembert whipped mousse flavored with truffle, served with a savory tuile. Strong culinary technique is also on offer, as can be seen in a dish of pigeon (from Bresse), precisely roasted and served with assorted wild mushrooms over truffled rice cooked in a mussel broth.

The trickery continues in a dessert called "fishbowl," where the "mussels" are dark chocolate, the bright red "coral" is sculpted white chocolate, and the "seaweed" is a savory cookie. **AH**

"The kitchen is alive … and those who devote themselves to it must learn how to listen to it."

Diego Guerrero, head chef of El Club Allard

⊼ A purple candle supports butterfish sashimi with three cauliflowers, truffle, and *tobiko* (flying-fish roe).

Casa Labra | An old-fashioned shopper's respite in the center of Madrid

Location Madrid   **Signature dish** Battered cod bites and sweet Spanish vermouth | ❸

Situated just seconds from Puerta del Sol, the center of Madrid and the point from which all distances in Spain are measured, Casa Labra is a hidden haven. Its location opposite a branch of the El Corte Inglés department-store chain means that it is also a favorite place for weary shoppers.

Yet Casa Labra has been a convenient point of reference for Madrileños and visitors to the city for more than a century. Founded in the nineteenth century, and resolutely old-fashioned in its appearance, with dark wood, tiled walls, and marble-topped walls, it offers a traditional taverna experience and reasonably priced tapas.

Head to the bar and order a thimble-sized glass of *vermut* (sweet vermouth) on tap. Then squeeze to the next counter to order a little tapas. The veteran staff know customers are passing through on a busy day, so service is quick and efficient. When it comes to what to order, the answer is simple. This Madrid institution has made its name for its way with cod, which it has been serving since it first opened. Opt for the trademark dishes: *tajada de bacalao*, a dainty piece of battered fish, with a crisp, golden-brown coating, or a *croqueta de bacalao* (homemade cod croquette), with its tasty, soft filling.

Casa Labra epitomizes the "eating-on-the-go" element of Spanish tapas. The servings are tiny and the prices, thankfully, are appropriately low, allowing clients to nip in and out, then continue with their day.

If a short pit stop in the bar (or outside on the street if the weather is nice) is not enough, head through to the sit-down restaurant for more cod, just served more elaborately. *Bacalao con setas y alcaparras* (a large piece of cod served in a sauce made of olive oil, leeks, wild mushrooms, capers, tomato puree, and orange juice) is the star dish there. **DC**

⬆ Locals flock to Casa Labra for its classic cod dishes.

El Brillante | Simply the best fried calamari in Madrid

Location Madrid   **Signature dish** *Bocadillo de calamares* (calamari baguette) | **$**

El Brillante belongs to a dying breed: a no-nonsense, napkins-on-the-floor, Spanish eating experience that takes pride in the quality of its dishes (one in particular), rather than its decor or surroundings. It is a classic, functional, working-class eatery, with a zinc-topped bar, tobacco-yellow lighting, constant hubbub of clattering plates, bellowing barman, and loudly conversing guests trying to make themselves heard over the racket.

Every item on the menu is a bona fide classic, *boquerones* (anchovies), *bonito* (tuna), *lomo con pimientos* (pork loin with green peppers), all prepared and served with frenzied efficiency. But most people are there for one thing: the *bocadillo de calamares* (calamari baguette). Forget rubbery calamari—squid rings got their fame from dishes like these. Freshly fried in a light yellow batter and served with a sprinkling of lemon, they are juicy, not chewy—a subtle marriage of flavors.

Clients order on one side and the food is prepared on the other: the gap is bridged by an almighty holler. The chef and the barman seem to be arguing—one is smiling, the other is not. Could they both be joking? It is hard to tell with these battle-hardened staff, all with the twenty or thirty years' of experience needed to keep a bar such as El Brillante in a semblance of order. They will not always acknowledge customers, even when they have heard them, as the time that might take could be better spent serving the next person.

Wash a meal down with a beer or try a *café asiático*. An invention from Cartagena in southern Spain that is rarely found in Madrid, *asiático* is a sweet concoction of coffee, brandy sweetened milk, Licor 43, cinnamon, coffee beans, lemon peel, and foamed milk. Another classic to enjoy. **DC**

⬆ A resolutely down-to-earth taste of Madrid at El Brillante.

Punto MX | Contemporary Mexican, delivering vivid flavors and corn tortillas prepared in front of guests

Location Madrid   **Signature dish** Baked marrow presented in the bone | ❺❺

"A Mexican restaurant that eschews preconceived ideas with its modern look and cuisine …"

Michelin Guide

⬆ Punto MX serves authentic Mexican regional cuisine in the Spanish capital.

Mexican chef Roberto Ruiz is a man on a mission. He wants to educate Europe about the cuisine of his home country. To this end, having previously run a restaurant north of Mexico City, Ruiz opened Punto MX in Madrid, his first venture outside Mexico.

Housed in a residential district of Madrid, the basement dining room, with its white walls and simple decor, is modern in style. Diners can enjoy Ruiz's Mexican cuisine, made with a commitment to high standards and innovation.

Dishes to enjoy there include those made with handmade tortillas. Shrimp with a *chipotle* (smoke-dried jalapeño pepper) sauce, for example, is served on a type of corn tortilla called *sopes*, a thick tortilla with pinched sides. The shrimp is tender, the *chipotle* sauce subtle, and the tortilla itself excellent—a world away from the industrial tortillas that are usually found in Europe's Mexican restaurants.

Another unusual dish is a well-balanced, nicely judged offering of tuna tacos, served with onions, avocado, and Serrano chili (a chili pepper originating from the Mexican regions of Puebla and Hidalgo) on a taco base.

The unusual emphasis on ingredient quality is seen in Wagyu beef tacos. The beef, raised in Spain, is excellent—tender and flavorful—combined to good effect and served with grilled onion, avocado, cilantro, grilled green tomatoes with jalapeño peppers, and shredded red bell pepper. The caramelized onions give a slight sweetness to the dish, nicely balancing the spiciness of the peppers.

As demonstrated by Punto MX, Ruiz is a great ambassador for the cuisine of Mexico. The ingredients used are of high quality, the tortillas made to order are a revelation, and the balance of the dishes is excellent. **AH**

De La Riva | Enjoy a leisurely lunch at this acclaimed restaurant

Location Madrid   **Signature dish** *Calamares en tinta* (squid in ink) | 💲💲

Packed with small, square tables and noisy with animated conversation, De La Riva is a taste of classic Spanish eating out—and that is before considering the expertly prepared traditional dishes.

Spain may have a contemporary reputation for the most colorful avant-garde cuisine, but there is also a popular hunger for classic-style dining experiences.

De La Riva is one of the most highly rated of these old-style restaurants in the capital. It has been serving top-quality Iberian dishes since 1932, when it was founded by Obdulia de la Riva, who was previously personal cook for Prime Minister Antonio Maura. In the twenty-first century, the decor is more sophisticated and the marketing more slick. The restaurant claims it is "preserving the gastronomic ecosystem," and customers love to hear background facts, like the owner cycles to market daily to buy fresh ingredients.

In true classic taverna style, there is no printed menu. Instead, the waiter recites what is available that day. This usually includes Iberian classics like suckling pig, homely seasonal stews, steak, veal, and grilled fish. Plenty of sophisticated flourishes emerge from the kitchen, too, like a sauce of green eels, calamari fried in anchovy oil, roast quinces, artichokes with ham, and innovative offal dishes.

The restaurant stands in the north of the city, near Real Madrid's Santiago Bernabéu stadium and is popular with fans on game days, and the rest of the time with businessmen, families, and politicians. It is not unusual to see a politician's bodyguards standing at the door while he or she eats inside.

Traditionally, Spaniards ate their main meal at lunchtime, which was followed by a long break from work. True to form, De La Riva serves lunch not dinner. Lunchtime customers, however, often linger well into the evening, drinking, and playing cards or chess. **SH**

El Tigre | Supersize portions of tapas—for free!

Location Madrid   **Signature dish** *Patatas bravas* (cubes of potato in a spicy, tomato sauce) | 💲

The word "tapa" comes from the Spanish word for "lid," originally used to cover a glass of wine with a slice of ham or cheese, chiefly to keep the flies out. Over time, tapas evolved to become more elaborate dishes served on small plates and, in most of Spain, rather than free nibbles served with a drink, they became something customers ordered and paid for.

El Tigre, however, has returned to the idea of free food and, with an admirable generosity of spirit, the plates of tapas there could cover punch bowls. With a round of drinks, expect three or four classics: *tortilla española* (Spanish omelet), *lacón gallega* (Galician dried ham), *patatas bravas* (cubes of potato in a spicy, tomato sauce), ham croquettes, cheese, Serrano ham,

---

"Buy a round of beers and get a plateful of delicious snacks to go with it …"

gadling.com

---

or *arroz caldoso* (a soupy rice dish). El Tigre's tapas are no gimmick—other bars like it exist, but this Chueca district classic is the best.

Do not presume that El Tigre sacrifices quality for quantity. The *lacón gallega* is always lean, juicy, and tender; the *patatas bravas* are cooked impeccably; and the ham croquettes are the creamiest ever, clearly homemade, and always fresh out of the fryer.

With the drinks so reasonably priced, it is a wonder El Tigre manages to stay in business, yet thankfully it does. Head there to enjoy the lively atmosphere, the excellent wine, and the free food. A visit to El Tigre to sample the supersize tapas is a Madrid rite of passage. **DC**

Sacha | Accomplished, imaginative food in a hidden gem

Location Madrid **Signature dish** Beef with bone marrow | ❸❸

With its tucked-away location in the north of the city, Sacha, founded in 1972, is one of Madrid's hidden culinary gems. Having found this well-established restaurant, however, the appealing surroundings—on a fine summer evening head for the terrace—and welcoming staff will make one feel glad to have made the effort to go off the beaten track. A number of the kitchen and waiting staff have worked in the restaurant for more than forty years. They have watched Sacha Hormaechea, the son of the owners, grow up here. Having trained in Catalonia, chef Sacha took over the ownership of the restaurant and can often be seen walking around the restaurant that his parents named after him.

> *"On a warm night, there may be no more pleasant place to sit in Madrid than on Sacha's leafy terrace."*
>
> The New York Times

There are two menus at Sacha: the traditional menu that has not changed since Sacha's parents owned the restaurant and the more extensive "today's specials," with a focus on seasonal ingredients. In fall, try "Caesar's mushrooms" made from thinly sliced mushrooms served raw with tarragon, lemon, and pine nuts; or a deftly cooked "lazy mushroom omelet" cooked on one side but not flipped, with the soft side of the dish garnished with a light vinegar and chive dressing.

Seafood is worth investigating, too. Fine-quality tuna, brought in fresh from the Cadiz village of Zahara de los Atunes, is paired with *tocino* (Spanish bacon) and Japanese flavorings. **DC**

El Pescador | The finest fish restaurant in Madrid

Location Madrid **Signature dish** *Merluza a la plancha* (grilled hake) or oysters from the bar | ❸❸❸

All the fish and seafood at Madrid's El Pescador, other than two types of French oyster, is fished in Spanish waters by Pescadarias Coruñesas, the fishing company that owns El Pescador: lobster and hake from the Cantabrian Sea; crayfish from San Lucar in Andalusia; shrimp from Huelva, Andalusia, and Denia, Alicante; and *angulas* (elver eels) from the Basque Country.

Twice daily, these catches are then packed in ice and flown to Barajas Airport in Madrid, where they are sorted and taken directly to market and to the El Pescador restaurant. Whether customers eat lunch or dinner, they can be sure the seafood has just arrived on the premises.

El Pescador is a fish restaurant. There are not even sprigs of parsley here; the fish come unadorned, as naked as the day they came out of the sea. Do not look for side dishes either: the only vegetable to be found is in the tomato and *ventresca de bonito* (white tuna belly meat) salad. However, there is a wide selection of fish and shellfish on offer, including turbot, sole, grouper, sea bass, shrimp, clams, blue crabs, lobsters, oysters, goose barnacles, and crayfish.

Instead of accompaniments, diners are offered a choice of styles for their fish. *A la romana* (lightly battered), *a la vasca* (in a clam and white wine sauce), *a la bilbaína* (shallow fried with garlic, lemon, and guindilla chili peppers), or *al horno* (oven baked with olive oil, vinegar, and garlic.) Traditionally, each fish is served in a particular style or two. El Pescador's waiters will always urge guests instead to go with the simplest option: *a la plancha*—grilled on a griddle with the slightest touch of olive oil and a sprinkling of sea salt, a method of cooking that allows the freshness of the fish and seafood to shine. **DC**

▣ El Pescador's seafood is fresh from the Spanish seas.

Casa Lucio | Homely restaurant acclaimed for fine versions of Spanish classics

Location Madrid　**Signature dish** "Lucio's fried eggs" | ❸❸

At the age of twelve, Lucio Blazquez began working at a long-established restaurant in Madrid. After serving there for almost thirty years, he managed to buy the restaurant from its owner. He promptly refurbished it, renamed it "Casa Lucio," and reopened in 1974. With the help of his four children, Blazquez's business has gained a reputation across Spain as an excellent traditional Spanish restaurant.

There is nothing chic or pretentious about Casa Lucio. Dark wooden double doors lead from a tiny street in the Latin Quarter into the dimly lit, bustling interior. The floor has terracotta tiles and a few framed paintings are dotted on the plain walls. All the wood is stained dark. Brick arches separating the restaurant sections are dark, too, while a panel of old decorative tiles behind the bar is obscured by a row of hanging hams. Old-school uniformed waiters serve dishes on crockery featuring the restaurant's name. The homely atmosphere is a perfect match for head chef Aurelio

Calderon's menu of Iberian classics. There is the predictable tripe, veal, suckling pig, robust seasonal stews, and tried-and-tested traditional desserts like rice pudding or egg custard.

The dishes may be familiar but the quality is not: Blazquez's kitchen sources the best ingredients and prepares them with skill and experience that has led to lines forming outside. Fans of Spanish classics appreciate that the baby eels come with the right amount of oil, garlic, and pepper; endives and tomato salad is dressed with cumin, garlic, and olive oil; local *cocido* stew includes the highest-quality beef, *chorizo* (spicy sausage), and black pudding; and the croquettes are made on site with a mild béchamel sauce. Not everything is by the book, and Blazquez is proud of his signature dish: a concoction of loosely fried free-range eggs on a bed of potato chips. **SH**

⬆ Dishes at Casa Lucio are lovingly prepared.

Casa Ricardo | Time-warp restaurant serving the freshest ingredients

Location Madrid   **Signature dish** *Gallina en pepitoria* (hen in an almond sauce) | ❸❸

After a bullfight in Madrid, cuts of meat from the bull's carcass, from entrecôte steak or tail, are brought by Casa Ricardo to be cooked and served in one of the tiny restaurant's exquisite beef dishes. Its unique selling point is its ingredients: fresh vegetables from specially selected *huertas* (vegetable gardens) and meats from some of the best suppliers in Spain.

A neighborhood restaurant with space for twenty covers, Casa Ricardo can be filled easily by a few discerning locals, and the atmosphere is suitably informal. Everyone knows everyone's name here. If someone wants to see what is cooking that day, he or she simply pokes his or her head inside the kitchen—there is no door—and sees the cooks at work.

For the daring, Ricardo specializes in *casquería* (tripe and offal). Regulars order dishes such as *sesos* (pig's brains), knowing both that the offal will be good quality and well cooked. For the more squeamish, there is Casa Ricardo's excellent range of classic

stews, slow-cooked using cuts such as *carrillera de ternera* (beef cheek) to flavorful, tender perfection. Something else not seen often in a contemporary restaurant is hen (as opposed to the more common chicken). Hen has a richer flavor than the male, with a darker, more intense meat. Casa Ricardo serves *gallina en pepitoria*, a traditional dish with an almond, egg, and white wine sauce, sticking with hen meat while other restaurants have long replaced it with chicken meat.

Casa Ricardo opened in 1932 (although the sign above the door says 1935, because it worked without a licence in the early days). And the interior has not changed since the restaurant opened: the bullfighting paintings are all original, as is the traditional Spanish tiling. Casa Ricardo does not try to return to the past because it never left it. **DC**

⊡ The interior harks from a bygone age.

Diverxo | Experimental and extraordinary modern cuisine

Location Madrid **Signature dish** Pork skin with black sesame brioche, salmon roe, and cherry sauce | 🍴🍴🍴🍴

David Muñoz's dishes at Diverxo are extreme examples of the most modern creative fusion cuisine that have become highly acclaimed. The restaurant stands in a suburban side street in Madrid. Inside, the restaurant is small and modern with squares of gray and glass along the walls, and a shiny black floor. Models of black butterflies and pink pigs with feathery wings are dotted around. And perhaps Muñoz's extraordinary food proves pigs can fly. It is served on plates that resemble canvases. Sauces are painted on with grave artistic intent. Ingredients are presented as if they were to be hung on a wall and admired, with the careful color schemes and precise arrangements of a graphic designer.

"… Diverxo's calm atmosphere belies a reported month-long waiting list …"

theworlds50best.com

The term "fusion" does not do it justice. The tiny elaborate dishes are much more than a mix of Asian and Iberian flavors; they are bizarre mixtures dreamed up in Muñoz's imagination. A glance through the menu shows a sequence of inspired pairings, like squid with strawberry, bacon ice cream with sherry vinegar, white chocolate with celery, coconut meringue and seaweed, duck tongue and avocado, herring with elk, and fish with mango chips.

The atmosphere is not the normal hush of Michelin reverence: chefs dash around in black outfits, adding ingredients to diners' plates as they eat. The culinary choreography includes dedicated implements to eat each dish, from chopsticks to a plastic spatula. **SH**

Juana La Loca | Gourmet tapas in Madrid's hip La Latina quarter

Location Madrid **Signature dish** Caramelized onion tortilla | 🍴🍴

A comparative newcomer on Madrid's tapas scene, Juana La Loca in Madrid's fashionable and popular La Latina quarter has become the place in which to eat adventurous and inventive tapas in the city. Instead of offering classic, traditional Madrid fare, the food draws its inspiration from Japanese, Chinese, and Mexican cuisines, as well as Spanish cuisine. The spirit of culinary exploration and innovation echoes the experimental cuisine of San Sebastian in the Basque Country and has found a receptive audience in the Spanish capital.

Juana La Loca is as much a local nightspot as it is a restaurant and, in the best Spanish tapas-bar tradition, it solves the question of whether to go out for drinks or dinner by offering both. The coolest, well-to-do, thirty-somethings meet there on a Friday night; they do not let a lack of tables deter them and simply stand while they eat. There is a general air of good-humored camaraderie among the staff and their regulars; do not be surprised to see a waiter downing a shot with a customer before serving some spinach crepe with baby eels.

Decor is stripped-down and minimal, which makes sense as all eyes are squarely on the menu and the bar-top tapas anyway. Juana La Loca's signature Spanish tortilla is unlike any tortilla found elsewhere; it is made using caramelized onions that give this classic tapas dish an unusual rich sweetness. Other popular dishes are the zucchini rolls filled with cod and the crispy duck pancakes that take the traditional Chinese restaurant starter to a new level, combining the crispest duck magret, sweet plum sauce, and the freshest, crunchiest vegetables.

On weekends, head to Juana La Loca for the fresh mussels, served with white wine and curry sauce. Such is the restaurant's popularity, however, that you should be prepared to stand. **DC**

Sergi Arola Gastro | Fine dining from
a talented modernist Catalan chef

Location Madrid   **Signature dish** Smoked veal *"al romero"* with morel ragout | ❸❸❸

Charismatic Catalan chef Sergi Arola has acquired a cult following for his trendsetting cooking. His career has included training with such legendary chefs as Ferran Adrià and Pierre Gagnaire, and he is regarded as a member of Spain's modernist school of chefs. His own Michelin-starred Madrid restaurant, Sergi Arola Gastro, with its sophisticated dining room, offers diners a chance to sample Arola's distinctly creative cuisine.

While inspired by Mediterranean cuisine, with ingredients such as salt cod and sardines among his favorites, his cooking departs from tradition. Given his culinary experience, it is not surprising that he has some kitchen tricks up his sleeve, as witnessed by a nibble of Caesar-salad foam, which tastes of the various components of the classic salad. One of Arola's signature dishes is a playful, contemporary take on that familiar tapas bar classic *patatas bravas*, which in Arola's hands is reimagined as little cylinders of potato containing *salsa brava* made from tomato, garlic, and chili topped with aioli, a stylish and tasty dish.

Arola's impressive technique allows him to deliver innovative dishes that both delight with their skill and impress on flavor with panache. During the meal customers might enjoy sardines cooked with a deep fried crispy egg (still with a liquid center), alongside a chanterelle salad and a little red wine sauce or an intense mousse of chanterelles topped with "rocks" made from olive oil, parsley, and garlic powder, garnished with a couple of shimeji mushrooms. The menu changes with the seasons, allowing Arola free rein for his inventive talents.

Desserts, similarly, demonstrate the kitchen's considerable abilities, combining several elements in one dish, always to good effect. The wines are impressive, with the chance to enjoy some lovely choices to accompany a meal. **AH**

> *"The wine list has more than 600 labels, mostly from small producers, all available by the glass."*

fodors.com

⬆ Chef Sergi Arola's culinary technique manifests itself in intriguing, innovative dishes.

Casino de Madrid | Modern cuisine from a disciple of Ferran Adrià

Location Madrid   **Signature dish** "False" risotto | ❺❺❺❺❺

With its splendid setting, dramatic decor, and accomplished cooking, Casino de Madrid offers a fine example of the level reached by contemporary high-end Spanish cuisine. The role of head chef is held by Madrid-born Paco Roncero, considered to be one of the legendary Ferran Adrià's, of El Bulli fame, most talented disciples. Roncero utilizes the amuse-bouche dishes, which are popular in modern cuisine, but keeps them firmly in the category of appetizers; there are no forty-nine-course meals here. On the taster menu, a selection of these culinary snapshots, including a black olive oreo and a goat cheese moshi, are followed by the three larger courses that old schoolers would consider a meal, giving both the gastronomic punch from the single-bite portions as well as satisfying larger offerings.

Dishes might be a deconstruction of something familiar such as a Bloody Mary, using the clear juice from the center of the tomato, a foam containing all the other ingredients that the cocktail normally includes, and a sprinkling of freeze-dried tomato flakes on top. It does not look like a Bloody Mary, it only tastes a little like a Bloody Mary, but it is a Bloody Mary. In other cases, what is on a plate looks like a classic dish and yet is something entirely different. Take the *risotto falso* (false risotto.) In every way, it looks like a risotto. But it is missing one thing: rice. Roncero has made chopped calamari resemble risotto's defining feature. It is with witty dishes such as this that Casino de Madrid plays with diners' eyes, taste buds, and conceptions of what a dish can be.

Not all dishes are so mischievous. Sometimes, as with his impeccable hake and seaweed, Roncero elevates the greens from a simple side to an integral part of the dish, balancing each mouthful to perfection. An elegantly creative eating experience. **DC**

⬆ Elegant sophistication at Casino de Madrid.

Botín | One of the oldest restaurants in the world and Hemingway's favorite

Location Madrid   **Signature dish** *Cochinillo asado* (roast suckling pig) | ❸❸❸

"We lunched upstairs at Botin's. It is one of the best restaurants in the world." These simple words are how Ernest Hemingway described Botín restaurant, where Jake Barnes and Lady Brett Ashley eat at the end of the author's most celebrated novel, *The Sun Also Rises* (1926). Reason enough to visit, one might think. But while most restaurants would be satisfied with one claim to fame, Botín has two of the very best. For not only was it Hemingway's favorite restaurant, but it is also featured in the *Guinness World Records* as one of the oldest restaurants in the world.

Botín does not just have box-ticking kudos, though. Jake and Brett went there to eat suckling pig, the same dish tourists, politicians, and artists have been going there for during nearly 300 years of business. Botín has been serving continuously since 1725, and the restaurant's signature dish has been on the menu since it first opened. Botín is spread over three small floors, giving more the impression of a country tavern than one of the finest restaurants in Madrid. The wood-beam-and-tile classic styling is modest and little changed over the centuries.

To get to their table, most guests will have to walk past the restaurant's centerpiece, its original 1725 wood oven, which sits proudly by the staircase. It contains racks of suckling pig at various stages of preparation and a cook tirelessly tending to the various meats, including lamb and chicken. Suckling pig is roasted over several hours before resting to allow the meat to tenderize. Serving it at the perfect moment is essential, so it helps to eat it at a restaurant where they serve so many.

Botín is owned by the Gonzalez family, who have been running it for three generations, bringing a feeling of a small family-owned restaurant despite all its attention-grabbing accolades. **DC**

⬆ Suckling pig is cooked in a centuries-old oven.

Viridiana | Characterful food and a charismatic chef

Location Madrid **Signature dish** Porcini puree with a fried egg and freshly grated black truffle | ❺❺❺❺

"All the dishes are sublime, and the inviting ambience makes you relax ..."

frommers.com

⬆ Viridiana is an intimate, characterful restaurant offering idiosyncratic Spanish cooking.

➡ Inventive dishes appeal to the eye and the palate, as in this dish of sardines with raspberry gazpacho.

It is just as well that Viridiana's owner, film historian and newspaper columnist Abraham García, has a good team in the kitchen, because he never seems to spend any time in it, instead walking among his guests, taking orders when his waiters are busy, and just generally entertaining. Setting the tone for the evening, García might greet a guest not with a hello, but with a joke about the small portions that were served at Ferran Adrià's El Bulli.

García is not one to tiptoe around his guests: he is more likely to dart in their direction to tell them an anecdote he has just remembered. This is a man who named his restaurant after a movie by the renowned Spanish surrealist director Luis Buñuel because he enjoys its atheist message. At Viridiana, as befits its name, García offers supremely irreverent takes on classic Spanish dishes to an appreciative audience.

The cuisine at Viridiana is inventive without being pretentious. Take its trademark dish, fried egg and porcini puree and freshly grated black truffle—it is brought out in a heavy skillet because that simple setting is where eggs look their most appetizing.

Other delights include swordfish in *salsa de huancaina* with a side of mango guacamole and asparagus, or the most spectacularly firm yet juicy foie gras possible, served to good effect with a nicely contrasting bitter-orange chutney and paired with Sauternes white wine from Bordeaux.

To round off a meal, in addition to the desserts, Viridiana offers a good selection of cheeses, including Idiazabal, made from unpasteurized sheep milk, which goes well with *membrillo* (quince paste).

The decor at Viridiana is stylish rather than overly formal. It is unusual to see screen shots from a black-and-white film lining the walls of an establishment of this caliber in Spain. The star of the show remains the memorable and creative food; reflecting the restaurant's owner, this is food with personality. **DC**

Malacatín | The place to sample Madrid's most famous dish

Location Madrid **Signature dish** *Cocido madrileño* (Madrid stew) | ❸❸

When visiting Madrid, there is one dish that stands out: *cocido madrileño*, or Madrid stew, a venerable, slow-cooked dish, which is thought to have Sephardi roots derived from the Jewish Sabbath dish *adafina*. The best place in Madrid to try *cocido madrileño* is at Malacatín.

Cocido madrileño consists of various cuts of pork, beef, and chicken, as well as chickpeas, cabbage, and *fideos* (a kind of pasta, like vermicelli) traditionally cooked in one giant pot, with the broth and pasta often served as the first course, and everything else served second. At Malacatín, using the same recipe that owner José Alberto Rodríguez's family has been using since his great-grandfather opened the restaurant in 1895, the dish is served in three courses. It needs to be, as otherwise there simply would not be enough room on the table. The dish is cooked in four stew pots, thus preserving the distinct flavors of each part of the meal.

At Malacatín, the *cocido madrileño* is prepared with the loving care and attention that a classic dish deserves. The meal begins with the broth from each separate pot, combined with noodles to create a tasty broth. Next come the chickpeas, the cabbage, and *tocino* (Spanish bacon). Pacing is key to enjoying a meal here. "Our servings are very generous indeed," explains the waiter. "We recommend you don't fill yourself on the soup or the second course, or you won't get to appreciate the meat."

With this in mind, be prepared for the generous plates of *morcillo* (beef shank), *manitas de cerdo* (pig's trotters), *chorizo* (spicy sausage), *morcilla* (black pudding), chicken, and *codillo* (pork knuckle) that comprise the main part of the meal. Do not worry about not eating it all: the restaurant gives leftovers to a local convent that then serves them to the poor. **DC**

⬆ Malacatín is noted for its *cocido madrileño*.

Santceloni | A gastronomic treasure trove in the Spanish capital

Location Madrid   **Signature dish** Banana, coffee, and whisky with tonka bean cream | ❸❸❸❸

This subtly elegant restaurant has an impressive culinary pedigree. It was set up in 2001 under the supervision of the late, great chef Santi Santamaria of the legendary, three-star Michelin restaurant. Oscar Velasco, the talented chef in charge of the kitchen here, worked for many years at Can Fabes, with Santceloni gaining two Michelin stars in 2005.

Bread is made from scratch in the kitchen, the selection of large loaves being presented to diners at the start of the meal before being sliced. The menu focuses on good-quality Spanish ingredients, as illustrated in the use of clams from Cadiz and Iberian pork. A meal might begin with a nibble of quail egg with paprika served in a little pastry case. The kitchen is happy working with unusual but logical flavor combinations, such as a chickpea salad with oxtail.

Modern cooking techniques are blended with traditional dishes; a leek and potato soup with eggplant caviar, accurately seasoned and having deep flavor,

with a piece of tender pork dewlap (neck) that has been cooked *sous vide* (under vacuum). Luxurious ingredients are used frequently, as seen with ravioli of smoked ricotta with Petrossian caviar.

Another unusual but successful flavor combination is smoked cuttlefish with vine shoots, served with roast tomatoes and pepper oil, the cuttlefish tender and having good flavor, the smokiness not dominant. In a dish of roe deer loin with endive confit, the flavorful venison is cooked rare, with the bitterness of the endive nicely balancing the richness of the meat. Santceloni is a sophisticated restaurant with technically assured cooking. Desserts are as accomplished as the rest of the cooking, with Velasco offering intriguing taste combinations—quince and wasabi, pear and rum—in beautifully constructed and delectable creations. **AH**

⬆ The modern, sophisticated decor is matched by the food.

Ramón Freixa | A chance to savor stylish artistry combined with culinary tradition

Location Madrid   **Signature dish** *Liebre a la Royal* (mixed plate of ice creams, gnocchi, and tapioca) | ❸❸❸

"Excellence in detail is my raison d'être, the very core of my being."

Ramón Freixa, chef and owner

⬆ Beautifully presented food is part of the appeal of dining at Ramón Freixa.

The considerable talents of chef Ramón Freixa are on show here at this elegant, eponymous restaurant, located in the Hotel Unico. Coming from a family heritage that included a grandfather who was a baker and a father who was a chef, food has always been an important part of his life. Freixa's experience of working at several European restaurants, including the acclaimed Comme chez Soi in Brussels and with chef Michel Bras in France, shows in the assured cooking on offer here, recognized and rewarded with Michelin stars, the first within months of opening in 2009 and a second gained in 2010. The modern, intimate dining room is a stylish setting in which to enjoy the food—aided by comfortable seating and tables spaced well apart—while the terrace, looking out over the garden, is an appealing addition.

The menu has a mix of traditional and modern Spanish dishes, so diners can choose the style they prefer, depending on their taste and mood. Traditional cooking is seen in cannelloni with three meats, in which chicken, veal, and pork are ground and combined, then seasoned and served inside delicate cannelloni pasta with a little cheese sauce.

The modernist side of the kitchen is seen in dishes such as a cube of pistachio and crab presented in a bowl, over which is poured a liquid "soup" of tuna. Within seconds, the soup solidifies into a jelly. Modernity may also take the form of suckling pig served with a topping of pork crackling, alongside several additional elements, including strawberry salad with celery leaves and vinegar, a little rhubarb soufflé with *xirivia* (parsnip) and long pepper, and pig trotter with foie gras and mushrooms.

Service is classy, with friendly, knowledgeable staff, and a fairly priced wine list with plenty of excellent Spanish wines. **AH**

Stop Madrid | Stop for classic Iberian ham and manchego cheese

Location Madrid   **Signature dish** Manchego cheese and Iberian ham | $

Stop Madrid is one of the oldest tavernas in Spain's capital, having opened its doors for the first time in 1929. Stop Madrid's location in Calle de Hortaleza finds itself at the border between two of Madrid's busiest barrios, the hipster Malasaña and fashionable Chueca. Life does not stop moving outside, but Madrid stops inside Stop Madrid. Here, the appealingly shady and fan-cooled bar keeps the noise and heat out and the flavors in, making it an excellent place in which to pass the hours.

Come in at 3.00 P.M. after the lunch rush and join the other diners relaxing companionably over a couple of plates of ham and cheese accompanied by a glass of wine, or sample canapés of goose pâté, caviar and crab, or Galician *lacón* (dried ham) and brie.

Stop Madrid is justly proud of its exceptional acorn-fed Iberian ham and cured manchego cheese, the classic ham and cheese combination that has been driving culinary visits to Spain for centuries. When it comes to Iberian ham and manchego, only one kind of each is offered.

When it comes to wine, however, the range is extensive and impressive. More than fifty kinds of wine are on offer, and all are available by the glass, with most at reasonable prices. The wines have been proudly and discriminatingly selected from throughout Spain: from the illustrious Ribera del Duero and Rioja regions to the lesser known *bodegas* (wineries) around Madrid.

The simple but good food, together with the excellent wine, and the friendly, accommodating service make Stop Madrid a relaxing respite in which to sit and enjoy a traditional, hospitable taverna experience in the heart of the busy city. This is a place frequented by locals as well as tourists seeking an authentic old-style bar. **DC**

El Figón de Eustaquio | Traditional Extremaduran classics

Location Cáceres   **Signature dish** *Salteado especial de verduras* (sautéed vegetables) | $$

El Figón de Eustaquio has long been a favorite among Cáceres locals. It is on Plaza de San Juan, just outside the medieval ramparts of the old city. Since 1947, three generations of the Blanco family have specialized in serving regional cuisine here, and now it is run by four Blanco brothers.

Look out for local Extremaduran classics like *migas* (crumbs), a great example of a kitchen using up leftovers to create a winning dish. It is a mix of old bread softened in water and flavored with garlic, paprika, spinach, fried sausage, and bacon. Even the signature dish of *salteado especial de verduras con torta del casar* is a simple mix of sautéed vegetables, truffles, and cèpe mushrooms, topped with a melting

> *"It is widely regarded as the best restaurant in Extremadura, with fantastic ingredients …"*
>
> José Pizarro, chef

creamy sheep cheese. Dishes like these are often served with chunks of bread as a communal starter for family groups. Inside, the setting of exposed beams, tiled floors, high-backed wooden chairs, and decorative plates hanging on the walls is as traditional as the food. In good weather, opt for one of the parasol-covered tables outside in the square.

The menu is packed with local ingredients, with lots of appearances of lamb and pork, plus venison, partridge, and trout, and usually accompanied with assorted varieties of asparagus, peppers, potatoes, and garlic. Specialities to look out for include honey soup, roast kid, truffles in cream, and local river trout wrapped in ham. **SH**

La Riuà | Family restaurant
serving classic paella in its heartland

Location Valencia   **Signature dish** *Paella valenciana* (vegetables, rabbit, and chicken with rice) | 💲💲

Spain's iconic savory rice dish, paella, traces its origins to eastern Spain, specifically to the rice fields around the Albufera lagoon, as a communal dish cooked by the laborers in the fields. Although regarded as a national Spanish dish, the classic *paella valenciana* carries a special charge of culinary history.

Here, in paella's heartland, the family-run La Riuà has been renowned as one of Valencia's top paella restaurants for more than thirty years. Found in the city center, the two-story building is unexceptional from the outside but inside is a large, lively dining area with a mezzanine upstairs. Service is brisk, the atmosphere relaxed, and decor is traditional, with scores of colored plates hanging from the walls.

"The walls are covered with … the gastronomic awards the restaurant has won over the years."

fodors.com

La Riuà's menu includes many regional specialties, like rabbit with garlic, stewed baby octopus, and sea bass baked in salt, but the award-winning paellas are the reason for the restaurant's enduring popularity. The signature *paella valenciana* features chicken and rabbit. To the locals, however, a perfect paella is all about the rice. It should be slightly al dente and never mushy, and cooked so that a caramelized crust forms on the bottom of the pan, called a *socarrat*. A paella in a traditional restaurant like La Riuà is served in the pan it was cooked in, with the precious *socarrat* still intact. Other paellas served feature combinations of fish and shellfish, including a grand lobster paella and an unusual cuttlefish and cauliflower paella. **SH**

Casa Montaña | Gourmet
tapas served among barrels

Location Valencia   **Signature dish** *Titaina* (tuna, tomatoes, and green bell pepper) | 💲

Casa Montaña does not look like it has changed much since it opened in 1836. The old arched door opens into a bar crammed with shelves of wine bottles, prices chalked on blackboards, and old bullfighting posters on the walls. As this wonderfully characterful bar fills with locals, tapas eaters squeeze between tall, oak barrels or escape to the less frenetic room behind.

Owner Emiliano García has built on the bar's long tradition to establish an extraordinary cellar with approximately 20,000 bottles representing some 1,000 labels, with an emphasis on Valencian vintages. Wine is available to sample by the glass.

For those looking to eat well, this old bodega does not disappoint. The tapas are so renowned that people travel from afar to sample them. Many similar dishes may be found all over Spain, but it is clear that great care is taken here with even the smallest tapas. Anchovies, for example, are purchased fresh from Santona in Cantabria. One specialist member of the kitchen staff carefully removes the bones and fillets the fish, which are then served in oil or fried.

Even simple ingredients like potatoes are sourced from a single harvest in October from the dry area of Guadalaviar in the mountains inland from Valencia. Their extra taste and texture enhances classic tapas such as *patatas bravas* (cubes of potato in a spicy, tomato sauce) and codfish croquettes. Fresh sardines and squid for grilling come straight from boats at nearby Castellon. Charcuterie is high quality, sourced from top producers. Ultra-local recipes are used to prepare *titaina* from Valencia's old fishermen's quarter, El Cabanyal; the dish comprises tuna, tomatoes, and green bell pepper. Cod croquettes are made in El Cabanyal-style, too, using pine nuts. **SH**

→ Casa Montaña is known for its wine cellar.

Nou Manolín | Grab a bar stool at this world-acclaimed tapas bar

Location Alicante **Signature dish** Sea bass ceviche | $$

Among the scores of tapas bars in the Costa Blanca city of Alicante, Nou Manolín is the highest rated. It began life before the Spanish Civil War as a simple local bar run by the Castello family. It happened to be in the childhood home of renowned writer Gabriel Miró. In 1972, the founder's grandson relaunched the bar as Nou Manolín and its reputation has grown steadily since. Lines often form outside before the bar opens and it fills quickly. Most customers vie to get a wicker-covered stool at the street-level bar—the best spot to see and try the tapas. The overspill tends to migrate upstairs to the more formal restaurant, with a printed menu and uniformed waiters. The dining room may be overshadowed by the champion tapas below, but it is an acclaimed restaurant in its own right, serving a fine locally based menu heavy on seafood and paella.

> *"... classical tapas—everything from shrimp in garlic sauce to batter-fried fresh anchovies."*
>
> frommers.com

The building looks grand from the outside, but the bar is a classic tapas venue, with a wood and tile bar, tiled floor, and tall windows in brick arches. Some people sit at tables, others around upturned barrels. Up to fifty different tapas are available, ranging from garlic shrimps to pig's liver, from fish and ham croquettes to smoked salmon and guacamole. There are classics like Serrano ham, and gourmet innovations such as sea bass ceviche with a blood-orange sorbet or a tuna burger. Little wonder that fans of Nou Manolín's tapas include world-famous chefs like Joël Robouchon. **SH**

El Faro | A pair of formal seafood restaurants on the Bay of Cadiz

Location Cadiz **Signature dish** Pasta with squid, shrimp, and garlic | $$

El Faro is made up of two restaurants on either side of the Bay of Cadiz. One El Faro stands in the growing town of El Puerto de Santa Maria, the other in the old town of Cadiz. El Puerto is famous throughout Spain as the departure point for Christopher Columbus' second voyage to the Americas. It has boomed since the 1980s, and is one of the region's largest towns. The original El Faro del Puerto was set up in 1987 by local chef Fernándo Córdoba. His high-quality seafood dishes served in a formal style have helped this El Faro become a popular local institution.

From the beetroot gazpacho to the homemade cream-cheese soufflé, expect a menu of Spanish classics, served with an infusion of modern flavors. So grilled tuna comes with a pineapple and mango chutney, flounder with garlic and asparagus, and mullet with roasted eggplant and tomato. The restaurant stands next to its own garden, supplying up to half the vegetables and herbs to the kitchen.

Across the bay, in the old walled city of Cadiz, however, the El Faro is slightly different. It is run by Cordoba's daughter Mayte. Through one door is a lively tapas bar; through the other, a more traditional seated restaurant. Both specialize in seafood and are served from the same kitchen.

The seated restaurant next door maintains a strict Spanish formality in this tourist hot spot. White-jacketed waiters serve Spanish classical seafood supervised by a classic maitre d' under high ceilings amid gilt-framed oil paintings and dark stained wood.

In contrast, the popular tapas area is perennially busy with customers standing, drinking, snacking, and talking. Although fish can be ordered from the bar and cooked to order, as is traditional, most customers opt for a sequence of small dishes like *tortillitas de camarones* (shrimp fritters) or fish cakes. **SH**

El Rinconcillo | Sample tapas at Seville's oldest and best-loved bar housed in a former convent

Location Seville **Signature dish** *Carrilleras de cerdo ibérico en salsa* (pork cheek stew) | **$**

Originally the refectory rooms of a convent, El Rinconcillo became a public restaurant and bar in 1670. That makes it the oldest tapas bar among an estimated 4,000 in Seville, the city known for its venerable tapas tradition.

It all started when Spanish bars used slices of ham or cheese as lids or "*tapas*" on glasses to keep flies out of the wine. The free snack proved to be a popular nibble with the drink. The tradition evolved over the centuries; in modern times, tapas are not usually free, but they are more interesting than a slice of cheese.

The sense of tapas heritage pervades the El Rincolcillo experience. It is as authentic a tapas venue as one could find in Spain's fourth largest city. Tucked away in the narrow streets of the Santa Carolina barrio, it is picturesque both from the outside and inside.

The bustling bar area features intricate decorative tiled walls, old glass fronted cupboards reaching to the high ceiling stacked with wine, and a forest of hams dangling from roof beams. Local dry sherry is served from barrels alongside gaudy religious images and an ancient stone floor acts as everyone's bin and ashtray. The waist-coated bar staff add up customers' tabs in chalk next to them on the broad wooden bar.

Expect plenty of the usual tapas dishes, like tortillas, spinach and chickpeas, fried anchovies, sardines, Russian salad, and garlic shrimp. But also look for specialties, such as *ortiguillas fritas* (fried sea anemones), fried saltcod croquettes, cod in tomato sauce, and the signature tapas: *carrilleras de cerdo ibérico en salsa* (a meaty pork-cheek stew).

Eat standing in the crowd at the bar or at a small selection of tables. Upstairs is an equally attractive restaurant with an à la carte, sit-down menu, but somehow it feels like one is missing the real fun that is going on downstairs. **SH**

"Time has allowed this place to build up an impressive range of little morsels …"

Lonely Planet

⬆ El Rinconcillo has been serving tapas for centuries.

El Cabra | Fresh fish caught locally at a beachside bar and restaurant with views out to sea

Location Malaga **Signature dish** *Marrajo* (shortfin mako shark) marinated in vinegar and fried in batter | $$

"One of the value spots is Manuel Cabra's Restaurante El Cabra ..."

Pauline Frommer's Spain

⬆ Dine on freshly caught fish right by the beach.

El Cabra is beach-bar-cum-restaurant in the old Malagan fishing area of Pedregalejo beach that specializes in fish and shellfish. It is an unpretentious place with plastic chairs, paper tablecloths, brisk but friendly service, and a relaxed ambience that marries well with the twin attractions of the stirring views out to sea and the briny-freshness of the fish. The philosophy of El Cabra, which started life in 1962, is simple: grab hold of locally caught fresh fish and serve.

Early each morning, a van leaves for the wholesale market on the edge of town and returns crammed with piscatorial plunder. As morning wears on, there is also activity on the waterfront, with the aroma of wood smoke drifting through the air as a small boat, its days at sea long over and now filled with shingle and sand, hosts a driftwood fire that smolders and glows all day long. Next to it stands a man whose daily job is to grill the sardines for which El Cabra is rightly famous. Ask a local who he is to be solemnly told that he has been doing the job all his life, and perhaps his father before him.

Even though Malaga's historic center is several miles to the south, El Cabra remains a locals' haunt. They rightly ooh and aah over the juicy, smoke-tinged silvery sardines as well as clams cooked in white wine sauce, deep orange-colored mussels in the shell, fried *boquerones* (anchovies), and *adobo*. The Spanish word *adobo* refers to the preparation of a small shark called the *marrajo* (shortfin mako shark), which is marinated in vinegar and then fried in batter. This treat is soft in the mouth with a vinegary and tangy bite alongside its mellow saltiness. Meanwhile, as one eats, the soundtrack is of the sea's soft susurration, gulls' high-soprano notes, and the low murmurs of appreciation from satisfied diners. **ATJ**

Son Amoixa Vell |
A stylish taste of the Mediterranean

Location Manacor **Signature dish** *Gambas son amoixa* (shrimp in spicy olive oil with garlic and herbs) | ❷❷

This grand old sixteenth-century Mallorcan farmhouse has been converted into a luxurious small country house hotel. Son Amoixa Vell stands among lush gardens and a 500-acre (202-ha) estate of fig, almond, orange, and lemon trees, near Manacor, on the eastern side of the island.

The rambling manor itself has been converted by its German owners into a romantic and stylish hotel stuffed with art and antiques. It offers everything from Champagne breakfasts to massages by the pool; but the award-winning food here is its forte.

Diners can enjoy fine Mediterranean-inspired cuisine using top-quality Mallorcan rural produce, in a perfectly relaxed atmosphere, surrounded by a typical agricultural landscape. Guests can eat outside, under huge cream parasols on the stone terrace surrounded by enormous plant pots, or in the cozy arched dining room, among bare stonewalls and dark wooden beams. Many ingredients are sourced from the surrounding farms and village markets, some are even picked from the hotel's herb garden and estate.

Chef Bruno Schulze, from Frankfurt, has been at the hotel for more than ten years, overseeing a daily changing menu that combines contemporary fine-dining dishes with local seasonal ingredients.

So the herb-crusted roast lamb and Rioja sauce is served with Mallorcan *patatas panaderas* (garlic potatoes) and the jumbo shrimp are served on the top of a Balearic salad of mango, papaya, and melon.

Dishes like sirloin of veal with jumbo shrimp in a sauce of black pepper and brandy, or tureen of lemon caramelized with cane sugar and strawberries, demonstrate this mix of influences. For dessert, note how the strawberries have been marinated in mint from the garden, and how often local nuts and berries appear in various guises. **SH**

Santi Taura |
A gem for imaginative Mallorcan fare

Location Lloseta **Signature dish** Cuttlefish risotto | ❷❷❷

Santi Taura is a small restaurant in a little-known Mallorcan village near the center of the island. This dusty back street is far from the tourist beaches. Only thirty-six diners can squeeze inside the small dining room, looking into the open kitchen. Yet this is one of the most acclaimed restaurants on the island, often booked up for months in advance.

The eponymous Santi Taura is the chef-patron, expressing his approach to cooking with verve. The concept is simple: diners are offered a set tasting menu of three starters, fish, meat, and dessert, with an optional Balearic farm cheese board. The menu is based on Mallorcan cuisine and ingredients, but presented in a modern, fine-cuisine style.

> *"Taura's style might best be described as modern market cooking, imaginative and clever …"*
> *GQ Magazine*

Such is Taura's creativity that the tasting menu varies constantly, with the chef seeking inspiration from the seasons and from ingredients he feels are at their best. So, for example, one week, the tasting menu might offer saltcod mousse, red bell pepper stuffed with ground pork and green tomato sauce, squid stuffed with piquant *sobresada* sausage, rabbit with liver and nuts in a fruity sauce, puff pastry tart with fig, and star anise ice cream. Another week, the Mallorcan chef serves grilled red bell pepper, smoked cod and black olive vinaigrette on toasted French bread, zucchini stuffed with meat timbale, cuttlefish risotto with bream and aioli, and grilled beef on potatoes and onions. **SH**

El Bungalow | Eat like a local islander at this much-loved humble beachside shack

Location Mallorca **Signature dish** Lobster paella with vegetables and rice | **$ $**

"Sit on the broad terrace close to the water's edge ... and order the day's catch."

Lonely Planet Mallorca

⤴ The beachside location offers a delightful vista.

An innocuous-looking, little, single-story café right on the beachside in the Bay of Palma? Along this coastline known for cheap-and-cheerful mass tourism, one might expect it to serve burgers, French fries, and ice cream. But do not rush to judge, because El Bungalow is one of the most acclaimed seafood restaurants on the island of Mallorca.

This humble restaurant stands about halfway along the long promenade between Palma and Arenal, in the Ciudad Jardin seaside district. It has an outside terrace shaded by a fluttering canopy, and diners can step right into the sand from the restaurant. Day or night, the tables have an uninterrupted view across the bay, with Palma's Cathedral in the distance.

The next good sign is that El Bungalow is always busy with locals. The fact that some of them are chefs from other restaurants is even better. This humble shack has become a Mallorcan institution that is renowned for its fresh fish, shellfish, and particularly for its paella. The views, south-facing aspect, and cooling sea breezes help. Perhaps the unpretentious image encourages regulars to sing its praises all the more. El Bungalow clearly occupies a great spot. It was a family beach house until 1985, when it was converted to a café. It has gradually evolved into an acclaimed restaurant since, although it is still run by the family.

The menu depends on the day's catch. Expect Mediterranean fish like bass and cod, and shellfish such as clams, squid, and mussels. Usually, fish is grilled or baked in a salt crust. Shellfish is steamed or used in paella. The rice dishes use a type of grain from the Ebro Delta on the mainland called *arroz de Calasparra*. Look out for the specialty lobster paella and the "rice with cauliflower and cod." **SH**

Ca Na Toneta | Rustic restaurant preserves Mallorca's old recipes

Location Mallorca   **Signature dish** *Tumbet* (fried quail's egg on eggplant and tomato) | 💲💲

The two Solivellas sisters run this humble little restaurant located deep in the Serra de Tramuntana mountain range in Mallorca. Maria is the chef, Teresa runs the front of house. And a house is what it looks like when one finally finds it in the back alleys of the village of Caimari. Ca Na Toneta is an old whitewashed stone country house. Inside, it is stylish in a rural minimalist way: there are two dining rooms and a small terrace with original wooden roof beams, old floor tiles, rough whitewashed walls, wooden shutters, and wickerwork chairs.

Maria helped found the Slow Food movement on Mallorca. Many of her ingredients come from the family small holding, where ancient rare indigenous varieties of plants like tomatoes are carefully cultivated from seeds obtained from the island's botanical gardens. Other produce comes from small, independent, ecologically sound farms and fishermen on the island. Many dishes are revived classics found in old family recipe books. The result is an acclaimed Mallorcan tasting menu at a reasonable price "inspired by the wise eating habits of our ancestors." It always comprises a soup, starter, fish, meat, and dessert, but varies with what is fresh and available.

A typical menu might include an earthenware pot of pea soup with a few loops of squid floating at the center, followed by a colorful tower of eggplant, pepper and tomato topped by a quail's egg fried in olive oil and served in its own tiny frying pan. Other courses might include roast lamb with mint, carrots, sweet onions, and couscous, or homemade ice cream with ginger cake.

Look out for the interesting traditional breads, too. Some come with caramelized onion and rosemary, while others come topped with thin zucchini, goat cheese, and tapenade. **SH**

MB | Dazzling haute cuisine in a contemporary Canary Island citadel

Location Tenerife   **Signature dish** Roast pigeon with wild mushroom marrowbone | 💲💲💲💲

The labyrinthine Abama Golf and Spa Resort on Tenerife does not seem a likely home of gourmet greatness, but its two flagship restaurants, MB and Kabuki, both have a Michelin star. MB is named for executive chef Martín Berasategui, who has a combined seven Michelin stars for restaurants scattered across Spain. It is headed by Erlantz Gorostiza, who skillfully executes star dishes from the mothership in the Basque Country alongside some of his own innovations.

MB is designed to cosset and comfort from the moment one enters, from behind a waterfall, to when one sips coffee in the moonlight on the terrace to the sound of the gentle wash of waves lapping up against

---

"With a wine cellar of over 500 of the finest global labels, diners get to sample Berasategui's … versatility."

Daily Mail

---

the shore. It is worth pairing the tasting menu with the Canary Island's sensational home-grown wines to get a real sense of place.

Much of the produce is grown at the hotel's organic farm, and the seventeen-course tasting menu is led by the seasons, starting with something to awaken the appetite: a foaming, passion-fruit whisky sour maybe, or a caipirinha drenched chunk of melon, followed by dishes intended to surprise. A silky Atlantic red shrimp carpaccio with espelette pepper, truffled, foie jelly, or a lightly pickled chunk of bonito with eggplant roasted in miso, finishing with desserts sweet and fresh. This is Berasategui at his best: clever flavor combinations and assured techniques. **TS**

Largo do Paço | Ambitious modern food in an historic setting

Location Amarante   **Signature dish** Bísaro | ❸❸❸

Amarante is situated on the Tâmega River, and with its pretty bridges is noted as one of the most beautiful towns in northern Portugal. Luckily for visitors, it has also always been famous for its restaurant scene, as home to popular restaurants specializing in the hearty food of the region. But there is one restaurant in Amarante that truly stands out: the Michelin-starred Largo do Paço.

To begin with, the restaurant boasts an impressive setting: it is housed within the Casa da Calçada, a sixteenth-century palace (*paço* is Portuguese for "palace"), with a rich history, which has been converted into a lovely hotel overlooking the river. Then there is the food. The chef, Vítor Matos, was born in Switzerland and studied there, but has been working in Portugal for most of his career. He retains touches of local heritage while using contemporary European culinary techniques, resulting in an à la carte menu with national roots and creative accents,

featuring intriguing dishes such as Bísaro suckling pig with Bairrada wine sauce or salted cod with chickpea foam, roasted peppers, garlic, and cilantro. Also on offer, as befits a Michelin-starred establishment, are some tasting menu options, offering the diner a chance to experience Matos' creativity and flair in full.

At the core of these recipes, once again, is Matos' passion for Portuguese produce and tradition: he uses meat from heritage Portuguese livestock breeds, such as flavorful pork from chestnut-fed Bísaro pigs or beef from Maronesa cattle, both from the Trás-os-Montes region. The wine list similarly aims to showcase the highlights of Portugal's wine tradition. Matos has been praised as one of the best young chefs in the country—when you taste his superb guineafowl and blue lobster stuffed with pistachios, truffles, and celery cream, you understand why. **CP**

⬆ A dish of salted cod with chickpea foam.

Pastéis de Belém | A sweet Lisbon institution

Location Lisbon　**Signature dish** *Pastel de nata* | $

The café Antiga Confeitaria de Belém, better known as Pastéis de Belém, is Lisbon's most iconic patisserie, as witnessed by the lines you find outside at any time. Its fame rests on a small pastry confection—the famous *pastel de nata* (round custard tart), which holds a special place in Portugal's affections. So famed are the pastries that, incredibly, this venerable café sells between 18,000 and 20,000 of them every day.

To go there is something of a tradition among the locals. Pastéis de Belém has been renowned for its own baked custard tarts since 1837, after they secured the recipe from the neighboring Jerónimos monastery. The café is located in a spot that was originally occupied by a sugar refinery, which provided all the sugar for the monastery (at the time, this was not as easy to find as today).

Although you can find a *pastel* in nearly every bakery across Portugal, the original is made here, following a secret recipe known only to a chosen few; you can taste the difference as soon as you get your first bite. They are distinctive, both for their crispy puff pastry and their light, velvety custard filling. Best eaten fresh from the oven, they are truly addictive: one is never enough.

The custard tarts can be enjoyed in the café's spacious rooms, some of which boast extremely old traditional blue-and-white *azulejo* tiles in geometric patterns or depicting scenery on the walls. Guests can also peek through the glass window to catch a glimpse of the tarts being made. There are also many other cakes and delicious savory snacks on offer, from spicy samosas to meat pies and *pastéis de massa tenra* (soft dough pasties). It is usually busy and quite crowded in the café; but, if you want to secure a table, do not let the long lines put you off. Many people order cakes at the counter to take away. **CP**

⬆ Pastéis de Belém is the home of the *pastel de nata*.

Ramiro | Quality seafood
in an unpretentious setting

Location Lisbon   **Signature dish** Garlic prawns;
prego sandwich | 💲💲

The atmosphere is noisy, and the busy waiters run from the counter to the tables as you would expect in a bustling *cervejaria* (beer and seafood restaurant). Ramiro is a haven for seafood lovers; but, in addition to superb clams and lobsters it is also famous for its *prego* (steak sandwich), which is considered one of the best in Lisbon. The steak is tender, seasoned only with garlic and sea salt, and served inside a fresh bread roll. Those in the know will enjoy a *prego* at the end of the meal, as a "dessert."

While lobster or jumbo shrimp can be costly, other dishes such as *gambas à la aguillo* (slightly spicy prawns with garlic sauce), *amêijoas à Bulhão Pato* (clams with garlic and coriander), or some fabulous

---

> *"Ramiro is highly rated by discerning Lisboetas ... it majors in shellfish, including lobster."*
>
> Condé Nast Traveller

Iberian *pata negra* ham from acorn-fed pigs, carefully sliced in front of you, are quite reasonable. Hungry customers will also find a plate of toasted, buttered bread already on the table.

Opened in 1956 by Ramiro Alvarez Alban, the restaurant began as a humble place. Over the years, its fame has spread, but it has kept the 1970/80s decor, which is part of its unpretentious charm. The fish theme continues with a tile panel by Viúva Lamego (a prestigious ceramic factory), depicting all kinds of seafood, and aquariums in the basement. A true Lisbon institution, this lively establishment brings in customers of all ages, including regulars who have been going there for many years. **CP**

Cantinho do Avillez |
Creative contemporary Portuguese food

Location Lisbon   **Signature dish** Selection of
petiscos | 💲💲

Belcanto may have the Michelin star, but Cantinho do Avillez has the fun. Chef José Avillez created both restaurants with success in the fashionable Chiado district of Lisbon. The two ventures are clearly different in style and prices, but it is hard not to fall in love with the charm of Cantinho, where Portuguese ingredients are at once cherished and reinvigorated. The restaurant is small (booking is always advisable) and the menu short, but this intimate spot is a great place to enjoy the culinary creativity of the talented Avillez.

The beloved national staple of *bacalhau* (salt cod) is cleverly reinvented: cooked at a low temperature and combined with "explosive" olives, it is paired with Avillez's version of *migas*, a traditional bread-based dish, while the traditional *peixinhos da horta* (green beans prepared tempura-style) are perfectly matched with a tartare sauce. Make sure to sample the *empadinhas de perdiz com bacon* (small partridge and bacon pies)—they are so irresistible that you will want a second portion. *Farinheira* (flour sausage) in cornbread crumbs or the traditional *prego* sandwich are also popular favorites.

The inspired selection of *petiscos* (Portuguese tapas) offer much scope for enjoyable grazing. At lunchtime, there is also a "dish of the day" available on special offer, so you can eat some of the best food in Lisbon for a very reasonable price. The sense of wit and style that suffuses the restaurant's cuisine extends to its decor, with eye-catching artwork made from old kitchen equipment by artist Joana Astolsi. The innovative cooking means that Cantinho do Avillez is steadily becoming one of the classic places in Lisbon that are not to be missed. **CP**

⊡ Cantinho do Avillez is a fashionable destination.

Vila Joya | Glamorous high-life dining on the Algarve coast

Location Praia da Galé, Albufeira **Signature dish** *Cataplana* | $$$$$

The location itself, overlooking a lovely Algarve beach, is a joy. And Vila Joya, which also comprises a 5-star hotel and spa, is home to a much-awarded restaurant, probably the most internationally celebrated (and Michelin-starred) Portuguese restaurant. Chef Dieter Koschina, from Austria, is behind the magic surrounding the restaurant, combining his northern European influences and techniques with the freshest local seasonal produce.

Each year, Vila Joya attracts top chefs for the International Gourmet Festival, also known as "Tribute to Claudia," which started in 2007 to offer homage to the late Claudia Jung, founder of the hotel and restaurant. If you get a chance to visit during the annual festival, you can experience the work of Michelin-starred chefs from around the world. If, however, you are looking for something more personal, book ahead for the chef's table: it only seats four and is a totally different, intimate experience, where you can see Koschina and his team working behind the scenes.

Koschina's menus are adventurous contemporary, creations, incorporating local Portuguese produce, although he also works with specially imported luxuries, including truffles in season. His flair for unexpected flavor pairings is amply demonstrated in dishes such as tempura of salmon roe and bacon, pork belly with *chouriço* (sausage) sauce and octopus, and caipirinha spheres or beetroot macaron with eel cream. Koschina also draws inspiration from traditional Portuguese cuisine, with his version of the *cataplana* dish (named after a lidded copper pan from the Algarve, which is used for cooking clams), which includes pork, clams, and lobster in a delicious sauce. The delicious, six-course tasting menu, the professional service, and the dreamy, romantic location are all part of an extraordinary experience that is well worth the expense. **CP**

"Vila Joya is superbly located . . . and star chef Dieter Koschina creates a first-class cuisine."

classictravel.com

↑ Sophisticated hors d'oeuvres are part of the exquisite menu at Vila Joya.

→ Outdoor dining with a fabulous view.

Botequim da Mouraria | Traditional Alentejo food made with love

Location Évora   **Signature dish** *Queijo no forno* | $$

"Local gastronomes believe this is Évora's culinary shrine ... a cozy spot serving the finest food."

Lonely Planet

⬆ Sliced Iberian ham with figs is one of the tasty starters on offer at Botequim da Mouraria.

The simple facade, with its white-washed walls, does not give any clues about the fabulous food that is cooked inside this tiny restaurant tucked away on a small street in the city of Évora, a Unesco World Heritage site. The restaurant is really very small; so, if you get a seat, you feel rather privileged. It does not accept reservations, so you just have to be there when the doors open at noon or six in the evening. The small room only has a counter with some stools and a few places by the window.

Once you have secured your seat, let the owner, Domingos, recommend a wine and some of his specialities for starters: *queijo no forno* (a dish of magnificent sheep cheese from Serpa in the oven, seasoned with oregano, and served with sliced radish), Iberian ham with figs, or the roasted Portuguese sausages *chouriço* or *farinheira*.

The *petiscos* (small plates) are cooked with flair by Domingos's wife, Florbela. As for the main courses, Iberian loin and *ensopado de borrego* (lamb soup with bread) are some of the top choices. All the dishes on offer are really a "labor of love," as this couple genuinely seem as in love with the food from Alentejo as with each other. Alentejo Region is a wide expanse in the south of the country, with beautiful landscapes of cork and olive trees, and many vineyards—Botequim da Mouraria stocks over 150 different wines from the region. Domingos loves to chat with the customers; and, if you get a seat at the counter, you will have the chance to listen to some of his stories and explanations of the dishes.

Altogether it is a real culinary experience, even by the high standards of Évora, which has become renowned for its excellent restaurants, and a popular destination for visitors and locals alike. There are no special effects here—only simple, honest cooking and a very warm welcome; you may never want to leave. **CP**

Peter's Café Sport | Unpretentious seafood in a cozy sailors' favorite

Location Horta, Faial **Signature dish** Wreckfish *cataplana* | ❺❺

Located almost 1,000 miles (1,600 km) from the mainland, the Azores are a traditional safe haven for sailors who cross the Atlantic. The harbor at Horta, on the island of Faial, is a particularly famous haven: the stone jetties are covered in hundreds of good-luck paintings left by departing crews.

A few yards from the harbor is Peter's Café Sport, a cozy seafarers' haunt going back more than 85 years. From currency exchange to meeting point, this family-run bar has become an Atlantic institution. Upstairs is a "scrimshaw museum" featuring the most intricate whalebone carvings made by whalers who used to live and work on the Azores. Downstairs, tourists, sailors, and locals mix in the bustling bistro bar amid dangling pennants, framed photographs of boats, and obscure whaling relics. In this cosmopolitan outpost, the food is surprisingly good and, less surprisingly, it is locally sourced.

The fresh seafood includes less familiar deep-sea varieties caught off the island, such as forkbeard, bluemouth rockfish, Atlantic wreckfish, and almaco jack, as well as the familiar tuna, octopus, and cod. *Cataplana* seafood stews with shrimps, clams, and mussels are often served as accompaniment. Fresh mackerel comes fried with a classic green sauce and sweet potatoes, while grilled sardines are served with a simple salad and maize bread.

Meat lovers are also catered to: look out for the sirloin steak marinated in a "pirate sauce" of rum and spices, with chestnut sauce, or the local speciality of black pudding and spiced sausage served with yams and orange from the islands. Cheese from Faial or San Jorge is served with chili paste, clams in the "Bulhão Pato" style (named after a poet), and cod in a chickpea stew. Much of the excellent local wine comes from the neighboring island of Pico, where a 600-year-old labyrinth of lava walls protects tiny plots of black volcanic soil for the grapes to grow. **SH**

"The mythical café continues to be a meeting place for sailors and travelers from the whole world."

Peter's Café Sport website

⬆ Peter's Café Sport is a popular Azores dining spot, complete with a museum of whalebone carvings.

U Fukiera | Fine traditional Eastern European cuisine amid bohemian decor

Location Warsaw **Signature dish** Baked carp with porcini mushrooms and cream | ❸❸❸❸

TV celebrity chef Magda Gessler is involved with at least a dozen top restaurants in her native Poland, but this is the one that is closest to her heart.

U Fukiera stands near the heart of the Old Town in Warsaw, and serves a fabulous menu of the finest Polish classics. What makes the restored 16th-century premises unique is the extraordinary decor—a mix of bohemian luxury and rococo indulgence. Once inside the restaurant, diners pick their way around enormous floral displays, quirky antiques, and artful arrangements of dangling ribbons, bread, fruit, and flickering candles, like ancient still-life paintings. Minimalist it is not.

Lush drapes, mismatched cushions, and quirky artefacts lurk in dark corners within a labyrinth that includes a romantic brick-lined cellar, rooms with florally painted arched ceilings, an intimate inner courtyard, and a summer terrace surrounded by colorful pot plants in the cobbled square outside.

The gilt-framed portraits, cabinets of eclectic glassware, and flower-draped crystal chandeliers form the backdrop to some of the most highly acclaimed versions of traditional Eastern European food available in the capital. Look out for red borscht from Ukraine; Hungarian goulash with peppers; Polish trout marinated in dill and cucumber; Russian crab with tomato and cognac sauce; Warsaw-style tripe on veal shanks with dumplings; Hungarian walnut and chocolate crêpes; and *Zupa nic*, the "soup of nothing"—a glamorous version of a Polish peasant dessert of berries, meringue, and Amaretto cream.

U Fukiera has catered to royalty (Queen Sofia of Spain, England's Princess Anne, and Denmark's Queen Margrethe), politicians (former U.S. Secretary of State Henry Kissinger and French President Jacques Chirac), and a host of celebrities, including artist Yoko Ono. **SH**

⬆ Potted plants frame the entrance to the restaurant.

Francouzská Restaurant | A Czech Art Nouveau masterpiece

Location Prague **Signature dish** Pigeon with black truffle sauce | ❸❸❸

In the spacious dining room of the Francouzská, it is as if someone has come along and sprinkled Art Nouveau gold dust all around: there are rich and deep *fin de siècle* tones of honey, deep maroon, and caramel cream daubed on the stucco moldings that adorn the walls and ceiling; separate booths allow for private eating. Glitteringly golden chandeliers hang from the ceilings and tall windows let in the light and give diners views of the comings and goings on Republic Square. Meanwhile, white-gloved waiters bustle around making sure that the silver cutlery gleams on the starched cloths that drape the tables.

As the restaurant's name suggests, French cuisine has an influence on the food created in the kitchen, where chef Jan Horky rules the roost. The menu is a vibrant synthesis of Gallic traditions with New World inventiveness and a touch of native Czech robustness. Starters might feature king crab in ginger jelly accompanied by palm hearts filled with coconut foam and coriander mousse, or sautéed rabbit kidneys with smoked bacon, shallots, and a veal glace. On the main menu, it could be pigeon with black truffle sauce or duck leg and breast alongside white and red cabbage accompanied by light and airy dumplings. For dessert, you could try the crème brulée.

This elegantly appointed restaurant is part of the Municipal Hall in the center of the Old Town next to the medieval Powder Tower. It, along with the hall, was opened in 1912, during the twilight years of the Austro-Hungarian Empire, when the idea of Czech nationhood was in the ascendancy—a time of hope, which is reflected in the magnificent patriotic paintings on the walls. After all this richness and history has been absorbed and the view across the square has given one a feel for the pumping heart of central Prague, it's time to eat. **ATJ**

⬆ The restaurant's gloriously opulent dining room.

Múzeum Café | Hearty but creative cuisine in a Belle-Epoque time capsule

Location Budapest **Signature dish** Whole roasted goose liver | ❸❸❸

"… dine in old-world style with a piano softly tinkling in the background."

Time Out

⬆ Hearty Hungarian dishes, served in style.

➡ Staff prepare the restaurant at the start of the day.

Múzeum Café reviewers who mention "stepping back in time" are understating the obvious. There's an atmosphere about this old central Belle-Époque Budapest restaurant that hasn't changed since Archduke Franz Ferdinand's day.

In fact, this place was in business long before the demise of the Austro-Hungarian Empire. The Múzeum has been serving fine food in Pest's historic center since 1885, and it seems that some of the decor hasn't changed since then.

Heels click on the shiny floor beneath cavernously high ceilings. The table linen is blancmange pink and, perched loftily on a vast tiled wall, hangs a lonely old clock. Huge arched windows keep the room light and airy, and the grand piano in the corner is sometimes played to diners by renowned local concert pianists.

The Múzeum Café is not chic, but it makes an apt setting for some perfectly conceived traditional mid-European classics. Roast pike, goose leg, duck breast, and veal must have been on the menu here for a hundred years. There is little sense of a contemporary international lightness of touch among the goulashes, potatoes, and cheeses. But look closer, and you'll see dishes that certainly demonstrate modern creative combinations of ingredients.

Veal steak comes with the restaurant's signature goose liver and mushrooms enlivened by a dill-paprika sauce. Also on the menu are lamb shank with clever vegetable dumplings, chicken with mashed potato and pear, and orange-flavored duck breast with almond cottage-cheese dumplings.

The place has been a haunt of politicians, writers, and artists since before the First World War. And it turns out that the timeless look is not a product of neglect or lack of resources. The Zsolnay porcelain wall tiles, hand-carved wood paneling and hand-painted ceiling frescoes have officially been declared protected Hungarian historic artifacts. **SH**

Archipelagos | Memorable and panoramic Greek island dining

Location Santorini **Signature dish** Seafood salad with mussels, shrimp, octopus, salmon, crab, and fish roe | ❸❸

As the sun sets across the Aegean Sea, diners at Archipelagos are gazing dreamily from an open terrace perched on the rim of an ancient volcano caldera. The tables look out across the seawater lagoon, toward the volcanic islands and the cruise ships anchored in the circular natural harbor below.

The restaurant's ultra-romantic setting is a converted sea captain's house, dating back to 1860. The interior is tastefully decorated with art and antiques, so the inside is almost as wonderful as the outside. Almost . . . because nothing beats that view, especially at sunset from a candlelit table.

The food at Archipelago faces tough competition from such a panorama, but it does introduce visitors to modern Mediterranean Greek cuisine with plenty of fresh local ingredients and Santorini wines. The volcanic soil is known to produce small but flavorsome vegetables, and many dishes come with the distinctive and diminutive Santorini cherry tomatoes and fava (small yellow split peas), as well as the capers that grow in the island's hedgerows. Look for these elements in the admirable collection of salads on offer, including rocket and *chloro* (a creamy goat cheese) with sun-dried tomatoes, or Anthohiro (a drier softer goat cheese) salad served with beetroot, apple, zucchini, and a walnut and honey vinaigrette.

Main courses, offering a modern twist on traditional Greek recipes, include lamb wrapped in vine leaves with artichokes, and shrimps in ouzo and cream sauce. Other local specialties include rabbit in wine sauce, goat cheese with fried eggplant, zucchini served with yogurt and spearmint, and *yiaourtlou*, a meat patty served with yogurt, onion, and spicy tomato sauce in pitta bread. But, for most diners, whatever they select, the most vivid memory will be that breathtaking view. **SH**

⬆ Diners can enjoy a truly spectacular sea view.

Strofi | A classic Greek tavern within view of the Parthenon

Location Athens **Signature dish** Kid goat cooked in parchment with gruyère and tomato | $$

At first glance, Strofi seems to be just another restaurant serving the dishes that might be expected in a thousand Greek tavernas. The menu, too, suggests that the dishes will be familiar, and it is only when they arrive at the table that you realize they are raised way above the norm by the quality of ingredients and attention to detail in the kitchen.

The neat and understated 1930s building that houses Strofi stands on a corner in the area directly below the Acropolis. You would not know it from below, but the roof terrace and balcony tables are among the most sought-after in Athens, thanks to their clear views of the Parthenon.

Many people go to Strofi after seeing shows at the nearby theater, and the walls are covered by autographed photos of performers who have dined there. The ballet dancers Rudolf Nureyev and Margot Fonteyn once ate there after a performance. Wherever you are sitting, expect the Greek classics, elevated to gourmet status. Starters include tzatziki, taramasalata, hummus, fried eggplant with feta cheese, stuffed tomatoes, stuffed vine leaves, grilled halloumi cheese, and moussaka. To follow, it is favorites like Greek salad, roast lamb with rosemary, and skewered pork. Look a bit closer to discover the extra touches: that feta cheese is lightly fried with honey and sesame seeds; the haloumi is grilled with fresh tomato and pine nuts; and the zucchini is baked with cheese and mint. A simple octopus starter is gently grilled, then drizzled with olive oil and served with chopped fresh herbs and beefsteak tomato.

By the time you have tackled the tender lamb steaks wrapped with cheese inside vine leaves, or the slow-cooked, parcel-wrapped kid goat with gruyère and tomato, you will understand why this restaurant is such a favorite with Greek celebrities and politicians. **SH**

[↑] The Parthenon provides a striking background.

Varoulko | Traditional Greek seafood cuisine, taken to another level by flair, creativity, and a sharp eye for detail

Location Athens **Signature dish** Greek barley risotto with langoustine | 💲💲

"All my childhood memories are linked with the sea, and this has always influenced my cooking."

Lefteris Lazarou, chef and owner of Varoulko

Varoulko chef and owner Lefteris Lazarou learned his trade while sailing the world working in the kitchens of cruise ships. Since launching his own seafood restaurant in 1987, he has tried to instill some of that maritime flavor in his progressive version of classic Greek cuisine. Lazarou has held a Michelin star since 2002, and Varoulko is now regularly judged to be the finest restaurant in Athens.

Lazarou visits the fish markets of Athens' port Pireaus every morning to find inspiration for the day's menu. His inventiveness has repeatedly transformed humble Greek staples into award-winning dishes. For example, sardines are given a thin layer of sourdough, flash-fried, and served with smoked eggplant puree and octopus is cooked in dessert wine with a mousse made from Greek trahanas pasta.

The building itself is neat and modern, if not in the most glamorous of areas. It houses two floors of very smart dining rooms, with floor-to-ceiling windows, plenty of bare oak, and walls and curtains of deep blue. The real star spot, however, is upstairs, where the wicker chairs of the roof terrace grant memorable views across the rooftops to the Acropolis.

Lazarou's inventive presentation of classic Greek seafood is impressive. His billfish may be delicately boned and the fillets braided together before serving in red-wine sauce; crayfish may be wrapped in sorrel leaves; squid may be served with basil paste; and red snapper may arrive with a black truffle and eggplant mousse. Creative combinations flow through the menu. Cretan rustic goat meat-flavored rice can be combined with chocolate; salmon with carob-tree bread; and smoked eel with granny smith apple. And be sure to leave room for one of the equally innovative desserts, notably Lazarou's extraordinary chocolate cigar, its ash made from cuttlefish and sugar, served in an ashtray contrived from sugar and squid ink. **SH**

⬆ Varoulko offers an elegant dining experience.

Amfora | Fresh fish in the vibrant heart of Zagreb

Location Zagreb **Signature dish** Grilled squid | ❺

Grilled squid, pliant and juicy; shiny, silvery sardines, fried in olive oil, the flesh falling off the bone, a hint of the briny Adriatic on the palate; mackerel, whiting, shrimp, octopus … people come to Amfora to wallow in all things piscatorial. Given that the restaurant is directly opposite the central Dolac market, known as the "belly of Zagreb," the fish served here is some of the freshest around, having been delivered to the market first thing in the morning after being landed the day before. Amfora is run by a couple of brothers, and the fact that one of them is a fishmonger ensures that only the best fish are brought to the table. Of course, there are other local specialties on offer, too, such as the Dalmatian ham and artisanal cheese from the island of Pag that make a delicious appetizer.

The restaurant itself is an unprepossessing looking place, hidden away within an arcade directly opposite the compact plaza that is home for the vegetable and fruit displays of Dolac (the fish hall is below). On warm days, the tables are laid outside in the cool shade of the arcade, giving customers opportunity for some lazy people-watching, while inside there is a small bar that feels more like a café; the main dining room is located upstairs. Amfora is a no-frills restaurant with simple tables and chairs and a hint of minimalism in its decor. The popularity of the place means that strangers are often asked to share tables, which adds to the fun.

Given Amfora's almost organic relationship with Dolac, it has the same opening hours, from 5 A.M. to 3 P.M. It is a case of getting there for lunch, or not at all. But even though you are eating in the bustling center of Zagreb, the fresh fish and even the name of this unpretentious restaurant conjure up some of the magic of the Dalmatian coast. For a moment or two, you can almost the smell the ozone-rich sea breezes and hear the murmurs of the sea. **ATJ**

Pod Gričkim Topom | Croatian cuisine served with passion

Location Zagreb **Signature dish** Beef *pasticada* | ❺❺

Regulars insist that Pod Gričkim Topom makes the best *štrukli* in town—high praise indeed given the ubiquity of this Croatian culinary icon in most of Zagreb's restaurants. *Štrukli* is a simple dish—dough filled with cottage cheese and then cooked in sour cream. But there is more to the menu of this surprisingly rustic, family-run restaurant than štrukli.

How about a John Dory bought fresh that day from the nearby Dolac market? Firm and yet juicy, it is accompanied by a rich garlic and butter sauce whose sweetness adds an adept counterpoint to the earthy spinach and potatoes served alongside. Those with a more carnivorous disposition might plump for the beef *pasticada*, a Dalmatian dish that takes two days to produce: the beef is marinated in red wine and then

---

"This cozy, endearingly rustic yet elegant restaurant … affords stunning views over the city."

fodors.com

---

slowly cooked. Dalmatian-born owner Ante Piljac, who is almost lyrical in the way he talks about food and wine, says that a glass of Croatian merlot, with its essence of berry fruits on the nose and palate, is an ideal companion to the *pasticada*. The dessert card is small, but apparently the passionate regulars love the chocolate cake, vanilla ice cream, and hot cherries.

Pod Gričkim Topom is a compact and intimate eaterie, perched halfway up the hill to the Upper Town, with extensive views of the red roofs of Zagreb below. The name loosely translates as "under the old town's cannon," and refers to the thirteenth-century Lotrščak Tower that is just above, from where a cannon booms out over the city every day at noon. **ATJ**

Proto | Excellent Dalmatian seafood in a Dubrovnik institution

Location Dubrovnik **Signature dish** *Brodetto* fish stew with polenta | $$

In the maze of ancient alleyways that form the heart of the old walled city of Dubrovnik, Proto has long been acclaimed for its fine seafood. Diners can choose to eat at tables under an awning outside the restaurant on the lively pedestrian street, or they may prefer the first-floor summer terrace, surrounded by plants, or the 1930s-style dining room.

When you come here, have a quick scan of your fellow diners, just in case—recent visitors have included jet-setters Bono of U2, Richard Gere, Francis Ford Coppola, and Novak Djokovic. And, many years ago, Edward VIII entertained Mrs. Simpson here. Proto is considered a national institution, and Croatia's President Ivo Josipovic was also a recent visitor. The atmosphere is elegant and traditional without pretention, although prices are considerable. Since 1886, the restaurant kitchen has been buying the best of the day's catch from Dubrovnik's fishermen and turning it into classic Dalmatian cuisine. In the present day, highlights of chef Bosko Lanac's menu might include fresh oysters from the nearby village of Ston, or a simple dish of local mussels in garlic, white wine, and parsley (you are provided with a bib). The restaurant's flagship dish is the traditional *brodetto* fish stew from the nearby island of Lopud. It is a hearty mix of white fish, mussels, shrimps, and squid, cooked with white wine, olive oil, lemon, garlic, tomatoes, and parsley, served with a chunk of freshly made polenta.

Many of the dishes change with the season and what has been caught that day, but you will often find sea bass on saffron rice; lobster risotto with wild rice, truffles, and mushrooms; and fresh local shrimps in saffron sauce. The dishes are presented with a simple charm, including the humorous touch of a smiley face drawn in balsamic vinegar on the side of a plate, and are accompanied by a choice of Croatian wines. **SH**

[↑] Alfresco dining at Proto in the old city of Dubrovnik.

L'Europe | Fusion and tradition in luxurious art nouveau surroundings

Location St. Petersburg **Signature dish** Thai-style barramundi | ❸❸❸

Elton John once ate at L'Europe and loved it so much that, after his meal, he got up on stage and performed an impromptu concert. That was in 1979. Now, diners relax to the sounds of a classical duo rather than "Rocket Man," while waiters in white shirts and black tails flit ghostlike between the tables. The menu demands careful consideration. Will it be the Beluga and Oscietra caviar taster with a fiery shot of vodka? Or maybe "egg in egg," a trio of eggs filled with truffled scrambled eggs and topped with caviar? Culture goes hand in hand with gastronomy at L'Europe, which is not surprising given that it is the main restaurant of St. Petersburg's historic five-star Grand Hotel Europe.

Standing just off the Nevsky Prospekt, the hotel was built in 1875, though L'Europe itself did not open until 1905. The restaurant interior is a striking example of art nouveau, with a stained-glass window of Apollo engaged in something godlike at one end. The tall dining room is bordered at an upper level by intricately carved wooden balconies and five private alcoves, one of which was reputedly popular with Rasputin for entertaining his lady friends.

In 2013, Australian Glen Cooper became the hotel's executive chef. One of his strengths is the ability to create new and exciting menu items from traditional dishes. His approach is to research the origin of a dish, modernize it, and re-introduce it to diners in new, exciting formats; one example is his innovative pairing of chocolate fondant with Thai curry ice cream. Cooper refuses to allow tradition to restrict his imagination. Alongside classic dishes like the rich, earthy borscht, diners might discover one of Cooper's earlier creations: Thai-style barramundi with soy sauce, ginger, lemongrass, and cilantro. After more than a century of political upheaval, revolution, and war, L'Europe continues to thrive. **ATJ**

⬆ The elegant art nouveau dining room at L'Europe.

Palkin | Spectacular Russian food served in an imperial setting

Location St. Petersburg **Signature dish** "Herring in fur coat" | $$$$

"If you want to splurge just once in St. Petersburg, do it here . . . Chefs research menus of past centuries."

frommers.com

↑ Dinner at the Palkin is a luxurious affair, complete with elegant tableware.

Forget the idea of dreary Soviet-era food. Since the collapse of communism, St. Petersburg has enjoyed a veritable restaurant boom, and the busy main boulevard, Nevsky Prospekt, boasts numerous eateries and dozens of contemporary designer restaurants. On a corner near the River Neva, Palkin takes things in a different direction— back in time.

The restaurant opened in 2002 on the site of a traditional restaurant dating back to the days of Chekhov and Dostoyevsky. The composer Tchaikovsky was also a regular at the original Palkin, which must have been an extraordinary emporium boasting as many as twenty-five dining halls, a room for playing pool, private booths, and a fabulous staircase adorned with exotic plants and a fountain. In Soviet times, the building was turned into a cinema.

The new Palkin is a smaller, slightly more humble take on that long-lost imperial style. The cooking is a fine blend of Russian-French tradition, and prices are considerable (particularly for the wine), but the views of Nevsky Prospekt and the aristocratic decor—created under the supervision of the Hermitage Museum—are worth it.

The menu is decadent, with luxury ingredients such as foie gras, truffles, caviar, and game featuring throughout. Dishes are researched from menus dating back to Catherine the Great and recreated with great fanfare. Main courses include chicken with morel sauce, venison with pine-nut marmalade, fillet of turbot with pistachio and curry sauce, and smoked salmon salad with oysters and Beluga caviar.

Service is suitably showy: some dishes are finished with blowtorches right in front of you, and spectacular clouds of liquid nitrogen are used to introduce many dishes; an impressive instant ice cream and dramatic flambées are also created at the table. The traditional Russian soup comes with a pie-crust lid covering the bowl and a shot of vodka on the side. **SH**

Café Pushkin | Dine like a pre-revolutionary aristocrat in a baroque mansion

Location Moscow   **Signature dish** Veal rissoles with roast potatoes and mushroom sauce | ❸❸❸

Café Pushkin is a grand eighteenth-century baroque mansion located not far from Pushkin Square in the heart of the Russian capital. It was once a library and a pharmacy, and has now been converted into a fine restaurant by Russian entrepreneur Andrei Dellos. Café Pushkin is Dellos's attempt to recapture the spirit of pre-revolutionary Moscow, when the famous poet Alexander Pushkin strolled the grand tree-lined boulevards of the city. It also recalls the pre-communist era of exceptional service, still a rarity in modern Russia. The staff dress and talk like the domestic servants of a wealthy family of the imperial era, and the menu looks like an old newspaper, written in archaic language that makes use of letters that are no longer part of the modern Cyrillic alphabet.

The final ingredient in this affectionate Tsarist time capsule is the food itself: authentic, fine Russian cuisine from traditional historic recipes. Look out for pre-Soviet classics, such as sturgeon, *blinchiki* (small savory pancakes), caviar, borscht, and *pelmeni* (meat dumplings). You may want to try other dishes that are less familiar outside Russia, such as roast marrow bones with gherkins and toasted honey bread or jellied pike with horseradish. An expensive wine list includes a range of fine vintages—but, in truth, for the real Russian experience, you should sample an impressive collection of vodkas throughout the meal.

The interior is characterized by high, ornate ceilings, elaborate wood paneling, and sparkling chandeliers. Each of the three floors serves a different purpose: the well-lit and busy cherrywood café bar is great for lunch, the quieter second floor ideal for more formal dining, and the cozy areas on the third floor for a late-night drink. In summer, you can also sit on the roof-top patio and enjoy regular performances by a string quartet. Café Pushkin is open around the clock, and also functions as a perfect after-clubbing breakfast haunt for the city's racier crowd. **SH**

"They treat you like a member of the landed gentry here … [they] really understand service."

Time

⬆ Café Pushkin's historic interior makes for an atmospheric setting in which to enjoy Russian food.

Hotel Metropol | Classic Russian food in a setting of opulence

Location Moscow   **Signature dish** Stolychny salad | 🅢🅢🅢🅢

Just minutes from Red Square and the Kremlin, and facing the Bolshoi Theater, the Hotel Metropol is at the very heart of the city of Moscow and is tightly bound to its history. When the opulent hotel opened in 1901, Muscovites would come in droves to gaze at its splendid facade and modern fittings. That was until the Russian Central Executive Committee took residence there in 1917. The Second House of Soviets, as it became known, was finally converted back to a hotel in the 1930s. Today, the Metropol is one of the most celebrated hotels of the world.

The Metropol is an outstanding monument to the Modernist era in Russian art and architecture, and nowhere is this more evident than in the hotel restaurant. Beneath the magnificent glass dome with its 2,500 panes, Shalyapin sang and Lenin made speeches; Bernard Shaw ordered vegetarian food; and Michael Jackson played the piano. From kings and Soviet leaders to modern-day presidents and pop stars, all have eaten there.

Today, the visitor can still dine like a czar, with the accent on classic Russian dishes, many of which have been handed down through generations of Metropol chefs. They include blinis (yeasted pancakes) heaped with caviar and a shot of ice-cold vodka; shchi (a traditional cabbage soup); solyankas (a soup made with meat or fish and salted cucumber); and borscht, the ubiquitous beetroot soup. Another Russian classic, Stolychny salad, comprising veal tongue, mayonnaise, quail eggs, cucumber, and salmon roe, is one of the Metropol's signature dishes. All does not rest in the glorious past, though. With a brigade of international chefs cooking for a global clientele, there is a demand for a broader brush.

Lucky enough to stay at the Metropol? Do not miss breakfast. The celebrated buffet runs the full length of the restaurant with every food imaginable. Vodka and caviar for breakfast, anyone? **EL**

> *"David Lean came with his crew to film scenes of Doctor Zhivago in the Metropol restaurant."*
>
> The Moscow Times

⬆ Lovingly restored and boasting a splendid glass ceiling, the Metropol restaurant is a wonderful sight.

Varvary | Creative and witty molecular gastronomy, Russian-style

Location Moscow   **Signature dish** Borscht with foie gras | 💲💲💲💲💲

Varvary is one of the finest restaurants in Moscow, yet is found in a surprisingly unassuming location in the city center. The single door and narrow corridor leading to the elevator belie the lavish interior decoration on the first floor and the superb roof terrace with views across the city. Tables groan under the weight of fine engraved silver cutlery, glassware, and crockery. The furnishings are rich and opulent.

Chef-owner Anatoly Komm does nothing by half. The Russian advocate of molecular gastronomy, he is much lauded for his culinary achievements, both within Russia and outside. His food is distinctly Russian, but in a new incarnation. The fifteen-course tasting menu is so complicated that it takes eighteen chefs all day to prepare for twenty-five diners.

The Varvary signature dish of borscht with foie gras is dazzling. Forget anything you thought you knew about the traditional Russian beetroot soup. First, bite-sized pieces of foie gras are served covered with shredded duck meat; alongside these is a frozen, hollow ball of sour cream studded with chives. The soup is then served, menacingly hot, from a weighty silver jug, causing the ball to melt and fuse with the glossy, intensely flavored soup.

Across the menu there are challenges, surprises, and much humor. One dish, "Herring under a fur coat," does not involve an animal pelt but slices of pickled herring, mixed with mayonnaise and topped with beetroot and carrot. In a particularly inventive touch, Komm has even borrowed a technology once used by the Soviets to make artificial caviar; he uses it to create tiny capsules of unfiltered sunflower oil, which he serves with many of his dishes.

The Russian word *varvary* means "barbarians," and the restaurant's shorter name is a play on the reputation Russians have for lacking sophistication in culinary matters. Given how much Komm has done to change all that, the name seems distinctly ironic. **EL**

"Varvary is an elegant affair, offering a sophisticated new take on familiar flavors."

Lonely Planet

⬆ A typically creative dish from the hands of Anatoly Komm, combining visual flair with striking flavors.

Africa

Food is a wonderful way to experience African culture. Whether savoring a romantic meal in a stunning Moroccan courtyard, feasting on fine food in the heart of South Africa's Kruger National Park while watching elephants and lions, or tasting local delicacies in central Cairo, the African continent offers abundant dining experiences.

← The view from La Table d'Antoine, Marrakech, Morocco.

Dar Roumana | French–Moroccan fusion in a courtyard setting

Location Fès **Signature dish** Braised rabbit in seeded mustard sauce with butter mash | $$

"Exclusive dining in a traditional Moroccan riad with panoramic views of the ancient medina."

Dar Roumana website

↑ The Bonnins offer an elegant fusion of North African and French cuisine in beautiful surroundings.

→ The serene, mosaic tile-clad interior of Dar Roumana.

Dar Roumana was one of the first luxury guesthouses to open in the Fès medina. When French chef Vincent Bonnin and his wife Vanessa took over management of the place a couple of years ago, they were determined to make their mark with the cuisine also. They chose to fuse classical French techniques with North African flavors, and the results are spectacular. Imagine impeccably executed French–Moroccan fusion in an elegant courtyard setting, coupled with faultless service and a carefully chosen Moroccan wine list—one that includes the eminently quaffable Perle de Sud sparkler from Essaouira.

A frequently changing menu draws on the native North African neighborhoods of Fès as its primary source, but embraces the whole of Morocco in terms of seeking out new and unusual ingredients; these include argan oil (pressed from the kernels of the endemic argan tree), date syrup from the south of the country, and rabbit, which originated in North Africa and southern Iberia. The dishes are cleverly conceived, too, with numerous local resonances. For example, Bonnin's chargrilled spatchcock with pomegranate molasses, served on pumpkin puree with rose petals, was inspired by the heady aromas of the spice souks (markets). The tart sweetness of the pomegranate molasses reflects the Moroccan love of blending sweet and savory in meat dishes; a sprinkling of pomegranate seeds pays homage to the venue (Dar Roumana means "House of the Pomegranate"); and rose petals, of course, evoke romance. The chef's pineapple carpaccio with ginger syrup, crystallized cilantro leaves, and mint granita is a nod to the country's favorite herbs, with the granita tasting like a pot of frozen mint tea with added peppery cilantro leaves, spicy ginger syrup, and sweet pineapple.

While a reverence for tradition provides the foundation of any cuisine, Bonnin showcases the best of two culinary cultures and transforms both. **TS**

The Ruined Garden | A secret garden serving contemporary street food

Location Fès   **Signature dish** Slow-roast shoulder of lamb with *ras-al-hanout* | 💲💲

A labyrinth to the first-time visitor, Fès medina is full of secret oases that are easily missed without a guide. The bucolic Ruined Garden restaurant, for example, seems to have sprouted from the foundations of an eighteenth-century riad (or traditional Moroccan house or palace) that has long since crumbled away. What remains is a faded courtyard, still with its zellige geometric terra cotta tile work floor, surrounded by sturdy external walls that provide a majestic frame for a garden lush with a huge variety of plants, including banana palms, Papyrus grass, and flowering hibiscus.

Here visitors can find shady corners in which to escape the frenetic activity and chatter of the souks. But they can also eat, and, with the Moroccan sky a lapis lazuli blue above, few places offer a more beguiling setting for al fresco dining. The relatively recent addition of a high-ceilinged lounge with a roaring wood fire makes The Ruined Garden a cozy bolt-hole on chillier days, too.

Opened in 2012, The Ruined Garden has fast become an essential stop during a stay in Fès. Visitors rub shoulders with resident expats over leisurely weekend brunches of home-smoked salmon and egg *svenge* (a savory fried donut), washed down with harissa Virgin Marys. The restaurant's creators—John Twomey, who also owns a pub in London, and Robert Johnstone, a designer, gardener, and cook who plans to develop an organic garden nearby—have painstakingly researched the culinary history of the region. Inspiration for the eclectic menu has come from local street food, such as popcorn *makouda* (potato cakes with a tomato-chili dipping sauce); Roman dishes, such as Volubilis Chicken, slow-roasted in Johnstone's version of garum; and classics such as *mechouia*-style barbecue. The result is a respectful reinterpretation of the classics that few can resist. **TS**

⬆ Delicious dishes are served in the idyllic garden.

Al Fassia | Sumptuous, traditional Moroccan fine dining

Location Marrakech **Signature dish** Lamb tagine with caramelized onions and tomatoes | ❸❸❸

Top-flight traditional Moroccan dining is not always easy to find, and Halima and Saïda Chabof, founders of the women's cooperative-run Al Fassia, set the bar high. Their Moroccan culinary heritage is channeled into a restaurant kitchen that has expanded to two sites, one in Marrakech's sophisticated Ville Nouvelle and the other in a boutique hotel in the countryside. The original venue, Al Fassia in Guéliz, is more atmospheric, with sumptuous antique textiles, banquettes piled high with cushions around low-slung tables, fresh flowers, and shimmering candles. However, the food at both is equally excellent.

In Morocco, a guest is considered the greatest honor to any household. The celebratory *diffas*, or banquet, treats guests to almost unimaginable hospitality, and so it is at Al Fassia. Going beyond the usual couscous and tagines, the restaurant's extensive menu of regional dishes showcases a much broader repertoire of serious feasting. Up to fifteen different salads include a sensational candied tomato salad, smoky *zalouk* (eggplant), tender steamed carrots brightened with cumin and paprika, and plump little fava beans with a sprinkle of salt. Flaky, savory pastries and slow-cooked stews, tagines, and roast meats are followed by achingly sweet desserts, fresh fruit, and the requisite mint tea. The pigeon *b'stilla*, a stuffed, wafer-thin pastry sprinkled with sugar and cinnamon, is superb, the slowly roasted, spice-rubbed lamb shoulder (for two people) is meltingly tender, and the classic chicken tagine with olives and preserved lemons is a prime example of the recipe.

It is little surprise that when thumbing through any of Paula Wolfert's wonderful books on Moroccan cuisine, the reader often finds recipes gleaned from these ladies. Al Fassia is recognized as one of the best traditional restaurants in Morocco and the world. **TS**

⬆ A classic chicken tagine with lemon and olives.

La Table d'Antoine | A taste of the future of Moroccan gastronomy

Location Marrakech   **Signature dish** Lemon-marinated tuna carpaccio; pineapple gazpacho | 💲💲

With eight different dining experiences on offer, the Palais Namaskar Hotel is fast becoming one of the most important gastronomic reference points in Marrakech. But it is La Table d'Antoine, the latest gourmet addition to the complex, that stands out as truly game-changing in Moroccan cuisine.

Head chef Antoine Perray has carefully sourced produce—including an exceptional selection of goat's cheeses from a small farm near Essaouira, ranging from sharp and crumbly to decadently mature and gooey—while updating traditional flavors and ingredients. Many of the fruits and vegetables are grown in the hotel's own organic gardens, and by adding sophisticated French techniques and a lightness of touch typical of Southeast Asian cooking, Perray created a menu that is part of a new wave in Moroccan cuisine (also referred to as "new Moroccan"): light, bright, and healthy, but with plenty of bold statement flavors.

Dining here is a real treat. Surrounded by soaring plaster arches that frame an aquamarine pool, the Palais Namaskar lives up to its name—it is truly palatial, with its expansive terrace and elegant but relaxed dining room (with sofas and easy chairs rather than traditional seating). The color scheme features muted grays and firy tones, and service is attentive.

The lunch menu is a bargain, but it is worth splurging to try dishes such as delicate artichoke tart with roasted foie gras, red peppers marinated in fragrant mint, *charmoula*-marinated sea bass with crunchy chestnut flour fries, and the sweetest Atlas figs with nougat ice cream. Gradually, this place is being discovered by more and more visitors who are happy to travel out from the center; it buzzes with an International mix of diners who are seduced by Perray's vision of the future of Moroccan cuisine. **TS**

⬆ **The terrace affords a spectacular view.**

Le Jardin | A hip new-wave Moroccan bistro

Location Marrakech **Signature dish** *Beldi* (country) chicken in saffron and honey, and Seffa semolina | $$

In Morocco, casual dining is a relatively new concept as far as Moroccan cuisine is concerned. The country's big cities have plenty of French bistros and cafés, Italian trattorias, and even the odd sushi restaurant; but, until recently, there have been very few places that could be said to have a strong, Moroccan identity.

That was before the arrival of the illustrious Kamal Laftimi, who opened his first business, the Café des Épices, in the Marrakech medina in 2006, followed swiftly by the Terrasse des Épices, a sleek, rooftop eatery. His most recent establishment is Le Jardin, an ultra-fashionable riad café designed as a jade-green oasis by Laftimi and color specialist Anne Favier. A pop-up boutique is included on one of the first-floor terraces and features updated local fashions.

Inspired by the Morocco of the 1960s, with vintage furniture and toys, and a number of resident tortoises, Le Jardin has become an all-day meeting point for locals and foreigners. In the morning, they come by for spicy espressos, strawberry and orange-blossom juices, and *m'semen* (Moroccan pancakes) loaded with honey. This leisure time can swiftly segue into lunch or even dinner as the conversation gets more animated and more people drop by.

Laftimi makes good use of medina products and draws produce from local organic farmers. There is even a small grocery store for stocking up on fresh ingredients to take home—a reminder that the place is located at the heart of Moroccan cuisine. Beet and citrus salad; Marrakchi-style marinated sardines redolent of preserved lemons and pink onions, and served on toast; a Halal burger piled high with lettuce, tomatoes, and cucumber; and caramelized pear with orange blossom are just a sample of the wide range of crowd-pleasing dishes. If there is such a thing as a truly Moroccan bistro, this place is surely it. **TS**

↑ Le Jardin offers a pleasant setting for all-day dining.

Abou Shakra | Egyptian international dishes in a family-run restaurant

Location Cairo **Signature dish** Royal Abou Shakra pigeon, *kofta*, and veal ribs | $

Located in the El Kair El-ani district near the Egyptian Museum, this is the original Abou Shakra restaurant, opened in the Egyptian capital in 1947 by catering entrepreneur Ahmed Abou Shakra. His family still owns and runs the well-respected business, which has grown considerably; it now operates eight restaurants in Cairo and Alexandria, but this is the original, and the one to which discerning visitors beat a path.

The overriding culinary concept is simple and involves marinating all the meat before cooking in order to add flavor. Each of the restaurants still operates its own kitchen, but as the business has grown Abou Shakra has established a central hub that enables the family to monitor quality and hygiene standards throughout the chain. A team at the organization's headquarters sources and prepares all the fresh, raw ingredients that are distributed to the individual restaurants. Most importantly, it is here that all the freshly slaughtered meat and poultry are marinated. This ensures the maintenance of standards throughout the Shakra empire.

Appetizers range from dips such as hummus to *sambousek* (cheese-filled pastries), but bear in mind what's to come. The specialities are noticeably generous portions of roasted and charcoal-grilled meats and poultry, so carnivores are well catered to. The laden kebab and *kofta* plates are also firm favorites with diners. Roasted lamb or veal arrives served with a bed of fatta made from crushed flatbread, while kofta meatballs are barbecued and served with tasty khalta rice, flavored with garlic, nuts, and spices. Other specialities include stuffed pigeon with *freekeh* (roasted green wheat) and roasted duck. Should you still have room, you can round off with classic Egyptian dessert *om ali*, a rich concoction of filo pastry with nuts, baked with milk and cream. **SH**

↑ The popular *kofta* are served on a bed of rice.

Abou Tarek | A humble eatery where street food achieves classic status

Location Cairo   **Signature dish** *Koshary* | $

A well-known landmark on a corner in Cairo city center, Abou Tarek specializes in *koshary*, a classic Egyptian creation made from rice, lentils, beans, macaroni, noodles, and chickpeas and flavored with crispy fried onions, spices, and a chunky tomato sauce. Locals claim that Abou Tarek's *koshary* is the best of its kind in the country.

The business started like many in Egypt, serving from a handcart in the street. Abou Tarek was later able to establish a small corner shop, which gradually expanded into its current three-story modern building. More crucially, Tarek has managed to turn an everyday humble street food outlet into a nationally recognized name. A large sign outside trumpets the rather unusual boast: "We have no other branches." The modern dining room upstairs overlooks a busy street below and the air-conditioned interior also boasts a bustling atmosphere. Abou Tarek is an unpretentious but popular eatery designed for locals in a hurry: the tables and chairs are bare metal, the lighting is bright, and there are aquarium tanks along the wall and fake plants suspended from the ceiling.

Waiters expect payment upfront, not after the meal. Customers simply have to decide whether to order 5, 7, or 10 Egyptian pounds-worth of the pre-cooked *koshary*, and which sauce to pour on the dish when it arrives. Pots of hot chili, lime, and vinegar, or garlic salt, are brought to the table to add as the diners see fit. Service is fast: typically no more than five minutes from order to delivery.

It's a very cheap, traditional meal that is simple yet satisfying, designed to fuel a hard working day. There are no frills or fancy touches. The koshary is the star of the show, served simply in a bowl to eat in the restaurant (with a spoon) or boxed to take away. **SH**

⤒ A dish of *koshary*, topped with fried onions.

Singita Lebombo Lodge | The ultimate bushveld
experience with panoramic views, wildlife, and great food

Location Kruger National Park **Signature dish** Horseradish and grape risotto with crispy-skin salmon | $\Theta\Theta\Theta\Theta\Theta$

"... contemporary safari living in completely glass-walled lofts with beautiful 'eagle's nest' views."

Singita Lebombo Lodge website

⬆ Contemporary South African food served at Singita Lebombo Lodge.

Among the ancient boulders of the Lebombo Mountains and overlooking the meeting place of two rivers is perched the enchanting Singita Lebombo Lodge. Home to fifteen loft-style suites, the lodge is surely one of the best and most beautiful in the Singita crown, especially when it comes to the food.

Lebombo Lodge is situated on Singita Game Reserve, a private concession in the Kruger National Park. It is an impressive structure, an assembly of wood, steel, and organic interiors encased in glass that makes the most of the incredible river views. The game viewing is unparalleled; expect to see black and white rhino, buffalo, elephant, hippopotamus, cheetah, leopard, and large prides of lions.

In terms of food, the focus at the Lodge's restaurant is imaginative, health-conscious cooking, making use of home-grown (and preferably organic) ingredients. Chef Archie Maclean and his team take inspiration from their surroundings and dish it up in a contemporary fashion. Maclean uses modern plating techniques while keeping the food simple. He believes that having too many flavors on a plate risks confusing the senses, and instead plays with interesting combinations, like horseradish and grape risotto with crisp-skin salmon, or salted caramel, lemon curd, and coffee ice cream. Breakfasts are bountiful and served with a panoramic view, lunches are light and healthy (with a side of indulgent desserts), and dinners are fancy affairs set in special locations, such as the veranda of your private suite, a carefully picked spot around the lodge, or in the bush.

As an aside, the Singita School of Cooking was established to develop culinary skills and provide employment opportunities among local youth. Students can gain a nationally recognized professional cookery qualification and commence work within a Singita lodge kitchen thereafter. **AG**

Roots | Fine dining at the Cradle of Humankind World Heritage Site

Location Krugersdorp **Signature dish** Springbok | ❸❺

About 30 miles (50 km) northwest of Johannesburg lies arguably one of the most significant World Heritage Sites, named the "Cradle of Humankind." It is the world's richest hominid site, and home to around 40 percent of known human ancestor fossils.

It is also the location of Forum Homini, a beautiful and luxurious boutique hotel set within a private game estate, where the history of mankind is weaved into the design and decor of the hotel's crowning glory, its award-winning restaurant, Roots.

The domain of executive chef Adriaan Maree, Roots offers an African and East Asian take on fine dining. The degustation menus, with their many small dishes, take the stress out of making decisions, and diners are left to enjoy the views, wildlife, and well-crafted plates of sophisticated food. Breakfasts and brunches are languid, five-course affairs; lunch has four courses, and dinners and Sunday lunches, six. That allows more than enough time to appreciate the chef's talent and the passing animal and bird life.

The inventive menus change every month, and can include anything from springbok served with a cocoa bean ragout and fillet with eggplant ash; duck from head to toe (breast, confit leg, tortellini, and foie gras foam); and kingklip (a cusk eel) with an almond crust, served with a clever turnip-and-lime flourish. There are lots of foams, airs, jellies, and savory meringues, and always at least one interesting sauce going around. A recent dessert highlight was chocolate torte with ginger soil and roast fennel ice cream, a gloriously clever combination that worked.

As one might expect, the cellar here is equally memorable, a showcase of the best of South Africa's rich wine scene. The best way to sip and savor the collection is to go for a per-course pairing. For maximum treat value, make your visit on a beautiful day and take a seat on the deck. **AG**

Wandie's Place | A spot on the tourist trail that is well worth a visit

Location Soweto **Signature dish** *mngqusho* | ❸❺

Soweto is probably the most famous township in South Africa. Bordering the mining belt of Johannesburg in the south, it has grown to become much more than just a city suburb. Soweto is infused with the history of the struggle against apartheid, and is energized by the fast pace of the "city of gold." Some say that Soweto represents the real South Africa.

In Dube, a suburb of Soweto, is Wandie's Place, a cozy township restaurant operating out of what used to be a typical four-roomed Soweto house. Since its humble beginnings as an illegal shebeen in the 1980s, it has evolved into a well-known restaurant that is popular with locals and tourists alike. Owner Wandile Ndala has turned it into a must-see on many a tour operator's schedule, and the restaurant has hosted

---

"Diners sit at long tables, creating closer bonds with their friends, and increasing the vibrancy."

Official website of the City of Johannesburg

---

the likes of Evander Holyfield, Jesse Jackson, Richard Branson, Will Smith, and Tom Cruise.

On offer is a feast of a buffet, with dumplings, *ting* (sour porridge), *mngqusho* (stamped corn and bean stew), *morogo* (wild spinach), and *mogodu* (tripe) accompanied by beef, sausage, and chicken. Salads include potato salad, coleslaw, and beetroot. Everything is topped with the omnipotent *chakalaka*, a simple, spicy vegetable relish made of onions, tomatoes, and often beans. The chatty waiters are able to serve anything you can think of to drink. It is a charming, unpretentious space where local singers like Miriam Makeba boom from the loudspeakers and regulars eagerly chat with new visitors. **AG**

Five Hundred | The finest of dining in glittering Johannesburg

Location Johannesburg **Signature dish** Pork with Jerusalem artichokes and pear and honey chutney | ❸❸❸❸❸

When it opened in 2012, this addition to the Johannesburg restaurant scene caused quite a stir. It is located in the city's luxury, boutique Saxon Hotel, and the name, Five Hundred, is the room number of the owner's suite, where the restaurant is now installed. At the culinary helm is award-winning chef David Higgs, who had made his name in the course of stints in and around Cape Town.

At the Saxon, Higgs was given the space to push the boundaries of contemporary modern cuisine and explore the complex emotive relationship between food, wine, and art. The result is a multi-sensory experience that would be hard to match elsewhere in South Africa. His team sources fresh seasonal ingredients from the Saxon's own vegetable garden, pairing it with handpicked artisan produce and the finest local and international wines. The result is intricate yet delicious plates of food. The "soup with nine lives" is a taste sensation of cucumber and horseradish, mushroom ceviche and yuzu, carrot and lavender, chocolate and beetroot, mandarin and tarragon, tequila and lime, blue cheese and walnut, all perched on a jellied camomile soup surrounding a fennel espuma. The mind-boggling pork, plated at the table, is served with Jerusalem artichoke, pear and burned honey chutney, and pine floor aromas.

Extraordinary care is taken to create an elegant, intimate environment and service is exceptional. The chefs appear to relish adding finishing flourishes at the table and are happy to discuss the thinking behind each dish. Everything about the restaurant appears to be done with a single goal: to make the statement that Johannesburg possesses a world-class restaurant incorporating South African flavors and produce. And that goal certainly has been achieved. **AG**

⬆ Sophisticated presentation is key at Five Hundred.

DW Eleven-13 | Contemporary culinary adventures

Location Johannesburg **Signature dish** Roasted chicken with braised lettuce | ❸❸

When Johannesburg started its assault on Cape Town's title as culinary capital of South Africa a few years ago, Marthinus Ferreira and his DW Eleven-13 led the pack. The energetic young chef brought to the Johannesburg dining scene what it desperately needed: innovative contemporary fine dining with a focus on simple, seasonal ingredients.

The compact menu changes often, but with luck will always include Ferreira's signature roasted chicken with braised lettuce, itself a testimony to his belief in not overworking dishes. But that is not to say that his food is not layered. Every dish on the tasting and à la carte menus consists of a variety of carefully considered parts, all beautifully presented. Take his seared Rougié foie gras (a favorite ingredient) with homemade duck prosciutto, port-poached pear, white pear puree, pickled pear cubes, Glühwein syrup, pistachio soil, and rendered chocolate: no one could claim that to be a simple dish.

Ferreira's main courses are equally impressive. Confit duck thigh with bacon lentil ragout, pan-fried marguet duck breast, and beetroot and orange puree sits alongside other flavorsome dishes, including fillet of grass-fed beef with roasted bone marrow, turnip puree, and rosemary dauphinoise potatoes. Desserts are fun and flavorsome and include Valrhona ganache with coconut sorbet, banana ice cream, chocolate–banana soil, milk tart macaroon, and salted peanut caramel sauce, and a delectable dark chocolate fondant, with mint ice cream, strawberry pannacotta, milk pillow, Turkish delight drops, and chocolate soil.

The setting, on the outskirts of a small shopping mall, and the somewhat bare modern decor, with touches of wood and leather, may perhaps seem unassuming—but ahead lies a Johannesburg culinary adventure second to none. **AG**

⬆ Dishes are carefully assembled from fine ingredients.

Café Bloom | Shabby-chic country dining

Location Natal Midlands **Signature dish** Fresh foods straight from the garden | **$**

"The mismatched chairs and characteristic barn-style red door make it an adorable café."

houseandleisure.co.za

Nestled between the vast Drakensberg and the scenic Natal South Coast are the magical Midlands. The roads are narrow and winding, the greenery and rivers abundant, and the valleys lush. And the food finds in this part of South Africa are spectacular.

One of the highlights is Café Bloom in Nottingham Road. Owned and run by ceramicist Michael (known as Mick) Haigh and his wife Sally, the eatery is a shabby-chic daytime joint set in an old converted barn. Comfortable couches and wooden furniture spill out onto a veranda overlooking beautiful gardens, and alongside an eclectic collection of art one finds Haigh's covetable ceramics. So desirable is his work that international decor stores such as The Conran Shop and Anthropologie have commissioned their own ranges.

Shopping aside, Café Bloom is a feast for the taste buds. The Haighs are longtime vegetarians, so the focus obviously lies in that area, although meat eaters need not worry. Mick Haigh claims that none of their dishes have names and that they seldom follow recipes, except when it comes to cakes. Their inspiration always starts in the garden.

What awaits guests at lunchtime is simply inspiring. The Haighs' pretty platters and bowls are piled high with freshly prepared foods. It might be lavish leek, parsnip, and parsley soup; creamy baby-marrow tagliatelle; a salad of rocket topped with caramelized cherry tomatoes and chickpeas fried with coriander, cumin, and fennel; kale mixed with nutty, slow-roasted mushrooms and creamy Danish feta cheese; or simply platters of cheese with pickled mushrooms, homemade chutneys, and breads. Whatever it is, it will taste very good. And when they do stick to recipes, they create masterpieces, too— witness the delectable cheesecake, carrot cake, polenta cake, scones, and lemon brioche. The perfect place to spend a lazy Sunday. **AG**

⬆ Even the simplest dishes, such as scrambled eggs, deliver on flavor at Café Bloom.

Cleopatra Mountain Farmhouse | A romantic gourmet getaway

Location Drakensberg   **Signature dish** Ginger chocolate soufflé | ❺❺❺❺❺

The KwaZulu-Natal part of South Africa's Drakensberg is a particularly beautiful part of the country—one that offers not only lush green and mountainous landscapes, but also incredible warmth and hospitality. Cleopatra Mountain Farmhouse is the epitome of this tradition, with the notable extra of an array of formidable food thrown into the mix.

The five-star lodge has only eleven rooms and is found in the beautiful Kamberg Valley close to Giant's Castle Game Reserve. The place is owned and run by Richard and Mouse Poynton, whose family has been coming to the farm since the 1940s. They are warm and inviting people, and have created what they call their dream hotel—an intimate gourmet getaway, run with charm and grace.

In these appealing, escape-from-it-all surroundings, guests can look forward to feasting on a different seven-course dinner every night, adjusted according to the availability of local produce and the season in Mouse's vegetable and herb garden. Richard's fascination with fine food has also led him to use imported luxurious ingredients, such as fine Italian cheeses and charcuterie. The food is rich and decadent, and expertly presented by the passionate Richard, whose enthusiasm for classic cooking techniques also informs the menu to excellent effect. On offer might be prawn and avocado with a piquant sauce, roasted quail, or trout timbale. The desserts are not to be missed, either; try the pear baked in pastry with a butterscotch sauce, or the legendary chocolate and ginger soufflé. These are delectable foods.

The dining rooms and lounge convey a sense of family, with photos, art, and quirky family collectibles scattered around. Make sure to take a walk before lunch or dinner at the adjacent Highmoor Nature Reserve; like Giant's Castle Game Reserve to the north, it is part of the Ukhahlamba Drakensberg Park, a World Heritage Site, and the views are breathtaking. **AG**

"At Cleopatra, the Little Mooi river runs through the property and it is stocked with brown trout."

uyaphi.com

⬆ The Farmhouse has an idyllic riverside setting close to the Highmoore Nature Reserve.

Capsicum | South Africa's homage to Indian curry

Location Durban   **Signature dish** Hot sugar bean curry | ❺

Alongside leg of lamb, samp and beans, *bobotie*, *melktert* (and a few even more obscure sounding dishes), the Durban curry is one of South Africa's most distinctive and celebrated local dishes. A variation on the already much varied and versatile Indian staple, the Durban curry comes in as many forms and flavors as the Asian original. And South Africans are willing to drive miles to find the perfect one.

For the curry aficionado, all roads in South Africa lead to the Capsicum Restaurant, located at the Britannia Hotel in central Durban. Built in 1879, this colonial-looking hotel had an unremarkable existence for its first century, attracting little attention. All that changed in 1983, when the Moodley family took over.

Since then, Capsicum has attracted an extremely loyal following. Not only does it offer the ultimate Durban curry, it also serves *bunny chow*, a much-loved, hugely popular local fast food, originating with Durban's Indian community, which consists of a hollowed out loaf of bread filled with curry. Although the menu also covers a range of Western foods—including a delectable dish of grilled prawns—and an array of East Asian delights, it is the curries that ensure that visitors from across the globe will keep coming back. The mutton *bunny chow*—tender, juicy meat served with the freshest of white bread and a carrot salad—is sublime, as are the hot sugar bean curry, the mouthwatering crab curry, and the lamb on the bone. Offal lovers will enjoy the tripe version, which is soft and full of flavor; even those who generally avoid tripe will make an exception once they have sampled it.

The surroundings are not hugely impressive—apart from the big light fittings—but that is not what is important here. Morning, noon, and night, Capsicum is packed, and mostly with extended local families; clearly, they are there for the food. **AG**

⬆ A plate of hake, shrimp, and calamari.

Oep ve Koep | Celebrating local ingredients in an unassuming setting

Location Paternoster **Signature dish** Maasbanker *bokkom*, pear, and shoreline herbs | ⓢⓢ

The mostly sleepy fishing town of Paternoster, on the West Coast of South Africa, is an unexpected place to find world-class cuisine. It is even more surprising when you see the humble restaurant that serves it. Situated alongside Die Winkel op Paternoster, the town's famous food emporium, itself known locally as Oep ve Koep, is a small, unassuming bistro that serves incredible food. Owner and chef Kobus van der Merwe (whose parents own and run the emporium) celebrates local produce on his ever-changing blackboard menu. And local means *really* local; Kobus is a master forager and finds many of his ingredients on the dunes and in the waters of Paternoster.

On the menu are interesting takes on South African favorites interspersed with clever inventions. The ingredients include dune spinach, sea lettuce, *veldkool* (a flower bud that looks like an asparagus spear), *vygies* (ice plants or midday flowers), *waterblommetjies* (Cape pondweed or asparagus), and

plenty of seafood, including local snoek, mussels and oysters from nearby Saldanha Bay, and *bokkoms* (salted air-dried fish) prepared by van der Merwe himself, using maasbanker instead of southern mullet. In winter, the menu is more likely to include red meat, such as springbok from a farm in Darling.

The ingredients may be rustic, but the plating and presentation are pure, multifaceted art: Saldanha Bay oysters served with gooseberries, green apple, and orange beurre blanc, or the same oysters with a salty, crunchy, local wild herb, samphire. Angelfish are encrusted with black sesame seeds and pan-fried, and served with nasturtium mashed potato, *waterblommetjies*, and dune spinach. If you are lucky, dessert will be honey panna cotta with preserved *naartjie* (mandarin) and wild sage. The wine list is a small selection of interesting Swartland estates. **AG**

⬆ A boat in the garden is used for growing vegetables.

Die Strandloper |

A rustic West Coast seafood fest

Location Langebaan **Signature dish** Flame-grilled snoek with potatoes and sweet potatoes | $$

Years ago, there was a trend for small fishing towns on the West Coast of South Africa to have rustic seaside restaurants—almost of a pop-up nature—offering large buffets of seafood, to be devoured in sittings half a day long. They took the local food scene by storm, and many a South African would plan weeks in advance to get to one of these spots. These days, the craze has died down a bit, but one restaurant that has stood the test of time is Die Strandloper ("the beach walker") in Langebaan.

A visit to Die Strandloper is the perfect family outing. All the West Coast favorites are there: *bokkoms* (salted air-dried fish), mussels in wine and onions, mussels with garlic butter, West Coast

---

"This beach restaurant has a view to remember—not to mention the unforgettable buffet …"

eatout.co.za

---

haarders (southern mullet), and fish curry. And those are just the starters. Main courses include flavorful flame-grilled snoek with potatoes and sweet potatoes, *waterblommetjiebredie* (a stew made of Cape pondweed and lamb), smoked angelfish, stumpnose, and crayfish. As with all good meals on the South African West Coast, there is also a good sweet offering: fresh farm bread, dollops of farm butter, and jam in huge jars. At the end of the meal, you get the obligatory big enamel mugs of *moerkoffie* (coffee brewed in a tin pot over the fire) and *koeksisters* (a doughnut-like sweet pastry dipped in syrup). When the chef announces the arrival of the next course, you had better grab a paper plate and fall in line. **AG**

Mzoli's Place |

The ultimate township food experience

Location Cape Town **Signature dish** Flame-grilled marinated sausage | $

Literally meaning "burned meat" in Zulu, *shisa nyama* is a term used in South African townships to describe a *braai* (barbecue) where friends gather to grill meat on an open fire. The event is usually organized by a butcher, and only meat bought from that butcher is allowed to be prepared on his *braai* (be it by the buyer or the butcher himself).

Mzoli's Place (also known as Kwa-Mzoli to the locals) is located in Gugulethu, a Cape Town township, and took *shisa nyama* to the foodie masses. Owned and run by Mzoli Ngcawuzele since the early 2000s, the eatery is frequented by a cosmopolitan crowd of locals, students, and tourists, often arriving in overloaded minibus taxis. The place is noisy and rowdy, and very basic (tables and chairs are plastic and cutlery is not always available), but the music is often live and well-known DJs make an appearance, accompanied by dancing locals. The music ranges from deep house and Cape jazz to kwaito and marimba. It's a fantastic spot to kick back and do some serious people watching. You may want to just check out the locals, but you will be bopping along in no time.

Visitors can handpick their meat and take it to be barbecued by the entrepreneurs running the *braai* stalls (massive fires). There isn't just one signature dish—anything done over the coals is bound to be good, from chicken wings and steak to lamb chops and sausage marinated in special sauce. Enjoy it with maize pap, steamed bread, and salads, and the delicious house *chakalaka* (a spicy vegetable relish). Mzoli himself is always on hand to make a recommendation. For even greater authenticity, wine and other drinks can be bought at the shebeen across the road. Visitors can book a shuttle to take them back after a long night of partying. **AG**

La Colombe | Classic techniques supporting the fusion of contemporary French and Asian fine dining

Location Cape Town **Signature dish** *Umami* broth with sea fog | $$

La Colombe is a stalwart of the South African fine dining scene, a wine estate restaurant with a succession of acclaimed chefs keeping standards high over the past two decades. The latest man in white is Scot Kirton, a talented if reserved young chef whose culinary philosophy centers around the combination of classic techniques, fresh seasonal produce, and uncomplicated flavors. The result is a menu in which contemporary French meets Asian fine dining, prepared with the best local South African ingredients. Perhaps most impressive of all is the tasting menu, where the kitchen team's artful plating and food theatrics are really celebrated.

Kirton is particularly adept with seafood and mixes it masterfully with other meats. He makes a very memorable dish of scallops and confit of pork belly in langoustine stock, and other menu stars include risotto bordelaise, beef *sous vide*, halibut miso yaki, and beetroot cannelloni and *umami* broth with steamed langoustine and miso scallops. And the theatrics? Well, if you are lucky, that umami broth will star on the menu for some time. It is an inventive, not to mention delicious, dish of samphire, seaweed, scallops, and langoustines, where a quick trick conjures up a cloud of sea fog rolling over the table.

The food is supported by great service and an amazing wine selection. On offer are Constantia Uitsig's own estate wines, and a very extensive list of both Cape and imported wines. Be sure to go for the recommended food and wine pairings.

The restaurant's interior has recently been renewed, but still leans toward an understated, light and classic atmosphere that is intimate and remarkably relaxed. In winter, try to get a place by the crackling fire. In summer, try dining on the veranda overlooking the courtyard garden and pond. **AG**

"A dish has to be understandable and have bold flavors . . . I'm always tweaking and refining . . ."

Scot Kirton, La Colombe

↑ Artful plating at La Colombe.

Carne SA | An Italian-inspired, inner-city temple for red-meat eaters

Location Cape Town **Signature dish** La Fiorentina beef |

"We wanted to create something exceptional from both a design and quality viewpoint."

Giorgio Nava, Carne SA restaurateur

⬆ Giorgio Nava serves prime meat from his own farm at his restaurant, ensuring maximum traceability.

➡ The dining area at Carne SA draws on a traditional Italian butchery for its distinctive, rugged look.

The robust Italian name of Carne SA suggests two important things about this Cape Town institution: it is all about meat, and it is grounded in great Italian cooking. Chef and proprietor Giorgio Nava hails from Milan, and brings with him a dedication to the best Italy has to offer (he also runs 95 Keerom, his Italian restaurant across the street). Nava owns a farm in the Karoo, arguably the home of South Africa's best lamb, and is committed to serving the best possible meat.

The meat on offer is spectacular. From the finest cut of Romagnola beef and Dorper lamb to a wild variety of game, it is all delicious, and can be traced back to its farm of origin. Smart, well-mannered waiters bring large trays of raw meat for diners to choose their dinner, letting them know of the day's specials, as well as the aging time of the meats and whether the animals were grass- or grain-fed.

The Italian menu (antipasti, primi, dalla griglia, secondi piatti, contorni, salse, and dolci) is clearly geared towards the carnivore, but there are hearty vegetarian options, too. Meat highlights are the hand-sliced, twenty-four-month, grass-fed sirloin beef carpaccio with rocket, Parmesan, and extra virgin olive oil and veal tongue carpaccio, with a poached tongue, salad, and salsa verde. Primi brings homemade ravioli of slow-baked lamb shoulder with sage butter and Parmesan cheese, and polenta gnocchi with a gorgonzola sauce.

For the main course, the La Fiorentina, a 2 lb 8 oz (1.2 kg), twenty-four-month grass-fed T-bone, more than enough to share between two, reigns supreme. Other options range from hangar steak, prime rib, and mixed game skewers to black wildebeest fillet.

Carne SA has won numerous awards, including that of Best Steakhouse at the Eat Out Restaurant Awards, and it really is no wonder: it is a modern, minimalist, magical temple where carnivorous South Africans go to worship their beloved red meat. **AG**

Panama Jacks | Seafood splendor in a harborside haven

Location Cape Town **Signature dish** Seafood platter | $

An unpretentious restaurant in a working harbor, clearly in desperate need of an overhaul of decor, menu, and probably the service staff, too, is not normally rated as one of the must-see restaurants in a city, let alone a country. Yet, Panama Jacks in Cape Town harbor is just such a place, and it is unmissable.

The seafood tavern, housed in what can best be described as a wooden shack, has been around for a gazillion years, hidden away in a not so attractive and busy part of the Table Bay harbor. It has a large contingent of regular diners and a few lucky newbies, all searching for the same thing: spectacular seafood.

The place is rough—slightly tacky furniture, low-hanging flags, fishing net and buoy decorations—but you need to look past that. You will find delectable and extremely affordable seafood, great service, and a very amenable atmosphere. The à la carte menu is straightforward and vast, and covers all the seafood bases. Starters include shrimp, a crayfish cocktail (with

sweet chili mayo, sesame seeds, and chopped green onions), classic Namibian oysters (served chilled on a bed of ice with fresh lemon wedges and Tabasco sauce), different takes on mussels (Portuguese-style, Thai-style, or with a creamy white-wine sauce), calamari, and even escargots, or land snails.

Main courses go further and wider, to include an impressive selection of crustaceans (West Coast rock lobster, wild abalone, jumbo shrimp, Mozambican langoustines, and more), a variety of line fish, and mixed seafood platters, as well as unexpected options like Hoi San sesame duck. On show are live lobsters and abalone in seawater tanks—perfect for keeping the kids entertained while the adults enjoy their pre-dinner garlic bread—and a small sushi kitchen. To round off the experience, the wine list is notably well priced and offers great seafood-friendly options. **AG**

⬆ Fresh seafood, including sushi, is Panama Jacks' forte.

The Test Kitchen | Where talent, skill, creativity, and fun collide

Location Cape Town   **Signature dish** Wild mushroom and duck liver with morel-glazed sweetbreads | 💲💲

If all the local kitchens were as exciting and innovative as this one, the South African food scene would be the hottest in the world. Hot, must-visit, and best are terms that are often used when speaking about the restaurant of chef Luke Dale-Roberts; and world-class it definitely is.

With British roots and an extensive international career under his belt, Dale-Roberts thinks and cooks global. His food, offered on five tasting menus—three-course, five-course, discovery, gourmand, and vegetarian—is ever-evolving and reflects his aim to enhance the natural flavors of seasonal fare with playful interpretations and imaginative combinations of fresh local produce. Best of all, you can watch the chef and his crew in action in the open kitchen.

Core ingredients range from foie gras, sweetmeats, and scallops to Chalmar beef fillet, veal tongue, and pig's head. Sauces and sides are pickled, poached, and pureed, with flavors ranging from wood-smoked and earthy to piquant, and embracing Asian elements, such as ginger, miso, and mirin.

Dale-Roberts' talent and skill is evident in his signature dish of wild mushroom and duck liver *chawanmushi* (egg custard) with morel-glazed sweetbreads. The chef manages to conjure up the "forest floor" character of the mushrooms while cooking the sweetbreads to perfection—not an easy feat. All dishes are paired to a wine by glass or bottle from an excellent selection of top South African labels.

The restaurant is right in the middle of Cape Town's burgeoning design district, in a warehouse that once formed part of an old biscuit mill complex. The unplastered brick walls, exposed piping, and wooden furniture make for a stylish, industrial-type setting, and displays of contemporary art emphasize the restaurant's commitment to creativity. **AG**

⬆ Luke Dale-Roberts at work in the kitchen.

Harbour House | Breathtaking ocean views and succulent seafood

Location Cape Town **Signature dish** Seafood ceviche | $$

Few seafood restaurants can boast of a more impressive setting than Harbour House in Cape Town. Built on the breakwater in the colorful Kalk Bay harbor, with windows from floor to ceiling, the chic, light, and white restaurant has exquisite views of False Bay and the mountains. It is perfect for appreciating the sunset or the frolicking whales—from late July, humpbacks and southern right whales come into the bay to calf.

But it is not just the view and the wildlife that make Harbour House a worthwhile destination. You can also taste some of the best and freshest seafood in Cape Town. The blackboard announces daily specials—mostly line fish and serving suggestions—while the standard menu offers a small selection of other seafood and meat options.

Be sure to start in elegant style, with either the marinated seafood ceviche—a light salad of fresh fish, shrimp, calamari, and mussels with a lime and cilantro dressing—or the Champagne oysters. The mains are overshadowed by the fresh line fish options, but always include sautéed paprika calamari and Mozambique-style tiger shrimp. The seafood platter comprises a whole grilled crayfish, tiger shrimp, line fish, West Coast mussels, and tender calamari tubes served on savory rice with aioli and fresh lemon. A favorite recommendation of the waiting staff, it is a great option that fully justifies its price tag.

The desserts are classics—examples are New York-style baked cheesecake, crème brûlée, lemon tart, and sorbet—and the wine list is equally sufficient, with a selection of well-known, good-quality wines that is just big enough to offer something to suit everyone's taste and the chosen dish. Once the sun has set and you have finished your dinner, you can carry on relaxing by popping in downstairs at Polana bar for a drink and some live music. **AG**

[↑] Great food with a side order of fantastic ocean views.

Jordan Restaurant | The perfect spot to enjoy the winelands

Location Stellenbosch **Signature dish** Mussels *en papilotte* | ❸❸

A breathtaking setting—mountains, vineyards, and a meadow-wrapped dam—might easily distract a chef from being totally focused on his restaurant's food. Not George Jardine. In fact, judging by the incredible food coming from his kitchen, you would think that he barely takes his eyes off it. This is especially impressive given that the open-plan kitchen and floor-to-ceiling windows make it nearly impossible to ignore the gorgeous panorama of the winelands.

Jardine has a gift for combining the best local produce with expert technique and a good shot of unpretentiousness to create seriously delicious food. This is fine dining without being overly fancy. The menu changes daily, and consists of a small selection of starters, mains, sides, and desserts and a menu du jour. Top of the list of must-eat starters is mussels *en papillote* (in parchment), made by steaming with Asian flavors like lemongrass, ginger, chili, and coconut milk and Oom Louis's Gemsbok ravioli, served with Jerusalem artichoke velouté, roasted Jerusalem artichoke, and forest greens. Mains like Chalmar beef fillet with marrow and morels are astounding, as is the roasted East Coast hake with brandade, creamed spinach, potato gnocchi, and crispy sage. The dessert options are all tempting; but, if there is a soufflé on offer, go for it. Whether it is honey and poppy seed, or pear with crème anglaise, order it.

The wine-estate setting ensures an endless supply of Jordan wines, supplemented by an ever-changing selection of handpicked wines from around the rest of the region and country. The highlight of every visit, however, is a wander around the cheese room. Mature cheddars, Witzenbergers, gorgonzolas, goat cheese—this is cheese heaven, and patrons are able to make their own selection for serving after their meal or simply to enjoy with wine. **AG**

⬆ An idyllic place for sampling exquisite food.

Makaron | Picture-perfect food and drink

Location Stellenbosch   **Signature dish** Forty-five-minute oysters | ❸❸❸

Part of Majeka House, a spectacular boutique hotel in an unassuming Stellenbosch neighborhood, Makaron is a feast for the senses. The decor and design set the scene. Recently renovated under the guidance of local design wunderkind Etienne Hanekom, the restaurant is a fusion of classic pieces, modern furnishings, and über-modern finishes. It is theatrical and fastastic, with an oversized black pig as a side table and large brass pendant lights.

The other near child genius at work here is chef Tanja Kruger. Young and hugely talented, she spends a month of every year working at top international restaurants, bringing back new influences and techniques. Her menu is therefore based on classic French cuisine, with touches of New World innovation. Ingredients are local—some as local as the hotel's own vegetable garden—and her combinations are imaginative. Best of all is the six-course set menu. Past winners include a starter of winter vegetables, rocket,

granola, and labneh; forty-five-minute oysters with herbs, flowers, soubise, and fennel veil; grass-fed veal with sweetbreads, cauliflower, thyme, and chive; and pork belly and cheek served with peas, pistachio, and green onion. Desserts are phenomenal, too, especially the cheesecake with hibiscus and plantation pepper and the apple tarte tatin.

Sommelier Josephine Gutentoft has compiled an excellent wine list to complement Kruger's food, and it is clear that the two women are partners in creativity. Have a drink in the chic MLounge, and, if you are staying over, be sure to give yourself enough time to recover before the spectacular breakfast the next morning. With gorgeous French canelés and the prettiest of other pastries on offer alongside the breakfast fruit, cheese, meats, and eggs, it might be even more spectacular than your dinner. **AG**

⬆ **Forty-five-minute oysters with herbs and flowers.**

Overture | Spectacular wineland views and innovative cooking

Location Stellenbosch **Signature dish** Pork fillet served with organic carrots and confit garlic | $$

Situated on the Hidden Valley Wine Estate, which nestles against the gorgeous Stellenbosch Mountains, the Overture restaurant pairs unparalleled views with equally spectacular food without taking on any airs and graces that might spoil the experience.

The lack of airs and graces probably has something to do with the person manning the kitchen. Chef and owner Bertus Basson is a bit of a rock star in the South African restaurant scene (not least because, during the heyday of the mohawk, he sported an extremely impressive one). He is young, energetic, outspoken, and brave when it comes to cooking. And his approach has paid off: Overture has been on South Africa's top ten list of restaurants since it opened in 2007.

The food echoes the chef's personality perfectly, being relaxed and unfussy but not shy on flavor. Basson likes to experiment with new techniques and trends, be it nose-to-tail eating, or smoking or cooking foods over an open fire. The menu changes constantly in response to seasonal availability.

Some top dishes include rabbit terrine, saffron linguine with fresh mussels, smoked hake with saffron and crispy squid, and Sweetwell pork fillet served with organic carrots and confit garlic. The soufflés are always a superb dessert option and are served at the table with ice cream and an accompanying sauce.

The fine dining service is outstanding, both relaxed and unintimidating, and the wine is on a par. In addition to the Hidden Valley wines, a small, carefully chosen selection is on offer. The sommelier will help you get the best match possible. Basson also owns one of the first food trucks in South Africa—Die Worsrol—which sells gourmet versions of the classic local *braai* (barbecue) dish, the *boerewors* (a type of hot dog). Clearly, there is no shortage of cool here. **AG**

↑ A beautifully presented dish at Overture.

Fyndraai | A celebration of heritage and horticulture

Location Franschhoek   **Signature dish** Wild rosemary-crusted rack of Karoo lamb | 💲💲

> *"Indigenous herbs are much sharper than normal herbs … so only small quantities work …"*

Shaun Schoeman, chef at Fyndraai

About 9 miles (15 km) outside of Franschhoek lies Solms-Delta, one of the wine estates that help to make this part of the Cape winelands the ultimate gourmet tourism destination. Wine has been produced at Solms-Delta for the past four centuries, but these days, it offers more than just unusual Cape blends. The estate is focused on celebrating and conserving various influences on the farm's history.

The crowning jewel here is Fyndraai, a restaurant built atop the remnants of a 1740 wine cellar. It is part of a larger conservation initiative on the estate called the Dik Delta Fynbos Culinary Gardens. Fyndraai offers a modern take on traditional Cape cuisine, the food exploring a diverse culinary heritage of African, Asian, and European flavors using local ingredients.

The result is magical. The fusion of tradition and creativity makes for incredibly interesting and decidedly delicious fare. Great starter options include West Coast mussels in Cape Malay tomato *bredie* (stew), pan-fried pickled ox tongue with dill cucumber cream, and seared spicy sea scallops with cauliflower puree. The main course brings, among other things, delectable wild rosemary-crusted rack of Karoo lamb served with braised *slaphakskeentjies* (a "salad" of small pickled onions), sautéed *spekboom* (a local succulent plant), and carrot custard; braised venison with wild herbs and typical traditional vegetables like sweet corn, stewed pumpkin, and buttered cabbage; and Cape line fish, topped with a lemon pelargonium crust and served with a crushed potato and crab meat salad and slow-roasted tomatoes.

Desserts include treats such as fridge tart with a *koeksister* (a traditional Afrikaans, syrup-coated, braided doughnut) and melon ice cream, or orange blossom crème brûlée with chilled fruit.

The foundations of the erstwhile wine cellar are exposed under a glass floor; but, if it is a beautiful day, sit outside instead and enjoy the mountain views. **AG**

⬆ Fyndraai's floor reveals 300-year-old foundations.

Pierneef à La Motte | Combining South African cuisine and art history

Location Franschhoek   **Signature dish** Cape *bokkom* salad with wild garlic vinaigrette | 🟢🟢

Pierneef à La Motte is situated on the picturesque La Motte wine estate, just outside the winelands town of Franschhoek. The fact that it is named for one of South Africa's greatest artists, Jacobus Hendrik Pierneef, is an indication that it explores the country's rich heritage, both in design and food.

The driving forces behind the unique food are chef Chris Erasmus and culinary manager and food historian Hetta van Deventer-Terblanche. Between them they have created dishes based on recipes used and modified in the Cape winelands for more than three centuries. The resulting seasonal menus are a marriage of Cape Dutch, Flemish, and French Huguenot fare, made from traditional herbs, nuts, dried fruits, artisan meats, and organic seasonal ingredients from the kitchen garden.

Erasmus' starters always include the signature Cape *bokkom* (mullet) salad, and might be supplemented by pickled ox tongue and a terrine of free-range chicken (served with smoked warthog and mushroom, yogurt blancmange, warthog bacon crunch, and onion and thyme marmalade). Mains include slow-braised smoked pork with mushroom croissant toast, creamed mushroom, apple, and Gruyère-flavored milk; grilled lamb *soutribbetjie* (salted lamb rib) with creamed peas and barley; or lemon-braised beef short rib with stewed fennel and roasted garlic pommes dauphine. Dessert is a feast of nostalgia and generally includes a reinvented old-fashioned roly-poly, and textures of chocolate (cacao custard, mud pie, and brownie ice cream).

The wines are spectacular: an excellent range of iconic labels from South Africa, France, and elsewhere, with rare vintages of the estate's own wines, too.

The restaurant itself is a gorgeous space, with designer furniture, chandeliers, and more than the occasional nod to its artist namesake. Relaxed and family-friendly, it is the ultimate Sunday lunch spot. **AG**

> *"Pierneef's work has been printed onto the lampshades hanging over the kitchen counter."*

Chris von Ulmenstein, hotelier

⭱ Artfully arranged fresh vegetables in a broth.

The Tasting Room | A playful celebration of South African ingredients

Location Franschhoek   **Signature dish** Surprise tastings of African seasonal foods | ❸❸❸

"My creations are nourished with exceptional African products, which are in constant evolution."

Margot Janse, chef at The Tasting Room

⬆ Innovative, seasonal food is a hallmark of The Tasting Room.

The reputation of Franschhoek as one of the hot spots on South Africa's food map owes much to The Tasting Room, the restaurant within Le Quartier Française, one of the anchor hotels of this winelands town. Never has a local restaurant, or indeed a local chef, garnered so many local and international accolades.

Margot Janse is a phenomenon. Dutch-born but now safely and solidly settled in South Africa, the much-lauded chef joined The Tasting Room in 1995, taking over as executive chef shortly after. Under Janse's watch, the restaurant has so far spent a decade on S. Pellegrino's list of the World's Fifty Best Restaurants. But The Tasting Room's awards are far from topping the list of reasons to dine there.

Instead of an array of options, diners have just two choices: the first is simple, whether to have the five-course or the eight-course tasting menu; the second involves selection of the accompanying wines. They then embark on a roller-coaster adventure through the culinary landscape of southern Africa.

What are the highlights of this ride? That question is difficult to answer, because the surprise menu changes daily and is just that, a surprise. What diners can expect, though, is a delightful combination of local ingredients like *buchu*, granadilla, *waterblommetjies*, and venison, masterly executed and beautifully plated.

Eating here is a celebration of the country and region, and the experience is a combination of the food on the plates and the stories that the service staff share with diners. You will learn about the winemaker and his dog, the things granny did with *buchu*, and why the baobab is called the upside-down tree.

Janse herself sums it up best: "When, at the end of the evening, I get thanked for a special experience and for all our guests learned about this amazing country, its culture, and indigenous produce—that's when I know we got it right." **AG**

Babel | Chic farm-to-fork eating at a designer destination

Location Franschhoek **Signature dish** Lamb shank marinated in harissa and buttermilk | ❸❸

Babylonstoren, one of the oldest Cape Dutch farms in South Africa, is not only home to a magnificent and enormous food garden, but also an award-winning, designer restaurant. Owner and local design doyenne Karen Roos transformed the farm's humble cowshed into a white, light, beautiful space that is the perfect backdrop for Babel's farm-to-fork cuisine.

The food is a celebration of luxurious offerings from the garden—freshly picked fruit, vegetables, and herbs, including several heirloom varieties. The food is simply presented, as befits the "pick, clean, serve" approach. The concise à la carte menu changes seasonally, with daily specials written on the tiled wall.

Salads are made according to their color—green, yellow, and red—and the season's offerings. In winter, the yellow salad might be a garden skewer of honey- and thyme-roasted pumpkin, carrot, sweet potato, pineapple, and fresh granadilla, on a carpaccio of guava and Satsuma orange, served with a citrus dressing and a toasted coconut, mint, and chili sprinkle; in summer, these make way for juicy mangoes, apricots, and white peaches.

For the main course, farmers of the district add meat to the bounty: fillet on the bone, lamb cutlets, and Franschhoek trout. The food is elegantly presented with the aid of farm-produced wine dressings, honey, and cold-pressed olive oil.

Meals are rounded off with stylish desserts to diners' tastes: bitter-sweet (dark chocolate fondant with clotted cream and shiraz drizzle); sweet–sour (orange blossom honey and lime crème brûlée with fruit); sour (baked lemon custard and sago pudding with citrus marmalade); or savory (sugar and salt guava membrillo with creamy gorgonzola).

The wine list is extensive and representative of the region, and the service warm and friendly. Not that one pays much attention to these details, because the farm and its food are overwhelmingly beautiful. **AG**

"This is what makes us tick. We love plants that have a sense of history and tell a story."

Karen Roos, co-owner of Babel

⬆ The tiled wall features a bull design and daily specials are usually written next to it.

Marianas | Honest, inspiring food off the beaten track

Location Stanford   **Signature dish** Chicken pie | 💲💲

"I owe my earliest awareness of food to a trio of women: my two grandmothers and my mother."

Mariana Esterhuizen, chef at Marianas

⬆ The peaceful village of Stanford is the home of Marianas restaurant.

An ordinary village home in the small, sleepy Overberg town of Stanford, a scenic two-hour drive from Cape Town, seems like an unlikely setting for culinary greatness. To be honest, the owners Peter and Mariana Esterhuizen even look like unlikely gourmands. But looks have rarely been so deceiving.

At the Esterhuizens' house, coming out of their small kitchen, the most phenomenal food is served to a handful of tables scattered around the house and terrace overlooking the back garden. Peter is maître d', sommelier, waiter, and general host, while Mariana and a tiny team make magic in the kitchen.

The food is inspirational, not just because it is delicious and beautifully simple, but also because it really is an ode to the season's bounty. Mariana's first port of call every morning is her vast kitchen garden, where she will wander through, check the produce, plan the day's delights, and pick what she needs.

The cooking is homely and deeply flavorsome, with more than the occasional nod to the Mediterranean. The day's offering is written on a mobile blackboard and presented in entertaining detail by Peter. If you are lucky, you will come across the old-fashioned chicken pie (made from the most liberated of free-range birds) or the lamb shoulder (served alongside last winter's pickling and that morning's pickings). Lighter options might include a fluffy gruyère soufflé, or a fresh mezze platter.

The sweet end of the scale goes straight back to homely, creamy, and indulgent: examples are berry cake, crème brûlée, or a cheese selection.

Marianas really is a magical place, where Peter's knowledgeable guidance through the wine list might well feel like that of an uncle cajoling you into trying the best from his handpicked collection. And Mariana? Well, the actual star of the show occasionally makes an appearance alongside tables to share a recipe or make a humble curtsey in response to praise. **AG**

Île de Païn | Heavenly breads and bakes

Location Knysna **Signature dish** Speciality breads and pastries | $

Some restaurants satisfy their customers on so many levels, and make them so incredibly happy, that they are tempted to just move in and live and feast there until the end of their days.

Île de Païn is such a place. Owned and run by husband and wife team Markus Färbinger and Liezie Mulder, this buzzing café was the first artisan, wood-fired-oven bakery in South Africa. The couple's philosophy of good craftsmanship, integrity, and simplicity is evident in every aspect of their project and is shared enthusiastically with old friends and new visitors alike. All customers, whether they are popping in to pick up freshly baked bread, stopping for a quick cuppa, or staying for a long lunch, are enticed by the pair's energy, obvious love of good food and great baking, and willingness to share what they know.

Dedicated baker and master chocolatier Färbinger patiently coaxes the best out of natural ingredients to produce incredible bread and pastries. On the one hand, there are breads—ciabatta, sourdough (rye and wheat), Vollkorn, Companio, crispy, nutty baguette and more—and, on the other, there are flaky croissants, delicate coconut *dacquoise*, absolutely delicious chocolate-chip cookies, and a variety of other creamy, fruity, and chocolaty treats. "Spoiled for choice" is an understatement.

Mulder is responsible for the rest of the food. With the help of handpicked local suppliers and farmers, she and her team create café basics such as burgers and Max Deluxe (toasted ham and cheese with a poached egg, cherry tomatoes, and mushroom sauce), as well as a varying menu of globally inspired street food like Indian curry, Israeli falafel, open-faced Danish sandwiches, and Mexican tacos.

As an aside, Färbinger has for the past few years trained many of the country's best bakers. Good though they may be, so far none has created a bakery for which it would be worth packing up your house. **AG**

"I love to cook simple food. I don't mean ordinary . . . but food that is made with love and integrity."

Liezie Mulder, restaurant owner

↑ Breakfast and lunch dishes make use of the best local ingredients.

Asia

The rich diversity of Asia's food cultures is sensational. The tradition of street food, from Singapore to India, is one wonderful element to enjoy. But you can also find highly refined dining experiences: enjoy Korean temple cuisine, delight in an atmospheric meal in a historic Beijing courtyard, feast in a magnificent Rajasthan fort, or savor sublime sushi prepared by an eminent master of Japanese cuisine.

← Food stalls on Jonker Walk, Malacca, Malaysia.

Chez Sami | Superb fish dishes enjoyed by the Bay of Jounieh

Location Maameltein **Signature dish** *Fattoush* (salad of arugula, thyme, purslane, tomatoes, and toast) | $$$

As befits an upmarket restaurant with a reputation for the excellence of its daily caught fish, Chez Sami is ideally located on a site overlooking the waters of the eastern Mediterranean. The restaurant itself, with its light and comfortable dining area, is an appealing combination of an old, traditional dwelling and a modern construction. Relatively new to the restaurant is its deck with bar and lounge, perfect for those who want to enjoy a swim and then lunch in the same spot. In good weather, make the most of the restaurant's wonderful setting by getting a table by the sea so that you can enjoy the sound of the breaking waves at first hand. But, indoors or out, all the tables are well placed to enjoy the mesmerizing view.

Once seated, customers are encouraged to pick out their own fish from the tempting array on the fresh fish counter; the prices are written above the fish. Seafood is Chez Sami's forte, so look out for octopus and calamari. The sultan ibrahim (fried red mullet) is accompanied by fried bread and the tahini sauce (sesame paste with lemon) favored by the Lebanese.

No written menu is offered, unless the client insists, but information is provided by the waiter. Begin your meal in leisurely style with two or three mezze dishes. A starter that should not be missed is *kibbet samak* (fish meat stuffed with walnuts, onion, and a touch of saffron). The signature dish of the house is *fattoush*, the classic salad made from arugula, fresh thyme, purslane, tomatoes, and toasted bread.

Meals are rounded off in hospitable style with an enticing complimentary dessert consisting of a bowl of *debs kharoub* (molasses) covered by plain tahini, Seville orange preserve, pistachio halva, and seasonal fruits. The dessert is often eaten scooped up with bread. All in all, a truly pleasurable seaside experience to be savored. **NS**

⬆ Tables at Chez Sami are set right by the water's edge.

Fadel | Classic Lebanese mezze among the pine trees

Location Bikfaya   **Signature dish** *Kibbeh* (meat with cracked wheat) | ❸❸❸

The family-run Restaurant Fadel, opened in 1976, is found at Naas, a charming area of the town of Bikfaya in the Matn district of Mount Lebanon. Naas, named for a spring that is said to have curative effects, is distinguished by the density of its pine trees.

In 1958, Emile Charabieh founded a much smaller premises in Bikfaya; it seated just ten people and offered four dishes to accompany his favorite tipple, the anise-flavored spirit arak. Today's restaurant still serves those four original dishes. The force behind Fadel is Charabieh's six children, brothers and sisters, who work tirelessly in assorted roles.

Fadel is entered via an arched pathway that leads to a wide garden terrace, abundantly surrounded by green foliage and white hortensias. Ornamental vegetation surrounds the restaurant, which is divided into an outdoor and indoor area, affording views of the pine trees all year around. The clientele range from Lebanese families enjoying an outing together to politicians and businesspeople; diners have also included Jimmy Carter and Prince Albert of Monaco.

The cooking is purely Lebanese, unaffected by trends. Lingering over mezze, such as parsley-rich *tabbouleh* or *shankleesh* (Lebanese cheese flavored with dried thyme and chili) is the way to dine. Be sure to try Fadel's signature dish, olive-shaped *kibbeh* (meat with cracked wheat), as well as the flavorsome sausages *makanek* and *soujouk* and the hearty *fattet al-hummus* (chickpeas, yogurt, and bread). The quality and freshness of the ingredients is remarkable. Most vegetables come from Fadel's backyard—the months of August, September, and October are particularly bountiful—or are sourced locally. Fadel is a fine example of the kind of restaurant the Lebanese flock to for Sunday lunch, as testified by its enduring popularity. **NS**

⬆ Enjoy some freshly prepared *tabbouleh* at Fadel.

Massaya | A bucolic dining experience in Lebanon's Bekaa Valley

Location Zahle **Signature dish** Vegetable salad with nuts | 🔴🔴

For a great experience of rustic cuisine, Massaya Vineyard and Restaurant, located 24 miles (38 km) from the ruins of Baalbeck in the fertile Bekaa Valley, is not to be missed. The owners, brothers Sami and Ramzi Ghosn, are passionate about nature and their land. After the Lebanese Civil War (1975–90), they returned in 1994 to revive their arak spirit, now considered to be one of the best. A few years later, they began to produce high-quality wine; then came the restaurant, overlooking the neatly aligned vines.

Offering a true taste of Lebanon, the food on offer here is prepared on the premises by women of the nearby villages. From 11.30 A.M., customers can enjoy an authentic brunch comprised of *man'ouchi* (flatbread) topped with either *za'atar* (a blend of dried thyme, sumac, sesame seeds, and olive oil) or *kishk* (cracked wheat and sun-dried yogurt). To observe the women deftly preparing the breads over the *saj* (a traditional iron-domed griddle, heated from below) is

a visual treat—while eating the breads is a gustatory one. After making a tour of the winery, visitors return to find a generous buffet of traditional dishes in large earthenware bowls adorning the restaurant's huge wooden table.

One dish is a mixed vegetable salad with nuts, a creation of the Ghosn brothers. Potato *kibbeh* (potato with cracked wheat) and eggplant dressed with pomegranate syrup are among the varied regional foods on offer. Hot dishes displayed next to the open fireplace include local *freekeh* (smoked green wheat), *shawarma* (spiced meat), and baked meat with cracked wheat. In winter, the menu changes to include dishes such as quail and sumac marinated in wine and cheese fondue with thyme. The vineyard is the perfect place to disconnect from the stress of daily life and spend a delightful day. **NS**

⬆ Diners can sit in the pleasant shade of the trees.

Al-Babour ve Hayam | Traditional and creative Palestinian delicacies

Location Acre **Signature dish** Kebab Al-Babour | 💰💰

Brothers Hussam and Nash'at Abbas, founders of the Al-Babour group of restaurants, were among the first to alert the Israeli public to the fact that authentic Palestinian cuisine went beyond hummus and the shish kebab. Their first restaurant, opened in 2000 at the entrance to Umm al-Fahem in the Arra Valley, introduced local diners to such delicacies as cooked salads made from wild edible plants; melt-in-the-mouth *mansaf* (a casserole of lamb shoulder slowly braised in yogurt); lamb neck stuffed with succulent rice; pine-nut pilaf; and kebab Al-Babour (grilled lamb patties baked with pitta dough in a terracotta dish).

Diners from near and far flocked to the restaurant, and within a decade there were three more Al-Babour restaurants in northern Israel, with pretty much identical menus, quality, and service. Al-Babour ve Hayam (Al-Babour and the Sea) has unique points in its favor. Situated in the beautiful and historic Old City of Acre, this sprawling restaurant offers breathtaking views of Haifa Bay and the ancient fishermen's wharf. Here, in addition to the dishes that made Al-Babour famous, the menu acknowledges the proximity of the sea with a wide selection of fish and seafood offerings.

Every meal starts with a dazzling array of mezze—more than a dozen little plates with fresh and cooked salads as well as creamy hummus and seasonal greens. Diners can easily eat their fill just with these starters alone, and that would be a shame because among the main courses there are many tempting options: *muhara* (a mix of fish and seafood baked in a terracotta dish); *saidiya* (a casserole of fish, rice, and vegetables); and an impressive selection of grilled meats, from lamb chops to kebabs. For dessert, go for *knafe*: sweet goat cheese cloaked in shredded filo pastry, doused with fragrant syrup, and garnished with crunchy pistachio nuts. **JGu**

⯅ *Mansaf* is served with rice and an array of side dishes.

Orna and Ella | Tel Avivian safe haven with a baking pedigree

Location Tel Aviv **Signature dish** Yam pancakes with chives and sour cream | ❸❸

Orna Agmon and Ella Shine were university students when they first met and started to moonlight as cake bakers for cafés and restaurants in Tel Aviv. In 1992, they opened their own neighborhood café on Shenkin Street, which at that time was the most happening place in town, replete with cutting-edge art galleries and fashion boutiques. The café was a huge success, and within a couple of years it morphed into a full-menu restaurant. It has since become one of the most beloved culinary institutions in Tel Aviv.

The decor is calm and minimalist—bare walls and tables clad in white linen. No background music is laid on, but the atmosphere is lively and the crowd refreshingly diverse; multi-generational families dine in the company of couples, large groups of friends, and a lot of artsy types. The fare, best described as comfort food with an elegant twist, features plenty of enticing vegetarian, vegan, and health-promoting items—the kind of food you want to eat every day.

Even though the selection changes seasonally, there are a few classics that the owners would not dream of removing from the menu. Most famous of all are the addictive yam pancakes, served with sour cream and chives. Then there is the "everything salad" (the waiters, tiring of reciting the goodies in the salad, simply stated that it had everything, and the name stuck). The "rice with vegetables" is a version of ratatouille served on a bed of white and wild rice and garnished with crunchy pumpkin seeds. Additional standouts include chicken curry in a yogurt and mint sauce and fig brioche with Roquefort cheese.

The baking background of the two proprietors is evident in the wonderful breads that are turned out daily in the restaurant kitchen, as well as the unmissable desserts, such as the creamy cheesecake and the lemon and raspberry tart. **JGu**

⬆ Orna and Ella serves delicious comfort food.

Manta Ray | Home of the perfect beachfront breakfast

Location Tel Aviv   **Signature dish** *Shakshouka* (eggs in a rich tomato sauce) with halloumi cheese | ⑤

No culinary tour of Israel would be complete without experiencing the Israeli breakfast—lavish, dairy-based, and featuring the ubiquitous chopped salad (Israelis seem to be the only people on the planet who have salad for breakfast). In Israel, quite a few fully fledged restaurants, as opposed to the more conventional hotels and cafés, offer breakfasts.

Manta Ray, already established as a popular beachfront fish and seafood restaurant, was one of the first to welcome customers at 9:00 AM and offer them a varied and delicious breakfast menu. And what better place to enjoy breakfast? The restaurant is airy and minimalist in design, and the Mediterranean Sea is literally a short stone's throw from the large, sea-gazing windows.

If the weather is fair (and there is plenty of sunshine in this warm country), book a table on the terrace, order a glass of freshly squeezed orange juice (or a Bloody Mary), and allow yourself to be lulled by the waves as you peruse the menu. You can opt for the classic "eggs-any-style" formula with Israeli salad on the side; but, if you are feeling a little more adventurous, try *shakshouka*, a spicy North African eggs-and-tomato dish that arrives at the table in a small iron skillet, topped off by a slice of melting halloumi cheese. Another delicious option, called "street morning market," consists of a puff-pastry *boureka* stuffed with cheese and olives, and served with a poached egg and a zesty tomato salad.

The bread basket that comes with every order is a veritable diet buster, and so is the accompanying array of sweet and savory spreads. For extra breakfast pampering, order a couple of mezze plates from the huge trays carried by waiters—the cured *matjes* (herring fillets) or roasted eggplant with goats' cheese are excellent. **JGu**

⊤ Order pancakes to round off an indulgent breakfast.

Raphaël | Creative and elegant dining with a North African slant

Location Tel Aviv **Signature dish** Lamb couscous with chickpeas, vegetables, and Maghreb spices | ❸❸❸

"... originality with French embellishments that only an adventurous chef could inspire."

cntraveller.com

⬆ A bowl of delectable couscous at Raphaël.

Raphaël is repeatedly nominated as among the best restaurants to be found in Israel, and here the biggest draw is the cuisine. A clue to the food's identity may be apprehended from the fact that there is always a dish of couscous on the menu—made from scratch, laced with butter, fragrant with spices, and dressed with succulent meats.

Chef and owner Raphi Cohen is very proud of his culinary heritage, and the couscous, among other offerings here, is an homage to his Moroccan-born grandmother, Aziza, who was his first cooking teacher and mentor. But that is not the whole story. Other dishes on the menu of this beautiful restaurant reflect the Jerusalem-born chef's love affair with French cuisine; witness the entrecôte for two with brown butter and marrowbone, or the Niçoise salad with grouper roe, toro tuna confit, and bottarga (salted, pressed and sundried roe of either tuna or gray mullet). Beyond that, Cohen has a strong connection with Middle Eastern cooking—the baby zucchini stuffed with rice and lamb and cooked in organic goat yogurt is a delicious example.

Raphaël's focaccia, oven-fresh and glistening with olive oil and salt crystals, has been imitated by numerous Israeli restaurants. Legend has it that it was born almost by accident. Cohen was mixing some dough for *sfinge* (Moroccan deep-fried donuts) when, on the spur of the moment, he decided to shape it as a loaf and bake it in the oven.

During the day this warm, welcoming, light-flooded restaurant offers a very reasonable fixed-price menu. In the evening, the prices go up, the lights go down, the music gets louder, and the ambience becomes upbeat and sexy. But whether you come for lunch or dinner, always leave room for desserts. At the very least, round off your meal with a plate of Cohen's dainty, jewel-like petits fours; they will go perfectly with your coffee. **JGu**

Toto | Seductive cuisine from one of the best chefs in Israel

Location Tel Aviv **Signature dish** Oxtail tortellini | $$

Toto was originally an Italian restaurant, under a different chef, and most guides still refer to it as such. It is true that its signature dishes include a decadent, thin-crusted pizza bianca with bacon and mushrooms, along with a few delectable pasta dishes; but, the cuisine eludes easy definitions, reflecting as it does the unique vision of Yaron Shalev, one of the most talented and original chefs in Israel.

Shalev had his first stint in a restaurant kitchen at the age of twelve. Having worked in some of the best restaurants in Israel, and a few Michelin-starred ones in Paris, he does not attempt to dazzle with molecular wizardry or extravagant plating. Instead, his presentation is stylish but effortless, the colors vibrant, the flavors bold and sensual. Behind this deceptive simplicity, there is brilliant technique and uncompromising devotion to quality ingredients.

The yellowtail *tabbouleh* is a good example of Shalev's cuisine. Nicely sized chunks of the freshest raw fish interplay beautifully with meticulously prepared crisp herb salad garnished with almonds, with a layer of creamy thick yogurt adding richness. Equally tempting are the red snapper served whole in a seafood broth perfumed with saffron, the legendary oxtail tortellini, and the chestnut gnocchi. Desserts are perfectly in tune with the rest of the menu—gorgeous, generous, and seemingly uncomplicated.

Toto is one of the few restaurants in Israel offering a truly extensive and exciting wine list (look out for the rare Burgundies). There is also a large selection of wines available by the glass and half bottle. During the day, the restaurant is mostly favored by businessmen and lawyers, while in the evening many celebrities and "beautiful people" may be spotted among the clientele. A full meal can be expensive, but there is always the option of having a pizza or a pasta and a glass of wine at the bar—a popular choice with Tel Aviv's pre- and post-theater crowd. **JGu**

"It's not quite Italy, not quite Israel—but one thing's for sure, you're definitely not in Kansas anymore."

unlike.net

↑ Dining informally at the bar is a popular choice at Toto.

Turkiz | Impeccable fish and seafood in a stylish space

Location Tel Aviv **Signature dish** Grouper kebabs with *matboucha* (tomato and bell-pepper sauce) | ❺❺❺

This restaurant is like the iconic "little black dress"—deceptively simple, fit for every occasion, and proudly transcending fleeting fads. Situated in a smart residential building at the northern tip of Tel Aviv, Turkiz is popular with both the local business elite and tourists in the know. The decor is warm, elegant, and unfussy, with an oversized wine cabinet dominating one of the walls, huge windows facing the sea, cushioned leather chairs, and a long and lively bar. Floor managers and waiters welcome patrons as if they were old friends (many of them come here so often that they actually are), but first-timers instantly feel at home, too.

The menu is equally friendly and offers something for everybody. Among the standouts in the first courses are Israeli salad chopped to order; asparagus with porcini aioli and pecorino; and tortellini filled with piquant cheese and spinach, resting in a pool of yellow cherry tomatoes and butter.

To choose your main course, it is best to have a chat with your waiter and inquire about the daily catch; the owners of Turkiz have a long-standing relationship with the local fishing fleet and are able to source the best and freshest fish and seafood. If you want to play it safe, go for the grouper (the king of Mediterranean fish), either pan-fried, oven-baked, poached in a spicy North African chrayme sauce, or ground and grilled in kebab form.

The wine menu is extensive and well chosen, and the service is at once polished and warm. Okay, all this excellence comes at a price—Turkiz is one of the more expensive restaurants in town—but the lunch menu is reasonable. Brunch is also served on weekends, at which time the place is invariably packed. **JGu**

◧ The magnificent sea view is part of the dining experience.

Abu Hassan | A must-stop eatery for hummus aficionados

Location Jaffa **Signature dish** *Messabaha* (warm hummus) | ❺

"If you only have one hour to spend in Israel, go to Abu Hassan. If you have only two, go there twice." This anonymous adage might seem to offer extraordinary advice to the visitor, but to those who love hummus it makes perfect sense. This deeply comforting concoction of chickpeas and tahini is a national obsession in Israel. It is best savored at a specialized *humusiya* (hummus restaurant), where it is prepared on the premises and served warm.

Abu Hassan is in a league of its own—on the menu of this tiny eatery perched above Jaffa Port there is nothing except hummus. You can choose between the classic (topped with tahini and whole chickpeas) and hummus topped with *ful* (a lemony

> *"Make sure you arrive for an early lunch, because once the hummus is finished the place closes down."*
>
> telavivguide.net

stew of fava beans)—both mopped up with fluffy pitta. But what has turned Abu Hassan into a legend is *messabaha*: this homey hummus variation contains whole chickpeas, cooked and slightly mashed, mixed with warm tahini sauce, and given a lift by *t'billa*, a spicy (cumin), lemony dressing—totally addictive.

Open from the early morning until the hummus selections run out (usually at around 2 P.M.), the place becomes packed at around noon. Early birds get to sit at one of the few tables in the small dining room, while the rest happily grab their plates with a couple of pitta and a soft drink, then cross the street and enjoy their fix of chickpea magic on a parapet offering pretty vistas of Old Jaffa. **JGu**

Mordoch | Jerusalem soul food at a place with a rapid turnover

Location Jerusalem **Signature dish** *Kubbeh* soup dumplings with *siske* (meat cured in fat) | $

Whether or not there is such a thing as Israeli cuisine, most would agree that there definitely is a Jerusalem cuisine, shaped by a turbulent history and the many communities that share this unique town. To savor typical Jerusalemite fare, visitors head to Mahane Yehuda market and look for little restaurants with long lines. Mordoch is one of the oldest and the best.

The menu of this no-frills, family-owned eatery offers a selection of standard Middle Eastern dishes such as stuffed vegetables and skewered meats, but the regulars are here for the place's signature dish: *kubbeh*. This is a one-dish meal, eaten in late morning or for lunch (loyal to this tradition, Mordoch closes down at 5 P.M. sharp). Kubbeh dumplings, distant relations of the Tibetan momo and Chinese won-ton, are made of bulgur wheat (and sometimes semolina), and stuffed with either ground meat, or *siske*, tiny, fat-cured chunks of meat. The dumplings are cooked and served in flavorful soups rich with vegetables. Mordoch offers three versions: red (with tomato and beet soup); yellow (slightly sour, with zucchini and lemon); and bright yellow, with *siske* filling. If you have only one chance, go for *siske*. Otherwise, try them all.

> *"You'll see rows of enormous pots . . . all filled with simmering Middle Eastern delicacies."*
>
> gojerusalem.com

Eating here is not a leisurely affair. If you come on Friday, there will be a line of people waiting for your seat. Twenty minutes and you are out of the door—slightly drowsy, your stomach full, daydreaming of generations of Jerusalem grandmothers. **JGu**

Machneyuda | Funky, creative cooking in a hip Jerusalem diner

Location Jerusalem **Signature dish** *Hamshuka* (hummus with ground meat) | $$

The name "Machneyuda" emulates the colloquial pronunciation of Mahane Yehuda, the famous Jerusalem *souk* (open-air market). Machneyuda advertises itself as an "authentic market restaurant," but it is actually something completely different, being modern, hip, and relatively expensive. Carefully designed to look undesigned, it projects a bohemian aura, with its rickety tables, vegetable crates, and charmingly mismatched china.

The three chef-owners share the smallish open kitchen, one taking the lead for a time while the other two work with the rest of the crew as line cooks. In the middle of a busy dinner service, with the restaurant packed and noisy, the whole kitchen staff might "spontaneously" break into singing, banging a rhythm on their pan-bottoms, and encouraging surprised diners to join in. But, make no mistake, in the midst of all this fun, some very serious cooking is taking place.

Assaf Granit, Uri Navon, and Yossi Elad are experienced and talented chefs, and they turn out delicious and creative dishes based on fresh produce from the neighboring market. The menu, prepared on a vintage typewriter and dotted with insider jokes, changes almost daily, so it is hard to recommend a specific dish; but, some of the standouts frequently on offer include *hamshuka* (a creamy, messy, and utterly delicious concoction of hummus and ground meat); soft polenta topped with mushroom ragout, asparagus, and oodles of Parmesan; and calf sweetbreads served on a pitta. To get the most of the Machneyuda experience, book a seat at the bar, directly facing the open kitchen, so you can watch the action, chat with the cooks, and perhaps have a taste from whatever is cooking right before your eyes. **JGu**

→ Machneyuda's charmingly bohemian dining space.

Fakhr-El Din | Lebanese food as enjoyed by Jordan's elite

Location Amman **Signature dish** Platter of raw lamb cuts with spices | ❸❸

Across the Middle East, Lebanese cuisine is regarded as the best. It's not considered strange, therefore, that the finest restaurant in Jordan's capital, Amman, should specialize in Lebanese food. Fakhr-El Din serves all the classic mezze. You'll normally start with a selection of small dishes. Some are familiar all over the world: hummus, *mouhamara* (a spicy mixture of nuts), dainty *sambousek* (meat-filled pastries), and finger-lickingly tasty *jawaneh* (grilled chicken wings with garlic sauce). Others are more hardcore: *noukha'at* (a salad of poached lamb's brains) and *thalat* (lamb spleen stuffed with parsley, coriander, and chili).

The restaurant's crisp linen and marble surfaces create a cool formality, but once seated everything is eaten in the normal communal, casual mezze style. It's the mix of fresh natural flavors that crowns the experience. A single table at Fakhr-El Din can contain the tastes of chicory, cumin, walnut, mint, lemon, and chili all at the same time. The restaurant is famed for its creativity within the meze format. Look out for less well-known flavors, spices like purple ground sumac and ingredients like palmetto, raw lamb's liver, and akkawi (white brine cheese).

Some dishes use adventurous combinations to take the traditional mezze formula into new territory: fried aubergine with grenadine, raw minced lamb with peanuts, or chicken balls with pistachio. Others are simply perfectly executed Levantine classics: *tabbouleh* with finely chopped parsley, tomatoes, lemon, mint, and onion flavoring the cracked wheat salad, or *fattoush*, with ground sumac adding a sour tang to the toasted pitta salad.

The restaurant is housed in a tastefully renovated 1950s villa in one of the smartest areas of the city. Tall arched art-deco style French doors open from the dining areas into a large garden with further tables. **SH**

⬆ Enjoy classic mezze dishes such as *fattoush*.

Pierchic | Sumptuous seafood at the end of a romantic wooden pier

Location Dubai   **Signature dish** Seafood platter for two | $$$$

Perched on stilts above the sea at the end of an 800-foot (250-m) wooden pier, Pierchic is a perfect engagement-ring-in-a-glass-of-Champagne kind of venue. Its fairy-tale setting batters cost-conscious cynics into submission with an over-the-top menu, even though the prices limit visits to special occasions.

Much of the restaurant's structure is wood, with the option to eat in the gentle sea breezes on the open terrace (heat and humidity permitting) or in the enclosed air-conditioned restaurant. For diners seated on the outside decks, Pierchic offers memorable views of Dubai's spectacular skyline.

From shucked oysters to poached trout, seafood is the main focus. The signature cold seafood platter demonstrates the culinary style on offer: this is a sumptuous collection of high-quality ingredients flown in from all corners of the globe. It is presented as a romantic sharing dish for two diners, but comes with an eye-watering price tag that merely prepares you for the wine list, which is extensive but very expensive, even by Dubai standards.

So this is definitely not the spot for simple grilled sardines or fish soup with crusty bread. Instead, even the most unadorned pan-fried fish dishes are served with accompaniments such as sugar snap pea puree, zucchini croquette potato and asparagus foam or mushroom mousseline, Portobello mushroom carpaccio, or a tarragon shallot salad. The menu features three different types of caviar and an exotic range of side dishes that include white truffle potato mash, wild rocket, and shaved Parmesan, or white and green asparagus in Castillo de Canena olive oil. In fact, fish soup does appear on the menu, but it is typically laden with luxurious ingredients: lobster bisque, for example, with seafood timbale and pistachio cream. **SH**

⬆ The light and airy dining room at Pierchic.

Seafire Steakhouse | Gulf great with its own Australian herd

Location Dubai   **Signature dish** Atlantis 12-oz (350-g) fillet steak | ❸❸❸❸

"The food was simple but expertly cooked, and it lived up to the setting: sophisticated."

Karen Pasquali Jones, *Friday Magazine*

⬆ The door to a beef eater's paradise.

It's hard for a restaurant to make a favorable impression when its premises are located on a marble corridor of designer stores in the depths of a massive tourist hotel complex. Thus the Seafire—which is situated between Dubai's Atlantis water park and more celebrated reataurants with Michelin stars—could be dismissed as one of the city's more moderate mainstream eateries. But prepare to be amazed, for Seafire steaks are often acclaimed as some of the best in the world.

How can this be true in a country without a single lush grazing meadow? The answer is that, in true Atlantis over-the-top opulent style, the Seafire Steakhouse rears its own dedicated high-quality beef thousands of miles away in Australia. Its Queensland herd has a carefully monitored ancestry and is fed on a scientifically evaluated mix of hay, barley, corn, and essential seeds, ensuring the even spread of fat through the animals' tissue. The results are noticeably tender and flavorsome.

Steak lovers can alternatively choose Black Angus beef from the United States or Japanese Wagyu meat. All are simply cooked on a charcoal grill, and come with a classic choice of sauces: Béarnaise, Gorgonzola fondue, forest mushroom, barbeque, black peppercorn, herb and shallot butter, or Bordelaise. Sides include all the traditional favorites, including onion rings, buttered corn, and, of course, French fries, which here come in the form of "smoked steak fries."

The American-style service means a lively first-name-term relationship with waiting staff, seriously generous portions, and accompanying razzmatazz that extends to huge leather bench seats, butter pats stamped "Seafire," and white plates so large that they could be mistaken for serving trays. As a final inducement to doubting gourmets, Seafire boasts the largest wine cellar of all the 17 restaurants in the Atlantis resort. **SH**

Ossiano | A memorable seafood experience in the midst of an aquarium

Location Dubai   **Signature dish** Grilled line-caught sea bass with clams | 🅢🅢🅢🅢🅢

Diners descend a long Cinderella-style winding staircase into a cool, dimly lit world beneath the bustling bright gloss of Dubai's Atlantis resort. Down here, in the muted blue glow, their eyes slowly adjust to an extraordinary restaurant with a huge aquarium.

Ossiano opened as three-star Michelin chef Santi Santamaria's first establishment outside his native Spain. Santamaria died in 2011, three years after Ossiano opened. His family no longer has a stake in the running of the restaurant, but the menu continues to embody the finest modern Mediterranean food. However, be aware that, like an overseasoned sauce, the restaurant's setting almost overpowers everything on the menu.

A delicate gazpacho made from fresh vegetables flown in from Spain may disappear unnoticed as a shark looms into view alongside your table. Crispy scallops with sautéed vegetables and lobster jus may be forgotten as a human diver holding a romantic message board appears alongside a neighboring table.

The Atlantis Lagoon aquarium is the centerpiece of the resort, housing more than 65,000 marine creatures. Yet, down here, it is a serious distraction from the very fine—and very expensive—cuisine.

Suitably, or maybe ironically, this is mainly seafood. It ranges from delicate appetizers such as apple and white fish mince or Gillardeau oysters in shallot vinaigrette, to more expansive mains, including crispy monkfish in a saffron and garlic emulsion and bouillabaisse with sourdough crutons.

Ossiano's dishes are not just locally sourced but also trawled from the better-known fish markets of the world. Diners are offered North Atlantic halibut, line-caught Brittany sea bass, Canadian lobster, and Loch Fyne salmon. The presentation is beautiful, particularly for the longer tasting menus, and, unusually for the United Arab Emirates, service is hushed and discreet. **SH**

"The food is absolutely, undoubtedly, a cut above nearly anything else you'll find in Dubai."

Daisy Carrington, *Time Out Dubai*

⯅ The fish are not for eating; they are just for show.

Kebabçi Iskender |
Where the döner kebab made its debut

Location Bursa   **Signature dish** The original Iskender kebab | $

A feast in Ottoman times usually meant whole pit-roasted lambs cooked in vertical ovens dug in the ground or lambs roasted on spits over an open fire. In 1867, Iskender Efendi, from the Western Anatolian town of Bursa, is said to have come up with a new method of cooking meat in a vertical spit with a coal barbecue. He invented a new, iconic way of cooking meat—and the legendary "döner" (the word means "turning"), now world-famous, was born.

Tender parts of meat are assembled by stacking thin slices to form a huge cone that is cooked by spinning slowly facing a low-heat source. Since the nineteenth century, the specific döner version named "Iskender kebab" has been especially renowned: fine

---

"A warning to anyone named Iskender: they even hold the trademark on your first name."

culinarybackstreets.com

---

shavings of perfectly roasted meat are served on top of soft pide bread and doused generously in sizzling butter, with a dollop of yogurt and a special tomato sauce. Nowadays, slices of meat served in various ways, tucked inside a loaf of bread, on top of sliced pieces of bread, or with rice, are found everywhere.

For visitors to Bursa, it is almost compulsory to sample this famous dish, and several places serve excellent versions. Haci Iskender, however, claims to be the only original and is still run by Iskender Efendi's heirs. It serves only the celebrated Iskender kebab as a main, but also offers lentil soup, salad and pickles, and dessert. Also try the *şira*, a slightly fermented dried grape drink matured in mulberry wood casks. **AT**

Hayat Lokantasi |
Turkish food taken to perfection

Location Bursa   **Signature dish** *Terbiyeli köfte* (meatball stew in an egg and lemon sauce) | $

Bursa, the second capital of the Ottoman Empire, located en route to the historical Silk Road, is also a hidden culinary gem. Hayat restaurant, literally meaning "life," started off as a modest place in 1947 near the city's main bus terminal. In 2008, when the old factory area of Merinos was turned into a park complex, the third generation owners, the Selek family, created a rehabilitation project in this new area. A renovated old storage building now houses a cheerful spacious restaurant with gardens both inside and outside the building, creating a feeling of dining inside a park. Although the restaurant is huge and can host up 600 people at a time, it offers a relaxed and friendly atmosphere, with families with children often among the diners.

The food is both tasty and plentiful, but note that alcohol is not served. You can sample traditional Turkish home cooking at its best, displayed "Turkish style" at the counter. When tasting *terbiyeli köfte*, a dish of small, round meatballs in a sublime egg and lemon sauce, the thought that pops into one's mind is that surely this is exactly the way this recipe should be executed. The pit-roasted tandoori lamb *tandir* is exquisite, while rice pilaf is prepared to perfection, just as it should be in a proper Ottoman kitchen. Diners often order the chef's plate, a selection of spoonfuls of the daily specials, which allow them to taste as many dishes as possible.

Desserts continue the high standard of the cooking. There is a whole range of typical Turkish sweets available: choose from milk puddings, a bright orange pumpkin dessert, and coral-colored baked quince, all served with a generous sprinkle of ground walnuts or a slab of clotted cream. However, one sweet is particular to Hayat: *süt tatlisi*, a delicate milk dessert. Come hungry. **AT**

Borsa | A great ambassador of classic Turkish food with multiple branches

Location Istanbul   **Signature dish** *Paça çorbasi* (sheep's trotter soup) | 💲💲

Borsa, which means "stock exchange" in Turkish, is a popular tradesmen's eatery turned fine-dining classic. An Istanbul institution since 1927, originally serving lunch only at the grain-produce stock exchange, Borsa is now an establishment, with three restaurant branches and several self-service eateries, each with its particular merits. Owner Rasim Özkanca aims to serve fine, classic Turkish food made with the best ingredients.

But Bogaziçi Borsa remains the iconic flagship restaurant, located near the Lütfi Kirdar International Convention and Exhibition Center, in a tranquil setting with a stylishly decorated indoor area and open terrace with a lovely view. The menu covers a wide range of Turkish classics and also features regional favorites such as Aegean vegetable dishes cooked in olive oil, especially rice- and herb-stuffed artichokes; grilled *adana* or *urfa* kebabs from the south-east; the famous, iconic Iskender kebab from Bursa; and wrapped cavolo nero leaves, or *kuymak*, a cheesy, fonduelike dip from the Black Sea. Each region of Turkey is represented with equal finesse, all ingredients are sourced locally, and all dishes are cooked true to their origins. Authenticity is very important here—there is a "housewife" who comes to the Borsa kitchen every single day to make the buttery layered pasta bake *su böregi*.

For a traditional meal, you might start with the smooth and satisfying sheep's trotter soup, progressing to one of the delicious mains, and round off the meal with a rich syrupy bread pudding with a cushiony slab of clotted cream. A Turkish feast at Borsa is a truly memorable culinary experience. All Borsa fine-dining restaurants (but not the self-service eateries) serve alcohol and hold an extensive list of top local wines. **AT**

"... the food is unquestionably worth the trip, even from London to Istanbul."

Financial Times

⬆ Borsa is an Istanbul institution offering a range of classic regional Turkish dishes.

Beyti | The best meat from the man who invented the original Beyti kebab

Location Istanbul   **Signature dish** Beyti kebab | ❸❸❸

"Serious meat lovers know that it's worth the trip … the meat dishes are extraordinarily good."

Lonely Planet

⬆ Diners can feast on Beyti's famous kebabs amid the restaurant's lavish interior.

For carnivores, Beyti has been an essential culinary haven since its establishment in 1945 as a tiny four-table place. Arguably the most succulent meat in the city is to be found here, hidden in the suburb of Florya in Bakirköy. The area was once a summer vacation hot spot before it was integrated into the ever-expanding metropolis, and it is still a serene, green spot.

The owner's name, Beyti Güler, is known all over Turkey because of the meat dish he invented, which bears his first name and is now served in almost all restaurants. Originally, the Beyti kebab was a fillet of tenderloin lamb rolled into a brochette encircled with a thin layer of fat that was marinated and grilled. But elsewhere, it has become more common to wrap a ground meat kebab in a thin layer of flatbread, which is then cut into round shapes to resemble the original Beyti brochettes.

Aside from all sorts of grilled meats imaginable, the restaurant also offers dishes that are suitable for vegetarians in its extensive menu. *Su böregi* (a golden-crusted, buttery cheese pastry), *zeytinyagli sarma* (rice-filled vine leaves), and artichokes and other vegetables cooked in olive oil are among the vegetarian highlights, as well as the classic Turkish desserts. The success of Beyti has been so phenomenal that the restaurant today is a notably airy, sophisticated, and spacious affair, housed over three stories with space for 450 diners. As befits a national icon, Beyti has also hosted a number of American celebrities and politicians, including Richard Nixon, Jimmy Carter, Arthur Miller, and Leonard Bernstein; but the restaurant remains very much a family affair, with Beyti's two sons running the business these days. Beyti himself still works every day, greeting customers with his big, warm smile. **AT**

Pandeli | A constant menu
of Turkish culinary highlights

Location Istanbul **Signature dish** *Dönerli patlican börek* (pastry with aubergine puree and döner slices) | ❸❸❸

Located on the upper floor of Istanbul's Spice Market, Pandeli provides an atmospheric experience as well as many gourmet delights. Established in 1901 by Hristo Pandeli, a Greek from the Central Anatolian town of Nigde, the restaurant moved to its present iconic, turquoise-tiled location in the late 1950s. Overlooking the Eminönü Square and Galata Bridge, with masses of people moving past, it is a calm haven. Pandeli harks back to the golden old days and never goes out of fashion; it is frequented by nostalgic residents as much as by visitors.

Every item on the menu is a safe choice and forms part of a kaleidoscope of old Istanbul tastes combined with late Ottoman cuisine and more "modern" elements. The retro menu could also be from decades ago and, in fact, Pandeli never changed its menu. Do not miss the *dönerli patlican börek* (pastry with aubergine puree and döner slices) for the warm entree and the *kagitta levrek* (sea bass baked *en papilotte*) for the main course, both signature dishes of the restaurant. The restaurant is also famous for its silky, smoky *patlican salatasi* (eggplant salad) and tender *fasulye pilaki* (white beans in olive oil). The appetizer plate is a little pricey, but includes luxurious "old Istanbul" delicacies such as caviar, *lakerda* (cured bonito), and *balik yumurtasi* (bottarga).

Other authentic traditional dishes worth trying are *kuzu tandir* (roasted lamb) and *hünkar begendi* (lamb stew with eggplant puree). Pandeli is also famous for its *visneli tirit* (bread pudding with sour cherries), and it serves one of the best *kazandibi* (creamy pudding dessert) in town. *Kabak tatlisi* (pumpkin dessert) is soft and not too sweet, and *güllac* (a traditional dessert made with milk, pomegranate, and pastry, here served with clotted cream and sour cherries) is also well executed here. **AT**

Haci Abdullah | A true taste
of Turkey in an Ottoman institution

Location Istanbul **Signature dish** *Patlicanli incik* (lamb shank with eggplant) | ❸❸

Haci Abdullah is a veritable Ottoman institution and Istanbul's first licensed restaurant. It started out in 1888, under the name "Abdullah Efendi," with the licence to conduct business issued by Sultan Abdülhamit, operating according to the "Ahi" tradition, where ownership is passed from master to apprentice. In the late nineteenth and early twentieth centuries, official envoys on a visit to Istanbul were taken here for a taste of Ottoman cuisine.

First located in the port of Karaköy, Haci Abdullah relocated to the fashionable district of Beyoglu in 1915. It changed its place and name a few more times, finally settling in its current location in 1958, where it stays serene amid the bustling crowds of Istiklal Street.

> *"The recipes reflect the best of traditional Turkish cuisine, serving substantial stews ... and lamb."*
>
> frommers.com

The interior has been redesigned, drawing inspiration from the Topkapi Palace, while maintaining the distinctive jumble of various preserves in large jars. Prepared dishes and marinated meats are on display—such food display is a ubiquitous feature at traditional Turkish eateries that often specialize in ready-to-serve, home-style dishes for lunch.

Here, the eggplant and slow-cooked lamb dishes stand out: *karniyariik*, split-belly eggplant stuffed with a minced meat and tomato filling, is as delicious as its cold, vegetarian equivalent, *imam bayildi*. Alcohol is not served, but you can order sherbets and choose from a wide range of fruit compotes that are also served as a beverage, just as in Ottoman times. **AT**

Mikla | A flying carpet of "new Anatolian cuisine" with a wonderful view

Location Istanbul **Signature dish** Crispy *hamsi* | ❸❸❸

Mikla is new and daring, but also classic and classy. Established in 2005, it started out as a modern fusion restaurant serving international cuisine, but then changed its approach to offer a unique blend of modern and traditional Anatolian cooking. The menu, the restaurant's setting, and its atmosphere reflect a combination of Scandinavian-style simple elegance and Turkey's vibrant diversity. Mikla is open only for dinner. Located on the roof top of Istanbul's Marmara Pera hotel, it affords a dazzling panorama of the heart of Old Istanbul and a bird's eye view of the Topkapi Palace and the Hagia Sophia.

Chef-Owner Mehmet Gürs has a Turkish-Finnish-Swedish background and relocated to Turkey in 1996. The name of the restaurant reflects his heritage: "Miklagard" means "Great Town," and is the Old Nordic name for Istanbul, abbreviated in Mikla. But the fine balancing act of opposing qualities does not end with the name. In 2012, Gürs embarked on a novel venture, conducting research on traditional Anatolian cooking techniques, ingredients, dishes, and produce. His team toured the whole of Turkey, rediscovering many old techniques and finding the finest producers.

The menu at Mikla is truly unique because of this profound reflective process about Anatolian cuisine. Furthermore, the dishes manage to be both urban and rural. Crispy *hamsi* (anchovies) is a witty interpretation of fish and bread, a popular local street food; Aegean grouper over foraged samphire, drizzled with sun-dried fig vinegar brings the salty breeze of the sea; and lamb shank with smokey eggplant and preserved yogurt echoes the deep-rooted, earthy flavors of Mesopotamia. The magical, refined atmosphere is enhanced by excellent, efficient service and a carefully selected wine list. **AT**

⬆ The stylish dining space also has a gorgeous view.

Ciya | A renaissance of long-forgotten regional recipes in home-style cooking

Location Istanbul   **Signature dish** Sour cherry kebab; stuffed lamb intestines | 🟡🟡🟡

Nowadays, Istanbul restaurants serving local cuisine from Anatolia are on the increase, but Ciya remains the ultimate pioneer for offering regional dishes from all over the country. For more than two decades, Ciya has brought the best-kept secrets of Turkey's cuisine to a wider public in a modest eatery.

As you walk through the Kadıköy market on the Asian side of Istanbul, with its many fruit vendors, fishmongers, delicatessen, and bakeries, the restaurant invites you in with its enticing steaming dishes. Ciya's zest for introducing hidden regional tastes and reviving forgotten recipes has generated so much interest that it has expanded to include three restaurants, facing each other on the same street. Two of them specialize in kebabs and the other one in what can be called "home-style cooking."

Owner Musa Dagdeviren was introduced to the world of food at his uncle's *lahmacun* (flatbread) bakery at the tender age of five. He then worked his way up steadily, embarking on a journey to discover traditional tastes and becoming a self-educated anthropologist of Anatolian food. He established his own supply chain for produce, with fresh foraged greens sent daily to Istanbul. Among the kebabs and meat dishes, those cooked with fruits stand out in particular as a living taste of historical Turkish cuisine that is almost impossible to find elsewhere.

Signature dishes include those featuring wild greens, seasonal fruit, and meat combinations such as sour cherry kebab or quince stew, or—for the more adventurous—lamb's intestine filled with minced meat and rice. The desserts feature delicacies such as candied walnuts, and, more unusually, baby eggplants and olives. Every day, new recipes with old roots are prepared at Ciya, varying according to the availability of ingredients. **AT**

⬆ Starters at Ciya include falafel and bulgur with yogurt.

Müzedechanga | Stunning, creative fusion
of traditional and contemporary elements

Location Istanbul **Signature dish** Slow-cooked lamb wrapped in vine leaves | ❸❸❸

"A beautiful, lush setting just a stone's throw from the Bosphorus … and a sophisticated ambience."

fodors.com

⬆ A dessert of spiced pear with candy floss.

Müzedechanga and its sister restaurant, Changa, have been at the forefront of introducing modern fusion cuisine to Turkey. Changa means "mix" in Swahili, and the menus here really dare to combine very different elements, merging classical Turkish cuisine with influences from Asia-Pacific. The two restaurants are the result of determined, persistent, and vigilant international team work: the acclaimed London-based New Zealander chef Peter Gordon, a pioneer of fusion cuisine, has been involved as a consultant since Changa opened in 1999, and the Turkish proprietors, Tarik Bayazıt and Savas Ertunc, have a great eye for detail combined with a bold enthusiasm. Flavors and techniques blend wonderfully at Müzedechanga, and inspiration is provided by the whole world or, more specifically, the art world.

Müzedechanga is housed in the verdant gardens of the Sakip Sabanci Museum, overlooking the Bosphorus and complete with an appealing, spacious open-air terrace with wonderful views. The food focuses on local produce and artisan ingredients, and inspiration is drawn from anywhere, even from the current exhibitions shown at the museum (the works of Anish Kapoor featured recently). Highlights include fried zucchini flowers stuffed with fresh curd cheese and basil with a sweet-sour sauce; crumbly-crusted, fried beef tongue; mushroom-filled dumplings; and clove-flavored meatballs. Do not miss the truly phenomenal slow-cooked lamb, grilled in vine leaves and served with yogurt and a sweet chili sauce, offering that exciting combination of flavors and textures that makes eating here such a treat.

Ingenious cooking, flawless organization and management, and friendly staff that go out of their way to provide perfect service—it is no wonder Müzedechanga has earned many global awards. **AT**

Konyali-Kanyon | From humble tradesmen's eatery
to flagship of the royal Ottoman court kitchen

Location Istanbul   **Signature dish** *Kuzu tandir* (slow roasted lamb); *Portakalli baklava* (baklava with oranges) | ❸❸❸

Konyali's story is one of a journey from humble beginnings to true grandeur: it started as a tiny eatery but later moved to the prestigious royal venue of the Topkapi Palace. Initially, Konyali was a minuscule and modest space, consisting of only four tables, in the trade district of Sirkeci. It was founded by a peasant from the central Anatolian town of Konya in 1897; but, by the 1940s, it had become one of the most renowned restaurants of Istanbul, visited by local and foreign celebrities alike.

Now run by the fourth generation of the family, Konyali expanded to include new branches, and the famous Topkapi Palace branch was established in 1967. Whereas Konyali-Topkapi is traditional and regal, the Kanyon branch has a stylish, urban chic to it and is one of the few places serving Ottoman palace cuisine in a fine-dining setting. Konyali-Kanyon is keen to embrace modern times, but also pays homage to the past, using the very same format of the 1940s typewritten menu from the defunct Sirkeci branch.

The menu seeks to revive classical Ottoman cuisine, rediscovering long-lost recipes such as fruit and meat stews and Ottoman sherbets. The honey-vinegar sherbet *sirkencübin* (known in ancient times as *oxymel*) is an intriguing, brave revival of a forgotten recipe that existed throughout history, in Roman, Persian, Byzantine, and Ottoman times. The slow-cooked tandoori lamb is memorably served with a royal pilaf studded with tiny morsels of fried liver, pine nuts, and currants, and perfumed with fragrant spices. The desserts cover a wide range of Ottoman classics, including delightfully soothing milk puddings, particularly *sütlac* (rice pudding), and a near-extinct variety of baklava with oranges that combines the buttery flakiness and syrupy sweetness of the pastry with refreshing citrus aromas. **AT**

"Crowds of shoppers, workers, and commuters pop in here to choose from the huge range of kebabs…"

Lonely Planet

⬆ Dining with a view at Konyali-Kanyon.

Ahdoo's | Kashmiri banquet food made to order

Location Srinagar **Signature dish** *Gushtaba* (velvet-textured meatballs in gravy) |

The restaurant known as Ahdoo's began its existence in the 1920s as a bakery shop before relocating in the 1940s to its present site on the banks of the Jehlum River in the heart of what used to be the British quarter of Srinagar, the summer capital of the Indian state of Jammu and Kashmir. Setting up a Western-style restaurant that served the food of a Kashmiri banquet was recognized at the time as a stroke of genius. Now, it is not only the oldest place to have done so, but also the most successful and the one that maintains its high quality most consistently.

Kashmiri banquets—known as *wazwans*—are prepared by cooks of a particular tribe who do so by hereditary right. The cooks work in the courtyard of the host, out in the open, on wood fires, slaughtering live sheep before rapidly transforming the carcasses into a feast fit for kings. A typical banquet consists of at least a dozen preparations of lamb, variously flavored with milk, curd, fried onion, and even apricot. Of course, lamb-based curries and kormas are easily produced in a restaurant kitchen, but the result does not compare to *wazwan* fare.

That is why Ahdoo's has acquired its formidable reputation: locals and visitors to Srinagar alike go back time and again for the quality of the cooking. Ahdoo's allows you to order as much or as little as you like (the wedding-feast cooking need not be eaten in wedding-feast quantities). The restaurant, charmingly shabby with threadbare carpets, is presided over by waiters who seem to have been in attendance since it first opened its doors. And the menu has not changed for the last several decades. Ahdoo's is one of the few restaurants where you can taste food that otherwise is only served at weddings and private family functions. What is more, you gain a peep into the "real" Kashmir, a world away from what is put on show for tourists. **MR**

⬆ A chance to sample Kashmiri *wazwan* cooking.

The Chinar | Fine cooking to savor in a spectacular landscape

Location Srinagar **Signature dish** *Waza seekh kebab* | 🅢🅢

There could not be a more picturesque location in the whole of India. The Chinar (the indoor restaurant at the Lalit Grand Palace hotel in Srinagar) provides outdoor seating in fine weather, and it is this that makes dining there a world-class experience. In the evening, with the warm glow of the setting sun, a hillside of pine trees, expansive lawns, and, after a drop of 50 feet (15 m), the Dal Lake shimmering in the distance, the setting is picture perfect. Even the chinar trees (another name for *Platanus orientalis*, or the oriental plane) marching around the gardens have a claim to history, because Mahatma Gandhi sometimes sat under the one where meals are served when he made visits to Kashmir. Here you can try fairly simple dishes from the cuisines of northern India, principally those of Jammu and Punjab. Expect the uncomplicated, earthy flavors of a lentil dish that has been gently smoked with a lighted coal, or those of a robust lamb curry.

Also available here are dinner-sized samples of the fabled Kashmiri *wazwan* multi-course banquet (you can specify how many or how few dishes you want by prior request). The *wazwan* mainly consists of lamb cooked in a multitude of ways: the ribs are shallow-fried with subtle spices; the fatty chest is cooked with tangy apricots; the hind leg is used to make *gushtaba*, a pounded, soft-textured meatball.

The Chinar has its own team of *wazas*, as the banquet cooks are called, who spring into action the day an order arrives. The concept of *wazwan* banquet catering is to use up an entire lamb in as many ways as possible, so it is considered uneconomical to order only a single dish; but, at a pinch, even that is possible. For its heady combination of unobtrusive service, great food, and a magical location, the Chinar is one of India's truly unmissable dining experiences. **MR**

⬆ A classic lamb dish served at The Chinar.

Karim's | Mughlai dishes in a venerable Delhi institution

Location Old Delhi   **Signature dish** *Nargisi kofta* (lamb and egg kofta curry) | **$**

Possibly the oldest restaurant in Delhi, Karim's was established in 1911 by one Haji Karimuddin at a tiny street stall near the south gate of the Jama Masjid mosque. Just two items were sold from the cart: dal (lentils) and lamb and potatoes in gravy. Business was so brisk that, two years later, Karimuddin opened up an eatery in a nearby building. It was the first local restaurant that the man on the street could afford and, a hundred years later, it still stands. More recent branches in New Delhi lack the cachet of the bustling, atmospheric parent branch, where you will see backpackers sharing tables with burka-clad ladies.

Now owned by the great grandsons of Karimuddin, Karim's offers a menu of mainly Mughlai

---

"You cannot fool the current generation. They understand value for money."

Zaeemuddin Ahmed, director of Karim's

---

dishes, the cuisine of the Mughal emperors who ruled India. Tandoori dishes include a whole lamb that has to be ordered twenty-four hours in advance and a seekh kebab of ground, spiced lamb that literally melts in your mouth. Karim's Mughlai cuisine originally came from a wide swathe from Central Asia to Persia, and you can discern the provenance of the dishes. While seekh kebab is elaborately prepared with subtle spicing, mutton burrah is the food of Central Asian horsemen of yore, who slaughtered lamb and barbecued it with a minimum of fuss. At Karim's, you will also find curries rarely seen elsewhere in the city, made by a long, slow, cooking process considered too painstaking by most rival establishments. **MR**

Indian Accent | Inspired combinations of India and the West

Location New Delhi   **Signature dish** *Galawat* lamb kebab with foie gras | **$$**

In a tree-lined avenue in a classy part of New Delhi is a most unexpected restaurant. Most of the city's grand restaurants are either in huge, deluxe hotels or in busy markets, but this one is tucked away out of sight. When you get to Indian Accent (by telling the taxi that you want to go to Friends Club, the nearest landmark), you are struck by how small and intimate the space is. The restaurant, part of a six-room boutique hotel, is the ultimate secret destination for gastronomes. Whether you sit in the small dining room, the private dining room, or on the verandah that overlooks the garden, you are treated to what many consider the finest modern cuisine in India, coupled with one of the most intelligently worked wine lists.

The presiding chef, Manish Mehrotra, previously worked in a series of pan-Asian restaurants, including one in London, where he says his exposure to the ingredients of the world grew. At Indian Accent, he effortlessly combines foie gras with a forcemeat kebab from Lucknow, pairing it with a strawberry coulis that has a hint of green chili. The chili and the kebab are quintessentially Indian; the other two ingredients are an interesting, quirky counterpoint. Some of Mehrotra's dishes rely on attractive presentation, others on verisimilitude to an international favorite. His smoked salmon with *thayir sadam* (curd rice) exemplifies his lighthearted look at food.

Nothing makes this irreverent chef happier than making his high-profile guests stare with disbelief at his intentional use of unfashionable vegetables and grains. Finger millet, amaranth, ridge gourd, and yam are avoided by most chefs, but all are grist to Mehrotra's mill. Indian Accent's glory, and his, too, lies in what he does with them. **MR**

⊡ Delectable morsels from chef Manish Mehrotra.

Bukhara | Cult kebabs in a game-changing Delhi restaurant

Location New Delhi   **Signature dish** *Murgh malai kebab* (chicken marinated with cream) | ❸❸❸

That Bukhara is the only restaurant in Delhi that does not accept table reservations after 8:00 PM is an indicator of its popularity. Ever since it opened its doors in 1977, Bukhara has been the maverick of Indian restaurants, breaking just about every rule in the book as it has gone from strength to strength. It was the first Indian eatery to feature an open kitchen, the first to have low seats (many without backrests), and the first not to provide cutlery. No other menu in the history of Indian fine dining was so short, either: just ten nonvegetarian and six vegetarian kebabs, a dal (lentil dish), and a few breads. Bukhara did away with curries completely and made few concessions to the all-important vegetarian diner. Detractors of the concept imagined early failure and rubbed their hands in glee.

More than three decades later, it is clear that Bukhara has been a visionary game changer. The idea of doing a kebab-only menu was a masterstroke, and

the kitchen has perfected its mastery of the tandoor. Each of the kebabs is a symphony of textures and spice mixes, combining flavor, succulence, and the trademark smokiness of the clay tandoor oven, in which the meat is grilled by hot charcoal.

Bukhara has been visited by several heads of state, including Bill Clinton during his tenure as U.S. president, yet everybody sits in the same space, within full view of other diners; private dining rooms would not fit with Bukhara's egalitarian spirit.

Bukhara is open for lunch as well, but there is no denying that it is a dinner restaurant: that is when the golden glow of its lights casts mysterious shadows around the warmly colored interior. The effect is strongly reminiscent of camping in India's rugged North-West Frontier Province, from where this inspired menu originated. **MR**

⬆ Diners can watch the chefs at work from their tables.

Dum Pukht | Memorable cuisine in the Lucknow tradition

Location New Delhi   **Signature dish** Kakori kebabs | ❸❸❸

The story goes that, in the seventeenth century, there was a *nawab* (Muslim ruler) of Lucknow who wanted to put in place helpful measures for his subjects during a crippling famine. When it was time to feed several tens of thousands after the day's work was done, by fortuitous chance a new style of cooking was discovered. Vessels of rice, lamb, and spices had been left to simmer for hours, and the lids had become sealed by dough. When mealtime arrived and the lids were pried open, wonderful aromas suffused the air and the ingredients were cooked to perfection. Because the method had involved long, slow cooking with sealed lids, it came to be known as "dum pukht" (cooked under pressure). The restaurant celebrates the use of "dum" (pressure) in its cooking.

Dum Pukht was always a grand restaurant in the quintessentially Lucknow tradition, presided over by a chef from that city; but, in 2011, it underwent a refurbishment. Its already distinctly Lucknavi

personality was enhanced further by arched niches studded with mirrors; trademark colors of navy, silver, and white; and cobalt goblets that make even plain water taste ambrosial. The service is formal and in the Western style, and there is a considered wine list.

While the food is always superlative, there are a few dishes that you should not miss. The first is the biryani—rice and meat cooked in a certain proportion with the most subtle aromatic spices. When the cooking vessel's dough seal is opened at your table, the cloud of fragrant vapor that rises from the biryani is enough to turn heads at neighboring tables.

The *kakori kebab*, using only tendon meat, is also a Lucknow invention, and you won't find a version that melts in the mouth quite as well anywhere else. The kormas and stews owe their provenance to the sealed cooking urn of three hundred years ago. **MR**

⬆ Arches and mirrors characterize the sumptuous interior.

Spice Route | Keralan specialities in visually rich surroundings

Location New Delhi   **Signature dish** *Appam* with stew | ❸❸

Famous as one of the world's ten most beautiful restaurants, Spice Route has interiors designed by a crafts impresario to approximate the various stages of man. The restaurant is right at the heart of New Delhi in Janpath, situated in the Imperial Hotel, itself an interesting art deco building with traces of the British Raj in its public areas and gardens.

Spice Route serves food from the south of the Indian subcontinent, including Kerala and Sri Lanka. The restaurant itself has nine divisions, all visible from one another. The walls, ceiling, and pillars have been profusely adorned with paintings and carvings executed in situ by craftsmen from Guruvayoor Temple in Kerala; the attention to detail is beyond description and the sheer spectacle of the restaurant is unparalleled. The space actually looks more like a temple or museum than a restaurant, but the surprising thing is that is works as a restaurant effortlessly. In fine weather, the open courtyard is the

first space to be booked—there is something soothing about dining under the stars with the sound of gurgling water. The next most popular area is the small, intimate "relationship" division of the restaurant, with its tables for two persons only.

Although the cuisine varies from Thai to Vietnamese to Malaysian, Kerala cuisine is well represented here, with creamy coconut milk-based stews that have to be mopped up with *appams*, lacy rice-flour breads that are made fresh and served hot at the table. There are mouth-puckeringly sour seafood curries, fiery beef stir-fries, and exotic vegetables like jackfruit, cooked with grated coconut and the fragrant spices for which the Kerala coast is so famous. So photogenic is the restaurant, and so appealing are the life-size boats and the teak wood pillars, that few leave without having themselves photographed. **MR**

⬆ The interiors boast intricate carvings and paintings.

Nosh | Atmospheric dining in the middle of the desert

Location Jaisalmer   **Signature dish** Jaisalmeri chicken with Mathania chili | 🅢🅢

Imagine lounging on a rug against bolsters in the desert, with not a sound or a human being for miles around: the only company you have is sand dunes. If it appeals to have folk musicians to entertain you while you tuck into the choicest kebabs, you can order a whole troupe of them. They will sing ballads in their native tongue, playing right in front of you. The staccato sounds of the castanetlike khartal and the powerful voices of itinerant musicians of the desert are magical. With your feet sinking into the cool sands, your palate is bedazzled with game meats like quail and hare, cooked in a coal brazier close to your table.

All this is possible at the Suryagarh resort hotel at Jaisalmer, a recreation of an eighteenth-century fort; its restaurant, Nosh (the name is Urdu for "a light meal"), overlooks the central courtyard, but the very concept has movability built into it. You can have dinner for two on a lonely terrace with a soulful balladeer singing for you, or be part of a larger party on a rocky outcrop just outside the ramparts, with lights enhancing the contours of the fairy-tale resort. You can have a picnic near a deserted lake a few miles away, with a butler to pour your Champagne, or breakfast on a ruined fort where two hundred peacocks are fed grain by the local administration.

It helps if you stay at Suryagarh, but all these services are available to outsiders, too, with advance notice. Nosh's food is nothing if not versatile. You can have a banquet of lamb dishes, including tongue and entrails if that is your preference, or the all-vegetarian food that the state of Rajasthan is so famous for—hardly any green vegetables, but plenty of beans, gramflour dumplings, millet, and sorghum, used in imaginative ways. Driving up to the enormous gates of this fort, you will feel like royalty. Dining at Nosh, you will be treated like a king. **MR**

⬆ **Choose from a wide range of dishes at Nosh.**

Grand Chanakya | Gloriously inventive Rajasthani vegetarian food

Location Jaipur **Signature dish** *Dal baati choorma* (breads served with lentils and sweet rice) | **$**

Jaipur is something of a tourist paradise, and, with the very interesting, unique, and largely vegetarian cuisine of the state of Rajasthan, it should be bursting with great dining options. That is not the case, however, and about the only option is the landmark Grand Chanakya in the city center. Generations have known this mid-level, well-appointed eatery that serves only vegetarian food. When it closed down for a few years, competitors were expected to leap in, but that did not happen. Now, Grand Chanakya is back with a bang and old-timers cannot seem to get enough of a cuisine that is hardly seen outside private homes.

Rajasthan is the desert state of India. Water is scarce and most vegetables refuse to grow there, so

---

"We are ... very nostalgic at the re-opening of iconic and heritage restaurant Grand Chanakya ..."

Ashok Odhrani, director of Chanakya Hospitality

---

the cuisine is based on dairy products and lentils in a multitude of forms. What is lacking in variety of ingredients, however, is made up for by imagination and sheer richness. A typical vegetarian meal may have sliced onion as its only vegetable component, or "ker sangria," pickled pods of the tree *Prosopsis cineraria*. There are gram flour dumplings (gatta) served with gravy or dry in a pulao; pieces of papad (wafer-thin, sun-dried lentil dough spiced with black pepper); sun-dried lentil balls called mangodi, added to curries; and sensational chili chutneys.

Grand Chanakya is an eminently civilized temple of gastronomy, and testimony to Rajasthan's imaginative triumph over Nature's shortcomings. **MR**

AD 1135 | Feast like a king within an authentic Rajasthani fort

Location Jaipur **Signature dish** *Junglee maas* (fiery red lamb curry cooked with chilis) | **$$**

There are many elements that go into the package that makes up the restaurant AD 1135. The first is its location: Amer Fort (pronounced and sometimes also spelled as Amber Fort) is one of Rajasthan's most visited historic fortifications, with magical palaces and temples sheltered by towering, honey-colored ramparts. Set in a lonely corner of the fortifications is this restaurant, which looks as if it has been here forever, but is, in fact, relatively new.

Another element is the difficulty of "discovering" it; no signage whatsoever is allowed, so it is quite a challenge to find. But with its plethora of terraces, courtyards, and grand dining rooms, AD 1135 is a Jaipur trip highlight, whether you are going in a group of twenty or just as a couple. In the first case, you will be made to feel like royalty; in the other, it is likely to be the most romantic evening of your trip to India.

Opt for the Sheesh Mahal private dining room—a mirror-mosaiced chamber with its own formal sitting room—or the Jaigarh View terrace for a romantic dinner for two. There's another terrace for two called the Amber View, and the Suwarna Mahal, with an outdoor courtyard. In all, AD 1135 is a one-of-its-kind royal space, in a fort that was built in the year 1135; hence, the choice of name. The owners could have got away with serving pedestrian food, but it is precisely for the food that many guests come.

There is an à la carte menu, but it is for the customized thalis that the place is best known. AD 1135 has gone to great lengths to procure recipes from all the royal families of Rajasthan. Quail is just one of the sought-after meats on offer. It is highly recommended that you call the management in advance and customize a meal of your choice. **MR**

➦ The sumptuous Sheesh Mahal private dining room.

Hanuwant Mahal | Dining to suit a Rajasthani maharaja

Location Jodhpur **Signature dish** *Junglee maas* (fiery red lamb curry cooked with chilis) | $$

"[Bali] flaunts a necklace with two tiger claws that once belonged to the maharaja of Bikaner..."

Mail Today

⬆ The restaurant has the feel of a maharaja's clubhouse, with crystal and antique trinkets.

Writing about Hanuwant Mahal, it is difficult not to fall into purple prose. First, consider the location. It is right below Umaid Bhawan Palace, also called the Chittar Palace, because it is built on Chittar Hill, Jodhpur's highest elevation. Hanuwant Mahal was once going to be made the residence of the Maharaja of Jodhpur, and the palace turned into a hotel. In the event, only part of the palace was converted, and His Highness stayed in one wing. Second, the view: sit on the restaurant terrace at dusk and you will see the entire city crowned by the magical palace. Third, the interiors of Hanwant Mahal take their cue from the palace itself. In fact, chef Sanjiv Bali, the man behind them, sought the help of his friend, the maharaja, in their making. Framed photographs and portraits in oils set off sage-green walls, and the palace stands serenely in front of the plate-glass windows.

This is not a place to bolt your food and charge out; indeed, that would be sacrilege. The staff, wearing colorful turbans with impressive "tails," offer Champagne on the terrace and set up a kebab station nearby. You can elect to remain there for a full service dinner under the stars, or make your way downstairs toward the intimate bar, the indoor restaurant, or the private dining room; the latter is a most impressive space, being a recreation of a royal table, complete with a gleaming forest of crystal and silver.

While the whole of Rajasthan is a desert, and Jodhpur the most arid part of it, paradoxically the region has the most highly rated cuisine in India. It is as if man's ingenuity has worked to overcome Nature's parsimony. It is in this region that the flavorful Mathania chili grows, and it is used liberally in the food. *Junglee maas* is an elemental preparation of chunks of lamb, chili, and clarified butter cooked on barely warm embers. It is ironic that a dish that was born from necessity is being served on the finest porcelain, but that is Hanuwant Mahal for you. **MR**

Vishalla | A simple but exquisite taste of Indian village life

Location Ahmedabad   **Signature dish** *Gotas* (Gujarati fried dumplings made with a special flour mix) | $

How to describe an iconic place that is more than thirty-five years old, that was once a rural getaway far outside the limits of Ahmedabad in Gujarat but has now been overwhelmed by the sprawling city? It is a rustic restaurant with no concrete and mortar to be seen, where diners eat under the stars, and where they are allowed—indeed, encouraged—to lie down on cots in the open, under the stars, after they have ambled around the crafts store, the tiny temple, and the utensils museum. This is Vishalla, the dream of one man with a vision.

From the start, Vishalla was conceptualized to resemble a village. Owner Surendrabhai Patel spent his childhood in just such a village, and, because of that, the touches are real rather than ersatz. Crucially, there is no electricity; one employee has the task of polishing the glass chimneys of a thousand kerosene lanterns all through the day, then lighting and placing them around the village at nightfall.

Guests pay a cover charge at the entrance, then wander about or simply laze around as the mood takes them. Dinner is served at the village equivalent of a trestle table. Because you have to sit on cushions on the floor, it is wise to be clad in long, loose garments; all eating is done with the fingers. The food is all vegetarian, and the utmost care is taken to source ingredients from all around Gujarat that have been grown organically. Perhaps Vishalla could be described as the first "green" restaurant in India, with the tiniest carbon footprint, but that would be seeing it from a Western perspective. Vishalla itself has never consciously sought fashionable labels, and that is what is so refreshing about it.

The folk-music performances (without sound amplification); the nearby museum of traditional utensils; the warm, friendly service; the unhurried village vibe of Vishalla; and pure food that also tastes great: there is not a phony note here. **MR**

"The dal, kadhi, and khichdi served with a generous helping of ghee are to die for…"

michaelswamy.wordpress.com

⬆ A multitude of vegetarian dishes is served banquet-style on a long table in metal bowls.

Bohemian | A creative taste of Bengali
cuisine with inventive surprises

Location Kolkata **Signature dish** Roast mutton with Bhuna sauce |

"Bengalis who have grown up with these flavors discover something new with every spoonful."

kolkatarestaurants.net

⬆ Chef Joy Banerjee creates unexpected delicacies.

On the whole, India is a fairly conservative country, with conservative tastes that also apply to its multitude of regional cuisines. Pushing the boundaries in cooking is often met with skepticism, because the average customer really does compare a dish in a restaurant to his mother's cooking. As a regional cuisine, Bengali food has never been subjected to much experimentation; but, at Bohemian, the interior, with its bright yellow walls, is already an indication that things are done a little differently.

The menu incorporates elements from English cooking, but not as affectation. Ever since Job Charnock landed in Kolkata in the sixteenth century, English food is regarded as the "default cuisine" among the city's cognoscenti. The chef, Joy Banerjee, sees English and Bengali food as two ends of a single continuum, and within this structure he does some rather interesting tweaking. Broccoli and baby onion with cheese does not sound particularly Bengali; but, with the tangy addition of green mango, the flavors suddenly change. Similarly, cauliflower and peas in lemon, chili, and coconut cream work together beautifully.

But Kolkata's cuisine encompasses far more than just Bengali cooking. It incorporates Armenian, Jewish, and even Mughal elements (the last documented Nawab from Lucknow ended his days in Kolkata), and a multitude of influences can be found at Bohemian: all the lamb dishes, for example, have their origins in ancient Muslim recipes.

Typical Bengali ingredients such as *kashundi* (a fiery mustard sauce), *bori* (sun-dried dumplings made with pounded lentils), several species of spinach greens, and the signature five spices that no meal is without, are used as elements in dishes that are studded with surprises. **MF**

Aaheli | Bengali cuisine
at its gloriously subtle best

Location Kolkata **Signature dish** *Chitol macher muitha* (clown knifefish in a special sauce) | ❸❸

Bengali cuisine is subtle and refined; its seasonings whisper rather than shout. Fish and shrimp are the stars in this particular firmament. The fish is steamed with yogurt or in a flaming mustard sauce, all wrapped in a banana leaf; shrimp are gently cooked inside tender coconut or in a gravy of coconut milk and red chilis (this dish is called *chingri* Malai curry, with "Malai" referring to Malaysia, from where the preparation originated). But for the ultimate fish dish, no effort is spared. *Chitol macher muitha* is made in several stages: the chitol fish (clown knifefish) is cooked, deboned, and formed into quenelles; these are steamed, sautéed gently, and then simmered in a sauce that is made separately. Unsurprisingly, due to its painstaking, multi-stage preparation, this is not a dish that is often made at home.

Aaheli offers modern conveniences—valet parking; a comfortable, air-conditioned environment; and possibly the best, most friendly, helpful service in all of Kolkata—blended with nice touches of tradition. Here one finds bell-metal tableware (notoriously difficult to maintain, which is why it has fallen out of favor); staff clad in traditional costume made of hand-loomed materials; and a menu studded with the finest, most interesting dishes of Bengali cuisine.

Most Indian cuisines shine either in their vegetarian dishes or in their treatments of meat and fish. Bengali food bucks that trend, because both have their attractions. At Aaheli, even the lentils in a meal are enlivened and given some textural contrast with bits of crunchy coconut, while an obscure vegetable—banana flower—is chopped and made into a superb cutlet with an interesting al dente bite. Best of all at Aaheli are the wonderful staff, who can be trusted to make helpful recommendations about what dishes to sample. **MR**

Trishna | Memorably
delicious spiced seafood

Location Mumbai **Signature dish** Butter-pepper-garlic crab | ❸❸

Right in the throbbing heart of South Mumbai, in the Kala Ghoda area with its interesting stores, museums, and art galleries, is the most famous seafood restaurant in the city. Yet Trishna was not always as prominent as it has been for the past decade. Indeed, the restaurant started out rather modestly, and might have remained below the gastronomic radar. But the unsurpassed excellence of its star dish, the butter-pepper-garlic crab, and its Hyderabadi fish ensured the restaurant's success.

Trishna serves traditional Mangalore food with a slight twist. Nobody is quite sure where exactly the butter-pepper-garlic concept came from, but it has certainly put Trishna on the culinary map and become

---

"People from all walks of life … throng the place for the butter-pepper-garlic crab."

Trishna website

---

a much-plagiarized dish all over the country. Trishna's menu beyond the crab has also become more ambitious. If you ignore the fanciful names of the dishes (the Hyderabadi fish bears little resemblance to that city's cuisine), you can have the time of your life.

Frequent visitors to the restaurant grumble about uncomfortable furniture and that the staff are three times the required number. But the seafood is irreproachably fresh and spices are used with a light, sure hand. Whether you order the *rawas Hyderabadi* (fillets of saltwater fish dusted with black pepper and salt, cooked in the tandoor oven) or one of the butter-pepper-garlic dishes—crab, squid, mussels, or oysters—you will get a meal made in heaven. **MR**

Swati Snacks | Appetizing street foods in a restaurant setting

Location Mumbai **Signature dish** *Bhelpuri* | 🅢🅢

Not ostentatious, and certainly not a hole in the wall, Swati Snacks flies defiantly in the face of stereotypes. The cuisine covers the territory that exists between light meals and heavy snacks, and is a combination of the rich, rather heavy, ghee-laden Gujarati food and its more austere counterpart from Maharashtra, whose capital is Mumbai. The large, airy eatery is found on a busy main road, opposite a hospital, and always has a crowd of people waiting patiently for a table. The interior is undeniably of the no-frills variety, sparse but clean and functional. Service is speedy: the aim is to serve as many people as quickly as possible.

The all-vegetarian menu is a revelation. The ingredients include a variety of carbohydrates: barley, millet, corn, rice, lentils, sago, wheat flour, and gram flour. These are cooked in a variety of ways to arrive at an array of simple, elemental dishes that are spiced to retain their natural textures. The variety of forms a handful of ingredients can be coaxed into is incredible, using only the bare minimum of seasonings and spices. By way of an example, gram flour, called besan, is made into a batter, fermented with a bit of sour curd, and then steamed. The product would taste like a rather dry, savory cake were it not for the drizzle of salted, sweetened liquid that is poured over it to give a dimension of juiciness. In the same way, cornmeal is coarsely pounded, seasoned lightly, and dusted with dill leaves; it is then poured between banana leaves and steamed. The resulting pancakes are eaten with chutney.

Swati Snacks celebrates the street foods of Mumbai and Ahmedabad, but provides them in clean surroundings; for the nervous visitor, it is an ideal introduction to the glorious tastes of Mumbai. The majority of the patrons cook this kind of food at home, yet come here for the extra pizzazz. **MR**

⬆ The streamlined interior of Swati Snacks.

Shri Thakker Bhojanalaya | Fantastic vegetarian Gujarati cooking

Location Mumbai **Signature dish** Vegetarian *thali* | ❸

Deep in the heart of a paper market is not where you would expect to find a restaurant that served absolutely stunning *thali* meals; but, then, the city of Mumbai always holds a trump card. Shri Thakker Bhojanalaya is a first-floor restaurant in the old district of Kalbadevi and, while the drive there is wildly atmospheric, it is a tough job finding it. Chaotic traffic, narrow lanes, trucks unloading unending reams of paper, and numerous fruit sellers cramping the narrow pavements with their colorful wares—Kalbadevi probably represents the "real Mumbai."

The busy paper wholesalers of Kalbadevi are from the largely vegetarian Gujarati community, and so the food at Shri Thakker is vegetarian. It is served in the *thali* format because that is the traditional way to consume all the food groups in a single meal. Also, the food cannot be priced above a certain limit because paper merchants are notoriously conservative

spenders. In other words, you are assured a spectacular, authentic meal at rock-bottom prices. The restaurant serves home-style food because customers come here several times a week and do not want to eat heavy, overly spiced food.

There is no menu, but you can certainly ask for additional helpings of whatever you choose: there are green vegetables, yogurt-based gravy thickened with gram flour, and fried crunchies on offer. You are served lentils and beans, and pickles, chutneys, and many different relishes, some made from vegetables you are unlikely to know, and a vast selection of different *rotis*. It can be tricky to find a good, varied vegetarian meal (although it is easier in India than in many other countries), but here vegetarians will be very happy indeed. The glory of a Gujarati *thali* is its motto: local, fresh, and seasonal. **MR**

⬆ **Many small dishes make up a classic** *thali.*

Casa Sarita | Goanese cuisine in luxurious surroundings

Location Goa   **Signature dish** Pork belly with onion-vinegar jam | ❸❸

Goa, India's smallest state, was ruled by the Portuguese for 450 years before being forced to relinquish sovereignty in 1961. The cuisine of the region is homely rather than haute. There are one or two showpiece dishes, but Goa's fish curries, and its vegetable preparations with dried shrimp, have been known chiefly for having a zero-kilometer carbon footprint. As a result of this low culinary profile, there are very few grand restaurants in Goa that serve the local food. Eateries that do serve Goan cuisine tend to be strictly functional establishments.

Casa Sarita, installed in the plush environs of the Park Hyatt Goa at Cansaulim, is the one glorious exception. Being part of a luxury resort, it cannot help but be grand, but there is more. The management has always procured the finest Goan chefs to head its kitchen, and also encouraged them to be innovative. The decor, too, might easily have been casual, but it is as formal as the service. Inside, an open kitchen and a few utensils and pickle jars from bygone days are on display. Window panes are made of mother-of-pearl shells, something of a time-honored tradition in Goa.

But it is the menu that is the star of this show. There is fish curry, redolent of coconut milk, cocum (a kind of mangosteen), and red chilis, eaten with the traditional, naturally red rice widely grown in Goa until a couple of decades ago. Also available are Goan chorizo sausages, although these bear little resemblance to the Spanish sausages of the same name. Every village family had its own pig, and once a year an orgy of sausage-making would take place, using huge quantities of a potent local vinegar, along with sea salt and Goan chilis. The tasting menu takes a rather bucolic cuisine out of the ordinary and serves it with a panache that would do any Mediterranean meal proud. **MR**

⬆ The sophisticated dining area includes an open kitchen.

Zaffran | Impeccable seafood kebabs by a Goan beach

Location Goa **Signature dish** Tandoori lobster | $$

Any visitor to India found biting into a succulent kebab is likely to be in the north of the country. Also, chances are that the kebab is either lamb or chicken. The clay oven in which kebabs are roasted came to northern India via Afghanistan and Central Asia, and grilling seafood has never been a tradition. Thus the idea of cooking seafood kebabs—with fish, shrimp, and lobster—has always been given short shrift in the landlocked cities of the north.

That is where Zaffran scores. Here, the freshest seafood undergoes an extremely well-judged marination, where you can still taste the ingredients through the whisper of light spices. Here, also, Punjabi food is done with a restrained hand, so that the flavors predominate and the heaviness is kept to a minimum. Zaffran is built on an open plan, like a cottage without walls, allowing you to watch the waves on the beach many feet below. It offers a near-perfect balance of casual interiors, impeccable service, and wonderful food. The backdrop of the Vagator Beach and the contrast between the casual, indolent air of Goa itself and the crisp service and almost formal presentations work together brilliantly.

In India, you can usually count on getting a great meal of the local food wherever you go, but regional cuisines tend not to travel well. Perhaps it is the difficulty of obtaining the right ingredients or chefs trained in that particular cuisine. But Zaffran is a textbook case of an exception proving a rule. It is open throughout the year; it is filled with regulars who holiday in Goa every year; it is visited by Indians and Western tourists; and its creamy *dal makhni* finds its way onto every table. Watching the sunset with a glass of wine and a plate of Zaffran chicken malai tikka, with the waves crashing on the beach below, is one of life's incomparable pleasures. **MR**

↑ Dine on exquisite seafood right by the sea.

Dakshin | A journey through the culinary glories of southern India

Location Chennai **Signature dish** *Vazhai shunti* (plaintain fritters) | ❸❸

Twenty-five years ago, young chef Praveen Anand started to research the food of his home state, Andhra Pradesh. Instead of just Hyderabadi cuisine, he discovered a wealth of micro-cuisines that changed subtly from one location to the next, depending on the geography and topography of the site. Because his work took him to Chennai, his research eventually took in the state of Tamil Nadu as well. Before he knew it, Anand's rather academic bent of mind and his love of poring over tomes in the local library gained him recognition as an authority on the cuisines of the south of India, including those of Kerala and Karnataka.

His employer, the Sheraton Park Hotel, Chennai, was interested in incorporating all the multitude of cuisines into a single restaurant, but the public greeted the idea with contempt. The concept of serving the vegetarian idlis and rasams of the Iyer Brahmins of Palakkad in the same physical space as the pork pandhi curry of the Kodavas of Coorg was too

revolutionary to be contemplated. However, not only was the idea adopted by what is now Dakshin at the hotel, it has also become the template for a style of restaurant: to juxtapose both well-known and obscure regional cuisines from southern India, where before no one single cuisine dominated.

The trademark sage-green walls of Dakshin, the polished brass accessories, the rich paintings, and the remarkably good food make for a grand occasion. But there is more. If there is a fish curry from coastal Tamil Nadu, a fisherman's spice mix will be flash-fried and added to the final product. Few grand restaurants would even know about the existence of *kari-vadagam* seasoning, let alone where it can be found, but that is Chef Anand's area of expertise. Effortlessly moving from rustic fishermen's hut to grand restaurant is Dakshin's success. **MR**

⬆ **The grand entrance to Dakshin restaurant.**

Kanua | Mangalore home cooking, served in a restaurant

Location Bangalore   **Signature dish** Chicken ghee roast | $

When an architect specializing in conservation decides to set up a restaurant, you know that food will not be the only thing on the agenda. Kanua is the name of a variety of rice that is now extinct, but was still clinging on while Rajesh Pai was growing up. Kanua, the restaurant, is pretty much one of a kind. It has no walls and only a tiled roof, of the kind you see in coastal Karnataka. Thanks to sly tricks of the architect's trade—such as double roofing—Kanua is cool throughout the year, without the aid of fans.

Kanua's cuisine is the coastal food of Karnataka, particularly of Mangalore, from where the owner and his cooks came. But the food of this unusual restaurant does not only acknowledge the region: it also celebrates the home cook. Many of the dishes follow "grandmother" recipes, particularly the signature chicken ghee roast. This dish appears on many restaurant menus but there is no doubt that Kanua's version is superior. That is because the ghee (clarified

butter) comes from a single artisanal supplier who makes it in the traditional way by "washing" the cream in several changes of salted water. It is this fastidious adherence to minor processes mistakenly regarded as obsolete that has made Kanua a byword for excellence in Bangalore's culinary circles.

You are guaranteed the time of your life just sitting in the restaurant for a couple of hours. All the accessories have been taken from old buildings in the region; overhanging eaves have space for owls to nest, which in turn impacts the ecosystem around the restaurant. You will see bunches of onions and garlic hanging from rafters to season, in just the way that traditional homes in the area have done it for centuries. Simple ingredients are presented with startling imagination—taste how bitter gourd and batons of sugar cane influence the flavor of a curry. **MR**

⬆ The tasteful interior has been put together with care.

Karavalli | A celebration of the riches of West Coast Indian cuisine in delightful garden surroundings

Location Bangalore   **Signature dish** Coorg fried chicken (chicken marinated with Coorgi garam masala spice mix and then fried) | **$$**

"What really makes for a spectacular end to a fabulous meal is the tamarind ice cream."

Michael Swamy, thehindubusinessline.com

⬆ Tucked away in the Gateway Hotel's garden, Karavalli offers a delicious taste of regional Indian cuisine.

An institution in Bangalore since 1990, Karavalli is a restaurant of the Gateway Hotel; its chief claim to fame used to be that it was built outside of the hotel building, making it something of an outhouse. That was offbeat enough in a deluxe hotel of yesteryear, but what made Karavalli decidedly raffish was the menu: red rice and meen pollichathu (pomfret fish baked in a banana leaf). Because of its odd location, inside yet outside of the hotel, it was always considered quirky, with its "not-quite-five-star" menu.

Recently, however, it was given a makeover. Not, one hastens to say, to become more mainstream, but to celebrate its angularities. Hence, the garden has opened up and the indoor part has taken the shape of a village dwelling. The plates are either black pottery or copper thali bowls, and the music sets the mood. Given Bangalore's famously temperate weather, opt to sit outside unless it is pouring rain; the garden is the most charming part of Karavalli.

The cuisine served here is the home-style food of several of the communities that live on the coast of southwest India, in three states: Goa, Karnataka (of which Bangalore is the capital), and Kerala. But more than that, it celebrates the food of particular communities: Kodavas of Coorg, Syrian Christians of Travancore, Brahmins of Mangalore, and Moplahs of the spice coast of Malabar. Further, the restaurant has picked just one or two representative dishes, so there are colocassia leaves layered with spice paste, folded like a Swiss roll and grilled, fish curry cooked in a terracotta pot on a wood fire, or the dryish Karavalli mutton with just about enough gravy to mop up an *appam* or two.

The portions are generous, the service is knowledgeable, the music is classical Carnatic, and an evening in the garden is just idyllic. **MR**

Paragon | Authentic Keralan cuisine—including breakfast

Location Calicut **Signature dish** *Moplah biryani* (chicken with rice) | ❺

The cuisine of North Kerala is undoubtedly one of India's finest, and the reason for that is obvious: the Malabar Coast is where Arab traders and spice merchants used to buy their pepper and cardamoms for a millennium, before taking them on the long journey to Europe. This flank of the state of Kerala already had a rich culinary heritage, to which the Arabs added another layer. Tree spices (pepper, cardamom, cloves, cinnamon, and nutmeg) may grow profusely in central Kerala, but they are used in the cuisine of north Kerala to their best advantage.

While the laid-back little town of Calicut may not have the charm to compete with towns and cities further south, you can eat superbly well here. And if you cross a narrow road with maniacal traffic, past the fly over, you will come to Paragon. The place is spotlessly clean and the food is excellent, no matter what you order. If you arrive at 6:30 AM for breakfast, you can opt for a hearty dish of boiled eggs in lashings of onion-based sauce, fiery red with chilis, accompanied by soft, flaky Malabar *parottas* (flat breads). Even at that early hour, many customers think nothing of ordering a spicy dish of shrimp, fish, or mussels, or even of chicken or lamb. There is also the option of a more conventional breakfast (by Kerala standards) of curried black grams (chickpeas) combined with a cylindrical roll of coarsely pounded red rice drizzled with coconut gratings.

In a town that is well known for its fresh seafood, Paragon leads the pack. It obtains its catch of the day from boats on the shore and buys just enough for one day. Order the mild, subtle fish *moilee*, tangy fish mango curry, or the signature Moplah *biryani* (the Moplah community are Muslim descendants of the Arab traders of yore), made with chicken. You can't reserve a table, but it is definitely worth the wait. **MR**

Bangala | A taste of home-style Chettiver hospitality

Location Karaikudi **Signature dish** *Chicken Chettinad* (chicken flavored with dagarful, a tree lichen) | ❺

The Chettinad region of Tamil Nadu is semi-arid; there are few villages and, had it not been for the cuisine, these would have decayed into obscurity. But in the largely vegetarian state of Tamil Nadu, the cuisine is startling: Chettinad food is full of meaty treats.

The villages do not have much in the way of entertainment, only the silent, shiplike mansions famously built in the eighteenth century by the Nattukottai Chettiars, a prosperous community of traders and bankers. Had it not been for initiatives like the Bangala, the glories of the Chettinad heritage might have passed us by completely.

The Bangala, one of the few hostelries in the region, is a "colonial" bungalow that was built as a

---

"Food is served on banana leaves instead of plates, which makes [it] even more tempting."

anothertravelguide.com

---

guesthouse for Westerners several decades ago. It is small and intimate, and the dining hall has always been its focal point; meals are at communal tables. Presided over by a Chettiyar dowager, it is the nearest thing to eating in a private house. A prior booking can secure a place at lunch or dinner, but nonguests should take into account that the nearest city, Madurai, is a two-hour drive away.

All the meals are fixed, and contain about seven courses. They include such homely fare as beetroot cutlets; *velai paniyaram* (similar to *idli*, a savory rice cake, but poached in sesame oil); and *chicken Chettinad*. Not only can you watch your food being cooked, you can learn how to prepare it, too. **MR**

Murugan Idli | Join the locals for some delicious breakfast

Location Chennai **Signature dish** *Idli* with chutney | $

> *"We get nearly 3,000 diners a day and for that ... we use up 880 lbs (400kg) of rice for the batter."*

S. Manorahan, owner of Murugan Idli

⬆ Creamy coconut chutney to relish at Murugan Idli.

Murugan Idli started out as a small shack—nowadays, it is a vast empire that includes over a dozen outlets across the country, and even an outpost in Singapore. The secret of its success is a fierce commitment to quality at rock-bottom prices. It helps that the restaurant is located in a part of India where the fragrant curry leaf—the key ingredient for Murugan Idli's signature chutney—grows in abundance. Wonderfully aromatic, it perfumes the entire banana leaf that it is eaten from.

Chutneys with *idli* are popular breakfast fare, so turn up early. It is best not to expect waiters to pull up chairs or even show you to a table: at Murugan, service simply means ensuring you get your banana leaf (there are no plates) within seconds of being seated at a shared table. By the time you have sprinkled water from your glass onto the leaf and gone through the motions of "cleaning" it, as is the custom, your food will have arrived.

First up are the four delicious chutneys: coconut, curry leaf, tomato, and tamarind will be expertly arranged on your leaf, without a drop being spilled. Then the *idlis* appear: savory cakes that serve as a base for the chutneys (and occasionally for other accompaniments). These *idlis* are what made the restaurant famous. A rice-and-lentil-flour batter is fermented just enough for the necessary aeration to take place, then the *idlis* are formed and steamed in order to reach the table hot, soft, and fluffy. Eaten on their own, they may not taste of much, but their purpose is to highlight the melange of sharp flavors in the various chutneys.

You might also wish to try the "country cousin" of the *idli*, the *dosa*, a griddle-fried crepe made out of variations of the same two flours, which tastes just as good with the chutneys as the *idli*. Washed down with some freshly ground coffee, this is the ideal breakfast; hence, its immense popularity with the locals. **MR**

Rice Boat | Cochin fine dining with a panoramic harborside view

Location Kochi **Signature dish** *Meen pollichathu* (fish coated in spices and wrapped in a banana leaf) | ⊗⊗

At the very southernmost tip of the Indian peninsula lies Kochi, formerly known as Cochin, a city that is at once a sleepy outpost, a natural harbor, and an exercise in time travel for the imagination. Here are the ghosts of Vasco da Gama and the thousands of unnamed sailors who docked their ships to collect the pepper, tea, and cardamom for which Kerala was so famous. Today, no galleons ride at anchor in the harbor; but, of course, there are modern ships, come to take away exactly the same cargoes that have departed from these shores for millennia.

The Rice Boat restaurant, created by and adjoining the Vivanta by Taj Malabar Hotel, literally consists of two historic rice boats lashed together. Aboard this stationary vessel, you can look out at what is pretty much the maritime history of the city. In front of you are Dutch trading posts, Portuguese churches, sprawling rain trees, and the shimmering waters of the bay. The magic is that here you can get wonderful, informed service, a good wine list, and the freshest seafood, and are able to dine next to the water.

Kerala is blessed with a network of backwaters, a lake, and the sea, and its seafood comes from all three sources. At the Rice Boat, there is one menu that is totally oriented toward Kerala cuisine and another that serves international favorites with a local spin, such as Malabar coastal fish broth and curried lobster bisque. The Kerala menu lists seafood by type: fish, crustaceans, molluscs, and so forth, and then goes on to list the styles of cooking, detailing dry varieties as well as curries. In a home-style meal in Kerala, the two types would go hand in hand; no one would eat three different types of curries together, or four different types of dry preparations.

The accompaniments here are as offbeat as any you are likely to find in India: steamed tapioca, red rice, and Malabar *parotta*, a flaky bread with as many layers as a shortcrust pastry, only whisper soft. **MR**

"Floor-to-ceiling glass walls and a curved cane ceiling make the best of its position right on the water..."

frommers.com

⊡ Diners sit looking out over the waters of the bay.

Green T. House Living | A "Neoclassical Chinese" tea experience

Location Beijing **Signature dish** "Field Dreams" | ❸❸❸

"If I am really enjoying it, there must be other people who will really enjoy it, too."

JinR, founder of the Green T. House Living concept

⬆ The food at Green T. House pleases the eye.

➡ Calm and serenity characterize the teahouse space.

The combination of a bathhouse and a fine-dining restaurant might seem too odd to succeed, but Green T. House Living pulls it off effortlessly. Winner of the Wallpaper Architectural Design Award, this bathhouse concept by Beijing designer and proprietor JinR enables guests to experience fine dining in a completely new way. Located among plush Beijing villas, the majestic 3.7-acre (1.5-ha) site features a stunning garden, a white pebbled courtyard, a glass-encased dining room covering 32,000 square feet (900 sqm) that seats only twenty-five people, and a luxurious modern bathhouse residence.

JinR, owner and creative force behind Green T. House Living, is simultaneously an artist, musician, tea connoisseur, and trendsetter. Born in Beijing, she underwent classical training in the *yang qin* instrument at the Central Conservatory of Music and then toured the world, becoming a musician of international renown. While traveling, she started to think about creating what she calls a "Neoclassical Chinese experience," one that blended her experiences of the modern world with her dedication to preserving the ancient spirit of tea.

JinR designed every facet of the Green T. House Living space, from its furniture and homeware to its original music sound track and menu items, many of which include tea as an ingredient. Her "Field Dreams" dish features fresh pear slices with homemade Green T. honey mustard and toasted walnuts and pecans, topped by goat cheese. Another signature dish is the "Curly Chicken": fried chicken slivers flavored with Sichuan peppercorns, sesame, and Parmesan on a bed of deep fried oolong tea leaves. Do not miss the Green T. dark and milk chocolate-encrusted bark, served in a bowl of crushed ice. After the meal, take "T." in the "Reflection" room overlooking a serene pagoda, or peruse the artful homeware and accessories for sale in the designer store. **JG**

Bao Yuan Jiaozi Wu | Absolute heaven
for dumpling lovers

Location Beijing **Signature dish** Traditional pork and fennel dumplings |

"There's so much more to dumplings than standard pork and veggie fillings at this joint."

fodors.com

⬆ The dumplings are shaped to resemble the form of old Chinese silver ingots.

The Chinese tradition of dumplings dates to more than 2,000 years ago. In the northern provinces where wheat is plentiful, dumplings are a mainstay on the dining table, and traditionally are consumed during the Chinese New Year over a reunion meal known as *tuan yuan fan*. This is always a festive affair, where everyone participates in rolling the dough, mixing the filling, and wrapping the dumplings.

Generally, fillings contain ground pork with napa cabbage and chives, but numerous other combinations exist, including shrimp, lamb, tomato, egg, celery, and fennel. In Beijing, where the winters can be excruciatingly cold, dumplings are popular at home, and in specialty restaurants dedicated to these warm and delicious little satchels.

Bao Yuan Jiaozi Wu is a family-run dumpling place with a legendary reputation for serving some of the freshest and tastiest dumplings in town. The restaurant is located near to the embassy district in Chaoyang and is frequented by locals, embassy staff, and even visiting heads of state. The dining room is low-key yet festive, with rows of red lanterns adorning the wooden ceiling beams. Friendly waiters serve clients, and the dumplings are made fresh to order, on the spot.

The menu can be overwhelming, with dozens of types of fillings such as smoked tofu, lotus root, cabbage, crispy rice, pork, and cilantro. The dumplings are wrapped in a silver ingot shape, which packs in more filling than regular crescent-shaped dumplings. The fun does not stop there—diners have the option of coloring their dough wrappers with vegetable juices including carrot, spinach, purple cabbage, and tomato, to produce rainbow-colored dumplings that are not only delicious to eat but pretty to look at, too. **JG**

Duck de Chine | Refined
roast duck tucked away in Sanlitun

Location Beijing   **Signature dish** Beijing roast duck |
❸❸❸

There is always fierce debate on where to go in Beijing to find the best roast duck. There are the traditionalists who prefer the Quanjude restaurant, with its traditional roasting methods and its one hundred years of history, while others laud Da Dong for its contemporary dining rooms and modernist cooking techniques. But for one of the most consistent and refined roast ducks in the city, one should go no farther than the entertainment district of Sanlitun.

A stylish and iconic roast duck restaurant, Duck de Chine is tucked away in a venue that is popular in its own right, a former factory and research facility built in 1949 that in 2008 was converted into a chic dining hub and given the name "Hidden City 1949." Duck de Chine is set within the former factory around a beautiful courtyard complex that also houses a stellar hand-pulled noodle bar, a wine bar, and a boutique art gallery. For many, the fact that the place is hard to find only adds to its appeal.

The restaurant has a skylight across the roof in the traditional style; inside, there is a dark wooden floor accented by warm brick walls. The two dining rooms are adjoined by an open kitchen, and customers can watch their ducks roasting in a custom-built brick oven.

The duck meat at Duck de Chine is moist and flavorful, its crispy skin roasted to perfection by a blend of fragrant fruit woods. The meat is served with paper-thin pancakes and *tian mian jiang*, a light, savory sauce made from fermented soybeans and flour. The duck soup is a rich elixir flavored with goji berries and herbs. Western-inspired dishes include duck confit and fusion duck tacos that combine roast duck, water chestnuts, and bell peppers served in a crispy taco shell. Wash everything down with a glass of bubbly from China's first Bollinger Champagne bar, housed at the restaurant entrance. **JG**

Mei Mansion | Romantic dining
dedicated to a famous opera singer

Location Beijing   **Signature dish** Mandarin duck chicken *congee* | ❸❸❸❸

One of the greatest Peking (Beijing) opera singers in modern times, Mei Lanfang helped make Beijing opera popular worldwide. He was also an epicure, with a taste for simple flavors and an appreciation of quality, seasonal ingredients.

Mei Mansion is a loving tribute to the singer's culinary persona located in a 200-year-old courtyard set in Beijing's ancient *hutong* alleys. The former home of a Qing dynasty concubine, in 2003 it was converted by Mei's son as a tribute to his father. It contains various memorabilia, marrying 1920s charm with a contemporary feel. Mei was famous for performing female roles and depicting idealized women on stage. He ate to maintain his pale complexion, feminine

---

> *"Diners receive a handwritten menu in Chinese calligraphy on a folded paper fan."*
>
> *Asia Tatler*

---

physique, and delicate voice, adopting a strict diet that was low in sugar, cholesterol, and sodium, but did not compromise on flavor. Mei Mansion offers a variety of his favorite dishes prepared by former apprentices to Mei's personal chef, Wang Shoushan. None of the dishes use chili because Mei saw the fiery ingredient as a threat to his white teeth, porcelain skin, and clear voice.

The restaurant's signature dish, and the one Mei ate before every performance, is the mandarin duck chicken *congee*. It takes forty-eight hours to braise the ground chicken until it reaches the consistency of the *congee* savory rice porridge, after which it is blended with a dash of vegetable juice. **JG**

Najia Xiaoguan |
A taste of traditional Manchu dining

Location Beijing   **Signature dish** Crispy fried
giant shrimp | ❸❸❸

As the center of economic and social activity in the ancient kingdom of China, various people migrated to Beijing. They took a wealth of diversity in culinary offerings with them, from simple snack stalls on the street, to large-scale sacrificial ceremonies made an imperial practice by the Manchus when they ruled from the Forbidden City during the Qing dynasty.

While the extravagances of Manchurian banquets have disappeared, one can still find interpretations of Manchu food in dedicated restaurants like Najia Xiaoguan. Opened by the grandson of an emperor's doctor in the Qing dynasty, its recipes are passed down from the doctor's *Golden Soup Bible*, a collection of dishes fit for an emperor. The Manchu tribe was

---

"There's a touch of the traditional Chinese teahouse to this excellent restaurant ..."

Lonely Planet Discover China

---

nomadic, and hunting was a royal pastime, so wild game features. Braised venison is a signature dish, as are diced venison in pancakes and venison fried rice.

Other exotic fare include braised ox with turtle and seahorses, shark's fin and abalone, and *huang tanzi*, a meaty soup cooked for at least eighteen hours in an earthenware pot. The thick, flavorful broth is made with chicken, duck, pork, and ham. But not everything is lavish, and there is always a dish of the house favorite, *mizi supi xia*—crispy fried giant shrimp with a sweet, golden glaze—on every table.

The setting is beautiful: a traditional two-story wooden house filled with natural light. Tables on the second floor look down onto a courtyard. **JG**

Huguosi Snack House |
Sample Hui halal snacks in Beijing

Location Beijing   **Signature dish** Beef *shaobing* |
❸

One of fifty-six recognized ethnic groups in China, the Hui people are a predominantly Muslim group who spread throughout the country in the seventh century along the Silk Road trading route. In the twenty-first century, there are approximately 10.5 million Hui spread out in Muslim communities in major cities such as Lanzhou, Xi'an, Changsha, and Beijing. Because of their faith, halal food is a defining part of Hui culture, and as the consumption of pork is prohibited in Islamic dietary law, beef and lamb are prominent in the cuisine. The characters *qing zhen*—Chinese for "halal"—mean "pure" and "true," defining the cleanliness and integrity of the food served in Hui establishments in the capital.

Such locales range from snack food stalls to grand banquet restaurants, where whole lambs are roasted and served. One of the most famous institutions to serve a variety of Hui traditional snacks is the Huguosi Snack House. A state-run enterprise favored by Hui clientele, it sells snacks, including *chatang*, or tea soup, a pale brown paste made from roasted ground millet, water, and sugar. Flavored with almond, lotus root, or mung bean, the comforting soup is especially popular in cold weather.

The Huguosi Snack House also offers a wide variety of baked and deep-fried pastries, including one of the city's best *shaobing*, a many-layered dough seasoned lightly with salt and ground Sichuan peppercorns, and baked with a sprinkling of sesame seeds on top. The *shaobing* flatbreads can be eaten alone, or as sandwiches filled with fragrant braised beef. Accompany the *shaobing* with deep-fried tofu ball soup, a fragrant lamb broth served piping hot with a sprinkling of cilantro on top. The Huguosi Snack House is perennially packed, so try to go early in the morning or mid-afternoon to avoid lines. **JG**

Han Cang | A chance to taste Hakka cuisine looking out over Qianhai Lake

Location Beijing **Signature dish** Foil-wrapped fish | ⓈⓈ

The Hakka people are a tribe of Han Chinese migrants from the Yellow River Valley region who dispersed and settled across southern China more than 2,000 years ago. Farther migrations took them as far as Sichuan in the west, as well as Taiwan and southeast Asia. As a result, the Hakka people do not have a geographic region to call their own. Despite the wide diaspora of the population, the Hakka people have maintained a strong sense of tradition and community, upholding a culture that includes a delicious, rustic cuisine evolved from thousands of years of nomadic living.

Hakka cuisine can be found in a handful of restaurants in Beijing, one of the most famous of which is Han Cang. Located on the picturesque east bank of Qianhai Lake, Han Cang opened in the 1990s and remains the city's top destination for rustic Hakka cuisine. Its bare concrete walls are dressed up with calligraphy scrolls. The view from the second floor is particularly pleasant, allowing diners to contemplate the calm and peace of the lake. In the summer months, it is possible to dine outside on the terrace. At Han Cang, it is easy to forget that the simple and tasty cuisine is the product of life in the most inhospitable environments where the Hakka people struggled to survive. Hakka women joined the men in the fields, doing laborious farm work that required hearty, filling, and salty foods. All parts of the animal were used and nothing wasted. Foods were salted, dried, and preserved to keep for long periods of time.

Han Cang's signature dish, *zhibaoyu*,—crisp, deep-fried whole fish baked in foil—reflects the Hakka cooking ethos. Other favorites include steamed *kailan* (Chinese broccoli) greens topped with intensely savory preserved olive leaves and *sanbei ya* (three-cup duck)—a hearty option of succulent duck meat braised in soy sauce, rice wine, and lard. **JG**

"… thick wooden tables on a granite floor emphasize the peasanty but arty look."

Time Out Beijing

⤒ Visitors to Han Cang can dine while enjoying the view of the spectacular Qianhai Lake.

Chuan Ban | Spicy Sichuan dishes served in a government restaurant

Location Beijing **Signature dish** Xiaochi |

"… raucous rather than romantic; expect loud talking, toasting, and clinking of glasses."

Time Out Beijing

⬆ Be sure to try the rice balls at Chuan Ban.

Of all the provincial government restaurants in Beijing, the most popular is Chuan Ban, a lively place inside the Sichuan representative office in Jianguomen, known for big flavors and even bigger lines. As officials from across the country come to the capital on business trips, they long for a taste of home, so chefs were dispatched from the provinces to cook authentic dishes from their hometowns. Aside from the boisterous patrons, there is little atmosphere as such in the restaurant, which features fluorescent white lighting and simple wooden furniture. But the food certainly delivers.

The menu consists of a good representation of classic dishes and a thorough repertoire of Chengdu's *xiaochi* (street snacks). Start with a dish of *kou shui ji*, a cold appetizer of poached chicken in a bath of red chili paste. One of the standout dishes is the *shui zhu yu*, a fish hot pot made from tender slices of carp cooked in chili oil, topped with a sea of red peppers, and green Sichuan peppercorns. The delicious *huiguo xiangxiangzui* is a Sichuan dish of twice-cooked pig's ears with a wonderfully crunchy texture and smoky aroma, balanced by freshly chopped scallions and green peppers.

Do not miss the classic *mapo* tofu, a simple dish of silken bean curd coated in a glistening red sauce made with broadbean paste, chili, and fermented black beans, topped with ground pork, and dusted with just the right amount of freshly ground Sichuan peppercorns—it is done to perfection here, with a fine balance of flavors. Be sure to mop up all of the sauce with an extra serving of white rice. Also of note are the traditional *hong you chao shou* red chili wonton snacks, the chewy *dan dan* noodles, and—for a break from the heat—the *lao zao tang yuan* glutinous rice balls in fermented rice wine. **JG**

Chengfu Courtyard |
Spectacular and exclusive dining

Location Beijing **Signature dish** Shaoxing wine-marinated chicken | 💲💲💲💲💲

Only a few steps from Tiananmen Square and Zhongnanhai—the walled compound that is home to China's top party officials—is the quiet, tree-lined Nanchang Road. Moving down this thoroughfare, it is easy to miss the doorway of No. 38, a small courtyard that houses one of Beijing's most exclusive restaurants, Chengfu Courtyard.

The establishment is named after its founder, Cheng Ruming, official chef to Zhongnanhai and one of China's sixteen "treasured culinary talents." In 1954, he became the personal chef to China's leader, Mao Zedong, and was responsible for preparing daily meals for Mao's family as well as elaborate banquets for visiting heads of state. Nowadays, Cheng's grandson Liu Jian runs Chengfu Courtyard, a small dining space with four private rooms seating thirty people.

Chef Liu sources the same organic ingredients that are delivered to Zhongnanhai. Devoted to historical accuracy, he favors recreations of dishes that featured in historic Communist Party banquets, such as when Mao entertained President Richard Nixon. Liu serves traditional Chinese dishes—including Mao's favorite red braised pork dish—alongside dishes influenced by Western cultural exchanges of the day. In a departure from the Chinese family-style meal, diners have their own place settings and are served individual portions.

There is no menu at Chengfu Courtyard; the banquet-style meals are based on what is fresh and in season. The signature dish is Shaoxing wine-marinated stuffed chicken; a fifteen-day-old chicken is deboned with its skin still intact, stuffed with a mixture of smoked sausage, mushroom, onion, chestnut, and glutinous rice, and then steamed in Shaoxing rice wine. **JG**

Zhanglaoerliangfen |
Sublime noodles in a snack house

Location Chengdu **Signature dish** *Tian shui mian* noodles (sweet and spicy noodles) | 💲

Opposite the famous Wenshu Buddhist temple in Chengdu, Zhanglaoerliangfen is one of the few old restaurants in the area that has withstood the test of time and maintained its traditional atmosphere. This hole-in-the-wall gem has been serving up some of the best noodles and snack foods in the area for decades. Extremely popular with both locals and tourists, it is well respected for its efficient service and bowls of cold, spicy noodles.

The restaurant holds a few tightly spaced tables, and its stools are never empty. Staff take diners' orders from a large menu written in Chinese on the wall. There are all the classics: red chili oil dumplings, wontons, and other snack foods. But a scan of the

"Hand-pulled noodles are a staple of Sichuan cuisine, but require extraordinary skill to create."

businessdestinations.com

surrounding tables quickly confirms that a bowl of *tian shui mian* sweet and spicy noodles, and *lu dou fen* mung bean noodles in chili sauce, cannot be missed.

Diners take tickets to the open kitchen counter, where their bowls are assembled on the spot. The textured noodles are ladled into a bowl, and the chef moves down a line of sauces and condiments, ladling the ideal amount of each into the bowl with masterful ease. The thick and chewy handmade noodles are the perfect canvas for the sauce, a balanced elixir of red hot chili oil, sesame seeds, ground Sichuan peppercorns, soy sauce, vinegar, and sugar. Served cold, the noodles make a refreshing afternoon snack on Chengdu's humid summer days. **JG**

Yu's Family Kitchen | The culinary laboratory of master chef Yu Bo

Location Chengdu **Signature dish** "Paint brushes with ink" | ❺❺❺❺

> *"I don't trade past experiences for new ones; I create new experiences with traditional ones."*

Yu Bo, chef and founder of Yu's Family Kitchen

⬆ Yu Bo's quirky dish of edible brushes and sesame ink.

Down a narrow alley in Chengdu, the capital of China's Sichuan province, an unmarked wooden door opens to reveal one of China's most revered restaurants. Yu's Family Kitchen has just six private rooms that are available for only one seating per night. Despite tremendous success over the years, the restaurant has not expanded.

Chef Yu Bo and his wife have operated the restaurant since 2006, when it was the first restaurant on Kuanzhai Lane. The place is a labor of love, from the miniature garden in the courtyard to the porcelain plates he designed himself. The chef celebrates the foundations of Sichuan cuisine in his cooking with technique and depth of flavor, but where he truly stands out is in the quality of his ingredients. Once a month, he and his wife will drive for hours out of Chengdu to handpick *huajiao* (Sichuan peppercorns), mushrooms, organic pork, bamboo, and artisanal soy sauce and vinegar.

Yu keeps his perspective fresh by traveling frequently to gather inspiration from abroad, keeping an eye on the trends and techniques of modernist cooking, and sometimes experimenting in his own kitchen. In his view, the humble Chinese tofu is just as much a feat of molecular gastronomy as anything that can be found in El Bulli's kitchen. His tasting menu might include a deceptive white gelée made of strained tomato juice. Another signature dish is an impressive, playful set of edible "paint brushes" that are made of a golden, flaky pastry, to be dipped in an "ink" of sesame paste.

Yu's Family Kitchen has the attention of Western media and international Michelin-starred chefs alike. It advances the perception of Sichuan food abroad and dispels the misunderstanding that the cuisine is only spicy, oily, and rich. Yu demonstrates that Sichuan food is harmonious and never flat, with an endless spectrum of flavor combinations. **JG**

Ming Ting | A top market restaurant that attracts diners like flies

Location Chengdu   **Signature dish** Pig's brain tofu | 💲

Cangyingguan (fly restaurants) are the essence of Chengdu cuisine. Centuries ago, street peddlers selling dumplings and snacks upgraded to tiny stalls with rickety stools and tables where people could devour afternoon snacks or morning tea. Such "hole-in-the-wall" food stalls exist in every neighborhood, and any passing local has a favorite fly restaurant he or she loves to frequent (and can recommend) for a good bowl of delicious no-nonsense food. Ming Ting is one of those.

Despite popular belief, the use of *"cangying"* (fly) does not refer to the restaurant's cleanliness or size. It is a nod to the residents of Chengdu, referring to how they can always follow their noses to find a good meal, no matter how hidden or unknown the restaurant. Flavor trumps all in the city.

One of the most famous fly restaurants in Chengdu, Ming Ting is located in the Cao Jia Alley outdoor market, near the town center. What started as just four tables has expanded and spilled out into the alley to accommodate droves of diners for lunch and dinner every day. People go to eat there as much for the lively atmosphere as for the innovative take on popular dishes.

A must-try is the house signature dish of pig's brain tofu, a twist on the much loved *mapo* tofu dish, which is made from bean curd and served with a spicy red sauce and pork. As an alternative to ground pork, crumbly chunks of pig's brain are used to top the tofu, making for a surprisingly smooth texture and slight offal taste. Another dish not to miss is the lotus-leaf steamed pork belly that comes out glistening, perfectly cooked, and gently fragrant of its lotus-leaf wrapping.

Before you go, remember to take a peek into the restaurant's industrial-size kitchen, where an army of young Sichuan chefs works an impressive assembly line of woks with speed and precision. **JG**

"Hidden down an alley … , it is always packed, as locals flock to it for specialities like pig's brain tofu."

Time Out Beijing

⬆ *Mapo* tofu served with a spicy red sauce.

Franck | The soul of a French bistro in the heart of Shanghai

Location Shanghai **Signature dish** *Côte de boeuf* | ❸❸❸

Franck Pécol's eponymous restaurant has maintained its status as the premier French restaurant in Shanghai, and arguably Asia, since its founding in 2007. Hidden away in Ferguson Lane, a tastefully developed enclave populated by cafés and art galleries, the intimate bistro is casual and unpretentious—a welcome surprise, given its exalted reputation.

Franck's menu is short and seasonal, written daily in chalk on easel-mounted blackboards carried to tables by affable and knowledgeable waiters. Based on what the chef finds in the wet market that day, offerings change almost daily, but the classics are constant. Try the rustic yet refined beef tartare, mussels, or *côte de boeuf* served with a rich Béarnaise

---

"I told myself … just do it exactly the same way you would do it if you were opening in Paris."

Franck Pécol, chef and founder of Franck

---

sauce and golden fries. The *grande charcuterie*, an elegantly presented platter of foie gras, smoked ham, and *saucisson*, finds welcome companionship with the impressive wine cellar, a collection of more than 300 mostly biodynamic wines from artisan French vineyards, some of which are carried exclusively at Franck.

Pécol notably deviates from his commitment to French traditional cooking in his adoption of Chinese "family-style" dining, whereby dishes are meant to be a shared experience, so expect the portions to reflect this. Resoundingly, a meal at Franck delivers the authenticity of the bistro experience as a perfect marriage of food, good company, and laughter. **JG**

Old Jesse | A legendary Shanghai restaurant with character

Location Shanghai **Signature dish** Codfish head with roasted scallions | ❸❸❸

Dinner at the original, so-called "Old" Jesse restaurant, one of a few restaurants in Shanghai that has achieved legendary status, is more than just a meal—it is a rite of passage and a true experience of the city. The setting is somewhat cramped, the staff can be brusque on occasion, and the lines snaking out the door are never-ending. But that does not stop dedicated patrons, visiting celebrities, and camera-toting tourists from piling in every night of the week.

Despite its popularity, Jesse has maintained a relaxed atmosphere. Located on quiet, tree-lined Tianping Road, at the western edge of the French Concession, the old house creaks with history. Treacherously narrow stairs twist up to an atticlike second floor. The room is packed with tables, and the dining experience is one of communal festivity. Such is the camaraderie among diners there that it is not uncommon for groups to strike up conversations and compare each other's dishes enthusiastically.

A quick survey of the tables will confirm the popularity of Jesse's signature classics, including the famous *hong shao rou* red braised pork, glistening in its clay pot, plates of "drunken" river shrimp that are still alive, and soft tofu topped with creamy crab roe.

One of the best signature dishes—codfish head with roasted scallions—must be ordered by telephone at least a day in advance. However, it is worth planning ahead: the fish is impossibly tender and comes on a giant plate submerged in finely slivered scallions that have been roasted in oil to release their intense flavor. Other items off the menu change with the seasons; it is worth calling to ask what is available.

To end a meal with a Shanghainese dessert, opt for a plate of sweet and sticky jujubes (Chinese dates) stuffed with glutinous rice. **JG**

Mr. & Mrs. Bund | A modernist French institution
offering exquisite dishes on the Bund

Location Shanghai **Signature dish** Truffle French toast | ❸❸❸

Paul Pairet's modernist French eatery on the Bund has done much to put Shanghai on the world culinary map, being recognized as one of the top ten restaurants in Asia and among the top one hundred in the world. Born in France, Pairet lived and cooked at a young age in Hong Kong, Sydney, and Jakarta before honing his skills under Alain Ducasse in Paris, developing a new French style.

Ultraviolet, his other restaurant in Shanghai, features a tightly controlled, fully immersive dining experience, but Mr. & Mrs. Bund is about "consensual cuisine" that caters to diners and their every whim. The foundation is French food, served family style, but the diner is encouraged to choose a theme and expand on it. For example, a craving for turbot can suggest turbot essential, turbot Béarnaise, or turbot truffle new Meunière.

By introducing menu items and potential sides and condiments as proposals, Pairet allows the diner to lead through the choices he or she makes—perhaps the signature truffle French toast, a piece of bread infused with a truffle mix before being toasted and topped with confit truffle slices and a nut-butter foam. Innovative Enomatic wine dispensers offer thirty-two bottles by the glass, allowing hyper precision in flavor pairings.

The casual, family-style approach extends to the service, with the denim-clad servers socializing with an eclectic group of diners, including Shanghai's glitterati, the jet-set crowd, gourmands, and oenophiles, creating a glamorous yet casual atmosphere that is hard to find on the Bund.

Open five nights a week until 4 A.M., Mr. & Mrs. Bund has become one of the few places to indulge in fine dining late into the night. Since opening in 2009, it has never looked back. **JG**

"Creative French dishes on a bewilderingly long menu, and the people-watching is top-notch."

Time Out Shanghai

⬆ Pairet's intensely flavored truffle French toast.

Mercato | Farm-chic Northern Italian fare by
Jean-Georges Vongerichten

Location Shanghai **Signature dish** Lobster ravioli | $$$$

"We try to be as artisanal as we can be [and] as sustainable as we can be."

Jean-Georges Vongerichten, chef and founder

⤒ Mercato's design plays on industrial materials.

French-born New Yorker Jean-Georges Vongerichten is no stranger to global success, having built a culinary empire that encompasses thirty-six restaurants in twenty-one cities. He has garnered three Michelin stars and his eponymous Manhattan outpost is one of the few restaurants in the city to earn a coveted four stars from *The New York Times*. His introduction to Shanghai was in 2004 with a signature outpost of Jean-Georges in the iconic Three On The Bund, followed by its more casual sibling, Nougatine, and then Mercato, his first foray into coastal Italian cuisine.

Taking over the entire sixth floor of Three On The Bund, the restaurant is spacious yet intimate. The space was designed by Neri&Hu, an award-winning architectural firm based in Shanghai that decided to draw on the chef's vision of creating an upscale yet rustic atmosphere, as well as the rich history of the Bund, from when it was an industrial hub. Stripping back to the building's structural elements revealed its steel columns. They are complemented with reclaimed wood and warm leather hues, creating an organic yet modern atmosphere.

Upon entering, one is greeted by a lounge-and-bar space surrounding an industrial-size Italian wood-burning oven. The menu reflects Vongerichten's signature style, balancing a seasonally inspired menu with dynamic texture and flavors, sourcing only the finest producers and freshest ingredients available. The lobster ravioli is a simple yet elegant dish, a fresh and lightly blanched lobster brined with herbs and drizzled in olive oil. Not to be missed are the signature pizzas, made with dough that is 70 percent hydrated and left to rise twice, creating a perfectly charred, light, airy texture. The wild mushroom, fresh ricotta, Fontina, and hen egg pizza—served while the yolk is still runny—is a highlight. **JG**

Fu 1088 | Refined Shanghainese in a stately mansion

Location Shanghai　**Signature dish** Egg-white custard with hairy crab　| 🅢🅢🅢

Fu 1088 is a must for visitors looking to experience the stately luxury and leisure of Shanghai's establishment. The menu at Fu 1088 is timeless, combining a core of traditional and perfectly executed Shanghainese offerings with a touch of the global sensibilities of its patrons. The dining experience is presented in tastefully furnished 1930s private dining rooms. There is no communal dining area at Fu 1088. Dinner is an elaborate affair, best enjoyed in good company.

Fu 1088 is tucked away from the bustle of the Bund in a quiet corner of the French Concession. Where other Shanghainese food institutions skew toward ostentation, Fu 1088 provides a perfectly measured experience of old-Shanghai opulence. Housed in a Spanish-style mansion, diners are greeted with gentle music from a grand piano, warm wood interiors, and decor evocative of a bygone time.

A classic restaurant must be measured against the canon of classic dishes, and, in this respect, Fu 1088 may be the most classic of all. Head chef Tony Lu's faithful interpretation of *hong shao rou* (red-braised pork belly) is a must for any visitor. Presented with bamboo shoots in an earthenware pot, Lu's pork belly is satisfying in a way that defies even the most ambitious imagination. The globally inspired offerings are novel but reserved. Consider the sake-poached goose liver or cocoa pork ribs. In September or October, make sure to try Fu 1088's seasonal egg-custard with hairy crab.

"Fu," meaning "fortune," is a prefix shared by several establishments in the city under the same ownership, such as Fu 1039, but the setting and offerings of Fu 1088 are without comparison. There is a mandatory minimum spend per customer but, given the intimate dining experience and iconic reputation of Fu 1088, that is reasonable. **JG**

Lin Long Fang | Sample some of Shanghai's best dumplings

Location Shanghai　**Signature dish** Crabmeat and roe *xiaolongbao* soup dumplings　| 🅢

Perhaps the dish Shanghai is most famous for, other than its *hong shao rou* red-cooked pork, is *xiaolongbao*, a soup dumpling that is hard to pronounce but easy to devour. The dumplings have various fillings, but the most popular variety consists of juicy pork and scalding hot soup wrapped in a thin, almost translucent, dumpling skin. Other fillings are minced crabmeat and roe or shrimp with egg. Dipped in black vinegar and topped with a few slivers of sliced ginger, the explosion of flavor is not easily forgotten.

One of the most long-standing but least well-known *xiaolongbao* restaurants, Lin Long Fang, is located south of the Xintiandi district, on a street corner at Jianguo Road. Behind a modest storefront, it

---

"The 1920s dark wooden accents allowed us to pretend we were in Old Shanghai for a bit."

shanghaiist.com

---

is frequented mostly by locals. Because of its location, it is rarely visited by the tourists that flock to its famed sister restaurant, Jia Jia Tang Bao. But aside from its name and color scheme, Lin Long Fang is identical; some might even say it is better.

All of the *xiaolongbao*s are wrapped and steamed to order, and customers can watch as the assembly line of cooks prepare them. The dining room is basic, with a few small tables and a number of backless stools. This place was designed to have customers feasting in less than 30 minutes. But, somehow, despite the plain decor, the atmosphere is not devoid of charm. It may have to do with the friendly staff, or simply the consistently delicious *xiaolongbao*. **JG**

Ultraviolet | The world's first multi-sensory dining experience

Location Shanghai **Signature dish** "Truffle burned soup bread" | ❺❺❺❺❺

"Paul Pairet, if anything, is trying to reverse-engineer a Proustian experience for you in real time."

blackinkmagazine.com

⬆ The superbly equipped kitchen at Ultraviolet reinforces the impression of culinary dedication.

➡ The ten-seat dining room is surrounded by screens.

Ultraviolet, called "the project of my life" by founder Paul Pairet, is almost famous enough to require no introduction. It is the world's first restaurant ever to attempt uniting food with multi-sensory technologies to create a "fully immersive" experience. In its making, the project required 30 tons of steel, 56 Sennheiser speakers, 7 projectors, 10 screens, 4,500 pieces of tableware, and one of the most advanced kitchens in the industry, featuring a custom-made, heavy-duty stainless steel Molteni stove—all for a cool $2.5 million (£1.6 million).

Expectations are high when a person steps into the ultraviolet-lit altar of Paul Pairet. If someone's name is on the list for one of the ten coveted seats at Ultraviolet, he or she has probably been waiting three months; that is how far in advance the restaurant is usually booked. The visit is likely celebrating a special occasion for which the expense is immaterial.

First, an e-mail directs one to rendezvous at Mr. & Mrs. Bund, Pairet's other modern French eatery on the Bund, at 6.30 P.M., to be shuttled to "a secret location." Once aboard, one sips on a glass of pear cider and sizes up the dinner companions for the evening, a group of immaculately dressed strangers. Down in a parking garage, the doors open, lights flash, the dramatic overture of *Also sprach Zarathustra* fills the room, and one starts to get an idea of the night ahead.

The journey that follows is absorbing, at times psychedelic, often parodic and playful. For an oyster course, one is transported to the seaside, surrounded by the sound of waves crashing and the smells of the ocean. Pairet's signature "truffle burned soup bread," consumed in a mystical forest surrounded by the smell of damp moss, is transcendent.

Often diners feel that nothing could possibly make the dish better—an affirmation of Pairet's ethos that "a dish is ready when there is nothing left to add or take away." **JG**

Whampoa Club | Intriguing new interpretations of traditional dishes

Location Shanghai **Signature dish** Smoked old-fashioned Shanghainese pomfret | ❸❸❸❸

"This nouveau Shanghainese joint has a 'wow' interior, replete with gilded chairs and a ... chandelier."

Lonely Planet

⤒ The spectacular interior of the restaurant features red lacquer and gilded wall decorations.

Named for the river that separates old and new Shanghai, the Whampoa Club aptly has culinary and atmospheric sensibilities that lie somewhere between the 1930s decadence of the Bund and the modern flair of Pudong. Situated in a traditional courtyard near the historical financial district, and with its mixture of art deco furniture, red lacquer, and colored glass, the Whampoa Club is somehow a bricolage of all the contradictions that make up Shanghai.

An institution in the city since it opened in 2004, the Whampoa Club was created by celebrity chef Jereme Leung. The varied influences of its design are recapitulated in the food. The current iteration of the kitchen, helmed by executive chef Hsu Mou Ki, is best described as "haute Chinese classical" with a contemporary twist. The menu is squarely Shanghainese traditional, although influenced by greater China in general and Hong Kong in particular.

Any visit to the Whampoa Club must include a sampling of Shanghainese smoked pomfret. The fish is served in crisp, bite-sized pieces that are, as with most eastern Chinese cuisine, more sweet than savory in preparation. Be sure to sample the delicious, if royally priced, hairy crab soup dumplings and glutinous rice cake with osmanthus.

Family-style dining, with large portions for groups to share, is the norm throughout China, and the Whampoa Club is no exception, so come in a large group (although there is an à la carte "Old Shanghai" *dim sum* brunch on weekends).

The Whampoa Club is perhaps distinguished from rivals most of all by its knowledgeable tea sommelier, who will help guests to navigate the menu of more than fifty premium Chinese teas. And for the complete Whampoa Club dining experience, waiters will advise customers on how to balance the elemental qualities of their food and drink in terms of hot, cold, dry, and wet. **JG**

28 HuBin Road | Ingredient-driven cooking on Hangzhou's West Lake

Location Hangzhou   **Signature dish** Dongpo pork | ❺❺❺

Hangzhou lies in the middle of the Lower Yangtze region, about 125 miles (200 km) southwest of Shanghai. Renowned for its West Lake, tea gardens, and history as a bastion of cultivated Chinese life, Hangzhou is now one of the largest and most prosperous cities in China. The surrounding region, colloquially known as "the land of fish and rice," has evolved a somewhat Spartan cuisine that refrains from many of the ingredients—oil, salt, seasoning, starch—that are used in other regions across China. Hangzhou's cuisine may not command the international reputation of Szechuan or Canton, but, within China, it is famous for its delicacy and healthiness.

A sterling example of Hangzhou's regional cuisine is found at the restaurant named 28 HuBin Road; the restaurant is located on the ground floor of the city's Hyatt Regency hotel and is named for the hotel's mail address. The restaurant's decor mixes Chinese traditionalism with modern global luxury.

Diners should take the opportunity to begin their meals with a tea ceremony. Hangzhou's famous Longjing tea may be paired with the appetizer platter, whose highlights include foie gras-stuffed quail egg with seasonal vegetables and enoki mushrooms. Chef Shen Liexing has a number of specialties, but make a point of ordering the Dongpo pork.

At 28 HuBin Road, the braised pork belly used for this classic is sliced impossibly thin and wrapped into a perfect pyramid. The dish is hearty, and strikes a fine balance between unctuous fat and subtle sweetness. "Beggar's chicken" is the other standout dish: a whole chicken is wrapped in layers of lotus leaf and cooked in a clay pot. Shen's masterful take on this Jiangsu classic is perfectly tender, and moderately flavored with rice wine, anise, and sesame. Round off the meal with a slow stroll around Hangzhou's beautiful West Lake. **JG**

"Many materials are from the West Lake, like vinegar fish and lotus root powder: very natural and healthy."

hangzhoutravel.org

⬆ The delicate soup dumplings at 28 HuBin Road are a fine example of regional Hangzhou cuisine.

Dragon Well Manor |

Organic cuisine in verdant tea fields

Location Hangzhou   **Signature dish** Young chicken with chestnuts | ❸❸❸

In a country where the provenance of food is so often a matter of faith rather than certainty, Dai Jianjun, owner and exacting proprietor of the Dragon Well Manor, has created a culinary sanctuary where food is local, meticulously sourced, and free of any of the industrial hazards attending modern Chinese life.

Dragon Well Manor is located in Hangzhou, described by Marco Polo as the most beautiful city on Earth. Like many regions of China, Hangzhou boasts its own culinary heritage. Dai Jianjun, already an accomplished restaurateur, decided in the early 2000s to create a space where Hangzhou's prominent residents could enjoy the finest offerings of the region. The restaurant, which is better described as a

---

"[My grandmother] instilled in me … that cooking was about ben wei, the essential tastes of things."

Dai Jianjun, founder of Dragon Well Manor

"gastro tea garden," has eight private dining rooms connected by stone walkways. The service team of more than one hundred is helmed by Dong Jinmu, the most accomplished chef in Hangzhou.

Meals are seasonal and dining is by set menu. The menu itself is determined ad hoc by the per-head spend of the dining group. Even at the minimum spend, diners can expect a ten-course experience, sourced entirely from local farms and foragers. Regardless of the season, do not miss the hand-ground soy milk or locally produced rice wine. Seasonal highlights include old-duck soup, young chicken with chestnut, and simple fineries such as baby pea shoots. **JG**

Lin Heung Teahouse |

Shabby but nostalgic dim sum parlor

Location Hong Kong   **Signature dish** Chinese sausage rolls | ❸

At this dim sum house, opened in 1928, all echelons of Hong Kong society may be found on stools at circular dining tables set over two floors. White-haired gentlemen rustle newspapers in favored corners earned by years of patronage, while newer generations of foodie thrill seekers pepper themselves around the rooms. Routine and tradition take precedence, and newcomers are initiated into the scrum, so think fast and enjoy the experience. Do not expect anything more than a cursorily pointed finger from the waiters—many of them old-timers themselves—as that is the most they will do to find seats for customers during the busy dim sum service from morning through to afternoon.

Seasoned diners seek out the best vantage points from which to observe the fresh batches of dim sum being rolled out on steel carts from the steamy kitchen. Inside, the carts are hardy bamboo baskets cradling both delicate and robust treats, many from a forgotten era. Tea—that vital fuel and palate cleanser between rich mouthfuls—is served in traditional lidded cups, or ordinary pots, a small nod to how the restaurant is dealing with changing times. The restaurant is cacophonous, a mix of the siren call of dim sum trolley waitresses and familial chatter. Bouncy, meaty *siu mai* dumplings are topped with triangles of pork liver, increasingly shunned by the metropolitan set but treasures to nostalgic dim sum hunters. Do not miss the fluffy steamed buns encasing preserved Chinese sausage imbued in rosé wine, another 1950s classic nearly extinct.

The beauty of Lin Heung is how it preserves a part of Hong Kong without resorting to superficialities, and, for that reason, it has become an indispensable part of the city's life for anyone hoping to either experience or recapture a flavor of the past. **CM**

Above & Beyond | Chic Cantonese grounded in tradition and elevated with innovation

Location Hong Kong **Signature dish** Sweet and sour pork with pineapple | ❸❸❸

The elevated dining room, which soars high above the waves and concrete, gives the Above & Beyond restaurant its name as much as its exceptional cuisine that transcends tradition. A Jenga block of perfectly caramelized pineapple, enveloped by the tender crunch of Iberian pork, is an encapsulation of fine Chinese food by design, created by chef Joseph Tse and his staff.

A parade of flawless Cantonese classics is available as hors d'oeuvre while admiring the magnificent Victoria Harbour vista. Perhaps intensely savory almond and pig-lung soup, just as grandma would have made it, or a steaming bamboo basket of sticky glutinous rice with grains pregnant with the essence of fresh oceanic crab. Take a moment to breathe in the surroundings housed in the uber-stylish Hotel Icon, which has blossomed under the blueprints of an international set of designers and architects. The setting is as much part of the experience as the food. The look of Above & Beyond was conceived by English designer Sir Terence Conran. It shows in the glossy lines, clever lighting, and occasional bright pops of color.

Classically trained Cantonese chef Tse is forthright in his cooking philosophy, adhering fiercely to the mantra of food as nourishment as well as luxury, whimsy, and an experience. His flavors are some of the cleanest in a city hell-bent on dramatic fusions or overt displays of opulence, and the use of froufrou ingredients such as black truffle or morels are incorporated seamlessly rather than dumped into the mix to add some zeros to the bill.

When a chef can create fireworks with the humble folds of silky bean-curd skin and verdant local vegetables, there is little doubt as to the quality of the rest of his menu. **CM**

"… to come for the views alone would be a pity, as the food is delicate, creative, and delicious."

Guardian

⬆ Sir Terence Conran helped to create a sophisticated modern feel at Above & Beyond.

The Chairman | Dine in luxury and champion flavorsome
and eco-friendly Cantonese cuisine

Location Hong Kong   **Signature dish** Steamed flower crab with Shaoxing wine and chicken oil | 🆂🆂🆂

"The restaurant celebrates a return to authentic Cantonese fare. Using only fresh, top-quality ingredients ..."

fodors.com

⤓ Crab is one of the many kinds of seafood served.

In a quiet cul-de-sac set among the quickly gentrifying Sheung Wan neighborhood, on the western end of Hong Kong island, a simple food revolution is taking place in the kitchens of a modest two-story building. The Chairman, a defiant name bringing with it conflicting emotions, is the work of a group of people in love with the natural bounty of the land and sea—something that is often forgotten in a city obsessed with luxury foreign imports and international celebrity chefs. Their manifesto is as stark as the surroundings, an almost ascetic setting of rice-white tablecloths and simple arrangements of modern art, blue glass panes, and retro patterned chairs.

The poultry and pigs used are raised in the Hong Kong suburbs, freshly slaughtered before their delivery to the heart of the city; local fishermen provide splashes of seafood; and vital condiments such as soy sauce and chicken oil are either sourced from trusted generations of old-school purveyors or made in-house. The team has gone as far as establishing its own farm in Sheung Shui, in the northern district of Hong Kong's New Territories, where organic vegetables grow, pickles are made, and meats cured and preserved

Taking control of the food used in the kitchen is no easy feat. The Chairman is commendable for a locavore philosophy that is more meaningful than hair shirt, and all the more delicious for it. This is no better exemplified than in the signature dish of lightly steamed flower crab resting in a viscous shimmer of aged Shaoxing rice wine and fragrant chicken oil, a powerful medley of ingredients, each standing out with its pronounced flavors, yet coexisting in a harmonious masterpiece of a plate. Simple, elegant, and ridiculously edible. **CM**

Kwan Kee | A favorite haunt of locals famed for its perfect rice

Location Hong Kong   **Signature dish** Clay pot rice | $

Quite often, the usual courtesies are not observed in the most traditional, well-worn, and much-loved institutions on Hong Kong's dining circuit. That is not to mean that the experience at Kwan Kee is left to the masochistic, but one should always be prepared to be in it for the long haul, starting with the usual lengthy wait for a table and the limited time for dawdling over menus or the bill.

It is an experience, certainly, and going armed with a cheat sheet of the restaurant's best hits—the eponymous clay pot rices, say, or the wok-fired seafood—will ensure a customer will be catapulted straight to the matronly owner's good side. The reason for this is that the clay pot dishes are all made to order, and since staff take no shortcuts with this most classic of winter-warmers—fanning the vessels slowly over a charcoal-fired flame, often a dozen at a time—it is no surprise that each table is peppered with the frantic questions of staff even before guests' seats have been warmed properly. A minimum of 20 minutes is required to cook each rice pot to perfection. It is a tricky feat, combining the elements of fire and water to adequately fluff up the grains of rice and create the all-important golden-brown crust at the bottom—the holy grail of clay pot rice alchemy.

The kitchen works wonders with fire, as evidenced in platefuls of smoky stir-fried emerald stalks of *gai lan* (Chinese broccoli), or—the fisherman's favorite—sea salty local clams cloaked in velvety black bean sauce. The clack of competing chopsticks and the scrape of steel spoons against weathered clay, mixing with the raucous conversation filling the tightly packed room, creates an experience uniquely Hong Kong and uniquely Kwan Kee. Visit often, go hungry, and try to make a reservation to avoid standing in line. **CM**

Kung Wo Soybean Factory | A totem to tofu

Location Hong Kong   **Signature dish** Silky bean curd dessert | $

A snapshot of a time where garish mosaic tiles, brash red lettering, and lazy ceiling fans were still in vogue, the Kung Wo Soybean Factory is a time capsule housing some of the best tofu products in Hong Kong's Sham Shui Po District. Open since 1893, Kung Wo is as much a part of the local culinary landscape as it is a part of the neighborhood's collective memories. Hidden behind market stalls on bustling Pei Ho Street—a rambunctious stretch of Kowloon known for its hawkers and knickknacks—this modest shop is synonymous with quality.

Out front, weathered workers cater briskly to the take-away crowd, who rubberneck each other, trying to get an eyeful of the best products on show. Piles of

> *"…[this is] definitely worth a visit if you love food made from soya bean!"*
>
> jaznotabi.wordpress.com

damp wooden palettes are stacked with wobbling pieces of freshly pressed tofu, ready to be included in the daily housewife grocery shop, and fierce tangles of snowy bean sprouts; flanking the walls are shelves filled with jars of fermented bean-curd cubes and bottles of freshly milled soybean milk. It is ramshackle, yes, but draw up a squat wooden stool and take in the scene while feasting on ethereally light tofu puffs filled with minced fish paste that is diligently fried to order, or a bowl full of smooth silken bean curd, glossy with a light sugar syrup—sprinkle over the salted duck yolk-yellow sugar for an extra hit of caramel. Fresh and bracing, with real bean flavor, truly the proof is in the pudding. **CM**

Kau Kee | A specialist in
beef brisket and noodles

Location Hong Kong   **Signature dish** Beef brisket
noodles | ❺

The "kau" in Kau Kee name refers to beef, and it is
bowlfuls of slow-cooked brisket and sprightly noodles
in a soul-soothing broth that have helped the
restaurant earn its place in the collective memory of
locals and travelers alike.

The setup at Kau Kee is like others of its kind in
Hong Kong: round tables and round stools, a cash
register out front with an impatient custodian, and
waiters in slightly grubby white button-downs
standing with their dog-eared notepads to scribble
out orders. Refreshingly, all strata of society dine here,
united by the knowledge that it offers some of the
best brisket in the city. The restaurant is in a
surprisingly central location on Gough Street, and it is

---

*"… the meat—served with
noodles in a beefy broth—
is definitely hard to beat."*

Lonely Planet

---

not unusual to spy pencil-skirted office ladies perched
alongside scruffier teens and business suits standing
among a sea of laborers. In the back corridor is
the kitchen, where the vast, bubbling vats of stock
simmer, along with tin pans holding the slabs of
cooked brisket and tendon.

Do not expect to eat at a leisurely pace. The
turnover is quick. Equally, do not expect anything
akin to pot roast or salt beef; in the Cantonese
style, the meat is braised slowly for hours in a herbal
broth until chopstick tender. While the herb-based
broth is the classic option for purists, the rich curried
beef brisket is of equal caliber, the mildly spiced sauce
cloaking each piece of melting brisket wonderfully. **CM**

Shun Kee Typhoon Shelter
Seafood on a small wooden boat

Location Hong Kong   **Signature dish** Stir-fried
crab | ❺❺

Relatively safe behind the breakwaters of one of Hong
Kong's many typhoon shelters, there is evidence of an
unusual restaurant renaissance—that of the wooden
boat diner, a relic of the mid-twentieth century.
Although the sea has defined much of the history and
legacy of city, and the culture of typhoon-shelter
restaurants is unique in its style, boat restaurants have
been battered by the tides of fashion and pragmatism.
By the 1990s, they had all but disappeared from the
harbor, but, in 2012, one particular descendant of
the boat-dwelling community decided to revive the
forgotten trade.

Shun Kee Typhoon Shelter is chef Leung Hoi's
tribute to his roots, and has gained a sizeable
following through word of mouth. A large
"mothership" kitchen vessel houses several wok
stations, at which a brigade of nimble-wristed chefs
toss fresh, sweet clams in an inky mix of black beans,
chili, garlic, and rice wine over a high heat; they also
gently boil saltwater shrimp until just pink, ready to be
peeled and dipped into a rudimentary mixture of soy
sauce, chili, and sesame oil. Diners sit at tables, each
mounted on its own small wooden boat, and are
rowed out to be docked with the kitchen vessel.
Seasoned waitresses hop effortlessly between the
boats with platefuls of steaming-hot seafood.

The food is a tasting menu of Hong Kong's best
marine fare, punctuated by fishermen's favorites
such as pig offal and roasted duck soup noodles.
But the star of the show will always be the hulking
platter of stir-fried crabs, lost under a dramatic and
fiery flurry of garlic, chili, and drapes of fresh green
scallions. With the gentle bob of the ocean beneath
one's feet, and the salty breeze mingling with the
arresting aroma of wok-fired seafood, there are few
places as intriguing as this. **CM**

Kimberley Chinese Restaurant | Cantonese classics
served with theatrical flair in a Kowloon hotel

Location Hong Kong **Signature dish** Roasted stuffed suckling pig | 💲💲

The visceral pleasure of tearing into a whole pig on a spit is taken to a higher level at the Kimberley Chinese Restaurant, the namesake kitchen on the mezzanine floor of The Kimberley Hotel in Kowloon. While the place is quiet on many evenings, the staff are experienced enough to brace themselves for the chorus of awe that reverberates across the cream-clothed tabletops, wood paneling, and tiled columns when the restaurant's signature dish is rolled out in all its porcine glory on a silver trolley topped by a well-used wooden chopping board.

The famed suckling pig, wrapped tightly around a rib-sticking log of glutinous rice speckled through with caramelized scallions, is roasted to order over charcoal flame until its skin becomes burnished and brittle, to crackle enticingly under the skilled knife work of the plastic-gloved waiters, who carve up the piglet nonchalantly using a sharp, heavy cleaver. There is an element of showmanship at this otherwise understated establishment, a place that has largely gone unnoticed among its more flashy, contemporary neighbors. In a tribute to the French *garçon* and his flourish of a silver cloche, waiters lift heavy lids from large, clay pots at the table to reveal sizzling, fragrant dishes such as salted chicken, its skin golden and crisp, or a steaming milky broth of the sweetest white turnips paired with silky, slow-braised pieces of oxtail.

There is an elegance and purity to the food at the Kimberley that can only be attributed to a kitchen dedicated to mastering the art of Cantonese cuisine and presenting it in a way that does not veer into the modernist trap. Equally, service harks from a simpler, friendlier era, where genuine and matronly advice wins out over a didactic approach. For Hong Kong cooking, few places keep tradition as alive as the Kimberley. **CM**

"Who can resist a copper-toned piglet stuffed with glutinous rice, rolled up into a … cylinder?"

e-tingfood.com

⬆ Whole roast suckling pig is a culinary tour de force at the Kimberley.

Yosokkoong | Eat like an aristocrat in a tranquil, historic setting

Location Gyeongju   **Signature dish** A course of noble cuisine | ❸❸❸

The town of Gyeongju, littered with ancient tombs and resplendent temples, is known as the "museum without walls." Itself a treasure of the town, the Yosokkoong restaurant stands on a site of a seventh-century palace of the Silla dynasty. The restaurant is named for princess Yosok, who once lived there.

The current structure is better known for its association with the noble Choi family, who settled here some four hundred years ago. Despite their riches, they came to be known for their charitable ideal of *noblesse oblige*. When Korea was subjected to Japanese imperialism, they harbored resistance fighters in their ample home. Today, Yosokkoong is found beside the old family seat, and it is the Choi family's cooking that gets people talking. Meals are based around the traditional, multi-plate *hanjeonsik* style favored by their ancestors, and the recipes they use have been passed from generation to generation.

The restaurant is more than two hundred years old, and its traditional features are still there—heavy wood, sliding screen doors, and plenty of pine trees on the grounds. Customers are ushered into one of the peaceful private dining rooms that run around a central courtyard. Servers are dressed in *hanbok*, a colorful costume, and the seating arrangements are also time-honored, with low tables and floor cushions.

The roll call of dishes appears to be never-ending. From *kimchee* (fermented vegetables) to *pajeon* (green onion pancake), *japchae* (stir-fried glass noodles), *galbijim* (beef rib soup), and *doengjang* (rice and bean-paste soup), the complex meal will leave even the biggest appetites sated. There is no better way to take in this area's historical heritage than to enjoy one of Yosokkoong's refined menus. **CP**

⬆ **The dining rooms face the central courtyard.**

Todam Sundubu | Traditional, handmade tofu served in a former barn

Location Gangneung   **Signature dish** *Sundubu jeongol* (spicy soft tofu stew) | $

In Chodang, a neighborhood so famous for its watery bean curd that it is known as "Soft Tofu Village," Todam Sundubu exemplifies everything that is good about this humble, artisanal product. Away from the busy tofu-making area of the main road, it has neither a fancy setting nor an elaborate menu, but the tofu that chef Su-Dong Gwak makes here is unparalleled.

Each day at 5.30 A.M., he starts the painstaking process of grinding, cooking, and straining soybeans before setting the milk naturally with purified seawater from the nearby East Sea. The resultant tofu is soft yet firm, and unbeatably light and creamy. His much sought-after *sundubu jeongol* (spicy soft tofu stew) is served in a wide earthenware bowl brimming with soft curds, simmered in their whey and mixed with Gwak's signature vibrantly red chili sauce. A generous handful of his excellent *kimchee*—vegetables fermented in giant earthenware pots at the entrance of the restaurant—adds an extra layer of complexity to the dish. One potful of the stew makes an ample meal for two. Other accompaniments might include sticky rice, spiced potato, seaweed, slow-cooked beef, and a few pickled vegetables. A plate of *mo dubu* (firm tofu) is no less enjoyable a treat, served simply with a soy sauce and scallion dipping sauce. More elaborate set meals (*baekban*) are also available.

Housed in a former barn, the rustic restaurant itself could not be more unassuming. Where the animals stalls would once have been, there are now heavy wooden tables—on one side of the room set traditionally with floor cushions and no shoes allowed, and on the other with benches. Behind Todam Sundubu's rustic simplicity lies real artistry in tofu-making and hospitality. **CP**

⬆ Todam Sundubu is famous for its exquisite bean curd.

Jung Sik Dang | Test bed restaurant of a chef at the cutting edge of the Seoul food scene

Location Seoul   **Signature dish** *Bibimbap* (sea-urchin spicy mixed rice) | 𝕊𝕊𝕊𝕊

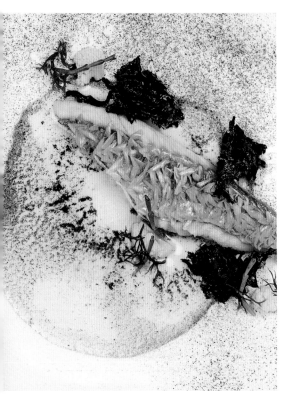

"The restaurant [offers] new items that break away from the stereotypes of Korean cooking."

visitkorea.or.kr

⬆ Innovative and cutting-edge Korean cuisine, aesthetically presented, at Jung Sik Dang.

When chef Jung Sik Yim opened the doors of Jung Sik Dang in 2009, he kick-started a trend for neo-Korean cuisine in Seoul. A fusion of traditional Eastern flavors with Western cooking techniques (including molecular ones), his food was a revelation.

Yim's tasting menus are filled with impressively sculptural plates of food. Each is meticulously constructed to bring out both the aesthetic and gastronomic values of its ingredients. The "design menu" is built around the notion of mixing and matching dishes to create your own bespoke five-course meal. For less choosy diners, there is also a tasting menu of six pre-picked signature dishes.

One fixture on the regularly changing menu is sea-urchin *bibimbap*. Laced with seaweed puree, toasted millet, and shredded fermented vegetables, then topped with urchin roe, this modern reworking of a classic dish packs a *umami* punch. Other highlights might include a salad resembling a miniature forest, its chive stalks and chervil leaves standing to attention like edible trees around a cluster of raw tuna slices and quails' eggs, or, for dessert, a chocolate and chestnut puree shaped like tiny *jangdokdae* or Korean fermenting pots—a clever nod to tradition—in a bed of chocolate soil. A meal ends with playful petit fours (cigarette butt-shaped meringues, anyone?) and a range of herbal teas.

Service is taken no less seriously than the food, and is polite, efficient, and faultlessly attentive. Yim trained at the Culinary Institute of America and worked in New York, and just two years after he opened Jung Sik Dang, Yim decided to take on the Big Apple with his second restaurant, Jungsik in Tribeca; by 2013, this had gained its second Michelin star.

But it all began with Jung Sik Dang in Seoul, and there is still nowhere better to experience new-wave Korean cuisine in all its innovative glory. **CP**

Byeokje Galbi | The best
beef barbecue to be found in Korea

Location Seoul   **Signature dish** *Saeng galbi* | ❸❸❸

There may be thousands of places offering barbecued beef in South Korea, but it would be hard to find one better that Byeokje Galbi. What makes it so special is the skill and knowledge of the team of chefs, many of whom have been working here for years. There is also the quality of every ingredient that goes into the dishes. Finally, it is the meat, and Byeokje Galbi's story really starts with its high-grade Korean beef.

Back in the 1980s, the restaurant's founder, Young-Hwang Kim, found himself thinking that Korean Hanwoo stock was every bit as good as Japanese Kobe, or any other premium breed for that matter. In 1986, he set out to prove it by opening this award-winning barbecue restaurant.

From farm to grill, the restaurant oversees every step of the process that its prize herd of organically fed Hanwoo cattle goes through. On a farm in Pocheon, to the north of Seoul, the animals are matured for up to thirty months before being expertly slaughtered and butchered. Once the beef, appropriately aged, arrives at the restaurant, the chefs use their experience to judge the exact moment when the meat will be at its best for the barbecue.

The result? Perfectly fat-marbled meat with exceptional flavor. The *deungsim* (sirloin) is so tender it melts in the mouth. The *saeng galbi* (rib) offers just the right amount of resistance as you chew, and it is scored with a latticelike pattern to ensure that it is evenly infused with smoke from the charcoal grill. The president of South Korea himself places orders for beef from Byeokje Galbi's herd.

Kim applies the same exacting standards to the other dishes on the menu, too, and these should not be overlooked, especially *Pyeongyang naengmyeon,* the chilled buckwheat noodle soup. Kim has a lot to be proud of at Byeokje. A meal here is more than just a memorable experience—it is a marvel. **CP**

Balwoo Gongyang | A rare
peek into ritualized temple cuisine

Location Seoul   **Signature dish** *Yeonip-bap* | ❸❸

Located across the road from the famous Jogyesa Temple in Insadong, Balwoo Gongyang takes its name from the meditative and ritualistic meal of Buddhist monks, and the set of four polished wooden bowls that are used. The restaurant is overseen by Venerable Dae Ahn, a monk herself, who is renowned for her promotion of temple cuisine. Here, the process of preparing food is also meditative, and no ingredient goes to waste, although it is still served in abundance.

Pretty pink and gray cubes of tofu, infused with chrysanthemum and black bean, arrive adorned with salt-pickled herbs. A rustic bowl of chewy, battered, spicy mushroom and capsicum chunks is scattered with nutritious pumpkin and sunflower seeds. Myriad other artful yet humble dishes follow. A meal might

---

"We take vegetables … picked from the mountains and prepare them with sincerity."

Venerable Dae Ahn, head of Balwoo Gongyang

---

include *yeonip-bap,* sticky rice with ginkgo, jujube, and black sesame seeds, wrapped in a wild lotus leaf. The accompanying soup is made with handmade bean paste from Geumsu Temple in the northeast. Using only natural produce, the kitchen staff strive to bring the best out of every ingredient—eloquently demonstrated by a platter of dainty wild vegetables and temple *kimchee*, made without garlic or onion.

The restaurant has a Zen-like quality, with patrons talking in hushed voices as they sit in the cleanly designed, modern space. Those lucky enough to get one of the more traditional private dining rooms are blessed with a view of the Jogyesa Temple as they feed body and soul with each delicate tidbit. **CP**

Ojang-dong Hamheung Naengmyeon | Regional North
Korean cuisine unraveled in a Seoul noodle bar

Location Seoul   **Signature dish** *Hoe naengmyeon* (chilled sweet-potato noodles with marinated stingray) |

"People did not cut the noodle in the past because lengthy noodles symbolized longevity."

english.seoul.go.kr

⬆ The restaurant is noted for its chilled sweet potato noodles, served in large metal bowls.

Like so many North Koreans, Seong-Hoon Mun's family took refuge in South Korea in the wake of the Korean War, bringing with them the food of home. Thanks to Mun's pioneering mother and others from Hamheung Province (to the northeast of Pyongyang), the Ojang-dong neighborhood of Seoul became the destination for Hamheung-style chilled sweet potato noodles (*naengmyeon*). These days the street on which the restaurant is located is so famous for the dish that it has been dubbed "Naengmyeon Alley."

Set up in 1955, Ojang-dong Hamheung Naengmyeon started with only a handful of chairs; but now it spans two floors that can accommodate 108 people—a testament to the quality of the cooking here. Each of the two long dining rooms in the restaurant is furnished with functional rows of battered blond tables. They are regularly packed with appreciative diners seated on the red floor cushions and happily slurping on the restaurant's specialty.

Served in large metal bowls, the springy, chilled, sweet potato noodles are served in three ways: topped with spicy marinated raw stingray (*hoe naengmyeon*); mixed with a delicious spicy sauce (*bibim naengmyeon*); or served in a refreshing beef broth (*mul naengmyeon*). The latter two are topped with slices of beef, shredded cucumber, and half a boiled egg. Each is served with a pot of consommé-like, clear beef broth infused with medicinal angelica root, to be sipped as you enjoy your noodles.

In Korea, there is a saying that good hands create good dishes, and Mun's mother, who started the restaurant, is said to have had excellent hands. Though she may no longer be in the kitchen, she trained the current chef, who has worked here for more than forty years, and he continues her impressive legacy. Those chilled, sweet-potato noodles are a delicacy that should not be missed. **CP**

Myeongdong Kyoja | A venerable handmade noodle establishment a cut above its rivals

Location Seoul **Signature dish** *Kalguksu* (wheat noodles in broth with dumplings) | $

The motto of this no-nonsense noodle joint in the affluent Myeongdong area of Seoul is that "sincerity is more important than science when making good food." The pared-down menu and simple decor make that message loud and clear.

Since 1966, Myeongdong Kyoja's impeccable *kalguksu* (hand-cut wheat noodles in chicken broth) have spawned many imitations. The restaurant's reputation stretches far beyond the Korean capital and it is not uncommon to see a line of expectant diners snaking out of the door of the two-floored restaurant. But it is worth the wait. People wax lyrical about the deep, *umami*-rich, and luxuriously thick chicken broth used to make the *kalguksu*, and how the soft, thick noodles become infused with meaty richness. The dish is completed with *byeonsi mandu* (subtly smoky pork dumpling triangles), mushroom slices, stir-fried ground beef, and garlic chives. Each ingredient is carefully sourced from within the South Korean peninsula to ensure the best of home-grown flavor. Still hungry? Top-ups of broth and noodles are free, as are bowls of sticky rice.

The other big draw is the steamed dumplings (*mandu*), which are stuffed with ground pork, garlic chives, and sesame oil, then crimped into pretty spherical parcels with a delicate, translucent wrapper. Be sure to accompany them with a few mouthfuls of the signature fiery *kimchee* (fermented vegetables) laced with plenty of pungent garlic.

As you might expect, the decor is functional: battered brown tables and chairs, white and beige walls. The service is swift and authoritative, and the waitresses have no problem corraling the hungry hoards into available seating, or letting them know if they are heading for the wrong place. Myeongdong Kyoja may be cheap, but it far from just any old noodle restaurant. It set the benchmark for *kalguksu*. **CP**

"A laughably small folding screen is placed between single diners [sitting] across from each other."

travel.cnn.com

⊡ Myeongdong Kyoja has become famous for its trademark *kalguksu* dish.

Samcheonggak |
Mountainside oasis with stories to tell

Location Seoul **Signature dish** *Sinseollo* | ❸❸❸

Set on picturesque, pine-covered Mt. Bugak, Samcheonggak ("Three Purity Palace") was built in 1972 by President Chung-Hee Park, not far from the Blue House, his own residence. For years, it was a place for high-ranking officials to be entertained. Today, the complex has become a public arts center showcasing folk performances, crafts, and Korean cuisine.

The large, pavilionlike main building has been transformed into a public performance hall where diners can enjoy traditional music and dance over a well-presented set meal. There is also a smart, traditional restaurant where wooden and paper screens are juxtaposed with glass and metal.

The food here fuses elements of old and new with a range of contemporary and classic tableware and

---

"One no longer needs to be a high-profile dignitary to enjoy the once-rarified atmosphere …"

english.seoul.go.kr

---

plating styles. A multi-dish set meal may include the likes of colorful pumpkin porridge; tangy water *kimchee*; slices of juicy marinated beef with earthy pine mushroom; and *sinseollo* (here with seafood), a classic royal court cuisine dish served in a kind of bundt pan, a metal hot pot with a coal-filled central funnel that keeps the food hot during the meal.

A post-meal trip to Samcheonggak's teahouse affords striking views of the fortress wall around the Blue House and the surrounding lush, wooded mountains. To truly savor this slice of Korean heritage, take a stroll around the artfully manicured gardens and imagine the negotiations of North and South Korean politicians that formerly took place here. **CP**

Gwangjang Market |
After-work hangout with street snacks

Location Seoul **Signature dish** *Nokdu bindaetteok* | ❸

This vibrant Seoul market may not be a restaurant as such, but it is a serious food destination. By day, locals come to the market, as to any other, to purchase fabric, secondhand clothes, and food ingredients. By night, one end of the market transforms into Seoul's largest food alley, with more than two hundred food carts, plus other more permanent stalls.

Snacking in the street is at the very core of Korean culture, and every evening hoards of hungry Seoulites of all ages congregate here. Perched on rickety stools around counters crammed with the market's delicacies, customers find it the perfect place to put the world to rights, eating with a bunch of friends in an atmosphere of lively bustle.

Top of the list of must-try dishes is *nokdu bindaetteok,* a thick, mung bean pancake the size of a dinner plate. There is no shortage of stalls selling it, but you can easily tell which are the most popular by the length of the lines—people will wait for more than thirty minutes to get their hands on the very best. Waiting in line leaves plenty of time to watch the red-apron-protected stallholders at work—grinding the beans, mixing the batter, and frying the crisp-edged disks on giant skillets swimming in oil; this is no dish for the calorie counters. Then it is time to find a seat and enjoy the spoils, dipped into the accompanying onion and soy-based sauce. Wash it down with a bottle of *magkeoli* rice wine (the classic accompaniment to any kind of *bindaetteok*), or *soju,* the fiery Korean distilled spirit.

Other popular eats range from *kimbap* (rice and seaweed) rolls) stuffed with *kimchee* and other vegetables, and barley *bibimbap*. Brave souls might try *jokbal* (simmered pig's trotter) and *sundae* (sausages stuffed with pig's blood and glass noodles). No visit to Seoul would be complete without an evening's stop-off at Seoul's oldest covered market. **CP**

Si Hwa Dam | Fine-dining restaurant combining the three noble arts of poetry, painting, and conversation

Location Seoul   **Signature dish** "The Sweet Potato Farm" (sweet potato rice cakes buried in crispy rice "soil") | ❸❸❸❸

In a bygone era of Korean history, the wealthy would pass the time together composing poetry, painting, and conversing. That lifestyle was the inspiration of fine-dining restaurant Si Hwa Dam, which takes its name from the three noble pursuits.

More than just an eating establishment, Si Hwa Dam is also a work of art. On the museumlike first floor it is astonishing to see ancient pottery from the Silla dynasty (57 BCE to 935 CE) displayed alongside contemporary pieces. On the upper levels are antique medicine chests, rows of china (the canvasses for the chefs' creations), and pristine open kitchens.

At Si Hwa Dam, no one has to eat with the masses, because groups are ushered into their own private dining rooms. Each room is named after a famous modern painter—Picasso or Matisse, perhaps—or inscribed with a line of poetry that sets out the ideals it embodies. A Si Hwa Dam meal is a journey of colors, flavors, and stories. Details of each of the eleven or so dishes are projected onto the wall to ensure that each diner understands its philosophy and provenance. In an approach that ensures the highest quality, everything prepared here is brought in fresh for each booking, and only from the finest suppliers.

In the fall, the menu might include the likes of delicate, sweet porridge made from handpicked chestnuts from Gangwondo Province, served with nectarlike chestnut tea. Next to arrive are morsels of fruit and shrimp, in a pine nut and mustard sauce designed to echo Matisse's color palette; and to follow, beef and pork meatballs stuffed with rice cakes and served over hot stones, along with the finest *songsunju* (aromatic pine liqueur). In a nod to tradition, the savory food concludes with rice, *doengjang* (fermented soybean paste soup), and a collection of twelve side dishes. For eating art on a plate in the lap of luxury, there is no better place in Seoul. **CP**

"You will be lulled by the beautiful sonata of Korean strings played by a gayageum performer."

magazine.seoulselection.com

⤒ Aristocratic aesthetics are celebrated at Si Hwa Dam.

Sandang | Culinary creativity and tranquility come together
at this food lovers' countryside retreat

Location Yangpyeong **Signature dish** "Crabs courting under a citron moon" | 🉐🉐🉐

Chef Jiho Im has garnered much recognition over the years for his distinctive use of natural and foraged ingredients and playful presentation. Despite a TV series in South Korea, and participation in numerous international food events, Im does not court fame. Instead, his focus is on food that is "medicine, science, and art." For more than forty years, he has been working by these criteria to create dishes that nurture both "body and soul." Sandang (Korean for "mountain village") is a perfect escape for Seoulites searching for a little peace in reach of the capital.

Start with a stroll around the grounds to admire the earthenware crocks of fermenting condiments, then head to the high-ceilinged dining room to sit on floor cushions by large windows that look onto the picturesque grounds. Each table is discreetly partitioned for an intimate experience.

The tasting menus on offer take you on a meandering journey through contemporary and classic Korean cooking. Pretty as a picture is a regal plate of *gujeolpan*: vibrant green pancakes framed by nine delicate mounds of ingredients with which to stuff them—orange pumpkin shreds, earthy burdock strips, dark morsels of cloud ear fungus, and more. Other showy dishes include mini deep-fried "crabs courting under a citron moon," and chestnuts served flaming in their prickly shells (the nuts are plucked from the tree at the entrance to the restaurant).

To conclude, Im produces *doenjang* (fermented soybean paste) soup, rice with ginkgo nuts, and a range of eight or so side dishes, including the popular soy sauce-marinated raw crab. Then you can go up to the airy second floor where, surrounded by artworks and views of the lush, surrounding landscape, you can pass the time with coffee and fresh fruit. A meal at Sandang is a veritable feast for all the senses. **CP**

"When I look at customers, I can feel what they will like for their meal."

Jiho Im, chef at Sandang

⬆ Bright green *gujeolpan* pancakes are served with a variety of fillings that you can add yourself.

Seoil Farm | An idyllic showcase of the best of Korean farm produce

Location Anseong **Signature dish** *Doenjang-jjigae* (soybean paste stew) | 💲

Fermented pickles and sauces are at the very heart of Korean cuisine, and Bun-Rye Seo, the owner of Seoil Farm, is a fierce champion and master of these quintessential ingredients. Set up almost thirty years ago in Anseong, to the south of Seoul, Seoil Farm is much more than just a restaurant. It is an organic farm and artisan producer of some of the finest Korean condiments you are likely to come across. From field to fork, almost everything served in the restaurant is grown, processed, and prepared on the farm. Even the water for the savory *ganjang* (Korean soy sauce) is drawn from a well on site.

For Seo, fermentation started as a hobby, but it has since become a passion and an obsession. Despite her expertise, she still feels that she has more to learn about the art of making traditional condiments. She is now passing on her skills to her daughter, who has worked by her side for the last fifteen years.

The menu in the serene restaurant is designed to show off the farm's produce and consists of just four items. Only simple, subtly flavored vegetables are used in the *doenjang-jjigae* (soybean paste stew) to allow the ten-year old paste's complex earthy flavor to sing. The lighter *cheonggukjang-jjigae* (quick-fermented soybean paste stew) is packed with firm tofu and rustic chunks of soybean. Both are accompanied by myriad delicate side dishes created from organic vegetables, herbs, nuts, and fruits. Effervescent with the flavors, Seo's *kimchee* (fermented vegetables) is also exceptional.

No visit to Seoil Farm would be complete without a tour of its sculpted lawns, majestic pine trees, and, of course, the army of *jangdokdae* (stout ceramic pots) filled with Seoil Farm's precious pastes and sauces. There is no better place to explore Korea's rich culinary tradition of fermentation. **CP**

Gogung | Superior food at the birthplace of the Joseon dynasty

Location Jeonju **Signature dish** *Bibimbap* (Jeonju spicy mixed rice) | 💲

Although Gogung only opened in Jeonju in 1996, the chef at this award-winning spot, Byung Hak Park, has more than fifty years of experience working with *bibimbap*, one of Korea's most iconic dishes. He claims that the secret of the spicy mixed rice combination is the quality of his home-fermented *gochujang* (chili paste); redolent with spicy, sweet, sour, and savory notes, it adds an extra dimension.

Bibimbap is said to be based on food from the royal court of the Joseon dynasty. Echoing the royal style, Jeonju *bibimbap* is served in a warmed, brass-colored bowl. There may be dozens of rainbowlike toppings, including dark brown bracken stalks; crunchy, green-rimmed cucumber disks; bitter, yellow

---

"The restaurant is decorated with the traditional, handmade paper for which Jeonju is famous."

visitkorea.or.kr

---

ginkgo nuts; chili-flecked radish strands; cooling mung bean jelly; sweet dates; bitter walnuts, savory ground beef, topped by an amber-yolked raw egg.

As well as the classic Jeonju variety, *dolsot bibimbap* (served in a heated stone bowl to create a crunchy layer of rice at the bottom) and *yuk hwe bibimbap* (with shredded raw beef) are also on offer.

To accompany the *bibimbap,* there is local mung bean sprout soup and eight or so side dishes. These may include the likes of potato slivers in pine nut sauce, simmered eggplant, mini *jeon* pancakes, and the ever-present *kimchee*—all free, of course. Without doubt, Gogung is the place to go to enjoy the full story of Korea's most popular mixed rice dish. **CP**

Dongnae Halmae Pajeon | Benchmark seafood pancake house

Location Busan **Signature dish** *Dongnae pajeon* (scallion and seafood pancake) | 💲

The Dongnae area was once a bustling market district with many sellers of *pajeon* (savory scallion and seafood pancakes). Every Dongnae *pajeon* maker would have his or her own distinctive recipe, balancing different quantities of rice and wheat flour for the batter that encases the scallions, seafood, and beef.

The recipe at Dongnae Halmae Pajeon has been passed down for four generations. While in other areas the savory pancake is fried to a crisp finish, here it is finished under a lid, which gives a softer, wetter result. You have to try it and see which you prefer.

Displayed on golden-hued metal plates, the thick, decorative pancakes are striped with green lines of sweet, local scallions. Each mouthful is packed with

---

"In the old days ... people solely visited the Dongnae market to eat Dongnae pajeon."

dynamic.busan.go.kr

---

shreds of beef and plump pieces of the freshest seafood (clams, mussels, oysters, and shrimp) plucked from the nearby coastline. There is no better accompaniment than a cup of the excellent local *dongdongju* (milk-colored rice wine).

Located at the current spot for more than forty years, the dining room at Dongnae Halmae Pajeon blends old and new. Cream walls are framed by dark beams and tables are made of chunky wood. On one side, a large window looks out onto lush greenery; on another, the *pajeon* makers are at work in the open kitchen. The current owner gracefully glides around the dining room in *hanbok* (traditional costume) while her efficient staff deliver the dishes. **CP**

Seok Da Won | Seafood taken from the seabed by female divers

Location Gujwa-eup, Jeju Island **Signature dish** *Jeonbok juk* (abalone rice porridge) | 💲

Kyung Jeo Choi, like generations of women before her, upholds the Jeju Island tradition of *haenyeo* (female seafood divers). Without the aid of an air tank, these brave women dive for a minute to a minute and a half at a time, scouring the seabed for abalone, turban shell, octopus, and more. Choi started while in elementary school and has been in this grueling profession for more than fifty years now.

Operating from street carts, shacks on beaches with only a tarpaulin sheet to cover them, or full-blown restaurants, many of the divers prepare and offer seafood to customers along the island's coastline. Choi herself started with a simple stall, but around eleven years ago, when a good road was laid along the black, volcanic stretch near Hado Beach where she dives, she set up a permanent restaurant.

Outside of the rustic, one-story building, a tank is filled with the day's catch. Inside, the wooden planks of the walls are dotted with appreciative notes from former customers and proud posters of Choi at work. At one end, a shamanistic talisman woven from straw alludes to the dangers of Choi's job (each year, the women perform ceremonies for a safe and abundant harvest). At the other end, Choi and her team prepare a selection of simple dishes in a basic kitchen.

The most famous dish prepared by the *haenyeo* is a savory rice porridge flecked with meaty slices of *jeonbok juk* (abalone); Choi's version is exceptional— soothingly savory and bursting with the rich, meaty flavor of the highly prized shellfish. It is accompanied by *kimchee*, made from home-grown vegetables and aged for six months. Also available are deep bowls of *kalguksu* (wheat noodles and mussels in broth) and sashimi. It does not get much better than this. **CP**

⬆ *Haenyeo* savory rice porridge with abalone and egg.

Okasei | Colorful plates of raw fish in a friendly seaside town

Location Onagawa   **Signature dish** *Onagawa-don* | ❺❺

In the wake of the tragic earthquake in the Tohoku region during March 2011, restaurants such as Okasei in the seaside town of Onagawa have come to be seen as symbols of hope. While the effects of the quake are still felt in much of Tohoku, the owners of this little restaurant worked hard to get back to business as soon as possible. For many affected by the tsunami, a trip to Okasei is a chance to remember what everyday life was like before the disaster. To see Okasei's bustling dining room and eat its seafood dishes makes them feel happy. People from all over Japan go there to show their solidarity with the inhabitants of Tohoku. Consequently, a trip to this friendly seafood spot is a way to show support for the people of Tohoku.

"We don't want to live where we can't see our boats … the sea hasn't changed"

Chikako Kimura, *Boston Review*

The area has always had a strong reputation for seafood, and, in terms of food, it is still the main draw. However, since the nuclear accidents caused by the earthquake and tsunami, all produce is checked meticulously to ensure it is free from contamination.

Okasei's menu features only what the local fishing fleet catches, and there are plenty of specialties on offer, including *Onagawa-don*. Topped with ten or more varieties of seasonal, raw fish, the *Onagawa-don* generous rice bowls are a veritable cornucopia from the sea. Another delicacy is the crab soup, which makes the palate sing. Of course, in a place with such good seafood, staff can prepare a colorful plate of sushi from the finest firm-fleshed fish. **AI**

Sekizawa | Enjoy rustic noodles in a peaceful country village

Location Nagano   **Signature dish** Soba noodle | ❺❺

There are various Michelin-starred soba noodle restaurants in Japan. But it is worth trying the more humble version of the noodles, too, and Sekizawa in the tiny village of Obuse in Nagano Prefecture is just the place to do so.

There are no real tourist attractions in Obuse. It is just a peaceful village in the Japanese countryside with rustic charm and generous inhabitants. "Peaceful'" and "generous" are also the perfect words to describe Sekizawa and its noodles. Both are thoroughly unpretentious. While some soba noodle specialists can be a little arrogant, with pushy chefs behind the counter telling clients how to eat their noodles, Sekizawa is quite the opposite and staff will never tell a guest what to do. Traditionally, soba noodles should be sucked up with an appreciative slurping noise, but no one at Sekizawa will bat an eyelid here if someone does not do so.

In the Nagano area, the delicate, cold noodles are made from buckwheat, and are generally eaten with a soy and vinegar dipping sauce. But there is a point of etiquette to be aware of if eating in overzealous noodle spots: do not immerse the noodles in the sauce for too long. However, Sekizawa's noodles have a bolder flavor, while its sauce is milder, so it is possible to disregard the rules.

Obuse is known for its organic vegetables, and staff serve plenty of them at Sekizawa. Rather than present them in rustic dishes, the staff transform the produce into a succession of sophisticated and attractive offerings to rival any smart restaurant. Sake fans are also in for a treat because they can order set menus at bargain prices to accompany a glass or two.

The perfect end to any feast at Sekizawa is the "Nakajo-peach" pudding, which is made with buckwheat, nectarines, and sake. **AI**

Turukou | Exquisite seafood gets high-class treatment at this traditional restaurant

Location Kanazawa   **Signature dish** Seafood *kaiseki*-style | ❺❺❺❺❺

Kanazawa city in Ishikawa Prefecture is nicknamed "Little Kyoto." Much of the city's scenery is traditional Japanese and, at first glance, it does appear similar to Kyoto. The two places share a lot of cultural similarities, too, including the food—both exclusive cuisine and more typical daily fare. Turukou's *kaiseki* cuisine is on a par with the great chefs of Kyoto's traditional fine-dining *ryotei* and *kappo* restaurants. However, when it comes to preparing fish, Kanazawa has a big advantage over Kyoto, and that is its geographic location. Like Kyoto, Kanazawa is surrounded by mountains, but it faces the Sea of Japan, which is one of the richest fishing grounds in the world. The Kanazawa fishing port is worthy of special mention, as is the city's fish market.

Turukou's menu offers magnificent seafood with all the elegance of Kyoto-style multi-course *kaiseki* cuisine. But Kyoto does not offer sashimi plates like the ones at Turukou, with eight to ten different pieces of fish on one plate. The fish is so fresh it shimmers like jewels in a crown. Kanazawa is the promised land for shrimp lovers, too. From *ama ebi* (sweet shrimp) to *botan ebi* (jumbo shrimp), or *shima ebi* (striped shrimp), the varieties are endless; and many of them only live on the Japanese coast of the Sea of Japan. Eating seasonal shrimp in Turukou is unforgettable. The staff know how to prepare this delicate seafood better than anyone else.

The style of Turukou's cuisine is traditional *kaga*, named after Kanazawa's historical name. A mixture of Edo-style (as Tokyo was once called) and Kyoto-style, *kaga* is a medley of rare and luxurious ingredients, all presented in sophisticated ways. In the past, Kanazawa was the gateway to China for trade, and a touch of Chinese influence is felt in local dishes. Turukou is at the crossroads for the two cuisines, which makes it all the more unusual and exciting. **Al**

"Ingredients from the area of Kaga must be used. Both in the broth or in dishes with rice."

Yasuo Kawada, chef

⊡ The *omakase* dinner at Turukou is a tasting of the freshest fish the chef has to offer.

Chanko Kawasaki | Eat like a sumo wrestler with a hearty *chanko* hot pot

Location Tokyo **Signature dish** *Soppe* (chunky chicken and soy sauce stew) | $$$

Sadly, samurai warriors no longer walk the streets of Japan. Like dinosaurs, they are an extinct species. However, spotting sumo wrestlers is much easier. Just go to Ryogoku in Tokyo, which is regarded as the heartland of sumo. Ever since the Ryogoku Kokugikan stadium for sumo was completed in 1909, several sumo training stables have been based in the area.

In Ryogoku, there are numerous *chanko* restaurants because *chanko* is the signature dish of the sumo wrestler. *Chanko* is a variety of *nabemono* or hot pot. Most *nabemono* take the form of stews and soups, which are served during the colder seasons and frequently cooked at the table in earthenware pots. Diners pick out the cooked ingredients they want from the pot, which can then be eaten with a dipping sauce.

Sumo wrestlers eat *chanko* as part of their weight-gain diet. They need to make their bodies extremely big, while maintaining their health. It may sound challenging, but *chanko* eaten in large quantities does the job. Rich in protein and packed with a mix of chicken, tofu, fish, noodles, and vegetables, diners who are not aiming to bulk up can still enjoy a bowl of the chunky chicken broth stew on a visit to Ryogoku.

Some of the restaurants are even run by former sumo wrestlers. Of all the *chanko* spots in the area, Chanko Kawasaki is most well known. It is also the oldest and was founded by a former sumo wrestler in 1937. An example of traditional *shitamachi* architecture, it looks like a samurai's house, decorated in an old-fashioned, Japanese style with tatami mat flooring and sliding panel doors. Stepping into the restaurant is like traveling back in time. Kawasaki's most famous *chankonabe* is *soppe*, made with a soy-sauce-based broth and filled with chicken chunks. The flavor is mild and cleansing. In fact, it is so good that it is easy to eat a bit too much—no wonder it is so popular with sumo wrestlers. **AI**

"For aficionados, though, there is only one place that truly matters: Kawasaki."

The Japan Times

[↑] *Chanko* pots include a multitude of ingredients.

Keika Ramen | Grab a steaming bowl of Japanese comfort food

Location Tokyo **Signature dish** *Taro-men (Kumamoto-*style ramen soup noodles) | $

Japan may be packed with restaurants serving all sorts of upmarket cuisines, but sometimes the simplest things can be the best. Steaming bowls of meaty broth filled with bouncy ramen noodles and plenty of toppings are a case in point. These warming bowls of Japanese comfort food top both sushi and soba noodles for popularity when it comes to eating out in Japan. Although noodles originally arrived in Japan from China, Japanese ramen soup noodles and Chinese lamian noodles in broth could not be more different. It is like comparing canned and fresh spaghetti, but it is for the individual to decide which one he or she prefers.

Ramen lovers take their passion seriously, too. There are more than a hundred guides to restaurants specializing in the noodle dish on Japanese bookstore shelves, and connoisseurs have heated arguments over which one does the best bowl. For the fanatic, the Keika Ramen chain would not be the first choice, but the soup noodles there have a rustic charm and bags of flavor; they are seriously addictive.

The chain first debuted in Tokyo in 1955. The best branch to visit is in the eastern wing of sprawling Shinjuku railway station. For anyone familiar with the film *Blade Runner,* the location will make them feel like Harrison Ford eating noodles in a messy downtown bar, because it is hard not to think about that scene while slurping noodles there.

To order, try *taro-men*—al dente noodles in a dense white soup, with roughly chopped raw, green cabbage. It is finished with a topping of meltingly soft, stewed pork belly, which makes diners want to come back for more. Similar to the milky *tonkotsu* broth, which has become so popular in the United States and Britain, this version from Kumamoto Prefecture in Kyushu has a stronger flavor. Be sure to drink every last drop of soup in a bowl here, because it is just too good to leave. **AI**

"Over the years [Keika] has ... satisfied innumerable diners in need of a pork-noodle fix."

The Wall Street Journal

⬆ A bowlful of Keika's addictively tasty ramen.

Kondo | An exquisite tempura experience in an unassuming office block

Location Tokyo **Signature dish** Vegetable tempura | ❺❺❺❺

Tempura made from seafood and vegetables dipped in a light batter, then deep-fried until light and crisp, is one of Japan's best known dishes. It is so well known that along with Mount Fuji and geisha girls, it has become a symbol of Japan. However, tempura arrived in Japan from Portugal during the Edo period. Before then, deep-fried, battered seafood was not part of Japanese cuisine.

Tokyo is famed for its tempura restaurants, with Kondo the most prominent of them all, making it one of the best in Japan. A person only has to eat at Kondo once to agree that this restaurant with two Michelin stars really is magnificent. Its unprepossessing location in an office block should not deter anyone visiting, and on arrival at the ninth floor of the building, customers enter a different world. The stripped-down surroundings are elegant yet simple, all the better to showcase the drama of the tempura. Diners perch at a long bar watching in anticipation as it is deftly prepared and skillfully fried before their eyes, and then placed on their plate to be savored.

Usually, the specialty of a traditional tempura restaurant is seafood—perhaps shrimp, squid, or conger eel. They are on offer at Kondo and cooked exquisitely. However, it is the seasonal vegetables that are especially worth sampling at Kondo, because they are heavenly and arranged in pleasingly original ways. The sweet potato and carrot tempura are famous. It is impossible to know the hidden depths of flavor contained in a carrot until a person samples one at Kondo. Despite the fact that this dish is deep fried, Kondo's tempura is gloriously crisp and ethereal. It is full of flavor and presence, yet impressively light. As chef-patron Fumio Kondo said: "Tempura is the best way to bring out the flavor of the raw ingredients."

Kendo is a food-lovers' shrine where dishes are prepared with considerable skill, and it should be visited for a revelatory tempura experience. **AI**

> *"At Kondo, tempura ...*
> *[delivers] the pure flavors*
> *of the finest ingredients."*

chow.com

⬆ Kondo is one of Tokyo's most famous tempura restaurants and was awarded two Michelin stars.

Midori Zushi | Superb sushi at remarkably reasonable prices

Location Tokyo   **Signature dish** Various sushi | 🅢🅢

Exclusive sushi restaurants can be hard to get into in Japan, but it is a shame to compromise by only eating budget sushi. To experience high-quality sushi, head to the flagship restaurant of the Midori Zushi chain at Umegaoka Honkan. Once a week, on Mondays from 11AM to 9PM, there is a sushi buffet, offering top-quality sushi at remarkably reasonable prices. The buffet is offered on the classic all-you-can-eat principle, with the only constraint being that diners should stick to a 90-minute time limit for their meals, which is ample time to enjoy a feast there. The service for the buffet is the same as in a restaurant, with customers free to order whatever they like individually, even the most expensive sushi creations.

Sushi's construction is made from two elements: the fish part and the rice part. In lower grade, budget sushi restaurants the trick of the trade is to slice the fish very thinly, bulking up the cheaper rice part of the dish. At Midori Zushi, however, the fish element of the sushi is bigger and thicker than the rice part. This is sushi as it should be: a luxurious dish to be enjoyed. There is no cheating—the excellent value sushi buffet retains the restaurant's usual high standards. There is a wide range of sushi from which to choose, including *anago* (conger eel), tuna, salmon, scallop, abalone, shrimp, sardine, cuttlefish, and sea urchin. Expect the rice to be cooked and seasoned perfectly.

Midori Zushi does not take reservations for the buffet and, given the quality of the food and reasonable pricing, it is best to go prepared to get in line. Despite a wait of possibly an hour, both locals and tourists who have been to Midori Zushi report that their patience was rewarded. However, if standing in line and time constraints do not appeal, then avoid the busy buffet by visiting Midori Zushi as a restaurant. Sushi is not the only good thing on offer here; it has a menu of cooked Japanese fish dishes, too. **Al**

"… they use a whole eel for one piece of anago sushi—you will never leave Midori Zushi hungry."

tokyofoodcast.com

⤒ Generously filled sushi is a hallmark of Midori Zushi

Kizushi | Sensational sushi prepared by a master

Location Tokyo   **Signature dish** Sushi | ❸❸❸❸

Sushi must be the most well-known food of Japanese origin. It is now available in countries around the world in take-outs, supermarkets, and restaurants. At first glance, it seems so simple—chopped fresh fish on vinegar-flavored rice. But, sushi is far from simple. Great sushi masters are like craftsmen with golden fingers, and hugely respected in Japanese society.

One such noted master is Ryuichi Yui of Kizushi. The third-generation proprietor and head chef, Yui is venerated by lovers of fine sushi. Sushi is such a talent of his that if he was compared to an actor, it could only be the lead in a Royal Shakespeare Company production of *King Lear* with rave reviews.

The best seats in Kizushi are the three simple stools near the front door. From there, it is possible to sit and watch how Yui, a handsome, slim, old man, makes sushi. His skillful handling of a sharp knife, the eloquent finger technique he uses to shape and create pellets of *nigirizushi* (fish-topped rice), and the drama of his gestures stir onlookers. The sense of anticipation mounts, a pleasurable preamble to what is to come. Then, when someone puts Yui's sushi into his or her mouth, after four or five chews, he or she is amazed. After eating Yui's sushi, no one continues to have any illusions that sushi is a simple food.

Friendly and down to earth, Yui reads his customers' moods and tastes perfectly. He is able to serve them exactly what they want—and what they need. It is best to just tell him: *"Omakase."* The phrase signifies "I'll leave it to you." And to do so means that a guest will experience an impressive meal under his guidance. Before starting on the sushi *omakase*, it is worth sampling a few starters, too. The stewed conger eel and Isobe razor clams are particularly good. It is impossible to see sushi, or seafood, in the same light again once you have tried these tasty creations. **AI**

⊤ Taste sublime sashimi and sushi at Kizushi.

Komuro | Culinary wizardry from a master of *kaiseki* cuisine

Location Tokyo **Signature dish** *Kaiseki* | ❸❸❸❸❸

Two Michelin-starred restaurant Komuro is tiny but pleasant. It has counter seating for eight people and a small private room for four guests—this style of restaurant is called *kappo*. Most *kappo* restaurants are relatively cheap but Komuro's cuisine is not standard *kappo*. Instead, it is closer to the Japanese haute-cuisine style of *kaiseki*. Komuro has one of the most acclaimed *kaiseki* chefs in Tokyo, Mitsuhiro Komuro.

Artistic and intricate *kaiseki* cuisine is the quintessence of Japanese restaurant food. Similar to a Western tasting menu, or degustation menu, there is no pre-set menu at Komuro. Instead, the chef will serve the finest produce he finds in the market. Tokyo is the capital city, and its food scene is rich and multifarious. Locals spend more money on eating out than New Yorkers or Parisians, and there are plenty of high-quality restaurants. However, *kaiseki* is more traditionally associated with Kyoto, and many Japanese people travel to Kyoto just to eat *kaiseki*.

So, Komuro's restaurant makes for a nice surprise. It may be difficult to get a reservation because of the diminutive size of the restaurant, but it is definitely worth it.

Kaiseki cuisine is undoubtedly a very personal style of cooking. The chef's talent and sensibilities are, perhaps, the most important factors. Mr. Komuro is very much a character, with a strong personality, and eating his food is a memorable experience. At a glance, some of the elements of the meal look deceptively simple—just baked or boiled. It is only when one takes the first delicious bite that one realizes just how special the food is. A lot of work goes into each dish, but it seems effortless. Often, the very best Japanese food is impressive without being overstated. Thanks to the modest Mr. Komuro, this restaurant is simply magical. **AI**

⬆ Memorably good food offered at Komuro.

Isetan | Head to the department store's food hall for a bento box

Location Tokyo **Signature dish** Bento box | $$

No Japanese department store would be complete without a basement food hall. Known as *depachika* (*depa* from department store and *chika* meaning basement), they are filled with concessions of food shops and restaurants from all over the world, picked carefully by the top buyers of each department store, who know how important their selections are. It is the *depachika* that lure customers into a store. They are a world apart from the food halls in a London or New York department store, and the Japanese love them.

Isetan has a reputation for having the best *depachika* in Japan in terms of both quality and quantity. The basement of the company's flagship store in Shinjuku is the best of all. It is a paradise for lovers of Japanese food, and it has more than 150 stalls offering many types of cuisine including Japanese, French, Chinese, and Indian. Isetan is aware of its status as an ambassador of foreign food culture, and no space is wasted in its food halls. When it comes to Japanese staples, a Japanese bento box makes a good choice to sample lots of dishes: a box has many compartments, each one filled with a different morsel. The version sold at Kamedo Masumoto is like a jeweled casket filled with attractive ingredients, while Jiyugaoka Aen's boxes are also excellent. For a more homely taste, Kanda Shinoda Zushi is the place to go for an old-fashioned sushi bento with no raw fish.

For dessert, it is possible to buy cakes from the world's best chocolatier, the multi-awarded French chocolate master Jean-Paul Hévin. To sample something more Japanese, try the pudding at Issui. Shinjuku is a hectic part of central Tokyo, but the Shinjuku Gyoen National Garden lies just ten minutes from Isetan. So, on a sunny day, shoppers might decide to enjoy their bento boxes in what is an oasis of tranquility among the city's skyscrapers. **AI**

[↑] Bento box—a lunchtime favorite at Isetan.

Obana | Succulent grilled eel at its very best

Location Tokyo   **Signature dish** *Unaju* | ❺❺❺❺

In the 1950s, eel was just a common river fish, eaten by ordinary people as a cheap source of protein. Similar to jellied eel in the U.K., it was thoroughly unpretentious. In the twenty-first century, it is seen as a smarter ingredient. *Kabayaki* has become the most common way of preparing *unagi* (freshwater eel) in Japan. The Japanese also believe eating eel has the same aphrodisiac effect as oysters or chocolate.

Kabayaki may have become common but the preparation is complicated. The fish is split down the middle, gutted, boned, butterflied, skewered, and dipped in a sweet soy sauce-based glaze before being grilled. The intricate preparation takes away any hint of the muddy river from which the eel came.

Such are the skills required to master the technique, it is said that an eel chef in Japan needs to do twice as long an apprenticeship as any other chef to qualify as a professional. The results, however, are worth the labor. Well-prepared *kabayaki* is not only delicious, it has a tantalizing aroma, too, because of having been grilled over charcoal. Obana in downtown Tokyo is an eel specialist, acclaimed for its *kabayaki*. The restaurant has a thoroughly traditional feel with tatami mat flooring and wood-paneled walls. The taste of the eel at Obana is truly excellent: unpretentious, sweet, rich, and savory.

The most popular item on the menu at Obana—and the one to make sure to order—is *unaju*. This dish consists of fillets *of kabayaki* on rice presented in a lacquered square box. The eel in *unaju* melts on the tongue like a fine terrine, and the texture of the delicately grilled eel is unlike that of any other fish. However, one *unaju* is not enough at Obana, and the more one eats, the more one will want. Other dishes on offer include *uzaku* (grilled eel in vinaigrette sauce) and *umaki* (grilled eel egg omelet). **AI**

⬆ *Unaju* is served in a shiny lacquered box.

Omiya Yogashiten | A slice of happiness in a Tokyo cake shop

Location Tokyo   **Signature dish** Strawberry shortcake | **$**

"There are many Japanese-style cakes, like strawberry shortcake, a symbol among cakes."

misojournal.blogspot.jp

⬆ Strawberry shortcake is popular in Japan.

The Omiya Yogashiten cake shop in Tokyo has more than a hundred years of history—and it does not just cover Japanese history either. In this one patisserie, visitors can see the history of Western cakes in Japan and how they have been adapted to become uniquely Japanese creations

Take, for example, the strawberry shortcake. The original British version is made with rich, buttery biscuits. But, in Japan, shortcake is a cream cake made with a soft, light, and slightly eggy sponge. Almost like a chiffon cake in texture, two sponges are sandwiched with whipped cream and strawberries, and then decorated with more cream and strawberries. Once completed, the strawberry shortcake is almost reminiscent of Cinderella's Castle at Disneyland. Such strawberry shortcakes are regular favorites among the Japanese for both their taste and beautiful aesthetic. From birthdays to weddings and even Christmas Eve, it is the cake that Japanese people love to eat. From the young to the old, it symbolizes happiness for all. Strawberry shortcake is sold in various shops, including French-style patisseries like Omiya Yogashiten, where that happiness will turn to ecstasy.

Omiya Yogashiten is like a holy shrine for cake-worshippers. Cakes of various colors and sizes fill the shop window tempting buyers inside. The shop's fourth-generation owner, Taro Yoshina, picks only the finest fruit for his creations. Each morning, he goes to the central wholesale market to pick the ripest, seasonal fruits that he can find, in order to give his cakes their distinctive flavors.

There is also a small café in Omiya Yogashiten, which serves tea, coffee, lovely old-fashioned sandwiches, savory breads, Russian soup, and a range of fantastic fruit juices. Cakes and drinks are served in a simple style on paper plates and in paper cups. But such modesty does not diminish the pleasure of eating a slice of "happiness" cake. **AI**

Sushizanmai Honten | A big fish for good value sushi in Japan

Location Tokyo   **Signature dish** *Maguro zanmai* (a selection of tuna sushi) | 🌑🌑

Conveyor-belt sushi is a worldwide phenomenon, and it is undoubtedly a fun experience. But a trip to Japan would not be complete without a visit to a proper sushi restaurant, even if on a tight budget. For anyone who wants to eat cheap and cheerful sushi, a trip to one of the 51 branches of the Sushizanmai restaurant chain is advisable. Each is open 24 hours a day—so they even satisfy late-night cravings. Even Lady Gaga is a fan of the chain, and it is easy to understand why after visiting an outlet.

The main branch is the Sushizanmai Honten in Tokyo. The fish is fresh, the staff are friendly, and there is plenty to choose from on the lengthy menu. It may not be the best sushi in Japan; but, for price, it is significantly better than anything found in a conveyor-belt sushi joint.

It is not only the excellent service, quality, and price that have led to Sushizanmai's fame in Japan. In January 2013, the restaurant chain also broke the world record for Bluefin tuna prices by spending ¥155.4 million (U.S.$1.76 million) on just one fish at the first tuna auction of the year at Tokyo's sprawling Tsukiji fish market. The fresh whole tuna weighed 489 pounds (222 kg) and was caught off northeast Japan. The transaction afforded the company a lot of media attention, and each year it prepares to up the bid if it means that it can secure the best fish of the season.

Sushizanmai buys quality tuna throughout the year. To try a decent assortment of tuna sushi, featuring all sorts of different cuts, order the *maguro zanmai*. The *tokusen hon-magurio don*—big rice bowls topped with sashimi fish slices—make a good choice, too. For decent sushi that will not break the bank, Sushizanmai is the place to go. The only slight problem is that, depending on the time of day, there may be a long line. Lunch times tend to be busy, and it is possible to wait an hour or so to get a table, so try to visit outside of peak hours. **AI**

"Sushizanmai has three restaurants in the area, of which the Honten main shop is the most atmospheric."

metropolis.co.jp

⬆ A tempting assortment of sushi.

Taimeiken | Enjoy Japan's take on British cuisine in a *yoshoku* restaurant

Location Tokyo   **Signature dish** *Omuraisu* (omelet rice) | $ $

"Established in 1931, this is a pioneering Western-style restaurant."

Time Out Tokyo

⤒ *Omuraisu* is a popular Japanese dish.

A distinctive strand in Japanese cuisine is *yoshoku*—the Western-influenced dishes dating back to the period in the late nineteenth century when Japan was absorbing information from the West eagerly. When it came to adopting Western cuisine, the Japanese government decided that Britain, rather than France or Italy, should be the major influence on *yoshoku* dishes. A typical example is curry, which in Japan was adapted from British rather than Indian versions. In modern times, Japanese curries almost equal sushi in popularity, striking a chord with many Japanese diners, and the odd expat Brit.

For a restaurant representing *yoshoku* cuisine, head to Taimeiken, a long-established locale with a loyal following. With white table cloths and dark wood features, the atmosphere and service evoke the experience of eating in a middle-class Victorian dining room. Make sure to try the beef curry. When it comes to choosing a side-dish, there are various retro options, such as the restaurant's much-loved cannned asparagus salad. The refreshing, mayonnaise-free "coleslaw" is also an excellent option.

The other famous dish is the *omuraisu*, which is one of the most popular dishes in every *yoshoku* restaurant. The dish's name comes from the combination of *om* (an abbreviation for omelet) and "rice." Usually, it consists of a tomato-flavored chicken or ham pilaf rice, wrapped in an omelet, then topped with ketchup.

But Taimeiken's style of *omuraisu* is different. Its version of the dish has a soft-cooked omelet, nestling on a bed of fried rice. Piercing the surface of the omelet to reveal its soft center is seriously satisfying and should not be missed on a visit to Taimeiken. The dish gained some international fame when it featured in the Japanese cult film *Tampopo* by Juzo Itami, where a tramp cooks Tampopo's son some *omuraisu*. **AI**

Aje | Impeccable barbecued beef in every form imaginable

Location Kyoto **Signature dish** *Hososhio* (grilled beef small intestine) | ❸❸❸

To enjoy quality beef at reasonable prices in Japan, grill restaurants where it is possible for guests to cook the meat themselves on tabletop barbecues are one of the best choices. Although this cuisine, called *yakiniku* in Japanese, has its roots in Korean cooking, it has become one of the most popular eating-out options, especially for Japanese youngsters. As Indian curries for the British, or Vietnamese food for the French, *yakiniku* is also a cuisine that has been adapted to local tastes.

The mecca for *yakiniku* is Tsuruhashi town in Osaka, which has the biggest Korean community in Japan. There are hundreds of *yakiniku* restaurants to be found there; but, with so much on offer, it can be hard to choose among them. Rather, head to Aje in the neighboring city of Kyoto, to avoid disappointment: it is a real paradise for meat lovers. The holy trinity of *yakiniku* beef cuts are *rosu* (loin), *karubi* (short rib), and *tanshio* (paper-thin slices of salted tongue), and all of them are executed well at Aje.

Another dish to try at Aje is *hososhio*. Taken from the small intestine, you might think that this cut is not much to look at—it is like a white blob—but once tried, it will likely make you see offal in a new light. When the white nuggets are placed on the hot wire netting of the barbecue, the luscious fat starts to melt into the grill. The flames rise up to envelop the meat, imbuing it with delicious charred and smoky notes. The texture is a little chewy, while the taste is rich and creamy. It is distinctive—and truly addictive.

Other must-try offal, or *horumon*, as it is known in Japan, include: *akasenmai* (abomasum, or reed tripe), *jomino* (rumen, or smooth tripe) and *tetchan* (large intestine). Aje always has long lines of people for dinner, but it is definitely worth waiting for *yakiniku* this good. **AI**

"Put your protein selections on the grill ... dip the cooked meat into the sauces provided, and enjoy."

Saveur

⬆ *Yakiniku* beef cooked on the grill.

Daiichi | Snap up a seat at this spot serving the Japanese delicacy of soft-shelled turtle

Location Kyoto   **Signature dish** *Marunabe* (soft-shelled turtle hot pot) | 💲💲💲💲💲

"[Turtle] tastes a little like chicken. If you're here for thrills, try the sake with turtle blood."

Time Out Kyoto

⬆ Samurai made slashes at the entrance door.

When thinking of Japanese cuisine, sushi comes to mind immediately. Then there are flavorsome bubbling *sukiyaki* and *shabu shabu* hot pots for dipping all manner of meats and vegetables. It is unlikely that soft-shelled turtle, or *suppon* as it is known, comes to mind, which is a pity because it has delicious ingredients, and is typically Japanese.

Turtle is not the kind of dish one eats every day, and it is not something people cook at home. The turtles used for *suppon* are not only expensive to buy, they are ferocious with a powerful bite, which is why they are also called "snapping turtles." So, to avoid losing any fingers, it is best to leave their preparation to the professionals.

The best *suppon* restaurants are found in Kyoto, and the cream of the crop is Daiichi. A truly magnificent restaurant, it has more than 330 years of history serving bubbling turtle hot pots (*marunabe*) to customers that have included the cream of Japanese feudal society, samurai warriors, and modern-day politicians including several Japanese prime ministers.

The current owner of the restaurant is 17th generation, and the restaurant's location is the same as ever. The classic wooden building must have been repaired hundreds of times over the years, but it is still standing and filled with charm. It is a place to sit down on the worn tatami mat floor in a private dining room and enjoy the feast of *suppon* dishes served by kimono-clad waitresses. Be sure to accompany the meal with sake.

Marunabe served in antique, ceramic *nabe* hot pots is undoubtedly the highlight of the meal. The consommé-like broth is dissimilar to anything else, with a rich and deep flavor that is also remarkably pure. Known for its rejuvenating qualities, *suppon* is also said to be an aphrodisiac. **AI**

Izuju | Try sushi as it used to be in Kyoto's famous exclusive geisha district

Location Kyoto   **Signature dish** *Sabazushi* (mackerel sushi) | 💲💲

Sushi has not always been made with raw fish. In the past, the fish could be boiled, steamed, marinated, or even stewed. Such "old-fashioned" sushi is still quite popular in Japan, especially in the Kansai region in the west of the country. Although the city of Osaka in Kansai is particularly well known for this style of sushi, Kyoto is famous for its old-style mackerel sushi (*sabazushi*), whereby lightly salted mackerel fillets are delicately marinated for a night in a vinegar mix, before being molded over sushi rice, and sliced into bite-sized pieces. Lots of Kyoto residents make *sabazushi* at home during festive seasons to share with neighbors or relatives as a token of gratitude.

The recipe for *sabazushi* might sound simple, but it is quite complicated to prepare. Consequently, it is also possible to find ready-made *sabazushi* in many places in Kyoto. Fishmongers, sushi restaurants, noodle bars, department stores, and even convenience stores sell it. But the best place to enjoy *sabazushi* is at the Izuju restaurant.

Founded in 1912, Izuju has been a favorite with Gion locals for more than a hundred years. One winning factor is its location opposite Yasaka Shrine in the majestic Gion district. The contrast between Izuju's atmospheric wood interior filled with historic ornaments and the view of the colorful shrine is guaranteed to impress. Another is the atmosphere: the space may be small, with only a handful of tables, but it is lively. The flavors at this little restaurant are also wonderful.

For more than the classic *sabazushi*, ask for *hakosushi* to receive a selection of pressed sushi squares, or *inarizushi* for sweet tofu pouches stuffed with vinegared rice and, in winter, scallions. No trip to Japan's ancient capital would be complete without sampling the iconic sushi from Izuju. **AI**

"This charming, century-old sushi shop specializes in Kyoto-style pressed sushi."

Frommer's Japan Day by Day

⬆ Izuju is noted for its renditions of traditional dishes.

Mishima-tei | A feast fit for a samurai at this
beef hot pot restaurant in Kyoto

Location Kyoto **Signature dish** *Sukiyaki* (beef and vegetable hot pot) | ❸❸❸❸

"Five generations of chefs have preserved the delicious sukiyaki recipe served here since 1873."

fodors.com

⤒ Mishima-tei is renowned for top-quality beef.

In 1963, a song about *sukiyaki* reached the top of the pop charts in Japan, which says a lot about the ethos of the era. The beef hot pot, with its sweet soy-based sauce, was the country's most famous dish at that time. For Japanese people, it symbolized "civilization and enlightenment" after the Meiji Restoration, which reopened Japan's borders to the rest of the world. As vegetarian Buddhists, the Japanese did not know how tasty beef was before 1868. In the twenty-first century, Japanese beef has become a well-established product. Rich, sweet, and meltingly tender, this fat-marbled meat is renowned throughout the world. It is quite different from the flavor and texture of French Charolais beef or Scottish Aberdeen Angus.

One of the best places to try Japanese beef in a dish of *sukiyaki* is Mishima-tei in Kyoto. Kanekichi Mishima, the founder of the restaurant, served as a samurai and mastered the art of cooking *sukiyaki* at that time. Then, when he came back to Kyoto in 1873, he opened this restaurant. On the first floor of the atmospheric wooden building, there is an impressive showcase of what is to come in the restaurant. Although they do not butcher the meat there, they sell a variety of cuts for making *sukiyaki* at home. Each is available in various grades, so clients can choose how much they are prepared to pay for quality.

Upstairs, there is a banquet hall and some cozy private rooms available for a *sukiyaki* lunch or dinner. Guests can choose the quality of meat for their hot pot from the menu, as well as the quantity—approximately 5.5 ounces (160 g) per person makes a good start. Then, lightly simmer the succulent Japanese beef and vegetables at the table, before dipping choice morsels into beaten egg. With the restaurant's evocative setting, it is possible to imagine what life was like for Japan's ancient noble class. **AI**

Tawaraya |

Top hospitality in Kyoto

Location Kyoto   **Signature dish** Tempura;
multi-course tasting menu | 🌑🌑🌑

Motenashi is a key word in the Japanese hospitality industry, yet it is hard to translate into other languages. It evokes the feeling of forgetting reality, truly being able to relax, and feeling restored. In Japan, making guests feel relaxed is more important than even the quality of the food or the facilities at a guesthouse.

Tawaraya is a well-known *ryokan* (traditional Japanese inn) in central Kyoto, where it is possible to truly come to understand the spirit of *montenashi*. Although people say happiness cannot be bought, a night at Tawaraya tells a different story. The rooms are impeccably decorated, the gardens ideal for quiet contemplation, and the staff have the knack of knowing exactly what guests need before they even do. There are even soothing wooden bath tubs for clients to take a refreshing dip in before dinner, plus 12-inch-(30-cm-) thick duvets to keep guests warm as they settle down into a cozy futon for the night. It is no wonder Tawaraya is so popular with celebrities and politicians, although this piece of happiness also has a very expensive price tag.

There are many places for a decent dinner in central Kyoto, but finding the service and atmosphere available at Tawaraya anywhere else is nearly impossible. Having a multi-course *kaiseki* meal filled with the spirit of *montenashi* is a remarkable experience rarely found even in Kyoto.

Toshi Sato is in charge of the operation, and she ensures that everything ticks along quietly behind the scenes to make sure a client's visit is every bit as good as it should be. Tawaraya would not be the same without her authority and sense of beauty. If a night at the *ryokan* seems too expensive, then visit its tempura restaurant, Tenyu, instead, to experience a sense of glowing hospitality. **AI**

Nakamura-ken |

Japanese sweets for every season

Location Kyoto   **Signature dish** *Wagashi*
(Japanese confectionery) | 🌑

While many Japanese dishes are available all around the world, there is one thing that is still not found easily outside of Japan: *wagashi*. The best place to get these Japanese sweets is Kyoto, and the people from there are picky about the quality of their confectionery. Created to balance the bitterness of the *matcha* green tea used in the *sado* (tea ceremony), it is little wonder *wagashi* is taken seriously in Kyoto because it is the Japanese capital in the art of the tea ceremony and renowned for the quality of its tea.

Although there are many high-quality Japanese confectionery shops in Kyoto, city center, a visit to the Nakamura-ken riverside shop in Katsura makes a pleasant escape from the hustle and bustle.

"Nowhere is the marriage of tea and wagashi as prevalent as in Kyoto, birthplace of sado ... "

The Japan Times

Built in 1913, Nakamura-ken's wooden building is located just behind one of Japan's most important large-scale cultural treasures, the Katsura Imperial Villa. Nakamura-ken is always busy, and it offers a different shape or flavor of *wagashi* for every season and occasion.

The main ingredient in *wagashi* is simmered and mashed red adzuki beans (*anko.*) For most Japanese people, *anko* is considered a treat. The foodstuff also has sacred links to Shintoism and seasonal traditions. For example, each year on June 30 for the *nagoshi-no oharae* (summer purification ritual), people eat *minazuki* (pounded sticky rice triangles topped with *anko*) to bring good luck. **AI**

Okina | Colorful plates of
raw fish in a family-run restaurant

Location Kyoto **Signature dish** Snapper sashimi
with crisp-roasted skin | 🅢🅢🅢🅢

One of the many appealing aspects of Okina restaurant is its tofu dishes. Kyoto is famous for its tofu cookery, and when it comes to tofu makers, the one who is considered the best is Morika. Naturally, the tofu used at Okina comes from Morika, which is located next to the restaurant.

But that is not the only reason to eat at Okina. The father and son team who run the restaurant are two chefs with an impressive talent for "free-style" *kaiseki* dishes. Working within the cuisine's tradition of intricately prepared, seasonal foods, the father's cooking is a real treat. It exemplifies the soul of the city's gastronomy. But perhaps the more eccentric of the two men is the son, whose style would

---

"The son occasionally goes to the mountains to pick wild vegetables …"

Michelin Guide

---

undoubtedly surprise any diner. Like an audacious translation of a classical text, he adds unorthodox ingredients to classic *kaiseki* cuisine, but his combinations truly work.

Unlike the son's dishes, the antique ceramic crockery is in classic *kaiseki* style. A combination of crisp, roasted red snapper skin with sashimi slices comes served on coil-patterned early *imari* ware. Slow-stewed yellowtail bone with icicle radish arrives on a restored piece of *sueki* stoneware from the Heian Period. Firefly squid with vinaigrette is presented in an antique, glass Baccarat bowl. The food is equally attractive: deep-fried, dried sea cucumber ovaries are arranged to look like a flower. **AI**

Kitcho Arashiyama |
Trendsetter for Japanese haute cuisine

Location Kyoto **Signature dish** Seasonal *kaiseki*
tasting menus | 🅢🅢🅢🅢🅢

Ask any Japanese person which is the best restaurant in Japan and invariably he or she will say Kitcho Arashiyama. Even people who have no interest in food have heard of the restaurant. With three Michelin stars and numerous other accolades, it is one of the best in the world, too.

The third-generation chef-owner there is Kunio Tokuoka, and although he may not be able to prepare every plate himself, he watches the other chefs with an eagle eye to ensure each meets his impeccable standards. So, clients can be confident that the quality will be sublime, with only the finest seasonal produce used. Each morsel in a multiple-course meal is like a work of art presented on attractive antique ceramics by charming staff.

Founded by Tokuoka's grandfather, Teiichi Yuki, quality has always been of the utmost importance there. Like a Japanese version of Auguste Escoffier, or Fernand Point, Yuki is not only the founder of a magnificent restaurant but also considered one of the founding fathers of post-Second World War Japanese restaurant cuisine. The style of cooking is *kaiseki*—an intricate and traditional meal with multiple courses, a little like a modern tasting menu.

When Yuki opened Kitcho Arashiyama, he started a culinary revolution by merging Japanese haute (*kaiseki*) cuisine with the Japanese tea ceremony. Although the styles are not so different in essence, their unity marked a new age for *kaiseki* cuisine. The style of restaurant is known as a *ryotei*. In the old days, *ryotei* were places to be entertained by geisha. They were exclusive spaces to conduct business or political meetings, and diners were accepted only by referral. Although clients may not need to be referred to gain a table at Kitcho Arashiyama, the prices ensure that it is still exclusive. **AI**

Hyotei | Enjoy an elegant breakfast in a restaurant steeped in history

Location Kyoto   **Signature dish** *Asagayu* breakfast | 💲💲💲

A *ryotei* is both a luxurious and traditional restaurant. It is a place which Japanese people visit for special occasions such as a wedding banquet, a significant birthday, or some other celebration; and Kyoto is, perhaps, the best city in which to enjoy a *ryotei*'s elaborate cuisine.

Hyotei is an exceedingly elegant *ryotei*, with a long history of acclaim. As well as gaining three Michelin stars, the restaurant's fourteenth-generation chef-owner Eiichi Takahashi has been designated as an Intangible Cultural Property of Japan. He is a master of innovation and an absolute perfectionist. His style is progressive, blending contemporary creativity with the utmost respect for the traditional spirit. This is what makes him the epitome of a Kyoto person—living a contemporary life in a city rich with history. In his cooking, Takahashi attempts to discover new tastes by studying those of the past.

A fine example of his approach is exemplified in Hyotei's famous breakfast. In the old days, a *ryotei* visitor would often come in early in the morning after a night out on the town, declaring, "I'm starving!" and be fed a simple breakfast. Hyotei, however, served the most amazing set meals for its breakfast. Rumors of how delicious the morning meal was spread like wildfire and people wanted to eat it, even if they had not been out all night. Obligingly, Hyotei added breakfast to the menu in 1868, and it is still there.

The morning *congee* (rice porridge) is a dish which Takahashi has worked to improve for contemporary tastes, yet without detracting from the original spirit of breakfast. High in protein and low in calories, it is a revitalizing dish that is beautiful to look at, enjoyable to eat, mild on the tongue, and easy to digest. It is a breakfast dish that everyone should sample at least once in his or her life. **AI**

"This 300-year-old restaurant first opened its doors as a teahouse to serve pilgrims ..."

frommers.com

⤒ Boiled eggs have been a speciality at the Hyotei restaurant for hundreds of years.

Uozuya | Minimal cuisine from a maverick chef

Location Kyoto **Signature dish** Seasonally changing, multi-course *kaiseki* tasting menus | 💲💲💲💲💲

Rather like Heston Blumenthal or Ferran Adrià, the owner of this one-starred Michelin restaurant is a maverick and a master of his craft. That is not to say that owner Kazuo Komori's cooking style is "molecular gastronomy," but his innovative dishes are on a par with any that those great chefs produce.

Although there are only twenty seats at Uozuya, it is comparatively easy to get a reservation. Run by Komori and his wife, it is a restaurant with personality. The dishes display the beauty of minimal presentation. There are no fancy decorations, or unnecessary adornments, and yet sampling them is a privilege. Like being invited to the home of a master musician for a private concert, it feels an honor to eat

---

"The owner-chef enjoys discovering the hidden tastes in ingredients … "

Michelin Guide

---

there. Each dish is presented on the best Japanese tableware. From precious antiques to studio pottery, the restaurant includes works by renowned potters Shoji Kamoda and Shiro Tsujimura. The combination of Komori's food and the ceramics is a feast for the eyes. The chopsticks are also special and are made by Ichihara, the best artisan chopstick maker in Japan.

At first, the taste of Komori's cooking seems minimal, but over time one realizes this is not true. The flavors and textures linger in the mouth and mind for a long time afterward.

To help guests remember the exquisite meal they experienced at Uozuya, they can take their chopsticks home as a souvenir. **AI**

Wontana | A taste of Kyoto's high-class culinary history at affordable prices

Location Kyoto **Signature dish** Seasonal fish dishes *kaiseki*-style | 💲💲

Japan is a popular destination for food lovers because of its rich culinary heritage. But, the prices are often seen as prohibitive. It is true that the high-end venues are not cheap, but eating in a Michelin starred restaurant in Japan costs less than the same experience in a Parisian three-starred restaurant.

In Kyoto, a city with a long gourmet history, high-quality cuisine is a quintessential element of everyday life. It is one of the best places in the world to visit for fine food. For those traveling on a tight budget in Kyoto, there is no reason to miss out. It is possible to try proper, high-end Japanese cuisine at more reasonable prices by visiting Wontana for lunch. The five courses on offer have visitors in ecstasy, and provide the best value in the city, making Wontana a place to visit more than once.

To try more of Wontana's excellent food, add a beautiful sashimi assortment to the five-course lunch for just a little more money. Of the other set meals, the ten-course *kaiseki* tasting menu is of remarkable value and quality. It is hard to imagine how prices can be so low at a restaurant in the center of Kyoto.

Those making a second visit to Wontana should try the à la carte menu, for which the specialty is fish. Owner Jun Yamamoto's family are fishmongers at Kyoto's central market, so it is unsurprising that he can source such good produce. Wontana also has a fantastic Japanese sake collection, and the fish and sake are a match made in heaven.

The service is friendly and the setting is impeccable, too. From the lighting to the temperature, the cutlery and toothpicks, Yamamoto ensures every last detail is taken care of in this appealing modern restaurant. **AI**

⇲ Kyoto has a venerable history of gourmet cuisine.

Sojiki Nakahigashi | An intimate insight into Japanese cuisine

Location Kyoto   **Signature dish** *Kaiseki* | $$$$

"Twelve counter seats are set around a stove and charcoal grill …"

Michelin Guide

⤒ Attention to detail is key at Sojiki Nakahigashi and each dish is presented beautifully.

To dine at Sojiki Nakahigashi is to be offered an insight into not only the high quality of Japanese food, but also its spirit. Such is the reputation of this diminutive restaurant in Kyoto that it is extremely difficult to get a reservation. But it is worth persevering because eating there is unforgettable.

Every morning, Sojiki Nakahigashi's owner-chef, Hisao Nakahigashi, goes out early to find his ingredients. All the ingredients he uses are organic and seasonal. Generally, chefs in Kyoto go to a central market, or the fantastic Nishiki Market—a place all food lovers should visit. Nakahigashi does not do this, however. Instead, this dedicated chef buys his vegetables from farmers. Then, equipped with a knife and a scythe, he goes to the mountains to pick herbs, wild vegetables like mushrooms and asparagus, and even flowers that he uses to decorate the restaurant.

Such blessings from nature are then cooked carefully in the restaurant's own spring water, or alternatively roasted, baked, or fried. Each ingredient is cooked with amazing precision. The taste of a meal at Sojiki Nakahigashi is that of Japanese earth, water, air, and fire in what is a celebration of all the elements.

Chef Nakahgashi is not interested in luxurious ingredients. There is no fancy fish on his sashimi plates. Instead, paper-thin slices of koi carp, or other humble varieties, are served adorned with twelve to fifteen different edible leaves and flowers. So exquisite is the presentation of his dishes that his sashimi resembles a colorful painting by Odilon Redon.

Sojiki Nakahgashi accepts telephone reservations just once a month, on the first day of the month, from 8am to reserve for the following month. Within just one hour, all the seats will be gone, and the restaurant is reported to have a five-month-long waiting list. When someone is lucky enough to get a seat in the restaurant, it is common to take a day off work to make the most of the experience. **AI**

Seto | Enjoy a chicken feast in a country village where timing is all

Location Kyoto   **Signature dish** Chargrilled chicken and *sukiyaki* (chicken hot pot) | ❺❺❺❺

Seto is outside central Kyoto but is accessible via a tram. After a thirty-minute journey to Ichihara Station toward the mountains in the northeast, take a tranquil fifteen-minute walk through the countryside to the restaurant. The effort and wait will all help build up a good appetite.

Once inside the Seto restaurant, guests are led to one of its cozy, private dining rooms. The centerpiece in each is a traditional open hearth, or *irori*. Filled with glowing charcoal, the heartwarming fire is a joy to watch while waiting for the food to appear. Chicken is slaughtered to order, just in time for guests' arrival, so it is best to be on time for a reservation.

Seto serves only the finest, free-range chicken, and the female owner, or *okami-san*, says there are many qualities that go into producing the best birds. Anything from the size of the bird to the weather condition or temperature can make a difference as to when each bird is ready to eat. As Seto's *okami-san* says: "Timing is the most important taste of all."

The restaurant host and her female staff cook in front of guests, while telling them which bits of the chicken meal to eat when. There is no menu available, so guests sit back and let the staff get to work on an impressive chicken feast.

Half of the bird is chargrilled. The other half is made into *sukiyaki*, which is a braise-style stew made in an iron pan. The vegetables that go into the stew are local, too. They come from a farm behind the restaurant that is owned by the proprietress, who is totally self-sufficient.

If a guest asks for extra green onions for *sukiyaki*, the *okami-san* will say: "Wait a second." Then, she goes to the farm's garden to pull them fresh from the ground. The green onions will be washed in the river that runs by the restaurant before being served. So, just like the chicken, the vegetables are timed to perfection as well. **AI**

> *"A whole chicken is used for each group, so best come in a party of two or three."*
>
> Michelin Guide

⤒ Seto specializes in stews and grills made from its own free-range chickens.

Nishiki Market | Savor the delights of Kyoto's "kitchen" one snack at a time

Location Kyoto **Signature dish** *Dashimaki* (rolled omelet) |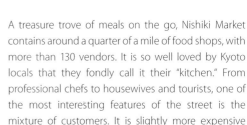

> *"If you want to see all the weird and wonderful foods that go into Kyoto cuisine, this is the place."*
>
> Lonely Planet

⬆ Locals, restaurateurs, and tourists all shop at Nishiki Market.

A treasure trove of meals on the go, Nishiki Market contains around a quarter of a mile of food shops, with more than 130 vendors. It is so well loved by Kyoto locals that they fondly call it their "kitchen." From professional chefs to housewives and tourists, one of the most interesting features of the street is the mixture of customers. It is slightly more expensive than average market prices, but the quality is good enough to match that of any restaurant.

Nishiki Market is also probably the busiest place in Kyoto, and for good reason. It is a place to have a snack, move on, snack again, and continue until sated. The quality and variety of food on offer, together with its lively atmosphere, have made it a tourist attraction.

Starting at the eastern entrance, visit Aritsugu. It is an ancient company that once made swords for Japan's Imperial family, which specializes in professional-quality kitchen knives. Next comes Tsunoki, where it is possible to sample some exceptional sake. The shop's owner, Teruo Fujii, is guaranteed to find something visitors will like.

Move on to Miki Keiran, where the must-try item is the Kyoto-style rolled omelet (*dashimaki*), which melts on the tongue. Okuniya is also remarkable, serving a charcoal-grilled eel recipe that has been handed down over three generations. At nearby Uoriki, broiled fish skewers and pike eel (*hamo*) cutlets are the specialties, and given it is possible to eat in there, it is a good place to pause if feeling tired. Farther on, Marukame sells more than fifty varieties of homemade, deep-fried fish cakes, which make a great street snack. Be sure to pass the exclusive greengrocer Kanematsu, too, where a basket of mushrooms can cost a few hundred dollars. There is lunchtime dining on the second floor, with lots of delicious vegetable dishes.

Finally, browse the selection of Japanese pottery at Pulau Deco before heading to the café at the back of the store for a well-earned cup of tea. **AI**

Yoshidaya Ryoriten | Fusing Kyoto flavors with the best of world cuisine

Location Kyoto **Signature dish** Summer rolls stuffed with fish tempura | $$$

Yoshidaya Ryoriten is a backstreet restaurant that is notoriously hard to find. Hidden at the end of a private alley, there is no noticeable sign or menu board on the façade of an old-fashioned building. Located near Kyoto's Imperial Palace (Gosho), reaching the restaurant is like trying to enter the castle in Franz Kafka's book of the same name. As a consequence, Yoshidaya Ryoriten is not the kind of place where chance customers just wander in without a booking. It is exactly this hideaway-like quality that makes the Yoshidaya Ryoriten such a popular hangout for famous artists and musicians.

Chef-patron Horoko Yoshina loves to travel, and her passion comes through in the flavors of her food. Exotic ingredients meet orthodox Kyoto cooking methods, and vice versa, to create dishes that are unique to Yoshidaya Ryoriten. Although Yoshina's cooking is essentially fusion, the term does not do her excellent creations justice.

An example of her innovation is Vietnamese summer rolls stuffed with classic Japanese conger eel, or Spanish mackerel tempura. And there is more: Korea and Mexico meet in her spicy tostadas, while local Kyoto *kujo* scallions are added to her omelets. Then there are mountain yam pickles flavored with pink peppercorns. Yoshidaya Ryoriten is a kaleidoscope of world food.

The location of Yoshina's restaurant may be understated, but that does not mean that she is necessarily shy of the limelight. As well as having written a couple of cookery books, she is also a TV chef and owns a beautiful old Japanese guesthouse. Nevertheless, she still finds time to spend every day in the kitchen at Yoshidaya Ryoriten cooking for her lucky diners. Happy to drink and chat with the customers, she is every bit as charming as the restaurant itself. For a bold meal in a discrete location, Yoshidaya Ryoriten really is the place to go. **AI**

"You would need a guide to find the place as it . . . doesn't even offer a sign to explain its whereabouts."

billy-kyoto.seesaa.net

[↑] Hidden in a backstreet, Yoshida Ryoriten is one of Kyoto's best kept dining secrets.

Hamatou |

A thrill-seeker's paradise in Osaka

Location Osaka **Signature dish** *Fugu tetchirinabe* (blowfish hot pot) | ❺❺❺❺

Why are some Japanese people obsessed with *fugu* or blowfish as it is known in English? The risk, of course. Famously, *fugu* is a poisonous fish. Wondering whether one will make it through the meal makes for a thrilling experience, but all the better to visit a trustworthy and reliable restaurant.

Japan has any number of *fugu* restaurants, but Osaka serves up 60 per cent of the country's haul. However, of the thousands of restaurants on offer here, Hamatou is the place to go for a bite of the infamous *fugu*. Open for around a century, there is no doubting its reputation for safety, because it would not have lasted so long. Hamatou's prices are also reasonable, although *fugu* is never a cheap option

---

"[Fugu contains] a poison called tetrodotoxin, which is 1,200 times deadlier than cyanide."

Time

---

because it must be prepared by a fully-licensed chef. So, generally, it is saved for special occasions. Hamatou's location is another big lure. Situated inside Kuromon Market, this vibrant street has been attracting food lovers since the early nineteenth century.

Hamatou's two specialties are blowfish hot pot (*tetchiri*) with tofu and vegetables and blowfish sashimi (*tessa*) sliced so thin it reveals the pattern of the plate below. Although characteristically firm, the *tessa* sashimi is not rubbery but filled with flavor and clammy sweetness. A meal of *fugu* at Hamatou is so rich, and packed with exciting tastes and textures, it makes for a filling meal—afterwards it can feel as if one has eaten a pot roast dinner. **AI**

Kissa Y |

Generosity abounds at this Osaka café

Location Osaka **Signature dish** Giant clubhouse sandwiches | ❺

Osaka's nickname is "Kuidaore" City, which means the city where you "eat until you collapse." The Kissa Y café is just the kind of place that has lent Osaka its unusual moniker. Kissa Y does not look like anything special from the outside, and appears to be just another ordinary corner café as you would find anywhere in Japan. But it does not take long before one starts to see what is different about this small spot.

Kissa Y is run by a charming woman, who greets guests with a warm smile as soon as they sit down at a table. Even when the place is full of customers, she will not take long to provide the menu—along with a plate of ham and eggs. If a guest looks puzzled at the plate of fried ham slices and huge pile of roughly scrambled eggs, she will smile and say: "This is just a starter. Enjoy!"

Ordering at Kissa Y is not about what is on the menu. It features all the usual Japanese curries, burgers, sandwiches, and lunch specials; but, the owner will make sure she serves guests all the best things on that day—whether they ask for them or not. If someone orders a curry, for example, he or she will not just get a large plate of curry with rice. The proprietress will also bring three or four other dishes, which can be anything from pork with ginger or beef and potato stew, to stir-fried vegetables, onion rings, or huge sandwiches, all at no extra charge.

The most popular dish at Kissa Y is the house special, a clubhouse sandwich. It is made with a whole loaf of bread, a dozen eggs, and half a pound of bacon. Although the dishes themselves are homely, the owner's generosity is exceptional. Even if a guest manages to finish his or her giant clubhouse sandwich, she will still ask if they want the same again for free. Such kindness has garnered Kissa Y a big fan base, which goes there for the atmosphere as much as the food. **AI**

Taiyoshi Hyakuban | Enjoy comfort food
in a kitsch former brothel

Location Osaka **Signature dish** Curry hot pot with udon noodles | ❸❺

If kitsch is a low-brow form of mass-produced art, then Taiyoshi Kyakuban in Nishinari-ku, Osaka, is the culinary equivalent. It serves all sorts of crowd-pleasing, but low-brow, mass-produced foods. However, the Japanese have a special place in their hearts for this kind of restaurant, which is known as "B-class gourmet."

There are all kinds of dishes to snack on at Taiyoshi Kyakuban, from German frankfurters to Chinese *shao-mai* dumplings. But, the specialty at Taiyoshi Kyakuban is a hot pot filled with chicken, pork, fish, shellfish, and vegetables in a curry-flavored stock that has a wonderful smell of cloves. One of the biggest treats is to add *udon* (thick, wheat flour noodles) to the remaining broth at the end of the meal. As the noodles cook, they pick up all the flavors left in the pan. Slurping the noodles is satisfying and an iconic "B-class gourmet" restaurant experience.

There is a raft of other Japanese comfort food dishes on the menu at Taiyoshi Hyakuban, too. Like in many other Japanese pubs, guests can choose anything from chips to *edamame* (fresh, boiled soybeans), sashimi, macaroni and cheese, or salad Niçoise—all at the same time.

Taiyoshi Hyakuban, however, is not a conventional pub, or *izakaya*, which is what makes it so interesting. It is located in a former brothel and opened as a restaurant in 1970. The kitsch interior has changed little since it was built as a brothel in 1918. The restaurant's façade is still outrageously flamboyant in the style of an old red-light establishment. Inside, the building's wooden structure is covered with drawings, paintings, reliefs, and Majolica tiles. In all its garish colorful glory, it is strangely beautiful, like the world in the animated film *Sen to Chihiro no kamikakushi* (*Spirited Away*, 2001). **AI**

"Many of its twenty-one rooms have changed little since its days as a brothel."

The Japan Times

⬆ Taiyoshi Hyakuban has become famous for its decor, which is typical of a period brothel.

Takoume | The perfect winter snack in an established Osaka restaurant

Location Osaka   **Signature dish** *Oden* | ❸❸

During the cold season in Japan, there is a distinctive smell emanating from any convenience store that comes from a steaming pot of broth in a square stainless cooker by the counter. The dish is *oden*. It is filled with boiled eggs, *daikon* (white radish), *konnyaku* (devil's tongue), and many varieties of processed fish cakes, all bathing in a soy-based broth. Each simmered chunk makes a perfect warming snack and is especially good dabbed with a little mustard.

To eat *oden* in a restaurant, try Takoume, which is the most famous spot for this dish. The taste of its mellow stew sets the benchmark for all other *oden*-makers in the country. But it is hard to imitate as the broth has not changed since 1844—it has kept on simmering through the Meiji Restoration and two World Wars, with regular top-ups from the diligent staff. It is impossible to create a stock quite like Takoume's, which is both complex in flavor and cleansing, and truly unique.

Sake is the perfect drink to accompany *oden*, and the sake at Takoume is particularly smooth. Takoume also serves another fantastic dish to eat with sake, *tako kanroni*, which translates as octopus sweet dew stew. It is a tender, boiled octopus tentacle glazed with sweet syrup. Served on a bamboo skewer, Takoume's *tako* helps to bring out the full flavor of the accompanying sake. It might not look like much, but it really is a treat. Even at lunchtime, it is difficult to resist a glass of hot sake to wash down some *oden* and *tako*.

For a hearty repast at lunchtime during the winter months, a set meal of five simmered pieces of *oden*, *tako kanroni*, a bowl of rice, and some miso soup should satisfy, even if it does not come with sake. Of course, part of the pleasure of the experience is feeling one is eating in an authentic eatery that has been loved by generations of locals. **AI**

⭱ *Oden* is made with fish cakes and boiled eggs.

Jan-Jan Alley | Eat filling Japanese "kebabs" in an Osaka food arcade

Location Osaka   **Signature dish** *Kushi-katsu* (breaded, deep-fried meat skewers) | $

Although Osaka offers all kinds of refined cuisines, including Michelin-starred establishments, it is also home to many places that serve more alternative foods. Among them are Tsuruhashi Korean Town, Kuromon Market Street, and the 509 restaurants and cafés of the Umeda underground shopping complex. But, Jan-Jan Alley is one of the most characterful spots of all. Built in 1912, the arcade used to be at the heart of an entertainment district. In the twenty-first century, it is more of a shopping street, but the 590 feet (180 m) of folk food restaurants it houses are great fun to visit.

Jan-Jan Alley's main dish is *kushi-katsu*. Akin to a kebab, *kushi-katsu* can be made from minced pork, shrimp, sausages, vegetables, or pretty much anything else that is edible. The ingredients are skewered, dipped in *panko* (Japanese bread crumbs), and then deep-fried in vegetable oil. Most of the *kushi-katsu* restaurants consist of an open kitchen with a handful of counter seats. Guests sit down and order

skewers, or just say how many they want and the chef will decide which ones to give them. Before eating, be sure to dip them in the beaker of black *kushi-katsu* sauce provided. Like a thicker, sweeter version of Worcestershire sauce, it is the perfect foil to the sticks

There are several *kushi-katsu* places to choose from in Jan-Jan Alley, but three of the best are Yae-katsu, Daruma, and Tengu. Prices are more or less the same at each. Between them, it is possible to find some thirty to forty different skewers from which to choose. It is well worth taking the opportunity to try unfamiliar ingredients here because the skewers are cheap as well as small, so it is easy to return and try something different if the unknown proves not to appeal to the palate after all. There are no strict rules in Jan-Jan Alley, bar one. To avoid being kicked out, never dip a skewer into the sauce more than once. **AI**

⊡ Deep-fried "kebabs" are served with *kushi-katsu* sauce.

Aragawa | Sumptuous chargrilled steaks made with the finest *sanda* beef

Location Kobe   **Signature dish** Chargrilled steak | ❺❺❺❺❺

It is rare for a steak house to be awarded more than one Michelin star, but Aragawa is not just any beef restaurant. Just as the French treat their wine production with great care, creating grading systems and strict controls to ensure the highest quality, the best Japanese cattle breeds are also raised with meticulous standards.

In terms of these high-class breeds, there is *matsuzaka* beef from Mie Prefecture, *oumi* beef from Shiga, and *yonezawa* beef from Yamagata—all of which are undoubtedly good. But, at Aragawa, the staff cook nothing but *sanda* beef from Hyogo Prefecture. Only 1,000 *sanda* beef cattle are sold to the market each year, and the best of all the *sanda* beef winds up at Aragawa. The restaurant exterior is plain, but the interior is more distinctive—like an old-fashioned country pub in the U.K. The smart restaurant service is smooth and efficient, and the atmosphere is composed but not too stiff.

As for the steaks, fillet, rib, aitchbone, and sirloin all come chargrilled. A bite of *sanda* beef does not come cheap, but each mouthful will intoxicate. The steaks are exquisitely tender and redolent, with a meaty flavor and texture that does not melt away too quickly. Be sure to savor each morsel while chewing.

More than just domestic cows, *sanda* cattle are bred and raised by dexterous craftsmen who produce exceptional beef. Once the meat arrives at Aragawa, the restaurant's master chef, Jiro Yamada, treats it with the greatest care. The meat is flavored with salt and pepper, and broiled on metal skewers in an oven fired with *binchotan* hardwood charcoal. But every ingredient at Aragawa is treated with respect, and this is the secret to Yamada's success. Even the tiniest salad is not overlooked. More than just a chef, Yamada is a true master of his craft. **AI**

⬆ Salads are prepared with as much care as the steaks.

Hinase Village | The best place in Japan for savory oyster pancakes

Location Okayama   **Signature dish** *Kaki-oko* (*okonomiyaki* oyster pancakes) | ❸

Okonomiyaki is a dish enjoyed all over Japan. Meaning "what you like, grilled," these thick savory pancakes are made from a batter of flour, water or broth, egg, and shredded cabbage filled with sliced pork, shrimp, squid, or all of them. Often, the mix is cooked at the table on hot plates, then brushed with a thick, tangy Worcestershire-style sauce, before being sprinkled with dried bonito fish flakes and seaweed powder.

Toppings and batters vary according to the region. For the classic variety, Osaka is undoubtedly the place, although Hiroshima has a special version stuffed with noodles, too. However, there is another kind of *okonomiyaki* that should not be missed and that is Okayama Prefecture's oyster pancakes, or *kaki-oko*. In the small fishing village of Hinase, about three hours by train from Osaka, oysters are a real specialty, and they pack at least two dozen small oysters into each *kaki-oko*. Naturally, they are beautifully fresh and filled with flavor. It is possible to find *kaki-oko* in other

prefectures, but they do not compare to the pancakes found in Hinase—for taste or price.

During oyster season, from October to March, many go to Hinase just to try this delicacy. When you bite into one of the *kaki-oko*, the springy oysters burst in the mouth before emitting a rich, heady taste of the sea. Combined with the tangy, brown sauce topping, the first experience of their bold taste is bound to be a memorable moment.

The village boasts eleven *kaki-oko* restaurants, and most people pick up a list from the tourist information center at the station before popping into three or four spots to sample their pancakes. So, if on a visit to the area at the right time of year, it is essential to join the hordes of *kaki-oko* appreciators doing the rounds in Hinase. In February, Hinase is especially busy because the town hosts its annual Oyster Festival. **AI**

⬆ *Okonomiyaki* is a popular dish across Japan.

Hinode Seimenjo |

Jostle for a seat at an udon factory

Location Sakaide **Signature dish** *Sanuki udon* noodles | $

Kagawa Prefecture is known as the "Udon Prefecture" in Japan. Locals love these noodles so much that there are some 657 udon restaurants in the area, which is three times more than the national average. No wonder locals are proud of the nickname. The texture of Kagawa's udon (known as *sanuki udon*) is completely different from the rest of Japan. They are springy but not undercooked, firm but not too hard, and chewy but not sticky—just perfect, according to many. People go to Kagawa on udon tours, eating four or five bowls a day during a noodle "pilgrimage."

Top of the list for udon fans is the noodle-making factory Hinode Seimenjo. The kitchen is only open for one hour a day from 11.30 A.M., and there are just twelve seats available, so competition is fierce. Those lucky enough to get in then choose how they want their udon—hot, cold, warm—and let the staff know at the counter. Guests pick the soup to put the noodles in at the table—hot, cold, thick (*bukkake*), or soy sauce. It is possible to add toppings, such as deep-fried fish cakes and boiled eggs. In the past, it was so DIY here that, if a customer asked for scallions, staff would point to a little farm behind the factory and say: "Help yourself."

> *"If you just mention Kagawa to anyone in the archipelago, they will probably lick their lips . . . "*
>
> gojapan.com

One particularly popular way of eating *sanuki* is piping hot straight from the pot mixed with a beaten raw egg. Known as *kamatama*, it tastes similar to spaghetti alla carbonara. The dish was popularized in the 2006 film *Udon*. **AI**

Tokugetsuro Honten |

Lavish dishes in a former geisha house

Location Kochi **Signature dish** *Bonito tataki* (seared bonito with herbs and citrus-soy sauce) | $$$$

Yokiro (*The Geisha*, 1983) is an iconic Japanese film. A cult classic, the movie gives an idea of what this restaurant—once home to the largest geisha house in Kochi—must have been like. Set in the 1930s, the film tells the turbulent story of an exceptionally talented and beautiful geisha girl, Momowaka, who worked at Yokiro, which was one of the best known geisha houses in all of Japan at the time. Anyone from politicians and moguls to yakuza mafiosi gathered there to play their power games. It was a place of intrigue and drama.

Since then, Yokiro has changed its name to Tokugetsuro and become a *kaiseki* restaurant specializing in Japanese haute cuisine. However, the architecture has changed very little, so it is possible to enjoy a fantastic local banquet surrounded by the splendor of an iconic geisha house with classic tatami mat floors and sliding panel doors.

Both the food and the architecture at Tokugetsuro are theatrical, and a meal there is guaranteed to take one's breath away. The most operatic dish at Tokugetsuro is a local specialty *sawachi*, whereby all of the courses are laid out together on a large plate. From sashimi to fish cakes, salad and fruits, all are beautifully decorated. The best variety of *sawachi* to order is called *kumimono*; it is the most traditional and spectacular combination of them all. It is well worth ordering *kumimono* in advance when making a reservation.

Also, be sure to ask for *tataki* to be included in the dish. A must-try delicacy, *tataki* is thick slices of seared bonito fish covered with plenty of herbs and seasonings and a Japanese citrus dip. It is one of the most famous dishes in the Kochi Prefecture, and the bonito fishing grounds of Kochi at Tosa Bay have an excellent reputation. **AI**

Hakata Yatai | Enjoy a snack at one of Hakata's famous street stalls

Location Fukuoka   **Signature dish** *Tonkotsu* ramen soup noodles | $

All Asian countries have their own street food culture, and Japan is no exception. In some countries, moveable stalls are set up at night for lively street markets. In others, they are bustling permanent fixtures in backstreet alleys or commercial districts. The most famous area for clusters of food carts and stalls in Japan is the Hakata area of Fukuoka in the southwest of the country.

Known as *yatai* in Japanese, more than 200 portable street stalls appear at night in Hakata, setting up among the modern buildings. In busy downtown areas such as Nakasu, Tenjin, or Nagahama, unassuming alleys and side streets take on an altogether different feel when the sun goes down. Their colorful signs, glowing lights, and bustling atmospheres are alluring for a quick bite at one of the long benches. They really are a lot of fun.

With so many to choose from, it is hard to say which is the absolute best, but a long line is often a clue. Perhaps more important is how to avoid the bad ones, and a good rule of thumb for that is to avoid anything raw; so do not opt for sushi. Instead, *tonkotsu* ramen soup noodles—a regional specialty—make an excellent choice. Made from long-simmered pork bones, a perfect bowl of milky *tonkotsu* broth is dense and intense, rich and creamy, yet not too heavy.

There are definitely some favored stalls among the connoisseurs: Yama-chan, Ichiryu, and Number One are the *yatai* to visit. The *tonkotsu* ramen at each has its own distinct taste, so it is best to try them all.

Try out a few of the other dishes, too—Yama-chan's *yakitori* (grilled chicken skewers), Ichiryu's *oden* (*dashi* fish broth hot pot), and Number One's *gyoza* (fried pork dumplings) are as popular as the noodles. But on any visit to Hakata, a trip to a *yatai* is an experience not to be missed. **AI**

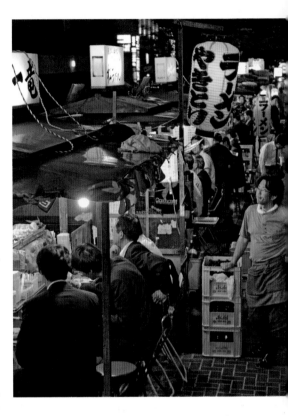

"The outdoor yatai, or street-side food stalls ... are the Fukuoka way to enjoy a late-night snack."

Frommer's Japan Day by Day

⬆ Trying dishes from the street food stalls in Hakata is an absolute must for food lovers.

Sansou Murata | Hot springs and high-class Japanese dining at an inn

Location Oita **Signature dish** Steak with roast vegetable juices | $$$$$

The tradition of enjoying hot springs with bathing facilities continues to be popular in Japan. The area of Yufuin in Oita Prefecture on Kyushu Island is noted for its hot springs, and has a number of *ryokan* (Japanese inns) that offer guests the chance to experience authentic Japanese culture.

One of the most highly regarded of these inns is Sansou Murata, a sophisticated establishment that has breathed new life into the area. Scenically located at the foot of Mount Yufu, it is noted not only for its hot spring spa, but also for the quality of the food it offers.

There is an appealing serenity to Sansou Murata. The decor is distinctly stylish. Rather, than displaying classic "Japanisms," the inn boasts postmodern design in both its interiors and its products. A similar philosophy is applied to the cooking. Ingredients are cooked precisely using classic methods. The kitchen does not aim to challenge the diners. Instead, it opts to concentrate on sourcing the finest local produce and working hard to bring out the flavors of the raw ingredients. Consequently, the meals at Sansou Murata are simply delicious.

The style of cooking at Sansou Murata is *kaiseki*, which is elaborate Japanese haute cuisine served in multiple courses that mirror the seasons. A highlight of a meal here is the plate of exquisite beef steak, served as a middle course. It is cooked without any fancy sauces, seasoned simply with salt and pepper, and then the juice of roasted vegetables is added as a relish. This is followed immediately with a plate of river fish such as char, served in classic Kyoto *kaiseki* style that is both elegant and understated.

Sansou Murata offers the kind of cooking that embodies the art of Japanese cuisine perfectly. Comfort food is always popular. And the chance to dine at this tranquil *onsen* (hot springs) villa is to enjoy Japanese comfort food at its most stylish and thoroughly flavorful best. **AI**

"Set amid pine-clad mountains ... the Sansou Murata ryokan *is a hidden gem."*

South China Morning Post

↑ Guests at Sansou Murata can enjoy the full *ryokan* experience.

→ Dishes are prepared according to what is in season.

Puong Thong | Hidden gem on the banks of the Ping River

Location Chiang Mai **Signature dish** *Moo tom khem* (slow-braised pork in soy sauce with spices) | ●

"Restaurant crawlers have an embarrassment of choice, but Puong Thong is on all their lists."

Roland Ings, food writer

⬆ Vivid flavors at Puong Thong include fish with chili.

In a very ordinary kitchen in an old Thai house in Chiang Mai, mother and daughter team Mali and Anchalee Ti Aree produce some truly extraordinary food. It's not the traditional regional cuisine that might be expected in the city sometimes known as "the Rose of the North," but classic, perfectly executed central Thai cuisine.

With a few tables set out along the banks of the Ping River, and Anchalee running back and forth with a huge smile serving dish after dish, this is a restaurant to enjoy at leisure—it's a small, family-run operation, so don't try to rush.

Highlights from its extensive menu include *yum kratiem* (a warm salad of tiny local garlic cloves, crisp dried chilis, cashew nuts, fried squid, and sautéed shrimp with a lime dressing); *pla neung manow* (steamed snake head fish served with a sharp, vibrant sauce of coriander, lime, and chilis); *kai yeow maa pad krapow* (1,000-year-old eggs stir-fried with chilis and crisp holy basil); *goong or bpu op woonsen* (giant shrimp or crab baked with Chinese celery, rice noodles, and spices in a claypot), and *moo tom kem* (tender pork, slowly braised for hours in soy sauce with spices). The last named is the the pièce de résistance, a dish that people travel from miles around to sample, so be sure to order it as soon as you arrive, if not the day before.

Mali makes all her curry pastes à la minute. This practice of preparing sauce in the same container as that used to make the main dish is generally associated with Michelin-starred restaurants; but, although Puong Thong has no such accolades, it offers comparably good food at around one-tenth of the price.

Beer and soft drinks are served, and you are welcome to bring your own whisky—the restaurant will supply ice and soda water. Bear in mind that you will need to pay in cash. **KPH & FH**

Samoe Jai | Quintessential Chiang Mai curried noodles and much else

Location Chiang Mai   **Signature dish** *Kow soi* | ❸

Located on the Thanon Faham Road, just downstream from Nakhon Ping Bridge (which carries the northbound crossing of the Chiang Mai ring road over the Ping River), Samoe Jai is widely regarded as the best place to sample the dish for which the city is renowned—*kow soi*.

Kow soi is a rich chicken noodle curry that varies from place to place but which is here served with a topping of crispy, deep-fried noodles, and accompanied by pickled cabbage, chopped fresh shallot, and segments of lime on the side, all to be added (or not) according to taste.

While this is the dish that takes pride of place on the menu, Samoe Jai has a wide range of other tasty regional specialities, including *laarp khua moo* (a northern Thai-style minced pork salad), *yum kanoon* (baby jackfruit salad), *sai oua* (Chiang Mai's local pork sausage, seasoned with turmeric, galangal, and chilis), and a range of grilled satays.

Samoe Jai is slightly off the usual tourist trail, but it is well worth seeking out. Don't expect any frills. The restaurant is housed in an open-sided, breeze-block supported barn; all the furniture and plates are plastic. But, as is so often the case in Thailand, the quality of the food cannot be extrapolated from the unprepossessing surroundings. This may come as a surprise to first-time foreign visitors accustomed to finding the quality of the food directly proportional to the opulence of the decor, but experienced travelers and locals alike flock to Samoe Jai, which serves thousands of them daily.

For foreigners, one of the joys of visiting Thailand is trying several different types of kow soi and making up their own minds which is the best. Anyone embarking on such a voyage of discovery would do well to start at Samoe Jai, because it provides a demanding benchmark against which subsequent meals can be measured. **KPH**

> *"[In] Chiang Mai's* kow soi *ghetto … is Samoe Jai.* Kow soi *foodies spend the day here."*
>
> Lonely Planet

⬆ A bowl of Samoe Jai's *kow soi.*

Laan Chula | Glorious central Thai cooking off the beaten track

Location Sukhothai   **Signature dish** *Gaeng ped hoi kom* (bitter snail curry) | ⓢ

Most people come to Sukhothai to visit its extraordinary ancient ruined city, founded in 1238 and now a UNESCO World Heritage Site. But few foreigners know that, just 7½ miles (12 km) away in the modern town, they'll find Laan Chula, an extraordinary restaurant specializing in the regional cuisine of Thailand's central plains.

Chefs Khun Tee and Khun Bangkom, both local celebrities thanks to their occasional appearances on Thai television, cook an expansive menu, with dishes ranging from their famous *gaeng ped hoi kom* (bitter snail curry) and *pad krapow gop* (frogs' legs with holy basil) to *pla tubtim nung manao* (ruby fish steamed with lemon, garlic, and chili) and local nam priks (fiery relishes). Be sure to try the *nam prik makarm*, which features the tart local tamarind, a memorably complex sour–sweet creation that is seriously addictive. All dishes star locally sourced produce, including seasonal kwang (wild venison).

On first impressions, Laan Chula can be rather overwhelming. To start with, there is the noise. This is far from being an oasis of calm. The cavernous, street-side dining room is cooled by rattling ceiling fans. Local soap operas blare from the TV. Cats wander the aisles hoping for scraps. But that's all a part of the fun. This is a place of discovery.

You come here for the extraordinary cooking of food that is explicitly Thai and profoundly local, yet far removed from the usual expectations foreigners have of Thai cuisine. And you come for the joy of the place and its chefs' contrasting personalities. The laconic Khun Tee plays off the exuberant Khun Bangkom's bundle-of-fun enthusiasm as, in a mixture of English and Thai (actually, mainly Thai), they guide you through a dauntingly extensive menu toward dishes you never thought to try and will never forget. **KPH & FH**

⬆ A dish of bitter snail curry, a popular Thai dish.

Soi Polo Chicken | Perfect deep-fried chicken and more

Location Bangkok **Signature dish** Deep-fried chicken with crispy garlic | $

Tucked away on the tiny Soi Polo (Soi Sanam Khli)—a side street off Bangkok's busy Wireless Road named for the polo club at one end of it—Soi Polo Chicken is a much-loved culinary institution. With two dining rooms, one open-fronted and the other air-conditioned, it serves a large menu of northeastern Thai or Issan specialities. But the highlight, which people travel from miles around to sample, is its *gai tod* (deep-fried chicken).

Crisp, golden, and smothered in deep-fried garlic (of which you can order extra on the side), this dish is moist, delicious, and perfectly cooked. It is served traditionally with sticky rice, a fresh *som tam* (green papaya salad), and fiery dipping sauces on the side. It is a simple yet totally satisfying combination of textures and flavors. Owned and run since the 1980s by Khun Jai Khee, Soi Polo Chicken is very much a family business. The decor is simple, bordering on the basic, with formica tables and metal stools. The servers are friendly and welcoming, the service is brisk, and the prices are reasonable. Such is the establishment's following that the dining room is frequently packed at lunchtimes with local office workers and staff from the many embassies along Wireless Road. It will also make deliveries to nearby hotels. Its popularity is simply unwaning.

While the chicken is the king, other stand-out dishes include an excellent *soop nor mai* (pickled bamboo shoot salad), *laarp pla dook* (warm catfish salad), *laarp woon sen* (warm duck salad mixed with glass noodles), and *tom sap* (spicy Issan hot pot), all nicely judged and well realized. There is nothing pretentious about this restaurant; its main virtues are the solid consistency that come from years of experience. It is a reminder that food does not have to be fancy; it just has to be good. **KPH & FH**

[↑] *Som tam* is the perfect accompaniment to the chicken.

Or Kor Tor Market |
Thai street food in a market setting

Location Bangkok **Signature dish** *Pad ped sataw* | **$**

Or Kor Tor is not a restaurant in the conventionally accepted sense of the term, but a market that sells ready-to-eat food as well as raw ingredients. It is renowned for its fresh fruit (particularly durians), seafood, and bags of multi-colored rice.

But we're here for something to eat, and at the back of the building is a food court, a plain place, almost a canteen, with tubular metal chairs, the sort that screech when scraped along the ground. Go closer to the counter, where in multi-colored metal containers stand almost innumerable curries, sauces, dishes, mounds of rice, and piles of noodles. Amid the murmur of diners, the sizzle of chopped-up duck being fried on a hot plate can be heard. The air is filled

> *"Or Tor Kor is Bangkok's highest-quality fruit and agricultural market ... culinary trainspotting."*
>
> Lonely Planet

with the spicy aroma of sauces and pastes all ready to be called into action.

The available selection is extensive. Favorite dishes include a bowl of red curry, its slices of pork submerged, with a helping of rice on the side. Also commendable are the portions of fried shrimp and grilled squid, served with a scorching chili sauce. Those in the know, however, usually plump for pad ped sataw (stir-fried spicy stink bean). This is a pungent, fiery dish whose saltiness is provided by the addition of dried shrimp (bits of pork also get a look-in).

Or Kor Tor is a market, but the great tastes of Thailand available onsite make it also a restaurant, albeit a highly unusual one. **ATJ**

Issaya Siamese Club |
Modern Thai food in a beautiful setting

Location Bangkok **Signature dish** Chili-glazed baby back ribs and banana blossom salad | **$$$**

Tucked away in a beautifully restored, neo-colonial-style house on a soi (side street) off Chua Pleong Road, the Issaya Siamese Club is chef Ian Kittichai's flagship Thai restaurant. With elegantly designed interiors by Hans Bogetoft Christensen and a relaxing garden scattered with colorful soft furnishings, Issaya feels chic and contemporary. But it's the food that you come for, and the food that will make you return.

From humble beginnings working at his mother's food stall, Kittichai has become one of Thailand's leading chefs. He uses ingredients of the highest quality—many of which come from Issaya's organic kitchen garden—to reinvigorate classic Thai recipes into an exciting, bold, and playful cuisine.

Issaya's very reasonably priced set menu includes the restaurant's signature dishes—succulent spice-rubbed baby back ribs with *kradook moo aob* sauce and *yum hua plee*, a gloriously piquant peanut and shallot-studded banana blossom salad.

Some of the other highlights include *kanom krok* (a savory take on a traditional coconut snack), *mussaman gae* (lamb shank massaman curry), *kow yum Bangkok* (sweet and tart rice salad with pomelo and tamarind), *hor mok goong mongkorn* (steamed Maine lobster in a lobster curry custard). Follow any of these dishes with one of Issaya's stand-out, not-to-be-missed desserts, such as jasmine-flower pannacotta, green curry macaroons, or *khanom kho prayuk* (sticky rice flour mochi filled with black coconut ice cream).

Issaya Siamese Club's food retains a profound connection with the traditions of Thai cooking, combining it with cutting-edge culinary flair and encapsulating the vibrancy and excitement of modern Bangkok. **KPH & FH**

▣ *Yum hua plee*, a delicate salad of banana blossom.

Bo.Lan | Ancient meets modern for the ultimate Thai "slow food"

Location Bangkok   **Signature dish** The Bo.Lan Balance tasting menu | ❸❸❸

"… perfectly deserves its reputation as one of the ten best restaurants in Bangkok."

bangkok.com

⬆ An elegant tasting plate at Bo.Lan.

Headed up by award-winning husband and wife team Duangporn "Bo" Songvisava and Dylan Jones, who both worked with David Thompson at Nahm, Bo.Lan restores Thai food to the heart of the Slow Food Movement. With a philosophy dedicated to the freshest seasonal produce and a proper understanding of traditional Thai farming and cooking rituals, Bo and Dylan have created a restaurant which both builds on Thompson's work and creates a modern Thai food based on the foundations of the country's ancient past.

Nowhere is this typified better than in the Bo.Lan Balance tasting menu. Designed to be ordered by the entire table of diners, it constructs a traditional and properly balanced Thai meal from five constituent parts: the *yum* or Thai salad; the *krueng jim* or relish; the *jan pad* or stir-fry; the *gaeng* or curry; and the *nam gaeng* or soup. The kitchen may also send out extras to complement these core dishes. And their platter of traditional Thai petit fours is outstanding. Note that the menu changes frequently, as Bo.Lan constantly strives to source the very best organic and artisanal ingredients from across the country.

Bo.Lan is also one of the few Thai restaurants that still make and serve *yaa dong*, a medicinal alcoholic drink that tastes like Fernet Branca.

If you plan to order à la carte, don't miss out on Bo.Lan's exceptional curries, which are made from pastes pounded fresh by hand to order. Particular favorites include *gaeng moo yang sai gluay dib* (a grilled pork and green banana curry) and *ngob gai* (a grilled red chicken curry wrapped in banana leaf).

Set in a beautifully restored and decorated mid-century Thai house tucked away on a residential street off Soi Sukhumvit, Bo.Lan offers a unique experience thanks to Bo and Dylan's exacting attention to detail. As they like to say, eating at Bo.Lan is "purely, essentially, and sincerely Thai." **KPH & FH**

Nahm | An exciting and refined taste of Thailand

Location Bangkok   **Signature dish** *Pla chorn* (snakehead fish curry) | ❸❸❸

Nahm is the brainchild of chef David Thompson, a world-renowned expert on Thai cuisine and the author of two best-selling books on the subject, *Thai Food* and *Thai Street Food*.

Thompson's first two restaurants were in Sydney in his native Australia. He then moved to Britain and created the original Nahm at the Halkin Hotel in London's Mayfair district. Within six months of its opening in 2001, it became the first Thai restaurant to be awarded a Michelin star.

In 2010, Thompson transferred himself to Bangkok, where he re-created Nahm in the city's Metropolitan Hotel. Here, his increased access to the best authentic Thai ingredients enabled him to raise his cuisine to an even higher level than he had previously attained.

Nahm's current setting, in a beautiful and glamorous room, may lead diners to anticipate a staid, traditional menu. But Thompson's creations are all refined and thrilling, from the first forkful to the last bite of dessert. In addition to the snakehead fish curry signature dish, stand-outs include pork cheek with smoky tomato sauce and jungle curry of salted beef with wild ginger, green peppercorns, and Thai basil.

When Thompson overheard a Thai member of his staff remark that the food was like her grandmother used to make, he was flattered. "Food from that older generation is better, stronger," he told *The Observer*. "To get those undulant tastes that strike a deep chord, rather than the superficial tastes you get with modern food, that for me is exciting. It's almost like I'm a culinary archeologist.

"Thai food ain't about simplicity. It's about the juggling of disparate elements to create a harmonious finish. Like a complex musical chord it's got to have a smooth surface but it doesn't matter what's happening underneath. Simplicity isn't the dictum here, at all." **NS**

"Some Westerners think it's a jumble of flavors, but to a Thai that's important."

David Thompson, food writer

⬆ Ma Hor: caramelized minced pork, chili, and coriander.

Chao Lay | Sumptuous Thai seafood at the water's edge

Location Hua Hin   **Signature dish** *Phu pad pong kari* (curried crab) | ❺❺

As befits its location, on a pier running off Naretdamri Road, not far from the fishermen's wharf in the town of Hua Hin, Chao Lay offers a prodigiously large seafood menu. Immensely popular with locals, out-of-town Thais, and foreigners alike, Khun Tip and Khun Dao's exactingly run restaurant provides a relaxed and easy-going dining experience, catering proficiently to raucous groups of work colleagues while simultaneously offering romantic, star-lit evening dining to courting couples.

Generally quiet at lunchtimes, Chao Lay really gets going after dark, when the cool evening breezes blow in off the Gulf of Thailand and the moonlight glitters on the waves. Patrons can either choose their dinner as they arrive from the huge tanks of fresh fish, crabs, and rock lobsters set out at street level or simply order at table. The latter option is normally preferred by those who don't want to know the exact provenance and back story of the food on their plates.

Standout dishes include *phu pad pong kari* (an excellent curried crab), *pla muk tod kratiem* (squid fried with garlic), *hoi chen pad cha*a (stir-fried sweet scallops), grilled rock lobster with a range of dipping sauces, and whole, deep-fried *pla kapong* (sea bass) covered with garlic. The seafood tom yum is widely credited as one of the best spicy soups of its kind. Orders arrive swiftly thanks to a well-orchestrated team of friendly waiters.

Chao Lay pulls off the unusual and difficult trick of providing intimate dining in a large setting. To arrive here is to be welcomed for a feast so good that one will certainly want to return. Three hours' drive from Bangkok, Hua Hin is one of Thailand's top beach resorts and the site of a royal summer residence. Chao Lay is not the town's only pier restaurant, but it is, in the view of most people, one of the best. **KPH & FH**

⬆ Be sure to try the signature curried crab.

Raya | Retro-Thai setting for nationally acclaimed, traditional food

Location Phuket   **Signature dish** Crabmeat and coconut milk curry with rice noodles | 🟢🟢

Housed in a restored, historic, two-story colonial house in Phuket Old Town, Raya has become an institution among locals and visitors alike. It is one of the most highly rated Thai restaurants in town. Owner Khun Kulab is held is such esteem that customers have included Thai royalty, prime ministers, and TV stars. Ultra-wealthy fans have even ordered Raya's dishes and had them flown to them in Bangkok. Many of the region's chefs learned their craft in Raya's kitchen, and visitors who wish to learn more about Thailand's vibrant cuisine can also take cookery classes here.

With its ornate balcony and wooden French doors with colored glass panels, Raya's vintage building is an appealing venue. Once inside, a charming old-world Thai atmosphere takes over. There are recordings of local ballads, overhead fans, and a simple decor featuring the original mosaic-tiled floor, open staircase in the middle of the restaurant, and exposed wooden ceiling. Portraits of Thai monarchs hang on the whitewashed walls. Bustling waitresses in black-and-white outfits rush multiple dishes to tables already laden with bowls of rice, salad, vegetables, dips, and sauces.

The restaurant is renowned for its creamy crab curry with huge chunks of crabmeat served with slender rice vermicelli noodles, a rich and glorious combination of flavors and textures. But diners have much to choose from as the menu includes a wide range of Thai dishes including dry crispy shrimps in chili sauce, spicy duck stir-fry, and sea bass in tamarind and lemon grass sauce. As with the best Thai cooking, the dishes offer a careful balance of chili hotness, sweetness, saltiness, and sourness. Dishes involve extensive and meticulous preparation behind the scenes, with Kulab careful to ensure that all this happens to the standards she requires. **SH**

⬆ **The charming old-world interior at Raya.**

Cuisine Wat Damnak |
Cambodian food with a French accent

Location Siem Reap **Signature dish** Sticky rice porridge with quail | 🟢🟢

Traditional Khmer cooking is one of the world's oldest and most influential culinary cultures. Its emphasis is on simple, fresh, local, seasonal ingredients, delicate spices, contrasts of texture, flavor, and temperature, and exotic presentation with herbs, flowers, or dipping sauces. Combine that with one of the finest Western gastronomic traditions, that of the French, and there is potential for some very sophisticated food. And that's the secret of Cuisine Wat Damnak's success. One of the of the country's highest-rated restaurants is the project of Joannès Rivière, a French chef who previously taught cooking to Cambodian children.

His restaurant, in a simple two-story traditional wooden house, offers a choice of two weekly changing, six-course tasting menus. These are designed to encourage customers to sample local specialties that they may not otherwise order. So Wat Damnak diners may try unfamiliar fruits such as ambarella, Java feronilla, and kuy fruit; eat local fish and shellfish unique to the Mekong and Tonle Sap lake; and sample fresh lotus seeds, wild lily stems, and edible flowers. The vast majority of ingredients are bought daily from local markets or are hand-picked wild ingredients, like mushrooms, wild mangosteen, and tromong leaves.

The outcome of all this is a series of imaginative modern dishes adding Gallic flair to Indo-Chinese classics. So a quail fillet may arrive at the table with a water mimosa salad; a perfect meringue may be stuffed with a purple dragon fruit.

Rivière's food is not cheap by local standards, but has become one of the most highly recommended restaurants for both tourists and locals. His wife Carole manages the front of house, which includes two floors of dining plus romantic candlelit tables in the tropical garden outside. **SH**

Foreign Correspondents' Club Restaurant | A bold mix

Location Phnom Penh **Signature dish** Salt and pepper calamari | 🟢

The Foreign Correspondents' Club in Phnom Penh was once one of only a very few safe havens in the whole of Cambodia for diplomats and journalists. The fall of the notorious dictator Pol Pot was reported to the world from this old French colonial villa. Today, the nation's capital is a bustling tourist destination, but the Club still retains some of the atmosphere of the old days. Usually referred to simply as "the FCC," or "the F," it is now a boutique hotel with a popular restaurant.

When the F first opened, it was a members-only retreat from the tense streets of the capital, where an uneasy peace was just taking hold. Writers and sources traded secrets in the shadows. Today, it's open

> *"The menu is Western and Asian fusion, with Cambodian curry taking its place beside pasta …"*
>
> travel.yahoo.com

to anyone, and more likely to be a retreat from the city's pushy vendors and noisy streets. From the veranda, diners can look out across the Mekong River.

The menu is an international mix: a few old journalists' favorites still feature, including beer-battered fish and chips and pizza. But Asian ingredients also appear, alongside more adventurous Western dishes, including grilled sea bass (with mildly spiced coconut curry infused with cloves, nutmeg, cardamom, roasted peanuts, and crushed potatoes) and sticky barbecue pork ribs (with baby bok choy and steamed rice). Explore the Asian side of the menu to find creative, locally inspired dishes such as pork dumplings with black vinegar and a garlic chive dip. **SH**

Pho 10 | Share a busy table for a bowl of Vietnam's famous beef noodle soup

Location Hanoi **Signature dish** Pho | ❸

Although the entrance to Pho 10 is often hidden behind a forest of motorbikes and scooters parked outside, the large illuminated orange sign above the doorway makes it hard to miss. There is nothing pretentious about this restaurant—it's a simple, efficient, and busy space in which to sample Hanoi's best-known street dish.

Pho, pronounced "fuh," is Vietnam's famous, flavorful beef noodle soup, usually bought from street vendors during the day and eaten as a snack. On a busy corner in the old quarter of Vietnam's capital, Pho 10 takes this street food into a comparatively comfortable environment. Its version of pho is highly acclaimed, and the restaurant has become a well-known institution in the city. The counters are bustling all day, so come prepared to line up for a seat at the communal tables. This is not a place to linger, though—bowls of pho are eaten quickly.

Huge vats of the broth steam all day in the open kitchen. Diners grab simple chairs at the tables, each of which has bins underneath for used tissues. The restaurant's laminated English and Vietnamese menu offers ten types of pho, involving combinations of different cuts of beef cooked to varying extents. These strips of meat are served in deep white bowls of spiced beef stock "soup" with smooth white noodles and clumps of fresh herbs.

Diners add flavor to their soups with a range of condiments and side dishes: the choice includes handfuls of chopped, fiercely hot chilis, crunchy bean sprouts, sprigs of aromatic herbs, slices of fresh limes, and a delicate homemade garlic vinegar. Many diners also order a plate of *guai*—crispy fried bread sticks that are dipped into the soup before being eaten. Pho 10 is a simple and satisfying experience that nobody should miss. **SH**

> *"No visit to Hanoi would be complete without sampling the famous dish [of] pho."*

Rosie Birkett, *Guardian*

⊡ A fragrant bowl of beef pho with noodles and herbs.

Cuc Gach Quán | A city restaurant offering
old Vietnamese country cooking

Location Ho Chi Minh City **Signature dish** Fried homemade tofu with lemongrass |

"It will come as no surprise that the owner is an architect … the decor is rustic and elegant."

Lonely Planet

⬆ The speciality of the house, tofu with lemongrass.

This charming restaurant hit the headlines after film stars Brad Pitt and Angelina Jolie visited it in 2010. Locals were already in on the secret, though. Cuc Gach Quán claims to focus on Vietnamese traditional cooking, but regulars realize it offers a lot more than that. The architect–owner has converted a French colonial-style family house in a residential side street into a quirky tribute to prewar Vietnam. Old local folk music is played on an ancient reel-to-reel recorder, and wall maps depict the city during French colonial days. The wine list is 100 percent French.

The house was converted with lots of recycled materials. With old wooden furniture, handmade hanging lanterns, and unmatched chipped earthenware bowls, the result is an authentic slice of traditional Vietnamese rural life within the nation's biggest city. There is even an indoor pond overhung by a flowering cherry tree.

The food from the open kitchen matches this ambience perfectly: the emphasis is on fresh local vegetables served in imaginative ways with traditional Vietnamese meat and fish. The enormous menu includes a list of 35 different vegetables, including bamboo shoots, sweet potato leaves, and morning glory. Diners decide the method of cooking, from a list including boiled, sautéed, and fresh salad. There is a similar menu of flowers, which are also "cooked the way it pleases you."

Even the flashiest dishes are inexpensive, but cooked with great skill and plentiful use of local flavors such as lemongrass and tamarind. Main courses include dazzling combinations: try the sea bass with passion fruit, or the beef with zucchini flowers, or the crispy pork with pickled vegetables. Condiments include jam jars of homemade honey and yogurt. **SH**

May | Classic Vietnamese family recipes in a grand colonial villa

Location Ho Chi Minh City **Signature dish** Pork stewed in a clay pot with duck eggs | **$**

French-Vietnamese entrepreneur Tu Tho established this restaurant to celebrate the traditional family recipes she grew up with. While the food is based on her grandfather's and father's recipes, the restaurant's building makes a rather grander statement. The white exterior of this former colonial villa gleams under its floodlights at night among the surrounding palm trees. Inside, the ornate plasterwork, impressive chandeliers, polished wooden floors, and shiny French-style bar create a dignified atmosphere in which to enjoy classic Vietnamese food.

As befits the surroundings, the menu offers elegant variations of traditional local cuisine. After a light starter (the fresh spring rolls are highly recommended), diners might move on to mains such as shrimp in a sweet and sour soup, or soft-shell crabs in tamarind sauce. The grilled dishes—including the classic *bo la lot* (beef wrapped in aromatic betel leaves) and grilled pork belly—are worth sampling. Ingredients such as morning glory, banana flowers, and water lilies are transformed into textured salads. The crockery is delicate blue-and-white china; the service unfailingly smooth and attentive.

May proudly boasts not only the usual mantra about using nothing other than the freshest ingredients, but also that there's "no monosodium glutamate" anywhere on the menu. Thus all the tofu is homemade and comes crisply fried on the outside, soft inside and cooked with fresh lemongrass and piquant chili. The signature dish—belly pork stewed for hours in a clay pot with garlic, fish sauce, sugar, aromatic spices, and hard-boiled duck eggs—is the traditional meal for Tet Nguyen Dán, the New Year holiday. Tho claims every family in Vietnam knows how to cook it. They are unlikely, however, to eat it in such grand surroundings as the May restaurant. **SH**

Com Nieu | Colorful Vietnamese dishes and flamboyant pot-smashing

Location Ho Chi Minh City **Signature dish** Com dap | **$**

The sign above the door of this contemporary two-story restaurant says simply "Vietnamese Gastronomy." Indeed, Com Nieu is renowned for serving dishes with all the creativity and color of indigenous street food, but in a stylish and spacious air-conditioned restaurant away from the hustle and bustle.

The late founder of the restaurant, the formidable Madame Ngoc, devised a unique catering gimmick that still keeps Com Nieu near the top of recommended restaurant lists for Vietnam's biggest city, and an endorsement by American celebrity chef Anthony Bourdain has helped spread the word. The restaurant's unique selling proposition involves a particular way of cooking rice, by baking it in clay pots

> *"Order the com dap, 'smashed rice', for the entertaining bowl-breaking, rice-throwing spectacle."*
>
> travel.yahoo.com

over a charcoal grill. A waiter then smashes the pot in front of the customers and throws the sizzling hot crispy rice cake over the diners' heads to another waiter, who deftly seasons it and adds sauce and scallions. By the end of every evening, the floor is littered with broken clay pots.

There is no doubt that it is the theatrical presentation of *com dap* (literally, "smashed rice") that has made the restaurant famous. However, the menu has as many as 300 items, from classic soft, shrimp-filled summer rolls with a dipping sauce, green papaya salad, and flavorful lobster in a sweet paprika sauce, to crabs stir-fried with basil, fish soup with tofu, and pork with tea-marinated, hard-boiled eggs. **SH**

328 Katong Laksa | An authentic taste of one of Singapore's most famous dishes

Location Singapore   **Signature dish** *Laksa* |

"Customers vote with their feet, and this place is full on a daily basis."

Gordon Ramsay, celebrity chef

⊞ A gloriously flavorful, spicy seafood noodle soup, *laksa* is a must-try dish.

Of the numerous rival candidates for the unofficial title of the national dish of Singapore, the one that is found most frequently in hawker centers and food courts throughout the island is *laksa*, which consists of thick rice noodles steeped in a spicy curry, thickened with chili paste and coconut milk and topped with cockles, shrimp, and fish cakes.

It was originally brought to the region by the Peranakan people, ethnic Chinese who immigrated several centuries ago to what was then a part of the British Straits Settlements. There are several regional variations on the recipe, but the version particularly associated with Singapore itself is *laksa lemak*, which is characterized by the use of a rich and thick coconut milk for a markedly different flavor that is more creamy than sweet.

In Singapore's Katong neighborhood, long a bastion of the Peranakan community, some of the most famous stalls have been serving up delicious bowls of laksa for decades. As more and more such outlets sprang up, the district's East Coast Road became the battleground for what became known as the Katong Laksa Wars.

Of the competing laksa stalls, one of the most lauded is 328 Katong Laksa at 51 East Coast Road, where the walls are lined with photographs of the numerous celebrities who have sampled its delights. The restaurant is small, with tables spilling out onto the sidewalk.

Here the soup is not too sweet, but rich and creamy with a kick of spice. It is served with cut-up noodles so that the dish can be consumed with only a spoon. The proprietor, Nancy Lim, explains that it is the quality of her ingredients that sets her soup apart, with only the freshest seafood and noodles used daily. The key ingredient of her addictive, creamy soup is the addition to the broth of a dash of evaporated milk. **JG**

Tiong Bahru Hawker Center | Lively market stall

Location Singapore **Signature dish** Chwee kueh | $

Hawkers sold their wares on the streets of Singapore from the days of the first colonial settlement of the island until after the Second World War, when the government built numerous complexes in an effort to move them all indoors. Today, there are hundreds of such buildings all around the island, and they have defined dining for generations of locals, who eat in them regularly. With no air-conditioning, these hawker centers are hot and sticky but are otherwise perfect environments in which to peruse endless stalls representing Singapore's multi-ethnic cuisines. Nothing is expensive in these places, and everything is brought to diners at the table.

One of the best examples of the type is the Tiong Bahru Food Market & Hawker Center, which is part of a larger market and dining complex in a lively neighborhood still characterized by a charming retro feel despite rapid modernization almost everywhere else on the island. This was Singapore's first neighborhood market, upgraded in 2004 to a two-story wet market and hawker center. One of the biggest on the island, it has more than 80 cooked food stalls, at least one-quarter of which have been there since the 1950s.

Any visit to Tiong Bahru must include a bite at old stalwart Jian Bo Shui Kueh, which sells a steamed rice cake called chwee kueh topped with spicy, stewed, fermented daikon (white radish) and a glistening dollop of chili paste. This uniquely Singaporean dish is a wondrous mouthful of textures, soft and delicately steamed into kueh (bite-sized snacks) and perfectly seasoned with garlic, soy sauce, and sesame. Other good outlets here include Hong Heng Fried Sotong Prawn Mee and Lee Hong Kee Cantonese Roasted, which both major in char siew and roasted pork, and Teochew Fish Ball Noodle, where the house speciality is handmade fish balls. **JG**

Ng Ah Sio | A decades-old bak kut teh institution

Location Singapore **Signature dish** Bak kut teh | $

Bak kut teh (BKT), the Hokkien dialect term for "meat bone tea," was introduced to Singapore and Malaysia in the nineteenth century by Chinese coolies, who took it as a tonic for their health. It is a strong, herbal soup boiled for hours with meaty pork ribs and bones. The tea in the name refers to the strong oolong that is usually served with it. Over the years, Teochew and Hokkien influences have created two different takes on the dish: the former is characterized by a lighter broth flavored with white pepper and garlic; the latter uses dark soy sauce.

There are numerous BKT stalls in Singapore, but one of the most famous and long-standing is the Ng Ah Sio Pork Ribs Soup Eating House on Rangoon Road. Extremely popular with a perpetual line out of

> *"In Singapore on the lookout for BKT, I soon learned that this is not the only place but it is the place."*
>
> Marguerite Zuiderduin, food writer

the door, the stall reportedly had to turn away Hong Kong's chief executive Donald Tsang in 2006 because it had run out of pork ribs for the day. Owner Ng Ah Sio started in the business by helping his father at his stall in the 1950s, and has seen it develop a cult following. He opened the current premises in 1988.

On most nights, the tables spill out onto the sidewalk, as patrons nosh on the intoxicatingly flavorful soup made from prime pork ribs, boiled in small batches throughout the day, with a secret blend of spices and herbs. Take your pick from the extensive tea list, and don't forget to pair the soup with freshly fried crullers and any of the excellent stewed dishes on the side. **JG**

Sin Huat Eating House |

Crab bee hoon with a side of attitude

Location Singapore **Signature dish** Crab *bee hoon* |
❸❸

In a city famous for restaurants serving crab, there is general, if sometimes grudging, agreement about the best of them all: Sin Huat Eating House, a garishly lit and slightly grimy-looking establishment where diners spill out of the dining room onto a sidewalk in the red light district.

Its signature dish—indeed, its *raison d'être*—is crab *bee hoon*, a platter of giant, meaty jumbo crustaceans from Sri Lanka, stuffed full of roe and piled atop a mess of rice vermicelli sticky with a "secret stock" of green onion, ginger, and chili. The flavor of the sweet crabmeat, with its intoxicating heat of spices, is intensified by the wok-hei preparation method and absorbed into the garlicky noodles.

"The best seafood in Singapore … as much as you're itching to criticize it, the food is fantastic."

Lonely Planet

So far, so good. What arouses the hostility of some patrons is the idiosyncratic approach to them of chef Danny Lee, who comes to the tables himself but, rather than take orders, prefers to tell diners what they're going to have, and in what quantities. (Sin Huat Eating House famously has no menu.) However, although Lee is pushy, he is not impervious to reason: you can get what you want if you're strong-minded.

Other notable dishes include flash-fried kai-lan (Chinese kale) flavored with garlic and light XO sauce; live bay scallops on the shell dunked in black bean sauce; and steamed giant shrimp blanched in garlic. In spite of Lee's combative personality, Singaporeans keep going back to him for more. **JG**

Andre | An impressive, impeccable gastronomic experience

Location Singapore **Signature dish** Octa-philosophy |
❸❸❸❸

André Chiang has been in the vanguard of global cuisine from the beginning of his working life. At the age of 15, he moved—with his mother's permission—from his native Taiwan to France to study at Pierre Gagnaire and L'Astrance in Paris and at Le Jardin des Sens in Montpellier.

Chiang's formative exposure to these ingredient-driven and technically supreme European master kitchens, combined with his reverence for the cuisine of Asia, inspired him to open in 2010 a self-titled (apart from the acute accent) restaurant in the heart of Singapore's Chinatown.

Dinner here is structured around the eight "universals" that Chiang regards as fundamental to a complete and perfect gastronomic experience. He labels the main tenets of this octa-philosophy as follows: texture, memory, pure, terroir, unique, salt, south, and artisan. The result is a set meal that wanders through the South of France, playfully recalls the comfort foods of childhood, and cerebrally employs technology to create unimagined flavor combinations.

These eight foundation stones are ever-present, but the ways in which they are manifested change with the seasons. Nonetheless, some standout dishes remain constant, including the artisan produce flown in from Chiang's personal garden in Taiwan, seafood stew tinted in Southern French style with pastis, and his molecular gastronomic desserts, notably a refigured take on the Snickers chocolate bar.

Andre seats only 30, and with a concentrated seven-member kitchen, dining there is an intimate and highly personalized experience. Chiang's restaurant is lauded, along with Iggy's, as one of Singapore's two premier kitchens. **JG**

▣ Dishes at Andre are stylish gourmet creations.

Iggy's | Contemporary cuisine and fine wine on Orchard Road

Location Singapore **Signature dish** Gillardeau oyster | ❺❺❺❺

Opened in 2004 and named after its founder, Ignatius (Iggy) Chan, this establishment is regarded as one of the best restaurants in the world. The current premises are hidden in the Hilton Hotel behind minimalistic wooden panel doors that slide open to reveal an elegant and dimly lit dining room. This is the second incarnation of Iggy's. Its first was as a 28-seater in the Regent Hotel, where it was the realization of Iggy's dream to serve great food in a small, intimate setting, with the finest seasonal ingredients sourced from the whole of Europe, Asia, and Australia.

In 2010, when Iggy's moved to this new space almost twice the size of the original location, the seating capacity was maintained while the kitchen doubled in size. It is here that Iggy now works with his culinary team, headed by chef Akmal Anuar, to create innovative new dishes based on his global travels and favorite flavor combinations. Iggy started his working career in 1989 at Fourchettes, the French restaurant in

the Singapore Mandarin Oriental Hotel. He then traveled extensively across Europe, working in French restaurants and wineries in Beaujolais, Burgundy, and Bordeaux before returning to Singapore.

His cuisine is rooted in his classical training and his fascination with Japan. His flavors are light and perfectly balanced, with dishes such as akamutsu with white bean, sea urchin, and okra and Gillardeau oyster with red cabbage and Cabernet Sauvignon vinegar.

Diners should ask Iggy and his team to pair each dish with a specially selected wine. As one of Chan's favorite grape varietals is Pinot noir, the wine list is built with a strong focus on Burgundies as well as more unusual choices such as sparkling sake. Some of the inclusions on any list of the world's best restaurants may be contentious, but everyone agrees that Iggy's is well worth its place. **JG**

⊡ A refined dish of cold *somen* noodles with caviar.

Wee Nam Kee | Chicken rice stalwart in Singapore with a focus on quality

Location Singapore   **Signature dish** Hainanese chicken rice | **$**

One of several contenders for the title of Singapore's national dish, Hainanese chicken rice has little to do with its namesake island off the coast of southern China, but rather has taken on an identity that is distinctively Singaporean.

It is difficult to avoid having a dish of chicken rice in Singapore—it is served in hawker stalls, food courts, high-end restaurants, and even by airlines. There are the legendary old stalwart purveyors such as Chatterbox, Yet Con, and Boon Tong Kee, all of which have established franchise outlets around the island. Then there are the chicken rice stalls that have become so iconic that they now represent Singaporean cuisine in other parts of the world. Wee Nam Kee is one of the latter institutions; it was founded in 1987, and has several stalls all around the island as well as in the Philippines capital, Manila. It frequently showcases its chicken rice at gourmet festivals as far away as Europe and Australia.

Hanging in every Wee Nam Kee display window are rows of glistening, succulent poached and roasted chickens. Walk by a store and you are engulfed by the intoxicating fragrance of rice cooked in chicken fat and the sharp aroma of minced garlic and freshly ground chili sauce. Traditionally, the chicken is steeped in sub-boiling pork and chicken stock, which is used again and again as per the Chinese master stock tradition. Then a separate chicken stock is used for the rice, producing oil-slicked grains with maximum flavor.

Most stalls use ready-made mixes and oils, but Wee Nam Kee makes everything from scratch. Oil infused with pandan leaf and herbs is added to the chicken stock used to cook the rice, instead of the chicken fat that is used in most stalls. Smothered generously in homemade chili and minced ginger sauce, Wee Nam Kee's chicken rice is a delight. **JG**

⬆ Hainanese chicken rice, a Singapore classic.

Line Clear Nasi Kandar | Historic stall in Penang's Little India

Location Penang **Signature dish** *Ayam goreng* | $

"One of the oldest nasi kandar *eateries left . . . a food trip wouldn't be complete without a visit."*

Time Out

↑ *Ayam goreng* is an unmissable dish.

The most important exotic influences on Penang's food came from the Tamils, who immigrated to the Malay Peninsula from South India and Sri Lanka in the late nineteenth century. They brought with them a range of herbs and spices that were new to Malaysia—among their contributions were cumin, fennel, and coriander. Before long, these found their way into the cuisine of the host nation, and aided the development of fusion favorites such as fish head curry, *mee goreng* (fried noodles), *roti canai* (a flatbread), and *nasi kandar* (rice with curries). Of these, *nasi kandar* has been widely acknowledged as a favorite since its early days as a cheap and filling source of nutrition for port workers and laborers.

In the Malay language Bahasa Melayu, *nasi* means "hawker" and *kandar* is the wooden pole that hawkers carried on their shoulders to support wooden baskets at either end, one of which typically contained rice, the other curries, and various side dishes. Over time, these itinerant sellers settled in fixed locations. Of all the thousands of nasi kandar outlets in Malaysia today, Line Clear is one of the most venerable still in operation, having opened in 1947 in a covered alley off Chulia Street. Open 24 hours a day, it is always teeming with customers, and at lunchtimes and weekends it is even busier than usual.

Join the line and select from the seemingly endless options of side dishes to go with your rice or nasi briyani. Among the best choices are the famous *ayam goreng* (golden fried chicken), curried shrimp, deep-fried fish head, squid, and okra, as well as whatever may be the special for the day. The finishing touch is a generous *campus* (mixture) of curry poured on the rice—this is known as *banjir*, from the verb "to flood." Many of these dishes are spicy and as hot as the normal daytime temperatures. To cool down after the meal, don't miss a glass of freshly squeezed lime juice or rose syrup water. **JG**

Heng Huat Kopitiam Char Koay Teow Stall | Food with attitude

Location Penang **Signature dish** *Char koay teow* | $

Of all the stall hawkers in Penang, perhaps none is as revered and as feared as Madam Soon Suan Choo, the formidable woman who doles out the food at the front of Heng Huat Kopitiam with a healthy dose of attitude. She serves mainly *char koay teow*, and it is from the initials of this dish of stir-fried rice-cake strips that she has acquired the name "Sister CKT."

Her reputation is based on her curt manners and strict ordering rules, which she enforces strictly and with impunity. Orders may be placed only in Hokkien—any attempt to communicate with her in another language will be ignored—and diners must be willing to wait for at least 45 minutes before any food arrives at their table. Add to all that her prices, which are around twice those of most other stores in Penang, and it may seem surprising that she remains in business, let alone merits an entry in this book. But customers keep coming back, and overlook the drawbacks because of the quality of the food.

Char koay teow is a speciality that evolved from Teowchew and Hokkien cuisine while Penang was a bustling commercial center under British rule and attracted merchants from all over the world. There are other versions of this dish in other parts of Malaysia and in Singapore, but it is generally agreed that *char koay teow* is best sampled in Penang, where fresh shrimp and cockles, *bak eu pok* (fried lard), *ku chai* (Chinese chives), and sliced *lap cheong* (Chinese sausages) are used.

The secret behind a great *char koay teow* is a very hot pan, and unlike those of her contemporaries who prefer the ease of a gas stove, Madam Choo still opts for charcoal, which she replenishes throughout the day. The noodles are fried in individual portions in order to maintain the optimal cooking temperature at all times. The result is an amalgamation of sweet and savory flavors, noodles charred ever so slightly at the edges, and a fragrance unlocked only by that ever-elusive quality known as "the breath of the wok." **JG**

"Taste: excellent . . . the seasoning was spot-on. It definitely had the wow factor."

Chen Jinhwen, *The Straits Times*

↑ *Char koay teow*—fresh rice noodles with seafood.

Hoe Kee Chicken Rice Ball | The oldest chicken rice ball shop in Malacca

Location Malacca **Signature dish** Chicken rice ball | **$**

"Their chicken is incredibly moist, succulent, and flavorful.... The soy-based sauce is to die for."

The Hungry Bunny

⤴ Rice balls with steamed white chicken.

➡ Food stalls line Jonker Walk (Jalan Hang Jebat) in Malacca's Chinatown.

As a major port on the Straits of Malacca, Malacca City has been visited by sailors and merchants from all over the world, and the cosmopolitan influence is now apparent in the local cuisine, which is a mixture of Peranakan, Malaysian, Portuguese, and Indian styles.

One of Malacca's most celebrated delicacies is the chicken rice ball, a variation on Hainanese chicken rice. The dish is now ubiquitous throughout the city and the hinterland state, but the Hoe Kee Chicken Rice Ball shop is the oldest and best place to eat it.

Located on historic Jonker Walk, the shop is immediately noticeable by the long lines snaking out the door. The founder, Chew Kim Por, started selling chicken rice in the 1960s with her eldest son. Most of the early customers were coolies at the dockyard. As these workers usually ate their lunch outdoors, Madam Chew decided to shape the rice into balls, which stayed warmer for longer and which could be eaten without cutlery. Today, these chicken balls have become a culinary symbol of Malacca. Hoe Kee has inspired several imitation chains around the city, but the original outlet remains the best.

Elegantly decorated to resemble an old Chinese home, the restaurant features traditional wooden beams and has a sky-lit courtyard at its heart. The food comes out steaming hot just moments after ordering. The signature dish, rice balls with steamed white chicken, may look simple, but such consistency and shape are difficult to achieve: the rice needs to be formed while still warm so that the starch can help bind its grains together. These days, a shortage of personnel with the right technique has forced the restaurant to offer loose rice to big eaters to supplement the balls. But the chicken meat remains as flavorful and tender as ever, with smooth, slippery skin perfect for dipping into chili sauce and minced ginger. Other must-try items are asam fish, fried cabbage, slow-cooked black bean soup, and lotus root soup. **JG**

Sardine | Stylish Balinese restaurant offering "sunshine cooking"

Location Bali   **Signature dish** Steamed barramundi wrapped in banana leaves | ❸❸

"Quite possibly Bali's most charming restaurant. Built entirely of bamboo with a stunning view."

frommers.com

⬆ Colorful ingredients make for stylish dishes.

Californian chef Michael Shaheen calls his work at Sardine "cuisine du soleil"—a menu of healthy, light food suitable for eating in hot climates. It's essentially a mix of the day's catches from fishermen in the nearby village of Jimbaran and the organic produce of the restaurant's own farm in a mountain village.

So Sardine diners will find dishes like sautéed kingfish with mountain potato and garden vegetable salad; grilled triggerfish with green papaya, clams, and shrimp; or pan-seared opakapaka with crisp vegetable and Asian herb salad. The accompanying light sauces may include lemon and rocket coulis, lime and virgin olive oil, cucumber raita, or Vietnamese green *nam jim* and sweet chili. And look out for surprise fresh local ingredients like squash blossom and hijiki seaweed, as well as more familiar Asian extras like soba noodles, ponzu sauce, and *sambal matah* relish. Desserts are European classics—pannacotta, crème brûlée, and sorbets—flavored with local ingredients such as ginger, coconut, or kaffir lime leaves.

These modern, delicate, international ingredients have helped Sardine soar up the island's restaurant ratings. Thanks are due to the owners, too: a former French chef and his Slovenian artist wife, who have ensured everything tastes and looks good.

Sardine customers eat under an open thatched bamboo pavilion overlooking a panorama of paddy fields, decorated with rows of pot plants, spectacular art, and dangling lanterns. Check out also the open-air lounge, where visitors relax on daybeds with cocktails or coffee right next to the rice fields.

Shaheen's credits include notable Californian kitchens, but here he has created a novel mix of culinary cultures. Some of his most successful dishes are steamed barramundi wrapped in banana leaves, black tea-cured salmon with Asian pear, and grilled Bali pineapple with raspberry and lime granita. This is tropical dining with a stylish contemporary twist. **SH**

Bebek Bengil | Finger-licking crispy duck in a Balinese institution

Location Bali **Signature dish** Crispy duck | **⑤**

"Bebek Bengil" may sound rather exotic to non-Balinese; but, in the local language of the Indonesian island it actually means "dirty duck." The restaurant was named after a group of the birds that waddled inside while it was being built.

At first, perhaps surprisingly, the diner didn't serve duck at all. It was only after it had been open for some time that it began to serve dishes better suited its name. Since then, the duck concept has taken over. The restaurant sign is now dominated by a duck, tables feature duck-shaped napkin holders, and the signature dish that draws the crowds is a Chinese-style crispy duck platter.

This Asian classic involves marinating the meat in Indonesian spices, then steaming and deep-frying it. The process releases much of the creature's abundant ingrained fat. Diners at Bebek Bengil get half a duck served with sautéed potato and salad, or rice and Balinese vegetables.

Bebek Bengil has become an institution and an unmissable port of call for all visitors to the town of Ubud in central Bali. It features scores of tables spread among a rustic complex of thatched pavilions dotted around a lush tropical garden of lotus, palms, and ornamental rice fields. Some diners squat at low traditional tables eating with their fingers, but most sit at Western-style tables. The "dirty duck diner" has been so successful that two offshoots have since been launched—one at Nusa Dua on Bali, the other in the Indonesian capital Jakarta.

Apart from duck, the eclectic menu includes garlic snails, Greek salad, guacamole, hummus, and fish and chips. There are, however, some serious Balinese dishes available for those who can see beyond the Western staples. Local specialities include babi guling (suckling pig) served with *urap* (a steamed salad with coconut); rijstafel, a feast of chicken curry, egg curry, sate, ginger chicken, and, perhaps inevitably, crispy duck. **SH**

"It is difficult to imagine a more beautiful, relaxed place to savor Bali's most famous dish."

John Brunton, *Guardian*

⌖ The tropical garden at Bebek Bengil.

There's a freshness and excitement to the dining out scene in Australia and New Zealand—a celebratory national pride in the wonderful local ingredients and the creative dishes made with them. From enjoying gloriously fresh produce in a New Zealand vineyard to dining on delectable seafood while looking out over Sydney's Bondi Beach, eating out in Oceania offers some very special occasions.

Oceania

← The view from Quay restaurant, Sydney, Australia.

Nautilus | Remarkable foods in a tropical utopia

Location Port Douglas   **Signature dish** Whole coral trout with green paw paw salad | ❸❸❸❸

Some people like to dine indoors; others much prefer to eat outside. Nautilus, in the small town of Port Douglas in the far north of Queensland, is a restaurant for the latter group. Their ceiling is a waving canopy of tropical palms, and the dining room is an open space of thoughtfully placed and carefully lit tables dotted among luxuriant vegetation. Nautilus creates clever dishes incorporating tropical produce, using masterly technique and achieving a delicate finish.

One dish of clever contrasts is a starter of crisp-skinned belly of pork with a soursop soufflé (soursop is a pulpy fruit similar to a custard apple), served against a sweet-and-sour glaze with lime and Sichuan pepper-salt. Another option is the lemon myrtle spanner-crab pot stickers (Chinese dumplings), unctuous and flavorful. Both dishes artfully combine native ingredients with traditional cooking.

Main courses include meats, such as the eye fillet of beef, served with crispy potatoes, a prawn butter Béarnaise, and mushroom jus. But in Great Barrier Reef country, it is naturally tempting to try the local fish, so see whether the local market has come up with any coral trout; this is an exquisite reef fish with a tender flake and mild flavor. At Nautilus, they dust it in light Asian spices, shallow-fry it, and serve it with green paw paw salad, along with a luscious, salty caramel dressing and an impressive chili jam.

Alternately, you may wish to indulge in another specialty, mud crab, sourced from the neighboring state of Northern Territory. Even when eaten plain, these crabs have a rich, buttery character with a hint of sweetness, and Nautilus enhances their flavor with either yellow coconut and kaffir lime, chili and lemongrass, or citrus butter. Surrounded by swinging lanterns, the hum of crickets, and the balmy tropical air, you will not wish you were anywhere else. **HM**

⬆ **Start the meal with pork belly with soursop soufflé.**

Berardo's | Australian beach dining at its most sophisticated

Location Noosa   **Signature dish** Hervey Bay scallops, spiced sea-urchin butter, apple, and leaves | ❸❸❸

Berardo's name has come to express the essence of Noosa, a stylish beach town in southeast Queensland. The restaurant has two offshoots: Berardo's Restaurant and a relatively casual bistro called Berardo's on the Beach. Between them, they give owners Jim Berardo and Greg O'Brien a significant reach throughout the town. By way of payback to the community, they host the much acclaimed Noosa Food and Wine Festival.

Dressed in white on white, the dining room of Berardo's Restaurant is a discreetly elegant affair. In these stylish surroundings, the owners showcase and celebrate the produce of the surrounding Sunshine Coast and its abundant seafood, as well as ingredients from inland areas such as Buderim and Maleny. Typical of the restaurant is a raviolo dish—one luscious pillow of pasta filled with local spanner crabmeat—or scallops from Hervey Bay (a town north of Noosa) that are finished with an intense sea-urchin butter.

Alternately, try the shrimp from Mooloolaba, fleshy and sweet and nicely balanced, with a serving of fennel and pink grapefruit.

Main courses include impressive fish dishes—often served with a dressing of green mango, chili, and sugarcane juice—but also treats for carnivores, such as slow-cooked Berkshire pork belly given a spicy edge with native Australian fruits and roasted duck breast with quinoa and blood orange. Classic desserts, such as pineapple tarte tatin or raspberry pannacotta, are light enough for the warm climate.

Waiters miraculously know what you want before you do, subtly suggesting additions to the menu that are always just right. The wine list is itself a celebration of Australia, with wines appropriate both for the subtropical heat of summer and the cool, hypnotic nights of winter. **HM**

⬆ Berardo's sophisticated white exterior.

The Spirit House | Accomplished, elegant, Asian-inspired cuisine

Location Yandina **Signature dish** Crisp pork belly with citrus caramel sauce | ❸❸❸

"At night hundreds of fairy lights and lanterns transform the landscape into something special."

Courier-Mail Goodlife Restaurant Guide

⬆ The decor of this serene restaurant draws inspiration from a traditional Thai spirit house.

The word "nirvana" means both a state of perfect happiness and an ideal or idyllic place. So peaceful is the Spirit House in the tiny town of Yandina, near the beach town of Noosa in southeast Queensland, that its guests describe it as a nirvana: that it serves wonderful food only reinforces the impression.

The picturesque setting is, quite literally, an escape, an exchange of Australia for Asia. The restaurant is set around a tranquill pond amid tropical gardens and trickling waterfalls. At nightfall, the gentle hum of crickets begins as you take a seat overlooking the water, to be served complex and thoughtful Asian-based dishes.

The broad brushstrokes of many Asian influences inform the menu. A signature dish of crisp pork belly with citrus caramel sauce offers gooey and sweet meat against the gentle acidity of citrus. Steamed salmon with ginger, shallots, green chili, and sesame oil has an elegance to its succulent flesh, heightened by the ginger and given a zing by the hint of chili. A yellow curry of duck is enlivened by punchy pickled paw paw and crispy lime leaves, and is carefully balanced by a fresh coconut and watermelon salad. For dessert, a caramelized pineapple cake with coconut sorbet and a sweetly spiced syrup is just the thing for rounding out the meal.

Time certainly slows down at the Spirit House. The waiters are present just as you need them, the perfume of the native trees drifts through the air, and the well-spaced tables give diners a sense of privacy.

Just as famous as the restaurant is the Spirit House Cooking School, at which you can learn how to make dishes from the restaurant's menu, or, alternately, take classes that explore Thai or Vietnamese cuisine. There is a store on the grounds selling Spirit House souvenir books and a wide range of sauces and chutneys. Before you leave, be sure to take a last look around; this is a restaurant that exists in its own nirvana. **HM**

Esquire | Creative culinary artistry on the Australian east coast

Location Brisbane **Signature dish** Air-dried beef with *kimchee* (fermented vegetables) | ❺❺❺❺

Ryan Squires, the chef behind Esquire, challenges his diners through his evocative and inspired menus. Brisbane was long considered a city unable to support great chefs or dining environments, but Squires has confounded the pessimists. By raising the culinary bar and the expectations of the Brisbane crowds, he has garnered their enthusiastic support.

The guest first encounters a more casual dining space, known as Esq., that overlooks the Brisbane River. Here, a business clientele enjoys a sandwich selection, perhaps spicy fish and pickles, or a vibrant starter of poached pork dumplings. The mains include lamb with cavolo nero, anchovy, and Jerusalem artichokes, and a rich selection of chargrilled dishes, such as rainbow trout, southern calamari, and marbled beef.

But enter Esquire proper and you will move onto another plane, one of extraordinary culinary artistry. Squires and his head chef, Ben Devlin, eschew flowery descriptions of their food, with the menu referring to dishes simply as "sardines, sweet potato, and almond milk" or "duck with cucumber." But what arrives are creations with each element heightened by the deft touches of Squires and Devlin. Flavors are pure and textures are playful: air-dried beef with *kimchee* (fermented vegetables) melts away on the tongue, with a clip of acid and bite from the *kimchee*. Southern squid has the delicate texture of butter and is given a depth of flavor by parsley and garlic. Desserts continue to surprise, with Campari, mandarin, and curds and whey providing a fresh, cleansing, and bittersweet finish to an extraordinary experience.

The restaurant occupies a room that is breathtaking in its Nordic simplicity—Ryan Squires spent time with René Redzepi at Noma, Copenhagen—and the service is knowledgeable and sharp. Squires challenges his customers, but he also delights in making them aware of the potential of ingredients, in an environment of comfort and style. **HM**

"Devlin creates food through … logic, while Squires paints with the brush of an artist."

foodservicenews.com.au

⬆ A dessert quenelle of Campari curds with orange and whey curd ice cream, Campari crystals, and mandarin.

Bills | An iconic and much-loved Australian café

Location Sydney   **Signature dish** Ricotta hotcakes with banana and honeycomb butter | 💲💲

> *"We had Nicole Kidman ...*
> *saying how Bills was her favorite*
> *breakfast place in Sydney."*

Bill Granger, chef and founder of Bills

⬆ A display serves as a reminder that many customers return to Bills for its superlative scrambled eggs.

If a visit to Sydney is in your plans, do not leave the Emerald City without first visiting Bills, as it is one of those rare venues that actually deserves the title of "institution." Bill Granger opened his first café on this site twenty years ago; it was an unassuming but beautiful place, serving generous portions of delicious dishes based on fresh local ingredients.

Crowds now stand in line for dishes that have become famous, such as Granger's scrambled eggs, a simple mix of eggs, cream, butter, and salt served over well-made sourdough bread. Somehow, using just the right measures of each ingredient has created a dish of such popularity that it will never be allowed to leave the menu. Equal billing is shared by ricotta hotcakes, which are light and fluffy, with the moist weight of fresh ricotta dotted through them, with banana and a sweet, decadent finish of honeycomb butter. The sweetcorn fritters (another permanent fixture on the menu) consist of pucks of corn kernels bound in a batter of onion and fresh cilantro, and dressed with a coarse avocado salsa.

But twenty years is a long time in this business, and tastes evolve. Those classics have been joined by brown rice and sweet white miso porridge with coconut yogurt and sweet red papaya, and crab, chorizo, and house *kimchee* with fried brown rice. At lunchtime, the inner-city Sydney crowd turn up for dishes such as the yellow fish curry, brown rice, and cucumber relish, as well as a playful take on an Australian classic, a pavlova made with brown sugar.

Bills was one of the first places in Sydney to put a communal table in the center of its small room: unusual at the time, it is now commonplace in cafés around the country. Bills is that kind of place: a trailblazer, a trendsetter, and a house of respite for its many regulars. The fact that he has also opened in the United Kingdom and Japan is testament to his foresight and his very good scrambled eggs. **HM**

Billy Kwong | Native Australian ingredients given a culinary twist

Location Sydney **Signature dish** Yolla bird with chili, crickets, and *shiro-shoyu* (white soy sauce) | ❺❺

Renowned Chinese–Australian chef Kylie Kwong joined forces with café king Bill Granger to open Billy Kwong. The restaurant hit the ground running in 2000, there were lines outside of its narrow frontage within its first week, and the pace has not slowed since. Granger is no longer a part-owner, but Kwong has since made a name for herself both as a very talented chef and as a vocal advocate of ethical and sustainable native Australian produce.

Kwong draws on her Chinese heritage and Australian upbringing to bring a broad spectrum of flavors and techniques to the Billy Kwong cuisine. She has introduced native produce—kangaroo, wallaby, and wattleseed—to her dishes, while keeping a note of welcoming familiarity in the daily changing menu.

Start with plump prawn wontons with sweet chili sauce, or freshly shucked oysters doused in biodynamic sesame oil. The caramelized chicken livers with sweet onion and lemon have a yin–yang, zingy balance, and, when you move on to the mains, you will find Kwong is adventurous in her kitchen, pushing boundaries and shifting perspectives. A dish of yolla bird (muttonbird, a native Australian seabird) is dressed in a sauce of chili and crickets combined with the smooth aromatic sweetness of *shiro-shoyu* (white soy sauce). Kwong also serves wallaby tail; the red-braised and caramelized tail is lifted with chili and given depth by black bean. A meld of bitter greens—organic milk thistle, amaranth, dandelion, warrigals, watercress, and silver beet—makes a rich vegetable side dish, with its light dressing of ginger and *shiro-shoyu*. There is always a dessert of the day, and, for those looking to feast, a banquet menu bringing dish after dish from the evolving menu.

This is a special restaurant; amid the clang of woks, the heady perfumes of aromatics, and the appealing decor, guests know, above all, that they will be served consistently good food of integrity. **HM**

"Food makes people happy; food connects people. You know, is it any wonder … that I'm into food?"

Kylie Kwong, chef and co-founder of Billy Kwong

⬆ Dishes such as crisp-skin duck with blood plum sauce are inspired by Kwong's Chinese and Australian heritage.

Mr. Wong | A shrewdly conceived, smooth-running Cantonese eatery

Location Sydney **Signature dish** Sweet and sour crispy pork hock | 💲💲

"More than anything, the food needs to be fun and be the kind people can eat every day."

Dan Hong, chef at Mr. Wong

⬆ Mud crab selected from the restaurant's tank is cooked Singapore-style with black pepper.

➡ The decor conjures the mood of 1930s Shanghai.

Set over two floors, Mr. Wong has a post-industrial edge that combines with retro Chinese decor to yield a clever mix of urban cool and easy comfort. The restaurant opened with a bang in the depths of the historic Establishment Hotel building in Sydney's central business district; since then, it has kept up its momentum with spot-on smart service, a killer wine list, and well-honed, contemporary Chinese food that has one foot firmly planted in Cantonese cooking and the other in modern Australian cuisine.

This is not East–West by any stretch, but it is a meeting of old and new incarnations of an ancient cuisine. Wunderkind chef Dan Hong is intuitive, feeding a public hungry for plump dumplings with splashes of black vinegar and chili, seafood chosen from the restaurant's tank, and duck and pork roasted to perfection. Scallop and prawn *shumai* (steamed pork dumplings) are trotted out by swift staff. Other favorites are the fresh and perky steamed cod dumpling with shrimp roe and a dish of intensely flavorful spring lamb *shumai*.

The quality of the produce sourced by Hong is impeccable. The sesame prawn toast, an old-fashioned idea that has never lost popularity, is paunchy with prawns; a wonton with Szechuan pork is made vibrant with asparagus; and a moreish spinach dumpling is given depth by morel mushroom. Sweet and sour crispy pork hock is a playful nod to Westernized Chinese food, and the *mapo* tofu is a wonderful jumble of ground pork, chili, and Sichuan pepper over steamed soy milk custard. Also great is the *chueng fun*, a steamed rice roll with prawn or barbecued pork, the slithery casing an excellent foil to the well-seasoned ingredients.

Once you are seated at Mr. Wong, the rush of busy staff, excited customers, plates and bowls, and exotic sights and smells will remind you why restaurants like this are so popular and so well loved. **HM**

Rockpool | Intelligent fine dining from a master of global cuisine

Location Sydney **Signature dish** Bo ssäm pork shoulder and wheat-infused soy beans | ❸❸❸❸

Sean's Panorama | A longtime favorite overlooking Bondi Beach

Location Sydney **Signature dish** Barossa chicken with parsnip puree and fava beans | ❸❸❸

If you relish the art and pleasure of dining out, you must try at least one of the restaurants run by accomplished chef and businessman Neil Perry, who has establishments in Sydney, Melbourne, and Perth. Perry is renowned at home and abroad for his unequivocal focus on using regional produce in simple, effective, and delicious ways. His flagship restaurant, Rockpool, in Sydney, is set in a beautiful, space with tall pillars and a lofty ceiling. The effect is dark and brooding, cleverly highlighted with lots of gray and black and warm wooden finishes.

Perry has a knack for bringing flavors and culinary techniques together in a sophisticated match that far exceeds fusion. His thoughtful, skilled repertoire may

> *"I love to taste the authenticity of a place, to find out what the regional food tastes like…"*
>
> Neil Perry, chef and founder of Rockpool

result in a menu carrying *chirashi sushi* (vinegared sushi rice) of bonito, snapper, and abalone next to a chicken parfait with "a one-thousand-layer pork tart." Such dishes of contrasting origins do not feel wrong on a menu by Perry. Main courses continue his successful tightrope walk of winning combinations: pigeon roasted pink with corn, scallops, and eggplant; rib and sirloin of beef cushioned against winter melon and braised gem lettuce.

The knowledgeable staff will describe dishes, tell the stories of producers, and steer guests toward an unforgettable dining experience. Perry is a master, and if you love food and wine as much as he does, visiting one of his Rockpool restaurants is a must. **HM**

Long, lazy Sundays at Sean's Panorama, with the sweet, salty scent of the sea rushing through the dining room and the big Sydney sky overhead—some might call that a clichéd idea of Australia, but the place itself is far from clichéd, despite its classic location, literally across the road from the surfers' paradise of Bondi Beach. Walking into the restaurant is like walking into a friend's dining room—the service is as welcoming as the sunshine, unpretentious but professional, with a knowledge of provenance and an instinct for helping the customer to relax.

Chef and co-owner Sean Moran (the Sean of the name) employs classic European technique to present dishes with a strong Mediterranean influence. The homemade bread with freshly churned butter is a must, and is part of an established fabric of signature dishes that express Moran's real sense of enjoyment. The menu, always written up on the blackboard, changes regularly, with favorite dishes being brought back and new ones always being tried.

Starters may include a textured zucchini salad with goat curd and walnuts, or cured kingfish (a vibrant, white-fleshed Australian fish) that is served against radish and daikon with finger limes. A main course of roast chicken from South Australia's Barossa Valley is a mainstay, roasted with oregano and perhaps served with a parsnip puree and fava beans.

There is an ad hoc feel to the room, with its scrawled food and wine boards and retro decor, but there is such a strong backbone of experience and skill that an immediate sense of calm is instilled on arrival—a calm that cannot be attributed to the ocean views alone. Moran and his business partners have created a glorious affirmation of an Australian stereotype, a pleasurable, mellow environment where good food can be thoroughly enjoyed. **HM**

Tetsuya's | Legendary Japanese cuisine created by a true master of his art in elegant surroundings

Location Sydney **Signature dish** *Kaiseki* | $$$$$

Tetsuya Wakuda is arguably the most famous Japanese chef in the world. His illustrious, eponymous restaurant, Tetsuya's, is a popular dining destination in Sydney. In a nation with a big integrated Asian population, it is natural that his kind of talent should emerge and make him such a prominent figure, although Tetsuya was, in fact, born in Japan and first came to Sydney at 22 years old. Tetsuya's first restaurant in Australia was small and modest, but his fame soon spread, and this current restaurant is a spacious, elegant affair, complete with a Japanese garden that includes bonsai and a waterfall.

Tetsuya's legendary reputation is fully justified. Such is the restaurant's appeal that you will have to be persistent to secure a reservation. But it definitely pays to persevere. The serene surroundings of the restaurant showcase Tetsuya's culinary skills to perfection. There is only one degustation menu on offer, comprising ten plates, but do not make the mistake of assuming that this is a simple selection of ten dishes. As you get started on the delicacies, you realize that each dish is connected to the next: the first plate makes the next even better, and then that plate serves as a foil for the next. Sometimes a great French menu recalls an orchestral symphony; the structure of Tetsuya's courses resembles Johann Sebastian Bach's *The Well-Tempered Clavier*, one of the most influential pieces of classical music.

Tetsuya's famous speciality, the grilled Huon Atlantic Salmon, is a truly memorable dish. The slow cooking works wonderfully as a method of locking the full flavor into the fish and giving it a distinct texture. The three different types of salty flavor—that of the of wild salmon, the caviar, and the seasoning salt—work in harmony, bringing out the sweetness of the salmon. **AI**

"It's worth getting on the waiting list . . . to sample the unique blend of Western and Japanese flavors."

fodors.com

↑ Tetsuya's is famous for its fish dishes.

Chiswick | An aesthete's delight and a gourmand's playground

Location Sydney **Signature dish** Wood-roasted lamb, chickpeas, *za'atar* herb mix, and mint | ❸❸❸❸

Sydney's Chiswick restaurant is an inviting visual mix of pretty and urban. There is a sense of being in a friend's home, so personable is the space with its large windows out to the kitchen garden, its lovely flowers, and the dining room with its gentle white hues and warm wooden finishes.

The kitchen garden is the heart of this lunch and dinner operation. In the 1,600-square-foot (150-sq-m) space, fruit, vegetables, and herbs are rotated seasonally to support the menu of co-owner and chef Matt Moran, who is well known in Australia for his commitment to provenance of quality produce. The full-time gardener at Chiswick works with Moran to plant ingredients and develop menus. The composition of each dish is breathtaking in its simplicity.

Rusticity and comfort are strongly accented in the menu, which changes monthly. Start with wood-fired bread with oregano and garlic while you nibble on pickled vegetables from the garden with a sprinkling of *dukkah* (an Egyptian mix of herbs, nuts, and spices), or snow crab made irresistible with Japanese Kewpie mayonnaise and gherkin. Moran's seafood includes hand-dived clams tossed with linguine, with the delicate vibrance of snow peas and a hint of chili, and a classic dish of battered fillets of flathead—a mild-flavored, well-textured Australian fish—served with fries and homemade tartare sauce.

Appropriately, for an environment that feels so much like a home away from home, there are seafood plates to share: roasted snapper fillets with mussels and gremolata and fish and shrimp tagine with couscous. Other shared dishes include roasted chicken with potatoes and mint and wood-roasted lamb from the Moran family's farm. The atmosphere of comfort extends to the professional service. Chiswick is luxury, well-crafted food, and warm hospitality. **HM**

⊡ Slow-roasted lamb shoulder at Chiswick.

Est. | Culinary talent on show in breathtaking surroundings

Location Sydney **Signature dish** Murray cod fillet, shaved abalone, snow peas, and black fungi | ❺❺❺❺❺

In the thick of Sydney's central business district, Est. is located in the Establishment Hotel, a beautiful, heritage-listed building that is itself enough to lure you here. The real draw of Est., however, is that here one finds Greg Doyle, one of the best chefs in Australia, creating a degustation menu that is contemporary in its execution and ingredients while being based on sound French culinary technique. To raise expectations even higher, the head sommelier and wine buyer, Franck Moreau, is an internationally renowned wine connoisseur with a finely tuned palate.

The food at Est. is as stylish as Kate Moss' wardrobe, always evolving and always fashionable. Never a follower, it sets its own standards. The discerning diners are treated to an ever-changing menu that keeps them returning. Here are dishes such as finely sliced ocean trout with *dashi* stock, next to the pop of tapioca and ocean trout roe, alongside puffed quinoa and lime, or grilled scallops with the crunch of white carrots, the sharpness of pickled pear, and the luxury of foie gras.

Doyle's signature dish, fillet of Murray cod (a native Australian fish with a wonderful element of fat to its flesh) is stylishly combined with shaved abalone, snow peas, black fungi, and ginger, dressed in a tangy green-shallot vinaigrette. He can do cold-weather comfort food, too, as witnessed by a saddle of venison, rich with black pudding, chestnuts, celeriac, and apple, set against semolina gnocchi.

Desserts maintain the same high standards. One beautifully balanced creation is a Valrhona chocolate delice with a crunchy wild-rice praline, caramelized pear, and toasted rice ice cream; far removed from being overly sweet, this is the thinking diner's dessert. The journey at Est. is worth every step and every course—so take it. **HM**

⬆ The dining room is light and airy.

Fish Market Café | Australia's rich seafood served ultra-fresh

Location Sydney **Signature dish** Platter comprising the best of the day's seafood catch | **$**

Sydney Fish Market is the third-largest fish market in the world, and its café serves some of the freshest seafood available anywhere in Australia. Even before the rising sun touches Pyrmont Bridge in inner Sydney, the café has had its pick of the freshest seafood, presenting it every day in simple, delicious, and irresistible ways. But do not expect fancy linen tablecloths or formally dressed waiters; this is a food experience that is focused on food.

Prominent is the seafood platter with whatever may be good that day: natural oysters just shucked, alongside traditional Mornay and Kilpatrick oysters; barbecued baby octopus so soft you would think it caught just moments before; fried calamari,

> *"Amid the hustle and bustle … this is a great little spot to sit and absorb the atmosphere."*
>
> truelocal.com.au

remarkably tender and gently seasoned; and pieces of grilled fish—fleshy, flaky, juicy bites of fish with tartare sauce for dipping. Bouncy battered prawns, firm to the bite, round out the platter; fries or rice provide a tasty but really rather superfluous adjunct.

To add to the myriad choices, there are Tasmanian scallops on the half-shell, bite-sized whitebait dusted with flour and served pan-fried with lemon wedges, and a diversity of fish from the varying waters of the north and south of Australia—blue grenadier, snapper, flathead—all just out of the water.

Some may think the café has a functional feel, but the staff is efficient and helpful, and the seafood makes the visit absolutely worthwhile. **HM**

Marque | Culinary stories told by a chef pursuing a personal dream

Location Sydney **Signature dish** Confit egg yolk with eggplant, licorice, and macadamia | **$$$$**

Chef Mark Best is a storyteller whose continuing narrative is his restaurant Marque in the Sydney suburb of Surry Hills. His story is one of determination, creativity, and intelligence; the former electrician put down his wirecutters and picked up a set of knives to follow his love of cooking. In the process, he changed the Australian dining landscape.

Best has a knack of bringing out the qualities of his ingredients through the techniques he uses and the combinations of textures and flavors he creates. His cooking is on offer each evening, showcased by a degustation menu of small, complex combinations. For example, in his dish of blue swimmer crab with almond gazpacho, almond jelly, sweetcorn, and avruga caviar, he tempers the sweetness of the crabmeat with the milky earthiness of the almond in its varying textures. While you wish that this spellbinding opening chapter would never end, you also cannot wait for the next installment. Does confit egg yolk with eggplant, licorice, and macadamia sound extraordinary? It is, with the yolk in its molten glory lifting its intensely flavored accompaniments into a rounded balancing act of deliciousness.

Best's story maintains its edgy elegance as you are served each dish by the articulate, knowledgeable staff. A fillet of blue eye trevalla fish with green tomato, verjus, potato paper, fish milk, and roe is a highlight, as is the Wagyu beef from the Darling Downs of southeast Queensland, served with fermented mushrooms. Coming to the end of the story, in the simply dressed room on a busy inner-city street, you will realize that the key to Best's narrative is that his food has nothing to do with trends: it is about an evolution of personal artistry and experience. **HM**

→ Marque's apple jelly, kaffir lime, and sherbet dessert.

Icebergs | Breathtaking views are only the beginning

Location Sydney   **Signature dish** *Fazzoletti con pesce azzurro* | ❸❸❸

The hackneyed phrase "ocean view" cannot do justice to what lies before you as you enter Icebergs restaurant, part of the Bondi Icebergs Swimming Club complex. With the building overlooking the great sweep of Bondi Beach, the description "a dramatic expanse of ocean" would be more accurate, as you are literally perched high on a cliff top overlooking the mesmerizing waves of the Pacific.

Icebergs is the stylish creation of Maurice Terzini, a respected restaurateur who started out in his hometown of Melbourne but moved to Sydney in 2000. There he opened Otto Ristorante before catapulting himself into the catering stratosphere with Icebergs. Excellent Italian food is Terzini's forte, and that is what you get here, cooked by talented chef Paul Wilson and inspired by Italy's Amalfi coast.

Returning from your dreamy contemplation of the horizon, you will find your attention caught by seafood starters such as fresh clams or freshly shucked Merimbula Lakes oysters. The emphasis on the quality of ingredients that has always been at the core of Italian cuisine is truly respected here. Local shrimp, lightly fried, arrive paired just with a robust aioli. The pastas are simple but excellent: linguine with zucchini and a zesty lemon sauce, or *fazzoletti con pesce azzurro* (pasta with sardines, olives, capers, and bread crumbs).

With Wilson, a master of cooking meats, in charge of the kitchen, it is hard to resist ordering the meat dishes. Try the salt-encrusted, rib-eye *bistecca* on the bone, a hefty 2-pound (1-kg) offering shared by two people. With its moist, flavorful flesh—nicely seasoned, cooked to perfection, and well rested—this is a carnivore's delight. The quality of the food is matched by the impeccable service that Terzini insists upon. In short, here is a restaurant that really does live up to its stunning location. **HM**

⬆ Iceberg's location and view are unbeatable.

Longrain | A feel-good restaurant offering a vivid taste of Thailand

Location Sydney **Signature dish** Eggnet, pork, prawns, peanuts, and cucumber relish | $$

Longrain, housed in a former warehouse in Sydney's suburb of Surry Hills, took the harbor city by surprise when it opened in 2000. Initially, the cavernous space with its lengthy wooden communal tables seemed daunting; but, once the heady scents of garlic, ginger, lemongrass, and cilantro permeated the room, it took on a more beguiling aspect.

Diners are pleased to discover the separate bar area, where charming bar staff muddle caipirinhas and pour caipiroskas for them as they wait for a table. The energy level, originally set at high, has been maintained here ever since, with a semi-religious devotion that has seen the restaurant become the blueprint and influence for many carbon copies around the country.

Some dishes have become known as being "very Longrain" and are staples of the menu. Betel leaf topped with Queensland spanner crab, curry powder, ginger, and chili is a perfect bite-sized appetizer—just wrap the leaf around the spicy ingredients and enjoy them in one vibrant mouthful. The eggnet filled with pork, prawns, peanuts, and cucumber relish is another immediately recognizable signature dish. Stunning to look at, with its clever crisscross of cooked egg, it envelopes a flavorful mix of tender pork and fleshy shrimp, given relish by a kick of vinegar and spice.

Behind the scenes, the kitchen certainly knows its stuff. Main dishes might consist of a Massaman curry of tender, slow-cooked lamb neck served over kipfler potatoes and lifted with pickled ginger, or an eye-catching whole fried snapper, with a tangy dressing of chili, lime, and tamarind.

There is a palpable verve to Longrain, in its flavors, its perky drinks, buzzy room, and flirtatiously energetic staff. This is a restaurant that has found a niche and kept the mood. Long live Longrain. **HM**

[↑] A dish of expertly prepared green papaya salad.

Momofuku Seiobo | An international chef brings his craft to Sydney

Location Sydney   **Signature dish** Eel dashi | ❺❺❺❺❺

"You just need to have a curious, insatiable appetite literally for knowledge and for the food."

David Chang, chef and founder of Momufuku Seiobo

⬆ David Chang's dishes are exciting combinations of flavors and textures, delivered with brio.

It is a long way to Australia from North America, but internationally recognized chef David Chang, who has restaurants in New York and Toronto, saw potential in Sydney's inner-city market and opened Momofuku Seiobo at the Star casino complex in Pyrmont.

Chang maintains the same table reservation system at all his outlets. Bookings can only be made online twenty days in advance. While that turns off some people, others routinely jump on the website to secure one of just thirty seats available per night.

The menu is constantly evolving and is a degustation based on local, seasonal produce. Its highly contemporary approach is steeped in Chang's Korean–American heritage while embracing the elegance and balance of Japanese technique.

Chang has created a stylish and simple setup that turns the focus onto the food. Operating the kitchen with studied precision, a sharp team meld seriousness with a sense of enjoyment and fun. The carefully chosen music—Beastie Boys, AC/DC, Led Zeppelin—is an important element of the experience. The seats at the bar that overlook the kitchen are much coveted for watching the chefs in action and taking in the noise, the buzz, and the Momofuku magic.

Dishes delve into layers of flavor and play with textures in a modern and approachable way. The meticulous balance of eel dashi, or perhaps the steamed buns with roast pork belly, may start your adventure. Beef with radish and black bean; marron (crayfish) with seaweed; or mulloway (a fleshy Australian fish) served with smoked roe and lettuce may arrive next. The wine list is an intelligent selection of small producers chosen for their myriad tastes.

To round out the Momofuku experience, the service is informed and thoughtful. It can take a while to get a table here, but when you do, it will become clearer why Sydney loves having a chef like Chang carving a place for himself on its culinary map. **HM**

Porteño | Seriously stylish dining backed up by Argentinian technique

Location Sydney **Signature dish** *Chanchito a la Cruz* (pork wood-fired for eight hours) | ❸❸❸

Sydney chefs and restaurant owners Ben Milgate and Elvis Abrahanowicz have gained a reputation as two of the more interesting innovators of Australia's current dining scene. Milgate and Abrahanowicz specialize in traditional Argentinian cooking and take an uncompromising approach to what they see as an authentic product. What they have created, initially at their eatery Bodega, and now at the larger and more "grown-up" Porteño, may not seem innovative at first glance, but it is the pair's creativity within their chosen cuisine that has put them on the culinary map.

The two chefs have their own particular sense of style; both wear tattoos, and they share a rockabilly sensibility that is clearly at the core of their DNA. Yet conservative diners unused to that aesthetic need only eat their food and experience the unusual environment they have created to realize that they are somewhere very special.

Milgate and Abrahanowicz cook their meats on a traditional Argentinian parilla (an elaborate barbecue) or an asador, which resembles the kind of campfire one might sit around, but here holding a splayed pig or lamb that is slow-cooked for eight hours over slow-burning ironbark wood before being served to share. Abrahanowicz's father, Adan, who grew up in Buenos Aires, tends to the fire and ensures its consistency. But Porteño's menu is not just a meat feast. Also featured is seafood—perhaps grilled South Australian calamari with three styles of cucumber—or vegetarian dishes such as homemade feta- and provolone-filled zucchini flowers, or broccoli and ricotta empanada.

Porteño is managed by Abrahanowicz's wife, Sarah Doyle, and the service here is excellent, bringing intelligence and substance to the task of ensuring that customers' needs are met. These are smart operators who own an impressive restaurant that oozes style, but they have gone way beyond that to create their own assertive identity and wonderful food. **HM**

"Cooking with fire is completely different. You get better flavor, better crust on the meat."

Ben Milgate, chef and cofounder of Porteño

⊞ Walls and leather-clad furniture in burgundy red add to a rockabilly take on an Argentinian interior.

Quay | Exceptional dining with incomparable views

Location Sydney   **Signature dish** Smoked and confit pig jowl, shiitake, and shaved scallops | ❻❻❻❻❻

"As a chef, you can't ever sit still; you have to keep reinventing to keep your customers … excited."

Peter Gilmore, chef at Quay

⬆ Executive chef Peter Gilmore exploits the fresh produce of kitchen gardens in his beautiful dishes.

➡ Quay directly overlooks Sydney Opera House.

Quay restaurant, with its glorious postcard views of Sydney harbor and the iconic Opera House, is an internationally recognized restaurant built on the strong ethos of local, seasonal, stunning produce served with great skill. Executive chef Peter Gilmore is one of Australia's most respected and revered practitioners, and the restaurant has featured in the San Pellegrino World's Fifty Best Restaurants list for five years consecutively.

Gilmore has been at Quay for more than a decade and is a trailblazer in terms of championing the potential of a kitchen garden in a commercially viable context. A passionate gardener, Gilmore has long established strong relationships with small-scale growers around the country, getting them to grow forgotten plant species exclusively for the restaurant. Building on these relationships, Gilmore has developed a repertoire of dishes that are strongly founded in skill and craftsmanship.

Expect much from Quay, and you will not be disappointed. The team here already expect much of themselves, and this is evident in the crisp, taut linen on the tables, the spotless floor-to-ceiling windows over the water, the articulate explanations of the cuisine, and the inviting presentation of the food.

You may find a dish of spring peas with garlic custard in chestnut mushroom broth, or smoked and confit pig jowl, with fleshy shiitake mushrooms and sweet shaved scallops, supported by savory Jerusalem artichoke leaves, bay, and juniper. Gilmore also cooks indigenous produce, perhaps wallaby tail slowly cooked in salted butter, golden orach, ice plant, bulrush, and agretti.

Quay is set apart by its attention to detail, not only in its presentation but also in its dedication to sourcing. Add compelling, soothing service and a wine list that is the envy of the country, and you have a unique Sydney, and global, dining experience. **HM**

Provenance | Australian food with a Japanese dimension

Location Beechworth **Signature dish** Tofu, marinated seafood, soy, pickled ginger, and salmon roe | ❸❸❸

Australian chef Michael Ryan creates Japanese-inspired food at Provenance, his beautiful restaurant in Beechworth, northeastern Victoria. The provenance of his ingredients is key to many of his creations, and he is a strong supporter of his local region and its producers. The restaurant sits in a former bank building, the elegant dining room dressed in artwork depicting plants and flowers. There is an intricacy to these portraits that translates to Ryan's plates; this is thoughtful food that, while it acknowledges regionality, also transmits his love of Japan.

Ryan makes his own silken tofu onsite, and serves it as an appetizer with marinated seafood, soy, pickled ginger, and salmon roe, the soft and meaty fish countered by pops from the roe. This dish demands one of the many *sake* rice wines available, with the option of matching one to each course.

Main courses are refined and complex, such as a *sake*-cured kingfish with roasted corn, corn custard, and a wood-aged soy dressing. Ryan continues to walk the cultural tightrope with dishes like local snapper with eggplant, sugar snap peas, tomato *dashi* (stock) and *shiso* (perilla), while the sweet complexity of roasted lamb ribs is amplified by support from pickled beetroot, smoked potato, and buttermilk from a butter factory in the local town of Myrtleford.

Ryan also displays his flair for combining ingredients in the dessert menu. He combines *sake kasu* (sake lees) ice cream with pickled strawberry salad and *shiso* sugar, or makes his own *fromage blanc* (fermented white cheese), served dusted in gingerbread crumbs with a dollop of lemon curd. His restaurant provides gloriously edible proof of the powers of provenance to deliver wonderful food. **HM**

◁ Ryan's venison, blood pudding, and beetroot.

Saint Crispin | Stylish and contemporary Australian cuisine

Location Melbourne **Signature dish** Veal cheek with hand-rolled macaroni and miso eggplant | ❸❸❸

Saint Crispin, in the northern suburb of Collingwood, Melbourne, has a pared-back decor of bare brick and white walls, with a room-length leather-clad banquette and a large, open kitchen, where the chefs and owners, Scott Pickett and Joe Grbac, can be seen creating their outstanding dishes. The two business partners met and became friends while working with chef Philip Howard at The Square restaurant in London, and their experience is obvious.

The menu starts with a list of lovely snacks: eel croquettes, salted cod, and the dangerously addictive, distinctly decadent, fried pork skin treat they call "Snack, Crackle, Pop," all of which titillate the appetite nicely in anticipation of more good food to come.

> *"There is always a welcomed element of surprise when your plate is brought to the table."*
>
> melbourne.concreteplayground.com.au

The set menu offers a choice of four entrees, mains, and desserts, with diners choosing two or three courses for a set price. If you want to try as many things as possible, there is a varied degustation that the chef will select from the menu.

The food is thoughtful, textured, seasonal, and beautifully presented. A pullet egg with mushroom, Parmesan, goat curd, and black rice is ripe with a velvety texture and savory flavors. The veal cheek with hand-rolled macaroni, miso eggplant, and almonds has quickly become a signature dish. A dessert of poached rhubarb, burned custard, and blood orange is a seasonal mix of sweet acid and slight bitterness. No wonder Melbourne has embraced Saint Crispin. **HM**

Rosetta | All the charm, style, and flavor of Italian cuisine

Location Melbourne   **Signature dish** Homemade ricotta with roasted tomato | ❺❺❺❺

Opened in 2012, chef Neil Perry's Italian restaurant Rosetta, in the Crown Casino complex overlooking Melbourne's Yarra River, has the beauty of Sofia Loren and the charm of Marcello Mastroianni, cleverly balanced with the comfort of excellent pasta.

The menu is broad; because he is not an Italian, Perry feels he has the freedom to express himself across various regions. Crudi and carpacci include a delicate Hiramasa kingfish with capers, tomato oil, and a touch of chili, as well as an antipasto dish of homemade ricotta with roasted tomato that is a stunning blend of creaminess and sweet acidity.

Pasta, handmade on the premises, is beautifully al dente. The tagliatelle with braised hare, red wine,

> *"Perry hopes to create dishes made the way you would want to eat them at the family table."*
>
> AgendaCity, Melbourne

tomato, and pancetta is earthy and rich; the garganelli with pork and fennel sausage, broccoli, chili, and garlic proves to be vibrant with balance and texture.

Main courses move through such favorites as a classic saltimbocca of pan-fried veal escalopes with prosciutto, sage, and polenta; slices of charcoal-grilled grass-fed fillet steak from Cape Grim, Tasmania, are given depth with parsley, garlic, and white beans.

With its plush red velvet banquettes and white drapes flowing from large windows, Rosetta is as comforting as it is sophisticated. That is not an easy balance to achieve, but Perry and his team have done it. They have founded a solid restaurant in the beautiful nuances of authentic Italian cuisine. **HM**

Café Di Stasio | An institution as famous for its ambience as its food

Location Melbourne   **Signature dish** Bread *maltagliati* with calamari and radicchio | ❺❺❺

Café Di Stasio has that certain, indefinable, intangible, something. The room of this well-established Melbourne institution feels as fresh as the St. Kilda beach located just across the road. The experience hinges on the moody lighting, the evolving Bill Henson photographs on the wall, and the waiters in starched white coats with flexible professional attitudes, many of whom know the customers who have been coming to this Italian restaurant since it opened. The owner, Rinaldo di Stasio, has maintained the magic through a menu that is traditional but relevant, leading to a stylish and satisfying experience.

Begin with a Negroni beer in the newly established adjoining bar, simply called Bar Di Stasio. If you are in the mood for casual dining—perhaps a quick bowl of pasta—or simply quaffing a bottle of Soave, this is an approachable meeting spot. Move into the handsome dining room, and you will see why Café Di Stasio has been here so long, and why it is so well loved by Melburnians—indeed, by all Australians.

A meal of exquisite execution begins with an entrée of chargrilled quail with mushroom, or oven-baked scallops with bread crumbs, Parmesan, and parsley, or a classic carpaccio of beef, fleshy and thin, with a simple lemon dressing. Pastas are all handmade on the premises; there may be bread *maltagliati* with calamari and radicchio, or silk-ribbon strips of linguine with fresh, meaty prawns.

Wild boar braised with wine and chestnuts is a hardy main course; alternately, the veal saltimbocca offers a lighter flavor, with salty-sweet prosciutto ham nicely setting off the buttery veal.

But it is the experience of Café Di Stasio as a whole that gives it longevity and iconic status. No wonder this delicious establishment has enjoyed a special place in Melbourne's heart for a quarter century. **HM**

Attica | Feasts for the eye as well as the palate from a chef who brings true artistry to his food

Location Melbourne   **Signature dish** King George whiting in paperbark | ❺❺❺❺❺

The simplicity of the dining room of this internationally renowned restaurant belies the beauty and complexity that is plated up by award-winning chef Ben Shewry. The room's black walls and thoughtful lighting make you feel as though you are sitting down in a theater, about to watch a show.

And Attica is certainly an experience. Shewry is a visionary and an artist, as well as being a very skilled chef. He takes the simplest of quality ingredients and highlights the subtlety of each one. Take, for example, his popular dish of King George whiting in paperbark. A single fillet of the delicate fish is brushed with butter, sea parsley and lemon myrtle are added, and thick Australian paperbark serves as the wrapping. Slow grilling over mallee root charcoal creates a buttery texture cut through by the perfectly pitched notes of tangy lemon myrtle and salty sea parsley.

There is always a seasonal set menu, and, one night a week, Shewry experiments with dishes and charges the customer less for sampling them. His symphony of flavors is an extraordinary testament to what is being grown locally. There is an emphasis on vegetable dishes, but Shewry will often work with indigenous meats such as wallaby, and with local producers of ethically raised pork and beef. The kitchen team has the use of a garden just a two-minute walk from the restaurant, where Shewry grows herbs and leaves not readily available in the marketplace, such as tansy, onion flower, and sorrel.

The wine list is a compelling tome, but you are well advised to hand the choosing over to the well-versed staff, who will challenge your perceptions of how food and the world's wines should be matched. Your confident guide will take you through an extraordinary experience that embraces both Melbourne itself and a global, ethical ethos. **HM**

"You work on something for a ridiculous amount of time… when you pull it off, [it] is incredible."

Ben Shewry, chef at Attica

⬆ Walnut shells, set on a bed of wood chips, are filled with rich walnut puree with snow peas and walnut oil.

Cumulus Inc. | Relaxed dining in a classy and central location

Location Melbourne **Signature dish** Shoulder of lamb (to share) | 💲💲

Cumulus Inc. opened in 2008 in the heart of Melbourne's central business district and immediately challenged preconceived ideas about eating out and what a dining room could offer to the city. A policy of not taking bookings got customers thinking about when they should arrive, and a flexible menu made the venue appealing for in-between mealtimes. Some of the customers could sit on stools to watch the chefs in action in the very open kitchen, and these stools became the most desirable seats in town.

The room at Cumulus Inc. is a stunning blend of off-white, dark, and pale woods, black metal, and enormous windows that allow natural light to bathe the room at every time of day. The menu changes with the seasons. The oysters, pert, plump, and plentiful, are shucked to order; a grilled octopus salad is earthy, with the velvety depth of smoked paprika, with a good dollop of aioli to give richness to the dish. The shoulder of lamb that is made for sharing has never

been taken off the menu; it is tender to the bite with a lush texture, perfect for a group or a hungry few.

A charcuterie selection includes house-smoked Wagyu pastrami, or *paletilla Ibérica de bellota Joselito* (a cured foreleg ham made from acorn-fed Spanish indigenous pigs), or perhaps a terrine of Aylesbury duck and smoked ham. This kind of food is approachable enough to eat regularly, yet special enough to make you feel that you have had a treat. The wine list supports the versatility of the menu, offering drinks from around the world, but also showcasing the vinous offerings of the state of Victoria—look at these, because there are some gems.

Cumulus Inc. gets to the core of what living in Melbourne is all about. It is a brilliant spot to start your personal history of Melbourne dining, and it is just as lovely a place to finish it, too. **HM**

⊤ The airy dining space affords a view of the kitchen.

The Town Mouse | Creative dining with a relaxed, neighborhood feel

Location Melbourne   **Signature dish** Slow-roasted red cabbage with prune, Parmesan, and red apple | ❸❸❸

This particular small restaurant space in Melbourne's suburb of Carlton has had many incarnations over the years, but the current owners have taken it to a whole new level as The Town Mouse. Named for the children's fable by Aesop, it is owned by New Zealand native and restaurateur Christian McCabe, his sister Tara, and her husband, Jay Comeskey. Their restaurant is aimed at all-day dining in a very relaxed environment, with bench seating, lots of black tiles, and a stunning dark wood and copper bar. The menu is by New Zealand-born chef Dave Verheul, who worked with Christian at Matterhorn, the chef's award-winning restaurant in Wellington.

A signature "snack" with which to kick off a meal here is the goat cheese profiterole with caraway, thyme, and honey, a sweet and savory explosion of varied textures. To combine ingredients with flair and imagination is characteristic of the cooking here. You may find smoked trout with pickled clams, radish, verbena, and wild onion, or duck breast served to contrasting effect with caramelized yogurt, sprouted wheat, and Chinese mustard leaves. And, if a humble vegetable dish can claim cult status, it might just be the slow-roasted red cabbage dressed in prune, Parmesan, and red apple. Desserts are also inventive, as in a combo of soured cream, pickled strawberries, white chocolate, lavender, and violet ice cream.

The Town Mouse was always designed to be a neighborhood restaurant and bar, and the locals are more than happy with the concept of a high-quality product pitched in an environment with an everyday feel. However, the extraordinary skill shown in each dish, and the detailed knowledge shown by the front-of-house staff, turn this into an experience that goes way beyond the usual neighborhood drop-in spot. It is plainly a very special dining room. **HM**

⬆ The bar forms part of the restaurant's cozy dining area.

Southern Ocean Lodge | Regional food in a wilderness setting

Location Kangaroo Island   **Signature dish** Seafood platter | ❸❸❸❸

Kangaroo Island lies 70 miles (110 km) southwest of Adelaide. More than one-third of its 1,750 square miles (4,500 sq km) are declared a national park, making it the third largest in Australia. Kangaroo Island is a quintessential Australian name, and the restaurant at the island's Southern Ocean Lodge has the quintessential spirit of an outstanding regional venue. The island is a haven for native fauna and flora, and there are many artisan producers and growers on the island working respectfully with their environment.

The restaurant in the lodge, used exclusively by guests, is renowned not only for its exacting standards but also for the work chef Tim Bourke does with producers on the island and in South Australia in nurturing a culture of local, seasonal, and sustainable food practices. Bourke's menu is testimony to the value of local ingredients and gentle handling.

Broccoli grown on the island may be used in a luscious soup, topped with goats' cheese, and finished with local olive oil; a salad of organic beetroot and apple with local sheep milk feta and a wild fennel custard is a tumble of textures, sweet and earthy. A tartare of Coorong black angus beef carries the bite of radish and watercress, supplemented by a free-range egg yolk and finished with a sprinkle of nasturtiums. The dishes at Southern Ocean Lodge are delicate, with the menu highlighting local producers and suppliers, such as Oyster Cove Shellfish, Island Pure Sheep's Milk Dairy, and Southrock Lamb.

Given its position, perched overlooking the magnificent Southern Ocean, the restaurant needs little adornment. Inside, glass walls invite the marine landscape into the room, and the service maintains the mood of tranquility engendered by the abundance of the location. Take time to visit Southern Ocean Lodge and celebrate this part of Australia. **HM**

⬆ Blissful dining with a view at Southern Ocean Lodge.

Sidart | A hidden gem with a truly innovative menu

Location Ponsonby **Signature dish** Roquefort ice cream, red wine poached pear, almond crumble, and red wine syrup | ❺❺❺

> *"Sidart presents the sublime essence of fine dining: art on a plate. A truly unique experience."*

The New Zealand Herald

⬆ Owner and chef Sid Sahrawat at work in the kitchen.

➡ Delicate dishes are artfully arranged.

A gem of a restaurant where owner and chef Sid Sahrawat produces innovative, sometimes daring, and perfectly balanced dishes with flavors and textures that play out to create a feast for eyes and mouth. At his "Tuesday Test Kitchen" night, he offers experimental dishes in a feast of eight courses that can become contenders for his regular menu. This is probably one of the best bargains of Auckland's sophisticated dining scene, with optional wine matches for an added fee. The rest of the week diners can choose from a five- or ten-course menu.

Diners need to negotiate their way through a bizarre mall entrance and up a set of winding stairs; but, once in the restaurant, they will find a comfortable haven on the otherwise busy Ponsonby Road restaurant strip. Dark and intimate, the restaurant offers stunning views of Auckland's downtown skyline and city center. Both the chef's table alongside the kitchen or one of the cozy banquettes provide the perfect setting for a fascinating succession of courses.

Dishes may include snapper, lychee, and *nim jam*, comprising a little jar with coconut puree with a chunk of *nim jam*-marinated, ocean-fresh snapper in tempura, and a tangle of bean sprouts and green onion, all topped with bright-flavored coriander and chili sorbet. Who would ever think of putting snapper in a jar? Then there is the Roquefort cheesecake that is so good it has been on the menu for several years: it has all the elements of a cheesecake, but then again—not cheesecake as you know it.

The waiting staff perform their duties in a warm and welcoming manner, helpfully guiding guests through all elements of dinner as well as the eclectic wine list, suggesting wines that may surprise and delight as much as the food. A magical, truly enchanting experience. **LJ**

Soul Bar & Bistro | Top of the list for food, wine, cocktails, and fun

Location Viaduct Harbour **Signature dish** Whitebait fritters with lemon butter sauce | ❸❸❸

"*Soul is the kind of place created for long lunches ... the wide-ranging menu has broad appeal.*"

Cuisine magazine

⬆ Dishes are made with fresh, seasonal ingredients.

Auckland embraces its beautiful harbor, yet only a few of the restaurants come into true contact with the shores or dockside. Soul Bar & Bistro, with its expansive, flower-decked terrace, superb views over tethered yachts, and easy walk-in access from the plaza and dockside, commands the prime position on the busy downtown Viaduct Harbour. The terrace is constantly filled with ladies who lunch, discerning food lovers, suited businessmen, and curious tourists who wander in to join the fun. Soul's sassy owner, Judith Tabron, oversees proceedings.

The food hits the mark, and Tabron states that it is Soul's customers who shape the menu. Head chef Gareth Stewart pitches his food perfectly, with no overly fussy, fluffy ideas. Diners often come to eat the same thing over and over, appreciating the modern fresh seasonal approach of the dishes.

Seafood is the strong point of the extensive menu. While most restaurants offer one fish choice—the catch of the day—Soul lists a wide variety of fresh fish, each cooked in a different style. Snapper, John Dory, tuna, or *hapuku* always feature as long as the fishing fleet has delivered a fresh catch. Accompaniments to the fish dishes change with the seasons: in winter, you might enjoy whipped cauliflower with blood orange *grenobloise* or chorizo with saffron potatoes and smoked paprika oil, while, in spring, asparagus and whitebait or green papaya, coriander, and mint salad with a mango dressing and toasted peanuts are on offer. Pasta, vegetarian dishes, and hearty beef, pork, and duck are all given the chef's fresh imaginative treatment.

Soul is also a place for sipping exotic cocktails, relaxing over a drink in the large bar, and enjoying many of the special events and promotions that Judith Tabron constantly offers. A large team of loyal staff seamlessly manage a restaurant that is fun and buzzy—the place everyone wants to be. **LJ**

Depot Eatery & Oyster Bar | Casual Kiwi fare with fun and flair

Location Auckland **Signature dish** *Hapuku* sliders, pickled lemon mayo, watercress | ❸❺

There has been a line of expectant diners standing on the pavement from the very first day chef Al Brown threw open the doors at Depot. Well worth the wait, this attendant experience is often as fun outside as the crammed dining within. Once your name is on the list, the friendly staff will ply you with on-tap wine and beer. Depot is also open all day, serving simple breakfasts and coffee with no lines.

Brown is the archetypal Kiwi, a hunting, shooting, and fishing type who has created a menu at Depot that reflects his love of land and sea. There is no artfully styled fancy food here, but you can feast on some of the freshest oysters and clams to be found anywhere, opened to order at the raw bar as you settle in to share small and large plates of locally sourced specialities. The New Zealand meat board is crammed with charcuterie sourced from the country's best artisan purveyors and is a must to nibble on to balance all the briny seafood.

Having spent time on the U.S. East Coast during his chef training and during subsequent travels, Brown incorporates New England and New York influences in this diner-style eatery. The most popular dishes are fish-based: tasty sliders filled with fresh *hapuku* (groper) and tangy lemon mayonnaise and cumin-battered fish tortillas with coleslaw and tomatillo sauce. Brown is the also the master of economical cuts of fish and meat, creating hearty dishes such as *hapuku* belly with eggplant *kasundi* (a type of relish), skirt steak with tobacco onions, or lamb ribs with *skordalia* (a garlic-based puree).

Waiting staff buzz happily about in the narrow space, which is furnished with heavy wooden tables and stools crammed together. The chefs work in full view, and a few lucky diners can perch near the kitchen, observing pans flashing and orders being called. The wine list extends beyond Sauvignon blanc on tap, with a wide choice of wines available by the glass. **LJ**

"… a fast-paced, fresh venue where you can drop in and enjoy perfectly cooked dishes."

The New Zealand Herald

⬆ Oysters are opened to order at the bar.

FIRST COURSE

French Country Terrine, pickled cherries 23
Sri Lankan Prawn Salad, coconut, curry leaves 24
Duck Salad, pomegranate, tahini, beets, pistachio 23
Twice-baked Goats cheese Soufflé 23
Soup: Tomato, fennel, cannellini bean 16
Risotto: Asparagus, peas, parsley, parmesan 21

MAIN COURSE

Veal Schnitzel, potato rösti, coleslaw, caper butter 32
Steak frites 'Hereford Scotch, maître D' hotel butter 35
Lamb rump, burghul pilav, baba ghanoush, harissa 34
Salmon fillet, lentils, buttered beetroot, dill crème 32
Chiang Mai Chook, coconut rice, tamarind, som tum 32
Hapuku, celeriac purée, fennel + pea broth, tapenade 34
SIDES: Fries, mayo 6 green Salad 7 Asparagus, hollandaise 16

CHEESE: bleu d'Auvergne
                Aged Gouda
50g/3 /15 'Ramara' washed rind

All
$15   DESSERT: Churros con Chocolate...
Summer berry tart, mascarpone, praline
Rose pannacotta, rhubarb, pistachio
Profiteroles, icecream, Chocolate sauce
Nougat glacé, saffron, Turkish delight
Handmade Valrhona Truffle 3.50 each

245

The Engine Room | An informal eatery with top notch food

Location Auckland   **Signature dish** *Churros con chocolate* | ❸❸❸

The menu shouts simplicity, with dishes such as flounder with potatoes, asparagus, and *sauce vierge*, or chicken leg with bread sauce, radicchio, and walnuts. Reading through, diners might think The Engine Room's food reminiscent of good old home cooking. But once the plates arrive, it becomes clear that there is no way any home cook could create such flavor or sophistication and make food this good.

Natalia Schamroth and Carl Koppenhagen scoured the city for months to find a site for their restaurant. They settled on an old post office building on Auckland's North Shore, not far from the downtown area, and have had a loyal following since they opened in 2006. Theirs is an informal and bustling, fuss-free eatery, where guests can feel really comfortable. As Natalia says, it's about "damn good honest food, cooked with heart and soul." The pair—both trained chefs—have worked together for many years and continue to travel frequently to draw on European and Asian influences for inspiration for their menu. To provide a seamless dining experience, Carl heads the kitchen while Natalia runs the front of house, offering diners a warm welcome.

The blackboard menu changes regularly, but some dishes, such as the untraditional but completely delicious *churros con chocolate*, the creamy twice-baked goats' cheese soufflé, and a simple veal Schnitzel (made with rose veal) with rösti, slaw, and caper butter have proved so popular that they have remained on the menu since day one.

The Engine Room also offers a tight selection of very well chosen wines, cocktails, and aperitifs. It's likely a wine will appear here well before it becomes trendy. In fact, that's exactly what The Engine Room is all about—delivering an excellent experience that puts it well ahead of most other places in Auckland. **LJ**

⬆ Dishes are announced on the blackboard.

The French Café | Consistently excellent food in an elegant setting

Location Auckland   **Signature dish** Spiced duckling with Asian greens, mandarine, and *kumara* | ❺❺❺❺

The awards bestowed upon this café reinforce its reputation as first choice for special-occasion dining, when you want a flawless experience. Chef Simon Wright and wife Creghan Molloy Wright, who oversees the dining experience, never rest for one minute in their relentless pursuit of excellence in food, wine, service, and classy atmosphere.

The pair took over this eclectic café more than 15 years ago and each year they added innovative details to make their restaurant a temple of fine dining. The exemplary service provided by staff turned out in impeccable style, the constantly reworked interior and exterior architecture, a snazzy outdoor courtyard planted with herbs and vegetables, and a stunning wine list make for a sophisticated, stylish experience.

The modern menu reaches back to Wright's classical British culinary training, and the experience he gained on travels to Asia, the Pacific, and back to Europe provide plenty of interesting influences.

Produce is sourced daily for playful dishes such as the "Fruits of the Sea," a frothy combination of native seaweed, oyster cream, samphire, and lemon oil, revealing delicious small sea creatures in the jellied broth, while caramelized pork belly is enhanced with langoustine, carrots, and the surprising flavors of almond and gingerbread. The duck is not to be missed, and is always paired with seasonal fare.

The tasting menu is highly recommended: ten courses of exquisite flavors, starting with a briny kingfish ceviche supported by apple jelly, verjus cucumber, crème fraîche, and caviar, and finishing with two desserts. Vegetarians are catered to with a separate tasting menu, including dishes such as barely-set egg yolk with smoked potato, mushrooms, rye, and fresh truffles. Dining in New Zealand does not get better than the French Café experience. **LJ**

⬆ Honey tones dominate the decor at The French Café.

The Sugar Club | World-recognized fusion food with spectacular views

Location Auckland **Signature dish** Laksa with duck, pumpkin, and "golden egg" | ❸❸❸

"Fusion food can create the most stimulating food you'll ever eat …It's fun and it's playful."

Peter Gordon, restauranteur

⬆ The Sky Tower affords breathtaking views of the city.

As you step out from the extraordinarily terrifying elevator that whisks you to the 53rd floor of the Sky Tower, the whole of the Auckland harbor stretches out below. But, within seconds, your attention shifts to the comforting, cosseting foyer and the cool, sophisticated, and very welcoming bar. Decorated in moody blues, with the most fascinating silk textured walls, it shrieks thoughtful design. A world-class setting for the father of modern fusion cuisine.

Chef Peter Gordon, a household name in New Zealand and other parts of the world where he consults on his unique Asian-European cross-culture cuisine, started out at the original Sugar Club in Wellington. He moved to London with that restaurant and now owns the popular Providores restaurant and tapas bar there. It was a master stroke on the part of the Sky City owners to call him home as consultant for their signature restaurant up in the clouds.

Peter jets back and forth from London almost as often as an Air New Zealand pilot. He works closely with his head chef, Neil Brazier, to create a menu that suits the surroundings. There are many classic Peter Gordon dishes and some, such as the beef pesto, hark back to his first foray into fusion: the beef is tenderly marinated in soy and spices, sautéed, and served with the fresh surprise of pesto on top. The laksa is deservedly famous: a spiced smokey version crammed with duck, pumpkin, and "golden egg." The *vattalapam*, an Asian-influenced dessert, is a must.

The Sugar Club offers weekend brunches and an express lunch menu, but the full dining experience, starting out as the sun sets and the city lights up at night is the best. The views almost steal the show from the refreshingly different, remarkably audacious food, which combines all the things people love about New Zealand and Asian ingredients. Staff are highly professional, and the small wine library offers a great selection to accompany the food. **LJ**

Black Barn Bistro | Tasty specialities from the Fruit Bowl region

Location Hawke's Bay **Signature dish** Za'atar crusted lamb with dauphinoise potatoes and minted pea puree | ❺❺

Surrounded by vines, with panoramic views overlooking the region known as New Zealand's Fruit Bowl, Black Barn offers an exemplary experience of vineyard feasting. Locals reserve well ahead for delicious weekend lunches and casual celebrations, and, through the summer months, the tables spill out onto a courtyard surrounded by topiary gardens underneath the trellised grapevines.

Andy Colthart and Kim Thorp, formerly a farmer and an advertising industry leader, respectively, are the two talented owners of Black Barn who oversee a small empire that encompasses the Black Barn Bistro and winery, an intimate summer season farmers' market, a classy art gallery, some self-catering luxury accommodation on superb sites around the bay, and an outdoor theater for jazz performances. Everything is accomplished with flair and style.

Chef Terry Lowe's well-conceived modern bistro menu has something for everyone, paying homage to local specialities such as the famous Hawke's Bay lamb matched to Black Barn Syrah, and succulent seasonal fruit and vegetables. Constantly changing, four or five starters are featured with six main courses, some rich desserts, and a delightful junior menu for the kids that includes a mini minute steak with salad and fries. Grown-up choices draw influences from Europe and Asia, as seen in dishes such as whole roasted baby chicken with jasmine rice, ginger, lime *ponzu*, and broccoli, or free-range pork belly with pineapple salsa, bok choy, kumara, and ginger mash in an Asian broth.

The bistro interior shouts country comfort, with polished wooden floors and walls shaded in pale grays to emphasize the bright light spilling through the expansive windows, complementing the carefully chosen artwork. Two stunning translucent panels emblazoned with blue flowers break up the airy space of the dining room. Service is friendly, and Black Barn wines by the glass are paired to every dish. **LJ**

"On a hilltop with fantastic views over the vines and beyond, the dining room is truly spectacular."

foodlovers.co.nz

⬆ Hawke's Bay lamb is a speciality at Black Barn Bistro.

Ortega Fish Shack | Fresh fish and a fun experience

Location Wellington   **Signature dish** Oysters served natural, crisply battered, or in a shot of Bloody Mary | 💲💲

With its pastel tiled floor, quirky ocean-themed collectibles, wooden tables and bentwood chairs, painted white timber walls, and seafood-dominated menu, you would almost think that Ortega Fish Shack was a fishing cabin on the Maine coast, not a small restaurant in the center of Wellington.

Owner Mark Limacher is one of the most respected chefs in the country and has mentored many bright young talents. Over the years, he has owned and worked this site in several guises. Working with his family, he created an ever-popular, casual, and fun dining experience.

The eclectic menu mostly concentrates on fresh fish that is sourced daily, but also strays into classic French provincial dishes. His sublime corn-fed duck liver pâté, steak with Café de Paris butter, and Catalan crepes with orange caramel sauce and vanilla ice cream are in great demand. The seafood dishes offer some surprises: a Scotsman wandering in would be puzzled by traditional kippers on the menu served with untraditional Edam-style goats' milk cheese, beetroot, and watercress. The local fish, terakihi, is roasted, smothered in Malay-style coconut gravy, and complemented by a refreshing shrimp, lime, and coriander salad, while the salmon sashimi is bathed in a Japanese-style dressing of togarashi, tamari, and lime. All dishes are well thought through and make the most of the variety of influences that make a meal here such an exciting culinary adventure.

A wide selection of tasty and diverse craft beers accompanies the well-selected wine list, and a jug or two of sangria goes down well in warmer months. Ortega's extensive bar is central to the restaurant, providing a perfect perching place for crowd-watching and downing an ale or two before feasting on some excellent food. **LJ**

⬆ The interior is decorated with sea-themed objects.

Logan Brown | A classical setting for modern cooking and fine wine

Location Wellington **Signature dish** Paua ravioli | ❸❸❸

There is an air of elegance about this restaurant, housed in a former bank in New Zealand's capital. It opened almost two decades ago and has hardly missed a beat as one of the most popular places where an eclectic mix of politicians, food lovers, and sports fans gathers. One of the original two partners remains in charge: Steve Logan, a master of hospitality, who heads for the outdoors when he is not directing his well-orchestrated team.

With its Gothic columns and dome, the space provides a comfortable spot in every corner of the room, where discreet conversations will not be overheard—no wonder it is the restaurant of choice for the nation's power brokers. The staff is very knowledgeable and offer genuine Kiwi hospitality.

The food takes center stage with some revered classics, a selection of wild game recipes, and a few unexpected twists by head chef Shaun Clouston. His cooking is firmly grounded in technique, with lovely combinations of top-quality New Zealand ingredients such as Rangitikei lamb served with spiced lamb cheek, local lentils, and a delightful smoked yogurt from local fresh cheese producer, Zany Zeus, or line-caught kingfish accompanied by Greek beans, smoked beet *skordalia*, and croquettes made with the famed Cook Strait crayfish.

A few dishes seem to have lingered on the menu forever: local paua (abalone) ravioli in a light and frothy lemon *beurre blanc* sauce and delicate red deer in some guise or other, according to season. Logan Brown is also recognized for its outstanding wine selection, with everything from top French Champagnes to fine examples of New Zealand varietals. Sauvignon blanc, chardonnay, and Pinot noirs are popular, and, for discerning diners, there are also bottles sourced from around the globe. **LJ**

⬆ The elegant dining space boasts high ceilings.

Herzog Restaurant | Destination dining with superb wines

Location Marlborough **Signature dish** Wild hare with quince and parsley | ❺❺❺❺

"Widely considered the best restaurant in New Zealand, Herzog has an old-world elegance."

concierge.com

⬆ A glass of sparkling wine overlooking the vineyard is the perfect start to a sophisticated dining experience.

This is destination and occasion dining at its best. Upon arrival, you walk through a display of carefully tended rose bushes, then take a relaxing sip of a pre-dinner drink while settling into a comfortable armchair overlooking Herzog's vineyard. In the dining room, the furnishings are luxurious, the space between the tables is generous, and there is an air of excitement and anticipation as you await an evening of culinary delights.

Therese Herzog gave up her high-flying corporate lifestyle in the capitals of Europe to follow her winemaking husband Hans to New Zealand. They bought land in Marlborough, the country's most prolific wine region, where Hans has proved to be one of the finest winemakers around. Therese then created a fine-dining restaurant to complement the stunning aromatic Hans Herzog wines. With a European flair and sensibility for fine hospitality, she attends to every detail to ensure that the surroundings, service, food, and wine provide a very special experience.

The kitchen is staffed with European-trained chefs who cook prime produce with sophistication and flair for the degustation menu. The menu explores local delights, including South Island salmon, wild game, local rock lobster, the famous local beef and lamb, and more. Each course is a little more than a tasting portion, expertly crafted to match the flavors of the accompanying Hans Herzog wine. Herzog's cheese trolley may be the best in New Zealand, accompanied by local organic nuts and homemade fruit chutneys.

But there is more. Herzog also has a fine cellar of precious European wines to choose from, a cigar room for post-prandial relaxation, and for those who want a more casual experience, Herzog Bistro next door, which overlooks the kitchen garden, is open all year and offers more hearty, informal fare. **LJ**

Pegasus Bay Restaurant | Rustic food in a country garden setting

Location Waipara **Signature dish** Venison carpaccio with cherries, horseradish, and Parmesan | ❸❸❸

A tranquil dining destination is not what you would expect at a busy working winery, but Ivan Donaldson and his wife Chris thoughtfully chose to situate their restaurant well away from the bustle and noise of their winemaking facility. Tables are placed in well-tended gardens with a stunning vista of the surrounding countryside for rural al fresco lunches. The only sound you can hear is the occasional crack of an air gun that shoos away pesky birds from the ripening vines. When the weather is chilly, the rustic dining room within offers comforting warmth.

It is no surprise to learn that Pegasus Bay has won the title of New Zealand's Best Winery Restaurant several times. Wine lovers who enjoy fine food pairings will find the 50-minute drive north from Christchurch well worthwhile, as considerable thought goes into sourcing ingredients to match the aromatic Pinot noir, Riesling, luscious dessert wines, and other varietals from both current vintages and library stock.

Three of the Donaldson sons are now involved in the business, taking responsibility as winemaker, marketer-manager, and general manager, respectively. Chris can often be found working in the gardens, and her rose border is one of the most beautiful in the area. Herbs, nuts, fruit, and vegetables from the property are destined for the restaurant kitchen, and, as the region is known for fine produce, it is likely that seasonal walnuts, olive oils, summer fruits, truffles, and vegetables will appear on the plate.

The food inspires lingering lunches, with a tasty platter of local specialities to nibble on for starters while choosing your meal. Two generous dishes designed to partner Pegasus Bay Pinot are worth trying: whole Muscovy duck with fig jus, with a melange of local vegetables and fruits and superb grass-fed Wagyu beef rib-eye with duck fat potatoes, salad, horseradish cream, and mustard (both to share). **LJ**

"The menu takes advantage of superb local produce and recommends appropriate wines."

Lonely Planet

⬆ The much-admired rose border creates a beautiful setting for an al fresco lunch.

Fleur's Place | Ruggedly rustic with fish straight from the boat

Location Moeraki, Otago   **Signature dish** Fresh muttonbird | 💲💲

Perched on a small finger of land that provides shelter for the local fishing fleet from the wild Southern Ocean, Fleur's Place oozes rustic charm. Fleur Sullivan, known to all as just "Fleur," presides over the kitchen and dining spaces in her little wooden house; she has become something of a cult figure on New Zealand's restaurant scene. Hers is the restaurant that world-famous chef and master of seafood Rick Stein chose when asked to name his ultimate seafood destination.

When Fleur opened her place, under local regulations, she had no way of purchasing fish directly from the local fishermen, but she set about the business in her unique style, making her peace with building inspectors, and now has special fishing licences and a quota for the many species of fish on offer. Eveything is cooked simply, and garnished with plain steamed vegetables, but guaranteed to be the freshest food that customers have ever encountered.

Smoked fish, when available, comes straight from the adjacent shaky smokehouse and is not to be missed. Smoked snapper or cod, bathed in a delicious spicy, salty marinade, are so tasty that diners lick their fingers. A particular speciality of the house is muttonbird, procured from Southern Ocean fishermen and rarely seen on New Zealand menus. A seabird that is extremely fishy with an anchovy-like flavor, for many this is an acquired taste.

Reaching the restaurant is quite a mission: Dunedin, the nearest city, is more than an hour's drive away to the south, and historic Oamaru 30 minutes to the north. But once you arrive, having negotiated the winding little coastal road from the main highway, you are in for a special fish meal that is sure to be fresh, wonderfully simple, and a fun experience. **LJ**

← The Kaimoana fish platter at Fleur's Place.

Fishbone Bar & Grill | The best fish and chips in town

Location Queenstown   **Signature dish** Crumbed blue cod with chips and pickled onion aioli | 💲💲

The fish is always fresh and the cooking so deliciously simple that you could eat at Fishbone every night of the week and never tire of the menu. The jaunty bar and grill occupies a small storefront on a busy shopping street in the heart of Queenstown, and oozes with the owners' passion for fresh food.

Former journalist turned chef Darren Lovell is living his dream, overseeing the kitchen and growing his own herbs, vegetables, and fruits. He also turned the entire yard of his home into a maze of plots, complete with a hen coop. The eggs are used in the Happy Hen Pavlova, a frothy concoction topped with lemon curd, kiwifruit, and fresh cream—a favorite of regulars and tourists alike.

> *"Wacky and colorful, the decorative, fish-filled interior is a joy. Fresh fish is sourced daily."*
>
> frommers.com

Queenstown, the "adventure capital of the world," is surrounded by majestic mountains, so the restaurant's focus on coastal fish may seem surprising. But Lovell rises early every day to ensure the best of the day's catch from Southern Ocean fisheries is whisked to his restaurant.

The menu features starters of mussel fritters, octopus, scallops, and clam chowder, followed by fresh fish prepared with influences from Asia and the Americas. Fish and chips are a Kiwi favorite, and Fishbone's version is the real deal: tender filets of sole or blue cod encased in a crunchy batter with hand cut fries and pickled onion aioli. The wines are carefully sourced to match the seafood. **LJ**

Index of Restaurants by Name

Contributors

Ray Avilez (RA)
is a prominent Venezuelan journalist with over twenty years of experience in TV journalism, radio hosting, and as contributor to lifestyle magazines. He is a serious foodie and sybarite. For ten years, he was the Venezuela correspondent for the U.S. TV show *Despierta América*.

Pascale Beale (PB)
is a California-based food writer, cookbook author, cooking instructor, and owner of Pascale's Kitchen, a Mediterranean-style cooking school. Her latest book, *Salade*, was published in 2014.

Cat Black (CB)
A member of the Guild of Food Writers and a Grand Jury member of the International Chocolate Awards, Cat is a chocolate and patisserie specialist. She writes on chocolatecouverture.com and contributes to *Cakes & Sugarcraft* magazine.

André Blomberg-Nygård (ABN)
A self-taught Norwegian chef, restaurateur, and all-around food connoisseur, André is famously unforgiving as the restaurant critic for Norway's largest newspaper. He hosts a weekly radio show and heads up the culinary think tank heltchef.no.

Amy Cavanaugh (AC)
is the Restaurants and Bars Editor of *Time Out Chicago*. She has also written about food, drink, and travel for *The Boston Globe*, *Chicago Tribune*, and *Saveur*.

Damian Corrigan (DC)
is a travel writer specializing in Spain. He is the Spain expert for about.com, and has lived and worked in the country for many years. He also runs a travel consultancy agency, advising travel companies in Spain.

Trish Deseine (TD)
A cookbook author, restaurant reviewer, and TV broadcaster, Trish has lived in and

around Paris since the 1980s. She is the author of several books, including *Je Veux du Chocolat* and *The Paris Gourmet*.

Mike Dundas (MD)
is a Los Angeles-based food writer and the co-founder and editor-in-chief of *Spenser* magazine, writing about reviving culinary traditions of the past and guiding readers in sourcing produce.

Richard Ehrlich (RE)
has been writing about food and drink for over two decades. He has reviewed restaurants for *Time Out* and *The Time Out Eating and Drinking Guide*, and is the author of seven cookbooks. He lives in London.

Karin Engelbrecht (KE)
Based in Amsterdam, Karin is the Dutch Food Editor for about.com. She also writes restaurant reviews and articles for *A-Mag*, the official English-language Amsterdam city magazine. She worked for *Time Out Amsterdam* for several years as Food and Drink Editor and restaurant reviewer.

Michèle Fajtmann (MF)
has lived in Brussels, New York, Warsaw, and London. She worked as a corporate lawyer for fifteen years before launching From My City, a boutique consulting and event management company that creates tailor-made arts events, tours, and networking events in unique venues.

Cyndi Flores (CF)
was born in Texas and moved to Washington, D.C., to obtain a degree in economics. There, she works in information technology management, which she spices up by engaging in and writing about travel, food, and culture.

Nathan Fong (NF)
is a regular food and travel contributor on *The Rush*, Vancouver's premier talk show, and a contributor to the *Vancouver Sun* and

Taste Magazine. He has also written for *Bon Appétit*, *Fine Cooking*, and *Men's Health*, and is a contributing editor of *Taste & Travel Magazine* and *Vancouver Boulevard* (a Chinese lifestyle publication), writing about food and travel.

Carole French (CFr)
A BBC-trained journalist, author, and member of the British Guild of Travel Writers, Carole French travels the world, including France, in search of inspirational stories and fabulous restaurants to feature.

Jenny Gao (JG)
Born in Chengdu, a UNESCO City of Gastronomy, Jenny is a food lover. She has appeared on the BBC documentary *Exploring China: A Culinary Journey* and the awarding-winning food show *Fresh Off the Boat*, and writes on the blog Jing Theory, which is dedicated to Chinese food culture.

Rozanne Gold & Michael Whiteman (RG & MW)
Rozanne is an award-winning chef, journalist, and international food consultant. A four-time winner of the prestigious James Beard Award, she is the author of twelve cookbooks and more than 500 articles on food. She was first chef to New York Mayor Ed Koch and worked as consulting chef to the Rainbow Room and Windows on the World. Her work has appeared in *The New York Times*, *The Wall Street Journal*, and *Bon Appétit*. Michael Whiteman is a journalist and lecturer, and one of the industry's leading restaurant and hotel consultants. He is the founding editor of *Nation's Restaurant News* and the president of Baum + Whiteman consultancy.

Matthew Gray (MG)
is a former chef and radio talk show host from Los Angeles. He now owns and operates Hawaii Food Tours in Honolulu and considers himself Hawaii's ambassador for those who love food and fun.

Anelde Greeff (AG)
is editor-in-chief of *Eat Out*, South Africa's foremost food guide, listing the country's definitive restaurants, food markets, and farms, and presenting acclaimed restaurant and produce awards. Not surprisingly, she spends most of her time eating fine food.

Roopa Gulati (RGu)
is a chef, food writer, and broadcaster. She has been a food editor with UKTV and scooped *Rick Stein's India* TV series for the BBC. She is an author and restaurant reviewer for *Time Out* magazine and guides.

Janna Gur (JGu)
is a food writer, editor, and cookbook author, and an expert on Israeli and Jewish cuisine. She is the founder and editor-in-chief of *Al Hashulchan*, the leading Israeli gastronomic monthly and the author of *The Book of New Israeli Food*.

Ellen Hardy (EH)
has covered restaurants in London, Paris, and Beirut for websites and publications ranging from fireandknives.com to *New York Magazine*. She started working with *Time Out* when living in Beirut, editing the magazine, restaurant guide, and city guide. She is now based in London, traveling back and forth to Paris as the Associate Editor of *Time Out Paris*.

Andy Hayler (AH)
is an author, broadcaster, and the restaurant critic for *Elite Traveler* magazine. He has eaten and written about every three-star Michelin restaurant in the world.

Simon Heptinstall (SH)
was a cider maker before becoming a professional writer, and worked in a bakery and a whole food cafe. He has since written about everything, from farming to travel, and reviewed restaurants for more than twenty years. He was a major contributor to *Taste Britain*, published in 2010.

Athico Ilye (AI)
was born in Kyoto, Japan, and now lives in London. He has published over thirty books in Japan, Korea, and Taiwan. He is a serious foodie.

Lauraine Jacobs (LJ)
is the food columnist for the *New Zealand Listener* and has written about restaurants, wine, and the New Zealand food scene for more than twenty-five years. She travels frequently in search of great food and has published several cookbooks. She is an advocate of simple food, beautifully cooked.

Dino Joannides (DJ)
is a London-based entrepreneur, food fanatic, and bon vivant. A true epicurean, he has traveled to and eaten at restaurants all over the world. Dino's first book, *Semplice*, about Italian cooking ingredients, was published in 2014.

Sybil Kapoor (SK)
is an award-winning food and travel writer and a regular contributor to the *Financial Times* and the *Guardian*, as well as a wide range of magazines. She is the author of seven cookbooks, including *Simply British*, *Taste* and *The Great British Vegetable Cookbook*.

Sam Kilgour (SKi)
has been writing about food for over a decade. A member of the Guild of Food Writers, she has served on the committee and judging panels for the Guild's annual awards. Her work has appeared in a range of publications, including *Gin & It* and the *Proceedings* publication of the Oxford Symposium on Food & Cookery.

Carol King (CK)
is a journalist and author with an interest in the arts and popular culture. A true Italophile, she spent years living in Sicily, enjoying the sun, the cuisine, and listening to Sicilians talk passionately about food.

Anne Krebiehl (AK)
German-born and London-based, Anne is a freelance wine writer who contributes to trade and consumer publications including *Harpers Wine & Spirit*, *The World of Fine Wine*, *The Drinks Business*, *Imbibe*, and others. She is an accredited member of the Circle of Wine Writers and the Association of Wine Educators. She has harvested and helped to make wine in New Zealand, Germany, and Italy.

Christiane Lauterbach (CL)
Born and raised in Paris, Christiane has reviewed restaurants in Atlanta since 1983. She is the publisher of *Knife & Fork*, the insider's guide to Atlanta restaurants, a popular public speaker and broadcaster, and loves food.

Elaine Lemm (EL)
is a former chef and restaurateur turned food writer and author. She writes for several leading magazines and newspapers, and her website, britishfood.about.com, is ranked as one of the most-visited food sites in the U.K.

Jenny Linford (JL)
is a London-based food writer. Her books include *Food Lovers' London*, a cosmopolitan guide to London's food scene, *Great British Cheeses*, *The London Cookbook*, and *The Creamery Kitchen*. She is always very happy in the presence of good food.

Erica Marcus (EM)
is a food reporter, blogger, and critic for *Newsday*, Long Island's daily paper. A graduate of Swarthmore College, she edited cookbooks and other books before joining Newsday in 1998. She lives in Brooklyn, New York.

Ben McCormack (BMcC)
is the editor of *Square Meal*, the leading website for restaurant and bar reviews

in London and throughout the U.K. He has been eating out for a living for fifteen years and sincerely hopes that his knowledge of the British food scene has expanded at the same rate as his waistline. He is also a regular contributor to *Marie Claire*, *Men's Health*, and the *Luxury* section of the *Telegraph*.

Barbara-Jo McIntosh (BM)

is an award-winning food professional with over twenty-five years' experience in the food and hospitality industry. Formerly the owner of Vancouver restaurant Barbara-Jo's Elegant Home Cooking, she opened Barbara-Jo's Books to Cooks bookshop in 1997.

Lauren England McKee (LM)

is a graduate student in Food Studies at New York University. She has done research and written for *Saveur* magazine, the James Beard Foundation, and several art publications. With academic interests in both gastronomy and the arts, she works as a curator and archivist for fellow contributor Rozanne Gold. She lives in Manhattan with her husband.

Hilary McNevin (HM)

worked front-of-house, managing restaurants and studying wine in both Australia and the U.K. for fifteen years before changing careers and becoming a food writer. She is the restaurant news columnist for *Epicure*, *The Age*, and goodfood.com.au, and contributes regularly to *Delicious* magazine, *Winestate*, and *The Weekly Review*. She lives in Melbourne with her two children.

Josimar Melo (JM)

is a Brazilian journalist working as a food critic for the *Folha de S. Paulo* newspaper and host of the *O Guia* program on the Brazilian National Geographic Channel. He also publishes the annual gastronomic guide *Guia Josimar*, writes about restaurants on his dedicated blog, and is a member of The World's 50 Best Restaurants international board.

Charmaine Mok (CM)

is a writer, editor, and flaneur. Based in Hong Kong, she is the online editor of *Hong Kong Tatler* and the *Hong Kong Tatler Best Restaurants Guide*. She is a full-time eater and part-time host for Little Adventures in Hong Kong, a company that organizes walks focusing on discovering the "real city."

Martin Morales (MM)

is the chef and restaurateur behind the award-winning Ceviche restaurant in London's Soho—which kick-started the Peruvian food explosion in the city— as well as the more recently opened Andina restaurant in East London. Passionate about food, he has been cooking since the age of 11. He is also the author of *Ceviche: Peruvian Kitchen*, published in 2013.

Marina O'Loughlin (MOL)

is a widely traveled, experienced restaurant critic cited by the *Sunday Times* and the *London Evening Standard* as one of the U.K.'s most influential people—but she still regards restaurants as just about the most fun anyone can indulge in.

Chris Osburn (CO)

is a freelance writer, photographer, dedicated blogger (tikichris.com), and avid foodie. Originally from the American Deep South, he has worked all over the world and has called London home since 2001.

Tanya Ott (TO)

was born and raised outside of Boston. She studied German and communications, and moved to Berlin in 1994, where she now works in TV and print media as, variously, producer, writer, translator, copy editor, and proofreader.

Simon Parkes (SFP)

has worked in journalism for over thirty years, specializing in food writing. He was an inspector for the U.K. Michelin Guide, a restaurant reviewer for British *Vogue*, and has also presented the BBC Radio 4 *Food Programme*.

Célia Pedroso (CP)

is a Portuguese journalist. Her work has appeared in *Metro International*, the *Guardian*, *EasyJet Traveller*, and other publications. She is the co-author of the book *Eat Portugal: The Essential Guide of Portuguese Food* and the co-founder of Eat Drink Walk tours in Lisbon.

Sudi Pigott (SP)

is a fanatical, discerning foodie and experienced travel and food writer, restaurant critic, and culinary trend consultant. She writes for a wide range of U.K. and international publications, and is the author of *How to be a Better Foodie*.

Celia Plender (CPl)

is a trained chef, writer, and food anthropologist who also works for *Time Out* magazine in London. Having worked at a traditional restaurant in Japan, and eaten her way all around South Korea, she regularly writes about the cuisines of these countries.

Fred Plotkin (FP)

is an expert on gastronomy, opera, and everything Italian. He has written for *The New York Times*, *Time*, and the *Financial Times*. He is also the author of *Italy for the Gourmet Traveler*, an exhaustive source for visitors who are interested in Italy's peerless food and wine heritage.

Kay Plunkett Hogge & Fred Hogge (KPH & FH)

Kay Plunkett-Hogge is a food writer and cook. She is the author of *Leon: Family and Friends*, *Make Mine a Martini*, and *Heat: Cooking with Chillies*. She also co-wrote *Bryn's Kitchen* and *For The Love of Veg* with chef Bryn Williams, as well as books with Chris Bianco and Stanley Tucci. Fred Hogge is a screenwriter and photographer, based in London, who likes a good restaurant.

Fran Quinn (FQ)

is an award-winning journalist and copywriter, who has written on everything from mushroom growing to chocolate making. She has a particular interest in

Sweden and Swedish cuisine, speaks the language fluently, and visits the country several times per year.

Hanna Raskin (HR)
is the food writer and critic for *The Post* and the *Courier* in Charleston. She previously worked as critic for the *Seattle Weekly* and the *Dallas Observer*.

Marryam H. Reshii (MR)
is a well-known restaurant critic and gastronomy writer based in Delhi. In her job, she has to travel frequently, both within India and overseas, and collecting bits of food-related wisdom and ingredients is her perfect hobby.

Lari Robling (LR)
A three-time nominee of the prestigious James Beard Foundation Award for Best Food Radio, Lari also writes for the *Philadelphia Daily News*. She is the author of the internationally acclaimed cookbook *Endangered Recipes* and writes on her website, endangeredrecipes.com.

Camille Rocca (CR)
is a writer based in Portland, Oregon, where she enjoys the unique culinary offerings of the verdant Pacific Northwest. The daughter of a Napa Valley winemaker and a frequent traveler herself, she appreciates any dish that is done well.

Kirsten Rødsgaard-Mathiesen (KRM)
is a Danish-born freelance journalist, based in New Zealand and working around the globe. She is the author of Denmark's best-selling guidebook to New Zealand and of *Passion, Pinot & Savvy*, a book about New Zealand women winemakers.

Raquel Rosemberg (RR)
is a true "porteña," living in Buenos Aires. She has a degree in social communication and works as a gastronomic journalist for *Clarín* newspaper and other media. She is passionate about food and flavors, and writes on her blog, saboresquematan.com, which is also the title of her first book. She is also chairwoman of The World's 50 Best Restaurants.

Tyler Rudick (TR)
After eating his way across the United States, culture writer Tyler developed a particular fondness for Gulf Coast cuisine. Following a seven-year stint in Houston, he currently resides outside Chicago with his wife, son, and shepherd mix.

Nada Saleh (NS)
is a nutritionist, food writer, and freelance restaurant consultant. She was shortlisted for the Andre Simon Memorial Fund Awards, for the books *Fragrance of the Earth* and *Seductive Flavours of the Levant*, and is the author of *Fresh Moroccan* and *New Flavours of the Lebanese Table*.

Michela Scibilia (MS)
has lived in Venice for over thirty years. A graphic artist and the author of four guidebooks, she promotes the city's culture, food, wine, and the work of its skilled artisans. She writes on her website, teodolinda.it.

David James Sheen (DJS)
Born and educated in England, David James Sheen now lives in Bologna, Italy, where he works as a translator, copywriter, and journalist. His publications include numerous magazine articles, fashion brand bibles, interviews for the BBC, and more than twenty children's story books.

Niamh Shields (NS)
is a London-based food blogger and writer. She spends her time traveling the world, exploring local cuisines and gathering recipes, and visiting restaurants, from fine dining places to street food stalls. She records her adventures on eatlikeagirl.com.

Christine Smallwood (CS)
is a food and travel writer. The author of *An Appetite for Umbria, … for Puglia*, and *… for Lombardia*, she tells the stories of the interesting people behind the gastronomy and food production of each Italian region.

Silvana de Soissons (SdS)
is an Italian cook and food writer living in England. She is also the founder of *The Foodie Bugle*, an online and print journal about food, and the Foodie Bugle Shop.

Tara Stevens (TS)
is a food writer and cook who splits her time between Barcelona and Fez. She is a contributor to *Condé Nast Traveler*, the *Guardian*, and *Fool* magazine, and is never happier than when out and about discovering new and delicious dishes.

Sue Style (SS)
is a freelance food, wine, and travel writer based in Alsace, France. She writes for several food and wine magazines, and is the author of nine books as well as a regular online contributor to zesterdaily.com and winetravelguides.com.

Aylin Öney Tan (AT)
is an architect, conservator, curator, and food writer, with columns in two national Turkish newspapers. In 2008, she received the prestigious Sophie Coe Prize in Food History at the Oxford Symposium on Food & Cookery conference, where she is a dedicated presenter.

Daisy Thompson (DT)
is passionate about food, cooking, and eating. Through her blog, daisysworld.net, she inspires readers to prepare gourmet food that is easy to make with fresh ingredients. When she isn't busy cooking in the kitchen, she loves discovering new restaurants.

Adrian Tierney-Jones (ATJ)
is an award-winning British journalist and writer who specializes in beer, food, and travel. He is the general editor of *1001 Beers You Must Try Before You Die*, and contributes to various magazines and newspapers in the U.K. and the United States.

Susan Wilk (SW)
is an avid cook, writer, eater, and blogger. Her blog, susaneatslondon.com, features original recipes and restaurant reviews from around the world. She currently lives in Seattle and returns to London whenever she can.

Picture Credits

Every effort has been made to credit the copyright holders of the images used in this book. We apologize for any unintentional omissions or errors and will insert the appropriate acknowledgment to any companies or individuals in subsequent editions of the work.

2 Pierre Monetta **20–21** Commander's Palace **22** Jeremy Koreski **23** Anthony Redpath **25** Anthony Metz **27** Blue Water Café **28** Raj Taneja **29** Christopher Morris / Corbis **31** The Pear Tree **32** The Pear Tree **33** Bearfoot Bistro **34** Langdon Hall **36** Bon Appetit / Alamy **38** Bosk **39** Photocuisine / Alamy **40** River Café **41** River Café **42** Gabriel Bertogg **44** Lee Brown / Alamy **45** Toqué **46** Guylain Doyle / Getty Images **47** Chez Boulay **48** 3660 on the Rise **49** Chef Mavro **50** Gayot **51** Rodolfo Arpia / Alamy **52** Salt Bar & Kitchen **52** David Reamer **54** Eric Wimberley **55** ildi.Food / Alamy **57** John Valls **58** Washington Post / Getty Images **59** Willows Inn **60** Meadowood **61** Meadowood **62** Acquerello **64** Greens Restaurant **65** Carlos Avila Gonzalez / San Francisco Chronicle / Corbis **66** ZUMA Press, Inc. / Alamy **67** Thomas Winz / Lonely Planet Images / Getty Images **68** Eric Wolfinger **71** Gary Danko **72** Andy Hayler **73** Kim Kulish / Corbis **74** Cephas Picture Library / Alamy **76** Foodcollection.com / Alamy **77** Freda Banks **78** Ed Anderson **79** Quince **80** Morton Beebe / Corbis **81** david sanger photography / Alamy **83** Bloomberg via Getty Images **85** ZUMA Press, Inc. / Alamy **85** lucydphoto / Getty Images **86** The French Laundry **87** The French Laundry **88** Cantus Artis **89** Green Leaf **90** Poppy **91** Bar Sajor **93** Nick Jurich **94** REX / Hans Kwiotek **96** Eric Wolfinger **97** Eric Wolfinger **99** Patrick Tregenza **99** Kodiak Greenwood **101** CUT **102** Joshua Resnick / Shutterstock **103** Dylan Ho **105** Ambient Images Inc. / Alamy **106** REX / Barry J Holmes **109** Ambient Images Inc. / Alamy **111** Rob Stark **112** LOOK Die Bildagentur der Fotografen GmbH / Alamy **113** David Crausby / Alamy **114** Bestia **115** Chef Demelogue **116** Brent Winebrenner / Getty Images **117** ZUMA Press, Inc. / Alamy **118** David R. Frazier Photolibrary, Inc. / Alamy **120** ZUMA Press, Inc. / Alamy **121** cobraphotography / Shutterstock **123** Twist **125** Full of Life Flatbread **126** Paolo Gallo / Alamy **128** Bonjwing Lee **130** Julie Soefer **131** Oxheart **133** David R. Frazier Photolibrary, Inc. / Alamy **134** Commander's Palace **135** Tyler Kaufman **136** Lew Robertson / Corbis **138** John Benson **139** Jose Moran Moya **140** Meadowood **141** REX / Martha Williams **143** LOOK Die Bildagentur der Fotografen GmbH / Alamy **144** Lisa Predko **146** Galdones Photography **147** Anne Petersen **148** Doug Fogelson **149** Clayton Hauck **150** Topolobampo **152** Jeff Greenberg "0 people images" / Alamy **155** Bacchanalia **156** James Camp **158** VIEW Pictures Ltd / Alamy **160** Husk **161** Andrew Cebulka **162** Hominy Grill **164** Albert Knapp / Alamy **166** Lee Foster / Alamy **167** Jason Colston / Getty Images **168** The Tabard Inn **169** The Tombs **171** Dusan Vuksanovic **172** Jason Varney **173** Franklin Fountain **175** Barbuzzo **176** Willow Street Pictures **177** Vedge / Alamy **179** Jose Moran Moya **194** Roberta's and Blanca **196** Serendipity 3 **197** Bloomberg via Getty Images **198** Francesco Tonelli **199** Francesco Tonelli **201** Gramercy Tavern **202** Gabriele Stabile **203** Gabriele Stabile **204** Oceana **205** Red Rooster Harlem **206** Jose Moran Moya **207** Daniel Krieger **209** Erica Marcus **210** The Four Seasons **212** Eric Laignel **213** Henry Hargreaves **215** Tanoreen **216** Anthony Bianciella **217** Per Se **220** Grand Central Oyster Bar **221** Peter Luger **224** Andrew Pini / Getty Images **225** Laissez Faire **226** Patti McConville / Alamy **227** The Standard Grill **228** The Spotted Pig **229** Patti McConville / Alamy **230** Foodie International **231** Dracisk **233** Brandon Rosenblum **234** Eric Striffler **235** Eric Striffler **236** Pat & Chuck Blackley / Alamy **237** LOOK Die Bildagentur der Fotografen GmbH / Alamy **241** Karyn R. Millet / Getty Images **242** Blox **243** Chris Osburn **244** Pujol **245** The World's 50 Best, sponsored by Cusqueña **246** Naomi Bishop **248** Shane Luitjens / Alamy **250** Marmalade **251** Michele Falzone / Alamy **252** Philippe Jacquet **253** Vladimir Godnik / Getty Images **254** guy harrop / Alamy **257** Danita Delimont / Alamy **260** Ray Avilez **261** Ray Avilez **262** Ray Avilez **263** Ray Avilez **264** Remanso do Bosque **266** Leo Soares **267** Hemis / Alamy **269** Robert Harding Picture Library / Alamy **270** The World's 50 Best, sponsored by Cusqueña **271** The World's 50 Best, sponsored by Cusqueña **272** Nicholas Gill / Alamy **273** Astrid & Gastón **274** Central **275** Chez Wong **276** La Mar **277** Maido **278** Wesley Rosenblum **279** Santiago Soto Monllor **280** The World's 50 Best, sponsored by Cusqueña **282** Holger Leue / Lonely Planet Images / Getty Images **285** The World's 50 Best, sponsored by Cusqueña **286–287** Pierre Monetta (Jules Verne) **288** INSADCO Photography / Alamy **289** Dirk Renckhoff / Alamy **290** Jimmy Linus **291** Jimmy Linus **292** Christopher Hauser **293** Martin Smedson **294** Fäviken **295** Per Anders Jorgensen **296** David Lebovitz **297** Fjäderholmarnas Krog **298** Daniel Berlin Krog **299** Per Anders Jorgensen **300** Atlantide Phototravel/Corbis **301** Lena Granefelt / Johner Images / Getty Images **302** Giovanni Tagini / Alamy **303** YLevy / Alamy **304** Mads Eneqvist **306** Ballymaloe House **308** Simon Heptinstall **309** Neil Juggins / Alamy **310** Gleneagles **311** sandy young / Alamy **312** The Kitchin **313** Travstock / Alamy **315** Bon Appetit / Alamy **316** Neil Setchfield / Alamy **318** steven gillis hd9 imaging / Alamy **319** Pipe and Glass **321** Hambleton Hall **322** Robert Young **324** Le Champignon Sauvage **325** Adrian Sherratt / Alamy **326** The Walnut Tree Inn **327** Justin Kase zninez / Alamy **328** Le Manoir aux Quat' Saisons **329** Tim Graham / Alamy **330** Hand & Flowers **331** The Royal Oak **332** Paul Winch-Furness **333** REX / Time Out **334** REX / View Pictures **335** Rules **336** Apsley's **337** Patricia Niven **339** The Ritz **340** Hakkasan **341** Le Gavroche **343** Simon Brown Photography **344** Hibiscus **345** Ottolenghi **346** Jonathan Lovekin **347** Pied à Terre **348** Petrus **350** Moro **353** The Ivy **354** The Ledbury **356** Dorchester **358** Gordon Ramsay **359** Gordon Ramsay **360** Andy Hayler **361** Andy Hayler **362** Locanda Locatelli **363** REX / View Pictures Ltd / Alamy **364** Fifteen **365** Berkeley **367** Koffmann's **368** Paul Winch-Furness **369** Pollen Street Social **370** Alex Seymour **371** The Square **372** REX / Geoffrey Swaine **373** The Waterside Inn **374** Neil Setchfield / Alamy **375** The Harrow at Little Bedwyn **377** Slawomir Fajer / Shutterstock **378** The West House **379** martin phelps / Alamy **380** Steve Speller / Alamy **381** Riverford **382** Jason Lowe **383** REX / Matt Austin **384** Marianne Outlaw **385** REX / Christopher Jones **388** Jack Hobhouse / Alamy **389** Star Castle Hotel **390** De Lindenhof **391** De Librije **394** De Kas **396** Hemis / Alamy **397** Hemis / Alamy **398** Lute **399** Caroline Rodriguez **400** In den Rustwat **401** Inter Scaldes **402** McAndrews, Chugrad / the food passionates / Corbis **403** Aux Armes de Bruxelles **404** Comme chez Soi **405** L'Idiot du Village **407** Jacobs **409** Gugelhof **410** W. Chodan **411** W. Chodan **412** Café Einstein **413** Eric Nathan / Alamy **414** Borchardt **415** Cookies Cream **416** Iain Masterton / Alamy **418** Juergen Henkelmann Photography / Alamy **419** Bon Appetit / Alamy **420** Coselpalais **421** Alte Meister **422** La Vie **423** Andy Hayler **424** Bloomberg via Getty Images **426** Andy Hayler **427** Amador **428** Leopold **429** sack / Getty Images **430** Berg **431** Wielandshöhe **433** Roman Boed **434** Schwarzwaldstube **435** Schwarzwaldstube **437** Dallmayr **438** Andy Hayler **440** Residenz Heinz Winkler **441** Residenz / Alamy **443** La Grenouillère **444** Restaurant Gill **445** Sa Qua Na **447** Arco Images GmbH / Alamy **449** Helen Cathcart / Alamy **450** Au Boeuf Couronné **451** John Sones Singing Bowl Media / Getty Images **452** Hemis / Alamy **454** Pierre Bonbon / Alamy **455** Raoul Dobremel **457** Pierre Monetta **458** Witold Skrypczak / Alamy **459** Paris by Mouth **460** Guy Savoy **462** Bloomberg via Getty Images **463** B.Lawrence / Alamy **464** Johnny Jones / Alamy **466** Le Jules Verne **467** David Arous **468** Andy Hayler **469** Le Dôme **470** Owen Franken/ Corbis **471** REX / Karl Blackwell **472** La Fontaine de Mars **473** Hemis / Alamy **475** Pierre Monetta **476** Directphoto Collection / Alamy **477** Hemis / Alamy **478** Jacques Gavard **481** Prunier **482** Matt Aletti **484** Cover / Getty Images **485** Andy Hayler **487** Gamma-Rapho via Getty Images **488** Septime **489** Verjus **491** imageBROKER / Alamy **492** Malcolm Bott **494** Espérance **498** Philippe Schaff **499** Loiseau des Vignes **500** Photocuisine / Alamy **502** Maison Troisgros **503** Maison Troisgros **504** Andy Hayler **505** GUIZIOU Franck / Hemis / Corbis **507** LOOK/Robert Harding **508** Café Comptoir Abel **509** Louis Laurent Grandadam / Corbis **511** Hemis / Alamy **512** La Tupina **513** Hemis / Alamy **515** David Bordes **517** Cubolmages srl / Alamy **518** Hemis / Alamy **519** La Colombe d'Or **520** Directphoto Collection / Alamy **522** Jean-Jacques Gelbart **523** Jacques Vieussens **524** Photocuisine / Alamy **525** Benjamin Haas **526** Chef Demelogue **528** REX / Sipa Press **530** LOOK Die Bildagentur der Fotografen GmbH / Alamy **531** AlphaAndOmega / Alamy **532** Steirereck / Stadtpark **533** Schwarzwaldstube **534** Nina Kissell / Alamy **535** Hôtel Georges Wenger **536** Hôtel de Ville **537** Prisma Bildagentur AG / Alamy **538** Didier de Courten **540** Trattoria Altavilla **541** Locanda dell'Isola Comacina **542** Al Sorriso **543** Piccolo Lago **544** Tips Images / Tips Italia Srl a socio unico / Alamy **545** Cubolmages srl / Alamy **546** Trattoria Visconti **547** Ristorante Baretto di San Vigilio **548** Da Vittorio **549** Da Vittorio **550** Toni del Spin **551** Giovanni Colosio **552** Ristorante Macelleria Motta **553** Ristorante Macelleria Motta **554** Due Colombe **556** Francesco Bolis **557** Il Ristorante Trussardi alla Scala **558** Il Desco **559** 12 Apostoli **560** Locanda Cipriani **561** Osteria Alle Testiere **563** Cubolmages srl / Alamy **564** Al Covo **565** Corte Sconta **566** Michela Scibilia **567** Widner **568** Mattia Mionetto **569** Mattia Mionetto **570** Quadri **571** Cubolmages srl / Alamy **573** Locanda delle Grazie **574** Del Cambio **575** Piazza Duomo **580** Andy Hayler **581** NBCU Photo Bank via Getty Images **583** Roberto Fumagalli / Alamy **584** LOOK Die Bildagentur der Fotografen GmbH / Alamy **585** Nigo Pezigo **587** Eco del Mare **589** Magnolia **591** Enoteca Pinchiorri **592** L'Erbhosteria **593** Cucinàa **594** Cubolmages srl / Alamy **597** Rupert Hansen / Alamy **600** Andy Hayler **601** Enoteca Ferrara **602** Zoonar GmbH / Alamy **604** Matassa, Mario / the food passionates / Corbis **606** Ken Field Photography Ltd. / the food passionates / Corbis **608** Ristochicco **608** Wieder, Frank / the food passionates / Corbis **609** Fiorenzo Ferreri **610** Antichi Sapori **611** Ristorante Bufi **613** Don Alfonso **614** Peter Forsberg / Europe / Alamy **615** Andy Hayler **616** Da Adolfo **617** Da Tuccino **618** Mikko Mattila - Travel, Italy, Campania / Alamy **619** Cibus **620** Carol King **621** Carol King **622** Casale Villa Rainò **623** Carol King **625** Terraliva **626** Il Duomo **627** Lorenzo-graph / Shutterstock **628** Branislav Senic / Alamy **629** Relais Torre Marabino **631** Caro / Alamy **632** Carol King **633** Andy Hayler **635** Xara Palace **636** Arzak **635** Arzak **636** Katya Flutes **637** Mugaritz **639** Akelare **641** Andy Hayler **642** Etxebarri **643** Horst Gottfried **644** Casa Marcial **647** Francesc Guillamet **649** Anna Gorchs **650** Andy Hayler **653** Kaiku **654** Jordi Sans **655** Bgn Appetit / Alamy **656** age fotostock / Alamy **660** Cinc Sentits **661** Cinc Sentits **663** Damian Corrigan **681** Damian Corrigan **682** Damian Corrigan **683** Jose Moran Moya **684** Damian Corrigan **685** Andy Hayler **686** Ramón Freixa **689** Casa Montaña **691** imageBROKER / Alamy **692** Diglogvi / Shutterstock **694** REX / Jonathan Cox **696** Largo do Paço **697** Célia Pedroso **699** Nuno Correia **700** imageBROKER / Alamy **702** Célia Pedroso **703** Alan Dawson Photography / Alamy **704** Anna Stowe/LOOP IMAGES/Loop Images/Corbis **705** Czech Tourist Board **706** B. and E. Dudzinscy **707** LOOK Die Bildagentur der Fotografen GmbH / Alamy **708** Mike Spence/Greece / Alamy **709** Strofi **710** REX / Karl Blackwell **712** LOOK Die Bildagentur der Fotografen GmbH / Alamy **713** Orient-Express Hotels Ltd **714** REX/Kommersant Photo Agency **716** Bernie Epstein / Alamy **717** Tim E. White / Alamy **718–719** Bon Appetit / Alamy **720** Hollis Bennett **722** The Ruined Garden **723** Bon Appetit / Alamy **724** Rob Crandall / Alamy **725** Le Jardin **726** Robert Harding Picture Library Ltd / Alamy **727** Simon Reddy / Alamy **728** Singita Lebombo Lodge **730** Five Hundred **731** DW Eleven **732** Café Bloom **733** Africa Media Online / Alamy **735** Jac de Villiers **737** La Colombe **738** Schoone Oordt **739** Carne SA **740** Panama Jacks **741** The Test Kitchen **742** Jordan Restaurant **744** Makaron **745** Overture **746** Fyndraai **747** Pierneef à la Motte **748** The Tasting Room **749** Babel **750** Marion Kaplan / Alamy **751** Île de Pain **752–753** El Katsumata / Alamy **754** Nada Saleh **755** Wyatt, Rawdon / the food passionates / Corbis **756** Massaya **757** Blaine Harrington III/Corbis **758** Orna and Elba **759** Orna and Elba / Al Hasulchan **760** Bon Appetit / Alamy **761** Toto **762** Eyal Nahmias / Alamy **765** Machneyuda **766** Cultura Creative (RF) / Alamy **767** Hemis / Alamy **768** REX/Image Broker **769** Kevpix / Alamy **771** Borsa **772** Beyti **774** Mikla **775** Steve Outram / AWL / Getty Images **776** Müzedechange **777** Konyali-Kanyon **778** Marryam H Reshii **779** The Chinar **781** Indian Accent **782** Bukhara **783** Dum Pukht **784** Spice Route **785** Marryam H Reshii **787** AD 1135 **788** Hanuwant Mahal **789** Lukaszewicz / Shutterstock **790** Bohemian **792** RMA Architects **793** Sean Sprague / Alamy **794** Ankur Panchbudhe **795** Zaffran **796** Dakshin **797** Kanua **798** Karavalli **800** Anubhavati **801** Vivanta Taj Malabar **803** Andrew Rowat **804** Studio Eye / Corbis **807** Lou-Foto / Alamy **808** Bon Appetit / Alamy **811** Eising Studio Food Photo & Video / the food passionates/Corbis **814** Matassa, Mario / the food passionates / Corbis **815** SOH Scott Wright of Limelight Studio **817** Scott Wright of Limelight Studio **818** Jenny Gao **821** REX / View Pictures **822** The Chairman **825** tomeats.com **826** Celia Plender **827** Todam Sundubu **828** Jung Sik Dang **830** Celia Plender **831** Celia Plender **833** Celia Plender **834** Celia Plender **837** JTB MEDIA CREATION, Inc. / Alamy **839** Turukou **840** Ronnarong Thanuthattaphong / Shutterstock **841** Keika Ramen **842** Nopparat Tosati / Alamy **843** Bon Appetit / Alamy **844** Atthico Ilye **846** HLPhoto / Shutterstock **847** amana images inc. / Alamy **848** amana images inc. / Alamy **849** Huw Jones / Alamy **850** Marie-Laure Tombini / Oredia / Corbis **851** Bon Appetit / Alamy **852** Janine Cheung **853** Izuju **854** MIXA / Alamy **857** Ruth Reichl **859** Deco / Alamy **860** Atthico Ilye **861** Atthico Ilye **862** Atthico Ilye **863** Atthico Ilye **865** Taiyoshi Hyakuban **866** Datacraft - Sozaijiten / Alamy **868** Datacraft - QxQ images / Alamy **869** Datacraft - Sozaijiten / Alamy **871** TONY MCNICOL / Alamy **872** B.S.P.I. / Corbis **873** Sansou Murata **874** rakratchada / Shutterstock **875** Piyato / Shutterstock **876** Thanapol Kuptanisakorn / Alamy **877** BaLL LunLa / Shutterstock **879** Issaya Siamese Club **880** REX / Mark Parren Taylor **881** Austin Bush / Lonely Planet Images / Getty Images **882** Sukpaiboonwat / Shutterstock **883** Willy Thuan **885** 2 / Iain Bagwell / Ocean/ Corbis **886** Bon Appetit / Alamy **889** Simon Reddy / Alamy **891** Andre **892** John Heng for Iggy's **893** MIXA / Alamy **894** Simon Reddy / Alamy **895** Simon Reddy / Alamy **896** travel images / Alamy **897** El Katsumata / Alamy **898** David Burden **899** Mark Coran / Alamy **900–901** Shane Rosario **902** Nautilus **903** Berardo's **904** The Spirit House **905** Jeong **906** Anson Smart **908** Ben Dearnley **909** Ben Dearnley **911** Lauryn Ishak / Corbis **912** REX / Newspix **913** EST **915** Marque **916** Rob Francis / Alamy **917** REX / Newspix **918** Lucy Deng **919** Porteño **920** Shane Rosario **921** Shane Rosario **922** Provenance **925** Attica **926** Cumulus Inc. **927** Flower Drum **928** Bill Bachman / Alamy **929** Moon Under Water **931** Simon Griffiths **932** The Town Mouse **933** LOOK Die Bildagentur der Fotografen GmbH / Alamy **934** Sidart **935** Sidart **936** Soul Bar & Bistro **937** Kieran Scott **938** Kieran Scott **939** The French Café **940** Manja Wachsmuth **941** Salman Javed **942** Ortega Fish Shack **943** Logan Brown **944** Ben Lewis / Alamy **946** LOOK Die Bildagentur der Fotografen GmbH / Alamy.

Books are always very much a team effort, especially one on this scale. My thanks to Jane Laing, Editorial Director at Quintessence, for thinking of me for this fascinating project, and to my editor, Katharina Hahn, for working with me on it so patiently and supportively. Thanks, of course, to my knowledgeable, gloriously greedy contributors. Finally, many thanks to my family, who lived with this book, too, while I worked on it!